Musical Instruments and Their Symbolism in Western Art

Musical Instruments and Their Symbolism in Western Art

Studies in Musical Iconology

EMANUEL WINTERNITZ

New Haven and London
YALE UNIVERSITY PRESS

Printed in the United States of America by The Murray Printing Co., Westford, Massachusetts.

Library of Congress Cataloging in Publication Data

Winternitz, Emanuel.
Musical instruments and their symbolism in Western art.

"Bibliography of writings by Emanuel Winternitz since 1940": p.
Includes bibliographical references and index.
1. Musical instruments in art. I. Title.
M185.W58 1979 704.94'9'78191 78-65482
ISBN 0-300-02324-3
ISBN 0-300-02376-6 pbk.

11 10 9 8 7 6 5 4 3 2

In memory of Alfred Schütz,
thinker, musician, and noblest of friends

Contents

Illustrations

b. Above: Zampogna (Italy, 19th century). Length of longest drone, 4 feet. *Below*: Musette (France, 18th century). Length of chanter, 9½ inches; of bourdon cylinder, 5½ inches. Metropolitan Museum of Art, Crosby Brown Collection.

25. *a.* Bock (Germany, 18th century). Length of chanter, 2 feet 5 inches; of drone, 5 feet 4 inches. Metropolitan Museum of Art, Crosby Brown Collection.
b. Bock with bellows (Germany, 19th century). Length of chanter, 1 foot 9 inches; of drone, 3 feet 6 inches; both are fitted with single beating reeds. Metropolitan Museum of Art, Crosby Brown Collection.

26. *a.* Musette player with other musicians, from Watteau's *L'Amour au théâtre français.*
b. Watteau, *Fête champêtre*, detail showing musette player.
c. Watteau, *L'Accordée de village*, detail showing musette and vielle played for dancing.
d. Engraving after Watteau, showing Chinese musician with a vielle.

27. *a.* Angel playing a three-stringed hurdy-gurdy (c. 1500). St. Thomas Altar, Cologne.
b. Van Dyck, *Portrait of François Langlois.* Private collection. Note the bellows straps on the right arm, and the single chanter.
c. Player with zampogna.
d. Street singer with hurdy-gurdy, from the case of a South Tyrolean psaltery (18th century). Metropolitan Museum of Art, Crosby Brown Collection.

28. *a.* Peter Bruegel, *Dance of the Peasants*, detail.
b. Engraving after Peter Bruegel, *The Fat Kitchen*, detail.
c. Vielle player from a woodcut (c. 1570) entitled *Les Noces de Michaud Crouppière: Histoire d'une drollerie facécieuse du Marriage de Lucresse aux yeux de boeuf et Michaud Crouppière son mary, avec ceux qui furent semouz au banquet.*

29. *a.* Page from Bordet's *Méthode raisonnée*, Paris, c. 1755.
b. Cornemuse with ivory pipes (France, 18th century). Length of chanter, 10 inches; of drone, 7 inches. Metropolitan Museum of Art, Crosby Brown Collection.

30. *a.* Plaque for the musical scholar Ercole Bottrigari (early 17th century).
b. Orpheus in Hades, after a bronze plaque by Moderno.

31. *a.* Examples of various lire da braccio and lire da gamba (after sketches by Disertori in *Rivista musicale italiana*, XLIV [1940]): (*a*) Lira da braccio, Brussels Conservatory, Mahillon Catalogue 1443. (*b*) Lira da braccio, Kunsthistorisches Museum, Vienna, Schlosser Catalogue 94. (*c*) Lirone, Heyer Collection, Kinsky Catalogue 780. (*d*) Lira da gamba, Heyer Collection, Kinsky Catalogue 784. (*e*) Lira da gamba, Brussels Conservatory, Mahillon Catalogue 1444. (*f*) Lira da gamba, Kunsthistorisches Museum, Vienna, Schlosser Catalogue 95.
g. Lira da braccio by Giovanni d'Andrea, Venice, 1511: front and back views (same as (*b*) above).
h. Lira da gamba by Wendelin Tieffenbrucker, Padua, c. 1590 (same as (*f*) above).

32. *a.* Bartolommeo Passerotti, *King David.* Galleria Spada, Rome.
b. Raffaellino del Garbo, *Musician.* National Gallery, Dublin.

59. From the Book of Hours of Jeanne d'Évreux, Metropolitan Museum, New York.
a. The Nativity. The main scene shows two angels with cymbals and a vielle; below is a monster plucking a jawbone.
b. Scene representing the education and chastisement of the young Saint Louis. At the bottom of the page, a youth sitting on a bearded monster is bowing a vielle.

60. From the Book of Hours of Jeanne d'Évreux, Metropolitan Museum, New York.
a. Page showing a monster with a triangle in the initial, and another with a harp below; a long-tailed monster is playing a mandola with a plectrum.
b. The Adoration of the Magi. Little angels in the background are playing a trumpet, bells, a psaltery, a vielle, and kettledrums. The scene below shows the Massacre of the Innocents.

61. From the Book of Hours of Jeanne d'Évreux, Metropolitan Museum, New York.
a. Page showing, in the initial, a monster wearing a monk's robe and plucking bellows with a plectrum; the little monk above him holds his music. In the lower right corner a long-tailed creature is playing a psaltery with his fingers.
b. Page showing, at left of Annunciation scene, a figure playing a mandola.
c. Initial with a monster playing a vielle in a rather awkward position.

62. From the Book of Hours of Jeanne d'Évreux, Metropolitan Museum, New York.
a. Initial with a woman playing cymbals.
b. A musician playing a bagpipe with a very large chanter and drone.
c. A mandola of medium size.
d. A tailed monster playing a bagpipe.
e. The 'training' of a bagpipe.
f. A fantastic creature playing a dog as a bagpipe, and another blowing a large shawm with a cowhorn bell.

63. From the Book of Hours of Jeanne d'Évreux, Metropolitan Museum, New York.
a. A snare drum and fife.
b. A rattle.
c. A monster blowing a bellows like a wind instrument.
d. A bellows played as a trumpet.
e. A triangle.
f. Bells and a reed pipe.
g. A snare drum.
h. A bell hit with a stick.
i. A goat bowing a jawbone with a rake.

64. Detail of Geertgen tot Sint Jans, *Virgin and Child.* Van Beuningen Museum, Rotterdam.

65. *a. Glorification of the Virgin.* Collection of Baron Heyl, Worms.
b. Geertgen tot Sint Jans, *Virgin and Child.* Van Beuningen Museum, Rotterdam.

66. Master of the St. Lucy Legend, *Ascension and Coronation of the Virgin.* National Gallery, Washington, D.C.

Preface to Second Edition

When this book was first published, a request to the Catalog Division of the Library of Congress to include among its subject headings the term *musical iconology* was refused because "such a discipline does not exist." Since then the situation has changed radically. Many scholars and students now devote themselves to the study of pictures as a gold mine of information about the practice of musical performance and other musical data. In 1971 the Research Center for Musical Iconography was established at the City University Graduate Center in New York, with Professor Barry S. Brook and myself as co-directors.

The text of the book is identical to that of the original edition. The reprint opportunity offered by Yale University Press does not permit additions or revisions, but it did allow for the inclusion of an appendix and a bibliography of my writings on iconology and related topics. These two new sections require an explanation. In the early 1960s, when I first compiled this book, there were many tempting topics to choose from. I selected those which permitted a demonstration of new methods of research or which suggested new, unexplored areas for iconological interpretation. I described the conflict between time-honored traditions in the shape of instruments and their novel musical functions, and the resulting atrophied patterns surviving and misunderstood for centuries. I also showed the advantage of describing gradual changes in the shape of instruments in cancrizans, that is, by gradually stepping backward through history, from the fully documented present to less documented past phases of culture. I interpreted the drolleries as evidence of the relation between the sacred and the profane in music as well as in art. I emphasized the practical value of writing parallel histories of instruments that are widely different in their mechanical structure but nearly identical in their emotional impact—for instance, the hurdy-gurdy and the bagpipe—because of their common drone principle. I called attention to Renaissance artists, devoted to the recovery of antiquity, who became successful archaeologists for the sake of the authentic classical style of their own works. I suggested the emergence of successfully standardized instruments such as the violin, not as products of sudden isolated rational planning, but as gradual crystallizations out of the turbulence of conflicting and converging shapes. Only a few problems could be treated in a book of moderate size. For other topics and a wider horizon of iconological themes, the student may consult my bibliography from 1940 to the present and the new appendix, which is an extract from a panel paper prepared for the Twelfth International Musicological Society Congress and RIdIM, Berkeley, 1977. RIdIM (Repertoire International d'Iconographie Musicale), under its president, Professor Barry Brook, has made a successful beginning in organizing the systematic collection of pertinent visual records on an international basis.

On these grounds it seemed appropriate to give my book a subtitle: Studies in Musical Iconology.

As for the plates, Yale University Press has kindly suggested that instead of mechanically reproducing them from the first edition, it would make the plates from new photographs. I wish to express my gratitude to Yale Press for this generosity.

Preface to First Edition

Most of the studies assembled here grew out of my work at the Metropolitan Museum of Art, for whose splendid collection of musical instruments I have, as Curator, been responsible since 1941. Preserving, repairing, and exhibiting instruments, studying purchases and gifts, and organizing museum concerts of forgotten masterworks using instruments of their periods, provided no end of incentive to research. Another stimulus came from the continual questioning by friends in the fields of the history of art and of music. In this age of intense interest in iconology, art historians seek information about instruments as traditional attributes of allegorical figures, as integral elements of mythical and religious beliefs and images, and as telling tools of social customs and traditions. In trying to answer these questions, it was necessary to view the instruments as objects invested with symbolic meaning beyond their musical significance. Music historians, in turn, having become increasingly familiar with the wealth of pictorial representations, have sought equivalent information for their purposes: more precise information about the nature of ensembles, playing methods, and practices of performance in general, in those many instances in which the answers could not be provided by surviving instruments.

This book does not aspire to be a comprehensive or systematic treatment of its subject. Nor is it only an anthology — that is, a conglomeration of essays chosen at random, unrelated to each other. When a selection from my articles on musical instruments was suggested to me, I was not sure that they would make a homogeneous group, but after some reshuffling, they seemed to fall into a natural order — reflecting what I suppose, or at least hope, has been an organic growth of thought.

That strange object the tool of music, a machine or technical contraption serving an art and often itself a work of art, pleasing the eye as well as the ear, opens up many vistas and approaches. It is obviously susceptible to investigation within its own esthetic realm, that of music. Among the problems to be studied here are: the function of the instrument in practical performance; the ever-changing rapport between the creative musician, striving for certain timbres, and the tools that best satisfied his imagination; and the ever-present antagonism between conservatism and the desire for change, and likewise between two other rival tendencies, individualization and standardization of musical instruments. But the interest in instruments is not confined to a consideration of them within a purely musical context. They carry meaning beyond their function as tools — that is, beyond their musical significance. And here we encounter aspects such as the function of the instrument within its social milieu, its role as bearer of allegorical thought, as product of the plastic arts, and so on. These aspects that are not strictly musical are, curiously, little investigated today, although much thought was given to them in earlier phases of culture — in the Renaissance and Baroque for instance — not only by scholars and poets, but also by artists. It was the painters, above all, who availed themselves of the symbolic character of musical instruments. A certain flute, or dragon trumpet, or drone fiddle, displayed in a mythological subject or *trionfo* or *fête champêtre* or genre scene, would often rapidly and accurately inform the initiated spectator of the meaning of the scene. It is for this reason that a large part of the articles selected for this book draw upon visual images as well as upon actual surviving instruments.

The function of the two introductory essays on the importance of co-operation between historians of art and those of music, hardly needs explanation here. The ensuing articles could perhaps be classified in three main sections, of which the first group, comprising Chapters 3 and 4, deals with the problem of evolution. In Chapter 3, 'The Survival of the Kithara,' some inconspicuous and non-functional elements of an instrument are revealed as atrophic remnants of parts that had been essential many centuries before, and the supposed revival of an ancient Roman instrument in the 15th century is seen as the final result of an actual survival. The chapter on 'Bagpipes and Hurdy-gurdies in Their Social Setting' is similarly concerned with gradual transformation: the strangely parallel history of instruments with wind and string bourdons is traced through the ages. Here the common bond is not their shape, but rather a functional musical device, the drone, whose characteristic sound possesses symbolic significance, especially within the bucolic and pastoral tradition.

The next group comprises studies of single instruments. Chapter 5, 'The Lira da Braccio,' deals with that exquisite improvisation instrument of the Renaissance. It is substantially an extract from an entry on the lira da braccio published in the German encyclopaedia *Die Musik in Geschichte und Gegenwart*, and I have placed it here as a focal point of factual information on this instrument, permitting me to eliminate repetitious references to its history and function in following articles, several of which touch on the lira da braccio. The sixth chapter tries to trace, in Lombard and Piedmontese pictorial documents, the still unknown early history of an instrument that was influenced by the lira da braccio — the violin. Chapter 7, the last of this group, seeks to interpret a fantastic harpsichord of Algardi's time as a typical Baroque allegory of two opposed branches of music, the learned and the rustic.

The remaining chapters deal with representations of musical instruments in various pictorial arts; most of these essays concern themselves either with the symbolic significance of the instruments for their time or with their significance as key to the interpretation of a particular work of art.

The index has been organized with special regard to iconological matters, and I hope that it may for this reason add to the usefulness of the book.

All the previously published articles assembled here were written during a span of twenty-two years: the first, '*Quattrocento* Science in the Gubbio Study,' in 1942, and the last, 'Muses and Music in a Burial Chapel,' in 1964. The chapter on 'The Knowledge of Musical Instruments as an Aid to the Art Historian' was written for this book. Some of the articles have been published in musical congress reports and in musicological journals and dictionaries. The greater part, those dealing chiefly with musical instruments represented in the visual arts, have appeared in periodicals that do not belong to the daily fare of musical connoisseurs: *The Metropolitan Museum of Art Bulletin*, *The Journal of the Warburg and Courtauld Institutes*, *The Art Bulletin*, and others. I sincerely hope that their appearance here will make them more readily accessible to students of music. The revision of the essays has consisted primarily in making excisions; occasionally, however, some repetition seemed unavoidable. My excuse — to borrow a phrase from William James — is that 'one cannot always express the same thought in two ways that seem equally forcible, so one has to copy one's former words.'

My sincere thanks go to Mrs. Eleanor Clark, my assistant at the Metropolitan Museum of Art, who with untiring devotion helped me in the preparation of my manuscript; to Mr. David Hamilton of W. W. Norton & Company, Inc., who brought to his editorial tasks the persistence of the gentle godfather towards the stubborn child; to Miss Mary McClane, for her assistance in compiling the index; and to the staff of Faber and Faber, especially Mr. Michael Wright for his supervision of the illustrations. I am also very much indebted to the John Simon Guggenheim Memorial Foundation for their generous grant, which made possible a substantial expansion of the picture section.

E. W.

Sources and Acknowledgments

Grateful acknowledgment is hereby made to the publishers of journals and books in which a number of the chapters in this book first appeared:

Chapter 1. *International Musicological Society Congress Report, New York, 1961.* Kassel: Bärenreiter Verlag, 1961.
Chapter 2. Published here for the first time.
Chapter 3. *Journal of the Warburg and Courtauld Institutes*, XXIV (1961), No. 3–4.
Chapter 4. *The Metropolitan Museum of Art Bulletin*, Summer 1943.
Chapter 5. *Die Musik in Geschichte und Gegenwart*, VIII, Kassel: Bärenreiter Verlag, 1960.
Chapter 6. *The Commonwealth of Music: Writings on Music in History, Art, and Culture, in Honor of Curt Sachs*, edited by Gustave Reese and Rose Brandel, New York: The Free Press, 1965.
Chapter 7. *The Metropolitan Museum of Art Bulletin*, February 1956.
Chapter 8. *Bericht über den siebenten internationalen musikwissenschaftlichen Kongress, Köln, 1958*, Kassel: Bärenreiter Verlag, 1958.
Chapter 9. *The Metropolitan Museum of Art Bulletin*, October 1942.
Chapter 10. *The Metropolitan Museum of Art Bulletin*, June 1958.
Chapter 11. *The Musical Quarterly*, XLIX (1963), No. 4.
Chapter 12. *Studies in the History of Art, Dedicated to William E. Suida*, London: Phaidon Press, 1959.
Chapter 13. *Mitteilungen des kunsthistorischen Institutes in Florenz*, XI (1965), No. 4.
Chapter 14. *Rendiconti della Pontificia Accademia Romana di Archeologia*, XXVII (1952–54).
Chapter 15. *The Burlington Magazine*, February 1958.
Chapter 16. *Les Fêtes de la Renaissance*, I, Paris: Éditions du Centre National de la Recherche Scientifique, 1956.

Musical Instruments and their Symbolism in Western Art

There's meat and music here,
as the fox said when he ate the bagpipe.
— *Gaelic proverb*

1 · The Visual Arts as a Source for the Historian of Music

The history of music has concentrated, ever since its beginning, and for obvious reasons, on the most immediate and reliable embodiment of music, its notation. Therefore, those times and regions and forms that had no written music, or from which no written documents have survived, have been greatly neglected. Areas thus slighted include folk music, music of so-called 'primitive' civilizations, and even some of the most subtle forms of occidental music, such as improvisation. Contemporary verbal description, by its very nature, can give but little information about such music; it can mention the instruments, ensembles, places and conditions of performances, but can, at best, give only a faint reflection of the music itself — especially since such descriptions are most often written by musical amateurs or by persons unfamiliar with those aspects of music that would interest the future student. One might hope to find more reliable information in the musical treatises of the time, yet these latter too often focus on problems of theory and pedagogy and give us little idea of what the music actually sounded like. Flagrant examples of this are the ancient Greek treatises, despite their elaborate information on theory of harmony and other matters, and the great Italian theoretical works of the Renaissance which, had no written music survived from that period, would leave us speculating as to the content and emotional impact of the music which they treat. In short, these treatises take for granted many things that to later times are by no means obvious or self-evident.

Instruments themselves are, of course, most valuable documents, but from many periods few, or none at all, have survived. Egypt, with its dry climate and sealed burial chambers, is one of the exceptions, but northern climates, or those with great fluctuations in humidity, are destructive. Moreover, most instruments, and above all string instruments subject to tension, need perpetual care and repair; when they fall from public favour they are likely to disintegrate, if they do not happen to be ornate showpieces or parts of a *Kunst- und Wunder-kammer* or other public or private collections. The bodies of many lutes and harpsichords have survived only because they were rebuilt into hurdy-gurdies and pianofortes.

In view of this situation, musical representations in painting, sculpture, and many other branches of the visual arts are of supreme documentary value to musical history.

It was not the historian of music who first indulged in the systematic collection of musical information from monuments of art. It was rather the artist himself who, during the early and high Renaissance, turned to the monuments of antiquity for models and inspiration, and borrowed what he needed for his own artistic purposes, including the images of ancient musicians and musical instruments. An enormous quantity of sketches and drawings of ancient Greek sculpture and Roman sarcophagi, many including musical subjects, have survived to our day from the 15th and 16th centuries. Raphael, to mention only one great name, employed draftsmen to obtain as many drawings as possible of ancient works of art, and he used the musical instruments of a Roman sarcophagus as models for those in his *Parnassus* in the Stanza della Segnatura.[1] Only later, when 16th-century humanism revived the ideal of recovering and, if possible, reconstructing ancient Greek music, did musical treatises begin to refer occasionally to Greek and Roman sculpture as authentic documents of ancient musical practice. At the same time, however, they referred also to contemporary — that is, Renaissance — works of art, sometimes naively crediting their creators with an exact understanding and imitation of the ancient originals. Ganassi (*Regola Rubertina*, 1542), in discussing whether the lute or the 'violone' is more ancient, refers to an ancient Roman marble relief in which one figure holds an instrument with a bow, 'una viola d'arco'(!), and the *Hiero-*

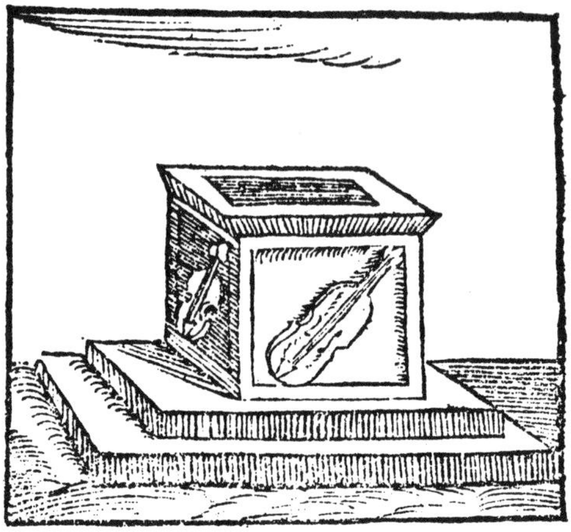

Fig. 1. Pseudo-ancient Roman altar with lire da braccio. Woodcut from Pierius Valerianus, *Hieroglyphica*, 1567.

[1] See Chapter 14 below.

glyphica (1567) of Pierius Valerianus includes a woodcut showing an 'ancient' Roman altar decorated on all four sides with lire da braccio in relief (see Fig. 1), a pseudo-archaeological imitation of an actual ancient Roman type of altar with four lyres, such as we find, for instance, in the Lateran Museum.[1]

Vincenzo Galilei, in his *Dialogo della musica antica e della moderna* (1581), repeatedly refers to the 'marmi antichi,' but he has few qualms about referring to works of art of his own time or of shortly before, trusting that these copies of ancient instruments were archaeologically correct, and being a true Florentine, he of course proudly refers to Florentine artists. In his chapter on the ancient lyre, he tells the reader to go to the court of the Medici palace, where he will find a statue of Orpheus, by Bandinelli, holding a lyre of ancient shape, and in his detailed discussion of the ancient plectrum, he cites the frescoes by Filippino Lippi in Santa Maria Novella, which include a large kithara flanked by two Muses, of which one is holding a plectrum. The Muses, by the way, had been copied by Filippino from a Roman sarcophagus.[2]

In the north, Praetorius, who obviously based the woodcuts of his *Organographia* (1618) on actual contemporary instruments, occasionally gives art objects as his source, as for instance in speaking of early kettledrums ('a type of kettledrum that is to be seen on old coins') and of one of the ancient lyres ('unknown and unusual types of lyres'; *Sciagraphia*, XL, 5; XLI, 9, 10).

Père Mersenne's *Harmonie universelle* (1636) also mentions the ancient Italian marbles and medals as important sources of information, but he broadens the horizon by at least mentioning the Egyptians (Bk. III, Prop. XXIV), and by including early Christian iconography. In his preface, Mersenne speaks of an illustration of the Redeemer in the character of a shepherd holding a 'seryngue' (or 'fleute pastorale'), which he found illustrated in a treatise called *La Roma soterranea.*

Kircher's *Musurgia* (1650) borrows, for one of its title pages, the schematic design of a lyre from an ancient gem, and a pseudo-ancient figure of Orpheus for another title page; but Book VIII contains a large engraving of a sort of filing cabinet with tabulations of the Greek *toni* and other theoretical information, as well as pictures of eleven instruments labelled 'Veterum Graecorum antiquis monumentis desumta,' though two Egyptian sistra are also included.

Buonanni, the learned student of Kircher, in his *Descrizione degli istromenti armonici* (1722), illustrates the instruments in a room contiguous to the Museo Kircheriano, today in the Collegio Romano in Rome. Buonanni's book is a curious mixture of lip service to the ancients from Pythagoras to Virgil and

[1] For more detailed information, see Chapter 14. Zarlino's *Istitutioni* (1558) confine themselves to mentioning that 'the Ancients had a statue of Apollo with a kithara on his knees' (Pt. II, p. 81).

[2] See Chapter 13 below.

astonishing carelessness in the illustrations. If he absorbed little from the Roman statuary in his immediate environment, ancient monuments are at least mentioned in his quotations from Mersenne, Kircher, and Strabo, who tells of having seen the statue of a kithara player in Calabria.

Padre Martini's classical *Storia* (1757–81) refers only occasionally to several 'Monumenta' (that is, illustrated editions of collections of classical antiquities), for instance that of Bernard de Montfaucon; and many of the charming vignettes with puzzle canons on Latin texts that are dispersed throughout his three volumes show musicians borrowed from ancient Roman reliefs. Volume III includes large engravings with ground plans of the Greek and Roman theatres.

Burney, manifestly affected by the English antiquarianism of his time, used his visit to Italy (1770) to good purpose. We may safely conclude, from his many explanations and illustrations of bas-reliefs, sculptures, vases, and frescoes, that he spent some time in Pompeii and Herculaneum, in museums at Rome, Portici, and Naples, and visited many of the Roman palaces that housed antiquities. Forkel's meagre iconographical references (*Allgemeine Geschichte der Musik*, 2 vols., 1788, 1801) are largely based on Burney.

As early as 1774, the first systematic exploration of medieval miniatures for the purposes of music history is found in Gerbert's *De Cantu et Musica sacra*, in which pictures from several codices are reproduced.

A review of 19th-century achievements would require an essay in itself, but among the most important contributions towards musical iconology there should be mentioned the works of Ambros (at home in the history of art as well as in that of music), Coussemaker, and the second volume of Viollet-le-Duc's *Dictionnaire raisonné du mobilier français* (1871).

Evidence of the rapidly growing interest in musical iconology, no doubt stimulated by the publication of illustrated art books and facsimile editions of illuminated manuscripts between 1900 and the outbreak of the First World War, are the many standard works of Buhle, Kinsky, Galpin, Schlesinger, Lütgendorff, Sachs, and the remarkable *Iconographie des instruments de musique*, organized by the Dutch collector of instruments, D. F. Scheurleer.[1]

Egypt and the ancient Near East abound in pictorial representations of musicians and instruments, and certain stylistic peculiarities in perspective and other mannerisms hardly hamper the recognition of actual shapes, fingerings,

[1] Readers interested in further information about the literature on musical instruments may consult the bibliographies given in the following:

Curt Sachs, *The History of Musical Instruments*, New York, 1940.

Nicholas Bessaraboff, *Ancient European Musical Instruments*, Cambridge, Mass., 1941.

Emanuel Winternitz, *Die schönsten Musikinstrumente des Abendlandes*, Munich, 1966; *Musical Instruments of the Western World*, London, 1967.

and embouchures, especially since so many depictions in reliefs and wall paintings are life-size or very nearly so.

Ancient Hebrew musical culture, with its disproportion between abundant references in the Scriptures and utmost scarcity of pictorial monuments, presents a problem too complex to pursue here.

The Greco-Roman world left us many visual records depicting musical scenes and instruments with admirable exactness. There are, above all, vase paintings, sculptures, reliefs, and coins, and from the Roman world an enormous quantity of frescoes, mosaics, and sarcophagi. Topics were mythological, as well as secular, including revelries, music lessons, and the like.

In the Middle Ages, subjects were for a long time limited to illustrations of the Scriptures (especially of apocalyptical themes), the Rex Psalmista, and the 150th Psalm. The apocalyptical subjects were:

(1) The seven angels with trumpets (Rev. 8: 2, 6).
(2) The seven holy men playing instruments in front of the Lamb ('numeri habentes cytharas').
(3) The two figures flanking each of the animals with the Lamb ('tenens cytharam' in Spanish Beatus MSS, represented with longnecked fiddles).
(4) The seven holy men 'stantes super mare vitreum habentes cytharas.'
(5) The twenty-four elders surrounding Christ in Glory (Rev. 4: 4; 7: 11; 14: 14). For the organologist this theme is by far the most rewarding of the apocalyptical scenes. Sometimes the elders are shown holding stereotyped, identical vielles (e.g., in the 11th-century Beatus MS of St. Sevère, Bibliothèque Nationale, Paris); later, the vielles often differ in shape and in the number of strings (Moissac); even later, other instruments, such as harps and organistrum, join them (Santiago di Compostela, Portico de la Gloria; Chartres, Portail Royal).

Carolingian illuminated MSS, above all the Utrecht Psalter, abound with portrayals of musicians (never angels) surrounding the Psalmist. These have been repeatedly — though not yet exhaustively — explored, especially in the works of Buhle, Schlesinger, and Panum. They represent an exceedingly complex problem in view of the fact that many of their illuminations are copied from, or at least influenced by, much earlier models, and therefore cannot be taken simply as depictions of contemporary practice. They may, however, throw new light on one of the great lacunae of musical history, the transition from the instrumental practice of late antiquity to that of the early Middle Ages, and especially on the rise, in the Occident, of instruments with fingerboards for stopping of strings, possibly due to the influence of performing practices in the Eastern Mediterranean.[1] Outstanding examples of the depiction of performance of secular music are the Manesse MS and, above all, the *Cantigas de Santa Maria*, with their enormous array of instrumentalists reflecting, side by side, both Christian and Moslem tradition. In Gothic art, when the sacred and the profane, even the vulgar, meet as close neighbours, a great number of wild and fantastic creatures, monsters, monks and nuns, jugglers and beggars, invade the margins of the pages of psalters, books of hours, and prayer books.[2] But while some of the instruments and ensembles are products of fancy, others are realistic depictions, rich in information about a period from which very few actual instruments have survived.

Musical angels, other than apocalyptical, enter the scene with the spread of the *Legenda aurea*, when legends of the saints and Marianic topics, especially the Assumption and the Coronation (the themes most conducive to the portrayal of large angel orchestras), prevail, and also appear later, chiefly in the Venetian realm, with the *sacre conversazioni* and their small ensembles or single angels playing the lute, the lira da braccio, and occasionally other instruments.

Of the biblical musicians, Renaissance imagery retains King David playing psaltery, harp, or, with the end of the 15th century, more often the lira da braccio. Of secular musical figures, the symbolic representation of Musica as one of the liberal arts is retained. At the same time, competing with the countless angel concerts, the mythological musicians of the ancient Greco-Roman world reappear on the scene: Apollo with the kithara; Hermes with the lyre he invented; Pallas Athena with her creation, the aulos;[3] Orpheus playing in Hades or for the beasts; and the Muses, particularly Erato, Euterpe, and Calliope. The publication of the *Ovidio metamorphoseos volgare* (Venice, 1497) stimulated countless portrayals of the contests between Apollo and his musical rivals Pan and Marsyas, in Lombard, Venetian, and Tuscan paintings, woodcuts, engravings, and plaquettes. The models for the instruments were found in ancient statues, sarcophagi, and other reliefs, greedily and systematically collected by the Renaissance connoisseurs, and copied, sometimes with great precision and thorough archaeological understanding, but more often misunderstood and distorted, or stylized and decorated with free pictorial fancy. True musical archaeology blended with strange misconceptions; Sappho, for instance, was credited with the invention of the fiddle bow, and etymology added to this confusion: 'lira' meant the ancient lyre as well as the lira da braccio,[4] and 'cetra' the ancient kithara as well as the contemporary cittern. Consequently,

[1] See Chapter 3 below.

[2] I have attempted an analysis of musical drolleries in the Hours of Jeanne d'Évreux, painted *c.* 1325 by Jean Pucelle, in Chapter 10 below.

[3] See Chapter 12 below.

[4] See Chapter 5 below.

Apollo, Orpheus, King David, and the allegorical Musica are now shown, more often than not, playing contemporary lire da braccio. Similarly, the diaulos is frequently replaced by contemporary wind instruments, usually double recorders, sometimes two shawms (as in a print by Giulio Romano), and the highest degree of pictorial fancy is reached in those paintings which evidently are renderings of scenes from stage plays or *intermedii*, and which portray fantastic instruments that are not functional, but rather, in all probability, stage props.[1] The greatest precision in the rendering of instruments is reached in the *sacre conversazioni* and the intarsias, the life-size portrayals of musical instruments in the choir stalls of Italian churches, in door panels of palaces, and especially in the studioli of Federigo da Montefeltro in Urbino and Gubbio.[2]

In reviewing 19th- and 20th-century achievements in musical iconology, it would be overly optimistic to believe that they are all better or more careful in method than their predecessors, although they are based on an incomparably greater wealth of source material. They often take pictures at face value, without critical discrimination between real and imaginary objects; without sufficient regard for successive styles, technical peculiarities, and mannerisms of pictorial representations; without an awareness of the artist's lack of freedom, during certain periods, in choosing his topic and often even in delineating his objects; without sufficient familiarity with the theological or political doctrines which controlled allegorical representation and therefore detracted from faithful adherence to the actual appearance of the object. Furthermore, they frequently take a pitiful handful of depictions as adequate evidence, ignoring the possibility that these may be atypical or that the rarity or profusion of certain pictorial representations may not at all correspond to the actual historical distribution of instruments and ensembles, or to actual performing practices. Last, but not least, they do not take sufficient account of the fact that the image of an object may not have been drawn directly from the object itself, but copied from a picture of it, and this again from another, resulting sometimes in a chain of successive copies reaching back, often through centuries, up to the point of complete denaturalization of the original object (see Pl. 1, a–d).

An enumeration of typical pitfalls and misunderstandings may help to illustrate these flaws in method.

In the interpretation of medieval illuminated manuscripts, two diverging

[1] See Chapter 16 below.

[2] See Chapters 8 and 9 below; also my article *Alcune rappresentazioni di antichi strumenti italiani a tastiera*, in *Collectanea historiae musicae*, II (1956), 465–73.

lines coming from a person's mouth, with a horned head issuing from the open end of the tube thus formed, have been taken for a wind instrument, when actually they symbolize a curse — in the fashion of the balloon in modern comic strips — and the horned head is none other than Satan's.

Likewise, in ignorance of traditional allegories, wind instruments have been seen in the four corners of illuminations in 12th-century Beatus MSS, where actually the artist was suggesting the airstreams issuing forth from the mouths of 'the four winds of the earth held back by angels' (Rev. 7: 1).

Angel orchestras depicted in *trecento* and *quattrocento* art have been accepted as true ensembles, whereas often the traditional requirements of compositional symmetry have led to the mirror-like duplication of such visually conspicuous shapes as trumpets, organetti, and the like. For instance, in Pl. 1e the representation of four trumpets pitted against a few soft string instruments should be taken *cum grano salis.*

Similarly, homogeneous angel orchestras consisting of musicians all playing the same type of instrument — for instance, all lutes, or all organettos — have been taken at face value, whereas actually the depiction was of an allegorical nature. Similar misconceptions were provoked by the frequent allegorical representation of Psalm 150, of which Luca della Robbia's cantoria in the Museo del Duomo in Florence is a famous example. There, the various groups of angels, one playing trumpets, another psalteries, and so forth, are literal illustrations of the verses of the psalm, 'Laudate eum in sono tubae, laudate eum in psalterio,' and have nothing to do with actual ensembles. Even the combination of portative, lute, and harp is only an illustration of the words 'Laudate eum in chordis et organo.' Nevertheless, Arnold Schering accepted this relief as the depiction of an actual ensemble.[1]

Sometimes even the most crucial questions of organology have been 'solved' by erroneous interpretation of pictorial evidence. A flagrant case in point is the attribution of the first fiddle bow in the Occident to the Carolingian period by Curt Sachs and, following his lead, Georg Kinsky and, still more recently, even *Die Musik in Geschichte und Gegenwart.*[2] The basis for this dating is the illustration of Psalm 108 in the Utrecht Psalter (Pl. 17a). Here the psalmist carries two instruments: a long-necked cittern in his left hand and a harp on his left shoulder. The long stick is not a bow, but a measuring rod — 'exsurge psalterium' (the harp) 'et cythara' (the long-necked cittern) 'et dividam Sicimam et convallem tabernaculorum dimeciar' (I will divide Sichem and mete out the valley of the tabernacles). Regrettably, the Latin text has been ignored, and the

[1] *Studien zur Musikgeschichte der Frührenaissance*, Leipzig, 1913, p. 59.

[2] Sachs, *Handbuch der Musikinstrumentenkunde*, Leipzig, 1920, p. 171; Kinsky, *Geschichte der Musik in Bildern*, Leipzig, 1929, p. 32; *Die Musik in Geschichte und Gegenwart*, IV, 158, Ill. 4.

incorrect interpretation made plausible by showing only one-third of the meting rod in the illustrations.[1]

The illustrations in the Utrecht Psalter, as well as in a great many other psalters and illuminated manuscripts, have also been erroneously accepted as evidence of 'contemporary' instruments, whereas these manuscripts are often links in a long chain of successive copies. The Utrecht Psalter, though written in Carolingian times, is derived from a manuscript pre-dating it by three hundred years. No botanist would uncritically accept literally the evidence of *herbaria* — again, copies of copies — but organologists do just this. Even today the precise dating of many early medieval manuscripts is controversial, and caution is required in accepting their illuminations as illustrations of contemporary life.

One might perhaps expect that this practice of copying copies, with its resulting accumulation of distortions, would have come to an end with the invention of the printing process, which offered, for the first time in the history of civilization, the means of reproducing visual statements with a high degree of accuracy. However, while this invention was of enormous value to scientific publications, it did not have the same impact on the arts for the simple reason that the exact repetition of a particular object or, in a more general sense, of so-called visual reality, is not necessarily the artist's goal. Even those prints which copied frescoes or paintings soon after their completion often simplified or distorted certain objects for the sake of popularization. I will mention here only two outstanding examples among many: Raphael, in his *Parnassus* in the Stanza della Segnatura, based the rendering of Sappho and the Muses on thorough archaeological research, and borrowed their instruments from the famous Sarcophagus of the Muses, which was long in the Palazzo Mattei and is now in the Museo Nazionale in Rome. But when Marcantonio Raimondi made an engraving of it, he preferred to replace the true ancient musical instruments with banal and stylized specimens.[2] Similarly, Raphael's famous painting of Saint Cecilia in San Petronio in Bologna appears distorted in Marcantonio's engraving and deprived of its original meaning. In Raphael's painting, the instruments lying at the feet of the saint have been broken and the angels in heaven engage solely in vocal music, while in the engraving, the instruments are intact and the angels blast away blithely with fiddle and harp.

Even after the invention of the printing process, distortions of illustrations

[1] Friedrich Behn's *Musikleben im Altertum und frühen Mittelalter*, Stuttgart, 1954, reproduces, in Tafel 95, a larger section of the page from the Utrecht Psalter, showing the whole length of the rod, which is substantially longer than the player himself. Nevertheless, in the text (pp. 162–63), he regards this as the first evidence of bowing in Europe; from the excessive length of the clumsy bow, he concludes that 'in the middle of the 9th century, that is, at the time of the origin of this Psalter, bowing had just been introduced.'

[2] See Chapter 14 below.

accumulated through successive copies, due to the fact that woodblocks and copper plates for engraving wear out and must be replaced or reworked; too, authors borrowing illustrations from earlier treatises had to employ draughtsmen, and their drawings were again inevitably altered by the engraver. Examples of this progressive distortion may be seen in Pls. 88a, 88b, 82a, and Fig. 2.

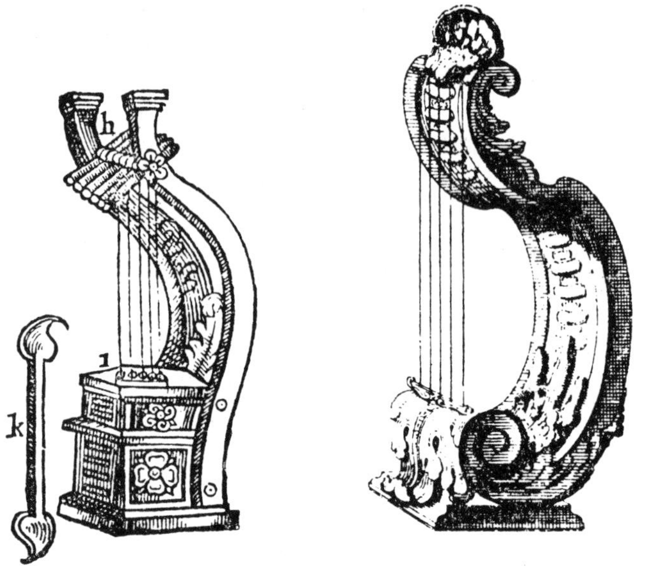

Fig. 2. LEFT: Kithara. From Mersenne, *Harmonie universelle*, 1636. RIGHT: The same kithara, in a later stylized version. From *Gravures en lettres, en géographie, et en musique*, in the *Encyclopédie ou dictionnaire raisonné*, 1751–65.

The study of Egyptian instruments and music through their pictorial representations has been comparatively free of such misinterpretations, because Egyptian archaeology began much later than classical archaeology, and with the immediate unearthing of an enormous wealth of precise representations in sculpture, relief, and wall paintings, as well as the excavation of a substantial number of well-preserved actual instruments from dry, sealed burial chambers. Of course, musicologists had been interested in the music of the Egyptians long before the large bulk of excavated treasures was available; Athanasius Kircher (*Oedipus aegyptiacus*, 1652, Bk. IV, Ch. 13, p. 426) mentions a 'lyra triangularis, von einem egyptischen Basrelief genommen'; and Burney, in his *General History of Music* (Vol. I, p. 204 ff.), includes a very large engraving of an Egyptian 'lute,' reporting that he had seen this instrument on the Egyptian obelisk lying in the Campus Martius in Rome, and that he had a drawing of it made under his very eyes. He also devotes almost two pages to the explanation of this instrument. This drawing then found its way into Forkel's *Allgemeine Geschichte der Musik*

(Vol. I, Ch. 2, p. 83). This 'lute,' however, is nothing else than a very common Egyptian hieroglyph, meaning 'good,' which uses an ideogram based on the shape of the windpipe joined to the heart!

One extremely frequent misnomer concerns ancient woodwind instruments. One can hardly blame classical archaeologists for calling ancient oboes 'flutes,' as they do when confronted with auloi and diauloi, but the same is often done by historians of music; even in Robert Haas's admirably illustrated *Aufführungspraxis der Musik*, Potsdam, 1932, double-reed pipes in Egyptian paintings are captioned 'Doppelflöte' (p. 5, Ill. 4; p. 9, Ill. 6).

Another source of bewilderment, a veritable *richesse d'embarras*, are pictures of early reed instruments, which are often interpreted as brass instruments — or, to use the more pretentious term, lip-vibrated aerophones — whenever the reeds are invisible. In the playing of early double-reed instruments with pirouettes, such as the shawms, the reeds were sometimes held, not between the lips, but rather in the cavity of the mouth, producing the same stiff tone that is peculiar to instruments with wind caps, such as the crumhorn. It is obvious that such a misinterpretation leads to a total misunderstanding of the timbre of these instruments.

Other frequent misunderstandings have arisen in the case of the flood of allegorical subjects in engravings of the late Northern Renaissance and the early Baroque, as for instance in the many religious musical allegories engraved by Antwerp artists beginning with the end of the 16th century, and above all, in the *Encomium musices* (Antwerp, c. 1595). Exact reproduction of the instruments is not the main concern of the draughtsman; the more striking or interesting the shape of the instrument, and the more varied and colourful the ensemble, the more attractive the composition. Yet such prints are frequently accepted as the gospel truth concerning both the instruments and their combination. Robert Haas reproduces one of these engravings, *Die Musik* by Philipp Galle, in his chapter on *Verzierungspraxis* (*op. cit.*, p. 115). The 'lutes' are downright fantastic; the 'zink' is no zink, but apparently a shawm, but with its protective cylinder in the wrong place, close to its bell; the harp has one of those undulating 'scrolliferous' frames, lacking any soundbox; and the strings care neither whence they come, nor where they go.

Finally, one of the most widespread misinterpretations of instruments in pictorial representations should be mentioned: that of small keyboard instruments. Surprisingly, this happens even with woodcuts and engravings, although as a rule the printmakers take the trouble to indicate such unmistakable features as the jackrail[1] of a virginal or spinetto and the typical curvature of the keys of

[1] See the *Musica* engraved after Frans Floris, reproduced in R. Haas, *op. cit.*, p. 132, Ill. 55, where the virginal is called a clavichord.

a fretted clavichord.[1] Amusingly enough, the reverse also occurs; an author, though himself entirely at home with the intricacies of a clavichord, employs for the illustration a draughtsman unfamiliar with the real mechanism, who copies another illustration and produces a jumble of incoherent curves (Fig. 3).

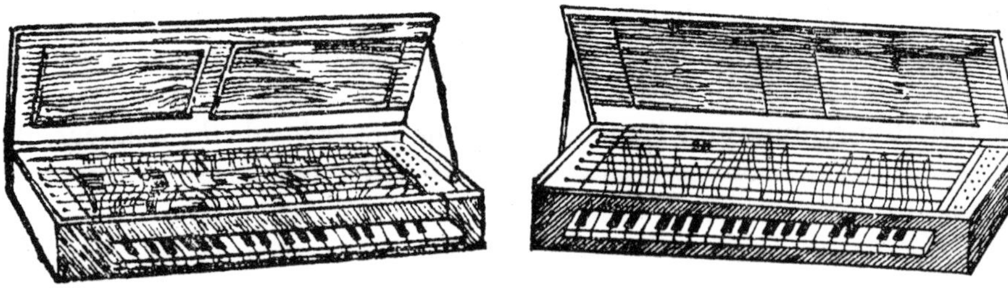

Fig. 3. LEFT: Woodcut suggesting a clavichord. From Virdung, *Musica getutscht*, 1511. RIGHT: Nonsensical copy of the same woodcut. From Martin Agricola, *Musica instrumentalis deudsch*, 1528, and used later as an illustration in Fétis, *Histoire générale de la musique*, 1869–76.

The information furnished by pictorial sources is by no means restricted to the field of performance practices, and, for the sake of brevity, a tentative tabulation of such data may not be amiss.

A) PERFORMANCE and PERFORMERS (Habits and methods of performance) — 1) Instruments, their shape and construction. 2) Playing methods. 3) Ensembles: *a*) vocal, instrumental and mixed groups; numerical proportions between the constituents; 'loud' and 'soft' instruments; the rules formulated for his time by Praetorius for the grouping of instruments in 'Accorts' or 'Stimmwerke' — these can be reconstructed to some extent by a comparative study of the visual sources. *b*) Use of written music for performance (choir books, part books, scores). *c*) Spatial disposition of performing groups (*cori spezzati*), polychoral music, placing of continuo instruments, etc. 4) Methods of conducting.

B) THE LISTENER — Placement of the audience in church or theatre; habits of acclamation; audience participation in the performance.

C) THE SITE OF PERFORMANCE AND THE ACOUSTICAL ENVIRONMENT — Here, pictures of rooms and halls, palaces and churches, theatres and even gardens no longer in existence are often the only source of information we have about the acoustical conditions of performance.

D) STAGE SETTINGS — Depictions of settings and decorations of church plays,

[1] See the admirably precise woodcut *Die Geschicklichkeit in der Musik* by Hans Burgkmair, in the book *Der Weisskunig* (*c.* 1516), in which the clavichord is seen chiefly from the back, yet sufficiently indicated by just a few curved lines for the keys.

intermedii, and operas are of significance to the modern performance and interpretation of these works.

E) SOCIAL STATUS AND ENVIRONMENT — 1) The social status of performers and instruments; social connotations of certain types of instruments and ensembles (typical high- and low-class instruments and ensembles).[1] 2) The role of the musician in society: court musicians, troubadours, minnesingers, jugglers, and beggars in early illuminations; the poet-musician, the humanist-reciter, and musician portraits in Renaissance art; the virtuoso as the centre of social circles in 18th-century and Romantic art; the professional, the amateur, the dilettante. 3) Types of ensembles and instruments associated by custom or tradition with various public occasions (weddings, funerals, receptions, festivals, *fêtes champêtres*, *serenate*, *notturni*, *cassazioni*, etc.) in contemporary imagery.

F) SYMBOLISM AND ALLEGORY (mystical, religious, erotic, political symbolism) — Here again, the overwhelming wealth of topics makes a systematic tabulation nearly impossible, but a few promising directions of research may be suggested: 1) Association of musical instruments with religious and cosmological beliefs; magical instruments in 'primitive' and Far Eastern art. 2) Instrumental concerts on the walls of Egyptian burial chambers. 3) Instruments symbolic of passion and reason in Greek mythology, philosophy, and educational doctrine (the instruments of Dionysus and Apollo; the symbolic implications of the musical contests between Apollo and Marsyas, Apollo and Pan, between the Muses and the Sirens; the significance of the invention of the aulos by Pallas Athena).[2] 4) Medieval and Renaissance representations of biblical musicians (King David and the elders, with their 'appropriate' instruments; King David with, successively, the lyre, rotta, harp, and lira da braccio). 5) The allegories of Musica from the late Middle Ages to the Baroque, and the instruments in the representation of the *Artes Liberales*; Pythagoras and Tubalcain with their instruments as traditional accompaniment of the allegorical Musica; the organ, clavichord, and harp as the instruments of Saint Cecilia in successive periods of painting.

Pervading all musical cultures is the erotic symbolism of musical instruments, especially of wind instruments and idiophones, traceable in their music and visual representations alike. The following are some outstanding examples: the aulos as the instrument of passion, urges, instincts; the aulos in the entourage of Dionysus, in the hands of satyrs, in drinking parties (Greek vase painting); the Dionysiac connotation of woodwind instruments (reed pipes, vertical flutes) in Renaissance art (as for instance in the woodcuts in the *Hypnerotomachia*; engravings by Marcantonio, Zoan Andrea, Girolamo Mocetto; numerous *trionfi*

[1] On instruments gaining and losing caste due to changing fashions, see Chapter 4 below.

[2] For a discussion of some of these questions, see Chapter 12 below.

d'amore; Francesco Cossa's Schifanoia frescoes in Ferrara; the numerous flute lessons, for instance in drawings by Lodovico Caracci (Uffizi), and other music lessons on the lute, theorbo, and virginal in Baroque genre paintings.

A special section of the broad field of the symbolism of musical instruments concerns their specific timbre as indicative of character, temperament, mood, and many other things. A few obvious examples are: 1) the timbre of reed instruments, often with drones, associated with the Nativity, both in painting and in music; 2) the 'heroic' connotation of the trumpet, traceable in the visual sources long before its absorption into oratorio, opera, and symphony; 3) the musical equivalent of the visible halo (for instance, Christ's halo suggested by string timbre in Bach's *St. Matthew Passion* and in the cantatas).

In many periods of art, the portrayal of the visible world, including musical scenes, is not a simple mirror, reflecting objects with photographic precision; rather, it renders or suggests them through various 'stylizations.' The artist is subject to many influences and factors that may interfere, in some measure, with the 'realistic' portrayal of the object. Some of these factors are of a psychological nature, others are rooted in traditions of technique or style, and still others are the result of the social environment in which the artist works. More precisely: 1) he is style-bound, born into a definite tradition with all its pictorial devices, tricks and mannerisms; 2) he is often limited in the choice of his subject, and in the manner of delineating it, by church or secular authorities and by the tastes and predilections of his sponsors and critics; 3) he is limited by his media and tools — stone or terra cotta, canvas or paper, brush or pencil, stained glass or needlework. Also, the two- and three-dimensional realms restrict 'realism' of portrayal in different ways. Depictions on the two-dimensional surface can represent the object from only one angle, and the various types of perspective used by different periods of art to create the illusion of depth must then be interpreted by the style-conscious beholder. Sculpture, on the other hand, does not easily permit the rendering of strings, the hairs of bows, and the like, and either omits these features entirely or suggests them in simplified form (Pl. 11b).

These are truisms, but perhaps worth repeating in view of a certain naiveté often betrayed in the 'reading' of pictures and the exploration of their 'objective content' by historians not steeped in the tricks of illusion that are part and parcel of the visual arts. The aim of the musical iconologist is to 'read' the work of art as a document, to concentrate on its material content and thereby see beyond the devices of stylization; to abstract, as it were, from the work of art just those elements which make it art. To formulate this paradox even more pungently, he should be an art historian, not for art's sake, but for the purpose of concentrating on the core and body of the image by consciously eliminating the subjective, 'disturbing' elements of style.

In selecting some outstanding examples of exact renderings of musical subjects in two-dimensional representations from the last five hundred years of Occidental art alone, one could mention the schools of Van Eyck and Memling; virtually all the Italian painters of *sacre conversazioni*, such as Giovanni Bellini, Carpaccio, Montagna, Fra Bartolomeo, and many more; Holbein's *Ambassadors*, with the famous likeness of a lute, in the National Gallery, London; Jan Bruegel's *Allegory of Hearing* in the Prado, with its nearly complete inventory of early 17th-century instruments; the many still-lifes by Baschenis composed entirely of musical instruments — not to mention the enormous wealth of Netherlandish genre paintings with their virginals, lutes, citterns, and theorbos. Though they all excel in their attention to minute detail and consistent use of linear perspective, they are yet surpassed, if this be possible, by the wood intarsias of 15th- and 16th-century Italy, with their many beautiful instruments.

The problem for the fact-finder is then to interpret the pictures 'correctly,' that is, for his practical purposes, and it may be useful to attempt an approximate tabulation of those factors which cause an image to deviate from 'reality.'

1) *Limitation of the medium of depiction.* For instance, in sculpture, strings are often not detached from the soundboard or fingerboard, or are omitted altogether. In woodcuts, the number of strings is frequently reduced, and other elements, such as pegs, are disproportionately large.

2) *Pictorial style of the period or of the individual painter.* An example would be the finger positions of the musician angels in the Isenheim altarpiece by Mathias Grünewald; an example of typical *chinoise* transformation can be found in Watteau's depiction of a vielle à roue (Pl. 26d).

3) *Carelessness or lack of mechanical or musical understanding.* Pseudo-lyres and harps, non-functional pipes, and many other acoustically impossible instruments, as well as ensembles composed at random and at the painter's fancy, are all too frequent.

4) *Requirements of pictorial composition.* One case in point is symmetry, often imposed by pictorial convention; for instance, the symmetrical duplication of instruments, particularly those of striking appearance such as organettos,[1] trumpets,[2] etc., or even of all instruments,[3] in order to achieve visual balance, at the expense of musical balance. Many examples are found in 14th- and 15th-

[1] As, for example, in the *Coronation* of P. and G. Veneziano (1358), Frick Collection, New York.

[2] As in the Florentine choirbook, *c.* 1350, in the Cleveland Museum, where the convincingly balanced string ensemble is overpowered by the flanking pairs of trumpets (Plate 1e).

[3] As in Bernardo Daddi's *Coronation of the Virgin*, Altenburg.

century angel concerts celebrating the Assumption and the Coronation of the Virgin.

5) *'Prettification.'* Rubens, who has no qualms in showing the puffed-out cheeks of a satyr playing the double recorder in his *Silenus* (National Gallery, London), prefers to show the fingers of Saint Cecilia elegantly hovering over the clavichord keys, rather than in the contracted position required. The problem confronting the painter in the conflict between the pleasant and the realistic was already clearly formulated by Giovanni Paolo Lomazzo in his *Trattato dell'arte della pittura, scultura, ed architettura* (1584; Bk. II, Ch. VIII). He recommends reckless realism at the expense of prettiness, an attitude quite remarkable in view of his manneristic leanings.

6) *Symbolic or allegorical significance of the painting.* This is a vast field, whose magnitude can only be suggested by a few examples. Number symbolism is frequent; Apollo's lira da braccio in Raphael's *Parnassus* has nine strings (7 stopped plus 2 open) instead of the customary seven (5 plus 2), thus alluding to Apollo's function as leader of the nine Muses, and possibly referring to the nine modes. Seven identical instruments are found in the hands of the apocalyptic angels and holy men. Number also plays a role in the numerous symbolic depictions of the nine angel choirs, and usually each of the nine groups is homogeneous — that is, devoted to singing or to playing the same type of instrument. In these paintings, the instruments are usually the exact images of contemporary ones, yet the 'homogeneous' ensembles offer no information as to usual ensemble practices. I have already mentioned the role of musical instruments as traditional attributes of mythological figures and saints; a main source of these symbolic connotations is the illustrated emblem books of the late Renaissance.[1]

Under this heading can also be grouped many of the allegorical and fantastic instruments and musical scenes in those paintings that represent or reflect actual stage performances (church plays, *intermedii*, etc.). The function of these instruments can frequently be clarified by the examination of contemporary instructions for the theatre workshop. Among the most important musical allegories in the visual arts are the representations of Musica, Poesia, Harmonia, and Auditus, all with more or less stereotyped attributes. To mention only one: a stag head made into a lyre in Filippino Lippi's *Allegory of Music* (Berlin Museum; Pl. 96b), evidently a variation on that traditional attribute of Musica, the stag, which symbolized velocity of sound.

7) *Archaic aims.* In periods of revival such as the Carolingian era and the 14th and 15th centuries, the artist will often fuse ancient models with actual objects taken from his contemporary environment. A characteristic case is that of the

[1] For the symbolism of the lira da braccio, see Chapter 5; for that of the bagpipe, see Chapter 4.

wind instrument held by Euterpe in Raphael's *Parnassus* (Plate 83). To comply with the archaeological ambitions of the time, it has the typical protuberances of the ancient Roman tibia, but at the same time it has the mouthcup and bell of a trumpet, the traditional attribute of Fama. This purposeful blending of two different mythological notions is, of course, acoustical nonsense.

8) *The fantastic.* Bizarre performances and instruments abound in the drolleries found in illuminated prayer books of 13th- and 14th-century Flanders, France, and England, and later in the Italian grotesques of the *cinquecento*. The works of Bosch and Peter Bruegel teem with demonic and humorous musicians and instruments. These depictions are often symptomatic of popular customs. One should also mention at this point musical caricatures, as well as satirical paintings and prints, pamphlets, and broadsides, some of which are full of information about the social status and political connotations of certain instruments.

In Italian Renaissance painting, especially in the large angel concerts, one often finds instruments that appear fantastic, and it sometimes requires more than a glance to establish whether they are: *a*) actual but rare instruments; *b*) common instruments, but smothered in Renaissance decor; *c*) instruments created *ad hoc* by the painter's brush, but nevertheless acoustically feasible (e.g. Pl. 21c); or, *d*) instruments which are grotesque inventions with no basis in reality. All of these types occur simultaneously, for instance, in Gaudenzio Ferrari's magnificent angel concert in the cupola of the Santuario in Saronno.

Other important factors that may blur the reliability of the visual document are spoiling due to time, and falsification due to inept restoration. Many telling details are often distorted or overpainted through a lack of understanding or a desire to 'prettify.' Unfortunately, the more famous the work of art, the greater the chance that it has been restored and possibly altered. The organologist in search of accurate documentation would often do better to go to out-of-the-way museums, which have less money for restoration, and see the correct shapes through layers of time-darkened varnish.

In addition to these factors impeding accuracy of portrayal, we must be aware that the popularity of certain instruments and musical practices is not necessarily reflected by their frequency of depiction in art. This is particularly true of periods in which most of the visual arts were of a religious nature. In such periods, folk music or secular court music had fewer chances of representation. Furthermore, large quantities of sculpture and painting have been destroyed by iconoclasm, war, and natural catastrophe.

In conclusion, and in view of the rapidly growing availability of pictorial sources, I should like to suggest at least a few *desiderata* for iconological research:

1) Critical interpretation with awareness of all the factors that might possibly have blurred the faithful delineation of the objects depicted.
2) Methodic evaluation of pictorial evidence, not in single isolated instances, but on the widest possible comparative basis, taking into account a reliable number of parallel cases, and making due allowance for contemporary local or regional variations in instrument building or playing habits.
3) Systematic distinction between functional and non-functional elements of instruments, and between those non-functional ones that are derived from decorative fashions or from atrophic remnants of once functional elements (carried through the centuries by the sheer force of habit or tradition).[1] Such distinction might help to pave the way for a morphological view of instruments throughout their gradual evolution.

Finally, I might suggest a few topics for research and discussion:

1) A comparative study of Near-Eastern parallels to the musical scenes in illuminations of the Carolingian period, especially in the Utrecht Psalter.
2) A new search for the origin of bowing in the Occident.[2]
3) The survival or revival of double-pipes in the Middle Ages and the Renaissance, and the question of the perpetuation of aulos practice in the double-oboe and double-recorder.
4) A study of the irruption of large and varied angel concerts into painting and sculpture with the rising popularity of Marian subjects (especially the Assumption, Ascension, Coronation, Mary in Glory), and a systematic investigation of the extent to which their instrumental ensembles are symptomatic of the contemporary evolution of polyphony.
5) The examination of Renaissance and early Baroque paintings to establish those scenes which are based upon actual or planned stage performances.
6) Re-investigation of the early history of the violin, especially through its documentation in frescoes and other art media, long before its regular production in more or less standardized shapes by the dynasties of the famous builders.

[1] I have tried to follow this method in Chapter 3 below.

[2] Since this was written, the excellent book of Werner Bachmann, *Die Anfänge des Streichinstrumentenspiels*, Leipzig, 1964, has filled this gap.

2 · The Knowledge of Musical Instruments as an Aid to the Art Historian

Nearly all the studies assembled in this book deal to one degree or another with musical instruments and instrumental practices as illustrated in painting and the other visual arts. In some instances, the paintings furnish valuable documentation for the organologist, showing instruments and the way in which they were played during periods from which few or no instruments have survived, or instruments which are valuable for comparison with specimens still existing. In other instances, the paintings permit us to draw conclusions about the current popularity of instruments, their religious significance, or their function as embodiments of symbolic meaning — for instance, the mythological connotations of certain instruments relating to Apollo, Dionysus, and others.

But whereas the visual arts present a gold mine of information for the organologist, the art historian, on the other hand, can draw manifold information for his purposes from the kinds of instruments, their players, their grouping, etc. Often the instruments represented provide trustworthy clues for dating a picture, since the invention of many musical instruments can be dated precisely — a fact which, fortunately, has been often unknown to even the most prudent and knowledgeable of forgers. One striking instance may be mentioned here. During the last war, the owner of a beautiful Dutch painting, apparently by Vermeer, came to my office at the Metropolitan Museum to ask advice about it. If anything was wrong with the picture, it was that it was too much Vermeer. It showed an old bearded beggar in a cloak whose folds half concealed a coiled metal horn. But the horn had valves, and valves, as any connoisseur of wind instruments knows, were invented in the 1830s. If the owner of the picture had publicized this information, the Van Meegeren scandal might have broken several years earlier than it did. Likewise, the inexpert stringing of a harp may contradict the attribution of a painting to an artist who is known to have been a connoisseur of music. Or the appearance of a drone string on a half-hidden instrument may reveal it as a lira da braccio, that aristocrat among polyphonic instruments — and reveal its player, dressed as a peasant, to be Apollo, participating in a pastoral masquerade. Or, to mention still another example, the appearance of pseudo-ancient instruments may prompt the interpretation of a Renaissance painting as one actually representing a stage performance of a mythological subject.[1]

An instrument depicted in a work of art may offer a clue to its interpretation if the instrument is an accepted attribute, or symbol, of the identity or status of a figure in the representation. Characteristic features of such instruments are often quite small or inconspicuous, but still, to the contemporary eye, the merest hint sufficed. We who come later need to acquire the knowledge that the artist took for granted. Beginning with the last decades of the *quattrocento*, most gods and heroes with a musical education, and likewise humanists and reciting poets, would have disdained anything other than the noble polyphonic lira da braccio. The same is true of the most elevated and sophisticated angels in the Venetian *sacre conversazioni*, and also of King David (King David with a psaltery, as in Raphael's *Disputà*, is one of the rare exceptions). There were many historical reasons for this, not the least important of which was the name 'lira,' harking back to the lyre of antiquity; in addition, its free-running, unstopped strings recalled those of the ancient lyre. The fact that bowing was unknown in Greek and Roman antiquity did not disturb Renaissance painters, stage designers, or musical historians because at that time the invention of the bow was attributed to Sappho; and did not statues and reliefs of Apollo and the Muses show them using large plectra — something, one might think, like bows?

The most outstanding functional characteristics of the lira da braccio are the drone strings (*bordoni*), which run outside the fingerboard and are held away from it by a little piece of wood that projects from one side of the peg box.[2] In Giovanni Bellini's *Feast of the Gods*, we can see only the small and rather inconspicuous shoulder of a string instrument held by one of the feasting peasants (Pl. 2). Yet the drone strings of a lira da braccio are clearly visible (Pl. 3a). No peasant plays a lira da braccio — the player must be Apollo, the only god who has this attribute. Thus a minute line, or a double line, can reveal a masquerade of the gods.[3]

In a drawing by Luca da Cambiaso (No. 13726F, Gabinetto dei Disegni, Uffizi), a naked youth holds a fiddle and a bow, the instrument only cursorily drawn and with no strings marked (Pl. 3b). But a short dark little line appears above the upper rim of its head. A word to the wise . . . ; it is the wedge for the

[1] See Chapter 16 below.

[2] See Chapter 5 below for a full description of the lira da braccio.

[3] See my article, *A Lira da Braccio in Giovanni Bellini's 'Feast of the Gods,'* in *The Art Bulletin*, XXVIII (1946), 114, where I tried to unfold the meaning of the whole painting as a feast of the gods, basing this interpretation on the presence of a lira da braccio. Later, two books concurred with my interpretation: Edgar Wind, *Bellini's Feast of the Gods*, Cambridge, Mass., 1948; and John Walker, *Bellini and Titian at Ferrara*, London, 1956.

drones of a lira da braccio. The youth is Apollo, since Orpheus is excluded for other iconological reasons.

If a little projection on the head of an instrument is the clue to its identification, this is because of the functional importance of this projecting part. But even a non-functional part of an instrument may be the salient feature for its correct symbolic interpretation. This is the case with a string instrument represented in Agostino di Duccio's reliefs in the Cappella delle Arti Liberali and the Cappella dei Planeti in the Tempio Malatestiano in Rimini. The instrument, a *quattrocento* cittern or cetra as revealed by the two little projections where the neck meets the body, appears in almost identical shape three times,[1] twice carried by gods and once by an allegorical figure, Musica.[2] One of the gods in the Chapel of the Planets is Mercury (Pl. 4a). Besides the cittern, he has all the attributes associated with him in traditional iconography:[3] the caduceus with the serpents, the winged feet, the rooster, and (less conventionally) the souls whose guide he is; they crawl between his feet and even try to climb the caduceus.

If we turn to the Chapel of the Liberal Arts, we find an instrument similar to that of Mercury, here held by Apollo (Pl. 4b). The god appears well equipped with his traditional attributes: bow and quiver, one arrow, and the birds. His instrument, however, differs in some respects from that of Mercury. Its head, decorated by a little carved *putto* face, is hidden by leaves, in fact by a whole cluster of laurel leaves, from which emerge the naked figures of the three Graces.[4]

Also in the Cappella delle Arti Liberali is the wonderful Allegory of Music. She is singing and holding two instruments, one a flute à bec and the other, again, a cetra (Pl. 5a). So here all the main realms of music are represented: voice, string instruments, and wind instruments. This cetra is the most elaborate and beautiful of the three represented in these reliefs (Pl. 5b). Its upper end terminates in a carved boy's head, and the soundboard is decorated in elegant,

[1] In the literature on Duccio, the instrument is not mentioned or is misunderstood, not only in Andy Pointner's *Die Werke des florentinischen Bildhauers: Agostino di Duccio*, Strasbourg, 1909, but also in the excellent description of Duccio's reliefs in Amico Ricci, *Storia dell'architettura in Italia*, Macerata, 1834. Pointner calls all these instruments, anachronistically, 'mandolins' (p. 97). Ricci calls them — in spite of their obvious identity — once a lyre in the shape of a viola (p. 467), another time 'cetra in forma di mandola' (p. 529), and finally simply 'mandola' (p. 533).

[2] Jean Seznec, in *La Survivance des dieux antiques*, London, 1940, p. 120, quotes from the *Comentarii* of Pius II the reproach directed to Sigismondo Malatesta about the paganism in the Church of San Francesco da Rimini (Tempio Malatestiano): 'He filled it with pagan works to such an extent that it appears to be a temple not so much of Christians as of infidels who worship demons' (*Comentarii*, p. 51).

[3] See, for instance, Natalis Comes, *Mythologia*, Bk. V, Ch. 5; Vincenzo Cartari, *Imagini dei dei degli antichi*, in the chapter 'Mercurius.'

[4] The Graces in Apollo's hand are taken over by Cartari, *Imagini*, 1571 ed.

extremely flat relief,[1] with tendrils among which are set two medallions having profile views of Sigismondo Malatesta and Isotta (whose glory, more than that of God, the whole temple appears to celebrate).

The iconologist, guided by the emblematic literature of the Renaissance and the results of modern scholarship,[2] may wonder what these strange little long-necked instruments have to do or to say when they appear in the hands of mythological personages, especially since they seem to be a world apart from the authentic and genuine instruments that were associated with certain gods and muses in antiquity — the kithara and the lyre. The cetra, as we have seen it in the hands of these three figures, was, in Duccio's time, a small instrument that, unlike the lute, had a shallow body made with a flat soundboard, a flat back, and side walls whose depth diminished from top to bottom. The body, in fact, recalled that of an ancient kithara, even to the projection at the lower end, corresponding to the more pronounced base of the kithara. The strings ran in pairs, and were usually struck with a plectrum. We mentioned above the two little projections at the shoulders, and one is tempted to ask what their function was. The answer is that they had no musical function whatever. They did not help in the playing nor in carrying the instrument. They are atrophic remains of the arms that carried the yoke or crossbar in the ancient kithara, and to which were fastened the upper ends of the strings.

It may seem strange, if not fantastic, to consider these two little pieces of wood as a sort of crystallized memory of a past at least nine centuries back. Yet an exploration of the history of the cittern, especially in its pictorial representations, reveals a gradual transformation of the arms of the ancient Roman kithara.[3] It was, in fact, a process of gradual shrinking, down to the inconspicuous remnants that survive in Duccio's citterns. These projections are not the only reminiscences of the ancient kithara. The instrument was struck by a plectrum, in the ancient kithara technique, and it often had a rudimentary base, as we mentioned above. Last but not least, there was the name, derived from the Latin 'cithara.' 'Cetra' thus meant cithara (kithara) to the *quattrocento*; a cetra in the hands of mythological persons was the legitimate substitute for the kithara, just as the lira (later, in the *cinquecento*, called lira da braccio) was the substitute for the lyre of the ancients.

[1] Such carving of the soundboard is not altogether imaginary. Actual instruments with such decoration existed, although there was always the danger that a soundboard thick enough for such modelling would not easily vibrate. An outstanding example, with no noticeable acoustical handicap, is the richly carved lira da braccio by Giovanni d'Andrea, now in the Kunsthistorisches Museum, Vienna (Pl. 31g).

[2] For the literature on iconology, see:

Erwin Panofsky, *Meaning in the Visual Arts*, New York, 1955; *Studies in Iconology*, London, 1939.

Jean Seznec, *La Survivance des dieux antiques*, London, 1940; English transl. by Barbara F. Sessions, as *The Survival of the Ancient Gods*, New York, 1953.

[3] For the history of the cittern, see Chapter 3 below.

If visual representations of musical instruments can be helpful in dating works of art, they share this quality with many other artifacts such as pottery, costumes, and carpets, all of which are reliable guides. But musical instruments can be helpful in still another way. They are often depicted not just as isolated decorative objects, but are held in the hands of players; and there are certain methods and fashions of blowing, plucking, bowing, and stopping strings or fingerholes, characteristic of various phases in the history of instrumental music. The contemporary painter is, of course, familiar with these methods; he may have been a musician himself, or have watched performers. Here I would recall the delineation of the bowing and stopping hands in Raphael's famous drawing of a player of the lira da braccio (possibly the famous virtuoso San Secondo; see Pl. 84b) as a study for the Apollo in the *Parnassus* of the Segnatura; or the finger position of the keyboard player in Titian's *The Concert* (Pitti Gallery, Florence).

One word of caution must be added here. 'Erroneous' instruments or playing methods can not always be taken as contradicting the authenticity or dating of a painting: one need only recall the mannered, theatrical, and highly 'unrealistic' way in which the angels in Mathias Grünewald's Isenheim altarpiece bow their fiddles, or the reversed shape of the beautiful organetto which seems to glide out of the hands of Saint Cecilia in Raphael's altarpiece in San Petronio in Bologna. (Normally the upper contour of an organetto descends from the longest bass pipe, at the left, towards the smallest treble pipe at the right, but this oblique line would have disturbed Raphael's composition.) Often, too, the art historian has to bear in mind that what looks unnatural to us may have been functional at some earlier time. A modern organist would never be called upon to bend his wrist sideways as players of Renaissance organettos do. They could not help it; in order to pump the bellows with the left hand, they had to hold one end of the instrument (that with the bass pipes) against their chests, and this in turn caused the awkward bend of the right hand pressing the keys or pushing the buttons, as in the case of the angel playing the organetto in Hans Memling's altarpiece for Najera.

The representation of a player's hand and fingers is a delicate task, requiring absolutely fastidious exactness and scrupulous observation; even a slight deviation in the design may result in functional nonsense. Unmusical distortions of this kind may be warning signals to the art critic, and perhaps lead to an investigation. An interesting allegorical painting attributed to Jan van Hemessen (Pl. 91) includes a musician with fiddle and bow. His right hand, holding the bow, is stiff and awkwardly bent, with the knuckles of three fingers resting on the ground and the index finger rigidly extended along the stick of the bow. No fiddler, even pausing in playing, would hold the bow in such a way. The suspicious art historian will look for an explanation, and with good fortune he will find that the whole figure is borrowed from that of the shepherd in Titian's *Three Ages of Man* (National Gallery, Edinburgh; see Pl. 90); there the shepherd, holding a little recorder, rests his right hand leisurely on the ground. Hemessen grafted the bow into a hand originally bent for quite a different purpose.[1]

Apart from musical instruments as mythological attributes, or as symbols of the social level (such as instruments belonging to angels, courtiers, peasants, beggars and jugglers), sexual symbolism is involved, especially with certain wind instruments. Such symbolism is based on their suggestive shapes, often on their intoxicating sounds, and frequently on both. From defloration and initiation flutes, taboo to women in the so-called primitive civilizations,[2] up to the intoxicating, reedy saxophone of our days (or nights), there runs an unbroken tradition of magic, religious, or poetic notions, all crediting certain wind instruments with sexual connotations and regarding them as symbols of fertility, birth, and rebirth.[3] The rapidly growing modern literature on primitive civilizations, especially on the ethnology of musical instruments and on folk music, is full of cases in point. The *locus classicus* in antiquity is Plato's warning against the use of the aulos in education.[4] And Hemingway, in *A Farewell to Arms*, reports on serenades in the Abruzzi in which flutes were forbidden: 'Why, I asked. Because it was bad for the girls to hear the flute at night.'[5]

Although these facts are well known and have been amply discussed, it seems curious how little modern iconology has drawn on them for the interpretation of paintings. The auloi in hundreds of scenes of revelry on Greek vases, and the countless vertical flutes represented in paintings of music lessons in Italian, French, and Dutch genre painting up to the Rococo, speak an eloquent and rather obvious language. But still, art historians have often misunderstood or even disregarded the meaning and importance of the flute in some very famous paintings of the Italian Renaissance. While the flute is not part of the official, conventional, pictorial idiom or language of symbols as codified in the iconological, mythographical, and emblematic treatises such as those by Ripa, Cartari, and Natalis Comes, it nonetheless appears so frequently as a conspicuous and unequivocal accessory in paintings with amorous topics that there can be no doubt about its connotation.[6]

[1] See Chapter 15 below.

[2] André Schaeffner, *Origine des instruments de musique*, Paris, 1936, p. 240 ff.

[3] See, for instance, Curt Sachs, *Geist und Werden der Musikinstrumente*, Berlin, 1929; the various investigations of Jaap Kunst; Schaeffner, *op. cit.*

[4] See Chapter 12 below.

[5] This passage was quoted in Curt Sachs's classic chapter on early flutes, in *The History of Musical Instruments*, New York, 1940, p. 45.

[6] 'Lascivious sound' has occasionally been imputed to other wind instruments as well; for instance, to the cornetto, a wind instrument that consisted of a wooden tube with side holes like a flute and a cup-shaped mouthpiece like that of a trumpet. Benvenuto Cellini, in his *Auto-*

Whether the representation of pipes implies an intentional borrowing from ancient sources, a case of humanist revival of ancient customs (as, for instance, instruments taken over from aulos scenes), is not an easy question to answer. Sometimes it is the aulos itself that appears in Renaissance painting and sculpture, copied from Roman sarcophagi. More often, this instrument is represented in mythological scenes by such substitutes as a pair of trumpets or a pair of *pifferi* (early Italian reed pipes) — that is, by instruments that were part of contemporary musical life in the Renaissance, but which could be arranged in the composition so that they gave the impression of double pipes diverging in aulos fashion.[1] They were represented as being played by two different people, or sometimes by a single person — which, in the case of trumpets, was of course nonsense. But most frequent of all substitutes for the aulos was the *flauto dolce* (also known as the recorder, or fipple flute), which happened to be a bucolic[2] as well as an art instrument.[3] We will restrict ourselves here to the flauto dolce and to three groups of examples that may interest art historians because they are well-known paintings: one of the Schifanoia paintings, Titian's Arcadian paintings, and an allegorical *tondo* by Veronese.

Among the *trionfi* from the frescoes by Francesco Cossa in the Palazzo Schifanoia, in Ferrara, is one of Venus.[4] It is filled to the brim with traditional astrological and mythological symbols, medieval as well as pagan — swans, rabbits, the Graces, Cupid — so many of them that it is almost surprising that they enhance rather than disturb the complex and graceful composition. In the foreground at the extreme right is a group of young people (Pl. 6a) — a pair kneeling in a tender embrace while the large group of their companions, young men and women, stand in a half-circle around them, watching seriously and curiously.[5] The girls at the extreme left and right each carry a lute, but the girl in the centre is holding, directly over the amorous couple, a pair of flauti dolci,

---

biography, reports that his father, an experienced maker of wind instruments, tried unsuccessfully to instruct his son in the use of the 'lascivissimo cornetto.'

1 See, for instance, Filippino Lippi (Pl. 94c), or the *tondo* showing a sacrificial scene by Giulio Romano in the Sala dei Venti of the Palazzo del Tè, Mantua, where two large pifferi, blown by two men side by side, produce the appearance of a double pipe.

2 See, for example, the satyr playing a recorder in double aulos fashion in Rubens's *Triumph of Silenus* (London, National Gallery).

3 On the recorder as an art instrument, see Sachs, *The History of Musical Instruments*, p. 302 ff. Sachs mentions that King Henry VIII, in 1547, left no less than 77 recorders in a collection of 381 instruments.

4 On the importance and symbolic content of the Schifanoia frescoes, see Aby M. Warburg, *Italienische Kunst und internationale Astrologie im Palazzo Schifanoia zu Ferrara*, in his *Gesammelte Schriften*, Leipzig, 1932, II, 471; and Jean Seznec, *op. cit.*, p. 175. However, neither author deals with the musical instruments.

5 Philipp Fehl, in a very interesting article, *The Hidden Genre: A Study of the Concert Champêtre in the Louvre*, in *Journal of Aesthetics and Art Criticism*, XVI/2 (Dec. 1957), 153, refers briefly to this

reminiscent of the auloi. The iconophile, confronted by the attributes of Venus in the same fresco, will not regard the flauti dolci as accidental.

Among bucolic scenes with flauti dolci are Titian's Arcadian landscapes and one of his paintings of Venus. In the centre of his Giorgionesque *Concert champêtre*, in the Louvre (Pl. 7), two youths in rich apparel are in conversation. In the foreground at their left and right are two nude women. The youth at the left holds a lute, but he is not playing it. Of the women, only the one on the right holds an instrument, a flauto dolce, and, again, she is not playing it. The young men do not pay any visible attention to the women.[1] It seems remarkable that it is one of the men who holds the noble lute, while the less decorous, not to say unladylike, wind instrument is held by a girl.

In Titian's *Three Ages of Man*, a pair of flauti dolci, in aulos fashion, forms the centre of the group in the foreground (Pl. 90). In the background an old man, sitting among skulls, symbolizes the evening of life. The infants at the right, in the middle ground, indicate the beginning. The two lovers in the foreground, gazing raptly into each other's eyes, represent the climax of life. Again, perhaps surprisingly, it is the girl who holds or plays a pair of flutes. Has the girl taken them from the young man? Vasari says that the girl offers the flutes to him,[2] but it would seem that he did not look closely enough. First of all, the young man himself has a flute, again a recorder, held in his right hand — a fact that has never been noticed by the interpreters of this painting and that alone excludes the assumption that the girl is offering her flutes to the boy. Furthermore, both of her recorders have their characteristic mouthpieces pointing upward towards her mouth, and she has the fingers of both hands on the fingerholes of the

group in the Schifanoia frescoes as 'an outing of young gentlemen in the company of courtesans' (p. 156). I would defend the young ladies against such a classification. This is, after all, a triumph of Venus; her power, we know, is irresistible, and making love in her presence is by no means a sign of professional activities.

[1] Philipp Fehl, *op. cit.*, p. 157, suggests that these women are 'not human but nymphs of the wood who, having been attracted by the music and the charm of the young men, have joined their concert. They are as invisible to the young men as they are, in the full beauty of the landscape which they represent, visible to us.' His explanation of the flute is that 'the music of the recorder recalls the sound of the birds' (p. 158), and that the recorder was an attribute of Poesia in the *tarocchi* (the Italian equivalent of the *tarot* cards). But the allegorical air of the *tarocchi* seems to me a world apart from the down-to-earth symbolism in the *Concert champêtre*. It is for similar reasons that I cannot quite concur with Patricia Egan's interesting interpretation of this painting [*Poesia and the Fête Champêtre*, in *The Art Bulletin*, XLI (1959), 303], in which she relates the two women in the painting to the *Poetics* of Aristotle and the Poesia of the *tarocchi*, and says that 'the meaning of the two nude figures must in some way have developed from that of the earlier one,' suggesting therefore as a title of the painting: *Allegory of Poetry*. If we take cognizance of all the girls with flutes in the pastoral scenes of the Giorgione-Titian orbit, it is hard to believe that these painters would have transplanted the respectable art of poetry into their sensuous Venetian Arcady.

[2] 'che gli offre certi flauti' (Vasari, *Le Vite*, ed. Milanesi, Florence, 1906, VII, 435).

instruments. Therefore, she must have just paused in playing. The flutes, connecting the two bodies as it were, have a twofold significance. They are the symbols of the amorous union; and the simultaneity of their sounds signifies the harmony of souls.[1]

The *Bacchanal*[2] in the Prado Museum (Pl. 8), Titian's rhapsody on wine, women, and song, has often been discussed and does not need a detailed description here. We will focus only on the role of music in it. The central place among the revellers is given to two women in the foreground (Pl. 9). In front of them, conspicuously in the middle, lies a music sheet with notation and the words 'Qui boyt et ne reboyt le ne scet boyre soit' ('He who doesn't have more than one drink doesn't know what drinking can be'). The music is a four-part canon.[3] However, no one is singing,[4] but each of the two women in the centre foreground holds a flute.[5] Curiously enough, the presence of these flutes, as far as I know, has not been given due attention before. The instruments are actually recorders, and those in the hands of the women are held so as to be in close and conspicuous proximity. A third flute is partially visible near the foot of the fair-haired woman in the centre.[6] Again, as in the other Arcadian pictures discussed, they are not being played. There can hardly be any doubt that these flutes symbolize an

[1] It is of this painting, and of the *Divine and Profane Love* (Villa Borghese, Rome), that Burckhardt says: 'Lastly, Titian painted two pictures without any mythological precedents, mere allegories, if you will, but of that rare kind in which the allegorical meaning that can be expressed is quite lost by comparison with an inexpressible poetry' (*Cicerone*, Basel, 1860, p. 975). One never turns to Burckhardt in vain. Although the genius of Titian seems 'inexplicable' to him, he is inspired to sum it up in perhaps the most monumental words ever written of a painter: 'The divine quality in Titian lies in his power of perceiving in things and men that harmony of existence which ought to be in them according to the natural tendency of their being, or which still lives in them, though dimmed and unrecognizable; what in real life is broken, scattered, and limited, he represents as complete, happy, and free. This is probably always the task of art; but no one any longer fulfills it so calmly, so unpretentiously, with such an appearance of necessity. In him this harmony was a pre-established one, to use a philosophical term in a special sense' (*Cicerone*, p. 967).

[2] Representing the feast of the Andrians after Philostratus (*Imagines*, I, 25), as Franz Wickhoff pointed out in *Venezianische Bilder*, in *Jahrbuch der königlich Preussischen Kunstsammlungen*, XXIII (1902), 118–20.

[3] It has been deciphered by Gertrude P. Smith in an excellent study, *The Canon in Titian's Bacchanal*, in *Renaissance News*, VI (1953), 52–56.

[4] Fehl, *op. cit.*, p. 167, attempts to identify the two youths in the left background as singers and points out the similarity of their dress to that of the two youths in the *Concert champêtre*. However, it is not quite apparent that they sing; they seem to be, rather, in quiet conversation with one another. Fehl does not mention the flutes.

[5] See also the sacrifice to Priapus in Francesco Colonna's *Hypnerotomachia Polyphili*, Venice, 1499, where three ladies accompany the cultic scene with wind instruments, two recorders and one piffero.

[6] This third recorder is difficult to make out in the shadows of Titian's canvas, but it is very clearly delineated in Castiglione's drawing after Titian (Bibliothèque Nationale, Paris), and Rubens's copy (Nationalmuseum, Stockholm).

utter abandonment to the senses. Also, by the way, a substitution of instruments for some of the four vocal parts of the canon would be quite in line with the performance practice of the time.

If we wish to focus on the symbolic connotation of the flute in the Italian Renaissance, we must deal with at least two different sources. One is of an intellectual and rational nature: the impact of the ancient authors, read, translated, and commented upon by the humanists. The other source is not humanist but human; not intellectual or literary; not an artificial graft. It stems not from a humanist revival of articulated legal, moral, or aesthetic preferences of the ancient world for certain kinds of music and instruments, but from the perennial underground stream of universal magic signs or symbols for elementary powers in human life.

These symbols are not attributes or conventional signs pedantically attached to the scene like explanatory labels, but are organic, self-evident elements of the life depicted by Titian. It is the golden glow of nostalgia for an Arcady far back in antiquity, and yet transposed into the vivid present; not an archaeological reconstruction, and not paying lip-service to the pagan past, but living fully, in a new harmony of lines and palpitating colours — the summer day of human existence, with the vibrating landscape and the sensuous flesh of the body all permeated by an inaudible music. And if this music is made visible by the representation of its tools, the musical instruments, these are organic elements of the magic substance conjured up by the master. Here we have no replicas of the pagan past, no renascence of ancient modes and moods of life, but a new unity of emotion — an artistic expression of *joie de vivre* stimulated perhaps by the recollection of ancient pictorial and literary models, but experienced in its fullness and in its own right. It is not a mosaic of humanist findings but a return into a paradise that was never wholly lost.

A study of flute symbolism should perhaps also include paintings which are not Arcadian or rural concerts in the strict sense of the word. Titian's *Venus and the Lute Player* (Metropolitan Museum of Art, New York) includes no less than four musical instruments (Pl. 10). The young cavalier sitting at Venus's feet plays the lute; Venus holds a recorder; a tenor viola da gamba leans against her couch; and, far back in the landscape, a bagpiper plays for the dancing crowd. Here we have no country girl, but a majestic woman bejewelled and crowned, with a winged *putto* in attendance. (This painting and a variant in the Fitzwilliam Museum in Cambridge are the only ones among a number of versions[1] that show so many instruments. The others have only one instrument, a large positive organ played by the cavalier.)

[1] Otto Brendel, in his very interesting study, *The Interpretation of the Holkham Venus*, in *The Art Bulletin*, XXVIII (1946), 65 ff., gives a complete list of all existing variants and old copies.

Of the instruments depicted here, only the viola da gamba has no player. Who played or is to play it — perhaps another admirer to whom Venus (if she is Venus at all) turns her far-away gaze? Or is it another instrument for herself? But no Venus is known to play a viola da gamba, or indeed any instrument.[1]

So much for flute symbolism in Titian's paintings, particularly the pastoral ones. A substantial number of contemporary engravings, though hardly suitable for reprinting, would readily confirm our interpretation of it. Thus, no literary evidence seems to be needed. The Greek and Roman bucolic literature was, of course, fashionable in the Renaissance. But apart from lip-service to the ancients, what description of actual life exists from that time? Living customs, like the air we breathe, were not usually topics of discussion or explanation. Cultural history is commonly written by later generations. Still, our problem of the etiquette of the flute was discussed at length, with humanist trimmings of course and yet with a half-hidden smile and in most elegant, suggestive language, by a great connoisseur of mores, Baldassare Castiglione:

> The human voice adds its charm and grace to all these instruments with which, I believe, the courtier should be acquainted. But the more he excels in them, the more he should stay away from those that once were rejected by Minerva and Alcibiades because they seem to have something disgusting about them.
>
> The appropriate time at which one can make use of that kind of music [the pipes] is, I believe, when a man finds himself in private and dear company and when he is not concerned with any other pursuits; but above all in the presence of women, because the appearance of these instruments softens the listener and makes her penetrable to the sweetness of this music and, at the same time, arouses the spirits of the one who makes the music. And, as I have said before, I like to avoid the crowds of indelicate people. But let it be understood that all this must be accompanied by tact and good judgement, for it is, after all, impossible to imagine all the things that can happen. . . .[2]

[1] Brendel, *op. cit.*, is rightfully puzzled by the fact that Venus holds a recorder, since this instrument is not among her attributes. In his search for the meaning of musical instruments and music, he quotes various passages from Marsilio Ficino, Leone Ebreo, Pietro Bembo, and Baldassare Castiglione on the relation between the different senses, specifically between that of the eye and that of the ear. They all concentrate on general aesthetic problems and do not seem to throw much light on the presence of a recorder in a nude woman's hand. The passage that Brendel quotes (p. 69) from Castiglione mentions the possibility that the woman may be a musician: 'Likewise with his [the courtier's] hearing let him enjoy the sweetness of her voice, the concord of her words, the harmony of her music (if his beloved be a musician). Thus he will feed his soul on sweetest food by means of these two senses. . . .'

[2] '. . . Dà ornamento, e gratia assai la voce humana a tutti questi instrumenti, de quali voglio che al nostro Cortegian basti haver notitia; e quanto più però in essi sarà eccellente, tanto sarà meglio senza impacciarsi molto di quelli, che Minerva rifiutò, et Alcibiade, perchè pare che habbiano del schifo. Il tempo poi, nel quale usar si possono queste sorte di musica, estimo io che sia sempre che l'huomo si trova in una domestica, e cara compagnia, quando

In passing, we should perhaps mention a symbolic flauto dolce in a Romanino fresco in the Castle of Trent (Pl. 11a). There we find an unmistakable antithesis between the allegories of sensuous love and chastity. Two representations are juxtaposed. The lower part of the fresco shows a beautiful woman, evidently Castitas, caressing a unicorn whose oblique horn is a conspicuous element of the composition. The upper part also shows a young woman in a pose parallel to that of Chastity. But this woman is extravagantly if not provocatively over-dressed; free strands of hair fall on her deep décolletage, and her expression is clearly seductive. All these features are eloquent enough to characterize her sufficiently as the opposite of Chastity. And to crown it all, there is one more piquant detail: the large recorder that she holds — but does not play — and which corresponds, within the composition, to the horn of the unicorn.

We should not conclude these remarks on the study of musical instruments as an aid to the art historian without citing an example of how a celebrated art historian, with considerable musical knowledge, managed to see in a picture things that are not visible, and to overlook others that were there. The art historian was Vasari, who was deeply interested in music. This interest of his appears not only in the cheerful frescoes with which he decorated his palazzino in Arezzo, but even more strikingly in his *Vite*, where he rarely misses an opportunity to refer to music whenever the painting he is describing gives him a chance. And he does not content himself by merely mentioning instruments or musicians, but often points out what only a connoisseur of musical practice would have known, describing accurately and with visible relish the musical importance of poses and gestures of players.[1]

How Vasari's musical knowledge helped him to describe and actually interpret — evidently from memory — a painting he could have seen only briefly during his visit to Venice, may be seen from his biography of Paolo Veronese (*Vite*, ed. Milanesi, VI, 373). The painting is Veronese's charming *tondo* for the

altre facende non vi sono; ma sopra tutto conviensi in presentia di donne, perchè quegli aspetti indolciscono di chi ode, e più, il fanno penetrabili dalla soavità della musica: et anchor svegliano i spiriti di chi la fà. Piacemi ben (come anchor ho detto), che si fugga la moltitudine, et massimamente de' gli ignobili. Ma il condimento del tutto bisogna che sia la discretione: perchè in effetto saria impossibile imaginar tutti i casi, che occorrono . . .' (*Il Cortegiano*, Book II).

[1] One good example of this is found in Vasari's life of Fra Bartolomeo, in the discussion of the latter's painting of the mystic betrothal of St. Catherine for San Marco in Florence (*Vite*, ed. Milanesi, IV, 185–86): '. . . two boys, one of whom plays a lute and the other a lira. The former is shown as he bends his leg to put the instrument on it, with one hand placed on the strings to stop them, an ear concentrating on the harmony, and his head turned up with the mouth slightly open, in such a manner that anyone who looks at him can almost hear the voice. In a similar way, the other boy, sitting next to him with one ear bent towards the lira, appears to perceive the harmony produced by the voice and the lute while he provides the tenor part; with downcast eyes, he listens to his companion who plays and sings. What an ingenious and understanding observer he is!'

old library of San Marco and which is to be seen today in the Palazzo Ducale (Pl. 6b). It is an allegory of music; we quote Vasari's lively description:

> There are depicted three beautiful young women; one of them, the most beautiful, plays a large lirone da gamba, looking down at the fingerboard of the instrument. Of the two women, one plays a lute and the other sings from a book. Near to the women is a cupid without wings who plays a gravecembalo,[1] showing that Amor is born from Music, or that Amor is always in the company of Music. And because Amor never tears himself away from her, he is shown without wings. In the same picture, the painter represented Pan, the God of shepherds according to the poets, together with certain flutes made of tree bark consecrated to him by the shepherds who had been victorious in the musical contest.

A comparison of this description with the picture reveals discrepancies. The lady with the 'lirone da gamba' (it is a viola da gamba rather than a lirone) gazes not down at its neck, but directly into the onlooker's eyes. The lady who 'sings from a book' has no book, or at least none appears in the painting. Likewise there is no 'gravecembalo' visible in front of the 'cupid without wings.' What we see is a small part of a box, and the awkward right hand of the cupid there does not give us a definite clue.

Yet Vasari's defective memory is not altogether wrong, and it is guided by a sound musical knowledge. The singer at the left, who evidently leads the three instrumentalists, appears to be reading her words and vocal part from a written page. Her glance seems to concentrate on a sheet or book hidden from our eyes.[2] A keyboard instrument would go well with voice, lute, and viola da gamba, and would conform to the musical practice of Vasari's time, although an instrument as large as a gravecembalo would less likely be found there in the open air than a spinettino. When Vasari saw the picture, he evidently perceived it in musical terms, and in his recollection pictured the ensemble as it could have been. (We won't argue too severely with him about the wingless cupid, although his reason for the absence of wings strongly recalls the assumption that the Egyptians must have had wireless because no telephones were found in their tombs! To dabble in mythology was fashionable in the *cinquecento*.)

Strange, however, is Vasari's attitude toward the flutes, and here he seems to have missed a point. The flutes may well be votive gifts from shepherds who were victorious in musical contests; indeed, Vasari knows his bucolica. But Pan would have welcomed a syrinx or two. The flutes in the picture are actually fipple flutes — recorders or, in the suggestive Italian term, flauti dolci. The

[1] Equivalent to clavicembalo, i.e. harpsichord.

[2] The seven instrumentalists in Veronese's *Marriage at Cana* (Louvre) all seem to be looking at written music, although only five have music books visible before them.

smaller is of square construction like a wooden organ pipe; the larger round one, in its oblique position, shows the fipple in profile. It does not require a Renaissance eye or imagination, nor a reminder of Giovanni da Udine's innuendoes in the fruit garlands of the Villa Farnesina or of the general fashion for more or less delicate pictorial allusions, to recognize here a discreet supplement to the figure of Pan-Priapus who, transcending his caryatid existence, squints amiably down at the ladies. Was the learned author of the *Vite* too solemn to mention frivolities, or was the serious Tuscan blind to Venetian mirth?

3 · The Survival of the Kithara and the Evolution of the English Cittern: a Study in Morphology

The history of the cittern, often called the English cittern, has been clearly traced back to Elizabethan times, when it was one of the most popular instruments, available in every self-respecting barber's shop for the convenience of the waiting customer.[1] England's claim to the invention of the cittern dates back to the Renaissance: as erudite a humanist and music historian as Vincenzo Galilei writes in 1581 in his *Dialogo della musica antica e della moderna*: 'fu la Cetera usata prima tra gli Inglesi che da altre nationi,[2] nella quale isola si lavorano già in eccellenza . . .' But Galilei cannot have read his Dante well, for in the *Divina Commedia*, *Paradiso*, Canto XX, the cetra figures in a wonderful metaphor comparing the formation of sound in an eagle's neck with that of a cittern:

Eccome suono al collo della cetra
Prende sua forma, e si come al pertugio
Della sampogna vento che penetra;

Cosi, rimosso d'aspettare indugio,
Quel mormorar dell'aquile salissi
Su per lo collo, come fossi bugio.

(And as the sound takes its form at the
cittern's neck, and as the vent of the
bagpipe enters its neck, so the sound
rose up through the neck of the eagle.)

Cetera (*cetra*) means here, of course, the cittern, not the kithara of antiquity (which was also called *cetera* in Dante's time, as it still is today), since the neck is described as the place where 'the sound takes form,' that is, where the stopping

[1] Thurston Dart, in his interesting essay *The Cittern and its English Music*, in *Galpin Society Journal*, I (1948), 46 ff., does not follow the literature of the cittern back further than the middle of the 16th century. He mentions the remarkable number of instruction books for solo cittern and suggest good reasons for the replacement of the lute by the cittern.

[2] Claims for Italy and for Flanders are mentioned in Dart, *op. cit.*, p. 50.

of the strings takes place. The metaphor could not be more telling! The names for old musical instruments are very confusing. The same instrument often had many names, and one name often indicated various instruments. The medieval vocabulary alone includes kithara, citola, cistôle, sitole, cuitole, sytole, cycolae, and later we find gittern, getern, kitaire, quitare, guiterne, guitarra. Which are actually the prototypes of the cittern and which those of the guitar? And are all of them children of the ancient kithara? Johannes de Grocheo (*c.* 1300), enumerating instruments, mentions the kithara and the gitarra side by side, and the *Speculum musices*, attributed to Johannes de Muris (1290–1358?), and recently to Jacques de Liège, groups together in a list of *instrumenta artificialia* cytharae, psalteria, and cycolae.

I will therefore confine myself chiefly to visual evidence; the representations of musical instruments in the visual arts tell a more reliable and, I trust, convincing story. I shall relate the story of the cittern in cancrizans, from its more recent, well-known forms back towards antiquity, on the assumption that it is certain non-functional features of an instrument — as of other artifacts — that reveal its evolution, if we can look at them from a sufficiently detached point of view. Musical instruments, like other tools, have to adapt themselves to constantly changing conditions and demands. They may develop new features and organs; usually, however, the outdated, useless features are not abandoned right away, but are retained through the centuries, and may survive, in atrophic form, for an incredibly long time. Instrument builders, and other artisans, like to continue to do what their fathers and grandfathers did, and so they preserve shapes, patterns, and features that once served a purpose, even though that purpose may now have disappeared, without giving the matter further thought. They may, of course, also be influenced by the fact that their customers expect the merchandise to have its traditional, time-honoured shape.

In Père Mersenne's *Harmonie universelle* (1636), although we find not a single word about the origin of the sistre — that is, our cittern — there are no less than three different woodcuts of citterns.[1] Mersenne concentrates on the different ways the instruments are tuned and played, but we are here more concerned with their shape. In Pl. 12a, showing the three illustrations, the middle instrument has a small, inconspicuous buckle at its shoulders, which otherwise rise smoothly enough from the neck. The cittern on the left has shoulders that terminate abruptly at right angles to the neck; the lower end of the body has a slight protuberance to which the strings are fastened. The cittern on the right has large scrolls at the shoulders and a larger projection at the bottom of the body which almost forms a base. All these minor features seem to be merely decorative; certainly they have nothing to do with the playing or with the

[1] *Harmonie universelle, Traité des instruments à chordes, Livre second,* Prop. XV, pp. 97, 98*r* and *v*.

musical function of the instrument. We find the same mysterious little buckles long after Mersenne, as for instance in Jan Steen's *Merry Company on a Terrace*, in the Metropolitan Museum of Art, New York, painted near the end of his life in the 1670s (Pl. 12b).

Tracing back the history of the instruments, we may single out certain specimens or depictions of citterns that have survived as examples revealing its evolution. Plate VII of the *Theatrum instrumentorum* in Michael Praetorius's *Syntagma* (*Tomus secundus de organographia*, 1618) shows two different citterns, the larger one with twelve double strings, the smaller with six double strings (Pl. 13a). Both are depicted in front and in side view and show clearly the small buckles. The same shape is shown in the cittern in the foreground of Frans Floris's famous allegorical engraving of *Musica*. Sebastian Virdung, in his *Musica getutscht* (1511), does not mention the cittern at all; nor does the versifier of Virdung's work, Martin Agricola, in his *Musica instrumentalis deudsch* (1528). Nevertheless, all throughout the 16th century the cittern was a fashionable instrument. One of the most beautiful and most lavishly decorated citterns to have been preserved is that made in 1574 by Girolamo de Virchis of Brescia (the town praised at exactly the same time by Vincenzo Galilei for its beautiful citterns), now in the Vienna collection (Pl. 12c). The buckles of this instrument have been skilfully absorbed into the Renaissance décor, while the neck terminates in a small figure representing Lucretia stabbing herself, and beneath her, at the rear of the neck, a fantastic mask impudently thrusts forth a large nose; this is the hook, which we will find now in larger and larger form, the farther back we go towards the early Renaissance.

Similar, but simpler, is a cittern in the collection of the Paris Conservatory. Here the nose of an animal head provides the hook, and the buckles stand out sharply from the smooth side walls of the shoulders. Several paintings of the early *cinquecento* (for instance, the little Giorgionesque painting of a boy in a landscape, attributed to Palma Vecchio, Lorenzo Lotto, Correggio, and others, now in the Munich Pinakothek) show citterns with more marked buckles and larger hooks.

The Italian *quattrocento* is an unparalleled gold mine for the organologist, for it abounds in extremely accurate depictions of instruments, often life-size or nearly so, in reliefs, in paintings of angel concerts and mythological scenes, and above all in the hundreds of intarsias in the choir stalls in Verona, Monte Oliveto Maggiore, in the doors of the Stanze of the Vatican, and many other places.[1] One of the most interesting representations of citterns is in the famous cantoria by Luca della Robbia (Pl. 13b). Since the panels of the cantoria all

[1] See Chapter 8 below; also my article *Alcune rappresentazioni di antichi strumenti italiani a tastiera*, in *Collectanea historiae musicae*, II (1956), 465–73.

illustrate the verses of the 150th Psalm, most of the panels are devoted to one instrument, which is then represented by several specimens, an allegorical grouping into ensembles which bears no relation to the actual grouping in performance. The relief with the citterns shows two specimens: in both of them the buckles are replaced, or rather 'preceded,' by large ears; the frets extend far out on one side of the neck; and the base has reached considerable dimensions.

These features are even more sharply defined in intarsias. One example is from the choir stalls in Monte Oliveto Maggiore, near Siena, made by the great *intarsiatore* Fra Giovanni da Verona. In the upper of the two half-opened shelves, there leans a large, bulky cittern (Pl. 13c) with a rather deep body of strongly curved outline, and a beautiful gothic sound-hole rose. The shoulders are set sharply away from the body, and two wooden 'wings' reach out from there into space. The seven frets are arranged in steps of slightly different height, and the hook behind the neck is emphasized in yellow-white wood. The strings are not depicted. Earlier in time is the other intarsia, or rather part of an intarsia, from the studiolo of Duke Federigo da Montefeltro, once in the ducal palace in Gubbio and now in the Metropolitan Museum of Art in New York.[1] This elegant cittern (Pl. 53a), casually resting upside down on a book, has a more shallow body with nearly straight sides that begin to curve near its lower end, and also a large base. Striking features are the large hook, the six frets in steps, and the nine strings minutely rendered in inlay. The horizontal line of the shoulders is much broader than that of the Monte Oliveto cittern and supports large 'wings.' If we turn this instrument over and rest it on its base, we can hardly fail to see behind its shape the spectre of the ancient kithara with its arms extending from the body: these arms have shrunk into the 'wings' of the more modern instrument.[2] Yet a thousand years still separate this *quattrocento* spectre of the ancient kithara from the time in late antiquity when the kithara was still in vogue. From now on visual evidence will be rarer and we must begin leaping from stone to stone.

We might well be tempted to think that our search ends here, and that the invention of the modern cittern should be ascribed to the early Renaissance, which took a direct interest in the culture and the arts of antiquity. Indeed the treatises of Renaissance archaeologists are full of theories about the ancient lyra and kithara. But rather than quote from treatises I would prefer to point out the impact of musical archaeology upon instrument building, as it is reflected in the visual arts. I shall cite only three or four examples out of hundreds of bronzes, reliefs, paintings, and prints. Sometimes the kithara shape is only slightly hinted

[1] See Chapter 9 below.

[2] The bulky, large-based cittern in the hands of Terpsichore in the frescoes by Spagna in the Pinacoteca of the Capitoline, Rome, also strikingly resembles the body of the ancient kithara.

at by indicating the 'ears,' as in the small pseudo-kithara held by the sorrowful Damon in the little Giorgionesque painting in the London National Gallery (Pl. 13d), or in a similar instrument with the 'ears' playfully suggested by the tips of decorative leaves in that largest of all angel concerts by Gaudenzio Ferrari in the cupola of the Santuario in Saronno (Pl. 14b). But this was only one of many ways in which the shape of the ancient kithara was borrowed and, with more or less fantasy, transformed by the artists of the *quattro-* and *cinquecento.* Filippino Lippi, who had deep archaeological interests and borrowed much from Roman sarcophagi, not only shows kitharas in his frescoes for the Capella Strozzi in Santa Maria Novella, Florence (Pl. 74c), but also invents lyre-guitars by adding a neck for the stopping of strings to the shape of a kithara (Pl. 74b); and Lorenzo Costa does the same in his mythological paintings now in the Louvre (Pl. 96a). A similar pseudo-guitar is seen in the hands of one of the angels in Raffaellino del Garbo's *Madonna* in the Dahlem Museum, Berlin (Pl. 14c).

The interest of artists in ancient instruments is manifest also in many drawings of such instruments taken from ancient statues, reliefs, and especially from sarcophagi: for instance, the drawing by Francesco di Giorgio of Erato holding an ancient kithara, in which both the instrument and the plectrum are rendered with the utmost accuracy. The model for this drawing is one of the Muses in the famous Sarcophagus of the Muses, formerly in the Palazzo Mattei, now in the Museo Nazionale in Rome. It was Raphael who later borrowed not only the figure of this Muse and her kithara but also all the other instruments for his *Parnassus* in the Stanza della Segnatura.[1]

As a matter of fact, this revival of ancient forms, and especially of the shape of musical instruments, in the *quattro-* and *cinquecento* was only one of many such revivals which have occurred throughout the evolution of occidental art. One, which we will discuss later, occurred during the Carolingian era. Another found expression during the first Napoleonic empire in the feminine vogue for instruments which were made to look like kitharas, but were actually played by stopping the strings against a fingerboard grafted on to the traditional shape (Pl. 14d).

These 'renaissances,' produced by deliberate and conscious selection from antiquity, are not the only form of borrowing from the past. There is also the hidden underground stream of tradition, unbroken since classical antiquity. And with this in mind, let us continue our voyage back towards antiquity.

The Queen Mary Psalter in the British Museum, dating from the early 14th century, illustrates numerous musicians, many of whom are playing citterns (called mandoras in the facsimile edition of 1912). We observe that the wings

[1] See Chapter 14 below.

are bigger again, and rounded now in true gothic style, while the bases take the form of the gothic trefoil shape. The instruments are plucked with a plectrum; this brings us one important step nearer to the ancient kithara. Pl. 14a shows one of these citterns side by side with a bowed vielle,[1] adequate proof of the absurdity of the old hypothesis that 'the cittern is probably a plucked descendant of the vielle of the tenth to twelfth centuries.'[2] We are fortunate in being able to compare this design with large representations of the cittern in sculpture. One of these, made about 1290, is in the middle section of the west portal of Strasbourg Cathedral (Pl. 15c). The fiddle played by the musician at the left in our illustration is a modern reconstruction; the cittern on the right, however, damaged though it is, corresponds exactly, with its large wings and trefoil base, to those in the Queen Mary Psalter. One century earlier, about 1180, we encounter the wonderful *David* by Benedetto Antelami in the Baptistery of Parma (Pl. 15d). David carries a large plectrum, and the shape of the whole instrument is now, except for the neck, precisely that of a small kithara. We have now reached the point where we can align this necked kithara with the type of instrument appearing in the Utrecht Psalter; the many string instruments illustrated in this Psalter were brilliantly analysed fifty years ago by Miss Kathleen Schlesinger in her studies of the precursors of the violin family.[3]

When we turn to the 10th and 9th centuries (the approximate date at which the Utrecht Psalter was written), we find rich pictorial evidence of the transformation of the ancient kithara into an instrument with stopped strings. The famous Bible of Charles the Bald, of the 9th century, shows in one full-page miniature King David surrounded by musicians. One of them plays a strange instrument (Pl. 15a): the bulky body has wings, and a neck over which run three strings. These wings carry merely decorative kithara arms, and the kithara yoke is replaced by a large ornamental and non-functional superstructure. The addition of a neck was one way in which to turn the open-string kithara into a stopped-string instrument; another way was to fill in the air space between the kithara arms with a massive solid wooden soundboard. One of the many examples of this latter form is in the Stuttgart Psalter of the 9th century, originating in northeastern France (Pl. 15b).[4] Here again the decorative superstructure is reminiscent of the yoke of the kithara, and the curving arms are retained in enormous ornamental wings. This, like the other illustrations of the Stuttgart Psalter, reflects contemporary musical usage; that is, native, barbaric — or, rather, pagan — tradition soon after it was modified by the

[1] Facsimile edition, London, 1912, Pl. 219.

[2] *Die Musik in Geschichte und Gegenwart*, II (1951), 1451.

[3] *The Instruments of the Modern Orchestra and Early Records of the Precursors of the Violin Family*, London, 1910.

[4] Facsimile edition, ed. Ernest De Wald, Princeton, 1930, f. 40r.

spread of the gospel, while our previous example from the Bible of Charles the Bald leans on earlier pictorial representation, thus reflecting an earlier stage of the transformation of the instrument.

The Utrecht Psalter is of the greatest value in this investigation because it depicts an unusually large variety of instruments, and also because it frequently shows the ancient kithara side by side with an instrument that has the body of a kithara, but a neck in place of the yoke; in other words, a cittern — that is, if we want to project this term as far back as the 9th century. The frets are usually carefully indicated on the neck, and the graceful curvature of the wings corresponds precisely to that of the arms of the kitharas near by.

Among the most important representations, we find:

a) in Psalm 147, the psalmist with a kithara urging numerous musicians, 'Psallite Deo nostro in Cythara'; on either side of him is a group of musicians, and in each of them appear both a kithara and a pseudo-kithara with fingerboard (Pl. 16a). On these fingerboards, or necks, one can clearly see the frets for stopping the strings.

b) in Psalm 150 (which we have seen before illustrated by Luca della Robbia, see Pl. 13b), on either side of the famous hydraulic double organ, are wind and string instruments, among which we again see these same instruments (Pl. 16b).

c) in Psalm 71, 'veritatem tuam . . . psallam tibi in cythara . . . ,' the psalmist himself holds the fingerboard kithara, and behind him a large kithara leans against what appears to be a roughly drawn hydraulis (Pl. 16c).

d) in Psalm 92, 'in deca cordo psalterio cum cantico in cythara . . . ,' we can relate the names of the instruments to the drawings: 'psalterium' indicates the harp, and 'cythara' our pseudo-kithara with fingerboard (Pl. 16d).

e) in Psalm 43, 'emitte lucem tuam et veritatem tuam . . . confitebor tibi in cythara . . .'; with only one instrument depicted (Pl. 17b), its identification as a 'cythara' is beyond doubt.

f) in Psalm 108, the psalmist carries two instruments: our fingerboard kithara in his left hand, and a harp on his left shoulder (Pl. 17a). The long stick is not a bow, but a measuring rod: 'exsurge psalterium [the harp] et cythara [our fingerboard instrument] . . . et dividam Sicimam et convallem tabernaculorum dimeciar' (I will divide Sichem and mete out the valley of the tabernacles). Regrettably, German organological literature has ignored the Latin text, and this incorrect interpretation is made plausible by showing only one-third of the meting rod in the illustration.[1]

As mentioned above, Miss Schlesinger has made a brilliant analysis of the instruments in the Utrecht Psalter, though I cannot follow her in considering these necked kitharas to be ancestors of the modern violin. At any rate, this

[1] See Chapter 1 above.

assumption seems less absurd than the hypothesis of Curt Sachs, still retained in *Die Musik in Geschichte und Gegenwart* and also followed by Friedrich Behn in his recent book, *Musikleben im Altertum und im frühen Mittelalter*,[1] that the cittern is probably a plucked descendant of the vielle of the 10th to 12th centuries. However this may be, the crucial question remains: do the drawings of the Utrecht Psalter reflect contemporary usage — that is, are these instruments of the 9th century? If they are, we now have reached the point where the technique — probably oriental — of stopping strings against a fingerboard had begun to rival and to replace the method of plucking open strings in kithara fashion. But, as is well known, the Carolingian era was an era of renaissance, of revival of 'classical' culture, and in all probability also of musical usage. On this basis, therefore, we would have to interpret at least the orthodox kitharas in the Utrecht Psalter not as a survival, but rather as a revival, of the Roman kithara abandoned centuries before.

However, there is still another, more convincing, possibility. Modern investigations have shown, with almost general consent, that the drawings of the Utrecht Psalter are based on much earlier models, probably Eastern and quite possibly Alexandrian, antedating the conquest of Alexandria. These drawings would then reflect, not 9th-century, but 6th-century or even 5th-century musical usage. This interpretation of the Utrecht Psalter, however, is based chiefly on the visual style of the drawings. If we had but one more reliable representation of a fingerboard kithara from the 6th century! It would not only push back the origin of the European cittern to the threshold of the ancient world, when kithara and lyre were still in use, as we know from other sources; it would also support the dating of the origin of the Utrecht Psalter in this earlier period. Recent work by British archaeologists has enabled me to find this missing link; an unmistakable cittern with atrophic kithara features (Pl. 17c) appears in one of the fifty panels in a large mosaic discovered in 1957 by the British School of Archaeology in Qasr el-Lebia, generally known today as 'Castle Libya,' fifty miles west of Cyrene, in Libya.[2]

This large mosaic occupied part of the nave of a church, but includes figures which are still quite un-Christian: for instance, a leaping satyr and the nymph Castalia. The panel which interests us here represents a musician holding an instrument with a long neck. The description in the supplement of the *Illustrated London News*, December 14, 1957, is perhaps a little naive: 'Everyday life is represented by a shepherd seated on a rock playing his lute, with a dog beside him, and his dinner-pot hung on a nearby tree. Despite the rusticity of the scene,

[1] See fn. 1, p. 33, above.

[2] I am indebted to Professor John Ward Perkins for kindly making available to me a photograph of this panel.

the musician uses a plectrum'! I won't argue with the dinner-pot, but I fail to see why an open-air occupation should exclude the use of a plectrum. Actually, the figure strongly recalls similar ones representing Orpheus. The instrument has four large pegs, although the mosaic technique allowed only two strings to be shown. What interests us most, however, are the atrophic wings curving away from the body in kithara fashion, and the large base. Thus, it is here, in the *6th century*, when the Roman kithara was still alive in Byzantine-Alexandrian civilization, that we can conclude our voyage, recognizing precisely the same atrophic features which puzzled us in the citterns of Mersenne and in 17th-century Dutch genre painting.

4 · Bagpipes and Hurdy-gurdies in their Social Setting

Every builder of musical instruments combines different roles: he observes, as an acoustical engineer, the invariant properties of vibrating matter, whether revealed by his own research or handed down by the tradition of his craft; he follows, wittingly or not, the vogue of his day; and, finally, he obeys his own personal taste, musical and decorative.

But these are not the only factors that determine the production of musical instruments. There are, also, different social levels: we see the instruments gaining and losing caste, passing from street singer or shepherd to courtier and perhaps back again. There is, moreover, the unequal pulsation of inventive life in the different dwelling places of men: centres of creative energy, courts and cities fermenting with competition and consequently with novelties, and quiet, remote mountain valleys where a hundred years are like a single day. There are, finally, the cultural migrations such as the infiltration of oriental civilization into Europe through its main gates, the Balkans, southern Italy, and Spain.

But above all, one is struck by the enormous influence that the beaten path of custom has. If the other factors form the fleeting and shifting surface pattern, the curls of foam, tradition is the regular beat of the heavy waves. Structural devices, playing techniques, even small decorative patterns such as the shape of soundholes are retained for centuries. Having seen a flute in an ancient Egyptian tomb, we recognize the same instrument in the hand of a fellah; just as we recognize in Torre Annunziata the very same wall scrawls, kitchen utensils, and children's toys that we had noticed half an hour before in Pompeii, four feet, or rather two thousand years, lower in the ground.

Among the most versatile instruments — at the same time stable and protean — are the bagpipe and hurdy-gurdy. Both are of remarkable age. Though at first glance they are as different as possible, after an adventurous history their fates intertwined, and they became so assimilated that they could replace each other in the same score. But before taking up their evolution, let us examine their structure.

In its simplest form the bagpipe consists of *a*) a bag, *b*) a short blowpipe through which the player inflates the bag with air, and *c*) one or more reed pipes through which the air leaves the bag, thus producing sound. The bag, which serves as a flexible wind reservoir, is made of the skin or bladder of an animal, usually a goat or a sheep; the pipes are inserted into the natural holes of the skin, where the animal's neck or feet were, by means of cylinders of wood (the so-called stocks) round which the skin is tightly fastened with a cord. The blowpipe, where it enters the bag, is fitted with a leather flap valve that prevents the air from passing back. The sounding pipes — primitive oboes or clarinets — differ in structure and function. One, called the chanter, is fitted with fingerholes that shorten the vibrating air column within the pipe and thus permit the playing of a melody. The other, which is usually larger, has no fingerholes and is therefore capable of only one tone — the continuous and invariable bass called the drone (a name also given to this pipe). The playing position of the bagpipe is well known: the player holds the blowpipe in his mouth, fingers the chanter in front of him like an oboe or clarinet, and squeezes the bag under one of his arms, thus regulating the air pressure (Pl. 20a).

The elements just described are only the minimum components of the typical bagpipe. Throughout its history the instrument has been subjected to various modifications, improvements, and complications: more drones have been added (producing the octave and the fifth of the first drone); the chanter has been doubled; the blowpipe, so hard on the lungs, has been replaced by the more comfortable bellows. In the British Isles even greater intricacies have been invented, one of the most complex instruments being the Uilleann pipe, also called the Irish organ.

As the bagpipe is an eccentric member of the woodwind family, so the hurdy-gurdy, being a sort of mechanized fiddle, is a capricious member of the great family of string instruments. The sound box may be that of a lute, guitar, or fiddle (Pls. 18a & 18b), but the strings stretched along it are neither plucked nor bowed, being set into vibration by a wooden wheel revolving in the middle of the sound box and turned by a crank at its tail end. The smooth edge of the wheel, which is coated with resin, serves as an endless bow. Like the pipes of the typical bagpipe, the strings differ in kind and function: there are stopped ones (the melody strings, or *chanterelles*) running along the middle of the sound box and open ones (the drones, or *bourdons*) running on either side. The melody strings are stopped by a primitive key mechanism, a set of stopping rods — naturals and sharps — equipped with little projections that press inward against the strings when the rods are pushed in (Pl. 19, and Fig. 4). Thus a full scale can be produced. When released, the rod falls back of its own weight. Consequently, as Pl. 20b shows, the hurdy-gurdy is played with the keyboard down. As the two melody strings are tuned in unison, each rod has two projections simultaneously stopping both strings. When there are two drones, they

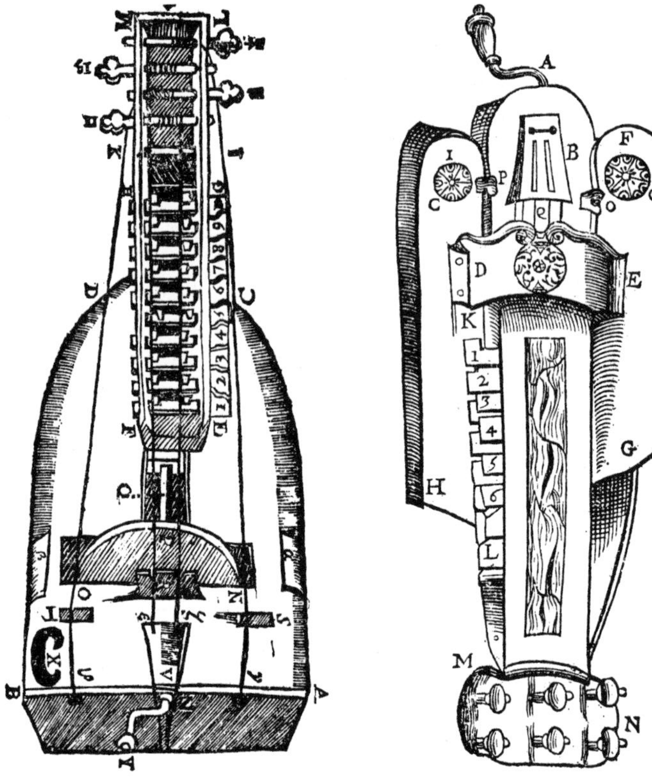

Fig. 4. Woodcuts from Mersenne, *Harmonie universelle*, 1636. LEFT: Hurdy-gurdy with open peg box and lateral pegs. RIGHT: Diagram of a hurdy-gurdy (compare with the identical instrument in Pl. 20b).

are tuned in octaves; when there are more, the octave is strengthened by an added fifth.

Thus it appears that our two instruments, so different in appearance and structure, have much in common musically. First, both are highly mechanized. In other instruments, such as the clarinet or lute, the player's lips or fingertips are in immediate contact with the heart of the instrument — that is, the agent of vibration: the reeds on the clarinet mouthpiece or the strings of the lute. But in our instruments mechanical devices intervene, the windbag in the bagpipe, the friction wheel in the hurdy-gurdy. True, this results in obvious handicaps: no such direct control of timbre and dynamics is possible as a clarinet or a lute permits, or even the bow of a violin, so responsive to the fingers. On the other hand, bag and wheel make possible something which neither lute or violin nor any pipes (at least in the Occident) can render — a continuous sound. This is the second analogy between our instruments: the bag overcomes the pauses between breaths, the wheel the pauses between the single strokes of plucking or bowing. The third, and musically the most important, analogy between the bagpipe and the hurdy-gurdy is that both employ the drone principle — that is, the accompaniment of a melody by an invariable bass. This principle is a very ancient one in the music of western Asia, where many instruments such as fiddles and pipes are based upon it. It has also played an important role in the development of occidental polyphony. We find it in the tuning of early occidental fiddles and, to mention the most notable example, in the open strings of the lira da braccio — the graceful instrument seen in the hands of Apollo and of so many angels in the Italian *quattro-* and *cinquecento.*

We have no means of knowing what emotional responses were evoked by music in distant periods; the habits of the musical ear follow the changes in musical styles. But the archaic contrast between a lively melody and a monotonously humming bass still affects us strongly and, strangely enough, with varying emotions. Sometimes it may be felt as restful, as in 19th-century music when it is used to convey a pastoral atmosphere, sometimes as exciting, as in the battle tunes of the Highland pipes. In the pedalpoints in classical and contemporary music there seems to be a similar ambiguity of expression.

It was particularly the principle of the drone that later brought about the most intimate relations between members of such distant families, but curiously enough neither the hurdy-gurdy nor the bagpipe had drones when they first appeared in occidental history. There is no mention of drone pipes before 1300. The hurdy-gurdy adopted drone strings even later — the precise date we do not know.

The bagpipe is much the older instrument of the two. The first traces of it go far back into remote antiquity in the Orient and in those parts of Africa which were subjected to the Persian-Arabian civilization. It seems that the idea of combining pipes with a bag must have been natural to herdsmen who had plenty of goats and little water and to whom the hide was familiar as a water bag.

Martial mentions the bagpipe, and from Suetonius we learn that Nero played the *tibia utricularis.* In the Middle Ages we find the bagpipe all over Europe, from the Mediterranean to Ireland, which indeed proudly claims to have invented the instrument independently of the Romans. Numerous manuscript illuminations bear witness to its popularity.

The hurdy-gurdy is exclusively the child of the Occident. When it first appeared in the 10th century, under the name of organistrum, it was an ungainly two-man affair (Pl. 23a), not less than five feet long and usually with three melody strings. The stopping mechanism was clumsier and slower than that described above for the later hurdy-gurdy. Instead of teeth, the small stopping rods had bridges which lay beneath the strings. To raise a bridge one had to take the end of a rod between his fingertips and revolve it a quarter circle. This was an awkward procedure, requiring two hands to achieve even a slight degree of speed, and thus a second player was needed to turn the crank. Moreover, with this method of stopping, the handles of the rods had to point upwards towards the player and so could not fall back of their own weight as in the later hurdy-gurdy.

It seems very likely that this stopping mechanism was an improvement on the

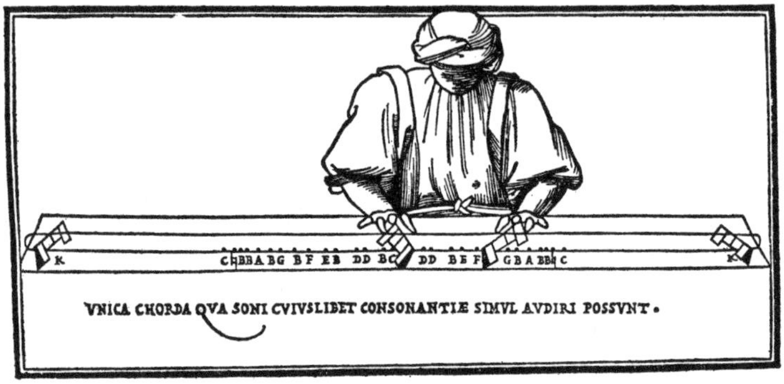

Fig. 5. Monochord for studying consonances; the two stopping bridges permit two tones to be produced simultaneously on a single string. Woodcut from Lodovico Fogliano, *Musica theorica*, 1529.

monochord, that venerable scientific instrument of the Pythagoreans and of the learned medieval monks for studying on one string the mathematical ratios of the consonances. The string of the monochord was originally stopped by means of a bridge that could be shifted back and forth. As this was awkward, several bridges were sometimes used (Fig. 5), and finally these were fixed in the proper positions to be raised by hand when necessary. One more improvement, the addition of handles to the bridges, would give us the key mechanism of the organistrum. It is worth noting that the great scholar and friend of Descartes, Father Marin Mersenne, found the hurdy-gurdy reminiscent of the monochord, which, of course, must have been an important tool in his acoustical experiments. In his *Harmonie universelle* (1636) he says of the melody strings that 'they act as an ever-ready [*perpétuel*] monochord, because they make all sorts of tones by means of the keys.' How the strings of the organistrum were tuned we have no detailed information, but there is reason to believe that the outer strings were tuned in octaves, the middle a fourth or fifth above the lower. This, at least, would be in line with the early forms of polyphony developed between the 9th and the 13th centuries. The beginnings of polyphonic music must have left their mark on the instruments of the time, particularly on their tuning. Unfortunately we do not know much more of that instrumental music than we can gather from depictions of the instruments. The early writers on polyphony deal mainly with vocal music. Their subject was the tabulation of rules for accompanying the traditional melodies of Gregorian chant with a second melody. Following those rules the singer had to improvise an accompaniment called the descant. The rules changed through history, but, very roughly, two main methods can be distinguished. One was the 'organum' found in the writings of the Flemish monk Hucbald (840–930); it prescribed an accompaniment in fourths and fifths — sometimes with the octave also added. The other, as found in Scotus Erigena (9th century) and again later in Guido d'Arezzo (about 1020), directed that the chant be accompanied by an improvised melodic line below, which started and finished in unison with the chant and often held the same note for some time with the chant moving above. The first method would correspond with the tuning of the organistrum described above, and the second method with the drone principle as found in bagpipes with drones. It might even be, though no documentary evidence exists, that at some time one of the strings of the organistrum was used as a drone, being touched by the wheel but not by the stopping bridges. This is the more probable as we know that early medieval fiddles had a drone string in the oriental tradition. It is worth noting in this connection that Scotus Erigena, the first writer on polyphony, was a son of Eire, where drones in bagpipes were supposedly used early. Indeed, Irish historians trace the beginnings of medieval polyphony directly to the Irish bagpipe. In any case, there is food for thought in the conjecture that the development of polyphony in theory and practice was connected with the introduction of drones to the bagpipe and hurdy-gurdy.

It was perhaps because of its harmonic, chordal capacity, as well as for its use in sacred music and in instruction in the cloisters, that the hurdy-gurdy was frequently given the place of honour in the assemblage of the twenty-four elders in so many French and Spanish tympanums of the 11th and 12th centuries. We find the organistrum with its two players at the summit of the 'rainbow' which — according to Revelation 4: 3–4 — arches over Christ, the organistrum thus being just above Christ's head (Pl. 23a). The elders, it seems, preferred the apparently nobler instruments, the stringed ones, perhaps because of the string instruments mentioned in Revelation 14: 2–3; as far as the writer can see, they did not touch a bagpipe.

In the 13th century the organistrum shrank to more elegant size and received the easier pushing rods, which could be managed with one hand, freeing the other for the crank. So we see it later in the hands of the graceful angel from the Saint Thomas Altar in Cologne (Pl. 27a). It is now called symphonia, or in old French, *chifonie*, from its being able to produce a concord of sound.

Hurdy-gurdy and bagpipe appear side by side in secular music and, if not in church music, at least in the hands of angels. Unlike the elders, angels seem to have no social prejudices whatever; like playful children they do not hesitate to take a juggler's or beggar's instrument for the greater glory of the Lord or his saints. In the *Glorification of Saint Francis* in Pistoia, by pupils of Giotto (Pl. 23b), we find several groups of angels before the throne of the saint, the middle group with string instruments, the flanking groups with winds. There is a bagpipe of considerable size, with an enormous oboe chanter and even a drone. To the right of the piper group an angel plays a hurdy-gurdy with six strings. It cannot now be ascertained whether this painting has been retouched, but if the six strings are authentic some must be drones, as the stopping rods could not very well have stopped six strings simultaneously.

We also find our two instruments in the miniatures of the *Cantigas de Santa Maria* of Alfonso the Wise of Castile (1252–84) in the Escorial. These form the richest collection of popular Spanish music of the 13th century and present important evidence of the influence of Arabic civilization, including music, on Christian Spain (though it should not be overlooked that Arabic music in its turn then carried a good deal of European, notably Byzantine, contagion). After having reconquered Seville from the infidels, King Alfonso became enthusiastic about the Moslem civilization and kept Moorish musicians at his court. Besides occasional musical scenes, the *Cantigas* contain a whole gallery of musicians — forty illustrations, most of them showing two players. In some of the pictures Moslem and Jewish musicians compete with Christian Spaniards. Lute and rebec still appear in their Arabic shape alongside instruments of occidental origin, such as the portative organ. The instruments and their manipulation are drawn with great care. Among them we find the bagpipe and the hurdy-gurdy. The latter is represented by two similar specimens (Pl. 22a). They have the form of oblong boxes, the stopping mechanism extending over the entire length of the box and the rods now placed away from the player, unlike those of the organistrum. Bagpipes appear here in an amazing variety. One form, the simplest (Pl. 22c), has only one chanter, elegantly decorated with a carved head and a slightly flaring bell, possibly of oxhorn. Another (Pl. 22d) is furnished with double pipes, of which the outer one seems to be a drone. This is the more probable as multiple pipes without a bag occur in other miniatures of this set. A third, the largest form (Pl. 22b), is fitted with two separate pairs of drones besides a double chanter — an unusually complex combination for a bagpipe of that time.

The Loutrell Psalter (14th century) also shows the bagpipe and the symphonia in friendly proximity (Pl. 21a). The symphonia has the form of a simple rectangular box. The stopping rods are of the older, clumsy type turned from above, though here with only one hand.

In the 15th century the hurdy-gurdy lost caste, but later it was still played by angels, as in the greatest angel concert ever painted, the famous fresco at Saronno by Gaudenzio Ferrari. Like his contemporary Leonardo, Ferrari was also a musician and, moreover, an imaginative inventor of instruments, as appears from the Saronno fresco and other paintings of his. Of the total of a hundred and sixteen angels glorifying God the Father, no less than fifty-seven play instruments. The fingering is depicted with the greatest precision and

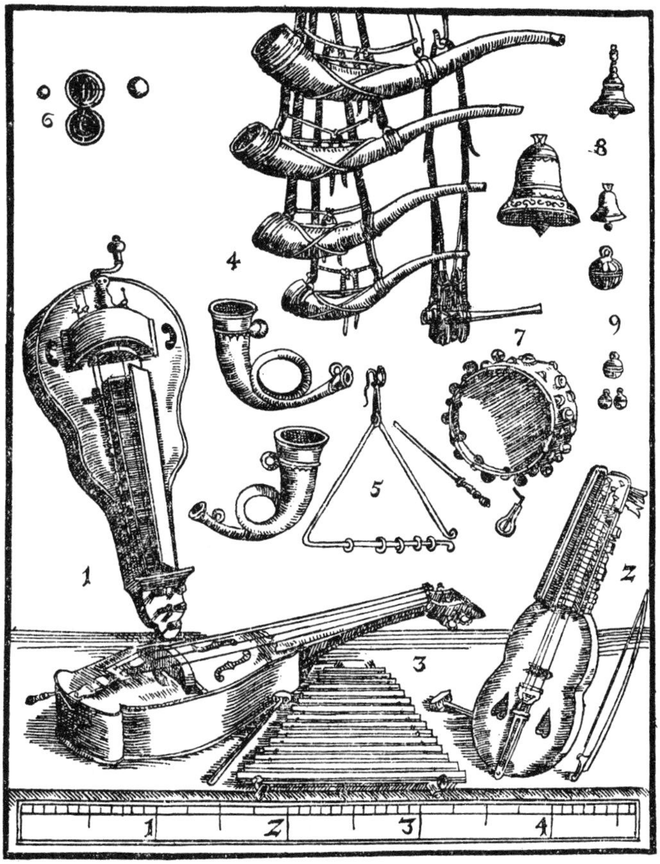

Fig. 6. Hurdy-gurdy and related instruments. From Praetorius, *Syntagma musicum*, 1618.

alone would reveal the hand of a painter musician. Plate 21b shows an elegant hurdy-gurdy, with three strings, to conclude from the pegs; Plate 21c a fantastic bagpipe with two one-hand chanters and two conical drones; it must have been capable of exceptional harmonic effects. A slightly later French woodcut, in the Rabelaisian vein, shows the hurdy-gurdy *déclassé* in the hands of a '*vielleur des maulx vestus*' (Pl. 28c).

It is interesting to observe how the earliest treatises on musical instruments evaluate the hurdy-gurdy. Sebastian Virdung in his *Musica getutscht und ausgezogen* ('Treatise on Music Put into German and Condensed'), published in

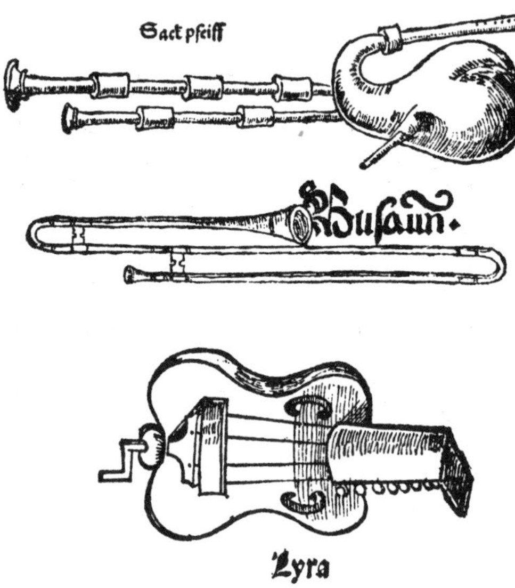

Fig. 7.
Woodcuts from Virdung's *Musica getutscht*, 1511.
ABOVE: Bagpipe.
BELOW: Hurdy-gurdy.

1511 in Basel, gives a woodcut of a four-stringed hurdy-gurdy (Fig. 7) but apparently does not consider it worth discussing in the text. The same is true of Martin Agricola, who reprints Virdung's woodcut in his *Musica instrumentalis deudsch* (Wittenberg, 1528), calling the instrument 'Leyer.' In the ominous year 1618, the first year of the Thirty Years' War, appeared the first comprehensive, systematic treatise on the subject, Michael Praetorius's *Syntagma musicum*, with many admirably precise woodcuts. Among them we find a five-stringed hurdy-gurdy (Fig. 6, upper left) and two of its relatives, a fiddle with a wheel but no stopping rods (lower left) and a keyed fiddle with a stopping mechanism but a bow instead of a wheel (right). The latter is still used as a folk instrument in Scandinavia under the name *nyckelharpa*. The caption for all three instruments says, somewhat deprecatingly, 'Some peasant lyres.' The text, without any discussion, merely mentions 'the peasants and vagabond women's lyre.' Shortly after this, in 1636, Mersenne expressed the same evaluation, though in more graceful and tolerant terms:

> If men of distinction usually played 'la Symphonie,' which is called *vielle*, it would not be as scorned as it is. But because it is played only by the poor, and especially by the blind, it is less esteemed than others that give less pleasure. This does not prevent my explaining it here, since skill does not belong to the rich more than to the poor and since there is nothing so base or vile in nature or in the arts as to be unworthy of consideration.

Two woodcuts from his *Harmonie universelle* are reproduced in Fig. 4, one showing an instrument identical with that in the hands of Georges de la Tour's *Hurdy-Gurdy Player* (Pl. 20b), the other interesting because of the open peg box with lateral pegs, a rather rare form obviously taken over from the rebec or the viol.

The bagpipe retained its status longer, particularly in the country of exceptions, the British Isles. We have reports that it enjoyed royal favour from Edward II to Henry VIII. On the Continent, too, it was used at courts and in the free cities, but on the whole it was the folk instrument which it has always been, played by beggars and at folk dances. The famous *Dance of the Peasants* (about 1568) by Peter Bruegel the Elder shows a large bagpipe with two drones (Pl. 28a). Its structure remains the same as that of the instrument played by Dürer's *Bagpiper* (1514) (Pl. 20a) and of the instrument illustrated by Virdung in 1511 (Fig. 7). A simpler instrument, with only one drone, is shown in Bruegel's *Fat Kitchen* (Pl. 28b). There can be no doubt about the social standing of the skinny piper, thrown out of the well-stocked kitchen by its well-fed inhabitants and their equally corpulent dog.

So far we have considered chiefly Western Europe and Italy; we should now glance at Eastern and Central Europe. There another type of bagpipe was in use and still prevails unaltered in the Balkans. It is the old Persian-Arabian type having a small double chanter formed of two cylindrical clarinets but no drones. Among the most striking decorative features are the animal horns attached to the chanter and serving as bells (Pl. 24a). Sometimes each pipe has its own horn, sometimes one horn embraces both pipes.

These East European instruments of old oriental type must have exerted a decisive influence in Central Europe, particularly in Germany, through the mediation of the Slavs. From a comparison of Virdung's (1511) and Dürer's bagpipes (1514) (Fig. 7 & Pl. 20a) with those in Praetorius (1618) (Fig. 8), it seems likely that this influence was exerted in the 16th century; for, besides the bagpipe shown in Virdung (Fig. 7), with a conical oboe chanter that reappears practically unaltered in Praetorius (Fig. 8, left, no. 7), we find there three new forms (nos. 6, 8, and 9) with small cylindrical chanters apparently identical with Eastern clarinet chanters. In Germany the instrument now underwent a strange transformation into the satanic grotesque. It grew, often into weird size; the hide retained its black fur; the pipes — not joined in the same stock but separated — were enormously expanded and with them the oxhorns which were attached as bells, the latter being sometimes lengthened even more by the addition of metal cones (Pl. 25a & b). This bagpipe was called the *Bock* ('billy goat'), and frequently the upper end of the melody pipe was fitted with a carved-wood head of a goat, which looked out convincingly enough from the dark fur. The old cloven-footed Pan, or as we might call him now, Satan, must have enjoyed this development. As the devil smelled of goat, so the bagpipe now smelled of the devil — 'Forthwith the devil did appear, for name him and he's always near.' The *Bock* played for peasant dances that must have been coarse enough. We recollect the even coarser dance of Walpurgis Night, when witches rode on goats to the Blocksberg to hold revels with the Prince of Hell in the

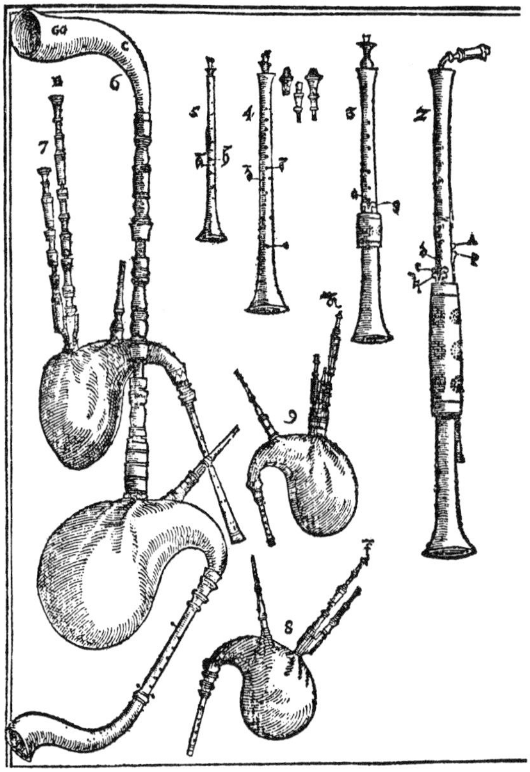

Fig. 8. Various bagpipes, From Praetorius, *Syntagma musicum*, 1618.

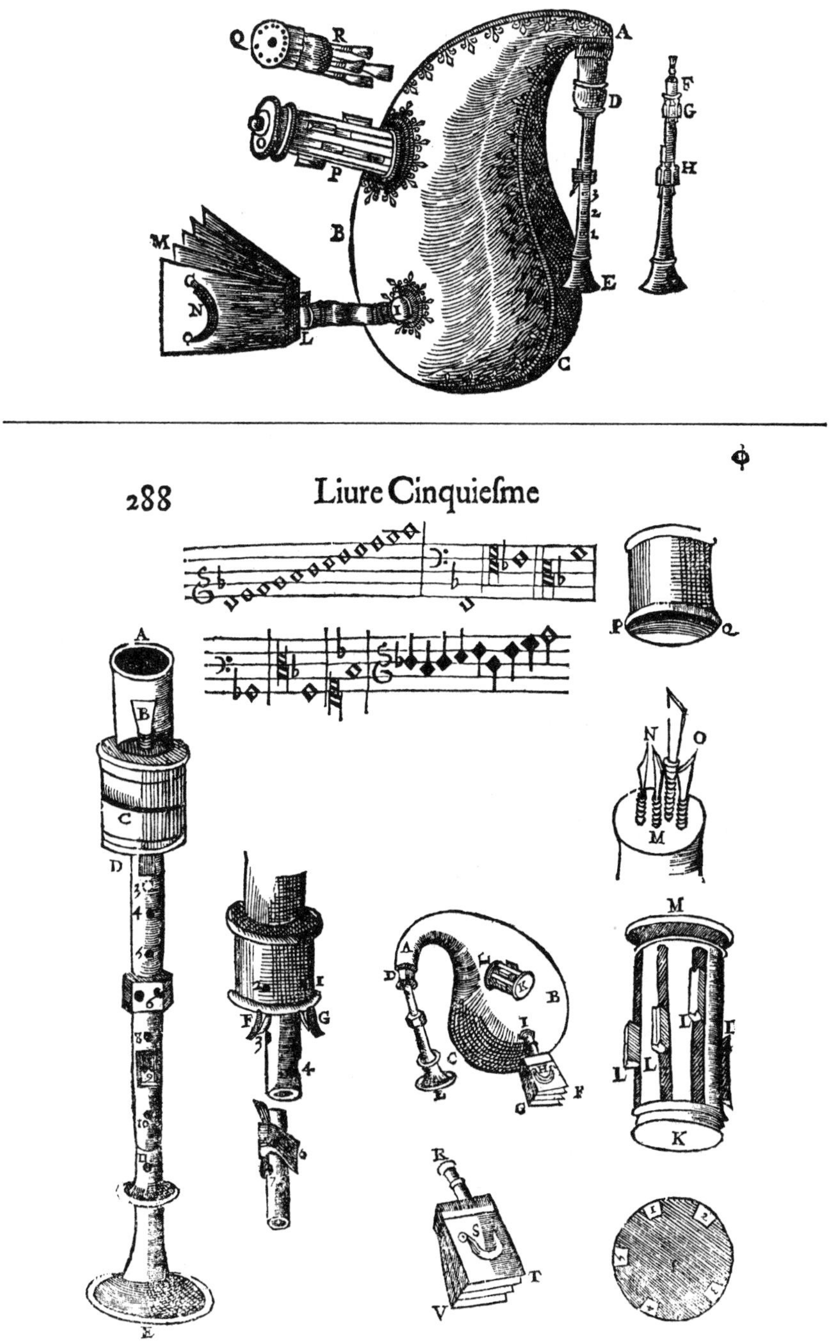

Fig. 9. Diagrams showing the construction of the musette. From Mersenne, *Harmonie universelle*, 1636. In upper diagram under R, and in lower diagram under N and O, note the four oboe reeds corresponding to the four drone channels concealed in the bourdon cylinder. In lower diagram, note the layettes marked L. The chanter shown is the form in use before Hotteterre's invention of the *petit chalumeau*.

guise of a gigantic goat — and all this in the heart of a Germany depaganized, we are told, long before.

The *Bock* had a sturdy life. Even in Viennese prints of Mozart's time we find street musicians with this instrument. Much earlier, in the time of the Reformation, the archfiend did not disdain to play the bagpipe himself. It was, however, a rather dainty one, a monk's head, apparently supposed to lure the faithful (Fig. 10). This woodcut is one of the grim political broadsides against the Church.

Turning again to Western Europe, we have to deal with one of the most decisive stages of the development leading to the assimilation of the bagpipe and hurdy-gurdy. It was the absorption into the pastoral fashion — or rather the pseudo-bucolic fashion — which put shepherd and peasant instruments in a refined and prettified form into the hands of the courtiers of Versailles. Two events at the end of the 16th century are of consequence for our story: the appearance of Giovanni Battista Guarini's pastoral drama *Il Pastor fido*, and the addition of bellows to the bagpipe.

The bellows is a very ancient tool; its story contains a good deal of the history of civilization. It was originally connected not with music but with fire, serving

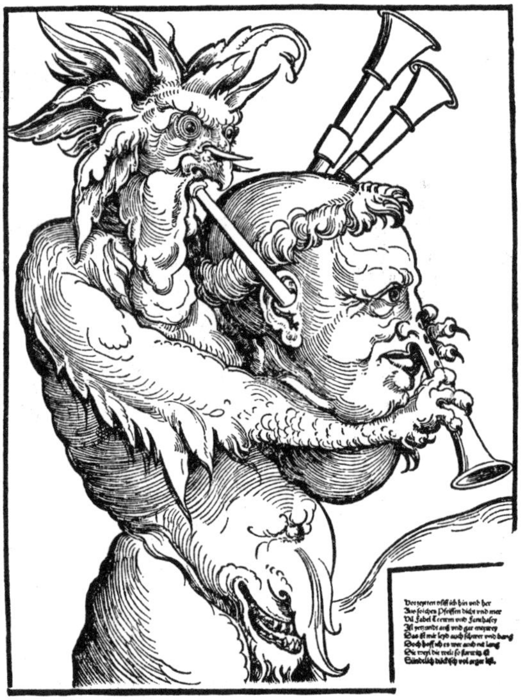

Fig. 10. German woodcut, c. 1535.

forges, furnaces, and foundries. It helped to melt metal in Thebes in 1500 B.C. Pyramidal bellows were known to the Romans. Bellows were added to bagpipes in the last quarter of the 16th century, either in Ireland, as the Irish claim, or probably before, in Central Europe, as a bagpipe with bellows still in existence is mentioned in the inventory of the collection of Duke Ferdinand of Tyrol (Schloss Ambras in the Tyrol) taken after his death. It may seem almost absurd that bellows found their way to the bag that late; they are so convenient and besides they had been connected with a musical instrument, the organ, for almost two thousand years. But technical inventions, as history proves, must be timely; if they do not fill a pre-existing need, they are not absorbed by their age.

This need, in our case the application of bellows to bagpipes, was brought about by the pastoral fashion in the Latin countries of Europe. The story of conventional bucolics cannot be written here: a few reminders must suffice. Nature as the subject of fashion is by no means peculiar to the 17th and 18th centuries. Every advanced epoch of urban civilization has had its *retour à la nature* as an antidote. Old Pan never died. It is the legendary herdsman, Daphnis, of whom Thyrsis sings to his goatherd in Theocritus's *Bucolics*. There is an almost uninterrupted chain of attitudes toward nature from Virgil's *Eclogues* to the French Rococo: mystical, philosophical, or merely recreational retreats to the innocence of nature. We may mention at random Saint Francis's praise of Brother Wind and Sister Water; Petrarch's wonderful descriptions of the Bay of Spezia and the woods of Reggio; Boccaccio's *Ninfale fiesolano*; the landscape backgrounds of Antonello da Messina, Giovanni Bellini, Filippo Lippi.

The most influential early work of the *poesia boschereccia* was Sannazzaro's *Arcadia* (1504). It presents contests on the *humile fistula di coridone* ('the humble pipe of Corydon') and, as an epilogue, a 'Farewell to the Zampogna' — the bagpipe of the South and Central Italian mountain people. Then follow in Western Europe, to mention only the most outstanding, Remi Belleau's *Bergerie* (1565), Tasso's *Aminta* (1573), Spenser's *Shepheardes Calender* (1579), and Cervantes's *Galatea* (1584). True, there is much imitation of the ancient classics in these works. But on the other hand we feel in them a good deal of real nostalgia for nature, just as we find it later in the Aeolian harps of the dying 18th century, the romantic horns of Weber's *Freischütz* and Mendelssohn's music for *A Midsummer Night's Dream*, French *plein-air* painting, and Debussy's *Après-midi d'un faune*. We cannot help recalling how much our own time is also imbued with an innocent longing for nature, to be satisfied, it is true, in the mill of mass amusement by *Ersatz*, by jungle and South Sea pictures and cartoons, by Tarzan and his Jane.

A quite different spirit permeated the French pastoral fashion of the 17th and 18th centuries. It was rustic life conventionalized as a pleasant game for the nobility. Its upbeat was Guarini's *Pastor fido* (1590), strangely enough the very same poem that was the finale of pastoral poesy in Italy. *Il Pastor fido* is a pastoral drama, its stage in Arcadia, but in it country life is far from being naive or innocent shepherdry. It is rather a slightly veiled satire contrasting the corruption of the court of Ferrara with blameless rural life, and it was this which made *Il Pastor fido* the enormous literary success that it was. It mirrored its time, decadent and dissolute, and became the textbook of feigned innocence, and probably it was no gross exaggeration for a contemporary voice to state that it had done more harm to Christendom by its blandishments than Luther by his heresy.

Of this brand was the rustic fashion that pervaded the court life of France. What a spectacle — a noble society that has conventionalized even its vices! There is some grandeur in it, no doubt: classical balance is carried to extremes, with Apollo entertaining Dionysus. It may be a triumph of civilization to rationalize even passion, but this triumph is dangerous, for moral boundaries are blurred when sins become socially acceptable.

The fashionable shepherds, smelling rather of perfume than of the stable, took over the pastoral bagpipe along with the hats and ribbons. This folk instrument, as it then was, did not, of course, fit the hands of courtiers. It had to be refined: its most awkward, heavy parts, particularly the drones, were reduced; the chanter became smaller in size and sweeter in tone and received more conveniently spaced fingerholes and, later, even keys; and, as mentioned before, the blowpipe, unbecoming to a lady's mouth, was replaced by bellows. Thus arose the musette, which remained in vogue from the early 17th century until almost the end of the *ancien régime*. The story of its gradual refinement would form a chapter in itself. How great a reduction in size took place one can realize by comparing the musette (Pl. 24b) with the gigantic Italian zampogna still played in the Abruzzi (Pl. 27c).

The contraction of the long drones of earlier bagpipes was achieved through the adaptation of an ingenious instrument, the rackett, also called ranket or sausage bassoon. This instrument, which can be traced back to the late Renaissance, consisted of a short wooden or ivory barrel within which a cylindrical bore of remarkable length was bent several times in U-shape and fitted with an oboe reed. Now it was constructed so as to enclose the drones of the bagpipe: instead of a single bore, there were several independent ones, each fitted with an oboe reed. This is the drone cylinder, or bourdon, which is found in the musette. Mersenne's woodcuts show four drones concealed in the bourdon (Fig. 9). Later the number grew to six. Each of the drones could be tuned by an ivory slide (*layette*) running in a groove along the bourdon. About 1650 Jean Hotteterre, the founder of a dynasty of instrument makers and virtuosos (flutists, oboists, and hurdy-gurdy players), added to the chanter of the musette a smaller chanter which ran alongside the other and extended its compass upwards. The chanters were now called *le grand* and *le petit chalumeau*. This fully developed form of the musette appears regularly in Watteau's *fêtes champêtres* (see Pl. 26a & b). The earlier form is found, for example, in Van Dyck's portrait of a French nobleman (Pl. 27b). Nothing was spared in decorating the musette with the finest material. The leather bag was covered with brocade or velvet; rosewood and ivory were used for the pipes; ribbons and tassels were added.

These refinements affected another, simpler type: the cornemuse, a bagpipe that still retained its blowpipe but reduced its drone, so that it lay alongside the chanter in the same stock (Pl. 29b).

The importance and diffusion of the musette were enormous and perhaps comparable to those of the saxophone and the jazz trumpet in our times. In *fêtes rustiques* and in the ballet it was indispensable. Lully soon took it into his opera orchestra. Its most rapid rise took place under Louis XIV: the king himself danced to the musette in the court ballet; it was used in the orchestra of the Grand Écurie. Learned treatises were written on it. The first systematic method appeared anonymously in 1672 in Lyons, the *Traité de la musette*, 'with a new method for easy and quick self-instruction.' Its author was the jurist Charles Emmanuel Borjon, 'avocat au parlement de Paris,' known for his *Compilations du droit romain, du droit français, et du droit canon*. A characteristic passage from the *Traité* runs as follows:

> There is nothing so common nowadays as to see the nobility, especially those who spend much time in the country, finding enjoyment in playing the musette. How many worthy men of science and affairs relax their minds by this charming exercise, and how many women make the effort to add to their other good qualities that of playing the musette.

Later, in 1737, there followed the *Nouvelle Méthode pour la musette* by Jacques Hotteterre Le Romain, the grandson of Jean Hotteterre, inventor of the *petit chalumeau*. The number of compositions for the musette is legion: it suffices to mention those of the three brothers Chédeville, who wrote for this instrument *concerts champêtres*, *symphonies*, *sonates*, *duos gallantes*, *fêtes pastorales*, *gallanteries amusantes*, as well as *Les Pantomimes italiennes dansées à l'Académie royale de musique, mises pour la musette, vielle, flute traversière, et hautbois*.

The rise of the hurdy-gurdy (in French, *vielle à roue*) followed that of the musette. The climax, it seems, came under Louis XV. Two wandering virtuosos,

Janot and La Rose, excited the nobility. The queen herself, Marie Leszczynska, was a famous amateur of the vielle. In the arts it is found even in chinoiseries; an engraving after Watteau shows a chinoiserie vielle probably never built in reality (Pl. 26d).

The vielle did not have to undergo such essential changes as the musette to become courtly and convenient. It had shrunk in size in the 13th century, as we have seen, but its range now had to be expanded. The famous virtuoso Charles Baton increased the number of stopping rods to twenty-three, that is, two tones less than two octaves. This made the range of the vielle equivalent to that of the chanter of the musette. In 1757 Charles Baton published a *Mémoire sur la vielle* in the *Mercure de France.* In 1741 the Abbé Terrasson, professor of Greek and Latin philosophy at the Collège de France, had published his learned *Dissertation sur la vielle.* In 1763 there appeared a *Méthode pour jouer la vielle, instrument agréable, brilliant et bon pour jouer seul et faire danser*, by Michel Corette. We have reports that innumerable lutes, theorbos, and guitars were rebuilt into vielles by adding a wheel and stopping mechanism. One can only guess how many magnificent Renaissance instruments fell victims to this fashion.

In Watteau we find occasionally the two drone instruments, vielle and musette, side by side (Pl. 26c), but their gradual convergence is evident from the increasing number of scores first with parts for both and later parts to be played by either one *ad libitum.* Already the great Antonio Vivaldi had composed *Il Pastor fido, Sonates pour la musette, vielle, etc.* (Op. XIIIa). About 1700 Esprit Philippe Chédeville, known as le Cadet, the second of the three brothers mentioned before, published *Les Déffis, ou l'Étude amusante pour la musette ou* [!] *la vielle.* We quote from the dedication:

> As for you, gentlemen, whom the god of war drafts to his colours, I have your applause if I have the ladies'. The clash of arms will not make you forget my concerts, and the blare of trumpets that proclaim your laurels will not render you insensible to the soft harmonies of the sweet musette.

How far is the pastoral musette of France from the martial bagpipe of Britain!

About 1755 there finally appeared a treatise that to a particular degree reveals the complete assimilation achieved between the vielle and the musette. This was the *Méthode raisonnée pour apprendre la musique d'une façon plus claire et plus précise à laquelle on joint l'étendue de la flute traversière, du violon, du pardessus de viole, de la vielle et de la musette. . . . Ouvrage fait pour la comodité des Maîtres et l'utilité des Écoliers*, by M. Bordet, 'Maître de flute traversière.' On page 23 of Bordet's book (Pl. 29a), the tuning and the compass of the two instruments are set against each other. At the left is shown the complete coincidence between the tuning of the drone strings of the vielle (*chanterelles*, *trompette*, *mouche*, *bourdon supprimé*, and *bourdon de sol*) and that of the drone pipes of the musette. At the right is shown the close analogy in the compass of the two instruments, which is now almost identical.

Before the French Revolution, the vielle had passed its zenith and returned to the street, where it had meanwhile maintained a humble existence (Pl. 27d). But at the same time, and for the last time, a great master wrote for it, Joseph Haydn. King Ferdinand IV of Naples, an ardent admirer of Haydn's art, had been inspired to play the vielle by a secretary at the Austrian Legation at the Court of Naples, Norbert Hadrava, who must have been one of those numerous and cultivated Czechs in the diplomatic service of the Austrian monarchy. Haydn, commissioned upon Hadrava's suggestion, wrote five concertos for the vielle and later several *notturni*, each of three movements, for two vielles and orchestra, magnificent pieces that found enthusiastic reception when they were performed again — with the vielle parts executed by flute and oboe — at the famous Salomon concerts Haydn gave in London. Even in the *notturni* the vielles are treated as typical solo instruments, successively alternating, imitating, and uniting. It was a magnificent finale for the vielle in art music.

But still the drone went on humming. Bagpipe and hurdy-gurdy had early been imitated by other instruments, such as the organ or the harpsichord, or by groups of instruments, whenever it was desirable to create a pastoral atmosphere. From many suites of the 17th and 18th centuries we know dance forms which were based completely or partly on a drone bass, often strengthened by its fifth. Among them was the graceful 'musette,' in calm three-four time. It had received its name from the bagpipe musette, just as about five hundred years earlier the organistrum had probably been named after the harmony it was fitted to perform, the organum. Another drone dance, in two-four time, was the 'tambourin,' derived again from the instrument of the same name, which is a stringed drum producing a drone bass in the tonic and dominant of the melody of a little one-hand pipe. There are countless 'musettes' and 'tambourins' in the harpsichord and orchestra suites of the Rococo. Anyone who wants a vivid idea of the vigour of the drone in typical tunes for the vielle may find imitations of this and other drone instruments in the *11ième Ordre* of Couperin's *Pièces de clavecin.* One of these is *Les Fastes de la grande et ancienne ménestrandise*, in five acts — a clever satire, by the way, on the clashes between the musicians' unions of that time. The second act is called *Bourdon* and carries the subtitle *Les Vielleux et les gueux.* It consists of two 'airs de vielle.' The third act, which introduces jugglers with their animals, is a characteristic pipe tune upon a drone bass in the tonic and dominant, suggesting a drum accompaniment.

The drone effect is also found in numerous pastorales of the middle of the 17th century. These are idealized shepherd tunes retaining the six-eight or twelve-eight rhythm and frequently the drone bass. Such tunes were played in South and Central Italy by the *zampognari* and *pifferari* who surrounded the cradle of the Child, a custom still alive. Thus it came about that pastorales were used in Christmas music, for example, the 6th movement of Corelli's *Concerto da Natale* and the *Sinfonia* in Bach's *Christmas Oratorio*. Handel must have heard the *pifferari* when he lived in Rome, and he used this effect in the *Sinfonia pastorale* of *Messiah*, in his oratorios *Semele* and *Acis and Galatea*, and in many other pieces. Other pastorales occur in works by the Scarlattis, Couperin, Pachelbel, Telemann, and so forth. One of the most famous is the great organ Pastorale in F major by J. S. Bach. Joseph Haydn, whose art was so deeply rooted in the fertile ground of folklore, employs drone tunes of all sorts, from literal quotations of bagpipe melodies to faintly suggestive uses of the drone effect. We mention only two examples, the finale of his Symphony No. 82, *L'Ours* (1786), based upon a real bagpipe tune, and the main theme in the finale of his 'London' Symphony, No. 104.

Not before Beethoven was there an entire symphony entitled *Pastorale*. In one of his sketch books it is called *Sinfonie caracteristica: Die Erinnerungen von dem Landleben*, or, as we might translate today, 'A programmatic symphony: Reminiscences of rural life.' Beethoven, moreover, took the utmost care to explain to the hearer what he wanted to express. Each movement is given a title suggesting the rustic scene it depicts. Was this necessary at the time? When the symphony started, with the violoncellos and violas droning the tonic and dominant as pedal point and the violins followed with their characteristic capering melody, the audience, we may safely assume, understood the connotation. In another mood, it seems that Beethoven himself took this response for granted, for a second note in his sketch book says, 'It is left to the hearer to find out the situations.' No doubt he did.

Today, however, a hundred and thirty years farther from the musette, the situation is different. Many listeners, more familiar with 19th-century music than with earlier music, may draw their interpretation of the drone as rustic from the mere fact that the drone occurs in a symphony which is entitled *Pastorale*.

Strange, indeed, are the mechanics of style. In the beginning there was a shepherd, his instrument the bagpipe, which happened to acquire a drone. The shepherd became fashionable; so did his drone. Thus the drone in art music became the symbol of the pastorale. Later generations, finding such effects used in music entitled *Pastorale*, learned its connotation from the name; they might never have seen a shepherd or heard a bagpipe. A short cut is formed: where grandfather knew the whole story, we react and interpret automatically. Thus a fashion hardened by tradition becomes second nature. So crystallize the habits of the ear.

The hurdy-gurdy as a folk instrument has not yet entirely died out. An imitation of a characteristic vielle tune is found in Schubert's melancholy *Der Leiermann*, the last song in the *Winterreise* cycle, ending with the words,

> Strange old man, say, will you go with me,
> Crank your lyre to my melody?

In our time it has been manufactured for the people of the Auvergne and Bourbonnais, of Berry, and of Savoy.

The bagpipe, however, is still very much alive, not only as a folk instrument in many mountain valleys of Europe but as a military instrument in the British Isles. The mechanical peculiarities of English and Irish bagpipes are beyond the scope of this article. They belong in a world of their own. Two facts only may be stressed: while the French musette symbolizes peace, for many centuries past the Highland pipes have led men to battle and still sound all over the globe where British troops are stationed. Secondly, the Scotch bagpipes reveal their oriental origin more strikingly than do other occidental bagpipes. It has been pointed out that the Piob Mor, the great Highland bagpipe, is not based on our equal-tempered scale, but that its scale, as determined by the spacing of the finger-holes on its chanter, is actually based on the Arabian. The sound of the Piob Mor on the North African battlefields during World War II thus closed a cultural circle of thousands of years.[1]

[1] In *The New York Times* for May 16, 1943, an American officer, First Lieutenant Daniel G. Kennedy, asked for bagpipes and discussed the value of this instrument for a soldier's morale. 'Even in the African campaign,' he said, 'they were reported to be a factor in the dogged, relentless drives at El Alamein and the Mareth line. Here at this infantry replacement center where the American doughboys train we have long wanted to add bagpipe music to our band.' Perhaps on some such occasion was heard again that fine old bagpipe tune so irresistible in 1702: 'The Day We Beat the Germans at Cremona.'

5 · The Lira da Braccio*

The lira da braccio was one of the most important string instruments of the High Renaissance, the instrument of the recitalists who improvised polyphonic accompaniments for their singing, and therefore one of the most characteristic implements of the intended revival of the rhapsodic art of the ancients. Its use remained primarily restricted to Italy.

In its fully developed form, the instrument consisted of a flat sound box with a broad fingerboard, a slightly rounded bridge, and a peg box on the front of which were seven pegs for fastening strings: five melody strings running over the fingerboard and two bass strings running parallel to the melody strings but apart from the fingerboard; there were no frets. Larger forms, such as the lirone and the lira da gamba, had a correspondingly greater number of strings, up to a total of fifteen, including four free-running strings.

Tracing our instrument in the treatises of the Italian Renaissance is no easy task, because it had a variety of names, some of which referred also to instruments of Greek or Roman antiquity, or were given indiscriminately to other different Renaissance instruments. Although sometimes also called 'lira da spalla,' it was generally called simply 'lira' in contemporary literature,[1] or occasionally 'lira moderna' to distinguish it from the ancient lyre; Ganassi speaks of the 'lira di sette corde.'[2] The invention of the lira was ascribed to the ancients by authors of the 15th and early 16th centuries, and even by Bernardi in 1581,[3] while 16th-century emblematic literature,[4] when discussing the lira, quotes indiscriminately from both ancient and contemporary sources, and regards both the 'lira con l'archetto' and the 'lira toccata dal plettro' as instruments of antiquity. Bronze plaques of the late 16th and early 17th centuries show Apollo with an ancient lyre and a modern bow. Ganassi describes a discovery of antiquities in Rome, among them the figure of a player

* The original article on the *Lira da Braccio*, published in *Die Musik in Geschichte und Gegenwart*, VIII (1960), contained several long sections concerning matters such as the morphological evolution of the lira da braccio, various methods of tuning, the history and evolution of its bow, various playing methods, the employment of the lira da braccio and of the lirone in intermedii, and others. Since these sections were of a predominantly technical nature, they did not seem sufficiently pertinent to warrant their inclusion here.

[1] For instance, in Giovanni Maria Lanfranco, *Scintille di musica* (1533), and Pietro Cerone, *El Melopeo y maestro*, Naples, 1613.

[2] *Regola Rubertina* (1543).

[3] *Ragionamenti musicali*, Bologna, 1581.

[4] E.g., P. Abb. Picinelli, *Del Mondo simbolico ampliato*, Bk. XXIII, Ch. V.

holding in his hand 'a viola d'arco, which should be called lira or lirone, rather than viola or violone,'[1] and Pierius Valerianus's *Hieroglyphica* (Basel, 1567) even illustrates an 'ancient' altar decorated with reliefs of lire da braccio (Fig. 1 in Chapter 1 above).[2]

This assumption that the lira da braccio was an ancient instrument was apparently based on several facts. The number of strings — seven — recalled that of the classical ancient lyre. Moreover, the lira da braccio had, in addition to its stopped strings, unstopped strings which always sounded their full length, just as did all the strings of the ancient kithara and lyre. Finally, it was widely believed that the ancient plectrum for the kithara and lyre was actually something like a fiddle bow, and it was only as late as 1581 that this assumption was energetically refuted by Vincenzo Galilei.[3]

For a long time, the lira da braccio was also called 'viola.' In the second half of the 16th century the usage still varied: Vasari, for example, speaks of the lira da braccio played by one of the angels in Carpaccio's *Presentation in the Temple* (Accademia, Venice; Pl. 33b) as 'una lira ovvero viola,' but calls the same instrument, in Fra Bartolommeo's *sacra conversazione* for San Marco in Florence, simply a 'lira.'[4] Galilei, in his *Dialogo*, maintains that only recently had the viola da braccio been called 'lira,'[5] and, in another passage, that it had been called 'lira' only in his own time ('modernamente').[6] The fact that earlier sources generally refer to the lira da braccio by the name 'viola' is not without importance in view of the many musicians with the nickname 'della viola'; as we know, during the reign of Alfonso II, the court of Ferrara employed Francesco di Viola, a pupil of Willaert, as chapelmaster, and also the madrigal composer Alfonso della Viola. Further evidence for the use of the name 'viola' for the lira can be seen in the terminology of the period, which frequently speaks of 'viols with frets' when referring to members of the viol family, obviously to distinguish them from the fretless lira da braccio; thus, Ganassi's *Regola Rubertina* speaks expressly of the 'viola d'arco tastada' in the title of its first part, and of the 'violone d'arco da tasti' in its second part, while Lanfranco's *Scintille* mentions 'violoni da tasti & da Arco.'

The names for the larger forms, with more than seven strings, were *lirone*, *lirone perfetto*, *lira da gamba*, and *arciviolatalira* (probably a corruption of *arciviola da lira*). The *Organographia* of Praetorius uses distorted names, *Arce violyra* and *Arce-viola telire*, while Mersenne calls the lira da gamba which he describes in his *Harmonie universelle* simply *lyre*.

[1] *Regola Rubertina*, Pt. I, Ch. VIII.

[2] For further information about this pseudo-archaeology, see Chapter 14 below.

[3] *Dialogo della musica antica e della moderna*, 1581, p. 130.

[4] *Vite*, Milan, 1564, III, 642. [5] *Dialogo*, p. 147. [6] *Ibid.*, p. 130.

The literary evidence from authors of the early and high Renaissance should be combined with what we can learn from extant specimens. Unfortunately only a very few pieces have survived, and of them hardly a handful are in their original or approximately original condition. The oldest, and certainly the most beautiful, is the magnificent instrument by Giovanni d'Andrea da Verona, dated 1511, now in the Kunsthistorisches Museum, Vienna (Pl. 31b & g). Its soundboard is of a warm brown colour, while the back and sides have a dark reddish varnish. The fingerboard and the string holder are decorated in typical North Italian style, 'alla certosina' — that is, by a colourful combination of ebony, ivory, bone which has been stained green, and brown wood. The most striking feature, however, is the carving of belly and back, which give the impression of human forms. The belly is shaped like a male torso and, correspondingly, the front of the peg box shows a grotesque male face. The back shows, in stronger relief, the form of a female torso with breasts and nipples strongly marked and, accordingly, the back of the peg box shows a woman's face. But this is not the end of the sculptural fantasy: acanthus leaves encroach upon the female torso and on its middle region is a large moustachioed *mascherone* that overlaps the undulations of the female form.

The sound-holes in the belly are unusually large, of tendril shape; the peg box can be closed, and it is remarkable how cleverly the pegs are inserted so as to disturb as little as possible the grimace of the grotesque face. A little ivory plaque inserted into the back bears the somewhat miswritten Greek inscription: '*ΛΥΠΗΣ ΙΑΤΡΟΣ ΕΣΤΙΝ ΑΝΘΡΩΠΟΙΣ ΩΑΗ*' ('Men have song as the physician of pain'). This is an adaptation of an ancient monostichon (326) in which, for obvious reasons, ᾠδή (song) replaced the original λόγος (*logos*), and in quoting it respect is paid to humanist learning, so important in Venetian culture of the time.

How far this masterpiece of applied sculpture is from the standardized forms of string instruments of later ages! And how much it helps us to visualize other Renaissance instruments, such as the lira da braccio that Leonardo built in the shape of a horse's skull — a shape so beloved by that great connoisseur of animal anatomy!

The Heyer Collection in Leipzig includes a lirone by Ventura di Francesco Linarol, Venice, 1577 (Pl. 31c). A lira da braccio in the Ashmolean Museum, Oxford, by Joan Maria, and a somewhat larger one in the Museum of the Brussels Conservatory (Pl. 31a) are undated, as are the following lire da gamba: one with four free and nine melody strings in the Vienna collection, by Wendelin Tieffenbrucker, Padua, *c.* 1590 (Pl. 31f & h), which is related by its complex contour to the lira da braccio shown in a painting by Bartolommeo Passerotti in the Galleria Spada, Rome (Pl. 32a); a later example in the

Brussels Conservatory Museum with a round sound-hole, nine melody strings, and frets (Pl. 31e); and a very late one from the mid-17th century in the Heyer Collection, which also has frets, a round sound-hole, and two free and fourteen melody strings. Two further examples in the Heyer Collection had been made into violoncellos before their restoration.

Since only very few examples, of comparatively late date, have survived, the pictorial sources for the lira da braccio are indispensable. There is a profusion of contemporary representations, especially in the art of Venice, Lombardy, and Tuscany — frescoes, paintings, woodcuts and engravings, sculptures, reliefs and plaques, wood intarsias, book vignettes, frame carvings, and so on. The most numerous depictions are in mythological and allegorical scenes, and in angel concerts.

In the mythological scenes, both Apollo and Orpheus are often shown playing the lira da braccio. Apollo appears both in his contests with Marsyas and Pan (of which the earliest illustrations are probably the woodcuts in *Ovidio*

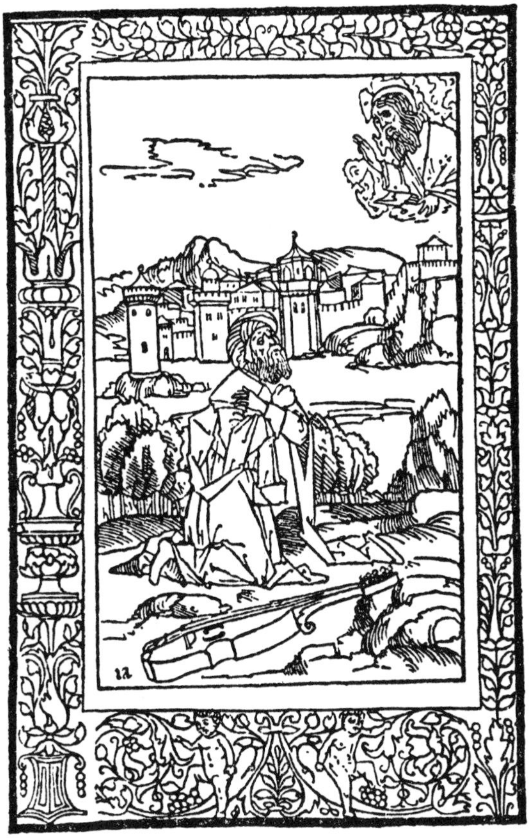

Fig. 11.
King David in prayer, with a lirone in the foreground. From a 1497 edition of the Office of the B.V.M.

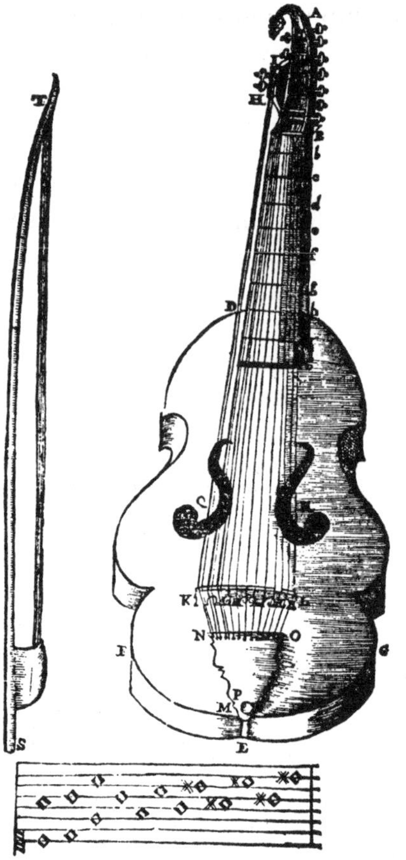

Fig. 12.
Fifteen-stringed bass lira ('lyre'), with bow and tuning. From Mersenne, *Harmonie universelle*, 1636.

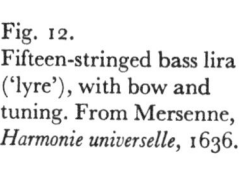

metamorphoseos volgare, Venice, 1497 and 1501; see Figs. 20 & 21 in Chapter 12) and as leader of the Muses (most notably in Raphael's *Parnassus* fresco in the Vatican, which was endlessly copied and varied; see Chapter 14 below). Orpheus appears playing among the wild beasts (as in the engraving of Benedetto Montagna), subduing the demons of hell (as in Signorelli's fresco cycle in the Chapel of San Brizio in the Orvieto Cathedral, and in Peruzzi's frescoed frieze in the Villa Farnesina in Rome), or leading Euridice (in Marcantonio Raimondi's engraving, for example). Concerts of the Muses, among them Tintoretto's numerous examples, also include the lira da braccio, and Homer and the royal psalmist David (Fig. 11) are frequently shown with it. It is, therefore, the celebrated recitalists of the ancient world and of the Old Testament who accompany their singing with the lira da braccio.

In angel concerts of the Renaissance, the lira da braccio appears both in the large instrumental ensembles surrounding the Coronation of the Virgin and in the small groups of angels (usually two or three, but sometimes only a single one) before the throne of the Madonna in the *sacre conversazioni*, especially those of the Venetian school (see Pls. 33, 35, & 37b).

Curiously enough, portraits of musicians with the lira da braccio are uncommon; an early one, attributed to Raffaellino del Garbo, is in the National Gallery, Dublin (Pl. 32b). Musical treatises contain few pictures of this instrument, and only from the last phase of its popularity; they are also sometimes unreliable, such as those in Praetorius's *Syntagma*[1] and in Buonnani's *Gabinetto armonico* (Rome, 1722). Mersenne's *Harmonie universelle* (1636) shows only one, a very precise woodcut of an atypical bass lira ('lyre'), with frets and side-pegs inserted in a sickle-shaped head (Fig. 12).

The accuracy of representation is greatest in the almost life-size depictions in Venetian altarpieces, and in the numerous, though heretofore largely ignored, still-lifes in wood intarsia (most importantly those at Monte Oliveto near Siena, in Verona, Padua, and the ducal palaces of Urbino and Mantua; see Pls. 34a, 52a, and Chapters 8 & 9 below), which excel in their use of accurate geometric perspective. The reliability of paintings is often impaired by inexpert restoration (ignorant restorers were likely to paint over the free strings), while often in sculpture and reliefs, for obvious reasons, the strings are simplified, their number is reduced, and the free strings are entirely omitted.

Pictures and reliefs often show lire da braccio of fantastic forms or with profuse ornamentation; among these are the lira in Cima da Conegliano's *tondo* in the Uffizi showing the contest of Apollo and Pan; that in the engraving by the Master of the Sforza Book of Hours, showing the Virgin with two musical angels; and the one in Gaudenzio Ferrari's *Madonna* in the Pinacoteca in Turin (Pl. 34b). The belief that the exquisite instrument shown in Passerotti's *King David* (Pl. 32a) really existed is made plausible by a comparison with the lira da gamba in the Vienna collection (Pl. 31g).

In general, one must keep in mind that it is not always easy to distinguish between the exuberant imagination of the painter and the decorative fantasy of the instrument maker, especially since the manufacture of musical instruments was by no means standardized at that time, and because solo instruments 'in the ancient manner' such as the lira da braccio were often built to satisfy the purchasers' desire for showpieces of unusual form and decoration; examples are Vasari's report of the lira built by Leonardo da Vinci in the form of a horse skull (not 'Pferdekopf' — horse head — as in much German art-historical literature, but 'Pferdeschädel'), and the lira of Giovanni d'Andrea described earlier.

[1] *Sciagraphia*, XVII, 4 and XX, 5.

In addition to its importance as a solo instrument, the lira da braccio and the lirone are frequently mentioned in reports of Renaissance intermedii, in which they were used for the accompaniment of madrigals, sometimes as a substitute for the harpsichord, or occasionally in such combinations as: 1 lirone, 4 violoni, and 4 tromboni.[1] Lire were also used in the famous Florentine intermedii of 1589; a solo madrigal was accompanied by a lute, a chitarrone, and an arciviolatalira, which latter was played by Alessandro Striggio himself. The performance of Peri's *Euridice* in 1600 used a 'lira grande' in the orchestra. Two short examples of tablature for the lira da gamba have been preserved: Mersenne reproduces three bars of a *Laudamus te* with an accompaniment of four- and five-part chords,[2] and a similar example is found in Cerreto's *Della prattica musica*.

It is characteristic of the great interest in archaeology prevailing in Italy that an instrument regarded — though erroneously — as a descendant of the ancient lyre achieved its greatest importance and popularity in the 'terra sacra'; outside Italy, the lira da braccio is seldom found. Mersenne emphasizes the scarcity of the 'lyre' in France.[3] Praetorius, in his *Theatrum instrumentorum*, specifically designates both forms illustrated as 'italienische,' and the few representations found in German art all seem to be derived from Italian models. This is the case

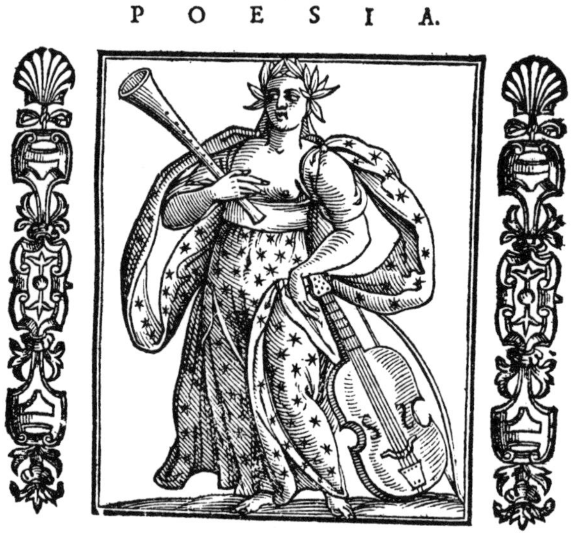

Fig. 13. Allegorical representation of Poesia with a lirone. From Cesare Ripa, *Iconologia*, 1618.

[1] For further information, see Otto Kinkeldey, *Orgel und Klavier in der Musik des 16. Jahrhunderts*, Leipzig, 1910, Chapter 6.

[2] *Harmonie universelle*, p. 207.

[3] *Ibid.*, p. 206.

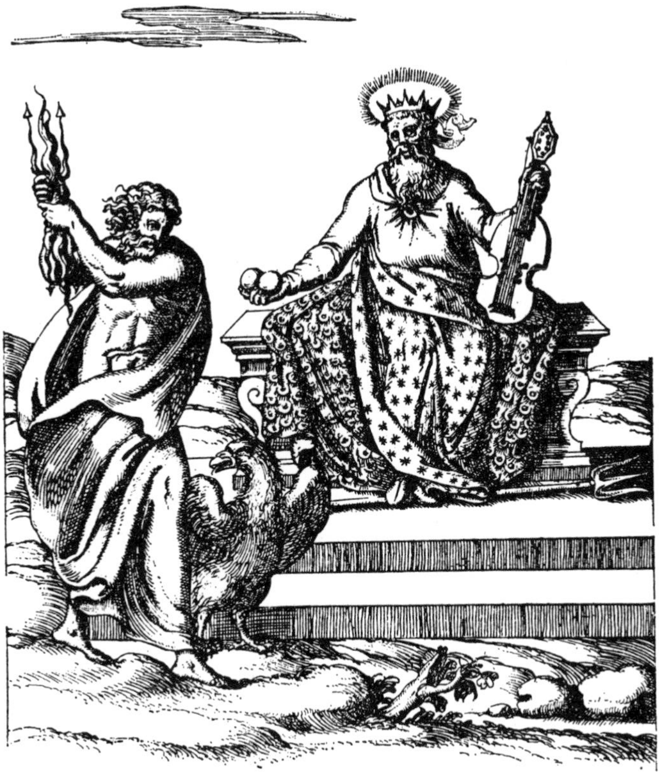

Fig. 14. Two representations of Jupiter, one holding a lira da braccio (described in the text as nine-stringed). From Vincenzo Cartari, *Le Imagini dei dei degli antichi,* 1580.

with Peter Vischer's Orpheus plaque, which is inspired by a similar plaque by Moderno (see Pl. 30b); a marginal vignette in Dürer's prayerbook for the Emperor Maximilian; and a small Orpheus playing the lira da braccio among the Muses, found in the decoration of a processional car for Maximilian illustrated among the woodcuts of Burgkmair. In Italy, the instrument seems to have survived until after 1600, and the larger forms even until after 1700; the inventory of instruments at the Medici court of 1716 includes three lire with twelve, thirteen, and fourteen strings — thus apparently bass lire — but not a single lira da braccio.

Although the lira da braccio was often, as mentioned above, referred to as 'viola' in the contemporary sources, it remained quite distinct, in structure, tuning, and playing technique, from the viola da gamba family which evolved at the same time. Occasionally, hybrid forms appeared, such as instruments combining the characteristic stringing of the lira da braccio with the scroll and lateral pegs of the viola da gamba; an example can be seen in the anonymous early 16th-century Italian portrait of a youth with a string instrument, in the Kunsthistorisches Museum, Vienna.

In shape, the later examples of the lira da braccio gradually approached that of the violin, and its characteristic tuning in fifths and lack of frets (as opposed to the viol family) clearly influenced the development of the violin. On the other hand, Gaudenzio Ferrari's cupola fresco in Saronno (*c.* 1534) shows a fully developed four-string violin alongside various forms of the lira da braccio, and therefore Hajdecki's hypothesis of a gradual but direct evolution of the violin from the lira da braccio cannot be maintained without some modification (see Chapter 6).

The musical treatises of the Renaissance that mention the lira da braccio focus primarily on technical questions such as tuning, rather than on its central position in the musical life of the period, a matter they take for granted. However, other writings give occasional hints to fill out a sufficient picture. Vasari, in his discussion of the musical interests of Leonardo, emphasizes the latter's predilection for the lira da braccio as that of a man 'who by nature possessed a spirit both lofty and full of grace which enabled him to improvise divinely in

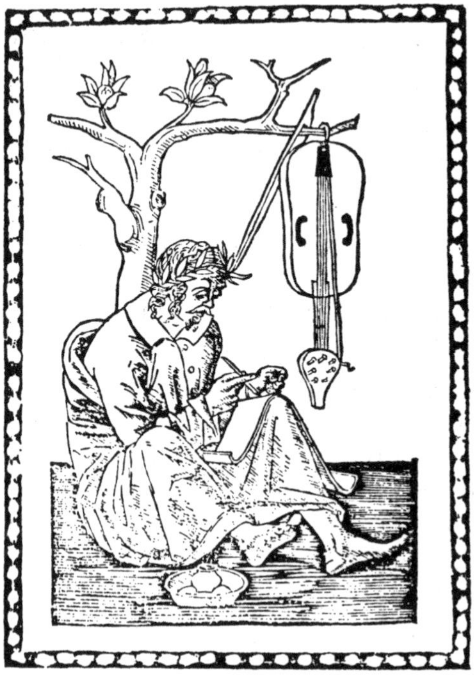

Fig. 15.
A poet with lira da braccio. From *Epithome Plutarchi*, 1501.

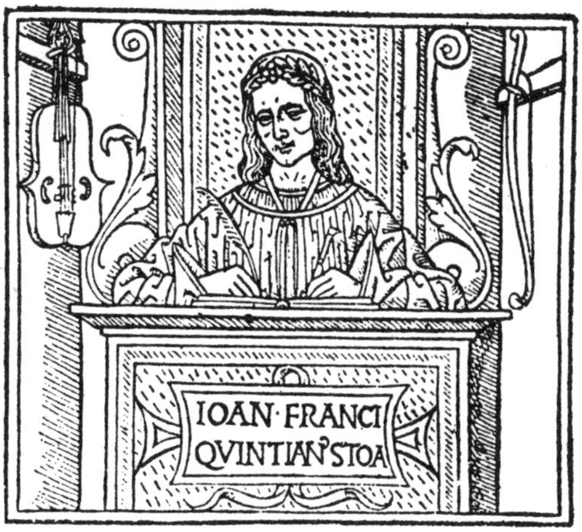

Fig. 16. A humanist with lira da braccio. From Quintianus Stoa, *De Syllabarum quantitate*, 1511.

singing and playing the lira da braccio,'[1] and a similar remark is applied to Raphael's teacher Timoteo Viti, who also played the lira da braccio.[2] Castiglione, in the second book of his *Cortegiano*, distinguishes between two forms of making music: 'Good music means to me singing well and securely and in good style from the score; but much more still the singing to one's own *viola* accompaniment'[3] — the 'viola' being the lira da braccio, which we find depicted several times in the ducal palace of Urbino, whose court and culture are the subject of Castiglione's treatise. Baccio Ugolino, the celebrated protagonist in the Mantua performance of Poliziano's *Orfeo* in 1471 and later bishop of Gaëta, earned the applause of Lorenzo de' Medici by his singing 'ad Lyram.' From these and many other passages emerges the significance of the instrument as a favourite of virtuosos and dilettantes. At the courts of Ferrara and Milan, virtuosos of the lira da braccio were employed. According to Vasari, Leonardo, when introduced to the Milanese court in 1494, was presented to the Duke as a player of the lira da braccio.[4]

As a rule, reports speak of 'cantare sopra' or 'su la lira,' which corresponds exactly to the conception that Renaissance musical archaeology had formed of ancient musical practice; Zarlino, for example, devotes an entire chapter in the

[1] '. . . che della natura aveva spirito elevatissimo e pieno di leggiadria, onde sopra quella cantò divinamente all' improvviso' (*Vite*, ed. Milanesi, IV, 18).

[2] *Ibid.*, IV, 498.

[3] 'Bella musica . . . parmi il cantar bene a libro sicuramente, et con bella maniera: ma anchor molto più il cantare alla viola'.

[4] *Vite*, ed. Milanesi, IV, 28.

fifth book of his *Istitutioni harmoniche* to the ancient poets and rhapsodists and their recitation to the 'lira' and 'cetra.' Sometimes the lira da braccio appears with the player not singing or reciting, particularly in depictions of angel concerts. In the larger ensembles shown in Coronations of the Virgin, it always appears only once, never doubled, while in *sacre conversazioni* it appears with one or two other instruments (lute, rebec, occasionally also a recorder or cromorne). There are, however, paintings in which it appears as the sole instrument; such a painting as Palma Vecchio's *Sacra Conversazione* in San Zaccaria, Venice (Pl. 36), where one angel sits alone before the throne of the Madonna and between the groups of saints playing the lira da braccio, is an eloquent testament to the rank and importance of the instrument.

More than any other instrument of the Italian Renaissance, the lira da braccio is associated with the attempted revival of ancient musical practice. The facts of its name, its supposed antique origin, and its specific or imagined similarities to the ancient lyre, mentioned above, all contributed to endow it with a kind of allegorical significance that is clearly mirrored in the visual arts and in the allegorical and emblematic literature of the period. As early as the *quattrocento*, it appears as the symbolic attribute of the great poets and musicians

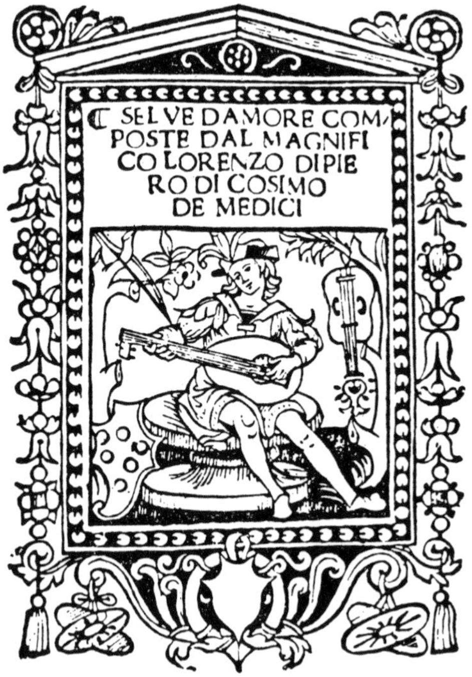

Fig. 17. Lute player, with lira da braccio in background. Title page of Lorenzo de' Medici, *Selve d'amore*.

of classical mythology and of the Old Testament: Apollo, Orpheus, Homer, King David — and also in the allegorical representations of Poesia, Musica, and Harmonia (see Fig. 13), in the famous mythological treatises of Lilio Gyraldi (*De Deis gentium varia et multiplex historia*, Basel, 1548), Vincenzo Cartari (*Le Imagini dei dei degli antichi*, Venice, 1556), Cesare Ripa (*Iconologia*, Rome, 1593), and others. In Cartari's book, even Jupiter is shown with a lira da braccio (see Fig. 14), while Valerianus, in his *Hieroglyphica*, 1567, shows it as an attribute of Mercury.

In the allegorical representations of the Liberal Arts, the lira da braccio frequently characterizes Musica, as in Pinturicchio's fresco in the Borgia Apartments in the Vatican, and in Pollaiuolo's decorations for the bronze tomb of Sixtus IV in St. Peter's. Later, even Tintoretto assigns it a prominent place in the foreground of his concerts of the Muses, and Jan Bruegel the Elder gives it the place of honour in the foreground of his *Allegory of Hearing* in the Prado (Pl. 37a), one of the last representations of the instrument.

In the numerous depictions of Apollo's contests with Marsyas and Pan, Apollo usually plays the lira da braccio, a symbol of the noble 'mathematical' music as opposed to the guttural and lascivious music of the various reed instruments played by his opponents (see Chapter 12); most of these use as their iconographical models the woodcuts of the first edition of the *Ovidio metamorphoseos volgare* (Venice, 1497). Later examples are found in the paintings of Schiavone, and in the picture by Correggio (or Bronzino?) in the Hermitage, originally the lid of a harpsichord. A small section of a lira da braccio can be detected in Giovanni Bellini's *Feast of the Gods* (National Gallery, Washington), a painting whose meaning can be deciphered by the presence of this very instrument (see Chapter 2).

In the miniatures and woodcuts of the late *quattrocento*, the lira da braccio begins to replace the harp and psaltery of King David, and the pictures and prints of the 16th century nearly always show him with this instrument (see, for example, the Passerotti painting in Plate 32a, and also Fig. 12).

Frequently, the number of strings is given symbolic significance — the number seven, for example, referring to the seven known planets (in Zarlino's *Istitutioni*, p. 21, and in Lanfranco's *Scintille di musica*). The nine strings of the instrument played by Apollo in Raphael's *Parnassus* evidently refer to the nine Muses and perhaps also to the nine Greek modes supposedly established by Gaudentius and later cited by Zarlino.[1]

[1] Zarlino, in the second table of contents for his *Istitutioni harmoniche* (Venice, 1558), states that 'Gaudentio filosofo numera nove modi nella Musica' and enumerates them in the text (part IV, p. 367) as follows: Mistolidio, Lidio, Frigio, Dorio, Hypolidio, Hypofrigio, Commune, Locrico, Hypodorio.

As an attribute of humanists, the lira da braccio appears in numerous book illustrations and frontispieces, to characterize the poet or philosopher, crowned with laurels and writing or teaching. Examples are the frontispieces of the 1501 Ferrara edition of Plutarch (Fig. 15), Quintianus Stoa's treatise *De Syllabarum quantitate* (Fig. 16), Lorenzo de' Medici's *Selve d'amore* (Fig. 17), and Pietro Aron's *Toscanello della musica* (Venice, 1523). On the back of a contemporary bronze plaquette (Pl. 30a) cast in honour of the Bolognese humanist Ercole Bottrigari, author of the treatise *Il Desiderio overo de concerti di varij strumenti musicali* (Venice, 1594), it appears among the traditional symbols of the *quadrivium*, and there are numerous other examples among treatises on astronomy, mathematics, and other subjects.

6 · Early Violins in Paintings by Gaudenzio Ferrari and his School

One of the great lacunae in the history of musical instruments is the question of the origin of the violin. This seems absurd, considering the increasing importance of this instrument for more than three hundred years. How different was the treatment accorded by musical historians to that other ruler among the tools of music, the pianoforte! We know almost everything about its origin and evolution, as it has been recorded in minute detail. True enough, the history of the pianoforte posed a much easier problem: one man, after a few years of experimentation, produced what the fashion of his time demanded — a keyboard instrument with a hammer action that enabled the player to perform crescendos and decrescendos, simply by modifying the pressure of his fingers on the keys. Thus a new keyboard style was at once made possible.

The violin, however, was not an 'invention.' Rather, it was the final product of a long and variegated process of development, a combination or fusion of many patterns and elements contributed by a number of different bowed instruments. Only when the great Lombard instrument-makers in Brescia and Cremona took over, after the middle of the 16th century, did something like a standard form emerge — standard, it is true, only in the sense of adherence to basic characteristics that still admitted countless variations of proportion, curvature, tonal quality, and so on. From that time on, we have something like a coherent history of the violin, told, if not in treatises, then by a considerable number of wonderful specimens that have survived to the present day.

A reliable account of the pre-history of the violin, and by that I mean the process of development mentioned above, has not yet been written, and a consultation of the modern books on the history of this instrument proves disappointing — they are vague or incorrect, or they simply avoid the problem.[1]

[1] a) George Hart, *The Violin*, London, 1884, pp. 24–25, refers to manuscript notes by Vincetto Lancetti that mention a three-stringed violin in the collection of Count Cozia di Salabue, in the form of the Italian viola, dated 1546 and attributed to Andrea Amati, but 'altered in the 19th century'! Then Hart continues: 'When or where the four-stringed Violin, tuned in fifths, first appeared in Italy is a question, the answer to which *must ever remain buried in the past*.'

b) Alexander Hajdecki, *Die italienische Lira da Braccio*, Mostar, 1892, p. 50, says: 'The Italian lira da braccio . . . is the mother of our violin. . . .'

So the origin of the violin is still obscure. Neither the alleged strict distinction between the families of the viola da gamba and the viola da braccio, nor the supposed direct evolution of the violin from the lira da braccio, conforms to its actual evolution,[1] and some attempts at condensation of its complex story have resulted in oversimplification. One cannot even blame the simplifiers, for the history of the violin is a process emanating from wide and wild experiments towards standardization, a standardization which is, in fact, almost unparalleled in the history of instruments. According to pictorial evidence, and contrary to the neat and departmentalized *Syntagma* of Praetorius, there were lire da braccio with 'violin' scrolls, violins with exuberant rebec sickles, violins with *C* holes, viols with bulging soundboards, and near-'violins' still with the flat peg leaf or peg box of the lira da braccio.

---

c) Laurent Grillet, *Les Ancêtres du violon . . .*, Paris, 1901, p. 9, refers to Lanfranco's *Scintille*, published in Brescia, 1533, and to an account from the same year of the 'dépenses secrètes' of Francis I, which mentions 'tous vyolons et joueurs d'instruments du Roy' and some later French sources (from after 1550), including Rabelais, that refer to 'joueurs de violon', but is silent about Italians before Andrea Amati, 1572.

d) The article in the *Encyclopaedia Britannica*, 11th ed., 1911, refers to a tenor viola 'bearing in general outline the typical features of the violin,' exhibited in 1872 in the Loan Exhibition of Musical Instruments at South Kensington, with the label 'Pietro Lanure, Brescia, 1509'.

e) W. Leo von Lütgendorff, *Die Geigen und Lautenmacher . . .*, Frankfurt-am-Main, 1922, cautiously credits Gasparo da Salò with 'the merit of having built the first violins and of having given them their definitive [*endgültige*] form' (Vol. I, p. 31).

f) Gerald R. Hayes, *Musical Instruments and their Music*, London, 1930, clearly reflects the embarrassing situation of the historian when he says (II, 160) that 'the violin is one of the very few important instruments of which it can be said that at a given date it was not at all, and that shortly afterwards it is found full-fledged in active life.' He very prudently refuses to decide whether Lanfranco's reference to the 'Violetta da Arco senza tasti' (*Scintille di Musica*, 1533) means rebecs or violins (II, 169).

g) Edmund van der Straeten, *The History of the Violin*, London, 1933, p. 35, refers to the well-known print showing a portrait of Gasparo Duiffoprugcar, dated 1562, which shows two early violins; and also to the description of a 'violin' in Philibert Jambe-de-Fer's *Epitome Musical*, Lyons, 1556, which mentions tuning in fifths, but does not say anything about the form of the instrument.

h) Francis Farga, *Violins and Violinists*, transl. Egon Larsen, London, 1950, regards Tieffenbrucker as the 'probable inventor of the violin' (Illus. XXVII) and says on p. 32: 'The violin is depicted in the paintings of some Bolognese masters towards the middle of the 16th century, for example, in a picture by Giulio Romano (*c.* 1550). There is also a picture by Pellegrino Tibaldi in the Vienna State Gallery which portrays St. Cecilia with two violin-playing angels. It is possible, therefore, that the violin originated in Bologna in the third or fourth decade of the 16th century.' He considers two violins by Andrea Amati with the year 1551 on the label as unquestionably authentic.

i) David D. Boyden, in his article on the violin in *Musical Instruments Through the Ages*, ed. Anthony Baines, London, 1961, carefully and prudently formulates the problem (pp. 110, 111): 'It is fruitless to try to attribute the "invention" of the violin to any one man or country. . . . The most impressive contributions were those of northern Italy where, shortly after the middle of the 16th century, the Italian school of violin-making dominated all others.'

[1] In Chapter 5 above, I have discussed these problems.

The situation is further complicated by the predilection of the curio collectors of the 15th and 16th centuries, who liked to commission unique and fantastic shapes as worthy additions to their *Kunst- und Wunder-kammern* or *Musikkammern*. The only straight and clear evolution in Renaissance string instruments, as far as I can see, was the gradual transformation of what pre-16th-century Italy called the 'viola' (a fiddle with a flat head and frontal pegs, with or without drones, such as was depicted, for instance, by the school of Giotto) into the full-fledged lira da braccio of about 1500, as shown in countless representations by Carpaccio, Giovanni Bellini, Cima da Conegliano, and others.

The veil that covers the origin of the violin may be lifted, at least a little if not wholly, by the evidence of pictures, and specifically by pictures that pre-date the time when the Cremonese masters created what appears in retrospect to be the first 'standardized' pattern of the violin. The first outstanding painter we have to consider in this connection is Gaudenzio Ferrari, whose creative years filled almost the whole first half of the 16th century. Very close in time and place to the great giants, Leonardo and Bramante, he achieved and maintained an astounding originality and independence. His frescoes and other paintings are characterized by vivacity and a great ease and variety of composition. His art is deeply rooted in his native soil, and many of the faces, figures, and gestures that he depicted can still be found today in Lombard and Piedmont villages.[1]

Apart from his glory as a painter, Ferrari was deeply interested in the other arts, including music. Several of his works contain representations of musical instruments, including violins: the frescoes and sculptures in and near Varallo; his altarpiece, *La Madonna degli aranci*, in the Church of San Cristoforo in Vercelli; the cupola fresco in the Santuario in Saronno; and others. A detailed study of these representations seems indispensable for the history of Renaissance instruments, and it is hardly too much to say that Gaudenzio's name is inseparable from the early history of the violin.

Now we turn to Ferrari's gigantic cupola fresco in the Santuario at Saronno,[2] one of his most important and original works. He received the commission for it in 1534 and worked on it throughout 1535. His idea of representing a large angel concert in a cupola had only one forerunner, Correggio's famous fresco of the *Assumption of the Virgin* in the cupola of the cathedral in Parma. We do not know

[1] This article is not the place for an evaluation of the importance to history of this great Lombard-Piedmontese painter, but I should like to refer here to one of the most lucid and concentrated studies of Ferrari's importance, recently written by Anna Maria Brizio as the introduction to her catalogue of the unforgettable exhibition in Vercelli, 1956, *Mostra di Gaudenzio Ferrari*, Milan, 1956.

[2] It was Karl Geiringer who first drew the attention of musical historians to this fresco, in 1927, in an excellent article, *Gaudenzio Ferrari's Engelkonzert im Dome von Saronno*, in the *Kongressbericht der Beethoven-Zentenarfeier*, Vienna, 1927.

whether Gaudenzio knew Correggio's fresco, which had been finished only a few years earlier, in 1530. In any case, Gaudenzio's composition is quite different and original; it represents the arrival of the Blessed Virgin in Heaven. Mary appears at the outer rim of the cupola, flanked by *puttini*; God the Father, in glory, is represented in stucco relief in the centre of the painting. The whole enormous, shallow, and circular vault between these two main figures is filled with angels, arranged in four concentric circles: the innermost circle next to God consists of thirty-one dancing *putti*; the other three circles are comprised of numerous large figures of angels, sumptuously clad in flowing robes. Some of them pray, some adore and exalt, but most of them play instruments. Of the eighty-six large angels, no less than sixty play or assist in playing instruments.[1]

There are, in all, fifty-six instruments. Among the bowed instruments we find several viols, several lire da braccio, rebecs, a Sicilian cane violin, a bizarre compound of fiddle with recorder, to be blown and bowed at the same time,[2] and, last but not least, a number of instruments that show most if not all of the basic characteristics of the violin.

But before concentrating on the violins, we should say something in general about the perspective in this fresco. The linear projection is far from being optically exact or — should we say? — pedantic. Even a quick glance convinces the beholder that most string instruments appear to be asymmetrical, with the bouts on either side not corresponding to each other. Also, the necks of instruments curve slightly upward so that their strings could not run parallel. Some of these irregularities are explained by the unevenness of the stucco surface in the cupola, and many spots are warped by fissures. But apart from that, Gaudenzio, with all his love for fancy detail, was not aiming here at photographic precision. He would, for instance, show the neck of an instrument with its sickle-head or scroll at a slightly different angle from that of the body, in order to insure identification of the instrument by its most characteristic feature. The scholar must be aware of this freedom in handling perspective 'con alcune licenze'; only then will he justly interpret the painted shapes, or rather 'reconstruct,' as it were, the actual instrument from its fanciful appearance in the painting. There is also another 'unrealistic' feature in the fresco: none of the stringed instruments, not even the lutes, citterns, harps, or psalteries, has its strings painted in.

[1] It was thanks to the late Fernanda Wittgens, the director of the Brera and the Sopraintendente delle Gallerie di Lombardia, that numerous detailed photographs of my favourite angels were made. I had visited the Santuario of Saronno so often that I was called by the sacristan and his family 'questo Americano pazzo,' and when, soon after World War II, I noticed rain damage in the cupola, 'La Fernandissima' lost no time in effecting repair and restoration. It was on that occasion that the photographs were taken which accompany this chapter.

[2] On this and other 'fantastic' instruments and their interpretation, see Chapters 1 and 16.

The suggestive position of the stopping, plucking, and bowing hands was evidently sufficient for the onlooker far down below.

To the left of a beautiful positive organ are four angels with bowed instruments (Pl. 38a). The one on top, which certainly has nothing to do with the violin, we may in the main disregard here. The angel plays a bizarre three-stringed instrument of very complex shape. Its curves project and, again, cut in deeply toward the centre of the body; its back is strongly bulging; and its broad rim is profusely decorated with intarsias. Its heart-shaped head with frontal pegs is typical of the contemporary lira da braccio.

The three other instruments, however, different as they are from each other, all have some features that can be related to the violin. Closest to our present-day standard violin is the alto-sized instrument played by a feminine angel at the right (Pl. 38b). There are the typical upper, middle, and lower bouts, and a shallow body with a bulging soundboard and projecting edges. There is also the narrow neck and fingerboard, and an elegantly shaped scroll. Inside the peg box, four stems are clearly visible.[1] Beside all these typical violin traits, however, there are other features that would perhaps seem abnormal today: the sound-holes, although they correspond fairly well to standard *f* holes, are placed very high, at the height of the middle bouts, which are extremely short and deep; the lower part of the body is much wider than the upper; and there are no purflings.

The bass (or tenor) instrument nearby, played by the sitting angel at the lower rim of the cupola, shares some elements of the violin with the alto instrument to its right: the outline, consisting of three bouts; the strong moulding of the soundboard; the shallowness of the body in comparison with that of a regular viola da gamba; the projecting edges; the long thin neck; and the scroll. On the other hand, there are many differences: the proportions of the body; the much less marked angle at which the shoulders meet the neck; the position and reversed shape of the sound-holes; the leaf-shaped string holder; and the position of the bridge, between the sound-holes and therefore much higher up. In fact, the differences are so remarkable that one hesitates to regard this second instrument as belonging to the same whole consort. The pegs are not clearly visible in the deep shadow, and the strings, as usual, are not drawn. The narrow fingerboard would probably not allow more than four strings, a number not contradicted by the position of the stopping fingers.

[1] I am aware of the fact that Curt Sachs, who referred to Ferrari's depiction in his *History of Musical Instruments*, New York, 1940, p. 357, calls this violin three-stringed, and indeed only three peg heads are visible. A close scrutiny, however, reveals that these heads do not precisely coincide with the four visible stems and that the somewhat shoddy perspective, attributable to quick fresco painting, or perhaps to a careless assistant, was intended to suggest a fourth peg hidden behind the juncture of the fingerboard and the sickle-shaped peg box. Certainly the painter would hardly have depicted the four stems without a factual base.

The smallest of our three pre-violins is somewhat hidden between the lute player and the player of the richly curved string instrument with the lira da braccio head. We see only half of its body, in a three-quarter back view, and the sickle-shaped peg box, without scroll, is turned with some freedom of perspective so that we can look into it. The middle bouts are obscured by the peg leaf of the lira da braccio in front of it but, as far as we can see under these circumstances, the proportions have some similarity to those of the alto instrument. The head, however, is much more primitive than the elegant scrolls of the other two instruments; it resembles, in fact, that of a rebec (which, by the way, is twice represented in this fresco). Three pegs are indicated.

In short, our three instruments, although they have several common features, are so different in proportions and in other respects that one again hesitates to consider any of them as part of one set or consort.[1] Certainly, if Gaudenzio had wished to design three sizes for one homogeneous set he would have expressed his intention more clearly. He actually did so in a drawing of playing angels (now in the Staatliche Graphische Sammlung in Munich), which is probably a study for the Saronno fresco and which shows an actual set of three musical instruments that differ only in size, from treble to tenor (Pl. 40a).[2] They are instruments of fantastic shape, with extremely long necks terminating in flamboyant sickle heads. Their bodies are of such complex curvature that one does better to avoid the danger of verbalizing a description. Out of their shoulders grow projections in spiral shape, similar to those on many Renaissance citterns — projections that were, in fact, a last atrophic reminiscence of the arms of ancient and Carolingian lyres and kitharas.[3] And even these fantastic instruments are not the last word in Ferrari's exuberant fantasy of form: among his many beautiful sketches of musical *putti* and *amorini*, there is one that is even richer in curves, a veritable orgy in spirals (Pl. 40b). The body is spade-shaped — its tail decorated with sculptured leaves (a frequent ornament not only of Gaudenzio's instruments but also of real instruments of the Renaissance); and the long neck ends in a giant spiral. The shoulders not only continue in side spirals, but also carry double scrolls that imitate, in reverse shape, the form of the *f* holes.

Oddly enough, since Karl Geiringer's reference to the Saronno fresco and Curt Sachs's pointing out the three angels (as playing '*violette da braccio senza tasti* with three strings in the true shape of the present violin family'), there has been no analysis of these representations, but only passing remarks, by historians

[1] Cf. Curt Sachs, *op. cit.*, p. 357.

[2] I should like to express my thanks to Prof. Degenhart, the director of the Staatliche Graphische Sammlung, for kindly providing me with a photograph of this drawing.

[3] See Chapter 3.

of musical instruments. It is even more curious that attention has never been called to another violin in the same fresco (Pl. 41b). This violin is in a section quite remote from the instruments mentioned before and is also somewhat obscured there by the surrounding instruments, two psalteries, a harp, a plater-spiel, and a lira da braccio. Our violin is shown face forward, presenting a top view of the soundboard, whose bulge is strongly marked by shading. The middle bouts are precisely in the centre of the sides — a position quite different from that on the alto instrument above; the sound-holes correspond in shape to those of the 'bass violin' but are much more finely drawn, terminating in delicate spirals; and there is a three-pronged string holder. The bridge is placed between the lower parts of the sound-holes, just where their curve affords maximum width; this arrangement is different from that on the alto instrument, on which the sound-holes converge toward the bottom of the instrument, causing the bridge to be placed extremely low. The neck is narrow, and the head, to the dismay of the organologist, is covered by the arm of an angel playing the lira da braccio. But from the small width of the neck it is quite clear that no lira da braccio was intended here, since that instrument had to accommodate five melody strings on its fingerboard, to say nothing of the two bourdons running outside.[1] The bow may seem short at first glance, but part of it is actually covered by an angel wing. From the position of the stopping fingers it appears that the angel is not playing at the moment, but is awaiting his turn.

We now turn from these violins in the Saronno fresco to one appearing in an altarpiece painted by Gaudenzio for the Church of San Cristoforo in Vercelli, in oil on wood. It is called *La Madonna degli aranci* because of the beautiful orange grove that forms its background, and it is reliably dated 1529 — that is, six years before the Saronno fresco (Pl. 39a). But we have chosen to defer discussion of it until now, since the variety of shapes and the free style of drawing and perspective apparent in the Saronno fresco have sharpened our eyes for the appreciation of the 'Aranci violin.' This violin differs in many ways from the Saronno instruments. Most striking are the proportions: its body is compact, very wide, and its upper half is almost mirrored by its slightly wider lower half; also, the double curve of the shoulders is repeated at the bottom of the body. This is a shape as different from all the Saronno fresco violins as it is from the modern violin. The marked bulge of the soundboard does not begin near the edges, but is confined to a rather narrow middle section. The *f* holes diverge slightly towards the neck; they are cut precisely into the rims of the strong middle bulge of the soundboard. There is a heart-shaped string holder. The long fingerboard terminates in a long peg box with a scroll and three pegs. The

[1] This can be seen, for instance, in the lira da braccio to the right of our violin. Pl. 41b shows only the bowing hand and a small section of the contour of the body.

instrument is played with the head pointing downward, the bow is short, and the bowing and stopping hands, with the thumbs visible, are depicted most carefully and convincingly.

The execution of the whole painting reveals the master's hand. There is no question here of assistants. The two *putti*, and especially the violin player with his tender and meditative expression, are of exquisite workmanship. The instrument itself appears in perfect perspective in front view, and is turned just a little to make one side wall and the projecting edges visible.

That the shape of this instrument was not just a passing idea of Ferrari's appears from the repetition of the same shape in his sketch for an *Adoration of the Child*, in the Palazzo Reale in Turin (Pl. 41a), although there the contours appear rather sketchy and perfunctory. It seems also significant that this same shape was taken over by Gaudenzio's school, especially by his long-time pupil and assistant, Bernardino Lanini.

There is no doubt that Gaudenzio had more than a profound interest in musical instruments; he must have been an expert player and, I am convinced, also a builder of instruments. His paintings reveal not only a deep familiarity with the forms of instruments (although there are occasional slips, probably committed by assistants), but also with their function — that is, their practical use. The attitudes of the musicians' bodies, the positions of arms and shoulders, the embouchures and finger positions in the wind instruments, and the truthful, lively rendering of hands and fingers in bowing, stopping, or plucking on the string instruments, are based on sharp observation. Telling, also, is the great variety of instruments shown, unsurpassed in any other angel concert and approximated only, perhaps, in a Northern painting: Geertgen tot Sint Jans' *Virgin and Child*, which shows virtually all the instruments existing in his time.[1]

Still more strikingly, Gaudenzio's profound acquaintance with instruments reveals itself in his crossing of the borderline between reality — that is, the exact portrayal of existing instruments — and free imagination — creating shapes that are functional enough but divergent from tradition even in a period that was remarkably little restricted by standardization. But in these fantastic instruments, such as a double bagpipe and a fiddle that could be both blown and bowed at the same time, Gaudenzio was not merely making wild creations of the brush for the sake of visual beauty; his instruments are functional — they could have been constructed and perhaps even were, for the fun of it, in a playful mood. In this they differ fundamentally from the many fantastic and scurrilous instruments that were created with sinister fantasy — the bird monsters with oboe beaks, etc., which a northern contemporary of Gaudenzio's,

[1] See Chapter 11.

Hieronymus Bosch, used in his hell scenes. But, of course, hell admits more of the grotesque than does heaven!

There is, finally, another fact that makes it seem probable that Gaudenzio built instruments himself: he was not only a painter, but also a sculptor, as we know from his expressive life-size figures at Varallo peopling many scenes from the New Testament.

Vasari (*Vite*, ed. Milanesi, IV, 652, and VI, 518) mentions Gaudenzio in a few laudatory words without going into detail; he was evidently not directly acquainted with Gaudenzio's work. Strangely enough, then, in the evaluation of the musical subjects painted by Ferrari, the most important biographical source has been entirely neglected, although it exists in a book often quoted by art historians: Lomazzo's *Idea del tempio della pittura* (1590?). Lomazzo, a painter and poet, was a nephew of Gaudenzio's, and his superlatives, with which he was never thrifty, should perhaps be taken *cum grano salis*: in his account of Gaudenzio's works in the *Trattato dell'arte della pittura scultura ed architettura* (1584), he calls Gaudenzio (p. 185) 'my old master Gaudenzio, not only an expert painter . . . but a most profound philosopher and mathematician. . . .' But he is more precise, at least as far as Gaudenzio's musical activities are concerned, in his *Idea del tempio*. There, in Chapter IX, entitled 'Fabbrica del Tempio della Pittura, e dei suoi Governatori' (p. 37 ff.), he establishes an analogy, in his fanciful poetic way, between the seven planets and the seven governors in the Temple of Painting, whose statues are to be erected in the temple. The governors are to be Michelangelo, Gaudenzio, Caravaggio, Leonardo, Raphael, Mantegna, and Titian (in that order). Of Gaudenzio, second only to Michelangelo, Lomazzo says: 'He was born in Valdugia, and was a painter, sculptor, architect, master of perspective, natural philosopher, poet, and performer on the lira and the lute.' The 'lira' was no doubt the lira da braccio.[1] Thus, on the basis of this information, Gaudenzio played the most noble and difficult bowed instrument of his time, a fact quite significant in view of his inclusion of violins in his pictures.

The basic shape of Ferrari's violin in the altar painting of *La Madonna degli aranci* was retained by his followers, especially by Bernardino Lanini. Lanini, who lived from about 1510 to 1583, had joined Ferrari's workshop in 1530 and was probably still assisting the master in the work on the Saronno fresco. As we shall see, Lanini was not deeply interested in musical instruments. Yet, since his many altarpieces included numerous representations of the Adoration of the Infant, the *sacra conversazione*, and the Assumption of the Virgin, the

[1] In Chapter 5 above, I have investigated the various names applied to this instrument and the resulting confusion, especially with reference to Vincenzo Galilei's explanation that the viola da braccio had begun to be called 'lira' only in what for him were modern times.

musical angels traditionally connected with these themes had to be represented.

Lanini repeated the broad and short pattern of the 'Aranci violin' in his altarpiece of the *Assumption* in the Church of San Sebastiano at Biella, in 1543, and also in his *Madonna with Saints and Angels* in the church of San Paolo, Biella, and the *Adoration of the Infant* in San Magno, Legnano. A surprising difference appears, however, in another instrument painted by him in a *sacra conversazione* (from the Cook Collection in Richmond, which later came to the Kress Collection in New York and is today in the Raleigh Museum in North Carolina; Pl. 39b).[1] There, one single *putto* plays a fiddle before the throne of the Virgin. At his feet are lying a lute, a recorder, and a jingle drum. The fiddle, although unmistakably a violin, with four strings and a strongly marked bulge in the soundboard, does not repeat the broad pattern of Lanini's other violins mentioned above, nor of Ferrari's 'Aranci violin', but is of an extremely long and narrow shape and shows purflings which, to my knowledge, had not been represented before. The painting reveals that Lanini, for all his good intentions and neat drawing, was not a player or connoisseur. The representation of the bridge disregards perspective to such an extent that it appears to be upside down, and the positions of the stopping and bowing fingers are so lifeless and perfunctory that they could have been drawn only by a musical ignoramus. But for just this very reason we must assume that this violin did not spring from Lanini's imagination, but portrayed an existing instrument; and this makes the painting an important record, especially since it is dated. To the left of the bow handle we read 'B.nardinus Laninus . Ucellen . F . 1552' (that is, thirty-two years after Ferrari's *Madonna degli aranci*).

Most treatises on the violin have pointed to Brescia and Cremona as the cradles of this instrument. But the great Brescian master, Gasparo da Salò, was only born about 1540 and would not have been constructing violins before the 1560s. And Andrea Amati, the founder of the Cremonese dynasty of Amatis, was born about 1535 (according to Lütgendorff, *Die Geigen und Lautenmacher*); his earliest known violins are dated about 1564, according to *Grove's Dictionary of Music and Musicians*, although some instruments dated '1551' are listed as authentic by Francis Farga (in *Violins and Violinists*).

But the violins represented in the paintings of Gaudenzio Ferrari and Bernardino Lanini point to another and considerably earlier root west of Milan or even to the Piedmont. They also add another little bit of information to the complex and fascinating story of the early violin: they show such a bewildering

[1] I am grateful to the Kress Foundation and Dr. Alessandro Contini-Bonacossi, who have made photographs of this picture available to me and permitted me to use them.

variety of shapes and proportions that one almost directly senses the morphological fermentation of which they were a part and which had not yet reached the point of crystallization into the more or less standardized patterns later created in Brescia and Cremona.

7 · The Golden Harpsichord and Todini's *Galleria Armonica*

One of the outstanding examples of baroque decorative art in the collections of the Metropolitan Museum in New York is a musical instrument, a gilded harpsichord of fantastic form (Pl. 42a). The wing-shaped body of the instrument is supported by three fishtailed tritons (Pl. 44b), gliding on softly swelling waves. Between them rise two sea nymphs, and riding behind is a *putto* (Pl. 44c), perched high on a sea shell and driving two dolphins. All these fishy folk move through the water with bold and cheerful gestures. The water itself, silvery green and shimmering, is enclosed by a massive ledge that repeats on a larger scale the outline of the harpsichord proper. And this whole oceanic phantasmagoria rests on lions' feet.

The right side of the harpsichord is decorated with an elaborate gilded frieze representing the triumph of Galatea (Pl. 42b). Sitting in a wheeled shell car drawn by fishtailed horses, Galatea travels over the waves; trumpeting tritons herald her approach and follow her carriage. *Putti*, some of them winged, ride sea horses, and everywhere one can see a gay medley of fins, spiralling tails, and agitated horses (Pl. 44a). Even the clouds in the background participate in the interplay of moving curves. On the extreme left, next to a span of three wildly excited horses yet quite removed from all the watery commotion, sits the only tranquil figure in the frieze, an idyllic youthful musician on a rock. In contrast to the other creatures, who blow on trumpets, he plays a string instrument, the noble lute.

The harpsichord in its basin is flanked by two life-sized figures, each sitting on a rock (Pl. 42a). Both, like the harpsichord, are made of gilded wood. The one on the left represents Polyphemus, the right Galatea. Polyphemus plays a bagpipe. Galatea's instrument is missing, but to judge from the position of her arms and fingers she probably had a lute. Here Polyphemus is not the ferocious man-eating and rock-throwing giant of the *Odyssey*, who devoured Ulysses' companions and crushed Galatea's lover with a stone, but the longing, unhappy shepherd, saddened and dandified by his unrequited love of the nymph, as we find him in Alexandrian poetry and particularly in Ovid's *Metamorphoses*, Book XIII:

> Behold, that savage creature, whom the very woods shudder to look upon, whom no stranger has ever seen save to his own hurt, who despises great Olympus and its gods; he feels the power of love and burns with mighty desire, forgetful of his flocks and of his caves. And now, Polyphemus, you become careful of your appearance, now anxious to please; now with a rake you comb your shaggy locks, and now it is your pleasure to cut your rough beard with a reaping-hook, gazing at your rude features in some clear pool and composing their expression.

The representations in art of this one-sided love affair would fill a museum. They range from Pompeian wall paintings to the grandiose Caracci frescoes in the Palazzo Farnese in Rome. In the east loggia of the Villa Farnesina Raphael painted his exuberant procession of Galatea (the frieze of the harpsichord is, as it were, a side view of the procession that Raphael depicted from the front). Immediately to its left is Sebastiano del Piombo's Polyphemus, sitting on a rock like our figure but holding a panpipe, or pastoral syrinx, in his right hand and gazing tenderly out to sea, that is, towards Raphael's Galatea.

The syrinx, made up of many small reed pipes, was the customary shepherd's instrument in classical times and was depicted as such in sculpture and painting. The bagpipe, known to antiquity as *tibia utricularis*, was not a pastoral but a sophisticated instrument. According to Suetonius it was, for example, played by Nero. It appears for the first time in the hands of shepherds in medieval miniatures, although in a more primitive form than that played by our Polyphemus (Pl. 46, left). What we see here is the elaborate *sordellina*, or musette, of the 17th century, equipped with one chanter and two drones. There is no blowpipe like that through which earlier pipers filled the bag with air; instead there are bellows attached by a leather belt to the right wrist. This was a technical improvement not found before the last quarter of the 16th century. One of the earliest examples of the improved form, an instrument mentioned as early as 1596 in the inventory of the Kunstkammer of Schloss Ambras in the Tyrol, is today in the Vienna collection of old instruments.

Such an impressive piece as our harpsichord, evidently designed by a first-rate artist, provokes curiosity. What was its origin and what is its history? The instrument entered the Metropolitan Museum in 1889 as part of the monumental Crosby Brown collection. It was known to have once been in the possession of Viscount Sartiges, who was the French ambassador to the Holy See in the 1860s, but here our information ended. However, two lucky discoveries have since provided answers to our questions.

In 1949 I heard various rumours about a very large private collection of musical instruments in Italy, brought together by Evan Gorga, the Rumanian tenor who performed the title role in the first performance of Mascagni's

L'Amico Fritz in 1891. I visited Mr. Gorga in Rome, and he told me enthusiastically about his collections of various objects. Before the Fascist period he had collected several thousand musical instruments and had later sold them to the Italian government. Much to his regret, they had never been exhibited, and he had only vague information about the places, mostly basements, where they were stored. He could, however, show me a mountain of photographs, all signed by Ottorino Respighi, who had taken part in the sale to the government, and also a small booklet that he had printed many years previously as a condensed description of the collection. Among its few illustrations there was one that, blurred and yellowed as it was, could be recognized at first glimpse as a model for our harpsichord. Mr. Gorga remembered that he had once owned such a model, made of clay, but had no idea what had become of it.

A little later, deeply saddened by the war damage in Subiaco and other old familiar hill towns, I revisited the Palazzo Venezia in Rome, whose director, Antonino Santangelo, kindly showed me storerooms where heaps of fragments salvaged from Genzano, Albano, and other bombed sites were temporarily stored. In one of these rooms was a wooden box filled with small reddish clay fragments. Among them I recognized a tiny bagpipe, about the length of a finger joint, closely resembling the sordellina of our Polyphemus. When the head of Polyphemus also emerged I was able to convince my slightly dubious host that this was a terracotta model closely related to our harpsichord. We quickly fitted the pieces together, and there was no doubt. A photograph taken at that time shows the half-assembled model (Pl. 43a). Soon afterwards, I sent photographs of our instrument to the Palazzo Venezia as a guide for the final reassembling of the fragments and received in turn pictures of the assembled model (Pl. 43b). Only minor details like fingers were missing, and still are today.

At first glimpse the little sculpture looks like a *bozzetto*, or model, made for the person who commissioned the instrument or as a guide for the woodcarvers who were to execute the real instrument. It is of the finest workmanship, elegant in its proportions and finished to the smallest detail. Yet, although it agrees with the instrument in the shapes of the figures and the relief, there are some puzzling divergencies. In the model the *putto* almost touches the end of the harpsichord, joining with the central mass of the body and its carriers, while the flanking figures sit so far away that the spaces between make symmetrical shapes. In the large sculpture these proportions are lost (Pl. 46).

There are even more subtle stylistic differences: the figures of the model have a soft roundness and a classical restraint lacking in the large sculpture, which shows more animation and 'baroque' exuberance. However, the problem of the relationship must be left open for the moment. One thing seems fairly certain: the large sculpture suggests the circle of Algardi, possibly his pupil Domenico

Guidi, or perhaps Ercole Ferrata.[1] Similar monumental wooden sculptures, designed as carriers, were not infrequent in Rome at the time. A pair of table supports in the form of winged tritons in the Palazzo dei Conservatori may be the work of the sculptor of our figures, or another of the same circle.

While the discovery of the model was a welcome surprise, it still left in darkness the history of the harpsichord. By good luck this has been clarified. In the library of the Palazzo Corsini I found one of the rare copies of the *Galleria armonica* by Michele Todini, published in Rome in 1676. The full title is *Dichiaratione della galleria armonica eretta in Roma de M. Todini Piemontese di Saluzzo, nella sua habitazione, posta all'Arco della Ciambella Roma 1676.* This amusing little book is the description of a museum of musical instruments by its enthusiastic founder and owner. The house that harboured this museum, in the Arco della Ciambella, a small street near the present Largo Argentina, does not exist anymore. But from the text of Todini's treatise we learn that it contained all sorts of music machines, which were extremely popular in the baroque period, not only in Italy but also in southern Germany and Austria. With understandable pride, Todini describes his treasures and his efforts to assemble them.

Todini, a Piedmontese, lived in Rome and made his living by playing the violone, the large bass fiddle of the time, in concerts and the trumpet in the wind band at the Castel Sant' Angelo. His real interest, however, was the construction of music machines. Some amusing details of his life are to be found in J. G. Walther's *Musicalisches Lexikon* (1732),[2] Filippo Buonanni's *Gabinetto armonico pieno d'istromenti indicati* (1722), and the first book of the *Phonurgia nova* (1673), by the versatile, learned Jesuit father Athanasius Kircher, who knew Todini.

For many years Todini designed and built musical clockworks, mechanical fiddles, novel types of organs, and harpsichords. He exhibited them in three large rooms of the Palazzo Verospi, probably to secure an income during his later life by charging admission. It was, as far as I can see, the first museum exclusively devoted to musical instruments. As he says in the preface of his book, he was urged by connoisseurs to publish a description of the objects in his collection and the difficulties he had to overcome in building his machines. Chapter 3 is called 'Descrittione della machina di Polifemo e Galatea' and is concerned with the second room of his museum, where the story of Galatea and Polyphemus was represented by a gilded harpsichord rich in carving and carried by

[1] After the first publication of this study, my colleague at the Metropolitan Museum, Dr. Olga Raggio, suggested very convincing reasons for an attribution to the circle of Filippo Parodi.

[2] Facsimile edition, Kassel, 1953.

life-sized Tritons, by large figures of Galatea and of Polyphemus 'in the act of playing a sordellina to please Galatea,' and by a *putto* driving two dolphins. He even mentions that the marine monsters in Galatea's procession carry *frutta di mare*, evidently referring to the fish, turtle, and large crab in the frieze of our instrument. He also states that Polyphemus was 'sitting on the slope of the mountain where he had his home.' Our figure has a flat back, which must have fitted against the background of the exhibition gallery. Thus it seems that our harpsichord was the central feature of a musical machine that, like each of the others, filled an entire room and that the whole decorative scheme was continued to the ceiling by means of stucco mountains and a painted landscape.

With these facts in mind we can now return to the clay model, in which the flanking figures are united to the instrument by the common base and by the harmonious design of the whole group. Why and when were the two figures separated from the central piece? If the little sculpture was a presentation or working model preceding the execution of the large group, we may assume that when the finished group came into Todini's possession he had it broken up to fit his scenic arrangement. Another possibility should perhaps also be considered: the model may have been commissioned by a visitor to the gallery who wanted a replica of the harpsichord and its figures for the music room of his palazzo or villa. Here we must leave the problem, trusting that future research may furnish more facts for its complete solution.

Todini's harpsichord group, like most of his machines, had a hidden mechanism that provided a surprise effect. Polyphemus's bagpipe played real music, sounding together with the harpsichord and thus achieving a combination of winds and strings. The one-man orchestra was an old dream of musicians that was realized over and over again in Renaissance and Baroque instruments, one example being the *claviorganum*. The sound of Polyphemus's bagpipe was actually produced by a set of pipes hidden in the mountain behind the figure and connected with a special keyboard concealed beneath that of the harpsichord. In his Chapter 20 Todini tells in amusing detail his troubles in building this mechanism and how difficult it was to get bagpipe experts to make metal pipes without cheating on the metal. Unfortunately, no illustration of the complete arrangement in the exhibition room has come to us.

However, another of Todini's tricky machines, described by him in Chapter 4, is also found in the *Appendix de mirifica phonurgia* to Kircher's book and is illustrated there as well as in Buonanni's *Gabinetto armonico*, Plate XXXIII. This was a group of no less than seven instruments, four with quills, two bowed, and one organ. The player of one of these instruments, the *archiclavicymbalum*, could make the other six sound from afar, or so it seemed to the listener. The engraving in Kircher's book (Pl. 45a) shows Todini playing the *archiclavicymbalum* at the left and three indefinite string instruments without keyboards standing freely in the middle before the organ. This schematic illustration was clearly not made on the spot but was done either from memory or hearsay. The engraving in Buonanni's book (Pl. 45b), however, seems to be a faithful portrait of the same machine, showing the three clavicymbals attached to the large organ case in the back. Still, Kircher complains in his awkward 17th-century Latin that Todini did not give his secret away, although we can say in retrospect that anyone familiar with late Baroque organs and their several compartments and complex tracker machinery would not have been puzzled. The baroque décor of the whole enormous structure reached to the ceiling, like the machine of Galatea and Polyphemus. On the organ case is the suggestion of a landscape, which according to Todini was painted by 'Gasparo Poussin,' evidently meaning Poussin's brother-in-law Gaspar Dughet, who was working in Rome at the time and who, by the way, also decorated a beautiful harpsichord in the Metropolitan Museum's collection.

Neither the artistic nor the musical aspect of Todini's machines exhausts our interest in them. For the historian of art they reflect a world passionately devoted to the theatrical effects inherited from the late Renaissance but vastly expanded through the new progress in the mathematical sciences. These are, however, only the artistic trappings, overlaying a deeper stratum of the mind. In a more profound sense, these musical machines were part and product of a world where — in theology and philosophy — the image of the automaton with its secret, hidden operator was often taken as the symbol of the Creator, mysteriously and incessantly imparting motion to the universe.

8 · The Importance of *Quattrocento* Intarsias for the History of Musical Instruments

As we have observed previously, music history for obvious reasons deals chiefly with music as it has survived in written form, and, for a long span, written music was prevailingly sacred vocal music. With this state of affairs, it is understandable that the wide realm of unwritten music remained for a long time a secondary field of interest for the historian of music. This area includes not only folk music in its narrower sense, but also some of the most subtle forms of instrumental music, such as the improvisations of the 15th and 16th centuries.

Where scores are lacking, it is the instruments themselves that are the main witnesses of this musical culture and its performance practice; and, where the instruments have not survived, we must rely on their representation in the visual arts. Georg Kinsky, Curt Sachs, Willibald Gurlitt, Hugo Leichtentritt, and others have pointed out the importance of these representations. Little noted, however, were the problems and difficulties inherent in the interpretation of these pictorial documents. Are the shapes of the instruments, the way they were played, and their combinations into ensembles reliably represented in paintings, frescoes, drawings, woodcuts, engravings, sculptures, embroideries, and the like? To what extent are these representations faithful portrayals of reality, and to what extent are they products of artistic imagination? And what are the reasons for which an artist would depart from accurate depiction? Any evaluation of the faithfulness of the representations presupposes intimate familiarity not only with musical matters, but also with the ever-changing aims and methods of expression through every period of the plastic arts.

I should like to draw attention to a still unmined treasure of pictorial sources: the Italian intarsias of the *quattrocento* and the first decades of the *cinquecento*. These sources are important for two reasons: first, the short-lived fashion of intarsias coincides with the famous improvisations, mentioned in numerous literary sources of the time, by the great virtuosos on the viola and the lira da braccio; and second, the instruments in the intarsias are rendered in life size or nearly so, and with such accuracy that they differ from real instruments only by their lack of a third dimension. The main aesthetic impulse for the intarsia fashion seems to have come from the refinement of theoretical perspective as a tool of the painter, above all through the treatises of Piero della Francesca and Luca Pacioli; the new technique of geometrical projection benefited, of course, the precision of representation.

There is no space here to discuss the dynasties of *intarsiatori*, the local characteristics of their style, the competition between the schools of Urbino, Monte Oliveto Maggiore, and Verona, or even to give a survey of the wealth of material; but I would like to give a few characteristic examples.

Some of the most interesting instruments in intarsias are to be found in the ducal palace of Urbino, the main residence of Federigo da Montefeltro. There, in the so-called *studiolo*, one of the great showpieces of the new technique of *quattrocento* linear perspective, we find a large clavichord (Pl. 51a) with no less than forty-seven keys — twenty-nine long and eighteen short ones, the former decorated with carved frontal slats of Gothic pattern. To these forty-seven keys there are twenty-two corresponding single strings; the instrument is, like all early clavichords, a 'fretted' one. The curvature of the keys and their tangents is drawn in precise perspective. A consistent application of foreshortening brings the strings so close to each other that the artist preferred to represent them not by wooden strips but by metal wires. An instrument of these remarkable dimensions and construction must have been the product of a long tradition. It is interesting that the earliest surviving clavichord, made in 1537 by Alexander Trasontinus and decorated with the complacent inscription 'Ut rosa flos florum ita hoc clavile clavilium'[1] (today in the collection of musical instruments in the Metropolitan Museum of Art in New York), has only thirty-six keys (twenty-one long and fifteen short ones) and an arrangement of bridges that is incomparably more primitive than that in the clavichord from the Urbino *studiolo*.

On the same wall of this *studiolo* we see a nine-string lute side by side with an early form of the lira da braccio, the latter with five strings: four stopped strings and one free bass string — equipment somewhat different from that which was customary later: five stopped strings and two free bass strings (Pl. 52a). Its peg box is still round and simple, its belly flat, and one can clearly observe how the side walls curve in between the strongly projecting edges of the belly and the back, a result of the fact that the side walls then were much thicker than those of the later violin; there were no blocks like those that help to hold the side walls of modern instruments to the belly and the back at the neck, bottom, and corners of the middle bouts. In the old instruments the broad upper and lower edges of the thick side walls were glued to the belly and back and then carefully hollowed out with a knife or chisel.

[1] 'Just as the rose is the flower of flowers, this is the clavichord of clavichords.'

Federigo da Montefeltro had, beside his gigantic palace in Urbino, a second residence in Gubbio.[1] The much smaller palace there also had a *studiolo* with wall intarsias; it is today one of the treasures of the Metropolitan Museum in New York. This *studiolo* is even richer in musical instruments than the one in Urbino. To mention one single example, there is a richly decorated positive organ with a double row of metal pipes: twenty-six in the first row, and a second row visible behind the feet of the pipes at the front (Pl. 47a). The keyboard consists of twenty-two long and thirteen short keys. Behind the organ, in one of the many cupboards of which the intarsias of these flat walls make believe to consist, we see a vielle with four stopped strings and one free drone string — thus an immediate predecessor of the lira da braccio in the *studiolo* of Urbino. During his years in Urbino, Raphael must have been familiar with these intarsias. In the upper section of the cupboard, a lute and two *cornetti curvi* of octagonal cross section are represented.

An interesting predecessor of the fully developed clavicembalo is found in the choir stalls of the cathedral of Genoa (Pl. 51b). The soundboard shows two sound-holes. Of special interest are the arrangement of the keys and the unusual form of the jacks, carrying quills cut from bird feathers.

A large lute of the high Renaissance, with eleven strings, is shown in daringly foreshortened perspective in a series of Bolognese intarsias, probably by Damian da Bergamo (*c.* 1545), also in the collection of the Metropolitan Museum (Pl. 47b). Nine strings are visible, but it would seem that there should be two more, since eleven pegs are indicated, of which some are of light and others of dark wood. Next to the lute on the complex tiled floor, of a type often seen in these intarsias, there is a music book: the open pages show a four-part and a seven-part canon which are both, curiously, without text.

The richest treasure of intarsias made for the decoration of churches is found in the choir stalls of the convent of Monte Oliveto Maggiore, not far from Siena. These intarsias come from the famous workshop of Fra Giovanni da Verona. Of particular interest is the bulky cittern seen in the upper section of one of the many half-open cupboards (Pl. 48a), with its characteristic hook behind the neck, its stair-shaped or terraced frets, and the peculiar ears protruding from its shoulders, atrophic rudiments of the arms of the late ancient and early medieval kithara.[2] The refinement of the whole composition attests to the elegant taste of the artist. The *trompe l'œil* effect (spatial illusion) is enhanced by the doors of the cupboards, which open at different angles, and by the way in which the neck of the lute protrudes out of the shelf towards the beholder. Exquisite also is the manner in which the geometrical and functional forms of the instruments themselves are accompanied by and contrasted to the spiral

[1] See Chapter 9 below.

[2] See Chapter 3 above.

curves of the music sheet, and the broken lute strings that also help to fill otherwise empty spaces in the composition.

Finally, there are several examples from the inlaid doors of the Stanza della Segnatura in the Vatican, which have, strangely, escaped the attention of art and musical historians — probably because these doors are always open with their inlaid fronts leaning against the wall. Here we encounter the most daring musical still-lifes in perspective ever created by the art of the *intarsiatori*. One panel shows two lutes (Pl. 48b) in unusual counterpoint, and again the undulations of the broken strings fill the empty spaces. There is a five-string viola da gamba, with sharp corners defining the middle bouts, quite unconventional sound-holes, and a massive bow (Pl. 50b); a set of five cromornes, together with a jingle drum (Pl. 49a); a harp, still of late Gothic shape, with a set of three recorders (Pl. 49b); and a spinettino of complex spherical contour, which floats so beautifully in space that, notwithstanding its precise rendering according to the *quattrocento* technique of geometrical projection, one is almost reminded of the spatial caprices of the Baroque (Pl. 50a).

These examples are a very small selection from the wealth of intarsias that have survived to our day, and that are not only of great interest for the history of musical instruments, but of immediate importance for the connoisseur of the improvisation practice of the *quattro-* and *cinquecento* and of the tools of the great virtuosos of the Renaissance.

They are objects of meditation and as such play a role in the early history of the still-life; they are reflections of actual musical activities at the Papal court, in palaces and churches of the time; they are remnants of the traditional allegories of the *quadrivium*; and, last but not least, they belong among the most fascinating showpieces demonstrating the new fashion of linear perspective.

9 · *Quattrocento* Science in the Gubbio Study

If any monument of art be an invitation to the past, an interior like the intarsia study of Federigo da Montefeltro now in the Metropolitan Museum of Art, has this appeal in an eminent degree. Sculptures have pedestals, paintings frames, leading from our everyday world to that of illusion; but here the illusion is complete, the visitor wholly enters the past. When we have accustomed ourselves to the spell of the warm, golden-brown dusk, the walls begin to speak. A graceful architectural setting becomes visible, its pillars framing cupboards with benches projecting beneath, all filled with books, musical and scientific instruments, armour, and library tools in pleasant order and variety. The illusion of depth is so great that we must make an effort to convince ourselves that we face two-dimensional pictures in inlay (Pl. 52b).

Was this little room a real study, a workroom for the learned Duke? Fill it in your imagination with the customary appliances of a private library of that time and you will see how the charm of the imagery upon the walls would be destroyed by any competition from actual objects. The Duke, we must suppose, had better taste. Besides, the balance of the decorative display, unbroken as it is, would only be disturbed by any outside intrusion. What then is the idea of this room? It is a witty play with the exciting new technique of strict linear perspective. It also pays homage to the Duke, with his various interests and activities. Finally, it is a mirror of the rich intellectual life at the court of which he was not merely the illustrious head but also the stirring heart.

Libraries have been written on Federigo da Montefeltro. His contemporaries called him the light of Italy. Statesman, warrior, scholar, and connoisseur in the arts, he stands out even against the background of his most versatile time as the embodiment of the practical, theoretical, and aesthetic gifts. In short, he approximated the ancient Greek ideal of harmony, well known to him from his beloved Aristotle. There was one trait of character, however, which distinguished this humanist *condottiere* from most of his fellows. This was his sense of justice and responsibility. That he, unlike most princes of the day, could dare to stroll unarmed among his subjects and be heartily greeted with 'Dio ti mantenga, Signore!' he owed above all to his celebrated system of taxation.

There is no image in the little study which does not celebrate the many interests of this universal man. The books, no less than fourteen, remind us of the library he built up in his main residence, Urbino. It was the greatest library of its time, containing in its wealth of items the catalogues of such libraries as the Vatican, San Marco, Florence, and Oxford. He preferred written to printed books and for many years employed thirty or forty writers, with an output of sometimes as many as two hundred books in twenty-two months.

Besides these compendia of the learned mind, we find the tools of the searching mind: a pair of dividers, a quadrant, a lever, a celestial globe. The latter particularly reminds us of the Netherlander, Paul von Middelburg, who was Federigo's court astrologist and mathematician.

The many arms depicted appear to be symbols of the art of war, in which the Duke was a learned and successful master. His authority in the rules of 'correct,' scientific warfare was undisputed, his victories famous, his new techniques, such as the use of heavy field artillery, epoch-making. He was a patron of all the sports of chivalry and loved to lead the evening contests of his young courtiers.

We next observe an amazing variety of musical instruments, fourteen in number, witnesses of the exquisite musical taste at Federigo's court. Besides percussion instruments, such as a tambourine and a tabor, we find plucked string instruments: two lutes, a cittern, a harp; bowed instruments: a rebec and a fiddle; wind instruments: two cornetti, a hunting horn, a pipe, and finally a magnificent portative organ. The cittern (Pl. 53a), similar to that of Fra Giovanni da Verona (Pl. 13c), shows some features lost afterwards, when the cittern became the fashionable instrument in the barbershops of Elizabethan England: namely, the characteristic hook at the neck and the sharp detachment of the neck from the body, which also occur in some fiddles of the same time (Pl. 53b). The pear-shaped rebec (Pl. 53c), leaning beside its bow, is clearly recognizable through the latticework of the cupboard door by its sickle-shaped peg box. Its box has not the usual cucumber or boat shape that is shown, for example, in the rebec played by an angel in a fresco by Pinturicchio in Santa Maria in Aracoeli, Rome (Pl. 54b), but rather a very long, thin fingerboard, tapering gradually into a broad sound box with a rounded profile. The almond-shaped fiddle (Pl. 53d) is depicted often in Renaissance painting, for instance by Signorelli in the Church of the Casa Santa at Loreto (Pl. 54a). The representation in our intarsias does not show its peg box, but it is easily recognized as a bowed instrument by its bridge, the form of its fingerboard, and the position and shape of the sound-holes. Besides its four melody strings, a drone is visible, foreshadowing the later transition into the lira da braccio, played in numerous Renaissance paintings by Orpheus, by Apollo, and by many angels. Characteristically, the string instruments, regarded as the nobler and favoured by Pallas and Apollo, outnumber the winds, the playing of which distorts the face, according to Plutarch (quoted in Book II of Castiglione's famous book on the courtier). What must have excited the inlay worker — the portrayal of wooden instruments in their natural substance but with their bulk reduced to two dimensions — is a sheer delight for the historian today. Old woodcuts of keyboard instruments caused many a headache to the connoisseurs before they discovered that the woodcuts had been reprinted in reverse. In our intarsias, the exact rendering of functional details, such as strings, frets, pegs, and so forth, in their natural dimensions, surpasses in exactness most other modes of illustration.

The multitude of the objects depicted, however, is not merely a reflection of the versatile personality of the Duke. There is a deeper bond between them. They are symbolic of the intimate connection among the arts at that time and between the arts and the sciences, and it is only of secondary importance to what extent this symbolism was intended by the maker of the study; he was a creature of his time. Both art and science in the *quattrocento* drew their inspiration from one strong impulse: the tendency toward rationalization, sweeping through all branches of natural science, aiming at calculation and control of nature by establishing its laws. The basic structure of nature was to be found in simple numerical formulas. This conception of natural science swept the artists along with it, but they were themselves pioneers in its development; in portraying nature 'correctly' they hoped to capture its secrets. Art was research into nature, the artist an experimental scientist, the canons of nature the canons or rules of 'correct' artistic creation.[1] Art was thus a sort of science, a body of knowledge dealing with the basic relations between phenomena, visible or audible. So, on the formula of the harmonic proportions were based, among other things, the standards for the human body and for architecture as well as the musical scale, and, as the most recent pearl on this string, the theory of linear perspective. The artist-scientists around Duke Federigo were among the most influential standard-bearers in this new adventure of the mind, and our study, looked at from this angle, is a monument and showpiece of the new achievements.

The main key to this interpretation of the study is found not so much in the objects depicted as in the manner in which they are depicted: it is a triumph of linear perspective. Problems of the utmost complexity are mastered here with playful joy and accuracy; no intricacies are avoided. To begin with trifles: the border patterns consist of strings of geometrical bodies, simulating three-dimensional forms (Pl. 56a & b). The turban ring (Pl. 56c) is only a slightly

[1] Leonardo: 'Those who are enamoured of practice without science are like a pilot who goes into a ship without rudder or compass and never has any certainty where he is going' (MS G, Institut de France, 8 r.). 'Perspective therefore is to be preferred to all the formularies and systems of the schoolman, for in its province the complex beam of light is made to show the stages of its development, wherein is found the glory not only of mathematical but also of physical science, adorned as it is with the flowers of both' (*Codice Atlantico*, 203 r.a.).

different version of one of the construction diagrams (Pl. 56d) described by Piero della Francesca in his famous treatise *De prospectiva pingendi*, dedicated in 1469 to Duke Federigo and most influential in the whole further development of theoretical and pictorial perspective, particularly on Luca Pacioli and Leonardo. The architectural details, such as the flutes of the pilasters and the mouldings of the architrave, burst forth with plastic life. The cupboard doors are open at all possible angles. Only a master of projective geometry could have designed the shadow of the lectern shaft, running over the complex mouldings of imaginary architecture (Pl. 54c). Particularly interesting is the border ornament around the cupboards which flank the window (Pl. 57c). It consists of little disks threaded on a small stick, a common frame pattern in *quattrocento* woodcuts, where it appears in cruder versions (Pl. 57a). But here what accuracy! If we sweep our eye upward along this string, we progress gradually from a top view to a bottom view of the disks. One disk shows its rim only and thus appears at eye level — it might have been the Duke's — and we remember Leonardo's advice to painters to take as the vanishing point the eye level of an average man. If, however, we run our eye along the horizontal ledge below the cupboard, no disk shows us only its rim; though these disks also appear in successive positions, it is clear that they are adjusted for an eye placed somewhat farther to the right than the disk at the extreme right corner. This requires an observer placed not in the window niche but more to the centre of the room. Thus the two rows of disks have a point of vision precisely determined as to its vertical and horizontal position.

Such a fixed position of the point of vision, as is possible for a single panel with its limited field, cannot be maintained for a whole interior: here the visitor turns around from wall to wall, continually shifting his point of vision. The complexity of this problem of a perspective interior may be shown by the following consideration: any three-dimensional object offers an infinite number of different two-dimensional aspects or images.[1] Only one of these images is chosen for a painting or any other two-dimensional representation, corresponding to one selected point of vision. Our intarsia room, however, is not a painting, or even a set of relatively independent images, but, like space itself, it continues and returns upon itself. Therefore, we might expect that, like any round object, it should offer to the observer, as he moves, a new aspect with every step, corresponding to his changing point of vision. But this it cannot do, being two-dimensional. Therefore, a sort of compromise is necessary to do justice to the observer in any possible position. How this compromise is approximated here without any loss in power of illusion constitutes an inexhaustible source of intellectual pleasure.

[1] Leonardo: 'Each body alone of itself fills the whole surrounding air with its images' (*Codice Atlantico*, 138 r.b.).

This problem of pictorial projection is made even more difficult by the further problem of the shadows. That the objects represented should throw shadows is obvious here where the highest degree of plastic illusion is aimed at. These shadows, particularly those of the balusters, are adjusted to two sources of light, the window and the door. Double shadows for one and the same object would have produced too confusing an effect. So in this too a compromise has been attempted. One has only to look at the corner formed by the small wall to the right of the door and the adjoining long wall to observe that the balusters at the small wall apparently receive their light and shadow from the window, while the long wall seems to be lighted through the door (Pl. 55a).

I am indebted to Cordray Simmons for an ingenious remark he made to me when I told him some observations made in the study. Being a painter and accustomed to constant shifting between one- and two-eye vision in his own painting, it occurred to him as he was helping to restore the study to wonder whether or not the one-eyedness of the Duke had anything to do with the particular character of the study as accomplished perspective illusion. The facts are that the Duke had lost his right eye in a jousting accident, and that the discrimination between a real object and its accurate portrait is much harder for one eye than for both. This defect in depth-sensation must have made the illusion even more perfect for the Duke.

The mastery of the visual reality by finding and formulating the numerical rules of space, that is, linear perspective, is only one aspect of the interfusion of creative art and science in the Renaissance. 'Practice,' in Leonardo's words, 'should always be based upon a sound knowledge of theory, of which perspective is the guide and gateway, and without it nothing can be done well in any kind of painting' (MS G, Institut de France, 8 r.). The first art to be founded on a grammar of this sort was not one of the visual arts but music. After the Pythagorean school discovered the precise dependence of the musical intervals upon certain arithmetical ratios of length of string, the search for a precise theoretical foundation of the arts and the conception of the scientist-artist never died out. Behind subjective beauty, an objective, rational grammar took shape, teachable and learnable, that of harmonic proportions. How amazing and at the same time reassuring — the chaos of sensations ruled by a simple and rigorous formula! Here a bridge was found, no less amazing, between the realms of the eye and the ear. From Vitruvius up to the last stragglers in the wake of Palladio, the theorists admonish the architects to borrow the rules of harmonic proportions from the musicians, who were the masters in this field. Leonardo, who, in his research on perspective, discovered the harmonic proportions in which a body withdrawing from the eye seems to diminish, regarded music as the 'sister of painting.'

It was for its strictly theoretical foundations that music was regarded as a science in antiquity and kept its place in the *universitas literarum*, beside rhetoric, geometry, arithmetic, dialectic, astronomy, and grammar, and that within the medieval classification of the arts into *artes liberales* and *artes mechanicae* it belonged to the first and nobler class, which imparted an elevated social position to its masters. This was by no means true of the visual artists; Plato ranked them with any other people exercising a skill, such as doctors, farmers, and sailors, and this was still the prevalent view in the *quattrocento*. No wonder the visual artists then, formulating the rules of their crafts, looked to music, where this formulation had been accomplished before. Besides, their social position could be improved by adding the same scientific rigour to their work as music enjoyed. Thus, after the model of music, the grammar of the visual arts was fashioned.

Viewed in this light the musical instruments in our study are of more than decorative importance; they are the tools of the most venerable 'science art.' The cittern mentioned above is flanked by a pair of dividers and an hourglass (Pl. 53a), the instruments for measuring space and time. True, they belong to the common paraphernalia of a Renaissance study, but the appearance of these metrical tools, side by side, and especially with a musical instrument, is perhaps more than accidental; and, indeed, these are the symbols by which, in the Renaissance theory, the mathematical foundations of music are indicated. A woodcut in Franchino Gaffurio's *Angelicum ac divinum opus musice*, Milan, 1496 (one of the standard musical treatises of that time), shows the author teaching, while to his left dividers and an hourglass remind us of the Pythagorean discovery that our scale, and hence harmony, is based on certain numerical relations, for instance, those of the lengths of strings or air columns producing sound (Fig. 18). These lengths are illustrated also by lines with their measurements added and pipes with the same proportion numbers. In woodcuts from Gaffurio's *Theorica musice*, Milan, 1492, it is old Pythagoras himself who works on chimes and glasses, strings and flutes, all with their proportion numbers added (Pl. 57b).

From here we do not have to pass far to other tools which we find in the cupboards, a celestial globe and a quadrant (Pl. 54d). There is no military leader from Alexander to Napoleon, and even beyond, who did not consult the stars. But the Pythagorean heritage, so vital in Federigo's time, points rather to the nobler sister of astrology, astronomy. The Pythagoreans had found the harmony of tones in the proportions of the planets and their orbits. This leading motif sounds throughout the history of astronomy from ancient Greek speculation to the famous title of Kepler's *De harmonice mundi* and the *Harmonie universelle* by the great musicologist and friend of Descartes, Father Mersenne. How unfor-

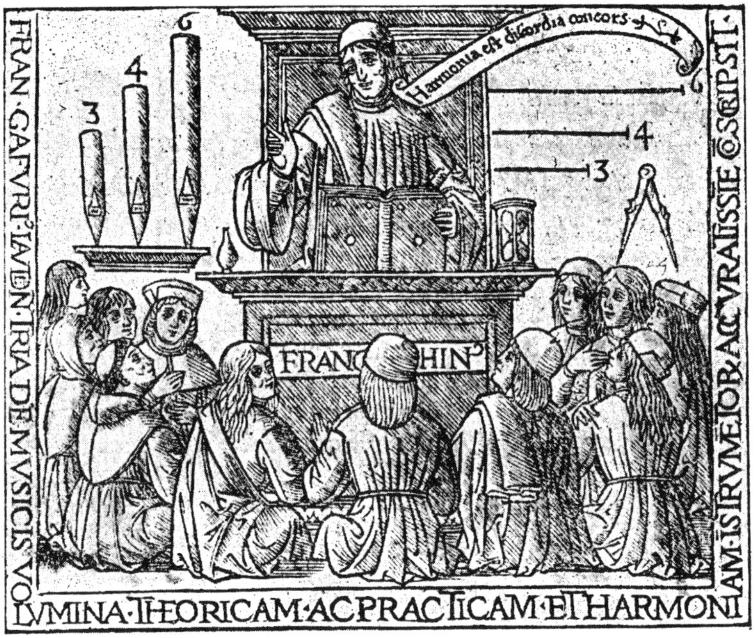

Fig. 18. Gaffurio teaching the theory of music. Woodcut from Gaffurio's *Angelicum ac divinum opus musice*, 1496. Compare the dividers and hourglass with those in Pl. 53a.

tunate that we cannot open the books above which the celestial globe is hanging, perhaps among them a treatise of the court astronomer, Paul von Middelburg!

There remains a last group of objects, the arms, evidence of a world apparently remote from the realm of science. But even warring, that exercise of sheer force, was carried on as an art in Federigo's time, art meaning skill based on science. War became a topic of scientific speculation and was subjected to conventional and technical rules, the rules of correct warfare. Federigo, the Gonfaloniere of the Church, was a celebrated master of the 'scienza militare.' His adviser in this matter, who built his castles and constructed his bombards and mortars, was the greatest military expert of the time, Francesco di Giorgio Martini,[1] whose *Trattato d'architettura civile e militare*, written in Urbino and dedicated to the Duke, had its influence as late as the time of Prince Eugene of Savoy and even Napoleon. The revolution in the technique of war of that time is marked chiefly by the use of heavy artillery and the adaptation of fortification plans to this new

[1] On the importance of Francesco di Giorgio Martini as theorist of military technique, see Leonardo Olschki's very instructive *Geschichte der neusprachlichen wissenschaftlichen Literatur*, Vol. II, Leipzig, 1922, p. 119.

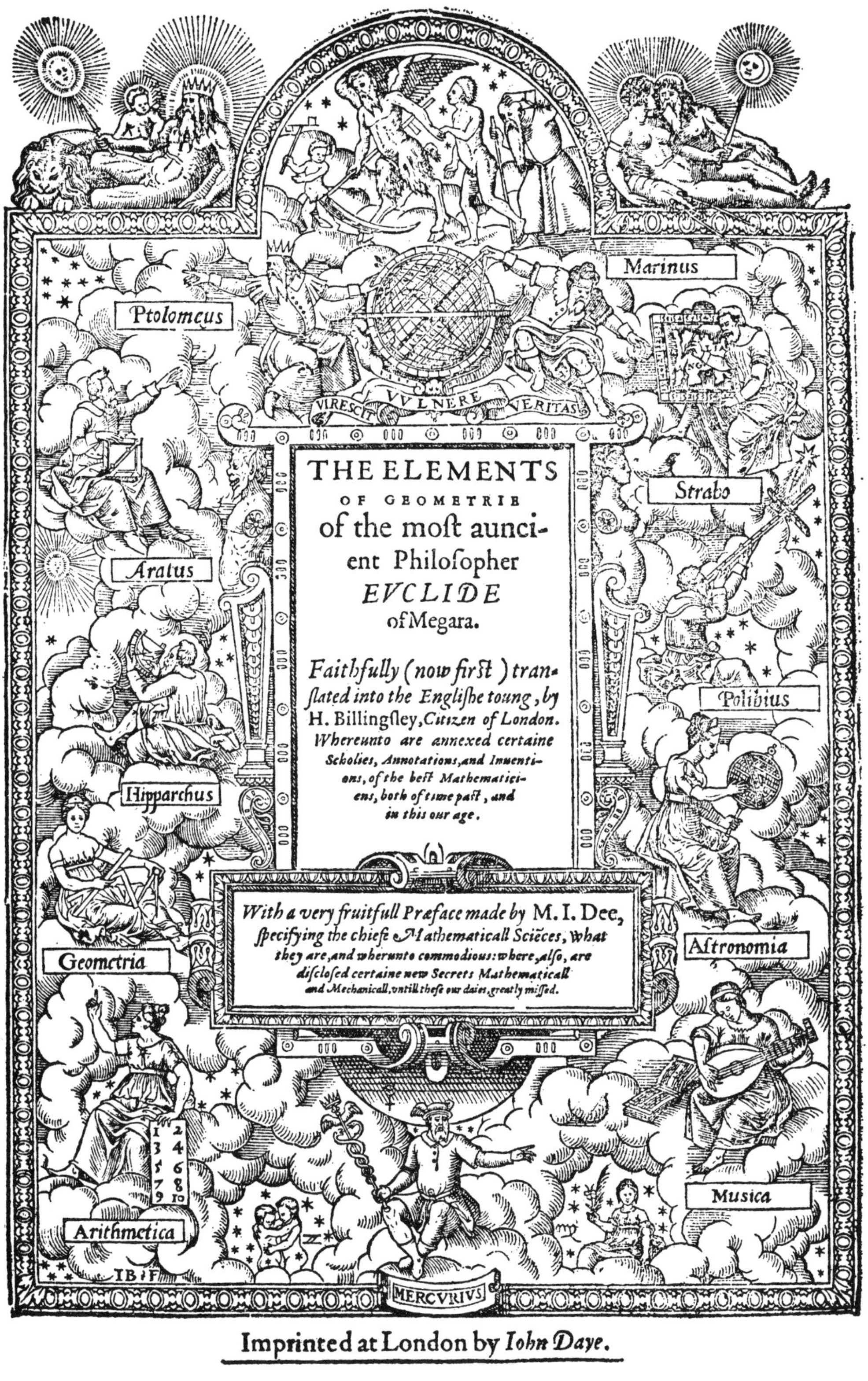
THE ELEMENTS
OF GEOMETRIE
of the most auncient Philosopher
EVCLIDE
of Megara.
Faithfully (now first) translated into the Englishe toung, by H. Billingsley, Citizen of London. Whereunto are annexed certaine Scholies, Annotations, and Inuentions, of the best Mathematiciens, both of time past, and in this our age.
With a very fruitfull Præface made by M. I. Dee, specifying the chiefe Mathematicall Sciẽces, what they are, and wherunto commodious: where, also, are disclosed certaine new Secrets Mathematicall and Mechanicall, untill these our daies, greatly missed.
Imprinted at London by Iohn Daye.
Ptolomeus
Marinus
Aratus
Strabo
Hipparchus
Polibius
Geometria
Astronomia
Arithmetica
Musica
MERCVRIVS
VIRESCIT VVLNERE VERITAS
IB F

Fig. 19. Title page of the first English edition of Euclid's *Elements* (London, 1570), illustrating the Pythagorean union between the sciences. In 1569 Urbino was visited by the English mathematician John Dee, who wrote the preface to the edition shown here.

weapon of attack. These arms, as well as the proper defences against them, demanded a more systematic control of space. Shooting with heavy cannon actually means practical mastery of space; levelling a gun implies thinking in terms of levels of space; scientific gunnery, or ballistics, as well as the technique of fortification against artillery fire, is nothing else but applied perspective, and it may very well be that the practical needs of the new gunnery contributed more to the 'rationalization of sight'[1] than is commonly supposed. Francesco di Giorgio, in a drawing for the treatise mentioned, illustrates one of his heavy guns levelled at a fortress by means of sights, which are also depicted in enlarged form (Pl. 55b). A glance at one of Dürer's woodcuts (Pl. 55c) shows that the aiming device for the gunner is basically akin to that used by the artist working on linear perspective. Although both contrivances serve quite different practical ends, they both assist in that calculation of which the factors are object, distance, image, the gunner starting from the image given and searching for the distance, the draughtsman defining the shape of the image with respect to a given distance. Both those operations are founded on the same mathematical principle, the precise proportions between the increasing distance of an object from the eye and its apparent diminution. Though the theoretical formulation of this principle is found first in Leonardo's writings, there seems to be no doubt that it had been practised before as a rule of thumb.

Thus, even the arms in the panels stand for a 'science art,' the theoretical conquest of space, brought about by the geometers, the portrayers of nature, and the military geniuses. This rational conception of space is based on numerical rules, the same divine harmony of proportions that is realized by the musical instruments and observed by the planetary orbits (Fig. 19). This is the great, the peremptory credo of the time: only by investigation into the blueprint of creation can one dare to portray it truly, to re-create it. In Leonardo's words, 'in Art we are grandsons unto God.' This belief, this search for the one in the many, the order in the chaos, the simple in the entangled is written not only in the treatises of the *quattrocento*, but, with considerable eloquence, on the walls of the study from Gubbio.

[1] To quote the title of Mr. Ivins' very original treatise on Renaissance perspective (*Metropolitan Museum Papers*, No. 8, 1938).

10 · Bagpipes for the Lord

The art of the drolleries in the Hours of Jeanne d'Évreux, acquired in 1958 by the Metropolitan Museum of Art, New York, belongs to those puzzling branches of medieval imagination where the sacred and the unholy are in close proximity. This is not the only branch of medieval art where these incongruous realms meet. In medieval church plays as well as in the architectural decorations of cathedrals, the untamed ocean of life, full of wild and fantastic creatures, pipes and drums, satyrs and nymphs, jugglers and beggars, foaming with sin and sex, surges, if not to the altar, at least to the portals of the house of God. The sacred and the profane, even the vulgar, meet as close neighbours. And while art in the Middle Ages — the visual arts almost completely and music to a large extent — means sacred art, the business of everyday life with its dreams and nightmares, its obsessions and fears, its games and amusements, was by no means banned from the sacred world. It is admitted in outspoken illustrations or in various allegorical guises and personifications as an integral part of this world. This is not to say that the devil is given free play, but his existence is more than acknowledged. He receives a limited concession for his business, and the demons of hell, together with other fantastic creatures, are permitted to perform their lusty games even under the watchtowers of the cathedrals.

Thus the pages of the Jeanne d'Évreux Hours, illustrated by Jean Pucelle, *c.*1325, admit a crowd of whimsical and funny creatures, laymen and clerics and dream-born compound animals such as lion-reptiles and snake-goats, dragons with monk heads and friars with the hind legs of beasts of prey, mingling with the innocent beasts of the woods and fields, hares and deer, birds and monkeys. There are also peasants, shepherds, knights, jugglers, and acrobats.

The wide margin beneath the text is peopled usually not by single figures but by whole ensembles performing little burlesque stage plays or buffooneries: dog-trainers, for example, with their audience astonished or pleased as the case may be.

Sometimes these scenes even ascend to fill the upper margins. And some form of fantastic life appears unfailingly in the space to the right of the text. Wherever the written sentence of the text leaves part of the line empty, monsters creep in to continue the black of the line up to the margin, and then widen out and expand in broader design on the border of the page. This, in a way, is a reversal of the position of gargoyles, which, for static reasons that are quite evident, adhere to the church walls with a broad, compact *derrière* and then thin out to reach far into the air with their long, slender necks. This high proportion of reptilian anatomy and long-tailed monsters is the only stereotyped aspect of Pucelle's otherwise boundless fancy, for the line left unfilled by the sacred text only leaves space for something long and thin — tails, if it is to be a living creature, and it inevitably is. Sometimes, however, these tails assume plantlike patterns and on occasion even the form of Gothic architectural decoration. Occasionally the artist must have become bored by all this monotony, for he frequently tries to wedge the body of a monster into an empty line space, with the tail then curving out unhampered into open space (Pl. 58b).

The effect, as I said before, is absurd and almost sacrilegious. An *averte iram tuam nobis* may end in a long-tailed goat, a *Deo gratias* in a reptile-man, or a *Gloria patri et filio et spiritu sancto* in a lion's tail with the top-heavy body of a hooded monk attached to it. Thus we have here a mingling of the most venerable words of the liturgy with the amusing, if not ridiculous and eery, creatures that are figments of the artist's imagination.

This specific irruption of the bizarre and farcical into the sacred, as happens in the Hours of Jeanne d'Évreux, is a Northern phenomenon confined chiefly to Flanders, France, and England. Yet one is tempted to look for a moment across a span of two centuries to a Southern fashion, the Italian grotesques of the *cinquecento*, beginning with Pinturicchio's famous vault decorations in the library of the cathedral of Siena, which, if not strictly parallel, still afford similar aspects from more than one point of view. Their habitat, of course, is walls rather than paper. Their immediate source is the ancient stucco and fresco decorations in the Thermae of Trajan and other buildings rediscovered at the time. Like the drolleries they spin a frivolous web of playful creatures around a centre of totally different significance, this time not a text of the Scriptures, however, but frescoes with sacred, mythological, or historical content. One recalls here combinations such as the rich fungus of grotesques sprouting all over the walls of Raphael's loggias in the Vatican, accompanying and crowding in the Biblical stories in the middle of the vaults. Here in the very centre of Western Christendom the satyrs and nymphs play their jolly games around the Deluge, the Birth of Christ, or the Last Supper.

To be sure, the single figures in the Italian grotesques, for all their fun and variety, are a rather domesticated brand of fantasy, and their symmetrical arrangement on the walls is largely dominated by their decorative function within the architectural frame. There is never any doubt that they are imitations — however free — of ancient models, while the medieval drolleries bear all the stamp of immediate, original, and inexhaustible imagination. If one were to look for a *cinquecento* parallel to our drolleries one would rather find it in Dürer's marginal drawings for the Emperor Maximilian's prayer book, which has that very same fusion of Northern exuberance and Latin clarity.

In the Hours of Jeanne d'Évreux a surprising number of the creatures, human or beastlike or compound, are engaged in playing musical instruments. Surprising, that is, to the spectator who is not familiar with the teeming, colourful musical life of the Middle Ages, and especially with the number and variety of musical instruments as compared with the standardized specimens which make up our modern symphony orchestra.

Illustrations of this kind are a true gold mine of information for the student of medieval musical instruments. They are an indispensable supplement to the occasional descriptions appearing in musical treatises and poetry, which necessarily lack the accuracy provided by illustrations as to the variety of types of instruments, of playing techniques, and their use in ensembles. Modern history of music has, with few exceptions, exploited these visual sources little — understandably so, for historians have concentrated above all on the music itself and thus on written music, which was chiefly sacred music. Therefore the music never confided to paper, that is, a large part of secular music, such as dances and the improvisations of solo performers, has remained somewhat outside the focus of musical history.

It is for this reason that the visual representations of instrumental performances assume great importance, providing an open window on secular music of the past. How important a role secular music played about 1325, when Pucelle decorated the Hours of Jeanne d'Évreux, may be hinted at here by one fact only. In 1321 there was established in Paris the Confrérie of Saint-Julien-des-Ménestriers, a guild — or, as we would call it today, 'union' — of French instrumentalists under a *roy des ménestriers*. This was the time of the *Ars nova*, when secular instrumental music in dances and arrangements of songs reached such heights that it in its turn began to influence the style of sacred music with its new inventions.

If we examine the various instruments depicted in the Jeanne d'Évreux Hours, we will find that some are playful caricatures while others are realistic depictions of actual instruments of the time, often portrayed with amazing precision considering the miniature size of these drawings.

We turn first to the wind instruments, which were prevalent from the Middle Ages until well into the Renaissance. Let us look first at the bagpipes, which appear in various forms on our pages. The bagpipe is one of the oldest instruments shown here; its history reaches back to antiquity. According to Suetonius and Dio Chrysostom, Nero played the bagpipe, though it is not reported whether he did this while Rome burned.

Some bagpipes on the margins of our pages are precise drawings of actual specimens, while others are burlesque versions. A large bagpipe is played by a musician perched cross-legged on a ferocious long-tailed beast (Pl. 62b). His thin legs and forearms form a strange pattern with the abnormally long chanter of the bagpipe, which ends in a carved animal head similar to that of the long-tailed monster. The bagpipe has an enormous drone reaching over the player's shoulder.

A smaller bagpipe is held — but not played — by a hooded reptile-monk who extends, as it were, the line of the text *spiritu sancto* (Pl. 62d). Here the drone is hardly longer than the chanter. The point where the chanter leaves the bag is decorated by a little crowned head. Such little wooden sculptures were quite common decorations on bagpipes of that time. This usage was retained for centuries, and the carved heads are still found in the powerful bagpipes played at the drinking parties painted by Jordaens, for example in the various versions of *Le Roi boît* in the museums at Brussels, Leningrad, and Antwerp.

On another page a bagpipe, this time without a drone, is the focal point of a little comedy scene (Pl. 62e). The small instrument is being trained as a dog. The little decorative dog head is that of a real bagpipe, but little dog feet appear under the bag. Two rustic characters are so overcome by the spectacle that they cavort with gestures of surprise. Even funnier is a canine bagpipe which decorates the page showing Christ before Pilate (Pl. 62f). Here two monstrous musicians compete in the production of noise. Both are half animal, with long, intertwining tails that sprout oak leaves. The right one, with puffed cheeks, blows a reed pipe that terminates in a large bell, possibly of cowhorn. This is a realistic picture. The other musician, however, employs a dog as a bagpipe, using its tail as a blowpipe and one of its hind legs as the chanter. One can imagine the sound.

While these three bagpipes have no inner relation to the spiritual content of the page, we find quite a different situation on the page illustrating the Annunciation to the Shepherds (Pl. 58a). The central scene overflows into the margin, where we see shepherds with all their attributes — sheep and crook and a dog — looking up in wonder. One of them plays the typical shepherd instrument, a small reed pipe (shawm or *chalumeau*). The reedy, bleating, guttural tone of the shawm, associated with the pastoral realm since time immemorial, has become symbolic in Christian iconology of the Nativity scene, one of the many strange ways in which musical and visual symbolism often mingle. Later the piffero and zampogna with their heavy drones appear for many centuries and still today as the inevitable attribute of the shepherds surrounding the Child in Italian *presepi*. The symbolic union between the sound of reed pipes and the crèche in the stable, or, in other words, of pastoral music with its characteristic drone and Christmas, pervades more than five hundred years of music up to the *Christmas*

Oratorio of Johann Sebastian Bach, and to Handel's *Messiah*, and still further. If, with this in mind, we look at the initial D of *Deus*, it does not seem altogether accidental that it is formed by a bagpipe player, for the bagpipe has the same reedy timbre as the simple pipe beneath. The only difference is the bag, a mere mechanical convenience that makes the player less dependent on the rhythm of his breathing.

Of other wind instruments in our Book of Hours we may mention in passing a transverse flute (Pl. 58b), several realistically drawn trumpets, and many specimens of the one-hand fife played together with a drum, according to age-old custom (Pl. 63g).

Turning now to string instruments, we find these represented in the Pucelle Hours by harps, psalteries, mandolas, and vielles, the first three instruments plucked, the last bowed. The harps are all small and have the characteristic rounded Gothic form. In Romanesque harps the three elements of the frame, that is, soundbox, neck, and pillar, were distinctly set off against each other, as they are in modern orchestral harps. The Gothic harp fuses the three elements into one curved design, as we see in the specimen plucked by the claws of a feathered monk-dragon in Pl. 60a.

The psalteries represented in our book all have the typical shape of a trapezoid with the two slanting side walls curving inwards (Pl. 61a). We find psalteries of this form in many angel concerts, both Northern and Italian, and they appear still in many illuminated manuscripts of the high Renaissance, in the hands of King David. In spite of the minute size of these illustrations, the hitch pins and the decorations of the sound hole have been indicated with great care.

The mandola, of Near Eastern origin like the psaltery, appears three times in our manuscript. All three forms have a lute-like body with a round sound-hole in the centre, and a characteristic long, thin neck passing into a widely curved sickle and terminating in a carved animal head. But our specimens differ in the shape of the soundbox. The smallest one has an almost circular corpus to which the neck is joined at a sharp angle (Pl. 61b). The larger one has a corpus of oval outline (Pl. 60a), and a third one of medium size shows the corpus gradually passing into the neck (Pl. 62c). Two of the mandolas are clearly plucked with a plectrum, with the plucking arm in a rather mannered, uncomfortable position.

The last of the string instruments — and the only bowed one — is the vielle, the typical fiddle of the time, depicted in countless Italian and Flemish paintings in the hands of angels and also in some secular manuscripts such as the Manesse Codex. One vielle appears on the lower margin of the page showing the education and chastisement of Saint Louis (Pl. 59b). It is played by a youth comfortably seated on the back of a monster. Since the youth resembles somewhat the young Saint Louis in the main scene, vielle-playing may have been shown here as part of his education. The instrument has the typical flat, leaf-shaped head so different from the scroll of the later violin; it has an elegant, shallow body with the side walls curving in slightly, already bordering on the shape of the Italian lira da braccio, a refined improvisation instrument which developed from the vielle and which we find, for instance, in the hands of Apollo playing to the Muses in Raphael's *Parnassus* in the Segnatura. The other vielle, played by a monster in an initial, is bulkier and is played in droll fashion, the right hand stopping the strings — or does it? — the left drawing the bow over the strings on the wrong side of the bridge (Pl. 61c).

Up to now we have observed only pictures of real instruments or caricatures of them, but the variety of existing instruments was apparently not sufficient for the imagination of our draughtsman; his comic sense supplied as instruments objects that are not instruments at all but other tools employed by his creatures for blowing or plucking or bowing. Among these, bellows play a large role. Now bellows are indispensable tools known to civilization ever since the technique of melting metal was invented. They even served as auxiliary gadgets for musical instruments; from antiquity, for example, they have provided air pressure for the wind chest of pipe organs. And they were added for a similar purpose to bagpipes when these instruments were transformed into the neat little musettes played by court ladies in the *fêtes champêtres* of Versailles, relieving these make-believe shepherdesses of the unbecoming act of blowing. But in the Évreux Hours the bellows themselves are exalted into tools of music. They are played as heraldic trumpets (Pl. 63c & d), or plucked with a plectrum by a monstrous monk, a sinister Orpheus who by his singing and playing entrances the creatures of the fields and woodlands (Pl. 61a). Another comic pseudo-instrument is, of all things, the jawbone. It appears twice in our drolleries. Once it is plucked by a lion-footed king, to the amazement of a dog, which may perhaps be more interested in the bone than in the music (Pl. 59a). Another time the jawbone is bowed with a rake by a billy goat, which is deterred somewhat from its performance by a ferocious, weasel-like creature attacking its tail (Pl. 63i). This brings to mind the Biblical jawbone of an ass, but one must be an obdurate iconologist to credit Pucelle with scriptural intentions here.

Besides wind and string instruments we find in the Hours of Jeanne d'Évreux a variety of percussion instruments, or, to use the scientific terms, sonorous substances and membranophones such as drums. The cymbals, an instrument going back to the ancient Orient and Rome, appears in our pages played by a monster in an initial (Pl. 62a). Its appearance in 14th-century illustrations is rather rare, but it is frequent in angel concerts of the 15th century, especially in Italy. Here each of the two disks has a simple form, curving gradually from the centre towards the rim, while later cymbals usually consist of a flat rim sharply set off from a central boss. Cymbals of the later type are shown in one of the reliefs by Luca della Robbia for the Singing Gallery, formerly in the cathedral at Florence, which illustrates a line from Psalm 150: *Laudate eum in cymbalis jubilationis*; they also appear in the angel orchestra surrounding the Madonna in the painting by Giovanni Boccati in the Pinacoteca Vannucci at Perugia.

Another noisemaker of metal is the triangle. It is played by a snake-tailed youth who suspends it with one hand while the other strikes it with a stick (Pl. 63e). The triangle in this illustration has several jingling rings that add a clattering noise to the sharp tones of the metal frame.

Bells — *tintinnabula* or *cymbala* — play a large role in the medieval instrumentarium. Our manuscript shows several forms: a youth perched on the shoulder of a monster plays a set of three bells with clappers; a hairy musician swings a set of bells with clappers while playing a small shawm with the other hand (Pl. 63f); and a bearded man strikes a large suspended bell with a stick (Pl. 63h). Chimes, so frequent in medieval illuminations, are for some reason absent from this book.

Of special interest is a rattle appearing in our pages, for rattles, especially of the form we have here, are rarely shown (Pl. 63b). We can clearly see a hammer attached to a horizontal bar. When this crossbar is shaken it is hit by the hammer. Rattles of this and other types played a large role in religious and folk customs of the Middle Ages and even of later times; they were used by night watchmen or by beaters in hunting, or to 'break the bones of Judas' on Good Friday. The Metropolitan Museum's collection of musical instruments also contains a medieval *crécelle*, a rattle of slightly different construction which according to custom was used to replace the sound of the church bells while they 'travelled to Rome' during the week before Easter.

Of single drums only one type is represented, a snare drum attached to the shoulders of the players (Pl. 63a & g). It has two drumheads, evident from the bracing cords that connect the two skins. In one case the player hits the drum with a large stick, playing at the same time, as usual, the one-hand fife. In the other case the player blows a larger pipe, stopping its holes with both hands, while the drum is behind his shoulders, possibly waiting to be pounded with the elbows. Such playing methods were by no means unusual. When I was a child in Vienna there were still musical beggars, veritable one-man orchestras, who played their many instruments at the same time with mouth and hands, knees and feet, head and elbows.

While up to now we have observed single instruments individually played, we also have two ensembles in our Book of Hours. The smaller one appears in the scene of the Nativity over the monumental cradle of the Child (Pl. 59a). One angel plays the cymbals, the other a large vielle.

The other and larger ensemble is an angel concert that significantly accompanies the page showing the Adoration of the Magi (Pl. 60b). The lower margin illustrates as fitting counterpoint the Massacre of the Innocents supervised by Herod himself. Musical angels invaded sacred imagery relatively late, during the second half of the 13th century, and most probably under the influence of Jacobus de Voragine's *Golden Legend*. The combination of loud instruments such as trumpets and drums with the fine silvery sound of small stringed instruments is by no means uncommon. In this heavenly orchestra we see a large psaltery in the centre similar to the one shown in Pl. 61a. The angel immediately right of it plays the vielle, while the one on the left side holds in each hand a set of bells with clappers. The flanking instruments, a trumpet and a pair of kettledrums, are old, inseparable companions throughout the Middle Ages and ever since. They have always been the attributes of high nobility since the Middle Ages, providing the musical equivalent to heraldic pomp and announcing with fanfares and flourishes the coming of princes and peers. And just as the shawm and the bagpipe accompanied the Annunciation to the Shepherds (Pl. 58a), trumpets and kettledrums here lend their majestic sound to the entrance of the three oriental kings.

It is here in the last-mentioned two pages from the Hours of Jeanne d'Évreux that the musical instruments make a deeply meaningful contribution to the spiritual content of the main illustrations. In this role they exceed their function elsewhere in the manuscript, where they merely provide an amusing and sometimes bizarre counterpoint to the scriptural text.

11 · On Angel Concerts in the 15th Century: A Critical Approach to Realism and Symbolism in Sacred Painting*

The historian of musical performance, especially that of early instrumental music, often has occasion to regret the sparseness of his sources of information. He draws on contemporary reports, but they are often vague and technically inaccurate. He draws on musical treatises, but they are usually devoted to pedagogical ideals rather than to descriptions of contemporary usage; understandably they take everyday routine for granted and thus leave untold what would interest him most.

There exists, however, another important and not yet systematically exploited reservoir of information in the form of representations of musical scenes in painting, sculpture, and the graphic arts. Such pictures are often likely to be more complete and detailed, and therefore presumably more reliable, than verbal descriptions. They too, however, present difficulties of interpretation. The farther back we go in the history of art — European or any other — the larger looms the role played by religious imagery. Apart from the twenty-four elders of Revelation and the well-known patrons of music, King David and St. Cecilia,[1] it is chiefly the angels who sing and play in sacred painting.

But in the heavens depicted in paintings, how much reliable information can we expect to find about secular music? Did the painters simply transfer earthly

* The principal ideas set forth in this study are the results of my preoccupation with the subject of angel concerts and of the lectures I have given on various aspects of this topic for many years at numerous universities and museums. Originally the present essay included an account of the history of angel concerts, tracing their iconology in doctrine, poetry, and the visual arts, as a prelude to the systematic examination of their value for the historian of musical performance. After completing my script, however, I saw the excellent book recently published by Reinhold Hammerstein, *Die Musik der Engel, Untersuchungen zur Musikanschauung des Mittelalters*, Munich, 1962, in which the author concurs independently with many of my own findings. To avoid duplication, I have restricted this study to problems that were approached differently or not at all in Hammerstein's book.

[1] A 'musical patron' only because of the misinterpretation of the phrase 'organis sonantibus,' describing her wedding.

ensembles, profane or ecclesiastical, into the celestial spheres? If so, were they not implying restrictions on the supernatural abilities of angels, restrictions based on the poorer range of human instrument-building and performance? Or were the painters straining their imaginations to compete with the mystic and poetic interpreters of the Scriptures, filling the heavens with fantastic shapes and other objects never seen on earth?[1] If the verbal interpretation of the Scriptures struggles with the corporeality of *pneumata*, what should the painter do?

The complex situation may be envisaged as a double process of symbolization, striving to make the invisible visible: first the text of the Scriptures themselves, creating verbal images of spiritual (i.e. incorporeal) creatures, such as the angels; second, the painter's translation of these verbal symbols into visual shapes. Actually the situation appears further complicated by the existence of exegesis which enriches the symbols found in the Scriptures by trying to reconcile evident contradictions or by filling lacunae through the establishment, for instance, of a systematic angelology.[2]

Paradoxically, the painter of sacred subjects for the Church is, at the same time, less free and freer than the mystic poet or exegete facing the same subjects. He is far less free inasmuch as he is usually not permitted to apply his full imagination to his subject. The interpretation of the Scriptures and other ecclesiastical texts is provided for him by the Church. He is in fact depending on the guidance and often on the strict instruction of the ecclesiastical authorities.[3]

Yet within these limits he enjoys the freedom inherent in his role as a painter. Where the poet or theologian uses words, the painter is privileged — and of course compelled — to specify and to detail, or to create a concrete sensuous appearance. Or, in Goethe's words:[4] 'Language cannot express the individuality

[1] Many examples of this are found in the paintings of Gaudenzio Ferrari, and especially in his fresco in the cupola of the Santuario in Saronno; see Chapter 6 above. On imaginary and fantastic musical instruments in sacred and profane art, see Chapter 10.

[2] I may point here only to Dionysius the pseudo-Areopagite, to whom a large part of early angel doctrine is due. It is remarkable and quite surprising to find that the same Dionysius who in grandiose mystic and poetic vision described for the first time the complete organization of the angelic hosts, uttered a warning against too beautiful and too sensuous images and pleaded for imperfect images since their imperfection would remind the worshipper of the spiritual essence behind the physical appearance. Thus the worshipper would never forget that the images are only symbols pointing at something beyond themselves.

[3] One of the most original and perceptive examinations of the relation between religious art and church doctrine is found in Rudolf Berliner, *The Freedom of Medieval Art*, in *Gazette des beaux-arts*, XXVIII (1945), 264–88. He discusses the question of how art could presume to represent certain themes in such a way that verbal descriptions of them are historically or dogmatically or intellectually acceptable, and comes to the conclusion that the freedom of art resulted from theological concepts of its role in the realm of religion.

[4] To Riemer, 1804.

of the phenomenon [*das Individuelle der Erscheinung*], the specific. Our words for the species are always general.'

Throughout nearly two thousand years of Christian art, methods of representing the supernatural did not remain unchanged. The invisible was made visible in many ways and forms, ranging in persistence from firmly ingrained and long-standing traditions, and even clichés, to the passing flight of fancy of an individual imagination. Familiarity with these iconographical traditions is often helpful and sometimes indispensable to the historian of music who turns to works of sacred art as documents of early styles of vocal and instrumental performance. Some problems implied in a critical interpretation of sacred painting may be illustrated by the following investigation, which will concentrate on a limited span of time in the late *quattrocento*. In that century, progress in the study of anatomy and the technique of linear perspective based on a strict mathematical method had brought about a new 'scientific' pictorial conquest of the visible universe centred around a new mundane concept of man. Consequently, even the heavens were then depicted in terms of the human world; angels were represented in the image of humans;[1] and — important to the historian of music — celestial musicians and ensembles appeared in the shapes of those familiar on earth. Heavenly liturgy was depicted not by dreams and visions, however standardized, but by a portrayal of the everyday routine on earth.

Naturally, this artistic interpretation went through many phases and did not conquer the North at the same time as it did Italy. Individual artists, moreover, still adhered to visionary representations. The paintings chosen here as examples are from this Janus-headed period of transition. They are approximately contemporary, yet remarkably different in their visualization of celestial music. Hence the difficulties for the historian searching for authentic records of *Aufführungspraxis*.

The first of our examples is a small picture of the Virgin and Child painted near the end of the 15th century by Geertgen tot Sint Jans, which only recently came to light in America and is today in the van Beuningen Museum in Rotterdam (Pl. 65b). Geertgen, not more than a dozen of whose works are known, was probably born in Leiden and died at the age of twenty-eight. According to Carel von Mander's famous biographical work on Northern

[1] The problem of depicting supernatural creatures and the gradual 'humanization' of angels in Renaissance painting is discussed by Jakob Burckhardt in his famous article *Das Altarbild*, in *Beiträge zur Kunstgeschichte von Italien*, 2nd ed., 1911, pp. 3–161. Some of his judgements have to be taken *cum grano salis*. His absorption in the Renaissance canon of anatomical proportions made him critical of 'unrealistic angels' in earlier and later periods of art. To indicate his bias we shall cite only his disapproval of Rembrandt's angel leaving the threshold of Tobit as anatomically so deficient that he is fortunate to be able to fly because he would not be able to walk — 'He departs in the most ridiculous manner, a real Flying Dutchman.'

painters, published in 1604, Geertgen lived and worked in Haarlem. His whole known *œuvre* dates from the decade between 1485 and 1495.

Geertgen's painting of the Virgin and Child is a visionary work of great originality, unforgettable to anyone who has ever seen it, because of its poetry and its miraculous luminosity. The bulky shape of the Virgin seems to be suspended in the centre of an oval of blinding light.[1] A closer look discloses beneath the heavy folds of her garment the two attributes of the apocalyptic Woman of the Sun, the crescent and the dragon (Revelation 12). At one and the same time, she is the idyllic young mother with the infant and the crowned queen of heaven in glory. The Child shakes two large jingle bells and is in excited motion, almost dancing, with His right leg up in the air and both large toes turned up.

The Virgin is surrounded by an enormous number of angels neatly grouped into several distinct concentric ovals. The innermost of these, which has the greatest luminosity, consists of fourteen adoring, many-winged cherubim and seraphim. In the next, somewhat darker oval, twelve angels carry the instruments of the Passion; and four angels around the head of the Virgin hold pennants inscribed with the abbreviated form of the word 'Sanctus.'[2] The outermost oval and the corners of the panel are filled with the largest group, consisting of twenty-three angels playing musical instruments. The instruments are: from the top, counter-clockwise — a lute, large shawm (without protective cylinder), vielle, flat handbell struck with beater, long pipe with snare drum, hurdy-gurdy, jingle-bells, small clapper, coiled trumpet, pair of handbells, another coiled trumpet, large clappers, curved trumpet, bagpipe, set of seven small jingles strung on a rope; left upper corner — positive organ played by one angel and held by another; left lower corner — clavichord played by one angel, while another holds music; below centre — cromorne; right lower corner — dulcimer, double shawm, pot; right upper corner — clavicytherium (?) played by one angel and held by another. This is a very rich and nearly complete instrumentarium of the time, including even the three contemporary keyboard instruments — organ, clavicytherium, and clavichord. Only the tromba marina, so frequent in Flemish paintings of the period, is absent. There is hardly any

[1] Geertgen's Virgin and Child preserves the basic form of the mandorla, but the hard linear shape is resolved in luminous concentric ellipses. The broad outline of the mandorla of Byzantine heritage had by this time been gradually softened by surrounding it and finally replacing it with rows of angels. Perhaps the most important landmark in this evolution is Orcagna's famous relief of the Death and Ascension of the Virgin, dating from before 1360, on the tabernacle in Or San Michele, Florence.

[2] The range of colours from the almost blinding yellow glare around the Virgin through the pink circle of cherubim to the darker red of the angels with the instruments of the Passion and the purplish black of the musical angels is strongly reminiscent of the moon-halo, very appropriate, of course, for the Virgin on the crescent.

need to state that Geertgen was not thinking of any actual ensemble. By depicting nearly all the instruments he knew, he gave an allegory of the loudest and richest possible sound.

The crowned Virgin, enshrined by dense crowds of angels, is the visual embodiment of a very old theme — the lauding and adoring angel choirs in heaven. Much has been written on the iconology of angel choirs. Here, it suffices to recall Dionysius the pseudo-Areopagite, St. Thomas Aquinas, and Dante. To determine to what degree Geertgen partakes in this pictorial tradition (not to say cliché), one has only to look at one of the many contemporary paintings of the same subject, for instance that by the Master of the Glorification of the Virgin (Pl. 65a; Worms, Collection of Baron Heyl). There too, the crowned Virgin rests on the crescent, surrounded by a multitude of angels. And there we even find angels with lute and vielle close to her and to the Infant, and in the lower corners there are two elaborate groups of musicians and instruments — on the left a portative organ and a psaltery, and on the right a little shawm and singers. Yet, what a difference from Geertgen's picture! In the Glorification of the Virgin, the angels crowd around her like a thick cluster of swarming bees, organized only by the application of a device as terrestrial as the gradual foreshortening from the nearer to the farther angels. All seem as heavy as any earthly creatures, and their earthliness is even more marked in the lower-corner groups, which are set firmly into the landscape.

Geertgen's painting is more ethereal; it seems to hark back to traditional notions which, during the Middle Ages, became curiously intermingled with the Christian doctrine of the angelic host, specifically the even more ancient idea of the celestial spheres developed in the writings of the Babylonians and the Pythagoreans, in Plato's *Timaeus* and *Politeia* and Cicero's *Dream of Scipio*, and still continued in the treatises of Kepler and Athanasius Kircher. Geertgen organized the angels into concentric rings or ovals, sharply distinct in their function, evidently alluding to the revolving spheres. One need only focus on the lower part of the ovals to see how the angels there, floating in nearly horizontal position, partake of the rotation.

This observation might help us still further to detect a deeper meaning, imparted to the picture by one striking and unique detail. As pointed out above, the Child shakes a pair of jingle bells with great animation. He looks down to the side and, in the line of His gaze, one of the musical angels in the outer ring is intently returning His glance (Pl. 64). It is the only angel whose eyes, notwithstanding the minuteness of the whole representation, are so distinctly rendered as to make their direction unmistakable. And it is this very angel who shakes a smaller pair of jingle bells towards the Child. An amusing little genre detail?[1]

[1] Such genre details occur later in the Venetian *sacre conversazioni*.

Perhaps so, although the unique mystic character of our picture and the thoughtfulness of the painter as manifested in other works may suggest a deeper interpretation, which is submitted here with the caution proper in the intricate field of pictorial symbolism: The *concentus* between the two pairs of bells reveals Christ as the leader or generator of the heavenly orchestra.[1]

Since Geertgen seems to have been familiar with the Areopagitic and Thomistic doctrine, one may assume also that the consonance of musical instruments — that is, the rapport between the two pairs of bells — is meant to represent God as prime mover of the universe, imparting the first impulse to the harmony of the spheres whose rotation is so vividly depicted here. This would be in line with Thomas Aquinas, *Summa Theologiae* I, *Questio* 105, discussing the problem whether God, as spiritual substance, can directly move a body, that is, corporeal matter; he states in Reply Obj. 1:

> There are two kinds of contact: corporeal contact (when two bodies touch each other) and virtual contact (as the cause of sadness is said to touch the one made sad). According to the first kind of contact, God, as being incorporeal, neither touches nor is touched. But according to virtual contact, He touches creatures by moving them but He is not touched. . . .[2]

So much for the Geertgen picture, which, rich as it is in theological and poetic symbolism, offers little to the historian of *Aufführungspraxis*.

Turning now to our second main example, we find a basically different attitude towards the representation of music and musicians, which stems from a different tradition and environment. This picture (Pl. 68), signed and dated 1474 and now in the Museum of Dijon, is a work of the Tuscan painter Zanobi

[1] Pseudo-Dionysius, in his *De divinis nominibus*, IV, 5, calls God 'the cause of consonance and clarity,' a statement commented on by St. Thomas Aquinas in *In Dionysii de divinis nominibus*, IV, lect. 5, nos. 340, 346, and 349. I am delighted to find in Reinhold Hammerstein's *Die Musik der Engel*, p. 118, two pertinent quotations: 1) According to Gregory of Nyssa, God generates the music of the universe; 2) Maximus Confessor defines the universe as music performed by God.— I may add that this notion is still alive in Athanasius Kircher's *Musurgia mirifica*, in which an engraving, Bk. VIII, p. 366, shows a big pipe organ, the instrument of the Creator, with several compartments, of which each is related to one of the days of creation according to Genesis.

[2] The existence of two similar pairs of bells and of the gaze exchanged between the infant Jesus and the angel has been pointed out by Daphne M. Hoffman in her article *A Little Known Masterpiece*, in *Liturgical Arts*, XVIII (1950), 44. There, this detail is explained by reference to the customary ringing of little hand bells during the Sanctus of the Mass. It is true that this custom originated before Geertgen's picture, in fact before 1400 according to J. A. Jungmann's *Missarum sollemnia, Eine genetische Erklärung der römischen Messe*, 1948, II, 160. Miss Hoffman's interpretation would seem convincing if only the angel were playing the bells. To have Christ Himself participating in the act of glorifying, which is the duty and function of the angels (according to Isaiah 6: 14; Ezekiel 3: 12, 13; later, Ambrose; and at the time of Geertgen, Tinctoris's *Complexus effectuum musices*, c. 1480), seems awkward and not consistent with the character of a painter as thoughtful and as familiar with doctrine as Geertgen. In any case, Miss Hoffman's interpretation would not necessarily exclude the presence of a deeper symbolism.

Machiavelli, one of the minor disciples of Benozzo Gozzoli. Zanobi was a provincial painter, but his work is no less interesting in composition and no less valuable for iconographical study than that of any of the 'great' masters.

The painting does not represent the Virgin with the Infant, but the Coronation, and it shows not the multitude of musician angels depicted by Geertgen, but rather a comparatively small number, in fact two ensembles of unequal size. This is by no means the rule within the Tuscan tradition, for the Coronation pictures of this school normally include — apart from earlier paintings of the Last Judgment — the largest aggregation of musical angels in all sacred painting.

Although we are in heaven, this heaven is not conceived in visionary free imagination, but is shaped after earthly models. The throne of Christ and Mary is solid, massive, strongly shaded, and firmly planted on a platform whose steps again solidly rest on a floor decorated with tiles shown in almost exaggerated linear perspective. The two central figures sit heavily; the four saints, John the Baptist, Francis, Mary Magdalene, and Peter, plant their feet firmly on the tiles, and the four angels in the foreground kneel weightily. All this heaviness is very 'realistic,' a characteristic of our everyday world, and different from the weightlessness and ecstatic floating in the Geertgen picture. No doubt our Tuscan painter felt all this as an achievement, as progress in the pictorial conquest of perceptible space through the increasingly refined technique of linear perspective. The size of the figures, too, is well planned according to the technique of foreshortening.

If all this implies a secularization or humanization through the use of new pictorial methods, we may consider whether this realistic attitude extends to the kind of music represented here. There are two ensembles depicted, one in the remote background, the other in front of the throne close to the spectator or rather the worshipper. The far group is large, consisting of nine musicians with their instruments: one bagpipe, one hand pipe with drum, two trumpets, a jingle drum, a pair of cymbals, and three more trumpets. Four of these five trumpets are arranged in pairs in strict symmetry on the left and right sides behind the pillars of the throne.[1]

This is indeed a noisy ensemble, consisting of winds and percussion only, and it would be difficult to select a louder or more shrieking group from the instruments available at that time. It could not have been a random choice of

[1] In paintings showing ensembles of musical instruments, the requirements of pictorial composition often led to a symmetrical duplication of instruments very much at variance with actual practice. Trumpets and organettos, especially, are often duplicated in this way, particularly in Italian 14th- and 15th-century angel concerts celebrating the Assumption and Coronation of the Virgin. Striking examples are found in the Coronations by Beato Angelico. For more examples, see Chapter 1 above.

instruments or a painter's whim. Pictorially it would have been more rewarding to show fewer and less-crowded players. The congestion in fact is such that the painter scarcely had space to hint at the angel wings, and he had to omit the haloes altogether. Yet this large ensemble could hardly be an imaginary or allegorical group such as the one in Geertgen. It seems in fact to be a very deliberate choice of timbres, particularly since some instruments such as organettos, psaltery, and dulcimer, regularly appearing in contemporary Italian angel orchestras to accompany the Coronation scene,[1] are absent. One is led therefore to look for parallels in actual orchestral ensembles of the time and to think of the typical outdoor wind bands that accompanied processions, dances, and out-of-doors festival occasions.

At the time of Zanobi's picture Tinctoris, in his *De inventione et usu musicae, Liber* III,[2] describes an ensemble similar to the one in this painting as typically producing 'loud music'; it consists of trombones and shawms, while in our picture the double-reed timbre is represented not by shawms but by a bagpipe. ('But as far as the lowest contra-tenor parts are concerned, and often also the other contra-tenor parts, one has to add to the shawm players: players of brass instruments and especially players of that kind of tuba which, as pointed out above, was called *trompone* in Italy and *sacque-boute* in France. The combination of all these instruments together is usually called "the loud music." ') In all probability the painter portrayed the band that had accompanied the Virgin in procession style on her rise towards the centre of heaven, to lend pomp to the act of coronation, as it would have been appropriate to do in representing any earthly ceremony.

To this wind and percussion band, the small group of four angels in the foreground presents the greatest possible contrast. The angel in the rear is clearly singing. The other three play a lute, a flauto dolce of treble size, and the six-stringed bowed instrument that the contemporaries of Zanobi called a viola and that, in retrospect, can be classified as an early form of the lira da braccio — its characteristic leaf-shaped peg box showing the rear ends of six pegs. The softness of the lute is proverbial, and that of the flauto dolce is revealed by its very name. Likewise, the lira da braccio produces a very soft tone; the very lax tension of the hairs of its bow is required by its polyphonic technique.[3] This little ensemble is of the softest possible silvery timbre, even if we assume that the players of the lute and the lira da braccio also join their voices with the instru-

[1] See Paolo Veneziano's Coronation, in the Accademia, Venice; Fra Angelico's coronation pictures in the Louvre and the Uffizi.

[2] Quoted by Anthony Baines in *Galpin Society Journal*, March 1950, p. 20 ff.

[3] On the technique of the lira da braccio and the use of this instrument in Italian angel concerts, especially in Coronations of the Virgin and in the *sacre conversazioni*, see Chapter 5 above.

ments. This group, then, distinguished by haloes and its central position, must be of nobler quality, devoted to the performance of pieces in three- or four-part polyphony. Here we find an anticipation of the small polyphonic instrumental ensemble in the foreground of many of the *sacre conversazioni* or the Madonnas of Gian Bellini, Carpaccio, Cima da Conegliano, Signorelli, and many others.

The simultaneous playing of both groups would make little sense, but each could well be thought of as an actual ensemble of the time; the big one for large court dances, banquets, or processions; the small one for more subtle music of polyphonic character, performed at intimate occasions permitting and requiring concentration on the intricacies of text and texture.

According to church doctrine, liturgical music is but an imitation of celestial liturgy. But in fact the painter, depicting the music of the heavens, has recourse to his own everyday environment. Thus his representation is often of great interest to the historian of musical practice. And his picture shows clearly the confrontation of two typical, standardized groups of the time — loud and shrill music versus soft and low (*haut* vs. *bas* or *douce*).[1]

Our third example is again a Marian subject. It is the Ascension and Coronation of the Virgin by the Master of the St. Lucy Legend, now in the National Gallery, Washington, D.C. (Pl. 66). The painter was Flemish,[2] and his dated works are from between 1480 and 1489. This picture was formerly in a convent near Burgos, Spain.[3]

The painting is of unique and highly complex composition in strict bilateral symmetry and of almost miraculously fine and accurate detail — even to the minute representation of the smallest feathers in the angels' wings, the brocade of the garments, the jewellery, and the decoration of the musical instruments, the playing hands, and the books and music sheets in the hands of the angels.

The tall and slender body of the Virgin, rising to heaven, forms the vertical axis of the picture. Beneath her in the human realm, a landscape rendered in finest detail with castles, trees, water, and bridges, showing even the small conch shell at the water's edge. The Virgin's feet rest on the crescent, just as they do in the paintings of Geertgen and the Master of the Glorification. Eight angels, four

[1] Edmund A. Bowles, in his *Haut and Bas: The Grouping of Musical Instruments in the Middle Ages*, in *Musica Disciplina*, VIII (1954), 115 ff., has accumulated many quotations from medieval poems and chronicles, mostly French, that attest to the standardization of ensembles of different sizes and their social functions. It might be wished that he would expand his collection to include the Renaissance and the Italian and Flemish orbit.

[2] The work has also been called Portuguese-Flemish, or said to be by a Flemish artist working in Portugal. The influence of Enguerrands Clarenton's famous Coronation of the Virgin at Villeneuve-lès-Avignon has also been suggested.

[3] I had the pleasure of seeing the painting before and during restoration in 1949, while it was still in the Samuel H. Kress Collection, when I was called upon to give some advice concerning the musical instruments represented in it.

large and four small, seem to carry her upward, although a slight touch of the graceful hands appears to suffice for the purpose. Two pairs of angels immediately above her head are singing, the two nearest her each holding a sheet of music and the other two peering over their shoulders to read also. The sheets in alto and tenor clef contain the beginning of an *Ave Regina* (Pl. 67). All along the left and right margins of the picture there are eight angels, four on each side: left, from bottom to top — organetto with two ranks of eighteen pipes each; a trumpet, of which only the mouthcup and the upper end of the coil are visible; a large (tenor?) shawm; a harp of typical Gothic shape. On the right side from top to bottom there are a medium-sized (alto?) shawm; a five-stringed vielle; a small (treble?) shawm; and a small nine-stringed lute.

We have an instrumental ensemble composed of loud instruments (one trumpet, three shawms) and soft ones (lute, vielle, harp, organetto) — that is, eight instruments against the small vocal body of four voices. The area occupied by Mary, the four singing, eight playing, and eight carrying angels, covers by far the greater portion of the painting. We may call it the middle region, or that of the outer heaven, in contrast to the landscape of the human realm below it.

But there is still another region. At the top of the painting the clouds have opened and, through the sharply defined circular rim that they form, the inner heaven becomes visible — the throne of the Trinity surrounded by another multitude of angels (Pl. 7). God the Father, crowned and sceptered, and God the Son hold between them a crown ready to place upon the head of the Blessed Virgin; above it hovers the Dove. Three blue-robed angels, following an old pictorial tradition, are holding the hanging behind the throne. Flanking it are two groups of angels. On the left are the singers, eleven in number, again divided into two groups, one of six angels and the other of five, each group singing from a book with music. It is curious that the singers of the foreground group are not winged; they appear to be older, and possibly they are entrusted with the lower voices. At the right of the throne are the instrumentalists, six in number, playing three recorders, a small lute, a dulcimer, and a harp — all 'soft' instruments. Like the eight instrumentalists in the outer heaven — and, of course, like 15th-century instrumentalists on earth — they have no need of written music.

So much for the visible facts. To what extent is the depiction of these ensembles, vocal as well as instrumental, 'realistic'; i.e. how does it correspond to Flemish practices at the painter's time? The music in the outer heaven presents questions regarding two subjects: the nature of the orchestra, and the possible relationship between it and the four singers. The first can only be answered with extreme caution. The five loud winds, including a trumpet, three shawms, and an organetto equipped with a double rank of metal pipes (not the considerably softer wooden pipes), would certainly overpower the three string instruments, a harp, a tiny vielle, and a small lute. This orchestra then, as in the Geertgen painting, may merely symbolize a great volume of sound. On the other hand, so many contemporary reports and pictures[1] tell us of medium-sized and even larger instrumental ensembles combining trumpets, trombones, and shawms with soft string instruments, that the effect of the orchestra shown here in the outer heaven would certainly have been less bewildering to 15th-century ears than it is to us today.

The second question, that concerning the relation between orchestra and singers, is again not easy to answer. The four singers would be drowned out by the eight instruments unless one may impute supernatural power to angel voices. However, in pictures of the Coronation of the Virgin, a combination of singers and instruments reflecting contemporary practice rarely occurs.[2]

In the inner heaven, the 'reality' of the instrumental group in terms of earthly practice is beyond any doubt. Numerous parallels are to be found in 15th-century paintings. And likewise, the composition of the vocal group corresponds to the usage of that period. Of the two books used by the singers in the Coronation by the Master of the St. Lucy Legend, the one in which the notation is visible cannot, unfortunately, be deciphered. But whatever the angels are singing, we have no secular evidence that would speak against the simultaneous performance of the vocal and instrumental groups. Significant, of course, is the superiority in numbers of the singers.

A simultaneous performance of the same music by the angels of the outer and inner heavens seems to be utterly beyond the intention of the painter. He could not have made the separation of the two realms more clear, and it may have been more than a mere whim on his part to show the singers of the outer heaven holding single sheets, perhaps needed only once for the singular event of the Ascension. The larger vocal groups in the inner heaven are using thick music books, possibly implying a rich and lasting repertory near the Lord.

A brief summary of the organological conclusions may be warranted here.

[1] For a small ensemble, see for instance the charming illustration of the authors of the psalms, in the Psalter of King René II of Lorraine (Paris, Arsenal Library) showing these instruments: dulcimer, harp, vielle, recorder, trumpet, organetto, and tabor (frame drum). Also along this line, if such a late example is permissible, is the title woodcut for the Orlando di Lasso *Patrocinium musices* (Munich, 1573), depicting a tenor viol, fiddle, lute, spinet, two transverse flutes, two cornetti, and two trombones. For a larger ensemble of this type, combining loud and soft, a miniature from the Mielich Codex showing Orlando di Lasso and his ensemble at the Munich court includes spinet, three viols, tenor fiddle, bass viol, lute, three boy singers, transverse flute, bassoon, bass trombone, straight cornetto, ranket, and curved cornetto.

[2] Among my collection of several hundred photographs of angel concerts in painting and sculpture, I have found only two altarpieces with a clear opposition of singers to a large orchestral group, and in each case the singers were also playing organettos.

Concerning the question of celestial musical practice, we are in the same plight as was the aged Gluck, who once told an Italian composer, seeking information as to whether the Redeemer would be singing tenor or baritone, that he did not yet have authentic information. None of the great connoisseurs of celestial ceremonial — Dionysius the pseudo-Areopagite and Thomas Aquinas, Jacques de Liège, Dante, and Jacobus de Voragine — informs us of the size and composition of the heavenly orchestra. A comparison with the human condition seems therefore inevitable. In each of the three pictures I have analysed, the instruments are depicted faithfully; there is not a single fantastic or imaginary instrument, such as those which Gaudenzio Ferrari invented a little later for some of his angels.

More complex is the question of the grouping of the angels in the ensembles shown in our paintings, and whether or not these correspond to contemporary usage. Here Geertgen provides no information; symbolizing a maximum of sound, he accumulates virtually all the instruments available. Zanobi represents two actually existing ensembles of different sizes, instruments, and purposes. The Master of the St Lucy Legend, like Zanobi, depicts the playing of loud, festive music with one group, the processional band in the outer heaven, although the inclusion of singers and softer instruments in this band may or may not reflect actual practice; and also, parallel to the small group in Zanobi's painting, his singers and players in the inner heaven correspond closely to the practice in intimate house music of the time.

There remains the delicate problem of the comparative distinction imputed to the ensembles. Zanobi, in accordance with similar representations of the time, clearly emphasizes the small and soft group as the superior one by placing it in front of the throne. But the larger and louder ensemble in the Zanobi painting is still so close to the throne that one might expect it to compete and alternate with the chamber group. In the painting by the Master of the St. Lucy Legend, however, the larger group seems to be only the transitory accompaniment to the Ascension of the Virgin, while the small and soft ensemble is the one worthy to perform perpetually in the presence of the Lord.

Two conclusions suggest themselves: the superior rank assigned to vocal music, evidently in keeping with the liturgical tradition followed by painters of the period, and the preference for soft instruments in the presence of the Lord.[1]

[1] In Hans Memling's triptych (1480) decorating the organ of the church of the Benedictines in Najera, the arrangement of the instruments seems to imply a graduation from loud to soft, with the loudest being nearest to the singers surrounding the Lord, as follows: left panel — shawm, trumpet, lute, tromba marina, psaltery; right panel — two trumpets, organetto, harp, vielle. Hammerstein (p. 242) sees in the relative distance from the central figure a difference in rank among the groups in this order: singers, *instruments hauts*, *instruments bas*. If Memling really had it in mind to represent a sort of celestial musical precedence, the symbolism implied would

Here we are reminded, and possibly the painters or their ecclesiastical advisers were too, of Elijah's experience as recorded in I Kings 19: 11, 12, and 13:

> And a great and strong wind rent the mountains, and brake in pieces the rocks before the Lord; but the Lord was not in the wind: and after the wind an earthquake; but the Lord was not in the earthquake: And after the earthquake a fire; but the Lord was not in the fire: and after the fire a still small voice: And it was so when Elijah heard it. . . .

---

be the reverse of that expressed in the inner heaven of the painting by the Master of the St. Lucy Legend except, of course, for the singers, who in both cases have the privileged place near the Lord.

12 · The Curse of Pallas Athena

The ancients had two legends about musical contests, one comical, the other deeply tragic. The comical one is the story of the contest between Apollo and Pan. Apollo's kithara easily triumphed over the syrinx of the goat-footed god, and the judge Tmolos had no trouble in according the victory to Phoebus. Pan was not punished, for he had not really irritated Apollo's pride or vanity. But the real joke is that a bystander was punished, the music critic King Midas. In spite of Tmolos' verdict, he had dared to consider Pan the better performer, whereupon Apollo transformed his insensitive ears into those of an ass.

More serious is the other contest, in which Apollo defeated Marsyas. Already the physiognomical appearance of Marsyas shows this; he is not a half-goat, but a satyr, quite human[1] except for a horse tail and slightly pointed ears (as we see him in countless Greek vase paintings and in sculpture). His *hybris* was incomparably more threatening to Apollo than that of Pan. He snatched the pipes that Pallas Athena, their inventor, had thrown away. The pipes,[2] still animated by the magic sparkle of the goddess, played as though by themselves, and the divine music so pleased Marsyas' compatriots, the Phrygians, that they considered it better than that of Apollo. Marsyas would not have been a professional musician if he had contradicted them. This was his undoing. Apollo insisted upon a contest, this time with the Muses as jury. Marsyas agreed and even accepted Apollo's condition that the winner could do as he pleased with the loser. All this seemed fair enough. For some time the Muses were inclined to favour Marsyas. Only then did Apollo resort to tricks. He played his instrument upside down[3] and challenged Marsyas to do the same, knowing well that the pipes could only be played from one end. He also sang, accompanying himself on the strings, and again the pipes could not match this feat. Finally, approaching

[1] Alkibiades in the *Symposium* (215) compares Socrates' appearance to that of Marsyas. The portrait busts of Socrates in comparison with the heads of Marsyas such as the one in the Museo Barracco, Rome, are an even more telling evidence.

[2] For generations archaeologists have chosen to call the aulos — and its Roman counterpart, the tibia — a 'flute,' that is, a pipe without reeds, whereas the aulos according to overwhelming literary and visual evidence is a reed pipe, or more precisely an oboe, that is, a tube fitted with a double reed.

[3] See the so-called Sarcophagus of the Via della Garbatella, Rome, Antiquarium del Governatorato; and Apollodorus, I, Vol. 4, p. 2.

sheer bribery he sang the praise of Olympus and Helicon, and the Muses did not fail to respond to this flattery.[1]

This then leads to the fatal conclusion. Marsyas is bound to a tree and flayed. Here the several versions of the myth diverge sharply: some authors, such as Apollodorus (I, 4, 2), Ovid (*Metamorphoses* VI), and Plutarch (*Alcib.* II), tell that Apollo himself did the flaying. Others such as Philostratus min. (*Imag.* 2) have the murderous act performed by a Scythian executioner, or describe the preparations such as the sharpening of the knife. There are also different versions about the transformation of Marsyas into a river: many hold that the river originated from the blood of Marsyas; in Ovid's *Metamorphoses*,[2] however, there is a more subtly poetical version relating that a river was formed out of the tears of the satyrs, nymphs, shepherds, and of Marsyas' pupil Olympus.

In their art the ancients significantly refrained from the portrayal of the flaying. The knife, however, often appears in the hands of the standing executioner[3] or of a squatting knife sharpener, who later became such an important motif for sculpture and painting, from the famous *Arrotino*, today in the Uffizi, up to Peruzzi's little monochrome on the ceiling of the Stanza delle Nozze in the Villa Farnesina. Even Philostratus the Younger did not go further in his description of the Marsyas painting than to describe the savage grin and glaring eyes of the barbarian whetting the knife.

In Hellenistic art the representation of Marsyas acquires a new dimension: the impertinent satyr rightfully punished for daring the god turns now into the outstanding image of tragic suffering. The face of a man hanging from a tree has now lost any traces of the satyr. Though furrowed and convulsed by pain, it is deeply human and pensive. Marsyas has become an image of the silently suffering creature, clearly the prototype of the crucified.

Numerous Greek myths, such as those of Prometheus, Pentheus, and Niobe, deal with *hybris* and its punishment, the merciless revenge of the offended god on the offender. Through the Middle Ages the Marsyas story remained familiar mainly as an allegory of temerity punished. But we also recall Dante's famous reinterpretation of the flaying in the first canto of the *Paradiso* as

[1] Lucian's irony in the *Dialogues of the Gods* formulates this sharply. 'Hera: "Isn't Apollo admirably clever? He, whom Marsyas would have skinned! If only the Muses had not been biased judges, since no doubt Marsyas was the better musician! But as it happened the poor, cheated fool became the victim of a rigged verdict. . . ." '

[2] Loeb ed., VI, 382; also *Fasti*, Loeb ed., VI, 703.

[3] See the wall painting showing Olympus begging clememcy for Marsyas from Apollo, repr. in J. A. Overbeck, *Atlas der Griechischen Kunstmythologie*, Leipzig, 1871–89, xxv, III, 13; and the ancient stucco decoration in the basilica of Porta Maggiore, reproduced in Ludwig Curtius, *Das antike Rom*, Vienna, 1944, p. 67. Raphael borrowed the motif of the standing executioner for his condensed representation of the contest on the ceiling of the Segnatura.

purification of the soul for the sake of its mystic union with God-Apollo.[1]

But the Marsyas story not only shows *hybris* punished but has a special flavour and message. It is a poetic condensation of an eternal conflict, the antagonism between two musical realms, between string and wind instruments. This means not only the difference between the serene and silvery sound of plucked gut strings and the bleating, shrill, guttural, exciting sound of a reed pipe, though this alone is sufficiently charged with symbolic meaning in primitive civilizations from the earliest times. It means in the rationalized form of the Greek myths the realm of inhibition, of reason, of measure — in the literal Pythagorean sense of measuring strings and intervals, and in the metaphorical sense of *mesure* — as opposed to the realm of blind passion: in short, the antagonism between Apollo and Dionysus.

This is not the place to give an elaborate picture of a problem as complex as the symbolism of musical sounds and of the instruments that produce them. A few quotations may suffice to show how strongly these feelings still run in later post-mythical Greek aesthetics and — significantly — in Greek education. Plato (*Gorgias* 501) considers 'aulos-playing an art which only pursues pleasure,' and declares (*Republic* III, 399) the instruments of Apollo 'preferable to those of Marsyas,' a statement that is much more than an aesthetic preference if we view it in the light of his suggestion that the traditional command of the Delphian god to his worshippers, 'Know thyself!,' be interpreted as 'Be temperate!' (*Charmides* 164). Aristotle denies moral standing to the aulos — it is too exciting and too emotional (*Pol.* VIII, 1341a, 20; 1342 6, 1) — but rationalizes the old myth of Athena's rejection of her invention, the aulos, by bending the myth into an educational precept: 'If the goddess threw the aulos away, it was not only because it made her face ugly, but because aulos-playing does not contribute anything to the mind' (*Pol.* 1341, 65).

Although the old orthodox antinomy between Apollo and Dionysus and their musical monopolies, Paean and Dithyrambus, has by now been blurred and undergone a gradual process of rationalization and reinterpretation in Aristotelian didactic philosophy, nevertheless within this process of rationalization the older and deeper-lying antinomy between the orgiastic, intoxicating 'low' music and temperate 'ethical' music has been preserved, and with it the differing symbolic characters of the kithara and the aulos, of the stringed and the wind instruments. Their symbolic and emotional function was too deeply rooted in mythical tradition — too much a part of immemorial usage to be diluted by such surface phenomena as the succession of philosophical systems

[1] Ghiberti (*Commentarii*, Book II) still misinterpreted the ancient carnelian with the three figures of Apollo, the bearded Marsyas, and the kneeling boy Olympus as an allegory of the three ages of man.

and educational doctrines. And their symbolic connotation has in fact not only outlived the ancient gods but persisted down through the ages. It is still firmly embedded in the undercurrents, for instance in the folk music of contemporary civilizations. And this is true especially of the orgiastic instruments, the reed pipes, which have preserved their exciting timbre and symbolic character from the Greek aulos through the Roman tibia, the medieval bagpipe and platerspiel, the shawm of the Renaissance, and the cornemuse and musette of the Baroque and Rococo, to the saxophone of our day.

However, it was not until the close of the *quattrocento*, with the vogue of great solo performers and improvisers, that the Marsyas myth as a musical contest recaptured the artistic imagination. The sudden crop of pictorial representations is enormous. And it is from this moment that these pictures become — or should become — of interest to the historian of music and especially of instrumental performance, because now in these pictures a variety of instruments appear in the hands of Apollo and Marsyas. They are frequently the ancient ones, aulos and kithara, borrowed from gems and sarcophagi in more or less stylized versions. But often they are replaced by their contemporary equivalents, by the lira da braccio or the viola for Apollo, and shawms or other pipes for Marsyas,[1] sometimes naively, but often also because a familiar instrument from daily life reveals its symbolism more directly to the beholder. Sometimes, too, contemporary instruments such as the lira da braccio and other bowed instruments were chosen because they were considered to be ancient ones; the invention of the bow, the viola, and the violin was attributed to Sappho even in *cinquecento* literature.[2]

One unusually rich and thoughtful representation of the Marsyas story appears on an Italian panel exhibited in the National Gallery, Washington, D.C. (Kress Foundation 433)[3] (Pl. 70a) and it certainly deserves more attention than has been bestowed upon it up to now, for it is one of the most original versions of the often depicted Marsyas story. It shows in narrative sequence several phases of the myth in an elaborate and variegated landscape. Of the five

[1] I know of only one painting where the challenger of Apollo has a string instrument: Cima da Conegliano's *tondo* with the contest between Apollo and Pan. While Apollo holds a stylized form of the lira da braccio, Pan has not his usual syrinx but a small rustic version of the rebec, evidently appropriate to the man from the woods.

[2] As for the Renaissance treatises on music attributing the invention of contemporary musical instruments to antiquity, see Chapter 14 below.

[3] The painting is labelled in the National Gallery 'unknown Florentine, sixteenth century.' As a historian of music I should leave dating and attribution to connoisseurs better qualified, but cannot refrain from suggesting an earlier and more northern origin — perhaps Brescian. The humid landscape, rich in water and mossy rocks, strongly suggests the foothills of the Alps rather than a Tuscan *ambiente*, and the whole composition, still breathing a spirit of the late *quattrocento*, may be placed not later than the first quarter of the *cinquecento*.

large figures, the central and dominating one is that of Apollo. With slightly opened lips, perhaps singing, and a serious expression in his languid, dreamy eyes, he bows his large fiddle. The other bow, his weapon, lies beneath his feet, discarded in favour of the musical bow. The quiver with the arrows is visible behind his right shoulder. Marsyas listens to him with an anxious, preoccupied, and worried face. He is a rustic character, with bare feet and thick, bushy hair, and holds a bagpipe in his lap.

We may just as well pause here to devote a few words to his musical instrument and that of Apollo, which after all are the real contestants and in a way the protagonists of the whole story. The bagpipe — or, as the *quattro-* and *cinquecento* would have called it, 'zampogna' or 'zamparella' — is in timbre the counterpart of the ancient Greek aulos or Roman tibia, for its sounding pipes, the chanter and the drone, are fitted with reeds like the aulos and produce a similar bleating 'reedy' timbre (these reeds are inside the bag). Yet bagpipes are extremely rare in Renaissance illustrations of the Marsyas story; we usually find simple reed pipes without a bag, like those in Perugino's drawing in the Accademia, Venice, or in the beautiful painting in the Hermitage attributed to Bronzino and Correggio, executed for the decoration of a harpsichord lid. In fact I know of only three artists who show bagpipes in the Marsyas story; one is the author of the woodcuts for the *Ovidio volgare* 1497; a second is Benedetto Montagna in his engraving (Arthur M. Hind, *Early Italian Engraving*, London, 1938–48, V, 186, No. 41); the last is Andrea Schiavone in his drawing of the flaying of Marsyas (Louvre), with a bagpipe in the foreground strangely paired with the ancient lyre. In his *cassone* painting of the contest in the Accademia, Venice, Schiavone again uses the bagpipe, played not by Marsyas, however, but by a small female figure near the margin.

The syrinx, composed ordinarily of seven pipes of different length, is usually the instrument of Pan in Renaissance painting,[1] as well as in ancient Roman sculpture,[2] but occasionally it also accompanies Marsyas.[3] In single cases the wind instrument is even replaced by a string instrument, as in Cima da Conegliano's *tondo*, in which Pan holds a rustic form of the rebec while Apollo bows a beautifully stylized and highly decorated string instrument, a version of the lira da braccio.[4]

[1] For instance, Tintoretto, *The Judgement of Midas*, National Gallery of Art, Washington, D.C.

[2] See the group *Pan and Daphnis* in the Museo Nazionale, Naples.

[3] See for instance the medallion with the flaying of Marsyas in Annibale Carracci's ceiling in the Galleria Farnese. In the sketch of Marsyas in the Louvre (No. 5923), attributed to Correggio, reproduced in A. E. Popham, *Correggio's Drawings*, London, 1957, Plate X, Marsyas plays an ancient syrinx; the same figure in the painting of the contest on the harpsichord lid in the Hermitage referred to previously shows the syrinx replaced by a large 16th-century shawm.

[4] Further about the lira da braccio, see Chapter 5 above.

The lira da braccio in our painting has four melody strings and one clearly visible drone string passing next to the thumb of the player's left hand (Pl. 69a). Its form is typical of the beginning of the *cinquecento*. This form is characterized by side walls consisting of two curves separated by a projecting point — as opposed to the later forms, which already approach the violin, with two projecting points resulting in a division of the side walls into upper, middle and lower bouts. Good examples of this type are to be seen in Lorenzo Liombruno's *Judgement of Midas*, before its destruction in the Berlin Museum; Perugino's *Coronation of the Virgin* in the Vatican; the Apollo in Raphael's *Parnassus* (Pl. 84a); Signorelli's Virgin in the Pinacoteca in Arezzo; and above all, the most beautiful depiction, in Carpaccio's *Presentation of Jesus in the Temple* in the Venice Accademia (Pl. 33b).

In the Italian literature of the *quattro-* and *cinquecento*, 'lira' means sometimes the ancient lyre, sometimes the contemporary lira da braccio. The numerous Renaissance treatises dealing with the music of the ancients and its relation to contemporary music make it quite clear that the name 'lira' was given at the time not only to the ancient lyre but also to the modern bowed stringed instrument, which sometimes is also called 'lira moderna,' as for instance, to mention only one source, in Vincenzo Galilei's *Dialogo della musica antica e moderna*, 1581, fn. pp. 136, 147.[1]

The left section of the painting shows the flaying (Pl. 69b). Marsyas is nude, his cloak and bagpipe at his feet, his right arm tied to the bare tree. His face is filled with horror and pain as he turns his head toward Apollo, who performs the cruel punishment himself, with a brutal gleam in his eye. This is quite rare. As I have mentioned, the Greeks in their innumerable representations have never shown the actual skinning.[2] It was in the Baroque, when art revelled in torture and martyrdom, that the act of flaying, frequently carried out by Apollo himself, became a generally accepted subject.[3]

[1] Vincenzo Galilei, the father of Galileo Galilei, was a famous composer, theoretician, and historian of music, and was deeply interested in ancient Greek music and the possibilities of reconstructing it.

[2] The preparation for the flaying is frequently symbolized by the standing or squatting figure of the Scythian executioner. The squatting figure was retained by Peruzzi in his frieze with the stories from Ovid's *Metamorphoses* in the third floor of the Villa Farnesina.

[3] Among the earliest scenes showing the flaying are Correggio's (Bronzino's?) painting on the lid of a harpsichord in the Hermitage, and Andrea Schiavone's painting, once in Andrea Vendramin's collection (Tancred Borenius, *The Picture Gallery of Andrea Vendramin*, London, 1923, pl. 59, fol. 71), and his drawing in the Louvre mentioned above. In all these representations, Apollo himself wields the knife. In Domenichino's fresco for the Villa Aldobrandini, later in the collection Lanckoronski, Apollo again does the flaying. The most elaborate vivisection, of almost Vesalian flavour, occurs in the painstaking engraving by Melchior Meier (after Martin Rota), Adam Bartsch, *Le Peintre graveur*, Leipzig, 1876, Vol. XVI, p. 246. There Marsyas under Apollo's knife appears as an anatomical showpiece, similar to Marco Agrate's statue of the

This brings us to the last of the five figures, a roundish and pretty young woman also playing the bagpipe at the edge of a pond (Pl. 69c). It is precisely the same kind of bagpipe which is held by Marsyas and lies at his feet in the flaying group. Who would guess at first glance that this bareshouldered and barefooted girl engaged in pastoral music is none other than Pallas Athena herself? But her attributes, the helmet, shield, and lance beside her foot, are clearly depicted; and, if there were still doubt, her pose would explain her function in the Marsyas story, for she takes no delight at all in her music, but bends forward anxiously to observe her reflection in the water. In short, we have here the representation of another myth, closely related to the Marsyas story. It is the story of the invention of the reed pipe by Athena. She invents the aulos and plays it at an Olympian banquet. Most of the gods are delighted, but Hera and Aphrodite smile at the distorted face and the puffed cheeks of Athena. The embarrassed Athena rushes into a Phrygian wood to look at her image in a pond, and, agreeing that her appearance is hardly improved by performing on the pipes,[1] she throws them away and curses them. When Marsyas snatches at them, she tries to prevent him,[2] but he takes them anyway and falls victim to the curse.[3]

---

skinned San Bartolomeo in the cathedral of Milan near the side entrance. In Titian's painting in the archiepiscopal castle of Kremsier, Apollo plays the lira da braccio while Marsyas, hanging down like one of the carcasses in Rembrandt's and Daumier's paintings, is butchered by the Scythian executioner and his assistant.

[1] See for instance, Athenaeus, Bk. 14, quoted in Natalis Comes, *Mythologia*, 1596 and 1616, Bk. VI, Ch. XV, 'De Marsya.'

[2] Illustrated in Myron's famous group (see Pausanias, I, 24, No. 1). The invention of the aulos itself by Athena — and, by the way, Hermes' creation of the lyre — was not illustrated, as far as I know, in Greek art.

[3] It is remarkable how this short myth reflects in a condensed form the ambivalent attitude of the Greeks towards the wind instrument (described above), and how attitudes common to primitive civilizations are rationalized in Greek myths, and parallel with this, in their arts. In primitive cultures the pipe is usually an initiation instrument and therefore under a taboo for women. In Greek writers the aulos is the instrument of passion, urges, instincts — in short, of what orthodox psychoanalysts would call the Id. Thus we find it in the entourage of Dionysus, in the hands of satyrs, and it is also the customary instrument in the hands of music-making girls in numerous scenes of drinking parties. But apart from this a woman would not ordinarily be shown with the aulos.— The Dionysiac connotation of the wind instrument is obvious in countless representations in Renaissance art, of which I mention here only a few characteristic examples from the late *quattro-* and early *cinquecento*: an engraving by Zoan Andrea, *Youth and Girl Embracing* (*c.* 1475) (Hind, *op. cit.*, V, 68, No. 18); engraving by Marcantonio, *Satyr and Nymph* (Henri Delaborde, *Marc-Antoine Raimondi*, Paris, 1888, No. 140), and its reinterpretation in the bronze *tondo* by pseudo-Antonio da Brescia, *Pan and Abundance* (A 395, 118 B., National Gallery of Art, Washington, D.C.); *The Sacrifice to Priapus* in the *Hypnerotomachia Polyphili*, with many wind instruments; the engraving by Girolamo Mocetto, *Metamorphosis of Amymone* (*c.* 1514) (Hind, *op. cit.*, II, 166), and the related drawing by Benedetto Montagna (Uffizi, Gabinetto dei Disegni 14589F); Luca Signorelli's famous *Pan and Attendants*, in the Berlin Museum until its destruction, with a syrinx and several pipes; Francesco Cossa's *Triumph of Venus* in the

As the patroness of crafts, Pallas Athena was credited with the invention of a tool as complex and delicate as the full-fledged aulos. Yet as a goddess revered as the embodiment of reason she could not favour an object charged with the connotation of passion, sex, and inebriation. But being the inventor of the instrument and the initiator of the whole chain of events she remains an important element of the story, and it is evidently for this reason that she is included in many of the larger representations of the contest between Apollo and Marsyas in Greek vase painting as well as on Roman sarcophagi. But she never acts; she is just present, just a bystander, and she does not hold an instrument.[1] It is in this passive function that she has been retained in most Renaissance and Baroque representations of the contest, that of Marsyas as well as that of Pan,[2] as for instance in the painting on the harpsichord lid in the Hermitage, mentioned before.[3] Athena's appearance in a musical contest as a main figure and even holding a musical instrument is of the utmost rarity, and if she does so in our painting it seems a poetic idea to round out the contest scene not only with its later tragic consequences but also by alluding to the origins of it all, the unlucky invention of the ill-fated pipes.

---

frescoes in the Palazzo Schifanoia, Ferrara (see Chapter 2 above); about the many pastoral girls with flutes in Titian, see Chapter 2 above.

While some of these scenes evidently pay lip service to ancient art, especially gems and sarcophagi, it is quite clear that the symbolic function of the wind instrument is contemporary in feeling. This tradition is continued in the numerous flute lessons (e.g., the drawing by Lodovico Caracci, Uffizi, Gabinetto dei Disegni 787E) and other genre scenes of the Baroque and even later. The clearest self-explanatory subject from antiquity is perhaps the combination of aulos-playing satyrs with the Dionysiac serpent baskets, for instance on the right side wall of the famous sarcophagus with Bacchus and Ariadne in the Louvre, and on the left side wall of the sarcophagus with the triumph of Dionysus in the Lyon Museum.

[1] I know of only one ancient representation of Athena playing the aulos: a first-century Roman sarcophagus in the Palazzo Barberini, once part of the famous collection Valle Capranica (Karl Roberts, *Die Antiken Sarkophag-Reliefs*, Berlin, 1890–1952, Vol. 3/2, p. 244, and Pl. lxiii), depicts, in three sections framed by *putti* that carry a garland, three phases of the Marsyas story, including in the first section Athena playing the aulos and watching her badly distorted face in the water. Also interesting in this connection is the myth of Athena as the inventor of aulos music as told by Pindar in his poem for Midas of Acragas, the winner in an aulos-playing contest (Pythian xii), a tale, by the way, of profound bearing on Greek aesthetics of instrumental music. According to this tale, Athena invented the aulos in order to imitate on this instrument the death cry of Euryale, the one of the three Gorgons who was beheaded by Perseus.

[2] The large canvas with the *Contest between Apollo and Pan* by H. de Clerck in the Rijksmuseum is an exception; there Pallas, in obvious ignorance of her traditional role in the ancient myths, counsels the playing Apollo.

[3] Mentioned in Vasari, *Vite*, ed. Milanesi, VI, 276; and in Raffaello Borghini, *Il Riposo*, Florence, 1584, Bk. IV. See also H. Voss in *Jahrbuch der Königlichen Preussischen Kunstsammlungen*, XXXIV (1913), 314 ff., and in *Die Malerei der Spätrenaissance in Rom und Florenz*, Berlin, 1920, p. 209 ff.; Hans Tietze and E. Tietze-Conrat, *Tizian-Studien*, in *Jahrbuch der kunsthistorischen Sammlungen in Wien*, Neue Folge, X (1936), 144 ff.; and A. E. Popham, *Correggio's Drawings*, London, 1957, p. 21 ff.

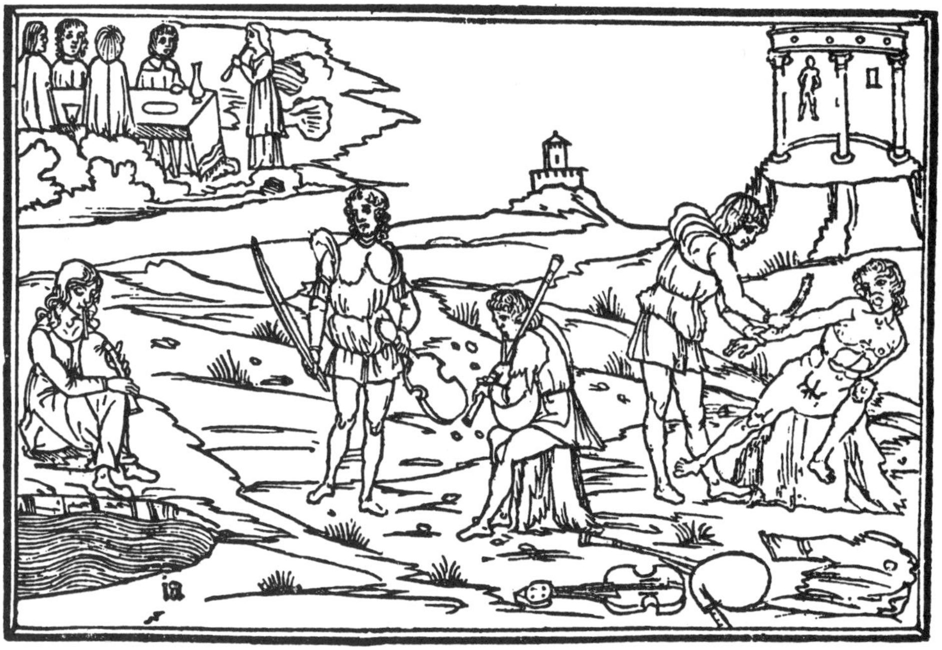

Fig. 20. *Contest between Apollo and Marsyas.* Woodcut from *Ovidio metamorphoseos volgare,* 1501, fol. 49v.

As the immediate source and inspiration for the master of our picture I should like to suggest the two woodcuts in the first edition of the *Ovidio volgare.*[1] The first of these illustrations (Fig. 20) shows in reverse all the five figures of our painting, all with the same instruments, the lira da braccio and the bagpipe. Here, as there, Athena looks at her reflection in the water, Apollo himself performs the flaying, and the musical instruments appear in the same number and order: the lira da braccio twice, in the hands of Apollo and discarded on the ground; the bagpipe three times, played by Athena[2] and by Marsyas, and again

[1] *Ovidio metamorphoseos volgare,* Venice, 1497 and 1501; leaf xlix verso in the 1501 edition with the contest between Apollo and Marsyas; and leaf cxxxxiii recto in the 1501 edition with the contest between Apollo and Pan.

[2] I know of only one other *cinquecento* representation in which Pallas Athena plays the bagpipe to study her appearance. It is in a *Judgement of Midas,* one of the two *cassone* paintings by Andrea Schiavone (Meldolla) in the Accademia, Venice (Pl. 71a). There the two contestants sit in the middle, Marsyas playing and Apollo listening. On the left are King Midas and Pan with his syrinx, and on the right margin in the middle ground is a small figure, Athena with a pipe in front of a pond. Marsyas, the 'villano' in the *Ovidio volgare,* wears a peasant straw hat. It is not without interest that Schiavone does not give the contemporary lira da braccio and bagpipe to the contestants but manifestly aims at archaeological accuracy: Marsyas plays the *diaulos* (double pipe), Apollo holds a stylized version of the ancient lyre — thus, instruments apparently

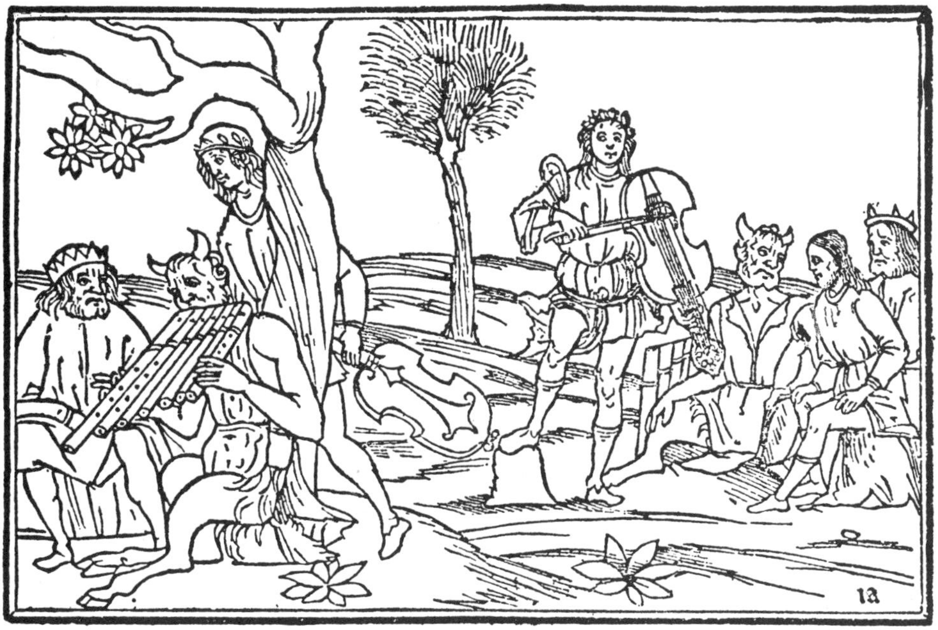

Fig. 21. *Contest between Apollo and Pan.* Woodcut from *Ovidio metamorphoseos volgare*, 1501, fol. 143r.

on the ground. The woodcut, however, shows two important additions necessary to do full justice to the text: Athena playing the pipe at the banquet of the gods, and the temple of Apollo where the skin of Marsyas is displayed.[1]

derived from ancient sarcophagi. This is the more curious since Athena retains the bagpipe, but evidently this is again a reminiscence of the *Ovidio volgare* illustration. Lili Fröhlich Bum in her description of this painting [*Andrea Meldolla, genannt Schiavone*, in *Jahrbuch der kunsthistorischen Sammlungen des Allerhöchsten Kaiserhauses*, XXXI (1913–14), 112] does not recognize Athena, but calls this figure 'eine fliehende Frauengestalt.' The arm which at a quick glance may indicate the resolute gesture of a fleeing woman is in fact reaching to hold the instrument. The larger canvas by Andrea Schiavone at Hampton Court, showing the contest between Apollo and Midas, includes Athena only as a witness of the contest.

[1]It is worth noting how much the Olympic scene and the little temple in the upper corners of this page differ from the main scenes below. The latter must have been drawn by a great master: a few sure economical strokes delineate Athena's absorption in her playing, and Marsyas' zeal as he plays eagerly like a puffed-up frog, and likewise his pain and horror in the flaying scene, and again the light and graceful posture of Apollo with the lira. And how sure and convincingly these five figures are placed in the wide landscape, intersecting the many horizontals enlivened rhythmically by tufts of grass. On the other hand, the Olympian banquet is stiff, almost childishly rough, the cloud rims hard, and the figures wooden and misproportioned. Similarly, Apollo's temple lacks any perspective. All this strongly suggests that the upper two scenes have been added by another hand, possibly to complete literally the references in the text to the banquet and the temple. The temple sketchily indicated in the woodcut has been

The display of the skin of Marsyas in Phoebus' temple is a crude popularization of the original versions of the myth, which were more subtle. Herodotus (VII, 26) quotes the Phrygians as saying that Apollo hung the skin of Marsyas near the source of the river Marsyas at the market place of the Phrygian town Kelainai, but Xenophon (*Anabasis*, I, 2.8) relates that the skin was hung in the cave whence the source of the river Marsyas springs, and Pliny (n.h.V, 106) adds that the river Marsyas disappeared into the ground and reappeared at the market place of Kelainai. There the hide moved when Phrygian tunes were played on the aulos. There is no evidence to suggest which of the ancient writers were directly known to the painter of our picture; we can only tentatively suggest that in his intentions the brook near the flayed man is connected with the river in the middle ground, and that the town far down in the deep plain is Kelainai.

There is, however, one notable discrepancy between this woodcut and our painting. In the painting Apollo actually plays and turns toward his rival who listens, while in the woodcut Apollo listens, holding bow and instrument in waiting position while turning away from his adversary, who eagerly plays the bagpipe. It seems more than likely therefore that the figure of the performing Apollo is borrowed from the second woodcut (Fig. 21), where Apollo bows the lira da braccio while Pan listens. The bearded Tmolus seated between Pan and Midas may also have lent his posture and preoccupied expression to the Marsyas of our painting.

The two woodcuts from the *Ovidio volgare* were also models for two engravings by Benedetto Montagna, one showing Apollo's contest with Marsyas (Hind, V, 186, No. 41) (Pl. 70b), the other with Pan (Hind, V, 185, No. 40) (Pl. 70c). Montagna in each of his engravings borrows only the central figures. Many details, such as the tunic of Apollo, twice girdled at the waist and at the hips, are repeated with great precision. This poses the question of whether the author of our painting also knew one or both of the Montagna prints. It is not improbable. In Montagna's representation of the contest with Pan, Apollo holds his lira against his left cheek, as in our painting, in a pose quite different from the one in the *Ovidio* woodcut. And in Montagna's representation of the Marsyas

---

retained — understood or not — in the Washington painting as the round tower above the flaying scene, and also in the Schiavone *Judgment of Midas* (Pl. 71a), where it appears behind the figure of Athena. In the latter case the significance of the temple has obviously not been understood, one of the innumerable examples of the persistence of elements after they have lost their original meaning.

On the subject of archaeological tendencies in the choice of musical instruments in Renaissance painting, see Chapter 14 below. Ulocrino, in his square plaquette with Apollo and Marsyas (C. L. M. E. Molinier, *Les Bronzes de la renaissance*, Paris, 1886, n. 252; examples in the British Museum, Victoria and Albert Museum, National Gallery of Art, Washington D.C., and other museums), is unusually cautious: he gives Apollo two instruments, a beautiful large specimen of the ancient lira, and a modern viola.

contest, Marsyas, characterized, by the way, as *villano* with the typical peasant straw hat, holds a bagpipe decorated with a checkered design precisely like that of Pallas and Marsyas in our painting.

The five figures are harmoniously spaced in the landscape, with Athena a little back toward the middle ground to suggest the origin of the events. The landscape, organized in near and far hills, is an admirable counterpoint to the chain of protagonists. Rocks, trees, and masses of foliage of varying densities form the background for the figures. Only the tree to which Marsyas is tied — though the rope is not visible — is bare. Between the hills of the middle ground far vistas open towards towns, one deep down in the plains, the other crowned

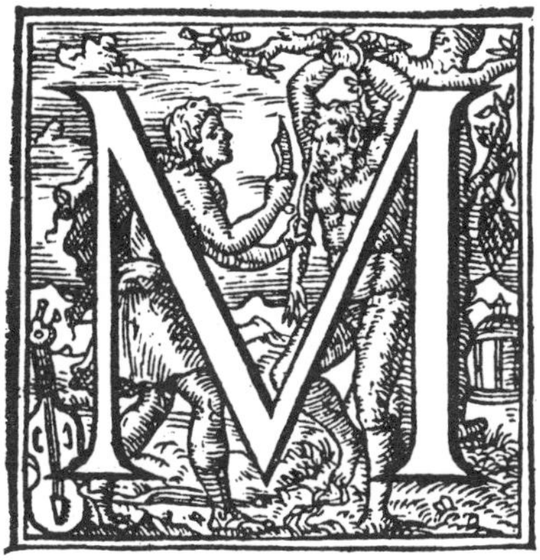

Fig. 22. *The Flaying of Marsyas.* Initial from Nicola Vicentino, *L'Antica musica ridotta alla moderna practica*, 1605.

by a castle on the rocks. Satyrs and humans are scattered over the paths, a pair of satyrs on the extreme left under the round tower run away, evidently terrified by the flaying.

There is also a rhythmical chain of significant objects scattered across the panel from the right middle ground to the left foreground, telling as it were the story in terms of instruments: passing from Athena's bagpipe over her divine attributes to the bagpipe played by Marsyas, rising to Apollo's lira da braccio, and falling to his shooting bow beneath his feet, the lira da braccio and the quiver laid aside by the god engaged in the flaying, and finally, sadly abandoned, Marsyas's bagpipe once more on the ground. Furthermore, in addition to this string of meaningful objects tying the picture together into a fateful sequence, there is also another symbolic device that frames the narrative: water as prologue and epilogue, the surface of the pond that by reflecting Athena's face led to the curse; and the brook trickling at the feet of the flayed one, indicating the river created by his blood. And when all is said it is perhaps not too far-fetched to consider also the two tufts of reeds in our painting as related to the symbolism of the whole scene. It is reeds that furnish the material for pipes, not only for the tubes,[1] but also for the small thin blades that make the air vibrate in 'reed pipes,' in the aulos as well as the shawms, oboes, and bagpipes of later times. One cluster of reeds is shown near the pond near which Athena placed the bagpipe, her recent invention. The other cluster appears near the water that trickles at the roots of the tree to which Marsyas is bound.

Thus Marsyas survives as a living stream, and the stream grows reeds, and the reeds turn into pipes again. Strabo (XII, 578) reports of his travels in Asia that the folk living on the banks of the Marsyas River were induced to make pipes by the growth of reeds there. The mighty stream of folk music flows on, hardly rippled by the quick vogues of art music; the reedy tunes are still heard in the shepherd pipes in the mountain valleys of Greece and the Near East, and in the *zampogne* and *pifferi* of the Apennines, and in the many forms of bagpipes in the British Isles. Marsyas's music, though cursed by Pallas, never dies.

APPENDIX

It seems appropriate to quote literally the account of Apollo's contest with Marsyas in the *Ovidio volgare*, together with the 'Alegoria' which there follows the narration. Not only is the retelling of the myth in folksy Boccaccio style extremely amusing, it is also interesting to observe how the illustrator of the *Ovidio* adheres with great precision to the story.

The following 'Alegoria' stemming from medieval moralizations is of course quite beyond pictorial illustration, at least in the late *quattrocento*. There is hardly an element of the story which is not invested with allegorical meaning: the two contestants are the images of the true and the false philosopher, the sophist. The reddish, swollen cheeks produced by aulos-playing signifies how the preachers of false philosophies appear swollen and blushing. The resonance of Apollo's kithara signifies the truthful resonance of arguments. In the flaying Apollo deprives the false philosopher of his false arguments, and by revealing his entrails shows 'how little brains he had in him.' And so on, not neglecting a particle of the story.

Sapiate disse colui che vuol contare e dire di Apollo: che Iove uno dì convitò tutti gli dei a mangiare: la dea Pallas per compiacere al padre tolse la zaramella e comincio a sonare: et cussi sonando gli sgonfiaron le guanze oltra modo et tanto si gli arosavano gli ochi che tuti gli dei cominciorono a ridere per forma

[1] See, for instance, Pliny, n.h. xvi, pp. 164–72, who explains the making of pipes out of cane.

che tuti gli denti gli sariano sta trati: che non haveriano sentito. Alhora Pallas si vergognò e partisse: et discese de cielo e venne sopra le palude de Tritone: et riguardando nelaqua cominciò a sonar: et alhora vide che le guanze gli se gonfiavano et pensò che gli dei avevano per questo riso: per la qual cosa gito via quella zaramella: e non volse più suonare. A poco tempo poi quello strumento fo trovato da uno villano el qual lo prese e cominciò a sonar. Intanto che per la longa consuetudine esso diventò uno buon sonatore: si che era tenuto famoso homo. Intanto che fo ardimento di chiamare Apollo ala prova del sono et contendea con Apollo dicendo: che meglio soneria con la sua zaramella chègli non faria con la sua citara: et cussi dicendo elesero uno iudice che giudicasse fra loro. Apollo disse 'io voglio che tra noi sia alcuna pena': disse lo villano 'a me piace'. Disse Apollo 'faciamo cussi: che quello che sarà vinto porta quella pena che piacerà al vincitore': et cussi fo fermato tra loro et cominciò Marsia a sonare con la sua zaramella tanto solennemente quanto più potè. Onde Apollo udendo tanto bon sono che feva Marsia: temete di non esser perditore: et perciò nel suono interpose la divinità. Et alhora Marsia fo vento: et fo data contra lui la sententia. Alhora Apollo havendo cussi vento chiamò Marsia e disse 'vien qui'. Disse Marsia 'che vuoi tu fare?' Disse Apollo 'io ti voglio scorticare'. Et cominciolo a scorticare. Marsia cominciò a gridare ma non potè tanto gridar che gli giovasse: onde Apollo lo scortico: e lo sangue andò in terra e tuto se convertì in aqua tanto che gli si vedeano le budelle et si cominciò uno fiume: el qual per lo nome di costui fo chiamato Marsia: el qual fiume va per la regione di Frigia dove è la cità di Troia. Da poi che Apollo hebe scorticato Marsia empì lo corio over la pelle et apicola ad alto nel tempio: a ciò che fosse exemplo a chi la vedea che niuna persona mai si ponesse per niuna cagione contra agli dei. Cap. LX

Alegoria: Pallas dice Ovidio che sonava la zaramella: per questo dovemo intender tute le cagione: le quali sono sofistiche: et perchè sonava dinanci agli dei. Intendo questa sola sofistica perciò che quella arte sola per se opando vale e non amaestra. Che gli se sgonfiassero le guanze: tanto vien a dire: questo che quando gli sofistici operano cotale cientia: si fano rossi et infiati. Che gli dei se credesero:[1] questo vuol dire che li savii homini se rideno e fano beffe di tale scienciati. Dice che Pallas discese del cielo: e andò a l'aqua dove conobe perchè gli dei havevano riso: questo non vuol altro dire: se non che poi che il sofistico torna in sua mente viene a la terra e a l'aqua; cioè ale scientie formate dali homini terreni e naturali: et cognoscendo lo suo errore gitta a terra quello istrumento: cioè quella intentione: et per Marsia che la trovò: intendo uno el quale sempre se regie e defendese in falacie. Et tanto è a dire Marsia in greco

[1] Probably should read 'ridessero.'

quanto che Ironio in latino: et questi cotali voglino disputar con Apollo: cioè con gli savii: ma Apollo gli vince con la cithara: cioè con gli veri argumenti resonanti: a corde e non a voce: & cio vuol dire p che la scientia viene da gli organi del cor(e): et ciò dimostra la cithara: La quale sonando se tiene dal lato manco apogiata al core: et cio dimostra che la vera scientia viene da li organi del core. Vento che fo Marsia dice che Apollo lo scorticò: cioè che gli spogliò le sue falacie et si gli assignò le vere ragione: et fece manifesto a la gente el poco seno ch'elli havia dentro da se, dove dice che gli se vedea le budelle: et dice che diventò uno fiume: per ciò che si come el fiume va palese per la terra: e sono perpetui cussi e palesato lo error dela lor scientia et divulgata e fermata la scientia de Apollo: cioè di savii: per la quale e soto la quale el mondo se regie e governa.

[TRANSLATION]

You must know this, says he who wishes to tell the story of Apollo. One day Jupiter invited all the gods for dinner. The goddess Pallas, to please her father, took her pipes and began to play; and while she thus played, her cheeks became greatly puffed up and her eyes became so red that all the gods began to laugh so hard that, if all their teeth had come out, they would not have felt it. Thereupon Pallas grew embarrassed and left; and she went down from heaven to the swamp of the Triton and, watching herself in the water, began to play. Then she saw that her cheeks became puffed up and she realized it was this that had made the gods laugh. For this reason she threw away her pipes and did not want to play any more. After a little while, this instrument was found by a rustic who took it and began to play; and by long practice he became such a good player that he was regarded as a famous man. So good was he that he dared challenge Apollo to judge the sound, and he competed with Apollo, saying that he would play better with his pipes than Apollo could with his kithara. Discussing this, they chose a judge who should decide between them. Apollo said, 'I want one of us to be punished,' and the rustic said, 'All right'; and Apollo said, 'Let's do it this way: the one who is defeated will suffer the punishment pronounced by the winner.' And so it was agreed between them, and Marsyas began to play his pipes as solemnly as he possibly could. Therefore Apollo, hearing the fine sound made by Marsyas, was afraid of being the loser, and imparted his divine power to his own sound. And so Marsyas was defeated and the judgement went against him. Now, since Apollo had won, he called Marsyas and said, 'Come here.' Marsyas said, 'What will you do?' Apollo said, 'I want to flay you.' And he began to flay him. Marsyas began to cry out, but all his screaming was to no avail. Therefore Apollo flayed him, and the blood ran into the ground and was all changed into water — one could see his entrails — and the water began to form a river. This river, after the name of the defeated man, was called Marsyas. The river goes through the region of Phrygia wherein is the city of Troy. After Apollo had flayed Marsyas, he cleaned the hide — or rather the skin — and hung it up high in the temple, to make an example for anyone who saw it there, so that no one, for any reason whatever, should put himself up against the gods.

ALLEGORY: Pallas, as Ovid tells, played the pipes. We must therefore try to understand the reasons for it, which are very subtle, and also why she played before the gods. The reason why the goddess played is that music is valuable for its own sake and does not teach anything. That her cheeks were puffed up: this means that when the learned employ such an art, they become red and inflated. That the gods laughed about it: this is to say that the wise people laugh and make fun of such scholars. Ovid says that Pallas went down from heaven and approached the water to find out why the gods laughed: this means nothing else than that the scholar turns to his own mind and arrives at earth and water, that is, the [positive] sciences made by earthly and natural man. Becoming aware of his error, he throws the instrument to the ground, thus abandoning his original intention. And Marsyas means: a man who always lives in error. And it is the same to say Marsyas in Greek and Ironius in Latin, since both of them wish to argue with Apollo — that is, the wise one. But Apollo defeats them with the kithara — that is, with real resounding arguments — with the strings and not with the voice. And this means that knowledge comes from the heart. This is proven by the kithara, which is played by being held against the heart; this shows that the true knowledge comes from the heart. That Marsyas was defeated and Apollo flayed him: this means he stripped him of his errors and assigned to him the truth, and made it clear to the people how little brains he had in him — at the place where Ovid says one could see the entrails. And Ovid says Marsyas became a river: this is because, as the river flows openly over the ground, the mistake of people like Marsyas is revealed, as is also the science of Apollo, that is to say, the wise people — the science by which the world is governed and ruled.

13 · Muses and Music in a Burial Chapel: An Interpretation of Filippino Lippi's Window Wall in the Cappella Strozzi

A wealth of musical symbols and allegories depicted in a burial chapel poses certain questions. These questions we shall try to answer in the following essay on one of the most interesting and profound creations of Filippino Lippi — the window wall of the Strozzi Chapel in Santa Maria Novella, Florence. In it there are several musicians and a number of ancient — or, rather, pseudo-antique — wind and string instruments; bone plectra draw sound from strings, but not a single singer appears. It seems almost absurd that the musical symbolism of the chapel, and the relation between death and music which it presents, has never been investigated in the literature on Filippino Lippi.[1] A study of it may, we hope, also throw some new light on the ancient models of some of the musicians depicted and complete our understanding of the numerous inscriptions scattered over the fresco, which have hitherto resisted coherent interpretation.

The design of the Strozzi Chapel's wall has been described repeatedly and therefore our description of it can be brief. As a muralist, Lippi had to take three immutable facts into account: the high Gothic shape of the chapel (Pl. 72); Benedetto da Majano's sarcophagus crowned by a massive semi-circular arch (Pl. 69d); and a high, narrow window. Lippi subdivided the available space by providing the strongest possible counterpoint to the Gothic elements, incorporating in his composition the powerful columns from the front of the Arch of Constantine. But only the two inner columns appear to project far out from the wall, as they do in the Arch. Lippi made them flank and frame the window in the chapel, as they do the middle door at the Arch, and here, as there, they rise from massive pedestals and support large figures above their high entablature.

[1] Some short but admirably precise and substantial comments on the Cappella Strozzi are found in Peter Halm, *Das unvollendete Fresko des Filippino Lippi in Poggio a Cajano*, in *Mitteilungen des Kunsthistorischen Institutes in Florenz*, III/7 (July 1931), 393. Neither Alfred Scharf, *Filippino Lippi*, Vienna, 1935, nor Katherine B. Neilson, *Filippino Lippi*, Cambridge, Mass., 1938, has focused on the problems of symbolism.

In the Arch of Constantine the pedestals were decorated with winged victories; Filippino adorned those in his fresco with the figures of Caritas and Fides (Pls. 74a & 75a). The entablature projecting over the columns of the Arch carried large statues of captive Dacian princes; in the fresco, giant angels carrying shields emblazoned with the Strozzi crescents decorate the frieze (Pl. 71b & c). The outer columns of the Arch have here become pilasters, scarcely projecting from the wall since now they form the transition to the side walls of the chapel, which are decorated with the miracles wrought by St. John the Evangelist and St. Philip.

If Lippi's composition is highly original, so also is his colour scheme. The only area with glowing colours is the stained-glass window, which seems to rise like a burning flame from the dark sarcophagus. It shows the Madonna (Pl. 73b) in its upper, and two saints, John the Evangelist and Philip (Pl. 73c), in its lower part. Jakob Burckhardt has called it the best Florentine window. Its intense luminosity almost suppresses the near-monochrome mural — so much so that one is reminded of the young Burckhardt's warning against concentration on stained glass: that the eye may not be weakened for the observation of murals.[1] But after readapting itself to the colour of the mural painting, the eye finds the fresco by no means monotonous or pale. Brown and blue tones are used — the wings of the figure of Parthenice (Pl. 74b) are dark blue; her large musical instrument, as well as the plectrum, is deep reddish-brown; some of the human figures show faint flesh tones which hold them in the twilight between sculpture and actual life. The gilding, used as highlights on certain small objects, chiefly those of symbolic importance, accentuates them in the design — a golden guide, as it were, for modern iconologists. Among these objects are the chalice, cross, and crown of Fides; the flaming crown of Caritas and the eternal flame at her feet; the large palm tree behind Parthenice; and most of the musical instruments depicted in the lower corners of the wall.

The gilding stimulates interpretation by inviting the eye to focus on points of symbolic interest, but there is a more direct attraction in the distribution all over the fresco of verbal allusions to the spiritual message of the window wall and perhaps of the whole chapel. Four of the inscriptions are connected by an elaborate system of ribbons on either side, which run from the top and go far down towards the allegorical figures. These ribbons or cords begin, garland-like, at the top of the Gothic window, continue to the large round plaques (Pl. 73a), and go from there through elaborate knots to the large angels standing on the entablatures of the Corinthian columns. Thence again, the ribbons continue diagonally towards two angels crouching on the entablature and from there, now divided into two thinner strands, go on down over the entablatures to hold

[1] *Cicerone*, Leipzig, 1925, p. 809.

the bulky oblong stone tablets (Pl. 75c) bearing Latin inscriptions. Yet even this is not the end of this suspension. Out of the sides of the tablet frames project harpies or woman-faced birds, holding other cords from which hang decorative objects. Weighty pieces of architecture suspended in mid-air, even if supported by angels, border on the burlesque, and Filippino makes it still more fantastic by counteracting the suspended fall with the figure of a grotesque little woman on either side, who seems to support the tablets easily with her outstretched hands while she herself blossoms out of weightless tendrils. The cords are not mere visual fancy, however; they connect (another easy guide for the 20th-century iconologist) the pieces of verbal revelation with the allegorical imagery in the lower part of the grisaille. The play of the floating ribbons, too jocular and airy perhaps for a chapel, clearly reflects Filippino's experience and participation in those magnificent though impermanent architectural displays fashionable in his time as important parts of *feste*: hanging tablets with inscriptions are, for instance, reported for the *Possesso* of Alexander VI in 1492 in Rome. I have not pursued the question of how far Filippino participated in its decor, but since he was working in Rome between 1488 and 1493 in the Caraffa Chapel, it would seem logical to assume that he was familiar with the *Possesso* and must have drawn on his knowledge of it when he helped to prepare the *feste* given in 1494 in Florence to welcome Charles VIII.[1]

As mentioned before, there are four inscriptions strung on the ribbons in the Chapel. High up, flanking the top of the window, we read inside circular tablets: SI SCIRES — DONUM DEI (Pl. 73a). These four words, being the largest in the fresco and so conspicuously displayed, might be expected to have profound bearing on immortality or another topic suitable for a memorial chapel, but they have never before been explained. The solution, however, is not difficult if we recall the conversation between Jesus and the woman of Samaria as recorded in Chapter 4 of the Gospel of St. John. Jesus asks the woman for water from the well and she at first questions him, wondering how a Jew could ask for a drink from a Samaritan ('for the Jews have no dealings with the Samaritans'); then (verse 10):

> Respondit Jesus, et dixit ei: *Si scires donum Dei*, et quis est, qui dicit tibi: *Da mihi* bibere, tu forsitan petiisses ab eo, et dedisset tibi aquam vivam.

The gift of God is the water of Life, or, as it is explained soon after, Eternal Life. This highly poetic metaphor of immortality becomes even clearer from the verses which follow:

[1] For an analysis of these *fêtes* and Filippino's participation in them, see the excellent study by Eve Borsook, *Decor in Florence for the Entry of Charles VIII of France*, in *Mitteilungen des Kunsthistorischen Institutes in Florenz*, X/2 (Dec. 1961), 106. On musical instruments in the *fêtes*, see Chapter 16 below.

Dicit ei mulier: Domine, neque in quo haurias habes, et puteus altus est: unde ergo habes aquam vivam?

Numquid tu major es patre nostro Jacob, qui dedit nobis puteum, et ipse ex eo bibet, et filii ejus, et pecora ejus?

Respondit Jesus, et dixit ei: Omnis qui bibit ex aqua hac, sitiet iterum, qui autem biberit ex aqua, quam ego dabo ei, non sitiet in aeternum:

Sed aqua, quam ego dabo ei, fiet in eo fons aquae salientis in vitam aeternam.

Dicit ad eum mulier: Domine, *da mihi hanc aquam*, ut non sitiam, neque veniam huc haurire.

Certainly no briefer or more pregnant motto than the four words 'Si scires donum Dei,' could be found for a burial place. In fact, Lippi himself used a longer quotation from these verses of the Gospel for an inscription on the tablet held by angels beneath his painting, *Christ and the Samaritan Woman*,[1] which is in the Seminary Museum, Venice (Pl. 76b). This inscription combines selections from verses 10 and 15: SI SCIRES DONUM DEI DA MIHI HANC AQUAM (a combination which seems a little strange since the first words, 'Si scires donum Dei,' are spoken by Jesus, and the following, 'Da mihi hanc aquam,' by the woman) Lippi or his learned advisers must have found the condensation into four words in the Strozzi Chapel clear enough for the 'initiati,' and of course this is not the only Renaissance example of an aristocratic preference for addressing the selected few.

Of the lower square stone tablets, that on the left is fully legible: SACRIS — SUPERIS — INITIATI — CANUNT. The one on the right is partially damaged and does not permit complete deciphering.[2] Here a happy coincidence helps to restore the complete text. An anonymous drawing in the Gabinetto dei Disegni of the Uffizi (No. 14587F), which is a fairly accurate copy of the two female figures in the lower right corner of Lippi's fresco, shows an elaborate inscription engraved on the broad base on which they are standing (Pl. 75b). On the fresco there appears only DEO — MAX. The copyist, however, found it appropriate to use a longer inscription: D. M. — QUONDAM . NUNC . DEO . OP . MAX . CANIMUS. There can be no doubt that he borrowed the inscription from the upper stone tablet of the Strozzi chapel mural, which in his time must still have been completely legible. It goes without saying that 'canere' (i.e. 'making music') also implies the playing of instruments.

Before turning to the lower part of the fresco with its allegorical figures, we must mention the two verbal messages in the stained-glass window. One is again on a stone tablet, which is suspended with cords and held by angels over the

[1] Painted about 1500, according to Alfred Scharf, *op. cit.*, p. 107.

[2] Halm, *op. cit.*, p. 416, reads it D. M. QUONDAM NVH . . . CANIMUS, and considers the last two words illegible.

head of the Blessed Virgin; it reads: MITIS ESTO (Pl. 73b), perhaps best translated as 'Be peaceful,' or 'Be without suffering.' The other inscription is on the pages of the book held open, toward the chapel, by St. Philip. It is not the only book there; St. John the Evangelist holds another, of which we can see only the back, and St. Philip reaches over with one hand towards St. John's book. The writing in St. Philip's book is today partly obliterated (Pl. 76a). Yet it clearly shows lines from the Apocryphal book of Ecclesiasticus,[1] or The Wisdom of Jesus the Son of Sirach. Actually, these lines are a free pasticcio from Ecclesiasticus with interpolations as well as omissions. The reader may compare the left page with Ecclesiasticus 44: 25, 26, and 27; and the right page with Ecclesiasticus 45: 3, 4, 6, and 9. Here is the text as far as I can decipher it:

(from *Ecclesiasticus* 44: 25, 26, 27)	(from *Ecclesiasticus* 45: 3, 4, 6, 9)
BEN(EDICTIONEM) — — —	— — — — — — — — (SU)AM
DOM(INUS) — — — — — — —	IN FIDE ET (LE)NIT(A)
(SUP)ER — — — — — — —	TEM (IP)SIUS SAN(C)
— USTI. IDEO DEDIT	TUM (F)ECIT ILLUM,
DOMINUS HERE(DI)	(E)T DE — — EUM EX OM
TATEM, DIVISIT ILLAM	NI CARNE. ET DEDIT
PARTEM IN TRIBUB(US)	(ILLI CORAM PRAECEPTA)
DUODECIM: ET INV(E)	(E)T LEGEM VITAE ET DI
NIT GRATIAM IN	(SCIPL)INAE (ET) EXCEL
COSPECTU REGU(M)	SUM (FE)CIT ILLUM — —
ET JUSSIT ILLI C(O)	— — — — — — (TEST)AMENTUM
(*RAM POPULO*) SU(O)	— — — — — — — — — (CIRCU)MCI
ET OST(ENDIT) — — —	— — — — — — — — — — (ZON)A

It is obvious that these pages have nothing to do with death and resurrection, but simply show a selection of phrases that seemed appropriate for the glorification of Filippo Strozzi, perhaps alluding to the beginning of Chapter 44: *Laudemus viros gloriosos, et parentes nostros in generatione sua. . . .*

We turn now to the allegorical figures in the lower section of the mural. The area next to the wide marble arch of the tomb represents the mortality of the flesh and its conquest by the Christian virtues. In the inscription over the centre of the arch, NI HANC DESPEXERIS VIVES (Pl. 74a), the mysterious 'Hanc' is not as enigmatic as it first appears if we relate it to the DONUM DEI in the right upper circular tablet, or rather to the latter's equivalent, HANC AQUAM.

[1] Halm, *loc. cit.*, mentions 'Eccl. 44: 25–27 und 45: 3–9 mit einigen Auslassungen.' The abbreviation 'Eccl.' is a little misleading since it points to the book of Ecclesiastes, whose sceptical text would hardly have been considered appropriate in a Dominican church.

The inscription thus implies a conditional promise: 'If you do not shun the water, you will live.' It is actually a paraphrase of 'Spes,' completing the three Christian virtues of which Caritas is shown at the left and Fides at the right. The tablet with this inscription partially covers a wall niche filled with human skulls. Other skulls are displayed by two winged angels: the right one holding a single skull aloft while stepping on another skull and a human bone; the left one holding up a skull and human bone while stepping on a single skull (Pls. 74a & 75a). The beautiful figures of Caritas and Fides, with their conspicuously gilded attributes, form the counterpoint — death overcome by charity and faith.

However beautiful the personifications of the virtues, and however striking their contrast to the hard, merciless angels, the iconology of this portion of the window wall does not transcend traditional imagery. But how different and how original is the symbolic role of the figures in its extreme corners — all musicians, as we shall see.

The group at the left is engaged in playing different instruments. Parthenice (Pl. 74b), a young woman[1] conceived *all'antica*, holds a string instrument. Two winged *putti* at her knees try their luck with wind instruments. The instruments represented here are a veritable gold mine for the collector of Renaissance misinterpretations of antiquity. Parthenice's instrument is, in today's terminology, a lyre-guitar, although Filippino himself certainly would have called it a 'lira' or 'cetra' (the Italian name for the ancient kithara).

In order to understand this instrument and its role in Italy around 1500, we must go a little deeper into organology, especially since connoisseurs of art are not always familiar with the radical metamorphoses of musical instruments, their changes of form, function, and name since late antiquity, and the puzzling renascences and pseudo-renascences to which they were subjected. One of the salient facts in the history of string instruments was the introduction of the fingerboard for the purpose of stopping strings, thus shortening their length and raising the pitch. Every musician or musical amateur is familiar with this device through knowledge of the violin and its family, or from the lute, guitar, or similar instruments. One of the great advantages of the fingerboard is that each string can be made to produce several tones. Yet in Greek and Roman antiquity the fingerboard technique did not exist or, at any rate, was exceedingly rare (confined largely to some long-necked instruments we find occasionally represented on sarcophagi, which are anachronistically called lutes by archaeologists). The string instruments that were most common by far, the kithara and the lira, had no fingerboards (Pl. 77b). They had sound boxes — a

[1] André Chastel, *Art et humanisme au temps de Laurent le Magnifique*, Paris, 1959, p. 391, fn. 2, was the first to point out, in relation to Filippino's Parthenice, that this name had been used as the title of one of the poems of G. B. Mantovano, celebrating the Mother of Christ (1488).

turtle shell or wooden bowl, or a box artfully constructed — from which sprang two arms carrying a yoke. The lower ends of the strings were fastened to the sound box and their upper ends to the yoke. Thus they ran freely through the air and could not be stopped against any surface.

Not before the Utrecht Psalter, written in the 9th century but based on models of the 6th or possibly even the 5th century, do we find string instruments with fingerboards firmly established; they have the shape of kitharas but their arms are non-functional, they have no yoke, and all their strings run over a long fingerboard and are fastened to its head. Significantly, these pseudo-kitharas with fingerboards are frequently depicted side by side with real kitharas (Pl. 16b). In 1960, through a fortunate accident, I became acquainted with a Roman mosaic from Qasr el-Lebia that includes a representation of a fingerboard instrument with rudimentary lyre arms (Pl. 17c). It is played by a youth among animals, probably a representation of Orpheus. We may call such pseudo-lyres (with a fingerboard) 'lyre-guitars,' not for want of a better name or in ignorance of their ancient one, but because of the French *lyre-guitares* of the late 18th and early 19th centuries, which became fashionable as ladies' instruments in the French Empire and throughout the Biedermeier period; they posed as ancient because of their lyre shape but were actually played like guitars.[1]

Between this Napoleonic Renaissance and the Carolingian Renaissance which produced the Utrecht Psalter had occurred the Renaissance of the *quattro-* and *cinquecento*, with its intense and immediate concern with the artifacts of Greco-Roman civilization. Absurdly enough, precisely this sincere archaeological concern, not to say passion, also produced a 'lyre-guitar.' It occurs frequently in paintings, prints, and sculpture with mythological and religious topics. One may ask why the ancient models, abundantly available in statues, reliefs and frescoes, were not strictly copied; strict adherence to the ancient models seems to have been the exception (one of the rare cases is the beautiful ancient kithara in the hands of Erato in Raphael's *Parnassus* — an instrument taken over, with admirable accuracy in every detail, from the Sarcophagus of the Muses that was once in the Mattei Collection and is now in the Museo Nazionale in Rome).[2]

The misinterpretation of ancient instruments by Renaissance artists was favoured by several circumstances, and their modification in pictures was hardly intentional. The ancient sculptures and reliefs could not, for obvious technical reasons, represent in marble the free-running strings of lyres, and thus the artist often resorted to making bands in which the strings were marked by incised lines. No wonder then that the *cinquecento* artists, in their drawings of statues or reliefs from sarcophagi, interpreted these bands as the solid fingerboards which

[1] See Chapter 3 above.

[2] See Chapter 14 below.

were familiar to them from contemporary instruments, and in line with the predominant playing technique of their time. Thus the lyres, copied with archaeological intention from ancient works of art, became 'lyre-guitars' by inevitable misunderstanding.

The wind instruments of the two *putti* are both *all'antica*. The syrinx, so big for the little musician that Parthenice must help him to hold it, is represented faithfully according to ancient models, with its seven pipes whose sacred number alludes to the planets and the harmony of the universe.

More problematic is the instrument of the other *putto*. It is a fantastic blending of various models, evidently influenced by ancient representations of the aulos (tibia). The two tubes with flaring bells vaguely recall the diaulos which, contrary to the terminology still common in archaeological literature, is not a double flute but a double oboe — that is, an instrument with double reeds. The unequal length of the two pipes, and the curving of one of them, recalls the Phrygian aulos. Also interesting to note are the little projections on the upper side of the main tube, which are seemingly operated by the left hand of the *putto*. The type of aulos usually represented on Roman sarcophagi, the tibia, had a special mechanism for adjusting the instrument to play in different modes: the fingerholes on the tube were covered by adjustable rings, which also had holes. By turning the rings, one could close the fingerholes either partially or entirely. In many tibias there were small cup-shaped projections attached to the ring-holes, which could enlarge the vibrating air column in the instrument by a small fraction and thereby lower the tone. One can see such cups in all well-preserved tibias in Roman sarcophagi. Raphael copied this device for the instrument of Euterpe in his *Parnassus*.

Unlike Raphael, Filippino — for all his archaeological penchant — could not have been a practising musician, for his pseudo-aulos is entirely non-functional. The *putto* blows into the tube between the fingerholes and the lower end of the pipes. It is curious that an analogous misunderstanding occurs in another contemporary Florentine representation of a fantastic instrument, the plucked and blown instrument in Pietro di Cosimo's *Liberation of Andromeda* (Pl. 92).

Finally, one notices another wind instrument at the foot of the *putto* on the right. Only a small part of the tube and the bell are visible, but the strong shadow on the stone base makes it conspicuous. It was probably meant to be another tibia.[1]

[1] Although we cannot be sure whether or not Filippino knew it, wind music, especially as represented by tibias, was a fitting accompaniment to funerals; see, for instance, Ovid, *Fasti*, VI, 659: 'cantabit sanis, cantabit tibia ludis cantabit moestis tibia funeribus' ('the flute played in temples, it played at games, it played at mournful funerals'; tr. by Sir James George Frazer, London, 1931).

One could profitably compare the instruments in the Parthenice group with Filippino's so-called *Allegory of Music*, now in the Berlin Museum (Pl. 96b). Here we again find the seven-pipe syrinx and, beneath it, what must have been intended to be a tibia. Here, with greater archaeological fidelity than in the Strozzi Chapel, two of the rings that close the side holes are shown, and each ring carries the little cup-shaped projections explained above. There is also a lyre, one of the numerous stag-head lyres of the *cinquecento*. Here we find the mixture of elements borrowed from ancient models with pseudo-archaeological elements. Archaeologically faithful are both the shape of the crossbars (although only one crossbar was employed in ancient lyres and kitharas) and the sacred number seven of the strings. But of course ancient lyres had — for acoustical reasons — sound boxes. In Filippino's lyre the strings never reach the stag head, which, in any case, could not have functioned to reinforce the sound. The *raison d'être* of the stag head is a symbolic one; as a symbol of the velocity of sound, the stag appears commonly with the Allegory of Music.

Coming back to the Strozzi Chapel fresco, we find that Parthenice, whose left hand assists one of the *putti* to blow the syrinx, holds with her right hand the lyre-guitar and a plectrum. This plectrum is quite different from those seen in the hands of Muses on Roman sarcophagi. It is made of bone, specifically the bone of a goat or deer foot; the hoof is clearly visible. Bone plectra occur occasionally in mythological paintings of the Renaissance. In one mentioned before, Filippino's *Allegory of Music*, a bone plectrum lies beneath the stag-head lyre.[1]

An interesting Florentine comment on this plectrum and on Filippino's faithfulness to the decorative language of the ancients is found, perhaps surprisingly, in a musical treatise of the 16th century — Vincenzo Galilei's *Dialogo della musica antica e della moderna* (Florence, 1581). Vincenzo, the father of Galileo Galilei, was a fertile, brilliant, and witty writer, and was steeped in the ancient authorities on music. His *Dialogo* is full of quotations from Aristoxenos, Aristides Quintilianus, Polibios, Pliny, Plutarch, and others. The book includes a detailed discussion of the difference between the modern bow and the ancient plectrum (p. 130 ff.); he illustrates the regular form of the plectrum by a woodcut, and explains the use of the deer-foot plectrum and the way it is fashioned, and then he reminds the reader of a good opportunity to see one (this entire passage is reprinted as an Appendix to the present chapter).

Of this account we must say that Vincenzo, in spite of his Florentine local

[1] On this and other attributes of Musica, see Chapter 16 below. A deer-foot plectrum can also be seen in a Florentine engraving of about 1470, showing a fat, vine-leaf-crowned player with a large deer-foot plectrum (Arthur Hind, *Early Italian Engravings*, London, 1938–48, A.IV.22, Vol. 2, Plate 150).

pride, must have neglected to refresh his memory by a visit to the chapel — the 'two women' are on the right side, and neither of them sings — but he obviously did mean that the figure on the left holds the *plettro alla zampetta*, described so vividly by him. The reference to Poliziano, as an expert in the musical practice of the ancient world, is not badly taken. Poliziano's *Fabula d'Orfeo* is full of stage directions as to the music to be sung and played during the performance, especially with reference to Orpheus playing the lira (although the latter, in the famous performances at Mantua, was without doubt a lira da braccio — that is, a bowed instrument).[1] The plectrum in Poliziano's *Fabula* acquires symbolic power when it rivals Pluto's sceptre. In the words of Pluto:

> *I' son contento che a si dolce plettro*
> *S'inchini la potenzia del mio scettro.*[2]
>
> (I am pleased that the power of my sceptre
> yields to so sweet a plectrum).

The two figures in the right lower corner of the chapel wall (Pl. 74c) are no doubt patterned after Muses from Roman sarcophagi, but no concrete model has ever been suggested.[3] The general type of these figures occurs, in slightly different versions, in numerous sarcophagi.[4] However, there is in my belief only one sarcophagus that offers an exact correspondence to our two figures. It is the sarcophagus with Muses, Apollo, and Minerva, from the Collection Giustiniani,[5] now in the Vienna Kunsthistorisches Museum (Pl. 77a & c; it was once in Rome, where it was drawn by the draughtsman of the Codex Coburgensis).

On its long side, this sarcophagus shows the nine Muses, Minerva, and Apollo. Minerva, in profile, is the central figure; on her left are five Muses, on her right four, and at the extreme right Apollo. The Muses that interest us are the first and third from the left. The third one has been directly taken over by

[1] See Chapter 5 above.

[2] On musical symbolism in Poliziano's *Fabula*, see Emanuel Winternitz, *Orpheus als Musikallegorie in Renaissance und Frühbarock*, in *Die Musik in Geschichte und Gegenwart*, X, Cassel, 1962, col. 412.

[3] If one considers how long and zealously historians of Renaissance art have searched for instances in which artists have borrowed literally from ancient models, it seems astonishing how little exact 'imitation' has been found in the works of the great *antichizzanti* such as Mantegna, Filippino Lippi, or Raphael. Fischel's *Raphaels Zeichnungen*, Berlin, 1913–41, for instance, does not establish any clear case. As for the Muses, I discovered one such case, which is discussed in Chapter 14 below.

[4] For instance, two sarcophagi in the Palazzo Mattei (Figs. I and II, *Monumenta Matthaeiana*); and one each in the Palazzo Farnese, the Louvre, the Berlin Museum, the British Museum (Cat. 2305), and the Museo Nazionale in Rome — the last two of the Sidamara type.

[5] Reproduced in an engraving in Vincenzo Giustiniani, *Galleria del Marchese V. Giustiniani*, Rome, 1631, II, Tav. 40, the sarcophagus has also been described and illustrated by Eduard Freiherr v. Sacken, *Die antiken Skulpturen des k.k. Münz- und Antiken-Cabinets in Wien*, Vienna, 1873, and (p. 41) 'the artistic value of the relief' judged as 'not considerable (*nicht erheblich*).'

Filippino Lippi. He has repeated her pose, with the elegant turn of the upper body towards her left and the gracefully turned left leg. Lippi's figure bends the head lower, towards the instrument, and her hair and robes flow in the wind. The plectrum in her right hand, which has the conventional Roman form on the sarcophagus, here becomes a bone. On the sarcophagus, her lyre rests in symmetrical position on a base,[1] which is only suggested in flat relief. The muse farthest to the left on the sarcophagus, with crossed legs and chin in hand — pensively listening — again is taken over by Filippino in precisely the same pose, except that the figure is reversed; hair and robes, as in the other figure, are dramatized. The *rotulus* in the left hand of the muse on the sarcophagus is turned by Filippino into a bone plectrum, so that in the fresco both figures become musicians with plectra.

An enormous transformation, however, takes place from the sarcophagus to the fresco in the representation of the musical instrument. In the relief it is the traditional kithara of the time, less than one-third the height of the player. In the fresco, between the two Muses, we find a magnificent lyre of gigantic dimensions on a high marble pedestal. It is strange that no attention has even been paid to this conspicuous instrument in the literature on Filippino, and that it has not even been recognized as a musical instrument.[2] This is even more curious in view of the fact that this lyre is distinguished, more than any other section of the fresco, by extensive gilding. Two high round columns carry a fantastic superstructure[3] crowned by a flaming lamp, which has perhaps given cause for misinterpreting the whole instrument as an altar. Only six strings are represented, not the sacred seven, and again Filippino reveals himself as uninterested in the acoustical and functional construction of instruments: the

[1] Of the other sarcophagi listed in fn. 4, p. 175, only one — that in the Berlin Museum — shows a base for the lyre of a Muse which resembles the one copied by Lippi. The second Muse on the Berlin sarcophagus, with chin in hand, is much less similar to the corresponding Lippi Muse than the one on the Vienna sarcophagus.

[2] Peter Halm, *op. cit.*, p. 414, and Alfred Scharf, *op. cit.*, p. 65, both speak of an altar.

[3] A similar superstructure on a fantastic lyre is shown in a drawing in the sketchbook of Amico Aspertini, in the British Museum. It is illustrated in Phyllis Pray Bober's invaluable book, *Drawings after the Antique by Amico Aspertini*, London, 1957, Pl. XLVIII, fig. 111 (Mrs. Bober speaks tentatively of a *putto* 'sitting on a skull before a fountain [?]'). The object and superstructure appear behind a *putto* sitting on a skull, opposite another mourning *putto* and beneath three Muses. The combination of mourning, skulls, Muses, and an instrument is too significant not to be compared with our fresco. The identification of the object with a fantastic lyre becomes even clearer if one compares it with an almost identical instrument held by one of the musicians surrounding King David in the Bible of Charles the Bald, Paris, Bibliothèque Nationale, MS Lat. I, fol. 215*v* (Pl. 15a). Without at all stressing a historical connection, this shows that non-functional elements in instruments easily become an opportunity for fanciful decoration. One should at least mention here Robetta's free fantastic version of Filippino's two musicians with the lyre, Robetta's lyre having a superstructure ornamented by grotesque half-moon faces and gryphons.

sound box, necessary of course for a string instrument, is suggested only by the sweeping curve on which the left column rests, and no real yoke holds the upper ends of the strings. In short, the whole thing is non-functional. But apart from these whimsical decorative details, the general design is solidly based on ancient models. Large lyres or kitharas on pedestals were frequent, and are often found represented on sarcophagi.[1] The famous 6th-century ivory diptych in Monza (Pl. 89b), with the poet and the Muse, shows the Muse with a large kithara on a base. And, at about the same time, Ammianus Marcellinus tells of lyres as large as horse carriages (*lyrae ad speciem carpentorum ingentes*).[2]

But examining the single inscriptions and allegorical figures is one thing; searching for a comprehensive and unified interpretation of the whole window wall is another. And thus we have to take up the question posed at the beginning of this study, and face the most unconventional aspect of the fresco — the proximity of death and music, the presence of Muses and instruments in the face of death. The appropriation by Renaissance artists of ancient images and mythological figures such as the Muses requires no comment here.[3] Libraries have been written about it. But was this absorption of ancient works of art always accompanied by a clear awareness of their ancient symbolism and of the spiritual atmosphere which had produced them? To what extent were the borrowings from ancient art paralleled by investigations into ancient literature? Our fresco here seems to present a good test case; for only a knowledge of ancient thought connecting death and music could vindicate a juxtaposition that otherwise must have been shocking to the visitors to the Capella Strozzi. Dirges and other sacred vocal music in church were not only acceptable but common; likewise, angels with instruments surrounding the dying or ascending Madonna (as in Carpaccio's *Death of the Virgin*, Accademia, Venice). But in a memorial chapel, inviting one to meditation, near to the tomb and the skull-bearing angels and the Christian virtues, what message could be conveyed by musicians and instruments?

[1] For instance: in the Villa Medici (M. Cagiano de Azevedo, *Le Antichità di Villa Medici*, Rome, 1951, Pl. XXIX, 45 [57]); in the Palazzo Mattei, two sarcophagi, one with the Muses and Pallas, and another with the Muses and a poet (both represented in the *Monumenta Matthaeiana*, Tav. XLIV); the sarcophagus with Muses in the Berlin Museum, which shows two pedestal lyres, one of them played by the third figure from the left (a Muse) and the other by the Muse on the extreme right. Pedestal lyres also occur in such representations as the statue of a Muse (Uffizi, No. 209) drawn by Dosio (cf. Christian Karl Friedrich Hülsen, *I Lavori archeologici di Giovannantonio Dosio*, in *Ausonia: Rivista della Soc. Ital. di Archeologia*, VII (1912), 41; and *Das Skizzenbuch des Giovannantonio Dosio*, Berlin, 1933, p. 28, Taf. LXXVIII); and, shown with an Apollo, in one of the medallions of the Arch of Constantine, so well known to Filippino.

[2] Ammianus Marcellinus, *Rerum gestarum libri XIX*, 6, 18.

[3] On Filippino as an imaginative heir of ancient imagery, see Chastel's excellent and comprehensive observations in his chapter 'Filippino Lippi: Les "singularités" du paganisme' (*op. cit.*, pp. 386–92).

These Muses certainly provide no dirge, nor would the instruments be suitable for consoling the bereaved. The meaning of the Muses here is on another plane and, we surmise, intimately connected with the topic of immortality.[1] It seems quite significant that behind Parthenice stands one of the symbols of eternity, the palm tree.[2] We can safely assume that Filippino and his advisers, in the Florence of Ficino and his Platonic academy, were familiar with the Platonic and neo-Platonic doctrine of the survival of the soul.[3] Immortality, according to Platonic doctrine, was not granted to every soul, but only to a certain selection. Plato's choice was the philosopher.[4] He had, by virtue of his profession, an intimate relation with death; in fact he pursued dying (*Phaedo*, 64). His desire to disengage himself from the body would make him rejoice in death (*Phaedo*, 68). His soul 'departs to the invisible world — to the divine and immortal and *rational* (φρόνιμος) — and forever dwells, as they say of the *initiated* (μεμυημένων), in company with the Gods.' I should like to point to the emphasis on the words 'rational'[5] and 'initiated' — to the latter in view of the 'initiati' in our fresco; to the former because it clarifies the principle according to which the choice is made. If the knowing ones, an intellectual élite, are chosen for eternal life, the

[1] For musical symbolism in Greek and Roman sarcophagi, see M. Henri Marrou, *ΜΟΥCΙΚΟC ΑΝΗΡ*, Diss. Univ. de Paris, Grenoble, 1937; and Franz Cumont's standard work, *Recherches sur le symbolisme funéraire des romains*, Paris, 1942.

[2] Pierius Valerianus, in his *Hieroglyphica*, Basel, 1567, p. 369, devotes a whole section, 'Temporis Diuturnitas,' based on Hesiod and Quintilian, to this topic. Also, the palm tree, no doubt as a symbol of resurrection, is frequently found on sepulchral urns, especially *kantharoi*, of which there are several examples in the British Museum.

[3] '... Is it likely that the soul, which is invisible, in passing the place of the true Hades which like her is invisible, and pure, and noble, and on her way to the good and wise God ... will be blown away and destroyed immediately on quitting the body...? This can never be ...' (*Phaedo*, 80).

[4] 'The soul, herself invisible, departs to the invisible world — to the divine and immortal and rational ... and forever dwells, as they say of the initiated, in the company of the gods' (*Phaedo*, 81). '... No one who has not studied philosophy and who is not entirely pure at the time of his departure is allowed to enter the company of the Gods, but the lover of knowledge only' (*Phaedo*, 82). Virgil, in his grandiose panorama of the netherworld (*Aeneid*, VI, 129), states: 'Pauci, quos aequus amavit / Juppiter aut ardens evesit ad aethera virtus, / dis geniti potuere....' ('Some few, whom kindly Jupiter has loved, or whom shining worth uplifted to the heaven, sons of the gods, have availed.') Plotinus expands the group of the selected in line with the Pythagorean doctrine of the harmony of the spheres and Plato's conception of love in his *Phaedrus*. Thus, Plotinus says (I, 3): 'The souls capable of ascending and escaping the realm of the senses are those of the musician, of the lover (ἐρωτικός) and the philosopher.' The Pythagorean heritage, with its doctrine of the harmony of the spheres, made its impact on Filippino's time above all through the 'Dream of Scipio' in Cicero's *De Republica*, Book VI, which through many copies, reprints, and comments became one of the most famous and influential treatises of the Renaissance; in art, it inspired the representation of the choirs of angels in Marian subjects (see Chapter 11 above).

[5] According to Aristotle, *Metaphysics*, I, 1070a, 26: 'Reason, not all of the soul, can survive death.'

role of the Muses as allegories of immortality becomes clear at once. For they, the daughters of Jupiter and Memory and the companions of Apollo-Logos, are the givers and protectors of knowledge,[1] the connoisseurs of the laws of the universe. It is because of this quality that they are represented on sarcophagi, often together with Apollo and Minerva, as sponsors of eternal life for the souls of the knowing ones.

The ardent interest in Roman archaeology and recently excavated works of art, among which were found many sarcophagi, coincided with the intensive revival of Plato's doctrine of the soul, above all in Ficino's *Theologia Platonica de immortalitate animarum* (1480). One of the inevitable problems of the time was to achieve a convincing reconciliation between the pagan and the Christian doctrines of immortality. The first centred on intellectual merit; the second on moral conduct and religion. The Christian Platonist, Ficino, attempted to reconcile these concepts through his theory of contemplation, i.e. the act of contemplation as a state of the soul that prepares for future existence.[2] But even this emphasis on contemplation retains the notion of the élite, the knowing, or in terms of Filippino's fresco, the 'initiati canunt.'[3]

One may argue that such a design, subtly blending pagan and Christian symbolism, may have been too complex for the understanding of the worshippers entering Santa Maria Novella. But easy intelligibility was certainly the least concern of the originator of this scheme, which was addressed to the 'initiati.' This is borne out by the character of the inscriptions, which, far from being explanatory labels, border on enigmas. Actually, subtle and unconventional iconological designs were generally admissable in chapels. They aimed at the humanist, the intellectual élite. Raphael once tried to endow one and the same object, the wind instrument in the hands of Euterpe in his *Parnassus*, with a double meaning: one for the humanist concerned with the ancient monuments and one for the naive beholder.[4] The combination of pagan Muses and ancient instruments with the Christian virtues and the promise of the water of Life may seem a trifle too pagan for a church under Dominican jurisdiction, especially in the days of Savonarola. But such an incompatibility simply did not exist. The Christian heaven had been widely opened to the invasion of pagan myths and images ever since Petrarch's time. Petrarch himself had not men-

[1] Virgil, *Georgics*, II, 489.

[2] *Opera omnium*, Turin, 1953, pp. 306, 385.

[3] Chastel, *op. cit.*, p. 391, relates this 'mystic' inscription to a passage in Ficino: 'Les mystères sacrés sont livrés à la foule sous des voiles et révélés aux disciples élus.' On his pp. 165–66, Chastel gives an interesting survey of the traditional styles of Tuscan funerary chapels, leading up to the Strozzi Chapel, but he does not attempt to solve the puzzle of the interrelation of the inscriptions in this chapel, nor of their combination with musical symbols into a homogeneous meditation on immortality.

[4] See Chapter 14 below.

tioned the Bible when he based his hope for immortality on the 'Dream of Scipio,' and it was not cynicism but the prevailing spirit of the times when he said that he did not hesitate as a Catholic to entertain a hope that he found proclaimed by the pagan authorities. And as for the Muses as sponsors of immortality, there was the authority of that great *anima naturaliter Christiana*, Virgil, who invokes the Muses as the great connoisseurs of stars and heaven, the guardians of the knowledge of the causes of things, a knowledge that conquers fear and fate and the noise of Acheron:

Felix qui potuit rerum cognoscere causas,
Atque metus omnis et inexorabile fatum
Subjecit pedibus, strepitum Acherontis avari.[1]

The long contract of 1487 entrusting Filippino with the work says nothing of the questions that interest us in this essay. Thus we may never know how strictly the artist was bound to a scheme devised by a 'litterato come da un pari del Poliziano,' to quote again Vincenzo Galilei. But even if a humanist programme had prescribed many details, there are countless ways, of course, of translating a verbal scheme into the realm of the visually concrete. For this, a poet was required — a poet with a painter's brush. And here Filippino, who was often no more than an imaginative story teller, surpassed himself. He certainly employed the Muses and their instruments in full awareness of their allegorical importance in antiquity and their relation to the doctrine of immortality. He spared no effort in designing them as faithfully and as 'ancient' in style as possible. Instruments seemed the surest way to characterize the Muses; possibly the employment of a majestic giant lyre was suggested to him. One likes to think that perhaps one among the Dominican[2] superiors of Santa Maria Novella, though officially committed to Aristotle and Thomas Aquinas, was a Platonist who treasured *Phaedo* and recalled the passage there about the lyre[3] and its incorporeal divine harmony as a metaphor of the soul; or perhaps he was under the spell of Ficino's astrological studies and thought of the Muses as fitting allegories of the harmony of the spheres.

However this may be, one must admire the way in which Filippino succeeded in fusing all the allegories and symbolic requisites into a convincing artistic

[1] 'Blessed is he who has been able to win knowledge of all things, and has cast beneath his feet all fear and unyielding fate, and the howls of hungry Acheron'; *Georgics*, II, 490, transl. by H. Rushton Fairclough, London, 1916.

[2] Filippo Strozzi had been prior of Santa Maria Novella for two years before commissioning his funerary chapel there. Filippino must have had excellent relations with the Dominicans since the Caraffa Chapel decorated by him is in the principal Dominican church of Rome, Santa Maria sopra Minerva.

[3] *Phaedo*, 86, 88, 92.

whole, a homogeneous visual meditation of profound poetry. He also added poetic touches that are not based on humanist archaeological tradition: the Muses have plectra made of human bones and it is these bones that draw music from the golden strings of the lyre, near to other bones held up or trodden upon by the angels of death. It is the music of the Muses, the harmony of the spheres, the music for the initiated, that confirms the Christian promise of the 'DONUM DEI' and the 'NI HANC DESPEXERIS VIVES.'[1]

APPENDIX

[From Vincenzo Galilei, *Dialogo della musica antica e della moderna* (1581), reprinted Rome, 1934, p. 130 ff.]

BAR: (Signor Giovanni Bardi). In qual maniera fatto & di qual forma credete per fede vostra che fusse il Plettro degli antichi Citharisti & Citharedi?

STR. (Signor Pietro Strozzi). Credo che egli fusse un'Archetto simile à quello che adoperano hoggi i sonatori di Viola da gamba, & da braccio, detta modernamente Lira.

BAR. Qui è tutto l'errore.

STR. Come di gratia.

BAR. Il Plettro degli antichi, era uno strumento lungo un palmo, ò un quarto di braccio in circa, della forma che qui vedete il disegno; di che (per quello ne sente Suida) fu autrice Saffo; la qual cosa non so come possa stare, avvenga che Homero che attribuisce l'inventione à Mercurio, fu avanti a Saffo del Mixolydio inventrice.

Il quale strumento s'impugnava con la destra, & con la sinistra si reggeva quella parte della Lira dove erano accomodati i bischeri; & l'altra dove erano attaccate le corde, che era come veduto havete al quanto più larga, si appoggiava al petto; à quella parte però che apportava comodità maggiore: ne tempi poi più bassi, quando si cominciò à sonare in consonāza come si disse che usava Epigonio & Aspendio, si posava in piedi sopra una tavola ò sgabello, & con le due linguette che avanzavano sotto & sopra al pugno ò da lati che ci vogliamo dire, si percotevano & non si secavano le corde di essa Lira; nella maniera che

[1] I know of only one other Renaissance chapel in which the relation between music and death is symbolized: it is Lorenzo Costa's *The Triumph of Death*, in the fresco of the Bentivoglio Chapel in San Petronio, Bologna. There, in front of the conventional procession of the dead, is a separate group of large figures standing (not marching) and listening in deep meditation to an Oriental (Orpheus?) who plays the lira da braccio. The quiet faces of the listeners are of unforgettable individuality. It would seem that here, in this counterpoint between music and death, an artist of little depth was inspired to outdo himself.

vi disse poco fa Vergilio & Ovidio: ha vendo altri & questi stessi Poeti, per mostrare maggior forza nel toccarle, usata questa voce; Ferire le corde, in vece di percuoterle. i quali strumenti si costumarono in quelli primi tempi, fare di quelli ossi che hanno le capre tra le ginocchia & l'ugne delle gambe dinanzi; lavorati & puliti al tornio ò in altra maniera; dàdogli gli artefici quella forma che havete veduta come più d'altra conveniente all'ufitio suo: ancora che alcuni altri vogliono, che l'ugna istessa servisse per percuotere le corde, inpugnando il Zampetto dopo l'essere staccato dalla capra & secco, & volendo vederne un ritratto molto simile, il quale non vedo mai senza mia maraviglia; ponete mente nel superbo tempio di Santa Maria Novella, nella cappella d'uno degli Avi nostri, dipinta da Filippo di Fra Filippo; in faccia della quale dalla parte sinistra, si vedono due femmine, una delle quali canta, & l'altra sostiene con la mano una Lira antica fatta secondo che di sopra vi ho dimostrato; & nella destra ha impugnato una cosa simile al disegno del Plettro mostratovi, quanto però alla forma & all'attezza dell'ufitio; dal che si può fare argumento, del gran giuditio di quello eccellente pittore; caso che in quel affare non fusse aiutato da alcuno litterato, come da un pari del Poliziano che fu in fiore nell'istesso tempo & luogo; il quale facilmente potette havere qualche lume di tale strumento, poi che litterato era, & della musica lasciò scritto in diversi suoi propositi alcune cose di momento, & comunicarlo à detto Filippo. & acciò che sappiate, non e più di due anni che tale certezza è pervenuta in cognitione di alcuni pochi particolari; mercè d'un Pilo antichissimo ritrovatosi ultimamente in Roma, il quale è hoggi nel Palazzo del Cardinale Santacroce; dove si vedono scolpite in basso rilievo le Muse, & in mano à una la forma di lui con lo strumento appresso, la cognitione & certezza del quale, fa hoggi che si scorge in più rovesci di medaglie, che era prima conosciuto per ogn'altra cosa che per un Plettro. un'altro ancore simile, se ne vede pur in Roma in una scultura antichissima; la quale è in una nicchia del cortile del Palazzo già del Cardinale Montepulciano, & hoggi de Cievoli Gentilhuomini Pisani; in mano d'una figura in habito di donna con uno strumento à canto. che le corde dell'antica lira si percotessero ultimamente, & non si secassero, ve lo confermo con l'essempio d'uno Evangelo Nobile Tarentino, raccontatoci da Luciano. . . .'

[TRANSLATION]

BAR. (Signor Giovanni Bardi). How and in what shape, in your opinion, was the plectrum of the ancient cithara players made?

STR. (Signor Piero Strozzi). I believe it was a bow, similar to that used today by the players of the viola da gamba and of the viola da braccio, called in modern times the lyre.

BAR. Herein lies the whole error.

STR. How so, if you please?

BAR. The plectrum of the ancients was a tool of about a palm's length, or approximately one fourth of an arm's length, in the shape which you can see in this illustration; and its inventor (as far as we can learn from Suidas) was

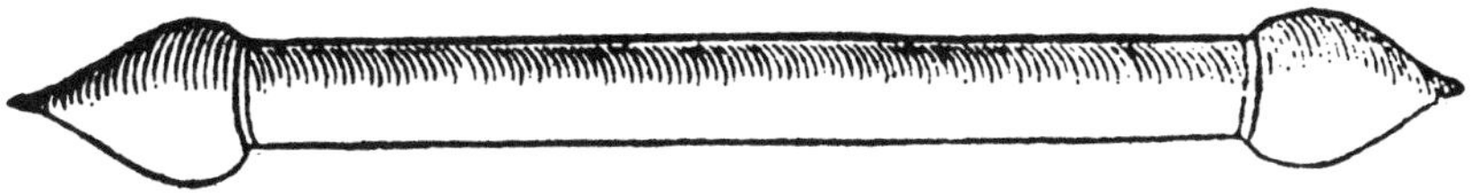

Fig. 23. Plectrum (see also Plate 88b).

Sappho; but I do not know how this could be, since Homer, who attributes the invention to Mercury, came before Sappho, who was the inventor of the Mixolydian mode.

The player grasped this tool in the right hand, while his left held that part of the lyre where the pegs are attached; the other and, as you have seen, much larger part of the lyre, where the strings are attached, was held against the chest where it was most comfortable; but in later times, when people began to play consonances, as allegedly did Epigonius and Aspendios, the lyre was placed upright upon a table or stool, with the two tongue-like ends projecting above and beneath the fist, or from its sides, so to speak; the strings of the lyre were struck — but not stopped — in the way we learned earlier from Virgil and Ovid: since they and other poets, in order to describe the greatest possible force in touching the strings, used the term 'wounding' the strings, rather than 'striking' them. In these early times, the plectra were usually made from those bones which goats have between their knees and the hoofs of their forelegs; they were fashioned and smoothed at the turning-lathe, or in some other way, so that they received from the craftsmen precisely the shape you have seen as most convenient for their function. Still, some others insist that the hoof itself was used for striking the chords, by taking the hoof after it had been removed from the goat and had been dried. And if you want to see a good likeness, which I can never look at without great amazement, then remember the church of Santa Maria Novella and the chapel of one of our forefathers decorated with paintings by Filippo di Fra Filippo; there on the main wall on the left two women can be seen; one of them sings and the other holds with her hand an ancient lyre shaped as I have explained above; and in her right hand she grips an object similar to the design of the plectrum that I have shown above, so adequately shaped for its function that one can draw conclusions about the expert knowledge of our excellent painter; unless he was helped in this matter by some humanist of the rank of Poliziano, who was flourishing at that time and place, and who could easily have had some information about such a plectrum, since he was learned and left us various important statements about music, which he might have communicated to our Filippo. And you must know, it was not more than two years ago that actual certainty was obtained in the knowledge of a few details, thanks to a very ancient sarcophagus recently found in Rome. It is now in the palace of Cardinal Santacroce, and on it in relief one sees the Muses; one of them holds in her hand, near the instrument, the object that we recognize today on the reverse sides of medals, which was earlier identified as something other than a plectrum. Another similar plectrum can be seen, also in Rome, on a very ancient sculpture, standing in a niche of the court of the palace formerly owned by Cardinal Montepulciano and now owned by the venerable gentleman from Pisa: there, it is held by the hand of a figure in female garb, with the instrument nearby. The fact that the strings of the ancient lyre were struck and not stopped in late antiquity, I can confirm by the example of a nobleman from Tarento, named Evangelo, as reported by Lucian.

14 · Musical Archaeology of the Renaissance in Raphael's *Parnassus**

The frescoes of the Stanza della Segnatura do not belong among the neglected works in the history of art, and about the *Parnassus* whole libraries have been written. Especially in the last generation, when the ancient models of Renaissance art were once again brought into focus, the *Parnassus* was examined as to its inspiration by Greek or Roman models. The results of these examinations are comparatively meagre. They are usually limited to such general statements as: 'antiquity is present in Raphael's compositions,' or, at best, they point concretely to some relationship or similarity between the pose or garb of a single figure in the fresco and that of an ancient statue.[1] The present study attempts to prove a direct relationship between the *Parnassus* fresco and a well-known Roman sarcophagus, a relationship that is not limited to certain small details of the figures or their garments, but is revealed by a considerable number of characteristic features taken over from that ancient monument because of the great interest of Raphael or his advisers in the musical instruments of antiquity and in the problem of their reconstruction. It is precisely through my studies in

* I wish to express my gratitude for most valuable help to Dr. Deoclecio Redig de Campos, the late Prof. Ludwig Curtius, Prof. Richard Krautheimer, Dr. Filippo Magi, the late Prof. Charles Rufus Morey, Dr. Olga Raggio, and the late Prof. Martin Weinberger, with all of whom I have had the pleasure of discussing various aspects of this study.

1 Oskar Fischel, *Raphaels Zeichnungen*, Berlin, 1913–41, p. 255: 'In Marcantonio's engraving, Apollo remained nearer to the ancient model, and the garb of the poets and Muses, after classical models, are not yet conceived in that timeless style which imparts so much poetic lightness to the fresco.' Fischel also calls attention to a similarity between the Muse at the right of Apollo (whom he calls Erato) and the girl playing a kithara on the sarcophagus in the Louvre, with the representation of Apollo in Skyros. Adolf Michaelis, *Geschichte des Statuenhofs im Vaticanischen Belvedere*, in *Jahrbuch des Kaiserlichen Deutschen Archaeologischen Instituts*, V (1890), 18 ff., observes, as did Passavant before him, a similarity between Raphael's sketch for Calliope in the Albertina and the statue known as Cleopatra in the Belvedere. I wonder whether Erato could not just as well be compared with the type of sitting figure that we find, for example, in the Palazzo dei Conservatori (catalogue by Settimo Bocconi, Rome, 1930, tav. 122). There is a great likeness not only in the pose but in several details of costume, especially if we look at Raimondi's engraving. Later Raphael transformed the whole figure into an image of intense listening and, at the same time, of nervous, passionate devotion, features particularly noticeable in the large sketch in the Albertina, where the ear is strongly accentuated and further emphasized by the encircling coil of hair (Fischel, *op. cit.*, Pl. 251).

the little-cultivated field of musical archaeology that I became convinced of the findings presented here.

To approach this problem, it will be necessary to look at the preliminary steps of the composition, especially Marcantonio's engraving (Pl. 79) and the copy of a compositional sketch in the nude at Oxford (Pl. 80), which are the most important surviving documents reflecting the earlier stages of the painting. An analysis will reveal that the instruments in the *Parnassus* were first treated quite differently, and that certain ancient (*antichi*) models entered the scene in the course of the work and decisively shaped the fermenting imagination of Raphael, at that time a most devoted student of antiquity. These models can all be identified as appearing in a Roman sarcophagus of the Asiatic type from the end of the 3rd century; a close comparison between the details of the sarcophagus and the fresco will reveal not only that all the musical instruments in the sculpture have been transplanted into the fresco, but also that Raphael borrowed other important details, such as the tragic and lyric masks, cloth motives, and coiffures. Thanks to some lucky discoveries, it will, I trust, not be too difficult to show that the sarcophagus was known at Raphael's time and to reconstruct its state of preservation at that time. We are then left with the most puzzling but, at the same time, the most thought-provoking problems: to explain the seemingly anachronistic introduction of Apollo's bowed instrument among those taken from antiquity; and to explain why the latter instruments differ from the ancient models in certain structural details, sometimes to the point of being functional nonsense. The reasons, we will find, are manifold: Raphael's allegorical aims; the blunders of the draughtsman when he copied from the ancient models; the beliefs — and mistakes — of contemporary students of ancient musical instruments; and, last but most revealing, Raphael's didactic intentions — his aim of combining features of modern instruments with those of ancient ones, to make his instruments appear truly antique (that is, archaeologically correct) and at the same time symbolically meaningful for the whole composition, which was to be seen and understood not only by the learned ones, by the Bembos and Castigliones, but by the public as well.

We begin with a quick preliminary look at the fresco itself (Pl. 78). There are five instruments depicted, some ancient, some contemporary, but all afflicted with strange and unorthodox features occurring neither in representations of the ancient instruments nor in the actual instruments of Raphael's day.

The nearest approach to an ancient model is the elaborate and ornate kithara held by Erato[1] on her lap (Pl. 82a). Its sound box actually consists of

[1] Or is she Terpsichore? The identification, or rather the naming, of the nine Muses on the basis of their attributes and their functions, according to the canons established by the art and

two boxes, the front of the lower box showing three slits. The arms, decorated with five knobs, curve up gracefully towards the yoke. The latter is inserted into the arms and can evidently be turned by the usual side disks, of which one is visible. Following Terpander's rule, there are seven strings, which spring from the lower box. The projecting rim of the upper box, functioning as a bridge, changes their direction, and at the point where they reach the yoke no fastening device is depicted. In fact, the usual sticks or rolls (*kollopes*; mentioned as early as the *Odyssey*, Bk. XXI), which help to attach the strings to the yoke and to vary their tension for tuning purposes, are absent here (see Pl. 77b, showing a Roman wall painting, for an idea of their shape and location).

No less problematic is the wind instrument held by Erato's counterpart, Euterpe (Pl. 83).[1] It is a single metal tube, swelling slightly towards the top and terminating first in a bulb and then in an unusually flat, small bell. The lower end shows clearly a cup-shaped mouthpiece, like those used in brass instruments of all periods. In short, this instrument would appear to be a trumpet were it not for the four strange protuberances on its right side, below Euterpe's arm; they make no sense in a trumpet or in any other brass instrument.

Most enigmatic is the string instrument held by Sappho (Pl. 82b). A curved sound box, shaped more like a turtle shell than an animal head, carries a complex machinery, a sort of frame with four side disks, three of which are visible. They seem to be of the same nature and function as those on Erato's kithara and thus would serve to turn the crossbar, or, more precisely, the two crossbars. But why two crossbars? Moreover, the way in which this machinery is attached to the turtle shell remains unclear. Certainly two arms grow from the shell, continuing its contour; it seems as if two animal horns are inserted into the two holes for the front feet of the turtle.

---

literature of the ancients, is no easy task. The literature on Raphael's *Parnassus* offers a diverting multiplicity of opinions. To cite one example, the two Muses flanking Apollo: Deoclecio Redig de Campos (*Le Stanze di Raffaello*, Florence, 1930, p. 26) calls the one at the left 'Calliope, la Musa della poesia epica,' and the one at the right 'Terpsichore, quella della poesia lirica,' while Fischel (*op. cit.*, p. 263) calls the former Euterpe — possibly with reference to Ausonius: 'dulceloquis calamos Euterpe flatibus urgit' ('the sweet-voiced Euterpe excites the pipes with her breath') — and the latter Erato — possibly with reference to the same poet: 'plectra gerens Erato saltat pede, carmine, vultu' ('bearing the plectrum, Erato, with expressive face, dances and sings'). But why criticize the modern scholars when even the ancients themselves did not agree? Terpsichore, according to Ovid, plays the *tibiam duplicem* — 'grataque Terpsichore calamos inflare paravit' ('the graceful Terpsichore was engaged in blowing the pipes') — while Ausonius has her play the kithara — 'Terpsichore affectus citharis movet, imperat, auget' ('Terpsichore, with her kithara, moves the passions, dominates and increases them'). Raphael, though full of respect for the iconography of the ancients, paid little attention to pedantries, and the Muse sitting at Apollo's left exchanged, without any apparent qualms, the syrinx that she held in Marcantonio's engraving for the more noble kithara of the Oxford sketch and the fresco.

[1] Terpsichore, according to de Campos (see preceding footnote).

At first glimpse, Sappho seems to hold one of those large plectra that are often depicted in ancient art. But a closer inspection shows that this large horn-shaped object is part of the instrument — without it, the instrument would fall down. Whether the instrument is connected to the bulge below the hand, or whether it is connected to a smaller bulge farther right (which may be another of the disks mentioned above), remains utterly unclear. No doubt the painter was not clear about it himself. The five strings spring from an elaborate string holder with a curved profile, and stop in mid-air shortly before reaching the fastening point, another symptom of the uncertainty of the draughtsman.[1]

There is a third Muse who holds a musical instrument, the wonderful figure with her back to the viewer, the farthest right of the Muses. Her instrument has scarcely been commented upon in the literature. Fischel[2] calls it a lute, and the shading indeed suggests a rounded surface similar to a lute's belly. But the belly of a lute was invariably made of staves, and that Raphael knew how to short-hand such a design is shown by his quick sketch of a lute player (Pl. 81b). In a study for the drapery of this Muse (Pl. 81a), the instrument rapidly jotted down resembles a cetra — that is, the Renaissance cetra rather than the ancient kithara, which was also called 'cetra' in Raphael's time. One might also be tempted to recognize, in the drawing, the front of the lute with the strings sketched in, but the strings of a Renaissance lute were attached to a frontal string holder, not to the tail end of the soundboard.[3] Among the enormous

[1] Numerous authors of the 16th century who wrote about the musical instruments of the ancients, and considered Raphael as the great authority in this field, found themselves in an embarrassing situation when they tried to translate obscure regions of a painting into the clear lines of a woodcut or engraving, where they were forced to resolve any confusions and uncertainties. In view of the well-known damage to the fresco (such as that inflicted during the sack of Rome in 1527) and the ensuing restorations, the reader may well inquire whether this section of the painting still retains its original surface, or whether the instrument has been changed by the hand of a well-meaning restorer. One could, in fact, draw up a long list of Renaissance works of art in which the musical instruments have been 'corrected' or 'modernized' in this fashion, for example by suppressing obsolete details such as bourdon strings or pegs. This kind of restoration is found above all in large museums and in famous works; in provincial collections and less famous churches, where zeal and money were lacking, paintings and frescoes have frequently remained intact. Fortunately, Sappho's instrument in the *Parnassus* shows no trace of restoration or overpainting. At this point, I wish to express my thanks to the Administration of the Vatican Museums, especially to Dr. Filippo Magi and Dr. Deoclecio Redig de Campos, who permitted me to spend many hours on scaffolds and to examine the sections of the fresco that were of interest to me. The unrestored condition of this particular section seems also to be confirmed by the words of Bellori, in his *Descrizione delle imagini dipinti da Raffaelle d'Urbino*, Rome, 1695: 'With her right hand Sappho reaches under the horn (*corno*) of the lyre,' a description that coincides perfectly with the instrument as we see it today.

[2] *Op. cit.*, p. 265.

[3] See, for example, the lutes depicted in Giovanni Bellini's altarpiece in the Accademia, Venice; Carpaccio's painting of the Virgin with Christ in Santa Maria de Frari, Venice; and Luca della Robbia's cantoria, in the Museo del Duomo, Florence.

number of extant lutes, and among those appearing in Renaissance painting, sculpture, and prints, I know of not one single exception. It will, perhaps, be better to leave this question open for the moment.

The last instrument to be mentioned is Apollo's. It is a lira da braccio and the only instrument which is being played; the others remain respectfully silent.[1]

So much for the instruments in the fresco. We can turn now to their representation in the engraving by Marcantonio and the drawing at Oxford. Fischel,[2] without directly establishing their chronology, simply states that 'in the grouping of the figures in the Oxford drawing, the composition already approached its final form.' But since this question is essential to my interpretation, we must pause to consider it.

At first glance the problem seems complicated, since Marcantonio's engraving shows seven more figures than the Oxford drawing, of whom most — with many or few changes — have been incorporated into the fresco. But closer inspection of the figures and their grouping reveals beyond doubt that the Oxford drawing is the immediate predecessor of the final work. All figures here have taken precisely the poses that they assume in the fresco: Apollo is seated as in the fresco; the extreme right Muse has turned around, now showing her back; the black-bearded poet on the right, often identified with Baldassare Castiglione, has turned towards the right. This similarity is apparent even in minutiae. In the Oxford drawing, as in the fresco, the seated Ennius is part of the smooth arc formed by Virgil, Homer, and Dante, and this rounded contour is continued through his right arm — quite different from the jagged contour in the engraving. The Oxford drawing also hides Euterpe's left forearm, fully shown by Marcantonio. A special case is the eloquent bearded elder in the right foreground; he appears in the engraving and also, in a more subtle and elegant version, in the drawing, but is omitted in the fresco (however, he reappears, slightly modified, in the right foreground of the *Disputà del sacramento*).

We arrive at the same conclusion if we compare the three compositions with respect to the grouping of the standing Muses. In the drawing, the heads in each group are so arranged that they form descending lines converging towards Apollo, and in the right group the two middle Muses are closely linked to each other and detached from the flanking ones. All this agrees precisely with the fresco but is markedly different from the engraving.

In addition to these incongruities, another aspect of the composition reveals that Marcantonio's engraving is a world apart from the fresco. In the engraving, the single groups are static, isolated from each other, and the figures are

[1] On the evolution and changing shapes of the lira da braccio, see Chapter 5 above.

[2] *Op. cit.*, p. 255.

firmly rooted to the ground. In the fresco all the poets are involved in a soft, almost imperceptible motion from the left foreground, over the hill, and down again.[1] It is like an eternal procession across the ages, from time immemorial and continuing into the future, suggesting the participation of all epochs in the beautiful. In contemplating this image, both profound and nostalgic, we are reminded — as perhaps was Raphael — of Petrarch's beautiful words:

E Greci e nostri, che son fatti eredi
Del monte di Parnaso e per quei gioghi
Mosser più tardo, non men presti, i piedi.[2]

Assuming, on the basis of this comparison, that the Oxford drawing represents a much later stage than Marcantonio's engraving,[3] we can turn to an examination of the musical instruments depicted in both of them.

To begin with the engraving: the same four figures as in the fresco (that is, Apollo and three of the Muses) have instruments, two string and two wind instruments in all. These evidently all pose as ancient instruments, but are not truly so; in fact, they have no more to do with Greek or Roman instruments than do the lyre-guitars, so fashionable for a short time in the French Empire. But these lyre-guitars could at least be played, whereas the vague, pseudo-ancient lyres were unfunctional, lacking, among other things, a sound box. In particular, the two lyres of Marcantonio, one with strings and a short base and the other without strings and with a larger base, are simplified stylizations for allegorical purposes. But one should not blame Raimondi for them; they may very well be Raphael's. These instruments are quite concordant with the usual pictorial representation of ancient lyres around 1500; Mantegna, in his *Parnassus*, gave Apollo a similar lyre,[4] and Raphael himself followed this usage in the decorative, stylized instruments that he gave to the Apollo defeating Marsyas on the ceiling of the Segnatura, to Poesia in the same work (called 'un suono antico' by Vasari), and to the large Apollo in the niche of *The School of Athens*. If one wishes

[1] In the literature on the *Parnassus*, only one writer points to this motion: De Campos, whose *Le Stanze di Raffaello*, in the form of a small guidebook, contains many valuable suggestions and original ideas.

[2] 'The Greeks and we Latins, who have inherited the mountain of Parnassus and have traversed these ranges — in later times, but no less swiftly' (*Trionfi*, III, 61; *altra redazione*, publ. in *Letteratura italiana, storia e testi*, VI, Milan, 1951, p. 575.

[3] There is no need to take up here *in extenso* the often-discussed question of whether Vasari's description of the *Parnassus* was based on Marcantonio's engraving or directly on the fresco. Both hypotheses have been maintained in the critical literature; I believe the solution lies in the middle. Vasari admires the *putti* ('an infinity of nude Cupids in the air'), which occur only in the engraving, but at the same time he speaks of the 'dotta Sappho,' who appears only in the fresco. It is more than probable, therefore, that Vasari, who certainly knew the fresco, used the engraving to refresh his memory.

[4] However, he copied Roman military instruments accurately enough for his *Triumph of Caesar*, now at Hampton Court.

to see how accurately Raphael depicts instruments familiar to him, one has only to look at the psaltery in King David's hand in the *Disputà* or at the lira da braccio of the *Parnassus* Apollo, both instruments that he must have seen and heard countless times in Urbino and Rome.[1]

Equally vague and conventional is the syrinx held by Erato. It is the typical pastoral instrument usually depicted at that time in the hands of shepherds, satyrs, and frequently Polyphemus (as, for instance, the languishing Polyphemus by Sebastiano del Piombo in the Farnesina, to cite an example from Raphael's circle). But the real syrinx — one beautiful example is held by the dancing faun of the Capitoline Gallery — has to be graduated, with tapering pipes, and there is no trace of this in Raimondi's print.

Finally, Euterpe's instrument, conspicuously held against the sky, is a typical trumpet, quite common at Raphael's time, and the traditional allegorical attribute of Fama. The mouthpiece is hidden, but the shape of tube and bell leave no doubt.

Thus none of the four instruments shown in Raimondi's print, though in line with the current allegorical conventions, have much to do with instruments of the ancients, nor, to say the least, do they stem from the observation of ancient monuments that became so important at the time of Raphael's work in Rome.

All this changes at once with the phase of Raphael's work that is represented by the Oxford drawing. No longer are there pseudo-ancient instruments: Euterpe holds a double pipe, clearly an indication of the ancient Lydian aulos, although the upper end is not delineated and the lower end is hidden behind the legs, as it was in Marcantonio's engraving. Erato now holds a kithara identical with the one in the fresco, except that her hand here grasps the nearer arm of the kithara. The Muse at the extreme right holds an instrument of which only the lower part is visible. It cannot reliably be identified, but it certainly is not the pseudo-lyre of the engraving; most probably, it is a contemporary cittern. Apollo, finally, has also replaced his pseudo-lyre with a cittern; it is very sketchily outlined, yet clearly recognizable from the characteristic ears that are non-functional yet inevitable features of *quattrocento* citterns, occurring first as large projections and then, towards the *cinquecento*, gradually degenerating into small scrolls.[2]

[1] He also must have seen daily the marvellous and minutely precise intarsia representations by Giovanni da Verona that decorate most of the lower sections of the doors leading into the Segnatura. These intarsias seem to be the last remnants of the decoration that covered the lower part of the walls of the room itself before it was given over to Raphael. The doors include exclusively contemporary instruments — a harp, a spinettino, recorders, krummhorns, a set of viols, and a lute, but not a single lira da braccio, psaltery, or brass instrument.

[2] See Chapter 3 above. Examining the persistence of such elements over the centuries, one could perhaps formulate a hypothesis of some sort of collective memory. And, although this is

This comparison between the fresco and the preliminary stages of its composition has produced a strange result: in the Oxford drawing, although it is, for the most part, merely a compositional study in the nude, two new instruments have been depicted, at a point close to the completion of Raphael's plans. They reveal, for the first time, an intimate observation of ancient Greco-Roman instruments. Where did this knowledge come from, and why did this archaeological interest not enter the work until this late stage?

It is a fact that most of the musical instruments represented in ancient art that could have served as models in Raphael's time have not survived up to our day, or survive only in severely damaged condition (as, for instance, the decorations of the Domus Aurea). Nor is the pre-1511 literature on ancient music very revealing for our problem, as it consists mainly of theoretical matters such as the explication of the ancient modes; there is little about the instruments themselves, and, above all, not a single illustration that might have served as a model for the painter or as a guide for his humanist advisers. Among actual monuments, we have chiefly gems and coins; of real lyres and kitharas little has been preserved. There are also wall paintings, but they were done with impressionistic verve. As for statues of Apollo and the Muses with instruments, almost none exist in which the delicate projecting parts are not broken or — usually incorrectly — restored.[1] These small delicate parts had their best chance for preservation in reliefs, and it is in fact a sarcophagus, almost completely preserved at Raphael's time, that furnished the exact models for the *Parnassus*. This sarcophagus is, I believe, the Mattei Sarcophagus in the Museo Nazionale in Rome (Pl. 85a), a work neither obscure nor unknown, having been published and reproduced repeatedly.[2]

This sarcophagus, one of the most beautiful specimens of the Asiatic Sidamara type,[3] shows the nine Muses with two poets — five Muses on the front and two

not the place to indulge in such theorizing, I should like to point out the strange coincidence that, just at the time when the fanatical revival of antiquity had reached its climax, Apollo, the player of the lyre in antiquity, was given an instrument equipped with an atrophic form of the arms of the ancient lyre.

[1] An example of expert and ingenious restoration is the Apollo Musagetes in the Sala delle Muse of the Vatican. The remaining stump of one of the two arms of the kithara showed, in relief, two small legs, up to the knees; the restorer has completed them by adding the entire body of the suspended Marsyas.

[2] Jakob Sponius, *Miscellanea eruditae antiquitatis*, Lyon, 1679–85; Bernard de Montfaucon, *L'Antiquité expliquée*, Paris, 1724, Tome I, Part II, Tab. LVI, p. 112; Ridolfino Venuti, *Vetera monumenta Matthaeorum*, Rome, 1779, Vol. III, Tab. XVI, XVII; Johann Joachim Winckelmann, *Monumenti antichi inediti*, 2nd ed., Rome, 1821, Lib. V, cap. 3, notes 25 and 37; also Lib. VIII, cap. 3; Edward Gerhard, *Ueber ein Musenrelief des Königlichenu Museums zu Berlin*, in *Archäologische Zeitung*, 1843, p. 115, n. 119; Friedrich Matz and Edward Friedrich Karl von Duhn, *Antike Bildwerke*, Leipzig, 1881–82, No. 3268, p. 406; Charles Rufus Morey, *Sardis*, Vol. V, Pt. 1: *The Sarcophagus of Claudia Antonia Sabina and the Asiatic Sarcophagi*, Princeton, 1924, p. 26, Plate XVI.

[3] For a comparison with other Asiatic sarcophagi, see Morey, *op. cit.*, pp. 49 ff.

Muses flanking a poet on each side. It is the front that interests us most, for here are all the attributes that characterize each of the five Muses and that, if my hypothesis is correct, must have interested Raphael: the musical instruments and the two masks, tragic and lyric, that emphasize the middle niche. The instruments correspond to those in our fresco, occurring in the same order from left to right: the left instrument was given to Sappho; the right one, an elaborate kithara, to Erato; the Lydian aulos, in a modified form which we will discuss later, to Euterpe, to the left of Apollo. And indeed the masks, too, have been transferred to the fresco in the same symmetrical arrangement, the bearded one carried by the extreme left Muse, the unbearded one by the Muse to the right of Apollo. The latter mask was already introduced in the Oxford drawing, but was there held by the first Muse on the right. The beautiful motif of the bare shoulder of the kithara player is repeated no less than three times in the *Parnassus*: in the figures of Euterpe, Sappho, and the Muse holding the lyric mask. But we look in vain for this motif in Marcantonio's engraving, which is one more proof that the motif was inspired by a subsequent acquaintance with the sarcophagus.

Yet, striking as these parallels may be, they still leave several questions open; not all the details tally. Sappho's instrument has a horn, while the corresponding one in the sarcophagus has none; Euterpe's strange trumpet is no aulos. Moreover, the instruments on the sarcophagus are damaged today — not to mention the four missing heads; in what condition were they when Raphael or his draftsmen saw them? And do we possess any evidence, besides its relation to the Segnatura fresco, that the sarcophagus was known before 1511? The art-historical literature, as far as I can see, does not contain a single word about this.

It is possible, and also advantageous, to answer all these questions together, for good luck makes it possible to refer to depictions of the sarcophagus in earlier, better-preserved states — at least one of them before Raphael's day.

Well known, of course, is the engraving of the sarcophagus in the *Monumenta Matthaeiana* (Pl. 85b). It is rather academic and conventional, but gives some important clues: the instrument at the extreme left has one horn with a hand touching it, as does Sappho's in the fresco; the aulos has four protuberances; the right arm and hand of the kithara-playing Muse and even the large plectrum are still intact. An amusing misunderstanding has afflicted the tragic mask; the fingers holding it by the chin have been misinterpreted by the engraver, so that the mask here spits the sleeve cloth of the Muse out of its mouth. More important is the fact that all the heads except the one at the extreme right are still extant. Although drawn schematically, they at least show the direction of the faces.

An earlier reproduction of the sarcophagus, the engraving in Jakob Sponius, *Miscellanea eruditae antiquitatis*, Sect. II, Art. IX, p. 44, is even more interesting and more precise. Here the original top is shown, with the medallion of the deceased couple, man and wife, which occurs in no other reproduction of the sarcophagus. Also, all the heads of the Muses appear, including the one of the farthest right Muse, which is missing in the engraving of the *Monumenta Matthaeiana.* The same engraving is repeated by Bernard de Montfaucon, *L'Antiquité expliquée et representée en figures*, Paris, 1724, Tom. I, Part II, Tab. LVI, p. 112 (Pl. 85c).

Let us now turn to still earlier evidence: the drawings. The drawing preceding Raphael's is by no lesser hand than that of Francesco di Giorgio (Pl. 88b; Uffizi, Gabinetto dei Disegni, 326 A.R.). Its subject and its relation to the Mattei Sarcophagus have so far not been recognized.[1] It is evidently a leaf from a travel sketchbook, containing ground plans of ancient buildings, with dimensions and an ancient inscription added. At the top left is the kithara-player from the Mattei Sarcophagus; further to the right are the heads of the other four Muses. Over the complete figure is the remark 'a san Pauolo', over the four heads again 'a san Pauolo.' The right head, graciously bent, evidently belongs to the extreme left Muse (compared with the engraving from the *Monumenta Matthaeiana*). Francesco was evidently particularly interested in the coiffure, and his shorthand is admirably precise, as we see if we compare the third head from the right with its model, the head of the centre Muse on the sarcophagus. This head has an elaborate double coiffure with a ribbon between the lower and higher part. Raphael, it seems, liked it too, and it found its way into the Oxford drawing, applied to the Muse at the extreme left; later, in the fresco, it was given to the standing Muse to the right of Apollo.

The full figure of the kithara-player is a model of delicate shorthand innuendo. No wonder Francesco was struck by the graceful pose of the lifted leg, and the smooth neckline with one shoulder exposed by the diagonal rim of the peplum. This figure was a favourite in antiquity and was used as a single figure, independent of the circle of the Muses. The right hand with the larger plectrum and, above all, the left hand plucking with strongly arched fingers are delineated with sharper, more determined strokes.

[1] A. S. Weller, *Francesco di Giorgio*, Chicago, 1943, p. 263, comments on this drawing: 'In the upper left corner is a sketch of a figure in transparent flowing drapery playing a lyre, labelled "*a sanpavolo.*" In the Uffizi Catalogue, Ferri says that this is an Apollo on a sarcophagus at San Paolo fuori le Mura. It appears, however, that the figure is no Apollo but one of the Muses. Four other female heads, in various attitudes, also appear. The heads have proportion lines added, in a fashion found also in many of the *Trattato* illustrations. . . .' R. Papini, *Francesco di Giorgio architetto*, Florence, 1946, Vol. II, fig. 26, reproduces only the upper part of the page, with the comment: 'Donna che suona la cetra, studii di teste e di una pianta di Villa.'

By a lucky coincidence, the other two Muses with instruments from the sarcophagus are also represented in a drawing, a page of the Wolfegg Sketchbook, attributed to Amico Aspertini.[1] This page shows in its four sections various scenes from ancient reliefs, all containing musical instruments, although this may not have been the principle of choice. The lower scenes are of maritime character; the upper ones have larger figures, evidently copied from sculptures in diverse places, for they are accurately labelled 'in santo paulo.' Interesting to us are the two figures in the upper left (Pl. 89c), evidently sketches after the left and middle Muses of the front of the Mattei Sarcophagus. The instrument of the left figure is sketched with considerable detail, and tallies in many details with Sappho's lyre in the fresco. But realistic observation and fantasy are mixed a little differently and less timidly than by Raphael. There is again the complex machine on top, but it includes the little *kollopes*. Thus we have to assume either that they were intact on the sarcophagus at that time or that the draftsman reconstructed them from the remains, which are still preserved today. Moreover, the instrument has only one horn, the one in the rear, as in the engraving of the *Monumenta*; the draftsman did not take the trouble to supply the other horn, the stump of which is still visible today. The player's hand does not hold the horn, as in the *Monumenta* engraving, but reaches down to the 'machine', and consequently the arm turned out much too long. The round sound-hole, drawn in by analogy with a lute, is sheer imagination. The three strings are drawn in, but they cross the horizontal projection of the soundboard and thus transform it into something like a bridge.

More reliable is the aulos; obviously, it was still preserved when the draughtsman saw the sarcophagus. The upper ends with the bulbous swellings are indicated, and so are the six cup-shaped protuberances, of which three still remain today while the other three are broken. The lower ends of the pipes beneath the left hand were neglected by the draughtsman, although they still survive today.

By comparing the drawings of Francesco di Giorgio and Aspertini, and the prints from Sponius and the *Monumenta* with the sarcophagus itself, the reader will now be able to reconstruct the successive states of preservation of the sarcophagus and acquire an approximate picture of the condition in which Raphael or his draughtsmen saw it; only now is it possible to judge how much

[1] Professor Richard Krautheimer, who kindly read the Italian version of this chapter, drew my attention to two articles, one by Cornelius von Fabriczy (*Un Taccuino di Amico Aspertini*, in *L'Arte*, 1905, p. 401), attributing the *taccuino* to Aspertini, and the other by Carl Robert (*Ueber ein dem Michelangelo zugeschriebenes Skizzenbuch auf Schloss Wolfegg*, in *Mitteilungen des Kaiserlichen Deutschen Archaeologischen Instituts, Römische Abteilung*, XVI, 237, n. 1); both articles suggest a relation between the Wolfegg sketch, the Mattei Sarcophagus, and the drawing by Francesco di Giorgio.

Raphael borrowed from the sarcophagus, and whether his deviations from this model resulted from damage, misunderstanding, or other reasons.[1]

Gathering together the results of our inquiry, we can now turn back to the instruments in the fresco. The simplest case is that of the kithara: it is an example of almost literal transplantation. The only functional differences between Raphael's instrument and that of the sarcophagus concern the *kollopes*: some of them have survived until today in the sarcophagus instrument (Pl. 88a). Francesco's drawing shows them all, and this was evidently the condition at Raphael's time, since he accurately depicts the front arm of the kithara with the side disk of the yoke (in both the Oxford drawing and in the fresco). Thus we have here simply a lack of technical-functional understanding, and Raphael's way out of the dilemma was to omit what he did not comprehend.

The problem is solved differently in the case of Sappho's lyre. Here too, the ancient model (Pls. 86 & 87b) is an accurate copy of a real instrument: the points where both horns broke off are still visible; the yoke, completely preserved, is the usual one; rudiments of the *kollopes* on both sides of the yoke are preserved. But evidently there was only one horn remaining in Raphael's time, and this must have perturbed the copyist, who interpreted it as a plectrum, without noticing that the Muse holds a plectrum in her right hand (Pl. 85a). In short, the result is a fantastic machine for 'la dotta Sappho,' and Raphael, embarrassed by this pictorial reconstruction, did not even dare to sling the strings around the yoke.

Much more complex is the case of Euterpe's trumpet. We observed at the beginning of this essay that the shape of the tube, and especially of the cup-shaped mouthpiece pressed against Euterpe's thigh, belongs clearly to a trumpet. But the bell is strangely small and flat, and even stranger are the bulb beneath it and the four dark protuberances growing out of the tube. Comparing this with the sarcophagus (Pl. 87a), the solution is obvious: the features, inexplicable in a trumpet, are taken from the aulos. The result is acoustical nonsense: no

[1] There are, of course, other sarcophagi with representations of the nine Muses, but only one of them, that from the Villa Montalto (now in the British Museum), is in many respects similar to that from the Mattei collection. Its front shows the Muses in niches: the central one in a small niche, the other eight, in pairs, in four larger niches. The Muse with the lyre at her feet is the third from the right; the one holding the tibia is in the centre; and the one with the kithara is on the right. All these Muses are strikingly similar to those of the Mattei sarcophagus, and the same is true of their instruments. Nonetheless, I do not believe it was this sarcophagus that inspired Raphael or the sketches of Francesco di Giorgio and Aspertini. The attire of the Muse with the lyre differs from that of the corresponding Muse on the Mattei sarcophagus, and the Wolfegg sketch corresponds perfectly with the latter and not with that from the Villa Montalto. Also, the Montalto Muse with the tibia raises her right hand up to head level, while in the Mattei sarcophagus and the Wolfegg sketch the hand reaches only to shoulder height. Finally, the Muse who plays the kithara bends backwards in the Montalto sarcophagus but slightly forward in the Mattei version and the sketch by Francesco di Giorgio.

trumpet had soundholes to be stopped by the fingers, while no aulos had a cup-shaped mouthpiece. Moreover, the aulos had its mouthpiece, with oboe reed and bulb, on top; the trumpet in the fresco had its mouthpiece on the lower end. Here ignorance can hardly be the explanation; instruments of the oboe type — and the aulos was a double oboe — were quite common at that time, and even double oboes were frequently depicted in angel concerts. Furthermore, not only contemporary double oboes were known; the ancient aulos itself was evidently well understood in the Raphael circle. Perin del Vaga, for instance, who had worked in the Segnatura to replace the intarsias of Fra Giovanni da Verona by more up-to-date frescoes,[1] made a drawing (now in the Gabinetto dei Disegni of the Uffizi) showing Muses with masks and musical instruments; one of the Muses holds a mask and two pipes, strikingly similar in shape to the instrument held by Euterpe in the *Parnassus* — but functionally correct and with the lateral protuberances sketched in. Still more important, Raphael himself, according to the Oxford drawing, depicted a double pipe, and therefore the apparent absurdity of Euterpe's instrument cannot be explained by ignorance. We must assume rather that functional logic was intentionally subordinated to allegorical aims. Up to now, we have called the Muse carrying the strange wind instrument Euterpe[2] because, according to ancient iconography, it was Euterpe who carried the aulos. But in the fresco there was also needed a heroic-epic Muse — 'Calliope gesta canens' — and her traditional attribute, at least in Raphael's time, was the trumpet. Perhaps, too, the presence of two wind instruments would not have been appropriate on the Parnassus that echoes with the silvery sound of Apollo's lira da braccio.[3] Thus the aulos was fused with the trumpet, and the appearance of archaeological authenticity was combined with allegorical persuasion: Euterpe merged with Calliope.

Apollo's instrument presents no archaeological problems;[4] except for the number of strings, it is a life portrait of the common lira da braccio (Pl. 84a). The body, the heart-shaped head with frontal pegs, the two drone strings, etc., are all of typical shape. The instrument is identical with the lira da braccio played by one of the angels in Raphael's *Incoronazione* in the Vatican Pinacoteca.

Raphael has often been criticized for including in the *Parnassus*, and

[1] See Vasari, *Vite*, ed. Milanesi, IV, 337, and V, 130. About the intarsias, see fn. 1, p. 191 above.

[2] See fn. 1, p. 186 above.

[3] With admirable logic and iconographical taste, Raphael also abandoned the all-too-bucolic syrinx that appears in Marcantonio's engraving.

[4] For the figure of Apollo, the Mattei sarcophagus offered no model. The Apollo of Marcantonio's engraving seems to bear some resemblance to the type of seated player (Apollo or Orpheus) in the centre of another sarcophagus reproduced in the *Monumenta Matthaeiana*, Tab. XIII, under the title 'Metropolis cum diis tutelaribus.' It is not without interest that this relief shows, in the group of figures that surround the player, two persons in profile, crowned with laurels and comparable to Virgil and Dante in Raimondi's engraving.

especially in the hands of Apollo, a contemporary instrument,[1] the more so because it is a bowed fiddle, and bowing was a technique unknown to Greco-Roman antiquity. But this anachronism is in fact specious, for was it not Raphael's purpose in the Segnatura, and especially in the *Parnassus*, to merge antiquity with contemporary life, to show the noble figures of the past in conversation with their followers, to show 'Greci ed Eredi' as strands of the very same fabric of history? Dante had no qualms about letting himself be guided by Virgil. Why should not Petrarch and Ariosto be assembled with Sappho? In *The School of Athens*, the fusion is even more intense: Plato appears in the likeness of Leonardo, Bramante as Euclid, Michelangelo as Heraclitus; and in the Stanza d'Eliodoro, Julius II opposes Heliodorus, while Aeneas, travelling in the other direction, saves Anchises from the 9th-century *Incendio di Borgo.*

Moreover, the lira da braccio is often mentioned in Renaissance literature as an instrument of the ancients. This was also believed of the viola and, later, of the violin; in fact, the invention of the bow was attributed to the ancients and frequently to Sappho.[2] This belief went as far as to include archaeological fakes. Sylvestro Ganassi's *Regola Rubertina*, Venice, 1542, Pt. I, Ch. VIII, refers to ancient statues as the source of information for bowed instruments in antiquity:

[1] One recalls, for example, Goethe's *Wilhelm Meisters Theatralische Sendung*, Bk. 6, Ch. 9. After praising the beauty of the violinist Horatio, the poet observes: 'and when he at last grasped his instrument, one forgave Raphael for showing his Apollo with a violin instead of a lyre.'

[2] Bernardi, *Ragionamenti musicali*, Bologna, 1581, p. 45: 'Il violino fu inventato da Orfeo, figliuolo d'Apollo, e di Calliope. Safo Erista Poetessa antica inventò l'Arco con li crini di Cavallo e fu la prima, che suonasse il Violino, e Viola, come s'usa hoggidi, e questa fu 624 anni avanti la ventura del Signor Nostro Giesù Christo.' ('The violin was invented by Orpheus, son of Apollo and Calliope. The ancient poetess Sappho invented the bow fitted with horsehair, and was the first to use the violin and viola in the way they are used today; and this happened 624 years before the coming of Our Lord Jesus Christ.') The emblematic literature of the 16th and 17th centuries, when speaking of the lira, frequently quotes ancient and contemporary sources indiscriminately, and, even where a distinction is made between the 'lira col archetto' and the 'lira toccata dal plettro,' both forms are said to be ancient (see, for instance, P. Abb. Picinelli, *Del Mondo simbolico ampliato*, Lib. XXIII, Cap. V). In an Italian plaquette of the late 15th century (E. R. D. McLagan, *Catalogue of the Plaquettes of the Victoria and Albert Museum*, No. 95, 1865, Pl. IX), Apollo contending with Marsyas plays the kithara, but also keeps a bowed fiddle in reserve. The question of whether antiquity actually knew the fiddle bow remained quite undecided until well into the 18th century; Leopold Mozart, in the introduction to his *Versuch einer gründlichen Violinschule*, Salzburg, 1756, after quoting Zarlino and Tevo, says sceptically: 'Und wenn endlich Merkur . . . das Recht zu seiner Leyer behält, solche auch nach ihm erst in die Hände des Apollo und Orpheus gekommen ist: wie lässt sich solche mit einem unserer heutigen Instrumenten vergleichen? Ist uns denn die eigentliche Gestalt dieser Leyer bekannt? Und können wir etwa den Merkur zu dem Urheber der Geiginstrumenten angeben. . . ?' ('And if, finally, Mercury . . . is left with his claim to the lyre, and if this instrument only after him comes into the hands of Apollo and Orpheus, how can we compare it with one of our modern instruments? Do we really know the actual shape of that lyre, and are we really entitled to consider Mercury the inventor of the fiddle?')

> Notice how the violone is made with six strings. I often wondered which was more ancient, the lute or the violone, when I wanted to describe its origin. Having discussed the question with various people, I recalled having seen among the antiquities of Rome, in a history with many marble figures, one figure who had in his hands a bowed viola similar to those mentioned above. There I immediately recognized that the violone was more ancient than the lute, on the evidence of the story of Orpheus, who is not mentioned as using the lute, but rather the instrument with strings and bow that is the lira, which with its strings and its bow is like the violone. But as to its name, it was lira or lirone, although most people call it violone. But it is more correct to call it lirone, and, in the plural, lironi, rather than violone or violoni; our evidence is based on Orpheus and his lyre. . . .[1]

Also Pierius Valerianus, in his *Hieroglyphica*, Basel, 1567, p. 346, includes, in an extensive chapter on the lira, a woodcut showing an ancient altar with a lira da braccio sculptured in relief on each of the four sides (Fig. 1 in Chapter 1 above),[2] evidently an imitation of the ancient type of altar with a lira or kithara on each of the four sides (such as that found in Vejo, now in the Lateran Museum). This confusion was no doubt facilitated by the name 'lira' and the presence of the two open strings. Accordingly, Pinturicchio's Musica in the Appartamenti Borgia and Pollaiuolo's Musica on the tomb of Pope Sixtus IV each hold a lira da braccio, as does a long line of Orpheuses, Apollos, King Davids, and countless angels in celestial concerts (for example in Perugino's *Assumption of the Virgin* in the Accademia, Florence). In all these cases — apart from the angel concerts, which follow their own iconographical tradition — the lira da braccio is the instrument of the solo player, usually accompanying his own song or recitation. This was precisely the case with recitation to the lyre or kithara in antiquity, and the Renaissance was fully aware of this. In this respect, Raphael was not deviating from convention.

But he was diverging in *one* respect: his lira da braccio has nine strings in place of the usual seven. The common *accordatura* consisted of five melody strings to be stopped against the fingerboard, and two open strings, running

[1] 'Nota bene come il violone è composto di sei corde, et più volte io pensava qual fosse più antico o il leuto o il violone per poter discrivere l'origine della cosa del che parlando con più persone sommi arricordato da uno haver visto nelle antighità di Roma in una historia di molte figure sculpite in marmo essergli una delle figure che haveva in mano una viola d'arco simile a queste, et subito conobbi ch'l fosse più antico il violone che il leuto per l'autorità ancora cavata d'Orfeo non si dice che lui usasse il leuto: ma ben lo istromento di corde, et arco che è la lira laqual è conforme di corde, et archetto come è il violone: ma ancora nel suo nome che è lira o lirone a ben che il più diceano violone: ma molto più è conforme al suo suggetto il nominarlo lirone et lironi molti insieme, che viole nè violoni: perchè l'autorità si cava di Orfeo per la sua lira. . . .'

[2] The text reads: 'huic autem a singulis angulis Lyrae appensae sunt, corymbis et sertis medio intervallo dependentibus. . . .'

outside the fingerboard and vibrating in their full length when plucked or bowed. We have mentioned above how familiar Raphael must have been with the lira da braccio, and thus a mistake concerning the number of strings is out of the question. The explanation can be found only on the allegorical plane: nine was frequently given as the number of Greek modes[1] as well as of the Muses. Baldassare Castiglione, if he was Raphael's adviser then, was probably too musical to symbolize the nine modes by nine strings; it would have been a superficial metaphor.[2] The Musagetes, inspiring the nine noble sisters, would not be beyond *cinquecento* concepts of allegorical numbers.

> *Mentis Apollinea vis has movet undique Musas,*
> *In medio residens complectitur omnia Phoebus.*[3]

In view of these problems, it seems less important whether Raphael, as has often been said, gave Apollo the likeness of Giacomo San Secondo, the famous virtuoso on the lira da braccio at the Court of Leo X. It is a fact that, at the time, solo players like San Secondo were among the most famous and most generously paid musicians,[4] but this, as far as I can see, is the only evidence

[1] Actually, different numbers are given in the ancient literature and, consequently, in the Renaissance writings. It is interesting that Zarlino in his *Istitutioni harmoniche*, Venice, 1558, p. 367, imputes to the philosopher Gaudentius the numbering of nine modes in music.

[2] In the Renaissance, symbolic significance was frequently attributed to the lyre. A long list of examples taken from ancient as well as modern sources is found in P. Abb. Picinelli, *op. cit.* (see fn. 2, p. 198 above). An example of number symbolism concerning the strings of the ancient lyre is found in Zarlino, *Istitutioni harmoniche*, Venice, 1573, p. 21: 'Questa tale harmonia troppo bene conobbero Mercurio et Terpandro; conciossia che l'uno havendo ritrovata la Lira, overamente la Cetra, pose in essa quattro chorde ad imitatione della Musica mondana (come dice Boetio et Macrobio) la quale si scorge ne i quattro Elementi, overo nella varieta de i quattro tempi dell'anno; et l'altro la ordino con sette corde alla similitudine de i sette Pianeti.' ('Such a harmony was well known to Mercury and Terpander, since the former invented the lyre or rather the cetra, and attached to it the four strings in imitation of the *Musica mondana* [i.e. the Pythagorean harmony of the universe] — according to Boëthius and Macrobius — that is, the music that we perceive in the four elements or in the difference between the four seasons; and the latter fixed it with seven strings, with reference to the seven planets.')

The same kind of symbolism is pointed out by Lanfranco (*Scintille di musica*, Brescia, 1533), who speaks of the correspondence between the seven strings of the lyre and the seven planets. Another kind of parallel we encounter in G. C. Capaccio, *Trattato delle imprese*, Naples, 1592, p. 23 verso: 'L'impresa di Napoli e rappresentata da una Sirena che si spreme latte dal petto con una lira da braccio in primo piano.' ('The emblem of Naples shows a Siren who squeezes milk from her breasts, with a lira da braccio in the foreground.' See Fig. 24 in Chapter 15 below.) The text explains that the lyre is symbolic, and that its six strings signify the union of 'cinque piazze di Nobili, e una Popolare' ('five piazzas of the nobility and one of the common people').

[3] Natalis Comes, *Mythologiae libri decem*, Padua, 1616, p. 583: 'The spirit of Apollo forcefully moves these Muses; residing among them, he embraces the universe.' See also Franchino Gafurius, *Theorica musice*, Bk. I, p. 2.

[4] On this point, see E. P. Rodocanachi, *La première renaissance, Rome au temps de Jules II et de Leon X*, Paris, 1912, p. 107; Jakob Burckhardt, *Die Kultur der Renaissance in Italien*, Leipzig, 1926, p. 342; Jan Lauts, *Isabella d'Este*, Hamburg, 1952, p. 55 ff.

proferred for this alleged identification.[1] A portrait of San Secondo has not survived, as far as I know, although the portrait of a musician in the Galleria Sciarra has occasionally been connected with San Secondo.[2]

It may be found surprising, by the way, that neither the *Parnassus* nor the *Scuola*, both so liberal in the inclusion of contemporary thinkers, admit any composers, though masters such as Ockeghem, Obrecht, Isaac, Josquin des Près, Pierre de la Rue, Brumel, Agricola, Orto, and Mouton were then in the flower of their glory. Two reasons seem probable: first, the great contemporary composers were famous chiefly for their *musica sacra*, which, as polyphony, could hardly have sounded well on Parnassus; as for the profane frottolas and madrigals, they were also polyphonic, as well as too light to be represented by composers of such fame. Secondly, Raphael's archaeological advisers may have felt, and rightly so, that ancient musical life gravitated around poetry and that it was the rhapsodists, the solo recitalists, who were the prototypes of the ancient musician. The allegorical figure on the ceiling of the Segnatura over the *Parnassus* shows the winged Poesia with a book in her right hand, a lyre in her left, and the bust of Homer decorating her throne.

In this gigantic allegory of the Beautiful, so radically and ingeniously departing from the traditional and still basically medieval cliché of Musica (as one of the *artes liberales*), Raphael, the Pope's new Superintendent of Antiquities, intuitively found his way back to the ancient conception. This was the first systematic attempt to employ ancient models with *intenzione antichizzanda*. It was not only an important step in pictorial symbolism, but also in humanist archaeology, long before the contemporary literature on the subject had advanced to this point, and before precise woodcuts or engravings have been made of the ancient instruments. Not before the literature of the Baroque was this subject tackled seriously and systematically, and wherever the instruments of the ancients are treated there, it is done with explicit references to the instruments in Raphael's *Parnassus*. But that is another story.[3]

[1] Such an identification must have already seemed suspect to Burckhardt, who wrote: 'Anyone who finds the violin objectionable should blame only Raphael himself; in no case is the present anachronism the result of an instruction to celebrate a famous contemporary virtuoso, who, by the way, is considered by some authors to have been also a valet of the Pope. In all probability, the violin offered the painter a more lively and telling motif than an ancient lyre' (*Cicerone*, Leipzig, 1925, p. 865).

[2] Cf. E. P. Rodocanachi, *op. cit.*, p. 108.

[3] As for the enormous impact made by Raphael's *Parnassus* on later painters, see above all the interesting study by A. P. de Mirimonde, *Les Concerts des muses chez les maîtres du Nord*, in *Gazette des beaux-arts*, March, 1964, which also deals with the problem of 'realistic' depiction of ensembles, complicated in concerts of Muses by the symbolic significance of instruments as attributes.

15 · The Inspired Musician: A 16th-Century Musical Pastiche

In the unending stream of combinations and recombinations that is the life of forms, two main types can be distinguished. An artist may borrow two or more images, combining them into a new composition, without however changing their content or significance. Or he may change a borrowed or inherited image to make it carry a new meaning. Both types occur frequently, but we do not often find a combination of both procedures, namely, a fusion of borrowed images into a new unity which is the carrier of a new message. Such a case can be seen in the picture which is the subject of this chapter (Pl. 91). It was evidently painted by an Italianate Dutch or Flemish artist towards the middle of the 16th century.[1]

A youth and a girl face each other against the background of a deep, luminous mountain landscape. Both have serious, deeply absorbed expressions, but, unlike lovers, avoid each other's gaze. The youth is evidently a musician, holding in his left hand a typical 16th-century viol, and in his right hand, with awkward grip, the bow. The girl, half-nude and crowned with laurel, also holds the viol with her left hand, while the right squeezes from her breast milk, which falls upon the instrument in four thin silver streams. This certainly is no love scene. Their glances do not meet, and the instrument separates them. The meaning is apparent: we have here an allegory of the creative artist together with the crowned Muse who inspires him by baptizing the instrument of his art with the nourishing liquid.

The allegory is quite unusual considering its date. It represents the inspiration of the artist, the musician in the act of receiving the divine afflatus at a time

[1] This picture was illustrated in *The Burlington Magazine*, Dec. 1950, p. 366, in the advertising supplement under 'Notable Works of Art now on the Market,' with the title '*Allegory* by Jan van Hemessen.' I was so intrigued by the allegory, its connection with Titian and other prototypes, and by the musical instrument, that I wrote to the owner, the Arcade Gallery Ltd., which kindly supplied me with a photograph. Since then I have found the painting in excellently cleaned condition in the collection of my former colleague at the Metropolitan Museum of Art, Mr. Theodore A. Heinrich, now Director of the Royal Ontario Museum, who attributes the painting to Jan van Scorel and dates it 1525–30. Earlier attributions which I encountered while studying the painting were to Gossaert, Massys, and Swart van Groningen; however, as a teacher of the history of music and curator of musical instruments I am in the fortunate position of being able to leave the crossing of the attributional Rubicon to others.

when it was not yet customary to depict a contemporary musician as an inspired being, as *ingegno*, as pioneering genius, as creator.

Images of Apollo, Orpheus, King David, with their various instruments — changing from period to period — come down through the centuries in an almost unbroken line from antiquity; the noble figure of Musica appears among the *quadrivium* as one of the *artes liberales*.[1] Mythological figures, such as the Muses, Pan, and Marsyas, became familiar again in the *quattrocento*. But it was not before the Romantic movement of the early 18th century and the age of Shaftesbury that musical genius — that is, a contemporary musician in the state of inspiration — became an accepted subject.

In other fields, the portrayal of inspiration is a different story: St. Matthew's stylus was inspired by the angel in countless medieval illuminations. The poet already appeared among the Muses on numerous Roman sarcophagi, a motif which is retained and intensified in the wonderful 5th-century ivory diptych in the cathedral of Monza, where in one tablet the poet is shown listening attentively to the music played on the kithara by the Muse in the facing tablet (Pl. 89b). Homer and Virgil, Dante and Petrarch, Ariosto and Pietro Bembo are admitted to the company of the Muses in Raphael's *Parnassus*, but no musicians, not even a Josquin or a Dufay; and the artisans — sculptors, painters, or architects — do not fare any better. Even Michelangelo could only make his appearance in Raphael's *School of Athens* when camouflaged as Heraclitus.[2] Similarly, Bramante needs the garb and pose of the prophet Joel to be admitted to the Sistine ceiling.

And when artists insert their self-portraits into frescoes or paintings to be near their painted saints or to secure visual immortality, they do so modestly. This is the case, for instance, with Ghiberti peering out of the frame of the Porta del Paradiso, with Masaccio in the Brancacci Chapel, with Orcagna who put his likeness into the marble relief of the *Death of the Virgin* on the tabernacle in Or San Michele, and with Raphael modestly sharing the company of the philosophers in the *School of Athens*. In these and many more cases it is the likeness of the artist which is immortalized, but he is never shown in the act of creation or in a state of inspiration.

It cannot, of course, be the purpose of this study to sketch the changing iconography of the inspired musician, but a few words may not be amiss on the ideas and the spiritual climate that determined the early formation of this image.

[1] There she is often accompanied by that bearded man with hammers who stands sometimes for Tubalcain, the inventor of musical instruments, sometimes for the blacksmith whose hammer sounds led Pythagoras to make his acoustical investigations, sometimes even for Pythagoras himself.

[2] See Deoclecio Redig de Campos, *Raffaello e Michelangelo*, Rome, 1946, p. 155.

The Pythagorean philosophy of numbers as modified by the Platonists and the Stoa conceived of Musica as the theory of proportions, as the rational science of the divine order of the cosmos, and therefore put music in the *quadrivium* together with arithmetic, geometry, and astronomy. In Augustine's famous definition of music as *scientia bene modulandi*, the term *modulari* signifies not only 'mode' as form of the musical scale, but also and chiefly the mathematical term 'modulus.' In the medieval treatises Musica retained — if not augmented — her noble position among the liberal arts. Or so one would believe if one reads in Giraldus de Cambrai that 'sine Musica nulla disciplina potest esse perfecta,' and finds in Aquinas that 'Musica inter septem artes liberales sola tenet principatum.' In fact this esteem had by that time increasingly become lip service: the Platonic-Stoic rational inquiry into the laws of the universe by investigating its mathematical proportions no longer had any place within Christian cosmology; the *ars musica* could no longer serve as a main road towards cognition of God and His creation, and therefore was gradually reduced to a theory of the musical intervals and to technical rules for making music *ad majorem Dei gloriam.*[1] This notion of Musica was absorbed by *quattrocento* humanism and — at least for sacred music — retained authority in the treatises of the theorists for more than two centuries and well into the Baroque.

The position of music in the *quadrivium* could not fail to give scholarly standing to the musicians — theorists, organists, and choirmasters. But it left little chance for a conception of the musician as creator in the deeper sense of this word. The emphasis was on the rules of composition, not on free creation. The customary musical images were the figure of Musica itself, usually depicted on her throne in the *quadrivium*; the twenty-four elders with their musical instruments; and above all the multitude of musical angels singing, dancing, and playing. King David, the musician, is an exception in that he is often shown as a solitary, sometimes even enraptured instrumentalist, but this is due in all likelihood to the affiliation of his early depictions with those of Orpheus in late antiquity. At any rate, it is significant that of the multitude of Renaissance portraits of musicians, hardly a single one shows more fire, let alone rapture, than would befit a master or teacher. Apart from the portraits, all with serious or pensive

[1] It is remarkable that the doctrine of the *quadrivium* had a quite different and in a certain sense contrary effect on the visual arts and the social status of the artists. While Musica as a science of proportion gradually lost her cosmological importance and thereby her central position in philosophical speculation, it was just the doctrine of proportions which became the preoccupation of the draughtsmen of the *quattrocento* and their rational-mathematically 'correct' portrayal of nature. Perspective became the new science-art and the vogue of the century, and consequently the painter ascended from the level of artisan to the rank of scholar. And Pollaiuolo merely put the seal on a completed evolution when — in need of an eighth figure for the decoration of the tomb of Sixtus IV — he added the figure of Prospettiva to the figures of the *quadrivium* and *trivium*.

expression, we find the master teaching, or at the organ, or offering his compositions to the Pope or to a secular patron. It would be grossly anachronistic to imagine a portrait of Palestrina in the transfigured pose that Gluck attains in Duplessis's grandiose painting, or in the pose that Ingres gives to Cherubini, with the monumental muse holding her blessing hand over the composer's head.

At the beginning of the Renaissance a new road opens toward the conception and depiction of the inspired musician through the direct turn to the mythological imagery of the ancients and the influence of neo-Platonic theories developed in Florence. Now pictures of Orpheus, Apollo, and Homer abound as allegories of poetic and musical inspiration. But characteristically this was not in the field of church music, where the medieval world of rules continues to prevail, but where invention and execution coincided: in the field of improvisation. It is no accident that the countless images of mythological musicians appear precisely in an age of celebrated virtuosi who improvise the accompaniment to their recitation on the lira da braccio or viol or lute. Understandably and lamentably not one note of their admired performances is preserved; neither do we know exactly how many paintings and prints of Apollo and Orpheus were portraits of actual musicians or poets of the day,[1] but in some cases the identity is established.[2] All the mythical musicians, however, whether they charm animals, or force the gates of Hades, or meditate, fiddle in hand, against the melancholy of the evening sky, are mere symbols of the power of music, and some, the solitary fiddlers and lutenists, possibly signify inspiration. Yet there is not another example of the scene shown in our painting, the allegorical baptism of the musician's instrument by the maternal muse.

If we find the content of our picture to be quite exceptional for its time, it may be even more surprising to find that this allegory is, in fact, composed of elements borrowed almost literally from other sources. One of these sources is evidently the famous mirror back, the *Patera Martelli* (Pl. 89a), or, more precisely, its right half. The correspondence between the bacchante there and our muse is quite obvious: the same profile view, the same nude torso with drapery falling from the right shoulder over the back, the same jets of milk. In the *Patera*, however, the milk flows into a drinking horn, evidently to be offered to the satyr opposite her. Streams of ink have been shed over the *Patera*, its meaning

[1] Raphael's enraptured Apollo playing the nine-stringed lira da braccio in the Segnatura has repeatedly been considered as a portrait of Giacomo San Secondo, the celebrated virtuoso on the lira da braccio at the court of Leo X, but this assumption has little basis in fact; see Chapter 14.

[2] See, for example, the print of the poet-musician Giovanni Filoteo Achillini playing the guitar, in Adam Bartsch, *Le Peintre graveur*, Vienna, 1802–21, Vol. XIV, 349, 469; Arthur M. Hind, *Marcantonio and Italian Engravers and Etchers of the 16th Century*, London, 1912, Pl. XI; Henri Delaborde, *Marcantoine Raimondi*, Paris, 1888, p. 252.

and its maker,[1] and this is not the place to augment this flood except to discuss two details that may have interested our painter. The *Patera* contains two musical instruments: the syrinx made of seven pipes in the centre and a small double oboe, the Lydian aulos, suspended beneath, both wind instruments and of Dionysiac connotation. The *Patera* also includes other symbols of generation and of the orgiastic realm of Dionysus: the little priapic herm and the *thyrsoi* tipped with pine cones behind the satyr and in front of the bacchante. Perhaps the gesture of the satyr's left hand[2] belongs to the same realm.

The artist who painted our picture was led to adapt the female figure to a new function. Laurel has replaced the vine, the animal skin has become a very civilized silk. The inclination of the head is less marked since her eyes are no longer fixed on the drinking horn. The left arm of the bacchante in the *Patera* was thrown back to enable the hand to squeeze the breast; now the upper arm falls so that the hand may grasp the viol.

The allegory of the muse inspiring the creative mind with her milk is of course an old one. Dante (*Purg.* XXII, 101) in the Poet's Limbo refers to no less a poet than Homer with the words, 'siam con quel Greco che le Muse lattàr più ch'altro mai,' and since then, it seems, this allegorical motive has lived on. Capaccio, *Trattato delle imprese*, Naples, 1592, p. 23, illustrates as the emblem of the city of Naples a siren squeezing milk from her breasts which falls on a lira da braccio (Fig. 24).[3]

[1] The *Patera Martelli* exists in several casts, of which the best belongs to the Victoria and Albert Museum (8717–1863). Another is in the Museo Nazionale at Florence (Pl. 89a). Its attribution to Donatello by Bode and others has been unanimously rejected in the last decades. The satyr and bacchante exist in separate Renaissance plaquettes: the Berlin Museum has plaquettes of both subjects (293, 294); the Victoria and Albert Museum, the bacchante (A48–1912). These plaquettes are copied after ancient models, a number of which still exist in various museums. (See *Catalogue of Italian Plaquettes*, Victoria and Albert Museum, London, 1924, p. 11.) I cannot exclude, of course, the possibility that our painter saw only a plaquette with the bacchante, although the connection with musical instruments and symbolism exists only in the *Patera*.

[2] Familiar still to Italians today as one of the protective magic gestures against *malocchio*.

[3] Capaccio's text explains the instruments as a symbol of Concordia: 'La Lira, significò la Concordia, che per quel celeste Simolacro se la dipingono propria i Napolitani in braccio d'una Sirena, e di sei corde, per l'unione di cinque piazze di Nobili, e una Popolare. Ma non parue a me buona mai l'Impresa di Sirena, mai di cosa buona significatrice, sempre fraudolenta, e che inganna; e direi che più tosto e Impresa per significar le delitie, e i gusti della Città, alludendo alla dolce, e delitiosa Partenope.' A true iconologist will not fail to consult his sacred books — Ripa, Cartari, etc.— and he will find direct relations not only with 'benignity,' but also with 'fecundity of the inventive mind.' Cesare Ripa, in his *Iconologia*, Rome, 1603, includes a woodcut showing Poesia, with the upper half of the body nude and with several musical instruments, among them a syrinx and a lirone (a large lira da braccio). The text explains that the breasts full of milk signify the wealth of ideas and inventions that are the soul of poetry ('mostrano la fecondità de' concetti & dell inventioni che sono l'anima della poesia'). In a similar pose, though with a different meaning, Charity (*Benignità*) is depicted and explained (see Ripa, 1618 ed., pp. 43, 66). I am indebted to Mr. Benedict Nicolson for drawing my attention to

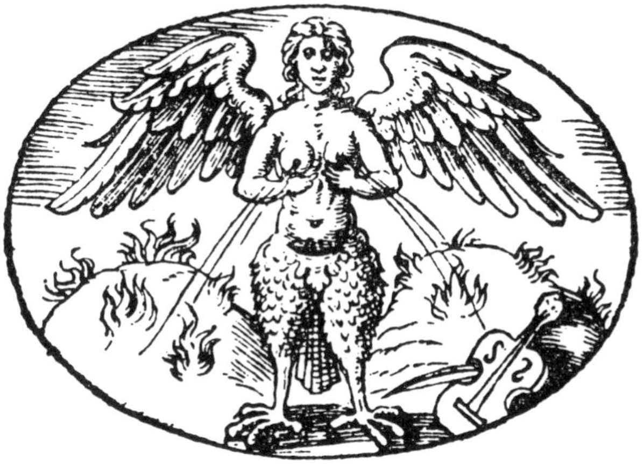

Fig. 24. Emblem of the City of Naples. From Capaccio, *Trattato delle imprese*, Naples, 1592.

While the right half of the *Patera* thus provided the model for the right half of the picture, one can hardly say the same of the left half, and it would probably be an over-estimation of the rejuvenating power of milk to relate the elderly satyr in the *Patera* to the youth in the picture. In any case it is quite obvious that the youth is not a free invention, but is borrowed from some other source. One has only to look at the unnatural position of the right hand that holds the bow. The model is apparently the naked youth at the left of Titian's *Three Ages of Man* in the Ellesmere Collection, exhibited in the National Gallery of Scotland (Pl. 90).[1] Here again, pose and contours, even the unruly hair, are almost identical; variations occur only so far as they help to adapt the figure to its new emotional and allegorical purpose. Complete clothing makes him a contemporary musician and therefore emphasizes the gap between a mortal musician and his mythological counterpart. The left arm now holds the viol, the right the bow. The right knee is lifted a little higher to support the instrument. One is tempted to assume that if the painter of our allegorical canvas did not see the

Giovanni Serodine's allegorical painting in the Ambrosiana as another possible example of lacteal baptism. On close inspection, I could detect only two very short stripes reaching upwards from the nipple of the right breast, but no trace of milk falling on the instrument. This instrument, by the way, is not a lute (as it is called in Schoenenburger, *G. Serodine*, Basle, 1957, p. 63), but a cittern (*cetra*), which sometimes has a symbolic connotation different from that of the lute.

[1] An attribution of our musical allegory to Van Scorel would coincide quite well with the date of Titian's *Three Ages*; Van Scorel went to Venice in 1520 and in 1522 to Rome, and Titian's *Three Ages* was painted early in his Giorgionesque period. Vasari dates the painting 1515. When I discussed the painting with Mr. Heinrich, I was glad to find that he also had related this figure to the Titian painting.

Titian painting itself, he was at least familiar with a print of it, and, though to my belief no print of it is known, one may assume that one existed because Titian's painting evidently served as a model through a print for other works of art — for example, the right side of an ivory relief of the *Infancy of Bacchus* in the Bavarian National Museum. Characteristically, the borrowed group appears there in reverse.[1]

Since our picture is a musical allegory and the musical instrument appropriately takes the centre of the scene (as the tool of a sacred art) between the symbolic figure and the artist from our world, a few words on the instrument itself and those in the *Patera* and in Titian's painting may be added.

As in our painting, in both the *Patera* and Titian's *Three Ages of Man* musical instruments are placed between the male and female figure. But these are wind instruments, while our painting shows a string instrument. This is quite in line with the symbolism connected with these instruments ever since antiquity and retained throughout the centuries in manifold modifications. The dichotomy between the two realms of strings and winds — with its emotional, aesthetic, religious, and social implications — is one of the most interesting chapters of the history of music and especially of musical instruments, and can only be hinted at here.[2] However, a few comments on the instrument in our painting and in its models may not be amiss and may even help to throw light on the allegorical intentions of our painter.

The syrinx and the aulos in the centre of the *Patera* do not appear in the two oval Renaissance plaquettes each of which shows separately one of the figures from the *Patera* (*e.g.* 645, 646 of the Berlin Museum).[3] It is evidently only in the original *Patera*, itself a *pasticcio*, that these two instruments appear, quite appropriately so between the satyr and the bacchante, together with other Dionysian attributes. The simpler of the two instruments is the syrinx, the traditional attribute of Pan, satyrs, shepherds, and the languishing Polyphemus of countless representations which were then adapted by *cinquecento* artists.[4]

[1] See Rudolf Berliner, *Die Bildwerke des Bayerischen Nationalmuseums*, Augsburg, 1926, IV, p. 93, Pl. 418 and 420.

[2] See Chapters 2, 4, and 14 above.

[3] See *Königliche Museen zu Berlin, Katalog, Bildwerke der christlichen Epoche*, Berlin, 1918, Pl. XLVII; *Catalogue of Italian Plaquettes*, Victoria and Albert Museum, 1924, xv.

[4] See, for example, the *Polyphemus* by Sebastiano del Piombo in the Villa Farnesina, and the one by Annibale Caracci in the ceiling frescoes of the Palazzo Farnese. Raphael, in one of the early stages of his *Parnassus* known to us in Marcantonio's engraving, gave the syrinx also to Erato, contrary to ancient tradition. Only later did he correct this deviation from ancient models when the strong current of humanist musical archaeology led him to borrow the instruments directly from an authentic ancient source, a Roman sarcophagus of the Muses, and to replace the syrinx by an aulos (see Chapter 14 above). Refer also to the seven-pipe syrinx carefully depicted by Filippino Lippi in his monochrome fresco on the window wall of the Cappella Strozzi in Santa Maria Novella. Strangely enough it is a musical treatise, Vincenzo

The more complicated instrument is the aulos (tibia), the attribute of Marsyas and the traditional requisite of revelry and Bacchic processions; in the Rome of the emperors it was also the never-absent accompaniment of animal sacrifice. Curiously, both the syrinx and the aulos of the *Patera* deviate in their design from their usual ancient representation. The syrinx, contrary to ancient tradition,[1] consists of two rows each of five pipes; in the two pipes of the aulos the fingerholes continue up the extreme end of each pipe, which acoustically is nonsense.

Small as these details may seem, they imply that the artist of the *Patera* was not entirely familiar with the ancient instruments he represented; an ancient sculptor would not have made such errors, even in a small background representation. But it is quite interesting that the Italian sculptor who united the two ancient figures in the *tondo* filled in the vacuum in the centre with appropriate ancient Dionysian attributes.

It is no less in the spirit of the ancients that Titian in his allegorical picture furnishes the loving couple with double pipes. The double pipes are not only symbolic of the vague association of Eros with music in a general sense, but actually link the two figures. He substitues 16th-century recorders for ancient oboes and thus is able to combine the seeming antiquity of the instruments with the actual contemporary technique of playing.[2]

Finally, our painting with the baptism by milk does not show an ancient instrument nor the reinterpretation of an ancient one, but represents instead a modern string instrument. It is a typical viol of the time, clearly recognizable by its deep body, its sloping shoulders, and its five strings. Viols of this shape with rounded contours without corners were not uncommon (specimens are preserved in the collection of the Vienna Kunsthistorisches Museum[3]), and the

---

Galilei's *Dialogo*, in a chapter on the plectrum of the ancients, which states that Filippino borrowed directly from ancient statuary and was advised by a humanist of no lesser stature than a Poliziano (see Chapter 13 above).

[1] See, for example, the bronze satyr from the Villa of Hadrian, now in the Museo Capitolino, who dances while the syrinx made of seven pipes hangs from the trunk of a tree. As one of many examples of the accurate use of the orthodox classical form of the syrinx in 16th-century symbolism, see Cartari, *Imagini*, 1581, with its beautiful woodcut of Pan holding a syrinx of seven pipes.

[2] This practice was quite common in the 14th and 15th centuries. One could enumerate a long line of examples, from Cossa's Schifanoia *Triumph of Venus*, in which a lady holds a double recorder in aulos fashion, to the double recorders in Rubens' *Triumph of Silenus* in the National Gallery, London. A similar adaptation is to be seen in Giulio Romano's *tondo* in Mantua in the Palazzo del Tè, Sala delle Medaglie, showing the sacrifice of a bull. Two musicians blow shawms which are so close to each other and held at such angles as to give the precise appearance of the two pipes of the aulos required by the ritual scene.

[3] See J. von Schlosser, *Die Sammlung alter Musikinstrumente*, Vienna, 1920, Nos. 71, 73, 74 (all 16th century). These specimens came from the famous Hapsburg Collection in the castle of Ambras in Tyrol.

four *C* holes also appear frequently, for instance in the viols played by angels in Grünewald's Isenheim Altar, in an engraving of a musician by Altdorfer, and in the instruments played by Apollo and one of the Muses in Luca Penni's *Parnassus*. The choice of a string instrument for our symbolical scene is quite significant, for these string instruments (lute, lira da braccio, viol) in the hands of the great virtuosi and *improvvisatori* were the tools of the most subtle and refined province of musical art.[1]

[1] On the subject of this article, see also my review of Günther Bandmann, *Melancholie und Musik, Ikonographische Studien* (Cologne, 1960), in *The Burlington Magazine*, April 1962; this work takes over the material of the present essay, but unfortunately with the addition of some misinterpretations.

16 · Musical Instruments for the Stage in Paintings by Filippino Lippi, Piero di Cosimo, and Lorenzo Costa

Italian feasts of the 15th and 16th centuries were full of music, both vocal and instrumental. Anyone who browses through the documents and *carteggi* will be overwhelmed by the profusion of details concerning the solo instruments and whole orchestras used in the *sacre rappresentazioni*, *intermedii*, and at many other festival occasions such as *trionfi*, weddings, funerals, and the spectacles that were the immediate precursors of the opera of the 17th century.

A concise interpretation of this material requires the synoptic study of numerous documents, such as records of the plans for spectacles and reports about them; the texts of plays; the visual material — paintings, drawings, and prints depicting the spectacles for posterity, as well as sketches made for their preparation; and the scores of the music that accompanied the spectacles. It may very well have been the complexity and variety of this material that has hampered systematic exploration. Often contemporary historians left detailed reports but no visual records came to us; in other cases, we have paintings or engravings that probably represent *feste* or were inspired by them, but we have no verbal reports by contemporaries to match them.

What the historian of music could hope to learn from this material would be the types of orchestras and ensembles used, the principles of alternation of vocal and instrumental groups, the fashions of accompaniment of solo singers and choirs, the various devices of *cori spezzati*, echo effects, and the like. With such ends in view, he could, for instance, approach such a painting as the Carpaccio *Ascension of the Virgin* (National Gallery, London), where we find no less than five different groups of angels with instruments distributed from the middle ground over the death bed up to the heavens, and relate it to reports such as that by Niccolò della Tuccia on the festivities of the Corpus Domini in Viterbo in 1462, where one could hear 'a singing of the hosts of the heavenly spirits, playing of magic instruments, frolicking, gesturing, laughter of all the heavens.'[1]

For the present study, we are interested only in a very small segment of this

[1] Sebastiano Ciampi, *Cronache e statuti di Viterbo*, Florence, 1852, Lib. VIII, p. 384 ff., quoted in Alessandro d'Ancona, *Origini del teatro in Italia*, Florence, 1877.

instrumental world: the bizarre instruments frequently represented in paintings of the *quattro-* and *cinquecento* that do not seem to fit into the gradual evolution of instruments from the *quattrocento* to the beginning of the Baroque. They are sometimes utterly fantastic in shape, sometimes more or less authentic reconstructions of ancient Greco-Roman instruments, and other times bastard forms between the latter and contemporary instruments. Some of the instruments so depicted seem unplayable, constructed by the painter's brush with no attention paid to functional or acoustical requirements; others, in spite of their unconventional nature, seem so well thought out that one has to consider them as instruments either portrayed after actual specimens or, at least, designed with so much musical and technological understanding that they might have been played.

For our purpose, we may single out paintings by Piero di Cosimo, Filippino Lippi, and Lorenzo Costa. The painting by Lippi that interests us here is his *Dance Before the Bull* (National Gallery, London), usually called — or, rather, misnamed — *The Adoration of the Golden Calf* (Pl. 93). This painting has provoked various iconographical interpretations.[1] One thing is certain: the dancing crowd adoring the bull is Oriental or Greek, judging by their garb, especially the turbans.[2] The numerous instruments represented are a strange mixture of contemporary and ancient shapes. The wind instrument at the left is a trumpet, coiled in S-shape, the form imported to Europe from the Near East and still frequently appearing in the *quattrocento* (for instance, in Fra Angelico's *Madonna dei Linaiuoli*, in the convent of San Marco in Florence). Likewise of oriental origin and frequent in the *quattrocento* is the pair of small kettledrums (*nacchere*) at the right of our painting; we find similar drums in the grandiose and, I believe, not sufficiently studied fresco of an angel concert by Michele Lambertini, in the large arch that separates the apse from the central vault in the Baptistery of the Cathedral of Siena. Another frequent *quattrocento* instrument is the tambourine or, more precisely, jingle drum, played in our painting by the second figure from the left. It is one of the few instruments that lived virtually unchanged from antiquity, where we find it depicted in numerous Bacchic sarcophagi, until the Renaissance and even later.

This leaves three instruments depicted *all'antica* but reconstructed with various degrees of reliability. The large coiled brass instrument towards the

[1] Katherine B. Neilson, *Filippino Lippi*, Cambridge, Mass., 1938, p. 153, gives a tentative interpretation of this scene; Otto Kurz, in his very interesting article, *Filippino Lippi's 'Worship of Apis,'* in *The Burlington Magazine*, LXXXIX (1947), p. 145 ff., explains the subject of painting as the adoration of Serapis by the Egyptians, as narrated in Petrus Comestor, *Historia scholastica, liber exodi*, Cap. IV (Migne, *Patrologia latina 198*, 1143).

[2] Greeks are frequently depicted with turbans; see the Pythagoras in Pinturicchio's fresco showing Musica, in the Borgia Apartments.

right (Pl. 94b) is a true Roman *buccina*, so accurately depicted in shape, proportions, and essential details, including its characteristic crossbar, that it must have been modelled after one of the Roman reliefs showing military processions. Roman military instruments were frequently depicted in the triumphs of the Renaissance, often with great archaeological precision, as for instance in Mantegna's *Triumph of Julius Caesar* (now in Hampton Court): '. . . when he painted in Mantua the triumphs of Julius Caesar, a rewarding topic for revealing the profound archaeological erudition he possessed in his time and his inclination to learn from ancient statuary.'[1] Another *Triumph*, following ancient models but with remarkable archaeological fidelity, is the relief made for Alphonso I, in the Castel Nuovo, Naples.

Much freer is the rendering of the kithara to the left of the buccina (seen also in Pl. 94b). While its design also stems fairly directly from ancient models (probably from sarcophagi of Muses or Marsyas), and while its functional character is evident, its shape has been simplified and, furthermore, it is embellished with typical Renaissance leaves.

The most puzzling instrument is the complex brass instrument played by the third figure from the left in the painting (Pl. 94c). This consists of two parallel metal tubes connected by two crossbars, both tubes ending in small bells; the player blows into the longer of the tubes. No instrument of this fantastic construction existed in antiquity or in the Renaissance. Still, the origin of the design can easily be detected. The instrument is a pictorial substitute for the ancient aulos, that double oboe required in ceremonial or sacrificial scenes. Similar more or less fantastic attempts to create the visual appearance of the aulos, which was not always functionally understood at that time, are quite frequent in Renaissance imagery. In Giulio Romano's *tondo* in the Palazzo del Tè, Mantua, representing the sacrifice of a bull, the appearance of an aulos is simulated by two large shawms played in the background by two different players, in such a way that the two tubes diverge at the same angle as the two pipes of an aulos usually do. A very subtle fusion of the aulos with the trumpet of Fama, for allegorical reasons, appears in Raphael's *Parnassus*.[2]

Yet the instruments depicted in Filippino's *Adoration of the Bull*, especially the 'ancient' ones, do not seem to be merely pictorial *staffage*, made to characterize the crowd as a musical one; they are painted with such a degree of realism that the spectator would expect to see their backs if he could only turn them around. One can hardly resist the belief that the painter must have seen them as real three-dimensional objects. Actually, such real instruments, however bizarre or fantastic, were used in the mythological plays or allegorical representations

[1] Milanesi, in his comments to his edition of Vasari, *Vite*, III, 458.

[2] See Chapter 14 above.

occurring in *intermedii, sacre rappresentazioni,* and other forms of theatrical display. Here, especially the kithara would point in this direction. Its simplified shape omits the resonating body; it could therefore have provided only very little volume of tone and was employed for its evocative appearance rather than for its sound.

The instruments are by no means the only details in Lippi's painting that remind us of the stage. The two symmetrical hills form stage wings, sharply dividing the foreground from the background and opening the vista on the distant sea. The straight line of dancers in the foreground, all equally near to the beholder, also strongly evokes stage design. Last but not least, the appearance of the bull in the sky corresponds strikingly to the numerous figures appearing in or descending from the sky that were quite routine in Renaissance stage machinery. It would have been easy to move the bull across the sky with the help of wires or ropes stretched between the two artificial hills, or with the help of unseen levers.

These strange features appear even more pronounced in Piero di Cosimo's famous *cassone* painting of *The Liberation of Andromeda* in the Uffizi (Pl. 92). This painting shows two successive phases of the liberation, with Perseus appearing in both. On the right, he is shown descending from the sky, in precisely the same manner as did many angels and deities on the Renaissance stage with the help of special machines (of which perhaps the most famous example is Brunelleschi's *macchina* devised for the descent of the Archangel Gabriel and eight other angels in the spectacles for the *Festa della Nunziata*[1]). In the centre of our picture, Perseus appears again, standing on the sea monster's shoulders[2] and reaching out to deliver the mortal blow. At the left, Andromeda is fainting, while the crowd averts its glance. At the right, however, we find the same crowd jubilant over her delivery and, in addition, there are two exotic musicians with strange instruments (Pl. 95a). The instrument at the left is held by a kneeling youth; it has a small sound box, which continues in an extremely long neck that termin-

[1] See Vasari, *Vite*, ed. Milanesi, II, 375 ff. Similar *macchine* were designed by Il Cecca for the *sacre rappresentazioni* on the Piazza del Carmine in Florence, where the cherubim and seraphim came down from heaven to announce to Christ 'il suo dover salire in cielo' (Vasari, *op. cit.*, III, 198). See also Sabbatini, *Pratica di fabricar scene e machine ne' teatri*, Ravenna, 1638, where these machines are explained in every technical detail, with illustrations, especially in Chapters 44 and 50.

[2] Similar sea monsters, dragons, and large serpents were extremely frequent on the Renaissance stage, and even outside, in processions such as the Provençal *tarrasca*. The *certamen pithicum* was a persistent element on the stage in Renaissance pageants. Gioseffo Zarlino, in his *Istitutioni harmoniche*, Venice, 1573, Pt. II, p. 79, mentions among the subjects recited by the ancients in their musical performances, 'la Battaglia di Apolline col serpente Pithone.' This combat was later the subject, for instance, of the third of the six *intermedii* performed in 1589 for the wedding of the Grand Duke Ferdinand I de' Medici to Christina of Lorraine, a spectacle of which we will speak later.

ates in a sickle-shaped peg box with side pegs. The upper end of the sound box tapers into a shape resembling the breast, neck, and head of a swan. Three strings run across the soundboard and over the neck to the peg box. This instrument, notwithstanding its fantastic shape, has a perfectly functional construction; its player is shown tuning it.

The other instrument, played by a dark-skinned musician in exotic garb, is much more complex: it has a large sound box, with seven strings running over two bridges. The upper end of the sound box continues in what seem to be two tubes, one short and the other a long one, bent back to run parallel to the side of the sound box. After this bend, the tube develops a bulbous extension in the shape of an animal head. Further down, we notice five side-holes and then a round bulb like that of a platerspiel (a simple form of bagpipe well known in the Renaissance; through its bulb, the tube receives air from the player's mouth by means of a short blow-pipe). While the left hand of the player plucks the strings, the right hand stops the fingerholes of the long tube. Curiously, the fingerholes are not between the blow-pipe and the mouth of the tube; thus the entire wind attachment is functional nonsense. However, as a combination of string sound with wind sound, it is only one example of a whole line of such instruments that seem to fulfil an old dream of musicians — the one-man orchestra.[1]

Piero's instruments, fantastic as they are, seem also to have been modelled after existing instruments, for which the obvious occasion may have been the *feste*. And, as in Lippi's painting, not only the instruments but the whole painting — its perspective, the theatrical dragon, the people shown both as a frightened and a jubilant 'chorus,' and the sky-born Perseus — indicates stage design. In this context it seems not unimportant that Piero was actively engaged in inventing and preparing *feste*.[2] And, what is even more important, there is evidence that painters of *cassoni* and similar decorative paintings were directly inspired by scenes from the theatre and from *feste*. It is, again, Vasari who, in a passage in his life of Dello Delli, emphasizes how widespread was the fashion to depict actual 'jousting, tournaments, hunts, *feste*, and other public entertainments. . . .'[3]

If, then, paintings like those discussed above are portraits of real *intermedio* scenes, or are at least influenced by actual stage performances, we should expect to find information on our fantastic and pseudo-ancient instruments in the

[1] Instruments blown and bowed at the same time appear in, for example, the recently restored angel concert by Gaudenzio Ferrari in the cupola of the Santuario at Saronno. In Praetorius's *Syntagma musicum*, Plate XXXI, an Arab spike fiddle is shown, the spike of which is a recorder (*flute douce*); the caption says: 'Monochordium, is a pipe and also has a string attached, which is bowed with a fiddle bow; common among the Arabs.'

[2] According to Vasari (*op. cit.*, IV, 135), he was the author of the *Carro della morte*.

[3] Vasari, *op. cit.*, II, 149.

literary reports describing such *feste*. In fact, these reports mention a bewildering number and variety of musical instruments designed for the stage. It is to this problem that we now turn.

One of the richest and most variegated spectacles of which we have a detailed report is the wedding of Francesco de' Medici and Giovanna d'Austria in Florence in 1565, described by Vasari.[1] A short analysis of the 'apparato' and of 'tutte le ceremonie ed effetti e pompe' may give us an idea of the manifold use of music and musical instruments. In Vasari's report we encounter, first of all, an enumeration of the decorations in various squares, streets, and bridges, and a description of the monuments such as portals, arches, obelisks, and equestrian statues, together with their surrounding scenery and with all the allegorical details employed. There is no lack of music and musical instruments in all these descriptions. Among the sculptures, we find that of a Muse with her flute, *amorini* singing odes, and other figures which appeared to sing, such as the three Graces ('pareva che cantassero con una certa soave armonia'), tritons blowing wind instruments (*buccine*), a whole choir of beautiful little angels engaged in singing, and so forth.[2] If Vasari considered it worthwhile to attribute these musical effects[3] to statues, we can easily imagine how many more musical activities were represented in all these decorations, and how much actual music was performed while the festival procession moved from one place to the next. But this was only the upbeat. The procession went to the Grande Sala del Palazzo, where an extraordinary spectacle was prepared for the guests. It was as if 'Paradise with all its angelic choirs had opened in this moment: an effect that was marvellously enhanced by a most sweet, masterly, and rich concert of instruments and human voices' (p. 572).

Then followed, as the main entertainment, d'Ambra's comedy *La Cofanaria*. Between the acts there were intermedii played, 'taken from that tender novel of Psyche and Cupid' by Apuleius. In the six intermedii, which were accompanied with real music by Corteccia and Striggio, we find a wealth of instruments. I will quote only some of the most interesting for the purpose of this study: the first intermedio showed Olympus with numerous Gods, which gave opportunity for 'soavissima armonia' (p. 573) and for 'un piacevolissimo coro' of the Hours and the Graces around Venus; in the second intermedio there appeared 'a little Cupid, who seemed to carry a lovely swan in his arms: in this swan, an excellent viol was hidden, and while the Cupid seemed to caress the swan with a swamp reed for a fiddle bow, it began to produce sweet music,' and soon after, the

[1] *Ibid.*, VIII, 519–622. [2] *Ibid.*, pp. 523 (Muse), 534 (*amorini*), etc.

[3] Vasari was a remarkable connoisseur of music, as one can judge from the numerous expert technical remarks in many of his *Vite*, and from the frescoes with which he decorated his own palazzino in Arezzo.

allegorical figure of music, 'recognizable by the musical hand [the symbolic Guidonian hand] on her head, and the rich garb decorated with her various instruments and various cards showing all the musical notes and tempos prescribed by her; but, even more, one could see her playing in sweet harmony a beautiful large lirone.'[1] Then four other cupids entered the stage, carrying 'four richly decorated lutes, also producing lovely sounds.' These cupids sang a madrigal describing the love of Amor and Psyche; the accompaniment was executed by 'lutes and many other instruments hidden backstage.' Thus we see here a variety of instruments. Some, like the lirone, are instruments *all'antica*; others are contemporary instruments, such as the violone, disguised for allegorical purposes, or beautifully decorated, such as the lutes.

The intermedii III, IV, and V used more dressed-up instruments. Intermedio III introduced Fraud and Deceit with their allegorical attributes, which could not help but produce a comical effect: 'they carried traps, fish hooks, or deceptive hooks under which were hidden, with singular ingenuity, curved pipes for the music they were supposed to produce'; and they also, like the cupids before them, performed a madrigal.

The description of the fourth intermedio mentions a rather subtle camouflage: two antropophagi or Lestrigones played trombones disguised as trumpets. In all probability, this especially interesting passage means that the martial significance of the trumpets had to be retained for the eye, although the ear was to be treated to the music of the much more flexible slide trombones.

Intermedio V included the most complex disguise. Four allegorical figures, Jealousy, Envy, Worry, and Scorn, had to defend themselves against four terrible serpents. Each grasped one of the snakes and beat it with thorny twigs. But, as soon as Psyche began to sing a madrigal, sweet instrumental music was heard; 'for in the snakes were cleverly hidden four excellent violins,' and in the twigs were four fiddle bows. In addition, four trombones furnished accompaniment from backstage.

The sixth and last intermedio brought Pan to the stage, with nine other satyrs, all 'holding various pastoral instruments beneath which other musical instruments were hidden.'

The intermedii were by no means the end of the festivities. They were followed by a 'Triumph of the Dreams,' which took place on the squares before Santa Croce and Santa Maria Novella. Here again, musical instruments were played, for instance, 'two beautiful sirens who, sounding two large trumpets instead of small ones, marched in front of all the others.' Then Fame appeared, with the customary attributes: 'carrying on her head a ball representing the

[1] For the lirone — the same instrument held by Armonia in one of the illustrations in Ripa's *Iconologia* of 1603 — see Chapter 5 above.

universe, and appearing to blow a large trumpet with three mouths.'[1] This fantastic trumpet reminds us somewhat of the brass instrument in Filippino Lippi's painting (Pl. 94c).

After the Triumph of the Dreams, there followed a procession of decorated cars, which had as their theme the genealogy of the gods. There were no less than twenty-one cars, of which I mention only those with interesting musical instruments. The fourth car, representing the Sun, showed, among many other figures, that of Orpheus, 'appearing to play a very ornate lira'; then the nine Muses, with various musical instruments; the tenth car again exhibited Fama, 'sounding a very large trumpet'; the fifteenth car showed Pan 'with a large *zampogna* of seven reeds.' *Zampogna* here does not mean a bagpipe, but the ancient syrinx (*syringe polycalume*). The twentieth car, devoted to Bacchus, was a boat of silver which carried, among other figures, several bacchantes and satyrs, 'playing various harpsichords and other similar instruments.'

The finale of the *festa* was a 'buffolata,' consisting of ten squadrons with various deities and allegorical figures. After all these secular spectacles in celebration of the wedding, there followed, in front of the Church of Santo Spirito, a performance of the traditional and famous *festa* of San Felice, as a religious finale to all the wedding festivities, 'with a very large apparatus, and with all the ancient instruments and not a few new ones added.' It is a pity that this interesting differentiation between old and new instruments is not elaborated by further details.

These occasional references by Vasari to instruments would in themselves permit us to judge what care must have been taken to make them appear convincing and realistic, and at the same time to adapt their shape to the allegorical meaning of the scene. And it goes without saying that wherever instruments *all'antica* were needed, they also were made to look realistic and, with the help of archaeological models and information, as authentic as some of those in Filippino's painting. In the case of disguised instruments, Vasari does not tell how the masking was actually done. Fortunately we find sufficient information on this point in the documents that report numerous details of the *feste* for the wedding of Grand Duke Ferdinand I de' Medici to Christina of Lorraine in 1589.[2] Artists of great reputation participated in the preparation of

[1] A four-pronged trumpet with four bells is blown by a winged Fama in a Flemish or northern French tapestry of the early 16th century, *The Triumph of Fama*, in the Metropolitan Museum of Art [A.N. 41.164.2].

[2] We selected the *Nozze* of 1565 for the description of the entire typical *feste* because they were more extensive and variegated, and because the reporter, Vasari, was a musical connoisseur. For details of performance, however, we prefer the *Nozze* of 1589, not only because of the excellent study of Aby M. Warburg (*I Costumi teatrali per gli intermezzi del 1589*, in his *Gesammelte Schriften*, Leipzig and Berlin, 1932, I, 259–300), with the important comments by Dr.

these spectacles: Giovanni Bardi as chief organizer, Emilio de' Cavalieri as stage and music director, Bernardo Buontalenti as stage architect and engineer of the theatrical machines, and Marenzio, Malvezzi, Peri, and again Bardi and Cavalieri, as composers. In addition to several comedies, a football game in costume, and animal fights on the Piazza Santa Croce, a *sbarra* (rope-dancing) and a *naumachia*, a *corso al Saracino*, and a masquerade of Rivers, there was a performance of six intermedii from the comedy *La Pellegrina*, 'nel gusto antico.' Unlike the six intermedii of 1565 described above, which represented in sequels one single theme — the story of Amor and Psyche — the intermedii of 1589 were only loosely connected, but all celebrated the power of music. Their titles were: 1) *L'armonia delle sfere* (The Harmony of the Spheres); 2) *Lo gara fra Muse e Pieridi* (The Contest of the Muses and the Pierians); 3) *Il combattimento pitico d'Apollo* (The Pythian Combat of Apollo); 4) *La regione dei demoni* (The Region of the Demons); 5) *Il canto d'Arione* (The Song of Arion); 6) *La discesa di Apollo e Bacco insieme col Ritmo e l'Armonia* (The Descent of Apollo and Bacchus with Rhythm and Harmony).

There is no need for a detailed analysis of these intermedii since they have been examined minutely from the iconographical point of view in Warburg's excellent study. What chiefly interests us here are the instruments, their types, their manufacture and, in many cases, their disguises. On this point we receive information from the *Memorie e ricordi* of Girolamo Serjacopi, Provveditore delle Fortezze di Firenze,[1] in which is contained, among other things, the technical instructions given by Bardi for each single instrument — instructions that were forwarded to the theatre workshop (*guarda roba*).

Stage instruments were disguised with papier-maché (*cartapesta*) or covered with veils, taffeta, or other cloth to fit the scenes and their allegorical functions. One of the instructions reads: 'other papier-maché to cover instruments' (*strumenti da sonare* — thus, real instruments!), and again, similarly: 'Decorate the instruments of the musicians with taffeta and veils.' The first intermedio (*L'Armonia delle sfere*) required instruments to fit (visually) the celestial rays: 'Decorate the harps, lutes, and other instruments so that they look the same as the celestial rays,' and 'Attach to the lutes, harps, and other instruments some ribbons and pieces of papier-maché or other material to make them look like rays of stars.' There was evidently much gilding.

In the second intermedio (*Lo gara fra Muse e Pieridi*), the instruments were adapted to the pastoral setting by covering them with foliage. The fourth intermedio, which presented Hell, required instruments posing as snakes.

Gertrude Bing (*ibid.*, p. 394 ff.), but also because there exists a great wealth of technical information on their stage details, including the musical instruments.

[1] Archivio di Stato, Florence, Arch. Magistrato delle Nove, fa. 3679.

Accordingly, viols[1] as well as trombones were camouflaged: 'Signor Bernardo says to give to the keeper of costumes the designs of the four viols that look like serpents . . . the wrapping of taffeta around the trombones to make them look like serpents is the duty of the keeper of costumes,' and also: 'four violoni should be covered with taffeta painted green, and scales, and gilded to look like serpents. . . .' The fifth intermedio, which introduced the singing Arion, required instruments appropriate for tritons and nymphs (following the ancient Roman representations, in the manner used before by Raphael and Giulio Romano), and wind instruments had to be masked as conch shells: 'Decorate the instruments of the goddess and the nymphs to make them look like sea shells, and do not forget the dolphin,' and 'it will be necessary to make the instruments look like sea shells and other things from the sea.'

These examples could of course be multiplied *ad infinitum*. It is not without interest that one can find many analogous ones in the *sacre rappresentazioni*. The abundance of instruments used there is documented, for instance by a text describing the transportation of the head of St. Andrew in Rome in 1462: 'one saw boys in the form of angels; some of them sang sweetly, others played organs; no instrument of the art of music was lacking. . . .'[2] The reports on the procession of the Corpus Domini, in the same year in Viterbo, mention the representation of paradise: 'singers, representing angels, intoned sweet chants . . . now one could hear lovely melodies sung by human voices, now delightful chords played by musical instruments. . . .' Later, in the course of the procession: 'sounded the trumpets, the organs, and innumerable musical instruments. . . .' And during the enacting of the Assumption of the Virgin, which was also part of the celebrations, there was 'a singing of the hosts of the heavenly spirits, playing of magical instruments, frolicking, gesturing, laughter of all the heavens. . . .'[3] Nor were the disguised instruments absent in the *sacre rappresentazioni*. D'Ancona[4] mentions 'una mascherata' in Florence, described in the diary of San Gallo (p. 153), having a representation of Hell and its devilish monsters: 'Thereupon came twelve standard-bearers on horseback, disguised as dragons . . . and trumpet players disguised as dragons with muted trumpets, and with wings, a fearful sight indeed.'

If we review these examples, we notice the careful attention given to the instruments in the course of the *feste*, and the precision with which they are adapted to the mythological or allegorical topics of the spectacles. These instruments can be classified into two main categories: on the one hand, instruments that are transformed into fantastic ones, thereby losing their musical

[1] In the fifth intermedio of the wedding of 1565, there were four serpent viols.

[2] Pius II, *Comentarii*, Rome, 1584, Lib. VIII, p. 365.

[3] Ciampi, *op. cit.*, VIII, 384 ff.

[4] *Op. cit.*, I, 273.

function, as in the case of the trumpet of Fame with its three bells; and, on the other hand, instruments that retain their function but are adapted to the scene by appropriate masking, as the violoni disguised as serpents and the bows disguised as twigs.

The subjects of the profane *feste*, whether intermedii or trionfi, were (almost without exception) mythological. Only the more vulgar spectacles, such as tournaments *a la Saracena* or animal fights, were free of classical influence. But for mythological subjects, the *gusto antico* demanded 'ancient' instruments for the stage, especially when protagonists such as Apollo, Orpheus, Amphion, and the Muses had to recite in the ancient manner, playing their own accompaniment. But the organizers of the spectacles found themselves in difficulties, for if they tried to follow the instructions given by the humanists and proceeded with archaeological precision, they must have realized that the 'ancient' instruments could not be played, because the playing technique of the Renaissance differed radically from that of the ancients. In fact, the ancient kithara and lyre were instruments with 'open' strings, each sounding their full length without being stopped against a fingerboard as is done on the lute or violin. The kithara and lyre, lacking a neck, had no fingerboard at all. The open-string technique of the Greeks, whether with plectrum or fingers, was totally different from the Renaissance stopping technique. And, in spite of all humanist research and attempts to rediscover and reconstruct Greek music, it was, after all, contemporary polyphonic or chordal music that was to be played in the *feste*. The interesting dilemma which resulted was solved in various ways.

The easiest way around the problem, and at the same time the most musically satisfactory way, was based on a falsification of history: this was the employment of the lira da braccio,[1] an instrument eminently suited by virtue of its five melody and two drone strings to polyphonic solo recital (*bicinia* and *tricinia*, according to Praetorius) and to recitation by singers who accompanied themselves. In texts of the Renaissance, this instrument is often called 'lira' and sometimes 'lira antica,' to distinguish it from the 'lira moderna.' According to a widespread belief, it was invented by Sappho and, in view of this, its appearance in the hands of countless representations of Apollo, Orpheus, and allegories of Music was not considered an anachronism. Even as late as the 17th century, the large statue of Apollo standing at the right of the left-hand Fontana dell Organo, in the garden of the Villa d'Este in Tivoli, holds a life-size lira da braccio. There is no doubt that the instrument was used in stage performances. Peruzzi, who gave the instrument to all the musical heroes in his frieze of Ovid's *Metamorphoses* in the Villa Farnesina, would certainly have had no qualms about having it used on the stage and in the plays that he helped to prepare.[2] It occurs often

[1] See Chapter 5 above.

[2] Vasari, *Vite*, ed. Milanesi, IV, 600 ff.

in paintings, with fantastic and elaborate decoration, as in the *King David* of Bartolommeo Passerotti, in the Galleria Spada (Pl. 32a). A lira da braccio decorated with plant-like curves and curls, in Gaudenzio Ferrari's *Virgin with St. Anne* (Pinacoteca, Turin; Pl. 34b), reminds us of the decoration of a lira 'alla boscareggia [*sic*]' mentioned in the description of the second intermedio in the *feste* of 1589. It is not without interest that two twigs spiralling away from the sound box in the latter example seem to suggest the arms of the ancient lira.

The second way out of the dilemma was to show unplayable instruments on the stage, instruments made to conform to archaeological standards or mythological tradition, and to supply the real sound by other instruments backstage.[1] We have encountered instruments of this type before, in the descriptions of *feste*, and we should here like only to refer to one example in painting, the stag-head lyre in Filippino Lippi's *Allegory of Music* (Kaiser Friedrich Museum, Berlin; Pl. 96b). Among the traditional attributes of Musica in the Renaissance were the swan and the stag. The latter, as traditional symbol of the speed of sound, is represented here not as a living animal (as it is in the allegory of Music engraved by Cornelis Floris), but only by its head, which serves as the body of an ancient lyre. This lyre is a strange mixture of completely fantastic elements and elements borrowed from ancient models with almost pedantic care. The yoke, with its elaborate form, and the strings — seven, with one of them broken — are archaeologically correct, as is the use of animal horns for arms to carry the crossbar. On the other hand, the second crossbar, beneath the first one, is sheer invention, and so is the way in which the upper and lower ends of the strings are attached. Last but not least, the instrument could not have produced much sound,[2] for the stag's head is not a real resonator or sound box. And even if it were, the strings do not reach it. Thus the instrument is entirely unfunctional, but, since it is conceived with the pretension of reality, it seems closely related to the theatrical showpieces used in the intermedii and other spectacles. The large bone plectrum beneath the lyre and the syrinx comprised of seven canes are faithfully copied after Roman sarcophagi, and the little pipe beneath the syrinx combines the appearance of a small contemporary shawm with that of an ancient aulos, for it has at least two of the rings with projecting cups that are the standard equipment of the fully developed Roman tibia. While this

[1] In pictorial representation, we often find instruments *all'antica* mixed indiscriminately with modern instruments. In a Flemish tapestry of about 1585 in the Uffizi (Pl. 95c), showing a festival given for the Polish ambassadors, we see Parnassus, upon which is Apollo with an ancient lyre, while the Muses beneath him play a *cornetto curvo*, a lute, and an ensemble of viols. Vasari, however, in his costume sketches, usually showed more archaeological ambition, and furnished Muses with even wind instruments *all'antica* (Pl. 95b).

[2] Leonardo's famous lira (Vasari, *Vite*, ed. Milanesi, IV, 18, 28, 29), shaped like a horse's skull and decorated in silver, was no doubt a lira da braccio used by him to accompany his recitation. See my article in *Die Musik in Geschichte und Gegenwart*, XIII, Kassel, 1966, col. 1664.

pseudo-aulos is not a functional instrument, it reveals the respect paid to the musical practice of the ancients.

This leads us to a third possible solution of the dilemma of combining archaeological precision with modern playing techniques: the invention of bastard instruments shaped to some extent after ancient models but incorporating modern functional elements that permitted the actual performance of Renaissance music. Here again, we find an example in the work of Filippino Lippi, namely in the wonderful grisaille frescoes on the window wall of the Cappella Strozzi (Pl. 74b) in Santa Maria Novella, Florence.[1] Of the four musical instruments depicted around the figure of Parthenice, the large string instrument held by Parthenice interests us most. Its lower part is precisely that of an ancient kithara: a large sound box with two gracefully curving arms that would normally carry the crossbar. But here they carry no crossbar, at least not directly; two columns are grafted on them, and it is only their capitals that carry the crossbar — or, rather, what poses as a crossbar, for the strings are attached not to it but to a three-leafed flat head that resembles the leaf-shaped flat head of the common lira da braccio. This head is connected with the sound box by a neck with fingerboard, and it is this fingerboard over which all the strings run. Thus we can say that this instrument is a kithara adapted to the Renaissance technique of stopping the strings by the addition of a neck like that of a lute, viol, or lira da braccio. Another contemporary feature is the round sound-hole in the soundboard, which resembles that of a lute. The bone plectrum in Parthenice's right hand follows ancient models. For want of a better term, we may call this instrument a lyre-guitar, simply because it resembles those lyre-guitars that became fashionable for a short time as ladies' instruments in the French Empire.

Thus this bastard instrument, constructed to reconcile Greek appearance with modern playing style, was a logical if fanciful compromise between the old and the new; and its inventor, whether Lippi or perhaps a stage designer before him, in fact repeated only the transitory stage in an evolution that took half a millenium, from late antiquity to the *trecento* — the gradual transformation of ancient string instruments into the fingerboard instruments of the Middle Ages. In this light it does not seem an accident that Lippi's lyre-guitar strikingly resembles the lyre-guitars in the Utrecht and Cambridge Psalters, where they are frequently depicted side by side with their immediate predecessors, the kitharas of antiquity.

This example of adaptation of ancient instruments to modern playing technique is by no means unique. We find such bastard instruments frequently in other paintings, and I believe they must have been used on the stage. Two of the

[1] See Chapter 13 above.

most carefully constructed instruments of this type are found in two mysterious paintings by Lorenzo Costa, both painted for the studiolo of Isabella d'Este in the Palazzo Ducale in Mantua, and now in the Louvre. It is not likely that these two paintings represent actual stage scenes, for we know the accurate and even pedantic instructions given by the Marchesa when she commissioned some of the other paintings for her studiolo from Giovanni Bellini and Mantegna, and in all probability similar instructions were also given for the two paintings by Costa. Nevertheless, if one examines these two paintings, one can hardly fail to be struck by their resemblance to actual stage sets; and, among the accessories, it is precisely the musical instruments which make us think of the theatre and can, in fact, hardly be explained if they are not considered as stage instruments. After all, Costa, like Piero di Cosimo before him, was engaged in the preparation of actual *feste*.[1] In all probability, he must have been familiar with the brilliant *feste* in Ferrara, such as those of 1503 which were honoured by the presence of Isabella d'Este and Lucrezia Borgia. Much ink has flowed concerning the meaning of these two allegorical paintings, but again we do not need to touch on their iconographical significance here, and may restrict ourselves to the instruments important to our study, the lyre-guitars in each of the two paintings.

In the painting frequently referred to as *The Court of the Muses of Isabella d'Este*, four musicians encircle the central scene. The two bearded figures nearer the front are evidently Greek or Oriental; their instruments can be seen only in part. The two figures towards the background, however, are evidently classical mythological figures. The left-hand figure (Orpheus?), enraptured, plays a lira da braccio. The one on the right (Sappho?) holds a lyre-guitar (Pl. 96a). Here the classical form of the kithara, with its arms, is precisely retained; but instead of one crossbar there are seven, and none of them is functional. A neck is grafted on to the sound box, ending in a long thin peg box with side pegs, and a square flat head with three additional frontal pegs. This instrument could certainly have been played in guitar fashion, although it may not have been comfortable to stop the strings on its neck, which could not be easily grasped. The other allegorical painting also contains a lyre-guitar, in addition to a lira da braccio, psaltery, syrinx, and other wind instruments. The lyre-guitar is held by a youth crowned with laurels (Pl. 96c), and consists, again, of the body of a kithara with a neck grafted on it. Here we have only one crossbar, but this penetrates the arms and the sound box at the middle and therefore cannot carry any strings, since the strings run the length of the soundboard and the neck. Costa is also not very consistent here: there are seven strings in all, but only six pegs on the flat head. Unlike the other lyre-guitar, this one has seven frets on the fingerboard.

[1] Vasari speaks of 'due trionfi, tenuti bellissimi, con molti ritratti,' in the frescoes for San Jacopo Maggiore in Bologna (*Vite*, ed. Milanesi, III, 135).

While my hypothesis that the instruments represented in the paintings discussed above, and possibly in many others, were actual stage instruments is, I believe, supported by some internal evidence, it would be immeasurably strengthened if real stage instruments of this sort had survived. Unfortunately, like most other tools designed for special use, these seem to have perished when their usefulness ceased. Francesco Sansovino, in his *Venezia, città nobilissima*, Venice, 1580, mentions, in the chapter on Venetian 'studi di musica,' the collection of Agostino Amadi, which included 'instruments not only *alla moderna*, but *alla Greca et all'antica*, in rather large numbers.' One would hardly be mistaken is assuming that these instruments *all'antica* were theatre instruments.

However this may be, we are lucky to find at least one instrument still surviving that could hardly have been anything but a theatre instrument. It is a curious bastard instrument (Pl. 94a), probably from the beginning of the 16th century, now in the Vienna Kunsthistorisches Museum;[1] it belonged to that part of the Habsburg collections that originally came from the famous Obizzi di Catajo collection. The body of this instrument, painted blue and gold, imitates in baroque patterns the form of the ancient kithara; like Costa's and Lippi's lyre-guitars, a long neck has been grafted on. This neck has eight divisions of brass and, like the contemporary chitarrone, two peg boxes — one for the six shorter strings and the other for the eight basses. The flat sound box produces only a limited sonority and this makes us think that it served largely a decorative function on the stage, at the same time permitting the illusion that it could be played.

We hope that the result of this little study may be of interest to the historian of music, since it may help to establish a clear distinction between functional and nonfunctional instruments — a line not easy to draw without relating instruments represented in paintings to those used on the stage, especially since even real and playable instruments were often cast in bizarre shapes and decorated in fantastic manners. Moreover, it may be of value to the historian of Renaissance music to find that the interest of the *quattro-* and *cinquecento* in antiquity extended also to the reconstruction of ancient instruments and to their representation in paintings as well as on the stage. A by-product of this study might be the suggestion that some Renaissance paintings that have not been connected with pageants for the stage should be considered as visual records of actual *feste*, or at least as closely related to theatrical imagination of the time, especially through the very instruments which appear in both.

[1] J. Schlosser, *Die Sammlung alter Musikinstrumente*, Vienna, 1920, item C. 94. In this catalogue, the instrument is called a 'Lyra-Cister.'

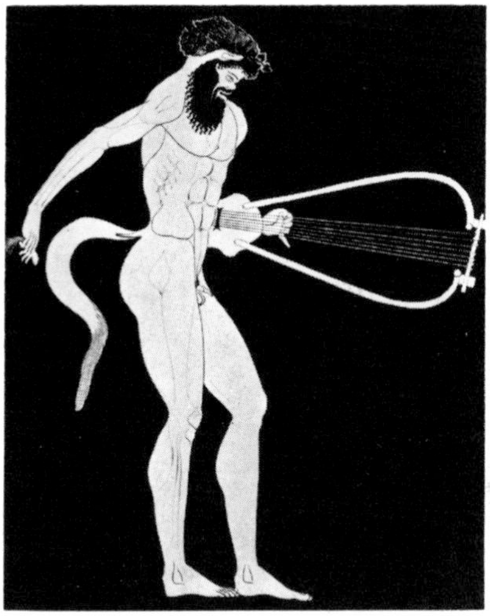

a. (*left*). Silenus with lyre, from red-figured Greek amphora, c. 490 B.C.

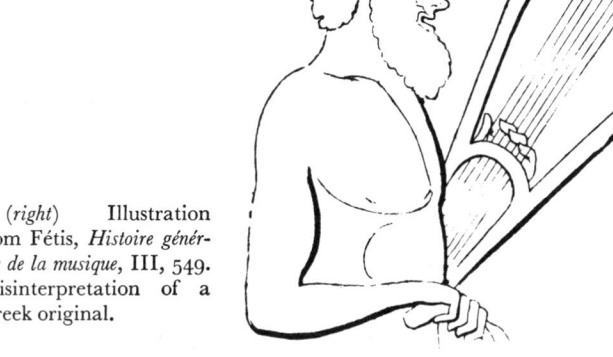

b. (*right*) Illustration from Fétis, *Histoire générale de la musique*, III, 549. Misinterpretation of a Greek original.

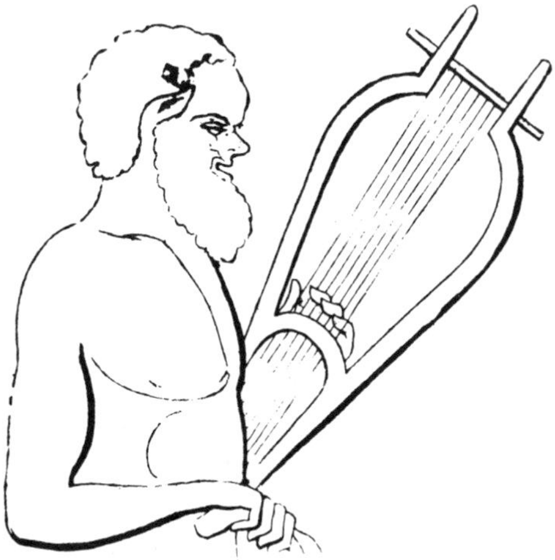

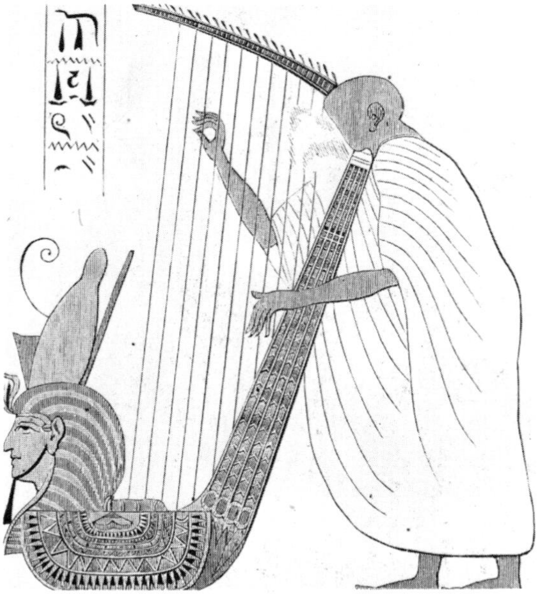

c. Illustration of a harp, from Fétis, *Histoire*, I, 255, after a reliable archaeological drawing of the wall painting in the tomb of Ramses III.

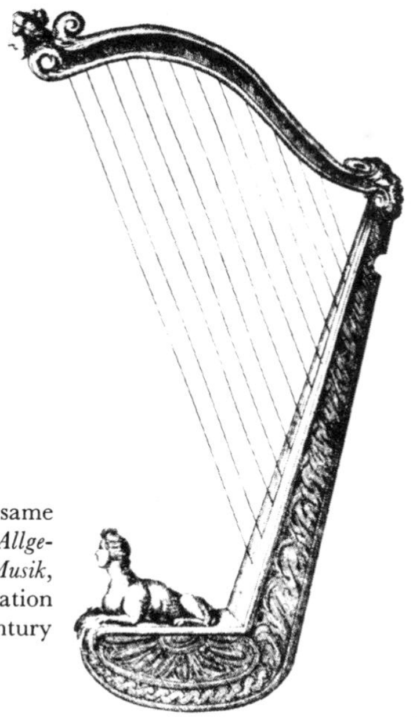

d. Illustration of same harp in Forkel's *Allgemeine Geschichte der Musik*, I, Tab. 5. An adaptation to please 18th-century taste.

e. Upper margin of an illustration from a Florentine choirbook, showing four trumpets in symmetrical duplication, overpowering the string instruments. Cleveland Museum of Art, J. H. Wade Collection.

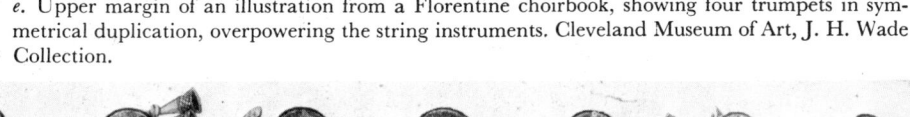

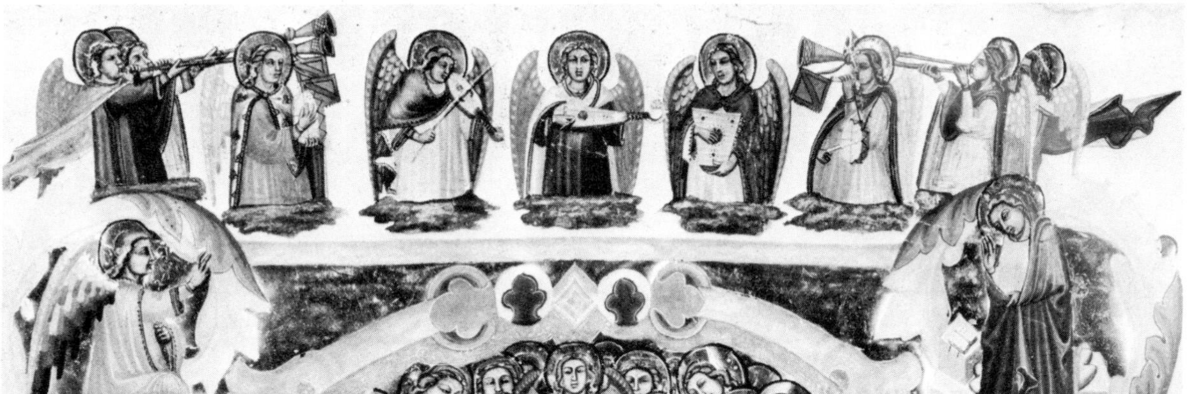

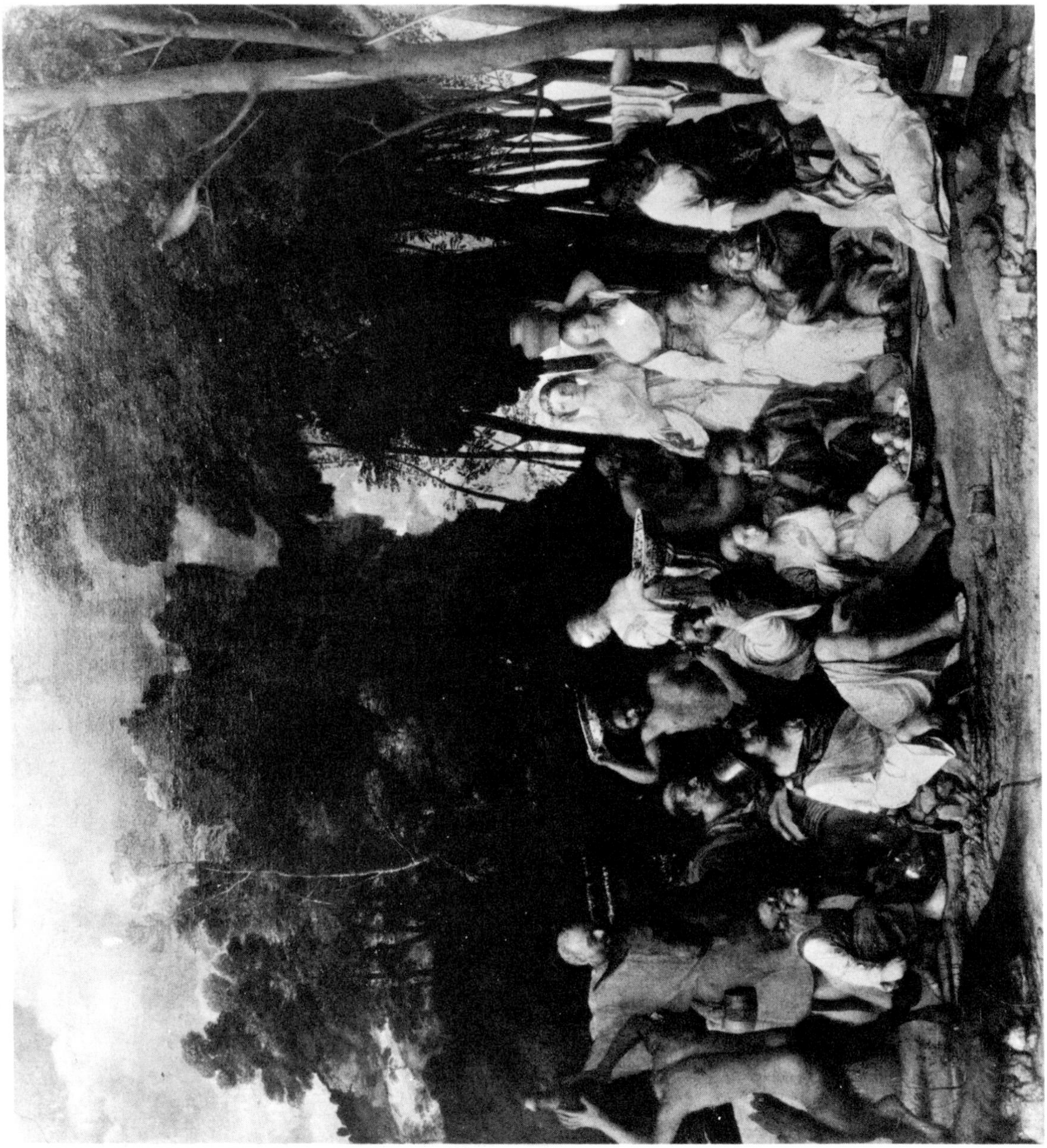

Giovanni Bellini, *The Feast of the Gods.* National Gallery, Washington, D.C.

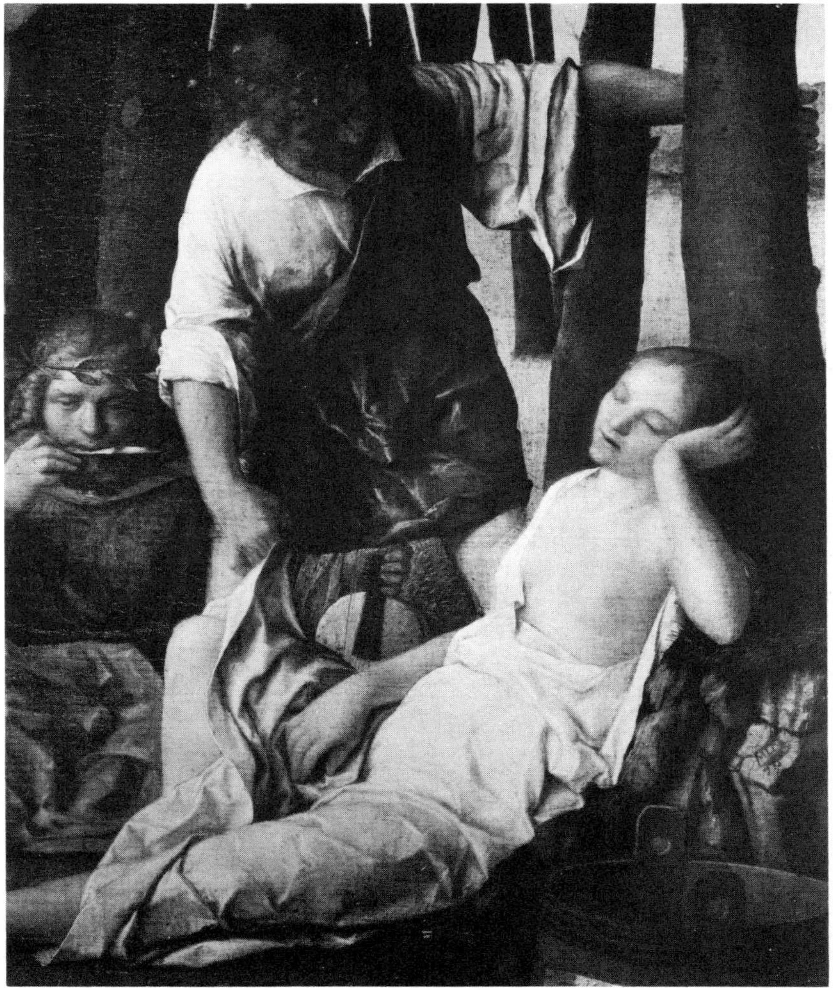

a. Detail of Plate 2.

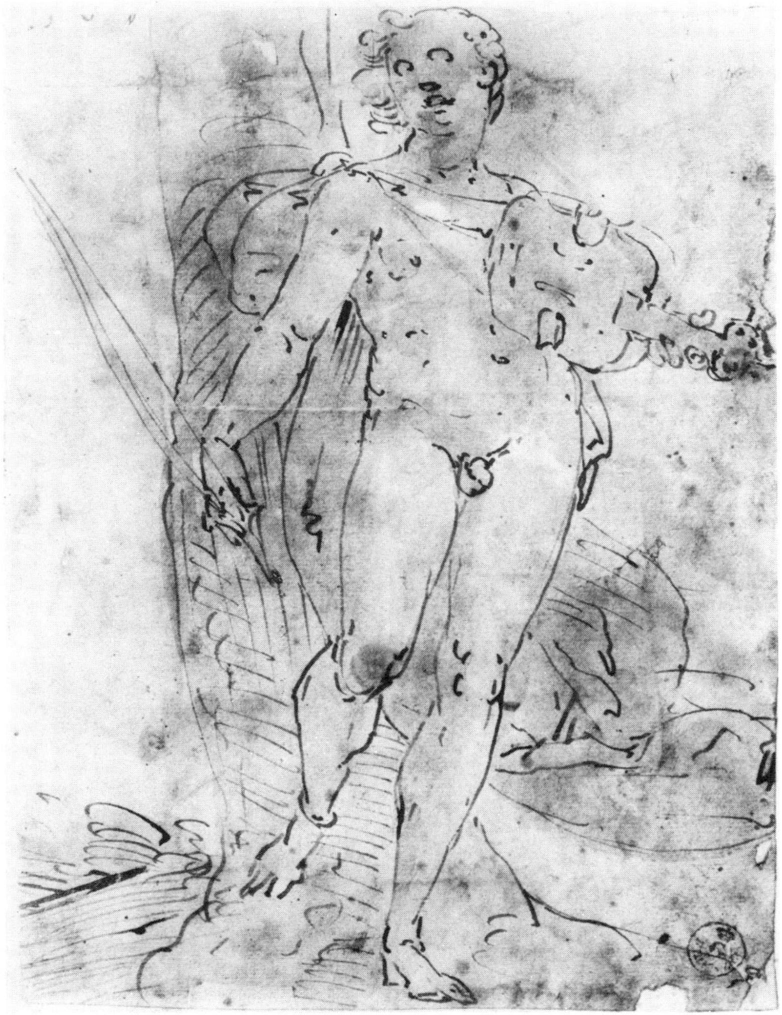

b. Luca da Cambiaso, *Lira da braccio player*. Uffizi, Florence.

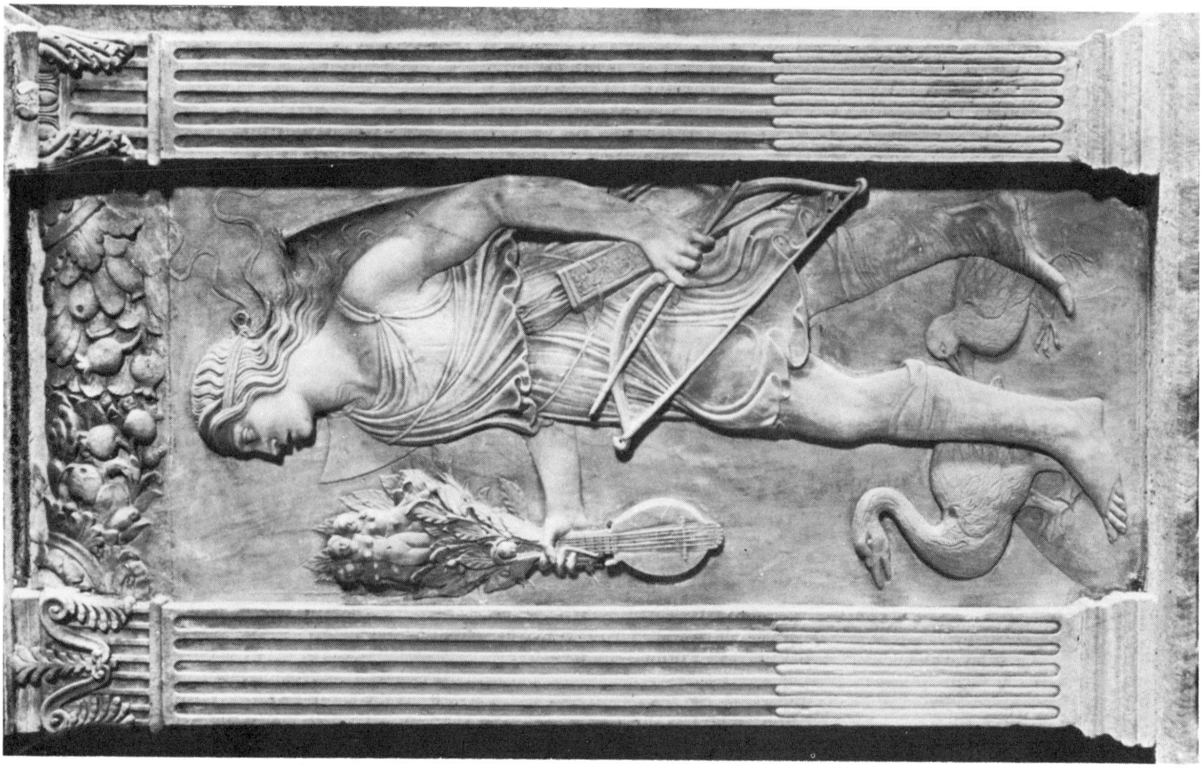

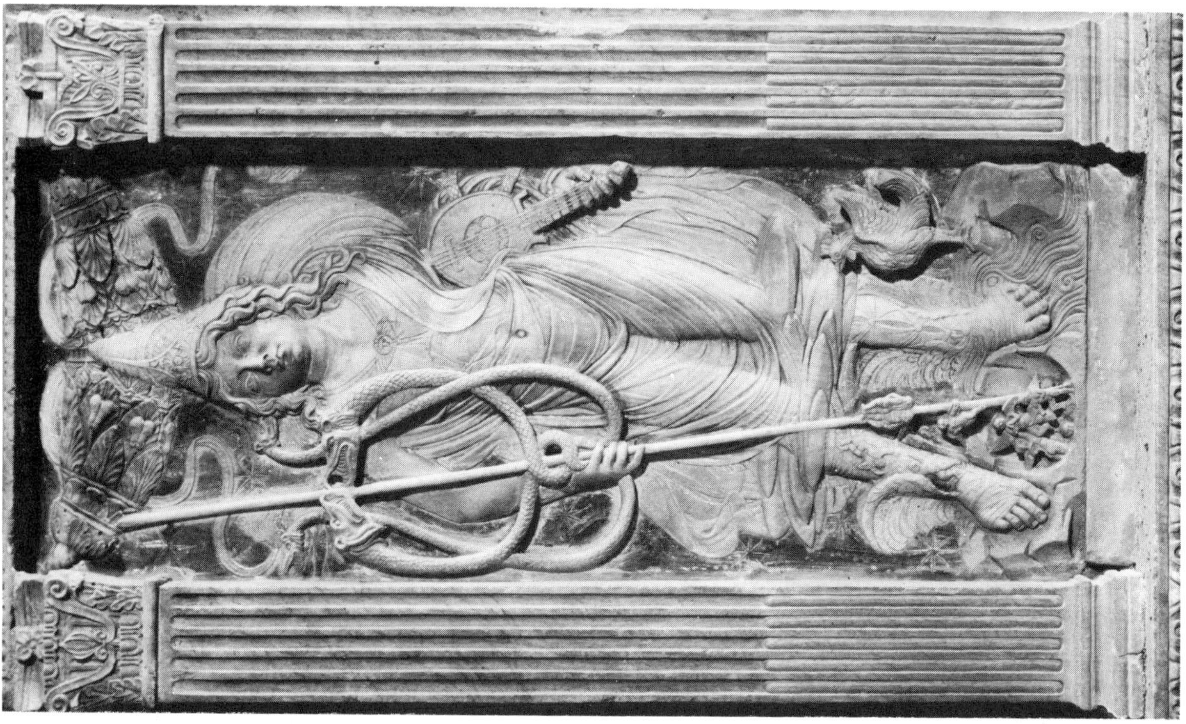

a. Agostino di Duccio, *Mercury*. Tempio Malatestiano, Rimini.

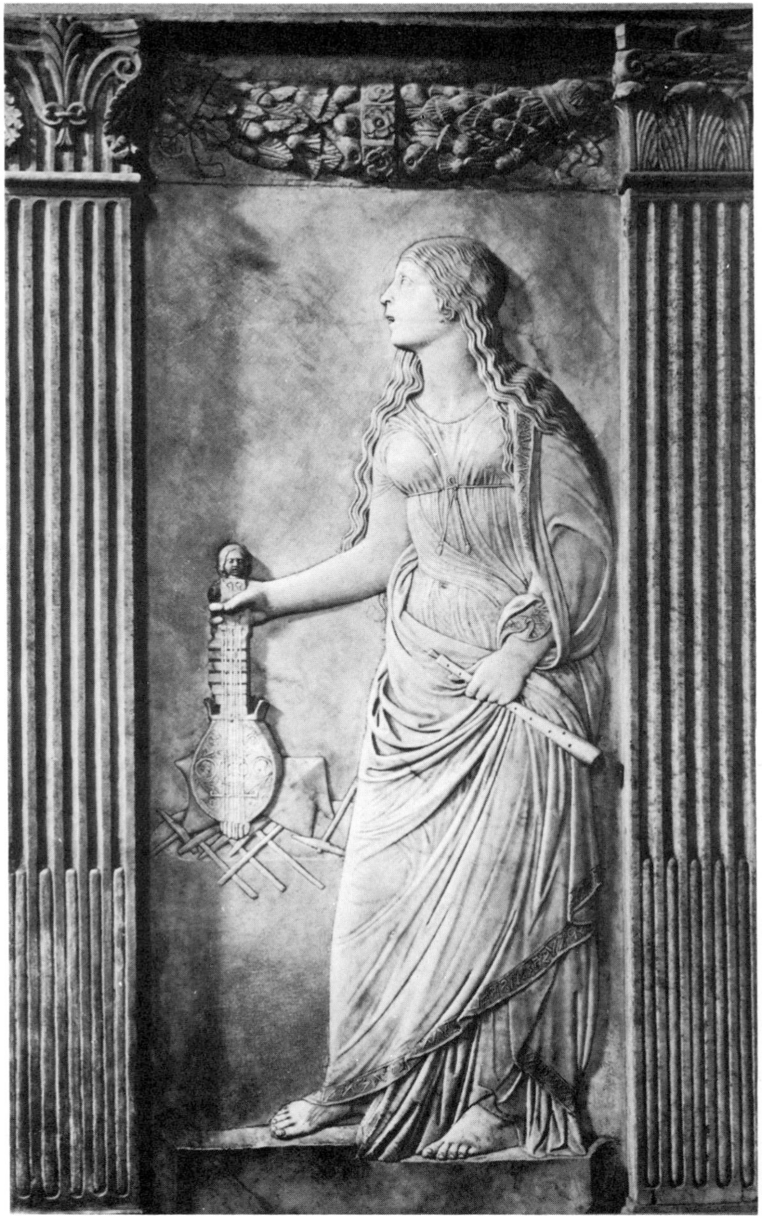

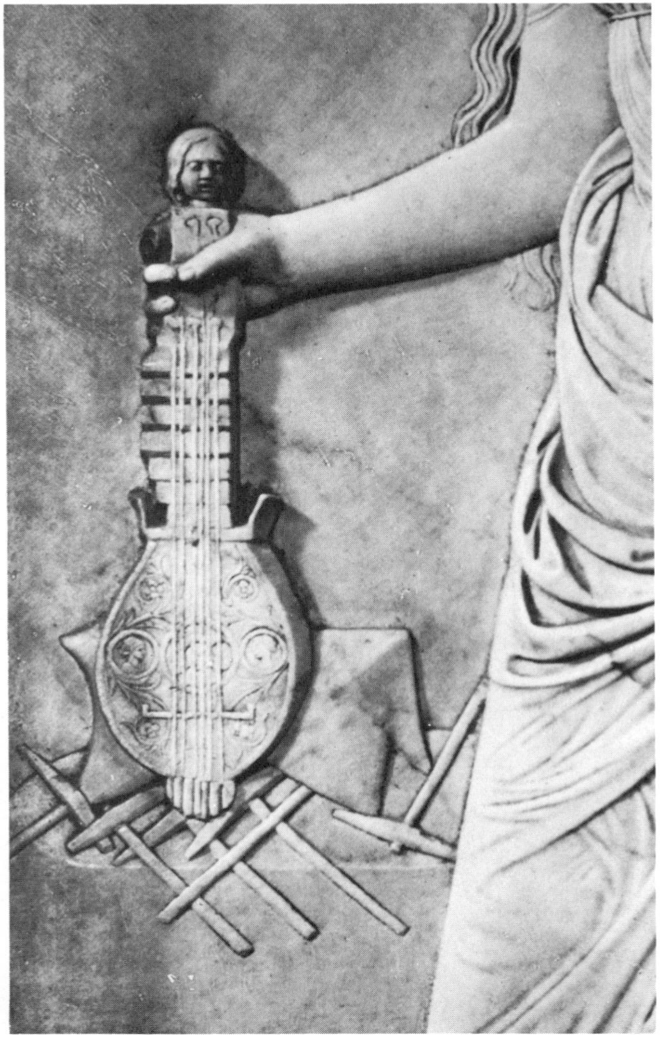

a. (*left*). Agostino di Duccio, *Musica*. Tempio Malatestiano, Rimini.

b. (*right*). Detail of Plate 5*a*.

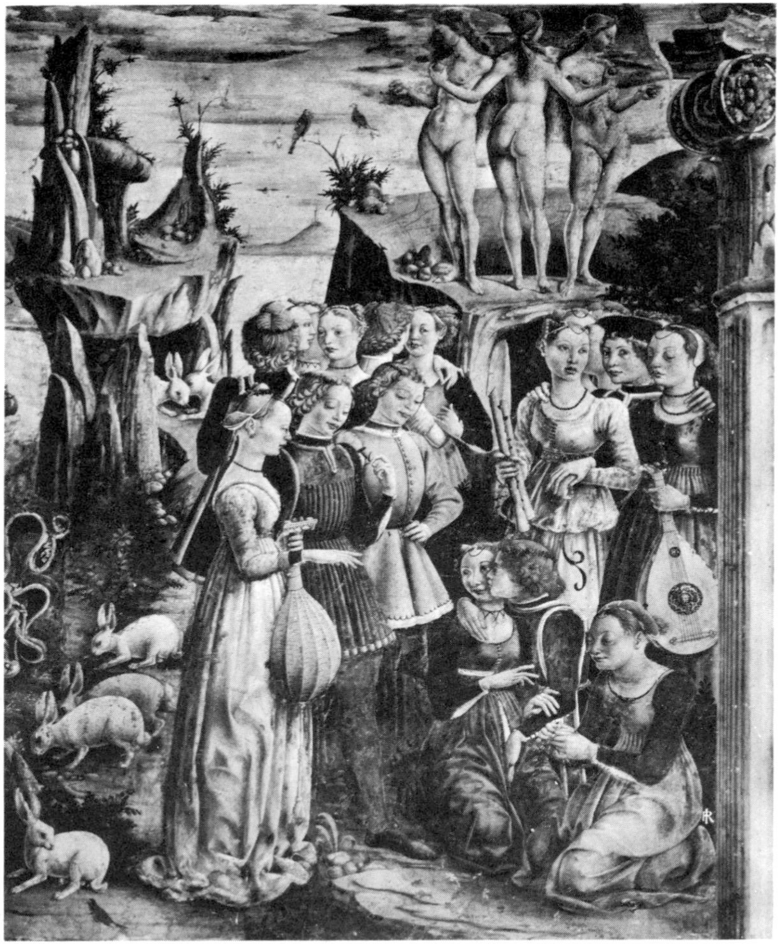

a. Francesco Cossa, detail from the frescoes in the Palazzo Schifanoia, Ferrara.

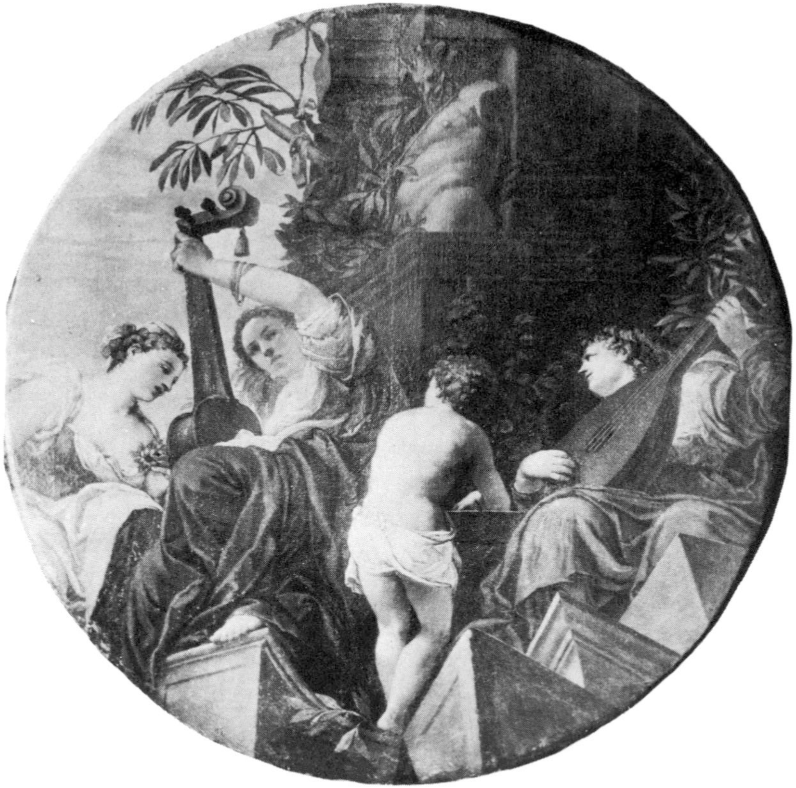

b. Paolo Veronese, *Allegory of Music*. Palazzo Ducale, Venice.

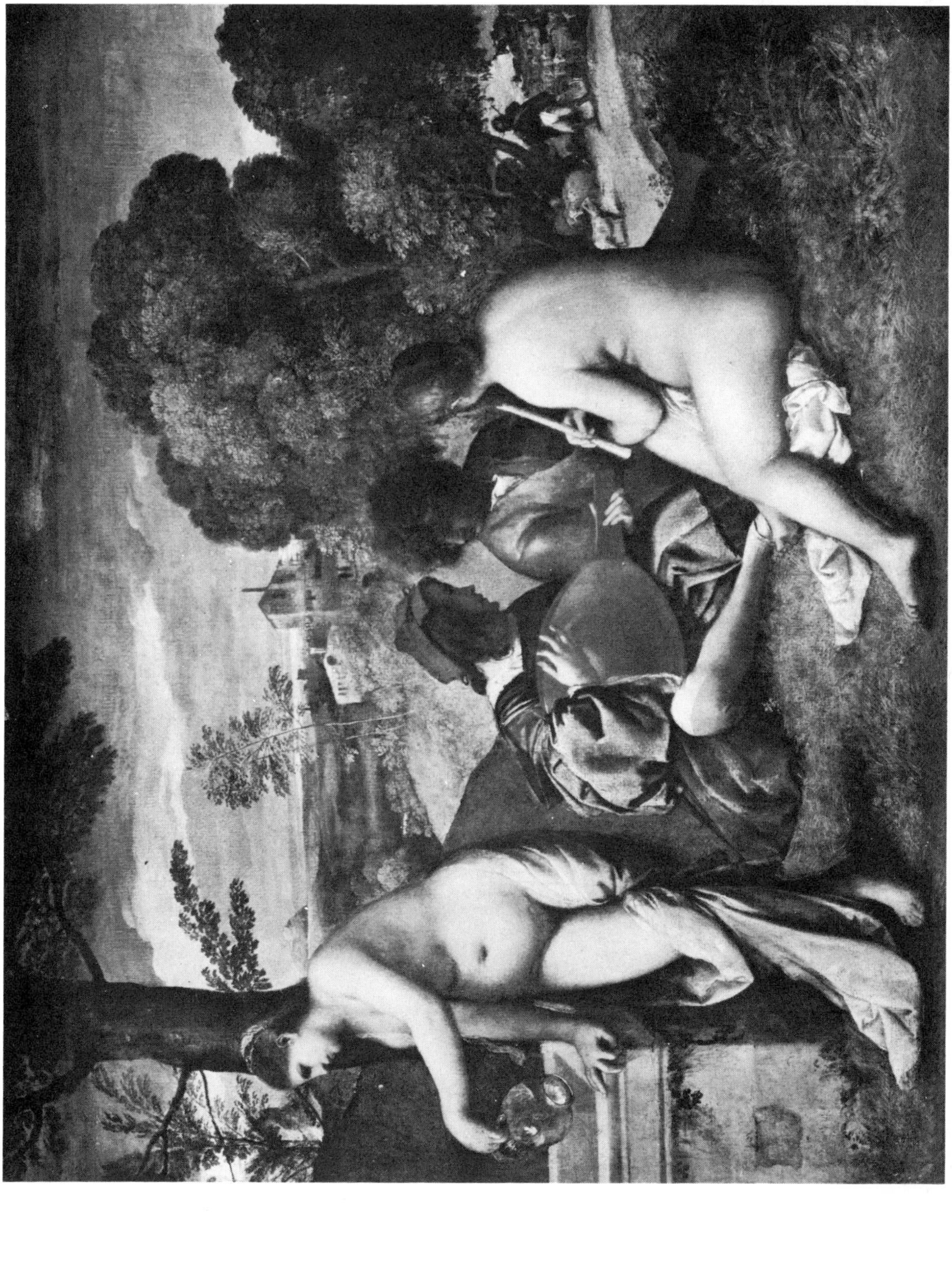

Titian (Giorgione?), *Concert champêtre*. Louvre, Paris.

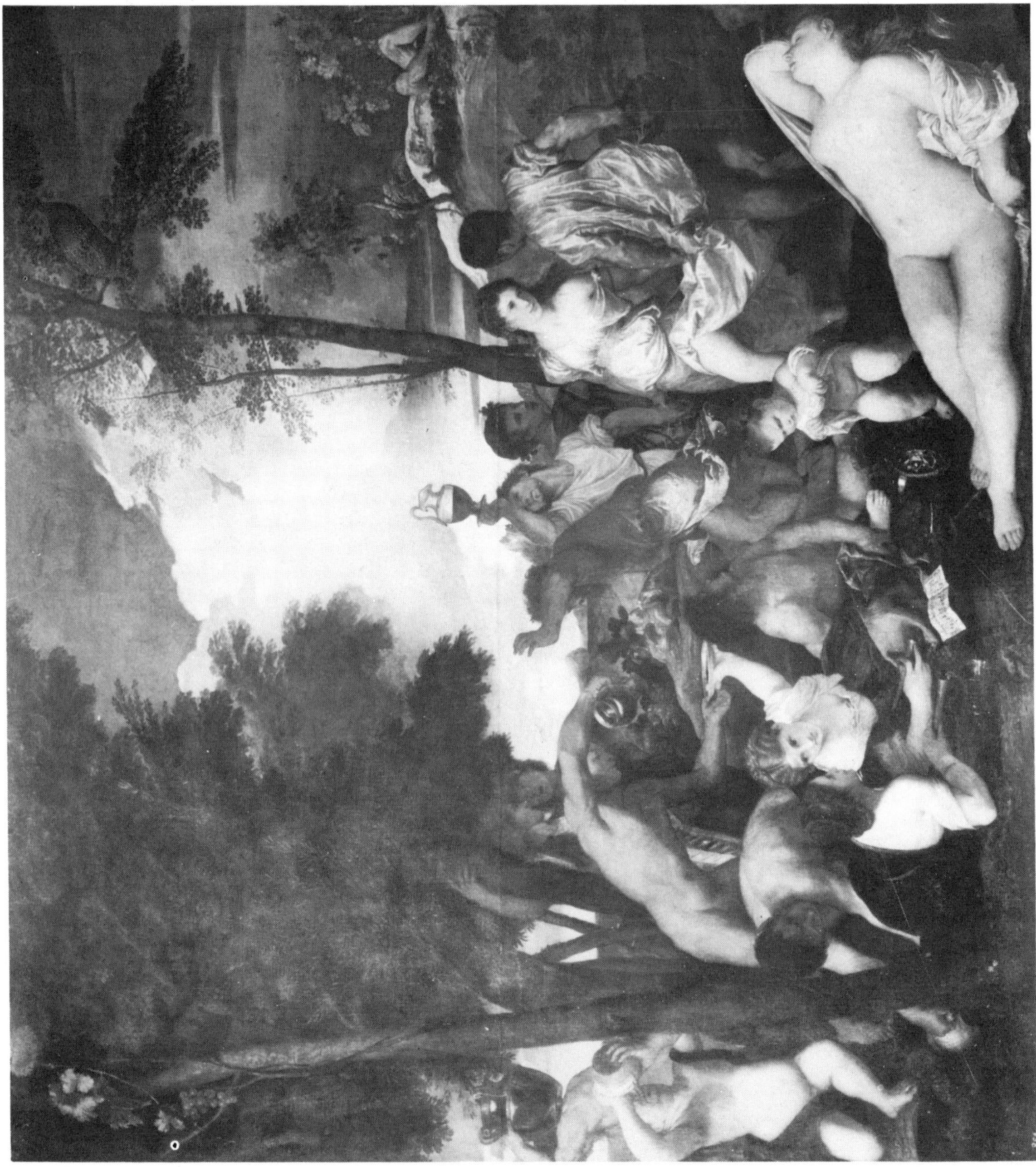

Titian, *Bacchanal*. Prado, Madrid.

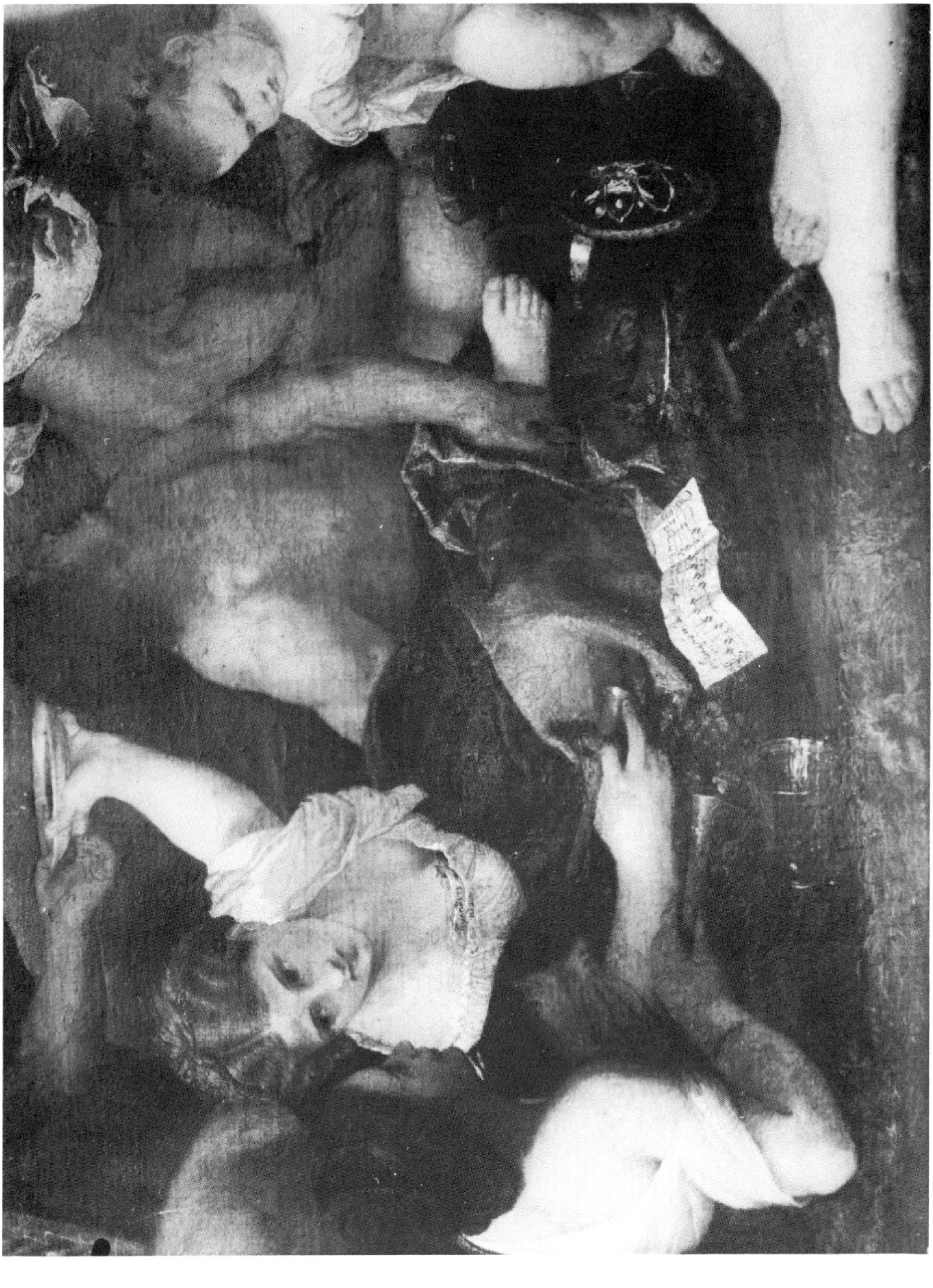

Detail of Titian, *Bacchanal*.

PLATE 10

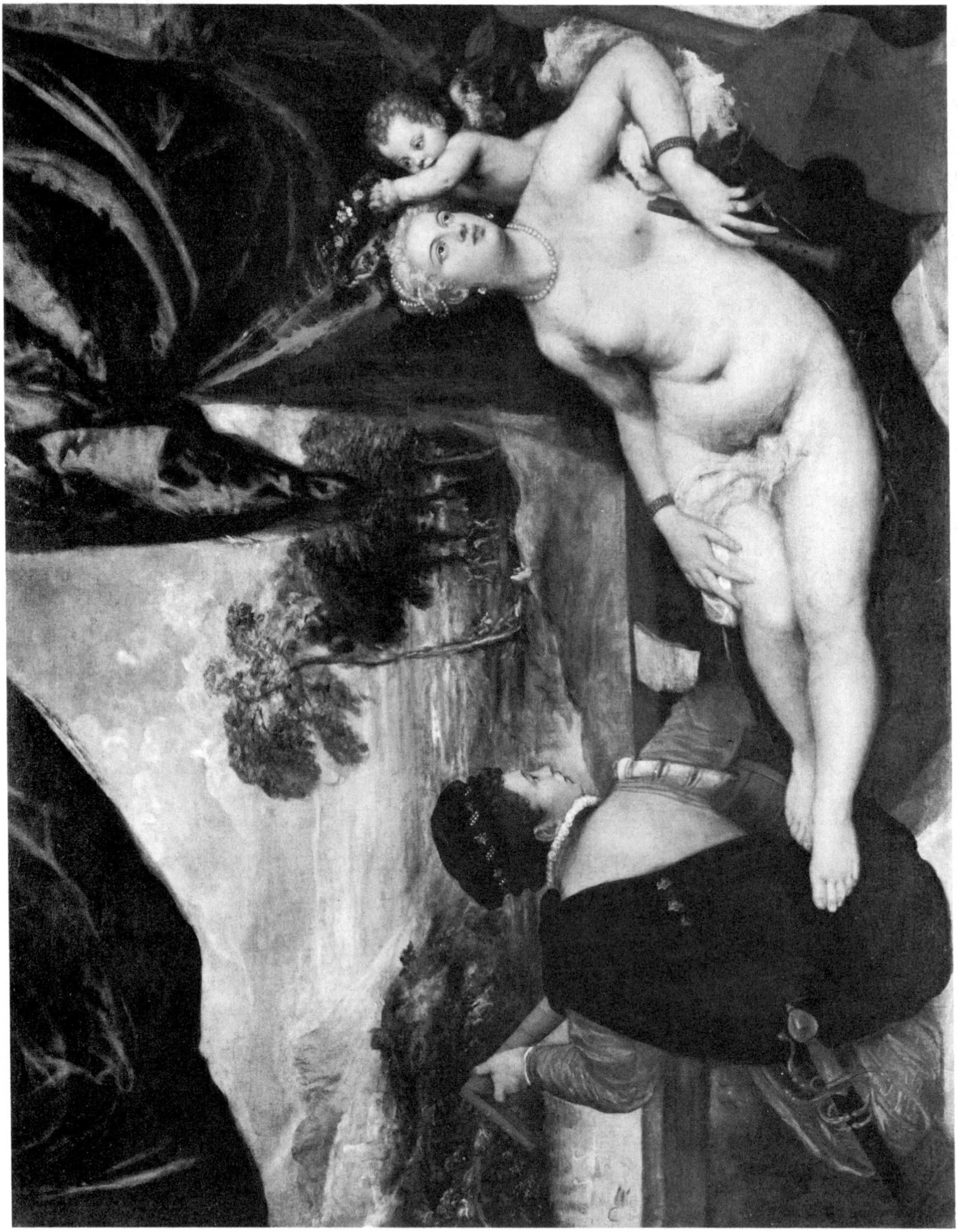

Titian, *Venus and the Lute Player*. Metropolitan Museum of Art, New York.

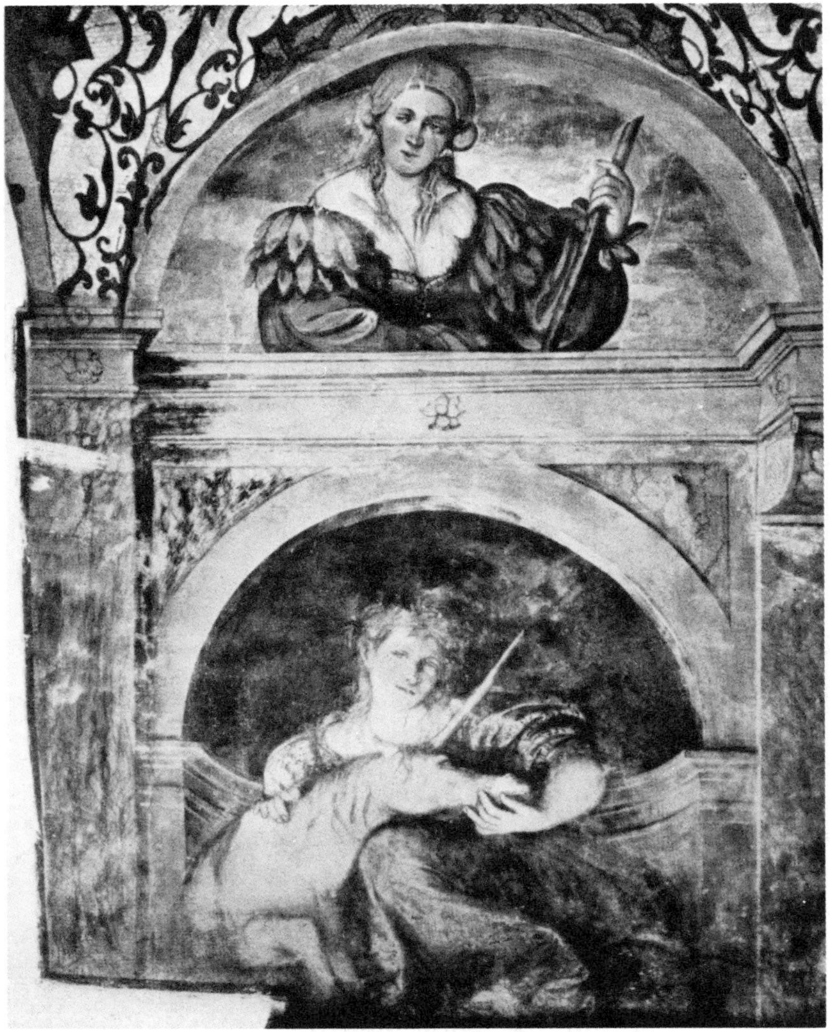

a. Romanino, detail of fresco in the Castle of Trent.

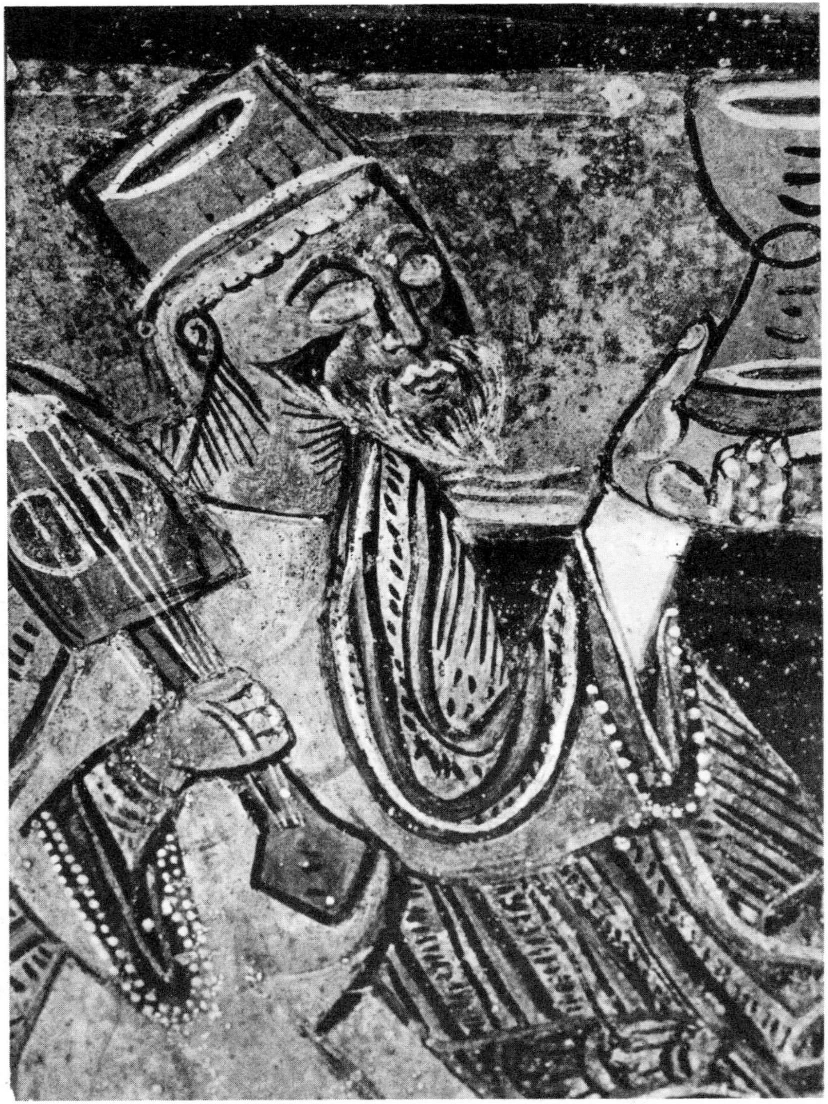

b. Apocalyptic elder holding a vielle, showing a bourdon not appearing in contemporary sculptural representations of the same subject. Detail from fresco in St.-Martin de Fenollar, Roussillon.

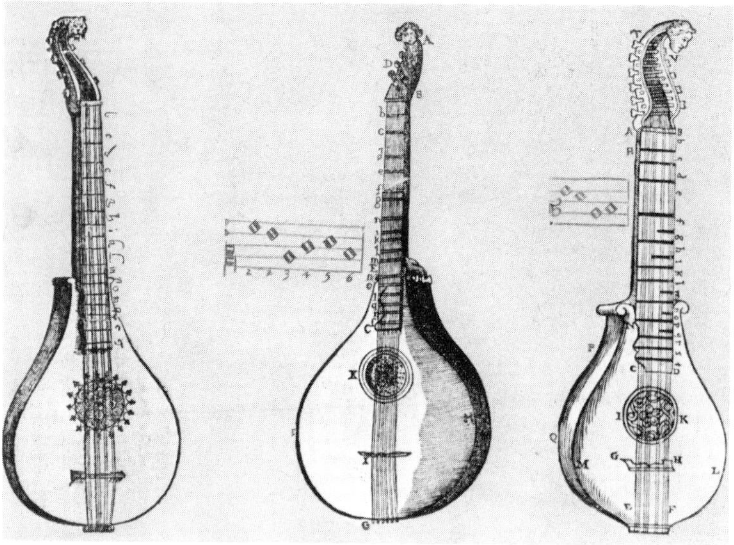

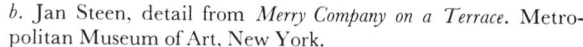

a. Three citterns, from woodcuts in Mersenne, *Harmonie universelle* (1636)

b. Jan Steen, detail from *Merry Company on a Terrace*. Metropolitan Museum of Art, New York.

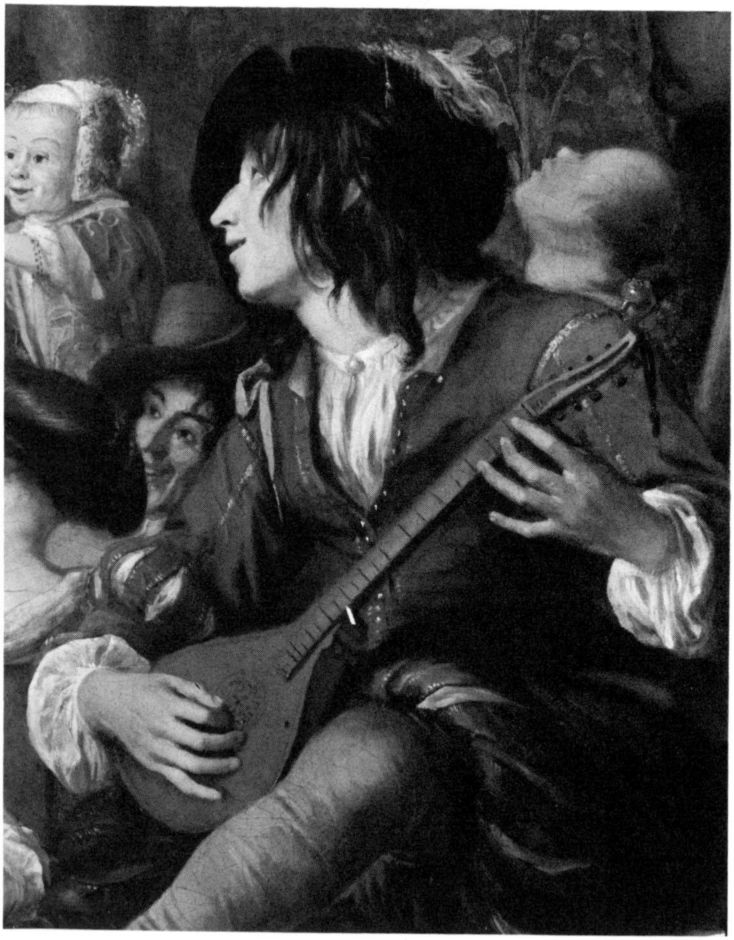

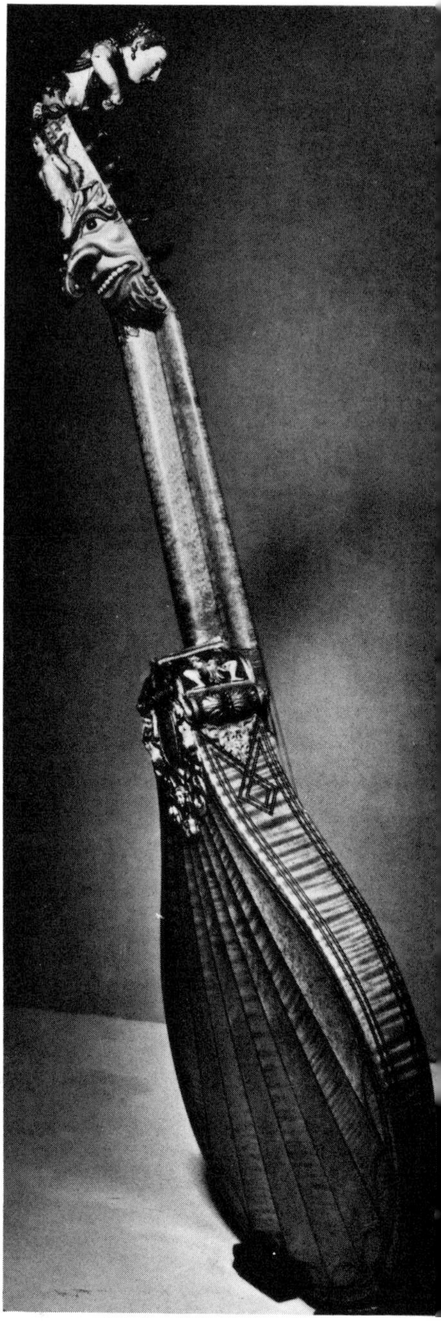

c. Cittern made by Girolamo de Virchis, Brescia, 1574. Kunsthistorisches Museum, Vienna.

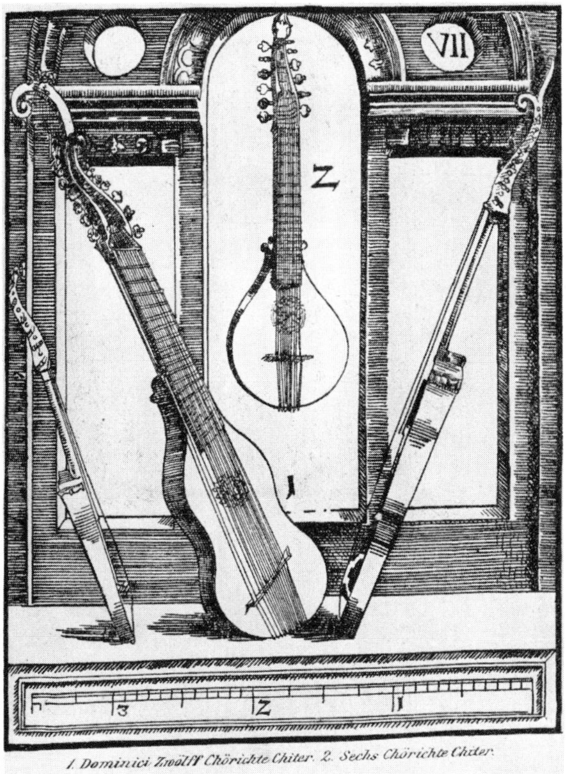

a. Two citterns, from Praetorius, *Syntagma*, *Theatrum instrumentorum* (1618).

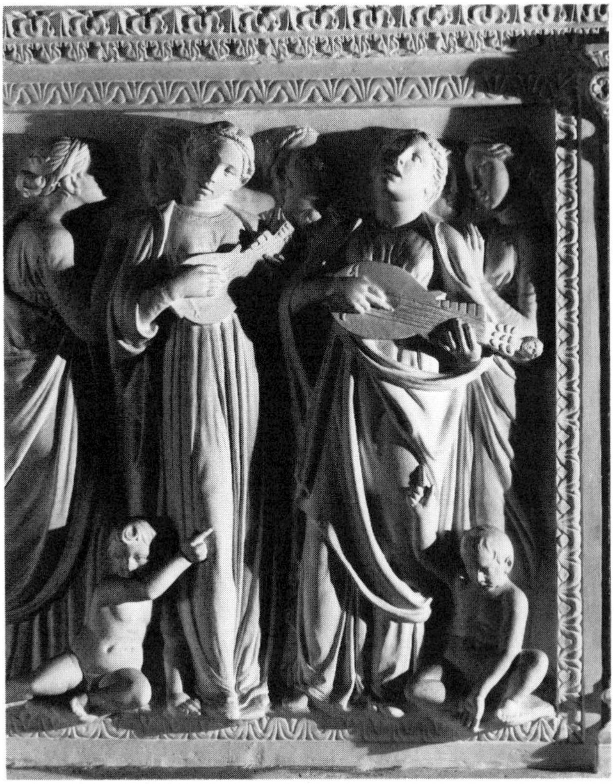

b. Luca della Robbia, *Cantoria*, detail of angels playing citterns. Museo del Duomo, Florence.

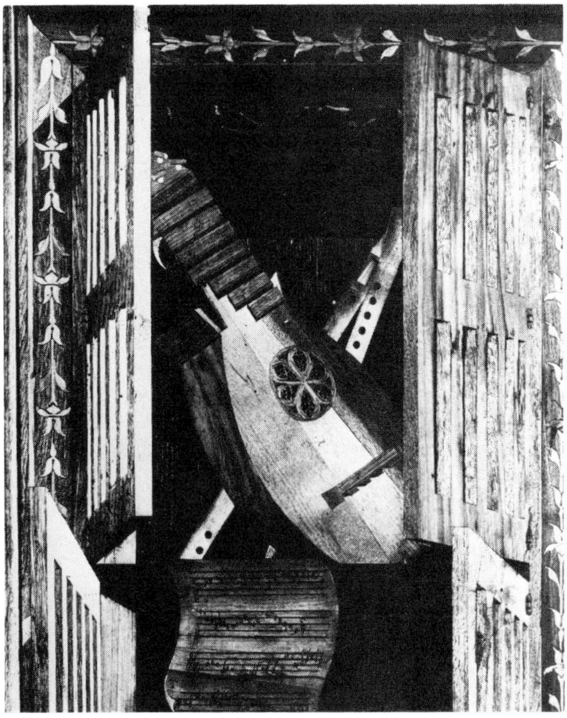

c. Fra Giovanni da Verona, cittern in intarsia. Choir stall, Monte Oliveto Maggiore, Siena.

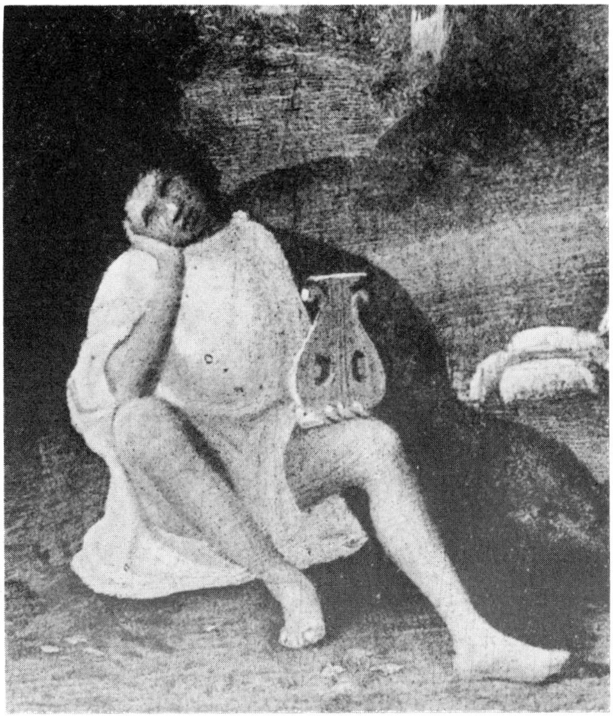

d. Andrea Previtali, detail from *Scenes from an Eclogue of Tebaldeo* (previously attr. to Giorgione). National Gallery, London.

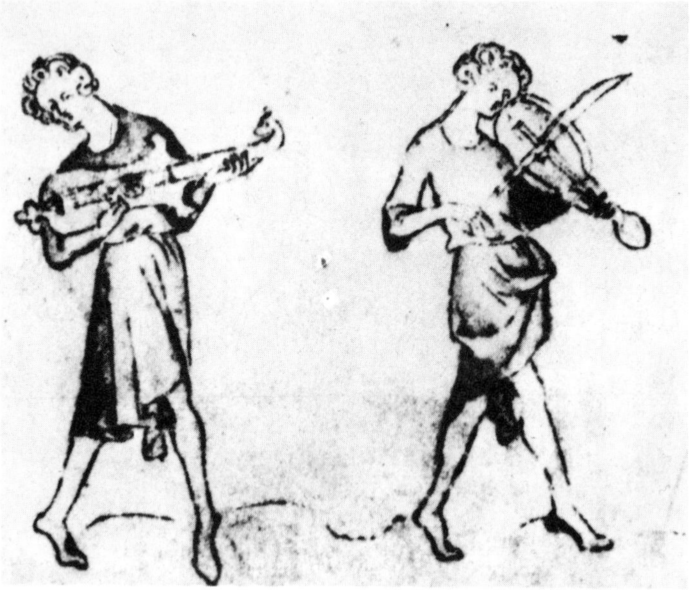

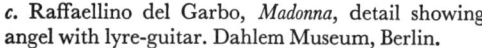

a. Musicians with cittern and vielle, from Queen Mary's Psalter. British Museum, London.

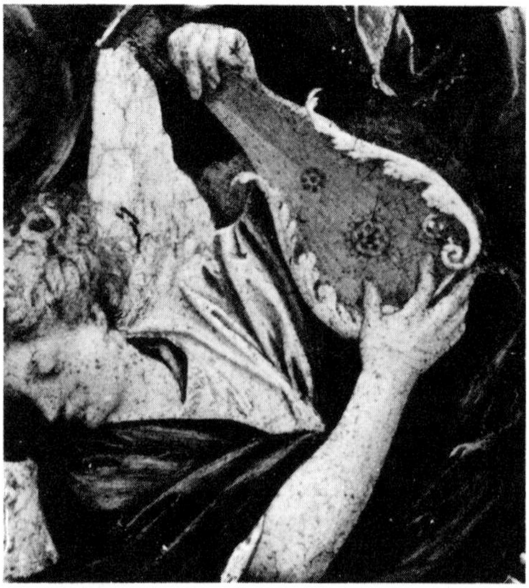

b. Gaudenzio Ferrari, detail from fresco, showing angel with cittern. Santuario, Saronno.

c. Raffaellino del Garbo, *Madonna*, detail showing angel with lyre-guitar. Dahlem Museum, Berlin.

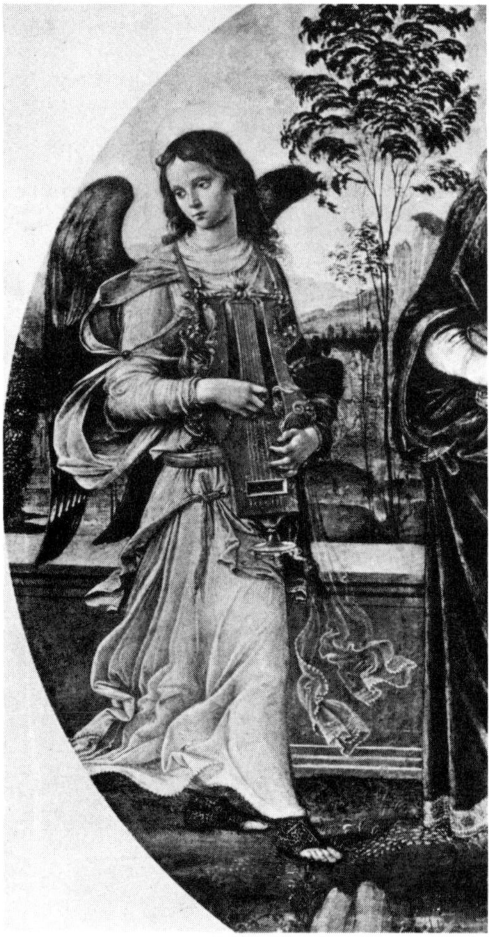

d. Lyre guitars. Metropolitan Museum of Art, Crosby Brown Collection.

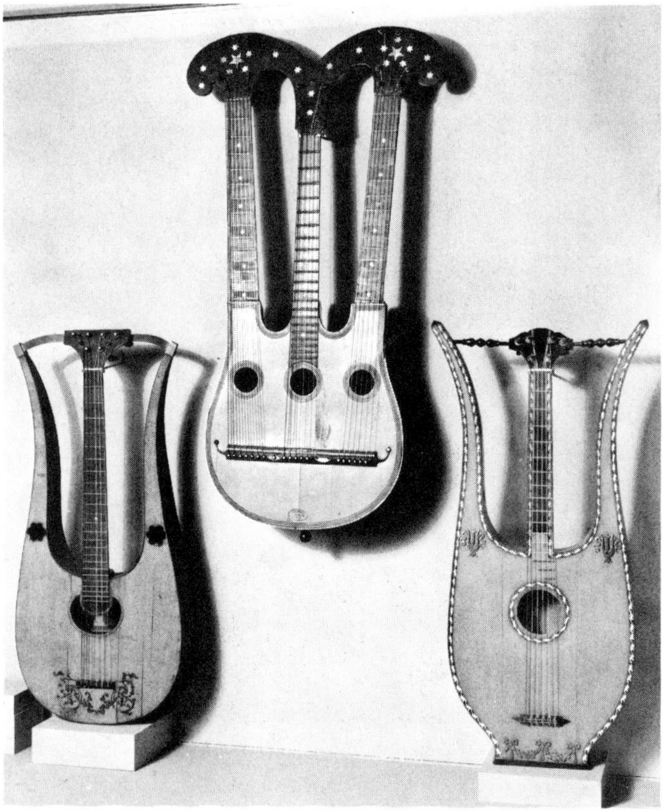

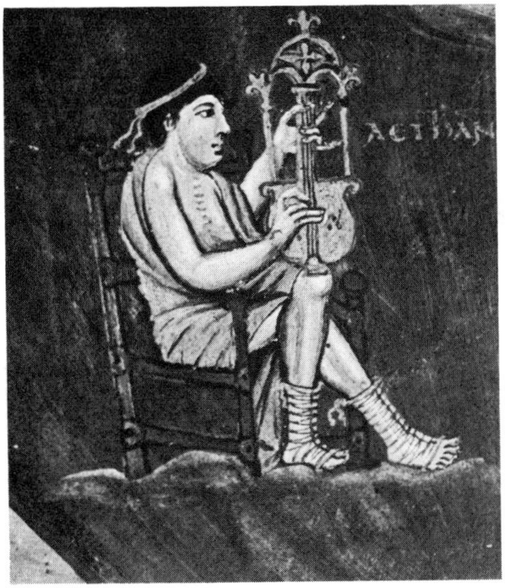

a. Musician, from Bible of Charles the Bald. Bibliothèque Nationale, Paris.

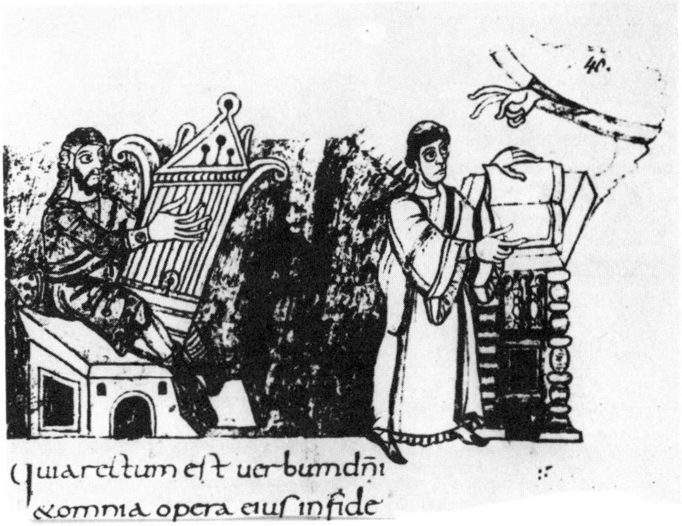

b. Detail from Stuttgart Psalter, f. 40r.

c. Musicians. Strasbourg Cathedral, west portal, middle section.

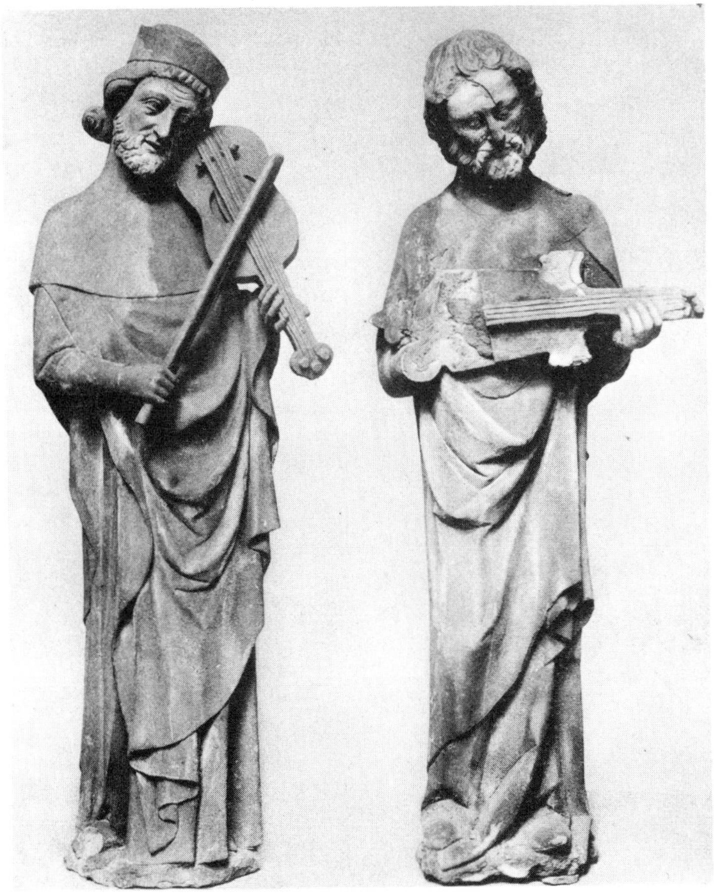

d. Benedetto Antelami, cittern player. Baptistery, Parma.

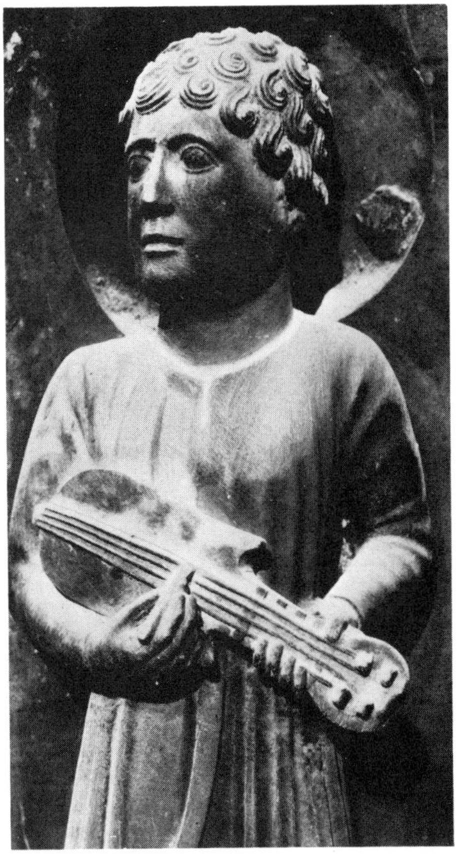

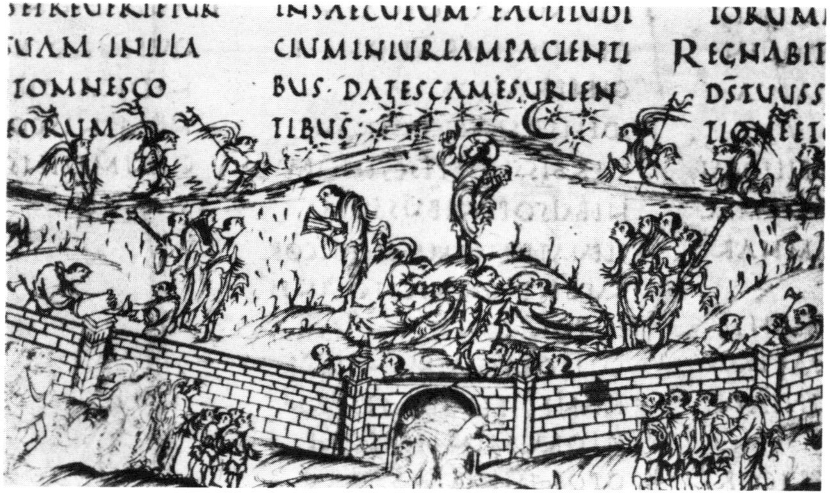

a. Psalm 147.

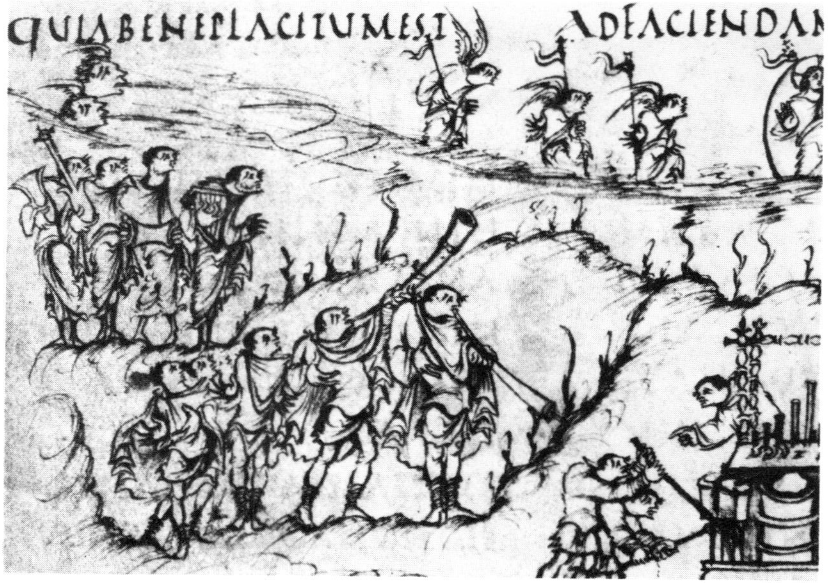

b. Psalm 150.

DETAILS FROM UTRECHT PSALTER

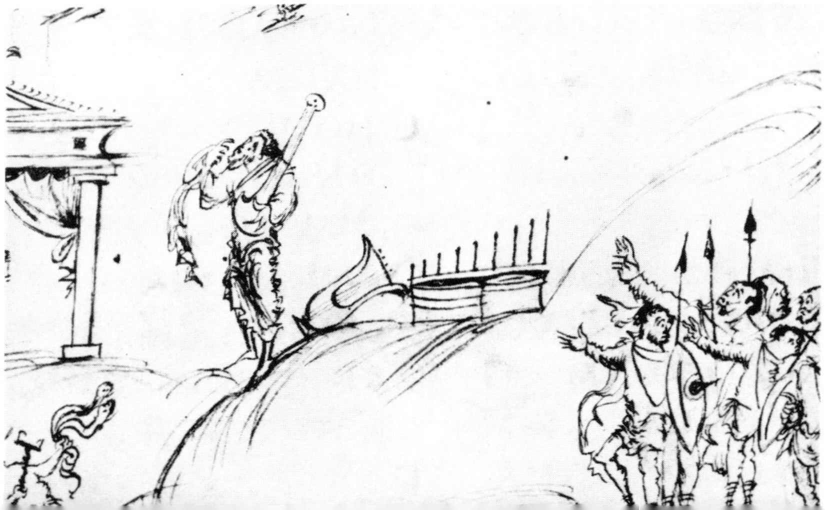
c. Psalm 71.

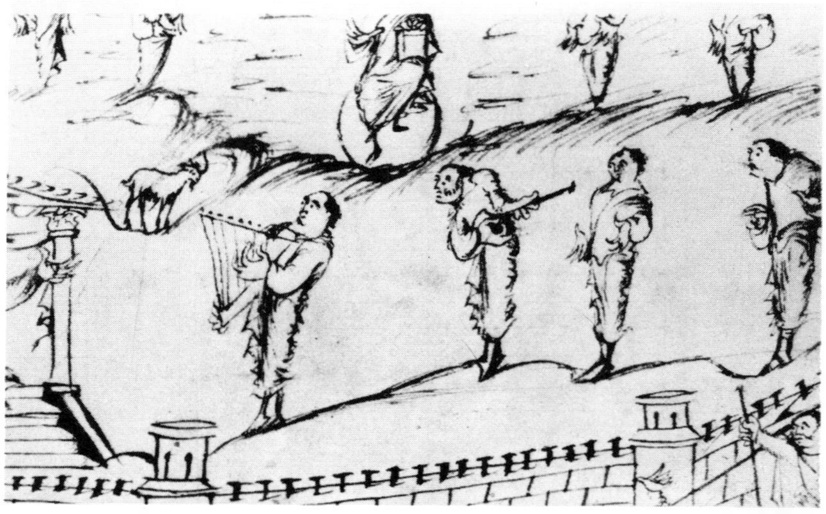
d. Psalm 92.

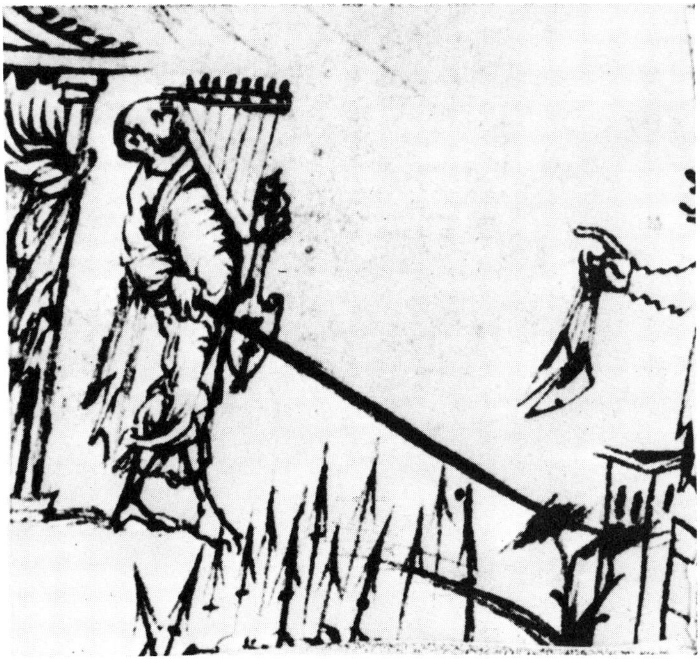

a. Detail from Utrecht Psalter, Psalm 108.

b. Detail from Utrecht Psalter, Psalm 43.

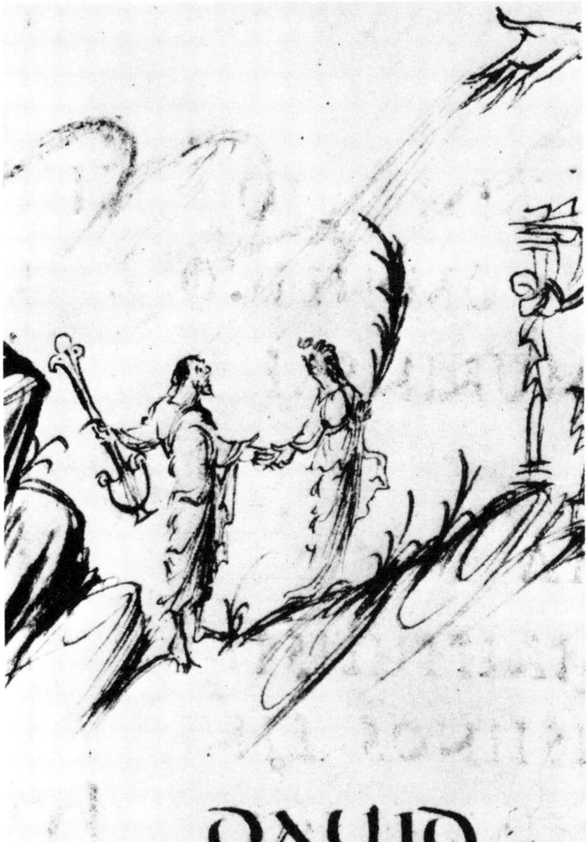

c. Detail from mosaic, Qasr el-Lebia.

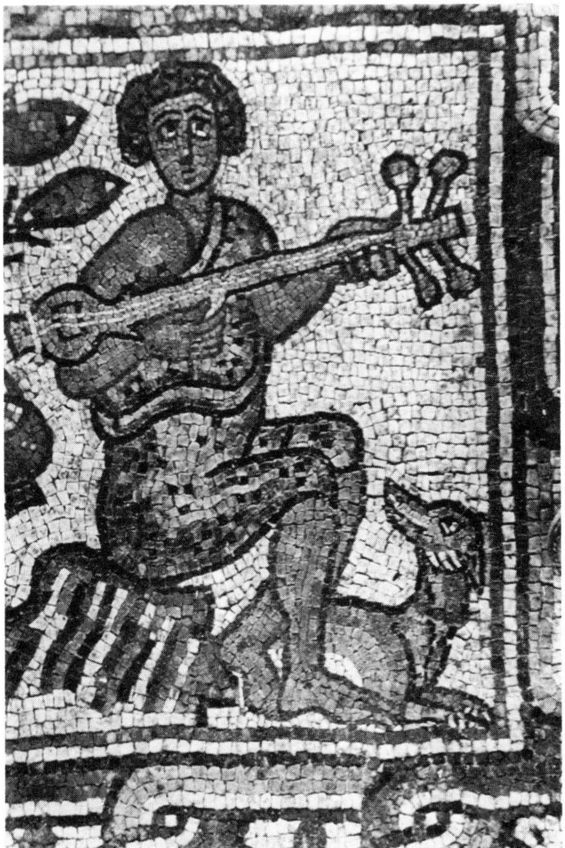

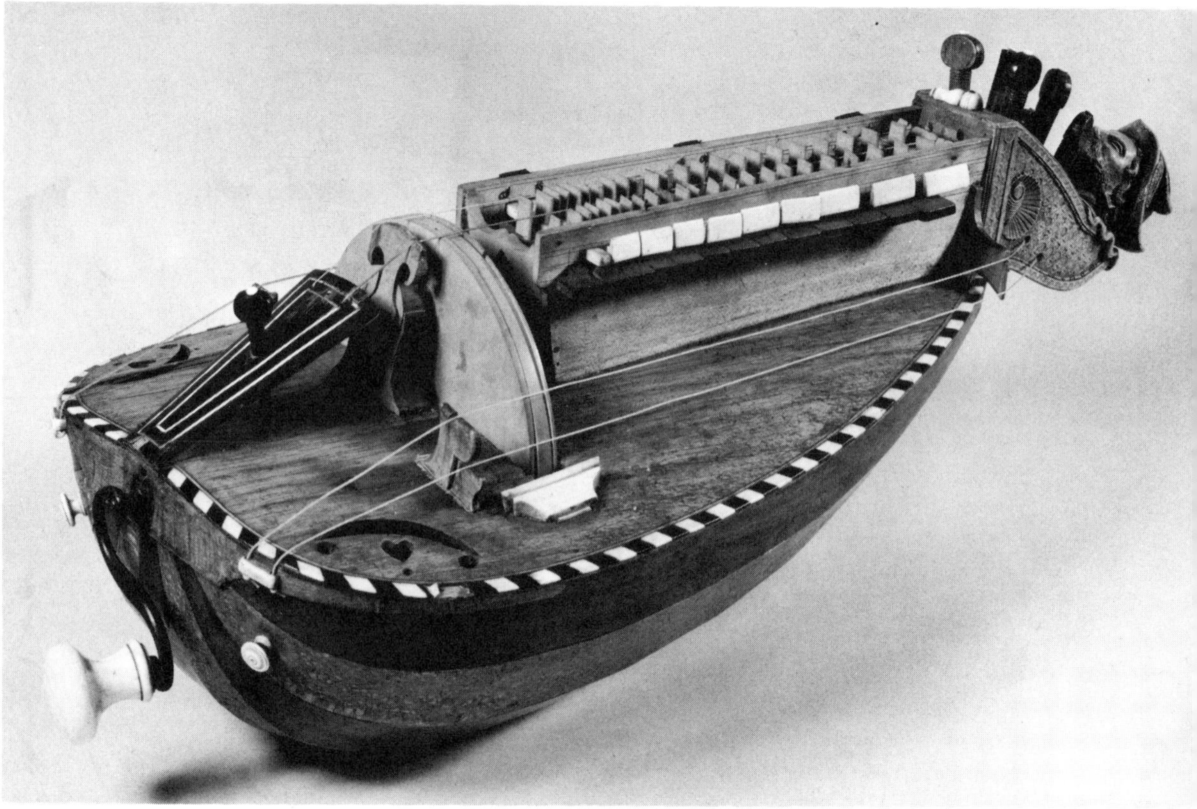

a. Hurdy-gurdy in lute shape (France, 18th century).
Metropolitan Museum of Art, Crosby Brown Collection.

b. Hurdy-gurdy in guitar shape (France, 18th century).
Metropolitan Museum of Art, Crosby Brown Collection.

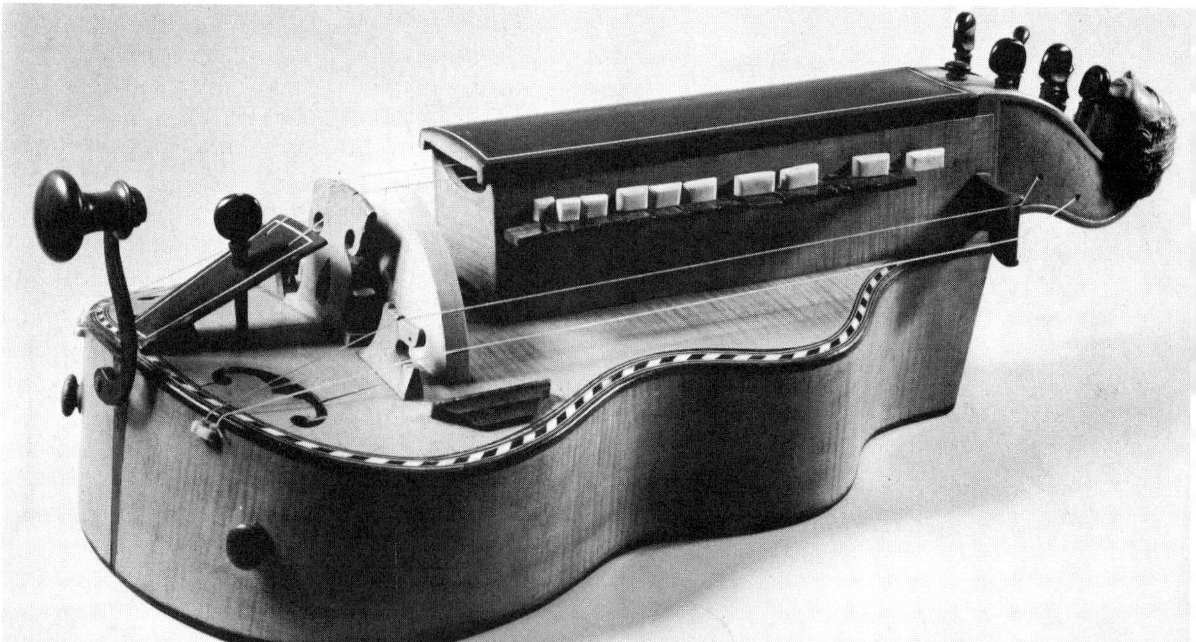

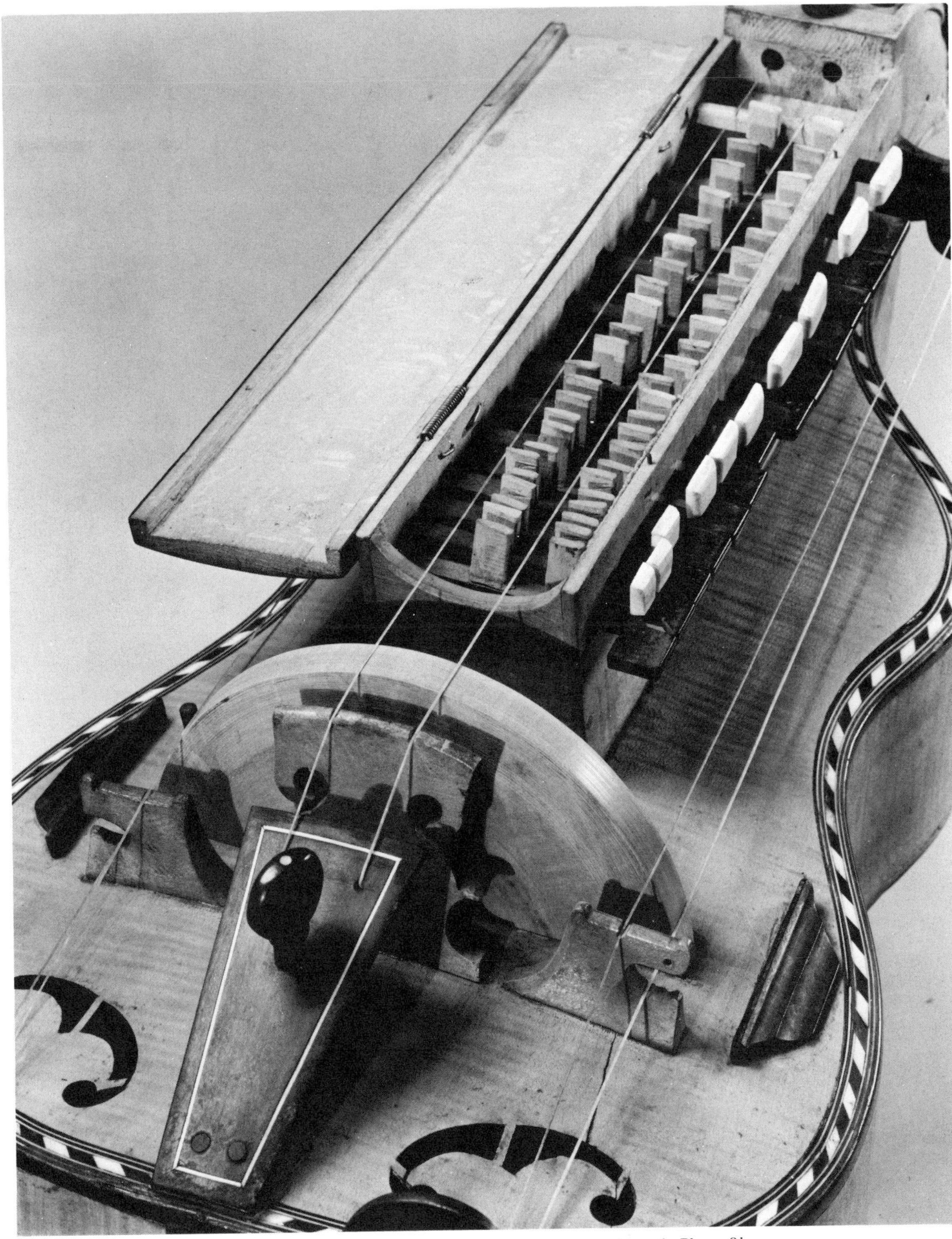

Wheel and stopping mechanism of the hurdy-gurdy shown in Plate 18*b*.

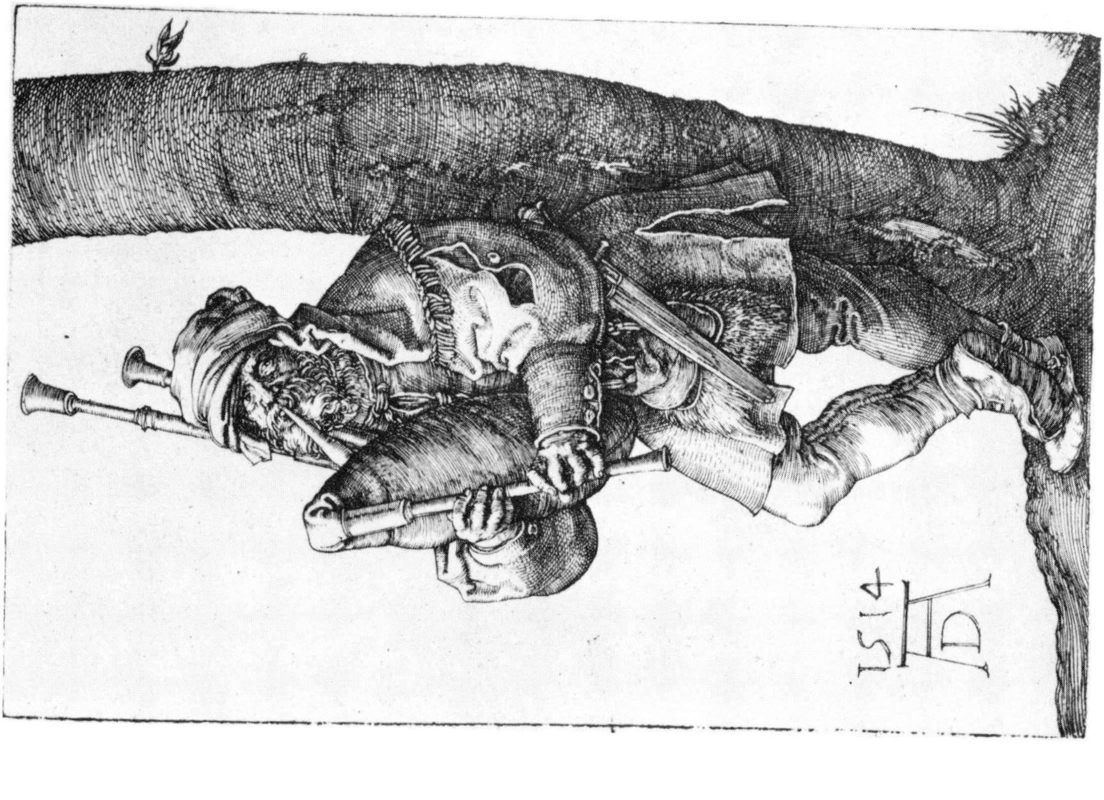

a. Albrecht Dürer, *The Bagpiper* (engraving).

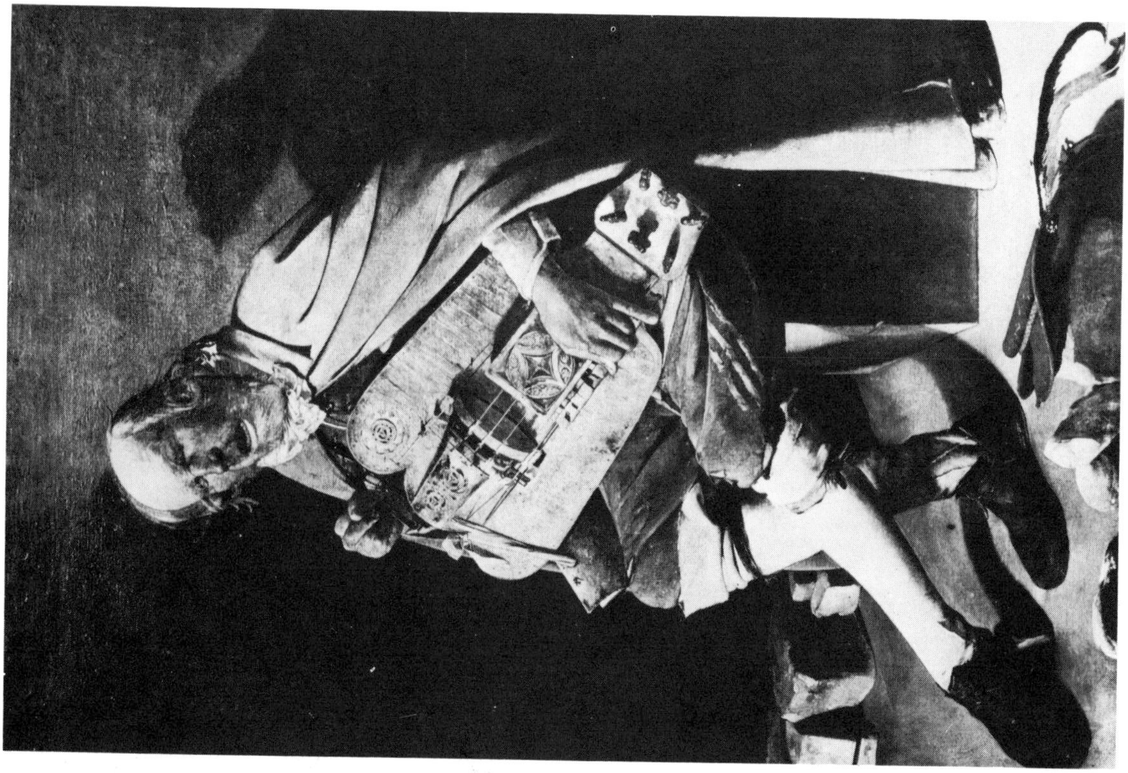

b. Georges de la Tour, *The Hurdy-Gurdy Player*. Nantes Museum.

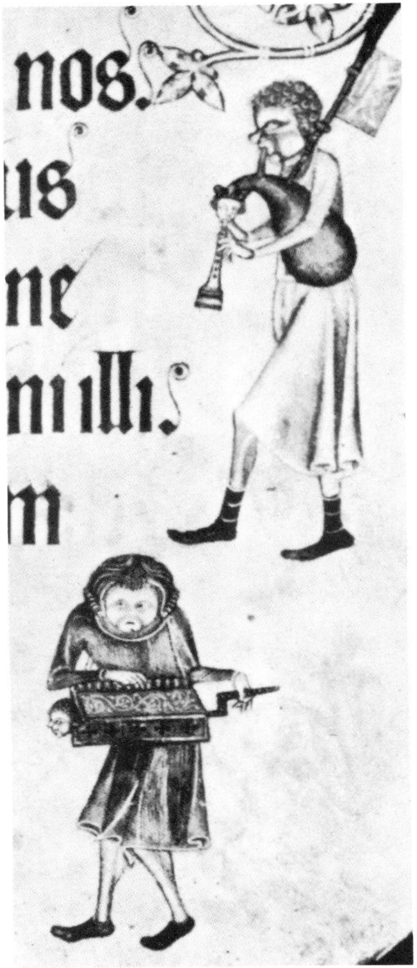

a. Musicians playing a bagpipe and a symphonia. Marginal illustrations from the Loutrell Psalter (14th century). Lulworth Castle, Dorset.

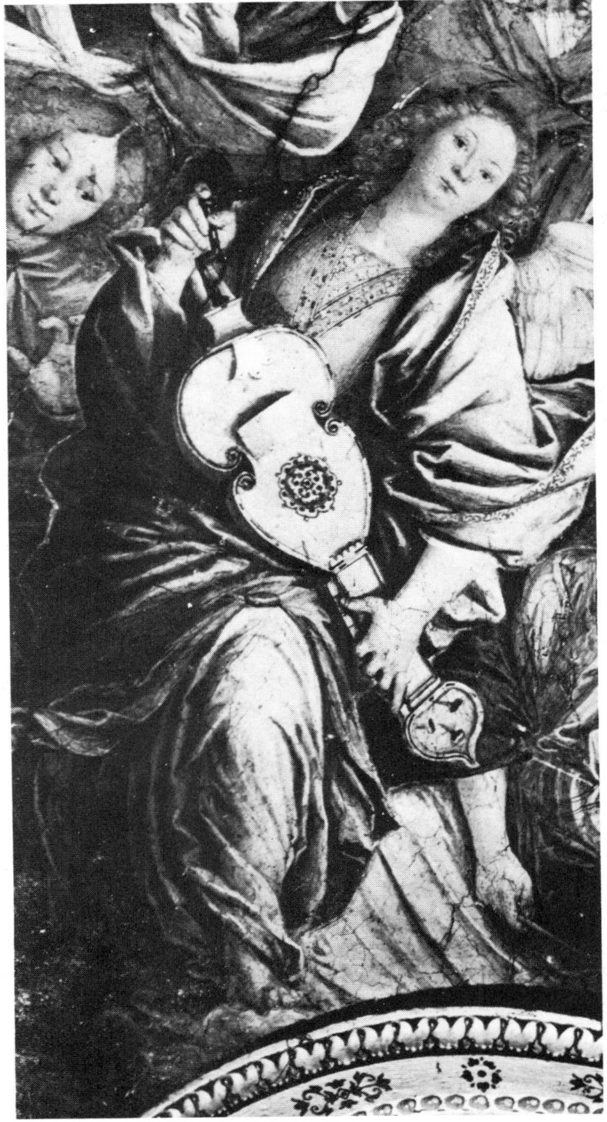

b. Gaudenzio Ferrari, detail of angel playing a hurdy-gurdy. Santuario, Saronno.

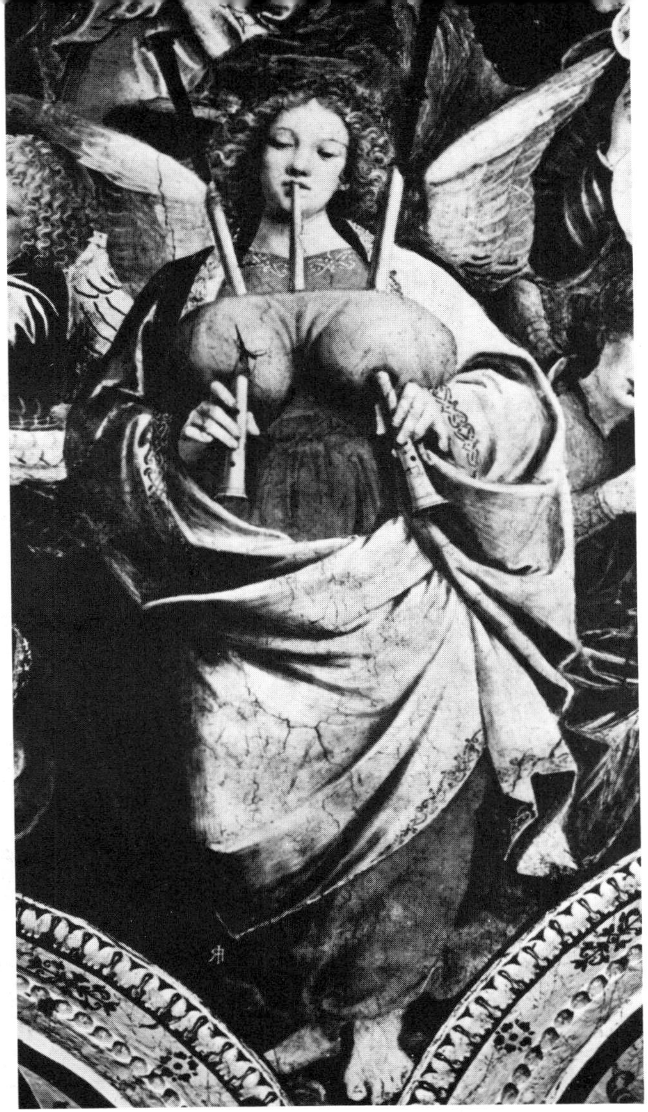

c. Gaudenzio Ferrari, detail of angel playing a bagpipe with two one-hand chanters and two drones. Santuario, Saronno.

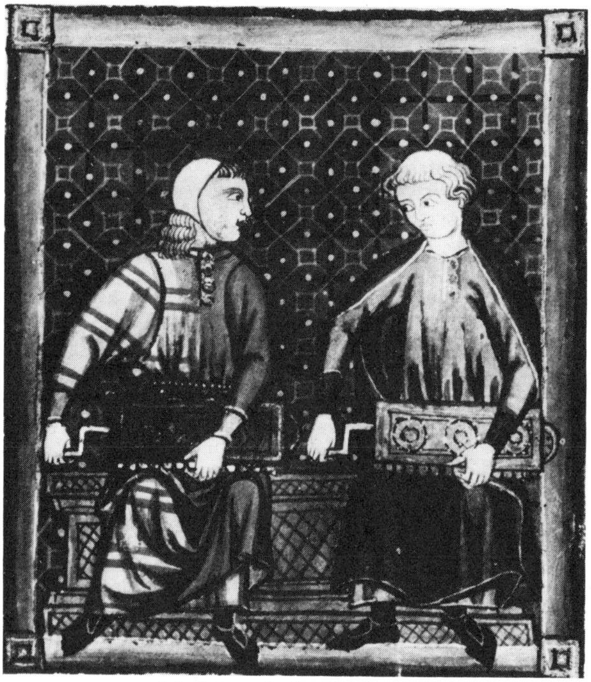

a. Musicians playing hurdy-gurdies.

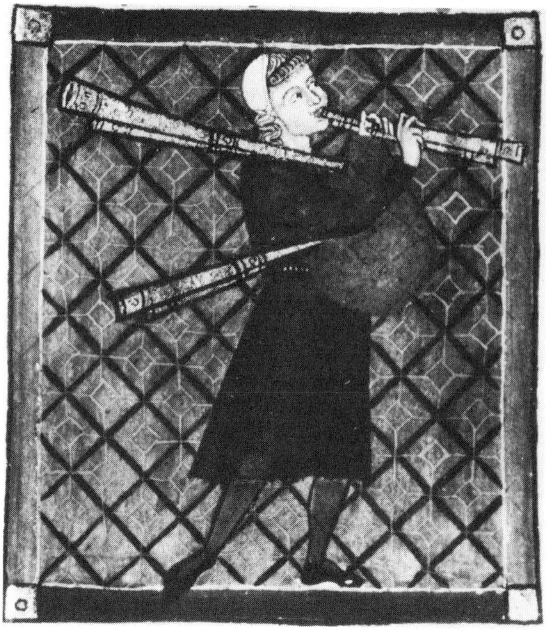

b. Musician playing a bagpipe with two pairs of drones and a double chanter.

MINIATURES FROM THE *CANTIGAS DE SANTA MARIA* (13TH CENTURY)

c. Musicians playing bagpipes with single chanters, no drones.

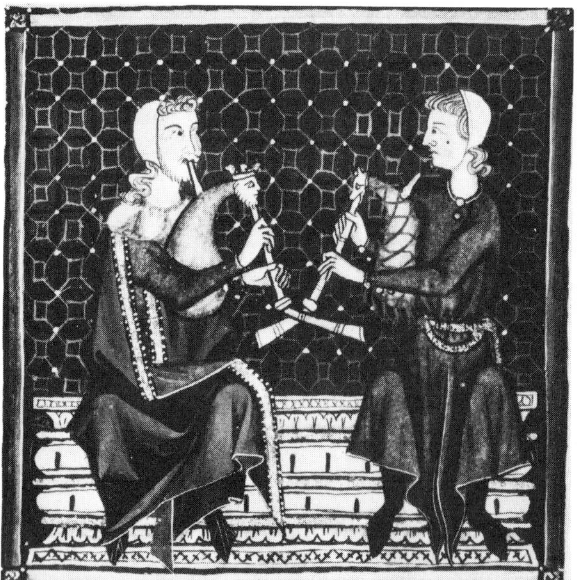

d. Musicians playing bagpipes with double pipes.

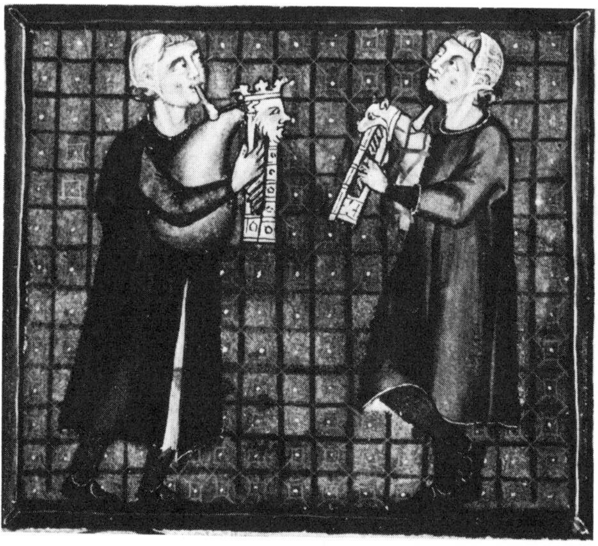

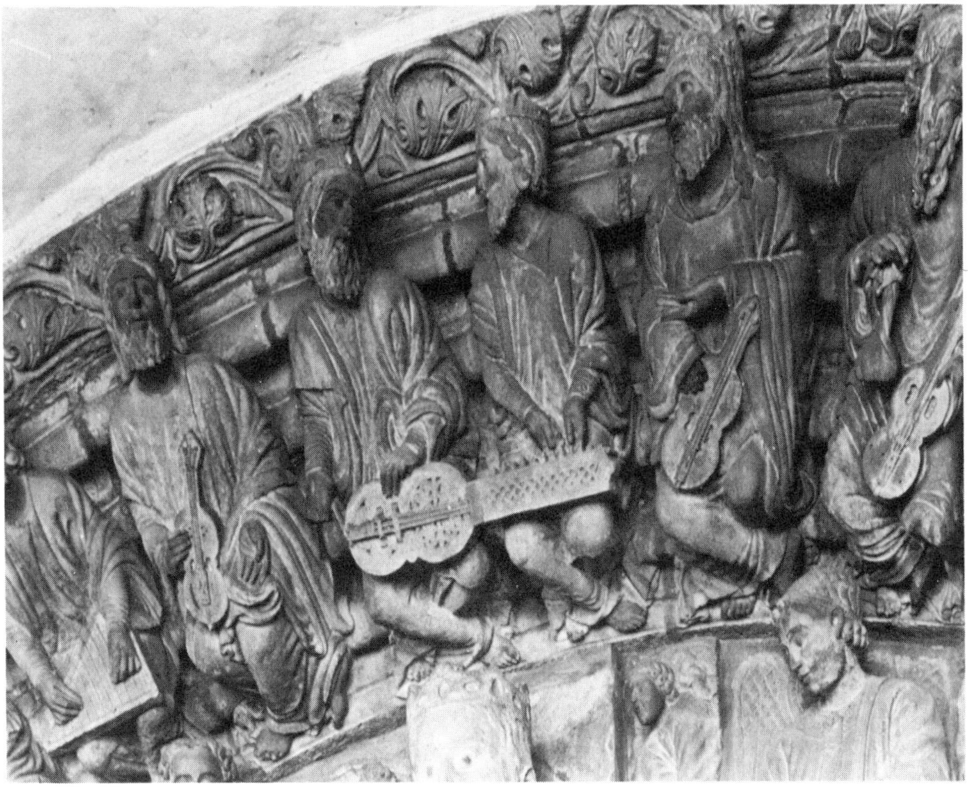

a. Organistrum played by two elders (end of 12th century). Portico de la Gloria, Cathedral of Santiago de Compostela.

b. School of Giotto, *Glorification of St. Francis,* detail. Church of San Francesco al Prato, Pistoia.

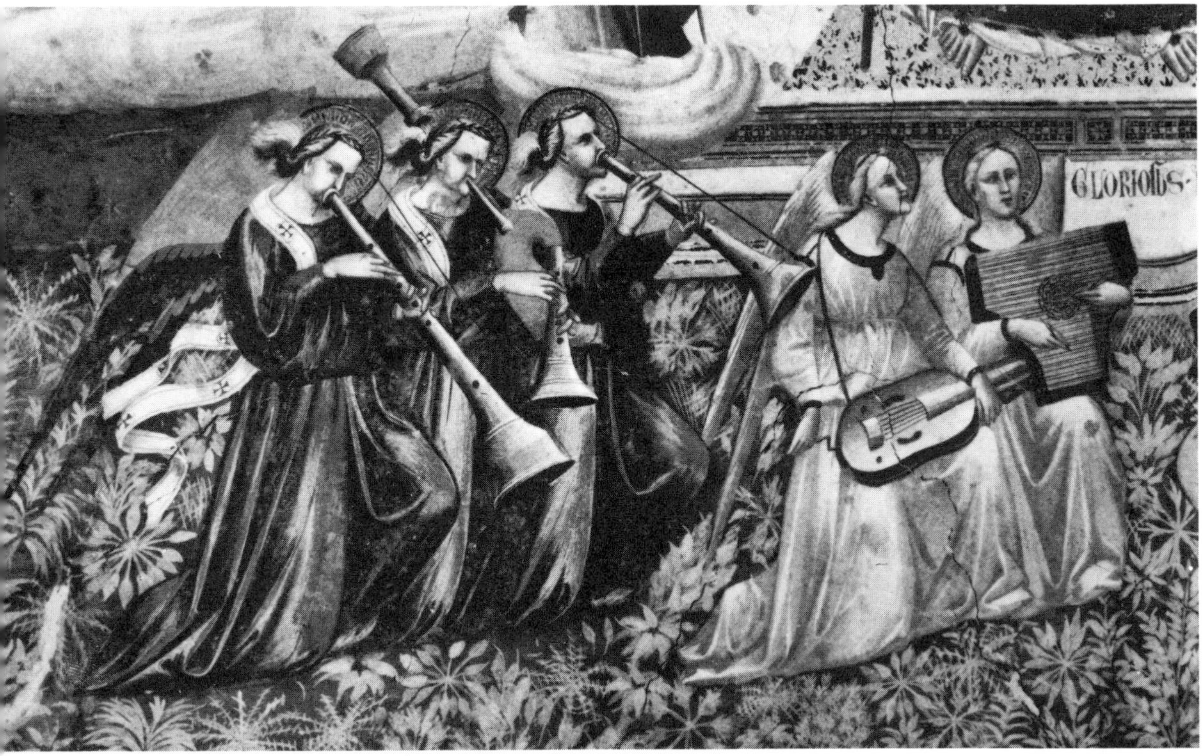

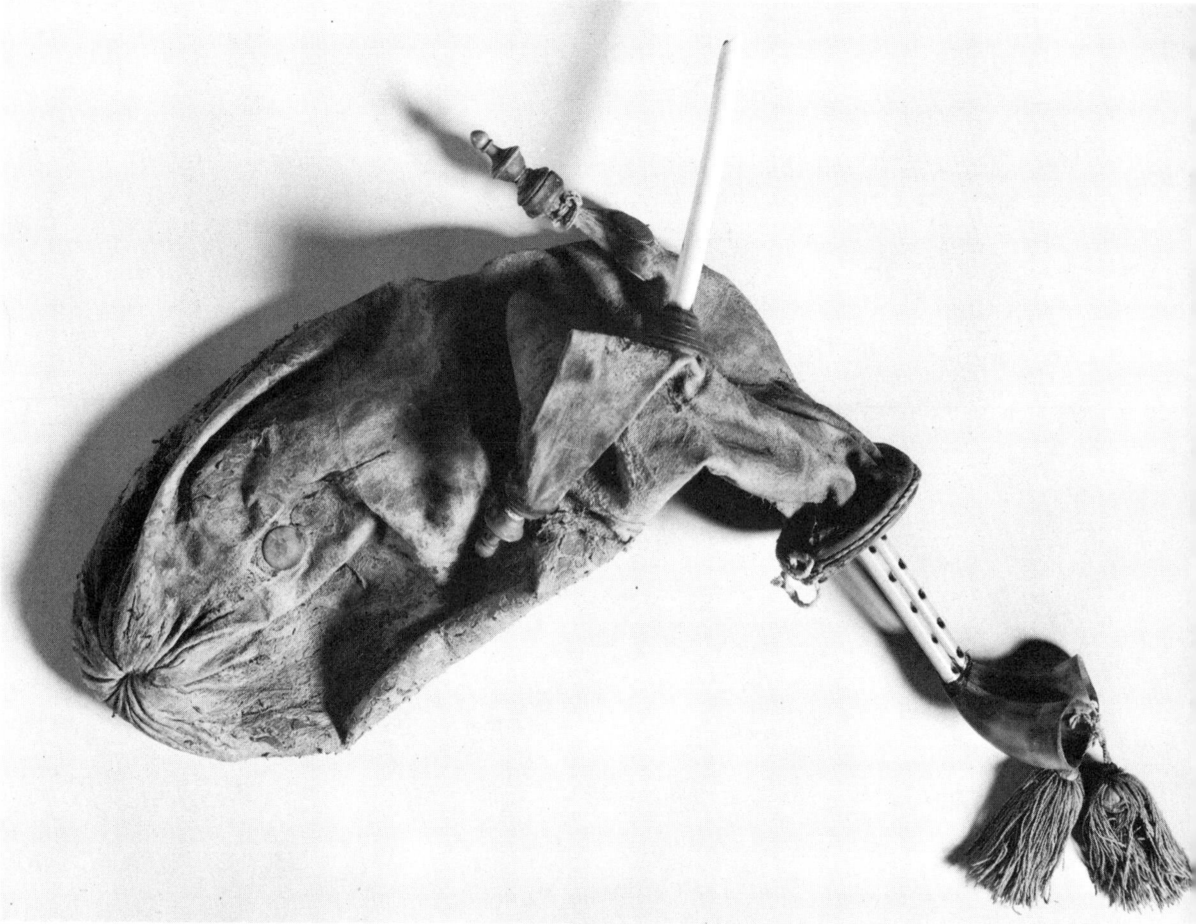

a. Bagpipe of Near Eastern type (Turkey, 19th century). Metropolitan Museum of Art, Crosby Brown Collection.

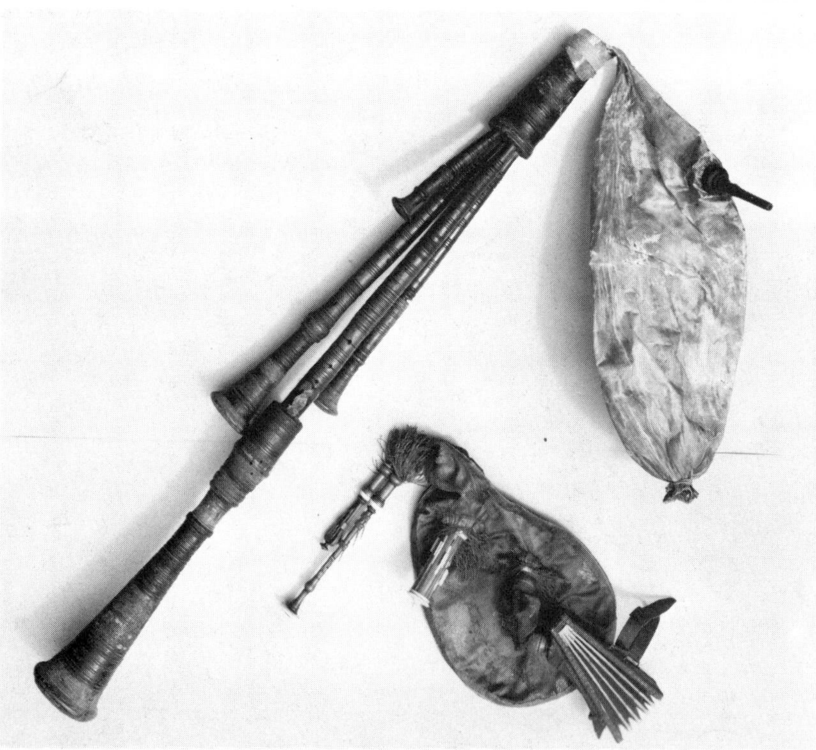

b. *Above*: Zampogna (Italy, 19th century). Length of longest drone, 4 feet. *Below*: Musette (France, 18th century). Length of chanter, $9\frac{1}{2}$ inches; of bourdon cylinder, $5\frac{1}{2}$ inches. Metropolitan Museum of Art, Crosby Brown Collection.

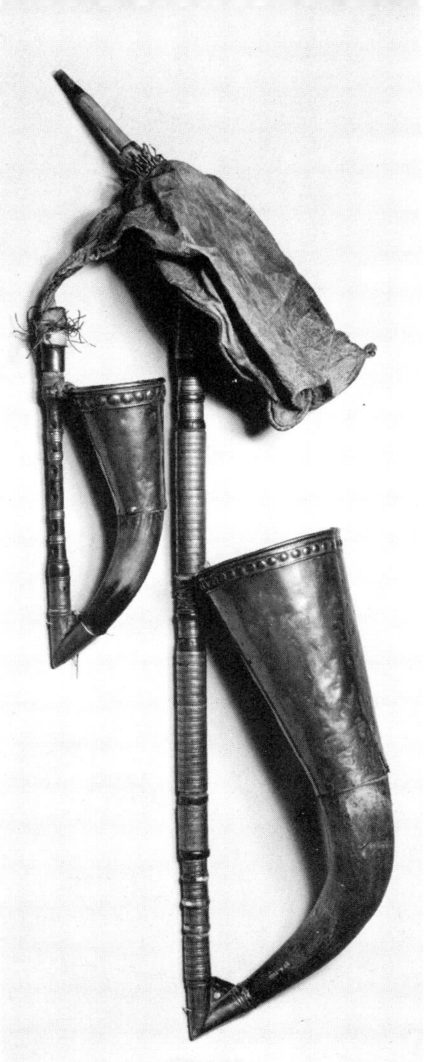

a. Bock (Germany, 18th century). Length of chanter, 2 feet 5 inches; of drone, 5 feet 4 inches. Metropolitan Museum of Art, Crosby Brown Collection.

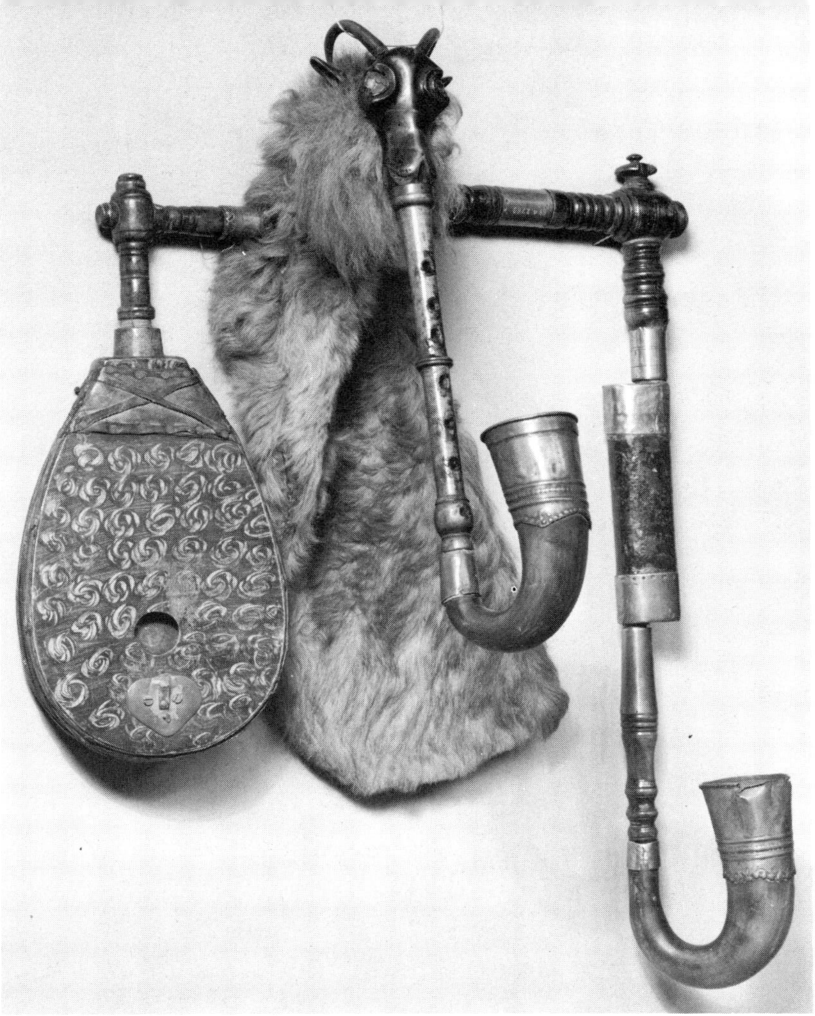

b. Bock with bellows (Germany, 19th century). Length of chanter, 1 foot 9 inches; of drone, 3 feet 6 inches; both are fitted with single-beating reeds. Metropolitan Museum of Art, Crosby Brown Collection.

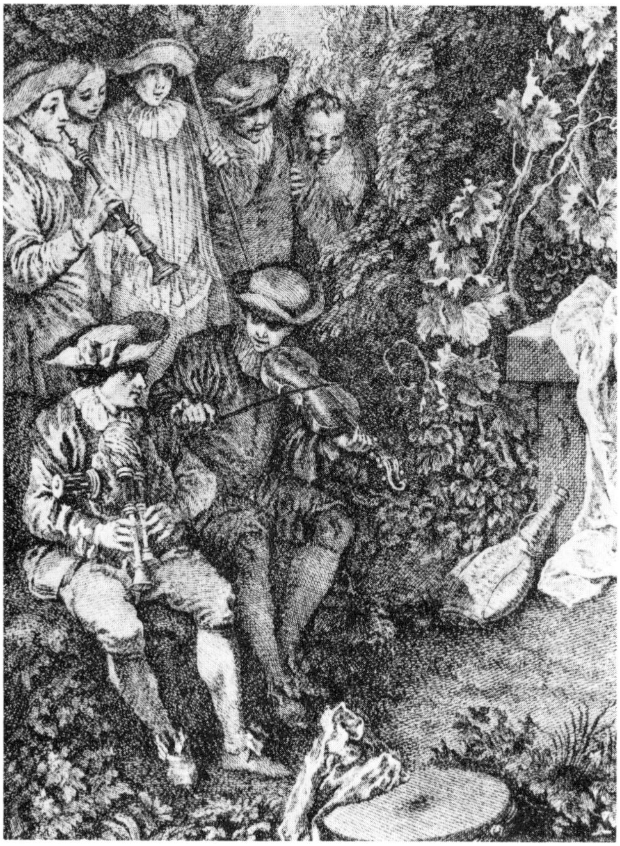

a. Musette player with other musicians, from Watteau's *L'Amour au théâtre français.*

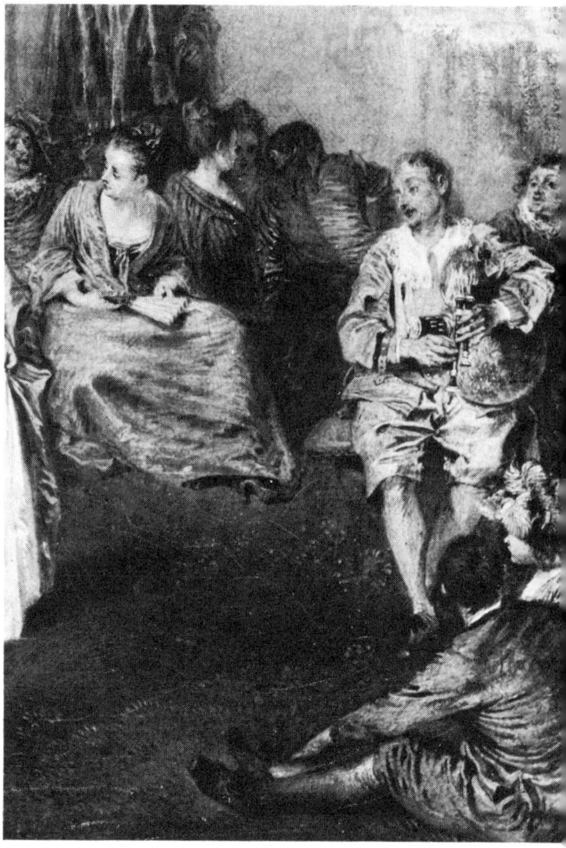

b. Watteau, *Fête champêtre,* detail showing musette player.

c. Watteau, *L'Accordée de village,* detail showing musette and vielle played for dancing.

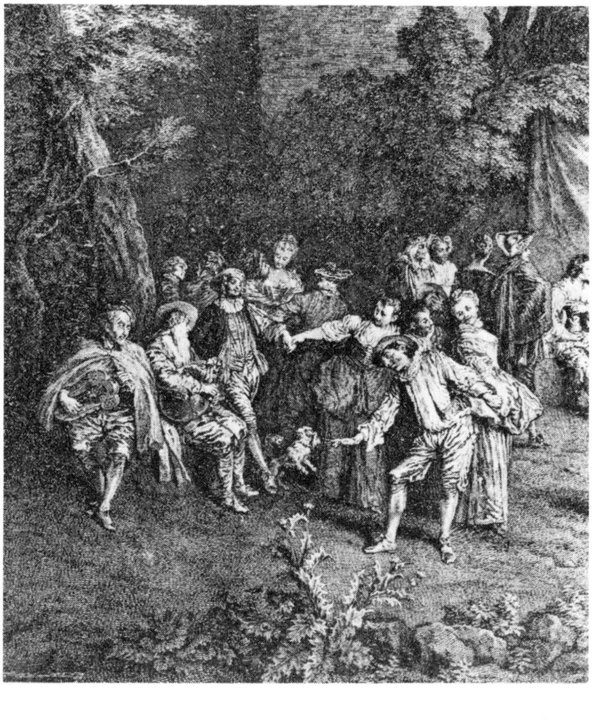

d. Engraving after Watteau, showing Chinese musician with a vielle.

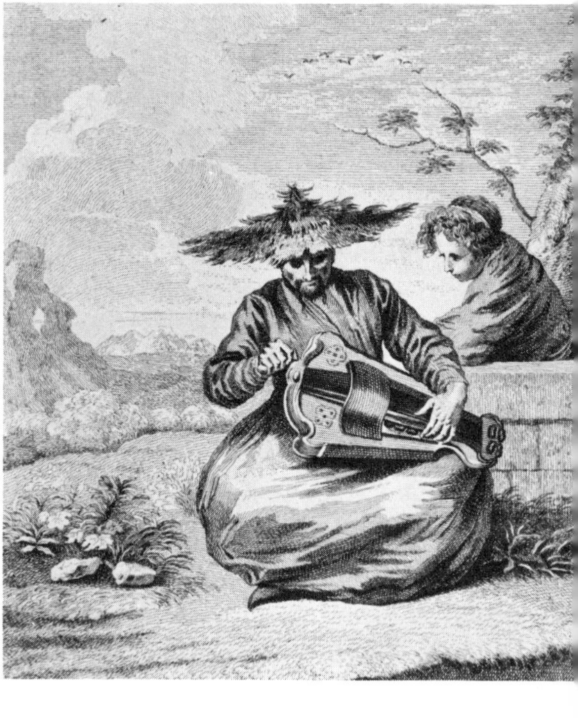

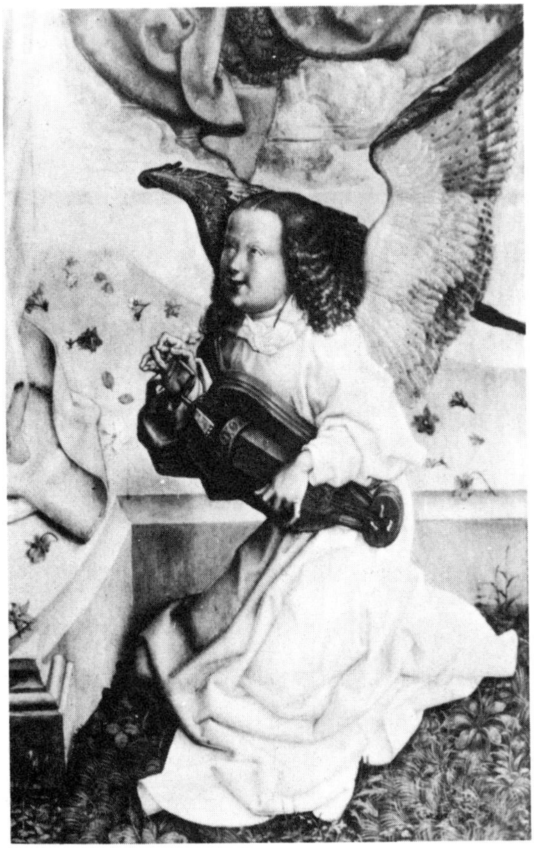

a. Angel playing a three-stringed hurdy-gurdy (c. 1500). St. Thomas Altar, Cologne.

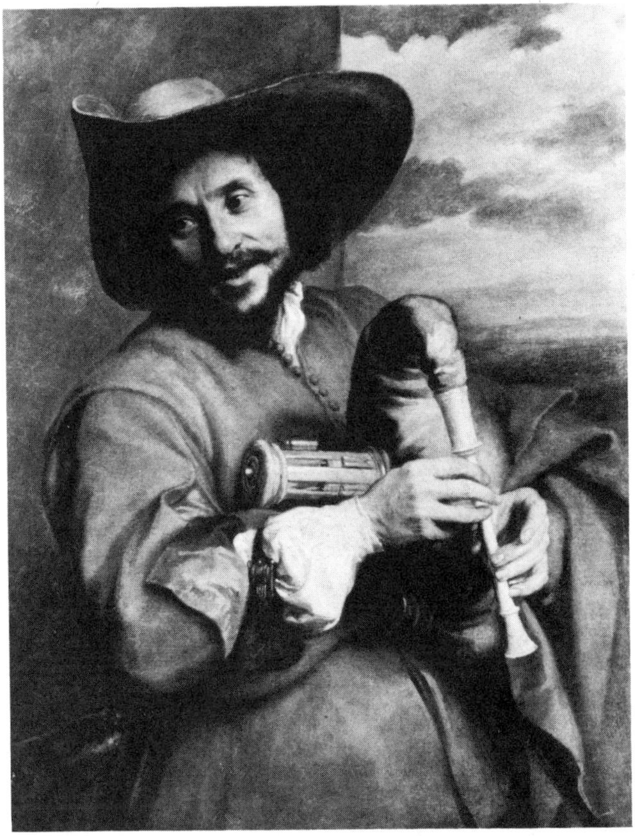

b. Van Dyck, *Portrait of François Langlois*. Private collection. Note the bellows straps on the right arm, and the single chanter.

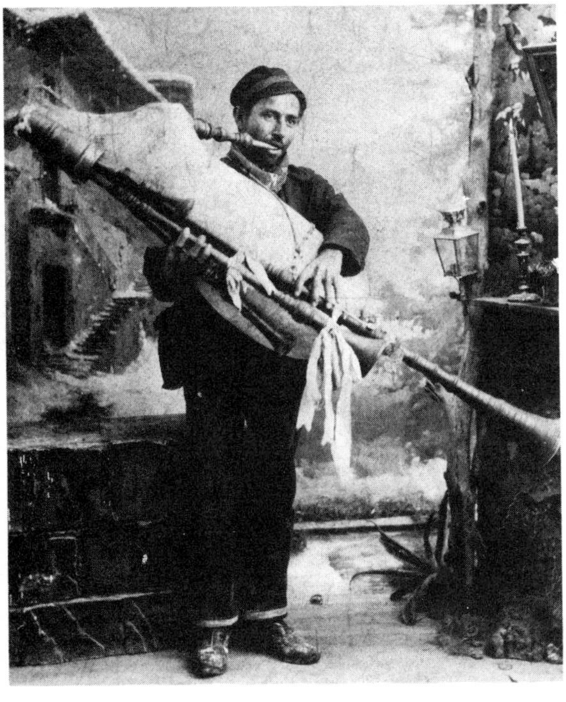

c. Player with zampogna.

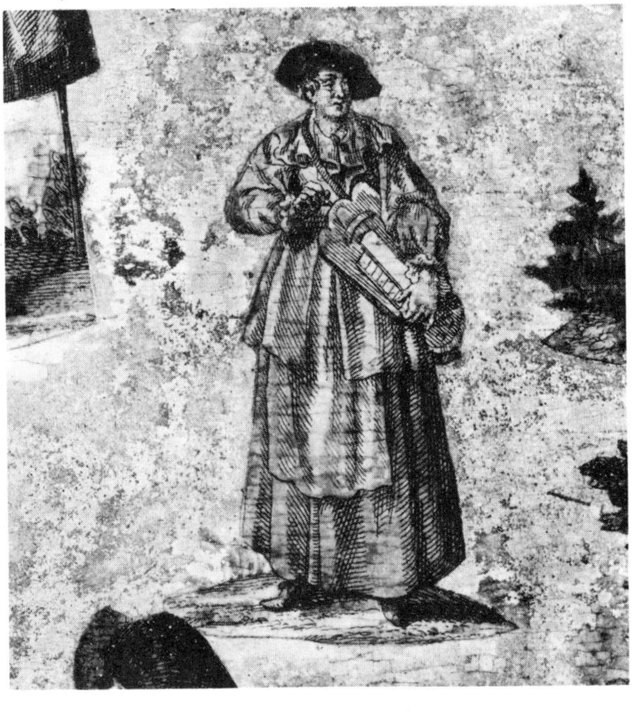

d. Street singer with hurdy-gurdy, from the case of a South Tyrolean psaltery (18th century). Metropolitan Museum of Art, Crosby Brown Collection.

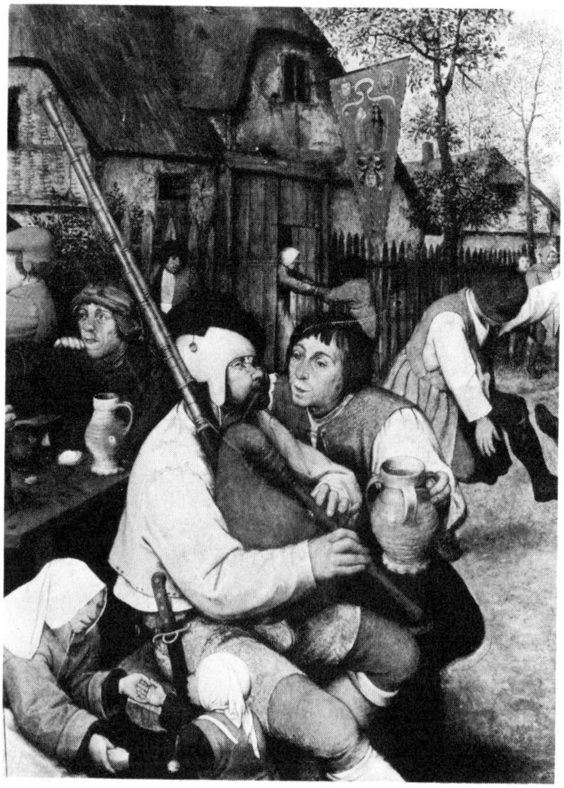

a. Peter Bruegel, *Dance of the Peasants*, detail.

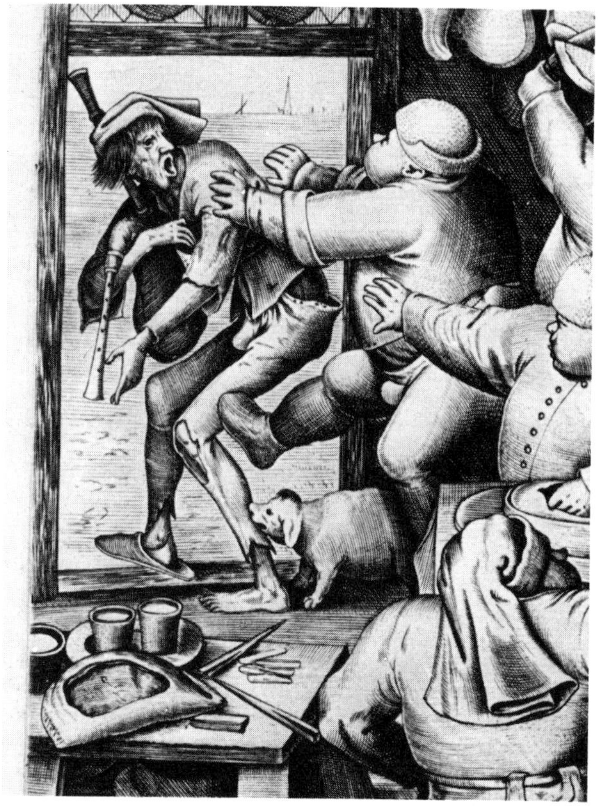

b. Engraving after Peter Bruegel, *The Fat Kitchen*, detail.

c. Vielle player from a woodcut (c. 1570) entitled *Les Noces de Michaud Crouppière: Histoire d'une drollerie facécieuse du Marriage de Lucresse aux yeux de boeuf et Michaud Crouppière son mary, avec ceux qui furent semouz au banquet.*

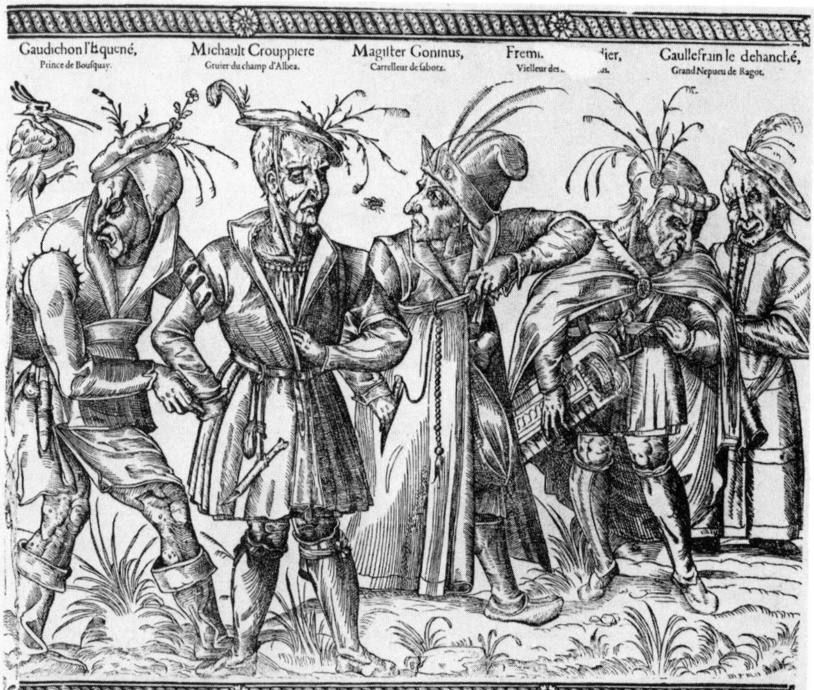

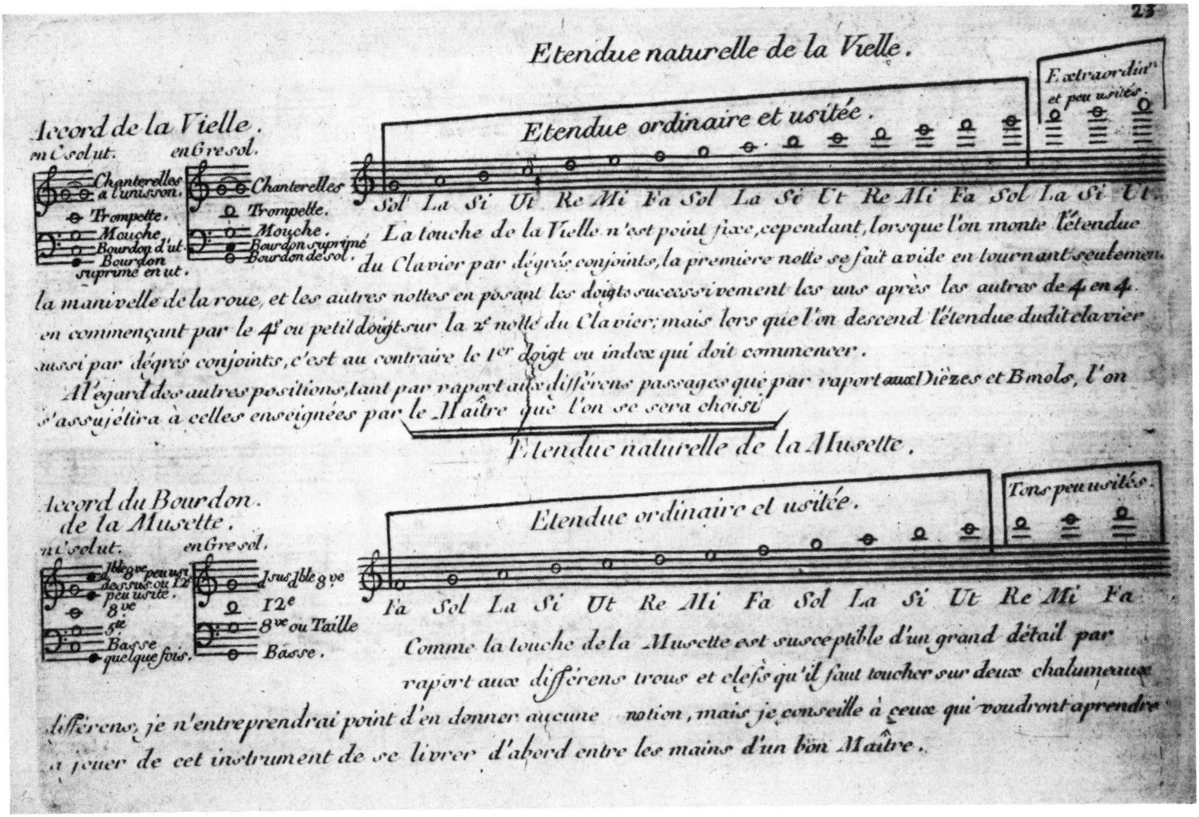

23

Etendue naturelle de la Vielle.

Accord de la Vielle. en C sol ut. en G re sol.

Chanterelles à l'unisson. Trompette. Mouche. Bourdon d'ut. Bourdon suprimé en ut.

Chanterelles. Trompette. Mouche. Bourdon suprimé. Bourdon de sol.

Etendue ordinaire et usitée. Extraordin.res et peu usités.

Sol La Si Ut Re Mi Fa Sol La Si Ut Re Mi Fa Sol La Si Ut

La touche de la Vielle n'est point fixe, cependant, lorsque l'on monte l'étendue du Clavier par dégrés conjoints, la première notte se fait a vide en tournant seulement la manivelle de la roue, et les autres nottes en posant les doigts successivement les uns après les autres de 4 en 4 en commençant par le 4.e ou petit doigt sur la 2.e notte du Clavier; mais lors que l'on descend l'étendue dudit clavier aussi par dégrés conjoints, c'est au contraire le 1.er doigt ou index qui doit commencer.

A l'egard des autres positions, tant par raport aux différens passages que par raport aux Dièzes et Bmols, l'on s'assujétira à celles enseignées par le Maître que l'on se sera choisi.

Etendue naturelle de la Musette.

Accord du Bourdon de la Musette. en C sol ut. en G re sol.

Ible 8.ve peu usité. dessus ou 12.e peu usité. 8.ve 5.te Basse quelque fois.

Ible 8.ve 12.e 8.ve ou Taille Basse.

Etendue ordinaire et usitée. Tons peu usités.

Fa Sol La Si Ut Re Mi Fa Sol La Si Ut Re Mi Fa

Comme la touche de la Musette est susceptible d'un grand détail par raport aux différens trous et clefs qu'il faut toucher sur deux chalumeaux différens, je n'entreprendrai point d'en donner aucune notion, mais je conseille à ceux qui voudront aprendre a jouer de cet instrument de se livrer d'abord entre les mains d'un bon Maître.

a. Page from Bordet's *Méthode raisonnée*, Paris, c. 1755.

b. Cornemuse with ivory pipes (France, 18th century). Length of chanter, 10 inches; of drone, 7 inches. Metropolitan Museum of Art, Crosby Brown Collection.

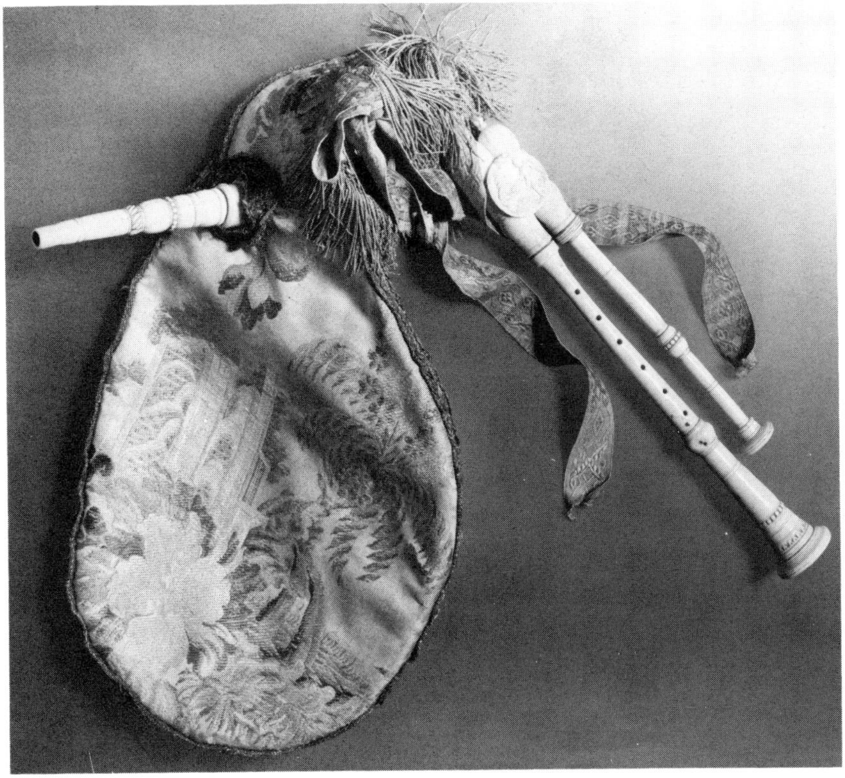

PLATE 30

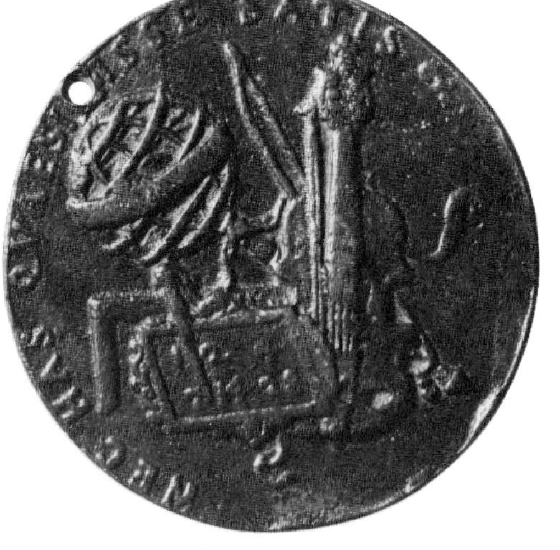

a. Plaque for the musical scholar Ercole Bottrigari (early 17th century).

b. Orpheus in Hades, after a bronze plaque by Moderno.

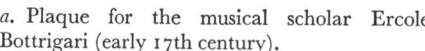

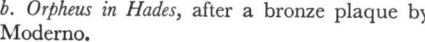

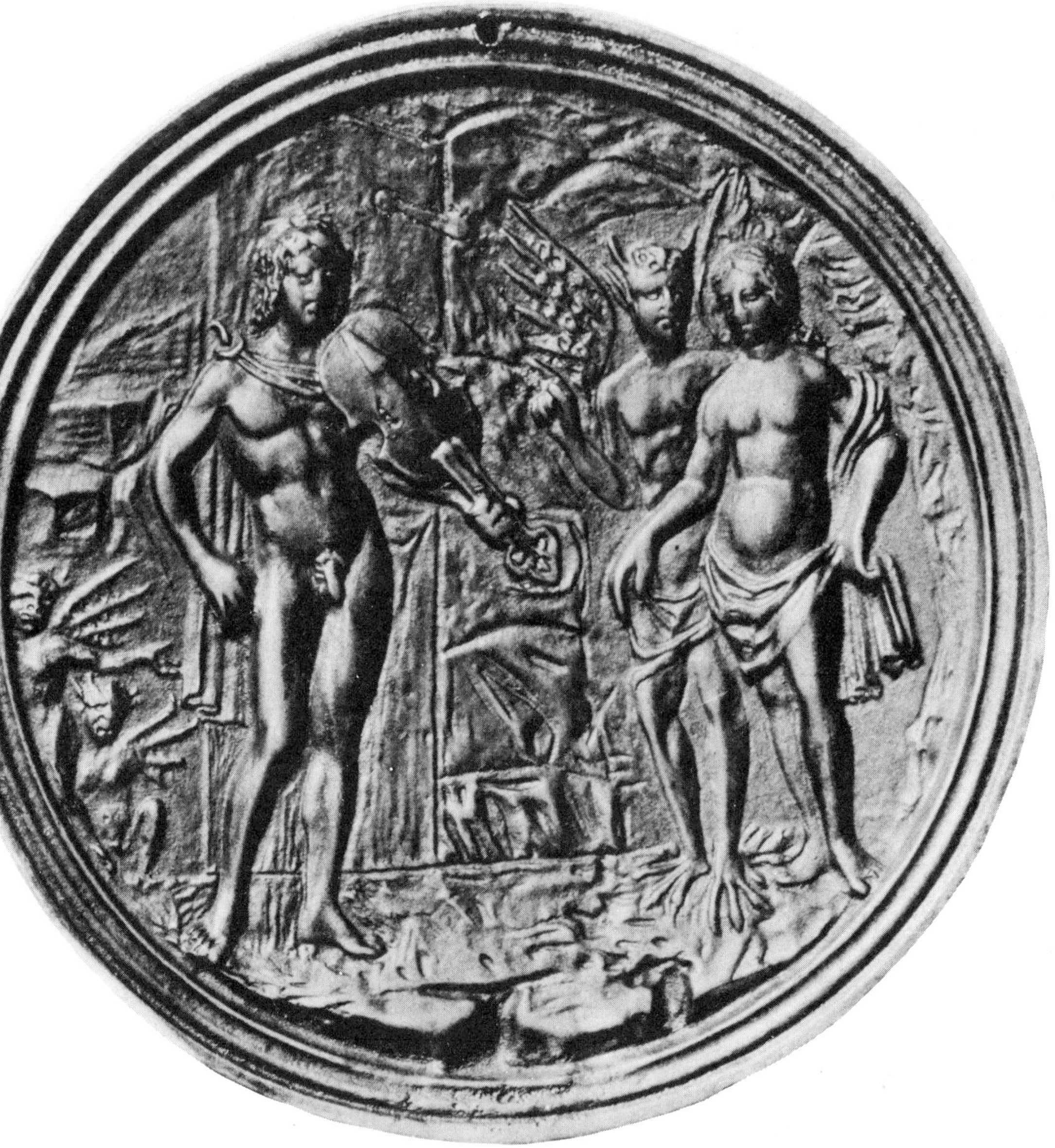

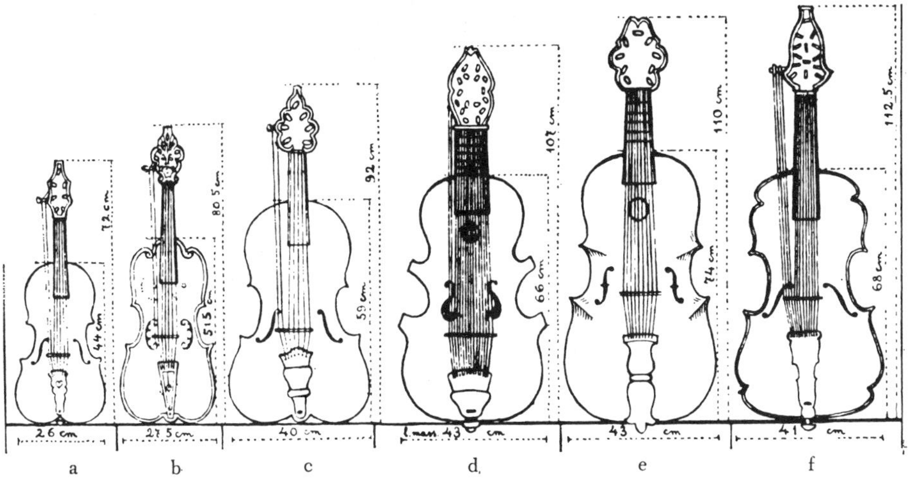

Examples of various lire da braccio and lire da gamba (after sketches by Disertori in *Rivista musicale italiana*, XLIV [1940]): *a.* Lira da braccio, Brussels Conservatory, Mahillon Catalogue 1443. *b.* Lira da braccio, Kunsthistorisches Museum, Vienna, Schlosser Catalogue 94. *c.* Lirone, Heyer Collection, Kinsky Catalogue 780. *d.* Lira da gamba, Heyer Collection, Kinsky Catalogue 784. *e.* Lira da gamba, Brussels Conservatory, Mahillon Catalogue 1444. *f.* Lira da gamba, Kunsthistorisches Museum, Vienna, Schlosser Catalogue 95.

g. Lira da braccio by Giovanni d'Andrea, Venice, 1511; front and back views (same as *b* above).

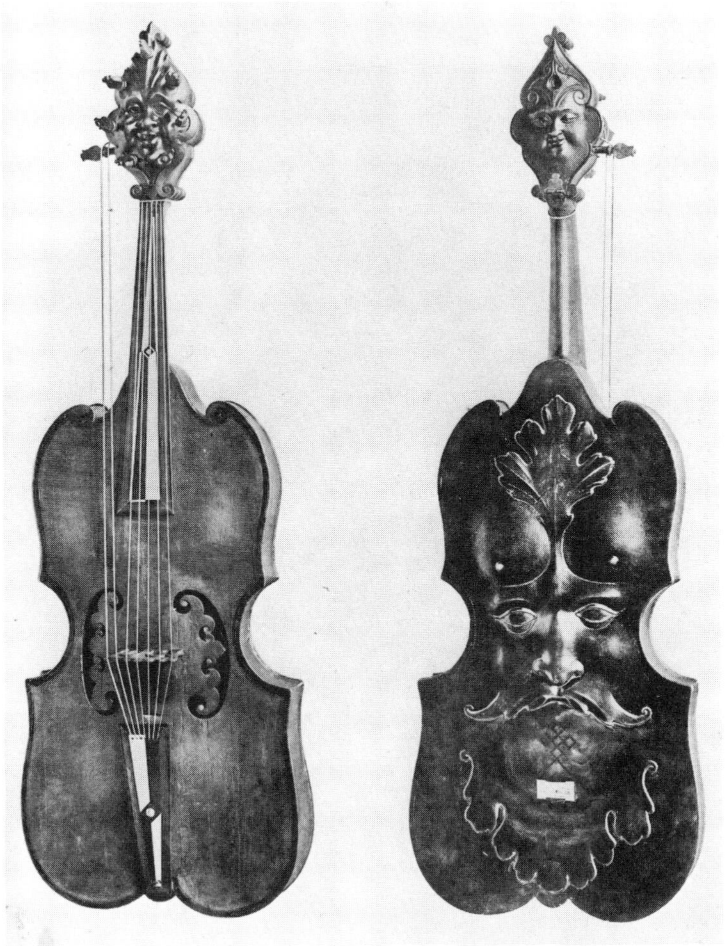

h. Lira da gamba by Wendelin Tieffenbrucker, Padua, c. 1590 (same as *f* above).

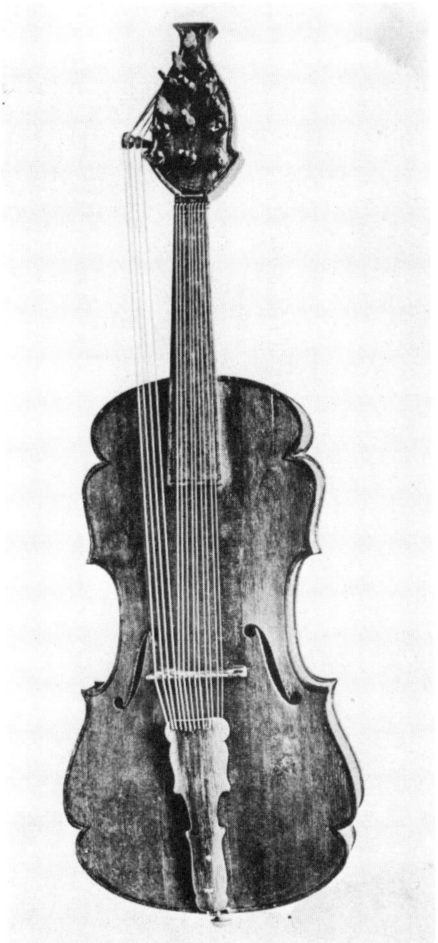

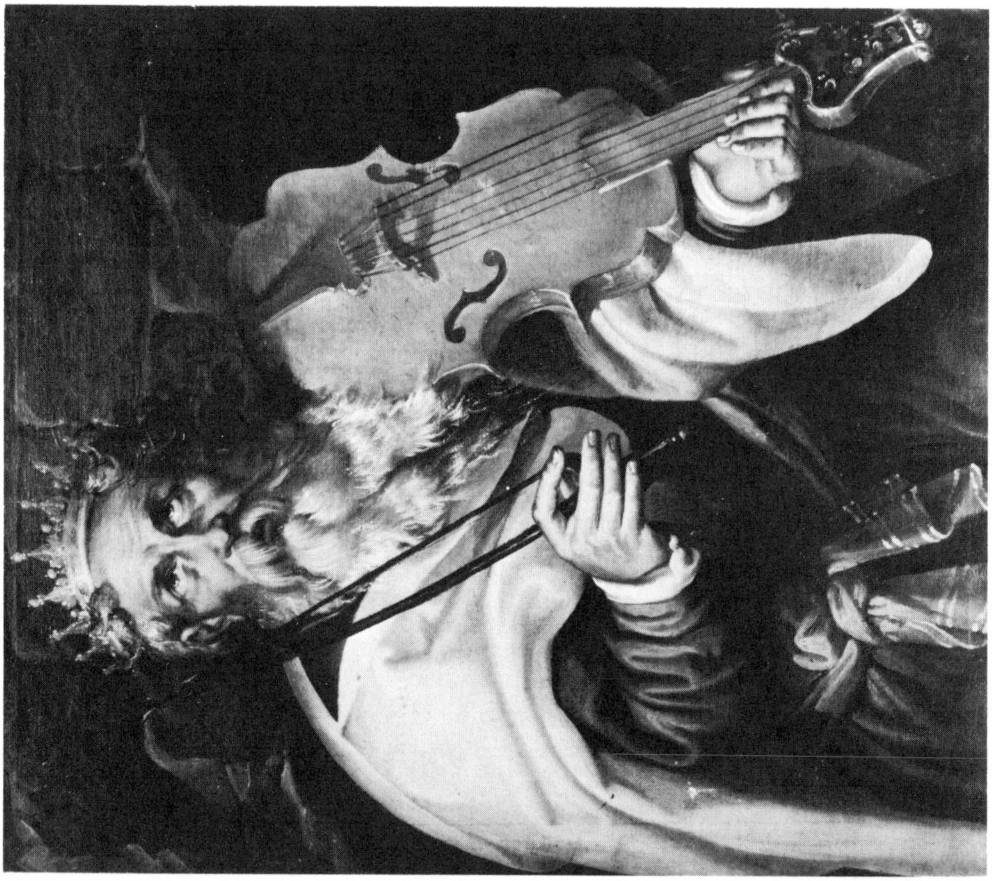

a. Bartolommeo Passerotti, *King David.* Galleria Spada, Rome.

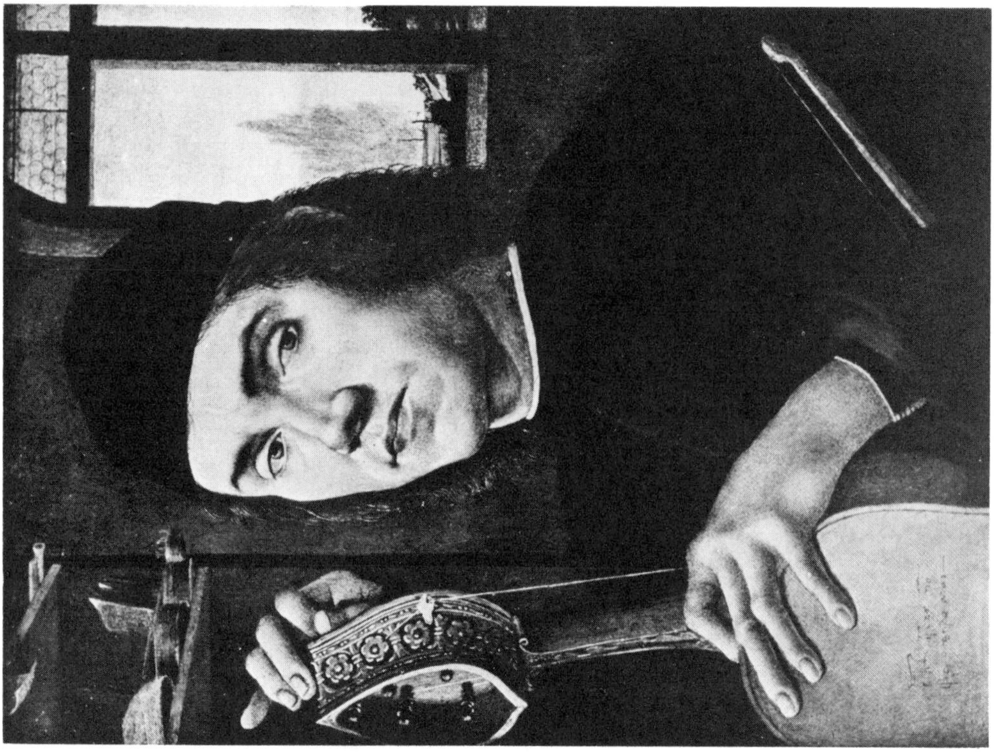

b. Raffaellino del Garbo, *Musician.* National Gallery, Dublin.

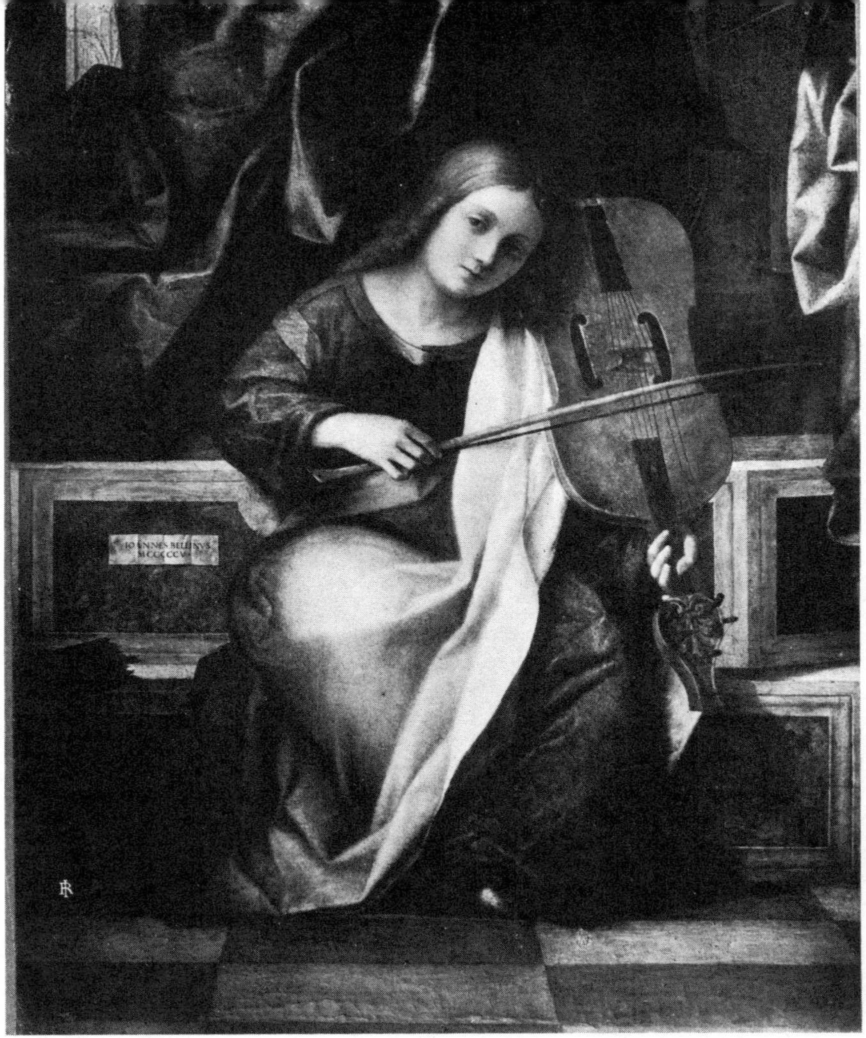

a. Giovanni Bellini, detail from altarpiece. San Zaccaria, Venice.

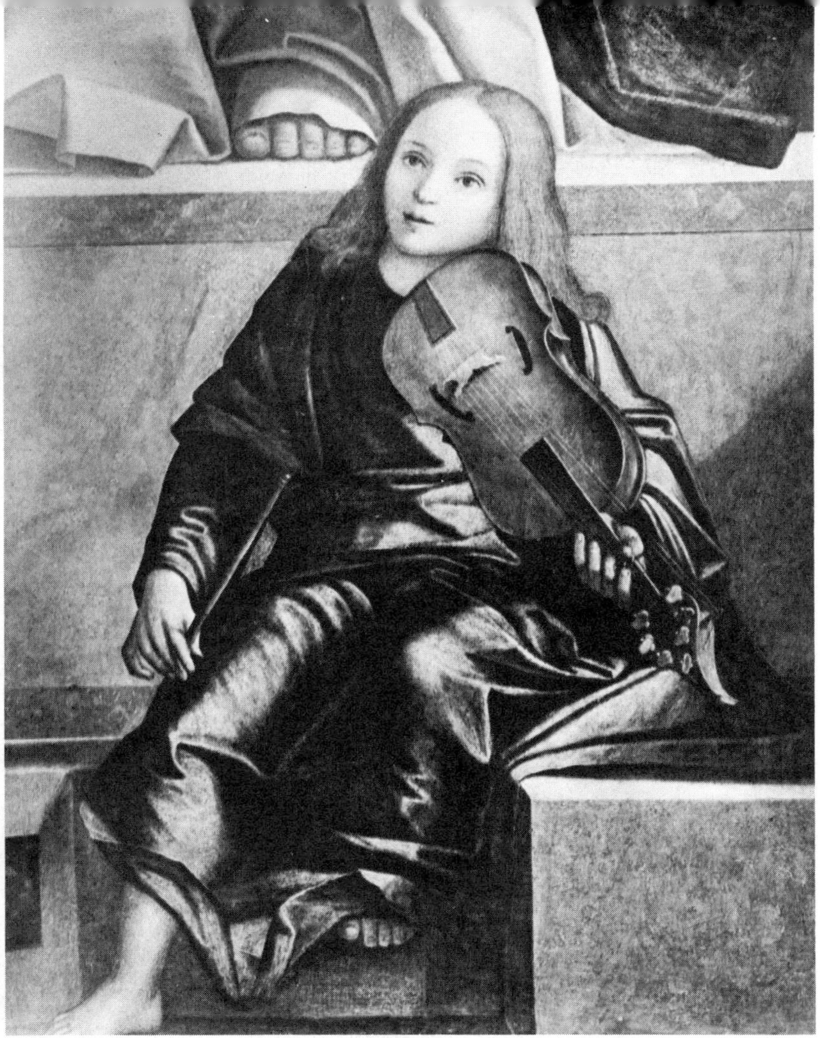

b. Vittore Carpaccio, *Presentation in the Temple*, detail. Accademia, Venice.

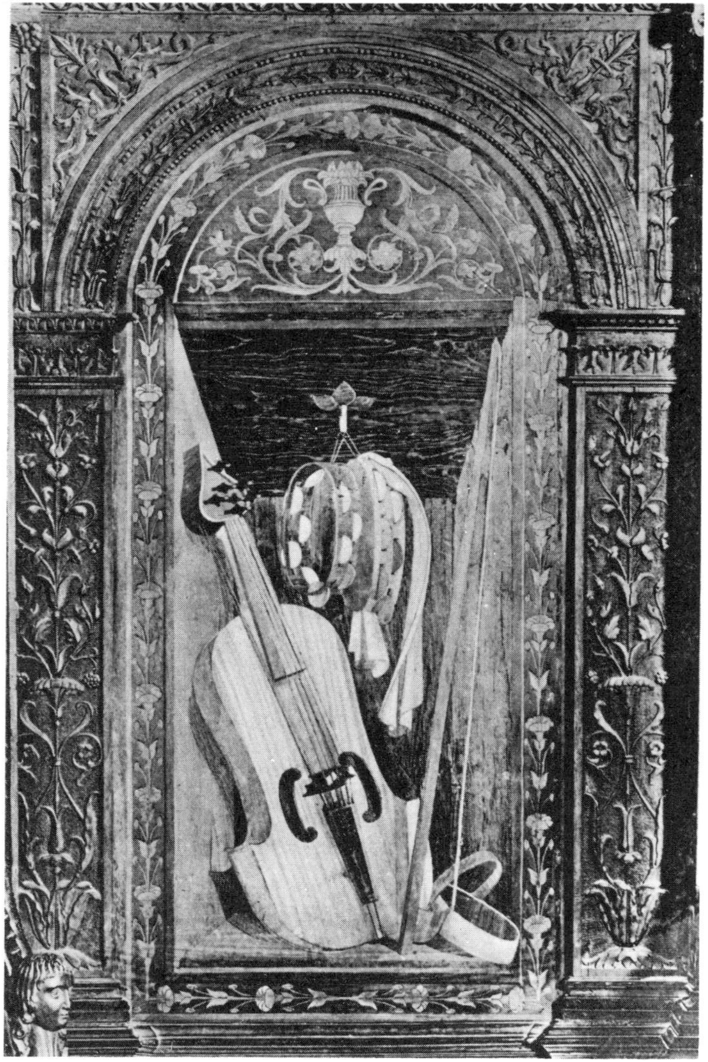

a. Lira da braccio in wood intarsia. Choir stall in Santa Maria in Organo, Venice.

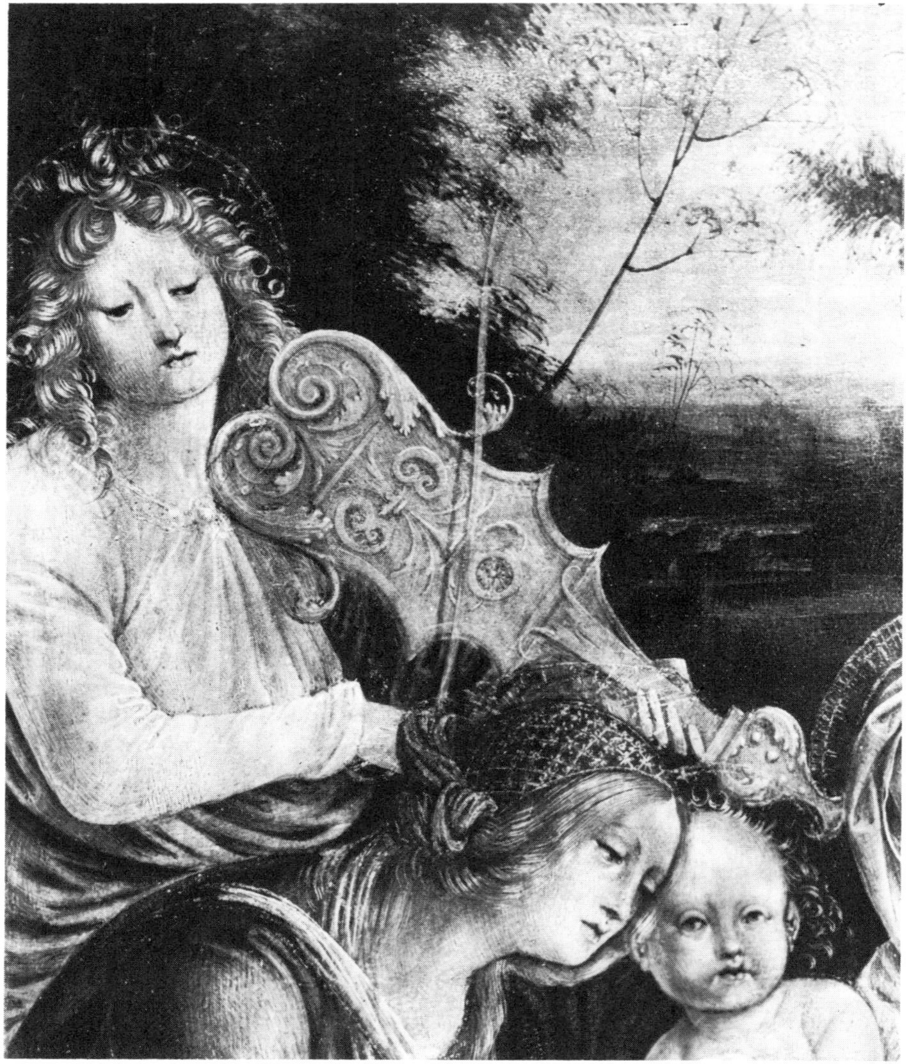

b. Gaudenzio Ferrari, detail from *Virgin with St. Anne*. Pinacoteca, Turin.

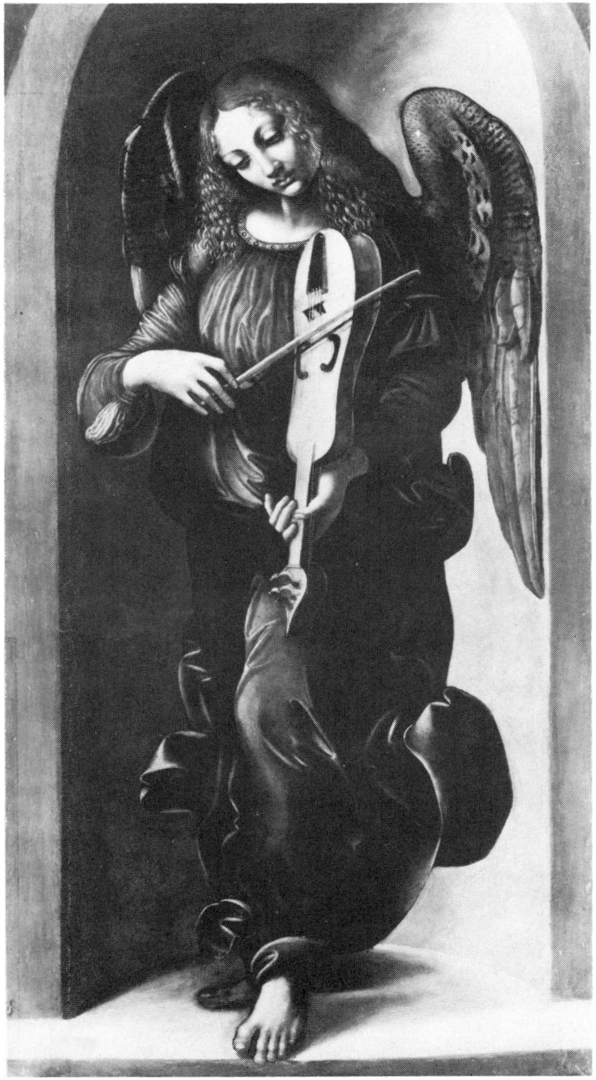

a. Ambrogio de Predis, detail showing angel with lira da braccio. National Gallery, London.

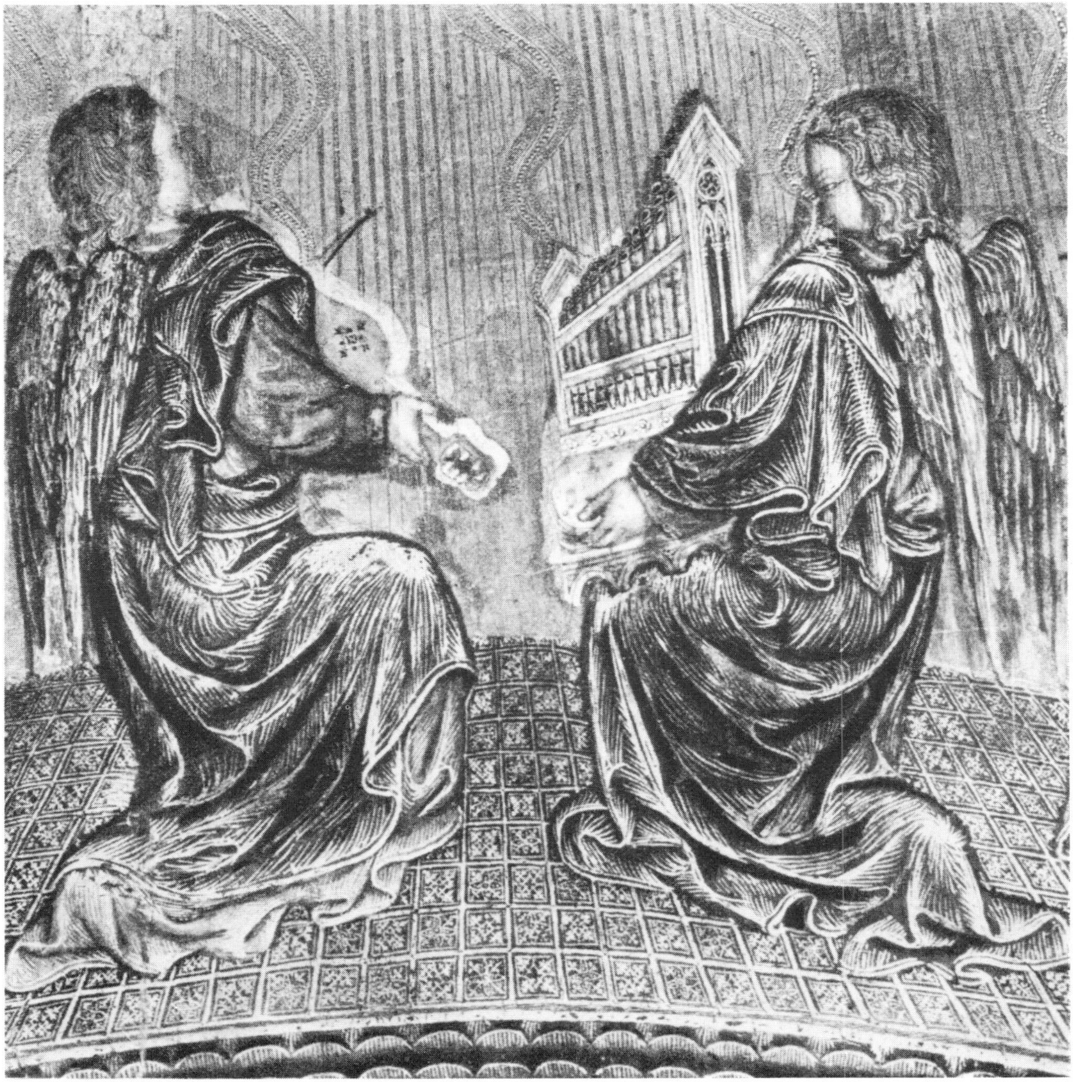

b. Gentile da Fabriano, detail from *Coronation of the Virgin*, showing angels with portative and early form of lira da braccio. Brera, Milan.

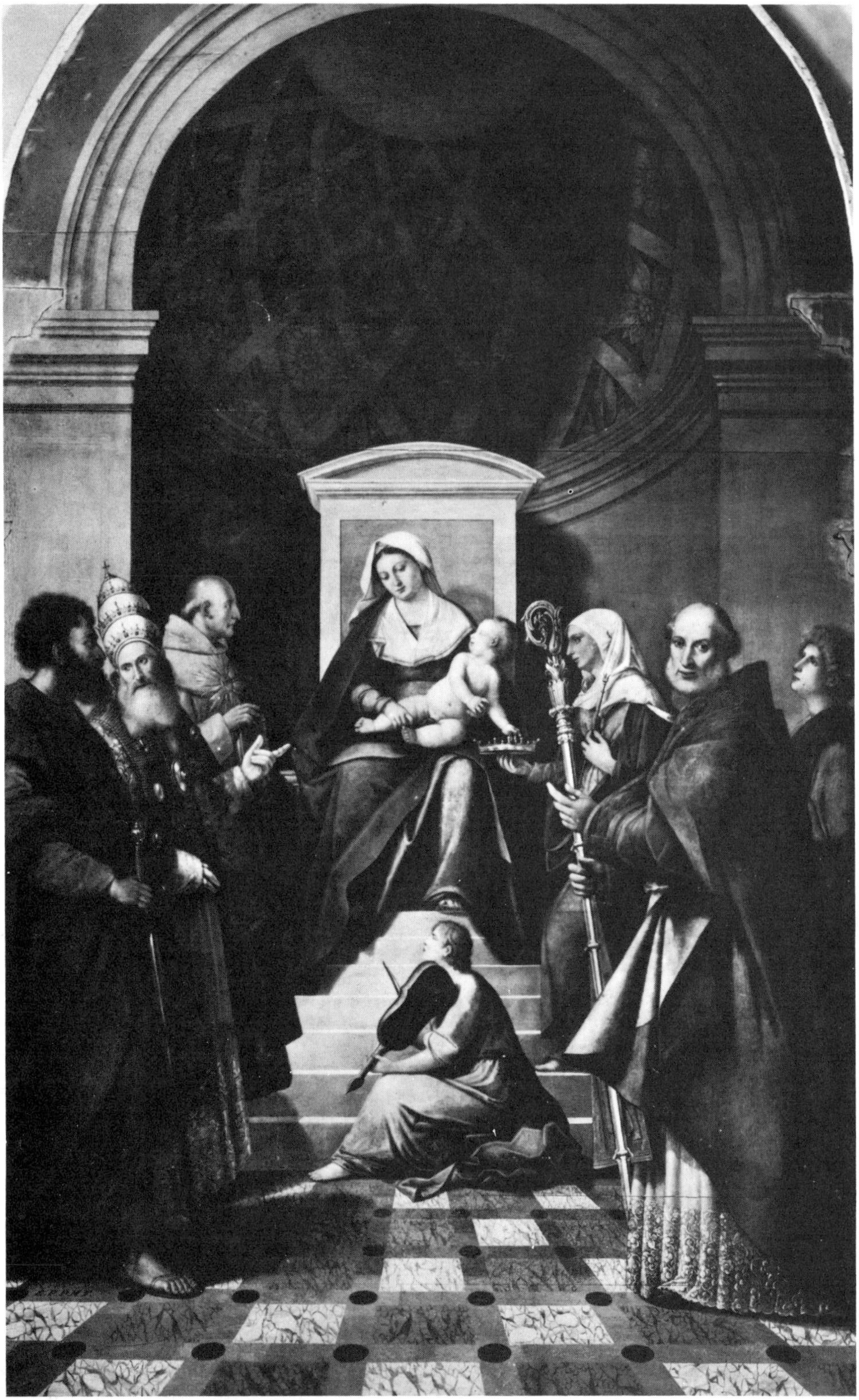

Palma Vecchio, *Sacra conversazione*. San Zaccaria, Venice.

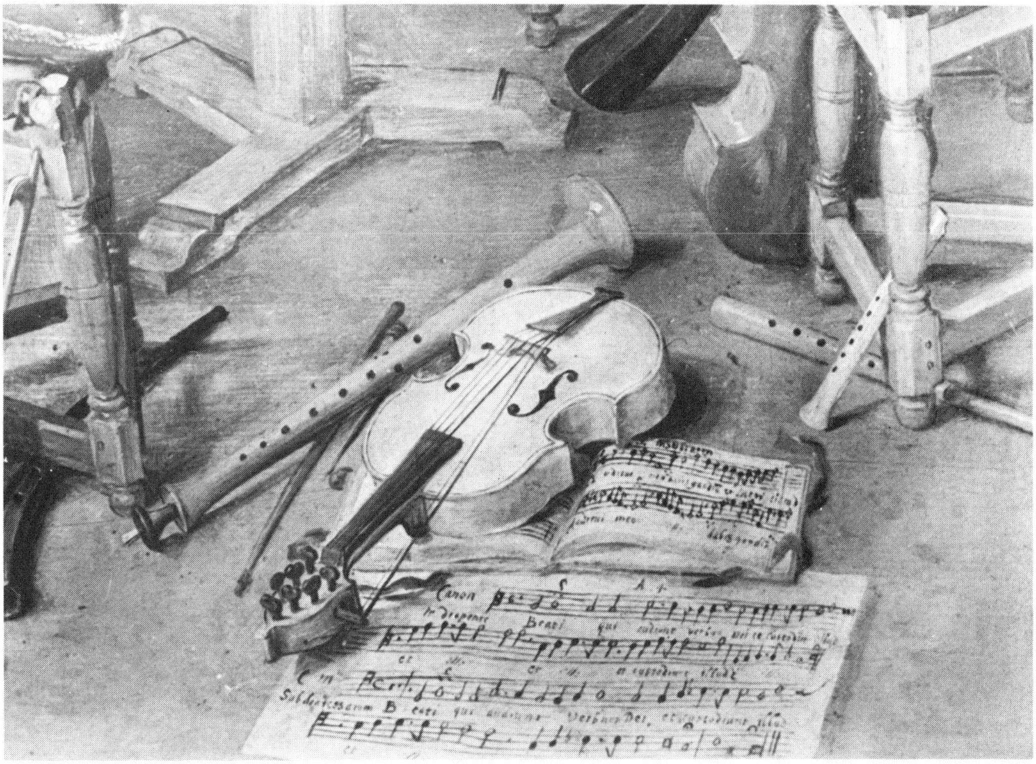

a. Jan Bruegel the Elder, detail from *Allegory of Hearing*. Prado, Madrid.

b. Luca Signorelli, detail from fresco, showing angel tuning lira da braccio. Cathedral, Orvieto.

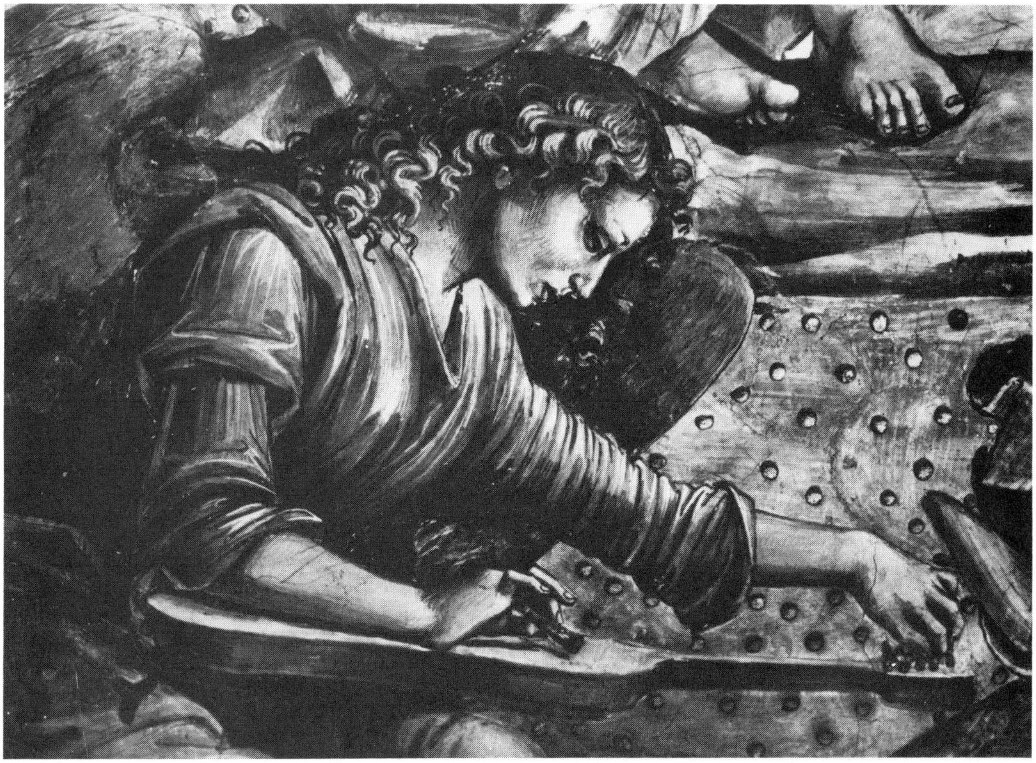

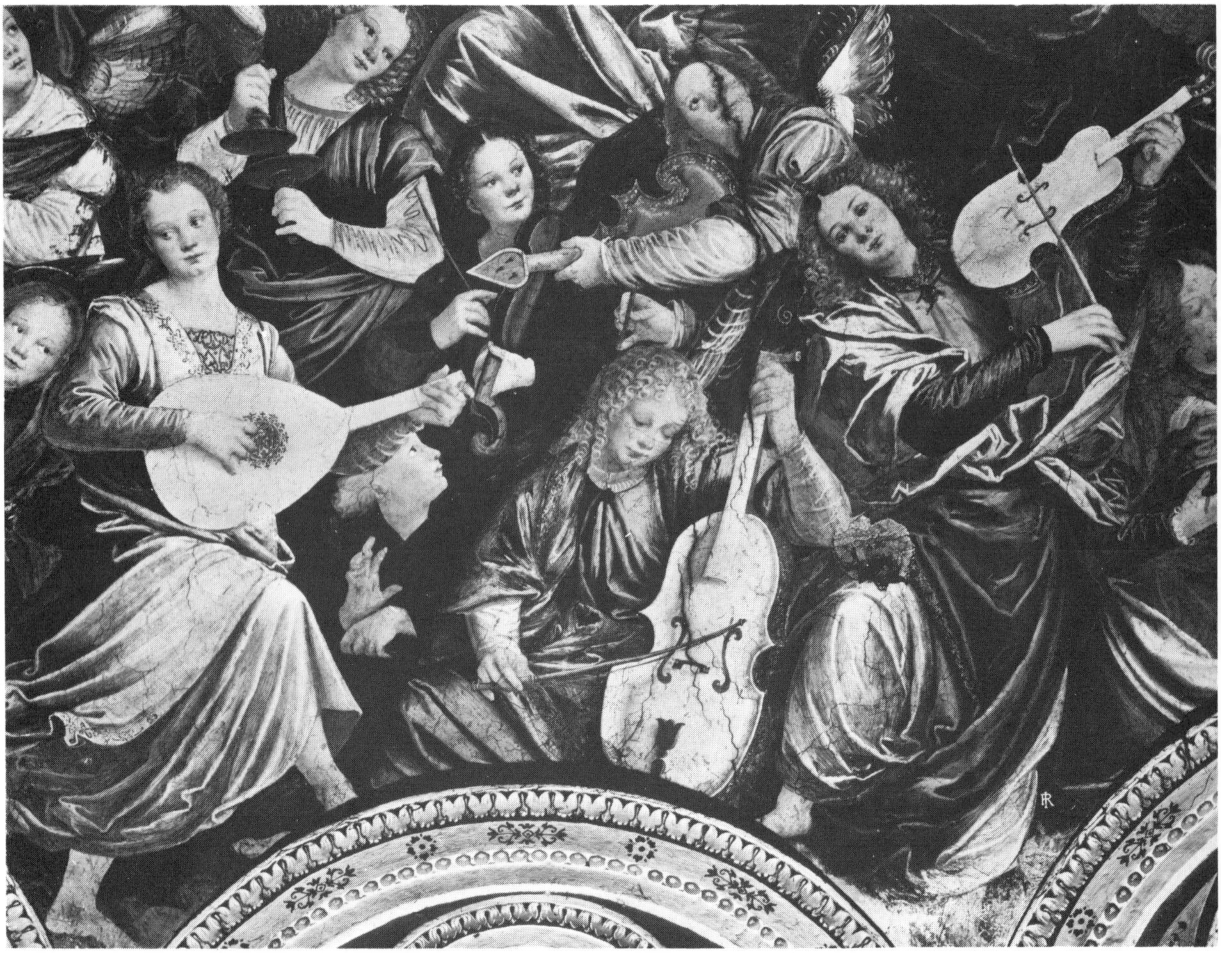

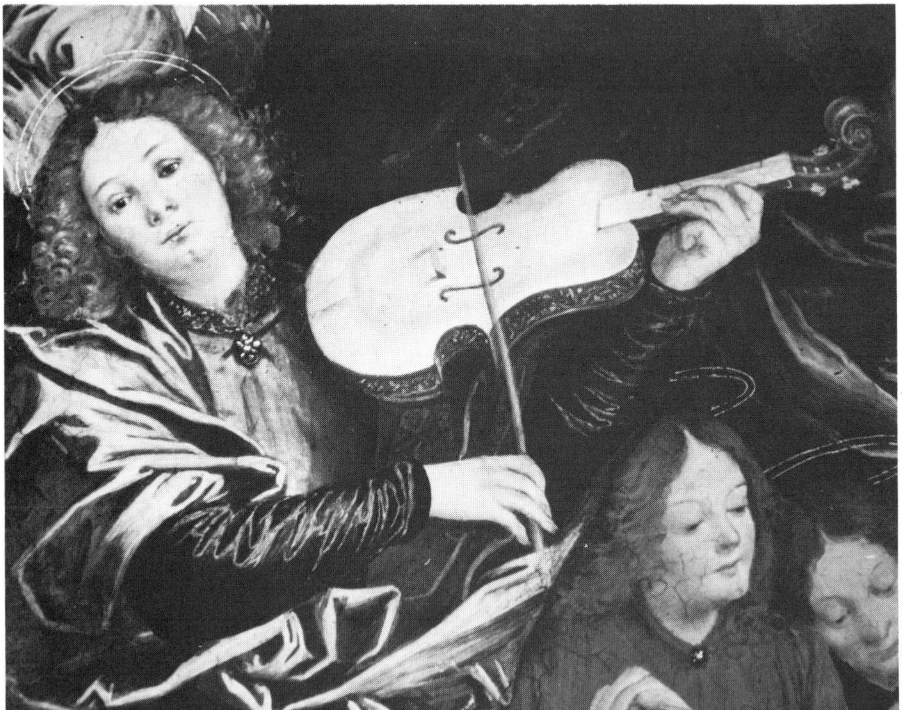

a. Gaudenzio Ferrari, detail from fresco. Santuario, Saronno.

b. Detail of Plate 38*a*.

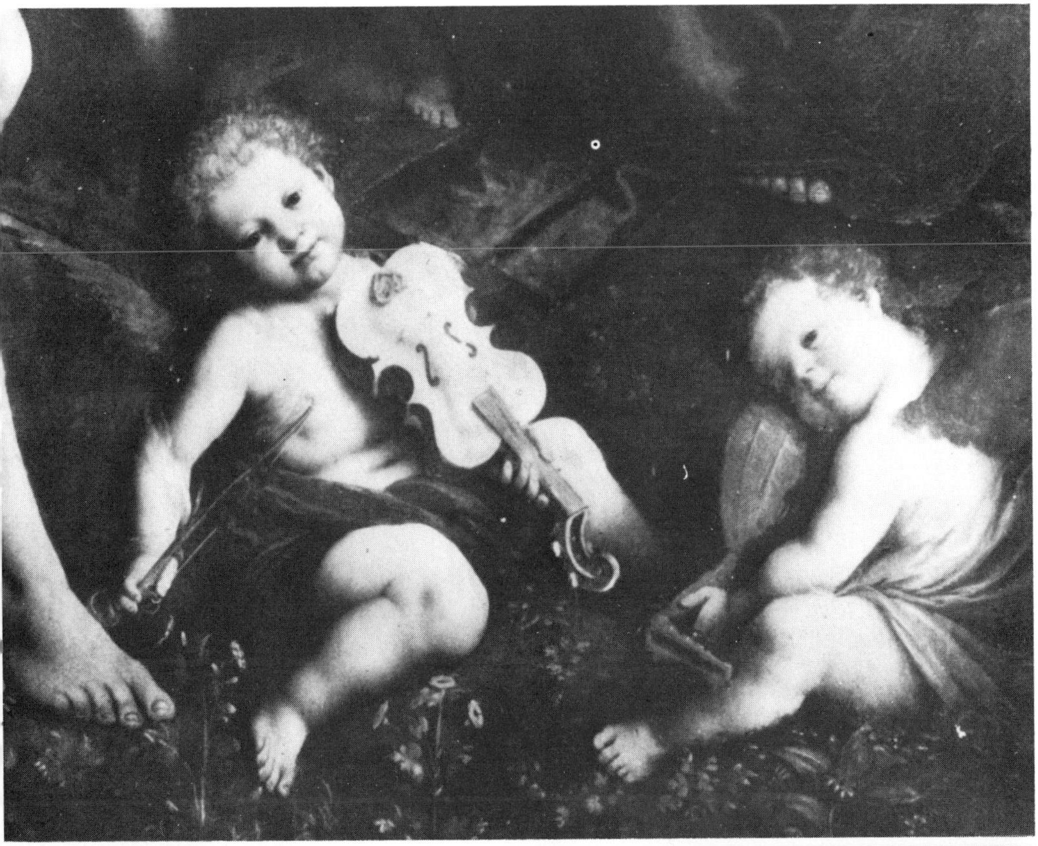

a. Gaudenzio Ferrari, detail of *La Madonna degli aranci*, Church of San Cristoforo, Vercelli.

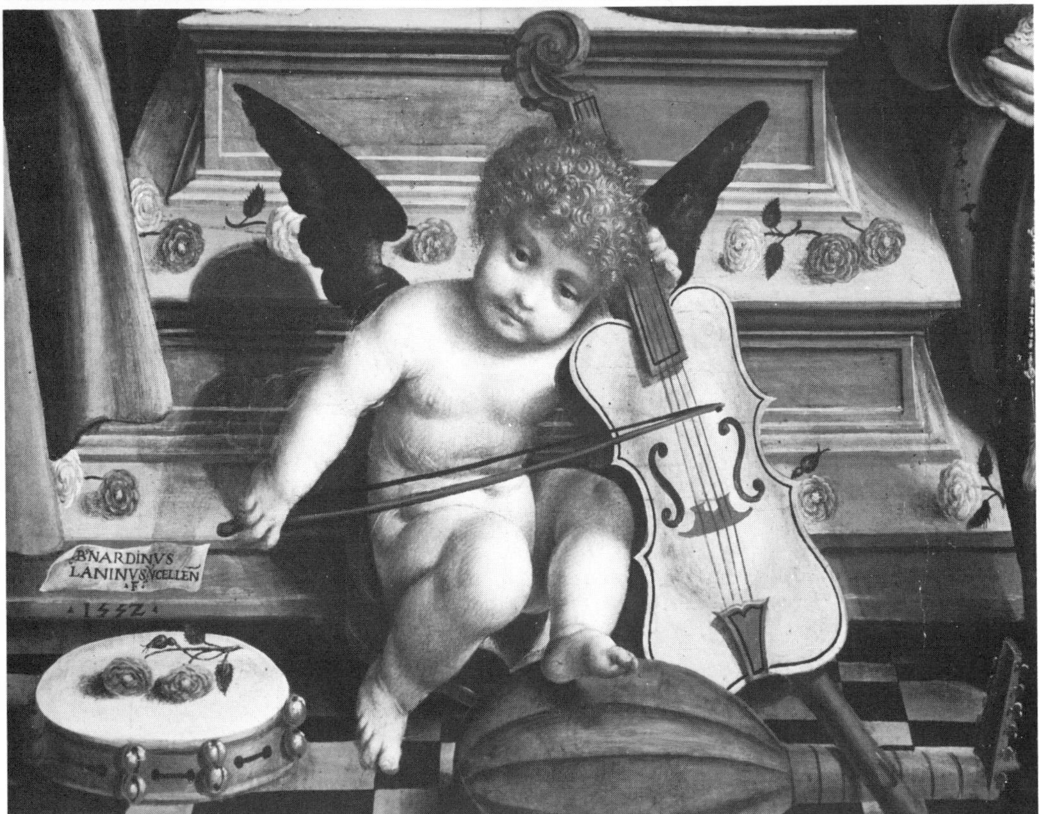

b. Bernardino Lanini, detail of *Sacra conversazione*, Raleigh Museum, Raleigh, North Carolina.

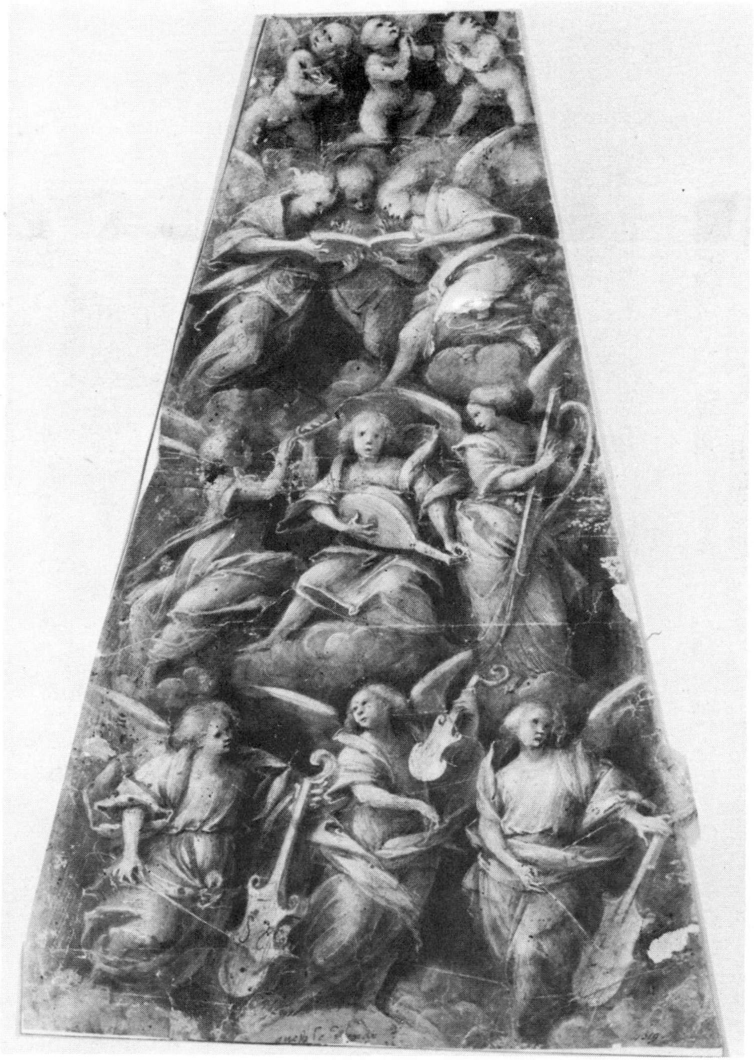

a. Gaudenzio Ferrari, study for an angel concert. Staatliche Graphische Sammlung, Munich.

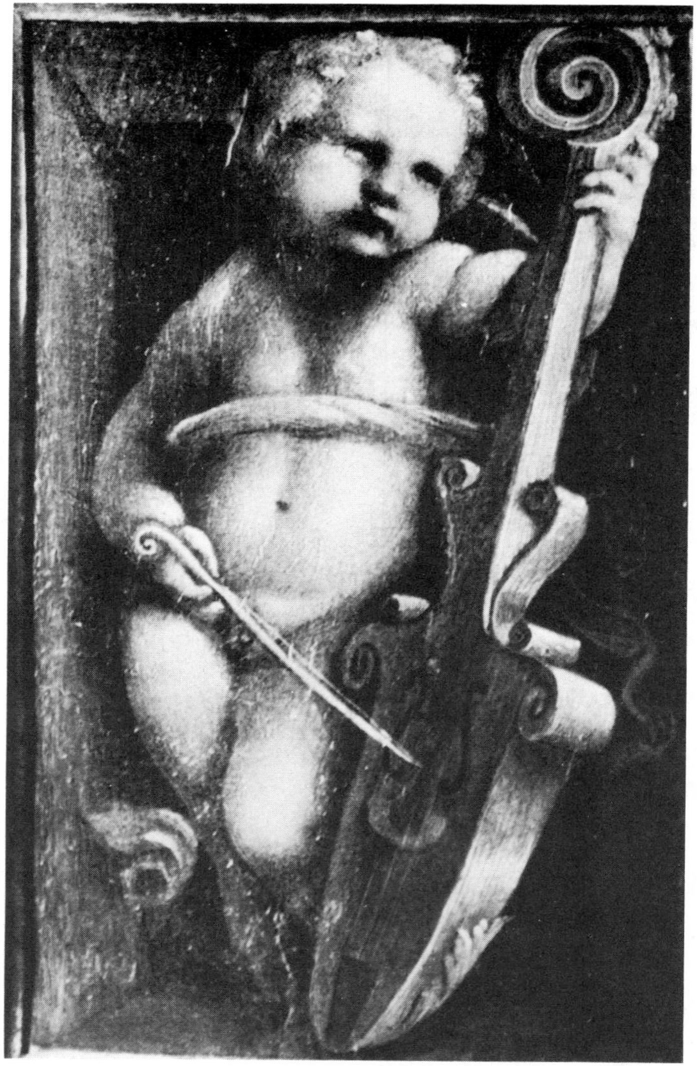

b. Gaudenzio Ferrari, *putto* with bowed instrument. Collection of E. Schweitzer, Berlin.

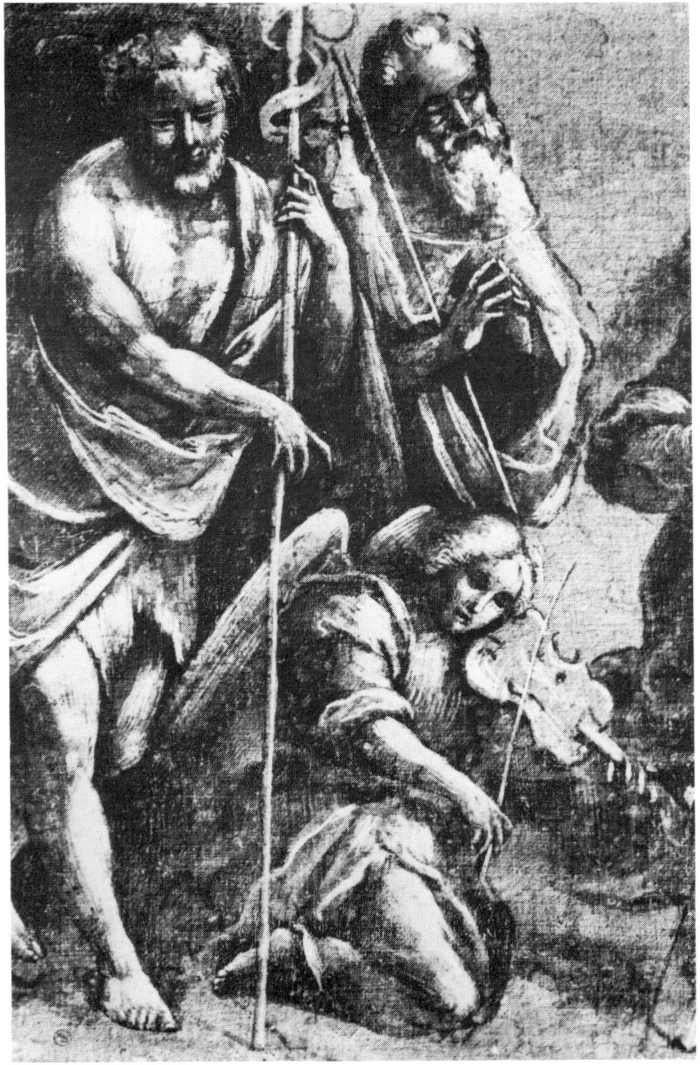

a. Gaudenzio Ferrari, sketch for an *Adoration of the Child*. Palazzo Reale, Turin.

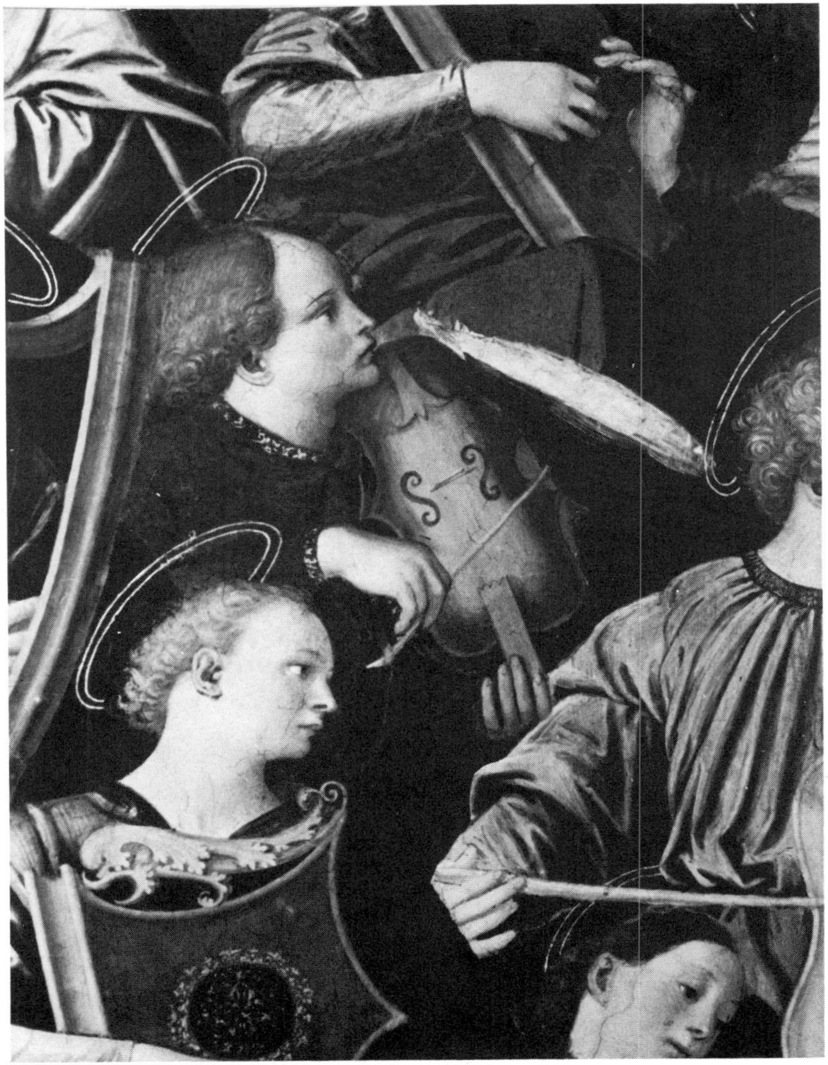

b. Gaudenzio Ferrari, detail from fresco. Santuario, Saronno.

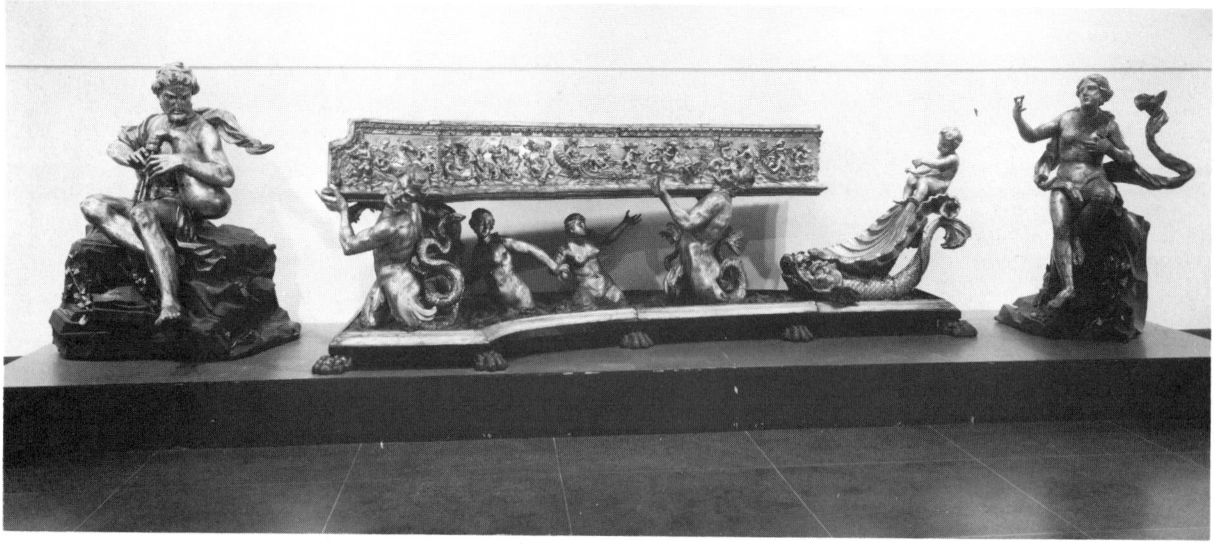

a. Harpsichord, supported by tritons and sea nymphs, with companion figures of Polyphemus and Galatea (Roman, 17th century). Metropolitan Museum of Art, Crosby Brown Collection.

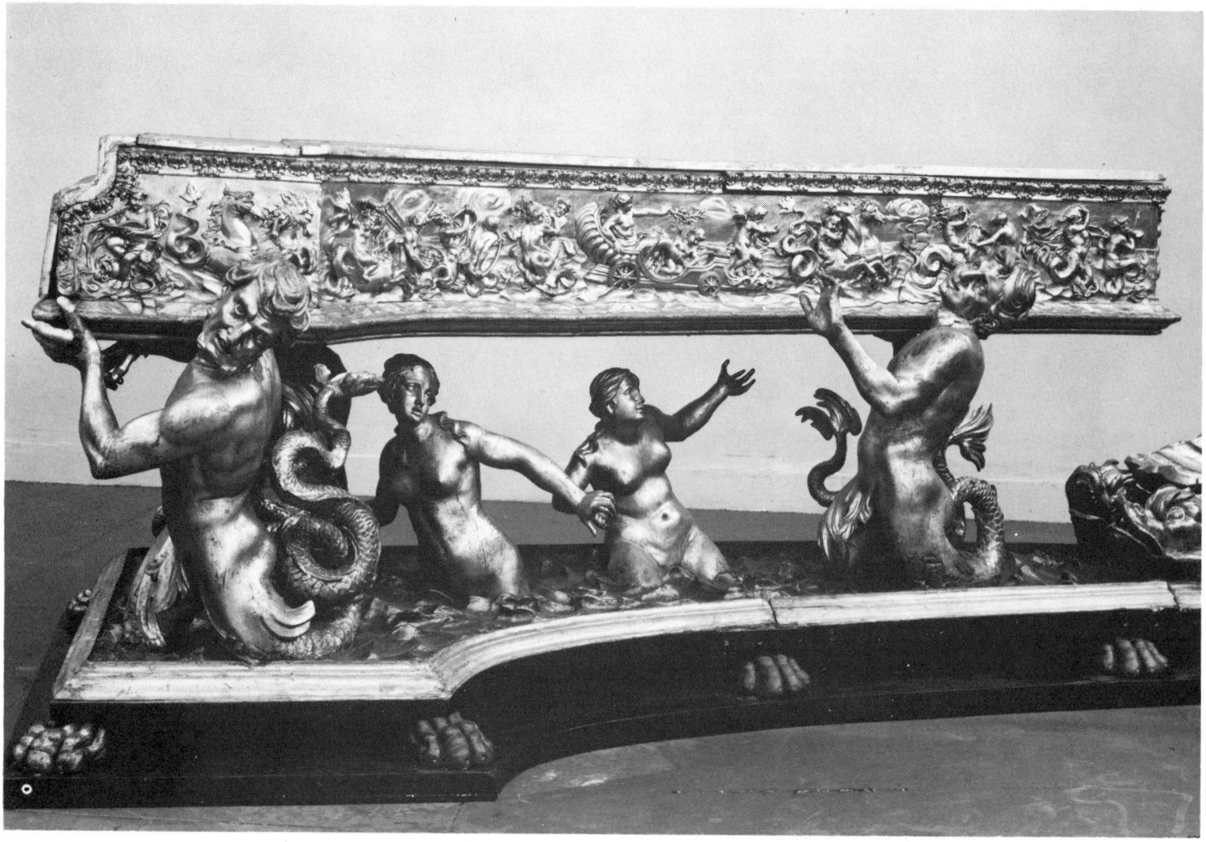

b. Detail of harpsichord, with frieze showing triumph of Galatea.

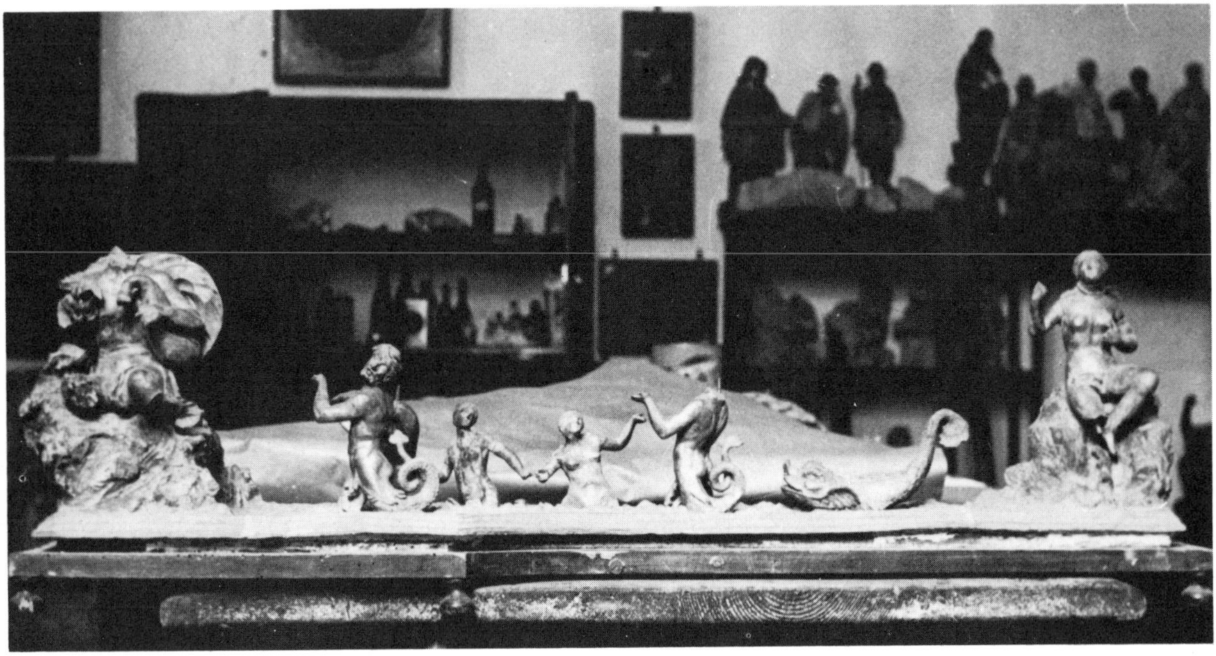

a. Small clay model of harpsichord, in partially assembled state. Palazzo Venezia, Rome.

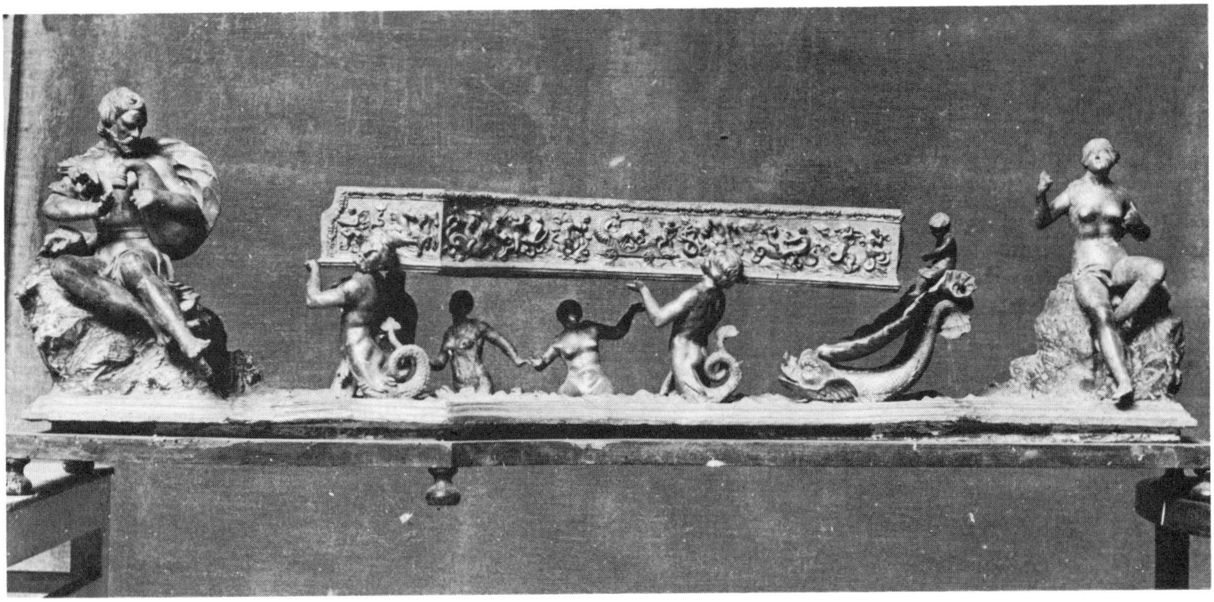

b. The model of the harpsichord, in completed state.

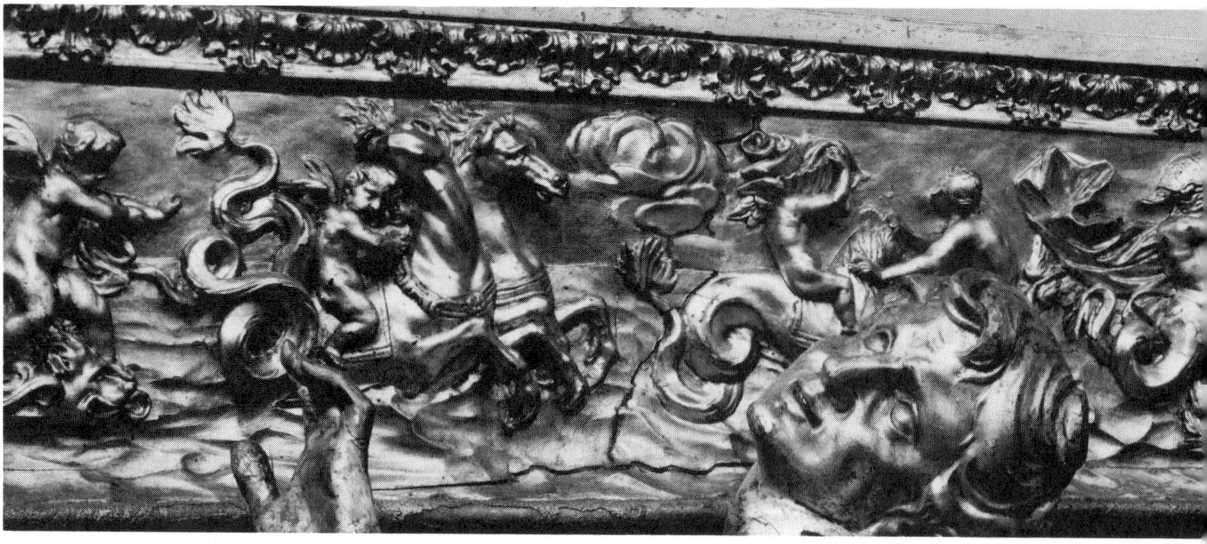

a. Detail of frieze on harpsichord.

b. One of the tritons at the front of the harpsichord, beneath the left end of the keyboard.

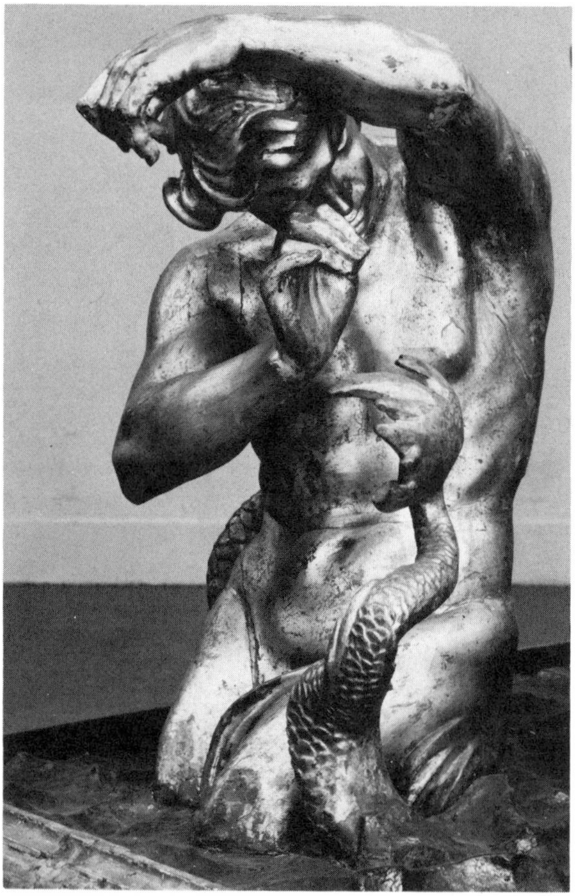

c. Putto riding sea shell, at end of harpsichord.

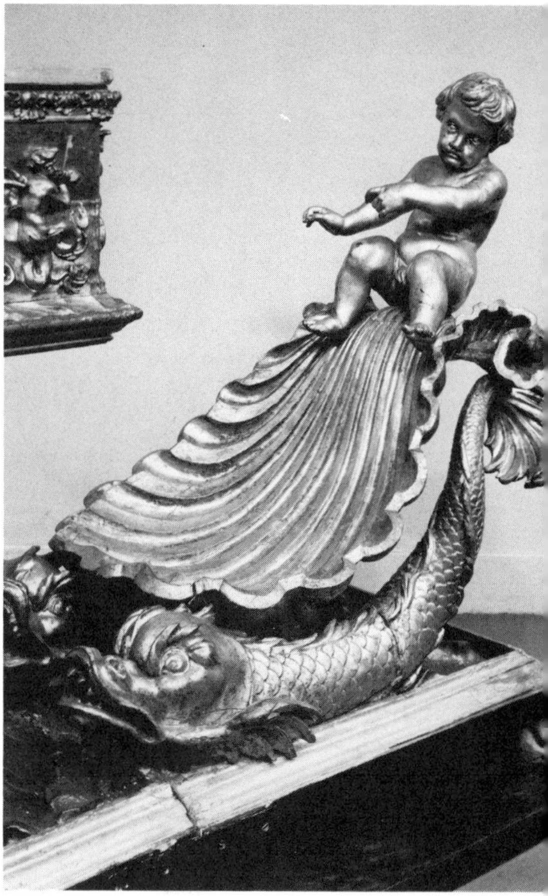

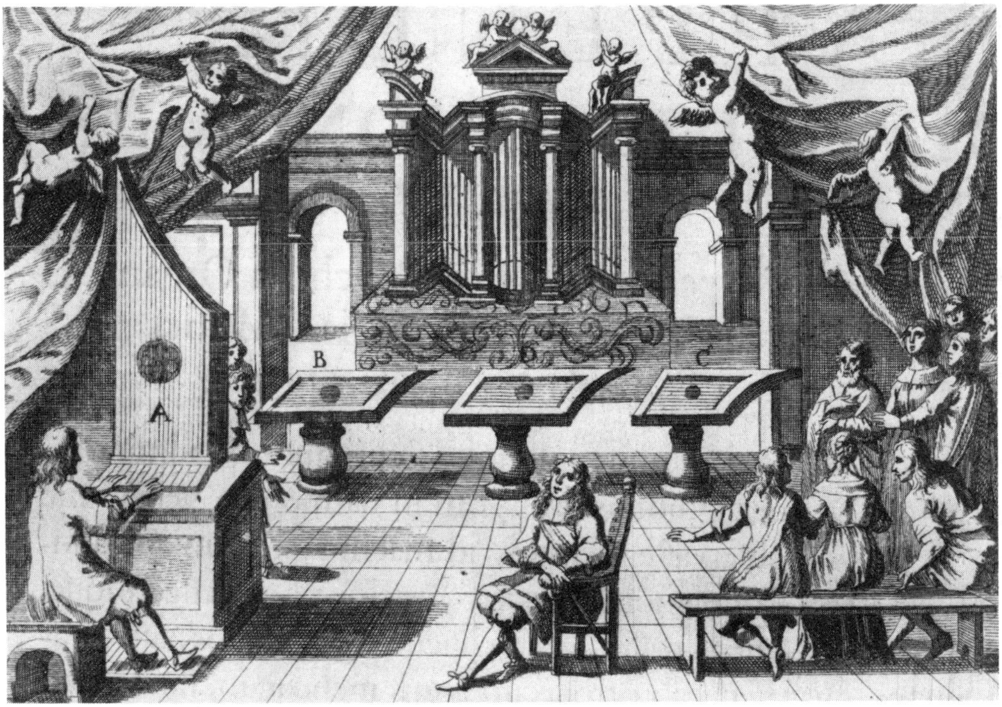

a. Schematic view of an exhibition room in Todini's music museum in Rome, with a musician (perhaps Todini himself) playing one instrument and, magically, three others at a distance. From Kircher's *Phonurgia nova*, 1673.

b. Another view of the same room, evidently drawn on the spot. Four keyboard instruments are attached to a structure hiding their mechanical connection. From Buonanni's *Gabinetto armonico*, 1722.

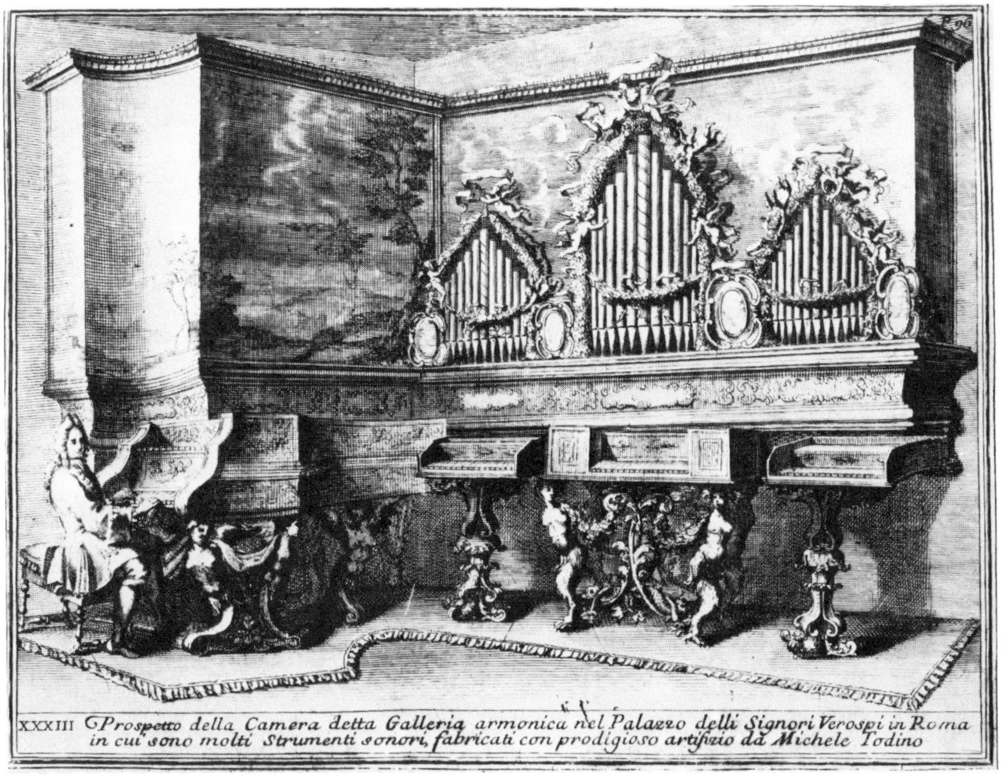
96
XXXIII Prospetto della Camera detta Galleria armonica nel Palazzo delli Signori Verospi in Roma
in cui sono molti Strumenti sonori, fabricati con prodigioso artifizio da Michele Todino

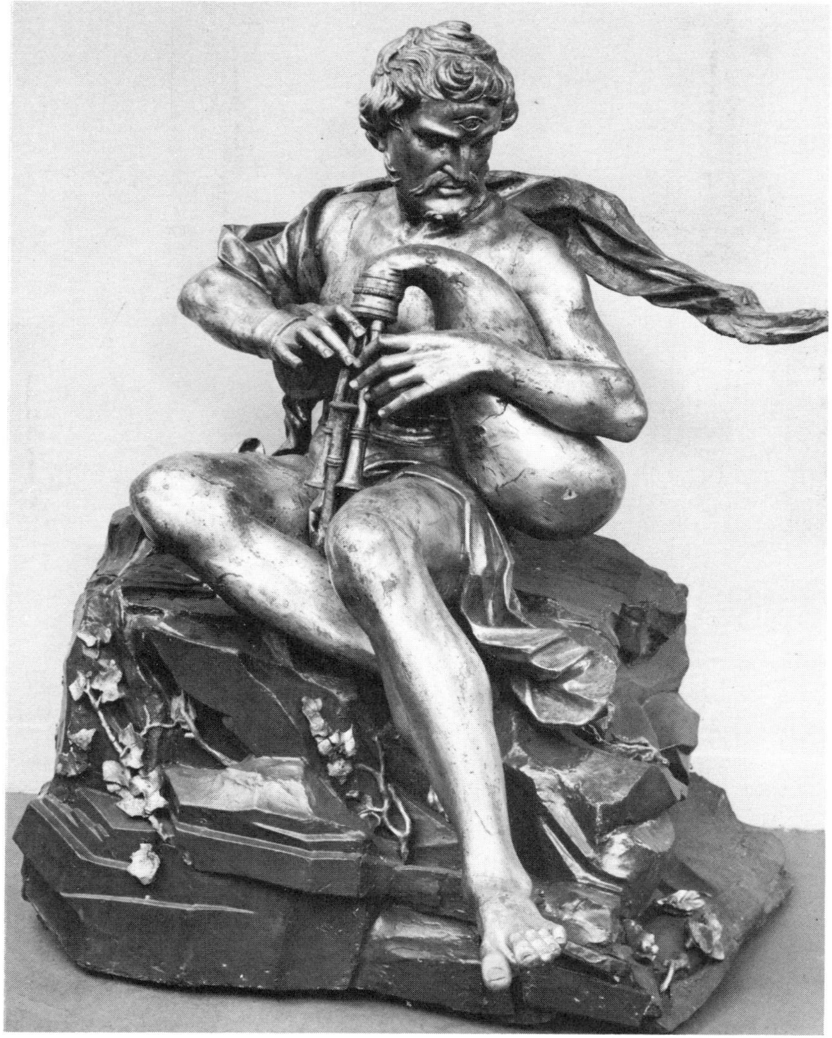

a. Figure of Polyphemus playing a bagpipe, from the harpsichord.

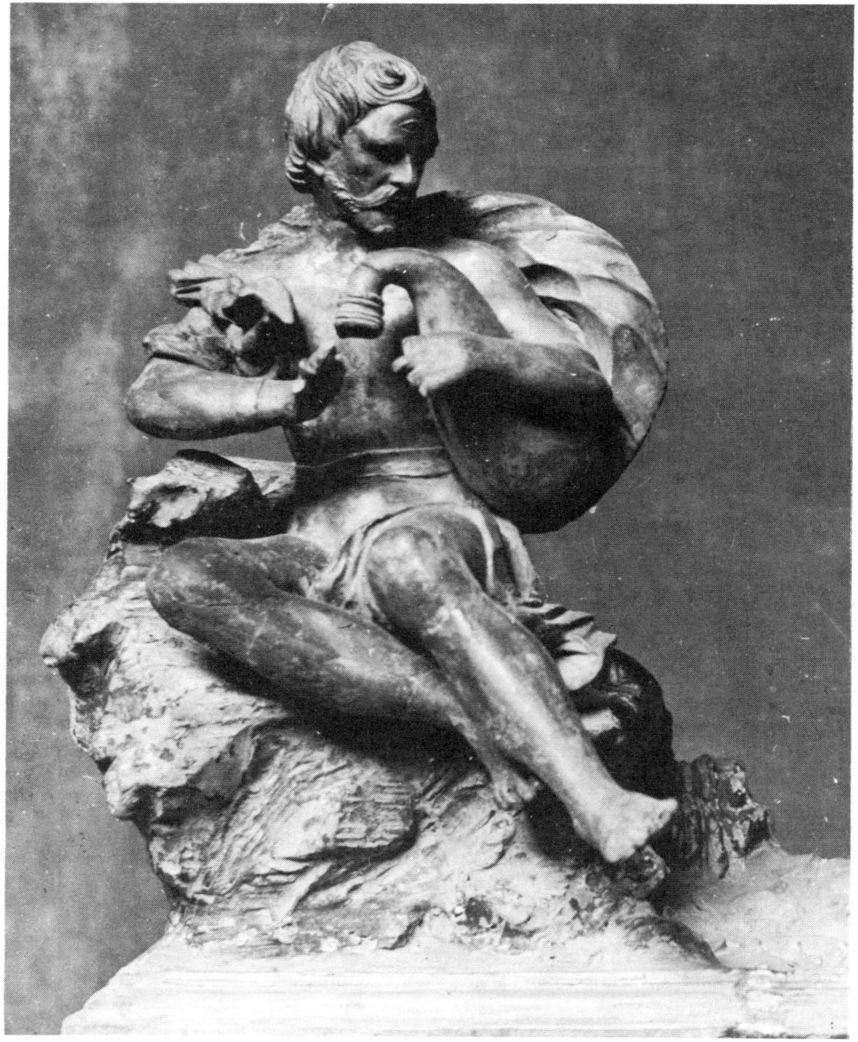

b. The same figure from the model.

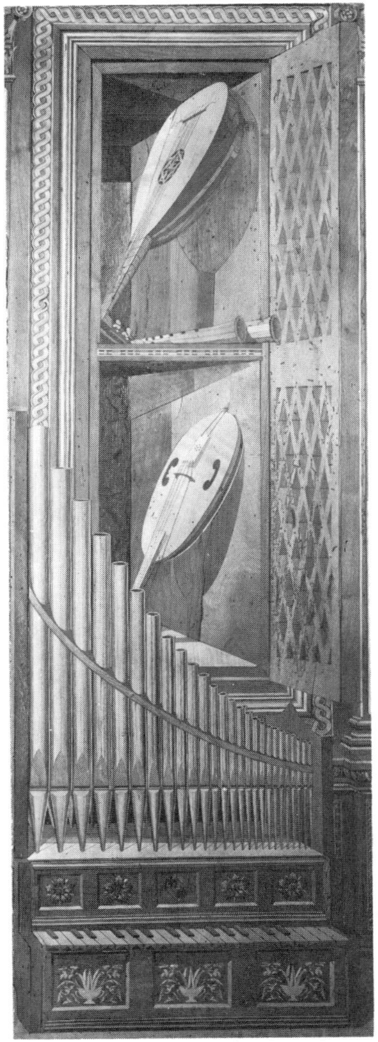

a. Intarsia of positive organ, vielle, and zinks, from the Gubbio Study, Metropolitan Museum of Art, New York.

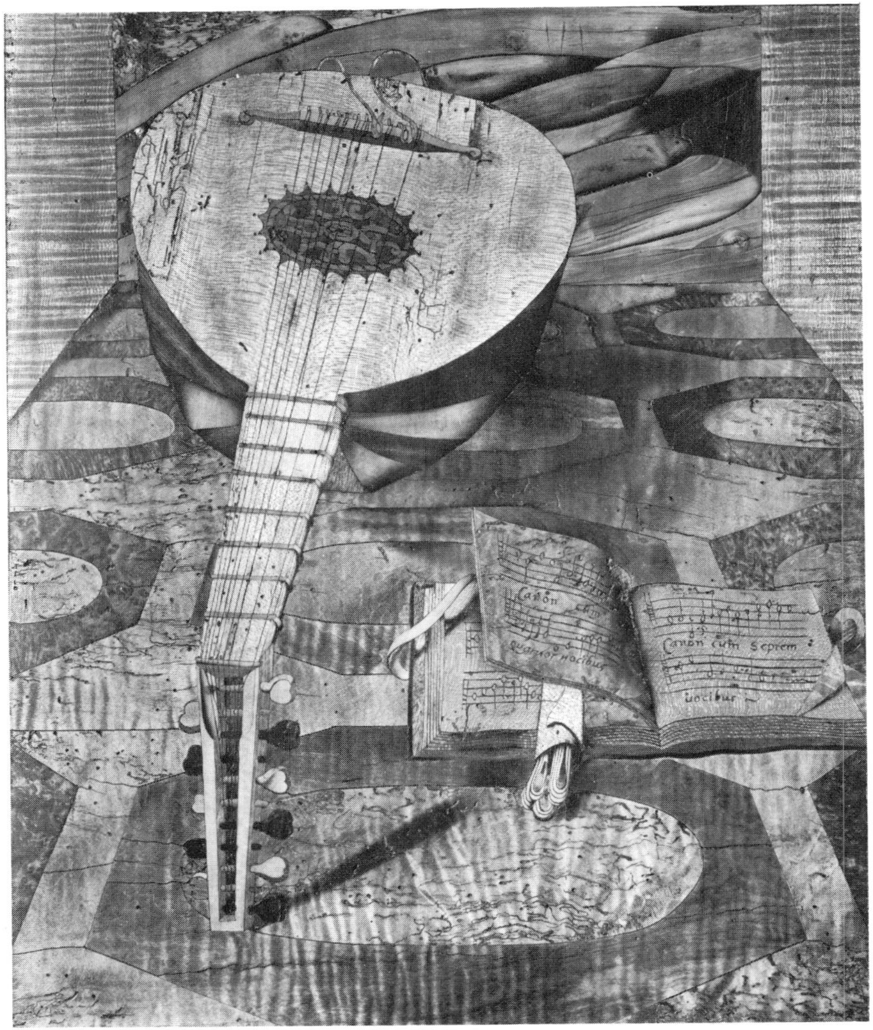

b. Renaissance lute, from a Bolognese intarsia. Metropolitan Museum of Art, New York.

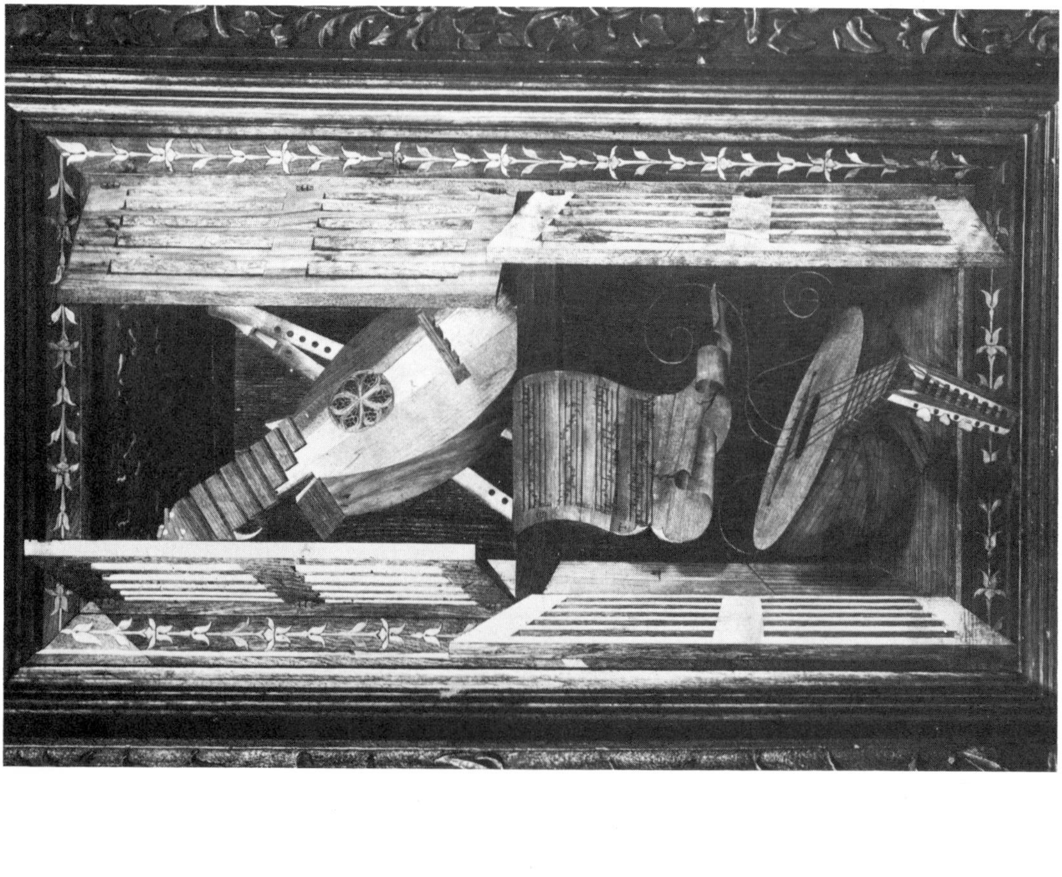

a. Intarsia of cittern, recorders, and lute. Monte Oliveto Maggiore, Siena.

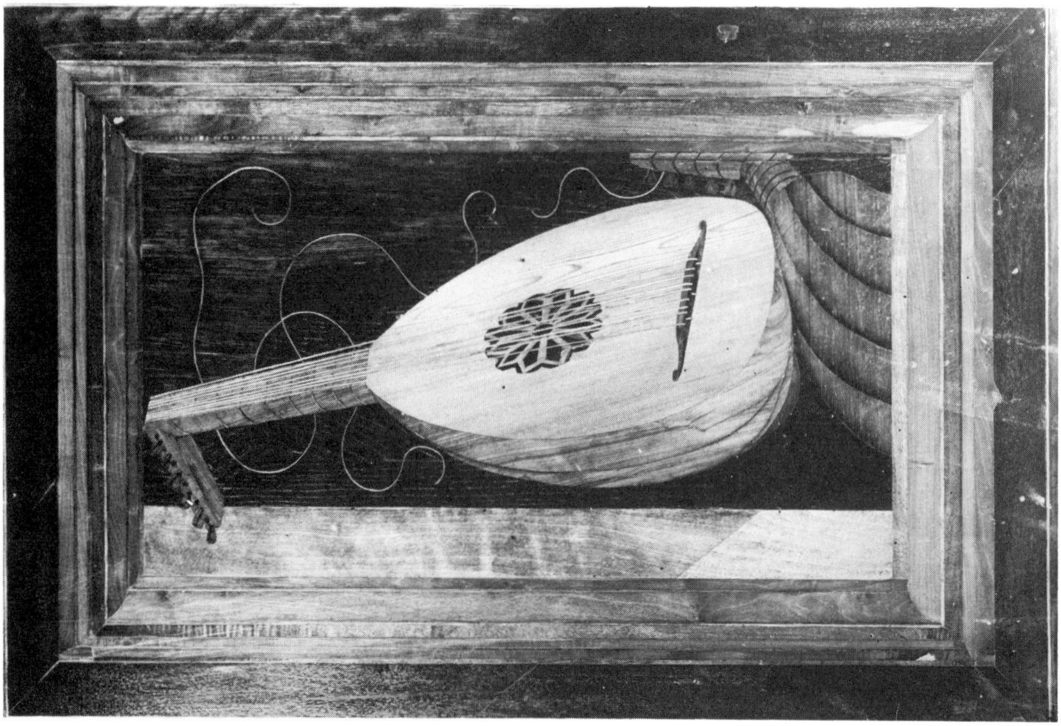

b. Intarsia of lutes. Stanza della Segnatura, Vatican.

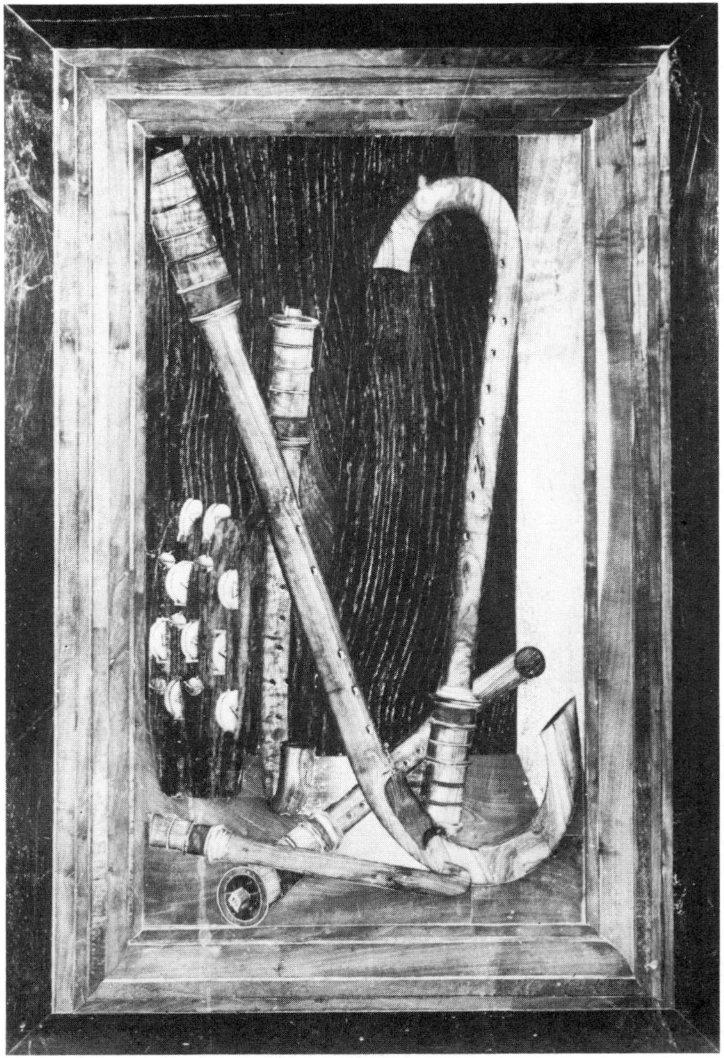

a. Intarsia of krummhorns and jingle drum. Stanza della Segnatura, Vatican.

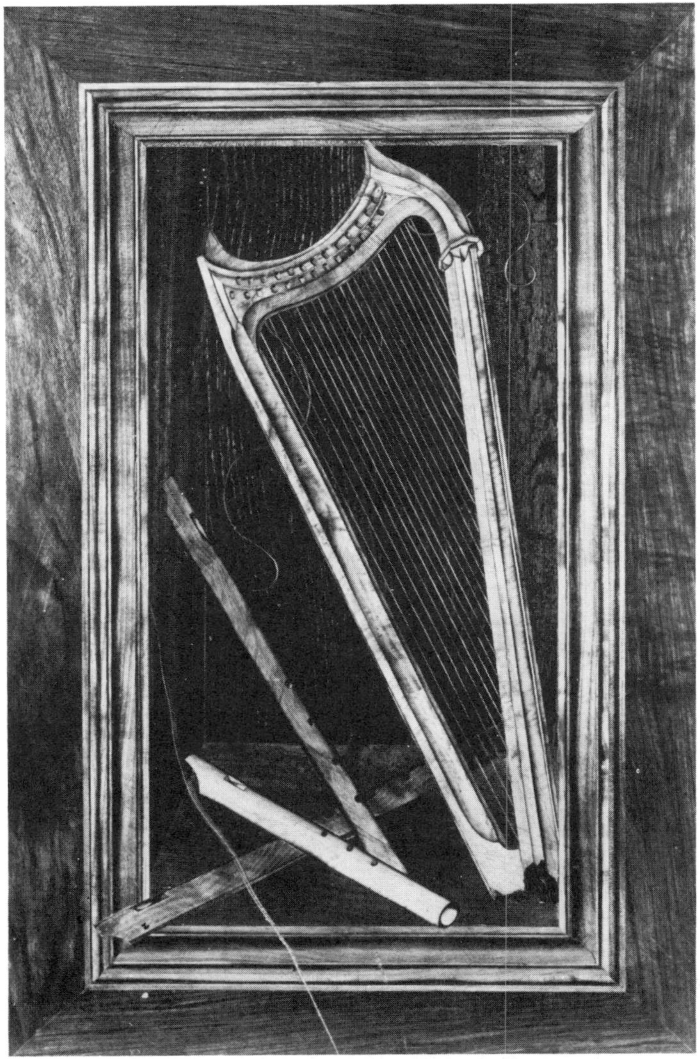

b. Intarsia of harp and recorders. Stanza della Segnatura, Vatican.

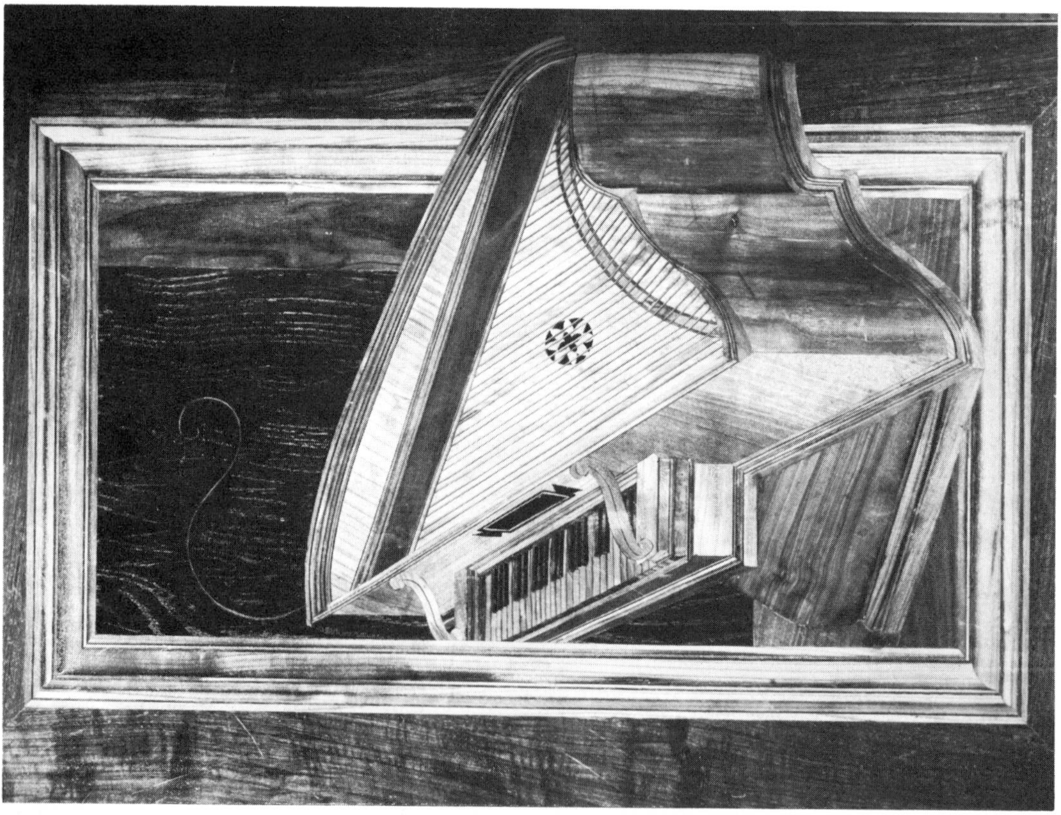

a. Intarsia of spinettino. Stanza della Segnatura, Vatican.

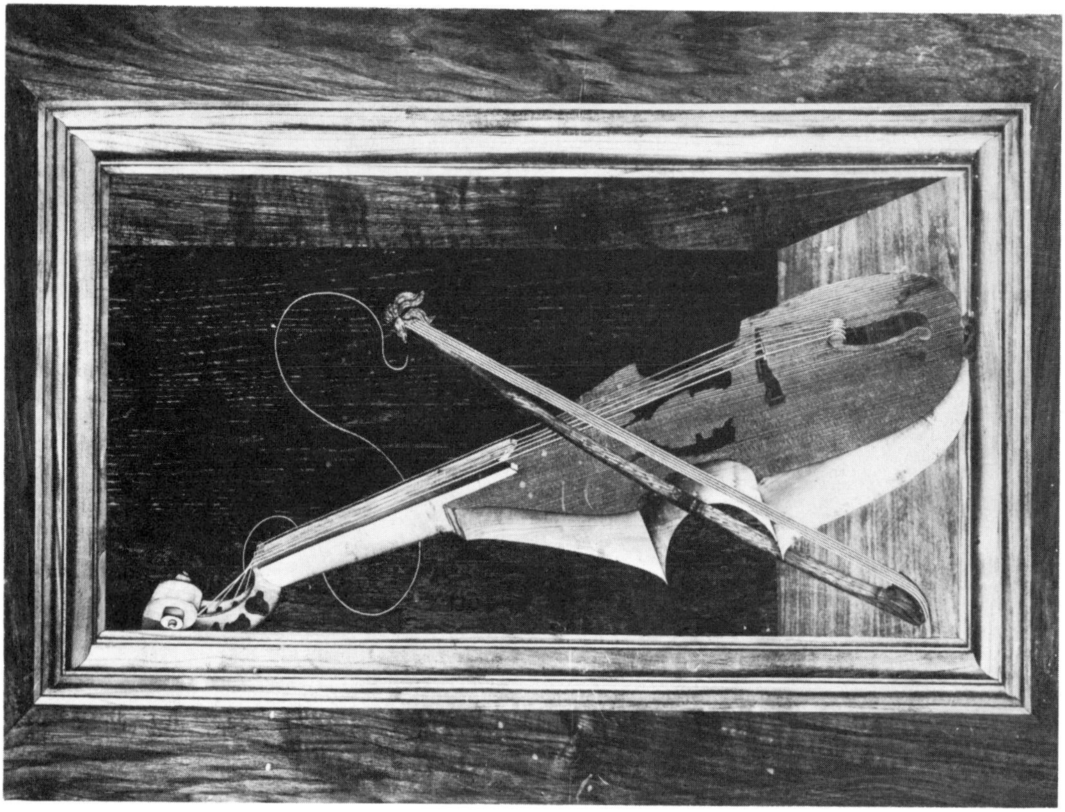

b. Intarsia of viola da gamba. Stanza della Segnatura, Vatican.

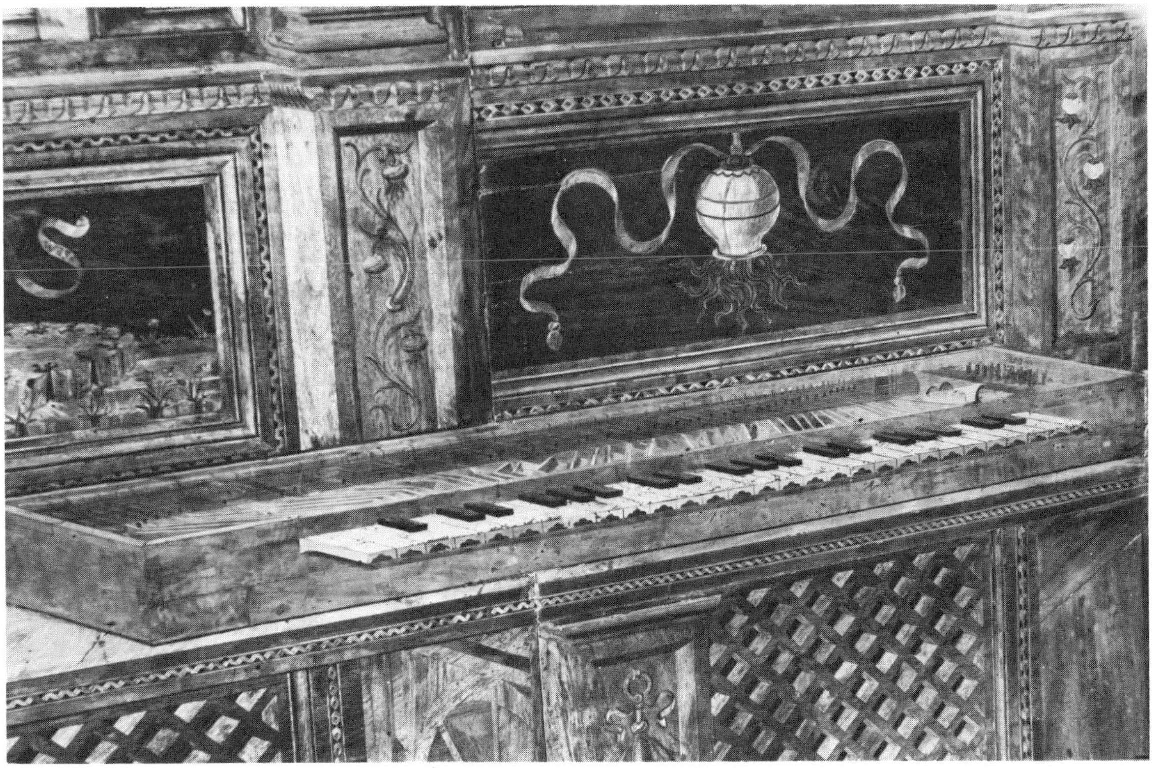

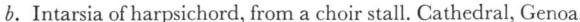

a. Intarsia of clavichord. Studiolo of Federigo da Montefeltro, Urbino.

b. Intarsia of harpsichord, from a choir stall. Cathedral, Genoa.

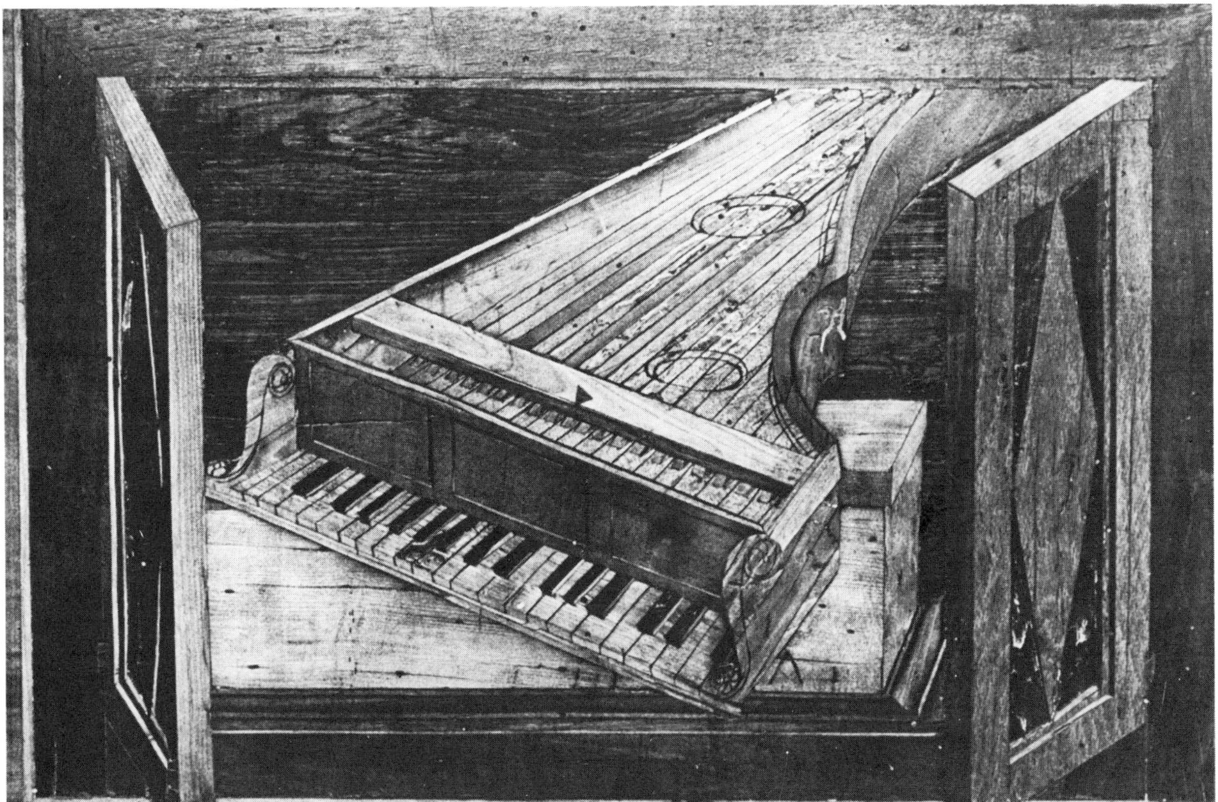

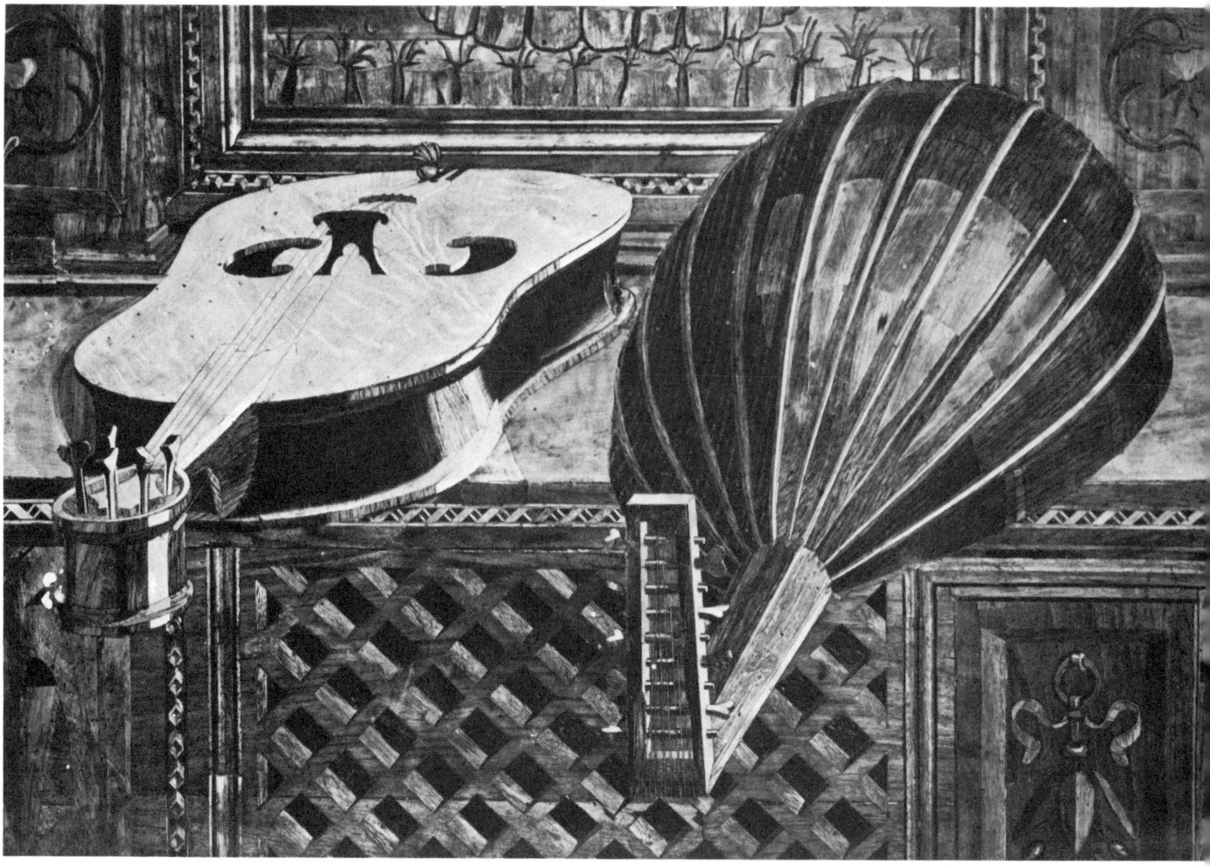

a. Intarsia of lute and lira da braccio. Studiolo, Urbino.

b. The Gubbio Study of Federigo da Montefeltre. Metropolitan Museum, New York.

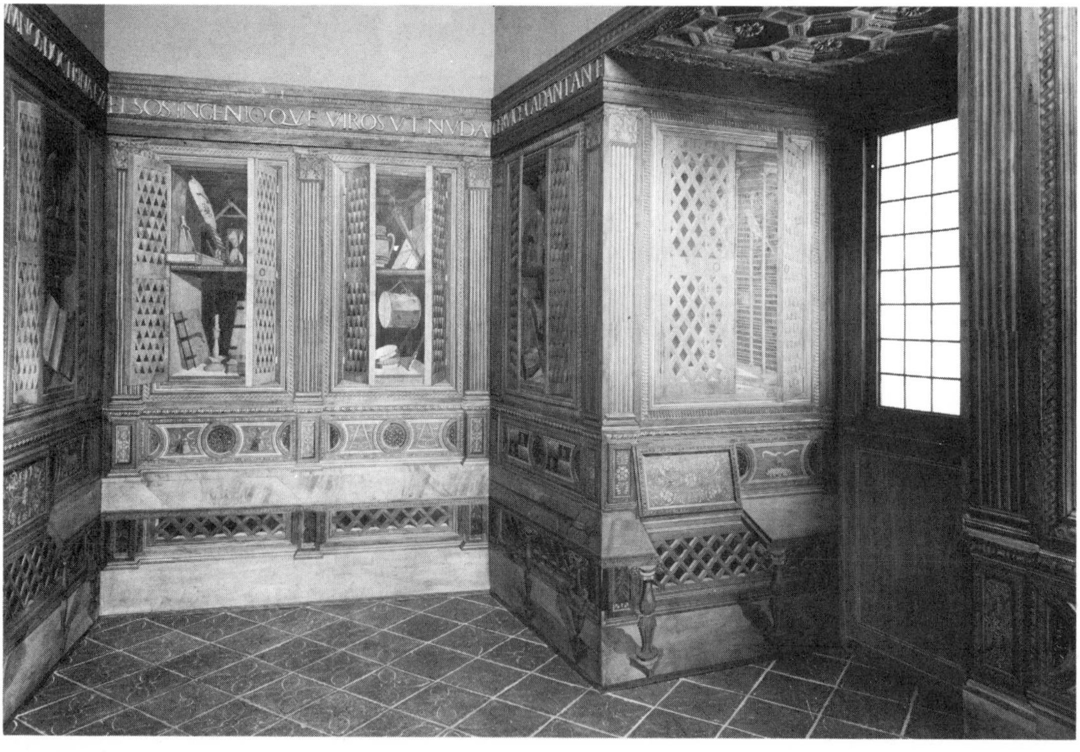

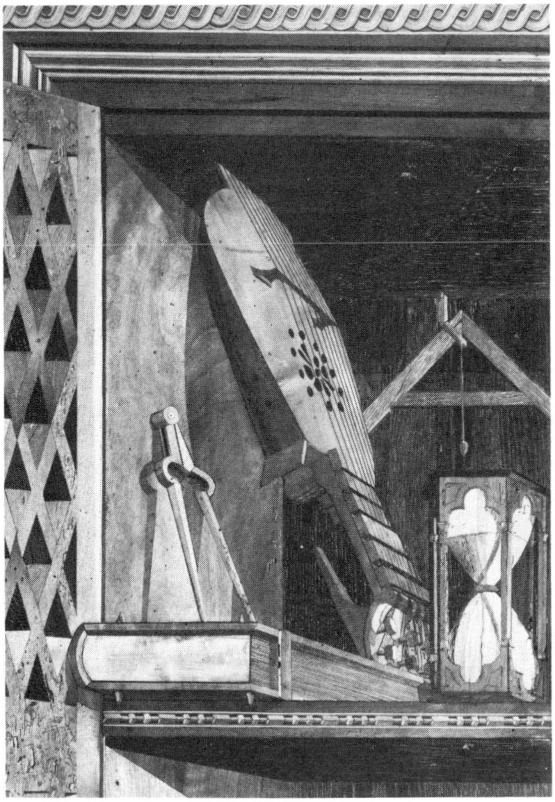

a. Cittern with pair of dividers and hourglass. In section 9 of the Gubbio Study.

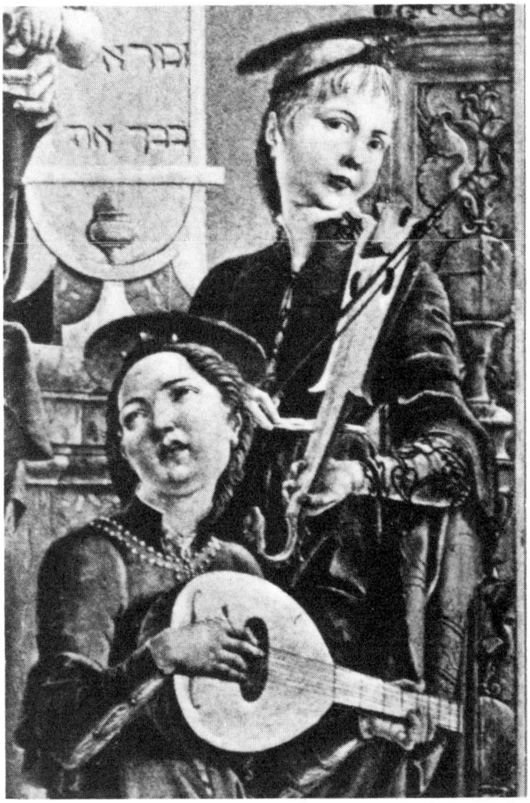

b. Cosimo Tura, detail of *Madonna and Child*. National Gallery, London.

c. Rebec and bow; the sickle-shaped peg box is partly visible. In Section 6 of the Gubbio Study.

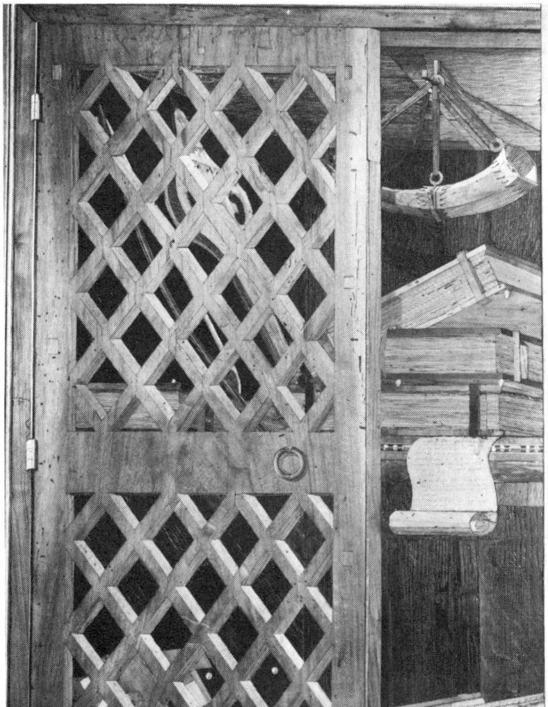

d. Fiddle with four melody strings and one drone. In Section 5 of the Gubbio Study.

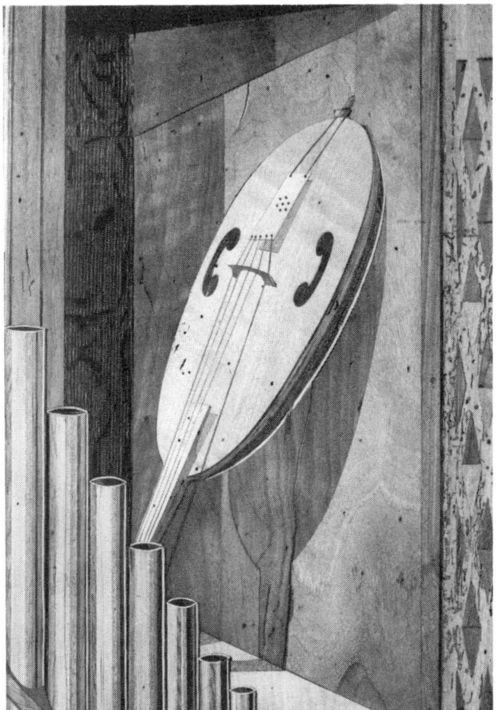

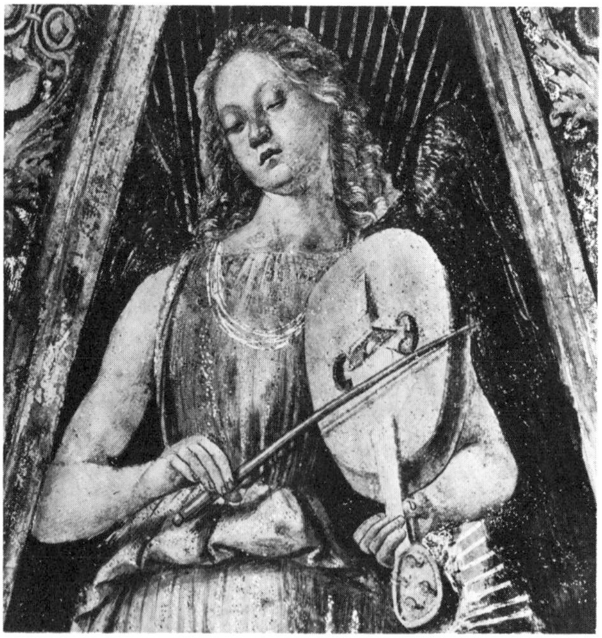

a. Signorelli, detail of a painting, showing an angel playing a fiddle. Church of the Casa Santa, Loreto.

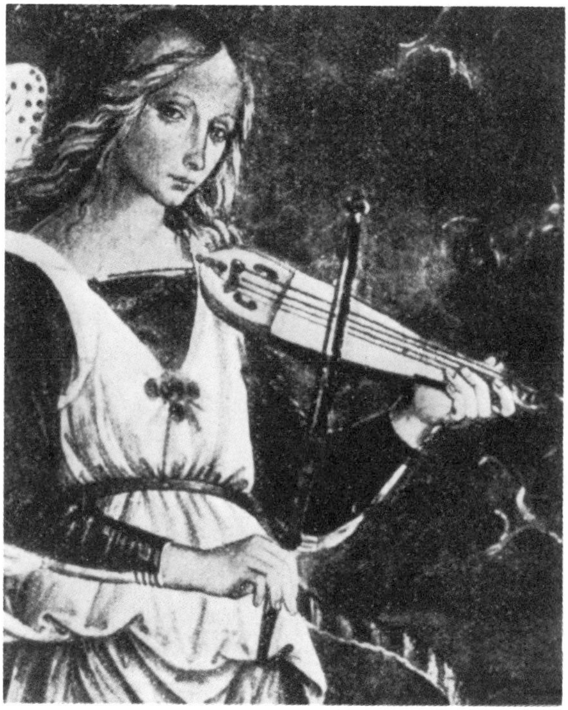

b. Pinturicchio, detail of a fresco, showing an angel playing a rebec. Santa Maria in Aracoeli, Rome.

c. Shadow cast on mouldings by the lectern. In Section 1 of the Gubbio Study.

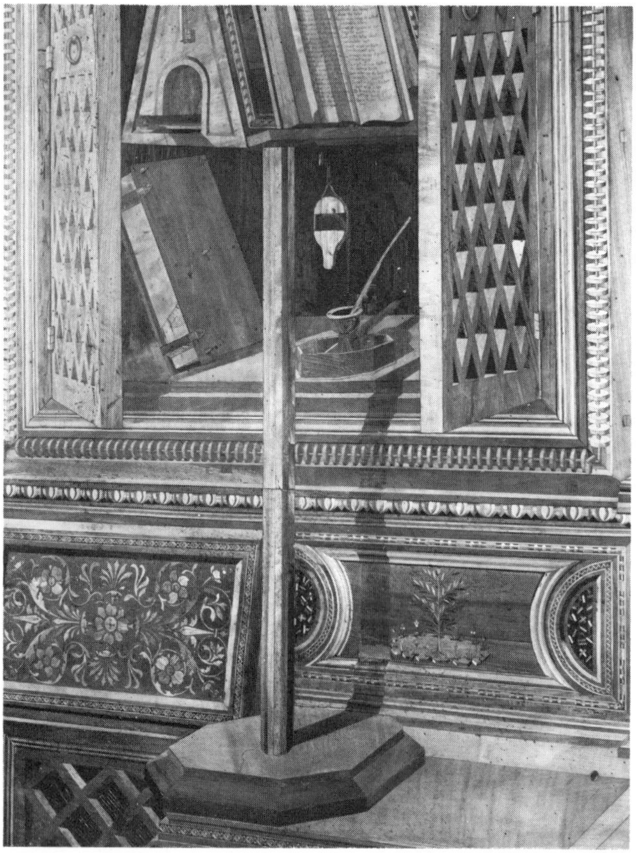

d. Celestial globe, books, and quadrant. In Section 2 of the Gubbio Study.

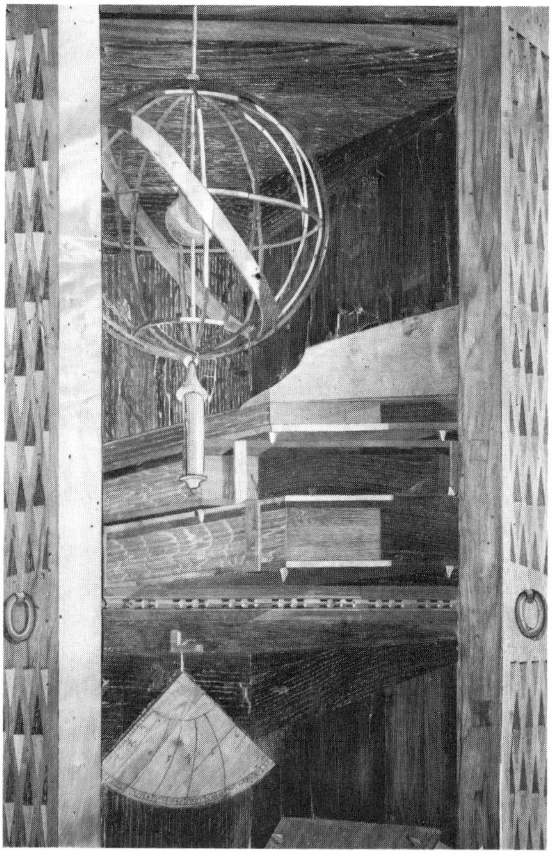

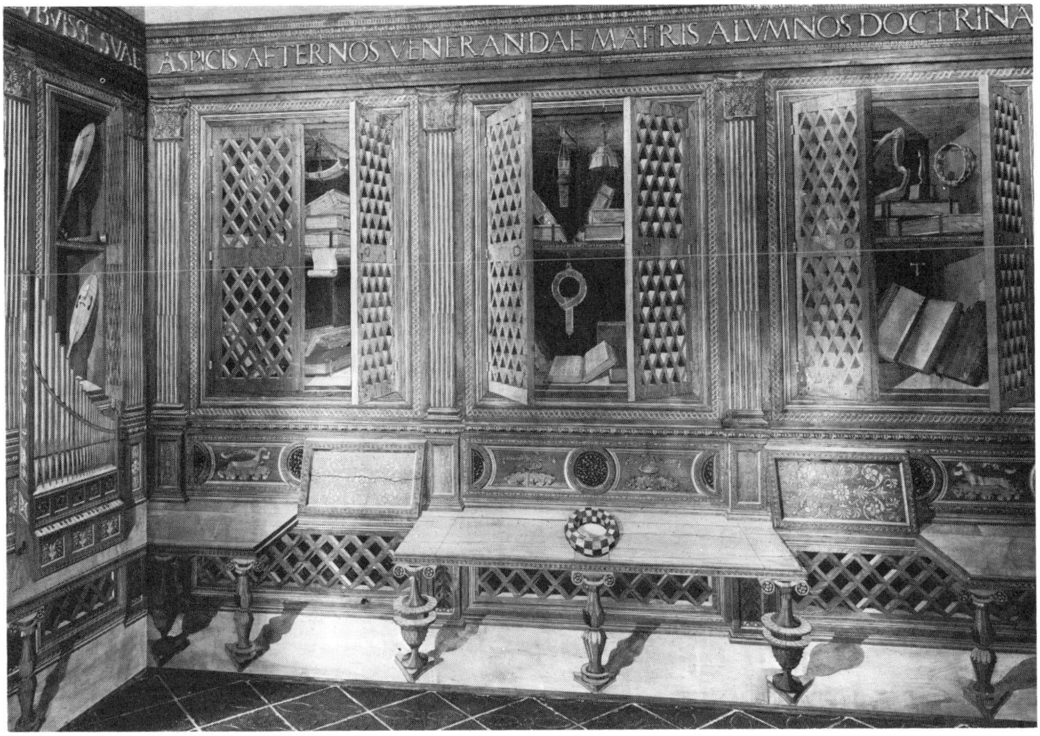

a. A corner of the Gubbio Study, showing the treatment of the baluster shadows.

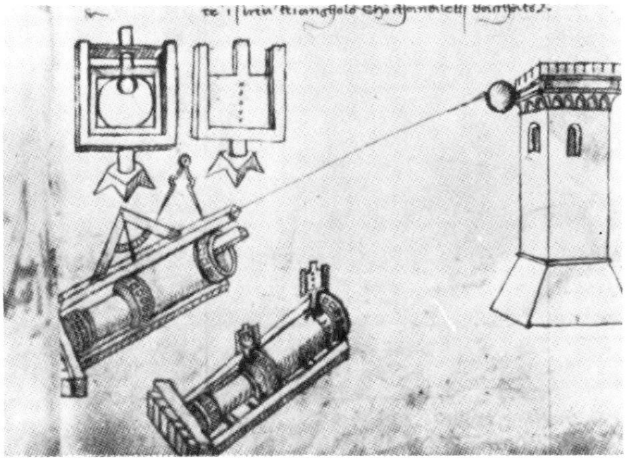

b. Francesco di Giorgio, drawing showing bombards and their sights. Ducal Library, Turin.

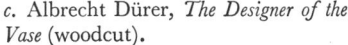

c. Albrecht Dürer, *The Designer of the Vase* (woodcut).

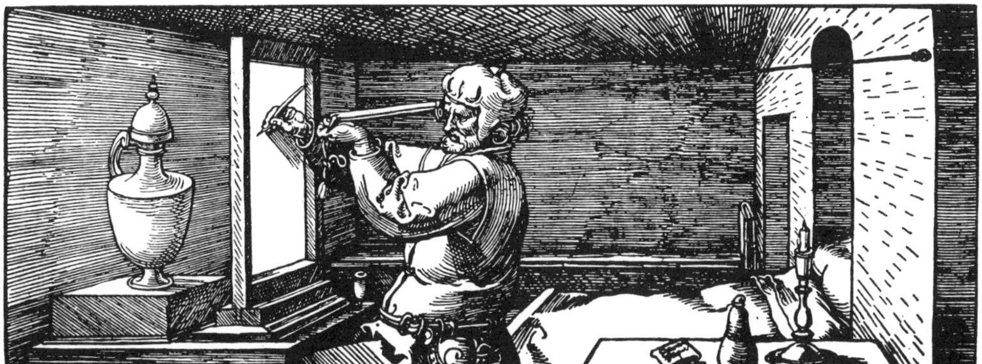

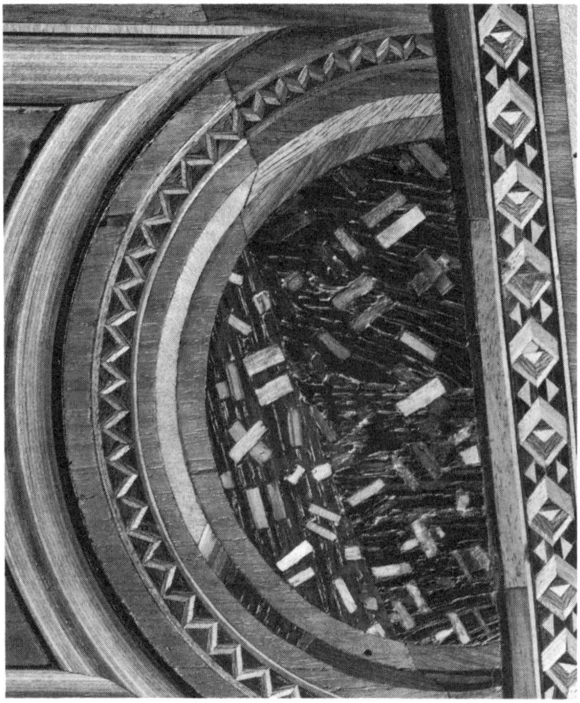

a. Border patterns with geometrical bodies. Centre wall of the Gubbio Study.

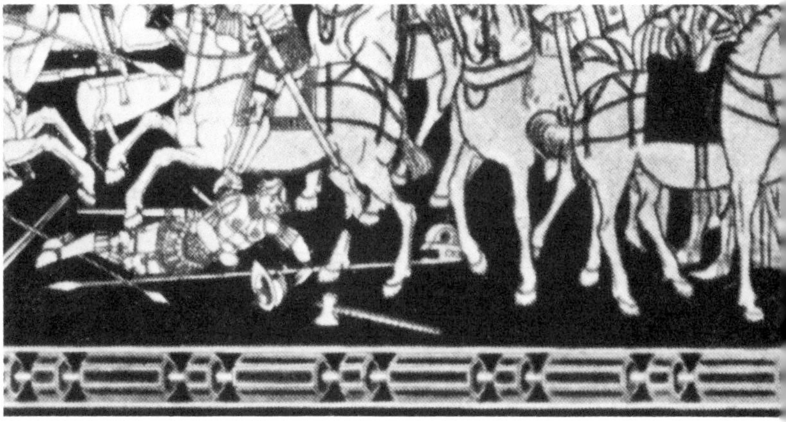

b. Geometrical border, from a panel attributed to Francesco di Giorgio. In the pavement of the Cathedral, Siena.

c. (*below*). Mazzocchio, or turban ring. On a bench in Section 7 of the Gubbio Study.

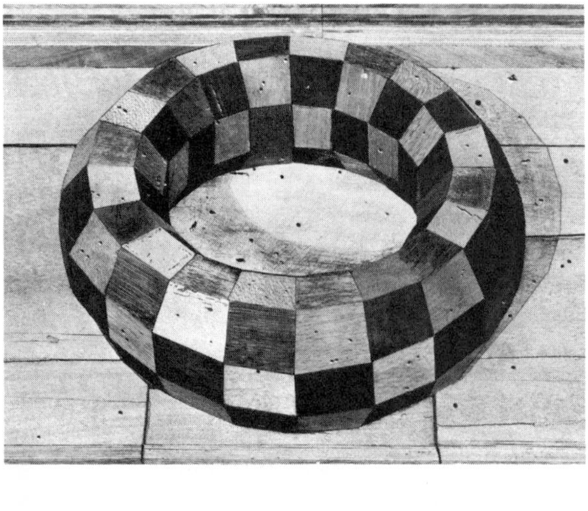

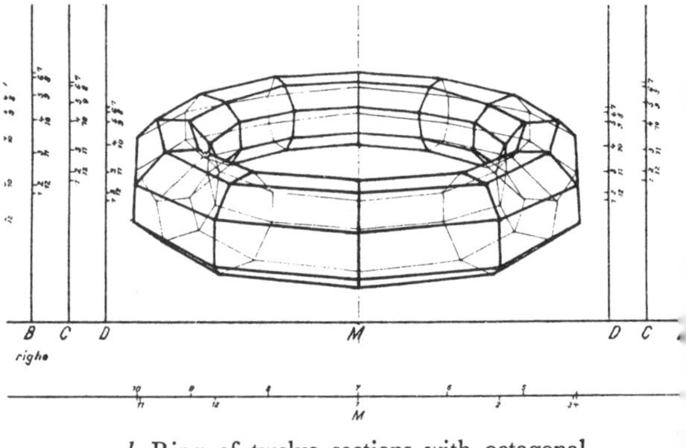

d. Ring of twelve sections with octagonal cross-section. From Piero della Francesca's *De prospectiva pingendi*, 1469.

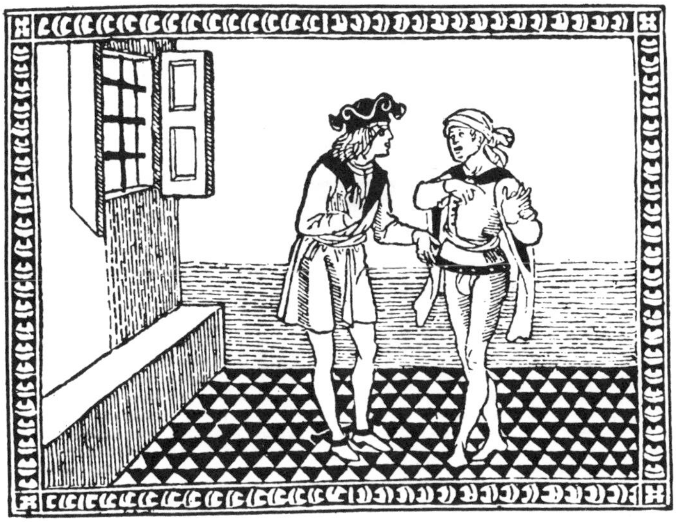

a. Florentine woodcut with disc border pattern, from *Il Savio Romano.*

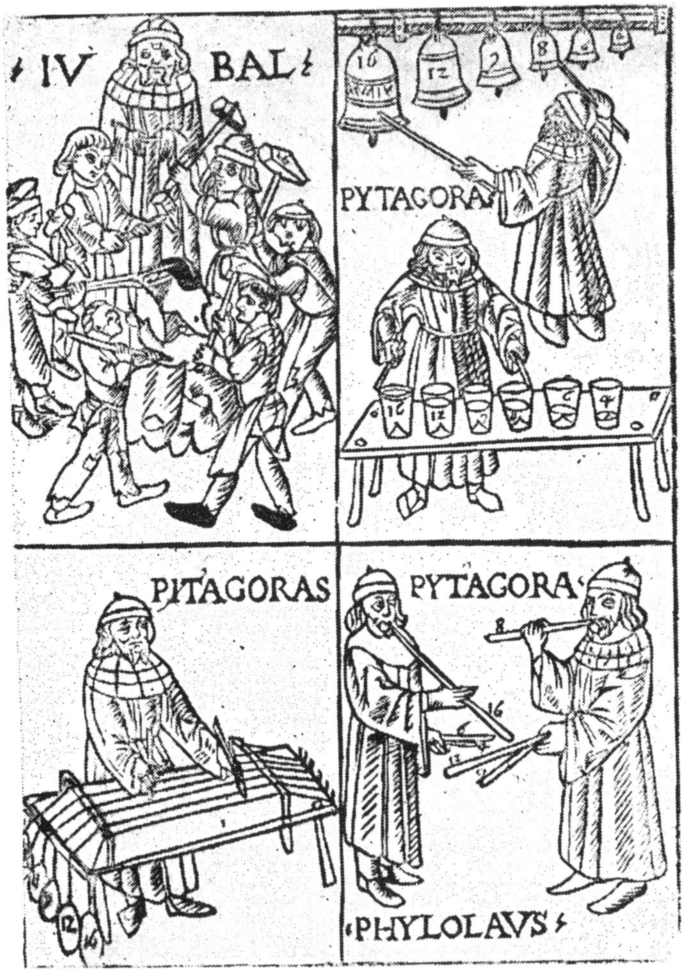

b. Woodcut from Gaffurio's *Theorica musice*, 1492.

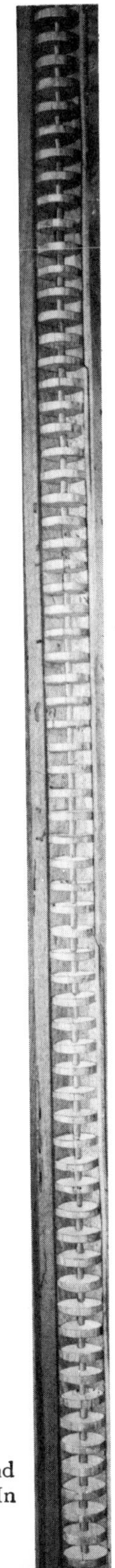
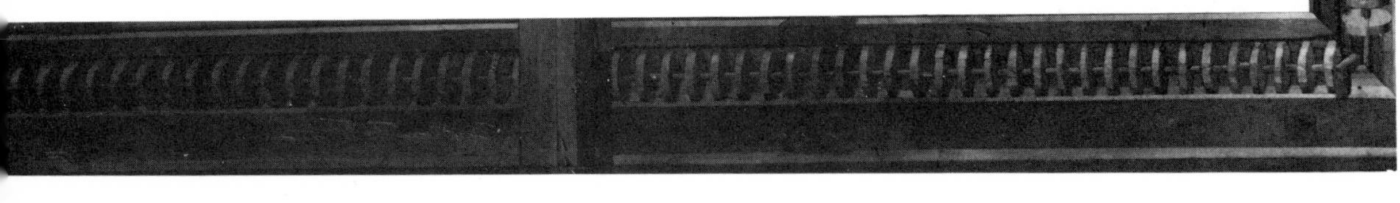

c. Border ornament around cupboards flanking window. In the Gubbio Study.

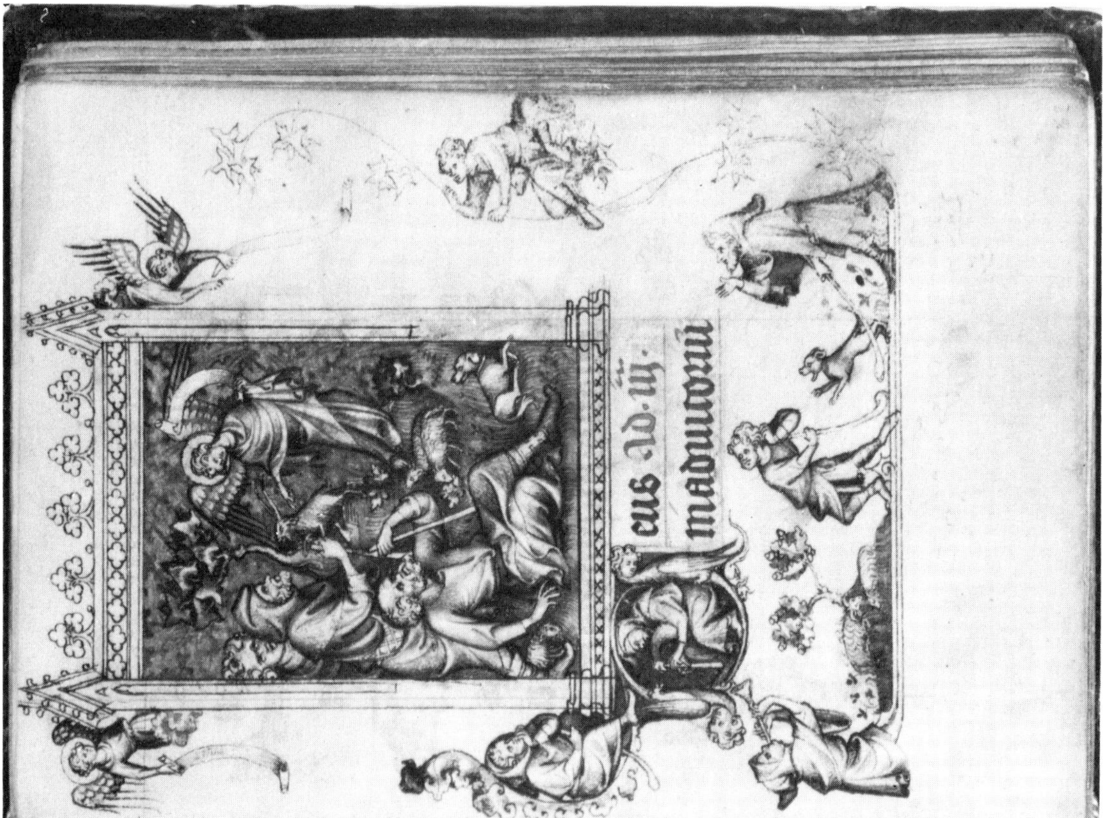

a. The Annunciation to the Shepherds. The musician in the initial is playing a bagpipe, the shepherd beneath him a pastoral shawm.

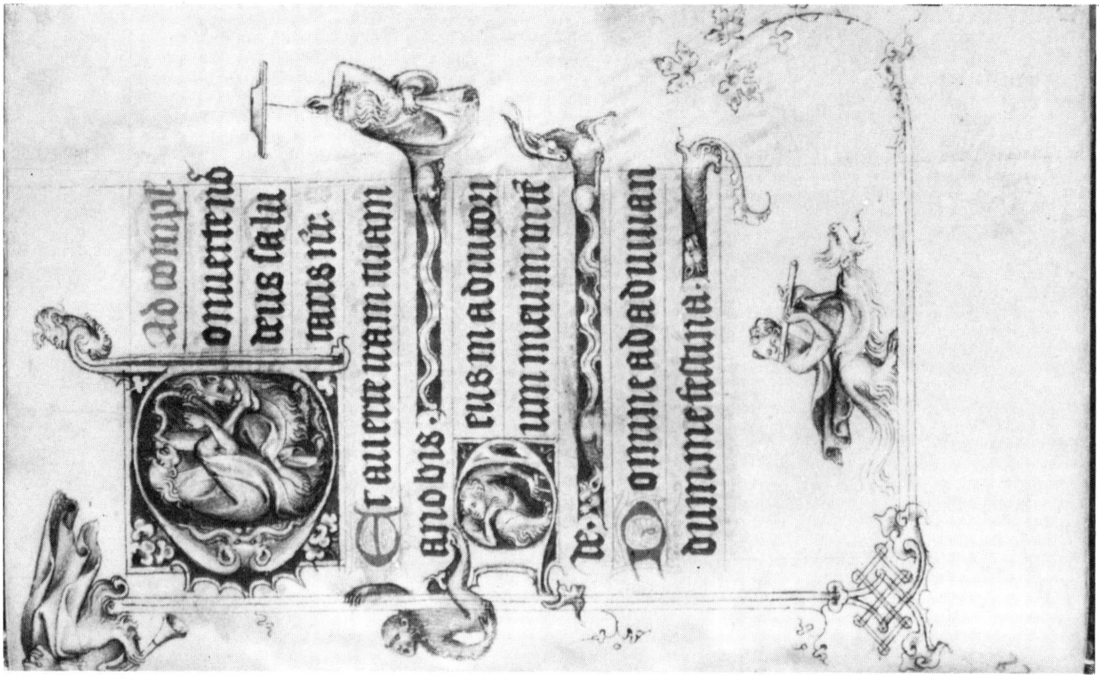

b. Page showing an old man with a harp in the large initial, and a monster playing a transverse flute in the space below the text.

FROM THE BOOK OF HOURS OF JEANNE D'ÉVREUX, METROPOLITAN MUSEUM, NEW YORK

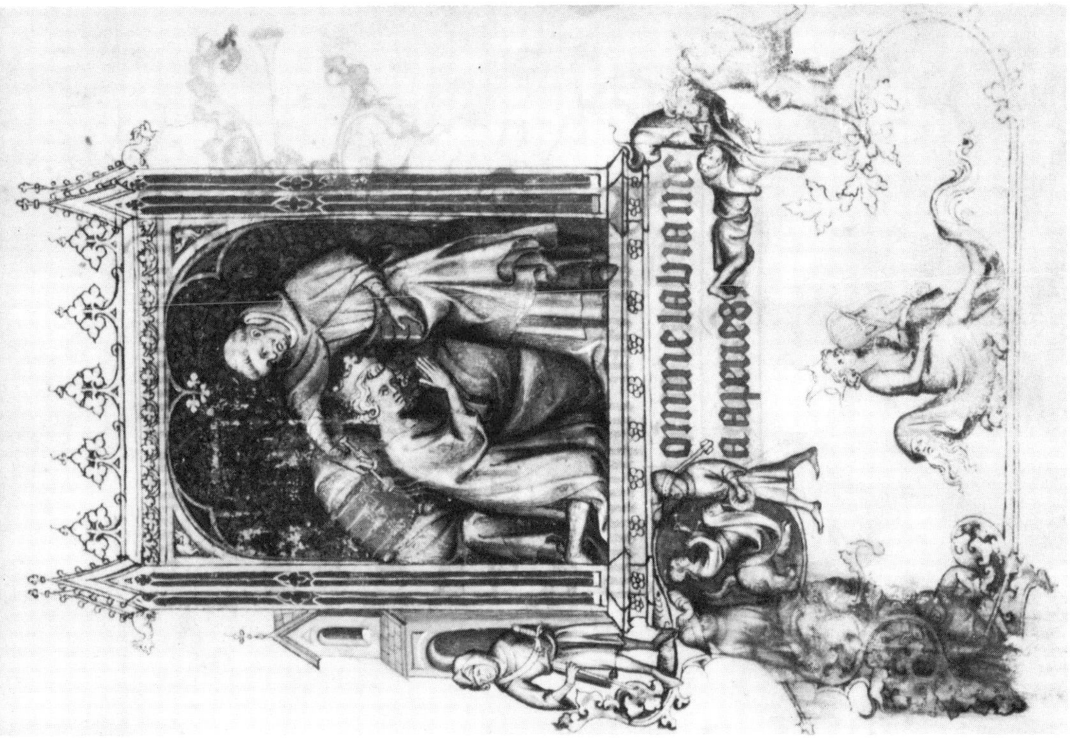

b. Scene representing the education and chastisement of the young St. Louis. At the bottom of the page, a youth siting on a bearded monster is bowing a vielle.

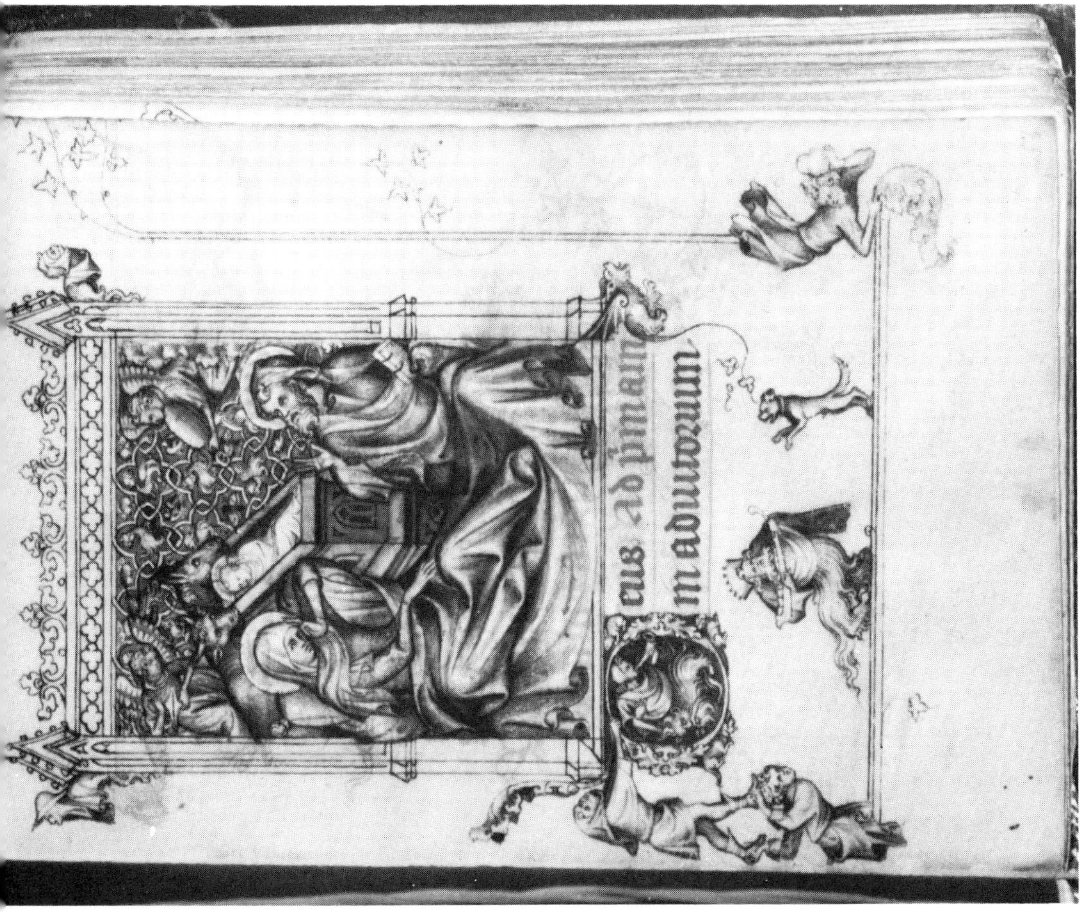

a. The Nativity. The main scene shows two angels with cymbals and a vielle; below is a monster plucking a jawbone.

FROM THE BOOK OF HOURS OF JEANNE D'ÉVREUX, METROPOLITAN MUSEUM, NEW YORK

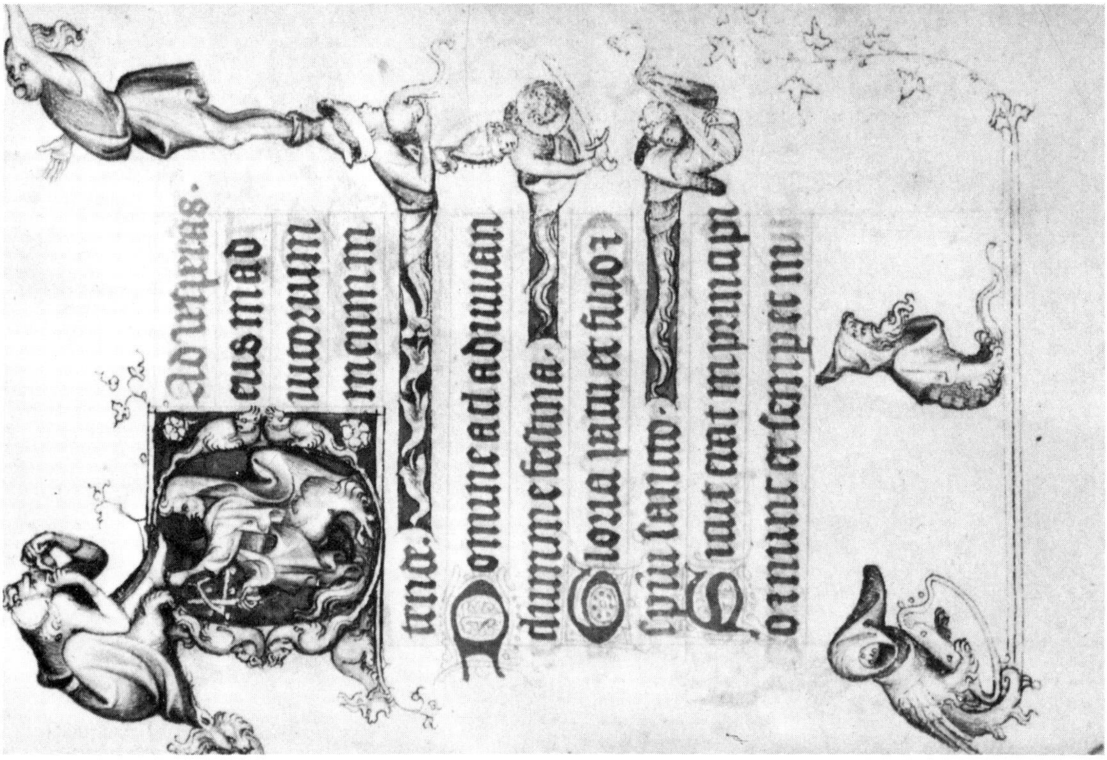

a. Page showing a monster with a triangle in the initial, and another with a harp below; a long-tailed monster is playing a mandola with a plectrum.

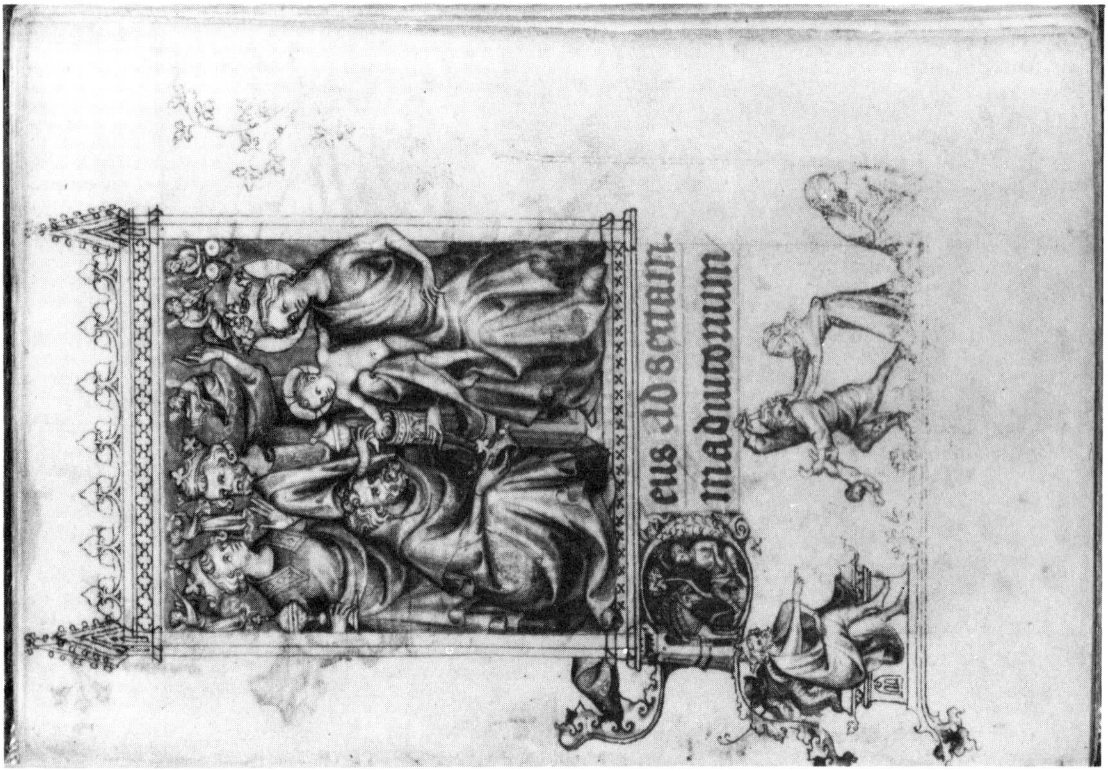

b. The Adoration of the Magi. Little angels in the background are playing a trumpet, bells, a psaltery, a vielle, and kettledrums. The scene below shows the Massacre of the Innocents.

FROM THE BOOK OF HOURS OF JEANNE D'ÉVREUX, METROPOLITAN MUSEUM, NEW YORK

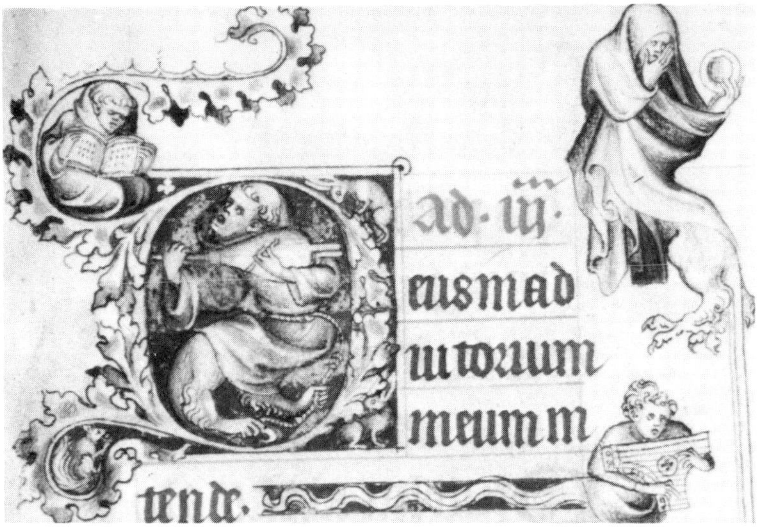

a. Page showing, in the initial, a monster wearing a monk's robe and plucking bellows with a plectrum; the little monk above him holds his music. In the lower right corner a long-tailed creature is playing a psaltery with his fingers.

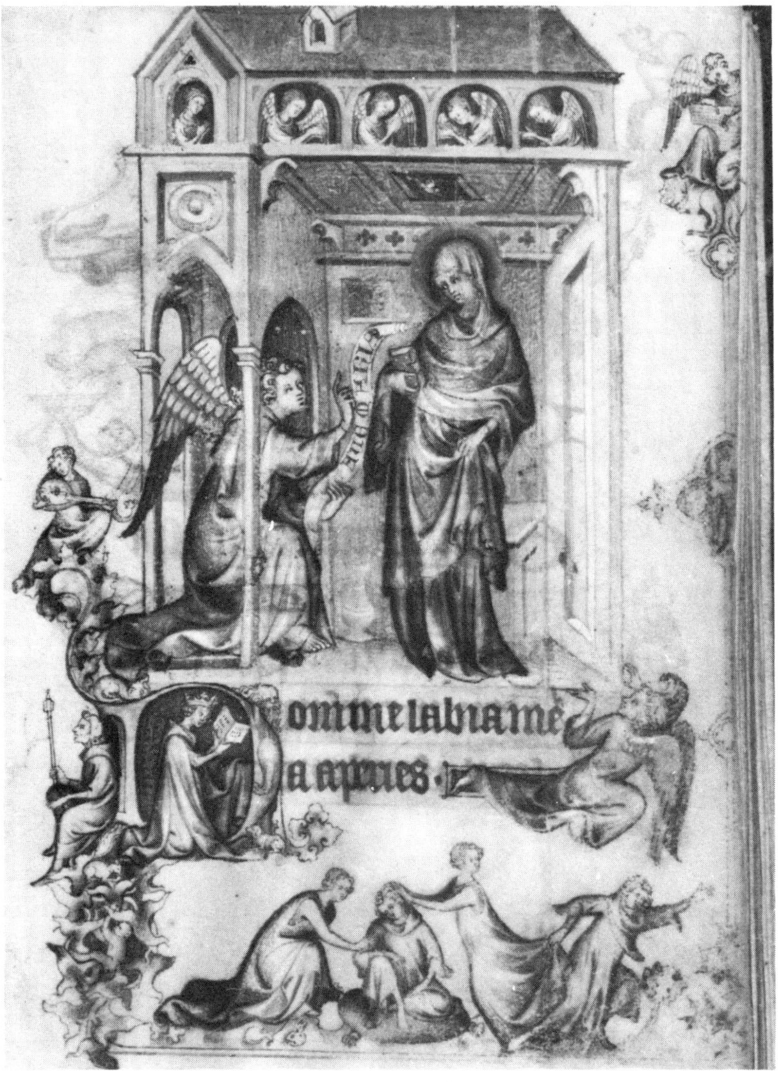

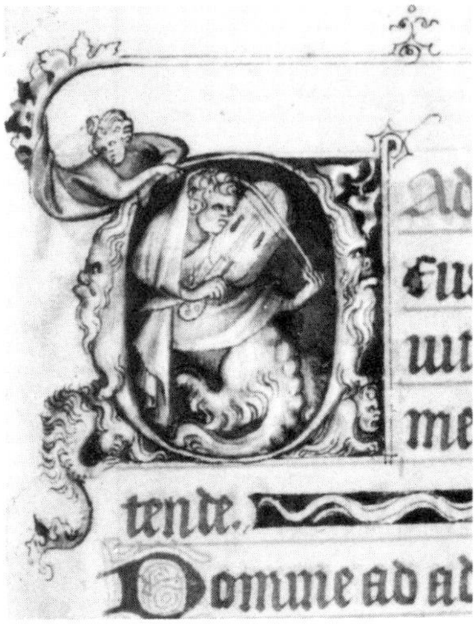

c. Initial with a monster playing a vielle in a rather awkward position.

b. Page showing, at left of Annunciation scene, a figure playing a mandola.

FROM THE BOOK OF HOURS OF JEANNE D'ÉVREUX, METROPOLITAN MUSEUM, NEW YORK

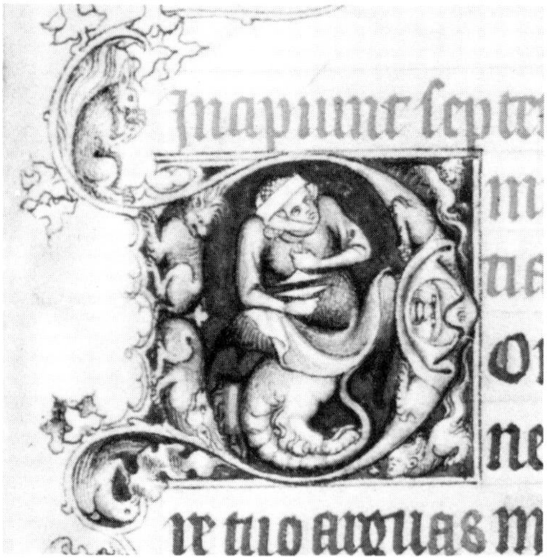

a. Initial with a woman playing cymbals.

d. A tailed monster playing a bagpipe.

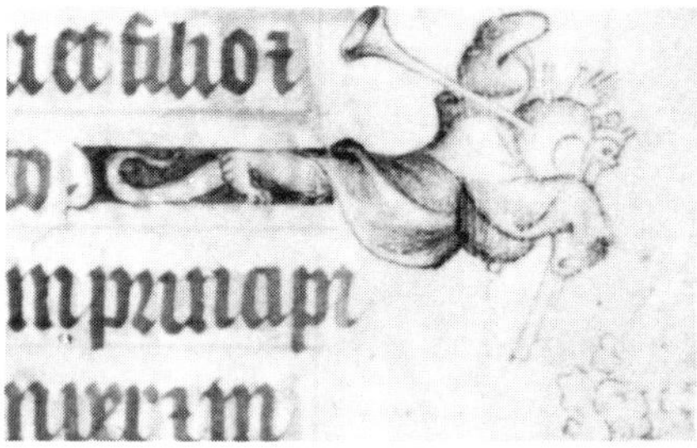

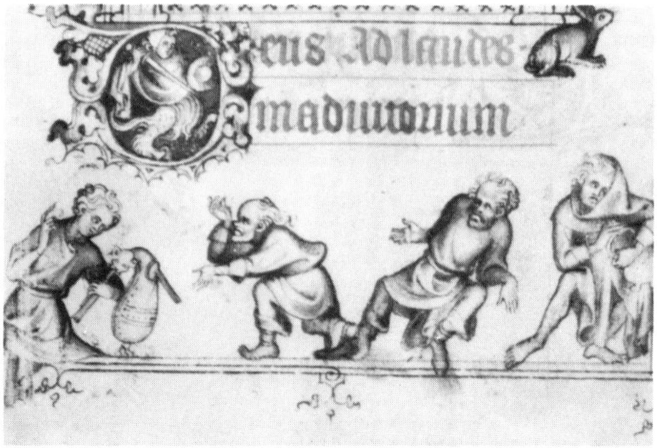

e. The 'training' of a bagpipe.

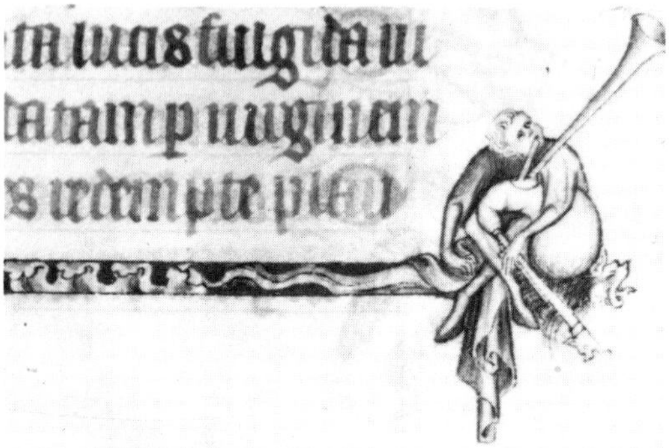

b. A musician playing a bagpipe with a very large chanter and drone.

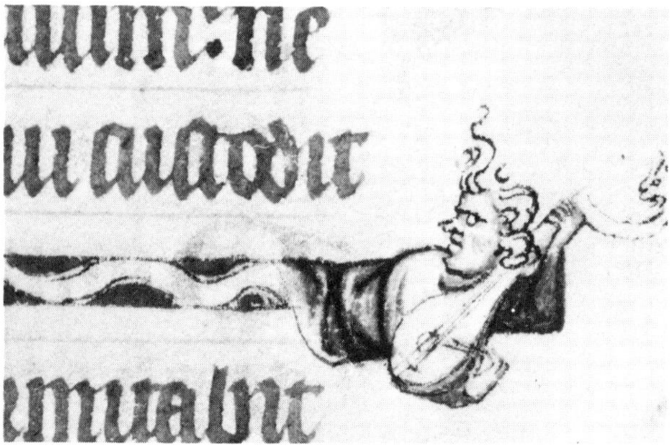

c. A mandola of medium size.

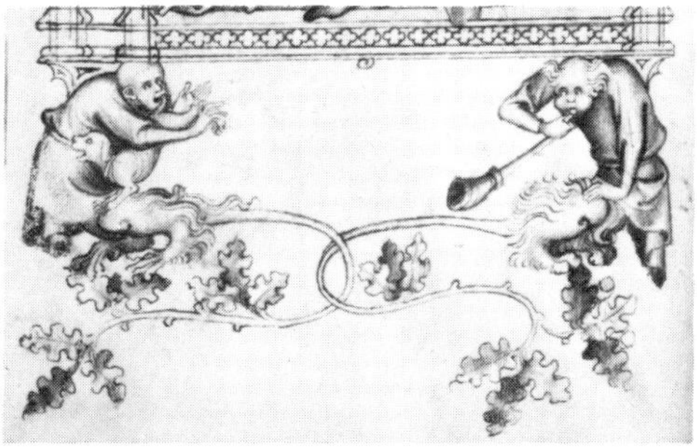

f. A fantastic creature playing a dog as a bagpipe, and another blowing a large shawm with a cowhorn bell.

FROM THE BOOK OF HOURS OF JEANNE D'ÉVREUX, METROPOLITAN MUSEUM, NEW YORK

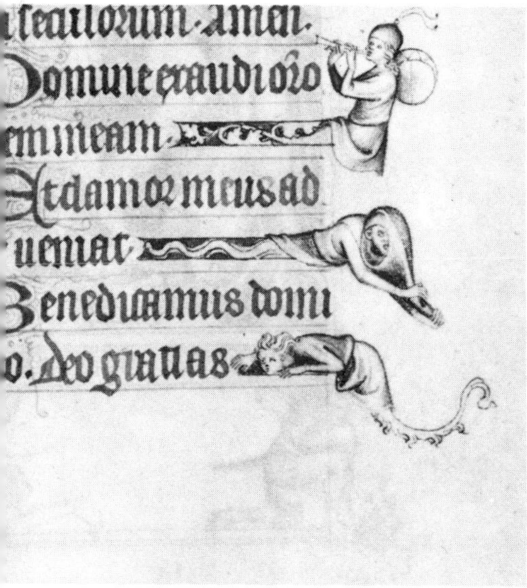

a. A snare drum and fife.

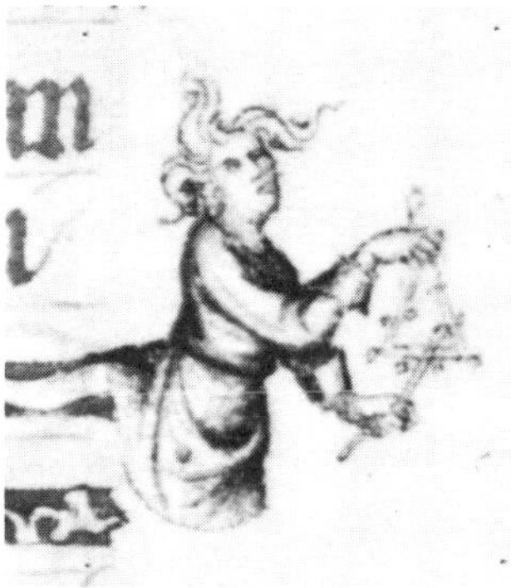

e. A triangle.

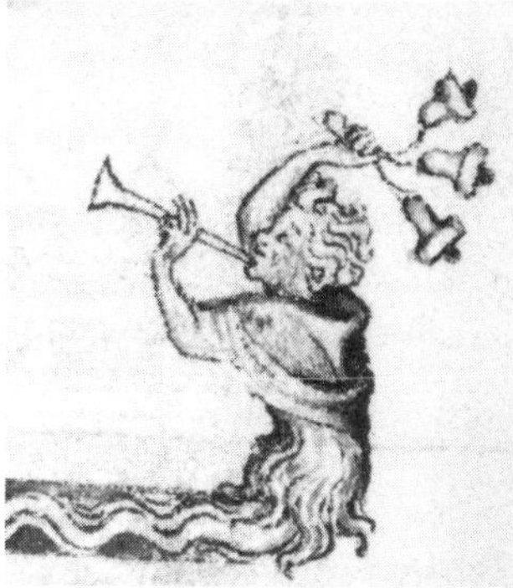

f. Bells and a reed pipe.

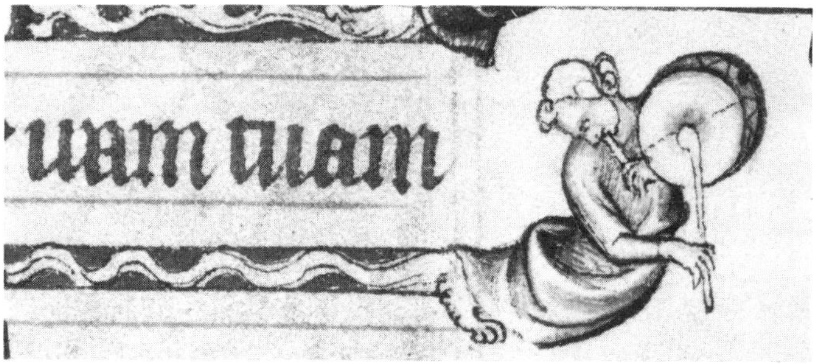

g. A snare drum.

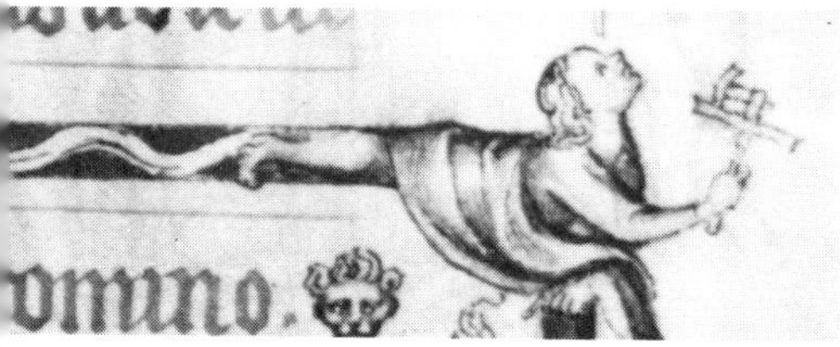

b. A rattle.

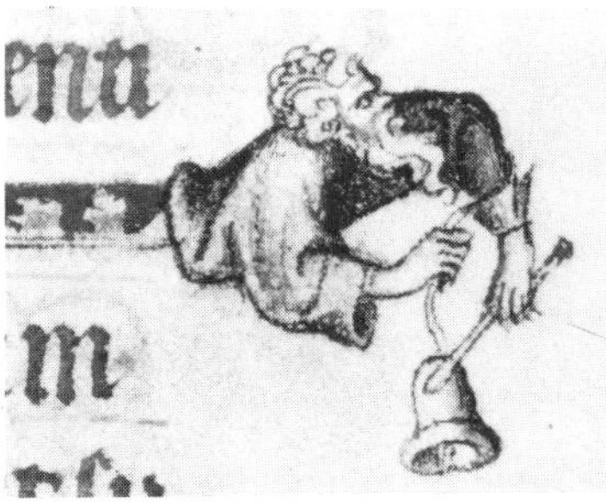

h. A bell hit with a stick.

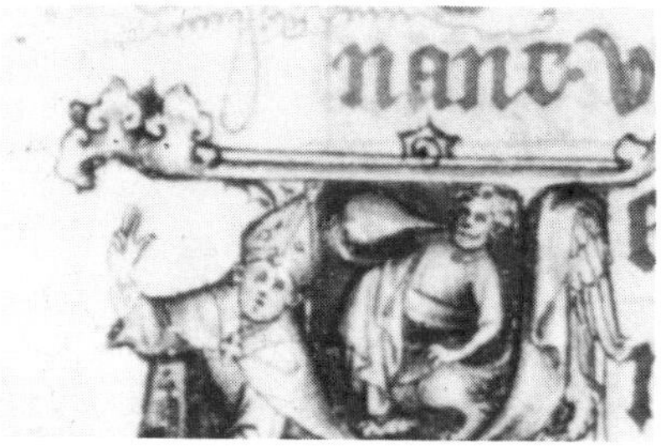

c. A monster blowing a bellows like a wind instrument.

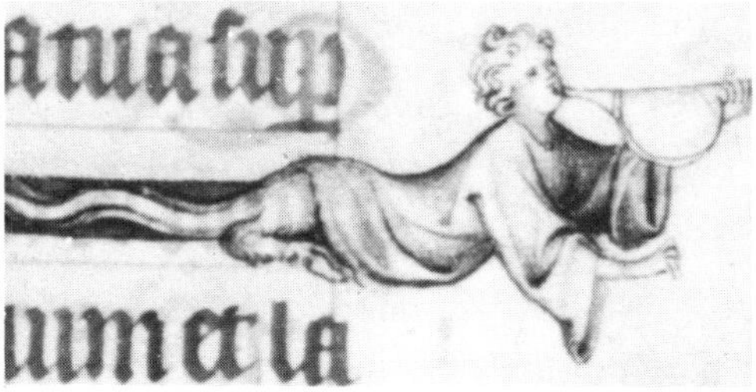

d. A bellows played as a trumpet.

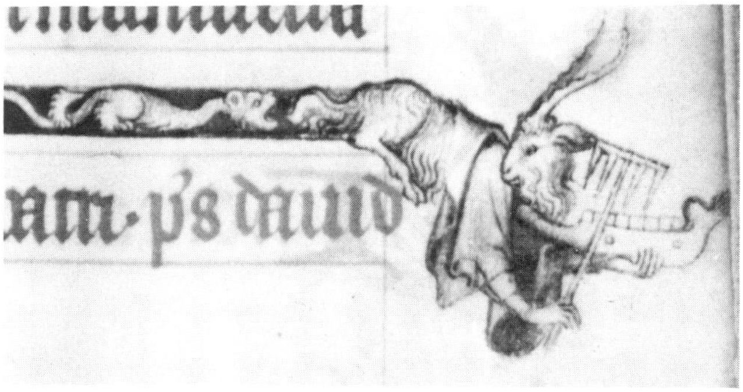

i. A goat bowing a jawbone with a rake.

FROM THE BOOK OF HOURS OF JEANNE D'ÉVREUX, METROPOLITAN MUSEUM, NEW YORK

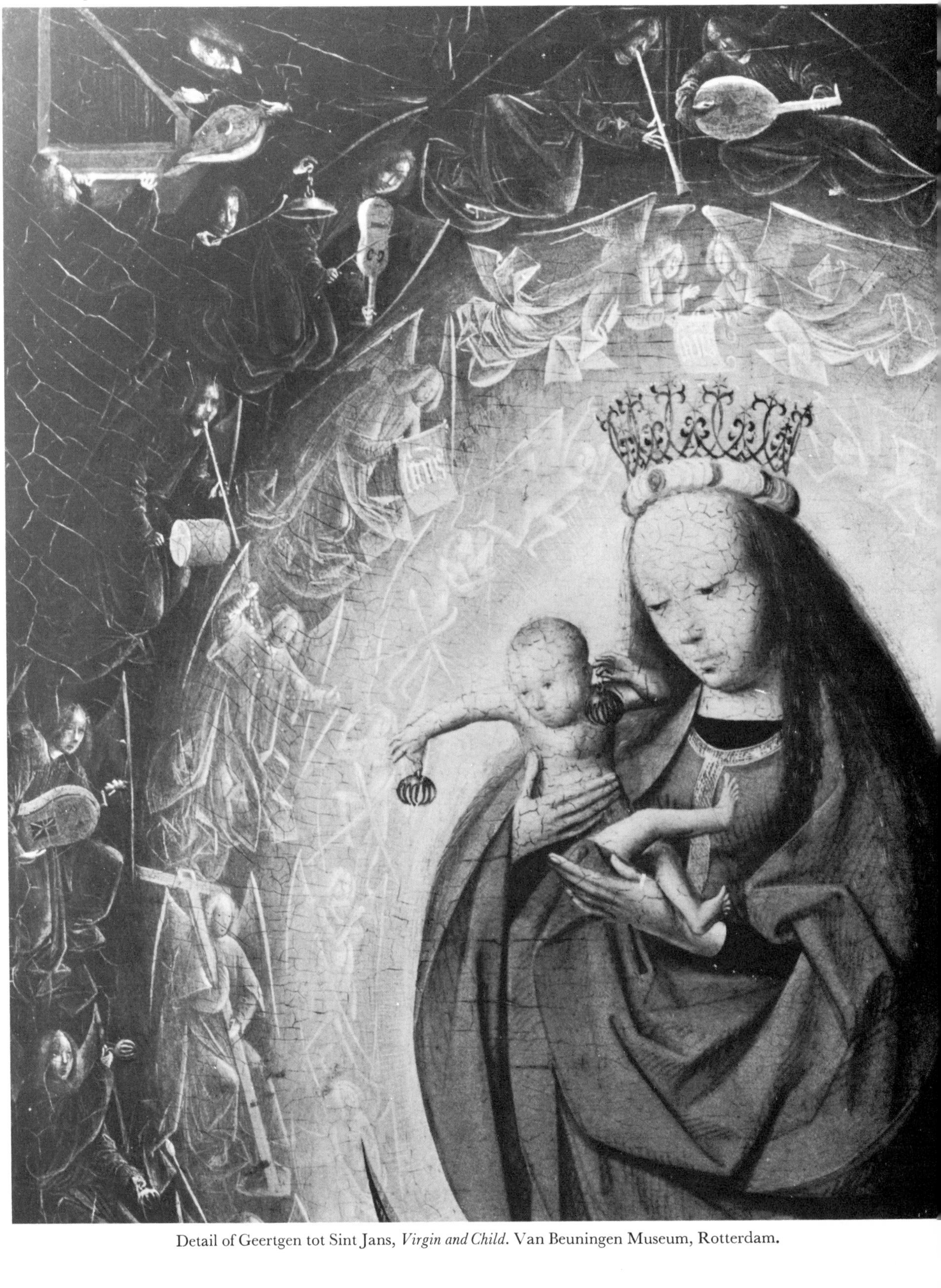

Detail of Geertgen tot Sint Jans, *Virgin and Child*. Van Beuningen Museum, Rotterdam.

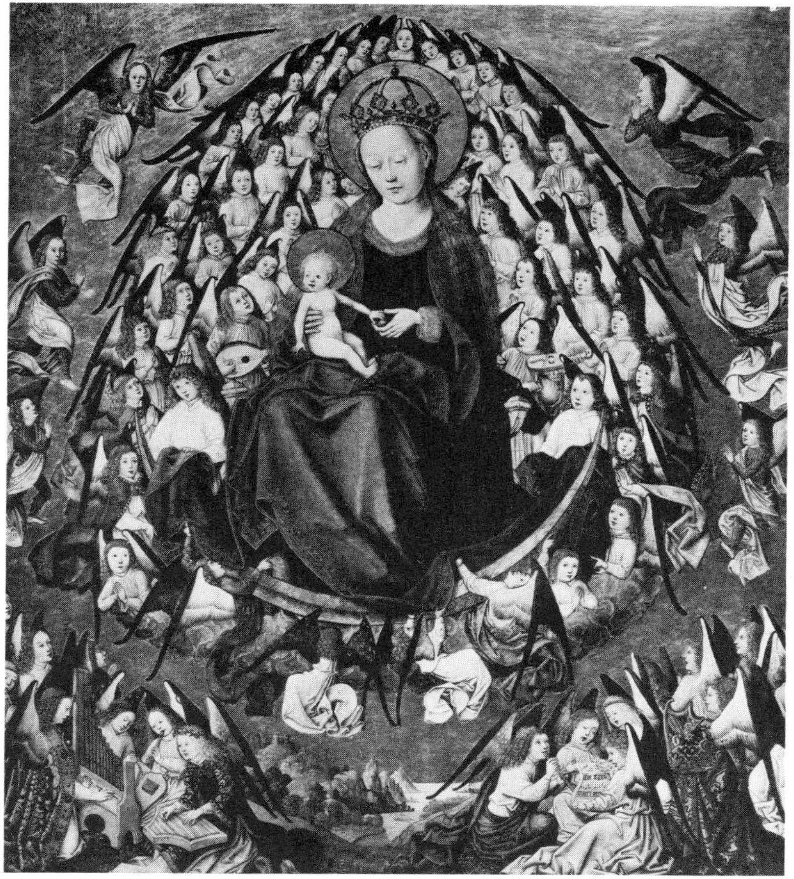

a. Glorification of the Virgin. Collection of Baron Heyl, Worms.

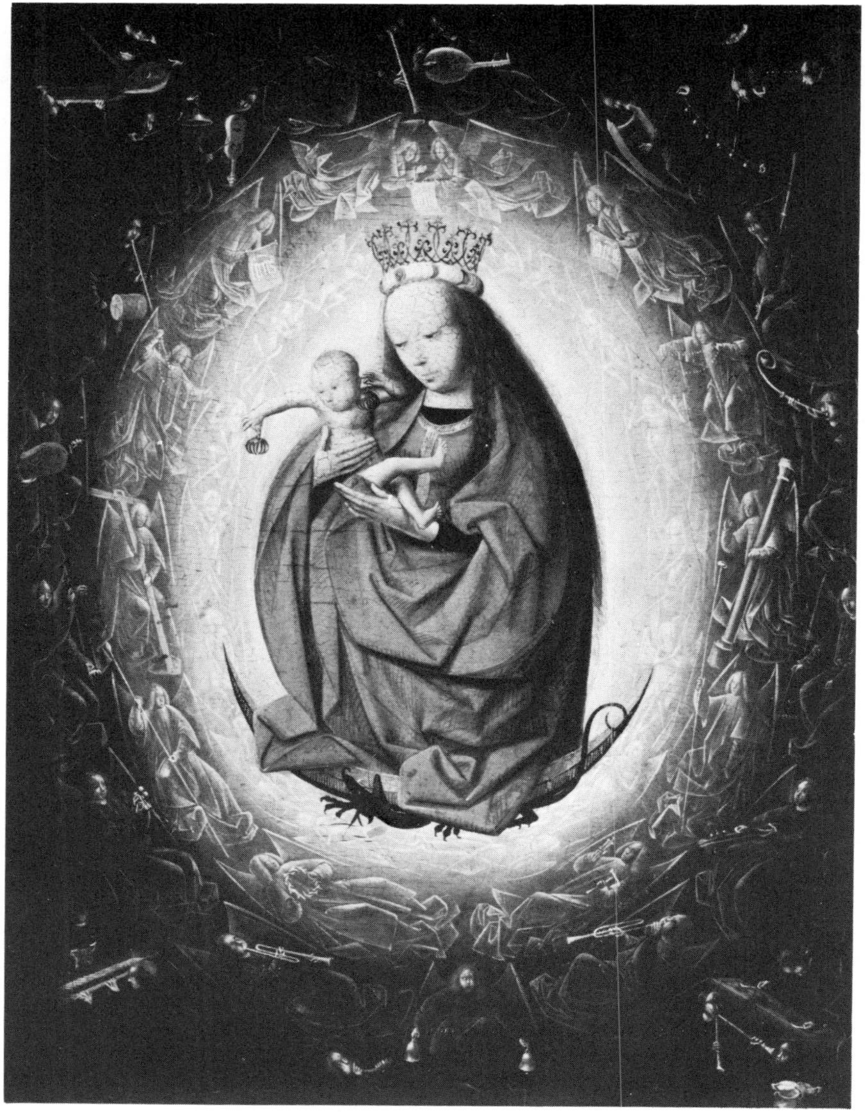

b. Geertgen tot Sint Jans, *Virgin and Child.* Van Beuningen Museum, Rotterdam.

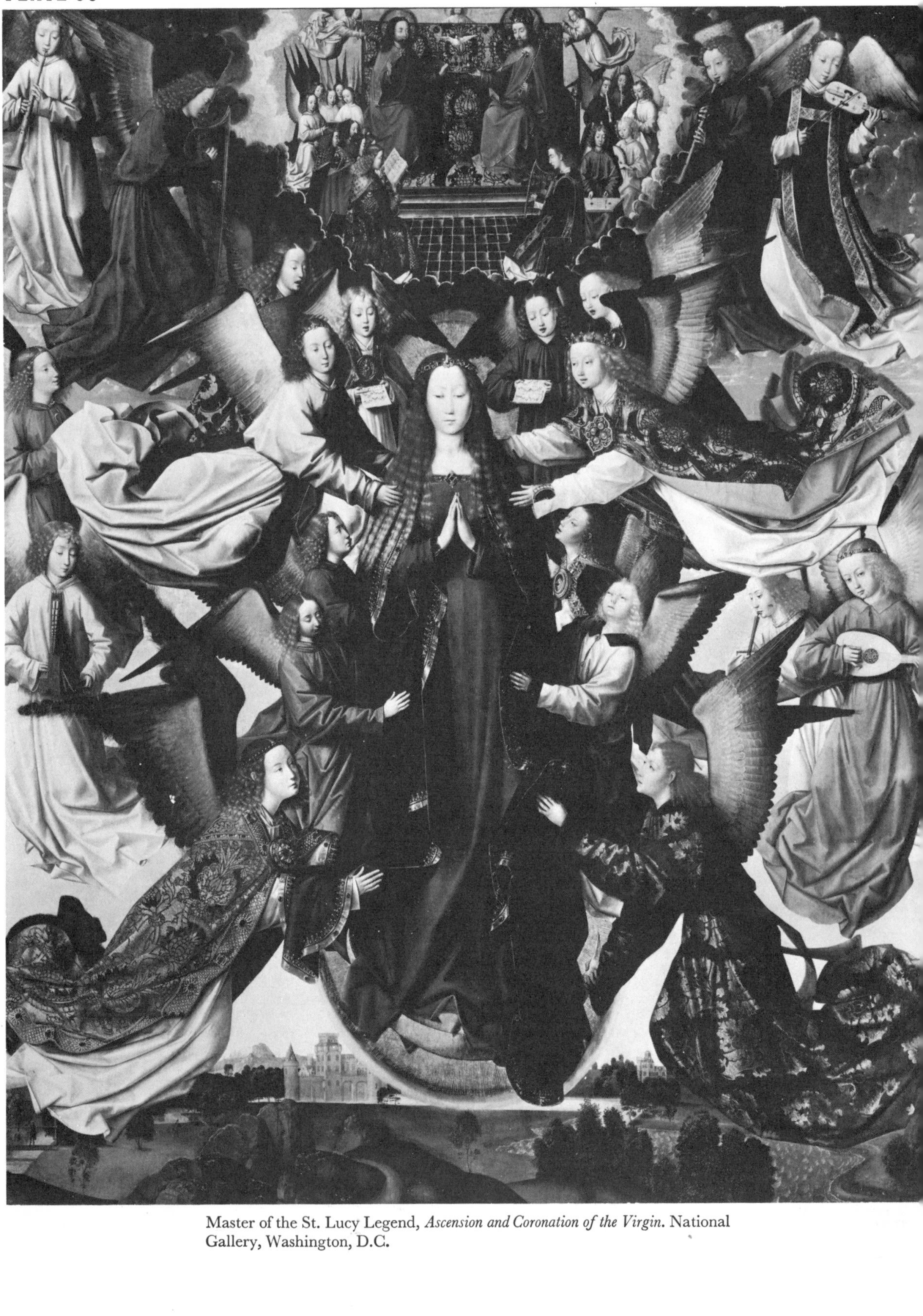

Master of the St. Lucy Legend, *Ascension and Coronation of the Virgin*. National Gallery, Washington, D.C.

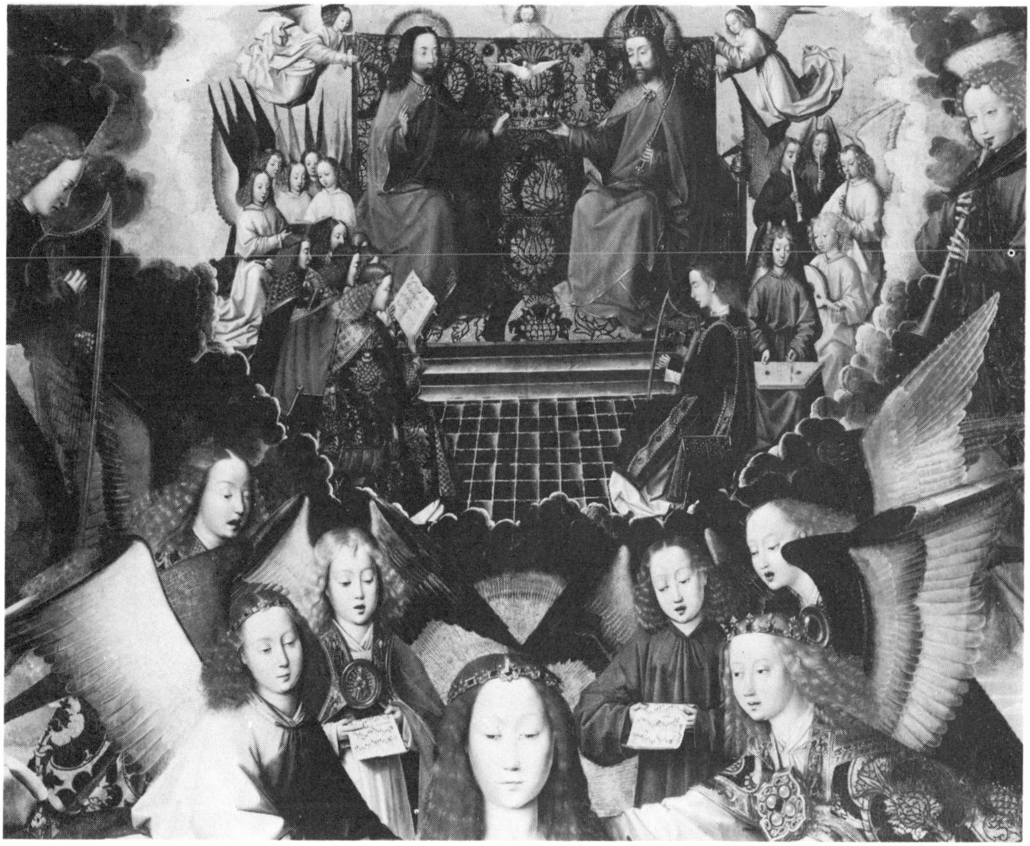

DETAILS OF PLATE 66

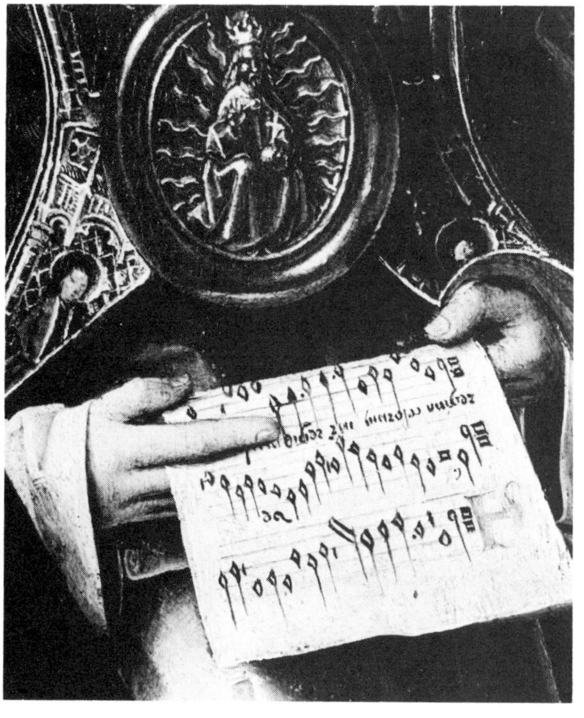

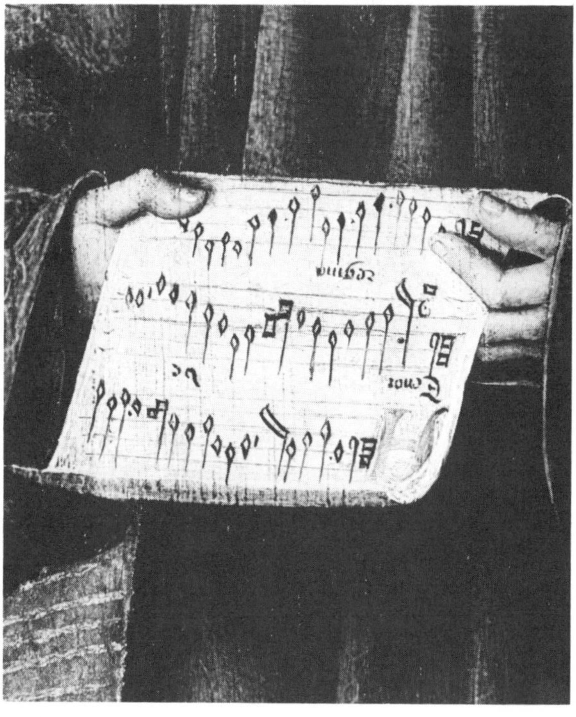

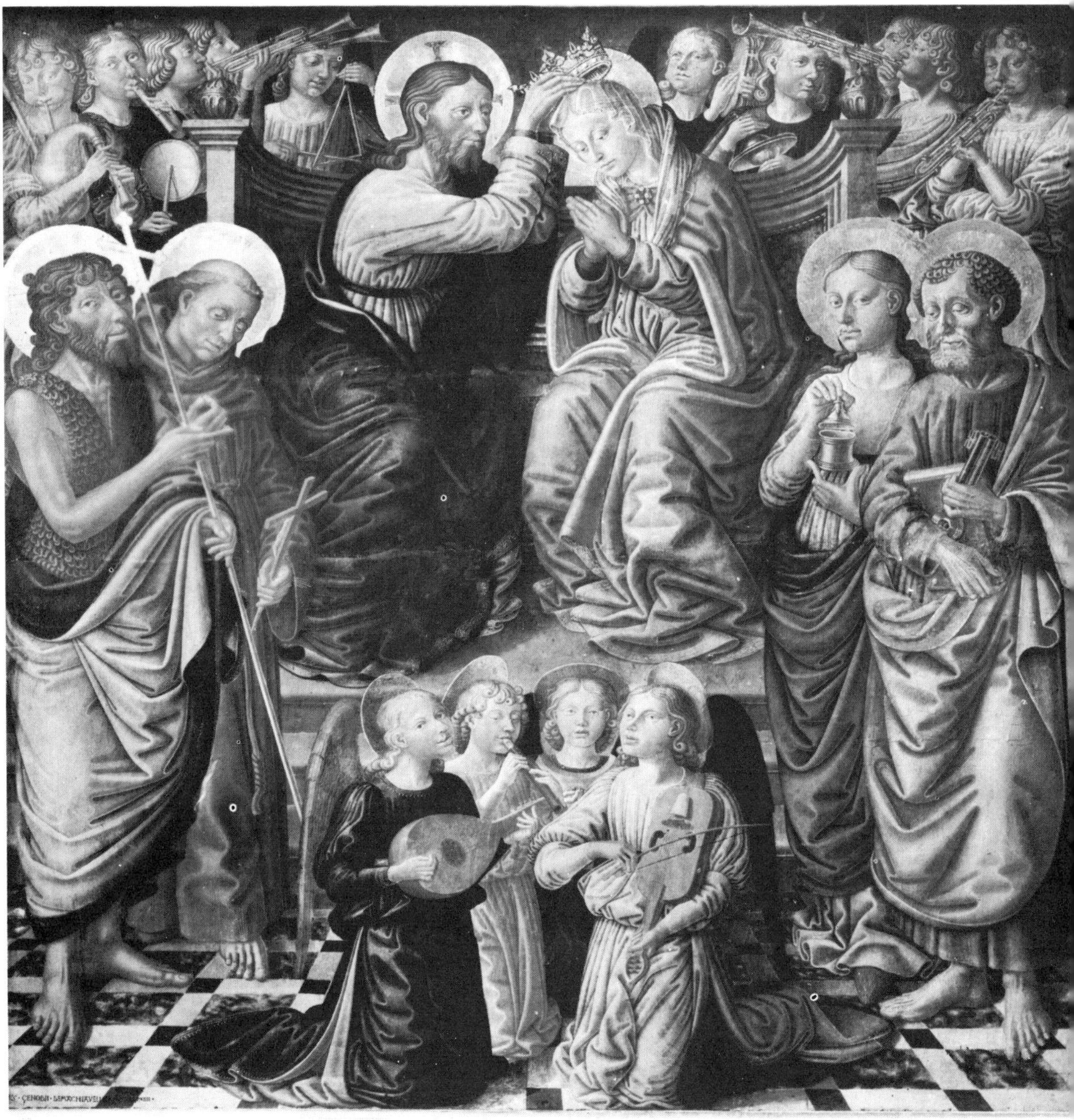

Zanobi Machiavelli, *Coronation of the Virgin*. Museum, Dijon

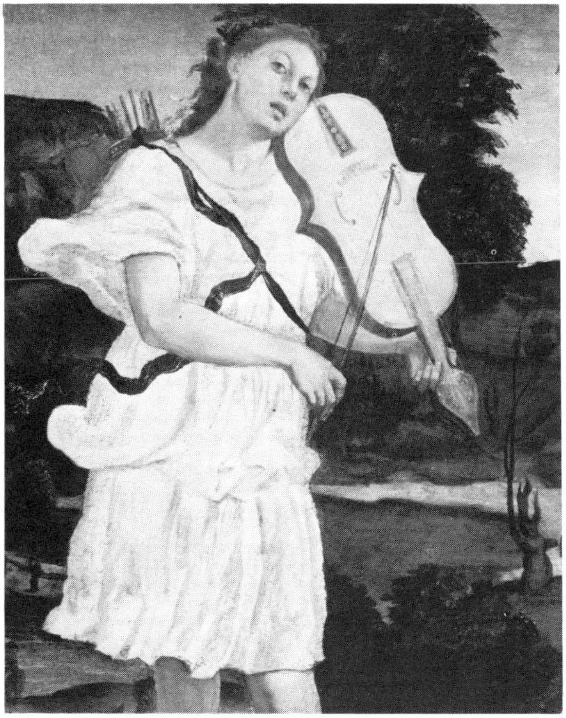

a. Detail of Plate 70*a*, showing Apollo.

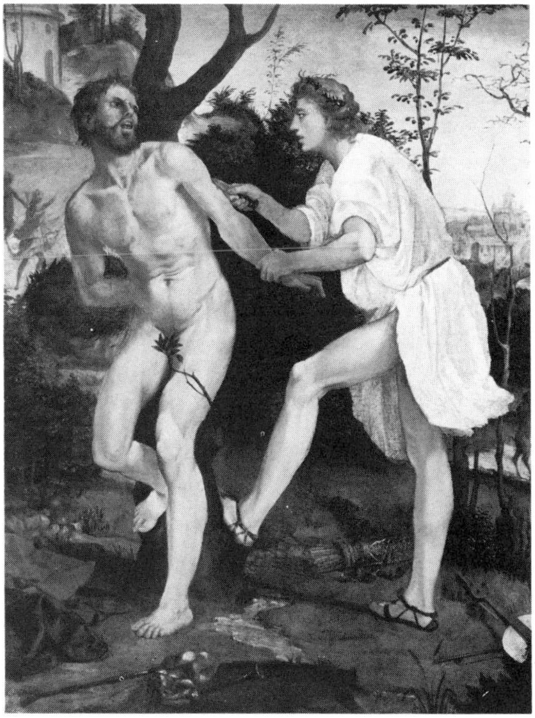

b. Detail of Plate 70*a*, showing Apollo flaying Marsyas.

c. Detail of Plate 70*a*, showing Pallas Athena.

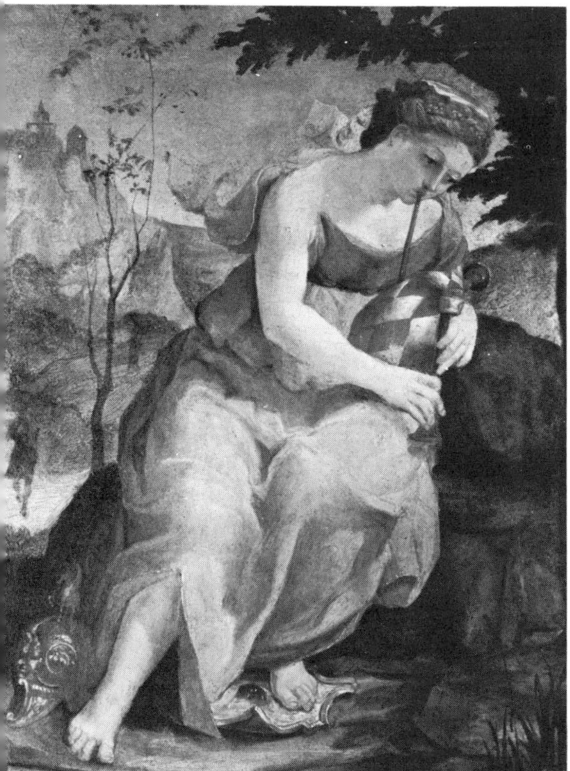

d. Benedetto da Majano, sarcophagus. Cappella Strozzi, Santa Maria Novella, Florence.

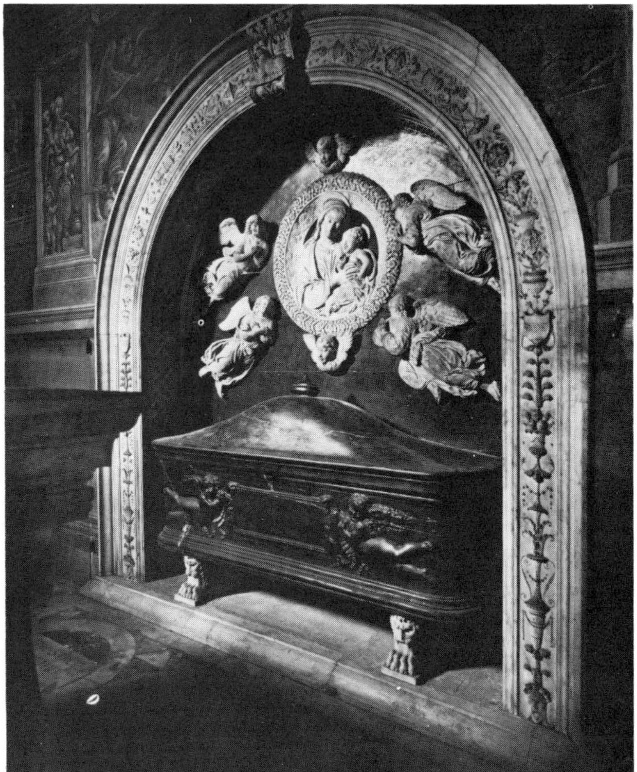

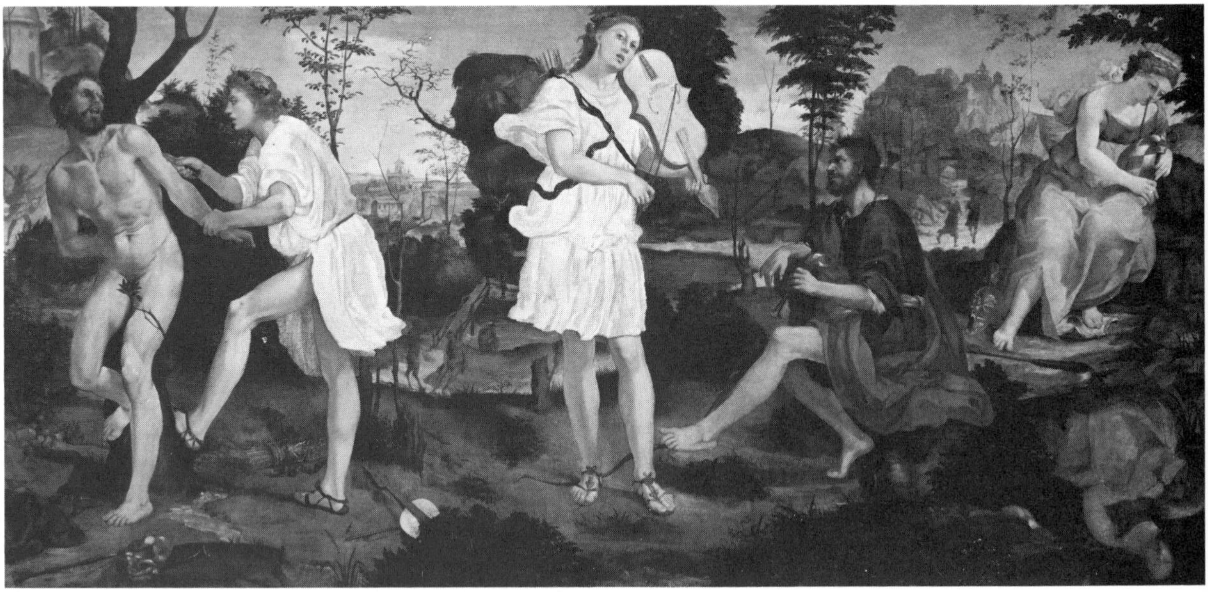

a. Contest between Apollo and Marsyas. National Gallery, Washington, D.C., Samuel H. Kress Collection.

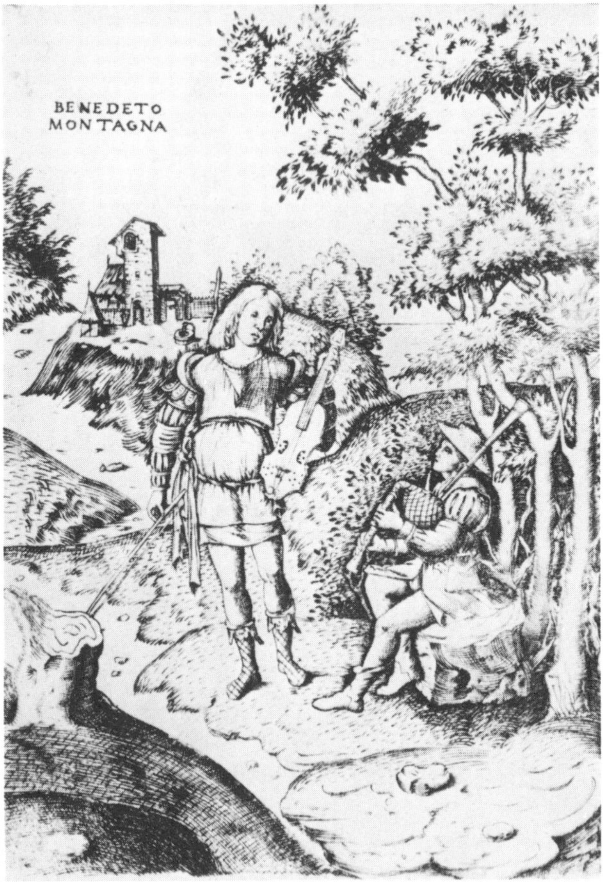

b. Benedetto Montagna, *Contest between Apollo and Marsyas* (engraving).

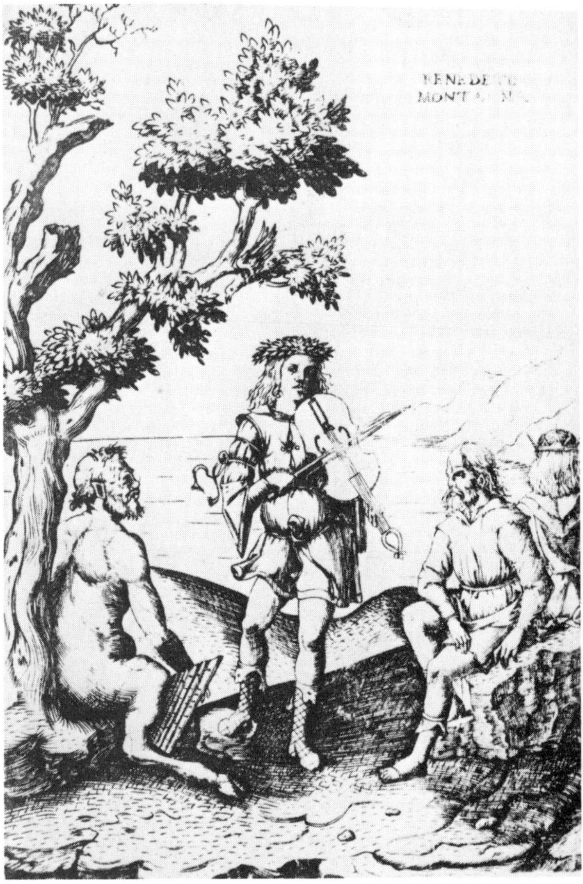

c. Benedetto Montagna, *Contest between Apollo and Pan* (engraving).

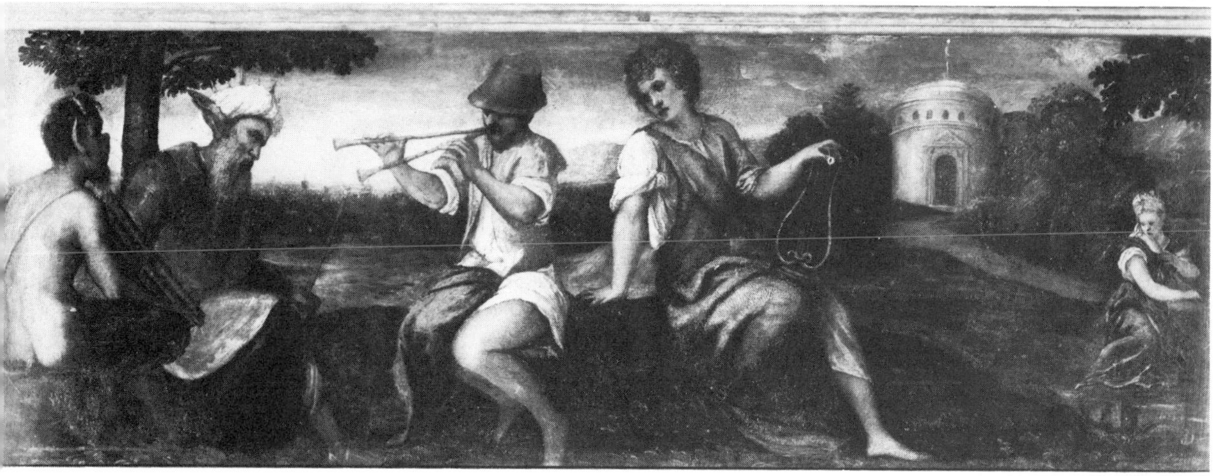

a. Andrea Schiavone, *The Judgment of Midas*. Accademia, Venice.

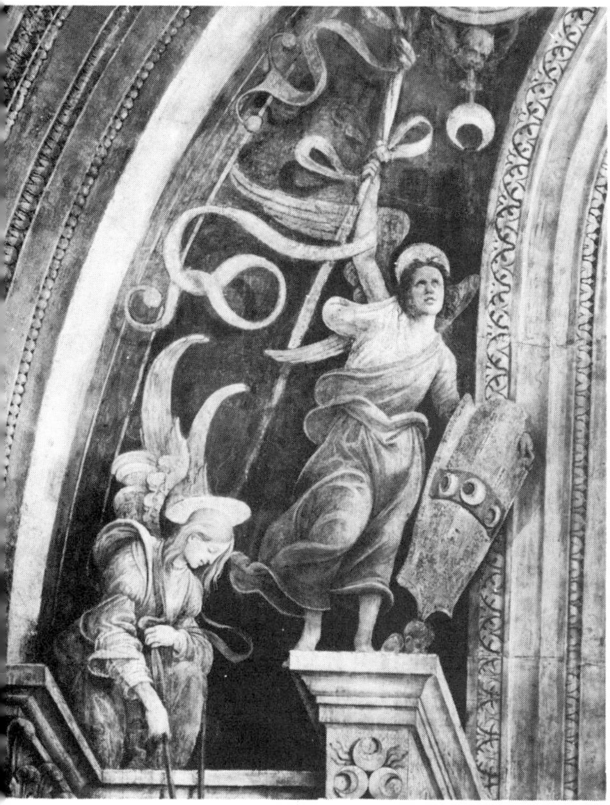

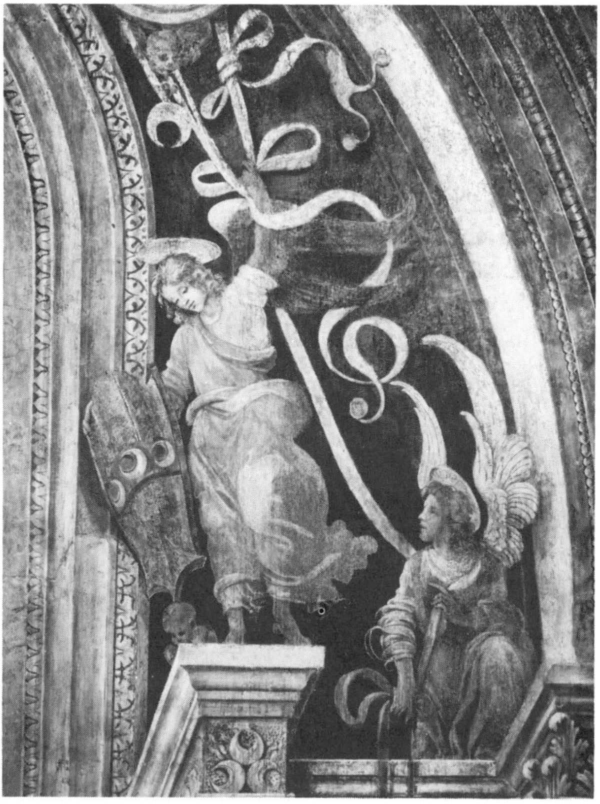

b. Details of window wall in Cappella Strozzi, Santa Maria Novella, Florence.

left: Angels to left of window.

right: Angels to right of window

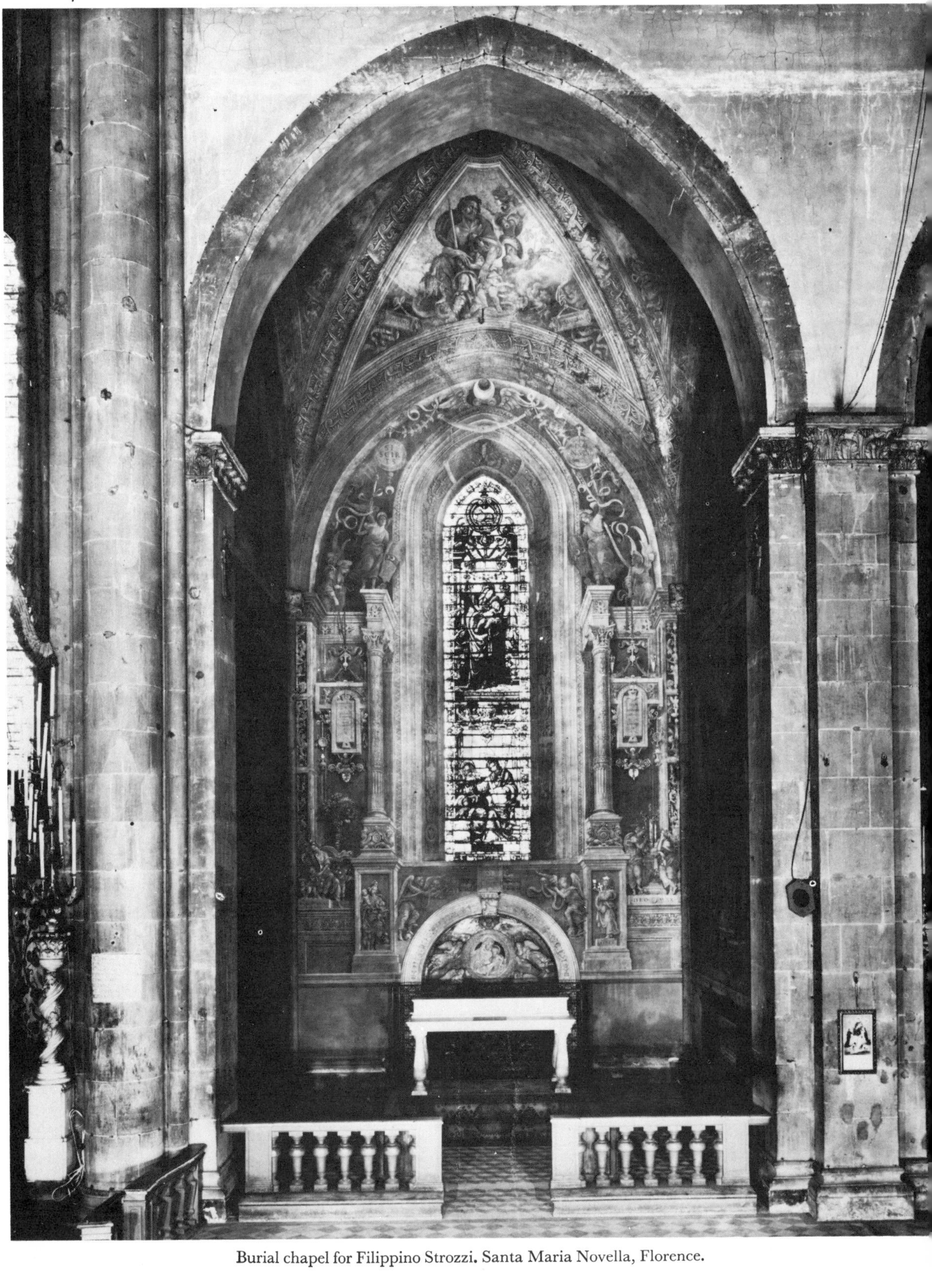

Burial chapel for Filippino Strozzi. Santa Maria Novella, Florence.

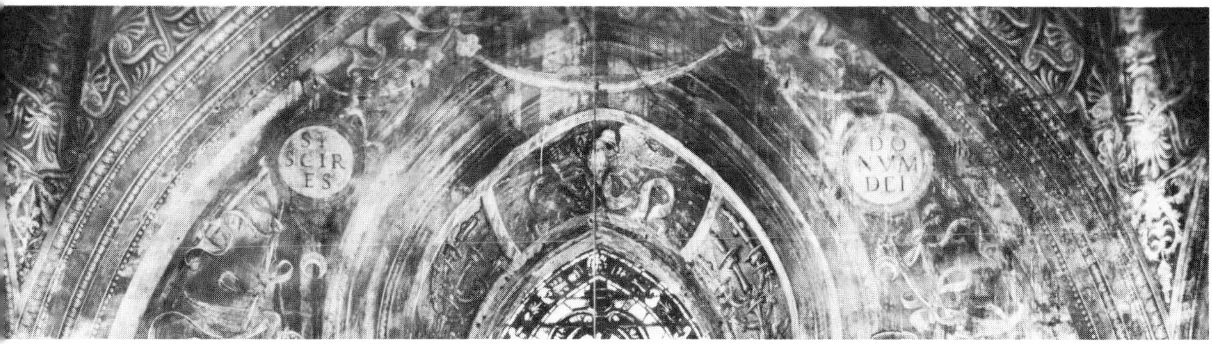

a. Window wall, showing round plaques at top.

b. Upper part of window: Madonna.

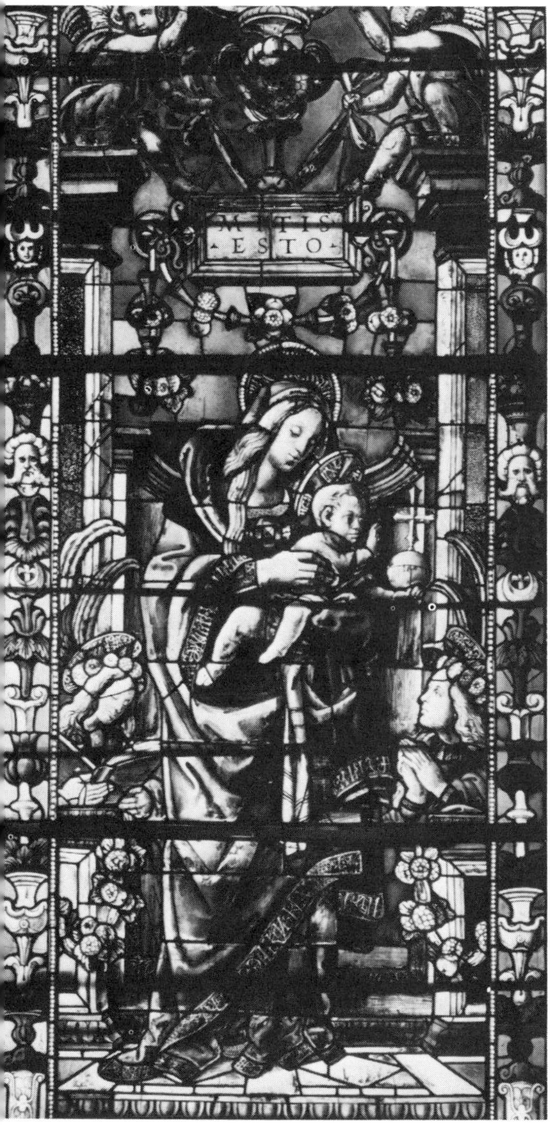

c. Lower part of window: St. John the Evangelist and St. Philip.

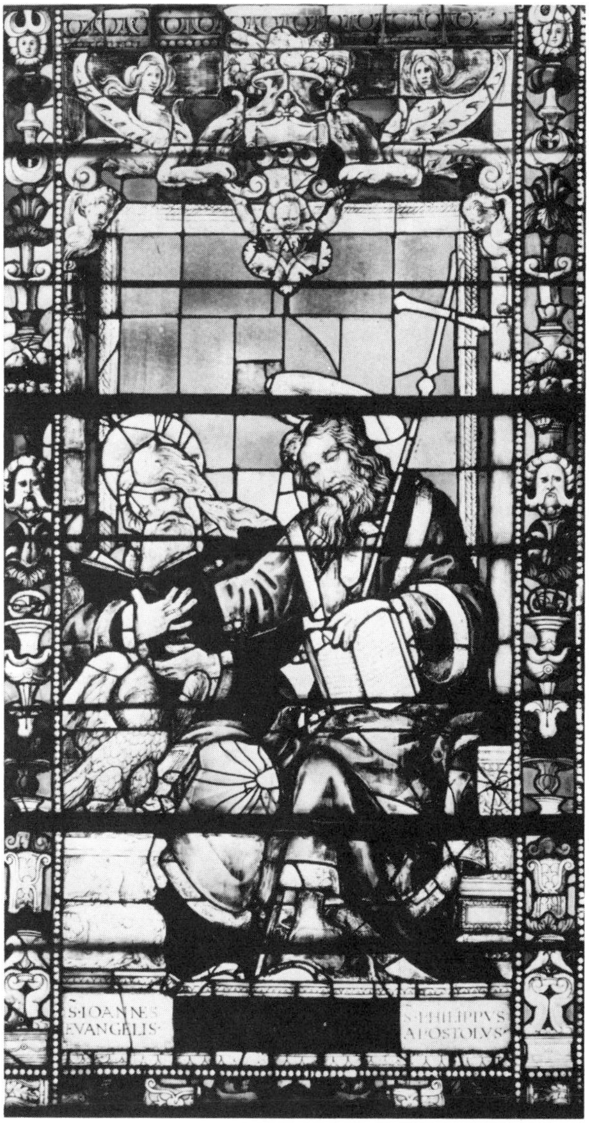

CAPPELLA STROZZI, SANTA MARIA NOVELLA, FLORENCE

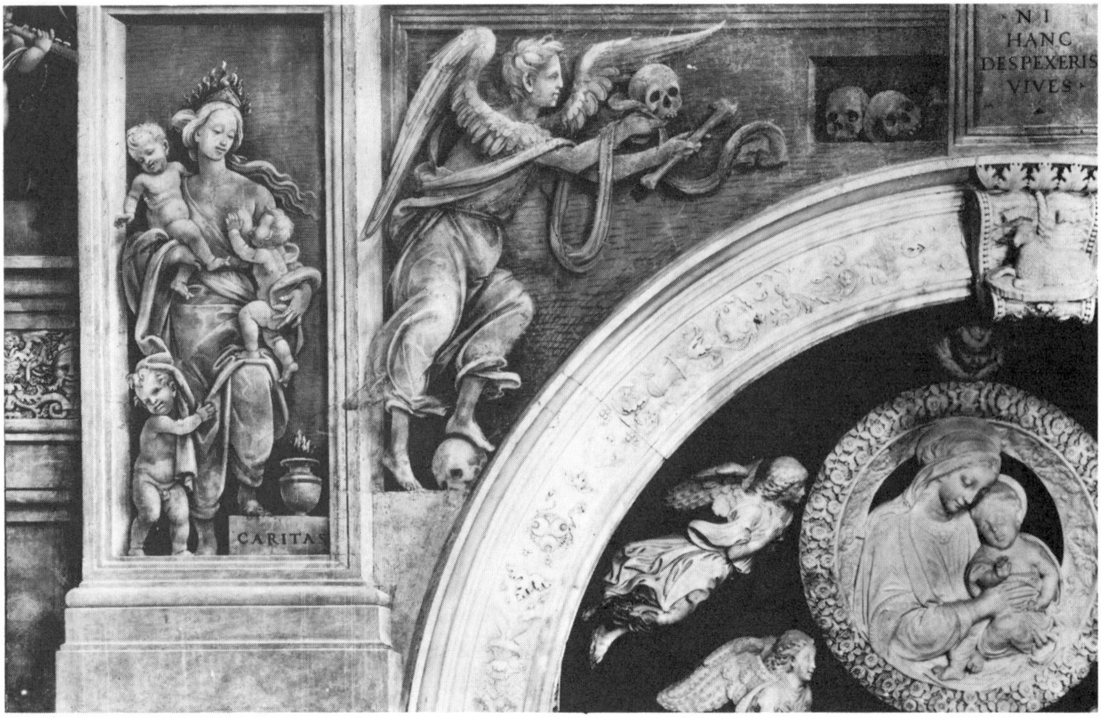

a. Detail of window wall in Cappella Strozzi, showing Caritas and angel.

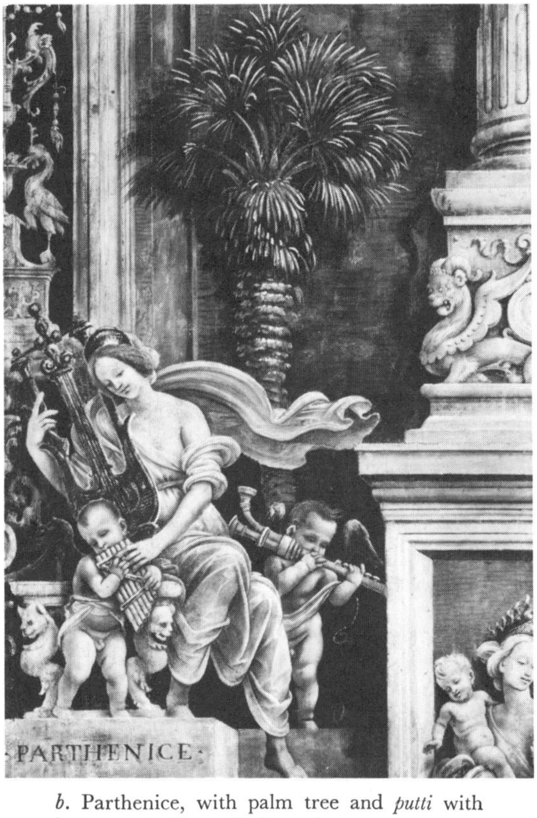

b. Parthenice, with palm tree and *putti* with instruments. Cappella Strozzi.

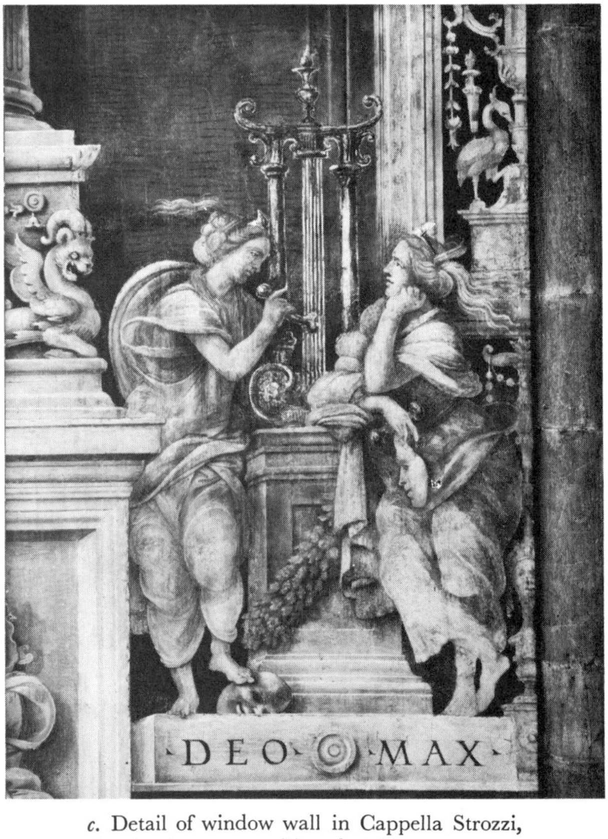

c. Detail of window wall in Cappella Strozzi, showing two muses with pedestal lyre.

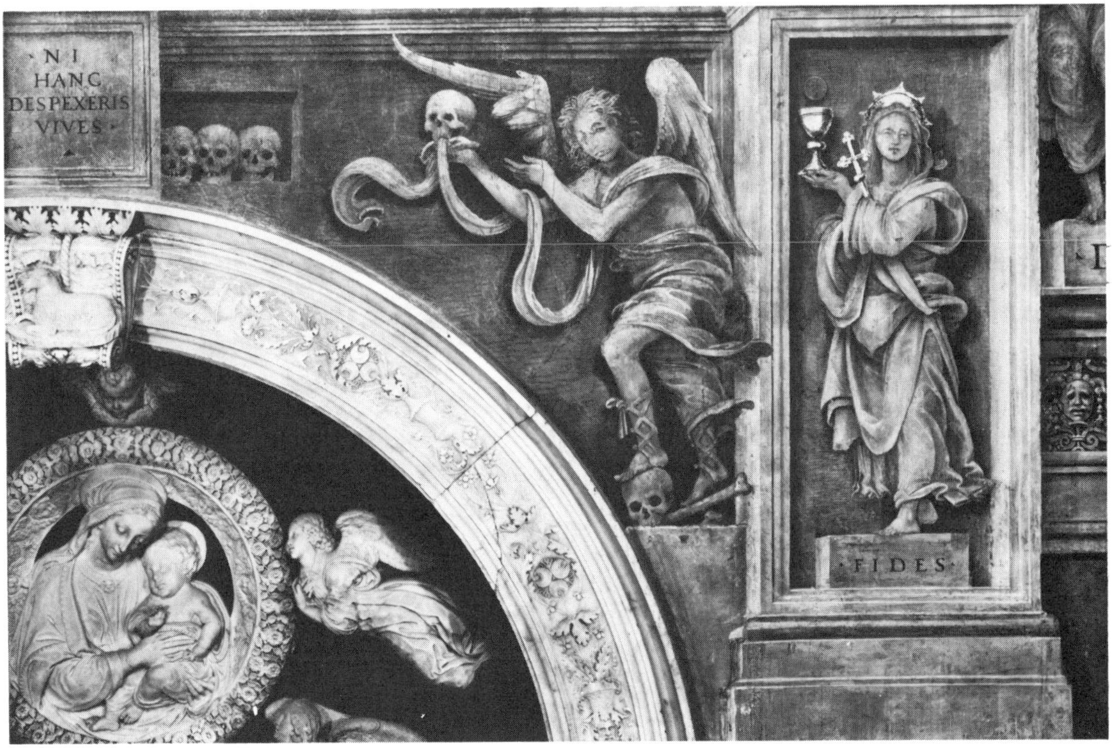
NI
HANC
DESPEXERIS
VIVES
FIDES

a. Detail of window wall in Cappella Strozzi, showing Fides and angel.

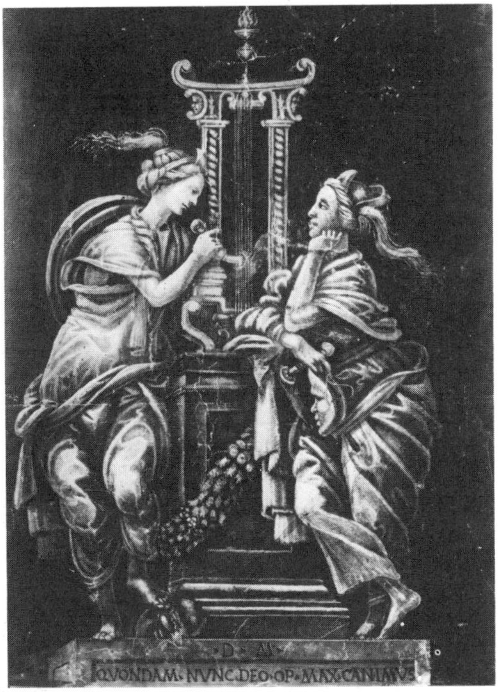
D M
QVONDAM. NVNC.DEO.OP.MAX.CANIMVS

b. Anonymous drawing of figures in Pl. 74*c*. Uffizi, Florence.

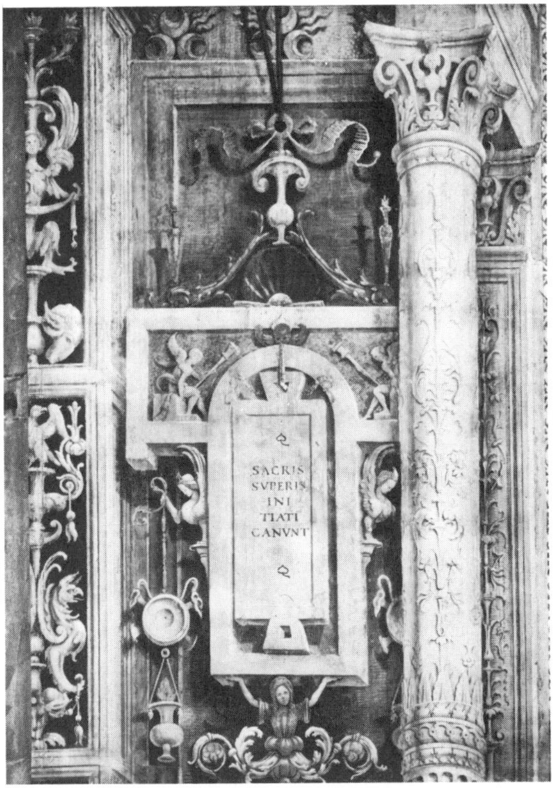
SACRIS
SVPERIS
INI
TIATI
CANVNT

c. Left tablet, with inscription. Cappella Strozzi.

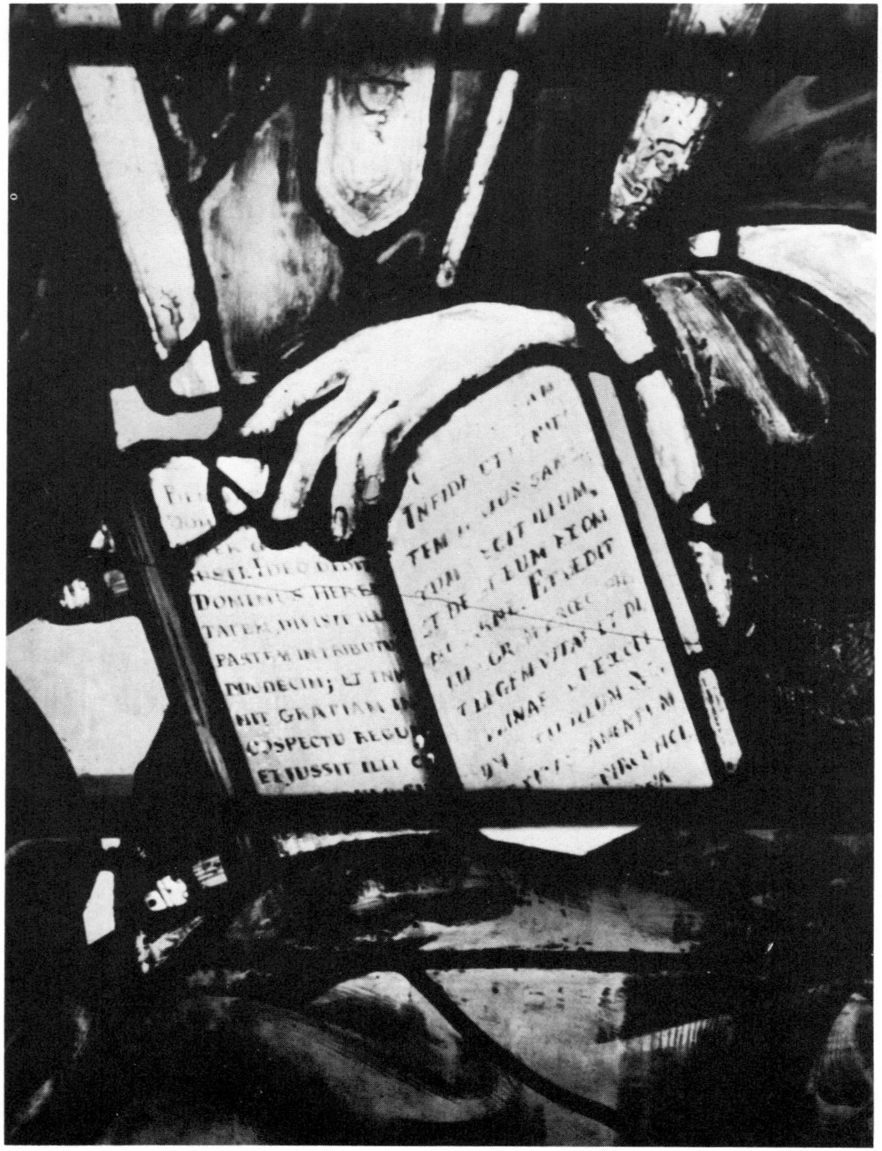

a. Detail of book held by St. Philip. Cappella Strozzi.

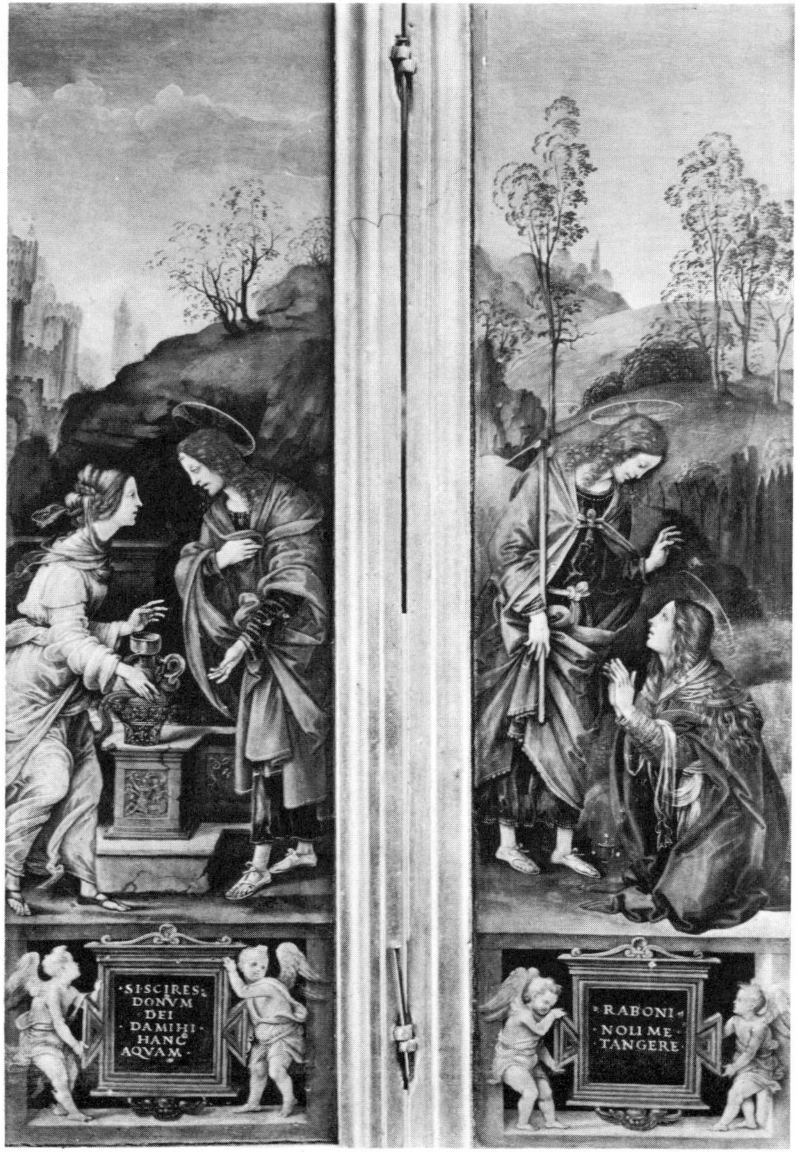

b. Filippino Lippi, *Jesus and the Woman of Samaria*. Seminario, Venice.

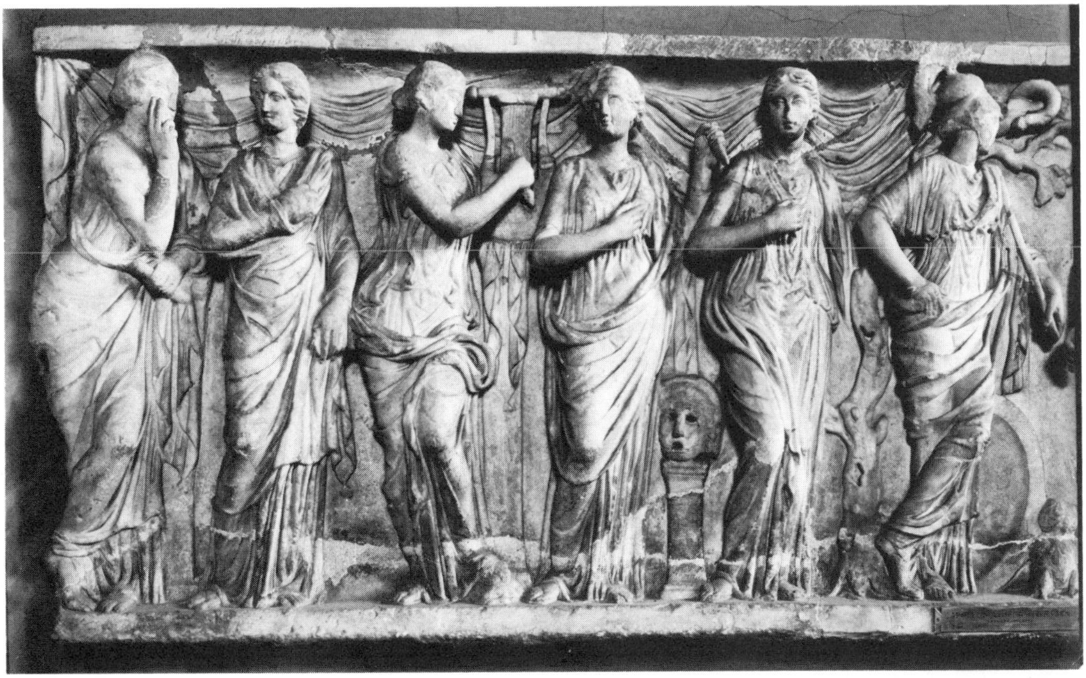

a. A sarcophagus of the Muses, showing left part of front. Kunsthistorisches Museum, Vienna.

b. (*below*). Kithara player, from Roman wall painting.

c. (*right*). Detail of Plate 77*a*.

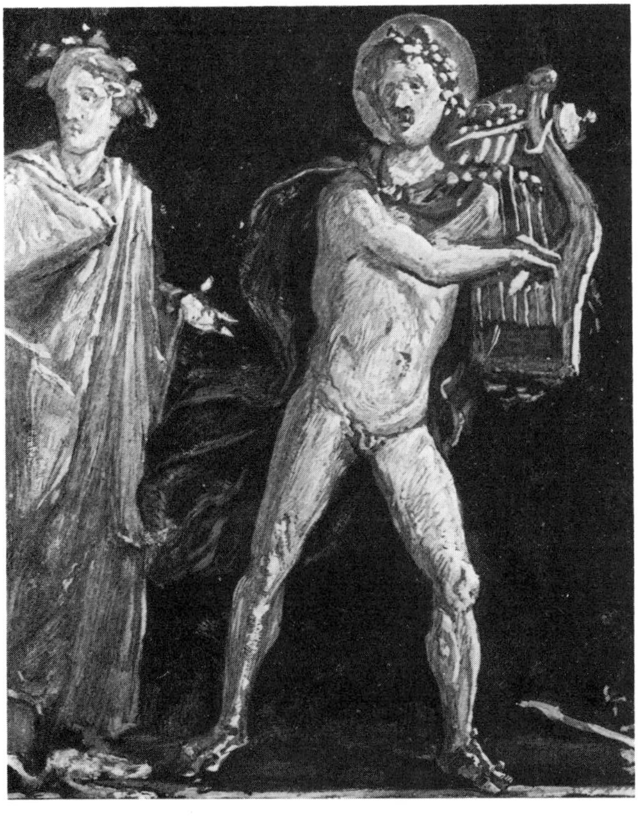

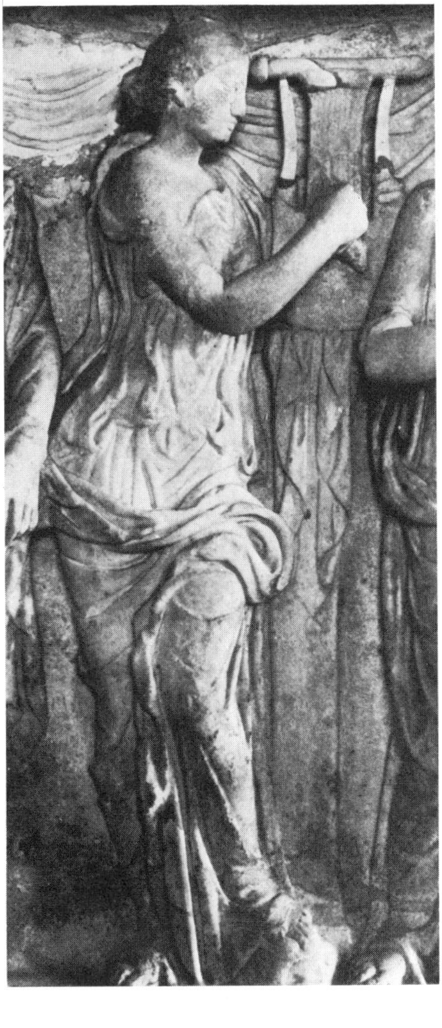

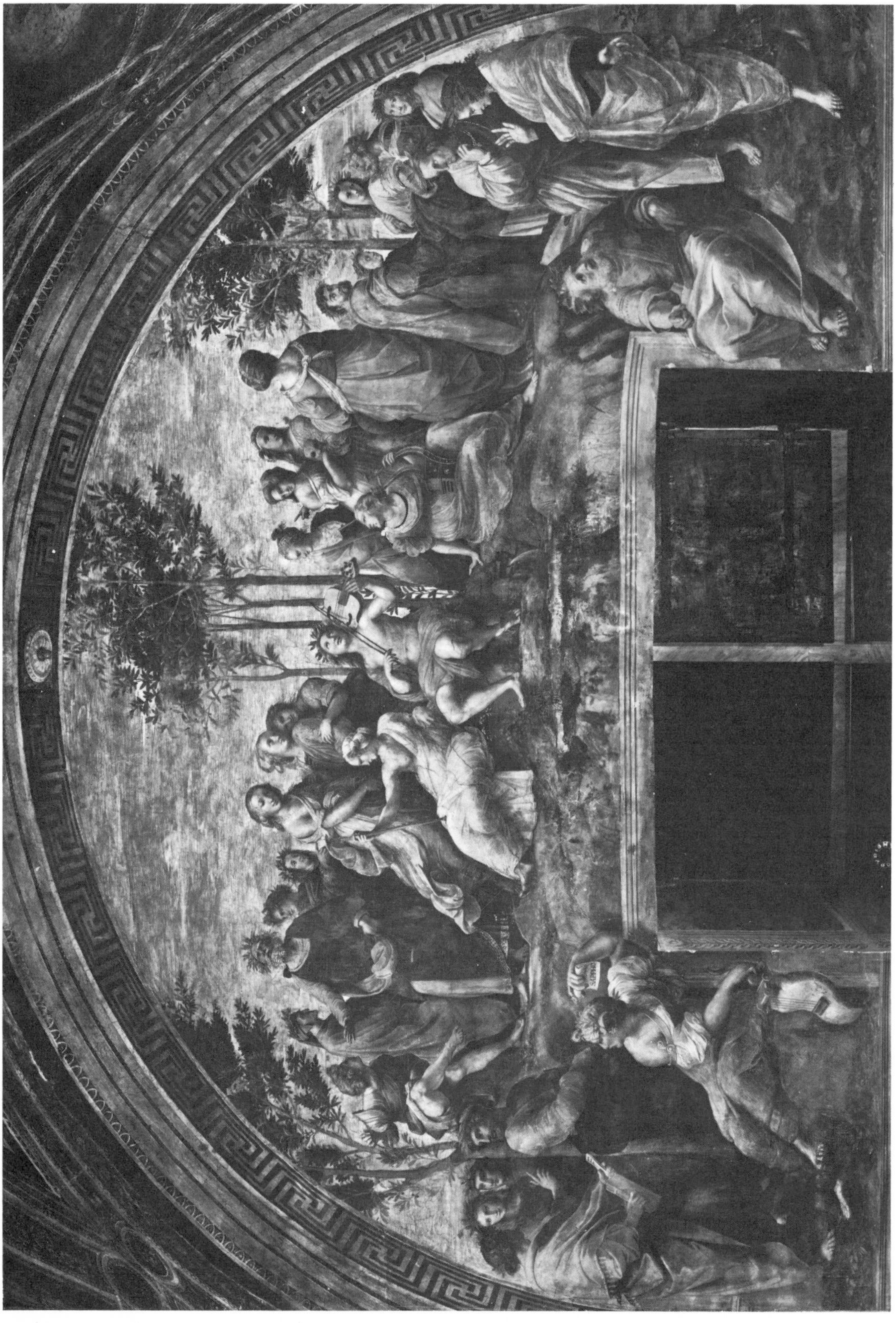

Raphael, *Parnassus*. Stanza della Segnatura, Vatican.

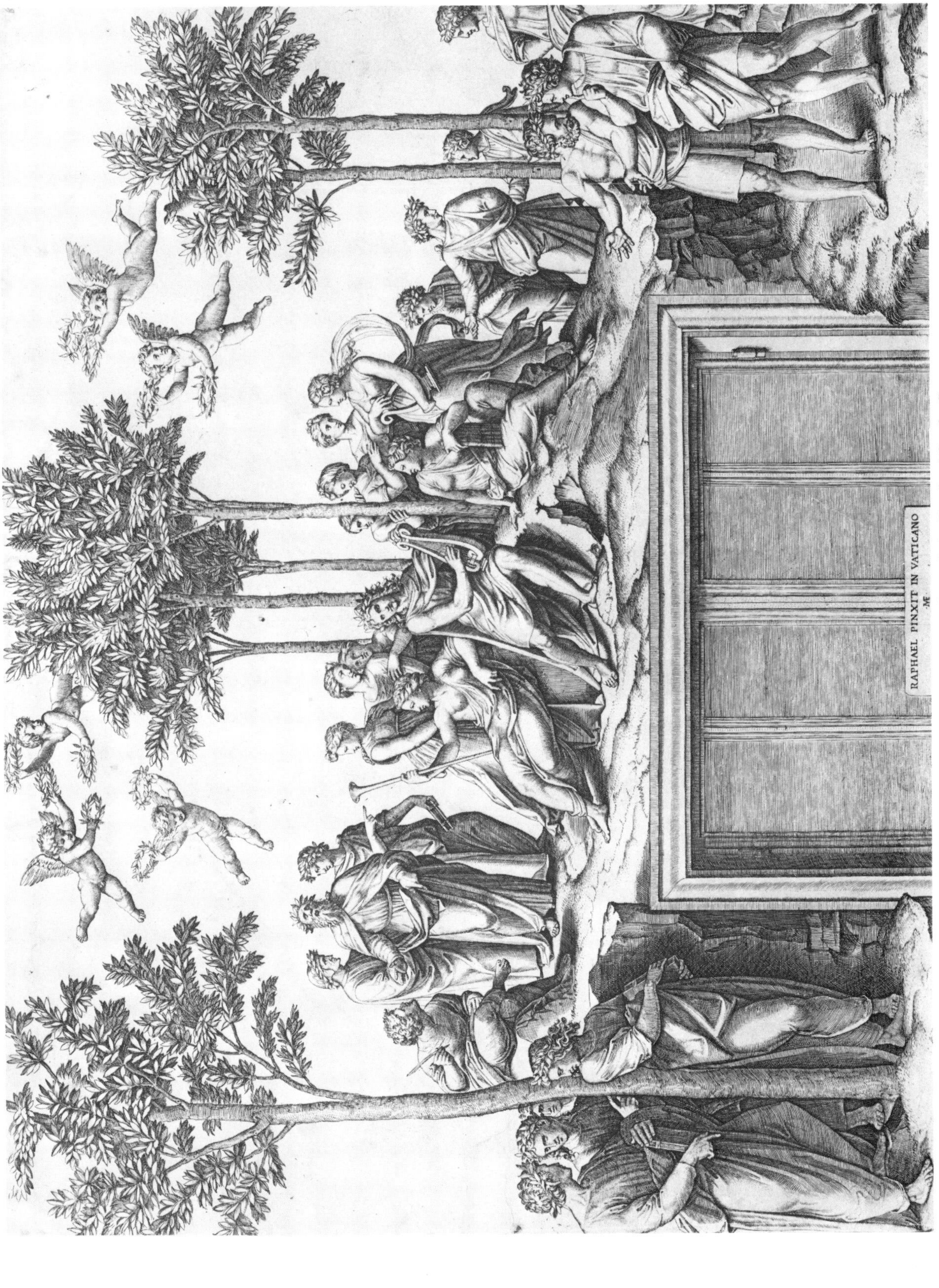

Engraving by Marcantonio, after an early study by Raphael for the *Parnassus*.

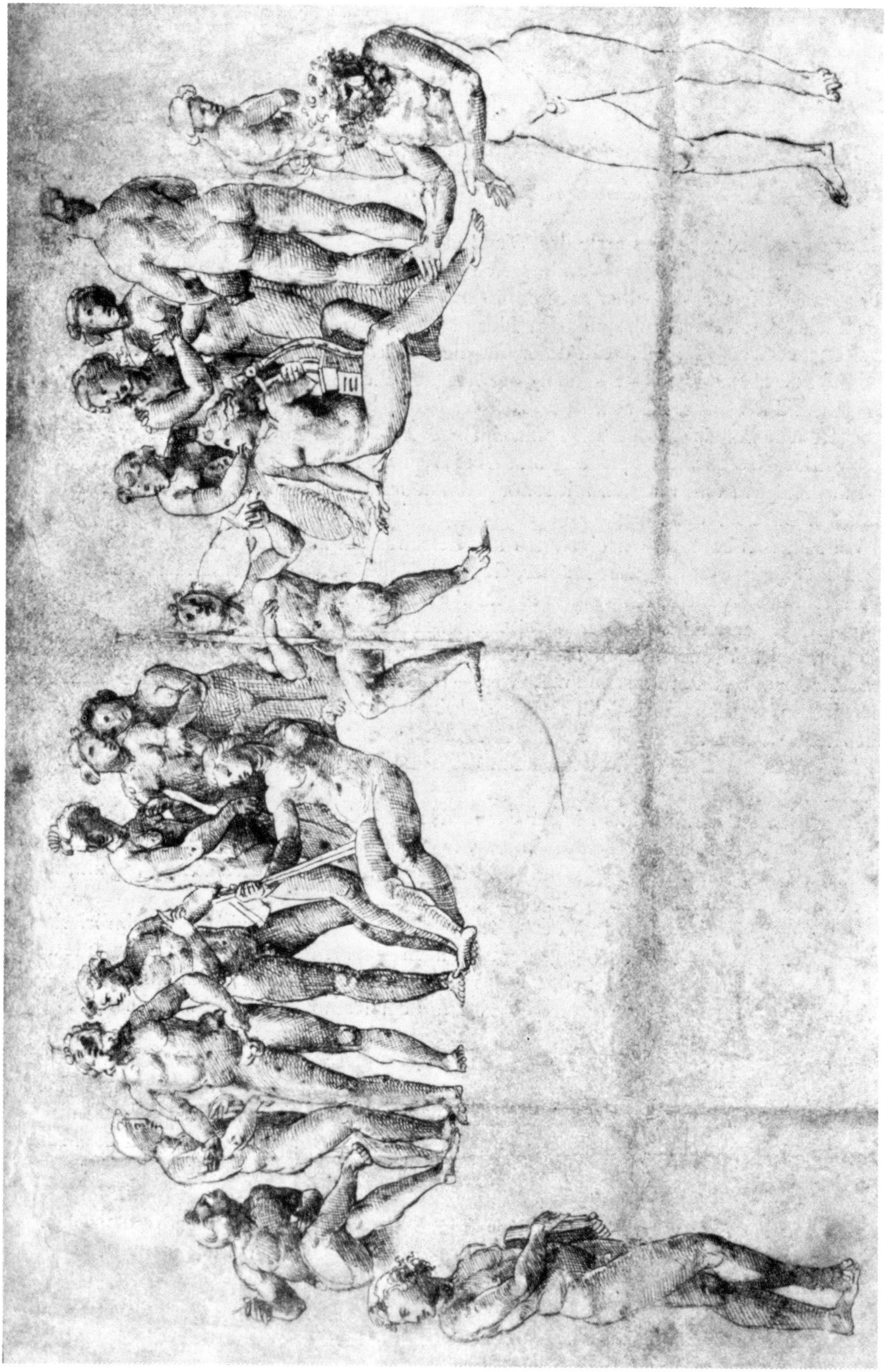

Early copy of a compositional sketch by Raphael for the *Parnassus*, Oxford.

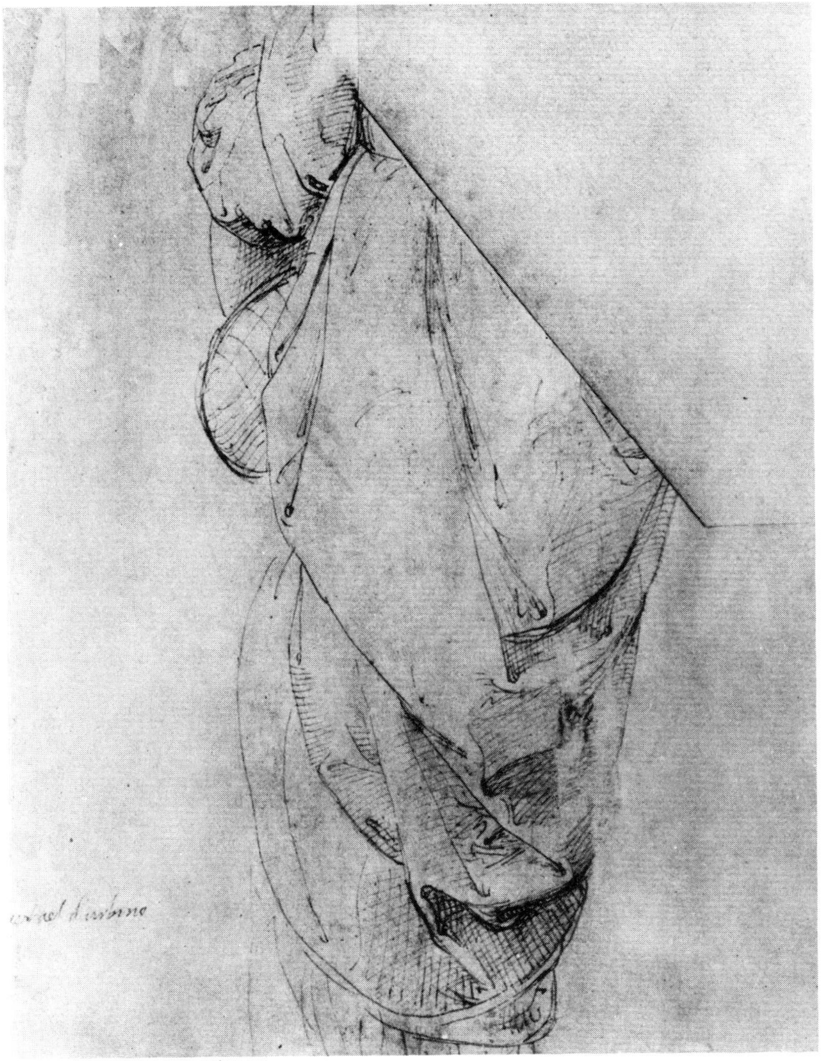

a. Raphael, sketch for the Muse at the right of Apollo. Albertina, Vienna.

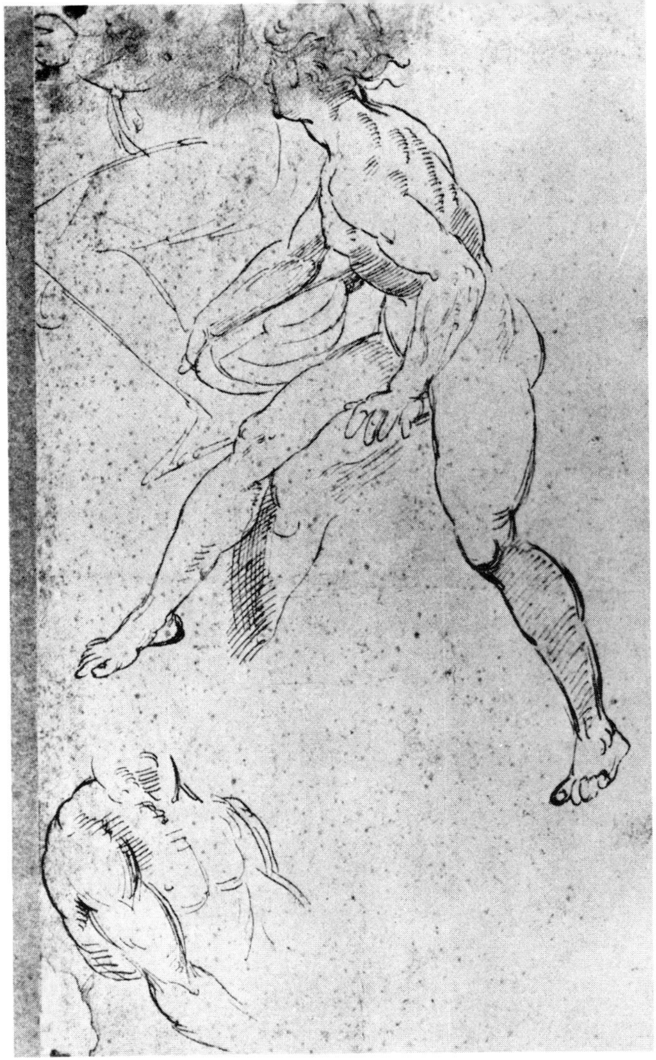

b. Early copy of a sketch by Raphael of a lute player. Chantilly.

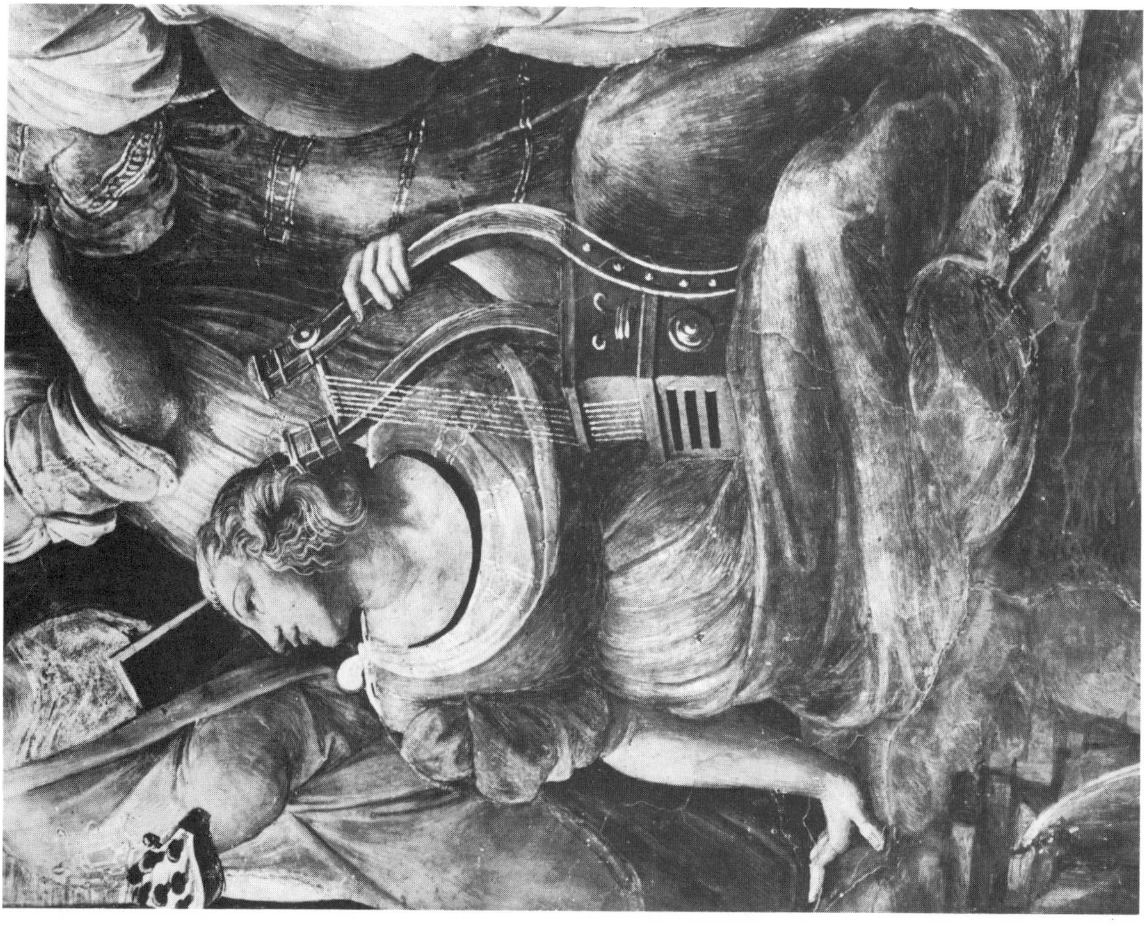

a. Raphael, *Parnassus*, detail showing Erato's kithara.

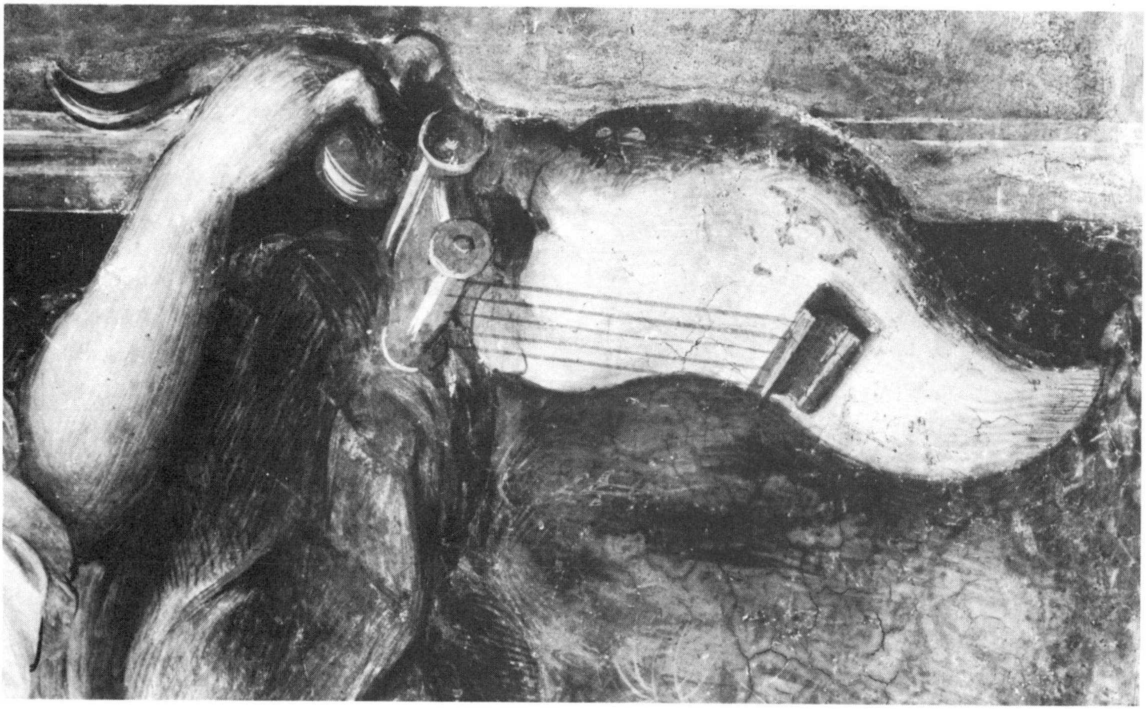

b. Raphael, *Parnassus*, detail showing Sappho's lyre.

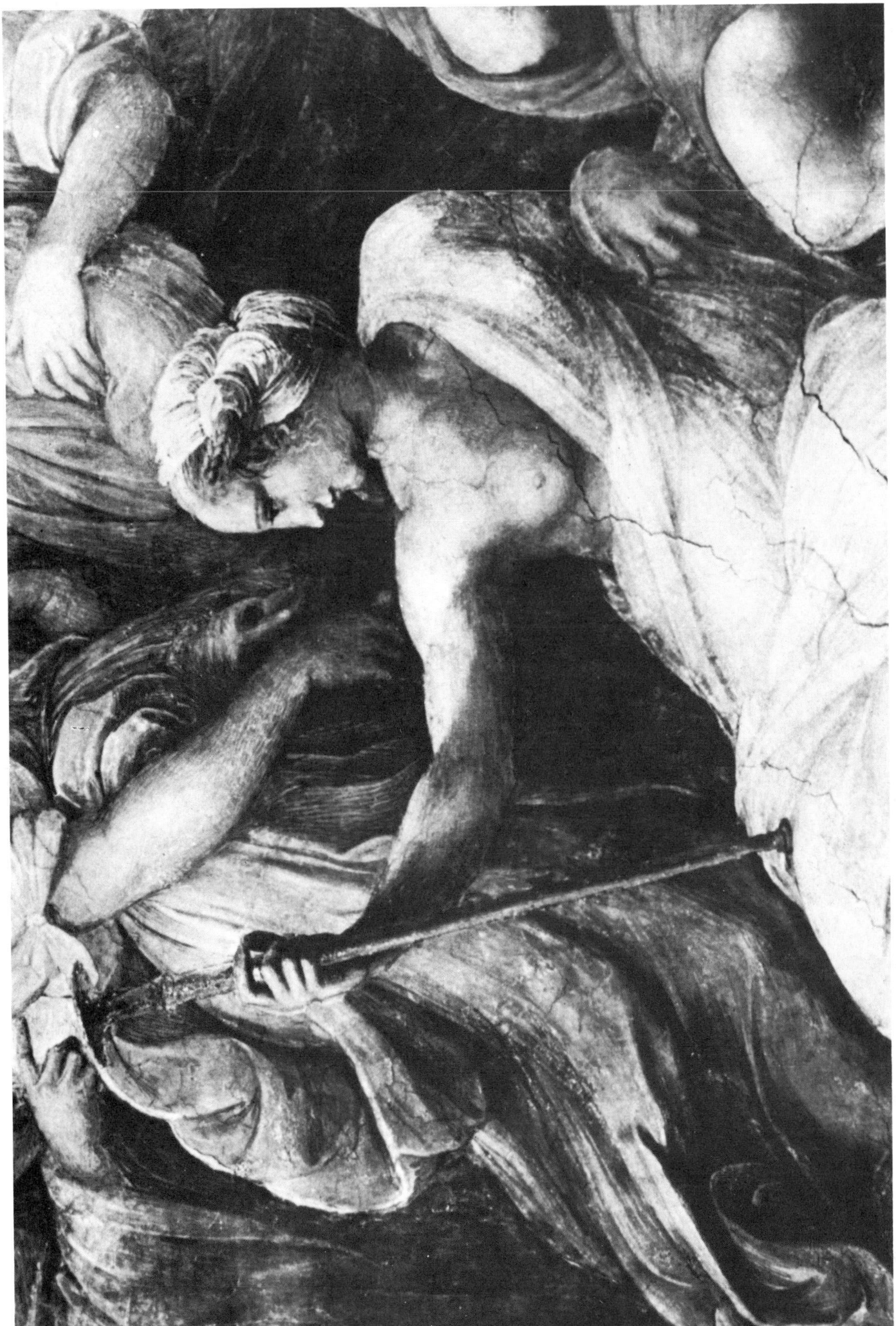

Raphael, *Parnassus*, detail showing Euterpe's wind instrument.

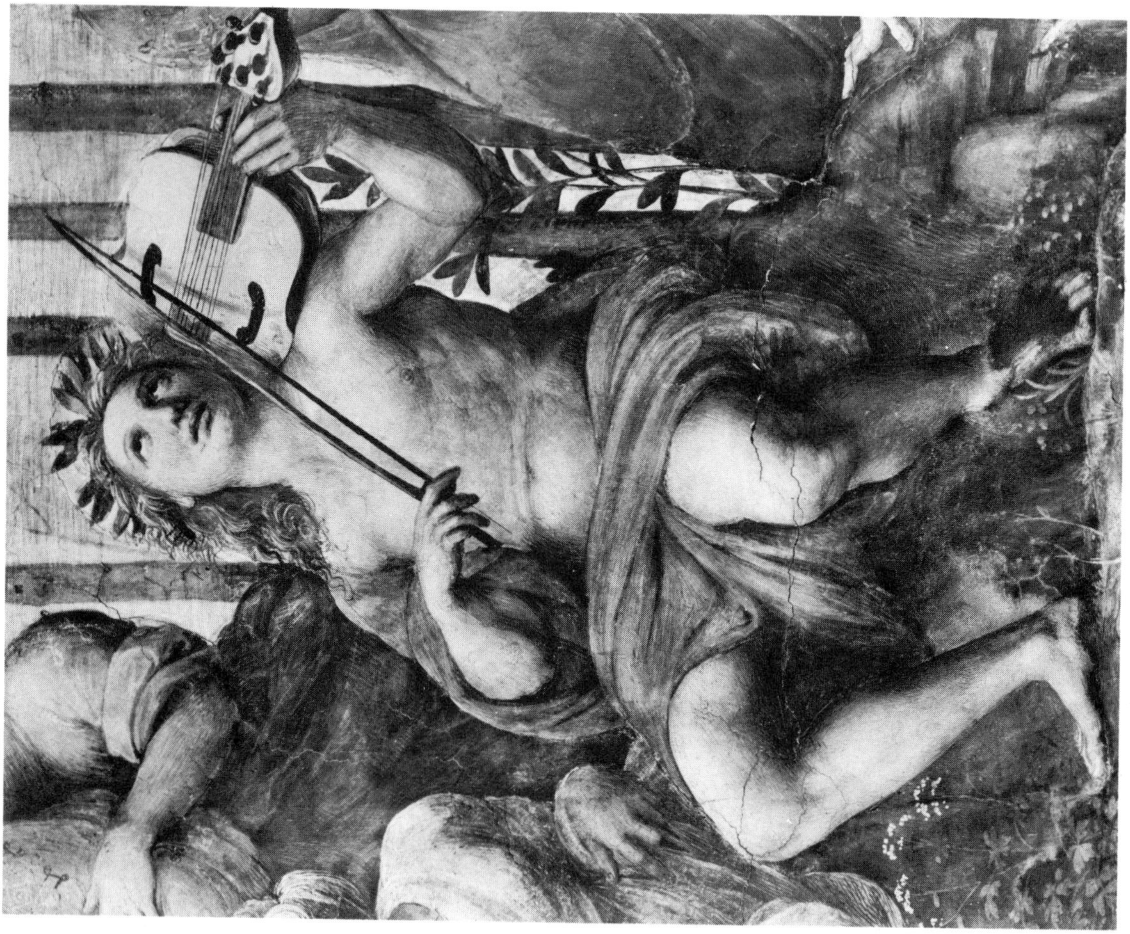

a. Raphael, *Parnassus*, detail showing Apollo.

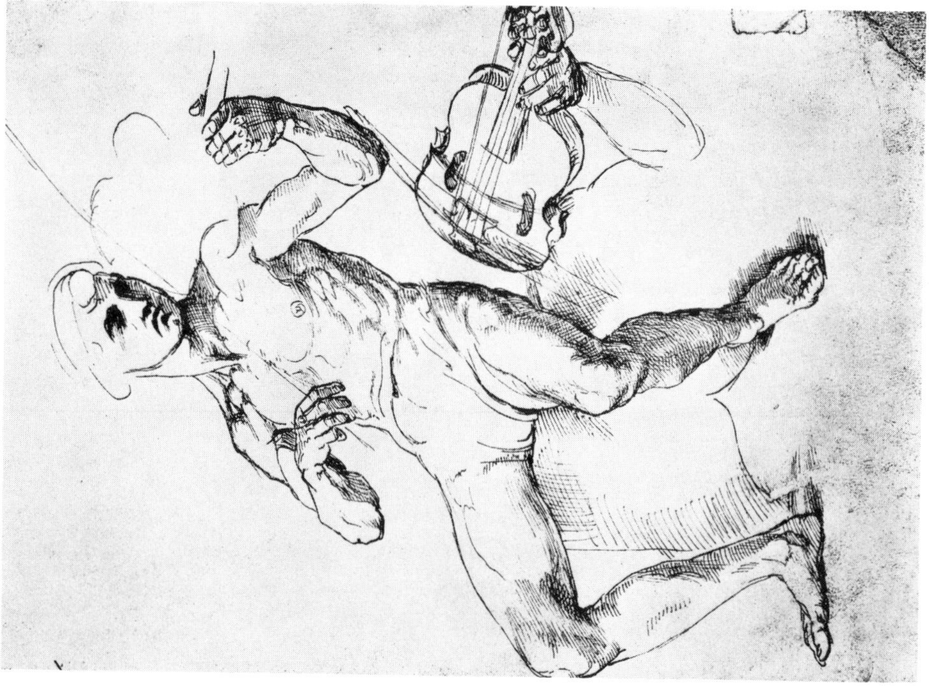

b. Raphael, sketch for the figure of Apollo playing the lira da braccio.

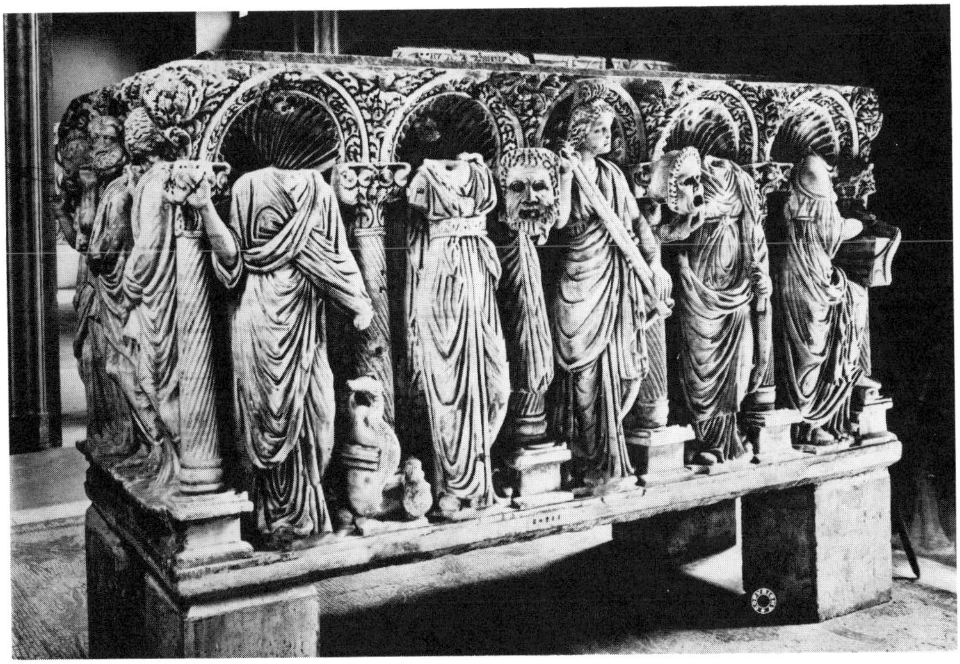

a. Sarcophagus of the Muses (formerly in the Mattei collection). Museo Nazionale, Rome.

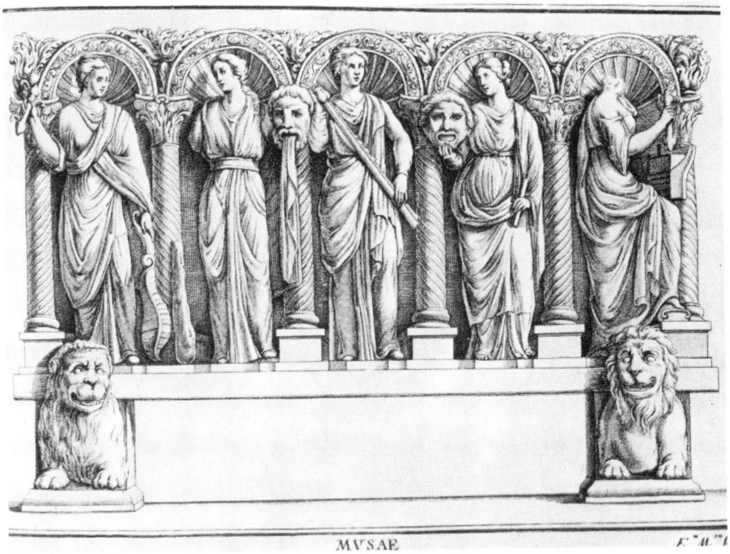

b. Sarcophagus of the Muses, in an engraving from the *Monumenta Matthaeiana.*

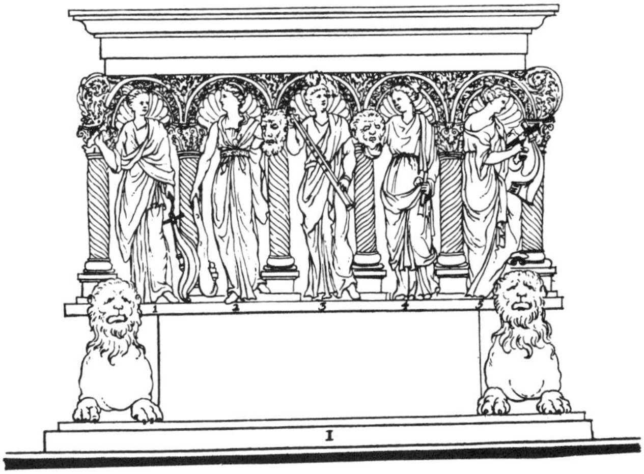

c. Sarcophagus of the Muses, in an engraving from Montfaucon, *L'Antiquité expliquée et representée en figures.*

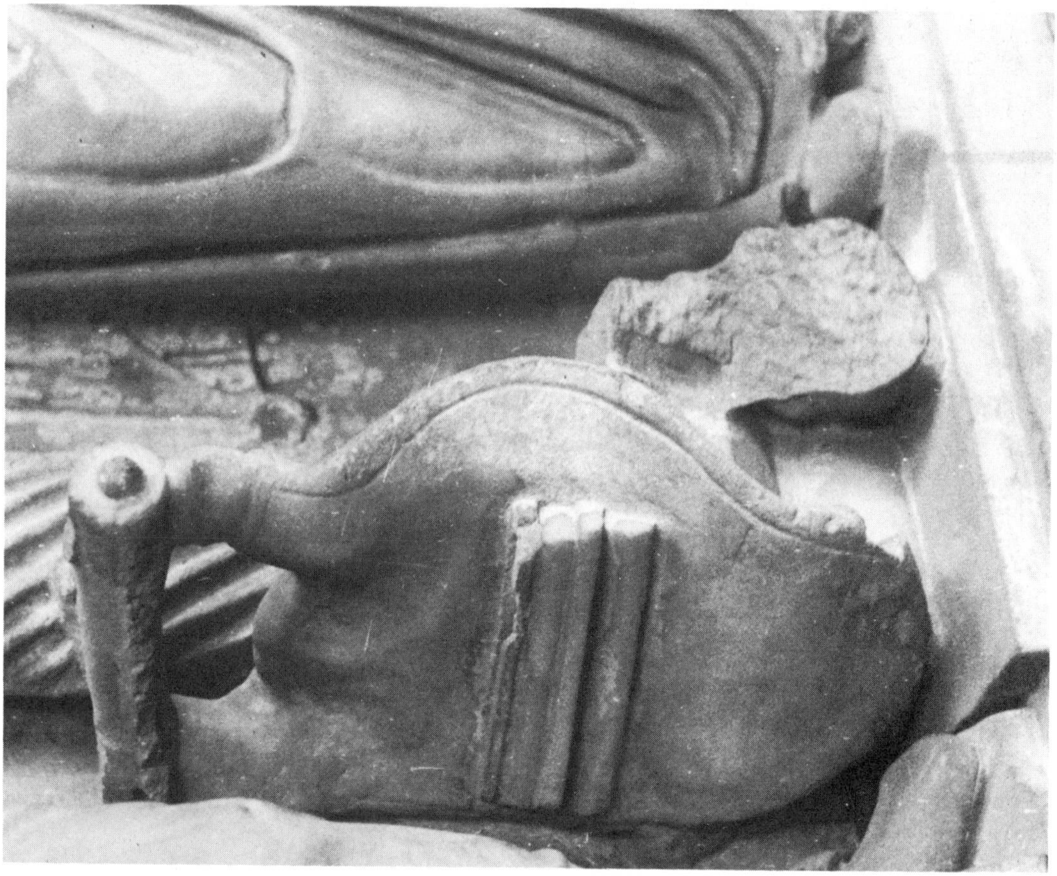

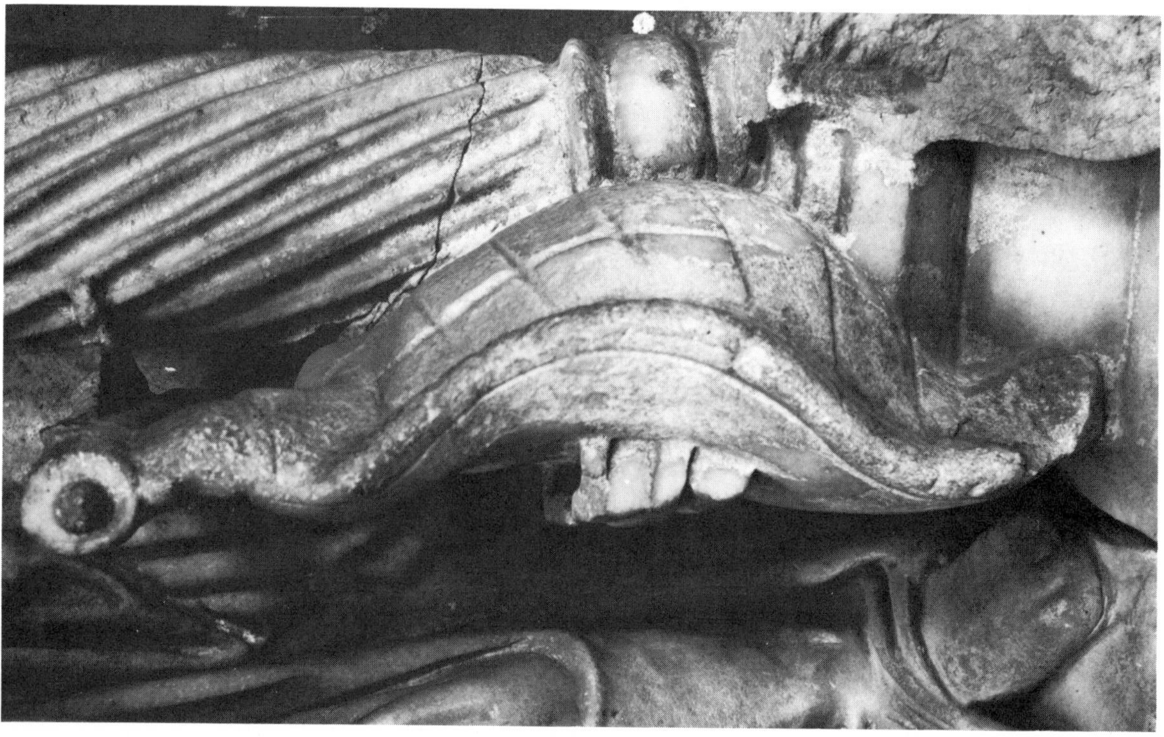

TWO VIEWS OF THE LYRE ON THE SARCOPHAGUS OF THE MUSES.
MUSEO NAZIONALE, ROME.

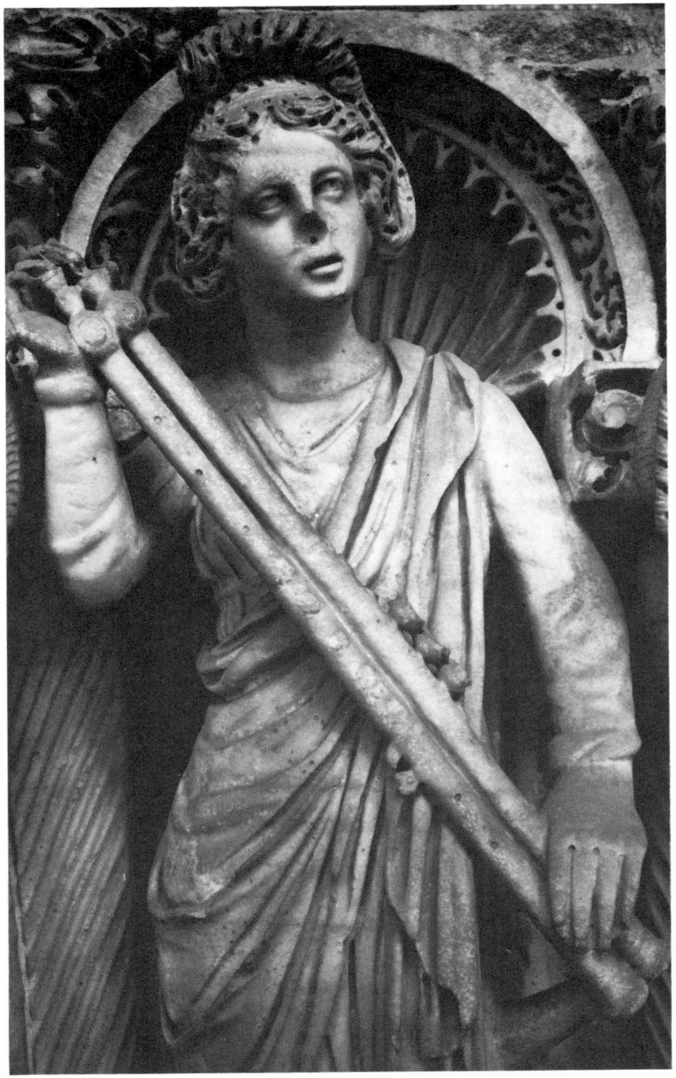

a. The tibia.

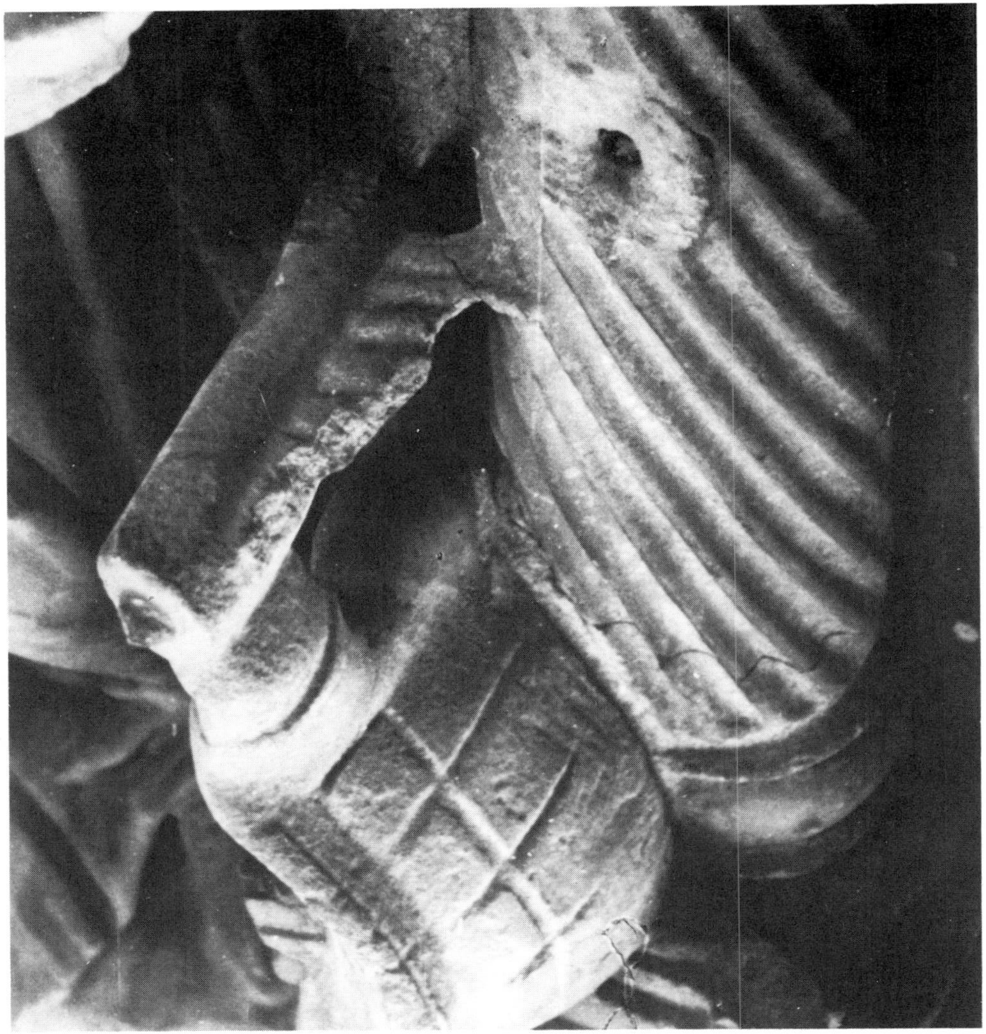

b. The lyre.

TWO DETAILS OF THE SARCOPHAGUS OF THE MUSES. MUSEO NAZIONALE, ROME

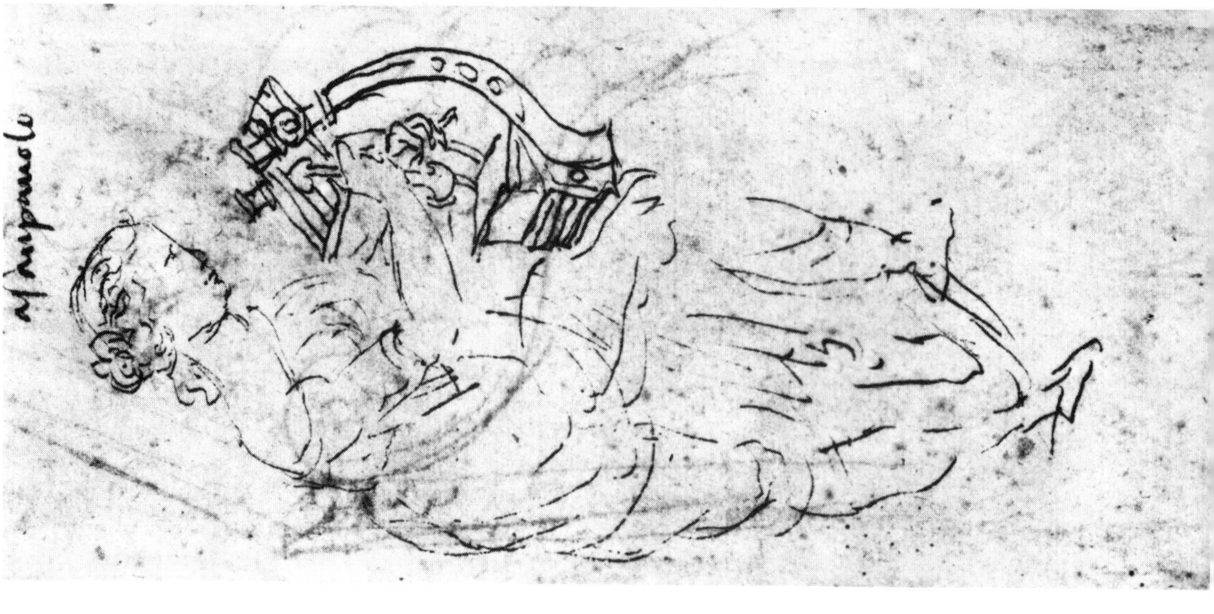

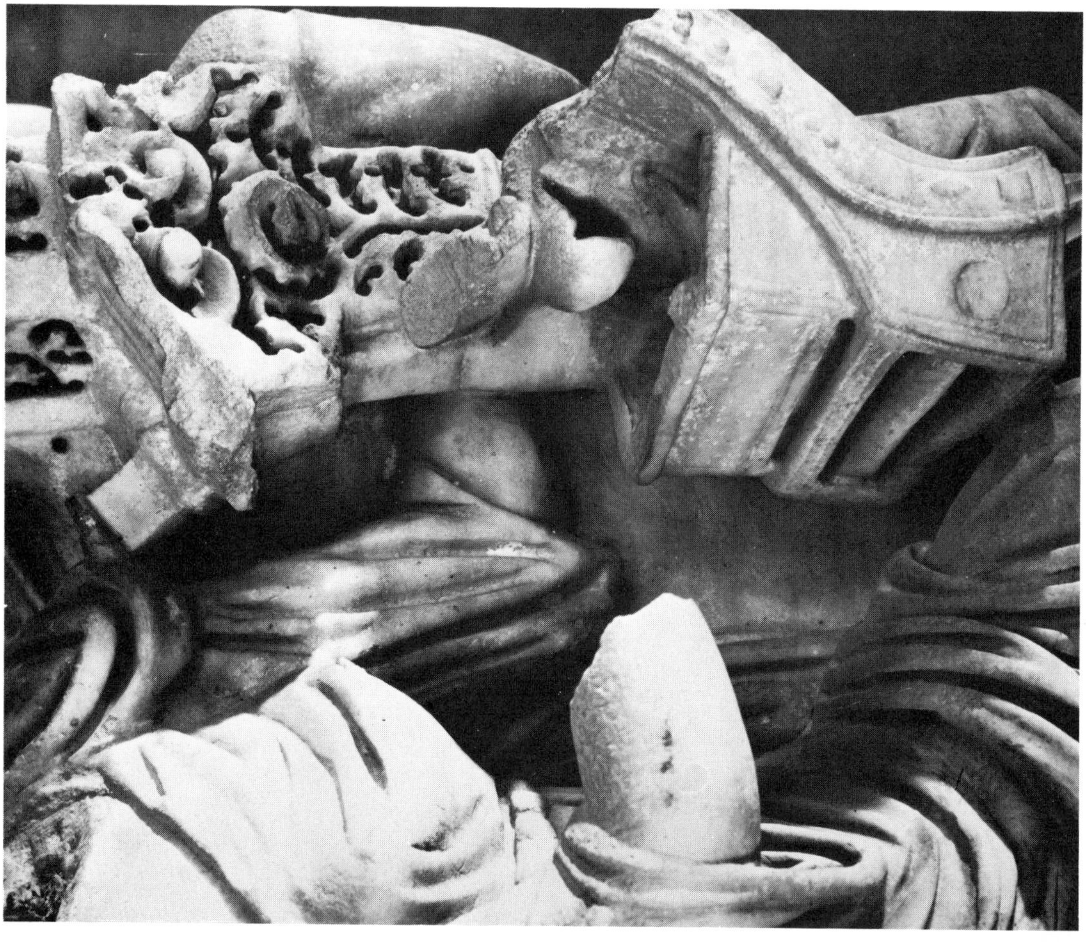

a. (*above*). Detail of the kithara on the Sarcophagus of the Muses. Museo Nazionale, Rome.

b. (*right*). Francesco di Giorgio, detail from a drawing. Uffizi, Florence.

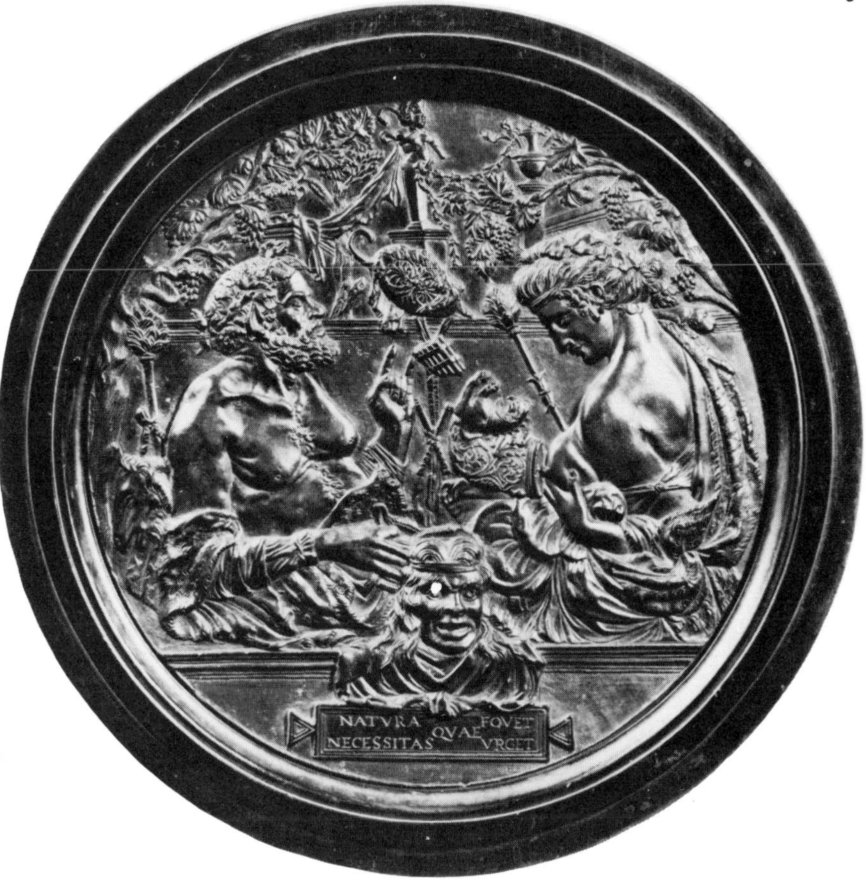

a. Patera Martelli. Museo Nazionale, Florence.

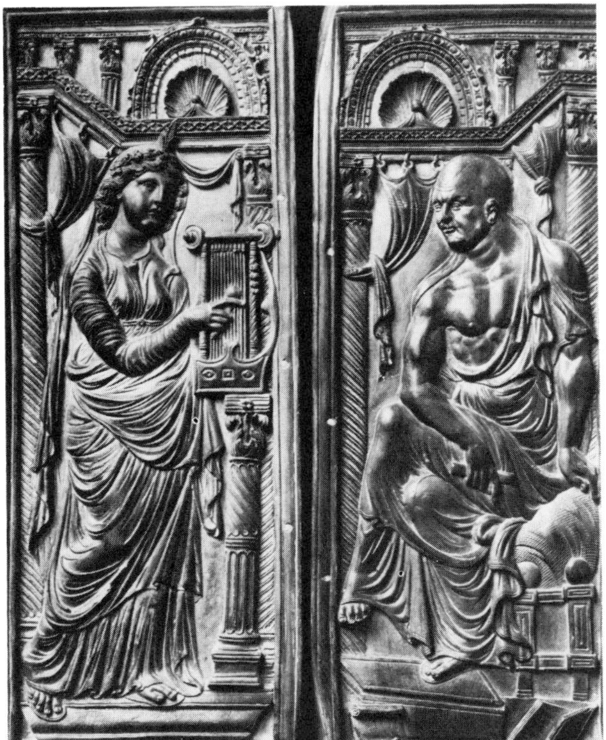

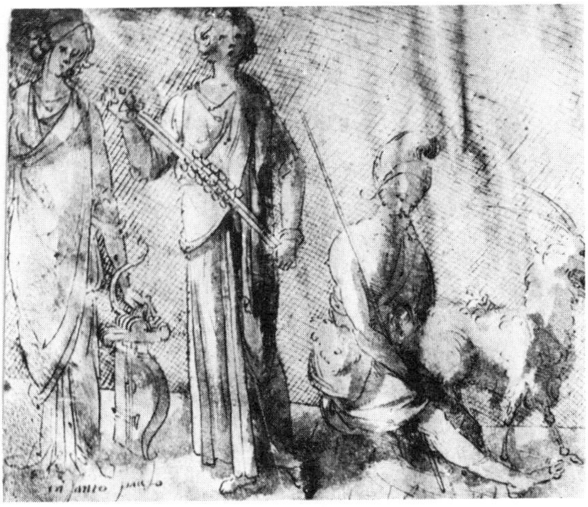

c. Amico Aspertini (?), detail from a drawing in the Wolfegg sketchbook.

b. The Poet and His Muse (ivory diptych, 5th century). Cathedral, Monza.

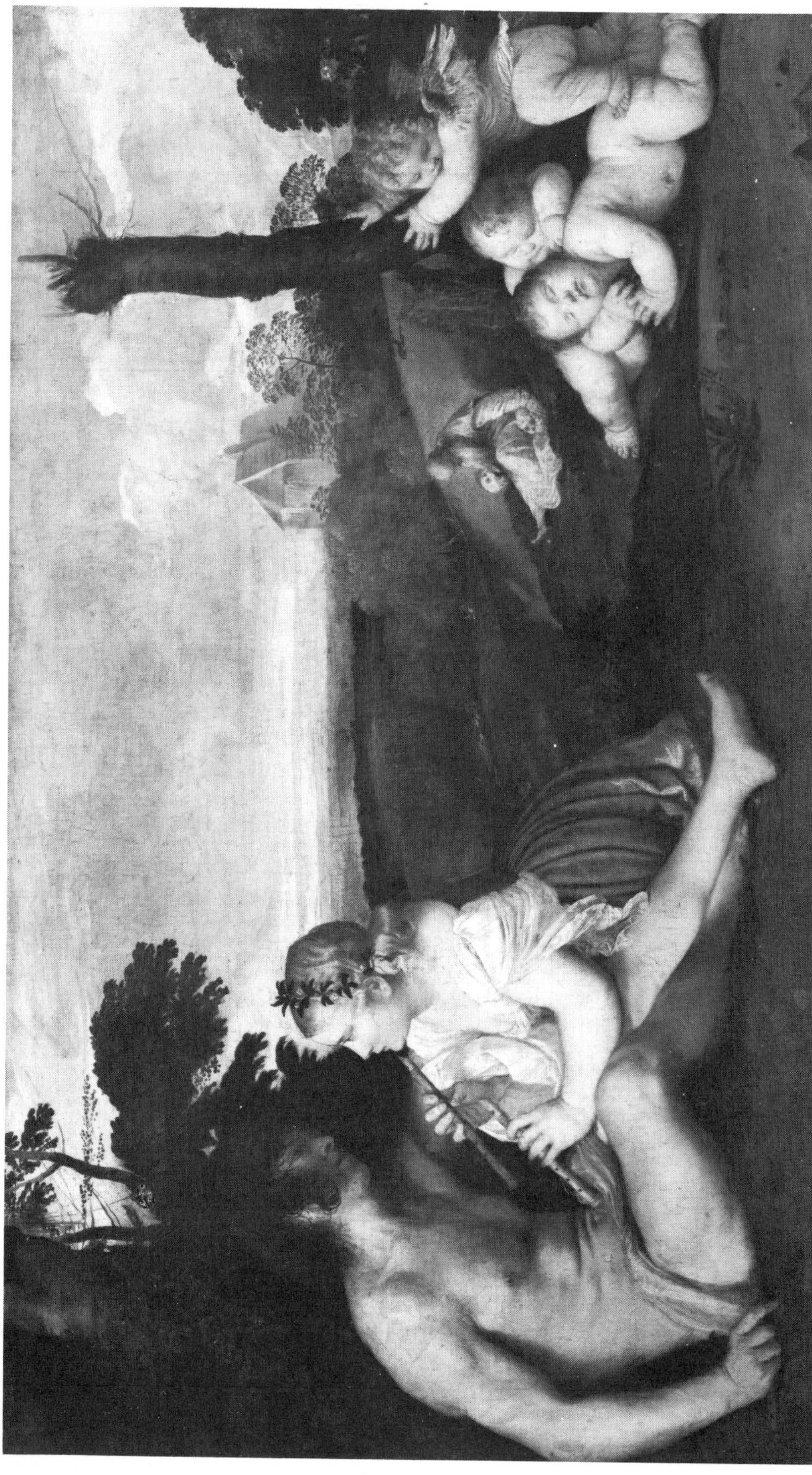

Titian, *Three Ages of Man*. Duke of Sutherland Collection, on loan to the National Gallery of Scotland.

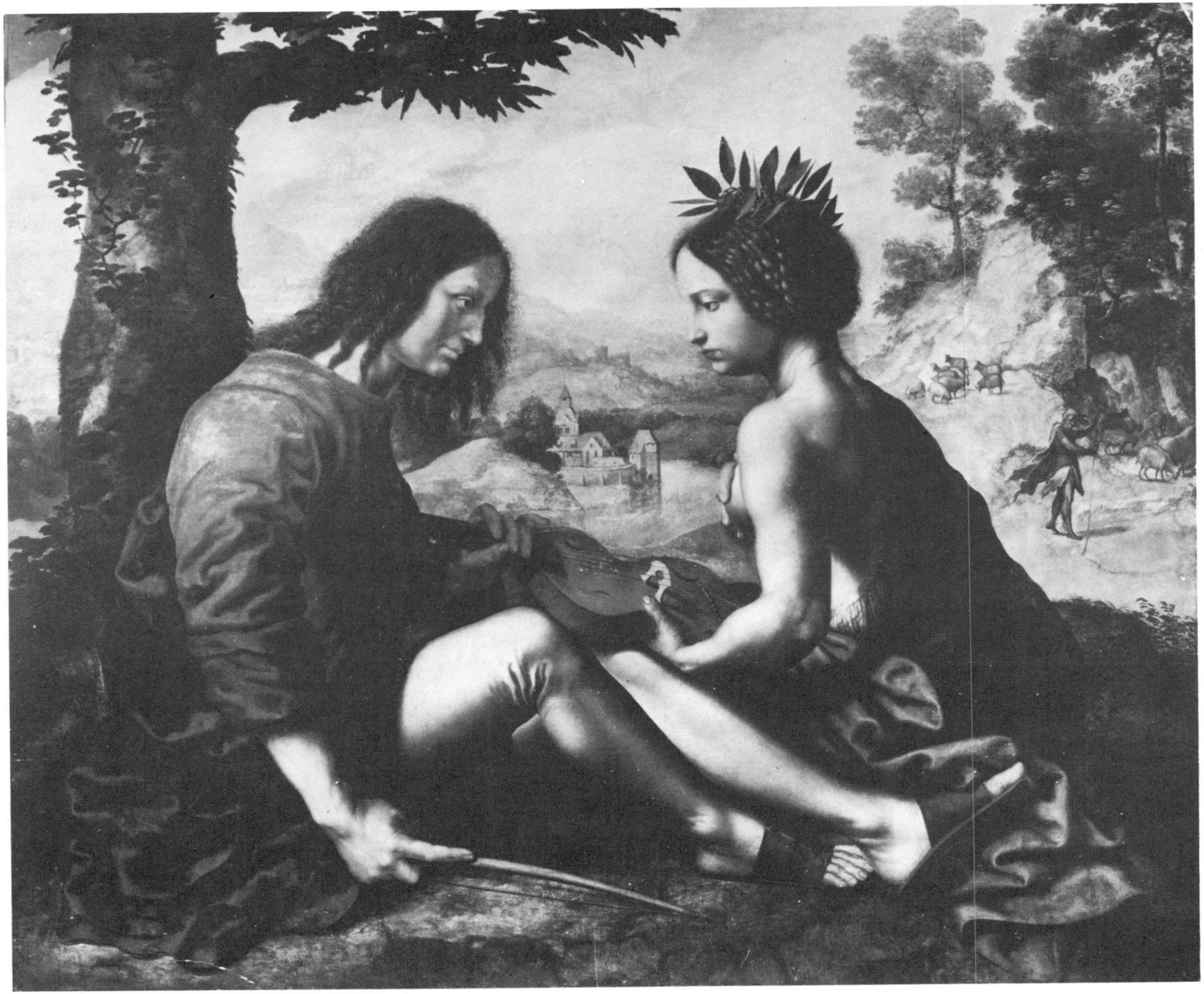

Allegory of Inspiration (Flemish, 16th century). Collection of Mr. Theodore A. Heinrich.

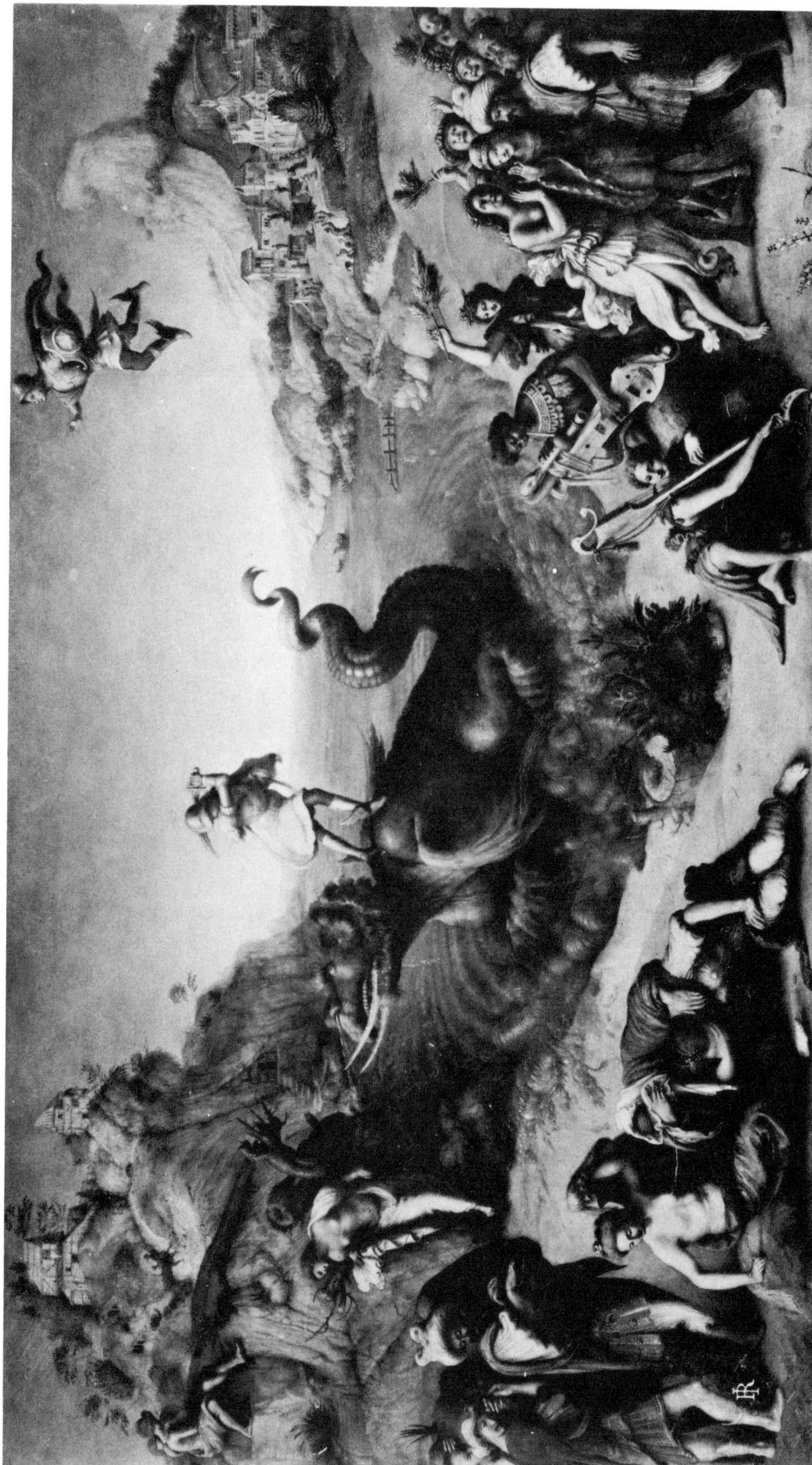

Piero di Cosimo, *The Liberation of Andromeda*. Uffizi, Florence.

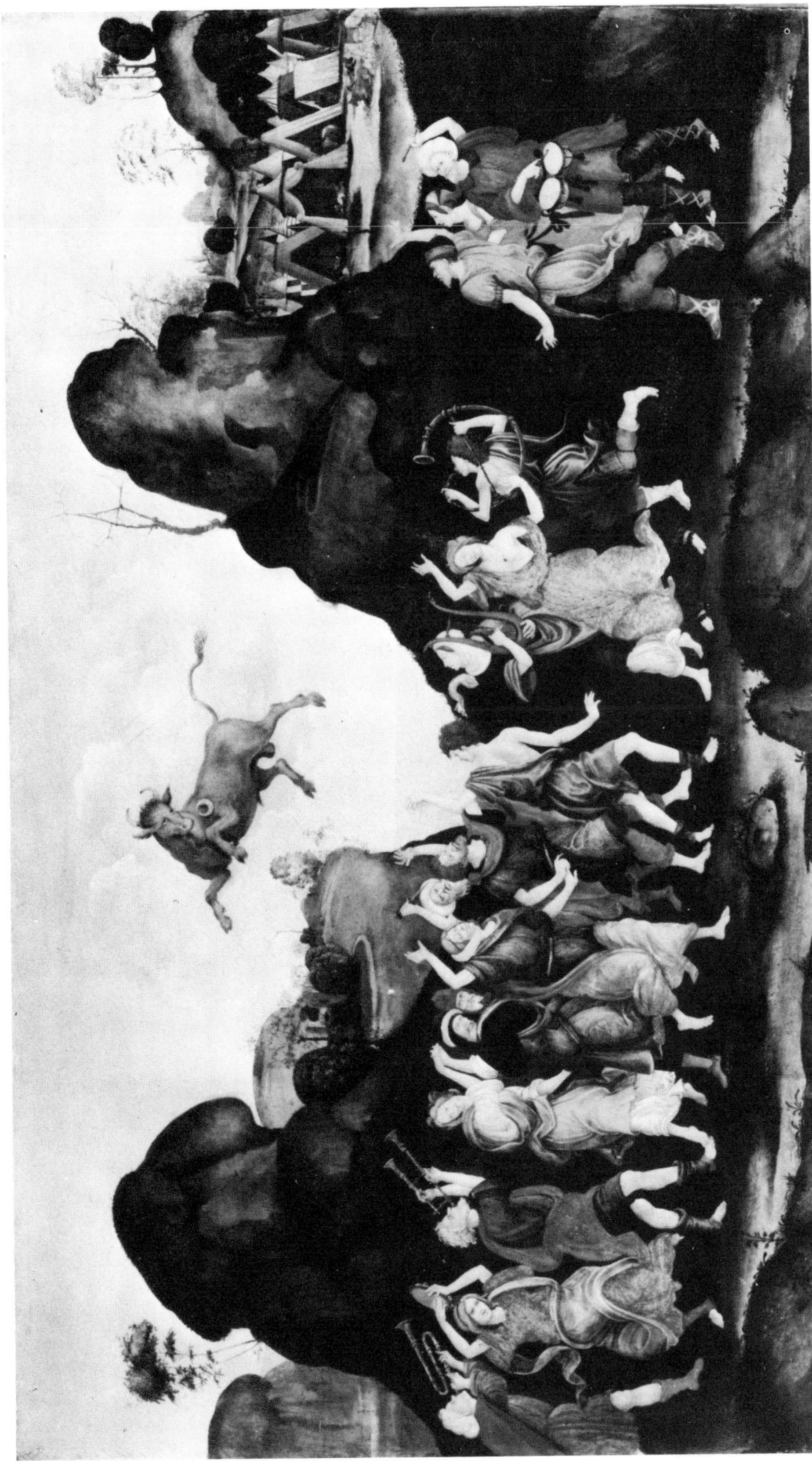

Filippino Lippi, *The Adoration of the Golden Calf*. National Gallery, London.

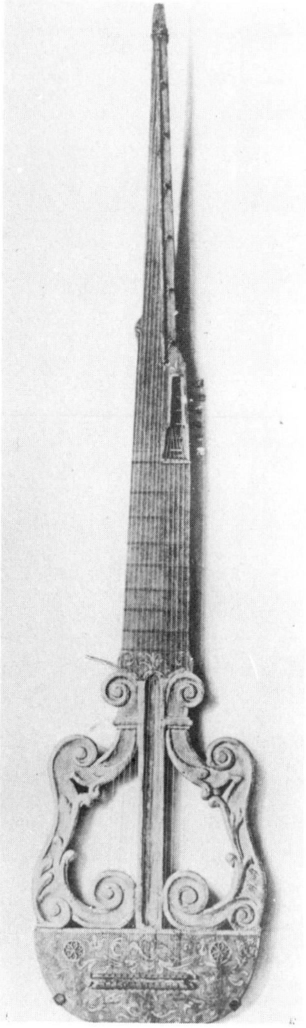

a. Theatre instrument. Kunsthistorisches Museum, Vienna.

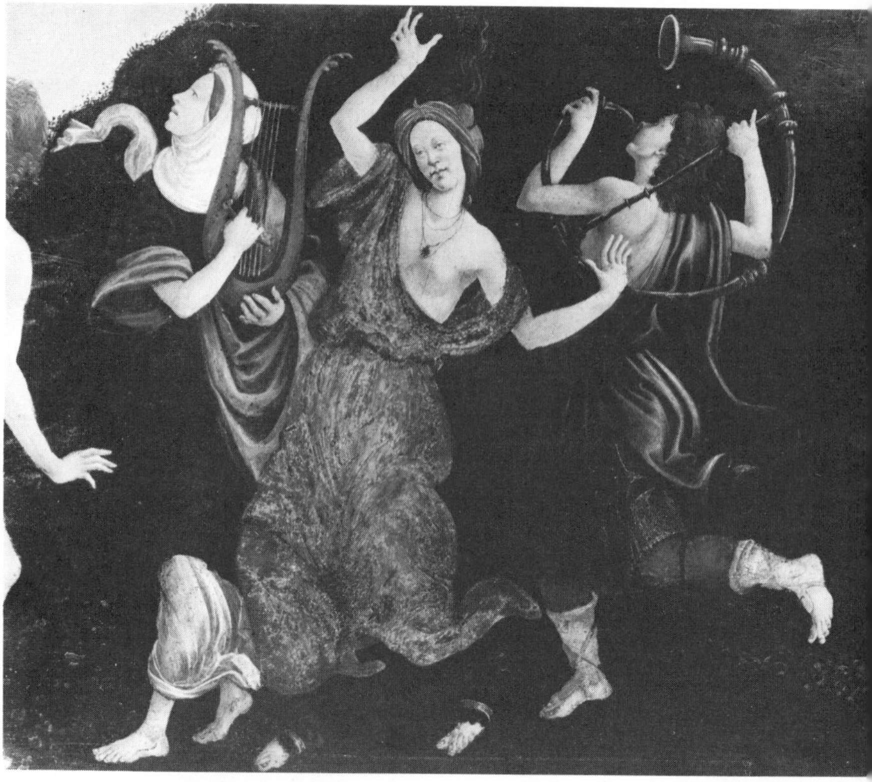

b. (*upper right*). Detail of Plate 93.

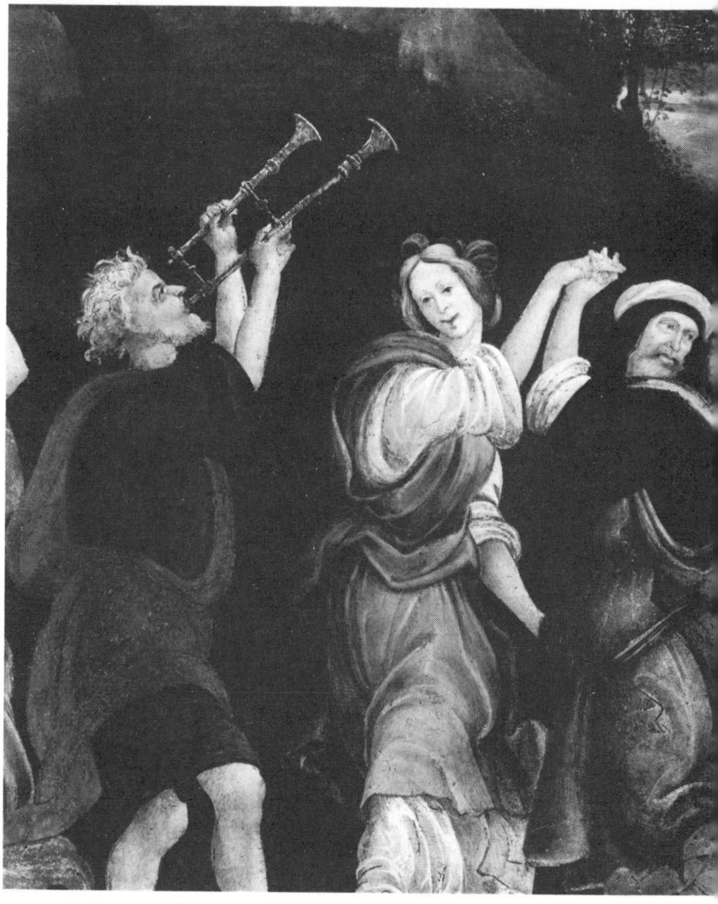

c. Detail of Plate 93.

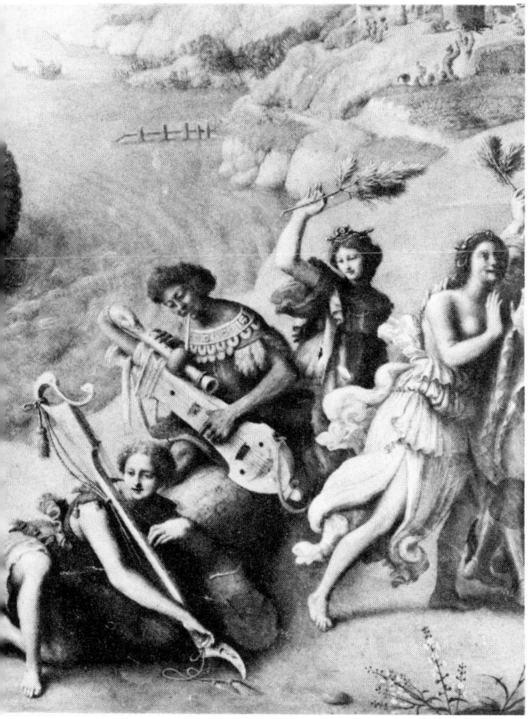

a. Detail of Plate 92.

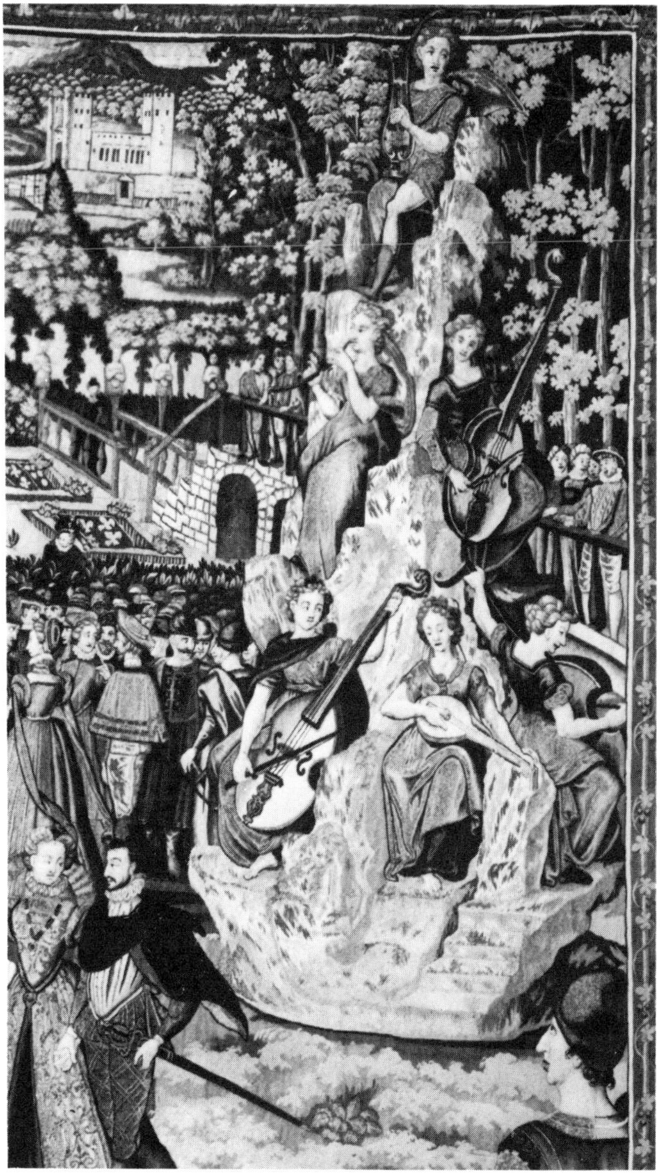

c. Parnassus, detail of a Flemish tapestry showing a fête in honour of the Polish ambassadors, c. 1585. Uffizi, Florence.

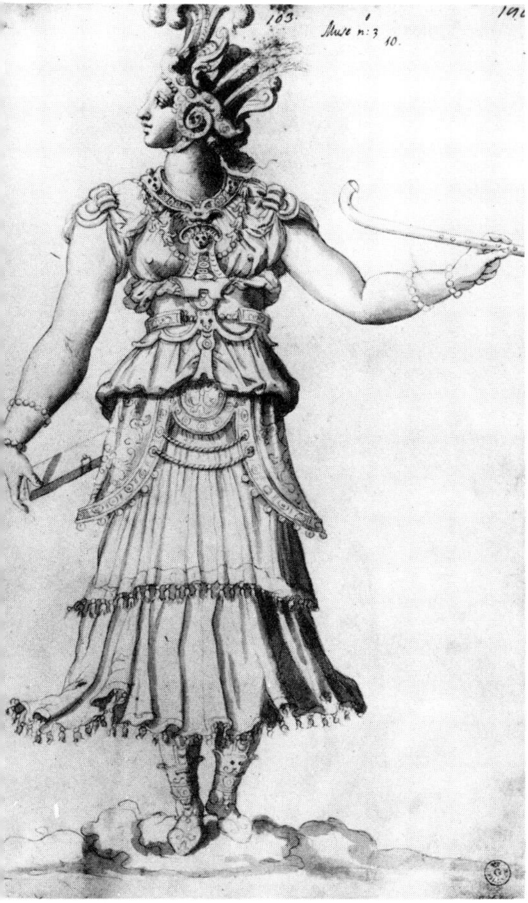

b. Giorgio Vasari, *Muse with Phrygian Aulos.* Uffizi, Florence.

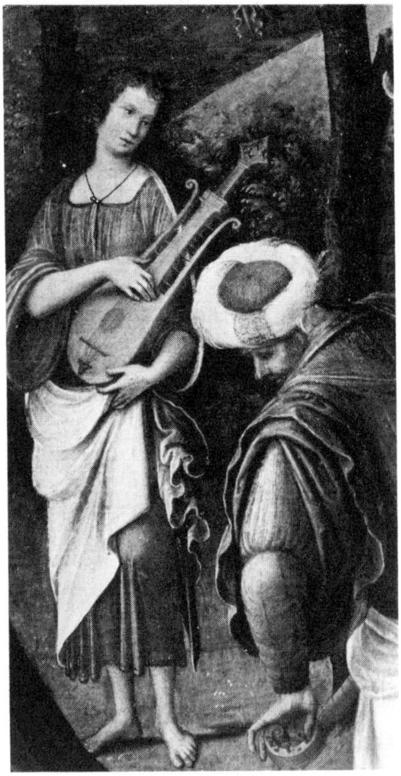

a. Lorenzo Costa, *The Court of the Muses of Isabella d'Este,* detail. Louvre, Paris.

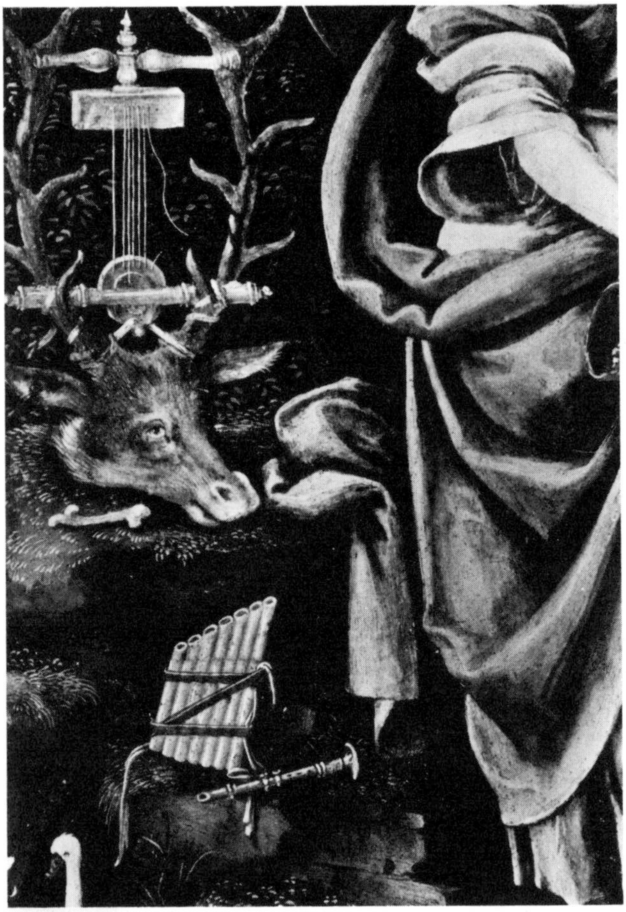

b. Filippino Lippi, *Allegory of Music,* detail. Kaiser Friedrich Museum, Berlin.

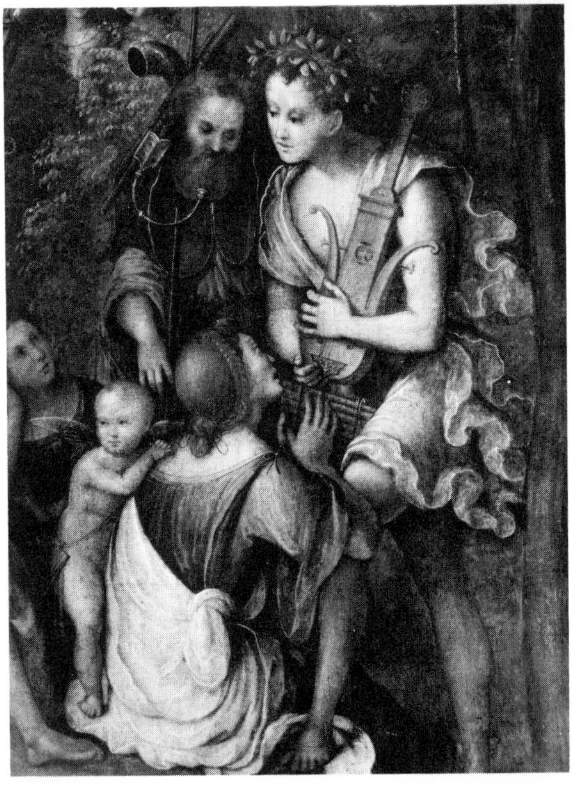

c. Lorenzo Costa, detail from an allegorical painting. Louvre, Paris.

Appendix: Images as Records for the History of Music

Iconology of music has stimulated great interest during our generation. In fact it had been practiced for many centuries, though not under its present name and not by historians of music, but by artists, in particular by Renaissance painters who studied and analyzed ancient Greek and Roman works of art for use in their own mythological paintings.

My interest in the subject springs from various roots. When one has been for many years curator of a large collection of musical instruments of many times and peoples, housed in one of the world's largest art museums, one develops strange habits. One begins to see the multifarious tools for producing organized sound against the rich background of ever-changing artistic cultures, and one comes to regard music as but one strand in the dense web of all the arts. The growing awareness of the incessant give and take between the visual and aural realms evokes new ideas.

One meditates about the interplay of form and function of tools, and the constant change of this relation through the ages; one inquires precisely how the instruments were plucked or bowed or blown or struck, who the performers were and what their relation was to the singers, what the social status of the musicians was and what the sites of performance were, how instruments developed in sacred and secular music and how they symbolize by their sound, as well as by their shape and decoration, the ultimate things, such as love, fertility, birth, death, and afterlife; and one wants to know how instruments acquired mythological connotations and became attributes of allegorical figures. One also begins to wonder about the strange force of tradition that determines the building and use of instruments through thousands of years. Today in Greece shepherds

Extract from a paper prepared for the Twelfth International Musicological Society Congress and RIdIM, Berkeley, 1977.

still play the bagpipe, its double-reed pipe producing the same exciting, shrieking tone that was produced by the ancient Greek oboe, the aulos, depicted in Dionysiac and revelry scenes on countless painted vases.

But, while curiosity grows, one discovers that a collection of even some 4,000 instruments represents only a small and accidental residue of the types that must have once existed. Climate, war, iconoclasm have all taken their toll. Moreover, fragile tools die not only by neglect but also simply from being played.

How, then, can we round out our fragmentary knowledge of past instruments? References in literature and treatises on music often disappoint us. Medieval treatises generally focus on problems of harmony and theories of musical proportions. They reveal little about performance. The techniques of performance were taken for granted. When they were described, the information is rarely exact. How does one describe precisely, for example, the curvature of fingers on the keyboard, or stopping strings, or holding a bow? How does one describe the shapes of an instrument, or of a singing mouth, or of the lips of a trumpet player? Here, pictures are better than words. One recalls the vivid pleasure of Goethe when he saw the lithographs of Delacroix illustrating scenes from his *Faust.* Goethe felt that his words had become more vivid, "translated" into pictorial details. As he said in 1804, "Language cannot express the individuality of the phenomenon (das Individuelle der Erscheinung), the specific. Our words for the species are always general."

The mass of images attainable as records for the history of music is of fearful yet promising immensity, a veritable *embarras de richesses* for fact finders not yet steeped in art history. The great cultures of the past differ radically in the quantity of their surviving visual records. Ancient Egypt and the ancient Near East abound in pictorial representations of musicians and instruments, and certain stylistic peculiarities in perspective and other mannerisms hardly hamper our recognition of actual shapes, fingertips, and embouchures, especially since so many depictions in reliefs and wall paintings are life-size or very nearly so. Ancient Hebrew musical culture presents a problem because of its disproportion between abundant references in the Scriptures and the utmost scarcity of pictorial documents.

The Greco-Roman world left us many admirably exact visual records of musical scenes and instruments in vase paintings, sculptures, reliefs, gems and coins, and, from the Roman world alone, in an enormous quantity of frescoes, mosaics, and sarcophagi. The topics are both mythological and secular, including revelries, music lessons, and the like.

In the Middle Ages, the topics were for a long time limited to illustrations of the Scriptures, especially of the Apocalyptical themes from Revelation, iv, vii, viii, and xiv, and the Rex Psalmistra. Curiously, Psalm 150 was not elaborately illustrated before Luca della Robbia's *Cantoria.* Carolingian illuminated manuscripts, above all the Utrecht Psalter, show many musicians, never angels, surrounding the psalmist with instruments that clearly reveal the transition of the ancient Greek and Roman technique favoring open strings to that of the early Middle Ages, which introduced fingerboards for stopping the strings, possibly as the result of Eastern influence.

Outstanding depictions of the performance of secular music occur in the Manesse Codex and, above all, the *Cantigas de Santa Maria,* with its enormous array of instrumentalists reflecting, side by side, the Christian, Muslim, and Jewish traditions. In Gothic art, when the sacred and the profane, even the vulgar, meet as close neighbors, a great number of wild and fantastic creatures, monsters, monks and nuns, jugglers and beggars invade the margins of the pages of psalters, books of hours, and prayer books. But, while some of the instruments and ensembles are products of fancy, others are realistic depictions, rich in information about a period from which very few actual instruments have survived.

Musical angels, other than Apocalyptical, enter the scene with the spread of the *Legenda aurea,* where legends of the saints and Marianic topics, especially the Assumption and the Coronation (the themes most conducive to the portrayal of large angel orchestras), prevail. They develop, together with the expansion of polyphony, and also appear later, chiefly in the Venetian realm, with the *sacre conversazioni* and their small ensembles or single angels playing the lute, the lira da braccio, and only occasionally other instruments.

Of the biblical musicians, Renaissance imagery retains King David playing successively different instruments: the psaltery, harp, or lira da braccio, among others. Competing with the countless angel concerts, the mythological musicians of the ancient Greco-Roman world reappear on the scene: Apollo with the kithara; Hermes with the lyre he invented; Pallas Athena with her creation, the aulos, subsequently appropriated by Marsyas; Orpheus playing in Hades or for the beasts; and the Muses, particularly Erato with her kithara, Euterpe and Calliope with their auloi.

Santa Cecilia is depicted with many instruments, including the organ and the clavichord, and allegories such as that of Musica as one of the liberal arts are retained. The greatest precision in the rendering of instruments is reached in the *sacre conversazioni* and the intarsias, the life-size portrayals of musical instruments in the choir stalls of Italian churches, in door panels of palaces, and especially in the *studioli* of Federigo da Montefeltro in Urbino and Gubbio, in Monte Oliveto Maggiore, and on one of the doors of the Segnatura in the Vatican.

Iconologia was used in 1593 as the title of Cesare Ripa's enormously popular book on visual allegories. Today's historians of music have taken over the names *iconology* and *iconography* from art history, specifically from the renowned teachings of Aby Warburg, Fritz Saxl, and Erwin Panofsky, although there they have quite a different significance: a specific direction of art-historical research, the study of the subtle change of meaning of images as their themes or topics pass from one artist to another.

Musical iconography and iconology are nothing of the kind. They do not focus on the meaning of the whole work of art but are concerned with images or any form of visual depiction that may yield factual information on the history of music. Also, iconography and iconology, as disciplines of the history of art, do not transcend the visual realm, whereas musical iconography and iconology, as handmaidens of musical history, turn to the visual arts as a storehouse of information.

In one respect, however, the musical historians could profitably borrow from art history: the distinction between iconography (from *graphein*) as a discipline chiefly devoted to identification and description (one could speak of fact finders) and iconology (from *logos*) as a systematic interpretation of the facts found (one could speak of interpreters). But in current practice the distinction between the suffixes is often not observed.

How old is musical iconology? Contrary to recent opinions, the interest of the musical historian in past images is not new. True, musical iconology was greatly stimulated by the publication of illustrated art books and facsimile editions of illuminated manuscripts between 1900 and the outbreak of World War I. Standard works like those of Buhle, Kinsky, Galpin, Schlesinger, Lütgendorff, Sachs, and the *Iconographie des instruments de musique,* organized by the Dutch collector of instruments D. F. Scheurleer, profited from this development. Yet already in the eighteenth century Charles Burney, who was evidently affected by the English antiquarianism of his time, used his visits to Rome, Pompeii, Naples, and Portici for studying bas-reliefs, sculptures, vases, and frescoes to illustrate in his *General History of Music.*

Even much earlier historians of music such as Vincenzo Galilei in his *Dialogo della musica antica e della moderna* (1581) refer to the "marmi antichi"—yet it was not the historians of music who first collected information from monuments of art but the artists themselves who, during the Early and High Renaissance, turned to the monuments of antiquity and borrowed what they needed for their own artistic purposes, including the images of ancient musicians and musical instruments.

A great number of sketches and drawings of ancient Greek sculpture and Roman sarcophagi have survived to our day from the fifteenth and sixteenth centuries. Raphael employed draftsmen to obtain as many drawings as possible of ancient works of art and used the musical instruments of a Roman sarcophagus of the Muses as models for those in his *Parnassus* in the Stanza della Segnatura. Likewise, Filippino Lippi copied Muses and their musical instruments from Roman sarcophagi to create his philosophical allegories in his frescoes for the Capella Strozzi in Santa Maria Novella. It was the investigation of Lippi's study of these ancient musical symbols that enabled me to unveil the secret of this burial chapel as a homage to the "Initiati" and to solve the many mysterious inscriptions (paper reprinted in the present text).

The iconographer can hope to extract from visual images facts pertaining to the history of performance practice: the shape and construction of instruments, the playing methods, the proportions and the grouping of ensembles, the use of written music for singers and players, the methods of conducting; facts pertaining to the listener: where he sat or stood in the church, theater, or concert hall, the acoustical environments of the performance, the stage settings, the social status of musicians and their audience; and facts about the symbolical and allegorical aspects of music and musicians, including mystical, religious, erotic, and political symbolism.

Here, naturally, the risk of misinterpretation is great. Which depictions are exact, which are fantastic, imaginary, or unreal? What can be taken at face value? Sculpture has difficulties in representing free strings; small woodcuts must reduce the number of strings; wall paintings from Egyptian tombs to the glorious cupola frescoes of Gaudenzio Ferrari show musicians and instruments in tricky distortions of perspective that have to be understood as such in "reading the pictures." There is the problem of pictorial symmetry: in the fourteenth- and fifteenth-century angel concerts, many artists achieved visual balance at the expense of musical balance. The idiosyncrasies and mannerisms of painters and sculptors have to be understood by the interpreter to reduce imaginary instruments and playing methods to their "real" core—in this connection one might consider the angel musicians in Grünewald's Isenheim altarpiece.

And then there is number symbolism: the twenty-four angel choirs corresponding to the spheres of heaven, the nine Muses, and Raphael's Apollo presiding over the Muses in the *Parnassus* while he plays the lira da braccio with nine strings, instead of the usual seven.

It is extremely difficult to assess the large angel concerts celebrating the Coronation of the Virgin. Are they fantastic depictions of celestial music or are they patterned after secular custom? Was the design determined by the imagination of the painter or by theological counsel? Are all combinations of players and singers to be viewed as working ensembles, or are some mere agglomerations to express majesty or grandeur? Here erroneous interpretations are frequent.

Often the bizarre is the main intention of the artist, as in the drolleries in the illuminated prayer books of the thirteenth and fourteenth centuries (Flemish, French, and English) and later in the Italian grotesques and the Spanish plateresque motifs of the cinquecento, teeming with demonic and jocular musicians and instruments. But these depictions often reflect popular customs, and as such they are of immense interest to the musicologist. Similar problems of sifting and comparing are encountered in the study of the many sketches of tools and musical instruments in Leonardo's notebooks: Which of them are diagrams for building real instruments, which are ideas for new types or improvements of existing ones, which are fantastic suggestions for feasts, intermedia, or masquerades, for allegories or caricatures? And what familiarity with Leonardo's intentions and his environment must the observer have to approach these questions?

The enormous task of assessing and interpreting the works of art and other visual records of musical interest in public and private collections is not without danger. Our gratitude is of course due to all those fact finders who compile the visual records. At the same time, one would like the iconographers to collect relevant material in proper perspective and to beware of sterile accumulitis. Checklists of illuminated manuscripts in libraries, indexes and lists of instruments represented in prayer books, manuscripts, and paintings often fail to indicate whether the instruments are real or fantastic, or whether they form ensembles among themselves or with vocalists. Such lists are of little help and also invite unnecessary duplication. The fact finder should from the start be equipped with solid critical discrimination to separate the wheat from the chaff. What can mechanical or quasistatistical collection methods establish? Perhaps that more bagpipes were played around the Virgin enthroned in Tuscan paintings than in Lombard ones, but if so, why? And this question could not be answered by statistics. It does not suffice to identify one by one the many instruments played by angels in the reliefs of Luca della Robbia's *Cantoria* without recognizing that in most of the groups the angels play identical instruments, thus not functioning as ensembles but literally illustrating the words of Psalm 150: "Laudate Dominum in sono tubae" (trumpets); "Laudate eum in psalterio" (psalteries) "et Cytharae" (citterns). It is also not helpful if different instruments embossed on separate buckles of a ceinture are listed mechanically as "quartet" or "quintet."

Separate teams of fact finders, one describing the instruments played by a group of musicians in Paolo Veronese's *Wedding at Cana* in the Louvre, another studying the chamber music group in the ceiling fresco in the Episcopal Palace in Würzburg by Tiepolo, would fail to see the connection unless some good memory were able to ignite a spark leaping from Cana to Würzburg. A comparison of the two versions of the same group of musicians would tell the art historian of an interesting borrowing habit of Tiepolo and would inform the historian of music of the fascinating change that happened in instruments during the 110 years between the two paintings.

Thus, fact finders and describers—in other words, iconographers—should be controlled by their awareness of the ultimate purpose of their work and should be familiar with at least some of the actual problems of musical history hitherto unsolved or with hypotheses that will have to be verified or discarded. In short, the iconographers should know a little iconology.

Looking to the future, I should like to make two pleas. The broadening of the accumulation process on an international basis is well under way. What is needed is an intense education of the fact finders in art history and the establishment of constant cooperation between the historians of the figurative arts and of music through teamwork, congresses, and common publications. My other plea is for concentration on fundamental unsolved problems of musical history, especially the filling of gaps in present historical information, problems that can be solved only with the help of visual records.

Bibliography of Writings by Emanuel Winternitz since 1940

BOOKS

Musical Autographs from Monteverdi to Hindemith. 2 vols. Princeton, New Jersey: Princeton University Press, 1955. Reprint. New York: Dover Publications, 1965.

Keyboard Instruments in the Metropolitan Museum of Art. New York: Metropolitan Museum, 1961.

Die Schönsten Musikinstrumente des Abendlandes. Munich: Keysersche Verlagsbuchhandlung, 1966.

Musical Instruments of the Western World (English and American editions of item immediately above). London: Thames and Hudson, 1967; New York: McGraw-Hill, 1967.

Gaudenzio Ferrari, His School, and the Early History of the Violin. Società per la Conservazione delle Opere d'Arte in Valsesia, Varallo, 1967.

Musical Instruments and their Symbolism in Western Art. New York: W. W. Norton; London: Faber and Faber, 1967.

ARTICLES

"On the Sense of Time in Teaching History." *Harvard Educational Review,* March 1940.

Letter to the Editor on the Relationship between Music and Art. *College Art Journal,* March 1942.

"Overspecialization and Art Education." *Association of American Colleges Bulletin* 28, no. 2, May 1942.

"Quattrocento Science in the Gubbio Study." *Metropolitan Museum of Art Bulletin,* October 1942.

"Bagpipes and Hurdy-Gurdies in their Social Setting." *Metropolitan Museum of Art Bulletin,* Summer 1943.

"Additions to the Collection of Musical Instruments." *Metropolitian Museum of Art Bulletin,* June 1946.

"A Lira da Braccio in Giovanni Bellini's 'The Feast of the Gods.' " *Art Bulletin* 28, no. 2, June 1946.

"Music for the Eye." *Art News,* June 1946.

"On Archlutes." *Guitar Review,* no. 9 (1949).

"Archeologia Musicale del Rinascimento nel Parnaso di Raffaello." *Rendiconti della Pontificia Accademia Romana di Archeologia* 27 (1952–54).

"The Evolution of the Baroque Orchestra." *Metropolitan Museum of Art Bulletin,* May 1954.

"The Golden Harpsichord and Todini's Galleria Armonica." *Metropolitan Museum of Art Bulletin,* February 1956.

"Instruments de Musique étranges chez Filippino Lippi, Piero di Cosimo et Lorenzo Costa." *Les Fêtes de la Renaissance I, Editions du Centre National de la Recherche Scientifique,* Paris 1956.

"Alcune Rappresentazioni di Antichi Strumenti Italiani a Tastiera." *Collectanea II.* Florence: Leo S. Olschki, Fall 1956.

"The Inspired Musician; a Sixteenth-Century Musical Pastiche." *Burlington Magazine,* February 1958.

"Bagpipes for the Lord." *Metropolitan Museum of Art Bulletin,* June 1958.

"The Early History of the Organ." In booklet accompanying phonograph record *The Organ,* Columbia Records (Columbia Masterworks DL 5288), September 1958.

"Gnagflow Trazom: An Essay on Mozart's Script, Pastimes and Nonsense Letters." *Journal of the American Musicological Society* 11, nos. 2–3 (1958).

"Quattrocento-Intarsien als Quellen der Instrumentengeschichte." *Bericht über den siebenten Internationalen Musikwissenschaftlichen Kongress Köln,* 1958.

"The Curse of Pallas Athena; Notes on a 'Contest between Apollo and Marsyas' in the Kress Collection." In *Studies in the History of Art, Dedicated to William E. Suida.* London: Phaidon Press, 1959.

"Lira da Braccio." *Die Musik in Geschichte und Gegenwart* 8 (1960).

Concert Program Notes for the Metropolitan Museum of Art concerts organized by Emanuel Winternitz from 1943 to 1960.

"The Survival of the Kithara and the Evolution of the English Cittern: A Study in Morphology." *Journal of the Warburg and Courtauld Institutes* 24, nos. 3–4 (1961).

"The Visual Arts as a Source for the Historian of Music." *International Musicological Society Congress Report, pp.* 109–20. New York: Bärenreiter Verlag, 1961.

"Orpheus" (-als Musikallegorie in Renaissance und Fruehbarock). *Die Musik in Geschichte und Gegenwart* 10 (1962).

"Musicali Strumenti." *Enciclopedia Universale dell'Arte* 9 (1963).

"On Angel Concerts in the 15th Century: A Critical Approach to Realism and Symbolism in Sacred Painting." *Musical Quarterly* 44, no. 4, October 1963.

"Keyboards for Wind Instruments Invented by Leonardo da Vinci." *Raccolta Vinciana,* Fasc. 20. Milan: Castello Sforzesco, 1964.

"Leonardo's Invention of the Viola Organista." *Raccolta Vinciana,* Fasc. 20. Milan: Castello Sforzesco, 1964.

"Melodic, Chordal and Other Drums Invented by Leonardo da Vinci." *Raccolta Vinciana,* Fasc. 20. Milan: Castello Sforzesco, 1964.

"The School of Gaudenzio Ferrari and the Early History of the Violin." In *The Commonwealth of Music* (writings in honor of Curt Sachs), edited by Gustave Reese and Rose Brandel. New York: Free Press, 1965.

"Muses and Music in a Burial Chapel: An Interpretation of Filippino Lippi's Window Wall in the Cappella Strozzi." *Mitteilungen des Kunsthistorischen Institutes in Florenz,* September 1965.

"Musicians and Musical Instruments in 'The Hours of Charles the Noble.' " *Bulletin of the Cleveland Museum of Art* 52, no. 3, March 1965.

"Theorbe." *Die Musik in Geschichte und Gegenwart* 13, col. 323 ff. (1966).

"Violine (Italienische Bildzeugnisse der Violine im 16. Jahrhundert)." *Die Musik in Geschichte und Gegenwart* 13, col. 1712 ff. (IV) (1966).

"Leonardo da Vinci." *Die Musik in Geschichte und Gegenwart* 13 (1966).

"Anatomy the Teacher—On the Impact of Leonardo's Anatomical Research on His Musical and Other Machines." *Proceedings of the American Philosophical Society* 3, no. 4, August 1967.

"Orpheus before Opera." *Opera News* 32, no. 15, February 10, 1968.

"A Spinettina for the Duchess of Urbino." *Metropolitan Museum Journal* 1 (1968).

"Hindemith Ludens." *Neue Zürcher Zeitung,* January 29, 1969.

"Strange Musical Instruments in the Madrid Notebooks of Leonardo da Vinci." *Metropolitan Museum Journal* 2 (1969).

"Rembrandt's 'Christ Presented to the People'—1665: A Meditation on Justice and Collective Guilt." *Oud Holland* (Rembrandt Tricentennial Issue) 84 (1969).

"Piccinni und Gluck." *Neue Zürcher Zeitung,* September 14, 1969.

"The Crosby Brown Collection of Musical Instruments—its Origin and Development." *Metropolitan Museum Journal* 3 (1970).

"The Role of Music In Leonardo's Paragone." In *Phenomenology and Social Reality* (Essays in Memory of Alfred Schütz), edited by Maurice Natanson. The Hague: Martinus Nijhoff, 1971.

"Music, Physician of the Soul." *Medicine, Mind and Music,* CBS Records Legacy Collection. New York, 1971.
"Iconology of Music—Possibilities and Pitfalls." In *Perspectives in Musicology,* edited by B. Brook, E. Downes and S. van Solkema. New York: W. W. Norton, 1972.
"Images as Records for the History of Music." *London Times Literary Supplement,* June 24, 1974.
"Leonardo and Music." In *The Unknown Leonardo.* New York: McGraw-Hill, 1974.
"Engelskonzert." *Die Musik in Geschichte und Gegenwart,* suppl. vol., col. 89 ff. (1975).
"Secular Musical Practice in Sacred Art." In *The Secular Spirit: Life and Art at the End of the Middle Ages.* New York: Metropolitan Museum of Art and E. P. Dutton, 1975.
"Leonardo da Vinci as a Musician." *London Times Literary Supplement,* April 1, 1977.

REVIEWS

Antonio Banfi, "La Fenomenologia e il compito del pensiero contemporaneo." *Revue Internationale de Philosophie* 1 (1939); *Philosophy and Phenomenological Research,* June 1941.
Henri Focillon, "The Life of Forms in Art." *College Art Journal,* March 1943.
"British Musical Instruments, An Exhibit in London." *Notes of the Music Library Association,* June 1952.
Otto E. Albrecht, "A Census of Autograph Music Manuscripts of European Composers in American Libraries." *Journal of the American Musicological Society,* Fall 1953.
Luigi Parigi, "I disegni musicali del Gabinetto degli 'Uffizi' " (Florence: Olschki, 1952). *Musical Quarterly,* October 1954.
Luisa Marcucci, "Mostra di strumenti musicali in disegni degli Uffizi" (Florence: Olschki, 1952). *Musical Quarterly,* October 1954.
Marziano Bernardi and Andrea Della Corte, "Gli strumenti musicali nei dipinti della Galleria degli Uffizi" (Turin: Radio Italiana, 1952). *Musical Quarterly,* October 1954.

Index

Woodrow Wilson

Woodrow Wilson

Essential Writings and Speeches of the

Scholar-President

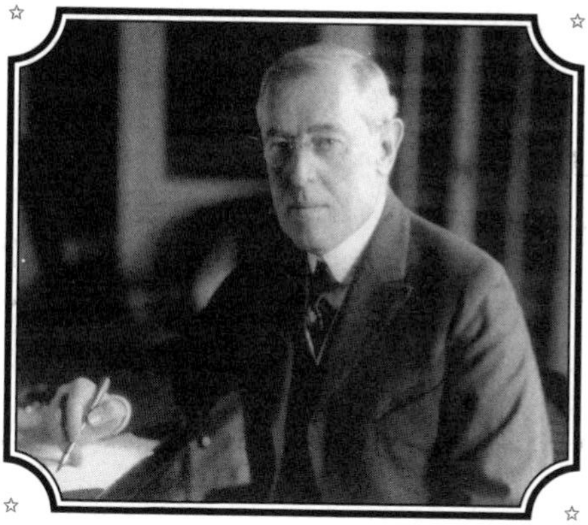

Edited and Introduced by Mario R. DiNunzio

New York University Press New York and London

NEW YORK UNIVERSITY PRESS
New York and London
www.nyupress.org

Library of Congress Cataloging-in-Publication Data
Wilson, Woodrow, 1856–1924.
Woodrow Wilson : essential writings and speeches of the scholar-president / edited and introduced by Mario R. DiNunzio.
p. cm. Includes bibliographical references and index.
ISBN-13: 978-0-8147-1984-8 (cloth : alk. paper)
ISBN-10: 0-8147-1984-8 (cloth : alk. paper)
1. United States—Politics and government—1913–1921. 2. United States—Foreign relations—1913–1921. 3. United States—Social conditions—1865–1918. 4. United States—Politics and government—1865–1933. 5. Wilson, Woodrow, 1856–1924—Religion. 6. Speeches, addresses, etc., American. I. Di Nunzio, Mario R., 1936– II. Title.
E660.W712 2006
973.91'3—dc22 2005037929

New York University Press books are printed on acid-free paper, and their binding materials are chosen for strength and durability.

Manufactured in the United States of America

10 9 8 7 6 5 4 3 2 1

To the Memory of Paul and Rene,
educators in the Wilsonian tradition

Contents

All illustrations appear as an insert following p. 208.

Acknowledgments

For her many, most helpful suggestions and for her tireless work as a talented editor, I am deeply in debt to Emily Park of NYU Press. I am most grateful for her generous patience and understanding throughout this project. Any flaws that remain are entirely my own. My thanks also go to Janet Masso and Keith Lewison for their timely assistance, and especially to Joan, Joseph, and Thomas for their persistent support and encouragement.

Chronology

1856	December 28, born in Staunton Virginia
1879	Graduated from Princeton University
1882	Admitted to the bar in Georgia
1885	June 24, married Ellen Louise Axson
1885 to 1888	Taught at Bryn Mawr College
1886	Received Ph.D. from Johns Hopkins University
1888 to 1890	Taught at Wesleyan University
1890	Appointed to professorship at Princeton
1902	Elected president of Princeton
1910	Elected governor of New Jersey
1912	Elected president of the United States
1914	August 6, death of Ellen Axson Wilson
1915	December 18, married Edith Bolling Galt
1916	November, elected to a second term as president
1917	April 2, appealed to Congress for declaration of war
1918	December, sailed to Europe for Versailles Peace Conference
1919	Awarded Nobel Peace Prize
1919	October 2, suffered paralyzing stroke
1921 to 1924	Lived in retirement on S Street in Washington
1924	February 3, died

Preface

Woodrow Wilson was the first and to date the only professional scholar to have served as president of the United States. With a Ph.D. from Johns Hopkins University, he launched a career in history and political science that carried him to distinction in university circles and won wide notice outside the academy. Prolific scholarship and the presidency of Princeton University made him a national figure years before he entered active politics. Through these varied labors as student, scholar, and statesman, he left a legacy of writings providing a rich repository of his ideas on religion, educational philosophy, politics, and history. They offer a window on his age, on American university education, on the Progressive Era, and on the emergence of the United States as a world power, and we read in them the thought of an acute observer, analyst, and actor in the drama of American life and politics.

Deeply religious, Wilson looked to his faith to guide his life and wrote candidly about the connection. Thoughtful and often elegant scholarly writing made him an academic star whose work would have enjoyed enduring notice even without the fame of high office. A passionate advocate of the importance of liberal learning, he broadcast his educational philosophy with missionary intensity and put his ideas to work at Princeton with the vigor of a dedicated reformer. These ideas continue to resonate today in debates about education and the role of the academy in the face of postmodern revisionism.

Wilson's scholarly analysis of American history and politics influenced several generations of students and scholars and remains useful in understanding the perspective of his contemporaries in a fruitful and productive period of American scholarship. In politics, Wilson journeyed from a rather conventional late-nineteenth-century conservative outlook on government to a progressive vision that transformed American politics in the new century. He developed both an appreciation for sustaining moral imperatives and a realism about the uses of power. In these works lie valuable insights for a world confused about both.

While governor of New Jersey, Wilson earned a reputation as a reformer that quickly made him a presidential contender. As president he led progressives to a triumph of political reform, and, with the two Roosevelts, he helped to reshape the character of government in the United States. His studies emphasized the importance of executive leadership. Those ideas, his experience as university president, and his own sense of mission guided his political career in times of peace and war. His voluminous writings across a large range of subjects give us uncommon access to the mind of this American leader.

This collection of Wilson's writing reveals the thought of a rare figure in American history, the scholar-statesman. Among the last of the presidents to write his own addresses, everything in the work is genuinely his. Included here are selections from all his major works, as well as occasional essays and key official statements. The selections were chosen and edited with the aim of distilling a voluminous body of writing into a compendium useful for a broad understanding of the life and thought of this important leader, and each document is introduced by a head note to place it in its proper context.

Unlike previous volumes, this collection is weighted toward Wilson's pre-presidential years. As a very young man Wilson struggled to understand his world in its religious, historic, and civic dimensions. Understanding his work as president would be incomplete without examination of the legacy of his thought from his religious formation through his work as a scholar, educational theorist, and reformist politician. These writings reveal the evolution of convictions, values, and analytical skills that informed the mind of Woodrow Wilson and guided his decisions as a leader in the academy and the nation. They show a mix of conservative reverence for the riches of tradition, both religious and intellectual, and a liberal openness to innovation and experiment. These qualities informed his character as scholar and president.

The book opens with selections from Wilson's writings on religion, which remained important to him from youth through his mature reflections in "The Clergyman and the State" (1910) and in "The Bible and Progress" (1912). A series of biographical sketches of famous men follows, highlighting the qualities of character and intellect in leaders who seem to have been models for Wilson and influential in his own development. From the start of his academic career, Wilson was concerned not only with the content but also with the process of a sound education. As a student, professor, and university president he thought deeply about the nature of liberal education, developed firm ideas about some of the worrisome changes emerging in American higher education, and wrote often as an advocate of his vision of learning. That vision prescribed not only preparation for vocation, but the cultivation of a breadth of intellect and molding of character. In chapter 3, writings from Wilson's early thought on education, as expressed in "True Scholarship" (1877), through an essay at the close of his academic career, "On the Importance of the Liberal Arts" (1910), reveal both continuity and development concerning the theory and technique of education.

As a professional scholar Wilson was both historian and political scientist, and the next two sections allow the reader to witness the development of both. The historian embraced a version of American exceptionalism, as in "The Course of American History" (1893), and illustrated both the professional consensus of his times and deep personal feelings about his native South. His interpretations of Civil War and Reconstruction history in "States Rights" (1899) and "The Reconstruction of the Southern States" (1901) have been much revised by modern scholarship.

Writing as a young political scientist in "Cabinet Government in the United States" (1879) and in his book *Congressional Government* (1885), Wilson argued his sympathies for the British parliamentary system, especially because it offered more effective executive leadership in shaping legislation than he could credit to the American congressional system of the nineteenth century. These studies, it can be argued, influenced his own hands-on, activist involvement in the legislative infighting both as governor and president.

When Wilson became more active in politics, even while still president of Princeton, he underwent a gradual transformation of political posture, moving steadily from conservative to more progressive stands on the issues of the day. Chapters 6 and 7 chart this trajectory from his early days as governor of New Jersey through the road to the White House. The Woodrow Wilson who wrote "The Government and Business" (1908), and the campaigning candidate and the new governor at his inauguration thought very differently about political issues. The continuing move to the left is documented in his speeches in the presidential campaign of 1912.

The book culminates with Wilson's presidential writings, from his inaugural address to his appeal for support of the League of Nations. Though never inclined to the radical, President Wilson's progressive New Freedom achievements brought important reforms to the nation and recast the role of the presidency and the federal government in American life. International affairs in Latin America absorbed the president in the early years of his administration. His statements on Latin American policy suggested hope for a new start in inter-American relations, a hope never fully realized during his presidency. World War I propelled Wilson onto the world stage. Much has been written about Wilsonian neutrality policy, the Versailles Treaty, and his role in the struggle to establish the League of Nations. Wilson's own writing on these matters testify not to a naive idealist with an unrealistic vision, but to an internationalist whose Fourteen Points set the agenda for much of the twentieth century. Arms control, freer trade, national self-determination, and an effective international organization for negotiation and peacekeeping have been and remain urgent objectives of international relations. For his vision of a more stable world, Wilson argued eloquently; the failures and tragedies of the twentieth century belong to others.

The works gathered here represent the best and the most important of Wilson's writings that retain enduring interest. Arranged topically, they reflect the range of his interests and ideas. Where necessary for appropriate focus and length, editing has been done with care to retain the original sense and spirit of his thought. Deletions are indicated by ellipses [. . .] for internal elisions and asterisks [☆ ☆ ☆] for omissions between sections.

PROVIDENCE COLLEGE

July 2005

INTRODUCTION

Woodrow Wilson

Scholar-President

The president stared at his audience in Pueblo, Colorado, in a momentary and inappropriate silence. He seemed unable to finish a reference to defeated Germany. The usually blasé reporters, who had listened to him every day of his long tour, suddenly came to attention. The president was never halting in addressing the increasingly enthusiastic crowds who came to hear his appeal for the American entry into the League of Nations. Struggling past the crippled sentence, he managed to finish his speech with a moving call for the nation to keep faith with those fallen men who would never return from the fields of France. Startled reporters and the assembly now saw the president weeping. Those close to him knew what they had feared from the start of the tour: Woodrow Wilson was terribly ill.

A few miles from Pueblo, the presidential train paused at a country crossroad. Wilson, his wife, Edith, and Cary Grayson, the president's physician, walked a short stretch, hoping the fresh air would help. It did for a time, but soon after the train resumed its trek, Wilson's head throbbed with pain, one side of his face contorted, and his speech was slurred. His wife and doctor pressed him urgently to end the tour against his insistence on continuing to Wichita. When his left arm and leg stiffened, Wilson finally agreed, and the train sped directly back to Washington. The cause had lost its champion, and the ailing scholar-president returned to the capital to witness the defeat of his dream at the hands of Henry Cabot Lodge and a resistant U.S. Senate.

Thomas Woodrow Wilson was born in Staunton, Virginia, on December 28, 1856, the son, grandson, and nephew of Presbyterian ministers. His identification as a southerner and a deep fidelity to his religious roots shaped his character and guided his action to the end of his life. His father was a strong, sometimes domineering figure in his life for many years, and the shy boy worked hard to please him. But Wilson was no prodigy and there were disappointments and early concerns for his family. Oddly for one who became a great scholar, Wilson seemed to learn slowly; he could not read very well until he was nearly twelve. He did not excel throughout his school days, and even years later failed to graduate with honors from his college, barely finishing in the top third of his class. His slowness to read may have been caused by a form of dyslexia. But intelligence and persistence were his, and they compensated for the slow pace of his early academic life.

Wilson enjoyed growing up in the South. After Staunton the family spent some time in the towns of Columbia, South Carolina and Wilmington, North Carolina. Wilson later studied law at the University of Virginia and practiced for a short time in Atlanta. His roots were deeply set in southern soil and he was conscious of himself as a son of the South. His father had been an ardent supporter of the Confederacy, and Wilson himself, in later years, wrote with great sympathy for southern life and especially for what he and most of his generation of historians believed was the great suffering of the South during the Reconstruction era. He once wrote that he yielded to no one in his love for the South, but added that *because* he loved the South, he rejoiced in the failure of the Confederacy. The young Wilson accepted romantic southern ideas about women, who should be honored and protected and should not demean themselves by engaging in practical matters. As president, he would be slow to support women's suffrage. He shared the white upper class's patronizing and paternalistic attitude toward blacks and was untroubled by the regimen of segregation. While he developed some modest sympathy for the idea of black civil rights, he believed black Americans ought not to seek "social equality" with whites. Through the years of his career as scholar, politician, and president, these attitudes changed little and influenced much.

Another great shaping force in Wilson's life was his religious faith. The Wilsons subscribed to a moderately liberal reformed Protestantism rather than the more fundamentalist evangelical movement. Given the intense religious commitment of his family, it is not surprising that he testified to a strong conversion experience in the summer of 1873 and formally joined his father's Presbyterian church. He read Scripture daily and remained faithful and devout throughout his life. It was during his second year at Princeton that Wilson published a series of essays in the North Carolina *Presbyterian*. They reveal an intensely religious personality and can be read like the sermons he might have delivered had he acceded to his father's wish that he enter the ministry. While there is little evidence of serious interest in theology, his moral vision was influenced by Calvinist doctrine, including a persistent belief in predestination. For Wilson the world was ordered by God from the beginning, a conviction that contributed to his personal sense of duty and destiny. His most important biographer, Arthur Link, argued that Wilson cannot be understood without weighing the profound influence of his religious faith on his ideas and motives. His politics and his own sense of purpose were in part derived from his faith in God and his embrace of the Christian ethic. For Wilson, religion illuminated and guided life and the two were inseparable. That guidance invested him with the supreme confidence he showed in his own judgment and perhaps with a reluctance to compromise and a tendency to dislike those who disagreed with him.

Religion undoubtedly guided his choice of colleges. In September 1873, he enrolled at Davidson College, and a year there served to prepare him for admission to Princeton in 1875. Both institutions were Presbyterian in the composition of their boards of trustees and of much of the faculty, at a time when such affiliation was taken seriously by American universities. Though not a top student, Wilson thrived in what he later described as the rich intellectual atmosphere at Princeton. Although he complained about boring and sometimes useless courses as a student, he later thought of his undergraduate years as "magical." In an active extracurricular life, he became a leader among his classmates. Debating and work on the student paper, *The Princetonian,* of which he became editor, took time from his studies but also fed his desire to write. For the student paper he wrote editorials on college athletics, which he favored greatly, and critical commentaries on Princeton educational policies, as in his essay "True Scholarship." More important were scholarly essays he published in various periodicals, including studies of William Pitt and John Bright, reflecting his interest in history and contemporary politics. Among these essays was a precocious analysis of cabinet government in the United States published in the prestigious journal, *International Review.* With it he marked out the area of his later academic specialization. In one of those wonderful oddities with which history teases, the editor who accepted Wilson's essay for the *Review* was a young Henry Cabot Lodge, his archenemy of the presidential years.

It is unlikely that Wilson, saddened at the thought of leaving Princeton on graduation in 1879, imagined that he would return to that happy place one day. For now his thoughts moved on to the study of law at the University of Virginia. He was unexcited by the law and quickly became active in debating and other campus activities, reliving undergraduate adventures. Perhaps because of his family's concern for his less than robust health, Wilson withdrew from the university six months short of taking his degree. This was no serious obstacle to the practice of law in those days of more relaxed barriers to the professions. In 1882, he joined Edward L. Renick, a Virginia classmate, in a joint practice in Atlanta. He found the practice of law no more satisfying than its study, and the partnership endured only briefly. During his stay in Georgia, two developments turned Wilson's life in a happier direction. The first was his decision to leave the practice of law to begin graduate studies at the new Johns Hopkins University in Baltimore in the fall. Then, on a visit to the town of Rome, Georgia, in the spring of 1883, he fell in love with and almost immediately proposed to Ellen Louise Axson, the daughter of the Presbyterian minister at the church he attended during that visit. By the end of summer the couple announced their engagement. They married in June 1885.

Meanwhile, he threw himself into the study of history and politics with great intensity. At Johns Hopkins he worked under renowned scholars Herbert Baxter Adams, Richard T. Ely, and John Franklin Jameson. These men quickly recognized Wilson's talent as a scholar and writer, and, given the rigidities of the German model of graduate study that dominated the university, they gave him unusual latitude to pursue his scholarly interests. His energy was prodigious. Within a year of enrolling, Wilson began work on *Congressional Government,* a critique of the American system, which was published by Houghton Mifflin in 1885. Publication by a prestigious house and the good reviews that followed were an enviable achievement for a student still short of his Ph.D. He took the degree after successful examinations in 1886, after he had begun his teaching career at Bryn Mawr College.

Wilson arrived at Bryn Mawr with his new bride in September 1885. He quickly became a popular teacher. It was a small college, and with few students and a humane schedule, Wilson continued writing and began to build a scholarly reputation beyond its halls. He enjoyed teaching and the notice his work brought him, reveled in the delights of his new marriage, and felt blessed with the birth of his first child, Margaret, born in April 1886. These were good times, and the future promised more. His days at Bryn Mawr were marred only by the unpleasantness of a contract dispute with its president. In 1887 Wilson received an offer from Wesleyan University in Middletown, Connecticut. He had signed a three-year contract with

Bryn Mawr, but claimed that the college had not fulfilled its terms, and so it did not bind him. After some tense exchanges, the president acquiesced and Wilson moved his family to Connecticut in the summer of 1888.

At Wesleyan, too, Wilson won high praise from students and colleagues and a growing reputation launched him on a fruitful sideline as a lecturer. Two more daughters brightened life in Middletown: Jessie was born in August 1887, and Eleanor arrived in October 1889. As the family grew, the work flourished. Always disciplined in his writing, he produced *The State* in 1889, the first textbook written on comparative government, which was widely adopted by universities for a generation and translated into several languages. His popularity as a teacher, his important publications, and the lecture circuit made Wilson an academic star not unnoticed by prestigious universities. Among these was his alma mater. Princeton offered a professorial chair and a salary of three thousand dollars. The salary Wilson thought too low, but the chair and Princeton were irresistible. Wesleyan was deeply disappointed to lose him, and the Wilsons had been happy in Middletown; but with only momentary sadness, they made a new start at Princeton in the fall of 1890.

For the next two decades, life at Princeton brought great achievement, praise nearing adulation among students and alumni, and, in the end, bitter controversy and frustrating defeat. It was a sequence Wilson repeated later in a larger theater. Both stories were marked by early triumphs.

Wilson's reputation preceded him to Princeton. In his first year, more than half the upperclassmen enrolled in his elective course in public law. His popularity as a teacher did nothing to distract his energies from scholarship. He wrote essays for scholarly and popular journals, and a study of the middle years of the nineteenth century, *Division and Reunion,* was published in 1893. *Mere Literature,* a collection of essays, included "The Course of American History," one of his important interpretative works. In it he broke with traditional interpretations of American development as an outgrowth of European models and emphasized American development as the product of the virgin environment of the New World. The idea is suggestive of the famous frontier thesis Frederick Jackson Turner published in 1893. Turner had been a student of Wilson at Johns Hopkins. Whether the idea was an independent if parallel development or the inspiration of one scholar by another is unclear. Though it brought fame to Turner in the historians' guild, there is no evidence of tension between the two men. In fact, Wilson so admired Turner's work that he tried to bring the historian into the Princeton faculty. His effort was spurned by the board of trustees on what to a later age seems the startling ground that Turner was a Unitarian and therefore unsuitable for Presbyterian Princeton. Wisconsin and later Harvard became the benefactors of Princeton's orthodoxy.

Wilson worked so hard that his health suffered. In May 1896 he suffered what in hindsight years later was diagnosed as a small stroke, which left his right hand stiff and cramped for some time. He dismissed the episode as writer's cramp from overwork, but it may have been the first of a series of strokes that afflicted him at about ten-year intervals, although this diagnosis from a distance is not definitive. His productivity in that decade was impressive. Publications, public lectures, and growing contacts made Wilson one of the most respected scholars in the American academy and forecast new directions for his life. His writing and lectures included ideas about the nature and goals of higher education and drew admiring attention and tempting invitations. Johns Hopkins asked him to accept a chair; the universities of Illinois and Virginia invited him to take the presidency. He was flattered by the attention, but his ties to Princeton were strong, and the matter was settled when the university, aware of the attempts to lure Wilson away, gave him a five-year contract and raised his salary to $6,500, making him its highest-paid professor. In 1900 he began a series of articles for *Harper's* that became the basis for a five-volume work, *A History of the American People.* Again he enjoyed friendly reviews, and the set remained in print for years through several editions. At this time, Wilson was planning a work on the philosophy of politics, which he intended to be his masterpiece. The book was never written. On June 9, 1902, the Princeton board of trustees unanimously elected Wilson to the presidency, the first layman chosen for the position. This new turn ended his serious work as a scholar. University administration and the political career that followed left little time for research.

Wilson's writing offers clues about the man and his future as a leader. Religion was centrally important to his life and thought, but less evident in his scholarly writing, which was so barren of religious argument that some questioned his Presbyterian orthodoxy. His work was marked by realism and was much influenced by the English political writer, Walter Bagehot. Wilson had studied Bagehot's work on the English constitution and drew liberally from it, including the idea that the British system brought greater efficiency to government than the American, which tended to scatter responsibility and diminish accountability. Wilson was unimpressed by the quality of men drawn to Congress and thought the American presidency a weak office. Less a political philosopher than a careful investigator, he aimed at a detached and objective analysis of the workings of practical politics—things as they were rather than as they were intended to be. He was concerned more with the uses of power and less with ideology. His purpose was to provoke useful ideas about the structure and operation of government and less to advocate specific reform ideas tied to political ideology. He did not emphasize economic influence in politics, and his political thought suggested a somewhat conservative inclination.

On important contemporary political issues Wilson expressed no sympathy for the Populists of his day and favored the "gold Democrat" position on the hot monetary dispute of the 1890s. He was concerned about the great power of the trusts, but skeptical about giving the government too much power. A firmly committed Democrat, he opposed the high tariffs protectively cherished by the Republican establishment for decades. Though not avidly anti-imperialist, he supported autonomy for Puerto Rico and the Philippines. Some of these views, including the relation of trust power to government action, would change in the new century when he developed greater appreciation for more progressive economic and political reform. By 1912 his political posture was very different from the conservatism of his earlier thought. But his developing commitment to reform never approached the impassioned crusading style of William Jennings Bryan or Robert La Follette. Wilson's academic success fed an already fulsome self-confidence, and, perhaps reenforced by his religious convictions, nurtured in him a sense of destiny. He was supremely confident in his own judgment, a quality that did not encourage great flexibility or lightly suffer opposition once his mind was firmly set. He confessed a temptation to engage in what he described as practical matters of worldly importance and had little difficulty imagining himself as a leader.

Election to the presidency of Princeton gave Wilson his chance to lead, and he took it ready with the ideas and will that would reshape the university. He strode into the office as a reformer disenchanted with the character and quality of American university training. He had already publicly criticized what he saw as excessive specialization and vocational concern and lamented inadequate devotion to the training of the mind and the pursuit of truth. The title essay "Mere Literature" in his book published in 1896 set out his educational philosophy. His intention was to create a modern academic design that could also preserve a respect for tradition. Contrary to the trend of the late nineteenth century, Wilson sided with

Matthew Arnold in advocating a humanistic undergraduate education over a more narrow technical regimen favored by a generation mesmerized by the rapid advance of technology. In his inaugural address, the new president of Princeton forecast his plans for the university. He saw the mission of Princeton and other universities to serve the nation, supplying enlightened men of broad learning. "The managing minds of the world . . . must be equipped for a mastery whose chief characteristic is adaptability, play, an initiative which transcends the bounds of mere technical training." The new emphasis on technical training was misguided, but there could be no return to a purer curriculum focused on the study of classical languages and literature. Those studies now had to take their place in a broad curriculum of science and the liberal arts.

Wilson reported to the board of trustees that Princeton could not hope to match the reputation of Harvard or Yale or Columbia without a great infusion of money. To execute the reforms necessary for Princeton, he would need $6 million at the start and more later. In turn-of-the-century dollars this was a stunning sum. Members of the board were expected to contribute and raise money, and Wilson personally campaigned for funds himself, speaking to alumni groups and seeking out and entertaining potential donors. His plans were appealing and he was persuasive; the money came. Beyond brick and mortar expansion, the agenda called for more money for faculty, who, he thought, were underpaid and overworked, a refrain still chanted by academics everywhere. He proposed establishing schools of science, engineering, and law and a graduate school. He was most passionate about the establishment of a preceptorial system of close contact between student and teacher, which he publicized in an essay in *Harper's Weekly.* By 1905, forty preceptors were added to the Princeton faculty for frequent sessions of one-on-one contact with students. The experiment was quickly hailed as a success and altered the character of the undergraduate experience at Princeton. Perhaps even more important than the preceptor system was Wilson's revision of the program of studies, for the teaching revolution was preceded by basic changes in the curriculum. By the end of his first year as president, Wilson won approval of a new program of studies that combined upper-class elective specialization and a set of required courses aimed at a rounded liberal education, which he thought ought to be at the heart of a student's college experience. Harvard and Yale shortly followed the Princeton lead in this kind of curriculum revision.

More innovation followed. The administration was thoroughly reorganized. The faculty was enlarged and better paid. Wilson appointed the first Jew and then the first Catholic to the faculty, and, in 1906, Princeton officially declared itself a nonsectarian institution. One Princeton dean, Henry B. Fine, surveying the work of his presidency, concluded that Wilson *made* Princeton. When he came, it could be compared with undergraduate colleges like Williams and Amherst; when he left, Princeton competed with universities like Harvard, Yale, and Columbia.

It was a record of great achievement, but there was trouble, too, and his troubles probably revealed more about Wilson than his successes. Wilson made few close friends. He demanded absolute loyalty from friends and subordinates, and sometimes mistook honest dissenting advice for disloyalty. In a pattern that continued most of his life, few men became intimate friends and most of those were sooner or later discarded. By 1906 his record of achievement had won universal praise on and off the campus from students, faculty, trustees, alumni, and an approving press. What little resistance developed to his reform ideas he brushed aside with ease. He brought Princeton and himself to the admiring attention of the country. This very success and the exhausting work that success demanded seeded trouble for Wilson, personally and professionally. Success fed his tendency to overconfidence, ill-disposed to concession or compromise; the overwork may have contributed to an attack that years later was diagnosed as another "stroke" episode. He was stricken late in May 1906, losing sight in one eye and leaving his right hand weak. The weakness passed, but he never fully regained sight in the left eye. A summer of rest and a vacation trip to England seemed to restore his vigor, and in the fall he took up his work again to continue the restructuring of Princeton, this time with less happy results.

Aiming at greater coordination of intellectual and social contacts among students, Wilson submitted a report to the board of trustees proposing new residence arrangements. The hottest of these ideas was his call for the abolition of the Princeton "eating clubs." Wilson charged that the clubs isolated upperclassmen from freshmen and sophomores, and, since membership required election to a club, they excluded about a third of the juniors and seniors. He painted the clubs as undemocratic and exclusive enclaves in an institution whose mission sought to foster a richer common life for students both intellectually and socially. The clubs had to go. He presented his "quadrangle plan" to establish residence halls with common dining and recreation facilities that would be open to all students. In June 1907, the board endorsed the idea and Wilson's troubles began. There had been no public discussion of the issue before the board approved, and club defenders accused Wilson of high-handedness in submitting such an important idea without consultation with important constituencies of the university. There was the expected anger of the clubs themselves, but alumni were also hostile to the plan, the faculty was divided, and even some on the board developed doubts. Not uncharacteristically, as opposition intensified, Wilson grew more firmly committed to his plan. He dismissed suggestions for compromise. He was convinced that the respect he enjoyed and his powers of persuasion would win approval for his scheme in the end. This confidence sharpened the bitterness of defeat when the board of trustees withdrew its approval for the quadrangle plan in October. Wilson felt betrayed and for a moment considered resigning the presidency. The humiliation did little to change Wilson's mind or his determination to continue the fight. He decided on a speaking campaign aimed at alumni, convinced their opposition was uninformed and that he could bring them to see the wisdom of his idea. The skeptics refused to convert. By spring 1908, even his loyalists recognized that the plan was dead, and an unhappy Wilson finally abandoned the effort.

This struggle over residence reform was a prologue to more controversy. Plans for development of a graduate school had been simmering since his inauguration. The trustees had authorized the development of a graduate school and appointed Andrew F. West as its dean. West prepared extensive plans, but Wilson's other initiatives took precedence and left the graduate dean deeply frustrated. Push and shove turned into war in 1909. The infighting between West and Wilson was not untypical of academic turf battles, nor has the academy fallen noticeably short of sensitive egos determined to have their way—usually little harm is done because usually there is really little at stake. At Princeton the graduate school issue became explosive, probably due more to prideful jousting than to the substantive matters of graduate study. At the heart of the struggle was a dispute about the location of the school. Wilson insisted the graduate school should be located on the Princeton undergraduate campus; West favored an off-campus site. Each side dressed its case with arguments that strained to tie location to pedagogical advantage. Looking back from a distance, it is hard not to conclude that this was more a clash of personalities (the two had never been friendly) and academic politics than high educational principle. West managed to engineer generous alumni grants in support of his position. For his part, Wilson again resisted all efforts of the less passionate to work a settlement. In June 1910, the trustees, too tempted by still more pledges of money for West's plan, decided on the off-campus site. This new insult to Wilson's leadership would probably have led him to leave the presidency, but that course had already been set by other events. By the time the graduate school question was finally decided, Wilson had already accepted the New Jersey Democratic gubernatorial nomination and a new career.

During the decade of his presidency of Princeton, Wilson continued his professional and personal interest in contemporary politics. He gave a series of lectures in 1907 that became the basis for his work *Constitutional Government in the United States,* and revealed some development in his thought. Observing Theodore Roosevelt in office was possibly influential, for he now saw more potential for presidential leadership and expressed more sympathy for dynamic government action, especially by the states, than he would earlier have conceded. But Wilson's political tilt still reflected the rather conservative posture he struck in the 1890s. He opposed the federal regulation of big business, calling it socialistic in principle. Malefactors should be punished by the law, but he feared too much government power that broad regulation would confer. Besides, big business was productive and efficient. Unions, on the other hand, interfered with the right to work and the freedom of contract. He criticized the muckraking critics of bankers, but also called on bankers to act more responsibly as "intermediaries between capital and the people." He had high praise for the conservative Grover Cleveland, the last Democratic president, but faulted Roosevelt as too impulsive, too bold, in pushing reforms. In 1908 a speech to the Commercial Club of Chicago in March ("Government and Business") and one to the New York Southern Society ("Conservatism: True and False") restated his still conservative views. Wilson was no point man for progressive causes—not yet.

Wilson became active in Democratic party politics during the decade. But he did not care to associate with the Bryan wing of the Democratic party and even avoided attending the same political gatherings with Bryan. His writing and his successes at Princeton had made him a national figure and even won him occasional mention as a potential candidate for office. In 1908 he visited England while the Democratic national convention was held and left firm instructions that his name was not to be mentioned in connection with a vice-presidential nomination on a Bryan ticket. There was little danger. During the campaign, he discouraged a Bryan appearance on the Princeton campus and refused to be active in the contest. He did, nevertheless, vote for Bryan in the election, his party loyalty rock-hard. After 1908 his political views gradually changed, perhaps as the idea of a political career grew in appeal. By 1909, in the last stages of his Princeton troubles, Wilson gave clear signs of interest in running for public office.

New Jersey was stubbornly resistant to the progressive reform ideas that had infected both political parties in much of the nation. A small progressive insurgency troubled the state's Republicans, and a smaller rebel movement annoyed the Democrats. The state was dominated by machine politics that did the bidding of the many large corporations chartered there, and which gave New Jersey an unenviable history of bipartisan corruption. A new face seen as independent and enjoying a respected reputation could serve the Democrats well. Wilson had appeal. His national stature and solidly conservative views caught the attention of Democratic leaders, and two party regulars, George B. M. Harvey and James Smith Jr., decided that Wilson could lead the party to victory. Harvey, editor of *Harper's Weekly,* had long admired the president of Princeton, and as early as 1906 had marked him as a potential presidential candidate. As a prelude, the New Jersey governorship would serve. Smith, boss of the Newark-Essex County Democratic machine, also saw the advantage in a figure like Wilson fronting the state ticket. Someone so broadly admired and whistle clean was what the party needed to fend off Republican attacks and the increasingly irksome progressive elements in New Jersey politics. Not incidentally, Smith's own campaign for the U.S. Senate would not suffer from such an association.

Early in 1910, Harvey tried to convince Wilson to become a candidate for governor. At first evasive, Wilson eventually agreed he would accept the nomination but would not actively campaign for it. That the graduate school fight was in its last stages and going badly probably weighed on Wilson. His candidacy was a blow to progressives of the party. His political views had gradually migrated to the left, but progressives were unimpressed. Their agenda included the establishment of a utilities commission, workers' compensation, direct primaries, and higher corporate taxes. Wilson seemed an unlikely champion for such a platform, and they were prepared to challenge his nomination, especially when Wilson refused to clarify his apparently contradictory political creed. Labor, too, was unhappy given what they knew of his anti-union statements. He did disavow his earlier views on labor, claiming they were being misrepresented in the press, and he argued that any criticism of labor in the past had been offered "as a friend."

At the state convention, reformers managed to win approval of the most progressive platform the New Jersey Democrats had ever adopted, but the regulars controlled the nomination polling, and Wilson was chosen on the first ballot. Accepting the nomination, Wilson made a kind of personal declaration of independence. He reminded those who had chosen him that he had not sought the nomination and had made no pledges or commitments of any kind. He declared his solid support for the platform, including its progressive planks. It is a testament to Wilson's power as a speaker that he captivated his party audience. Even the so recently skeptical progressives rose to cheer, and the campaign that followed brought most of them solidly to his side. Among the progressive converts was Joseph Tumulty, who became the governor's private secretary in 1911 and remained a trusted colleague for the rest of Wilson's life.

Declining to stump the state, Wilson scheduled a brief series of speeches that became more and more progressive in tone and substance, a source of increasing anxiety for the regulars who had lured him into the race. They saw the Democratic candidate winning such broad popular support that victory looked increasingly likely. Perhaps they could manage him once in office. By election day, Wilson was pointedly speaking as the leader of the state Democrats and promising a thorough reorganization of the party. The outmaneuvered Smith and his friends could do little but watch and hope that their influence on Wilson did not dissolve completely. The election was a triumph. Wilson won 54 percent of the vote and carried a Democratic House into office with him in a state that had given Taft and the Republicans a landslide victory only two years earlier.

The new governor wasted no time in drawing the strings of party control to himself. Using his own instincts, and having Tumulty by his side to fill in the more occult details of state politics, Wilson maneuvered to push the old-line party men aside. One of the first victims was James Smith, who had done so much to make him governor. Wilson refused to support Smith's bid in the legislature for a seat in the U.S. Senate. Smith was successfully challenged in a nonbinding primary by a perennially unsuccessful office seeker, James E. Martine, a Bryan Democrat for whom, incidentally, Wilson had little respect. In part because of his public support of primary elections and in part as a showdown with Smith for party control, Wilson backed Martine and conducted a successful campaign of lobbying legislators for support. What might have been seen as a parochial battle was, in fact, an important victory for Wilson. The old party horses were startled into attention by his political skill and obvious public influence; progressives cheered a new champion against the bosses, and the country began to notice.

Although it had been a necessary step to sever his ties to the old regime, more important for Wilson were the achievements of his first year as governor. Early in January 1911, even before his inauguration, the governor-elect announced a program of reforms. It was a progressive wish list not likely to have won the blessing of the younger, more conservative Princeton political scientist. The list began with an election reform law to eliminate voting fraud and other election abuses. Wilson combined a program of public speeches and quiet lobbying of legislators to generate support. Despite opposition from the leadership of both parties, the Geran election reform law passed both houses in April by close votes, bringing together progressives of both parties into what amounted to a ruling coalition. This victory opened the gate for the rest of the reform program. As the governor's popularity and power expanded, the opposition retreated. A corrupt-practices law that struck at a host of dishonest practices and fueled the old political machines passed easily. Then the Osborne-Egan law created a public utilities commission with real authority to investigate and regulate a broad list of industries. The same legislative session passed a workmen's compensation law that forced employers to assume some decent obligation toward workers injured on the job. With Wilson's encouragement, progressives also passed a law allowing New Jersey municipalities to adopt commission government, thought at the time to be a way around boss control in the cities.

For progressives in New Jersey, this legislative session was an astonishing success and Wilson was their hero. That such reforms had come in New Jersey—notorious for its association with corrupt bossism—magnified the achievement, focused national attention on the governor as a new force in American politics, and wakened thoughts of higher office. The *New York Times* saw "obvious" implications for the future in Wilson's success. Soon after the legislative session ended, Wilson embarked on a speaking tour of western states and returned with a touch of presidential fever. Wilson-for-President clubs popped up in New Jersey by summer. With one eye on such flattering signs, the governor turned his attention to tightening his control over the state party, anticipating the fall elections. He and his progressive allies organized their own party machine across the state. Nevertheless, the fall elections were disappointing. Republicans returned to control both houses, in part because of defections and subversion in the old boss-controlled strongholds. Wilson could wring little out of the new legislative session, with Republicans reluctant to boost his reputation and perhaps a presidential bid.

But the western tour had, in fact, already launched Wilson's presidential campaign. In July 1911, a Wilson headquarters opened in Manhattan, and Wilson clubs organized around the country. Expressions of encouragement and support streamed in steadily; a few were less enthusiastic. Some old-line party leaders in states like New York and Illinois had reservations about promoting a man to the presidency who had made his reputation by crushing political machines. That kind of opposition generated more support. Gradually, key figures in the party began to strike their positions. William Jennings Bryan, long disdained by Wilson, had kind words for the governor; Wilson's attitude toward Bryan mellowed proportionately. Two key figures joined the bandwagon in the summer of 1911: William Gibbs McAdoo and Colonel Edward M. House. Both became important to Wilson's political and personal life. McAdoo served as one of the managers of the presidential campaign, joined the administration as secretary of the Treasury, and married Wilson's daughter Eleanor. On a trip to Texas in October, Wilson met House for the first time. There was an immediate bond between the two, and House, holding no official post, became Wilson's special assistant, closest adviser, and intimate friend.

The race for the Democratic nomination in 1912 was especially hot. As the minority party in national registration, the Democrats had long been underdogs in presidential elections, but 1912 looked more promising than the past. The Republicans were divided by the ideological battle between President William Howard Taft and Theodore Roosevelt, who was now leading a progressive charge against the old guard. When the Republicans quarreled in 1884, the Democrats elected Cleveland. Now there was more than quarreling; a party split was possible, and hungry Democrats could taste victory. There was, then, no shortage of candidates. The Wilson campaign organization continued to build support, with Wilson himself crisscrossing the country, hunting delegates. But as the Baltimore convention approached, the Wilson engine slowed down. When the convention came to order on June 25, Champ Clark, of Missouri, then the Speaker of the House who could boast of a long-standing progressive record, had emerged as the leading contender. Clark had won a number of primaries and the support of William Randolf Hearst, and came into the convention with nearly a majority of delegates. Wilson forces came to town with a few more than two hundred solid commitments. The tireless maneuvering of his managers, who labored past exhaustion, and the two-thirds rule that governed Democratic nominations worked in Wilson's favor. What followed is difficult to imagine in a day of nominating conventions slickly orchestrated for television. The first ballot on June 28 confirmed Clark's lead of 440 delegates to Wilson's 334, with a scattering of votes among six other candidates. Five days and a numbing forty-six ballots later, the convention named Woodrow Wilson the Democratic candidate for president of the United States.

The presidential election of 1912 was one of the most important of the century for its drama, and especially for the upheaval of political alignments. Theodore Roosevelt, having swung steadily to the left through his presidency and especially after leaving office, was itching to lead the country with what many Republicans regarded as a radical program of reform. The old guard, loyal to Taft and disdainful of Roosevelt's evolution as a reformer, dominated the party and its convention. Although primary elections, where they were held, favored Roosevelt, the convention nominated Taft. Roosevelt claimed he had been cheated by the manipulations of Taft forces and was therefore justified in bolting to a third party. His exit from the Republican party drew much of its progressive or liberal element to the new "Bull Moose" Progressive party. Many of those liberals were not inclined later to return to a Republican establishment dominated by the old guard conservatives who insisted on Taft over TR, nor were they especially welcomed to return. Progressivism had been a bipartisan phenomenon. After 1912, conservative domination of the Republican party drove the progressively inclined toward the Democrats and set the complexion of American politics for much of the twentieth century.

The election served as a referendum on reform. On the far left, Eugene V. Debs represented the most radical change with his socialist program. He led the Socialist party to its best showing ever that year with nearly 7 percent of the vote. American politics has never been congenial ground for radicals, even those as benign as Debs. On the right, Taft appealed to voters who thought minimal government best, and change—almost any change in the direction of reform—was unnecessary, costly, and dangerous. An unfettered capitalism had made America prosperous and should not be tampered with. Debs had no realistic chance for election, and Taft, with an uninspired campaign effort, faded quickly. The American mood in

1912 inclined strongly to reform; the question was whether the changes would be driven by Theodore Roosevelt or Woodrow Wilson.

Roosevelt's New Nationalism, inspired by the progressive critique of Herbert Croly and by his own inclinations, shifted antitrust strategy to argue that most trusts were efficient and productive and ought not to be dissolved. They should, however, be controlled by a government strong enough to regulate their activities for the national good. Strong leaders should direct a strong government for the general welfare of the people and the fulfillment of the nation's destiny. In this role, Roosevelt was ready to serve. With his entry into presidential politics, Wilson migrated still farther from his earlier conservatism to a vigorous advocacy of progressive ideas. But even in 1912, Wilson's New Freedom campaign harbored a Jeffersonian suspicion of strong central government. Perhaps Roosevelt's powerhouse government would bring good results in harnessing the power of capital and providing for humane social transformation. But what if it failed or abused its power? Once created, would such a powerful regime allow itself to be dismantled? Despite the ideological argument, the New Nationalism and the New Freedom bore many similarities and presented progressives with a difficult choice. Roosevelt was impassioned, hot, podium thumping, and always attractive to voters. Wilson was thoughtful, cool, and measured, but could also excite a political audience with a deceptively seductive rhetorical style. Together they produced an exciting election campaign.

Progressive Democrats crafted a platform that reflected Bryan's continuing influence in the party. The agenda called for lower tariffs, antitrust action, business regulation, support for an income tax, popular election of senators, banking reform, and an exemption for labor from the injunction provisions of the Sherman Act, which was aimed at trusts but often hit unions. Progressives of both parties had long favored these planks, and some ideas, which had been dubbed radical when the raucous Populists waved them, now, coming from middle-class progressives, seemed sanitized. Even with its cautions about big government, Wilson's New Freedom campaign embraced the program. To help, he drew into his circle one of the nation's leading authorities on trusts and corporate regulation, Louis D. Brandeis, for advice on turning his New Freedom ideas into concrete proposals. Brandeis became an invaluable counselor during the election and after.

In 1912 the country voted for change. The three candidates who advocated reform ranging from liberal to radical polled over ten million votes.

Taft, representing the conservative status quo, finished a weak third, drawing a few less than 3.5 million stalwart Republicans. Wilson's 6,293,454 votes was not a majority of those cast, but decisive over Roosevelt's 4,119,538. Democrats won majorities in both houses, and among the Republicans elected were progressives whose votes for liberal measures could be had. The election was a mandate for reform, and it was the once conservative Woodrow Wilson who carried progressive hopes into the White House.

Wilson's scholarship in political science had emphasized the importance of executive leadership. The absence of an effective executive was a key to his critique of the American system and explained his admiration for the British parliamentary system. His study of politics, his experience at Princeton, and his own sense of mission shaped his philosophy of leadership. In the governorship, he had honed his rhetorical skill in raising public consciousness and support for important issues. Unfettered by obligation to any party faction or economic interests, the president-elect drew men of talent to his administration. Ironically, Brandeis, who had been so helpful in the campaign, was not among them. Brandeis was bitter and party progressives were disappointed when he was not named to the cabinet. Wilson wanted him as attorney general, but pressure from Brandeis enemies in and outside the party killed the appointment. Nevertheless, he remained a valued adviser and key actor in shaping banking and antitrust legislation, and his reward would come later. (To the outrage of conservatives, Wilson appointed Brandeis, one of the country's leading critics of big business, to the Supreme Court in 1916.) Service and status as a party giant dictated the appointment of Bryan as secretary of state, and, contrary to expectations, he served tirelessly and made important contributions to domestic and foreign policy. Only when his inclination toward pacifism clashed with Wilson's neutrality policy did the relationship dissolve. Wilson gave cabinet officers wide latitude in their own areas, but remained characteristically somewhat distant in his relations with the cabinet. When persistent and unwelcome leaks followed close on cabinet meetings, those gatherings became perfunctory, and important policy issues were avoided.

For those matters Wilson relied more on his inner circle, especially McAdoo, Tumulty, and, on matters large and small, Colonel House. McAdoo was an extremely able politician and among the most strongly committed progressives in the administration. Tumulty, secretary to the president, was less polished but no less knowledgeable about party politics. He served as a kind of political point man and often deflected heat away from Wilson. Sadly suggestive of a less tolerant era, Tumulty was the subject of frequent protests to Wilson because he was a Roman Catholic and therefore not to be trusted in a position so close to the exercise of power. Wilson testily rejected the attacks as absurd. House was Wilson's right hand. Having won Wilson's trust during the campaign, House soon became the president's closest confidant outside his family. Without portfolio, he shaped policy, especially in foreign affairs, by guiding and at times manipulating his friend.

Wilson's New Freedom pledges during the campaign promised quick action on three issues of central concern to progressives: tariff reductions, banking reform, and antitrust legislation with more teeth than the Sherman Act of 1890. The new president was determined to deliver on his promises. He threw himself to the task with great energy, broke precedent, and acted out his ideas about effective executive leadership. He surprised legislators and the country in April with an address to a joint session of Congress, a practice he continued throughout his presidency. Not since Jefferson abandoned the practice had a president delivered his messages to Congress in person. He lobbied legislators, visited the Capitol to stir up support, and lashed out at lobbyists seeking to undermine his program. His efforts were productive; in his first two years in office he compiled a record of legislative success unmatched by past presidents.

Action on the tariff brought the first victory. Progressives, consumers generally, and farmers especially had long complained that high tariffs raised the cost of living and reflected big-business greed and power over the economy. Import duties had been kept at high levels since the Civil War, and what posed as an effort to lower rates, the Payne-Aldrich tariff of 1909, actually raised the cost of imports still higher. Now at Wilson's urging, the Underwood-Simmons Tariff Act proposed a dramatic reduction in rates. By September 1913, having brushed aside the resistance of business lobbyists, Congress passed the act by large majorities and gave Wilson and the progressives a double victory. In that simpler day the government met most of its obligations with income from import duties—income the new law would cut drastically. A rider attached to the act by Congressman Cordell Hull solved the problem by enacting a graduated income tax, now constitutional with the recent ratification of the Sixteenth Amendment. The tax provision levied a 1 percent tax on incomes over $4,000, the rate rising to a maximum 6 percent on incomes over $500,000. In 1913 this left most of the country untaxed but satisfied another progressive objective for a modest redistribution of income. The victory elevated Wilson to a commanding position as leader of his party and the nation.

Conservatives had denied the need for tariff reform, but nearly everyone agreed on the urgency of banking reform. What kind of reform was less clear. There had been no major banking legislation since the Civil War, and no central banking agency existed to deal with financial crises. A congressional investigation in 1913 revealed the charges that a money trust was controlling the nation's economy were not entirely fictitious. The probe showed that a small clan of Wall Street bankers, including J. P. Morgan and John D. Rockefeller, controlled a pyramid of interest in over one hundred major corporations valued at more than $22 billion. Even those untroubled by Wall Street's influence hoped for legislation that might encourage greater stability in financial markets. The problem had been under study since 1908, and Republican senator Nelson Aldrich of Rhode Island presented a central bank plan congenial to the banking community. Progressives were hostile to the Aldrich scheme, which still left too much control in the hands of Wall Street. The alternative, the Glass-Owen Act, won Wilson's support, but did not satisfy either side completely. The legislation that followed created the Federal Reserve System of fifteen regional banks controlled by member banks. A Federal Reserve Board appointed by the president was to govern the system. Wilson urged passage in another address to a joint session, and in December, despite objections by some progressives who favored more government control and some conservatives who wanted less federal influence, Congress gave its approval. The banking issue reflected the ambiguity of Wilson's relations with the more intensely progressive. His realism at times fell short of their ideals, and while he often encouraged them, he could on occasion be neutral or even hostile toward their efforts.

Progressives pressed Wilson for a stronger version of an antitrust law, the third leg of his campaign program. Wilson had reservations about exempting unions, frequently harassed by the Sherman Act as combinations in restrain of trade, from the provisions of the new law. In the end, he relented and signed the Clayton Anti-Trust Act in October 1914. The act also gave the government more leverage in trust prosecution and banned interlocking directorates and other practices restricting competition. American Federation of Labor leader Samuel Gompers hailed the act as labor's "Magna Carta," and Wilson, despite his earlier reluctance, reaped the advantage of labor good will. With a push from the trusted Brandeis,

Wilson argued for creation of a Federal Trade Commission to regulate a wide range of business practices. With passage of the Fair Trade Act in September 1914, the New Freedom moved closer to the Roosevelt-Croly vision of a more activist federal government.

Along with these major initiatives, Wilson's domestic achievements boasted an array of progressive changes in American law, and the record added still more strength to the president's already ample store of self-confidence. When complete, the list included Federal Farm Loan Banks, the Seamen's Act to ease the brutal conditions forced on merchant sailors, the Adamson Act, providing an eight-hour day for railroad workers, the Keating-Owen Child Labor Act (struck down by the Supreme Court in 1918), and the woman suffrage Nineteenth Amendment. When first pressed by suffragists, the president hedged and withheld his support, but in 1917 he reversed himself and supported passage. Wilson directed this great surge of progressive change intended to adjust the role of the American government confronting the demands of social justice and the realities of modern capitalism. Three presidents accomplished the transformation. Theodore Roosevelt had set the precedents for federal action, Wilson expanded them, and under the massive reforms of Franklin Roosevelt the process was largely completed.

This was a record of great domestic achievement, but in the cause of justice, neither the progressives nor Wilson responded well to the racism suffered by black Americans. Indeed, during his years in office, conditions for African Americans became worse rather than better. Five of the ten cabinet appointees were southerners, and the president did nothing to prevent their introducing the systematic segregation of federal employees in Washington and elsewhere. Postmaster General Albert Burleson of Texas was especially diligent in this task. Many black federal employees in southern states were dismissed or demoted. Leaders of the NAACP appealed to the president to establish a National Race Commission to investigate the condition and status of African Americans. Wilson declined. In 1915, he allowed a private screening of the Klan-glorifying, D. W. Griffith film, *Birth of a Nation,* at the White House, an event backers tried to turn into a public endorsement of their film. Joseph Tumulty rescued Wilson from that embarrassment with a timely statement to the press denying the president's approval of the film. Reflecting his own southern background, Wilson had long believed that separation of the races was proper and did not contradict his notions of civil equality. To protests by leaders of the recently organized NAACP and the northern press, he responded weakly that separation of the races was in the best interests of blacks. The period from 1890 to 1920, though marked as the "progressive" era, stands as the worst period of race relations in American history after the Civil War. Court-supported Jim Crow laws, disfranchisement, lynching, and race riots made a strange backdrop to the progressives' struggle for economic and social reform. Racial justice was a long road away.

Nevertheless, given the realities of the age, Wilson accomplished much and proved his political and leadership skills. Unlike his last years at Princeton or the League of Nations battle to come, on domestic issues he was flexible, open to persuasion, and capable of compromise. As always, he threw himself into this work of the presidency with an inexhaustible drive, still managing to sustain a warm family life. But before long, Wilson faced a family crisis.

The Wilsons had enjoyed a long and happy married life. In marrying Wilson, Ellen abandoned without regret what might have been a promising career as an artist. Separations dictated by academics or politics produced a voluminous correspondence over the years, and the letters clearly record a deep and passionate love. Wilson's letters often contained only thinly disguised references to intimate pleasures sadly postponed. There were love poems and the warmest expressions of affection, uncharacteristic of the cool and reserved public persona he projected as scholar and politician. Arriving in Washington as first lady, Ellen preferred to avoid the social circuit of the city's elite. At her request there was no inaugural ball; she thought such affairs were too often ostentatious. Though she shared her husband's convictions about the social separation of the races, she assisted in the distribution of food and clothing to the poor of Washington and pressed congressmen she met on the need for action to improve the deplorable housing conditions suffered by African Americans in the city.

Barely settled into life at the White House, Ellen Wilson began to feel a certain loss of strength, but the illness did not become obvious until 1914. Early in March she collapsed in her bedroom. At first it was taken simply as a fall, but in the weeks that followed she failed to regain her strength. The problem was Bright's disease, a malady of the kidneys assaulted by nephritis. By July, Ellen was failing steadily as her anguished husband watched helplessly. On August 6, she died with the president and her daughters by her bedside. Wilson was inconsolable. In his grief he wondered if he could continue the work of his office and confessed to Colonel House that he no longer wished to live. It took all the strength of the disciplined life he had always led to confront the daily business of a presidency in the course of a great legislative campaign and troubled foreign affairs. The president's physician Cary Grayson thought his health was visibly declining after Ellen's death. As the weeks passed, his prescription was to throw himself into the details of his work with even more than his usual fervor. The cure was only partial; political successes did little to ease the pain of his loss and loneliness.

Woodrow Wilson had always enjoyed the company of women, and female company in or out of the family unfailingly made him more relaxed and cheerful. When a new woman came into his life, the president was able to shake off his mourning and enjoy life again. His cousin, Helen Bones, who was serving as the widowed president's hostess, introduced him to her dear friend, Edith Bolling Galt, in March 1915. She had much to appeal: attractive, sophisticated in dress and manners, member of a family of long Virginia lineage. Widowed in 1908, she managed a comfortable living from the Washington jewelry store she inherited from her husband. Tea at the White House on that March afternoon was followed by dinner a few days later, and the president was smitten. Usually with Cousin Helen accompanying, the couple met frequently in the weeks that followed, and early in May, Wilson declared his love and asked a somewhat shocked Edith to marry him. Her immediate response was to decline; she was flattered, but it was all too fast. They had known each other less than two months. The president was not to be deterred. Flowers, daily notes, and frequent visits followed, and her appearance by his side at several official functions tipped off even casual observers to the presidential romance. His ardor and a few months' time wore down her resistance, and the public announcement of their engagement was given to the press on October 6.

Those close to Wilson were pleased, having witnessed the change in him since meeting Edith . During the courtship, he traded depression for joy and came alive again. But there were some reservations among his political associates. Who could measure the political consequences of the marriage after so short a courtship, and one which began less than a year after the death of his wife? House saw danger; Tumulty feared disaster. Even before the engagement announcement, cabinet and other party leaders discussed the problem. Wilson, of course, was too deeply in love to be deflected by politics. While there were undercurrents of public criticism, he was undoubtedly pleased when, on a visit to New York with Edith, crowds cheered the couple arriving at the rail station and again later at the theater. On December 18, in the parlor of Edith's home, surrounded by family and a few close friends, they married and set out for a honeymoon in Virginia. Edith brought Wilson a love and strength that sustained him literally "in sickness and in health" for the rest of his life.

When the Wilsons returned to Washington, the news of the loss of two American lives on a British ship sunk in the Atlantic by a German submarine stunned the president and the country. When he became president, Wilson focused on the New Freedom and expected that his time in office would be devoted principally to domestic affairs. With Europe's explosion into war in August 1914, all changed. The war in Europe took more of the president's time now. Relations with warring parties demanded carefully crafted policy and exquisite diplomacy. Troubles with Latin America, including even the possibility of war, added to the burdens of office already deeply engaged in domestic reform. With extraordinary agility, Wilson steered his administration through the legislative labyrinth and the diplomatic minefields. To deal with Congress, he brought with him some political experience, but nothing in his political career or his studies had prepared him for the complexities of international relations across the Atlantic and below the Rio Grande.

Progressives and anti-imperialist elements had hoped that the new Democratic administration would make a new start in Latin American policy. Wilson did repudiate the "dollar diplomacy" of the Taft years and spoke of cultivating friendship and mutual respect, though he added the caveat that he had no sympathy for revolutionaries. He encouraged advocates of a new policy when he agreed to pay Colombia an indemnity of $25 million to assuage that country's bitterness over the heavy-handed role of the United States in engineering independence for Panama. Theodore Roosevelt, on the other hand, let loose a blast of invective at the implication that his actions had to be atoned for. Wilson and Secretary of State Bryan shared similar foreign policy views, though neither were expert in the conduct of foreign relations. Both believed the United States should be a beacon for democracy and freedom. But their confidence that they knew what was good for other people more than their own leaders dimmed that vision. The result was contradictory action and hostility. Bryan, ahead of his time, did suggest a program of economic assistance for Latin America through low-interest loans, but Wilson thought this would be regarded as too novel and radical. In the end, despite the Colombia treaty and the commitment to establishing decent relations, the record of dealings with Latin American nations was tainted by heavy-handedness and more interventions than previous administrations. Promises to the contrary, significant differences from the "dollar diplomacy" were difficult to discern.

In January 1914, revolution broke out in Haiti. American bankers, their investments threatened, called for action to restore order. The situation grew worse when revolutionary factions set to fighting each other. Wilson ordered American marines into Haiti, and troops remained there until Franklin Roosevelt's Good Neighbor Policy took effect in 1934. Chaos in Santo Domingo led to American military occupation until 1924. To support Wall Street banking investments, Nicaragua was forced into protectorate status in 1915. Beyond economic motives, the administration was concerned for the safety of the canal and intent on dominating the Caribean, especially to avoid possible European interventions in the unstable region. State Department ineptitude and recourse to military incursions ignited anti-American sentiment in some Latin American quarters. But the most dangerous hemispheric adventures of the Wilson administration concerned Mexico.

Revolutionary turmoil had afflicted Mexico since 1910 with repeated coups d'etat, in one instance punctuated by murder. By 1913 the contest for control of Mexico was being fought by competing factions, including the forces of Venustiano Carranza, who offered some hope of decent government, and Victoriano Huerta, the most recent usurper and a murder suspect. Wilson looked for an opportunity to intervene on behalf of Carranza, and it came in April 1914. American sailors, ashore at Tampico to purchase gasoline, were arrested by forces commanded by Huerta. They were quickly released with apologies, but the commander of the American squadron off-shore, with Wilson's approval, insisted that Huerta raise the American flag on shore and offer a twenty-one-gun salute or face grave consequences. Huerta refused and, at the president's request, Congress passed a joint resolution supporting the use of arms in Mexico. Before military action could be set in motion, a new front opened. Hoping to intercept a German shipment of arms to Huerta forces, Wilson ordered an invasion of Vera Cruz on April 21, and a quick victory left the United States in control there. Wilson had hoped that intervention would meet little resistance and lead to the fall of Huerta, a naive miscalculation. The action outraged Mexicans, including Carranza. In the face of criticism at home and the probable need for prolonged occupation and perhaps enlarged operations, Wilson abruptly made a more realistic assessment of conditions and called a halt to further action. In a fortunate turn, Carranza forces dislodged Huerta in August, and with the new government in power, the crisis and the threat of war seemed to pass.

The hope of better relations with a triumphant Carranza soon gave way to more tension and confusion. Francisco Villa, once a cattle rustler and outlaw, had supported Carranza's cause but was soon plotting against him and acting as a kind of war lord in northern Mexico. In March 1916, Villa crossed the border to loot and burn the town of Columbus, New Mexico, killing seven American soldiers and eight civilians, and other raids followed. The Carranza government agreed to allow an American expedition to enter Mexico in pursuit of Villa. General John J. Pershing and an army eventually numbering over six thousand troops crossed into Mexico. At one point Pershing proposed occupying the state of Chihuahua, bordering on the United States, and seizing its railroads. The idea shocked Wilson, who knew it would mean war. The president made clear that his purpose was to capture Villa, not to compromise Mexican sovereignty. As weeks passed Carranza insisted the threat from Villa had diminished and no longer warranted such an American presence on Mexican soil. He insisted the Americans should leave lest Mexico be forced to defend its territory. Troop presence in Mexico inevitably led to unfriendly contacts with Mexican contingents and a series of ugly incidents that threatened to spark a war. Even so, with few exceptions in the yellow press, editorial and public opinion in the United States strongly opposed war. Wilson responded. On June 30, 1916, he told a press gathering in New York that force by a strong country against a weak neighbor could not "reflect distinction upon the United States." He was not in office, he said, to serve the interests of the investors in Mexico, but to serve the nation. The speech was widely praised and marked a turning point in administration policy toward Mexico. In July, the two countries agreed to establish a joint commission to arrange the evacuation of American forces, and they were withdrawn in February 1917. Tensions eased, but bitter memories persisted in Mexico for decades.

Economic and strategic interests alone do not explain Wilsonian Latin American policy. In Mexico and elsewhere, the administration hoped to establish order and stable governments, a solid motive clumsily executed. Misjudgment of local sentiment, incompetent performance by diplomats and administration officers, and the hubris that usually accompanies absolute power created a nightmare of tragic miscalculations and errors. On the other hand, particularly in regard to Mexico, Wilson was generally wiser than his lieutenants, restrained at crisis moments, and ultimately successful in avoiding war. War came from another direction.

The assassination of Austrian Archduke Franz Ferdinand at Sarajevo on June 29, 1914, set the world on a slide toward war that a month of frantic diplomacy could not halt. The war shocked most Americans, but an arms race, imperialist competition, distrust, and the naive idea that war would be brief and decisive blinded the great powers of Europe. Interrupting the vigil at his dying wife's bedside, Wilson announced to the nation that the conflict was a European affair and Americans should remain impartial in thought and action. Most agreed. There existed broad sympathy in the administration and in the country for the democratic Allies over an autocratic Germany invading a helpless and neutral Belgium on the way to France. But there was also general agreement that neutrality was the proper posture. The affirmation of neutrality was easy; sustaining it proved extremely difficult. Two developments challenged the American diplomacy of neutrality.

First, the British declared a blockade of Germany and reminded the United States that His Majesty's government had respected Lincoln's blockade of the southern coastal cities during the Civil War. The blockade meant American shipping could not reach Germany, and British domination of the ocean surface kept German merchant ships away from the United States. American trade with Germany evaporated, while trade with Britain and France grew by leaps. This did not violate the laws of neutrality but clearly benefited the Allies. Wilson also allowed American banks to lend money to the Allies, eager to borrow and spend in America for food and war supplies. Germany, of course, protested, and it might seem that impartiality should have accompanied neutrality: no trade with Germany, no trade with the Allies. Aside from the economic cost, such a policy would have handed victory to Germany in a matter of months. The Germans could draw supplies by land from the center of the continent. Britain was an island, and France was cut off from the rest of Europe. Without American supplies the two most vibrant democracies of Europe would have faced defeat. Germany would likely have demanded the cession of arms and key imperial possessions and emerged as an unchallenged world superpower, an uncongenial prospect for the United States. As the fighting bogged down into a trench-war stalemate, Wilson hoped neither side would overwhelm the other so that he could lead the United States as the mediating force for a just peace. As early as September 1915, Wilson sent House to Europe to deliver his first offer of mediation. None of the belligerents accepted; they pretended interest and made excuses, but only to avoid giving offense to the United States.

A second challenge to neutrality policy arose from a change in the technology of warfare. The Germans had built a submarine fleet. The accepted rules of warfare dictated that a warship overtaking a merchant ship or passenger liner of the enemy must make provision for the safety of the passengers and crews of these unarmed vessels before sinking them or after ushering them into port. This was possible for large, surface warships, but a submarine was a small and fragile vessel. Even a small hidden gun on the deck of a merchant ship could destroy a sub if it surfaced to signal a capture. In the case of passenger ships, what was a submarine to do with a thousand or more passengers in midocean? Submarines could not safely play by the old rules, but play they did. German submarines attacked British and French merchant ships without warning. Incidents involving the United States were inevitable. In March 1915, an American citizen was killed when a U-boat attacked a small British liner. On May 1, an American tanker was mistaken for British and torpedoed. On the same day, the Germans claimed that the British were illegally stowing arms in holds of passenger liners and warned in newspaper advertisements that travelers should avoid British ships. That was the day the *Lusitania* left New York. On May 7, off the Irish coast, a U-boat fired a single torpedo into the liner. A huge explosion followed, and the ship sank in less than twenty minutes. Twelve hundred people died; 124 were Americans. Neutrality faced its most serious test.

Wilson drafted a protest note to Germany in language so strong that Secretary of State Bryan thought it risked war and could not in conscience deliver it. True to his pacifist-leaning religious convictions, Bryan had urged the president to prohibit Americans from traveling on passenger ships of any country at war. Wilson refused to surrender the right of Americans to travel unmolested on unarmed ships. Now Bryan had no choice but to resign. State Department counselor Robert Lansing replaced Bryan and sent the protest note. Germany at first defended her action, claiming the *Lusitania* was carrying contraband, which was true. But in the face of Wilson's strong words, the Germans pledged to do all they could to avoid American casualties. There was no war hysteria in the United States, but now public opinion became more sharply anti-German as the *Lusitania*'s sinking seemed to confirm the claims of British propaganda about the German capacity for atrocity. The attack did convince Wilson that military preparedness, not yet begun, was now prudent. Progressives, who counted many pacifists among their number, were reluctant to support the president in his call for defense spending; some actively opposed the policy. Bryan made a series of speeches calling military preparations a menace to peace. After intense debate and new incidents at sea, Congress eventually sided with Wilson.

An uneasy calm into the summer did not last. On August 19, a German submarine attacked without warning and sank the *Arabic*, a British ship carrying over four hundred passengers. Forty-four people, including two Americans, were killed. Again the United States protested, and again Germany retreated, claiming the submarine commander had exceeded his instructions and pledging to desist. The months that followed brought no new American casualties. Then, on March 24, 1916, in violation of their *Arabic* pledge, the Germans attacked the *Sussex* in the English Channel, killing eighty people and injuring four Americans. Now Wilson threatened to break off relations with Germany. In the diplomatic exchange that followed, the Germans again pledged to avoid passenger liners and unarmed merchantmen, but there was a qualification. They reserved their freedom of action if the United States did not persuade the British to observe what they called the laws of humanity. By this they meant an easing of the blockade, which by then was causing shortages and suffering in Germany. Wilson accepted the pledge without the conditions. Again with some dissent from pacifists, German-language newspapers, and some Republicans with an eye on the coming election, most press and public opinion seemed to support the president.

The British, too, sparked Wilson's anger and tested his patience with violations of American neutral rights. They blacklisted American businesses, which they claimed were trading with the Central Powers through neutral ports. British war ships intercepted American merchant ships at sea, opened mail packets to search for useful intelligence, and confiscated cargoes they suspected were destined for Germany. Wilson was outraged by these actions and protested repeatedly. There was, however, a critical difference between British and German violations. The British carefully compensated American businesses for lost cargo, and, however blatant the violations, no Americans died. When the Germans acted, people were killed and there could be no adequate compensation. As insulting as the

British offenses were, it was difficult for the Americans to threaten extreme action over a load of cotton. Wilson navigated these shoals of neutrality troubles with skill and patient restraint.

Wilson's objective was not war, but a role in a negotiated peace. He tried repeatedly to maneuver the belligerents to a truce. In the continuing effort to stop the fighting, House sailed for Europe for the second time in December 1915. He stopped first in England. The British again pretended interest in a truce, which House took as genuine. He and Lansing, Anglophiles with a strong desire for an Allied victory over Germany, frustrated Wilson's effort for judicious neutrality on more than a few occasions with independent actions and press leaks. House moved on for talks with the French and the Germans and returned to England ready to draft a proposal. The result was the House-Grey Memorandum. Edward Grey, the British foreign secretary, agreed that Wilson should call for a truce. The Allies would agree, but if the Germans declined, the United States would enter the war on the side of the Allies. When Wilson later read the memorandum, he carefully added the word "probably" to the statement about entering the war. House was delighted with his success, but Grey pleaded that, given the current battlefield circumstances, a quick truce would leave the Allies at a great disadvantage. He promised that he would signal Washington at the opportune moment. Wilson could then make his call for a cease-fire and the Allies would accept. The signal never came; the British had cleverly encouraged House and Wilson with no intention of following through. The Germans, perhaps, lost an opportunity. Had they accepted House's offer of a mediated truce and the Allies did not, they would have appeared to be taking the moral high ground with telling effect on American diplomacy. But in fact neither side was interested in peace without victory. It was one of the ugly ironies of war that the combatants could not stop fighting because too many men had already died. None of the warring governments dared face their people after all the sacrifice and death with anything but victory. While Wilson waited, the United States entered the election season.

As the election approached, Wilson organized his campaign from a position of strength. Progressive reforms were popular, the economy, with a boost from Allied spending in agriculture and industry, was prospering, and the nation was still at peace. But reelection was not to be an easy ride. Outside the South, many more voters were registered Republicans than

Democrats, and the Republican party was whole again. If most were grateful for peace, others thought Wilson's responses toward neutrality violations and Mexican turmoil were too weak. Critics charged that preparedness came too slowly and too late; others saw military preparation as making war more likely. At the St. Louis Democratic Convention in June, the party trumpeted the record of progressivism and peace and nominated Wilson by acclamation. Fears of a party split evaporated when Bryan, despite his differences with the president, announced his endorsement to the assembled Democrats. The most enthusiastic cheers at the convention and during the campaign came in response to the slogan, "He kept us out of war." In Chicago, the Republicans could not forgive Roosevelt's defection in 1912 and turned instead to Supreme Court justice Charles Evans Hughes to lead their ticket. He had served two terms as a reform governor in New York, and Taft raised him to the court in 1910. His judicial decisions were often aligned with the liberal dissenters on the court, and he was not hostile to social and economic reform. Though nominated by a now firmly conservative party, Hughes was not an old guard warrior and there were misgivings among the leadership; but it was hoped he might draw votes away from Wilson.

It was a hard-fought campaign. Republicans, like Roosevelt, now returned to the fold, and Senator Henry Cabot Lodge labeled Wilson's foreign policy in regard to Mexico and the war in Europe as cowardly. Democrats charged Hughes with courting anti-British and pro-German votes. Wilson's aides worried about rumors circulating about an illicit affair between Wilson and Mary Allen Peck, a widow whom Wilson had met on vacation in Bermuda while president of Princeton. At first clearly platonic, the friendship probably led to a brief romantic episode. The two remained friends for years, and Mrs. Peck visited with Ellen and Wilson on several occasions. Wilson confessed to Edith in 1915 to a folly "loathed and repented of." Now a whispering campaign became election fodder but never reached the level of public discussion. More vicious among the whispers was the slanderous charge that the president had pushed Ellen down a flight of stairs causing an injury that led to her death. Neither rumor decided the outcome of the election. Despite reservations about neutrality policy, progressives rallied to Wilson. Even Herbert Croly, editor of the progressive *New Republic* and a Roosevelt champion, now favored Wilson's election, convinced that the New Freedom had been set aside for a design closer to the kind of government envisioned by the New Nationalism. A majority of the committee that drafted the Progressive Party platform in 1912 now publicly announced for Wilson on the grounds that he had seen to the enactment of much of what they had called for in their platform.

The election was one of the close contests of American presidential history with a most dramatic finish. Hughes swept the eastern states, and newspapers there declared him the winner. By the end of the night the president, too, was convinced he had lost. But overnight returns showed Wilson strong in the West, casting the outcome in doubt. Not until late morning did returns come in from California, giving Wilson the state and the election. He polled 9.1 to 8.5 million for Hughes and took the electoral vote 277 to 254. Besides crucial California, he carried all of the South as expected and most of the usually Republican farm states. Democrats retained control of both houses of Congress, but by small majorities.

Having campaigned emphasizing peace and taking reelection as a mandate, the president redoubled his effort to bring the war to an end. Wilson realized, perhaps later than he should have, that he had been had by the British pretense for a truce. Fearful of being drawn into war by the uncontrollable action of others, the president decided to act unilaterally. In December he asked the warring parties for terms on which a truce could be established and peace talks begun. House and Lansing, still clearly pro-British, were fearful that Germany might accept, frustrating chances for an Allied victory. Peace groups in the country hailed Wilson's note, but Lodge called it pro-German, and Roosevelt, with characteristic restraint, used words such as "preposterous" and "immoral" to describe the president's initiative. The British and the French were irate, and the Germans declined to state peace terms and spurned Wilson's mediation, expressing interest only in a conference among the belligerents. Wilson pressed on.

In January he addressed the Senate, outlining U.S. policy and calling for a negotiated peace, a peace without victory. He warned that only a peace among equals could last. The foundation of that peace was to rest on a set of principles including national self-determination, freedom of the seas, arms reduction, and open diplomacy without entangling alliances. He called these "American principles, American policies." The speech also proposed a "concert of nations" to oversee and defend the peace. The Senate thundered its approval, and the overwhelming public response moved Wilson deeply. Less gratifying was Republican criticism led by Lodge, who had not long ago favored the idea of a league of nations, but now thought it would compromise American sovereignty. The warring powers, with victory their irreducible objective, were unmoved. The decisive response from Germany came at sea.

By now the blockade was causing great hardship in Germany. The military, arguing that the war had to be won soon or not at all, proposed a final strategy. The plan called for unrestricted submarine attacks on all shipping, including the vessels of neutral countries heading for the Allied ports. The naval war was to be coordinated with a massive land offensive in France. They realized this would mean sinking American ships and war with the United States. But they reasoned that by strangling supply lines to the Allies, Germany could win the war before the Americans could reach France with a significant force. The assaults began early in February with the sinking of the USS *Housatonic.* Even then, to Lansing's distress, Wilson showed remarkable restraint. He broke diplomatic relations with Germany but stopped short of calling for war.

In the lull that followed, a bizarre incident, not untypical of clumsy German diplomacy with the United States, darkened the prospects for peace further. British intelligence intercepted and forwarded to the Americans a note from German foreign secretary Arthur Zimmerman to his minister in Mexico. The note directed the German minister to offer an alliance with Mexico if the Americans entered the war. In return, the note promised that Texas, New Mexico, and Arizona would be restored to Mexico. Wilson still tempered his reaction. Holding the note secret, he asked Congress to authorize the arming of merchant ships and other actions to defend American commerce. When filibuster threatened against such broad authority, the president released the Zimmerman note. National outrage forced the retreat of much of the antipreparedness sentiment, even among some pacifists. More German attacks eliminated virtually all doubts.

On March 12, the *Algonquin* was sunk, and a week later three more American merchant ships were torpedoed within a twenty-four-hour period. After conferring with the cabinet and some agonizing private thought that fed him no good alternative, Wilson summoned a special session of Congress for April 2. In an emotion-filled speech, he asked for a declaration of war. He ended his address invoking God's help for America for "she can do no other." At the close, the chamber burst into fervent cheers and applause. Wilson later told Tumulty how strange he thought it was that a message that meant the death of young men should be applauded. Approval was massive, but not unanimous. On April 4, the

Senate, after a night's debate, passed the president's resolution 82 to 6. Two days later, on Good Friday, the House, by 373 to 50, voted for war.

Wilson administration neutrality policy remains a topic of great controversy among historians. Was it the right policy? Was it properly executed? Was the United States too partial to the Allied cause? Did the Anglophile prejudices of so many in the administration steer decisions? Among the actors in this tragic play, Woodrow Wilson was consistently the most judicious and restrained. He saw pitfalls and opportunities more clearly than any of his subordinates. He hated the thought of war and felt anguished and guilty sending men to die. In the end, he had little choice. Germany had, in fact, already launched a war against the United States, counting on victory before the Americans could be ready to fight.

The Germans miscalculated. They challenged the United States in the area of its greatest strength, the ability to produce and move goods. The first troops arrived in France in weeks, a great lift for Allied morale. In little more than a year, a million trained and equipped Americans were in France. Despite heavy shipping losses, armed convoys with sub-killing destroyers delivered enough supplies to keep the Allies fed and their armies fighting. Meanwhile, at home, despite the fact that there was little mobilization for war before 1917, Americans produced materiel sufficient to equip and train enough men to raise army strength from 200,000 troops at the start to nearly 4 million before the war ended. Wilson led his administration in organizing for war. This demanded raising more than $30 billion, harnessing industry to war production, and sustaining the normal operations of government. There were mistakes and inevitable waste in an enterprise so vast, but the necessary objectives were reached with competence and timeliness. Less commendable was the degree of repression thought necessary in time of war. Postmaster General Burleson was draconian in blocking from the mail material he deemed subversive. Wilson was embarrassed, but only once intervened to lift a ban on *The Nation* magazine. The government prosecuted almost three thousand people, many on thin warrant, under espionage and sedition acts passed by Congress. Eugene Debs was sentenced to ten years in prison simply for speaking out against the war. In one of the more heartless decisions of his presidency, Wilson refused to pardon an old and ailing Debs when the war was over. That kindness fell to Warren Harding.

One potential recruit for the war was Theodore Roosevelt. The old Rough Rider was desperate to relive the glory of combat. He loathed "the schoolmaster" and was unrelenting in his public criticism of Wilson, especially for his restraint toward Germany. Privately, words like "coward," "lily-livered skunk," and "that gray rat in the White House" slipped easily from his lips. Brushing his venom aside, he begged a meeting with Wilson a week after the declaration of war. Praising Wilson's address to Congress and marshaling an array of arguments, be beseeched the president to let him raise a volunteer regiment for the fighting in France. The meeting was surprisingly cordial, and Wilson later confessed there was a "compelling sweetness" in the man. At the time, Roosevelt was a year short of sixty and blind in one eye. For those reasons and for reasons of state and politics, Wilson refused to set the colonel on his path to glory. A bitter Roosevelt never forgave.

After early gains, the 1917 German offensive stalled, buying the Allies valuable time to build strength. In the spring of 1918, after Lenin pulled Bolshevik Russia out of the war in the east, the Germans transferred troops to the western front and launched a new offensive. By then, American troops were arriving in force. In midsummer the tide turned; a recent German advance slowed and in September turned into retreat. Now the Germans sought a cease-fire, but beaten and exhausted, they were forced by the Allies to accept what was, in effect, a surrender on November 11, 1918.

In the months after Americans joined the fighting in Europe, Wilson refined his thinking about the postwar peace. In January 1918, he once again addressed the Congress to announce a set of war aims and postwar objectives—what came to be known as the Fourteen Points. Reiterating some earlier principles, he listed the abolition of secret diplomacy, freedom of the seas, reduction of international economic barriers, arms reduction, a somewhat vague item about colonial adjustments, various territorial and border settlements, including the reestablishment of an independent Poland, and, most important to him, the establishment of a league of nations to work for peace and collective security among countries large and small. The response was electrifying. Translations in pamphlets and books were broadcast around the world and Wilson was cast as a moral leader. At home and abroad he was a hero. What scarce dissent there was came from the governments of Britain and France who understood that a Wilsonian just peace could well interfere with their vengeful desires to punish Germany. After the armistice, Wilson broke precedent with the stunning announcement that he would personally go to Paris as the head of the American delegation to the peace conference.

Early in December, Wilson sailed for Europe aboard the *George Washington.* On arrival he was greeted with undisguised joy. On a preconference tour to the great capitals—London, Paris, and Rome—cheering crowds lined the rail lines as his train passed. Governments soon worked to discourage the enthusiasm, fearing his stature as hero might interfere with the demands they planned to wring out of the conference. The momentum was his, but troubles lay ahead, some of his own making. In the American delegation, Wilson did not include any important Senate Republican. In that preatomic age, unembarrassed partisanship still ruled even in important foreign affairs. The Republicans had won majorities in both houses of Congress in November, giving them control of the Senate Foreign Relations Committee, which Wilson had to know would act on any treaty submitted to the Senate. Worse, Lodge was to be its chairman. In December, Lodge and Roosevelt exchanged ideas on strategy to defeat the league idea even before the details of the treaty had been negotiated.

In Europe, British and French leaders were unmoved either by their rescue by the United States or by Wilson's moral stature. French Premier Georges Clemenceau is supposed to have said, "Mr. Wilson bores me with his Fourteen Points; God Almighty only had ten." At the conference they quickly insisted on looting German resources and annexing her colonies. Wilson knew that an unjust peace would only lead to new war, and resisted doggedly. On the colonial question, he did manage to force the adoption of what became the mandate system of the league, holding the promise of eventual independence for subject peoples. But time and realism demanded compromise, and the Allies wrung territorial and material concessions inconsistent with Wilson's model for an enduring peace. The result was a treaty marred by revenge that left an embittered Germany in its wake. Without Wilson's restraining voice, it would undoubtedly have been worse. The president knew he could not win every point, but he pinned his hopes on the league to right injustices and sustain the hope for peace. He would not compromise on the league. By the middle of February he was able to address a plenary session of the conference and announce the approval of the Covenant of the League of Nations. The conference then recessed so that Wilson could return to the United States to deal with congressional action passed in his absence.

Before departure, the president sent a message to the Congress requesting the courtesy that debate on the league be delayed until he arrived to respond. As he sailed the Atlantic, the Senate, unconcerned with courtesy, began the debate, opponents of American participation in the league taking the lead. Shortly before Wilson returned to Paris, Senator Lodge introduced the Republican Round Robin, a letter signed by thirty-nine members of the Senate expressing opposition to the League Covenant. The number was significant. If sustained, it was sufficient to block ratification. In Europe it appeared that the president's own legislature had repudiated him. Led by British Prime Minister Lloyd George and Clemenceau, the victors now redoubled their demands for booty, and Wilson fought them to exhaustion. In the first days of April he fell ill with the flu, suffering acute symptoms, including a high fever. There were, of course, no antibiotics then, and the world was suffering the great influenza pandemic which took more lives than the war. Though seriously ill, the president continued to negotiate from his sickbed, resisting the demands he knew would damage the Treaty of Versailles. Wilson almost single-handedly kept the treaty from being more severe than it was. The Germans, powerless now, could do no more than protest its terms. Late in June, in the Hall of Mirrors at Versailles, the treaty ending World War I was signed. Wilson was unhappy with the final result but still hoped American influence in a league of nations could soften its impact. He sailed for home determined to win the fight for ratification.

In the Senate, Lodge organized the opposition. In the partisan political culture of the day, Republicans, out of office since 1913, were loath to give a Democratic president a great victory so near the election of 1920. For all of his political life, Lodge was an internationalist who labored persistently to enlarge American power and its role in world affairs. He was convinced by Alfred Thayer Mahan's work on the influence of sea power that no nation could hope to be a great power without a great navy. With Theodore Roosevelt and others, Lodge had lobbied for increased naval forces since the 1880s. He wrote of the need for some kind of international organization, not unlike Wilson's league, years before the Fourteen Points were promulgated. But the league was Wilson's idea now, and, as he admitted to Roosevelt, Lodge hated Wilson. Lodge had been a scholar in earlier years, but Wilson became an academic star. He had enjoyed a very successful political career, but not the presidency. His daughter later confessed that reservations he claimed he had were a sham, that her father intended from the start to kill the league proposal. Now he was determined that Wilson's creation would not leave the Senate. The tactic he settled on was to claim the United States should join the league only if certain reservations were incorporated into the charter. On this matter the Senate divided into four groups. Forty-three Democrats and one Republican were ready to vote for the peace treaty as written. About a dozen Republicans and one Democrat, called the irreconcilables, opposed involvement in the league under any circumstances. Standing between these was a group of senators expressing mild reservations and another that joined Lodge in claiming they would vote for the peace treaty only if the league charter were amended to satisfy their strong reservations. As chairman of the Foreign Relations Committee, Lodge selected the ten majority members; he chose six irreconcilables. When the treaty was presented to the Senate, there was clear popular support for the league provision. Polls, newspaper editorials, and resolutions passed by over thirty state legislatures favored the president. Lodge calculated that public opinion might pressure the Senate to ratify; he needed time for opposition to build. The chairman ordered that the entire peace treaty be read aloud in the committee chamber, a pointless exercise that took two weeks with a clerk reading to a virtually empty room. This was followed by six weeks of hearings that accomplished little but delay.

At the center of concern was Article X of the league's charter by which signatories pledged to respect and defend the territorial integrity of member states. In theory, this collective security commitment was intended to deter any aggressor power, knowing it would face the united response of league members. Dissenters argued such a commitment might draw the United States into a conflict in which it had no vital interest and compromise American sovereignty. Lodge played on these fears and insisted on changes in the treaty. Wilson was adamant; there could be no amendments, which, he argued, would require new international negotiations.

As the summer wore on, support for the treaty eroded. Pacifist groups saw in it the potential for another war. Various immigrant groups were hostile when they learned that their former homelands had not been well served by treaty provisions. Domestic turmoil in 1919, strikes, race riots, and the first red scare, distracted public attention. At one point in late August, it seemed Wilson might accept "interpretative" reservations. A now confident Lodge was not interested. Fearing defeat, Wilson decided to take the issue to the people, hoping to revive public enthusiasm and pressure on the Senate. The strain of the peace conference and the weeks of struggle with the Senate showed on Wilson. Those close to him feared for his health, but he told the protesting Cary Grayson, his physician, he could not let his safety or his health outweigh his duty. On September 2, ignoring the fears of Grayson and a worried Edith, Wilson set out on a month-long speaking tour that was scheduled to take him to California and back. As the tour moved west, the press began to report larger and more enthusiastic crowds. It seemed for a time that the president might succeed in recovering public support. By the time the presidential train turned east again, leaving California, Wilson was pleased but obviously exhausted. Then, outside Pueblo on September 25, a stroke abruptly cut short the tour. Tumulty broke the news to the press that the president was ill and returning to Washington. In the days that followed, Wilson regained the use of his left arm and leg, but remained in pain. Back at the White House, on the morning of October 2, he collapsed and lost consciousness. When Grayson arrived, he determined the president was completely paralyzed on his left side. The cause had lost its champion.

While Wilson struggled to recover, the Senate continued to debate the treaty, with Republicans attempting to add a long list of reservations that Wilson insisted would cripple the treaty. He stubbornly resisted even when cabinet members and other Democrats suggested some compromise might be possible. The final vote on the treaty totaled forty-nine ayes and thirty-five nays, a majority in favor but seven votes short of the two-thirds of the Senate required for ratification. Tumulty recorded Wilson's reaction. The United States could have taken the leadership of the world, "and soon we shall be witnessing the tragedy of it all." He predicted, with terrible accuracy, another war within twenty-five years.

For weeks after his collapse, Edith allowed no one to see the president except medical aides. All through his illness, tears came easily to him. The strokes had not impaired his intellect, but his body's response to treatment was painfully slow. Bills from Congress were brought to him and signed or, as in the case of the Volstead Act, vetoed, but his name was scrawled in a way that ignited rumors about whether the signature was truly his. With Tumulty's help, essential government business continued, although Edith, who never liked him, limited even his access to the president. Bills became law without his signature, much mail went unanswered, including letters from House, from whom Wilson was now estranged. Edith received cabinet officers and told them what the president wanted done. Senator Albert Fall, later secretary of the interior and a culprit in the Teapot Dome scandal and the first American cabinet secretary to go to jail, railed in the Senate about "petticoat government." Wilson slowly regained some strength. By March 1920, he was able to go for a drive, and in April he presided haltingly over a cabinet meeting. In a judgment undoubtedly clouded by his illness, Wilson thought briefly of running for reelection, but that possibility was clearly past. When the election came, Wilson, against all informed opinion, insisted that Democrat James Cox would win because of the league issue. Warren Harding swept the election, and the prospect of the United States joining the league was dead. Happier news came in December, when Wilson learned he had been awarded the Nobel Peace Prize.

Preparing to leave office, the Wilsons purchased a house on S Street in Washington, where they led a very private life for the next three years. There were rides in the country, visits mostly from family and the closest friends, and very rare appearances in public. The president's vigor never returned; movement was halting, and serious writing was beyond reach. Late in January 1924, he grew very weak. The faithful Grayson again attended him. Wilson knew he was dying and referred to himself as broken machinery. The president lingered for a few days and died on February 3. As the country mourned, President Coolidge offered the help of the government for the funeral. The Senate suspended its business and named a funeral delegation that included Senator Lodge. Edith Wilson communicated to Lodge that his presence would not be welcome, describing the funeral as a private and not official event. On the day of the ceremony, Lodge's office announced that illness would prevent the senator's attendance.

After a solemn and moving service before an overflowing crowd at the National Cathedral in Washington, Woodrow Wilson was laid to rest. His remains lie in a bay on the south side of the nave of the cathedral.

1

On Religion

Early Religious Essays

During the summer of 1873, seventeen-year-old Woodrow Wilson experienced a powerful religious awakening, a conversion experience. Thereafter, what had been a matter of routine observance became a shaping force in his life. A committed Calvinist Presbyterian, Wilson saw God's hand in the destiny of men. During his sophomore year at Princeton, Wilson wrote a series of notes for publication in the Wilmington, North Carolina *Presbyterian.* In these brief essays, a young Wilson emphasized militant faith, duty, and orthodoxy, commending them to all and particularly to the statesman. "Christ's Army" embraced the language of warfare to describe the struggle of the Christian for righteousness against satanic temptations. There is little sympathy for the lukewarm here, for those with "folded arms," and a heavy emphasis on individual responsibility. Wilson allows "no middle course, no neutrality." The primacy of religion marked his advice to the statesman, who should be a Christian and a gentleman according to biblical standards. As he did throughout his religious writing, in "The Positive in Religion" Wilson held the Bible as the unfailing and essential guide toward uncompromising obedience of God's commands. The theme of struggle was again evident in "Christian Progress," in which he described progress in life as the progress of the soul. These essays appeared in issues of the *Presbyterian* published from August to December 1876.

Christ's Army

One of the favorite figures with sacred writers in their references to the inhabitants of this world is that of representing mankind as divided into two great armies. The field of battle is the world. From the abodes of righteousness advances the host of God's people under the leadership of Christ. Immediately behind the great Captain of Salvation come the veteran regiments of the soldiers of the cross with steady tread, their feet shod with the preparation of the Gospel of Peace, girt about with truth, their breast-plates of righteousness glittering beneath the bright rays of their Master's love, each one grasping the sword of the Spirit. Later come the younger troops all eager for the fray. From the opposite side of the field, advancing from the tents of wickedness, come the hosts of sin led by the Prince of Lies himself, riding upon death's horse. Behind him a mighty army marshaled by fiends under the dark banners of iniquity. The object of the warfare on the part of the first is to gain glory for their Great Leader as well as the best good of the conquered by persuading them to leave the ranks of the evil one and enlist under their great Redeemer; that of the other to entice as many as will listen to them to go with them by the alluring paths of worldliness to everlasting destruction. The foes meet—upon the great battle field of every-day life. With one sweeping charge the Christian band falls upon the overwhelming numbers of the Prince of Darkness and are met with a cloud of fiery darts from the hands of the Evil One. The battle waxes fierce. Some of the Christian leaders faithfully and eagerly press onward, rallying their broken ranks more vigorously upon every repulse. Others stand with folded arms, only now and then languidly issuing an order or encouraging their followers, and ever incurring the displeasure of their gracious Master by failing to carry out his orders or properly marshal and encourage his forces. The followers of the former, fight manfully, with only here and there a laggard or coward; those of the latter partake of the spirit of their leaders and do little towards gaining the battle. The hosts of sin, ever and anon charging, break through the weak portions of the opposing battalions, and then again quail before the uplifted swords of the Spirit. Here, the plumes streaming from the glistening helmets of salvation are seen among the retreating brigades of sin; there, Satan leads his followers to victory over the dead bodies of many a soldier of the Cross. Thus the battle of life progresses and the army of Saints ever gains ground under divine generalship; now slowly, now rapidly, driving before them with irresistible force the broken ranks of the enemy.

Surely in this great contest there is a part for every one, and each one will be made to render a strict account of his conduct on the day of battle. Will anyone hesitate as to the part he shall take in this conflict? Will anyone dare to enlist under the banners of the Prince of Lies, under whose dark folds he only marches to the darkness of hell? For there is no middle course, no neutrality. Each and every one must enlist either with the followers of Christ or those of Satan. How much more glorious to fight for the divine Prince of Peace, under whose glorious standards, whose shining folds are inscribed with *Love to God,* he will advance to sure victory and an everlasting reward! All professing Christians are, no doubt, more or less enthused by such thoughts as these, and hope that they can feel themselves soldiers in Christ's great army; but they do not *know* that they are such. Why should they not know? If they would be assured of the fact that their names are in the great Roll Book, let them fight for Christ. Ah! but how do this? As you would fight for any other cause. You know your enemies. They are evil thoughts, evil desires, evil associations. To avoid evil thoughts altogether is, of course, impossible. But whenever one of these subtle warriors of evil attacks you, do not fear to test your breastplate; wield with power the sword of the Spirit and with skill the shield of faith. Overcome evil desires, those powerful and ever present enemies, by constant watchfulness and with the strong weapon of prayer, and by cultivating those heavenly desires which are sure to root out the evil one. Avoid evil associations, evil companions. No one can make a good soldier who keeps company with the emissaries and friends of the enemy. These companions can be avoided by avoiding the places where they are to be found and seeking the more congenial and pleasant company of the good and upright, whose companionship will strengthen you in the struggle by making you feel that you are not alone in it. In every minor thing watch yourself and let no fiery dart enter your soul. One who thus faithfully does his duty and purifies himself in the smallest things has little to fear from the foe, and, if he withal leads others by his example and precept to do likewise, and fears not to warn the enemies of the Cross to turn from the error of their ways, he may rest assured that his name is enrolled among the soldiers of the Cross.

A Christian Statesman

There is a growing tendency to confine religion to certain walks of life. To the minister of the Gospel, it is of course considered essential; he must be pure in all his dealings, and his life must be a model of Christian consistency; his conversation must be free from all vanity, and he must in all things set his people a godly example. As the conditions and occupations of life differ more and more from those of the minister, and men's duties diverge more and more from the duties of a pastor, less and less of religion is generally considered necessary. Religion is thought out of place in the business office; it is thought wonderful for a soldier to be a true Christian; a lawyer is too often justified in a lie; and we would be tempted to smile at hearing of a praying statesman. This belief is in direct opposition to the Scripture views of religion. In the Bible a saving faith in Christ is represented as an ornament and help to the business man; an unfailing aid to the soldier who is fighting in a just cause; the true dignity and motive of the lawyer, causing him to uphold truth and justice, and always to strive to deal out the law with an equal hand; and above all, as the first requisite for a statesman, upon whom rests so heavy a responsibility, both to God and man. This last phase of the subject, is the one we wish to present to thoughtful minds by a very brief statement of the principles bearing upon it.

Although there are principles of duty to his party and to the cause he has espoused, still no statesman should allow party feeling to bias his opinions on any point which involves truth or falsehood, justice or injustice. He should search for truth with the full determination to find it, and in that search he should most earnestly seek aid from God, who will surely hold him responsible for the course he pursues. When he has arrived at what he is convinced is the truth, he should uphold that truth, both by word and deed, irrespective of party. In no case should he allow expediency or policy to influence him in the least, if the support of the measures which seem expedient or politic, involves a support of untruth or injustice. And let no statesman think that by silence or refraining from acting on any subject or question, he can escape responsibility. When he does not actively advocate truth, he advocates error. Those who are not for truth are against it. There is here no neutrality.

On the other hand, when the statesman has become convinced that he has arrived at the truth, and has before his mind the true view of his subject, he should be tolerant. He should have a becoming sense of his own weakness and liability to err, and, while supporting with the utmost vigor what he considers to be the truth, he should treat his opponents with due forbearance, and should avoid all personal attacks, which show a want of real argument, and which will only engender useless and unchristian enmity.

In short, let his faith be in Christ his Saviour, let his truth be truth which is in accordance with the Bible's standard, and let his whole conversation and life be such as becomes a Christian and, therefore, a gentleman.

The Positive in Religion

Decision of character has always been most justly admired. A man is universally praised for being earnest in whatsoever undertaking he engages, and we are even sometimes attracted to the character of one who is determined in the pursuit of evil, who seems to be wrapped up in his wicked calling. We find ourselves instinctively admiring the bandit or highwayman who dies courageously and who not only does not give any sign of repentance, but even maintains his innocence to the last. Up to modern times the Christian who was a Christian "not in word only but in deed and in truth" was much admired. In this age of ours there is a growing tendency to depreciate all positivism in religion. Men say that the harsh tenets and severe doctrines of our fathers should now be replaced by more loving principles and milder teachings—that we should be allowed to put our own interpretations upon the teachings of the Bible, and simply to follow the dictates each of his own conscience. Men are apt to style this so-called "harsh" Christianity of our fathers and of the early saints of the church puritanism, whereas it was the true Christianity in which alone safety rests and salvation is sure; the Christianity of which puritanism was the mockery. No one can conceive of a more lovely and gentle character than that of Christ, and yet no one ever enforced God's commands—the commands which are now called harsh—with more vigor. We are not misinterpreting the commands of the God of Love when we say that his every command is to be obeyed in every particular, and that his severest commands are not inconsistent with his attribute of love. In every instance of disobedience which the Bible has given for our warning and instruction, the offender has been punished for not obeying God's commands to the very letter, even when his pretexts and excuses were more plausible and just than those of modern free-thinkers. Nothing is more injurious than the efforts of some men to prove that the service of Mammon is perfectly consistent with the service of God, and that, when God says "ye cannot serve God and Mammon," he means that you can. The key to the whole gospel lies in this promise: "Who will render unto every man according to his deeds: to them who by patient continuance in well doing seek for glory and honor and immortality, eternal life." Can we think that we are conforming ourselves to the image of Christ while we are endeavoring to conform ourselves more and more to the image of the world? Can we think that we are continuing patient in well doing when we are making the actions of the world the criterion by which to judge of the propriety of our daily walk and conversation as Christians? No; he is not a Christian who is one outwardly, but he is a Christian who is one inwardly, whose praise is of God and not of man. Nor is this view of religion by any means a gloomy one. By carrying sour faces, throwing out texts of Scripture upon all occasions appropriate or inappropriate, by making religion thus an offensive thing, we offend God. A gloomy and despondent Christian is as strange a sight as a criminal mourning over a pardon, and is just about as sincere. When positivism again characterizes religion we are safe, and then only.

Christian Progress

Addison, in his thoughtful essay on the immateriality of the soul, has made use of this beautiful figure: "The soul considered with its Creator, is like one of those mathematical lines that may draw nearer to another to all eternity without a possibility of touching it: and can there be a thought so transporting as to consider ourselves in these perpetual approaches to Him, who is not only the standard of perfection but of happiness." In this essay, which forms one of the most pleasing numbers of the Spectator, this genial writer seems to view the soul in its relations to its creator, rather in a philosophical light than in the light of revelation, and in its more specially religious bearings. He takes a pleasing glance at the possibilities and noble resources of the soul, and views it as something which was meant for, and is capable of almost infinite development in power and virtue. To a thoughtful reader, however, he suggests many a thought pregnant with deep meaning. He suggests that approximation to the divine character which is possible to every Christian who molds his life after the perfect pattern with which our Lord has furnished us. But he does not seem to realize the difficulty which attends soul-progress. Turning to our Bibles we can study this subject by the aid of the light of inspired teachings. The Bible everywhere represents the Christian life as a progress, a progress of the soul. But, although it always speaks of the Christian's journey as a pleasant one, since it is the only road in which true happiness can be found, it never describes it as a path strewn with flowers, but rather as one attended with and obstructed by many difficulties. In order to advance, the Christian must needs strain every muscle. This strain, though necessary at all times, is not, of necessity irksome, as God's all-powerful arm is ever around us, and the darkness which surrounds us is seldom so dense as to shut out the radiance of the Almighty's loving smiles. We can conceive of no more constant or eager striver after perfection than the apostle Paul, and yet even he said: "Brethren, I count not myself to have apprehended: but this one thing I do, forgetting those things which are behind, and reaching unto those things which are before, I press toward the mark for the prize of the high calling of God in Christ Jesus." All through his epistles he expresses this same distrust of himself, and gives vent to fears, lest his carnal mind should gain the mastery. In one place he says: "But I keep under my body, and bring it into subjection: lest that by any means, when I have preached to others, I myself should be a castaway." If this mighty soul, whose chief and only aim was to "walk worthy of the high vocation wherewith he was called," was troubled by such fears as these, what should be the feeling of the listless, half-souled follower of Christ! As the followers of this mighty Prince of Light we are ever under the stern necessity of fighting for our own safety, as well as the general advance of Christian doctrine. He who pretends to fight under the great banner of Love, should rejoice that there is no armor for his back, that to retreat is death, and should thus go forward with an eagerness and will which no slight cause can turn from their object.

The Clergyman and the State

At the General Theological Seminary in New York in April 1910, Wilson offered a meditation on religion and politics. As his own conversion to progressivism in politics advanced, he saw the need for religion to supply a "clear standard of moral judgement" to political thought. The Church, he thought should set the standard of behavior for statesmen and offer a guide for reform. In this he was not alone; the Social Gospel was one of the strong roots of the Progressive movement, and religious influence in American reform movements had a long history. The new demands of modern life, he thought, dictated an important role for the Church. Wilson wrote of "the Church" here in the broadest sense, embracing both Protestant and Catholic in a kind of ecumenical appeal for all clergymen to stand in judgment and to hold society to the highest moral standards. He was not receptive, however, to Christian Socialism, a significant movement among some American churches during the Progressive era. Wilson's thoughts were printed in *The New York Churchman.*

It is evident to us all that within the past few years there has been an extraordinary awakening in civic consciousness, and, beyond this, an extraordinary awakening of the public mind with relation to the moral values involved in our national life. We are now witnessing the dawn of a day when there will be a universal revaluation of men and of affairs. There is no mistaking the present dissolution of political parties; no mistaking the fact that you cannot restore the enthusiasm of our existing parties by turning backward in any respect and merely recalling the formulas, or shouting the slogans, of past campaigns and past transactions. The Nation is not looking over its shoulder, nor acting in retrospect; it has its eyes on the future.

And because of this, the Nation has to grapple, on an extraordinary scale, with the newness of the day in which we live. The elements of our modern life are so new that we are bewildered when we try to form moral judgments regarding them. For example, how difficult it is now to assess an individual, in view of the fact that he does not now act as an integer, but as merely a fraction of modern society, inextricably associated with others in the conduct of business, and dominated by corporate responsibility. It is impossible that he should exercise, except within a very narrow circle, independent judgment. And therefore the old forms of moral responsibility we find it very difficult to apply. For, in order that we should be morally responsible, there must be freedom of individual choice, and that is so much circumscribed, narrowed, and confined by the divisions of modern life that we are groping to find a new basis, a new standard, and a new guide of responsibility, by which we shall walk, and to which we may hold our consciences square.

☆ ☆ ☆

Every pulse ought to be quickened by such an age; and it is in the guidance of such a day that the clergyman's obligations lie. Every age has had its own misgivings about the Church. The prevailing temptation, the persistent temptation of the Church, is to ally itself with certain social interests. The temptation has been not to be democratic in its organization, in its sympathies, in its judgments.

In looking back through the history of political society, I have often been struck by the circumstance that the polities of the middle ages would certainly have broken down for lack of administrative capacity if it had not been for the Roman Catholic Church. It supplied administrative ability to all the chancelleries of Europe during that long period when Europe was aristocratic, and not democratic. For the Church in that period was democratic in that it had its rootage in the common people. No peasant was so humble that he could not become a priest; no priest so obscure that he might not rise to be the Pope of Christendom. All sources of power were supplied in the organization of the Church. The political capacity of Europe renewed itself constantly by drawing upon that all-inclusive institution. While aristocracy was decaying, the people were feeding fresh blood into the great Church.

So long as the Church—any Church—retains this conception, keeps the sources of its strength open, it will not only serve itself, but will serve society as perhaps no other organization could conceive of serving. It will then keep true to its fundamental conception, the fundamental conception of Christianity: that there is no difference between man and man in respect to his relationship to his God. We do not arrange the pews of our churches on this principle. We do not arrange the worship of our churches on this principle; and in proportion as we do not, we lose, and deserve to lose, the confidence of the great mass of the people, who are led by our practices to believe that Christianity is not for the obscure, but for the rich and prosperous and contented.

It seems to me perfectly clear that an extraordinary opportunity is afforded by the present day to the Church; to the whole Church, whether Protestant or Catholic, an opportunity to supply what society is looking for; that is, a clear standard of moral measurement, a standard of revaluation, a standard of re-assessment, of men and affairs.

When I ask myself how the Church is going to do this, the first thing that is apparent is that the Church must do it through the example of her ministers. They must devote themselves to those ideals which have no necessary connection with any form or convention of society whatever, but which take each human soul and make it over and weigh it in the scales of revelation. I have known a good many ministers in my day who were very careful of the social connections they formed. I have known a great many who did not afford to society an example of that general, universal sympathy and contact with all sorts and conditions of men which was afforded by our Lord and Master Himself, who did not make any social distinctions in His choice of, associates. I have not seen the ministers of our churches, as a rule, follow His example in that respect.

I have, it is true, seen them do, under a sudden and temporary impulse, things which they supposed were equivalent to this. For instance, I have known ministers to frequent places where they ought not to go, and where no self-respecting man ought to go, under the impression, apparently, that what Christ allied Himself with was places, not human souls. What He sought out was the individual spirit, not its environment. It is not necessary to go to saloons in order to make one's self the friend of a man who drinks. The best way to serve such a man is not to find him in such surroundings, but to lead him into better; not to find him there, but to draw him thence, by counsel and sympathy.

☆ ☆ ☆

The Church can in its definite teaching contribute to the enlightenment and guidance of our, for the time being, bewildered society. The Church ought to expound the difference between individual responsibility and corporate responsibility. The Church ought to discover the individual in modem society. The great temptation to every man in business affairs in our day is that he can so easily run to covert in some organization. That is the great difficulty also, with our political organizations. We have so divided up responsibility that we cannot put our finger on the man who ought to be held responsible. Tom Nast, the famous cartoonist, drew a picture, you remember, of the Tweed Ring as a circle of men, each pointing his thumb to his neighbor and saying, "Twan't me." The imperative necessity of politics is to obtain a "Tis you!" form of government. The Church ought to assist society to pick out individuals. It ought to show, in its administration and discipline, that it will not tolerate for a moment men who have been responsible for demoralizing our corporate life.

I dare say every man who has aided to demoralize society finds refuge and harborage in some Church; and so long as the Church harbors these men, it cannot afford society the standard for which society longs. I mean that in the case of all such individuals the Church should make them realize that absolute reformation is the price of their continuing to consort with the members of the Church. Full opportunity to repent, but the absolute obligation of reformation must be the program of regeneration, an absolute unhesitating, uncompromising analysis of what it is that they have done, and what they have imperilled and then absolute insistence that they square their conduct with the standards of the Church. They should be dealt with with sympathy and tenderness, but given no absolution. If the Church with any degree of unanimity should undertake this, the dockets of our courts would not be so full. It would not be necessary to set the majesty of the law in operation, if the majesty of opinion were first set in operation. Men are not afraid of the penalties of the law; but men are afraid of the look into the accusing eyes of their friends and acquaintances. The most terrible punishments are spiritual punishments; the heart-breaking thing is that the people who trusted you have ceased to trust you, and that you are not free of their company on any terms except those which show utter repentance. What rules the heart is what molds society; and the standards of opinion are the standards of private conduct.

Then it seems to me that the Church could, in the administration of all its affairs, in handling its congregations, in the conduct of its charitable work, in all those things in which it reaches out to touch and raise society, show to society that it is acting upon unworldly standards, and not upon worldly ones; that it does not matter to it whether it have properly appointed churches and parish houses or not; that the work will go on through its love of men whether the proper instrumentalities be afforded it or not; and that it will be conducted upon an absolutely democratic principle which distinguishes man from man by his spiritual, and not by his social position.

The Church ought to make itself in every respect a society of mutual self-sacrifice and self-abnegation; and then it will have afforded society that standard of which it is in search. I know, to my cost, that society is in search of standards; because what society now wants more than anything else is disinterested advice. It is resorting to the colleges for this sort of advice. It takes it for granted that a college teacher is not a self-seeking person, or he would not have been foolish enough to go into an underpaid profession. It believes that he is likely to know what he is talking about, and can be counted upon to speak it, because presumably free from those obstacles to candor which so embarrass the lips of other men. So college professors are appealed to, here, there and everywhere; not because they are specially able, but because they at least are supposed to be disinterested. It is as if society were now calling upon the colleges to do what it ought to call upon the Church to do. It ought to be a matter of course that the priest, the minister, has devoted himself to unworldly objects, and that he can be counted on to speak his mind without fear of man, or any other fear except to transgress the law of God.

The attitude of ministers to the State, if what I have been saying is even in part true, is a matter susceptible of the most rigid analysis. The minister ought to be an instrument of judgment, with motives not secular but religious; who conceives in his mind those reforms which are based upon the statutes of morality; who tries to draw society together by a new motive which is not the motive of the economist or of the politician, but the motive of the profoundly religious man.

"Christian Socialism" I believe to be a contradiction in terms. The motives of the pure Socialist are clearly Christian motives; but the moment you translate Socialism into a definite program, into which you are going to force men by a universal social compulsion, it ceases to be a spiritual program. Socialism as a program of organization is the negation of Socialism as a body of motives. I can understand Christian anarchism; for Christian anarchism means a state of society where no government will be needed, because each man will live within the law of an enlightened and purified conscience. But "Christian Socialists" are contending that a certain political, material and economic program will be the best for all spiritual interests. If true, it would be the millennium. I understand all descriptions of the millennium to be descriptions of that Christian *anarchism* in which every man will be a law unto himself, but every man's will

will be purified and rectified by being centered not upon himself, but upon Christ; anarchism not meaning disorder, but that broadest of all order which is based on self-sacrifice, charity and friendship. The program of the minister, therefore, is a program of devotion to things always outside of himself, never centered upon himself.

☆ ☆ ☆

It is the minister's first vocation so to find himself, and to devote himself to a common interest, which may or may not be his own private or selfish interest. It is the duty of every priest to do what it is the duty of the whole Church to do, to judge other men, with love but without compromise of moral standards; uncompromisingly to assess what they have done, without ceasing to love them for having done it; so as to let no man escape from full reckoning of his conduct. That is a task too great for the courage of most ministers. I am not criticizing. It is the hardest thing in the world to do. I am not saying for a moment that I would have the grace to do it. But that is one reason why I have kept out of the ministry.

To pass further than that the minister ought to make those with whom he is dealing realize that he holds the integrity of souls higher than any other kind of prosperity; higher than fortune, wealth, social position—than any other kind of success. I believe as the profoundest philosophy in the world, that only integrity can bring salvation or satisfaction; can bring happiness; that no amount of fortune can, in a man's own consciousness, atone for a lost integrity of the soul. Beyond question, a minister lets down all the levels of morality in the would by compromising with his own or any other man's conscience. The moral levels of the world are to be maintained by him, or they will collapse with a general subsidence of all that is steadfast in the universe. If you are going to admit fear into you calculations, then the world is infinitely imperilled. The Church is the mentor of righteousness, and the minister must be the exemplar of righteousness.

The central force that makes for righteousness is the fountain of it all. The Church, when it uncovers those waters which alone can quench the thirst of mankind, will prove to have been the source of all the life-giving influences that kept weary men alive. For she is the guardian of that sure belief that there are things beyond this life, when we shall see face to face, shall know as we are known.

The Bible and Progress

On a national tour in anticipation of the 1912 election year, Wilson stopped in Denver, Colorado, on May 7, 1911, to address a religious meeting marking the three-hundredth anniversary of the publication of the King James Bible. Twelve thousand people heard his address tying the guidance of Scripture to personal and civic progress and to political reform. He made an unequivocal association of Christianity and the nation and linked American destiny to the guidance of Scripture. Progress, he argued, could not be divorced from religion, and the Bible should serve as a kind of handbook for reform and human progress. It seems clear that he believed political action was a kind of religious vocation and required religious guidance and inspiration. Wilson revealed an intimacy with the Bible that daily readings throughout his life had produced. The speech offered a clear explication of Wilson's powerful religious convictions on the eve of his presidency.

The thought that entered my mind first as I came into this great room this evening framed itself in a question—Why should this great body of people have come together upon this solemn night? There is nothing here to be seen. There is nothing delectable here to be heard. Why should you run together in a great host when all that is to be spoken of is the history of a familiar book?

But as I have sat and looked upon this great body of people I have thought of the very suitable circumstance that here upon the platform sat a little group of ministers of the gospel lost in this great throng.

I say the "suitable circumstance," for I come here tonight to speak of the Bible as the book of the people, not the book of the minister of the gospel, not the special book of the priest from which to set forth some occult, unknown doctrine withheld from the common understanding of men, but a great book of revelation, the people's book of revelation. For it seems to me that the Bible has revealed the people to themselves. I wonder how many persons in this great audience realize the significance for English-speaking peoples of the translation of the Bible into the English tongue. Up to the time of the translation of the Bible into English, it was a book for long ages withheld from the perusal of the peoples of other languages and of other tongues, and not a little of the history of liberty lies in the circumstance that the moving sentences of this book were made familiar to the ears and the understanding of those peoples who have led mankind in exhibiting the forms of government and the impulses of reform which have made for freedom and for self-government among mankind.

For this is a book which reveals men unto themselves, not as creatures in bondage, not as men under human authority, not as those bidden to take counsel and command of any human source. It reveals every man to himself as a distinct moral agent, responsible not to men, not even to those men whom he has put over him in authority, but responsible through his own conscience to his Lord and Maker. Whenever a man sees this vision he stands up a free man, whatever may be the government under which he lives, if he sees beyond the circumstances of his own life. . . .

Our present life, ladies and gentlemen, is a very imperfect and disappointing thing. We do not judge our own conduct in the privacy of our own closets by the standard of expediency by which we are daily and hourly governed. We know that there is a standard set for us in the heavens, a standard revealed to us in this book which is the fixed and eternal standard by which we judge ourselves, and as we read this book it seems to us that the pages of our own hearts are laid open before us for our own perusal. This is the people's book of revelation, revelation of themselves not alone, but revelation of life and of peace. You know that human life is a constant struggle. For a man who has lost the sense of struggle, life has ceased.

☆ ☆ ☆

No man can sit down and withhold his hands from the warfare against wrong and get peace out of his acquiescence. The most solid and satisfying peace is that which comes from this constant spiritual warfare, and there are times in the history of nations when they must take up the crude instruments of bloodshed in order to vindicate spiritual conceptions. For liberty is a spiritual conception, and when men take up arms to set other men free, there is something sacred and holy in the warfare. I will not cry "Peace" so long as there is sin and wrong in the world. And this great book does not teach any doctrine of peace so long as there is sin to be combated and overcome in one's own heart and in the great moving force of human society.

And so it seems to me that we must look upon the Bible as the great charter of the human soul, as the "Magna Charta" of the human soul. You know the interesting circumstances which gave rise to the Magna Charta. You know the moving scene that was enacted upon the heath at Runnymede. You know how the barons of England, representing the people of England, for they consciously represented the people of England, met upon that historic spot and parleyed with John, the king. They said: "We will come to terms with you here." They said: "There are certain inalienable rights of English-speaking men which you must observe. They are not given by you, they cannot be taken away by you. Sign your name here to this parchment upon which these rights are written and we are your subjects. Refuse to put your name to this document and we are your sworn enemies. Here are our swords to prove it."

The franchise of human liberty made the basis of a bargain with a king! There are kings upon the pages of Scripture, but do you think of any king in Scripture as anything else than a mere man? There was the great king David, of a line blessed because the line from which should spring our Lord and Savior, a man marked in the history of mankind as the chosen instrument of God to do justice and exalt righteousness in the people.

But what does this Bible do for David? Does it utter eulogies upon him? Does it conceal his faults and magnify his virtues? Does it set him up as a great statesman [as he] would be set up in a modern biography? No, the book in which his annals are written strips the mask from David, strips every shred of counterfeit and concealment from him and shows him as, indeed, an instrument of God, but a sinful and selfish man, and the verdict of the Bible is that David, like other men, was one day to stand naked before the judgment seat of God and be judged not as a king, but as a man. Isn't this the book of the people? Is there any man in this Holy Scripture who is exempted from the common standard and judgment? How these pages teem with the masses of mankind! Are these the annals of the great? These are the annals of the people, of the common run of men.

The New Testament is the history of the life and the testimony of common men who rallied to the fellowship of Jesus Christ and who by their faith and preaching remade a world that was under the thrall of the Roman army. This is the history of the triumph of the human spirit, in the persons of humble men. And how many sorts of men march across the pages, how infinite is the variety of human circumstance and of human dealings and of human heroism and love! Is this a picture of extraordinary things? This is a picture of the common life of mankind. It is a mirror held up for men's hearts, and it is in this mirror that we marvel to see ourselves portrayed. How like to the Scripture is all great literature! What is it that entrances us when we read or witness a play of Shakespeare? It is the consciousness that this man, this all-observing mind, saw men of every cast and kind as they were in their habits as they lived. And as passage succeeds passage we seem to see the characters of ourselves and our friends portrayed by this ancient writer, and a play of Shakespeare is just as modern today as upon the day it was penned and first enacted. And the Bible is without age or date or time. It is a picture of the human heart displayed for all ages and for all sorts and conditions of men. Moreover, the Bible does what is so invaluable in human life, it classifies moral values. It apprizes us that men are not judged according to their wits, but according to their characters, that the test of every man's reputation is his truthfulness, his squaring his conduct with the standards that he knew to be the standards of purity and rectitude.

How many a man we appraise, ladies and gentlemen, as great today, whom we do not admire as noble! A man may have great power and small character. And the sweet praise of mankind lies not in their admiration of the smartness with which the thing was accomplished, but in that lingering love which apprizes men that one of their fellows has gone out of life to his own reckoning, where he is sure of the blessed verdict, "Well done, good and faithful servant."

☆ ☆ ☆

Let every man pray that he may in some true sense be a soldier of fortune, that he may have the good fortune to spend his energies and his life in the service of his fellow men in order that he may die to be recorded upon the rolls of those who have not thought of themselves but have thought of those whom they served. Isn't this the lesson of our Lord and Savior Jesus Christ? Am I not reminding you of these common judgments of our life, simply expounding to you this book of revelation, this book which reveals the Common man to himself, which strips life of its disguises and its pretenses and elevates those standards by which alone true greatness and true strength and true valor are assessed?

Do you wonder, therefore, that when I was asked what my theme this evening would be I said it would be "The Bible *and* Progress"? We do not judge progress by material standards. America is not ahead of the other nations of the world because she is rich. Nothing makes America great except her thoughts, except her ideals, except her acceptance of those standards of judgment which are written large upon these pages of revelation. America has all along claimed the distinction of setting this example to the civilized world, that men were to think of one another, that governments were to be set up for the service of the people, that men were to be judged by these moral standards which pay no regard to rank or birth or conditions, but which assess every man according to his single and individual value. That is the meaning of this charter of the human soul. This is the standard by which men and nations have more and more come to be judged. And so, reform has consisted in nothing more nor less than this: in trying to conform actual conditions, in trying to square actual laws with the right judgments of human conduct and human liberty.

That is the reason that the Bible has stood at the back of progress. That is the reason that reform has come, not from the top but from the bottom. If you are ever tempted to let a government reform itself, I ask you to look back in the pages of history and find me a government that reformed itself. If you are ever tempted to let a party attempt to reform itself, I ask you to find a party that ever reformed itself.

A tree is not nourished by its bloom and by its fruit. It is nourished by its roots, which are down deep in the common and hidden soil, and every process of purification and rectification comes from the bottom, not from the top. It comes from the masses of struggling human beings. It comes from the instinctive efforts of millions of human hearts trying to beat their way up into the light and into the hope of the future.

Parties are reformed and governments are corrected by the impulses coming out of the hearts of those who never exercised authority and never organized parties. Those are the sources of strength, and I pray God that these sources may never cease to be spiritualized by the immortal subjections of these words of inspiration of the Bible.

If any statesman sunk in the practices which debase a nation will but read this single book he will go to his prayers abashed. Do you not realize, ladies and gentlemen, that there is a whole literature in the Bible? It is not one book, but a score of books. Do you realize what literature is? I am sometimes sorry to see the great classics of our English literature used in the schools as textbooks, because I am afraid that little children may gain the impression that these are formal lessons to be learned. There is no great book in any language, ladies and gentlemen, that is not the spontaneous outpouring of some great mind or the cry of some great heart. And the reason that poetry moves us more than prose does is that it is the rhythmic and passionate voice of some great spirit that has seen more than his fellow men can see.

I have found more true politics in the poets of the English-speaking race than I have ever found in all the formal treatises on political science. There is more of the spirit of our own institutions in a few lines of Tennyson than in all the text-books on governments put together:

"A nation still, the rulers and the ruled,
Some sense of duty, something of a faith
Some reverence for the laws ourselves have made,
Some patient force to change them when we will,
Some civic manhood firm against the crowd."

Can you find summed up the manly self-helping spirit of Saxon liberty anywhere better than in those few lines? Men afraid of nobody, afraid of nothing but their own passions, on guard against being caught unaware by their own sudden impulses and so getting their grapple upon life in firm-set institutions, some reverence for the laws they themselves have made, some patience, not passionate force, to change them when they will, some civic manhood firm against the crowd. Literature, ladies and gentlemen, is a revelation of the human spirit, and within the covers of this one book is a whole lot of literature, prose and poetry , history and rhapsody, the sober narration and the ecstasy of human excitement, things that ring in one's ears like songs never to be forgotten. And so I say, let us never forget that these deep sources, these wells of inspiration, must always be our sources of refreshment and of renewal. Then no man can put unjust power upon us. We shall live in that chartered liberty in which a man sees the things unseen, in which he knows that he is bound for a country in which there are no questions mooted any longer of right or wrong.

Can you imagine a man who did not believe these words, who did not believe in the future life, standing up and doing what has been the heart and center of liberty always, standing up before the king himself and saying, "Sir, you have sinned and done wrong in the sight of God and I am his messenger of judgment to pronounce upon you the condemnation of Almighty God. You may silence me, you may send me to my reckoning with my Maker, but you cannot silence or reverse the judgment." That is what a man feels whose faith is rooted in the Bible. And the man whose faith is rooted in the Bible knows that reform can not be stayed, that the finger of God that moves upon the face of the nations is against every man that plots the nation's downfall or the people's deceit; that these men are simply groping and staggering in their ignorance to a fearful day of judgment and that whether one generation witnesses it or not, the glad day of revelation and of freedom will come in which men will sing by the host of the coming of the Lord in His glory, and all of those will be forgotten, those little, scheming, contemptible creatures that forgot the image of God and tried to frame men according to the image of the Evil One.

You may remember that allegorical narrative in the Old Testament of those who searched through one cavern after another, cutting the holes in the walls and going into the secret places, where all sorts of noisome things were worshiped. Men do not dare to let the sun shine in upon such things and upon such occupations and worships. And so I say there will be no halt to the great movement of the armies of reform until men forget their God, until they forget this charter of their liberty. Let no man suppose that progress can be divorced from religion, or that there is any other platform for the ministers of reform than the platform written in the utterances of our Lord and Savior.

America was born a Christian nation. America was born to exemplify that devotion to the elements of righteousness which are derived from the revelations of Holy Scripture.

Ladies and gentlemen, I have a very simple thing to ask of you. I ask of every man and woman in this audience that from this night on they will realize that part of the destiny of America lies in their daily perusal of this great book of revelations, that if they would see America free and pure they will make their own spirits free and pure by this baptism of the Holy Scripture.

2

Biographical Sketches

William Earl Chatham

Wilson won an essay prize with this sketch of William Pitt (1707–78) in the October 1878 edition of the *Nassau Literary Magazine.* An earlier effort on Bismarck appeared in 1877 but failed to take the prize. Written while he was a senior at Princeton, the essay displays a confident command of language and maturity of style untypical in an undergraduate. Pitt was the great leader who did much to engineer the British victory over France in the Seven Years War, hugely expanding the size of the empire. Unpopular with the new king, George III, he was forced to resign on the eve of victory and was fiercely critical of the Treaty of Paris in 1863. He thought the imposition of the Stamp Act on the American colonies was a mistake, and as trouble with the colonies mounted, he unsuccessfully urged a policy of conciliation. This character sketch is little concerned with historical events, but delivers intelligent insights about and undisguised admiration for its subject. Wilson especially admired those qualities of resolute will and pursuit of high goals which, indeed, would mark Wilson's own career. The essay also balances his praise for Pitt with realistic assessment of his flaws of character, especially pride and arrogance. An admirer of British Prime Minister William Gladstone, Wilson apparently could not resist the opportunity here for a swipe at his rival, Benjamin Disraeli.

Beneath Westminster Abbey's arched roof, with commanding mien, haughty features, and gesture of authority, stands the statue Chatham. Visitors to the venerable oɪd church may see in the hard lines of the cold marble the lifeless yet life-like reproduction of the striking form of the great statesman; but to all who have learned, in the pages of history, to comprehend the character and work of Chatham, this piece of stone must seem to fall very far short of bringing before their imaginations the real person of the Great Commoner. A skillful sculptor might trace the lines of cunning policy and of secret scheming, the habitual air of authority upon the face of a Metternich, and we would recognize the man himself in his effigy; he might chisel the marks of cruel purpose, of uncurbed and defiant ambition, of pitiless despotism upon the spare visage of a Richelieu and we could wish for no better reminder of the man; he might preserve the deep-cut wrinkles that spoke of thought, the firmly-set mouth that indicated an inflexible determination, upon the open countenance of a Hampden; but the marble must have the warmth of life infused into it by the hand of God before it could resemble the dwelling of Chatham's high-wrought, passionate, many-sided nature.

It is indeed the diversity of his genius which first strikes us as we look back to the elder Pitt. In him consummate powers kept company with small weaknesses, strong wisdom stood side by side with weak folly, truthfulness and earnestness were contrasted with affectation and pedantry. To the careless student of history Pitt's character, made up as it was of qualities the very opposites of each other, might at first seem to have been inconsistent with itself. But it was a character of great power, because in reality of singular unity. His many talents, his capacity for good, his capacity for evil, his wisdom, his folly, his strength, his weakness, apparently at war among themselves, were reconciled and brought into harmony by the concentrating power of strong convictions. Prior to a thoughtful investigation of the history of his times, however, there would seem to be some cause for surprise that such a man as Pitt should have risen to the head of the state when he did; for few men's tempers ever clashed more roughly with their surroundings, ever sympathized less with the tastes and tendencies of the day, than did the temper of the great Commoner. Indeed he harmonized with his age in nothing but in affectation, and even his affectation had an earnestness and a frankness about it which did not belong to the all-pervading affectation of the society around him. He was in everything enthusiastically earnest, and his age laughed at earnestness; he was vehement, and his age affected coldness and indifference; he was sternly virtuous, scorning corruption, and his age was skeptical of virtue, nursing corruption; he had eager, burning beliefs and was actuated by a warm love for principle, and his age delighted in doubtings and questionings, was guided by no principle save that of expediency; he was used constantly and confidently to appeal to the higher, brighter, purer instincts of human nature, and his age doubted the existence of any such instincts, nay, even argued from its own experience that all human nature was low and pulseless. He stood, in fact, almost alone—above the masses who, from sheer admiration, supported him, and in their enthusiasm idolized him; separated by all his tastes and sympathies from those classes of society with which he was naturally thrown by virtue of his high public station.

That a man thus isolated from his fellows should wield undisputed power over them seems at first beyond explanation. But as we study his character more closely the mystery which hangs around his ability to exercise unquestioned authority over those who were entirely out of sympathy with him clears rapidly away. The elements of his power are not far to seek. They lay almost altogether within himself. Outwardly he was every inch a leader. Every attitude, every gesture, each play of feature, each tone of voice bore witness of a will that must be master. And men were speedily convinced of the depth and strength of the nature thus outwardly shadowed forth. They bowed to a will which itself bent to no obstacle; they feared, even while they sneered at, the personal purity which gave such a keen edge to his attacks upon corrupt opponents. Their hearts instinctively warmed toward a man whose patriotism was so real. Selfish policies fell beneath the onsets of a man whose great intellect gave such resistless force to the convictions he so boldly avowed.

Pitt's nature was so passionate as to be almost tragic, rendering his career an essentially dramatic one. Passion indeed was the ground-work of his character; and because, led on by ardor, he trod, steadily onward toward the ends he had marked out for himself, the name of Chatham has become to Englishmen a synonym of the highest statesmanship. And certainly, if we conceive of statesmanship as being that resolute and vigorous advance towards the realization of high, definite, and consistent aims which issues from the unreserved devotion of a strong intellect to the service of the state and to the solution of all the multiform problems of public policy, Pitt's statesmanship was of the highest order. His devotion to his country's service was as intense as it was entire; and the intellect whose every power he brought to bear upon the direction of her affairs compassed its duty with a vigor commensurate with its colossal proportions. To enquire why Pitt so completely identified himself with the fortunes of England would be an invidious task. The motives which prompt to great deeds are often as hidden as the deeds themselves are conspicuous. Pitt's self-love was boundless, and small men can, therefore, see nothing in his high aims but an inordinate desire to gratify ambition, to exalt self. But to those who believe that there is some nobility in human nature, and especially to those who can see how small a part of his real character Pitt's egotism constituted his ardent, absorbing patriotism is sufficient cause for the belief that there was much of true disinterestedness in his great career.

Each quality of Pitt's mind bespoke the ardor of his nature. Even his affectation and his pedantry, like his love and determination and pride, had caught the hue of passion. It was impossible for such a man to espouse any cause with coldness. With him every act must be an act of warm enthusiasm. His mind was strong and clear, his will was unswerving, his convictions were uncompromising, his imagination was powerful enough to invest all plans of national policy with a poetic charm, his confidence in himself was implicit, his love for his country was real and intense. Of course, then, he entered into the realities of public life with all the vigor of a large and earnest soul, with all the keen interest imparted by a vivid imagination, and it is not strange that his policy was well-defined and determined, straightforward and brilliant. The startling, far-reaching results of his administration, molding the future history of the world, were such as appealed to the admiration and won the approbation of a people the very marrow of whose nature is a spirit of adventure, enterprise, conquest. What could be more impressive than a policy which, in winning India for the English Crown, built a great empire in the far East; in driving the French from America, made our great republic a possibility in the far West; and, in lending constant and effective aid to Prussia's great Frederick, prepared the destiny of her greater Bismarck? Such having been the work of the elder Pitt, Englishmen may justly regard him as high among the greatest statesmen of a great race. And yet his errors were many and grave. They were, however, such as are incident upon a policy whose authors seek, with whole-souled ardor, with keen enthusiasm, to carry out great principles in all their integrity. Such a policy is always admirable in the abstract, but, in practice, is seldom safe. In a free government, founded upon public opinion, the governmental machinery is so nicely balanced, opposite parties, opposing forces of thought, generally exercise powers so nearly equal, that great principles must be worked out cautiously, step by step, seldom attaining triumphant ascendency by a course of uninterrupted success—by only a few bold and rapid strokes. Public opinion must not be out-stripped, but kept pace with. Time, indeed, has traced out to their end all the greater lines of policy which, in their beginnings, bore indications of the strokes of Pitt's decided hand. But he had lain in his grave many years before some of the most prominent measures which he had advocated were carried out in their fulness; and during his lifetime, while he was still a power in the state, even his towering influence fell powerless when he sought to force his country to follow the paths of foreign policy which he had cleared for her, and which he had shown to be the only roads to honor and safety. The enormous strain which war had brought upon the Treasury was thought to be cause for serious alarm; and the reaction thus brought about, seconded by the sinister influence of an unscrupulous king, thrust a ruinous peace upon the country. Pitt left the Cabinet to be re-stricken by the disease which finally sapped the strength of his imperial intellect. His life drew rapidly toward its close; but he had done enough to set a seal to his fame—enough to mark *that* as the highest type of statesmanship which, with conscientious purity, by an undeviating course, with cool judgment and prompt determination, with a bright hope and a passionate patriotism, overpowering opposition, subordinating party to national interests, constantly and confidently seeks to build a great policy upon broad, deep, homogeneous principles. Such, with all its small follies and minor inconsistencies, despite disfiguring arrogance and overbearing pride, was the statesmanship of William Pitt.

If, because his statesmanship was whole-souled and dazzlingly successful, we do not wonder that William Pitt has been considered worthy of a place among the very first of English statesmen, still less can we be surprised that he has been called the first of Parliamentary orators. If the passionate intensity which entered so largely into the texture of his character lent so much of force, so much brilliant boldness, to his plans of administration, what masterly power must it have imparted to his oratory! Passion is the pith of eloquence. But it alone cannot make the consummate orator; for while it gives strength, it may be rugged and cumbersome. Imagination must be present to give it wings and a graceful flight. And one of the most striking features of Pitt's mind was "a poetic imaginativeness" which set his words fairly aglow with beauty. While vivid passion blazed out in his orations, the reality of the convictions he so fearlessly uttered hid the exaggeration of his diction transfiguring all that was bombastic and ungraceful, and clothing with real grace his theatrical airs. Unfortunately our only trustworthy information concerning his oratorical powers comes from meager tradition. Those who had seen his noble figure in striking action, his eagle eye alight with the thoughts that stirred within him have left us only some scanty outlines of his more brilliant thoughts and most memorable flights of rhetoric. The main bodies of all his great speeches, those thoughts which constituted the warp and woof of his masterly statements of political truths and his moving appeals in behalf of a broad, patriotic, and consistent state policy are irretrievably lost to us. But, aside from the unanimous testimony of his contemporaries, the fragmentary utterances which we know to have fallen from his own lips bear ample witness to his unrivaled powers, being laden, even for us, with much of their old potency. Even upon the printed page, the echo of his impassioned accents seems yet to linger about his words. Although in his youthful studies of Demosthenes he had failed to catch the great Athenian's purity of style, he recognized, as the movings of a kindred spirit, his burning vehemence. Athens had at times responded as one man to the rapid, vehement, cogent sentences of Demosthenes; the British Parliament, the English nation, harkened with glad eagerness to the organ tones of Pitt's eloquence, and dared not disobey.

William Pitt was the second of that long line of great commoners of which gifted, wise, unscrupulous Robert Walpole was the first, and which has molded English policy down to the day of shrewd, fickle, brilliant, plausible Benjamin Disraeli. In one respect Pitt resembled the now exalted Jew: he had an unhesitating, almost boundless confidence in himself, in the wisdom of his own aims. But Beaconsfield loves and has confidence in himself alone; Pitt loved and trusted the English people as well—for he was himself an Englishman!

With Pitt's acceptance of an earldom not only his official power but also much of his innate greatness passed away. Disease had unmanned him, and he refused to aid his country at a time of sorest need, thus, in a moment of folly, well nigh undoing the great work of a memorable lifetime. William Pitt was a noble statesman; the Earl of Chatham was a noble ruin. But in his death we catch a faint glimmer of his old manhood. Under the deepening shadow of a gathering storm we obtain a last glimpse of Chatham, as he stands, himself a wreck, holding up before a blind Ministry a picture of the dark ruin which was awaiting them. With some of his old haughtiness the austere old man rises to answer one who had dared to reply to him, and falls, never to rise again.

John Bright

As a law student, Wilson continued his interest in writing for publication. This essay in praise of British reformer John Bright (1811–1889) appeared in the *Virginia University Magazine* in March 1880. There are suggestions here of Wilson's own early thought on politics and history. Bright served in Parliament for over forty years and as president of the Board of Trade in the cabinet of William Gladstone. His fame as a reformer began when he was a founding member of the Anti-Corn Law League, fighting against the price protection he thought unjustly granted to British landed interests. As a follower of the Manchester School of economics, he passionately supported free trade and laissez-faire economic policies. Bright was a key figure in the campaign for a more democratically representative Parliament and saw success with the passage of the Reform Bill of 1884. Wilson's praise for Bright's stand on free trade reflects a view he would sustain through his career. His rejection of empty formulas and impractical speculations in politics echo again in this writing. Also in this essay, the young Wilson, in a brief diversion, reveals his sympathy for the Confederacy, his belief in the "purity" of its purposes, but also his conviction that its ultimate defeat was best for the South.

In every effort of comprehension we are made painfully conscious of the narrow compass of man's boasted powers of mind. As, when we stand before some one of the greater masterpieces of architecture and bestow our admiration upon its grand outlines, its multiform and uniform strength and grace, its swift and high-bending arches, its massive supports, its slender summits, we miss the careful carving of its cornices, the laborious polish of its marbles, or the modest beauty of the exquisite forms of stone, which in cold counterfeit of man, guard its portals or stand their solemn, silent sentry on its towers—so, when we contemplate the great movements of recorded history and attempt to take in the broader scope of events and follow the main lines of civilization's "journey with the sun," we overlook, in our wide survey, the inner lives of individual nations, the special workings of separate forces, the events of individual epochs, the controlling influence of individual men, in our endeavor to put ourselves in sympathy with *mankind,* we have ceased to sympathize with *man.*

It is, then, under peculiar advantages that we undertake an examination of the character and career of John Bright. Certainly no man ever won for himself a more definite position or a more certain place than has he. He has attained to honored age, absolutely without deviation from the principles of his youth. His life has inseparably interwoven itself with all the greater events of later English history. His name has become synonymous with liberalism. Since his entrance into public life, no great political reform has been accomplished which he has not powerfully helped to triumphant completion. Not since then has there been any considerable scheme of political reformation which has not been set to the music of his eloquence, or any great cause of advancement which has not been at some point carried on the shoulders of his strength.

From his very birth he has imbibed free political principles. He was born some sixty-nine years ago in the busy village of Rochdale, and was bred in the most thriving parts of thrifty Lancashire, the modern home of liberal politics in England. For modern English liberalism seems to have been born in the manufacturing districts, in the inner heart of Britain, in those busy counties in which Nottingham, Sheffield, Leeds, Manchester and Liverpool are clustered. Nothing could have been more natural than that the clouds of conservative prejudice should have first broken away in these homes of industry. As civilization advances and the steps of commerce quicken, men are more and more massed in great centers of industrial enterprise; and it is in these, where similarity of occupation, activity of intercourse and community of feeling kindle quick sympathy among large bodies of men and rouse to active intelligence whole classes of society, that broad and generous ideas of governmental polity find their firmest rootage and their sunniest seasons. It were next to impossible that such principles should find their earliest acceptance in agricultural communities or rural neighborhoods. There, where every condition of disintegration, and not one of union, is present, combined and aggressive action is looked for in vain. Political purposes are not there easily communicated; new political doctrines are not there readily sown. There men's thoughts run as slowly as their plows; men's purposes are as sluggish as their beasts of burden. It were perhaps equally idle to look for political impulse to come from the mining districts. There, where every day is spent away from the light of the sun, men's minds seem as ill-lighted as the deep galleries in which they wearily ply the pick. Their only reform is in riot. They crave license, not liberty.

Trade, indeed, is the great nurse of liberal ideas. Men who deal with all the world *cannot* sympathize with those whose thoughts do not reach beyond the limits of their own immediate neighborhood. The ordinary English farmer knows no world greater or more remote that the nearest market town. The English manufacturer sells his goods in Calcutta, in Valparaiso, in Hong Kong, it may be. When he wishes to buy, the cheapest market is the nearest; when he desires to sell, the dearest is the nearest. Accordingly when we see the cotton-printers and spinners of Manchester the first to uphold the doctrines and spread the gospel of Free Trade, we find no room for surprise. The earliest stirring of the great agitation which looked towards the establishment of Free Trade, were felt about the year 1836. Manchester and her industrial sisters had recently been enfranchised by the Reform Act of 1832, and the famous Anti-Corn-Law-League was one of the first and greatest manifestations of the potential influence which the manufacturing and trading classes were beginning to assume. This stupendous Free Trade movement found its ablest directors and its foremost leaders amongst the merchants of Manchester and its vicinity—leaders who afterwards became the doctors of what came to be known as the

"Manchester School" of politicians. Zeal for rational principles of trade changed simple unambitious men of business into diligent politicians, transformed them into orators, exalted them into statesmen. Foremost among these, by reason of zeal, by reason of worth, by reason of intelligence, was Richard Cobden, a cotton-printer of Manchester. His exalted character and persuasive eloquence made him the directing genius of the great drama of agitation set afoot by the League. In economical legislation his talents proved themselves beyond comparison brilliant and sovereign. But it was not permitted him long to survive the great League he had so successfully led. His life ended suddenly upon the triumphant completion of his life-work. He died the greatest apostle of Free Trade, and men now scarcely remember that he was anything else.

The name of John Bright was scarcely less prominently connected with the work and mission of the League than that of Cobden. *His* first step in public life was, like Cobden's, a step to the leadership of the forces of Free Trade. It were not possible or desirable upon this occasion to consider in detail, or even in general outline, those Corn Laws against which the League organized its forces. Suffice it to say that, passed in 1815, their effect had been virtually to exclude all foreign corn from the markets of Great Britain, under the silly pretense of "protecting" home produce, and that it was against this short-sighted policy that the forces of Free Trade made their determined stand. Never before or since has peaceful political agitation been more thoroughly organized or more shrewdly conducted. Every mailbag that left Manchester was full to overflowing with Free Trade tracts; no conceivable method of schooling the people in the doctrines of sound economy was neglected. From channel to channel, from Tweed to Thames, its principles were preached with all the dint of demonstration, all the power of persuasion, all the energy of eloquence. Immense bazaars evidenced its enterprise and contributed to its wealth. Unrivaled fairs and unnumbered mass-meetings drove its designs to completion. It was a vast movement of thought. Every day added to its increasing strength. Every wind brought news of its accumulating triumphs. It was in this work that Mr. Bright first tried his mettle. It was in this cause that he first developed his genius for affairs. His singleness of aim and energy of purpose and nobility of conception first discovered themselves in the direction and control of this stupendous machinery of propagandism. His character is of strong and elastic fibre such as is toughened and strengthened by every test. It partakes of all the sober thoughtfulness, the warm and intense earnestness, and the noble straightforwardness of that sturdy sect, the Quakers, from whose loins he is sprung, that sect which long ago, under the energetic leadership of that sterling pioneer and singularly genuine man, William Penn, penetrated the wilds of our thriving northern neighbor and laid the first foundations of that illustrious commonwealth whose unsurpassed industries are driving European manufacturers from their won markets. Mr. Bright carried to the public platform and into Parliament a political creed no less simple and no less openly avowed than the religious creed of his sect. And this creed was perfected before it was promulgated. Not until his thirtieth year did he actively participate in public affairs. His liberalism was then mature. His opinions were full grown and fruiting. His convictions were rooted and grounded in his very nature. And these convictions are vivid beliefs such as constitute the very essence of practical statesmanship, when united, as they are in him, with an undeviating purpose and a will which knows no discouragement and no defeat. These are rare gifts to be crowned with the rarer gift of eloquence. The campaigns of the League were preeminently speech making campaigns. The gospel of Free Trade was a preached gospel. Every public hall in England had rung with the appeals of its heralds and the cheers of its disciples. In this school was Mr. Bright trained. In the proclamation of this gospel were first developed his marvelous powers of public speech—powers which were first manifested in broken sentences and harsh tones, giving little promise of those grand passages of eloquence and that voice of unrivaled sweetness, variety and strength which have since won for him a place among the very greatest of English orators. These powers were not slow of growth. They grew with his energy and kept pace with his purposes. No orator ever more signally illustrated the truth that eloquence is not of the lips alone. Eloquence is never begotten by empty pates. Groveling minds are never winged with high and worthy thoughts. Eloquence consists not in sonorous sound or brilliant phrases. *Thought* is the fibre, thought is the *pith*, of eloquence. Eloquence lies in the thought, not in the throat. It was as the expression of his high impulses and strong purposes and sagacious plans and noble courage that John Bright's oratory became a tremendous agency in the world of politics. It is persuasion inspired by conviction.

☆ ☆ ☆

Mr. Bright's diction is as self-restrained as the orator himself. It is characterized by simple dignity and supple strength. It has none of the superb imagery or the sublime plenitude of Burke's gorgeous rhetoric; it has none of the pithy passion and "pregnant brevity" of Chatham's oratorical sword-thrusts; it has none of the smiling smoothness of Canning's bright sentences. But it has the Saxon bone and sinew. It is lithe and muscular. It is straight forward and natural, but not rugged. It is scholarly, but never pedantic. His refined taste and natural good sense put him above the silly affectation of mere rhetorical glitter. He has escaped that error which so many have allowed to possess them, the error of confounding sound with sense, of reckoning eloquence by the number of syllables. His sentences have the easy, spontaneous flow of conversation; yet they follow each other in close connection, hastening the progress of the thought and clearing the way for the apprehension. The power of his style is indisputable. Even upon the printed page it retains its sovereignty. One has but to read it to feel its charm. The periods are often unskillfully turned. The clauses are sometimes loosely thrown together. There is no dash or swiftness in the movement of the style. And yet, although you cannot always admire it from an artistic point of view, you must always allow its power to engage the attention and to lead the thoughts. It is, undoubtedly, what he says, rather than his manner of saying it, that gives him his supreme control over his hearers and his readers. Yet we are fain to admit, that nobility of sentiment seems all the more noble, strength of principle all the stronger, and mastery of thought all the more masterful when conveyed in a style of such simplicity and clearness that not crystal itself could transmit the light of thought more cloudlessly.

Mr. Bright never received a classical education. In breadth of scholarship he cannot, of course, be for a moment compared with Mr. Gladstone, with acrid Robert Lowe, with Sir William Harcourt, or with several of the more prominent and gifted Conservatives. But his attainments as an *English* scholar are preeminent. Our own language has been the special object of his untiring study. The rich stores of our own English literature he has explored with careful research. The Bible, Milton, and Shakspere have been his most constant companions. And is not this fact pregnant with suggestion? From these noble sources have come, no doubt, his simplicity of creed, his earnest morality, his singleness of principle, his steadfastness of purpose, his breadth of sympathy. From the Bible his unhesitating truthfulness and exalted sentiment; from Milton, his quiet, brave integrity; from Shakespeare, his knowledge of English human nature and his touching eloquence! His character illustrates with peculiar aptness that striking remark of Richter's: "Feelings come and go like light troops following the victory of the present; but principles, like troops of the line, are undisturbed and stand fast."

As I have already said, Mr. Bright's liberalism had attained its growth before he entered public life. His convictions were matured. His purposes were definitely formed. He started, consequently, some forty years in advance of his age, and this fact exposed him to the flings of the unthinking, to the ridicule of the majority of his countrymen, who could not keep pace with his thoughts or sympathize with his designs. Like all who have dared to anticipate the growth of wisdom, or ventured to hasten on before the slow-advancing forces of public opinion, he was assailed with the bitter taunt of *radicalism.* To this day you may hear the echoes of the fierce accusations which were long ago hurled at him by haughty, hating Tories whose hatred was born of fear. You may hear heedless observers even *now* speak of John Bright as "the great radical." His voice was raised at first, as now, always in behalf of the people, and men were quick to call him "agitator" and "demagogue." No one, however, who knows anything clearly about the actual history of events in England since the formation of the Anti-Corn-Law League can now seriously entertain any other opinion of Mr. Bright than that his statesmanship has been as consummate as his oratory. Take down a volume of his speeches and look over the table of subjects upon which he has most frequently and most powerfully spoken. He has identified himself with every enlightened and subsequently triumphant view of policy both at home and abroad. Free Trade, an extended and purified suffrage, a just and liberal land system, a perfected finance, a worthy, manly, Christian foreign and colonial policy; all have found in him a steady friend and an unwearied advocate. Look further than the index to his speeches. Follow the lines of his eminently statesmanlike plans of administration, plans, almost all of which have now come to their full harvest, and then tell me if you do not find in these at once the seeds and fruits of an enlightened *conservatism.* Wisdom is always conservative. John Bright a demagogue and a radical! If constant and consistent support of the policy dictated by a clear-sighted liberalism, if a strenuous and unyielding opposition to the encroachments of power, and the oppressions of prejudice, and the tyranny of wealth, be demagogy, then has he indeed been the chiefest of demagogues! If an early and clear recognition of those principles of administrative reform which have now received the sanction of law and the vindication of experience be radicalism, then has he indeed been the fiercest of radicals. It is a matter of demonstration that he has uniformly been found among the earliest and most ardent supporters of all those great measures which are now regarded as the most admirable fruits of the legislation of Great Britain during the last forty years. And his view has gone still further. He has looked beyond the present even and has from the very beginning of his career been eager to urge and powerful to prove essential such a change in the laws regulating the tenure of English land as would remove the unhappy restraints of primogeniture and facilitate the breaking up of the vast single estates which now damn England to agricultural stagnation, such a change as would make possible the creation of numerous small estates and the existence of a large and enlarging class of small land-owners, a yeomanry not less glorious than that of bright days of power long gone by: days when stout bowstrings sped victorious arrows on many a field of battle, a yeomanry such as would build up old England in strength, infuse new youth into her political system, and secure to her a fresh lease of power and influence. Such a change must come, if England is not to die: and its coming will be but a fresh vindication of John Bright's political prescience and far-reaching statesmanship. He is always pressing on to those great reforms which he knows the future must bring forth.

Well, his countrymen are tardily coming to understand Mr. Bright. Now that they have come to think in most points as he has all his life been thinking, they cannot well *help* understanding him. He has been translated into their own thoughts and desires. The "Times" newspaper, for many years his most uncompromising foe and loudest denouncer, has now much generous praise for the man and much genuine respect for his opinions. But it exclaims with impatient self-complacency, that he is still bigoted, intolerant of everything that savors of opposition to the hitherto triumphant progress of liberal ideas! He cannot, it complains, give his opponents their due meed of credit and praise. He can see nothing good in whatsoever comes from the Conservative party. The "Times" is not far wrong. Mr. Bright is positive and obstinate in his opposition to the policy of the present conservative government, to the Beaconsfieldism of these later days of brilliant failure abroad. . . . Absolute identity with one's cause is the first and great condition of successful leadership. It is that which makes the statesman's plans clear-cut and decisive, his purposes unhesitating; it is that which makes him a leader of States and a maker of history. I would not for a moment be understood as seeking to lend any color of justification to that most humiliating and degrading precept, "Party, right or wrong." This is the maxim of knaves, or of fools. . . . With wicked folly such as this Mr. Bright most assuredly cannot be charged. Never until very recent years has he acknowledged fealty to either of the great parties which divide English public opinion. Hitherto he has himself led a small detached party of progress. Only within the last few years has he announced his adherence to the Liberal party. That great party has come to adopt all the greater of those principles whose promotion has been his life-work, and now that his principles are its principles he is a Liberal.

☆ ☆ ☆

But I am conscious that there is one point at which Mr. Bright may seem to you to stand in need of defense. He was from the very first a resolute opponent of the cause of the Southern Confederacy. Will you think that I am undertaking an invidious task, if I endeavor to justify him in that opposition? I yield to no one precedence in love for the South. But *because* I love the South, I rejoice in the failure of the Confederacy. Suppose that secession had been accomplished? Conceive of this Union as divided into two separate and independent sovereignties! To the seaports of her northern neighbor the Southern Confederacy could have offered no equals; with her industries she could have maintained no rivalry; to her resources she could have supplied no parallel. The perpetuation of slavery would, beyond all question, have wrecked our agricultural and commercial interests, at the same time that it supplied a fruitful source of irritation abroad and agitation within. We cannot conceal from ourselves the fact that slavery was enervating our Southern society and exhausting to Southern energies. We cannot conceal from ourselves the fact that the Northern union would have continued stronger than we, and always ready to use her strength to compass our destruction. With this double certainty, then, of weakness and danger, our future would have been more than dark; it would have been inevitably and overwhelmingly disastrous. Even the damnable cruelty and folly of reconstruction was to be preferred to helpless independence. All this I can see at the same time that I recognize and pay loving tribute to the virtues of the leaders of secession, to the purity of their purposes, to the righteousness of the cause which they thought they were promoting, and to the immortal courage of the soldiers of the Confederacy. But Mr. Bright viewed the struggle as a foreigner. He was not intimately enough acquainted with the facts of our national history or with the original structure of our national government to see clearly the force or the justice of the doctrine of States Rights. That doctrine to him appeared a mere subtlety, a mere word-quibble. He saw and appreciated only the general features of the struggle. Its object was none other than the severance of a union which he saw was essential to the prosperity of the South no less, nay, even more, than to the progress of the North, its severance for the avowed purpose of perpetuating an institution which *we* now acknowledge to have been opposed to the highest interests of society. Surely we cannot say that he erred in withstanding a suicidal course such as this. . . .

I am fully aware that I have laid myself open to the charge of having pronounced an eulogy upon John Bright. I have not stopped to display those small faults of temper and those minor deflections from principle which mar his life as like faults mar every human life. I have allowed myself to believe that these things may be left out of our estimate of the great orator and statesmen without violence to justice or infidelity to truth. . . . The lesson of his life is not far to seek or hard to learn. It is, that duty lies wheresoever truth directs us; that statesmanship consists, not in the cultivation and practice of the arts of intrigue, nor in the pursuit of all the crooked intricacies of the paths of party management, but in the lifelong endeavor to lead first the attention and then the will of the people to the acceptance of truth in its applications to the problems of government; that not the adornments of rhetoric, but an absorbing love for justice and truth and a consuming, passionate devotion to principle are the body and soul of eloquence: that complete identification with some worthy cause is the first and great prerequisite of abiding success. Such are the crowning ornaments of the character of him in whom the elements are so mixed, "that Nature might stand up and say to all the world, This was a man." Such are the gifts and graces we must foster; such is the panoply of moral strength we must wear, we who are the builders of our country's future, if we are to preserve our institutions from the consuming rusts of corruption, to shield our liberties from the designs of enemies within the gates, and to set our faces towards the accomplishment of that exalted destiny which has been the happiest, brightest dream of generations lately passed away, and which may, we still may trust, be the crowning experience of generations soon to wake.

An Old Master: Adam Smith

Originally a lecture delivered at Johns Hopkins University in 1884, this essay documents Wilson's interest in educational technique through a discussion of the classroom lecture. Published while he was enjoying great teaching success at Wesleyan University, it slaps at teaching styles that offered "a science brief of data and bibliography" and stoutly defends the lecture that is well crafted to instruct and inspire. It is a discussion not unknown in current academic circles. Using Adam Smith as his exemplum, Wilson combined a commentary on Smith as a powerful lecturer with a tribute to his enduring influence. As a teacher, Smith inspired students who flocked to his lectures. Wilson reminds us that as a philosopher Smith intended *Wealth of Nations* only as one part of a project of encyclopedic scope. His method was the method of the Enlightenment, concentrating on observation of human behavior and the collection and analysis of factual data. Acknowledging Smith's debt to others, particularly to French Enlightenment thinkers, Wilson credits the "master" with transforming the data into effective and useful theory of enormous influence. The essay appeared in the *New Princeton Review* in September 1888.

Why is it that no one has ever written an essay on the art of academic lecturing and its many notable triumphs? In some quarters new educational canons have spoken an emphatic condemnation of the college lecture, and it would seem to be high time to consider its value, as illustrative of an art about to be lost, if not as exemplary of forces to be retained, even if modified. Here are some of the questions which thrust themselves forward in the topic: Are not our college class-rooms, in being robbed of the old-time lecture, and getting instead a science-brief of data and bibliography, being deprived also of that literary atmosphere which once pervaded them? We are unquestionably gaining in thoroughness; but are we gaining in thoughtfulness? We are giving to many youths an insight, it may be profound, into specialties; but are we giving any of them a broad outlook?

There was too often a paralysis of dullness in the old lecture, or, rather, in the old lecturer; and written lectures, like history and fashion in dress, have an inveterate tendency to repeat themselves; but, on the contrary, there was often a wealth of power in the studied discourse of strong men. Men bent upon instructing and inspiring—and there were many such—had to master that central secret of literature and spoken utterance, the secret of style. Their only instrument of conquest was the sword of penetrating speech. Some of the subtlest and most lasting effects of genuine oratory have gone forth from secluded lecture-desks into the hearts of quiet groups of students; and it would seem to be good policy to endure much indifferent lecturing—watchful trustees might reduce it to a minimum—for the sake of leaving places open for the men who have in them the inestimable force of chastened eloquence. For one man who can impart an undying impulse there are several score, presupposing the requisite training, who can impart a method; and here is the well-understood ground for the cumulating disfavor of college lecturing and the rapid substitution of "laboratory drill:" but will not higher education be cut off from communion with the highest of all forces—the force of personal inspiration in the field of great themes of thought—if you interdict the literary method in the class-room?

I am not inclined, however, to consume very many words in insisting on this point, for I believe that educators are now dealing more frankly with themselves than ever before, and that so obvious a point will by no means escape full recognition before reforming methods of college and university instruction take their final shape. But I also believe that it is very well to be thinking about the matter meanwhile, in order that this force may be getting ready to come fully militant into the final battle for territory. The best way of compassing this end would seem to be the studying of the old masters of the art of learned discourse. With Lanfranc one could get the infinite charm of the old monastic school life; with Abelard, the undying excitement of philosophical and religious controversy; with Colet, the fire of reforming zeal; with Blackstone, the satisfactions of clarified learning. But Bec and Paris and Oxford have by no means monopolized the masters of this art, and I should prefer, for the once at least, to choose an exemplar from Scotland, and speak of Adam Smith. It will, no doubt, be possible to speak of him without going over again the well-worn ground of the topics usually associated with his great fame.

☆ ☆ ☆

He was not, perhaps, a companionable man; he was much too absent-minded to be companionable; but he was, in the highest sense, interesting. His absent-mindedness was of that sort which indicates fullness of mind—a mind content, much of the time, to live within itself, indulging in those delights of quiet contemplation which the riches of a full mind can always command. Often he would open to his companions his mind's fullest confidences, and, with a rare versatility, lavish upon topics the most varied and diverse a wealth of information and illustration, always to the wondering delight of all who heard him.

☆ ☆ ☆

The breadth and variety of the topics upon which he chose to lecture, and the felicity, strength, and vitality of the exposition he gave them (we are told by one who had sat under him), soon drew to Glasgow "a multitude of students from a great distance" to hear him. His mastery of the art of academic lecturing was presently an established fact. It appears clear to me that his success was due to two things: the broad outlook of his treatment and the fine art of his style. His chair was Moral Philosophy; and "moral philosophy" seems to have been the most inclusive of general terms in the university usage of Scotland at that day, and, indeed, for many years afterward. Apparently it embraced all philosophy that did not directly concern the phenomena of the physical world, and, accordingly, allowed its doctors to give very free play to their tastes in their choice of subjects. Adam Smith, in Glasgow, could draw within the big family of this large-hearted philosophy not only the science of mental phenomena, but also the whole of the history and organization of society; just as, years afterward, John Wilson, in Edinburgh, could insist upon the adoption of something very like *belles-lettres* into the same generous and unconventional family circle.

Adam Smith sought to cover the field he had chosen with a fourfold course of lectures. First, he unfolded the principles of natural theology; second, he illustrated the principles of ethics in a series of lectures, which were afterward embodied in his published work on the *Theory of Moral Sentiments;* third, he discoursed on that branch of morality which relates to the administration of justice; and, last, coming out upon that field with which his name is now identified, he examined those political regulations which are founded, not upon principles of justice, but upon considerations of expediency, and which are calculated to increase the riches, the power, and the prosperity of the state. His own notes of his lectures he himself destroyed when he felt death approaching, and we are left to conjecture what the main features of his treatment were, from the recorded recollections of his pupils and from those published works which remain as fragments of the great plan. These fragments consist of the *Theory of Moral Sentiments,* the *Wealth of Nations,* and *Considerations Concerning the First Formation of Languages;* besides which there are, to quote another's enumeration, "a very curious history of astronomy, left imperfect, and another fragment on the history of ancient physics, which is a kind of sequel to that part of the history of astronomy which relates to ancient astronomy; then a similar essay on the ancient logic and metaphysics; then another on the nature and development of the fine, or, as he calls them, the imitative, arts, painting, poetry, and music, in which was meant to have been included a history of the theater—all forming part, his executors tell us, 'of a plan he had once formed for giving a connected history of the liberal and elegant arts'"; part, that is (to continue the quotation from Mr. Bagehot), of the "immense design of showing the origin and development of cultivation and law; or . . . of saying how, from being a savage, man rose to be a Scotchman."

☆ ☆ ☆

It is interesting to note that even this vast miscellany of thought, the *Wealth of Nations,* systematized though it be, was not meant to stand alone as the exposition of a complete system; it was only a supplement to the *Theory of Moral Sentiments;* and the two together constituted only chapters in that vast book of thought which their author would have written. Adam Smith would have grouped all things that concern either the individual or the social life of man under the several greater principles of motive and action observable in human conduct. His method throughout is, therefore, necessarily abstract and deductive. In the *Wealth of Nations,* he ignores the operation of love, of benevolence, of sympathy, and of charity in filling life with kindly influences, and concentrates his attention exclusively upon the operation of self-interest, and expediency; because he had reckoned with the first-named motives in the *Theory of Moral Sentiments,* and he would not confuse his view of the economic life of man by again lugging these in where selfishness was unquestionably the predominant force. "The philosopher," he held "is the man of speculation, whose trade is not to do anything, but to observe everything"; and certainly he satisfied his own definition. He does observe everything; and he stores his volumes full with the sagest practical maxims, fit to have fallen from the lips of the shrewdest of those Glasgow merchants in whose society he learned so much of the uses of his theories. But it is noticeable that none of the carefully noted facts of experience, which play so prominent a part on the stage of his argument, speaks of any other principle than the simple and single one that is the pivot of the part of his philosophy with which he is at the moment dealing. In the *Wealth of Nations,* for example, every apparent induction leads to self-interest, and to self-interest alone. In Mr. Buckle's phrase, his facts are subsequent to his argument; they are not used for demonstration, but for illustration. His historical cases, his fine generalizations, everywhere broadening and strengthening his matter, are only instances of the operation of the single abstract principle meant to be set forth.

When he was considering that topic in his course which has not come down to us in any of the remaining fragments of his lectures, the principles of justice, namely, although still always mindful of its relative position in the general scheme of his abstract philosophy of society, his subject led him, we are told, to speak very much in the modern historical spirit. He followed upon this subject, says the pupil already quoted, "the plan which seems to have been suggested by Montesquieu; endeavoring to trace the gradual progress of jurisprudence, both public and private, from the rudest to the most refined ages, and to point out the effects of those arts which contribute to subsistence, and to the accumulation of property, in producing corresponding improvements alterations in law and government." In following Montesquieu, he was, of course, following one of the forerunners of that great school of philosophical students of history, which has done so much in our own time to clear away the fogs that surround the earliest ages of mankind, and to establish something like the rudiments of a true philosophy of history. And this same spirit was hardly less discernible in those later lectures on the "political institutions relating to commerce, to finances, and to the ecclesiastical and military establishments," which formed the basis of the *Wealth of Nations.* Everywhere throughout his writings there is a pervasive sense of the realities of fact and circumstance; a luminous, bracing, work-a-day atmosphere. But the conclusions are, first of all, philosophical; only secondarily practical.

It has been necessary to go over this somewhat familiar ground with reference to the philosophical method of Adam Smith, in order to come at the proper point of view from which to consider his place among the old masters of academic lecturing. It has revealed the extent of his outlook. There yet remains something to be said of his literary method, so that we may discern the qualities of that style which, after proving so effectual in imparting power to his spoken discourses, has since, transferred to the printed page, preserved his fame so far beyond the lifetime of those who heard him.

Adam Smith took strong hold upon his hearers, as he still takes strong hold upon his readers, by force, partly, of his native sagacity, but by virtue, principally, of his consummate style. The success of his lectures was not altogether a triumph of natural gifts; it was, in great part, a triumph of sedulously cultivated art. With the true instinct of the orator and teacher, Adam Smith saw—what every one must see who speaks not for the patient ear of the closeted student only, but also to the often shallow ear of the pupil in his class-room, and to the always callous ear of the great world outside, which must be tickled in order to be made attentive—that clearness, force, and beauty of style are absolutely necessary to one who would draw men to his way of thinking; nay, to any one who would induce the great mass of mankind to give so much as passing heed to what he has to say. He knew that wit was of no avail, without wit's proper words; sagacity mean, without sagacity's mellow measures of phrase. He bestowed the most painstaking care, therefore, not only upon what he was to say, but also upon the way in which he was to say it. Dugald Stewart speaks of "that flowing and apparently artless style, which he had studiously cultivated, but which, after all his experience in composition, he adjusted, with extreme difficulty, to his own taste." The results were such as to offset entirely his rugged utterance and his awkward, angular action, and to enable the timid talker to exercise the spells of an orator. The charm of his discourses consisted in the power of statement which gave them speed, and in the vigorous, but chastened, imagination which lent them illumination. He constantly refreshed and rewarded his hearers, as he still constantly refreshes and reward his readers, by bringing them to those clear streams of practical wisdom and happy illustration which everywhere irrigate his expositions. His counsel, even on the highest themes, was always undarkened. There were no clouds about his thoughts; the least of these could be seen without glasses through the lucid atmosphere of expression which surrounded them. He was a great thinker, and that was much; but he also made men recognize him as a great thinker, because he was a great master of style, which was more. He did not put his candle under a bushel, but on a candlestick. . . .

It is this power of teaching other men how to think that has given to the works of Adam Smith an immortality of influence. In his first university chair, the chair of *Logic,* he had given scant time to the investigation of the formal laws of reasoning, and had insisted, by preference, upon the practical uses of discourse, as the living application of logic, treating of style, of the arts of persuasion and exposition; and here in his other chair, of Moral Philosophy, he was practically illustrating the vivifying power of the art he had formerly sought to expound to is pupils. "When the subject of his work," says Dugald Stewart, speaking of the *Theory of Moral Sentiments,* "—when the subject of his work leads him to address the imagination and the heart, the variety and felicity of his illustrations, the richness and fluency of his eloquence, and the skill with which he wins the attention and commands the passions of his hearers, leave him, among our English moralists, without a rival."

Such, then, were the matters which this great lecturer handled, and such was the form he gave them. Two personal characteristics of the man stand out in apparent contrast with what he accomplished: he is said to have been extremely unpractical in the management of his own affairs, and yet he fathered that science which tells how other people's affairs—how the world's affairs—are managed; he is known to have been shy and silent, and yet he was the most acceptable lecturer of his university. But it is not uncommon for the man who is both profound and accurate in his observation of the universal and permanent forces operative in the life about him, to be almost altogether wanting in that sagacity concerning the local and temporary practical details upon which the hourly facilitation and comfort of his own life depend; nor need it surprise any one to find the man who sits shy and taciturn in private, stand out dominant and eloquent in public. "Commonly, indeed," as Mr. Bagehot has said, "the silent man, whose brain is loaded with unexpressed ideas, is more likely to be a successful public speaker than the brilliant talker who daily exhaust himself in sharp sayings." There are two distinct kinds of observation: that which makes a man alert and shrewd, cognizant of every trifle and quick with every trick of speech; and that which makes a man a philosopher, conscious of the steady set of affairs and ready in the use of all the substantial resources of wise thought. Commend me to the former for a chat; commend me to the latter for a book. The first will sparkle; the other burns a steady flame.

Here is the picture of this Old Master: a quiet awkward, forceful Scotchman, whose philosophy has entered everywhere into the life of politics and become a world-force in thought; and impracticable Commissioner of Customs, who has left for the instruction of statesmen the best theory of taxation; an unbusiness-like professor, who established the science of business; a man of books, who is universally honored by men of action; plain, eccentric, learned, inspired. The things that strike us most about him are, his boldness of conception and wideness of outlook, his breadth and comprehensiveness of treatment, and his carefully clarified and beautified style. He was no specialist except *in the relations of things.* Of course, spreading his topics far and wide in the domain of history and philosophy, he was at many points superficial. He took most of his materials at second hand; and it has been said that he borrowed many of his ideas from the French. But no matter who mined the gold, he coined it; the image and superscription are his. Certain separate, isolated truths which served under him may have been doing individual, guerrilla warfare elsewhere for the advancement of science; he marshaled them into drilled hosts for the conquering of the nations. Adam Smith was, possibly, somewhat indebted to the Physiocrats, but all the world is indebted to Adam Smith. Education and the world of thought need men who, like Adam Smith, will dare to know a multitude of things. Without them and their bold synthetic methods, all knowledge and all thought would fall apart into a weak analysis. Their minds do not lack in thoroughness; their thoroughness simply lacks in minuteness. It is only in the utterances of such men that the mind finds such exhilaration and exaltation as come with the free air that blows over broad uplands. They excite you with views of the large aspects of thought; conduct you through the noblest scenery of the mind's domain; delight you with majesty of outline and sweep of prospect. In this day of narrow specialties, our thinking needs such men to fuse its parts, correlate its forces, and center its results; and our thinking needs them in its college stage, in order that we may command horizons from our study windows in after days.

The breadth and comprehensive of treatment of characteristic of the utterances of such a teach are inseparable attributes of his manner of thought. He has the artist's eye. For him things stand in picturesque relations; their great outlines fit into each other; the touch of his treatment is necessarily broad and strong. The same informing influence of artistic conception and combination gives to his style its luminous and yet transparent qualities. His sentences cannot retain the stiff joints of logic; it would be death to them to wear the chains of formal statement; they must take leave to deck themselves with eloquence. In a word, such men must write *literature,* or nothing. Their minds quiver with those broad sympathies which constitute the life of written speech. Their native catholicity makes all minds receive them as kinsmen. By reason of the very strength of their humanity, they are enabled to say things long waiting to be said, in such a way that all men may receive them. They hold commissions from the King of Speech. Such men will not, I am persuaded, always seek in vain invitations to those academic platforms which are their best coignes of vantage. But this is not just the time when they are most appreciated, or most freely encouraged to discover themselves; and it cannot be amiss to turn back to another order of things, and remind ourselves how a master of academic inspiration, possessing, in a great power to impart intellectual impulse, something higher than a trained capacity to communicate method, may sometimes be found even in a philosophical Scotchman.

Edmund Burke: The Man and His Times

Among Wilson's heroes out of history, Edmund Burke (1729–1797) ranks among the highest. Burke has remained an icon of conservatism. As a member of Parliament he was critical of British colonial policy in America (which Wilson read as a conservative posture) and of imperial injustices in India. His enduring influence lay in his defense of traditional institutions, despite his support for a number of British reform causes. His most famous work, *Reflections on the Revolution in France* (1790), correctly predicted that chaos would be the fruit of what he thought was the too rapid abandonment of traditional political and religions traditions. That work remains a classic statement of conservative political philosophy. As in biographical sketches of other men he admired, Wilson was careful to mark his subject's shortcomings and failures here. The young Wilson shared Burke's conservative view of government. Even in his "progressive" incarnation as governor and president, he favored organic change, emphasized more effective administration rather than structural changes, and was generally more restrained than many of his supporters. His political writings and his leadership reflected, as Burke advised, practical solutions aimed at conciliation rather than conflict. This sketch of Burke originated as a lecture and was printed in revised form in his collection of essays, *Mere Literature.*

There is no man anywhere to be found in the annals of Parliament who seems more thoroughly to belong to England than does Edmund Burke, indubitable Irishman though he was. His words, now that they have cast off their brogue, ring out the authentic voice of the best political thought of the English race. "If any man ask me," he cries, "what a free government is, I answer, that, for any practical purpose, it is what the people think so, and that they, and not I, are the natural, lawful, and competent judges of the matter." "Abstract liberty, like other mere abstractions, is not to be found. Liberty adheres in some sensible object; and every nation has formed to itself some favorite point, which by way of eminence becomes the criterion of their happiness." These sentences, taken from his writings on American affairs, might serve as a sort of motto of the practical spirit of our race in affairs of government. Look further, and you shall see how his imagination presently illuminates and suffuses his maxims of practical sagacity with a fine blaze of insight, a keen glow of feeling, in which you recognize that other masterful quality of the race, its intense and elevated conviction. "My hold on the colonies," he declares, "is in the close affection which grows from common names, from kindred blood, from similar privileges, and equal protection. These are the ties which, though light as air, are as strong as links of iron. Let the colonies always keep the idea of their civil rights associated with your government, they will cling and grapple to you, and no force under heaven will be of power to tear them from their allegiance. But let it once be understood that your government may be one thing and their privileges another, that these two things may exist without any mutual relation, and the cement is gone, the cohesion is loosened, and everything hastens to decay and dissolution. So long as you have the wisdom to keep the sovereign power of this country as the sanctuary of liberty, the sacred temple consecrated to our common faith, wherever the chosen race and sons of England worship freedom, they will turn their faces towards you." "We cannot, I fear," he says proudly of the colonies, "we cannot falsify the pedigree of this fierce people, and persuade them that they are not sprung from a nation in whose veins the blood of freedom circulates. The language in which they would hear you tell them this tale would detect the imposition; your speech would betray you. An Englishman is the unfittest person on earth to argue another Englishman into slavery." Does not your blood stir at these passages? And is it not because, besides loving what is nobly written, you feel that every word strikes towards the heart of the things that have made your blood what it has proved to be in the history of our race?

These passages, it should be remembered, are taken from a speech in Parliament and from a letter written by Burke to his constituents in Bristol. He had no thought to make them permanent sentences of political philosophy. They were meant only to serve an immediate purpose in the advancement of contemporaneous policy. They were framed for the circumstances of the time. They speak out spontaneously amidst matter of the moment: and they could be matched everywhere throughout his pamphlets and public utterances. No other similar productions that I know of have this singular, and as it were inevitable, quality of permanency. They have emerged from the mass of political writings put forth in their time with their freshness untouched, their significance unobscured, their splendid vigor unabated. It is this that we marvel at, that they should remain modern and timely, purged of every element and seed of decay. The man who could do this must needs arrest our attention and challenge our inquiry. We wish to account for him as we should wish to penetrate the secrets of the human spirit and know the springs of genius.

☆ ☆ ☆

I would not be understood as saying that Burke's speeches were impartial. They were not. He had preferences which amounted to prejudices. He was always an intense party man. But then he was a party man with a difference. He believed that the interests of England were bound up with the fortunes of the Rockingham Whigs; but he did not separate the interests of his party and the interests of his country. He cherished party connections because he conceived them to be absolutely necessary for effective public service.

☆ ☆ ☆

Certainly there were no party prizes for Burke. During much the greater part of his career the party to which he adhered was in opposition; and even when in office it had only small favors for him. Even his best friends advised against his appointment to any of the great offices of state, deeming him too intemperate and unpractical. And yet the intensity of his devotion to his party never abated a jot. Assuredly there was never a less selfish allegiance. His devotion was for the principles of his party, as he conceived and constructed them. It was a moral and intellectual devotion. He had embarked all his spirit's fortunes in the enterprise. Faults he unquestionably had, which seemed very grave. He was passionate sometimes beyond all bounds: he seriously frightened cautious and practical men by his haste and vehemence in pressing his views for acceptance. He was capable of falling, upon occasion, into a very frenzy of excitement in the midst of debate, when he would often shock moderate men by the ungoverned license of his language. But his friends were as much to blame for these outbreaks as he was. They cut him to the quick by the way in which they criticized and misunderstood him. His heart was maddened by the pain of their neglect of his just claims to their confidence. They seemed often to use him without trusting him, and their slights were intolerable to his proud spirit. Practically, and upon a narrow scale of, expediency, they may have been right: perhaps he was *not* circumspect enough to be made a responsible head of administration. Unquestionably, too, they loved him and meant him no unkindness. But it was none the less tragical to treat such a man in such a fashion. They may possibly have temporarily served their country by denying to Burke full public acknowledgment of his great services; but they cruelly wounded a great spirit, and they hardly served mankind.

They did Burke an injustice, moreover. They greatly underrated his practical powers. In such offices as he was permitted to hold he showed in actual administration the same extraordinary mastery of masses of detail which was the foundation of his, unapproachable mastery of general principles in his thinking. His thought was always immersed in matter, and concrete detail did not confuse him when he touched it any more than it did when he meditated upon it. Immediate contact with affairs always steadied his judgment. He was habitually temperate in the conduct of business. It was only in speech and when debating matters that stirred the depths of his nature that he gave way to uncalculating fervor. He was intemperate in his emotions, but seldom in his actions. He could, and did, write calm state papers in the very midst and heat of parliamentary affairs that subjected him to the fiercest excitements. He was eminently capable of counsel as well as of invective.

He served his party in no servile fashion, for all he adhered to it with such devotion. He sacrificed his intellectual independence as little as his personality in taking intimate part in its counsels. He gave it principles, indeed, quite as often as he accepted principles from it. In the final efforts of his life, when he engaged every faculty of his mind in the contest that he waged with such magnificent wrath against the French revolutionary spirit, he gave tone to all English thought, and direction to many of the graver issues of international policy. Rejected oftentimes by his party, he has at length been accepted by the world.

His habitual identification with opposition rather than with the government gave him a certain advantage. It relaxed party discipline and indulged his independence. It gave leave, too, to the better efforts of his genius: for in opposition it is principles that tell, and Burke was first and last a master of principles. Government is a matter of practical detail, as well as of general measures; but the criticism of government very naturally becomes a matter of the application of general principles, as standards rather than as practical means of policy.

Four questions absorbed the energies of Burke's life and must always be associated with his fame. These were, the American war for independence; administrative reform in the English home government; reform in the government of India; and the profound political agitations which attended the French Revolution. Other questions he studied, deeply pondered, and greatly illuminated, but upon these four he expended the full strength of his magnificent powers. There is in his treatment of these subjects a singular consistency, a very admirable simplicity of standard. It has been said, and it is true, that Burke had no system of political philosophy. He was afraid of abstract system in political thought, for he perceived that questions of government are moral questions, and that questions of morals cannot always be squared with the rules of logic, but run through as many ranges of variety as the circumstances of life itself. "Man acts from adequate motives relative to his interest," he said, "and not on metaphysical speculations. Aristotle, the great master of reasoning, cautions us, and with great weight and propriety, against this species of delusive geometrical accuracy in moral arguments, as the most fallacious of all sophistry." And yet Burke unquestionably had a very definite and determinable system of thought, which was none the less a system for being based upon concrete, and not upon abstract premises. It is said by some writers (even by so eminent a writer as Buckle) that in his later years Burke's mind lost its balance and that he reasoned as if he were insane; and the proof assigned is, that he, a man who loved liberty, violently condemned, not the terrors only, that of course, but the very principles of the French Revolution. But to reason thus is to convict one's self of an utter lack of comprehension of Burke's mind and motives. . . .

From first to last Burke's thought is conservative. Let his attitude with regard to America serve as an example. He took his stand, as everybody knows, with the colonies, against the mother country; but his object was not revolutionary. He did not deny the legal right of England to tax the colonies (*we* no longer deny it ourselves), but he wished to preserve the empire, and he saw that to insist upon the right of taxation would be irrevocably to break up the empire, when dealing with such a people as the Americans. He pointed out the strong and increasing numbers of the colonists, their high spirit in enterprise, their jealous love of liberty, and the indulgence England had hitherto accorded them in the matter of self-government, permitting them in effect to become an independent people in respect of all their internal affairs; and he declared the result matter for just pride.

☆ ☆ ☆

"All government, indeed every human benefit and enjoyment, every Virtue and every prudent act, is founded on compromise and barter. We balance inconveniences; we give and take; we remit some rights, that we may enjoy others; and we choose rather to be happy citizens than subtle disputants." "Magnanimity in politics is not seldom the truest wisdom; and a great empire and little minds go ill together."

Here you have the whole spirit of the man, and in part a view of his eminently practical system of thought. The view is completed when you advance with him to other subjects of policy. He pressed with all his energy for radical reforms in administration, but he earnestly opposed every change that might touch the structure of the constitution itself. He sought to secure the integrity of Parliament, not by changing the system of representation, but by cutting out all roots of corruption. He pressed forward with the most ardent in all plans of just reform, but he held back with the most conservative from all propositions of radical change. "To innovate is not to reform," he declared, and there is "a marked distinction between change and reformation. The former alters the substance of the objects themselves, and gets rid of all their essential good as well as of all the accidental evil annexed to them. Change is novelty; and whether it is to operate anyone of the effects of reformation at all, or whether it may not contradict the very principle upon which reformation is desired, cannot certainly be known beforehand. Reform is not a change in the substance or in the primary modification of the object, but a direct application of a remedy to the grievance complained of. So far as that is removed, all is sure. It stops there; and if it fails, the substance which underwent the operation, at the very worst, is but where it was." This is the governing motive of his immense labors to accomplish radical economical reform in the administration of the government. He was not seeking economy merely; to husband the resources of the country was no more than a means to an end, and that end was, to preserve the constitution in its purity. He believed that Parliament was not truly representative of the people because so many placemen found seats in it, and because so many members who might have been independent were bought by the too abundant favors of the Court. Cleanse Parliament of this corruption, and it would be restored to something like its pristine excellence as an instrument of liberty.

He dreaded to see the franchise extended and the House of Commons radically made over in its constitution. It had never been intended to be merely the people's House. It had been intended to hold all the elements of the state that were not to be found in the House of Lords or the Court. He conceived it to be the essential object of the constitution to establish a balanced and just intercourse between the several forces of an ancient society, and it was well that that balance should be preserved even in the House of Commons, rather than give perilous sweep to a single set of interests. "These opposed and conflicting interests," he said to his French correspondent, "which you considered as so great a blemish in your old and in our present Constitution, interpose a salutary check to all precipitate resolutions. They render deliberation a matter, not of choice, but of necessity; they make all change a subject of *compromise,* which naturally begets moderation; they produce *temperaments,* preventing the sore evil of harsh, crude, unqualified reformations, and rendering all the headlong exertions of arbitrary power, in the few or in the many, forever impracticable. Through that diversity of members and interests, general liberty had as many securities as there are separate views in the several orders; whilst by pressing down the whole by the weight of a real monarchy, the separate parts would have been prevented. from warping and starting from their allotted places."

☆ ☆ ☆

It is not possible to escape deep conviction of the wisdom of these reflections. They penetrate to the heart of all practicable methods of reform. Burke was doubtless too timid, and in practical judgment often mistaken. Measures which in reality would operate only as salutary and needed reformations he feared because of the element of change that was in them. He erred when he supposed that progress can in all its stages be made without changes which seem to go even to the substance. But, right or wrong, his philosophy did not come to him of a sudden and only at the end of his life, when he found France desolated and England threatened with madness for love of revolutionary principles of change. It is the key to his thought everywhere, and through all his life.

It is the key (which many of his critics have never found) to his position with regard to the revolution in France. He was roused to that fierce energy of opposition in which so many have thought that they detected madness, not so much because of his deep disgust to see brutal and ignorant men madly despoil an ancient and honorable monarchy, as because he saw the spirit of these men cross the Channel and find lodgment in England, even among statesmen like Fox, who had been his own close friends and companions in thought and policy; not so much because he loved France as because he feared for England.

It was to keep out infection and to preserve such precious stores of manly tradition as had made that little world "the envy of less happier lands" that Burke sounded so effectually that extraordinary alarm against the revolutionary spirit that was racking France from throne to cottage. Let us admit, if you will, that with reference to France herself he was mistaken. Let us say that when he admired the institutions which she was then sweeping away he was yielding to sentiment, and imagining France as perfect as the beauty of the sweet queen he had seen in her radiant youth. Let us concede that he did not understand the condition of France, and therefore did not see how inevitable that terrible revolution was: that in this case, too, the wages of sin was death. He was not defending France, if you look to the bottom of it; he was defending England: and the things he hated are truly hateful. He hated the French revolutionary philosophy and deemed it unfit for free men. And that philosophy is in fact radically evil and corrupting. No state can ever be conducted on its principles. For it holds that government is a matter of contract and deliberate arrangement, whereas in fact it is an institute of habit, bound together by innumerable threads of association, scarcely one of which has been deliberately placed. It holds that the object of government is liberty, whereas the true object of government is justice; not the advantage of one class, even though that class constitute the majority, but right equity in the adjustment of the interests of all classes. It assumes that government can be made over at will, but assumes it without the slightest historical foundation. For governments have never been successfully and permanently changed except by slow modification operating from generation to generation. It contradicted every principle that had been so laboriously brought to light in the slow stages of the growth of liberty in the only land in which liberty had then grown to great proportions. The history of England is a continuous thesis against revolution; and Burke would have been no true Englishman, had he not roused himself, even fanatically, if there were need, to keep such puerile doctrine out.

If you think his fierceness was madness, look how he conducted the trial against Warren Hastings during those same years: with what patience, with what steadiness in business, with what temper, with what sane and balanced attention to detail, with what statesmanlike purpose! Note, likewise, that his thesis is the same in the one undertaking as in the other. He was applying the same principles to the case of France and to the case of India that he had applied to the case of the colonies. He meant to save the empire, not by changing its constitution, as was the method in France, and so shaking every foundation in order to dislodge an abuse, but by administering it uprightly and in a liberal spirit. He was persuaded "that government was a practical thing, made for the happiness of mankind, and not to furnish out a spectacle of uniformity to gratify the schemes of visionary politicians. Our business," he said, "was to rule, not to wrangle; and it would be a poor compensation that we had triumphed in a dispute, whilst we had lost an empire." The monarchy must be saved and the constitution vindicated by keeping. the empire pure in all parts, even in the remotest provinces. Hastings must be crushed in order that the world might know that no English governor could afford to be unjust. Good government, like all virtue, he deemed to be a practical habit of conduct, and not a matter of constitutional structure. It is a great ideal, a thoroughly English ideal; and it constitutes the leading thought of all Burke's career.

In short, as I began by saying, this man, an Irishman, speaks the best English thought upon the essential questions of politics. He is thoroughly, characteristically, and to the bottom English in all his thinking. He is more liberal than Englishmen in his treatment of Irish questions, of course; for he understands them, as no Englishman of his generation did. But for all that he remains the chief spokesman for England in the utterance of the fundamental ideals which have governed the action of Englishmen in politics. "All the ancient, honest, juridical principles and institutions of England," such was his idea, "are so many clogs to check and retard the headlong course of violence and oppression. They were invented for this one good purpose, that what was not *just* should not be *convenient.*" This is fundamental English doctrine. English liberty has consisted in making it unpleasant for those who were unjust, and thus getting them in the habit of being just for the sake of a *modus vivendi.* Burke is the apostle of the great English gospel of Expediency.

The politics of English-speaking peoples has never been speculative; it has always been profoundly practical and utilitarian. Speculative politics treats men and situations as they are supposed to be; practical politics treats them (upon no general plan, but in detail) as they are found to be at the moment of actual contact. With reference to America Burke argues: No matter what your legal right in the case, it is not *expedient* to treat, America as you propose: a numerous and spirited people like the colonists will not submit; and your experiment will cost you your colonies. In the case of administrative reform, again, it is the higher sort of expediency he urges: If you wish to keep your government from revolution, keep it from corruption, and by making it pure render it permanent. To the French he says, It is not *expedient* to destroy thus recklessly these ancient parts of your constitution. How will you replace them? How will you conduct affairs at all after you shall have deprived yourselves of all balance and of all old counsel? It is both better and easier to reform than to tear down and reconstruct.

This is unquestionably the message of Englishmen to the world, and Burke utters it with incomparable eloquence. A man of sensitive imagination and elevated moral sense, of a wide knowledge and capacity for affairs, he stood in the midst of the English nation speaking its moral judgments upon affairs, its character in political action, its purposes of freedom, equity, wide and equal progress. It is the immortal charm of his speech and manner that gives permanence to his works. Though his life was devoted to affairs with a constant and unalterable passion, the radical features of

Burke's mind were literary. He was a man of books, without being under the dominance of what others had written. He got knowledge out of books and the abundance of matter his mind craved to work its constructive and imaginative effects upon. It is singular how devoid of an direct references to books his writings are. The materials of his thought never reappear in the same form in which he obtained them. They have been smelted and recoined. They have come under the drill and inspiration of a great constructive mind, have caught life and taken structure from it. Burke is not literary because he takes from books, but because he makes books, transmuting what he writes upon into literature. It is this inevitable literary quality, this sure mastery of style, that mark the man, as much as his thought itself. He is a master in the use of the great style. Every sentence, too, is steeped in the colors of an extraordinary imagination. The movement takes your breath and quickens your pulses. The glow and power of the matter rejuvenate your faculties.

Benjamin Franklin

Wilson used this introduction to craft a tribute to Franklin, arguing for the redemption of the author from charges of pettiness which critics have and on occasion still level at the *Autobiography.* Wilson understood Franklin as a practical reformer and dismissed interpretations of the book as a work of self-serving egoism. Franklin critics often label him as the father of a materialist entrepreneurial ethic, and his writing is contrasted with the more idealist outlook of an Emerson or Thoreau. That reading misses the importance of Franklin's advocacy of philanthropic causes and his promotion of public service as well as civic and social responsibility. Wilson also offered an interesting critique of the eighteenth-century Enlightenment mentality, especially in its French incarnation. He saw it as full of "pettifogging difficulties" that "missed the secrets of the very things it meditated upon." Acknowledging Franklin as a man of the Enlightenment, Wilson absolved him of the French excesses and paid tribute to his leavening of abstract rationalism with common sense and prudence. With a keen ear for language, Wilson also offered high praise for Franklin's power as a writer. This essay was written for an edition of the *Autobiography* published in 1901.

This famous book needs an introduction as little as any I know. Its frank pages reveal the man who wrote them more vividly, more completely, more naturally than any comment could reveal him. It is not even necessary to set a stage upon which to place him; you catch the air of the world in which he lived from his own sentences, and see the affairs he handled as he saw them. You meet him here as you might have met him in some Philadelphia coffee-house a hundred and twenty years ago, and your curiosity as to what he was and what he concerned himself with is satisfied out of his own talk. Here is his authentic flavor, to be had for the tasting.

And yet there is something more to be said. It is not easy to leave off when once you have begun to speak of Benjamin Franklin. When you have closed the book and he is gone, the genial figure lingers in your thought. Half peasant, only half man of the world, and yet a statesman, philanthropist, scientist, man of letters, his broad, plain, sunny nature fertile in every part of whatsoever is fit to nourish or be serviceable to the race, his thought running always upon conduct or upon affairs or upon the forces of the physical universe, the door is hardly shut upon him before we fall to comment and comparison, praise and thoughtful assessment.

Such a man, we say, could hardly have been born or brought to the full light of fame anywhere but in America. He is racy of the soil and of the institutions, not of Northamptonshire nor even of Massachusetts, but of the English colonies in America. In England, we feel (can we be mistaken?), he might have been, such another as his uncle Thomas, the "ingenious" scrivener, who was "a chief mover of all public-spirited undertakings for the, county or town of Northampton and his own village"; but hardly the chief figure of a whole nation for sagacity and for all the thoughts that make for enlightenment and quiet progress. Such a career bespeaks a country in which all things are making and to be made. No one who reads these pages can doubt that Franklin had the literary gift: you cannot mistake the career he describes or the country whose affairs set it about. For all it is so plain in diction and keeps in so businesslike a way to the quiet path of narrative, the book has flavor, smacks of men and things, and is touched throughout not only with the originality and the distinctive personal qualities of the man himself, but also with the qualities of a country and a time. All his writings attest Franklin a man gifted in no common measure with the power of expression. The firm, clear strokes define and clarify everything he touches. His sentences assemble with admirable precision, support one another without hesitation or confusion of movement; and when he is done the field clears at once, and you perfectly understand what you have seen. He can convince with excellent cogency; he can persuade with an art you shall not easily escape. And yet there is nowhere in what he writes any note of distinction. You tread always, while you walk with him, the levels of the ordinary world. The path does not rise; the air stirs with no breath from distant uplands or the vast extended sea. It is always the street or the counting-house, the country road, or the council-chamber, the laboratory or the tradesman's counter that lies before you, and the man who speaks is intent upon the business of the place, not upon principles so much as upon transactions and upon all the means, great and small, by which men may be led to take part in them.

Is not this lack of the full flavor of letters, this air of being always engaged upon some new piece of business, one of the characteristics of the man which make us think of him as distinctively a product of America? American letters have so far lacked the full-throated power and the amplitude of tone which have made the literatures of many other countries rich and various and full of the qualities that move and refresh. The writings of Franklin do not, indeed, stand for all. There have been men amongst us who greatly excelled him in the range and efficacy of their power in letters. We have had among our writers men of unmistakable charm, men of power fit for the handling of great themes, men of vision, men who had caught not a little of the music of our mother-tongue. But in candid moods we are fain to admit that there has been, on the whole, a certain tameness in our better authors, something less than an easy mastery of theme and manner, a certain thinness where we could have wished for richness and depth of tone.

If we desired an explanation, we might turn to Franklin for it. Our genius has been of the practical type demanded of us by our tasks. We have had to subdue a virgin continent from sea to sea, construct institutions suitable for life upon it, whether as wilderness or settled countryside, get sustenance from its soil, and the resources of our wealth from its forests and mines and quarries. The task has not dulled our wits; it has quickened them, rather; but it has not been a business to stir our imaginations deeply. It has made us thoughtful of means, ingenious, inventive, men to look before and after and make good every stroke of constructive work; but we have accomplished the thing we set ourselves to do, not in armies under command, under no master's eye, with no breath of large plans, consciously thought out and perfected, in our nostrils, but singly, rather, each man for himself, hand and thought close to the immediate task, by an instinct and mastery which operated from day to day, upon one thing at a time, no one keeping the whole pattern of the complex business in his eye the while, or directing with authority how it should be completed and brought to perfection. And our writing has matched our life and circumstances. Franklin's writing stands typical and significant of our whole intellectual history as a nation. It is letters in business garb, literature with its apron on, addressing itself to the task, which in this country is every man's, of setting free the processes of growth, giving them facility, and speed and efficacy. It speaks in phrases of exposition and counsel, of debate, analysis, discussion. It looks upon the world, as a laboratory and upon thought and the expression of it as a scientific, not a creative, process.

One is struck by nothing in this book so much as by the all-round efficiency of the man who wrote it. He was as practical, as thorough, as businesslike, as successful, in supplying General Braddock with wagons and teamsters for his ill-fated expedition against Duquesne as in organizing fire companies or a circulating library or a Philosophical Society; kept the same cool business head and the same shrewd eye upon individual men in diplomacy that had made him so sure of success in his printing-office and his book-shop; approached nature and got her secrets from her as calmly and easily as he dealt with governors or with subscribers, using as simple means, a common kite to draw the electricity from the clouds, and kept the exact and quiet mind in everything. His success lay, by an almost accidental choice, in the staid town of Philadelphia, and the things he did were the things natural sagacity and quick insight into human nature suggested in such a place, where the common interests of an ordered community waited to be served; but he would have succeeded anywhere in America, on the frontier as readily as in the settled town. Indeed, that is the characteristic and final test for a man of whom we say that he was a typical American. Would he have been fit for the frontier; would he have made as great a figure out in the forests or upon the untilled plains, where the rough first work of civilization was to be done? No one can doubt the answer in Franklin's case. The work would have been less rough and less slow for his presence. He would have studied and captained it like a scientist and a master.

And yet Franklin was no provincial, but belonged in many a characteristic to the whole large world of his time as well as to America. It was the man's range and variety that made him great. Nothing that he does or says, but only his plain dress, marks him a man out of place even in a Parisian drawing-room. Indeed, it is odd to see how close kin the man seems to the French savants and thinkers of his day, and yet how different he is. He unmistakably belongs in thought and life to the European eighteenth century no less than to the American. He has all the cool rationalism of the time, dissents without passion, surmises without enthusiasm, makes reason, not belief, the guide and critic of conduct, enacts a list of virtues and a set of maxims as his code of morality, is above all things speculative, and fills his days with little scrutinies and ingenious tests of thought and practice. There were not many heart-searching doubts in the philosophy of the eighteenth century. It abounds in pettifogging difficulties and cool dissents; its motive is curiosity, its method criticism and amateur experiment, its only enthusiasm for those who have none. The Reason which the French would have enthroned at their Revolution was not the reason of the fully sentient mind, but a thing as abstract, as separate from life and the real forces that must ever move the world, as the word-puzzles of the schoolmen in an age gone by and among the French despised. They played at laying all the elements of mind and nature bare in cold analysis, and missed the secrets of the very things they meditated upon. Franklin salted their philosophy with sound American sense and a practical sagacity not easily to be misled, used it for the most part only upon the objects it was really suited to elucidate, made it an instrument of practical prudence, and left its vagaries to the French who invented them.

☆ ☆ ☆

No doubt in its day the plain-spoken book served that purpose, and many a man steadied his life by means of its precepts and took heart from its example. But we feel, as we read it now, that its usefulness in that kind is no longer very great or very vital. Prudence is at best a dull motive. Only men of the eighteenth century or still under its spell and influence could dwell with unction upon those saving details of moral commonplace or take inspiration from the precepts of expediency. Of course prudence and expediency are not all that Franklin has to offer to support his principles of morality. A motive played through his life at once noble and deeply moving, the desire to serve his fellow-men, to turn them to a better way of living, to higher comforts and more elevated interests, to a life of thought and aspiration, of civic virtue and domestic honesty, as well as of toil and the heaping up of goods. But there is something singularly cool in his attitude toward it all. Mere increase of knowledge and of material comfort and convenience plays a noticeably large part in his conception of welfare, seems oftentimes, indeed, to constitute the whole of it. Men do not take fire from such thoughts, unless something deeper, which is missing here, shine through them. We are not content to order our lives by maxims or square our prudence by the saws of "Poor Richard's Almanac." There seems to us now something very pale and thin about the morality which is founded upon them. What may have seemed to the eighteenth century a system of morals seems to us nothing more vital than a collection of the precepts of good sense and sound conduct, the old-time "wisdom of the world."

What redeems it from pettiness in this book is the scope of power and of usefulness to be seen in Franklin himself, who set these standards up in all seriousness and candor for his own life. His little precepts take dignity from their author. Had he been a man no greater than Lord Chesterfield was, his morality might have seemed as shallow as Chesterfield's, the mere perfected good judgment of a practiced man of the world. But Franklin was a really great man. You shall find yourself deeming him such, as you read, even in the midst of trivial passages and unpleasing disclosures. He was no mere philosopher walking among men to dole out shrewd comment and kindly suggestion. He was a practical master in the mechanics of society, as well as in the mechanics of the material universe and in the sophistries of the human mind. He was in nothing greater than in the achievement which comes by organization and from the concerted effort of many men moving in voluntary accord. He not only conceived projects that would better society, but also persuaded men of their utility, drew them together to carry them out, and gave to their action a vitality which did not flag when his hand was withdrawn. He had that saving sense of what is practicable which makes reformers no reformers at all, but effectual leaders, rather, who can quicken progress at will. Reformers will often convince you that they are right; but leaders will take hold on you and persuade you to action, will point out to you practicable modes of achievement, will begin with what a few can do, and wait for enterprises to get their natural and wholesome growth. Probably no man ever better understood how to handle a subscription paper or how to give a society its first organization and sufficient impulse than Franklin did. This is the power in him that takes your imagination, this power to rule other men. This is his incommunicable secret. This is the field of achievement which no maxims good for business behind a counter can bound or contain.

The whole essence and object of this book is to explain, for the instruction of others, how Mr. Franklin, the son of a tallowchandler of Boston, came to cut so notable a figure in the world. "My father," says he, "having, among his instructions to me when a boy, frequently repeated a proverb of Solomon, 'Seest thou a man diligent in his calling? he shall stand before kings; he shall not stand before mean men,' I from thence considered industry as a means of obtaining wealth and distinction, which encouraged me, tho' I did not think that I should ever literally *stand before kings*, which, however, has since happened; for I have stood before *five*, and even had the honor of sitting down with one, the King of Denmark, to dinner." How priggish and self-satisfied such a sentence sounds thus divorced from its context and set off by itself; how essentially self-laudatory the whole motive of such a narrative of one's own success! And yet the surprising and delightful thing about this book is that, take it all in all, it has not the low tone of conceit, but is a stanch man's sober and unaffected assessment of himself and the circumstances of his career. Here is the nicest possible test of how generous, large, and substantial the real bulk of the man's character and achievement was. He was cool, sober-minded, judicious enough to be trusted to look at himself objectively, without affectation of modesty, without excess of self-appreciation. There could be no finer or more conclusive proof of sanity and perfect balance. No just critic can call this book a piece of vanity; no man of right judgment can lay it down without esteeming Franklin, not less, but more.

Moreover, the undisguised personal equation is the chief charm in writing of this kind. The salt of Franklin's own good sense keeps the matter sound and untainted. Another man, as great, as large of mind, as sane, might have done such a piece of biography exceeding ill, to the deep offending of all good taste. A more intense man, a more ponderous mind, a less detached and nicely poised nature, unable really to hold aloof from itself and look at its own acts in the temper of the scientific observer, might have bungled sadly this delicate task of self-assessment. Franklin had just the right equipoise and temperament. The book, as a consequence, is flavored to the taste of the most critical and judicious. It is by common consent a classic in its kind, and must ever charm those who read it with its authentic image, intimate and from the life, of a figure which all men must account one of the most distinctive and notable in an age of creation and achievement.

Abraham Lincoln: A Man of the People

In this tribute to Lincoln, Wilson examined the nature of political leadership and concluded with a description of the kind of political leader a nation should seek. He recommended a leader who is not "hot" but "cool," one who can "withdraw himself" and "see the stage." It is not an impossible stretch to read these remarks as a reference to the recently concluded administration of Theodore Roosevelt, who has rarely been describes as a "cool" leader. Wilson's admiration for Lincoln as a man and as a leader was unrestrained in this speech, but, unlike most Lincoln tributes, he made no reference to his subject's role in the emancipation drama and only obliquely to the Civil War. Wilson had written in the past in defense of the Southern "cause," though he conceded the final outcome was best for the South and the nation. Perhaps, for Wilson, a tribute to Lincoln was best delivered without reference to what were still powerfully emotional memories. The piece was written on the eve of his campaign for governor of New Jersey, at the start of his new career in politics. The reader wonders if Wilson had himself as well as Lincoln in mind when writing of a cool leader who can see the stage. The address originated as a Lincoln Day address in Chicago and was printed in 1909 and reprinted in a collection of tributes to Lincoln in 1910.

My earliest recollection is of standing at my father's gateway in Augusta, Georgia, when I was four years old, and hearing some one pass and say that Mr. Lincoln was elected and there was to be war. Catching the intense tones of his excited voice, I remember running in to ask my father what it meant. What it meant, you need not be told. What it meant, we shall not here today dwell upon. We shall rather turn away from those scenes of struggle and of unhappy fraternal strife, and recall what has happened since to restore our balance, to remind us of the permanent issues of history, to make us single-hearted in our love of America, and united in our purpose for her advancement. We are met here today to recall the character and achievements of a man who did not stand for strife, but for peace, and whose glory it was to win the affection alike of those whom he led and of those whom he opposed, as indeed a man and a king among those who mean the right.

☆ ☆ ☆

Have you ever looked at some of those singular statues of the great French sculptor Rodin—those pieces of marble in which only some part of a figure is revealed and the rest left in the hidden lines of the marble itself; were there emerges the arm and the bust and the eager face, it may be, of a man, but his body disappears in the general bulk of the stone, and the lines fall off vaguely? I have often been made to think, in looking at those statues, of Abraham Lincoln. There was a little disclosed in him, but not all. You feel that he was so far from being exhausted by the demands of his life that more remained unrevealed than was disclosed to our view. The lines run off into infinity and lead the imagination into every great conjecture. We wonder what the man might have done, what he might have been, and we feel that there was more promise in him when he died than when he was born; that the force was so far from being exhausted that it had only begun to display itself in its splendor and perfection. No man can think of the life of Lincoln without feeling that the man was cut off almost at his beginning.

And so it is with genius of this kind, not singular but universal, because there were uses to which it was not challenged. You feel that there is no telling what it might have done in days to come, when there would have been new demands made upon its strength and upon its versatility. He is like some great reservoir of living water which you can freely quaff but can never exhaust. There is something absolutely endless about the lines of such a life.

And you will see that very fact renders it difficult indeed to point out the characteristics of a man like Lincoln. How shall you describe general human nature brought to its finest development?—for such was this man. We say that he was honest; men used to call him "Honest Abe." But honesty is not a quality. Honesty is the manifestation of character. Lincoln was honest because there was nothing small or petty about him, and only smallness and pettiness in a nature can produce dishonesty. Such honesty is a quality of largeness. It is that openness of nature which will not condescend to subterfuge, which is too big to conceal itself. Little men run to cover and deceive you. Big men cannot and will not run to cover, and do not deceive you. Of course, Lincoln was honest. But that was not a peculiar characteristic of him; that is a general description of him. He was not small or mean, and his honesty was not produced by any calculation, but was the genial expression of the great nature that was behind it.

Then we also say of Lincoln that he saw things with his own eyes. And it is very interesting that we can pick out individual men to say that of them. The opposite of the proposition is, that most men see things with other men's eyes. And that is the pity of the whole business of the world. Most men do not see things with their own eyes. If they did they would not be so inconspicuous as they consent to be. What most persons do is to live up to formulas and opinions and believe them, and never give themselves the trouble to ask whether they are true or not; so that there is a great deal of truth in saying that the trouble is, that men believe so many things that are not so, because they have taken them at second hand; they have accepted them in the form they were given to them. They have not reexamined them. They have not seen the world with their own eyes. But Lincoln saw it with his own eyes. And he not only saw the surface of it, but saw beneath the surface of it; for the characteristic of the seeing eye is that it is a discerning eye, seeing also that which is not caught by the surface; it penetrates to the heart of the subjects it looks upon. Not only did this man look upon life with a discerning eye. If you read of his youth and of his early manhood, it would seem that these were his only and sufficient pleasures. Lincoln seemed to covet nothing from his business except that it would give him leisure enough to do this very thing—to look at other people; to talk about them; to sit by the stove in the evening and discuss politics with them; to talk about all the things that were going on, to make shrewd, penetrating comments upon them, to speak his penetrating jests.

I had a friend once who said he seriously thought that the business of life was conversation. There is a good deal of Mr. Lincoln's early life which would indicate that he was of the same opinion. He believed that, at any rate, the most attractive business of life was conversation; and conversation, with Lincoln, was an important part of the business of life, because it was conversation which uncovered the meanings of things and illuminated the hidden places where nobody but Lincoln had every thought of looking.

☆ ☆ ☆

I know some men can see anything they choose to see, but they won't say anything; who are dried up at the source by that enemy of mankind which we call Caution. God save a free country from cautious men;—men, I mean, cautious for themselves,—for cautious men are men who will not speak the truth if the speaking of it threatens to damage them. Caution is the confidential agent of selfishness.

This man had no caution. He was absolutely direct and fearless. You will say that he had very little worldly goods to lose. He did not allow himself to be encumbered by riches, therefore he could say what he pleased. You know that men who are encumbered by riches are apt to be more silent than other. They have given hostages to fortune, and for them it is very necessary to maintain the *status quo*. Now, Mr. Lincoln was not embarrassed in this way. A change of circumstances would suit him just as well as the permanency of existing circumstances. But I am confident that if Mr. Lincoln had had the gift of making money, he nevertheless would not have restrained his gift for saying things; that he nevertheless would have ignored the trammels and despised caution and said what he thought. But one interesting thing about Mr. Lincoln is that no matter how shrewd or penetrating his comment, he never seemed to allow a matter to grip him. He seemed so directly in contact with it that he could define things other men could not define; and yet he was detached. He did not look upon it as if he were part of it. And he was constantly salting all the delightful things that he said, with the salt of wit and humor.

☆ ☆ ☆

Lincoln was a singularly studious man—not studious in the ordinary conventional sense. To be studious in the ordinary, conventional sense, if I may judge by my observation at a university, is to do the things you have to do and not understand them particularly. But to be studious, in the sense in which Mr. Lincoln was studious, is to follow eagerly and fearlessly the curiosity of a mind which will not be satisfied unless it understands. That is a deep studiousness; that is the thing which lays bare the map of life and enables men to understand the circumstances in which they live, as nothing else can do.

And what commends Mr. Lincoln's studiousness to me is that the result of it was he did not have any theories at all. Life is a very complex thing. No theory that I ever heard propounded will match its varied pattern; and the men who are dangerous are the men who are not content with understanding, but go on to propound theories, things which will make a new pattern for society and a new model for the universe. Those are the men who are not to be trusted. Because, although you steer by the North Star, when you have lost the bearings of your compass, you nevertheless must steer in a pathway on the sea,—you are not bound for the North Star. The man who insists upon his theory insists that there is a way to the North Star, and I know, and every one knows, that there is not—at least none yet discovered. Lincoln was one of those delightful students who do not seek to tie you up in the meshes of any theory.

☆ ☆ ☆

Lincoln was of the mass, but he was so lifted and big that all men could look upon him, until he became the "model for the mass" and was "singly of more value than they all."

It was in that sense that Lincoln was "a man of the people." His sources were where all the pure springs are, but his streams flowed down into other country and fertilized other plains, where men had become sophisticated with the life of an older age.

A great nation is not led by a man who simply repeats the talk of the street-corners of the opinions of the newspapers. A nation is led by a man who hears more than those things; or who, rather, hearing those things, understands them better, unites them, puts them into a common meaning; speaks, not the rumors of the street, but a new principle for a new age; a man in whose ears the voices of the nation do not sound like the accidental and discordant notes that come from the voice of a mob, but concurrent and concordant like the united voices of a chorus, whose many meanings, spoken by melodious tongues, united in his understanding in a single meaning and reveal to him a single vision, so that he can speak what no man else knows, the common meaning of the common voice. Such is the man who leads a great, free, democratic nation.

☆ ☆ ☆

Why was it that Mr. Lincoln was wiser than the professional politicians? Because the professional politicians had burrowed into particular burrows and Mr. Lincoln walked on the surface and saw his fellow-men.

Why could Mr. Lincoln smile at lawyers and turn away from ministers? Because he had not had his contact with life as a lawyer has, and he had not lectured his fellow-men as a minister has. He was detached from every point of view and therefore superior,—at any rate in a position to becoming superior,—to every point of view. You must have a man of this detachable sort.

Moreover, you must not have a man, if he is to be a man of the people, who is standardized and conventionalized. Look to it that your communities, your great cities, do not impose too arbitrary standards upon the men whom you wish to use. Do not reduce men to standards. Let them be free. Do not compel them by conventions. Let them wear any clothes they please and look like anything they choose; let them do anything that a decent and an honest man may do without criticism; do not laugh at them because they do not look like you, or talk like you, or think like you. They are freer for that circumstance, because, as an English writer has said: "You may talk of the tyranny of Nero and Tiberius, but the real tyranny is the tyranny of your next-door neighbor. There is no tyranny like the tyranny of being obliged to be like him,"—of being considered a very singular person if you are not; of having men shrug their shoulders and say, "Singular young man, sir, singular young man; very gifted, but not to be trusted." Not to be trusted because unlike your own trustworthy self! You must take your leaders in every time of difficulty from among absolutely free men who are not standardized and conventionalized, who are at liberty to do what they think right and say what they think true; that is the only kind of leadership you can afford to have.

☆ ☆ ☆

The tasks of the future call for men like Lincoln more audibly, more imperatively, than did the tasks of the time when civil war was brewing and the very existence of the nation was in the scale of destiny. For the things that perplex us at this moment are the things which mark, I will not say a warfare, but a division among classes; and when a nation begins to be divided into rival and contestant interests by the score, the same is much more dangerous than when it is divided into only two perfectly distinguishable interests which you can discriminate and deal with. If there are only two sides I can easily make up my mind which side to take, but if there are a score of sides then I must say to some man who is not immersed, not submerged, not caught in this struggle, "Where shall I go? What do you see? What is the movement of the mass? Where are we going? Where do you propose you should go?" It is then I need a man of the people, detached from this struggle yet cognizant of it all, sympathetic with it all, saturated with it all, to whom I can say, "How do you sum it up, what are the signs of the day, what does the morning say, what are the tasks that we must set our hands to?" We should pray, not only that we should be led by such men, but also that they should be men of the particular sweetness that Lincoln possessed.

The most dangerous thing you can have in an age like this is a man who is intense and hot. We have heat enough; what we want is light. Anybody can stir up emotions, but who is master of men enough to take the saddle and guide those awakened emotions? Anybody can cry a nation awake to the necessities of reform, but who shall frame the reform but a man who is cool, who takes his time, who will draw you aside for a jest, who will say: "Yes, but not today, tomorrow; let us see the other man and see what he has to say; let us hear everybody, let us know that we are to do. In the meantime I have a capital story for your private ear. Let me take the strain off, let me unbend the steel. Don't let us settle this thing by fire but let us settle it by those cool, incandescent lights which show its real nature and color."

The most valuable thing about Mr. Lincoln was that in the midst of the strain of war, in the midst of the crash of arms, he could sit quietly in his room and enjoy a book that led his thoughts off from everything American, could wander in fields of dreams, while every other man was hot with the immediate contest. Always set your faith in a man who can withdraw himself, because only the man who can withdraw himself can see the stage; only the man who can withdraw himself can see affairs as they are.

And so the lesson of this day is faith in the common product of the nation; the lesson of this day is the future as well as the past leadership of men, wise men, who have come from the people. We should not be Americans deserving to call ourselves the fellow countrymen of Lincoln if we did not feel the compulsion that his example lays upon us—the compulsion, not to heed him merely but to look to our own duty, to live every day as if that were the day upon which America was to be reborn and remade; to attack every task as if we had something here that was new and virginal and original, out of which we could make the very stuff of life, but integrity, faith in our fellow-men, wherever it is deserved, absolute ignorance of any obstacle that is insuperable, patience, indomitable courage, insight, universal sympathy,—with that program opening our hearts to every candid suggestions, listening to all the voices of the nation, trying to bring in a new day of vision and of achievement.

3

On Education and Scholarship

True Scholarship

Throughout his life as an educator, Wilson consistently argued for broad general education *over* narrow specialization for undergraduates. One of the earliest expressions of this theme was published in the university periodical *The Princetonian* in May 1877, during his sophomore year. This brief essay reflected a student perspective on Princeton, but also a mature critique of the superficiality and narrowness of both student efforts and the "system" of undergraduate education in his day. Much remains the same. While always extremely careful in his own writing, Wilson had no patience for style over substance in education.

A comparison of American scholarship, as represented in our institutions of learning, with that of Germany and England, is very discouraging. It is true that every College can boast of hard students, but with the greater number of them the highest motive is grade, and far be it from us to honor with the title "scholar" the man who has no higher end in view than this.

While the mere student works with the spirit of a slave, the scholar seeks wisdom because he is inspired with a love for it, and to him no exertion seems too great to obtain it. He is genuine, not superficial. Instead of making a good recitation his highest motive, he is constantly training all his powers in the most perfect discipline; the judgement in selecting fields for exploration from the vast territories of knowledge which lie open to him; his industry and perseverance to assist in untiring efforts in gathering and storing away the precious truth, and his memory in holding them in constant readiness for future use.

When true scholarship offers so grand an opportunity for the exercise of our noblest faculties, we marvel that it should be so neglected. On the part of the student, misguided energy and an insufficiency of enthusiasm are at fault; but we must believe that to our collegiate system a large part of the blame can be attached. Nothing is so utterly destructive of true scholarship as what is technically called "cramming." To abolish the practicability of this operation should be the basis principle in the College regime.

But so far is this from being the case, that it would be impossible to devise a method better adapted to encourage and reward it than our present arrangement and style of examinations. Hay is much more likely to be made while the sun shines, if the shower is constantly impending, and the College work would be much more faithfully performed if the students knew not when they would be called to account.

But one great reason why scholars are so few and held in such low repute is, that the highest ambition with many of men of excellent talent is to be able and polished writers. We are too prone to forget that knowledge is power, and that without a well-filled mind, our highest literary efforts can never be of much worth. They may even be tinctured with genius, and, without the restraining and correcting power of learning, be mere effusions. Then, too, the characteristics of mind which especially mark the scholar, are, to a large extent, the same with those which make the writer. Thus in both, the secret of success is the power of mental vision, of deep, thorough, condensed thought. Nothing so hampers the writer as a wandering mind. To comprehend his subject fully and justly, to hold it before his mind in all its shades and ramifications, and to reproduce it, requires the utmost concentration.

Further, the scholar who is versed in all literature is capable of drawing apt illustrations from science and art, and of leaving everywhere the impress of his own originality. If Princeton is to hold a high rank in literature, she must produce scholars; and if we are fired with an ambition for fame and for the glory of our alma mater, no pathway is nobler than true scholarship.

On the Study of Politics: Address to Princeton Alumni

Wilson was one of the pioneers of the discipline of political science. American higher education was changing rapidly. Graduate study on the European model was growing, and changes in curricula gave rise to new academic departments now familiar in the landscape of the university. Wilson was a leader in the move to stimulate the realistic study of politics and to establish political science as a separate academic discipline. In a speech to the Princeton alumni of New York, he made a plea for colleges to add professors of politics to their faculties. He described politics as an experimental art, something more than the rational application of ideas to society. The teaching of politics should dissect government as a "living organism." He pressed the need to study the gritty stuff of politics as actually practiced, to shed light on the "unsavory parts" of politics. Remarks about socialism and the "unpunished crime" of ward politics offer clues to his own political thought. The address was delivered in March 1886, while he was a member of the Bryn Mawr faculty.

There is an old subject called "the scholar in politics"—a theoretical subject of much interest, and admitting of endless treatment. It exerts its fascination upon the mind of the college-bred man at a very early stage in his career—indeed principally at that stage. And this for a very simple reason. In this country, at least it is a subject for speculation rather than for laborious investigation. It is surrounded by the bewitching light of Utopia.

The "working hypothesis" of this subject is a proposition which is true only if understood in just the opposite sense from that in which it is generally used by the undergraduate—and, for the matter of that, the graduate—authorities upon this great topic. That proposition is that the scholar in politics, if a true scholar, is different from anybody else in politics. The inference is that he is better equipped for his business than any other politician; and it is this inference which needs to be reversed. His equipment for public service is different from other men's—and it is much larger. But it is more likely to be an incumbrance than an aid. The average college man goes into public life with a certain stock of ideas about politics: the more thoroughly a college man he is, the stiffer and more absolute those ideas. I cannot enumerate them: but I can describe them. Taken in the bulk, they may be said to be *reasoned politics;* politics stripped of its rages of humanity, washed of its dust, and soberly attired in the cap and gown of academic logic.

Now the world, I admit, is governed by logic in the long run; but representative government—the only govt. we ever talk about—is conducted not by long runs but by short. It is a matter of persuading a great many people to take hold of certain objects just at hand—not run after certain distant objects on the logical horizon. There is nothing that the logician more abhors than prejudice; nothing seems so contemptible in his eyes as slow expediency. And yet prejudice elects more candidates and passes more bills than logic—and expediency, I cannot help thinking, is of greater dignity in politics. There are no parts of Burke upon which I more love to dwell than those in which he defends prejudice against the assaults of the rational and expediency against the haste of the radical. "We are afraid," he says, "to put men to live and trade each on his own private stock of reason, because we suspect that his stock in each man is small, and that the individuals would do better to avail themselves of the general bank and capital of nations and of ages. Many of our men of speculation, instead of exploding general prejudices, employ their sagacity to discover the latent wisdom which prevails in them. If they find what they seek, and they seldom fail, they think it more wise to continue the prejudice with the reason involved, than to cast away the coal of prejudice, and to leave nothing but the naked reason; because prejudice with its reason has a motive to give action that reason, and an affection which will give it permanence. Prejudice is of ready application in the emergency; it previously engages the mind in a steady course of wisdom and virtue, and does not leave the man hesitating in the moment of decision, skeptical, puzzled, and unresolved. Prejudice renders a man's virtue his habit, and not a series of unconnected acts. Through just prejudice, his duty becomes a part of his nature."

What is this but a commentary on much of modern socialism? The program of the average labor organization, made up of distorted bits of economic truth; mixed with many of the cut and dried formulas of rationalistic socialism, represents an attempt to replace in the mind of the laborer the virtues of patient industry and of reverence for law which had taken such deep root there with calculated policies which ignore law and would substitute the natural rights of man. It is a perilous attempt to train the unlearned and the undisciplined to "live and trade each on his own private stock of reason." Its success is due to the fact that it uses these theories of natural right which chime in with selfish desire and so establishes passion at the same time that it overthrows habit. If that success is to extend, it would seem as if the crew of our ship of state must succeed in wrecking her under the idea of thereby escaping the hardships of navigation.

But we must not conclude that because in this case passion masquerades in the garb of reason the carnival is to be broken up by logic. The scholar's stock of ideas, profound and rounded as they are, belong to that category of the things that are not seen—and cannot be seen by those whom we most want to have see them. The only gateway to a solution of such difficulties is knowledge of affairs. The logic of events will always convince men of folly: the statesman must prepare the way for that logic to operate by temperate concession to intemperate demands. Politics is an experimental art. As a scholar Mr. Gladstone defends the union of church and state; as knowing affairs, he disestablishes the church in Ireland and forecasts disestablishment in England. The logic of Cobden and Bright, backed by the thunders of every political economist then esteemed, had to wait to be assisted to the repeal of the Corn Laws by a famine in Ireland. Logic is much too stiff a thing to fit into the grooves of the world. It must be made flexible by expediency.

You have seen already, of course, the conclusion to which I am coming. It is not that the college is, but only that it might be, a great direct aid to government. Its indirect contribution to good institutions is of course inestimable. It has been the gymnasium of which men's minds have received the agility and the strength which have steadied them for the higher exercises of government as for the greater undertakings in all other spheres of thought. But the college might do more than merely prepare men to understand *anything*. It might give them some preliminary drill in the practical thought of this great *particular* thing, government. And to some extent it is doing so. But in every college there is missing a professor of politics. (Of course I am speaking roughly: every speech like this must be as broad as it is short.) There is instruction almost everywhere, of one sort or another, in history, and in many institutions instruction in political economy, jurisprudence, and constitutional law sets the student in the way of understanding most of the permanent relations of modern political society. The largest endowments and most advanced administrations even provide lectures on current topics of governmental policy: and such lectures are within the province of the future professor of politics. But that person himself is not yet in any of our faculties. Presently I shall describe the functions of such a teacher as I foresee them. First let me say that we are afraid of the word politics. We fear that it would make prudent parents stare and pish to see it in our catalogues. Some of the more earnest of us even nerve ourselves to adopt the uncouth word "civics" amongst the respected words of our vocabulary. Or we seek to stow politics away in disguise under the broad but elegant "umbrella" of "political science." Perhaps this is part of the prejudice of logic. Politics is largely an affair, as I have said, of management and expediency—of much else besides reason—and it may seem to some that nothing which does not rest entirely—or at least mainly—on reason ought to find a place in a college curriculum. But the management and expediency of general politics is not necessarily the management and expediency of ward politics. The secrets of the ward politician would find their proper relations of place and treatment in a work on criminal jurisprudence; under the heading, unpunished crime. To let them assume exclusive title to the Aristotelian word "politics" would be to sin against all philosophy.

It would be one of the chief services of the professor of politics that he would by his very title reclaim this word from its unmerited disgrace. It would be his duties to know and expose these unsavory parts of his subject: but only as some of the vicious forces which had to be understood only to be overcome by the higher management of the political art. It would be his whole duty to throw the light both of theory and of practice upon the art of government: to expound government as an historical development and to dissect it as a living organism. Let me be more explicit. I understand politics as a subject for instruction to include the history of political institutions and of speculative thought about such institutions, but to include these, not as sufficient in themselves to supply precepts for present political action, but only as indispensably introductory to inquiry, through every available channel, as to the real forces now at work in politics and the actual operation of the governments of the world. This would be, not a study of systems merely, but also of the circumstances and spirit which make each system workable in its own country and amongst its own people. Sir Henry Maine's striking volume on popular government recently published, comes within this sphere of the professor of politics, though it knows rather too much of the outer and rather too little of the inner history of national life to touch the real springs of democracy.

Of course the professor of politics may easily get lost in the immense field which I have vaguely set apart for him—just as the political economist of the new, "all-the-facts" school may get lost in his boundless universe of statistics and particulars. To the subject of politics as I have defined it, there belongs a limitless world of human circumstances: it must have Shakespeare as well as Mill . . . for its text writer. But there are sane and possible methods for threading even such a labyrinth: and there will always be much to say against the political education sought to be furnished by our colleges so long as they confine themselves to the detached subjects of political economy and constitutional law and do not seek to penetrate to the heart of the nation's—if possible, of each nation's—being, laying bare the springs of action and the intricacies of acquired habit, political morality as well as political forms, political prejudice and expediency, as well as political reason and rigid consistency.

Perhaps it is too early in the history of our colleges to speak of such an addition to their faculties: but it is certainly not too early in the history of our politics. The practical difficulties of popular government, as well as of governments of all other sorts, have so enormously increased that study which does not elucidate the practical conditions and aptitudes of government contributes almost nothing to the political life of the nation. Our politics are too narrow, our politicians too egotistically content with learning only from themselves. There is no channel through which to avail ourselves of the lights of comparative politics, of the general bank and capital of nations in the exigencies which threaten. It would help greatly if we could have in our colleges chairs of politics which should bridge over the gulf between close doctrine and rough, everyday practice. I ask you to drink to the future professor of politics: may he be no less a scholar for being studiously a man of the world!

Mere Literature

This essay was Wilson's response to the increasingly positivist, "scientific" direction of scholarship of the late nineteenth century. The phenomenal progress of science in the nineteenth century encouraged a utilitarian vision of learning that led many to conclude that ideas that were not "scientific" or quantified were not worth serious attention. The result in education was an increasing emphasis on technical training in fields useful in the "real" world and a concomitant decline in respect for less immediately profitable disciplines. For the kind of scientific mind to which Wilson referred, "mere" was a word of impatient dismissal. He attacked the narrowness and lack of vision in the trend and revealed an appreciation of the importance of literature to human understanding. One could often learn so much more of a people from their poetry than could be understood through the study of the narrow details of their sociology or politics. Originally published in the *Atlantic Monthly* in December 1893, it became the title piece for a book of his essays published by Houghton Mifflin in 1896.

A singular phrase this, "mere literature,"—the irreverent invention of a scientific age. Literature we know, but "mere" literature? We are not to read it as if it meant sheer literature, literature in the essence, stripped of all accidental or ephemeral elements, and left with nothing but its immortal charm and power. "Mere literature" is a serious sneer, conceived in all honesty by the scientific mind, which despises things which do not fall within the categories of demonstrable knowledge. It means nothing but literature, as who should say, "mere talk," "mere fabrication," "mere pastime." The scientist, with his head comfortably and excusably full of knowable things, takes nothing seriously and with his hat off except human knowledge. The creations of the human spirit are, from this point of view, incalculable vagaries, irresponsible phenomena, to be regarded only as play, and, for the mind's good, only as recreation,—to be used to while away the tedium of a railway journey, or to amuse a period of rest or convalescence; mere byplay, mere make-believe.

And so very whimsical things sometimes happen, because of this scientific and positivist spirit of the age, when the study of the literature of any language is made part of the curriculum of our colleges. The more delicate and subtle purposes of the study are put quite out of countenance, and literature is commanded to assume the phrases and the methods of science. It would be very painful if it should turn out that schools and universities were agencies of Philistinism; but there are some things which should prepare us for such a discovery. Our present plans for teaching everybody involve certain unpleasant things quite inevitably. It is obvious that you cannot have universal education without restricting your teaching to such things as can be universally understood. It is plain that you cannot impart "university methods" to thousands, or create "investigators" by the score, unless you confine your university education to matters which dull men can investigate, your laboratory training to tasks which mere plodding diligence and submissive patience can compass. Yet, if you do so limit and constrain what you teach, you thrust taste and insight and delicacy of perception out of the schools, exalt the obvious and the merely useful above the things which are only imaginatively or spiritually conceived, make education an affair of tasking and handling and smelling, and so create Philistia, that country in which they speak of "mere literature." I suppose that in Nirvana one would speak in like wise of "mere life."

The fear, at any rate, that such things may happen cannot fail to set up anxiously pondering certain questions about the systematic teaching of literature in our schools and colleges. How are we to impart classical writings to the children of the general public? "Beshrew the general public!" Cries Mr. Birrell. "What in the name of the Bodleian has the general public got to do with literature?" Unfortunately, it has a great deal to do with it; for are we not complacently forcing the general public into our universities, and are we not arranging that all its sons be instructed how they may themselves master and teach our literature? You have nowadays, it is believed, only to heed the suggestions of pedagogics in order to know how to impart Burke or Browning, Dryden or Swift. There are certain practical difficulties, indeed; but there are ways of overcoming them. You must have strength so that you can handle with real mastery the firm fibre of these men; you must have a heart, moreover, to feel their warmth, an eye to see what they see, an imagination to keep them company, a pulse to experience their delights. But if you have none of these things, you may make shift to do without them. You may count the words they use, note the changes of phrase they make in successive revisions, put their rhythm into a scale of feet, run their allusions—particularly their female allusions—to cover, detect them in their previous reading. Or if none of these things please you, or you find the big authors difficult or dull, you may drag to light all the minor writers of their time, who are easy to understand. By setting an example in such methods you render great services in certain directions. You make the higher degrees of our universities available for the large number of respectable men who can count, and measure, and search diligently; and that may prove no small matter. You divert attention from thought, which is not always easy to get at, and fix attention upon language, as upon a curious mechanism, which can be perceived with the bodily eye, and which is worthy to be studied for its own sake, quite apart from anything it may mean. You encourage the examination of forms, grammatical and metrical, which can be quite accurately determined and quite exhaustively catalogued. You bring all the visible phenomena of writing to light and into ordered system. You go further, and show how to make careful literal identification of stories somewhere told ill and without art with the same stories told over again by the masters, well and with the transfiguring effect of genius. You thus broaden the area of science; for you rescue the concrete phenomena of the expression of thought—the necessary syllabification which accompanies it, the inevitable juxtaposition of words, the constant use of particles, the habitual display of roots, the inveterate repetition of names, the recurrent employment of meanings heard or read—from their confusion with the otherwise unclassifiable manifestations of what had hitherto been accepted, without critical examination, under the lump term "literature," simply for the pleasure and spiritual edification to be got from it.

An instructive differentiation ensues. In contrast with the orderly phenomena of speech and writing, which are amenable to scientific processes of examination and classification, and which take rank with the orderly successions of change in nature, we have what, for want of a more exact term, we call "mere literature,"—the literature which is not an expression of form, but an expression of spirit. This is a troublesome thing, and perhaps does not belong in well-conceived plans of universal instruction; for it offers many embarrassments to pedagogic method. It escapes all scientific categories. It is not pervious to research. It is too wayward to be brought under the discipline of exposition. It is an attribute of so many different substances at one and the same time that the consistent scientific man must needs put it forth from his company, as without responsible connections. By "mere literature" he means mere evanescent color, wanton trick of phrase, perverse departures from categorical statement,—something all personal equation, such stuff as dreams are made of.

We must not all, however, be impatient of this truant child of fancy. When the schools cast her out, she will stand in need of friendly succor, and we must train our spirits for the function. We must be free-hearted in order to make her happy, for she will accept entertainment from no sober, prudent fellow who shall counsel her to mend her ways. She has always made light of hardship, and she has never loved or obeyed any save those of her own mind,—those who were indulgent to her humors, responsive to her ways of thought, attentive to her whims, content with her "mere" charms. She already has her small following of devotees, like all charming, capricious mistresses. There are some still who think that to know her is better than a liberal education.

There is but one way in which you can take mere literature as an education, and that is directly, at first hand. Almost any media except her own language and touch and tone are non-conducting. A descriptive catalogue of a collection of paintings is no substitute for the little areas of color and form themselves. You do not want to hear about a beautiful woman, simply, how she was dressed, how she bore herself, how the fine color flowed sweetly here and there upon her cheeks, how her eyes burned and melted, how her voice thrilled through the ears of those about her. If you have ever seen a woman, these things but tantalize and hurt you, if you cannot see her. You want to be in her presence. You know that only your own eyes can give you direct knowledge of her. When once you have seen her, you know her in her habit as she lived; nothing but her presence contains her in her habit as she lived; nothing but her presence contains her life. It is the same with the authentic products of literature. You can never get their beauty at second hand, or feel their power except by direct contact with them.

☆ ☆ ☆

It is so with all essential literature. It has a quality to move you, and you can never mistake it, if you have any blood in you. And it has also a power to instruct you which is as effective as it is subtle, and which no research or systematic method can ever rival. It is a sore pity if that power cannot be made available in the classroom. It is not merely that it quickens your thought and fills your imagination with the images that have illuminated the choicer minds of the race. It does indeed exercise the faculties in this wise, bringing them into the best atmosphere, and into the presence of the men of greatest charm and force; but it does a great deal more than that. It acquaints the mind, by direct contact, with the forces which really govern and modify the world from generation to generation. There is more of a nation's politics to be gotten out of its poetry than out of all its systematic writers upon public affairs and constitutions. Epics are better mirrors of manners than chronicles; dramas oftentimes let you into the secrets of statutes; orations stirred by a deep energy of emotion or resolution, passionate pamphlets that survive their mission because of the direct action of their style along permanent lines of thought, contain more history than parliamentary journals. It is not knowledge that moves the world, but ideals, convictions, the opinions or fancies that have been held or followed; and whoever studies humanity ought to study it alive, practice the vivisection of reading literature, and acquaint himself with something more than anatomies which are no longer in use by spirits.

☆ ☆ ☆

It is doubtless due to the scientific spirit of the age that these plain, these immemorial truths are in danger of becoming obscured. Science, under the influence of the conception of evolution, devotes itself to the study of forms, of specific differences, of the manner in which the same principle of life manifests itself variously under the compulsions of changes of environment. It is thus that it has become "scientific" to set forth the manner in which man's nature submits to man's circumstances; scientific to disclose morbid moods, and the conditions which produce them; scientific to regard man, not as the center or source of power, but as subject to power, a register of eternal forces instead of an originative soul, and character as a product of man's circumstances rather than a sign of man's mastery over circumstance. It is thus that it has become "scientific" to analyze language as itself a commanding element in man's life. The history of word roots, their modification under the influences of changes wrought in the vocal organs by habit or by climate, the laws of phonetic change to which they are obedient, and their persistence under all disguises of dialect, as if they were full of a self-directed energy of influence, is united with the study of grammatical forms in the construction of scientific conceptions of the evolution and uses of human speech. The impression is created that literature is only the chosen vessel of these forms, disclosing to us their modification in use and structure from age to age. Such vitality as the masterpieces of genius possess comes to seem only a dramatization of the fortunes of words. Great writers construct for the adventures of language their appropriate epics. Or, if it be not the words themselves that are scrutinized, but the style of their use, that style becomes, instead of a fine essence of personality, a matter of cadence merely, or of grammatical and structural relationships. Science is the study of the forces of the world of matter, the adjustments, the apparatus, of the universe; and the scientific study of literature has likewise become a study of apparatus, of the forms in which men utter thought, and the forces by which those forms have been and still are being modified, rather than of thought itself.

The essences of literature of course remain the same under all forms, and the true study of literature is the study of these essences,—a study, not of forms or of differences, but of likenesses, likenesses of spirit and intent under whatever varieties of method, running through all forms of speech like the same music along the chords of various instruments. There is a sense in which literature is independent of form, just as there is a sense in which music is independent of its instrument. It is my cherished belief that Apollo's pipe contained as much eloquent music as any modern orchestra. Some books live; many die: wherein is the secret of immortality? Not in beauty of form, nor even in force of passion. We might say of literature what Wordsworth said of poetry, the most easily immortal part of literature: it is "the impassioned expression which is in the countenance of all science; it is the breath of the finer spirit of all knowledge." Poetry has the easier immortality because it has the sweeter accent when it speaks, because its phrases linger in our ears to delight them, because its truths are also melodies. Prose has much to overcome, its plainness of visage, its less musical accents, its homelier turns of phrase. But it also may contain the immortal essence of truth and seriousness and high thought. It too may clothe conviction with the beauty that must make it shine forever. Let a man but have beauty in his heart, and, believing something with his might, put it forth arrayed as he sees it, the lights and shadows falling upon it on his page as they fall upon it in his heart, and he may die assured that beauty will not pass away out of the world.

☆ ☆ ☆

Scholarship gets into literature by becoming part of the originating individuality of a master of thought. No man is a master of thought without being also a master of its vehicle and instrument, style, that subtle medium of all its evasive effects of light and shade. Scholarship is material; it is not life. It becomes immortal only when it is worked upon by conviction, by schooled and chastened imagination, by thought that runs alive out of the inner fountains of individual insight and purpose. Colorless, or without suffusion of light from some source of light, it is dead, and will not twice be looked at; but made part of the life of a great mind, subordinated, absorbed, put forth with authentic stamp of currency on it, minted at some definite mint and bearing some sovereign image, it will even outlast the time when it shall have to deserve the acceptance of scholars,—when it shall, in fact, have become "mere literature."

Scholarship is the realm of nicely adjusted opinion. It is the business of scholars to assess evidence and test conclusions, to discriminate values and reckon probabilities. Literature is the realm of conviction and of vision. Its points of view are as various as they are oftentimes unverifiable. It speaks individual faiths. Its groundwork is not erudition, but reflection and fancy. Your thoroughgoing scholar dare not reflect. To reflect is to let himself in on his material; whereas what he wants is to keep himself apart, and view his materials in an air that does not color or refract. To reflect is to throw an atmosphere about what is in your mind, an atmosphere which holds all the colors of your life. Reflection summons all associations, and they throng and move so that they dominate the mind's stage at once. The plot is in their hands. Scholars, therefore, do not reflect; they label, group kind with kind, set forth in schemes, expound with dispassionate method. Their minds are not stages, but museums; nothing is done there, but very curious and valuable collections are kept there. If literature use scholarship, it is only to fill it with fancies or shape it to new standards, of which of itself it can know nothing.

True, there are books reckoned primarily books of science and of scholarship which have nevertheless won standing as literature: books of science such as Newton wrote, books of scholarship such as Gibbon's. But science was only the vestibule by which such a man as Newton entered the temple of nature, and the art he practiced was not the art of exposition, but the art of divination. He was not only a scientist, but also a seer; and we shall not lose sight of Newton because we value what he was more than what he knew. If we continue Gibbon in his fame, it will be for love of his art, not for worship of his scholarship. We some of us, nowadays, know the period of which he wrote better even than he did; but which one of us shall build so admirable a monument to ourselves, as arts, out of what we know? The scholar finds his immortality in the form he gives to his work. It is a hard saying, but the truth of it is inexorable: be an artist, or prepare for oblivion. You may write a chronicle, but you will not serve yourself thereby. You will only serve some fellow who shall come after you, possessing, what you did not have, an ear for the words you could not hit upon, an eye for the colors you could not see, a hand for the strokes you missed.

Real literature you can always distinguish by its form, and yet it is not possible to indicate the form it should have. It is easy to say that it should have a form suitable to its matter; but how suitable? Suitable to set the matter off, adorn, embellish it, or suitable simply to bring it directly, quick and potent, to the apprehension of the reader? This is the question of style, about which many masters have had many opinions; upon which you can make up no safe generalization from the practice of those who have unquestionably given to the matter of their thought immortal form, an accent or a countenance never to be forgotten. Who shall say how much of Burke's splendid and impressive imagery is part and stuff of his thought, or tell why even that part of Newman's prose which is devoid of ornament, stripped to its shining skin, and running bare and lithe and athletic to carry its tidings to men, should promise to enjoy as certain an immortality? Why should Lamb go so quaintly and elaborately to work upon his critical essays, taking care to perfume every sentence, if possible, with the fine savor of an old phrase, if the same business could be as effectively done in the plain and even cadences of Mr. Matthew Arnold's prose? Why should Gibbon be so formal, so stately, so elaborate, when he had before his eyes the example of great Tacitus, whose direct, sententious style had outlived so many hundred years the very language in which he wrote? In poetry, who shall measure the varieties of style lavished upon similar themes? The matter of vital thought is not separable from the thinker; its forms must suit his handling as well as fit his conception. Any style is author's stuff which is suitable to his purpose and his fancy. He may use rich fabrics with which to costume his thoughts, or he may use simple stone from which to sculpture them, and leave them bare. His only limits are those of art. He may not indulge a taste for the merely curious or fantastic. The quaint writers have quaint thoughts; their material is suitable. They do not merely satisfy themselves as virtuosi, with collections of odd phrases and obsolete meanings. They needed twisted woods to fit the eccentric pattern of their thought. The great writer has always dignity, restraint, propriety, adequateness; what time he loses these qualities he ceases to be great. His style neither creaks nor breaks under his passion, but carries the strain with unshaken strength. It is not trivial or mean, but speaks what small meanings fall in its way with simplicity, as conscious of their smallness. Its playfulness is within bounds, its laugh never bursting too boisterously into a guffaw. A great style always knows what it would be at, and does the thing appropriately, with the larger sort of taste.

This is the condemnation of tricks of phrase, devices to catch the attention, exaggerations and loud talk to hold it. No writer can afford to strive after effect, if his striving is to be apparent. For just and permanent effect is missed altogether, unless it be so completely attained as to seem like some touch of sunlight, perfect, natural, inevitable, wrought without effort and without deliberate purpose to be effective. Mere audacity of attempt can, of course, never win the wished-for result; and if the attempt be successful, it is not audacious. What we call audacity in a great writer has no touch of temerity, sauciness, or arrogance in it. It is simply high spirit, a dashing and splendid display of strength. Boldness is ridiculous unless it be impressive, and it can be impressive only when backed by solid forces of character attainment. Your plebeian hack cannot afford the showy paces; only the full-blooded Arabian has the sinew and proportion to lend them perfect grace and propriety. The art of letters eschews the bizarre as rigidly as does every other fine art. It mixes its colors with brains, and is obedient to great Nature's sane standards of right adjustment in all that it attempts.

You can make no catalogue of these features of great writing; there is no science of literature. Literature in its essence is mere spirit, and you must experience it rather than analyze it too formally. It is the door to nature and to ourselves. It opens our hearts to receive the experiences of great men and the conceptions of great races. It awakens us to the significance of action and to the singular power of mental habit. It airs our souls in the wide atmosphere of contemplation. "In these bad days, when it is thought more educationally useful to know the principle of the common pump than Keats' Ode on a Grecian Urn," as Mr. Birrell says, we cannot afford to let one single precious sentence of "mere literature" go by us unread or unpraised. If this free people to which we belong is to keep its fine spirit, its perfect temper amidst affairs, its high courage in the face of difficulties, its wise temperateness and wide-eyed hope, it must continue to drink deep and often from the old wells of English undefiled, quaff the keen tonic of its best ideals, keep its blood warm with all the great utterances of exalted purpose and pure principle of which its matchless literature is full. The great spirits of the past must command us in the tasks of the future. Mere literature will keep us pure and keep us strong. Even though it puzzle or altogether escape scientific method, it may keep our horizon clear for us, and our eyes glad to look bravely forth upon the world.

Inaugural Address as President of Princeton

At his inauguration as president of Princeton, academic dignitaries were joined by celebrities from the arts, politics, and business. In the audience were Grover Cleveland, Booker T. Washington, Mark Twain, William Dean Howells, and J. P. Morgan. In that august company the new president of Princeton used his inaugural address to expand upon his vision of higher education, properly providing a broad, catholic education to its students. The "pursuit of the particular" he thought had been excessive. He pleaded with the specialists themselves not to abandon undergraduate education, in later years so often consigned to graduate assistants by too many universities. Wilson envisioned a university in which professional scholars pursuing advanced study worked closely with young students to guide them to moral and intellectual development for service to the larger community. The address refers to his dream of locating the planned graduate school at the center of the undergraduate college. He was of course unaware that the geography of the graduate school would become one of the great controversies and disappointments of his presidency. When he became its president, Princeton was still officially Presbyterian. Here Wilson emphasizes the importance of religion, and specifically Christianity, informing the work of universities. That view would not broadly endure. Wilson was inaugurated on October 25, 1902.

Six years ago I had the honor of standing in this place to speak of the memories with which Princeton men heartened themselves as they looked back a century and a half to the founding of their college. Today my task is more delicate, more difficult. Standing here in the light of those older days, we must now assess our present purposes and powers and sketch the creed by which we shall be wiling to live in the days to come. We are but men of a single generation in the long life of an institution which shall still be young when we are dead, but while we live her life is in us. What we conceive she conceives. In planning for Princeton, moreover, we are planning for the country. The service of institutions of learning is not private but public. It is plain what the nation needs as its affairs grow more and more complex and its interests begin to touch the ends of the earth. It needs efficient and enlightened men. The universities of the country must take part in supplying them.

American universities serve a free nation whose progress, whose power, whose prosperity, whose happiness, whose integrity depend upon individual initiative and the sound sense and equipment of the rank and file. Their history, moreover, has set them apart to a character and service of their own. They are not mere seminaries of scholars. They never can be.

Most of them, the greatest of them and the most distinguished, were first of all great colleges before they became universities; and their task is twofold: the production of a great body of informed and thoughtful men and the production of a small body of trained scholars and investigators. It is one of their functions to take large bodies of young men up to the places of outlook whence the world of thought and affairs is to be viewed; it is another of their functions to take some men, a little more mature, a little more studious, men self-selected by aptitude and industry, into the quiet libraries and laboratories where the close contacts of study are learned which yield the world new insight into the processes of nature, of reason, and of the human spirit. These two functions are not to be performed separately, but side by side, and are to be informed with one spirit, the spirit of enlightenment, a spirit of learning which is neither superficial nor pedantic, which values life more than it values the mere acquisitions of the mind.

Universities, we have learned to think, include within their scope, when complete, schools of law, of medicine, of theology, and of those more recondite mechanic arts, such as the use of electricity, upon which the skilled industry of the modern world is built up; and, though in dwelling upon such an association of schools as of the gist of the matter in our definitions of a university, we are relying upon historical accidents rather than upon essential principles for our conceptions; they are accidents which show the happy order and system with which things often come to pass. Though the university may dispense with professional schools, professional schools may not dispense with the university. Professional schools have nowhere their right atmosphere and association except where they are parts of a university and share its spirit and method. They must love learning as well as professional success in order to have their perfect usefulness. This is not the verdict of the universities merely but of the professional men themselves, spoken out of hard experience of the facts of business. . . . The modern world nowhere shows a closeted profession shut in to a narrow round of technical functions to which no knowledge of the outside world need ever penetrate. Whatever our calling, our thoughts must often be afield among men of many kinds, amidst interests as various as the phases of modern life. The managing minds of the world, even the efficient working minds of the world, must be equipped for a mastery whose chief characteristic is adaptability, play, an initiative which transcends the bounds of mere technical training. Technical schools whose training is not built up on the foundations of a broad and general discipline cannot impart this. The stuff they work upon must be prepared for them by processes which produce fibre and elasticity, and their own methods must be shot through with the impulses of the university.

It is this that makes our age and our task so interesting: this complex interdependence and interrelationship of all the processes which prepare the mind for effectual service: this necessity that the merchant and the financier should have traveled minds, the engineer a knowledge of books and men, the lawyer a wide view of affairs, the physician a familiar acquaintance with the abstract data of science, and that the closeted scholar should throw his windows open to the four quarters of the world. Every considerable understanding has come to be based on knowledge, on thoughtfulness, on the masterful handling of men and facts. The university must stand in the midst, where the roads of thought and knowledge interlace and cross, and building upon some coign of vantage, command them all.

☆ ☆ ☆

Probably no one is to blame for the neglect of the general into which we have been led by our eager pursuit of the particular. Every age has lain under the reproach of doing but one thing at a time, of having some one signal object for the sake of which other things were slighted or ignored. But the plain fact is, that we have so spread and diversified the scheme of knowledge in our day that it has lost coherence. We have dropped the threads of system in our teaching. And system begins at the beginning. We must find the common term for college and university; and those who have great colleges at the heart of the universities they are trying to develop are under a special compulsion to find it. Learning is not divided. Its kingdom and government are centered, unitary, single. The processes of instruction which fit a large body of young men to serve their generation with powers released and fit for great tasks ought also to serve as the initial processes by which scholars and investigators are made. They ought to be but the first parts of the method by which the crude force of untrained men is reduced to the expert uses of civilization. There may come a day when general study will be no part of the function of a university, when it shall have been handed over, as some now talk of handing it over, to the secondary schools, after the German fashion; but that day will not be ours, and I, for one, do not wish to see it come. That masters who guide the youngsters who pursue general studies are very useful neighbors for those who prosecute detailed inquiries and devote themselves to special tasks. No investigator can afford to keep his doors shut against the comradeship of the wide world of letters and of thought.

☆ ☆ ☆

The age has hurried us, has shouldered us out of the old ways, has bidden us be moving and look to the cares of a practical generation; and we have suffered ourselves to be a little disconcerted. No doubt we were once pedants. It is a happy thing that the days have gone by when the texts we studied loomed bigger to our view than the human spirit that underlay them. But there are some principles of which we must not let go. We must not lose sight of that fine conception of a general training which led our fathers, in the days when men knew how to build great states, to build great colleges also to sustain them. No man who knows the world has ever supposed that a day would come when every young man would seek a college training. The college is not for the majority who carry forward the common labor of the world, nor even for those who work at the skilled handicrafts which multiply the conveniences and the luxuries of the complex modern life. It is for the minority who plan, who conceive, who superintend, who mediate between group and group and must see the wide stage as a whole. Democratic nations must be served in this wise no less than those whose leaders are chosen by birth and privilege; and the college is no less democratic because it is for those who play a special part. I know that there are men of genius who play these parts of captaincy and yet have never been in the classrooms of a college, whose only school has been the world itself. The world is an excellent school for those who have vision and self-discipline enough to use it. It works in this wise, in part, upon us all. Raw lads are made men of by the mere sweep of their lives through the various school of experience. It is this very sweep of life that we wish to bring to the consciousness of young men by the shorter processes of the college. We have seen the adaptation take place; we have seen crude boys made fit in four years to become men of the world.

☆ ☆ ☆

There are two ways of preparing a young man for his life work. One is to give him the skill and special knowledge which shall make a good tool, and excellent bread-winning tool of him; and for thousands of young men that way must be followed. It is a good way. It is honorable, it is indispensable.

But it is not for the college, and it never can be. The college should seek to make the men whom it receives something more than excellent servants of a trade or skilled practitioners of a profession. It should give them elasticity of faculty and breadth of vision, so that they shall have a surplus of mind to expend, not upon their profession only, for its liberalization and enlargement, but also upon the broader interests which lie about them, in the spheres in which they are to be, not breadwinners merely, but citizens as well, and in their own hearts, where they are to grow to the stature of real nobility. It is this free capital of mind the world most stands in need of,—this free capital that awaits investment in undertakings, spiritual as well as material, which advance the race and help all men to a better life.

And are we to do this great thing by the old discipline of Greek, Latin, Mathematics, and English? The day has gone by when that is possible. The circle of liberal studies is too much enlarged, the area of general learning is too much extended, to make it any longer possible to make these few things stand for all. Science has opened a new world of learning, as great as the old. The influence of science has broadened and transformed old themes of study and created new, and all the boundaries of knowledge are altered. In the days of our grandfathers all learning was literary, was of the book; the phenomena of nature were brought together under the general terms of an encyclopedic Natural Philosophy. Now the quiet rooms where once a few students sat agaze before a long table at which, with a little apparatus before him, a lecturer discoursed of the laws of matter and of force are replaced by great laboratories, physical, chemical, biological, in which the pupil's own direct observation and experiment take the place of the conning of mere theory and generalization, and men handle the immediate stuff of which nature is made. Museums of natural history, of geology, of paleontology stretch themselves amidst our lecture rooms, for demonstration of what we say of the life and structure of the globe. The telescope, the spectroscope, not the text book merely, are our means of teaching the laws and movements of the sky. An age of science has transmuted speculation into knowledge and doubled the dominion of the mind. Heavens and earth swing together in a new universe of knowledge. And so it is impossible that the old discipline should stand alone, to serve us as an education. With it alone we should get no introduction into the modern world either of thought or of affairs. The mind of the modern student must be carried through a wide range of studies in which science shall have a place not less distinguished than that accorded literature, philosophy or politics.

But we must observe proportion and remember what it is that we seek. We seek in our general education, not universal knowledge, but the opening up of the mind to a catholic appreciation of the best achievements of men and the best processes of thought since days of thought set in.

☆ ☆ ☆

I should dread to see those who guide special study and research altogether excused from undergraduate instruction, should dread to see them withdraw themselves altogether from the broad and general survey of the subjects of which they have sought to make themselves masters. I should equally despair of seeing any student made a truly serviceable specialist who had not turned to his specialty in the spirit of a broad and catholic learning,—unless, indeed, he were one of those rare spirits who once and again appear amongst us, whose peculiar, individual privilege it is to have safe vision of but a little segment of truth and yet keep his poise and reason. It is not the education that concentrates that is to be dreaded, but the education that narrows,—that is narrow from the first. . . .

We mean, so soon as our generous friends have arranged their private finances in such a way as to enable them to release for our use enough money for the purpose, to build a notable graduate college. I say "build" because it will be not only a body of teachers and students but also a college of residence, where men shall live together in the close and wholesome comradeship of leaning. We shall build it, not apart, but as nearly as may be at the very heart, the geographical heart, of the university; and its comradeship shall be for young men and old, for the novice as well as for the graduate. It will constitute but a single term in the scheme of coordination which is our ideal. The windows of the graduate college must open straight upon the walks and quadrangles and lecture halls of the *studium generale.*

In our attempt to escape the pedantry and narrowness of the old fixed curriculum we have, no doubt, gone so far as to be in danger of losing the old ideals. Our utilitarianism has carried us so far afield that we are in a fair way to forget the real utilities of the mind. No doubt the old, purely literary training made too much of the development of mere taste, mere delicacy of perception, but our modern training makes too little. We pity the young child who, ere its physical life has come to maturity, is put to some task which will dwarf and narrow it into a mere mechanic tool. We know that it needs first its free years in the sunlight and fresh air, its irresponsible youth. And yet we do not hesitate to deny to the young mind its irresponsible years of mere development in the free air of general studies. We have too ignorantly served the spirit of the age,—have made no bold and sanguine attempt to instruct and lead it. Its call is for efficiency, but not for narrow, purblind efficiency. Surely no other age ever had tasks which made so shrewdly for the testing of the general powers of the mind. No sort of knowledge, no sort of training of the perceptions and the facility of the mind could come amiss to the modern man of affairs or the modern student. A general awakening of the faculties, and then a close and careful adaptation to some special task is the program of mere prudence for every man who would succeed.

And there are other things besides material success with which we must supply our generation. It must be supplied with men who care more for principles than for money, for the right adjustments of life than for the gross accumulations of profit. The problems that call for sober thoughtfulness and mere devotion are as pressing as those which call for practical efficiency. . . . The final synthesis of learning is in philosophy. You shall most clearly judge the spirit of a university if you judge it by the philosophy it teaches; and the philosophy of conduct is what every wise man should wish to derive from his knowledge of the thoughts and affairs of the generations that have gone before him. We are not put into this world to sit still and know; we are put into it to act.

It is true that in order to learn men must for a little while withdraw from action, must seek some quiet place of remove from the bustle of affairs, where their thoughts may run clear and tranquil, and the heats of business be for the time put off; but that cloistered refuge is no place to dream in. It is a place for the first conspectus of the mind, for a thoughtful poring upon the map of life; and the boundaries which should emerge to the mind's eye are not more the intellectual than the moral boundaries of thought and action. I do not see how any university can afford such an outlook if its teachings be not informed with the spirit of religion, and that the religion of Christ, and with the energy of a positive faith. The argument for efficiency in education can have no permanent validity if the efficiency sought be not moral as well as intellectual. The ages of strong and definite moral impulse have been the ages of achievement; and the moral impulses which have lifted highest have come from Christian peoples,—the moving history of our own nation were proof enough of that. Moral efficiency is, in the last analysis, the fundamental argument for liberal culture. A merely literary education, got out of books and old literatures is a poor thing enough if the teacher stick at grammatical and syntactical drill;

but if it be indeed an introduction into the thoughtful labors of men of all generations it may be made the prologue of the mind's emancipation: its emancipation from narrowness,—from narrowness of sympathy, of perception, of motive, of purpose, and of hope. And the deep fountains of Christian teaching are its most refreshing springs.

☆ ☆ ☆

I have studied the history of America; I have seen her grow great in the paths of liberty and of progress by following after great ideals. Every concrete thing that she has done has seemed to rise out of some abstract principle, some vision of the mind. Her greatest victories have been the victories of people and of humanity. And in days quiet and troubled alike Princeton has stood for the nation's service, to produce men and patriots. Her national tradition began with John Witherspoon, the master, and James Madison, the pupil, and has not been broken until this day. I do not know that the friends of this sound and tested foundation may have in store to build upon it; but whatever they add shall be added in that spirit, and with that conception of duty. There is no better way to build up learning and increase power. A new age is before us, in which, it would see, we must lead the world. No doubt we shall set it an example unprecedented not only in the magnitude and telling perfection of our industries and arts, but also in the splendid scale and studied detail our university establishments: the spirit of the age will lift us to every great enterprise. But the ancient spirit of sound learning will also rule us; we shall demonstrate in our lecture rooms again and again, with increasing volume of proof, the old principles that have made us free and great; reading men shall read here the chastened thoughts that have kept us young and shall make us pure; the school of learning shall be the school of memory and of ideal hope; and the men who spring from our loins shall take their lineage from the founders of the republic.

The Princeton Preceptorial System

Addressing a national audience, Wilson described his plans for a preceptorial system that transformed undergraduate education at Princeton. He proposed a system of close contact between preceptors and small groups of student outside the formal atmosphere of the lecture hall and emphasizing extensive reading and discussion. Wilson successfully raised sufficient funds to recruit several dozen young teachers for the program, including well-qualified men from Harvard, Columbia, Johns Hopkins, and other major universities. The program was quickly judged a success, and the innovation ranked as one of his great achievements as president of the university. Explaining the advantages of the new regimen, this essay appeared in the *Harper's Weekly* in the summer of 1905.

The object of the preceptorial system is to prevent the disintegration of the university, its disintegration in that essential feature of all vital teaching, the intimate acquaintance and contact of pupils and teacher. Mere increase of numbers separates them. As a university grows in numbers professors and students draw apart, have hardly a speaking acquaintance with one another. Lectures bring them into the same room, but not into vital touch. No matter how strong and interesting a lecturer may be, his contact with his hearers is not personal: They are only an audience, and get only such flavor of is personality as may inevitably get into the sentences he utters, into the tone and manner in which he utters them. Even when he meets his classes in small sections for quizzes, recitations, oral tests, the contact is hardly more intimate. There is a stiffness about the intercourse, a formality, a restraint: He sits behind a desk upon a dais; they sit in rows in front of him, and are prodded to expose their ignorance.

The small college escapes this difficulty, in large part by very reason of its smallness. The total number of its students is small; the instructors generally meet their pupils in many different classes; teachers and pupils become personally known to each other by constant contact and daily meetings in many places. The vitality and fruitfulness of their contact arise out of their acquaintance with one another, the impression the personality of the teacher makes upon the pupil, and the direct appeal the pupil's needs makes to the teacher's interest and sympathy: the profit is not derived from the formal intercourse of the class-room so much as from the personal touch and the mutual understanding which exist because of their knowledge of each other outside of the class-room.

The large university, teeming with hundreds of growing youngsters, ought not to forego this fruitful process of comradeship if it can possibly get the advantage of it by any feasible arrangement. The other advantages of the large university are so great, its larger library, its greater variety of gifted men, its quickening life amidst the hosts of its graduates and undergraduates, its ampler resources, and completer equipment; it should find a way by which its students may be given an intimate use of these things instead of being held off at arm's length, as if their very multitude made the full use of the university by them impossible. Intimate access to their teachers is the first and chief step by which to bring this about. Graduate students have it already; undergraduates should have it too.

It is Princeton's plan, with this object in view, to add at once to her teaching force, to add fifty "preceptors,"—as she will call them, for want of a better name,—whose special duty it shall be to deal with their pupils outside of the class-room. The preceptors are to be members of the faculty, not distinguishable from the rest in rank and privilege, and the present members of the faculty are to undertake preceptorial work in order that the new and closer contact may be brought about all along the line; but for the new men the preceptorial work will be the chief function. It will be their duty to take the students in the several departments, either singly or in groups, and by every serviceable method give them counsel, guidance, and stimulation in their work. Dull men and very bright and ambitious men they will probably have to take singly. Groups will have to be made up by careful classification, combining men of like training, acquirements, and aptitudes. But the object will be always the same,—not to hear "recitations" on fixed textbooks, but to discuss, to sift, to test the reading done by the men in their several courses, so that the men may feel that the preceptors are in some sense their fellow students and friendly guides in their outside reading, the reading by which lectures are to be supplemented and the more formal discussion of the class-room broadened and made part of an independent scheme of study. By such means college work may be made to seem something more than a sublimated kind of school work, and may be made to rest not upon the dictum of the teacher in the class-room or of the author of a particular textbook, but upon something like first-hand acquaintance with the chief authorities on the several subjects studied.

It is the tutorial system of Oxford adapted to American conditions and to the traditions of American colleges. The lecture and the formal class exercise are not to be abandoned, but they are to be very much less relied on, are to be considered only a part, and that not the chief part, of the process of college instruction. The chief part is to be the reading done with the preceptors.

There will naturally be a great deal of written work connected with it. The preceptors will certainly find that the most serviceable way of ascertaining what reading the men are doing, and with how much thoroughness and intelligence they are doing it, is to require written reports of the them, brief, it may be, but definite, critical, at once a collation of what they have been reading and a commentary upon it. These reports will incidentally be judged as pieces of English, as well as with reference to their adequacy and accuracy. If they are incorrectly or inelegantly written, they will be given back to be rewritten; and if any man cannot express himself accurately and with some degree of propriety and elegance, he will be handed over to the English department for fundamental drill. It is one of the reproaches of American colleges and universities that their graduates are not trained in the correct use of their mother tongue. "Theme writing"—that is, constant, deliberate exercise in English composition,—does not seem to supply the training that is necessary. Its most radical defect is that it is a means for making men write for the sake of writing, for the sake of the language and the style. The object of the use of language, the only legitimate object of the development of style, is the release of ideas, the clear statement of fact, the adequate embodiment in words of some image or conception of the mind. The reports of the students to their preceptors will furnish at least a natural motive for expression, and will furnish, besides, a great variety of themes which must be taken seriously. When every piece of written work done in the university, examination papers included, is required to be in correct English, the English department of the university can afford to give over its laborious addiction to "themes."

Another thing which is expected to give naturalness to the preceptorial system is that the preceptors are not to set the examinations, but are to read with their men in subjects upon which their colleagues set the tests; and the examinations are to be upon subjects, not upon a particular course of lectures merely, delivered by the examiner. The lectures are to be only one means of setting forth the subjects, one means of stimulating interest in great fields of study: the chief means is to be conferences with the preceptors, following no cut-and-dried routing, limited to no single textbook or view, but intended to give the men at least an introduction to the literature of the subjects considered.

The rule, moreover is not to be that for each subject a man will have a particular preceptor. At Princeton the students select "departments" of study, and the "departments" are as inclusive as "philosophy," "history and politics," "classics," and "modern languages." Each undergraduate is to be assigned to one preceptor for all the courses or studies of his department, in order that he may have at least an adequate conception of their co-ordination, their connection, their vital union as *body* of studies.

Such reading, so free from artificial trammels and done in constant conference with helpful scholars, ought to impart to study a new reality, ought to give college men a sense of having been emancipated from school and mere tutelage, and given the responsibilities as well as the opportunities of maturity. They are challenged to read, to look about them in great subjects, and discover the world of thought. No doubt more work will be done under the new stimulus than is done now, but it will not, if properly directed, be burdensome, dull, a task, a matter of reluctance, as too much college work is now. It is really a pleasure to use your mind, if you have one, and many a man who now never dreams what fun it is to have ideas and to explore the world of thought, may be expected, in his intercourse with his preceptors, to find learning a rare form of enjoyment, the use of his faculties a new indulgence. He may even discover his soul, and find its spiritual relations to the world of men and affairs.

My Ideal of the True University

In one of his best essays on the nature of the university, Wilson reaffirmed his commitment to broad education in the liberal arts and sciences. But here he moved on to discuss the nature of learning, scholarship, and the relationship among the divisions of the university to each other and to the whole. The character of the university, he thought, had to be formed in large part outside the classroom, where learning could be stimulated by contact between young and old, specialist and novice, graduate and undergraduate, and across disciplines. Wilson understood the purpose of university education to include the preparation of the young for the full responsibilities of citizenship, which was vital in a democratic society. He was realistic about the march of specialization in higher education, but he insisted that an education would be incomplete and seriously flawed without exposure to broad liberal learning. When he complained of the distance between faculty and undergraduates in many American colleges, he cited a problem that has not disappeared from the academy. This work appeared in the journal *The Delineator* in November 1909.

The word "university" means in our modern usage, so many different things that almost every time one employs it, it seems necessary to define it. Nowhere has it so many meanings as in America, where institutions of all kinds display it in the titles they bestow upon themselves. School, college and university are readily enough distinguishable, in fact, by those who take the pains to look into the scope and methods of their teaching; but they are quite indistinguishable, oftentimes, in name. They are as likely as not all to bear the same title.

But practice is always the best definer; and practice is slowly working out for us in America a sufficiently definite idea of what a university is. It is not the same idea that has been worked out in England or Germany or France. American universities will probably, when worked out to the logical fulfillment of their natural development, show a type distinct from all others. They will be distinctive of what America has thought out and done in the field of higher education. Those which are already far advanced in their development even now exhibit an individual and characteristic organization.

The American university as we now see it consists of many parts. At its heart stands the college, the school of general training. Above and around the college stand the graduate and technical schools, in which special studies are prosecuted and preparation is given for particular professions and occupations. Technical and professional schools are not a necessary part of a university, but they are greatly benefitted by close association with a university; and the university itself is unmistakably benefitted and quickened by the transmission of its energy into them and the reaction of their standards and objects upon it. As a rule the larger universities of the country have law schools, divinity schools and medical schools under their care and direction; and training for these, the "learned," professions has long been considered a natural part of their work. Schools of mechanical, electrical and civil engineering have of late years become as numerous and as necessary as the schools which prepare for the older professions, and they have naturally in most cases grown up in connection with universities because their processes are the processes of science, and the modern university is, among other things, a school of pure science, with laboratories and teachers indispensable to the engineer. But the spirit of technical schools has not always been the spirit of learning. They have often been intensely and very frankly utilitarian, and pure science has looked at them askance. They are proper parts of a university only when pure science is of the essence of their teaching, the spirit of pure science the spirit of all their studies. It is only of recent years that we have seen thoughtful engineers coming to recognize this fact, preach this change of spirit; it is only of recent years, therefore, that technical schools have begun to be thoroughly and truly assimilated into the university organization.

There is an ideal at the heart of everything American, and the ideal at the heart of the American university is intellectual training, the awakening of the whole man, the thorough introduction of the student to the life of America and of the modern world, the completion of the task undertaken by the grammar and high schools of equipping him for the full duties of citizenship. It is with that idea that I have said that the college stands at the heart of the American university. The college stands for liberal training. Its object is discipline and enlightenment. The average thoughtful American does not want his son narrowed in all his gifts and thinking to a particular occupation. He wishes him to be made free of the world in which men think about and understand many things, and to know how to handle himself in it. He desires a training for him which will give him a considerable degree of elasticity and adaptability, and fit him to turn in any direction he chooses.

☆ ☆ ☆

We have misconceived and misused the college as an instrument of American life when we organized and used it as a place of special preparation for particular tasks and callings. It is for liberal training, for general discipline, for that preliminary general enlightenment which every man should have who enters modern life with any intelligent hope or purpose of leadership and achievement. . . . Its "liberalizing" influences should be got from its life even more than from its studies. Special studies become liberal when those who are pursuing other studies—studies of many kinds, pursued from many points of view. The real enlightenments of life come not from tasks or from books so much as from free intercourse with other persons who, in spite of you, inform and stimulate you, and make you realize how big and various the world is, how many things there are in it to think about, and how necessary it is to think about the subjects you are specially interested in their right relations to many, many others, if you would think of them correctly and get to the bottom of what you are trying to do.

The ideal college, therefore, should be a community, a place of close, natural, intimate association, not only of the young men who are its pupils and novices in various lines of study, but also of young men with older men, with maturer men, with veterans and professionals in the great undertakings of learning, of teachers with pupils, outside the classroom as well as inside of it. No one is successfully educated within the walls of any particular classroom or laboratory or museum, and no amount of association, however close and familiar and delightful, between mere beginners can ever produce the sort of enlightenment which the lad gets when first he begins to catch the infection of learning. The trouble with most of our colleges nowadays is that the faculty of the college live one life and the undergraduates quiet a different one. They are not members of the same community; they constitute two communities. The life of the undergraduate is not touched with the personal influence of the teacher; life among the teachers is not touched by the personal impressions which should come from frequent and intimate contact with undergraduates. The teacher does not often enough know what the undergraduate is thinking about or what models he is forming life upon, and the undergraduate does not know how human a fellow teacher is, how delightfully he can talk, outside the classroom, of the subjects he is most interested in, how many interesting things both his life and his studies illustrate and make attractive. This separation need not exist, and, in the college of the ideal university, would not exist.

It is perfectly possible to organize the life of our colleges in such a way that students and teachers alike will take part in it; in such a way that a perfectly natural daily intercourse will be established between them; and it is only by such an organization that they can be given real vitality as places of serious training, be made communities in which youngsters come fully to realize how interesting intellectual work is, how vital, how important, how closely associated with all modern achievement—only by such an organization that study can be made to seem a part of life itself. Lectures often seem very formal and empty things; recitations generally prove very dull and unrewarding. It is in conversation and natural intercourse with scholars chiefly that you find how lively knowledge is, how it ties into everything that is interesting and important, how intimate a part it is of everything that is "practical" and connected with the world. Men are not always made thoughtful by books; but they are generally made thoughtful by association with men who think.

The present and most pressing problem of our university authorities is to bring about this vital association for the benefit of the novices of the university world, the undergraduates. Classroom methods are thorough enough; competent scholars already lecture and set tasks and superintend their performance; but the life of the average undergraduate outside the classroom and other state appointments with his instructors is not very much affected by his studies; is almost entirely dissociated from intellectual interests.

It is too freely and exclusively given over to athletics and amusements. Athletics are in themselves wholesome, and are necessary to every normal youth. They give him vigor and should give him the spirit of the sportsman—should keep him out of many things of a very demoralizing sort which he would be inclined to do if he did not spend his energy out-of-doors and in the gymnasium. Amusement, too, is necessary. All work and no play makes Jack not only a dull boy, but a very unserviceable boy, with no spirit, no capacity to vary his occupations or to make the most of himself.

But athletics and amusement ought never to become absorbing occupations, even with youngsters. They should be diversions merely, by which the strain of work is relieved, the powers refreshed and given spontaneous play. The only way in which they can be given proper subordination is to associate them with things not only more important, but quite as natural and interesting. Knowledge, study, intellectual effort, will seem to undergraduates more important than athletics and amusement and just as natural only when older men, themselves vital and interesting and companionable, are thrown into close daily association with them. The spirit of learning can be conveyed only by contagion, by personal contact. The association of studies and persons is the proper prescription.

Turn from the college, which lies at the heart of the university, to the graduate and professional schools which lie about the college and are built upon it, and you are discussing and entirely different matter, looking for different principles and methods. Their right relationship to the college, moreover, is a very difficult question to determine. Both the college and the high school are trying to do two things at once—two things not entirely consistent with each other. The majority of pupils in the high school—the very large majority—do not intend to carry their studies any further. They must get all the schooling they are going to get before they leave the high school. They must be given the best training, the completest awakening within the field of knowledge that the school can give them, for that is to be their final preparation for life. A small minority must be handled, in such circumstances, in different ways, and it is very hard indeed to arrange the courses of study in a way that will be suitable for both. The high school is clearly justified in shaping its policy and its methods to the needs, first of all, of the majority. Exceptional arrangements must be made, if possible, for the minority.

Similarly, in the college the great majority of undergraduates mean to go at once from their courses there into some active practical pursuit; do not mean to go on to more advanced university studies. A minority, on the other hand—a larger minority than in the schools—do intend to go further, will enter the graduate schools to become teachers and investigators, or the technical and professional schools for some calling for which a special training is necessary. The difficulty of the college is to arrange courses and adopt methods which will serve both these classes. It does so, generally, by offering a much larger choice of studies than it is possible or desirable to offer. But the majority must determine its chief characteristics and adaptations. Its chief object must be general preparation, general training, and all-round awakening.

It is evident, therefore, that the college, while it should be the foundation of the professional schools, not only stands below them, as their support and feeder, but also alongside of them; would be necessary if it did not exist; furnishes the only introduction our young men desire or need get to the wider fields of action and experience which lie beyond it. It is, first of all and chiefly, a general fitting school for life. Its social organization and influence are almost as important as its classrooms. It is not a subordinate school, but the chief, the central school of the university. For the professional schools it is, at the same time, an indispensable foundation. That profession is clearly impoverished which does not draw to its special studies men bred to some thorough school of general training. In these higher schools the atmosphere is changed; another set of objects lies before the student; his mind has already begun to enter upon tasks which will fill the rest of his life. He can not, there, seek the things that will connect him with the more general fields of learning and experience.

What is called the graduate school in our universities is not, strictly, a professional school. As a matter of fact most of its pupils will be found to be looking forward to the profession of teaching; but graduate schools of the higher type do not keep that profession in mind. Their object is to train scholars, whether in the field of literature, or science, or philosophy, or in the apparently more practical field of politics. They carry the college process a stage father and seek to induct their students into the precise, exacting methods of scholarship. They not only carry the college process farther, they also alter it. Their students are thrown more upon their own resources in their studies; are expected to enter on researches of their own, strike out into independent lines of inquiry, stand upon their own feet in every investigation, come out of their novitiate and gain a certain degree of mastery in their chosen field, their professors being little more than their guides and critics. They are not taught how to teach; there is no professional tone in the life of the school. They are taught how to learn, thoroughly and independently, and to make scholars of themselves.

Schools of medicine, law and theology, on the other hand, while also, when upon a proper plane, schools of scholarship, are professional schools, and have in all their instruction the professional point of view. Their object is not only to introduce their students to the mastery of certain subjects, as the graduate school does, but also to prepare them for the "practice" of a particular profession. They devote a great deal of attention to practical method—to the ways in which the knowledge acquired is to be used in dealing with diseases, with disputes between men over their legal rights, and with the needs and interests of men who should be helped with spiritual guidance. They are frankly and of necessity professional. The spirit of the doctor's or of the lawyer's office, of the pulpit and of the pastor's study, pervades them. They school their men for particular tasks, complicated and different, and seek to guide them by many practical maxims.

Similarly, the technical schools are professional schools, their objects practical, definite, utilitarian. Their students must not only know science and have their feet solidly upon the footing of exact knowledge, but must acquire a very thorough mastery of methods, a definite skill and practice, readiness and precision in a score of mechanical processes which make of them a sort of master-workmen. The practical air of the shop pervades the law school. They are intent upon business, and conscious all the time that they must make ready for it.

In the professional schools of an ideal university nothing of this practical spirit would be abated, for such schools are, one and all, intensely and immediately practical in their objects and must have practice always in mind if they would be truly serviceable; but there would always lie back of their work, by close association with the studies of the university in pure science and in all the great subjects which underlie law and theology, the impulse and the informing spirit of disinterested inquiry, of study which has no utilitarian object, but seeks only the truth. The spirit of graduate study, and of undergraduate, too, would be carried over into all professional work, and engineers, doctors, ministers, lawyers, would all alike be made, first of all, citizens of the modern intellectual and social world—first of all, university men, with a broad outlook on the various knowledge of the world, and then experts in a great practical profession, which they would understand all the better because they had first been grounded in science and in the other great bodies of knowledge which are the fountains of all practice. That is the service of the university owes the professional schools associated with it. The parts should be vitally united from end to end.

The professional schools, in their turn, do the university this distinct and very great service that they keep it in conscious association with the practical world, its necessities and its problems. Through them it better understands what knowledge, what kind of men, what scholarship, what morals, what action, will best serve the age for whose enlightenment and assistance it exists. Our universities should be "ideal" chiefly in this—that they serve the intellectual needs of the age, not in one thing, not in any one way only, but all around the circle, with a various and universal adaptation to their age and generation. America can never dispense with the enlightenment of general study, and should wish to have as many of her young men as possible subjected to its influences. She should demand that her professional schools be grounded in such studies in order that her professional men may see something more than individual interest in what they do. It is best, therefore, that professional schools should be closely associated with universities, a part of their vital organization, intimate parts of their system of study. That very association and inclusion should make them more thorough in their particular practical tasks. They should be the better schools of technical training. The ideal university is rounded out by them, and their roots are enriched by her fertile soil of catholic knowledge and inquiry. The ideal university would consist of all these parts, associated in this spirit, maintained always in this relationship.

On the Importance of the Liberal Arts: Address to the Association of American Universities

At the close of his academic career, Wilson examined the problem of how education could prepare people for a world of change in which mere knowledge could become rapidly obsolete. His concern was for an ideal curriculum that would provide students with the skills and training needed in such a world. The ideas were consistent with the philosophy of education he had cultivated since his undergraduate days and championed as president of Princeton. He warned against making education a commodity and reviewed the elements that should make up a model curriculum. The training of the mind, the habits of learning, were more important than the mastery of a particular body of information. The speech was printed in the *Journal of Proceedings* of the association's conference in 1910.

I think that it is best to start out with certain ideas that seem to be preliminary to the whole discussion. It seems to me that all specialism—and this includes professional training—is clearly individualistic in its object. I mean that the object of professional training is the private interest of the person who is seeking that training. He is seeking to prepare himself for a particular profession. He is seeking to make himself ready for a particular performance in the work which will be the means of his own support, and, it may be, of his own private distinction. His point of view, therefore, is centered in himself. His purpose is to make himself efficient for the life which he wishes to lead; and I suppose that is the object of all special training, whether it be called professional or not.

There is a very interesting and suggestive passage in Mr. Chesterton's book on *Orthodoxy* which seems to me to illustrate a portion of this subject. He says that it is not true to say of a man who has won success and position in the world that "you can't bribe a man like that." He says it is true only in this sense, that he had already been bribed. He has won his success by particular processes supplied him by the world as it stands. He is therefore bribed to see that the world as it stands is not changed, for fear the conditions of his success should be altered. His is under bonds to stand by the *status quo.* The *status quo* is his opportunity. To change it would be to alter his opportunity, and his whole point of view, centered as it is upon one special interest, is the point of view of that special interest.

You do not need to be told how practically all the difficulties of our national life, all the difficulties in the field of statesmanship, I mean, arise out of the jealousies and the competitions of special interests and the lack of understanding between them or of a common project. My own experience in conversing with distinguished lawyers or distinguished bankers or distinguished manufacturers is that with each one of them I have to approach the subject we are discussing from a special point of view, namely, his own, and try, if it is possible, to draw his thought and vision out to the broader field which he has for the time being overlooked and forgotten, but which, nevertheless, is the field with which he must relate himself successfully if his business is not to draw him into courses which will be against the general interest. It is this specialization of interest which constitutes the danger, I mean the intellectual danger as well as the economic danger, of our times.

☆ ☆ ☆

The question we have to ask, therefore, is as to the relative value, on the one hand, of a discipline whose object it is to make the man who receives it a citizen of the modern intellectual and social world, as contrasted, on the other hand, with a discipline whose object is to make him the adept and disciple of a special interest. I think that is not an unfair statement of the subject that is to be discussed.

When you come to a discussion of the special terms of the subject, there is an initial difficulty. There is no arts course, if you use the term in the singular. If you look our colleges over, you will find that there is nowhere an arts course—almost nowhere. There is a miscellany of courses whose object is not professional or semi-professional. This miscellany of courses is not arranged with any organic connections. It is not arranged in any fixed sequence. It is not organized with regard to any particular congruity between its several parts. And therefore we are in the position of those who would ask, "Is it possible to have an arts course? And if it is possible, is it desirable? If it is desirable, upon what grounds is it desirable?"

Not withstanding the fact that we have no arts courses, I suppose that when we use that term we have substantially the idea which I have tried to outline already. I suppose we mean a body of studies whose object is not individualistic, but whose object is a general orientation, the creation in the mind of a vision of the field of knowledge, in some degree, at any rate as a whole, the development of a general, catholic, intellectual sympathy, the development of a power of comprehension. I do not believe, for my own part, that the object of an arts course is knowledge. If it were, we would have to acknowledge a practically universal failure, for we all recognize the fact that a graduate of any one of our colleges, after he is ten years out, has practically forgotten all he studied as an undergraduate. If it is the knowledge that was valuable to him, he has lost it, and the value has gone out of it. What he was taught to do with his mind in receiving the knowledge, however, what he was taught to see, what he was taught to discriminate, what he was taught to sympathize with, what he was enabled to comprehend, is what he has got out of it. And if he shall have got that out of it, he has got everything out of it; for the knowledge itself is the mere material upon which these habits are formed, the habit of looking facts so steadily in the face that the atmosphere disappears from them and you see them cold as they are; the habit of stating things with precision, of reasoning with exactness, of reasoning with fearlessness, of moving from premises to conclusion like those who desire to see the truth and desire not to be deceived: these are some of the things that a man gets out of this kind of discipline. . . .

Moreover, it seems to me that this orientation has in it a moral content as well as an intellectual. I believe that the object of the kind of discipline which we mean when we speak of an arts course is to cultivate in those who receive it a correct moral appreciation, a correct appreciation of moral values; so that they must not be allowed to confine themselves to the field of the exact sciences, for example, where sympathy is neither here nor there, where moral perceptions are involved only in so far as the student divests himself of prejudice and sincerely seeks the truth. There the subject-matter itself is non-moral, whereas the subject-matter of life is saturated with moral perception. The facts of history may escape our memory, but the morals of history, the operations of character, the play of motive, the distinction of integrity, may leave their lasting impression upon us.

☆ ☆ ☆

We have to ask ourselves then, "What are we to do in this field of almost unlimited choice?" For, while it is true that you can name a definite content for the older curriculum and a definite, though miscellaneous, content for the varied newer curricula, it is not true that it is possible to combine out of the two a single curriculum which will give you the discipline which you need in order to be citizen of the modern intellectual and social world. We have, therefore, to resort to a choice of elements, rather than to a choice of subjects, and we have to remind ourselves before we make that choice what it is that we are seeking to do.

In the first place, we are seeking to impart discipline; and for my part, it seems to me that hat is the particular thing which in our modern schemes of study we have forgotten and neglected. We have sought with a diligence which was pathetic the best means of information, but we have not sought with any degree of intelligence the best means of discipline. We have not sought to subject the mind to the processes which it needed for its undeveloped powers, but we have sought to indulge it in the use of its developed powers or of those powers the instinct and beginnings of which were already appreciated by those who possessed them. We have not sought, in other words, to find out in any systematic way whether the mind had received the proper intimations and acquired the proper habits with regard to the processes of the modern intellectual world.

☆ ☆ ☆

Very well, then, if these be our objects, to communicate discipline, to afford enlightenment, to make a man free of the modern world so that he will not be a yokel and a provincial and will really come out upon a stage where he can look about him and see, we must select the things that give him the characteristic discipline of the modern world. That leads us to the point where we seek to pick out the elements of an arts course—I mean the fundamental elements. I do not mean the particular subjects and studies, but the fundamental elements, and they seem to me to be only four—unless I have been led very much astray in my analysis.

In the first place, you must give the mind a thorough drill in some part of pure science. I use the word pure, of course, as contrasted with professional science or applied science. You must give the mind the discipline which is so characteristic of the modern world, which enables it to follow the processes and appreciate the results, and produce the results, of modern scientific thinking, in the realm of nature; the elements of pure science, not elaborated, but dwelt upon in their essential elementary conceptions and processes so long, so intensively, so insistently, that the mind can never afterward shake off the prepossessions of scientific inquiry. . . .

Then it seems to me that you must have the elements of pure philosophy, by which I mean an explanation of nature and human life which seeks to include all the elements. That is a large order, and so far as my reading goes I do not know where to look for such a coordination and explanation; but I do know that a very interesting thing has been happening in our day, something which has its direct influence upon the administration of universities. It used to be possible for men, without any twinges of conscience, to devote themselves exclusively to a particular science. They cannot do so any longer, because the frontiers are being obscured. I cannot now find anybody who can trace a scientific frontier between mathematics and physics, between physics and chemistry, or between chemistry and biology. It is clear enough in the center of the province where you are, but not clear on the frontiers where you are, whether you are in chemistry or physics, whether you are in physics or in mathematics; and as these boundaries disappear, you observe what is happening. Our mind is sweeping through an organic whole. We do not know when we cross from one province to another; which means that there are no natural boundaries, that the boundaries are artificial, boundaries of convention, agreed upon by treaty and not arranged by nature. There is no mountain range piled there, no great river has dug its pathway there. There is no natural, obvious boundary. You do not know, except by convention and if you carry a map in your hand—and then you are not certain—when you have crossed from one to another.

And when you have swept this apparent circle through, you find that there is a segment lacking, a segment the lack of which all men of science are becoming aware of, and that is the spiritual segment. There is something inexplicable in it all unless you insert into this circle the segment of philosophy, in the broad sense in which I have tried to indicate it here. Until you have explained the universe in terms of spirit, you have not explained the universe at all. You may have catalogued it, you may have arranged it, you may have made a museum of it, you may have enabled us to employ the processes of it and understand how nature does this, that, and the other particular thing, but you have not explained it. That is the task, the tremendous task, of the philosopher. The modern philosopher is not trying to think merely in terms of metaphysics; he is trying to think in terms of physics, he is trying to think in terms of physical universe, interpreted by the human spirit. Science will be impoverished as a body of thought until that is accomplished.

It seems to me, therefore, that it is indispensable, in this general discipline which we are seeking to outline theoretically, that the mind should be led at any rate to perceive the lack of an explanation, and to understand the main attempts which have been made to explain. That is what I mean by pure philosophy: the fact that there is something to explain, the definite appreciation of just what it is that is to be explained, and so much of the history of philosophy as is necessary to know what attempts have been made to explain it. You cannot be a citizen of the modern world of thought unless you have an introduction, and something more than an introduction, a familiar companionship, with aims of that sort, and there cannot be familiar companionship unless the process is continued for a long time.

☆ ☆ ☆

Then I should say that there must be the elements—always the elements; you do not have to cover the wide field; you must go by a single road in each of these cases—the elements of pure literature. The only delight in literature, so far as I can see it, is the delight of enlargement. I suppose we read books of travel because we cannot travel thither ourselves. If we could, I would very much prefer to go than to read another man's travels. I suppose we venture into fields of reading which are not distinctively our own because we would like to be so many things that we are not, because the world is so narrow in our little piece of it, because we want the adventures of life and cannot have them all, because we want to experience the thrills which have stirred other minds than our own, and have moved within the spirits of other men but not within our own. We want to take the walls down from the room and sweep the horizon and know what airs are astir that we did not originate, and have as yet never breathed.

And these visions of the mind, the whole realm of poetry and creative prose, the realm of insight and interpretation, are the regions in which we refresh ourselves and breathe an upper air which keeps our lungs fit for the more sedate and mundane things we have to do. I pity the man who cannot get this dissociation and removal from the actual world occasionally, this refreshment on the uplands, which are ready to his mere desire, if he only entertain it. For my own part, I must say that in my own studies, in the field of politics, I have found more true political interpretation in the poets than I have every found in the systematic writers of political science. The systematic writers on political science will tell you a great many interesting things, but they interpret almost nothing for you, and some sudden light flashed in a single line of poetry will sometimes interpret more politics to you than you can find in the bound volumes of the political science library; because the poet has suddenly seen what the human heart is striving for out there in the field of politics, has uncovered that; and after you have seen it you know what the significance of your study is.

☆ ☆ ☆

And then, I dare say, we would all admit that the field of history and politics is a necessary part of a lad's introduction into the modern world. I shall not swell upon that, because perhaps it is my own prepossessions which lead me to think that is one of the necessary elements, but I dare say that is obvious enough.

☆ ☆ ☆

I would conclude by this suggestion, that professionalism in learning has the same effect upon the intellectual world that professionalism in sport has on the world of sportsmanship. The minute professionalism enters sport it ceases to be sportsmanlike. The minute professionalism enters learning, it ceases to wear the road and genial face of learning. It has become a commodity; it has become something that a man wishes to exchange for the means of support. It has become something that a man wishes to use in order to get the better of his fellow-men, to enhance his fortunes, to do all the things that center in and upon himself. It is professionalism that spoils the game, the game of life, the game of humanity, the game of co-operation in social undertakings, the whole handsome game that we are seeking to throw light upon by the processes of education.

This, then, seems to me the position and the importance of the arts course as distinct from the professional and semi-professional courses.

4

The Historian

On the Writing of History

Wilson began his academic career at a time when history and political science were not yet clearly distinct disciplines. His study of congressional government was heavily historical, and many of his published works throughout his academically productive years were histories. Always interested in scholarly technique, he often wrote about the process of scholarship with emphasis on the importance of style as well as precision and analysis. Much has been written debating the character of history as a science or as a literary art; Wilson saw no incompatibility in the historian's struggle for the objectivity of science *and* the need for graceful presentation. With a glance at the methods of Macaulay, Gibbon, Carlyle, and Green, Wilson here made the case for the writing of history as both art and science. He distinguished between the "investigator" and the historian whose task is not merely to uncover facts but to "recover" the past. Many modern historians have followed that model; more than a few have not. This essay appeared in *Century Magazine* in September 1895.

"Give us the facts, and nothing but the facts," is the sharp injunction of our age to its historians. Upon the face of it, an eminently reasonable requirement. To tell the truth simply, openly, without reservation, is the unimpeachable first principle of all right living; and historians have no license to be quit of it. Unquestionably they must tell us the truth, or else get themselves enrolled among a very undesirable class of persons, not often frankly named in polite society. But the thing is by no means to easy as it looks. The truth of history is a very complex and very occult matter. It consists of things which are invisible as well as of things which are visible. It is full of secret motives, and of a chance interplay of trivial and yet determining circumstances; it is shot through with transient passions, and broken athwart here and there by what seem cruel accidents; it cannot all be reduced to statistics or newspaper items or official recorded statements. And so it turns out, when the actual test of experiment is made, that the historian must have something more than a good conscience, must be something more than a good man. He must have an eye to see the truth; and nothing but a very catholic imagination will serve to illuminate his matter for him; nothing less than keen and steady insight will make even illumination yield him the truth of what he looks upon. Even when he has seen the truth, only half his work is done, and that not the more difficult half. He must then make others see it just as he does; only when he has done that has he told the truth. What an art of penetrative phrase and just selection must he have to take others into the light in which he stands! Their dullness, their ignorance, their prepossessions, are to be overcome and driven in, like a scouted troop, upon the truth. The thing is infinitely difficult. The skill and strategy of it cannot be taught. And so historians take another way, which is easier; they tell part of the truth, the part most to their taste, or most suitable to their talents, and obtain readers to their liking among those of like tastes and talents of their own. . . .

The trouble is, after all, that men do not invariably find the truth to their taste, and will often deny it when they hear it; and the historian has to do much more than keep his own eyes clear; he has also to catch and hold the eye of his reader. It is a nice start, as much intellectual as moral. How shall he take the palate of his reader at unawares, and get the unpalatable facts down his throat along with the palatable? Is there no way in which all the truth may be made to hold together in a narrative so strongly knit and so harmoniously colored that no reader will have either the wish or the skill to tear its patterns asunder, and men will take it all, unmarred as it stands, rather than miss the zest of it?

It is evident the thing cannot be done by the "dispassionate" annalist. The old chroniclers, whom we relish, were not dispassionate. We love some of them for their sweet quaintness, some for their childlike credulity, some for their delicious inconsequentiality. But our modern chroniclers are not so. They are, above all things else, knowing, thoroughly informed, subtly sophisticated. They would not for the world contribute any spice of their own to the narrative; and they are much too watchful, circumspect, and dutiful in their care to keep their method pure and untouched by any thought of theirs to let us catch so much as a glimpse of the chronicler underneath the chronicle. Their purpose is to give simply the facts, eschewing art, and substituting a sort of monumental index and table of the world's events.

The trouble is that men refuse to be made any wiser by such means. Though they will readily enough let their eyes linger upon a monument of art, they will heedlessly pass by a mere monument of industry. It suggests nothing to them. The materials may be suitable enough, but the handling of them leaves them dead and commonplace. An interesting circumstance thus comes to light. It is nothing less than this, that the facts do not of themselves constitute the truth. The truth is abstract not concrete. It is the just idea, the right revelation of what things mean. It is evoked only by such arrangements and orderings of fact as suggest meanings. The chronological arrangement of events, for example, may or may not be the arrangement which most surely brings the truth of the narrative to light; and the best arrangement is always that which displays, not the facts themselves, but the subtle and else invisible forces that lurk in the events and in the minds of men—forces for which events serve only as lasting and dramatic words of utterance. Take an instance. How are you to enable men to know the truth with regard to a period of revolution? Will you give them simply a calm statement of recorded events, simply a quiet, unaccentuated narrative of what actually happened, written in a monotone, and verified by quotations from authentic documents of the time? You may save yourself the trouble. As well make a pencil sketch in outline of a raging conflagration; write upon one portion of it "flame," upon another "smoke"; here "town hall, where the fire started," and there "spot where fireman was killed." It is a chart, not a picture. Even if you made a veritable picture of it, you could give only part of the truth so long as you confined yourself to black and white. Where would be all the wild and terrible colors of the scene: the red and tawny flame; the masses of smoke, carrying the dull glare of the fire to the very skies, like a great signal banner thrown to the winds; the hot and frightened faces of the crowd; the crimsoned gables down the street, with the faint light of a lamp here and there gleaming white from some hastily opened casement? Without the colors your picture is not true. No inventory of items will even represent the truth: the fuller and more minute you make it, the more will the truth be obscured. The little details will take up as much space in the statement as the great totals into which they are summed up; and the proportions being false, the whole is false. Truth, fortunately, takes its own revenge. No one is deceived. The reader of the chronicle lays it aside. It lacks verisimilitude. He cannot realize how any of the things spoken of can have happened. He goes elsewhere to find, if he may, a real picture of the time, and perhaps finds on that is wholly fictitious. No wonder the grave and monk-like chronicler sighs. He of course wrote to be read, and not merely for the manual exercise of it; and when he sees readers turn away, his heart misgives him for his fellow-men. Is it as it always was, that they do not wish to know the truth? Alas! Good eremite, men do not seek the truth as they should; but do you know what the truth is? It is a thing ideal, displayed by the just proportion of events, revealed in form and color, dumb till facts be set in syllables, articulated into words, put together into sentences, swung with proper tone and cadence. It is not revolutions only that have color. Nothing in human life is without it. In a monochrome you can depict nothing but a single incident; in a monotone you cannot carry truth beyond a single sentence. Only by art in all its variety can you depict as it is the various face of life.

Yes; but what sort of art? There is here a wide field of choice. Shall we go back to the art of which Macaulay was so great a master? We could do worse. It must be a great art that can make men lay aside the novel and take up the history, to find there, in very fact, the movement and drama of life. What Macaulay does well he does incomparable. Who else can mass the details as he does, and yet not mar or obscure, but only heighten, the effect of the picture as a whole? Who else can bring so amazing a profusion of knowledge within the strait limits of a simple plan, nowhere encumbered, everywhere free and obvious in its movement? How sure the strokes, and how bold, how vivid the result! Yet when we have laid the book aside, when the charm and the excitement of the telling narrative have worn off, when we have lost step with the swinging gait at which the style goes, when the details have faded from our recollection, and we sit removed and thoughtful, with only the greater outlines of the story sharp upon our minds, a deep misgiving and dissatisfaction take possession of us. We are no longer young, and we are chagrined that we should have been so pleased and taken with the glitter and color and mere life of the picture. Let boys be cajoled by rhetoric, we cry; men must look deeper. What of the judgment of this facile and eloquent man? Can we agree with him when he is not talking and the charm is gone? What shall we say of his assessment of men and measures? Is he just? Is he himself in possession of the whole truth? Does he open the matter to us as it was? Does he not, rather, rule us like an advocate, and make himself master of our judgments?

Then it is that we become aware that there were two Macaulays: Macaulay the artist, with an exquisite gift for telling a story, filling his pages with little vignettes it is impossible to forget, fixing these with an inimitable art upon the surface of a narrative that did not need the ornament they gave it, so strong and large and adequate was it; and Macaulay the Whig, subtly turning narrative into argument, and making history the vindication of a party. The mighty narrative is a great engine of proof. It is not told for its own sake. It is evidence summed up in order to justify a judgment. We detect the tone of the advocate, and though if we were just we must deem him honest, we cannot deem him safe. The great storyteller is discredited; and, willingly or unwillingly, we reject the guide who takes it upon himself to determine for us what we shall see. That, we feel sure, cannot be truth which makes of so complex a history so simple a thesis for the judgment. There is art here; but it is the art of special pleading, misleading even to the pleader.

If not Macaulay, what master shall we follow? Shall our historian not have his convictions, and enforce them? Shall he not be our guide, and speak, if he can, to our spirits as well as to our understandings? Readers are a poor jury. They need enlightenment as well as information: the matter must be interpreted to them as well as related. There are moral facts as well as material, and the one sort must be as plainly told as the other. Of what service is it that the historian should have insight if we are not to know how the matter stands in his view? If he refrain from judgment, he may deceive us as much as he would were his judgment wrong; for we must have enlightenment—that is his function. We would not set him up merely to tell us tales, but also to display to us characters, to open to us the moral and intent of the matter. Were the men sincere? Was the policy righteous? We have but just now seen that the "facts" lie deeper than the mere visible things that took place, that they involve the moral and motive of the play. Shall not these, too, be brought to light?

Unquestionably every sentence of true history must hold a judgment in solution. All cannot be told. If it were possible to tell all, it would take as long to write history as to enact it, and we should have to postpone the reading of it to the leisure of the next world. A few facts must be selected for the narrative, the great majority left unnoted. But the selection—for what purpose is it to be made? For the purpose of conveying an *impression* of the truth. Where shall you find a more radical process of judgment? The "essential" facts taken, the "unessential" left out! Why, you may make the picture what you will, and in any case it must be the express image of the historian's fundamental judgments. It is his purpose, or should be, to give a true impression of his theme as a whole—to show it, not lying upon his page in an open and dispersed analysis, but set close in intimate synthesis, every line, every stroke, every bulk even, omitted which does not enter of very necessity into a single and unified image of the truth.

It is in this that the writing of history differs, and differs very radically, from the statement of the results of original research. The writing of history must be based upon original research and authentic record, but it can no more be directly constructed by the piecing together of bits of original research than by the mere reprinting together of state documents. Individual research furnished us, as it were, with the private documents and intimate records without which the public archives are incomplete and unintelligible. But separately they are wholly out of perspective. It is the consolation of those who produce them to make them so. They would lose heart were they forbidden to regard all facts as of equal importance. It is facts they are after, and only facts—facts for their own sake, and without regard to their several importance. These are their ore, very precious ore, which they are concerned to get out, not to refine. They have no direct concern with what may afterward be done at the mint or in the goldsmith's shop. They will even boast that they care not for the beauty of the ore, and are indifferent how, or in what shape, it may become and article of commerce. Much of it is thrown away in the nice process of manufacture, and you shall not distinguish the product of the several mines in the coin, or the cup, or the salver.

Indeed, the historian must himself be an investigator. He must know good ore from bad; must distinguish fineness, quality, genuineness; must stop to get out of the records for himself what he lacks for the perfection of his work. But for all that, he must know and stand ready to do every part of his talk like a master workman, recognizing and testing every bit of stuff he uses. Standing sure, a man of science as well as an artist, he must take and use all of is equipment for the sake of his art—not to display his materials, but to subordinate and transform them in his effort to make, by every touch and cunning of hand and tool, the perfect image of what he sees, the very truth of his seer's vision of the world. The true historian works always for the whole impression, the truth with unmarred proportions, unexaggerated parts, undistorted visage. He has no favorite parts of the story which he boasts are bits of his own, but loves only the whole of it, the full and unspoiled image of the day of which he writes, the crowded and yet consistent details that carry, without obtrusion of themselves, the large features of the time. Any exaggeration of the parts makes all the picture false, and the work is to do over. Test every bit of material, runs the artist's rule, and then forget its origin and the dross from which it has been freed, and think only and always of the great thing you would make of it, the pattern and form in which you would lose and merge it. That is its only high use.

It is a pity to see how even the greatest minds will often lack the broad and catholic vision with which the just historian must look upon men and affairs. There is Carlyle, with his shrewd and seeing eye, his unmatched capacity to assess strong men and set the scenery for tragedy or intrigue, his breathless ardor for great events, his amazing flashes of insight, and his unlooked-for steady light of occasional narrative. The whole matter of what he writes is too dramatic. Surely history was not all enacted so hotly, or with so passionate a rush of men upon the stage. Its quiet scenes must have been longer—not mere pauses and interludes while the tragic parts were being made up. There is not often ordinary sunlight upon the page. The lights burn now wan, now lurid. Men are seen disquieted and turbulent, and may be heard in husky cries or rude, untimely jests. We do not recognize our own world, but seem to see another such as ours might become if peopled by like uneasy Titans. Incomparable to tell of days of storm and revolution, speaking like an oracle and familiar of destiny and fate, searching the hearts of statesmen and conquerors with an easy insight in every day of action, this peasant seer cannot give us the note of piping times of peace, or catch the tone of slow industry; watches ships come and go at the docks, hears freight-vans thunder along the iron highways of the modern world, and loaded trucks lumber heavily through the crowded city streets, with a hot disdain of commerce, prices current, the haggling of the market, and the smug ease of material comfort bred in a trading age. There is here no broad and catholic vision, no wise tolerance, no various power to know, to sympathize, to interpret. The great seeing imagination of the man lacks that pure radiance in which things are seen steadily and seen whole.

It is not easy, to say truth, to find actual examples when you are constructing the ideal historian, the man with the vision and the faculty divine to see affairs justly and tell of them completely. If you are not satisfied with this passionate and intolerant seer of Chelsea, whom will you choose? Shall it be Gibbon, whom all praise but so few read? He, at any rate, is passionless, it would appear. But who could write epochal history with passion? All hot humors of the mind must, assuredly, cool when spread at large upon so vast a surface. One must feel like a sort of minor providence in traversing that great tract of world history, and catch in spite of one's self the gait and manner of a god. This stately procession of generations moves on remote from the ordinary levels of our human sympathy. It is a wide view of nations and peoples and dynasties, and a world shaken by the travail of new births. There is here no scale by which to measure the historian of the sort we must look to see handle the ordinary matter of national history. The "Decline and Fall" stands impersonal, like a monument. We shall reverence it, but we shall not imitate it.

If we look away from Gibbon, exclude Carlyle, and question Macaulay; if we put the investigators on one side as not yet historians, and the deliberately picturesque and entertaining *raconteurs* as not yet investigators, we naturally turn, I suppose, to such a man as John Richard Green, at once the patient scholar—who shall adequately say how nobly patient?—and the rare artist, working so like a master in the difficult stuffs of a long national history. The very life of the man is as beautiful as the moving sentences he wrote with so subtle a music in the cadence. We know whence the fine moral elevation of tone came that sounds through all the text of his great narrative. True, not everybody is satisfied with our doctor angelicus. Some doubt he is too ornate. Others are troubled that he should sometimes be inaccurate. Some are willing to use his history for didactic uses, hesitate how they shall characterize him, and quit the matter vaguely with saying that what he wrote is "at any rate literature." Can there be something lacking in Green, too, notwithstanding he was impartial, and looked with purged and open eyes upon the whole unbroken life of his people—notwithstanding he saw the truth and had the art and mastery to make others see it as he did, in all its breadth and multiplicity?

Perhaps even this great master of narrative lacks variety—as who does not? His method, whatever the topic, is ever the same. His sentences, his paragraphs, his chapters, are pitched one and all in the same key. It is a very fine and moving key. Many an elevated strain and rich harmony commend it alike to the ear and to the imagination. It is employed with an easy mastery, and is made to serve to admiration a wide range of themes. But it is always the same key, and some themes it will not serve. An infinite variety plays through all history. Every scene has its own air and singularity. Incidents cannot all be rightly set in the narrative if all be set alike. As the scene shifts the tone of the narrative must change: The narrator's choice of incident and his choice of words; the speed and method of his sentence; his own thought, even, and point of view. Surely his battle pages must resound with the tramp of armies and the fearful din and rush of war. In peace he must catch by turns the hum of industry, the bustle of the street, the calm of the country-side, the tone of parliamentary debate, the fancy, the ardor, the argument of poets and seers and quiet students. Snatches of song run along with sober purpose and strenuous endeavor through every nation's story. Coarse men and refined, mobs and ordered assemblies, science and mad impulse, storm and calm, are all alike ingredients of the various life. It is not all epic. There is rough comedy and brutal violence. The drama can scarce be given any strict unbroken harmony of incident, any close logical sequence of act or nice unity of scene. To pitch it all in one key, therefore, is to mistake the significance of the infinite play of varied circumstance that makes up the yearly movement of a people's life.

It would be less than just to say that Green's pages do not reveal the variety of English life the centuries through. It is his glory, indeed, as all the world knows, to have broadened and diversified the whole scale of English history. Nowhere else within the compass of a single book can one find so many sides of the great English story displayed with so deep and just an appreciation of them all, or of the part of each in making up the whole. Green is the one man among English historians who has restored the great fabric of the nation's history where its architecture was obscure, and its details were likely to be lost or forgotten. Once more, because of him, the vast Gothic structure stands complete, its majesty and firm grace enhanced at every point by the fine tracery of its restored details.

Where so much is done, it is no doubt unreasonable to ask for more. But the very architectural symmetry of this great book imposes a limitation upon it. It is full of a certain sort of variety; but it is only the variety of a great plan's detail, not the variety of English life. The noble structure obeys its own laws rather than the laws of a people's life. It is a monument conceived and reared by a consummate artist, and it wears upon its every line some part of the image it was meant to bear of a great, complex, aspiring national existence. But, though it symbolizes, it does not contain that life. It has none of the irregularity of the actual experiences of men and communities. It explains, but it does not contain, their variety. The history of every nation has certainly a plan which the historian must see and reproduce; but he must reconstruct the people's life, not merely expound it. The scope of his method must be as great as the variety of his subject; it must change with each change of mood, respond to each varying impulse in the great process of events. No rigor of a stately style must be suffered to exclude the lively touches of humor or the rude sallies of strength that mark it everywhere. The plan of the telling must answer to the plan of the fact—must be as elastic as the topics are mobile. The matter should rule the plan, not the plan the matter.

The ideal is infinitely difficult, if, indeed, it be possible to any man not Shakespearian; but the difficulty of attaining it is often unnecessarily enhanced. Ordinarily the historian's preparation for his task is such as to make it unlikely he will perform it naturally. He goes first, with infinite and admirable labor, through all the labyrinth of document and detail that lies up and down his subject; collects masses of matter great and small for substance, verification, illustration; piles his notes volumes high; reads far and wide upon the tracks of his matter, and makes page upon page of references; and then, thoroughly stuffed and sophisticated, turns back and begins his narrative. It is impossible, then, that he would begin naturally. He sees the end from the beginning, and all the way from beginning to end; he has made up his mind about too many things; uses his details with a too free and familiar mastery, not like one who tells a story so much as like one who dissects a cadaver. Having swept his details together beforehand, like so much scientific material, he discourses upon them like a demonstrator—things too little in subjection to them. They no longer make a fresh impression upon him. They are his tools, not his objects of vision.

It is not by such a process that a narrative is made vital and true. It does not do to lose the point of view of the first listener to the tale, or to rearrange the matter too much out of the order of nature. You must instruct your reader as the events themselves would have instructed him had he been able to note them as they passed. The historian must not lose his own fresh view of the scene as it passed and changed more and more from year to year and from age to age. He must keep with the generation of which he writes, not be too quick to be wiser than they were, and look back upon them in his narrative with head over shoulder. He must write of them always in the atmosphere they themselves breathed, not hastening to judge them, but striving only to realize them at every turn of the story, to make their thoughts his own, and call their lives back again, rebuilding the very stage upon which they played their parts. Bring the end of your story to mind while you set about telling its beginning, and it seems to have no parts: beginning, middle, end, are all as one—are merely like parts of a pattern which you see as a single thing stamped upon the stuff under your hand. It is a dead thing dissected.

Try the method with the history of our own land and people. How will you begin? Will you start with a modern map and a careful topographical description of the continent? And then, having made your nineteenth-century framework for the narrative, will you ask your reader to turn back and see the seventeenth century, and those lonely ships coming in at the capes of the Chesapeake? He will never see them so long as you compel him to stand here at the end of the nineteenth century and look at them as if through a long retrospect. The attention both of the narrator and of the reader, if history is to be seen aright, must look forward, not backward. It must see with a contemporaneous eye. Let the historian, if he be wise, know no more of the history as he writes than might have been known in the age and day of which he is writing. A trifle too much knowledge will undo him. It will break the spell for his imagination. It will spoil the magic by which he may raise again the image of days that are gone. He must, of course, know the large lines of his story; it must lie as a whole in his mind. His very art demands that, in order that he may know and keep its proportions. But the details, the passing incidents of day and year, must come fresh into his mind, unreasoned upon as yet, untouched by theory, with their first look upon them. It is here that original documents and fresh research will serve him. He must look far and wide upon every detail of time, see it at first hand, and paint as he looks; selecting as the artist must, but selecting while the vision is fresh, and not from old sketches laid away in his notes—selecting from the life itself.

Let him remember that his task is radically different from the task of the investigator. The investigator must display his materials, but the historian must convey his impressions. He must stand in the presence of life, and reproduce it in his narrative; must recover a past age; make dead generations live again and breathe their own air; show them native and at home upon his page. To do this, his own impressions must be as fresh as those of an unlearned reader, his own curiosity as keen and young at every stage. It may easily be so as his reading thickens, and the atmosphere of the age comes stealthily into his thought, if only to take care to push forward the actual writing of his narrative at an equal pace with his reading, painting thus always direct from the image itself. His knowledge of the great outlines and bulks of the picture will be his sufficient guide and restraint the while, will give proportion to the individual strokes of his work. But it will not check his zest, or sophisticate his fresh recovery of the life that is in the crowing colors of the canvas.

A nineteenth-century plan laid like a standard and measure upon a seventeenth-century narrative will infallibly twist it and make it false. Lay a modern map before the first settlers at Jamestown and Plymouth, and then bid them discover and occupy the continent. With how superior a nineteenth-century wonder and pity will you see them grope, and stumble, and falter! How like children they will seem to you, and how simple their age, and ignorant! As stalwart men as you they were in fact; mayhap wiser and braver too; as fit to occupy a continent as you are to draw it upon paper. If you would know them, go back to their age; breed yourself a pioneer and woodsman; look to find the South Sea up the nearest northwest branch of the spreading river at your feet; discover and occupy the wilderness with them; dream what may be beyond the near hills, and long all day to see a sail upon the silent sea; go back to them and see them in their habit as they lived.

The picturesque writers of history have all along been right in theory: they have been wrong only in practice. It is a picture of the past we want—its express image and feature; but we want the true picture and not simply the theatrical matter—the manner of Rembrandt rather than Rubens. All life may be pictured, but not all of life is picturesque. No great, no true historian would put false or adventitious colors into his narrative, or let a glamour rest where in fact it never was. The writers who select an incident merely because it is striking or dramatic are shallow fellows. They see only with the eye's retina, not with that deep vision whose images lie where thought and reason sit. The real drama of life is disclosed only with the whole picture; and that only the deep and fervid student will see, whose mind goes daily fresh to the details, whose narrative runs always in the authentic colors of nature, whose art it is to see and to paint what he sees.

It is thus, and thus only, we shall have the truth of the matter: by art—by the most difficult of all arts; by fresh study and first-hand vision; at the mouths of men who stand in the midst of old letters and dusty documents and neglected records, not like antiquarians, but like those who see a distant country and a far-away people before their very eyes, as real, as full of life and hope and incident as the day in which they themselves live. Let us have done with humbug and come to plain speech. The historian needs an imagination quite as much as he needs scholarship, and consummate literary art as much as candor and common honesty. Histories are written in order that the bulk of men may read and realize; and it is as bad to bungle the telling of the story as to lie, as fatal to lack a vocabulary as to lack knowledge. In no case can you do more than convey an impression, so various and complex is the matter. If you convey a false impression, what difference does it make how you convey it? In the whole process there is a nice adjustment of means to ends which only the artist can manage. There is an art of lying; there is equally an art—an infinitely more difficult art—of telling the truth.

The Course of American History

In 1893, the same year in which Frederick Jackson Turner published his famous thesis, *The Significance of the Frontier in American History,* Wilson wrote an essay titled "The Course of American History." Though not as detailed or fully developed as Turner's seminal work, the ideas are remarkably similar. Turner had been a student of Wilson at Johns Hopkins, and he had tried to bring Turner to Princeton, but his effort was frustrated by the board of trustees. It is possible that the two scholars had discussed the frontier idea, but whether the idea came to them coincidentally and which man hit on the theory first have not been determined. Wilson reflected his southern roots in this work, challenging the New England perspective of much historical writing about the American past. He was also much concerned here with the influence of different interests among the sections of the nation, an interest about which Turner also wrote extensively. This essay was included in his collection, *Mere Literature.*

Our national history has been written for the most part by New England men. All honor to them! Their scholarship and their characters alike have given them an honorable enrollment amongst the great names of our literary history; and no just man would say aught to detract, were it never so little, from their well-earned fame. They have written our history, nevertheless, from but a single point of view. From where they sit, the whole of the great development looks like an Expansion of New England. Other elements but play along the sides of the great process by which the Puritan has worked out the development of nation and polity. It is he who has gone out and possessed the land: the man of destiny, the type and impersonation of a chosen people. To the Southern writer, too, the story looks much the same, if it be but followed to its culmination, to its final storm and stress and tragedy in the great war. It is the history of the Suppression of the South. Spite of all her splendid contributions to the steadfast accomplishment of the great task of building the nation; spite of the long leadership of her statesmen in the national counsels; spite of her joint achievements in the conquest and occupation of the West, the South was at least turned upon on every hand, rebuked, proscribed, defeated. The history of the United States, we have learned, was from the settlement at Jamestown to the surrender at Appomattox, a long-drawn contest for mastery between New England and the South, and the end of the contest we know. All along the parallels of latitude ran the rivalry, in those heroical days of toil and adventure during which population crossed the continent, like an army advancing its encampments. Up and down the great river of the continent, too, and beyond, up the slow incline of the vast steppes that lift themselves toward the crowning towers of the Rockies, beyond that, again, in the goldfields and upon the green plains of California, the race for ascendancy struggled on, till at length there was a final coming face to face, and the masterful folk who had come from the loins of New England won their consummate victory.

It is very dramatic form for the story. One almost wishes it were true. How fine a unity it would give our epic! But perhaps, after all, the real truth is more interesting. The life of the nation cannot be reduced to these so simple terms. These two great forces, of the north and of the South, unquestionably existed, were unquestionably projected in their operation out upon the great plane of the continent, there to combine or repel, as circumstances might determine. But the people that went out from the North were not an unmixed people; they came from the great Middle States as well as from New England. Their transplantation into the West was no more a reproduction of New England or New York or Pennsylvania or New Jersey than Massachusetts was a reproduction of Old England, or New Netherlands a reproduction of Holland. The Southern people, too, whom they met by the western rivers and upon the open prairies, were transformed, as they themselves were, by the rough fortunes of the frontier. A mixture of peoples, a modification of mind and habit, a new round of experiment and adjustment midst the novel life of the baked and untilled plain, and the far valleys with the virgin forests still thick upon them: a new temper, a new spirit of adventure, a new impatience of restraint, a new license of life, these are the characteristic notes and measures of the time when the nation spread itself at large upon the continent, and was transformed from a group of colonies into a family of States.

The passes of these eastern mountains were the arteries of the nation's life. The real breath of our growth and manhood came into our nostrils when first, like Governor Spotswood and that gallant company of Virginian gentlemen that rode with him in the far year 1716, the Knights of the Order of the Golden Horseshoe, our pioneers stood upon the ridges of the eastern hills and looked down upon those reaches of the continent where lay the untrodden paths of the westward migration. There, upon the courses of the distant rivers that gleamed before them in the sun, down the farther slopes of the hills beyond, out upon the broad fields that lay upon the fertile banks of the "Father of Waters," up the long tilt of the continent to the vast hills that looked out upon the Pacific—there were the regions in which, joining with people from every race and clime under the sun, they were to make the great compounded nation whose liberty and mighty works of peace were to cause all the world to stand at gaze. Thither were to come Frenchmen, Scandinavians, Celts, Dutch, Slavs, men of the Latin races and of the races of the Orient, as well as men, a great host, of the first stock of the settlements: English, Scots, Scots-Irish, like New England men, but touched with the salt of humor, hard, and yet neighborly too. For this great process of growth by grafting, of modification no less than of expansion, the colonies, the original thirteen States, were only preliminary studies and first experiments. But the experiments that most resembled the great methods by which we peopled the continent from side to side and knit a single polity across all its length and breadth, were surely the experiments made from the very first in the Middle States of our Atlantic seaboard.

Here from the first were mixture of population, variety of element, combination of type, as if of the nation itself in small. Here was never a simple body, a people of but a single blood and extraction, a polity and a practice brought straight from one motherland. The life of these States was from the beginning like the life of the country: they have always shown the national pattern. In New England and the South it was very different. There some of the great elements of the national life were long in preparation: but separately and with an individual distinction; without mixture, for long almost without movement. That the elements thus separately prepared were of the greatest importance, and run everywhere like chief threads of the pattern through all our subsequent life, who can doubt? They give color and tone to every part of the figure. The very fact that they are so distinct and separately evident throughout, the very emphasis of individuality they carry with them, but proves their distinct origin. The other elements of our life, various though they be, and of the very fibre, giving toughness and consistency to the fabric, are merged in its texture, united, confused, almost indistinguishable, so thoroughly are they mixed, intertwined, interwoven, like the essential strands of the stuff itself: but these of the Puritan and the Southerner, though they run everywhere with the rest and seem upon a superficial view themselves the body of the cloth, in fact modify rather than make it.

What in fact has been the course of American History? How is it to be distinguished from European history? What features has it of its own which give it its distinctive plan and movement? We have suffered, it is to be feared, a very serious limitation of view until recent years by having all our history written in the East. It has smacked strongly of a local flavor. It has concerned itself too exclusively with the origins and Old-World derivations of our story. Our historians have made their march from the sea with their heads over shoulder, their gaze always backward upon the landing-places and homes of the first settlers. In spite of the steady immigration, with its persistent tide of foreign blood, they have chosen to speak often and to think always of our people as sprung after all from a common stock, bearing a family likeness in every branch, and following all the while old, familiar, family ways. The view is the more misleading because it is so large a part of the truth without being all of it. The common British stock did first make the country, and has always set the pace. There were common institutions up and down the coast; and these had formed and hardened for a persistent growth before the great westward migration began which was to reshape and modify every element of our life. The national government itself was set up and made strong by success while yet we lingered for the most part upon the eastern coast and feared a too distant frontier.

But, the beginnings once safely made, change set in apace. Not only so: there had been slow change from the first. We have no frontier now, we are told, except a broken fragment, it may be, here and there in some barren corner of the western lands, where some inhospitable mountain still shoulders us out, or where men are still lacking to break the baked surface of the plains and occupy them in the very teeth of hostile nature. But at first it was all frontier,—a mere strip of settlements stretched precariously upon the sea-edge of the wilds: an untouched continent in front of them, and behind them an unfrequented sea that almost never showed so much as the momentary gleam of a sail. Every step in the slow process of settlement was but a step of the same kind as the first, an advance to a new frontier like the old. For long we lacked, it is true, that new breed of frontiersmen born in after years beyond the mountains. Those first frontiersmen had still a touch of the timidity of the Old World in their blood: they lacked the frontier heart. They were "Pilgrims" in very fact, exiled, not at home. Fine courage they had: and a steadfastness in their bold design which it does a faint-hearted age good to look back upon. There was no thought of drawing back. Steadily, almost calmly, they extended their seats. They built homes, and deemed it certain their children would live there after them. But they did not love the rough, uneasy life for its own sake. How long did they keep, if they could, within sight of the sea! The wilderness was their refuge: but how long before it became their joy and hope? Here was their destiny cast; but their hearts lingered and held back. It was only as generations passed and the work widened about them that their thought also changed, and a new thrill sped along their blood. Their life had been new and strange from their first landing in the wilderness. Their houses, their food, their clothing, their neighborhood dealings were all such as only the frontier brings. Insensibly they were themselves changed. The strange life became familiar; their adjustment to it was at length unconscious and without effort; they had no plans which were not inseparably a part and a product of it. But, until they had turned their backs once for all upon the sea; until they saw their western borders cleared of the French; until the mountain passes had grown familiar, and the lands beyond the central and constant theme of their hope, the goal and dream of their young men, they did not become an American people.

When they did, the great determining movement of our history began. The very visages of the people changed. That alert movement of the eye, that openness to every thought of enterprise or adventure, that nomadic habit which knows no fixed home and has plans ready to be carried any whither, and the marks of the authentic type of the "American" as we know him came into our life. The crack of the whip and the song of the teamster, the heaving chorus of boatmen poling their heavy rafts upon the rivers, the laughter of the camp, the sound of bodies of men in the still forests, became the characteristic notes in our air. A roughened race, embrowned in the sun, hardened in manner by a course life of change and danger, loving the rude woods and the crack of the rifle, living to begin something new every day, striking with the broad and open hand, delicate in nothing but the touch of the trigger, leaving cities in its track as if by accident rather than design, settling again to the steady ways of a fixed life only when it must: such was the American people whose achievement it was to be to take possession of their continent from end to end ere their national government was a single century old. The picture is a very singular one! Settled life and wild side by side: civilization rayed at the edges, taken forward in rough and ready fashion, with a song and a swagger, not by statesmen, but by woodsmen and drovers, with axes and whips and rifles in their hands, clad in buckskin, like huntsmen.

It has been said that we have here repeated some of the first processes of history; that the life and methods of our frontiersmen take us back to the fortunes and hopes of the men who crossed Europe when her forests, too, were still thick upon her. But the difference is really very fundamental, and much more worthy of remark than the likeness. Those shadowy masses of men whom we see moving upon the face of the earth in the faraway, questionable days when states were forming: even those stalwart figures we see so well as they emerge from the deep forests of Germany, to displace the Roman in all his western provinces and set up the states we know and marvel upon at this day, show us men working their new work at their own level. They do not turn back a long cycle of years from the old and settled states, the ordered cities, the tilled fields, and the elaborated government of an ancient civilization, to begin as it were once more at the beginning. They carry alike their homes and their states with them in the camp and upon the ordered march of the host. They are men of the forest, or else men hardened always to take the sea in open boats. They live no more roughly in the new lands than in the old. The world has been frontier for them from the first. They may go forward with their life in these new seats from where they left off in the old. How different the circumstances of our first settlement and the building of new states on this side the sea! Englishmen, bred in law and ordered government ever since the Norman lawyers were followed a long five hundred years ago across the narrow seas by those masterful administrators of the strong Plantagenet race, leave an ancient realm and come into a wilderness where states have never been; leave a land of art and letters, which saw but yesterday "the spacious times of great Elizabeth," where Shakespeare still lives in the gracious leisure of his closing days at Stratford, where cities teem with trade and men go bravely dight in cloth of gold, and turn back six centuries, nay, a thousand years and more, to the first work of building states in a wilderness! They bring the steadied habits and sobered thoughts of an ancient realm into the wild air of an untouched continent. The weary stretches of a vast sea lie, like a full thousand years of time, between them and the life in which till now all their thought was bred. Here they stand, as it were, with all their tools left behind, centuries struck out of their reckoning, driven back upon the long dormant instincts and forgotten craft of their race, not used this long age. Look how singular a thing: the work of a primitive race, the thought of a civilized! Hence the strange, almost grotesque groupings of thought and affairs in that first day of our history. Subtle politicians speak the phrases and practice the arts of intricate diplomacy from council chambers placed within log huts within a clearing. Men in ruffs and lace and polished shoe-buckles thread the lonely glades of primeval forests. The microscopical distinctions of the schools, the thin notes of a metaphysical theology are woven in and out through the labyrinths of grave sermons that run hours long upon the still air of the wilderness. Belief in dim refinements of dogma is made the test for man or woman who seeks admission to a company of pioneers. When went there by an age since the great flood when so singular a thing was seen as this: thousands of civilized men suddenly rusticated and bade do the work of primitive peoples, Europe *frontiered!*

Of course there was a deep change wrought, if not in these men, at any rate in their children; and every generation saw the change deepen. It must seem to every thoughtful man a notable thing how, while the change was wrought, the simplest of things complex were revealed in the clear air of the New World: how all accidentals seemed to fall away from the structure of government, and the simple first principles were laid bare that abide always; how social distinctions were stripped off, shown to be the mere cloaks and masks they were, and every man brought once again to a clear realization of his actual relations to his fellows! It was as if trained and sophisticated men had been rid of a sudden of their sophistication and of all the theory of their life, and left with nothing but their discipline of faculty, a schooled and sobered instinct. And the fact that we kept always, for close upon three hundred years, a like element in our life, a frontier people always in our van, is, so far, the central and determining fact of our national history. "East" and "West" an ever-changing line, but an unvarying experience and a constant leaven of change working always within the body of our folk. Our political, our economic, our social life has felt this potent influence from the wild border all our history through. The "West" is the great word of our history. The "Westerner" has been the type and master of our American life. Now at length, as I have said, we have lost our frontier: our front lies almost unbroken along all the great coast line of the western sea. The Westerner, in some day soon to come, will pass out of our life, as he so long also passed out of the life of the Old World. Then a new epoch will open for us. Perhaps it has opened already. Slowly we shall grow old, compact our people, study the delicate adjustments of an intricate society, and ponder the niceties, as we have hitherto pondered the bulks and structural framework, of government. Have we not, indeed, already come to these things? But the past we know. We can "see it steady and see it whole"; and its central movement and motive are gross and obvious to the eye.

Till the first century of the Constitution is rounded out we stand all the while in the presence of that stupendous westward movement which has filled the continent: so vast, so various, at times so tragical, so swept by passion. Through all the long time there has been a line of rude settlements along our front wherein the same tests of power and of institutions were still being made that were made first upon the sloping banks of the rivers of old Virginia and within the long sweep of the Bay of Massachusetts. The new life of the West has reacted all the while—who shall say how powerfully?—upon the older life of the East; and yet the East has molded the West as if she sent forward to it through every decade of the long process the chosen impulses and suggestions of history. The West has taken strength, thought, training, selected aptitudes out of the old treasures of the East, as if out of a new Orient; while the East has itself been kept fresh, vital, alert, originative by the West, her blood quickened all the while, her youth through every age renewed. Who can say in a word, in a sentence, in a volume, what destinies have been variously wrought, with what new examples of growth and energy, while, upon this unexampled scale, community has passed beyond community across the vast reaches of this great continent!

The Making of the Nation

In this wide-ranging article published in the *Atlantic Monthly* in July 1897, Wilson reviewed the historical tension between nationalism and sectionalism throughout American history. Among the many historical disputes concerning the Civil War has been the question of whether the war was avoidable or inevitable. It is clear here that Wilson believed that the fundamental tension between North and South could only have been resolved by conflict. He also took the opportunity to present again his own theory of the long absence of and urgent need for strong executive leadership to weld effective national policy.

The making of our nation seems to have taken place under our very eyes, so recent and so familiar is the story. The great process was worked out in the plain and open day of the modern world, statesmen and historians standing by to superintend, criticize, make record of what was done. The stirring narrative runs quickly into the day in which we live; we can say that our grandfathers builded the government which now holds so large a place in the world; the story seems of yesterday, and yet seems entire, as if the making of the republic had hastened to complete itself within a single hundred years. We are elated to see so great a thing done upon so great a scale, and to feel ourselves in so intimate a way actors in the moving scene.

Yet we should deceive ourselves were we to suppose the work done, the nation made. We have been told by a certain group of our historians that a nation was made when the federal Constitution was adopted; that the strong sentences of the law sufficed to transform us from a league of States into a people single and inseparable. Some tell us, however, that it was not till the war of 1812 that we grew fully conscious of a single purpose and destiny, and began to form policies as if for a nation. Others see the process complete only when the civil war struck slavery away, and gave North and South a common way of life that should make common ideals and common endeavors at last possible. Then, when all have had their say, there comes a great movement like the one which we call Populism, to remind us how the country still lies apart in sections: some at one stage of development, some at another; some with one hope and purpose for America, some with another. And we ask ourselves, Is the history of our making as a nation indeed over, or do we still wait upon the forces that shall at last unite us? Are we even now, in fact, a nation?

Clearly, it is not a question of sentiment, but a question of fact. If it be true that the country, taken as a whole, is at one and the same time in several stages of development, not a great commercial and manufacturing nation, with here and there its broad pastures and the quiet farms from which it draws its food; not a vast agricultural community, with here and there its ports of shipment and its necessary marts of exchange; nor yet a country of mines, merely, pouring their products forth into the markets of the world, to take thence whatever it may need for its comfort and convenience in living, we still wait for its economic and spiritual union. It is many things at once. Sections big enough for kingdoms live by agriculture, and farm the wide stretches of a new land for the aid of money borrowed from other sections which seem almost like another nation, with their teeming cities, dark with the smoke of factories, quick with the movements of trade, as sensitive to the variations of exchange on London as to the variations in the crops raised by their distant fellow countrymen on the plains within the continent. Upon other great spaces of the vast continent, communities, millions strong, live the distinctive life of the miner, have all their fortune bound up and centered in a single group of industries, feel in their utmost concentration the power of economic forces elsewhere dispersed, and chafe under the unequal yoke that unites them with communities so unlike themselves as those which lend and trade and manufacture, and those which follow the plough and reap the grain that is to feed the world.

Such contrasts are nothing new in our history, and our system of government is admirably adapted to relieve the strain and soften the antagonism they might entail. All our national history through our country has lain apart in sections, each marking a stage of settlement, a stage of wealth, a stage of development, as population has advanced, as if by successive journeyings and encampments, from east to west; and always new regions have been suffered to become new States, form their own life under their own law, plan their own economy, adjust their own domestic relations, and legalize their own methods of business. States have, indeed, often been whimsically enough formed. We have left the matter of boundaries to surveyors rather than to statesmen, and have by no means managed to construct economic units in the making of States. We have joined mining communities with agricultural, the mountain with the plain, the ranch with the farm, and have left the making of uniform rules to the sagacity and practical habit of neighbors ill at ease with one another. But the whole, the scheme, though a bit haphazard, has worked itself out with singularly little friction and no disaster, and the strains of the great structure we have erected have been greatly eased and dissipated.

Elastic as the system is, however, it stiffens at every point of national policy. The federal government can make but one rule, and that a rule for the whole country, in each act of its legislation. Its very constitution withholds it from discrimination as between State and State, section and section; and yet its chief powers touch just those subjects of economic interest in which the several sections of the country feel themselves most unlike. Currency questions do not affect them equally or in the same way. Some need an elastic currency to serve their uses; others can fill their coffers more readily with a currency that is inelastic. Some can build up manufacturers under a tariff law; others cannot, and must submit to pay more without earning more. Some have one interest in a principle of interstate commerce; others, another. It would be difficult to find even a question of foreign policy which would touch all parts of the country alike. A foreign fleet would mean much more to the merchants of Boston and New York that to the merchants of Illinois and the farms of the Dakotas.

The conviction is becoming painfully distinct among us, more-over, that these contrasts of condition and differences of interest between the several sections of the country are now more marked and emphasized than they ever were before.

☆ ☆ ☆

There is no longer any danger of a civil war. There was war between the South and the rest of the nation because their differences were removable in no other way. There was no prospect that slavery, the root of those differences, would ever disappear in the mere process of growth. It was to be apprehended, on the contrary, that the very processes of growth would inevitably lead to the extension of slavery and the perpetuation of radical social and economic contrasts and antagonisms between State and State, between region and region. An heroic remedy was the only remedy. Slavery being removed, the South is now joined with the "West," joined with it in a stage of development, as a region chiefly agricultural, without diversified industries, without a multifarious trade, without those subtle extended nerves which come with all-round economic development, and which make men keenly sensible of the interest that link the world together, as it were into a single community. But these are lines of difference which will be effaced by mere growth, which time will calmly ignore. They make no boundaries for armies to cross. Tide-water Virginia was thus separated once from her own population within the Allegheny valleys, held two jealous sections within her own limits. Massachusetts once knew the sharp divergences of interest and design which separated the coast settlements upon the Bay from the restless pioneers who had taken up the free lands of her own western counties. North Carolina was once a comfortable and indifferent "East" to the uneasy "West" that was to become Tennessee. Virginia once seemed old and effete to Kentucky. The "great West" once lay upon the Ohio, but has since disappeared there, overlaid by the changes which have carried the conditions of the "East" to the Great Lakes and beyond. There has never yet been a time in our history when we were without an "East" and a "West," but the novel day when we shall be without them is now in sight. As the country grows it will inevitably grow homogeneous. Population will not henceforth spread, but compact; for there is no new land between the seas where the "West" can find another lodgment. The conditions which prevail in the ever widening "East" will sooner or later cover the continent, and we shall at last be one people. The process will not be a short one. It will doubtless run through many generations and involve many a critical question of statesmanship. But it cannot be stayed, and its working out will bring the nation to its final character and role in the world.

In the meantime, shall we not constantly recall our reassuring past, reminding one another again and again, as our memories fail us, of the significant incidents of the long journey we have already come, in order that we may be cheered and guided upon the road we have yet to choose and follow? It is only by thus attempting, and attempting again and again, some sufficient analysis of our past experiences that we can form any adequate image of our life as a nation, or acquire any intelligent purpose to guide us amidst the rushing movement of affairs. It is no doubt in part by reviewing our lives that we shape and determine them. . . .

The colonies which formed the union were brought together, let us first remind ourselves, not merely because they were neighbors and kinsmen, but because they were forced to see that they had common interests which they could serve in no other way. "There is nothing which binds one country or one State to another but interest," said Washington. "Without this cement the Western inhabitants can have no predilection for us." Without that cement the colonies could have had no predilection for one another. But it is one thing to have common interests, and quite another to perceive them and act upon them. The colonies were first thrust together by the pressure of external danger. They needed one another, as well as aid from oversea, [*sic*] as any fool could perceive, if they were going to keep their frontiers against the Indians, and their outlets upon the Western waters from the French. The French and Indian war over, that pressure was relieved, and they might have fallen apart again, indifferent to any common aim, unconscious of any common interest, had not the government that was their common master set itself to make them wince under common wrongs. Then it was that they saw how like they were in polity and life and interest in the great field of politics, studied their common liberty, and became aware of their common ambitions. It was then that they became aware, too, that their common ambitions could be realized only by union; not single-handed, but united against a common enemy. Had they been let alone, it would have taken many a long generation of slowly increased acquaintance with one another to apprise them of their kinship in life and interests and institutions; but England drove them into immediate sympathy and combination, unwittingly founding a nation by suggestion.

The war for freedom over, the new-fledged States entered at once upon a very practical course of education which trust its lessons upon them without regard to taste or predilection. The Articles of Confederation had been formulated and proposed to the States for their acceptance in 1777, as a legalization of the arrangement that had grown up under the informal guidance of the Continental Congress, in order that law might confirm and strengthen practice, and because an actual continental war commanded a continental organization. But the war was virtually over by the time all the reluctant States had accepted the Articles; and the new government had hardly been put into formal operation before it became evident that only the war had made such an arrangement workable. Not compacts, but the compulsions of a common danger, had drawn the States into an irregular cooperation, and it was even harder to obtain obedience to the definite Articles than it had been to get the requisitions of the unchartered Congress heeded while the war lasted. Peace had rendered the makeshift common government uninteresting, and had given each State leave to withdraw from common undertakings, and to think once more, as of old, only of itself. Their own affairs again isolated and restored to their former separate importance, the States could no longer spare their chief men for what was considered the minor work of the general Congress. The best men had been gradually withdrawn from Congress before the war ended, and now there seemed less reason than ever why they should be sent to talk at Philadelphia, when they were needed for the actual work of administration at home. Politics fell back into their old localization, and every public man found his chief tasks at home. There were still, as a matter of fact, common needs and dangers scarcely less imperative and menacing than those which had drawn the colonies together against the mother country; but they were needs and perils of peace, and ordinary men did not see them; only the most thoughtful and observant were conscious of them: extraordinary events were required to lift them to the general view.

Happily, there were thoughtful and observant men who were already the chief figures of the country, men whose leadership the people had long since come to look for and accept, and it was through them that the States were brought to a new common consciousness, and at last to a real union. It was not possible for the several States to live self-sufficient and apart, as they had done when they were colonies. They had then had a common government, little as they like to submit to it, and their foreign affairs had been taken care of. They were now to learn how ill they could dispense with a common providence. Instead of France, they now had England for neighbor in Canada and on the Western waters, where they had themselves but the other day fought so hard to set her power up. She was their rival and enemy, too, on the seas; refused to come to any treaty terms with them in regard to commerce; and laughed to see them unable to concert any policy against her garrisons from the Western posts which lay within the territory belonging to the Confederation; but Congress had promised that British creditors should be paid what was due them, only to find that the States would make no laws to fulfill the promise, and were determined to leave their federal representatives without power to make them; and

England kept her troops where they were. Spain had taken France's place upon the further bank of the Mississippi and at the great river's mouth. Grave questions of foreign policy pressed on every side, as of old, and no State could settle them unaided and for herself alone.

Here was a group of commonwealths which would have lived separately and for themselves, and could not; which had thought to make shift with merely a "league of friendship" between them and a Congress for consultation, and found that it was impossible. There were common debts to pay, but there was no common system of taxation by which to meet them, nor any authority to devise and enforce such a system. There were common enemies and rivals to deal with, but no one was authorized to carry out a common policy against them. There was a common domain to settle and administer, but no one knew how a Congress without the power to command was to manage so great a property. The Ordinance of 1787 was indeed bravely framed, after a method of real statesmanship; but there was no warrant for it to be found in the Articles, and no one could say how Congress would execute a law it had had no authority to enact. It was not merely the hopeless confusion and sinister signs of anarchy which abounded in their own affairs—a rebellion of debtors in Massachusetts, tariff wars among the States that lay upon New York Bay and on the Sound, North Carolina's doubtful supremacy among her settlers in the Tennessee country, Virginia's questionable authority in Kentucky—that brought the States at last to attempt a better union and set up a real government for the whole country. It was the inevitable continental outlook of affairs as well; if nothing more, the sheer necessity to grow and touch their neighbors at close quarters.

Washington had been among the first to see the necessity of living, not by a local, but by a continental policy. Of course he had a direct pecuniary interest in the development of the Western lands, had himself preempted many a broad acre lying upon the far Ohio, as well as upon the nearer western slopes of the mountains, and it is open to any one who likes the sinister suggestion to say that his ardor for the occupancy of the Western country was that of the land speculator, not that of the statesman. Everybody knows that it was a conference between delegates from Maryland and Virginia about Washington's favorite scheme of joining the upper waters of the Potomac with the upper waters of the streams which made their way to the Mississippi—a conference held at his suggestion and at his house—that led to the convening of that larger conference at Annapolis, which called for the appointment of the body that met at Philadelphia and framed the Constitution under which he was to become the first President of the United States. It is open to any one who chooses to recall how keen old Governor Dinwiddie had been, when he came to Virginia, to watch those same Western waters in the interest of the first Ohio Company, in which he had bought stock; how promptly he called the attention of the ministers in England to the aggressions of the French in that quarter, sent Washington out as his agent to warn the intruders off, and pushed the business from stage to stage, till the French and Indian war was ablaze, and nations were in deadly conflict on both sides of the sea. It ought to be nothing new and nothing strange to those who have read the history of the English race the world over to learn that conquests have a thousand times sprung out of the initiative of men who have first followed private interest into new lands like speculators, and then planned their occupation and government like statesmen. Dinwiddie was no statesman, but Washington was; and the circumstance which it is worth while to note about him is, not that he went prospecting upon the Ohio when the French war was over, but that he saw more than fertile lands there, saw the "seat of a rising empire," and, first among the men of his day, perceived by what means its settlers could be bound to the older communities in the East alike in interest and in polity. Here were the first "West" and the first "East," and Washington's thought mediating between them.

The formation of the Union brought a real government into existence, and that government set about its work with an energy, a dignity, a thoroughness of plan, which made the whole country aware of it from the outset, and aware, consequently, of the national scheme of political life it had been devised to promote. Hamilton saw to it that the new government should have a definite party and body of interests at its back. It had been fostered in the making by the commercial classes at the ports and along the routes of commerce, and opposed in the rural districts which lay away from the centers of population. Those who knew the forces that played from State to State, and made America a partner in the life of the world, had earnestly wanted a government that should preside and choose in the making of the nation; but those who saw only the daily round of the countryside had been indifferent or hostile, consulting their pride and their prejudices. Hamilton sought a policy which should serve the men who had set the government up, and found it in the funding of the debt, both national and domestic, the assumption of the Revolutionary obligations of the States, and the establishment of a national bank. This was what the friends of the new plan had wanted, the rehabilitation of credit, and the government set out with a program meant to commend it to men with money and vested interests.

It was just such a government that the men of an opposite interest and temperament had dreaded, and Washington was not out of office before the issue began to be clearly drawn between those who wanted a strong government, with a great establishment, a system of finance which should dominate the markets, an authority in the field of law which should restrain the States and make the Union, through its courts, the sole and final judge of its own powers, and those who dreaded nothing else so much wished a government which should hold the country together with as little thought as possible of its own aggrandizement, went all the way with Jefferson in his jealousy of the commercial interest, accepted his ideal of a dispersed power put into commission among the States, even among the local units within the States, and looked to see liberty discredited amidst a display of federal power. When the first party had had their day in the setting up of the government and the inauguration of a policy which should make it authoritative, the party of Jefferson came in to purify it. They began by attacking the federal courts, which had angered every man of their faith by a steady maintenance and elaboration of the federal power; they ended by using that power just as their opponents had used it. In the first place, it was necessary to buy Louisiana, and with it the control of the Mississippi, notwithstanding Mr. Jefferson's solemn conviction that such an act was utterly without constitutional warrant; in the second place, they had to enforce an arbitrary embargo in order to try their hand at reprisal upon foreign rivals in trade; in the end, they had to recharter the national bank, create a national debt and a sinking fund, impose an excise upon whiskey, lay direct taxes, devise a protective tariff, use coercion upon those who would not aid them in a great war, play the role of masters and taxgatherers as the Federalists had played it, on a greater scale, even, and with equal gusto. Everybody knows the familiar story: it has new significance from day to day only as it illustrates the invariable process of nation-making which has gone on from generation to generation, from the first until now.

Opposition to the exercise and expansion of the federal power only made it the more inevitable by making it the more deliberate. The passionate protests, the plain speech, the sinister forecasts, of such men as John Randolph aided the process by making it self-conscious. What Randolph meant as an accusation, those who chose the policy of the government presently accepted as a prophecy. It was true, as he said, that a nation was in the making, and a government under which the privileges of the States would count for less than the compulsions of the common interest. Few had seen it so at first; the men who were old when the government was born refused to see it so to the last; but the young men and those who came fresh upon the stage from decade to decade presently found the scarecrow look like a thing they might love. Their ideal took form with the reiterated suggestion; they began to hope for what they had been bidden to dread. No party could long use the federal authority without coming to feel it national, without forming some ideal of the common interest, and of the use of power by which it should be fostered.

When they adopted the tariff of 1816, the Jeffersonians themselves formulated a policy which should endow the federal government with a greater economic power than even Hamilton had planned when he sought to win the support of the merchants and the lenders of money; and when they bought something like a third of the continent beyond the Mississippi, they made it certain the nation should grow upon a continental scale which no provincial notions about the state powers and a common government kept within strait bounds could possible survive. Here were the two forces which were to dominate us till the present day, and make the present issues of our politics: an open "West" into which a frontier population was to be thrust from generation to generation, and a protective tariff which should build up special interests the while in the "East," and make the contrast every sharper and sharper between section and section. What the "West" is doing now is simply to note more deliberately than ever before, and with a keener distaste, this striking contrast between her own development of that of the "East." That was a true instinct of statesmanship which led Henry Clay to couple a policy of internal improvements with a policy of protection. Internal improvements meant in that day great roads leading into the West, and every means taken to open the country to use and settlement. While a protective tariff was building up special industries in the East, public works should make an outlet into new lands for all who were not getting the benefit of the system. The plan worked admirably for many a day, and was justly called "American," so well did it match the circumstances of a set of communities, half old, half new: the old waiting to be developed, and new setting the easy scale of living. The other side of the policy was left for us. There is no longer any outlet for those who are not the beneficiaries of the protective system, and nothing but the contrasts it has created remains to mark its triumphs. Internal improvements no longer relieve the strain; they have become merely a means of largess.

The history of the United States has been one continuous story of rapid, stupendous growth, and all its great questions have been questions of growth. It was proposed in the Constitutional Convention of 1787 that a limit should be set to the number of new members to be admitted to the House of Representatives from States formed beyond the Alleghenies; and the suggestion was conceived with a true instinct of prophecy. The old States were not only to be taken out of their self-centered life, but were even to see their very government changed over their heads by the rise of States in the Western country. John Randolph voted against the admission of Ohio into the Union, because he held that no new partner should be admitted to the federal arrangement except by unanimous consent. It was the very next year that Louisiana was purchased, and a million square miles were added to the territory out of which new States were to be made. Had the original States been able to live to themselves, keeping their own people, elaborating their own life, without a common property to manage, unvexed by a vacant continent, national questions might have been kept within modest limits. They might even have made shift to digest Tennessee, Kentucky, Mississippi, Alabama, and the great commonwealths carved out of the Northwest Territory, for which the Congress of the Confederation had already made provision. But the Louisiana purchase opened the continent to the planting of States, and took the processes of nationalization out of the hands of the original "partners." Questions of politics were henceforth to be questions of growth.

For a while the question of slavery dominated all the rest. The Northwest Territory was closed to slavery by the Ordinance of 1787. Tennessee, Kentucky, Mississippi, Alabama, took slavery almost without question from the States from which they were sprung. But Missouri gave the whole country view of the matter which must be settled in the making of every State founded beyond the Mississippi. The slavery struggle, which seems to us who are near to it to occupy so great a space in the field of our affairs, was, of course, a struggle for and against the extension of slavery, not for or against its existence in the States where it had taken root from of old, a question of growth, not of law. It will some day be seen to have been, for all it was so stupendous, a mere episode of development. Its result was to remove a ground of economic and social difference as between section and section which threatened to become permanent, standing forever in the way of a homogeneous national life. The passionate struggle to prevent its extension inevitably led to its total abolition; and the way was cleared for the South, as well as the "West," to become like its neighbor sections in every element of its life.

It had also a further, almost incalculable effect in its stimulation of a national sentiment. It cleared throughout the North and Northwest a passion of devotion to the Union which really gave the Union a new character. The nation was fused into a single body in the fervent heat of the time. At the beginning of the war the South had seemed like a section pitted against a section; at its close it seemed a territory conquered by a neighbor nation. That nation is now, take it roughly, that "East," which we contrast with the "West" of our day. The economic conditions once centered at New York, Boston, Philadelphia, Baltimore, Pittsburgh, and the other commercial and industrial cities of the coast States are now to be found, hardly less clearly marked, in Chicago, in Minneapolis, in Detroit, through all the great States that lie upon the Lakes, in all the old "Northwest." The South has fallen into a new economic classification. In respect of its stage of development it belongs with the "West," though in sentiment, in traditional ways of life, in many a point of practice and detail, it keeps its old individuality, and though it has in its peculiar labor problem a hindrance to progress at once unique and ominous.

It is to this point we have come in the making of the nation. The old sort of growth is at an end, the growth by mere expansion. We have now to look more closely to internal conditions, and study the means by which a various people is to be bound together in a single interest. Many differences will pass away of themselves. "East" and "West" will come together by a slow approach, as capital accumulates where now it is only borrowed, as industrial development makes its way westward in a new variety, as life gets its final elaboration and detail throughout all the great spaces of the continent, until all the scattered parts of the nation are drawn into real community of interest. Even the race problem of the South will no doubt work itself out in the slowness of time, as blacks and whites pass from generation to generation, gaining with each remove from the memories of the war a surer self-possession, an easier view of the division of labor and of social function to be arranged between them. Time is the only legislator in such a matter. But not everything can be left to drift and slow accommodation. The nation which has grown to the proportions almost of the continent within the century lies under our eyes, unfinished, unharmonized, waiting still to have its parts adjusted, lacking its last lesson in the ways of peace and concert. It required statesmanship of no mean sort to bring us to our present growth and lusty strength. It will require leadership of a much higher order to teach us the triumphs of cooperation, the self-possession and calm choices of maturity.

☆ ☆ ☆

The making of a nation has never been a thing deliberately planned and consummated by the counsel and authority of leaders, but the daily conduct and policy of a nation which has won its place must be so planned. So far we have had the hopefulness, the readiness, and the hardihood of youth in these matters, and have never become fully conscious of the position into which our peculiar frame of government has brought us. We have waited a whole century to observe that we have made no provision for authoritative national leadership in matters of policy. The President does not always speak with authority, because he is not always a man picked out and tested by any processes in which the people have been participants, and has often nothing but his office to render him influential. Even when the country does know and trust him, he can carry his views no further than to recommend them to the attention of Congress in a written message which the Houses would deem themselves subservient to give too much heed to. Within the Houses there is no man, except the Vice-President, to whose choice the whole country gives heed; and he is chosen, not to be a Senator, but only to wait upon the disability of the President, and preside meanwhile over a body of which he is not a member. The House of Representatives has in these latter days made its Speaker its political leader as well as its parliamentary moderator; but the country is, of course, never consulted about that beforehand, and his leadership is not the open leadership of discussion, but the undebatable leadership of the parliamentary autocrat.

This singular leaderless structure of our government never stood fully revealed until the present generation, and even now awaits general recognition. Peculiar circumstances and the practical political habit and sagacity of our people for long concealed it. The framers of the Constitution no doubt expected the President and his advisers to exercise a real leadership in affairs, and for more than a generation after the setting up of the government their expectation was fulfilled. Washington was accepted as leader no less by Congress than by the people. Hamilton, from the Treasury, really gave the government both its policy and its administrative structure. If John Adams had less authority than Washington, it was because the party he represented was losing its hold upon the country. Jefferson was the most consummate party chief, the most unchecked master of legislative policy, we have had in America, and his dynasty was continued in Madison and Monroe. But Madison's terms saw Clay and Calhoun come to the front in the House, and many another man of the new generation, ready to guide and coach the President rather than to be absolutely controlled by him. Monroe was not of the caliber of his predecessors, and no party could rally about so stiff a man, so cool a partisan, as John Quincy Adams. And so the old political function of the presidency came to an end, and it was left for Jackson to give it a new one, instead of a leadership of counsel, a leadership and discipline by rewards and punishments. Then the slavery issue began to dominate politics, and a long season of concentrated passion brought individual men of force into power in Congress, natural leaders of men like Clay, trained and eloquent advocates like Webster, keen debaters with a logic whose thrusts were as sharp as those of cold steel like Calhoun. The war made the Executive of necessity the nation's leader again, with the great Lincoln at its head, who seemed to embody, with a touch of genius, the very character of the race itself. Then reconstructions came, under whose leadership who could say?—and we were left to wonder what, henceforth, in the days of ordinary peace and industry, we were to make of a government which could in humdrum times yield us no leadership at all. The tasks which confront us now are not like those which centered in the war, in which passion made men run together to a common work. Heaven forbid that we should admit any element of passion into the delicate matters in which national policy must mediate between the differing economic interest of sections which a wise moderation will assuredly unite in the ways of harmony and peace! We shall need, not the mere compromises of Clay, but a constructive leadership of which Clay hardly showed himself capable.

There are few things more disconcerting to the thought, in any effort to forecast the future of our affairs, than the fact that we must continue to take our executive policy from presidents given us by nominating conventions, and our legislation from conference committees of the House and Senate. Evidently it is a purely providential form of government. We should never have had Lincoln for President had not the Republican convention of 1860 sat in Chicago, and felt the weight of the galleries in its work, and one does not like to think what might have happened had Mr. Seward been nominated. We might have had Mr. Bryan for President, because of the impression which may be made upon an excited assembly by a good voice and a few ringing sentences flung forth just after a cold man who gave unpalatable counsel has sat down. The country knew absolutely nothing about Mr. Bryan before his nomination, and it would not have known anything about him afterward had he not chosen to make speeches. It was not Mr. McKinley, but Mr. Reed, who was the real leader of the Republican party. It has become a commonplace amongst us that conventions prefer dark horses, prefer those who are not tested leaders with well-known records to those who are. It has become a commonplace amongst all nations which have tried popular institutions that the actions of such bodies as our nominating conventions are subject to the play of passion and of chance. . . .

It has not often happened that candidates for the presidency have been chosen from outside the ranks of those who have seen service in national politics. Congress is apt to be peculiarly sensitive to the exercise of executive authority by men who have not in some time been members of the one House or the other, and so learned to sympathize with members' views as to the relations that ought to exist between the President and the federal legislature. No doubt a good deal of the dislike which the Houses early conceived for Mr. Cleveland was due to the feeling that he was an "outsider," a man without congressional sympathies and points of view, a sort of irregular and amateur at the delicate game of national politics as played at Washington; most of the men whom he chose as advisers were of the same kind, without Washington credentials. Mr. McKinley, though of the Congressional circle himself, has repeated the experiment in respect of his cabinet in the appointment of such men as Mr. Gage and Mr. Bliss and Mr. Gary. Members resent such appointments; they seem to drive the two branches of the government further apart then ever, and yet they grow more common from administration to administration.

These appointments make cooperation between Congress and the Executive more difficult, not because the men thus appointed lack respect for the Houses or seek to gain any advantage over them, but because they do not know how to deal with them, through what persons and by what courtesies of approach. To the uninitiated Congress is simply a mass of individuals. It has no responsible leaders known to the system of government, and the leaders recognized by its rules are one set of individuals for one sort of legislation, another for another. The Secretaries cannot address or approach either House as a whole; in dealing with committees they are dealing only with groups of individuals; neither party has its leader, there are only influential men here and there who know how to manage its caucuses and take advantage of parliamentary openings on the floor. There is a master in the House, as every member very well knows, and even the easy-going public are beginning to observe. The Speaker appoints the committees; the committees practically frame all legislation; the Speaker, accordingly, gives or withholds legislative power and opportunity, and members are granted influence or deprived of it much as he pleases. He of course administers the rules, and the rules are framed to prevent debate and individual initiative. He can refuse recognition for introduction of measures he disapproves of as party chief; he may make way for those he desires to see passed. He is chairman of the Committee on Rules, by which the House submits to be governed (for fear of helplessness and chaos) in the arrangement of its business and the apportionment of its time. In brief, he is not only its moderator, but its master. New members protest and write to the newspapers; but old members submit, and indeed the Speaker's power is inevitable. You must have leaders in a numerous body, leaders with authority; and you cannot give authority in the House except through the rules. The man who administers the rules must be master, and you must put this mastery into the hands of your best party leader. The legislature being separated from the executive branch of government, the only rewards and punishments by which you can secure party discipline are those within the gift of the rules, the committee appointments and preferences: you cannot administer these by election; party government would break down in the midst of personal exchanges of electoral favors. Here again you must trust the Speaker to organize and choose, and your only party leader is your moderator. He does not lead by debate; he explains, he proposes nothing to the country; you learn his will in his rulings.

It is with such machinery that we are to face the future, find a wise and moderate policy, bring the nation to a common, a cordial understanding, a real unity of life. The President can lead only as he can command the ear of both Congress and the country, only as any other individual might who could secure a like general hearing and acquiescence. Policy must come always from the deliberations of the House committees, the debates, both secret and open, of the Senate, the compromises of committee conference between the Houses; no one man, no group of men, leading; no man, no group of men, responsible for the outcome. Unquestionably we believe in a guardian destiny! No other race could have accomplished so much with such a system; no other race would have dared risk such an experiment. We shall work out a remedy, for work it out we must. We must find or make, somewhere in our system, a group of men to lead us, who represent the nation in the origin and responsibility of their power; who shall draw the Executive, which makes choice of foreign policy and upon whose ability and good faith the honorable execution of the laws depends, into cordial cooperation with the legislature, which, under whatever form of government, must sanction law and policy. Only under a national leadership, by a national selection of leaders, and by a method of constructive choice rather than of compromise and barter, can a various nation be peacefully led. Once more is our problem of nation-making the problem of a form of government. Shall we show the sagacity, the open-mindedness, the moderation, in our task of modification, that were shown under Washington and Madison and Sherman and Franklin and Wilson, in the task of construction?

States Rights

A southerner by birth and sentiment, Wilson brought his perspective on the cause of the Civil War to this essay written in 1899. As the title suggests, it was states rights that led the South to secession and war, with slavery establishing the occasion for the broader issue. His comment on slavery as "not so dark a thing" and his picture of slaves as generally well treated and "happy" in their condition do not survive modern scholarship, but such conclusions were not uncommon among historians of his generation. In Wilson's day, what is referred to as the Dunning School of historiography, centered at Columbia University, was deeply influential on histories of the Civil War and Reconstruction. Those histories tended toward great sympathy for the South and encouraged the vision of the suffering South at the hands of vengeful northern radicals. That perspective distorted the history of the era for decades until distance and data began to unravel the story. Wilson clearly shared the Dunning consensus.

When the historian of the United States reaches the year 1850, he finds himself at a point at which it is convenient, at which it is indeed necessary, that he should pause and "look before and after," in order that he may reckon the forces amidst which he stands and scan the whole stage of affairs. The "Compromise of 1850" settled nothing; but it was compounded of every element of the country's politics and may be made to yield upon analysis almost every ingredient of the historian's narrative. Its object was the settlement of all urgent questions. Texas has been admitted to the Union with disputed boundaries which needed to be definitely determined; territory had been acquired from Mexico, by conquest and purchase, for which it was requisite to provide a government; opinion in one section of the country was demanding that the slave-trade should be excluded from the District of Columbia, the seat of the national government, and slavery itself from the new territory; opinion in another section was demanding, with an air almost of passion, that the question of slavery in the Territories be left to those who should settle and make States of them, and that property in slaves should everywhere be adequately protected by effective laws for the apprehension and return of fugitive negroes. It was the question of the extension or restriction of slavery that made the adoption of a plan of organization and government for the new Territory perplexing and difficult, and the determination of the boundary of Texas a matter of critical sectional interest; and yet the rapid growth and development of the country rendered it imperative that action should be taken definitely and at once. Something must be done, and done promptly, to quiet men's minds concerning disturbing questions of policy and to keep parties from going utterly to pieces. That was the object of the "Compromise of 1850."

It consisted of a series of measures framed and introduced by a committee of which Henry Clay was chairman, and urged upon Congress with all the art, energy, and persuasiveness of which the aged Kentuckian was so great a master, even in those his last days. It was agreed (1) that Texas should be paid ten million dollars to relinquish her claim upon a portion of New Mexico; (2) that California should be admitted as a State under a constitution which prohibited slavery; (3) that New Mexico and Utah should be organized as Territories without any regulation in respect of slavery, leaving it to the choice of their own settlers whether there should be property in slaves amongst them or not; (4) that the slave-trade should be excluded from the District of Columbia, but be interfered with nowhere else by federal law; and (5) that the whole judicial and administrative machinery of the Federal government should be put at the disposal of the Southern slave-owners for the recovery of fugitive slaves found within the Free States.

☆ ☆ ☆

No one could deny the South has all along played a part in the control of parties which was altogether out of proportion to her importance in wealth or population. But every year relaxed her hold upon affairs and more definitely and obviously threatened her mastery with destruction. The country was growing away from her. It had grown away from her in the years which preceded the coming in of Jackson and the rough Western democracy which despised tradition; but the fact had not been upon the surface in those days. In 1850 it was plain to see. During the twenty years which had passed, the country had grown at an infinitely quickened pace, and in ways which could escape no man's observation, while the South had almost stood still. Her order of life was fixed and unchangeable. She could not expect manufacturers to make their home with her; she could not induce immigrants to settle on her untilled lands. Diversification of industry was for her, it seemed, out of the question. She had begun to perceive this twenty years ago, and had been deeply moved by the discovery. She could not forget the controversies which had raged about the tariff legislation of 1828 and 1832, or rid herself of the painful impression of what had been done and said and threatened when South Carolina made her attempt at "nullification." Time had but made the issues of that conflict more distressingly plain and significant.

The South could not compete with the North in the establishment of manufacturers because she could not command or maintain the sort of labor necessary for their successful development; nor could she compete with the North in the establishment of agricultural communities and the building of new States in the West, if her people were to be forbidden to take their slaves with them into the national territories. Her statesmen had felt a great enthusiasm for national expansion at the first, had favored moderate tariffs and the diversification of industry, had spoken like men of a race, not like men of a section, until they saw at last how the very organization of the communities they loved best and most passionately seemed to shut them out from sharing in the great change and growth which were to command the future. Then, as was but natural, they began to draw back and to doubt as to the course they had taken. To put tariff-charges on imports in order that manufacturers might get higher prices for their goods in the markets of the States, was, they said, when viewed from the side of the effects it would have upon their own people, only an indirect way—and not a very indirect way either—of making the South, which could not engage in manufactures, support of the people of the North, who could. It would curtail the commerce of the Southern ports and markets without furnishing any countervailing advantage to offset the loss.

That had been the ground of South Carolina's "nullification." Calhoun had not led her into that singular course: he had followed her into it. He had hitherto held his mind to a national scale of thinking; but the distress of his own people swung him about, to study the causes of their disquietude. He accepted, when it was pressed upon him, their own explanation of the decline of their commerce and the falling off in the price of their cotton. He believed, as they did, that these things were due to an inequitable distribution of the burdens of federal taxation: that the South was being made to pay for the maintenance of manufactures in the North. He accordingly supplied them with weapons of defense, with constitutional arguments which went the whole length of an absolute refusal to obey oppressive and unequal laws, with the full-wrought doctrine of nullification.

Calhoun did not invent the doctrine of nullification. It had been mentioned and urged in South Carolina again and again before he had been brought to accept it—mentioned very explicitly and urged very passionately. He had turned very reluctantly from national plans to sectional defense; and only because men who were his intimate friends and close political associates at home, as well as events happening under his own eyes at Washington, convinced him of the critical peril of the Southern States. But when he did turn it was with eyes wide open and with all the passion of his nature, and with the passion of his mind also, that singular instrument of power, which gave order, precision, and a keen and burning force to whatever it touched. The doctrine of States Rights, which other men had used for protest, for exhortation, for advantage in debate, he used as if for legal demonstration. He made of it a philosophy of right, a statesman's fundamental tenet. The very coolness and precision of his way of reasoning seemed to make the doctrine a new and wiser thing. In every sentence, too, there was added to the sharp lines of reason the unmistakable glow of conviction. Once convinced of the necessity of this his new line of action, he followed it with the zest of a crusader.

☆ ☆ ☆

The disturbing effects of all this upon the composition and aims of parties, and upon the action of the general government in affairs of domestic policy, were enhanced by the disappearance of the old party leaders. Calhoun died in March, 1850, the central month of the great Compromise debates—died stricken at heart, as it must have seemed to all who observed him closely, because forced in those last days to see with his keen eye of prophecy what the years to come must inevitably bring to pass. He had told those about him that the South was stronger now than she could ever be again, and must insist now or never upon what she considered her rights under the Constitution; that she had yielded too much when she consented to the Missouri Compromise of 1820, and must utterly lose the game of power if she conceded more; that the preservation of the Union depended upon the maintenance of an equilibrium between the Slave States and the Free, and that the Union must go to pieces unless that equilibrium, already destroyed, should be restored. He knew in those last sad days that it could not be restored, and that the Union he had loved and lived for must enter on its struggle with death. His own hand, more than any other man's, had wrought to bring the struggle on, because what he deemed his duty had bidden him to the work. He had drawn out the plot of the tragedy; but must have thanked God he was not to see it played out. He had designed it to be a warning: it had turned out to be a prophecy.

Webster and Clay survived him two years. Clay died in June, 1852, and Webster followed him in October. They had employed all their remaining power in the task of maintaining peace between the parties under the Compromise of 1850. Webster had gone about the country reproving agitation, speaking of the compromise measures, in his solemn and impressive way, as a new compact, a new stay and guarantee of the Constitution itself, the pledge and covenant of domestic peace. He had, indeed, sacrificed a great deal to effect the adjustment he so earnestly defended. He had lost many a friend and had infinitely saddened his own old age by advocating accommodation between the contending forces of North and South. Many thought this accommodation an utter abandonment of the gallant position he had taken in 1832, when he had faced Senator Hayne so successfully with his confident vindication of the sovereign authority of the general government. Men who had once trusted him to the utmost now denounced him with cutting bitterness as an apostate and an enemy of the Union. But he endured the shame, as he thought, so that the Union might be saved. Clay also cried out to the last for peace, for good faith in the acceptance and fulfillment of the Compromise, for a steady allegiance in the maintenance of the old parties and the old programs, against discontent and uproar and disquieting agitation. Both men passed from the stage before they could know what the outcome would be, hoping for the best, but doubting and distressed, their veteran heads bowed as if before a breaking storm.

☆ ☆ ☆

The parliamentary *regime* had broken down because there was no organized method of leadership in Congress and no responsible ministry at the head of a dominant party and of the law-making Houses. The President's "cabinet," though in the early years selected from among men who had seen service in Congress and were the known and acknowledged leaders of their party, had never had a place on the floor of Congress. Congressional committees had for many years after the foundation of the government accepted the suggestions of the President and his advisers in matters of legislation; bills had often been framed in the executive departments which the houses showed themselves very ready to adopt; and the early Presidents had counted upon exercising a guiding influence in legislation as a natural prerogative in view of their position as accepted representatives of the nation. But Congress had by degrees broken away even from this private connection with the executive, this connection of advice and common counsel; and there had never been any public connection whatever. The Houses looked more and more exclusively to their own committees or to their own private members for the bills which they were to act upon, and grew more and more jealous of "outside" suggestions or assumptions of parliamentary leadership. There was still always a nominal "Administration" party, and always a party also of the "Opposition," in the House and Senate; but the "Administration" party had grown every session more and more disposed to dictate to the President rather than submit to his leadership; and Congress was not homogeneous enough to follow distinct or consistent lines of action. It was itself a miscellaneous body, made up, as the nominating conventions were made by, by the free, non-co-operative choice of separate and differing localities. There was no responsible leadership either in Congress or out of it. And so irresponsible leadership was substituted, the leadership whose function was in the electoral districts, in local campaign committees, in newspaper offices, in the management that was private and away from the forum of debate where questions of statesmanship seemed the determining factors in affairs.

☆ ☆ ☆

It was such a process that the virtual dissolution of parties was being made evident in the years which preceded and followed the year 1852; and the question of slavery was the chief dissolvent.

☆ ☆ ☆

It was the independent groups of thinking men who had made up their minds to resist the extension of slavery that began the work of disintegration which by 1852 had gone so far. At first they deliberately avoided the formation of an independent political party. They were of both parties,

Whigs and Democrats; they felt the compulsion of party allegiance still strong upon them, and rejected with unaffected distaste every proposal to break away from and oppose their old associates, whose creed and practice alike they still relished and sympathized with in most things. They realized, too, the weakness and probable instability of a party whose existence was founded, and staked, upon a single issue. For long, therefore, they contented themselves with questioning individual candidates for Congress, named by the regular parties, concerning their opinions and purposes upon the slavery question, and gave or withdrew from them their support according as their replies pleased or displeased them. It was only when they saw how ineffectual this must prove, how casual, unsystematic, haphazard, that they found themselves at length constrained to take independent action. Then at last they held their own conventions, and even ventured their own independent nominations for the presidency, assuming the role of a national organization, a distinct Free-Soil party. Democrats and Whigs alike joined them at first; but as time went on it turned out that they were to draw their strength from the Whig rather than from Democratic ranks. The Democratic party depended for its organization and leadership upon the South much more than the Whig party did. It formed its purposes with regard to slavery, therefore, much more readily and confidently, and kept up its spirit much more naturally and spontaneously in the face of the accumulating difficulties of the time: so that timid and busy men, and men accustomed to follow leaders and take their cue in politics from the clearest and most confident voices, left off doubting and searching for a party and followed it, electing Pierce and leaving the Whig party to go to pieces at its leisure.

☆ ☆ ☆

Politics moved upon a confused stage during the next eight years, years of critical interest every one of them; but determining events followed each other in quick, unbroken succession. A storm gathered and burst, and the crisis all had waited for and dreaded came at last. For a little while it seemed as if the presidential and congressional elections of 1852 had cleared the air and restored a certain calm to affairs. If other parties had been broken and thrown into confusion, the Democrats at least were united and in full possession of power. The Free-Soilers had lost, not gained, in strength. President Pierce made William March his Secretary of State, a man who exercised authority as a member of the "Albany Regency," a group of astute politicians in the State of New York who understood better than any other men in the country the new art of organizing conventions, and of turning local majorities not only to local but also to national use. Jefferson Davis of Mississippi had become Secretary of War, and brought to the support of the new Administration the great southern wing of the victorious party. The new heads of the government seemed established in the confidence of both sections of the country, supported alike by perfected party machinery and by a decisive general sentiment, and served and guided by capable, masterful men familiar with the movements of opinion. Both in Congress and at the executive mansion the Democrats took heart to be very bold, and to show their mastery.

Before the year of his installation was over, President Pierce had purchased still more territory from Mexico, in the region to which it seemed most likely that slavery would ultimately be extended. He had really little choice in the matter. Mexico still claimed a considerable tract of land in the far south-west which the United States deemed included in the cessions of the treaty of Guadalupe Hidalgo, a tract of more than forty-five thousand square miles lying to the South of the Gila river; and a Mexican army, under the notorious Santa Anna, had actually entered the region, as if to renew the war if Mexico's claim were not admitted. Pierce rightly thought it a prudent act of statesmanship to purchase the disputed territory for ten million dollars. The purchase was effected through Gadsden, of South Carolina, in December, 1853; and the anti-slavery men everywhere noted the transaction with profound chagrin.

But worse was to follow. Bad as it seemed to Northern men to purchase new lands which must stand open to slavery, under the compromises of recent legislation, at any rate until the day when States should be erected upon them, it was of course infinitely worse to abandon those compromises altogether, and deliberately open every part of the country not yet formed into States to the spread of the fatal institution. And yet that was what Stephen A. Douglas actually proposed and carried through Congress before the end of May, 1854. He was one of the senators from Illinois, and was but forty-one years of age, full of the rude, straightforward strength and audacity which showed him to have been bred in the free communities of the Western country. He had been born in Vermont, but had gone West as a lad to make his way, and had there grown into the short, square, coarse-fibered, thick limbed, aggressive, vehement, eloquent man who seemed in the Senate a sort of dwarfed giant, compact of the energy and daring of the West. He confidently deemed himself, what many accepted him to be, the spokesman and leader of his party in Congress. He more boldly and explicitly than any other man pronounced the question of the extension of exclusion of slavery where the Western lands were filling up a thing to be determined by the settlers themselves, upon a free principle of self-government with which Congress and the federal authorities ought not to interfere. And there was a particular part of the Western country to which he wished to see his principle applied at once. This was the broad "Platte country" which lay within the Louisiana purchase to the northward and westward of Missouri. Across it ran the direct overland route to the Pacific, along which frequent wagon-trains moved to and fro between California and the East. There was some danger that it might be assigned as a reservation to the Indians and closed to settlement; and ever since 1843, when he was a member of the House of Representatives, before the days of the Mexican cessions, Douglas had been urging the erection of this great stretch of prairie into a Territory, not as a road to the Pacific—for in those days no one knew of the gold in California—but as a new home for settlers and commonwealths.

Early in January, 1854, being chairman of the Senate's Committee on Territories, and seeing his own party in power, he returned to his favorite scheme and introduced a bill which provided for the creation of a Territory to be called Nebraska in the Platte country. Every previous proposal for the erection of Territories within the region covered by this bill had assumed, as a matter settled and of course, that slavery was to be excluded from it, under the Compromise of 1820; for it lay north of the southern line of Missouri; but this bill explicitly provided that the States subsequently to be formed out of the new territory were to be left to decide the question of the introduction of slavery for themselves, in accordance with what Senator Douglas called the principle of "popular sovereignty." His opponents called it the doctrine of "squatter sovereignty." The bill was presently withdrawn and amended. When reintroduced from the Committee on January 23, it provided for the creation of two Territories instead of one—a Territory of Kansas, west of Missouri, and a Territory of Nebraska, north-west of the old compromise State. But the "Kansas-Nebraska Bill" did not differ from the measure for which it was substituted in the matter of slavery. It was declared in the new bill to be the "true intent and meaning" of the Act, "not to legislate slavery into any Territory or State, nor to exclude it there from, but to leave the people thereof perfectly free to regulate their domestic institutions in their own way, subject only to the Constitution of the United States." It extended all laws of the United

States, including the Fugitive Slave Law, to the new Territories, but explicitly excepted "the eighth section of the Act preparatory to the admission of Missouri into the Union,"—the compromise section, which had been considered one of the foundations of national politics. That section it pronounced "inconsistent with the principles of non-intervention by Congress with slavery in the States and Territories, as recognized by the legislation of 1850," and expressly "declared inoperative and void."

It was certainly an astonishing measure, conceived in the true spirit of the school of statesmen to which Senator Douglas belonged. No doubt its very audacity was what chiefly commended it to Douglas; no doubt, too, he believed it strategically as wise as it was daring. The Southern men had never dreamed of demanding a measure which should repeal the now venerable Missouri Compromise, and open all the Territories to slavery; parties wanted nothing so much as rest and oblivion of past excitements, if that might be had; a session of ordinary routine would have been welcomed on all hands as a pleasing program of peace. But to the party leaders who hearkened to Douglas' counsels it seemed best to use their present power to have done with compromises and make all the future plain by the adoption of the simple, obvious, and consistent principle of "squatter sovereignty." Unexpected and revolutionary as the Bill was, it of course pleased the slavery men extremely, and majorities were found for it in both Houses. In the Senate 37 to 14 was the vote; and in the House 113 to 100. Forty-four Northern Democrats voted against the measure in the House; but as many more were ready to follow Douglas. Nine Southern members looked askance at the new thing and voted "No"; but most of them received it gladly. On May 30 the President signed the Bill, and it become law. He had been consulted beforehand about it, as it seems, and had expressed his approval of it, saying that he thought it founded "upon a sound principle, which the Compromise of 1820 infringed upon," and to which he was willing to return.

☆ ☆ ☆

There was no longer debate; that was ended, and argument gave place to action. Kansas became the theater of a perilous appeal to fact, which turned out to be an appeal to force. A Slave State lay neighbor to it on the east, and slave-owners were the first to pour across its borders and occupy it against the day of final settlement; but, though the men out of the Free States came later, they came in hosts and companies when they did come;

they had behind them the organized assistance of societies and large funds subscribed in the Free States of the North and East; and they came bringing arms as well as tools. The country almost held its breath as it waited to hear what news should come out of Kansas; and it had not to wait long before it knew. Within two years the demoralizing game for power there had been played and lost and won—won by the settlers out of the Free States; but not before blood had been shed and federal troops sent in to prevent anarchy. The Missouri settlers, being first on the ground, had very promptly acted upon their initial advantage; had organized a territorial government; and had enacted stringent penal laws against whosoever should in any way interfere with the introduction of perpetuation of slavery. But the Free-State settlers, pouring in from the North, ignored what the Missouri men had done and attempted to set up a government of their own. When they found that course forbidden by the federal authorities, they took the other, of sending majorities to the polls where a new territorial legislature was to be chosen. Partisans on both sides went armed; there were fatal riots at the voting places; blood was shed deliberately and by plot as well as in the heat of sudden brawls, fearful days of embittered passion in the distracted Territory made men everywhere presently talk of "bleeding Kansas"; but out of the fire came a definite enough settlement at last. A Free-State majority established "squatter sovereignty" very effectually; and by midsummer of 1856 the House of Representatives had passed a bill, which the Senate rejected, for the admission of Kansas into the Union under a constitution which forbade slavery.

Here was evidence plain enough for any man to read of the beneficent operation of Douglas' pretty theory of popular right in the organization of Territories and the formation of States. The country saw with sad forebodings what it meant; partisanship everywhere was inflamed and put in a mind to go any lengths of violence; individual passion broke through all restraints; and prudent men were sore put to it to keep their comrades in affairs to the sober ways of moderation and law. It was in May, 1856, that Preston Brooks, a young Carolinian member of the House of Representatives, strode into the Senate and assaulted Sumner where he sat, for words of personal bitterness uttered in debate, striking him to the floor insensible; and it was one of the unhappiest signs of the times that such an act of blind anger and passionate folly was condoned and even applauded, not condemned, by the constituents of the man who had done it. No wonder excitement gathered head and statesmen grew infinitely uneasy when such things could happen.

The year 1856 brought another presidential election. It was a year, therefore, when every force that was astir came into the open and added to the manifest and perplexing confusion of affairs. There had been signs beforehand of what was coming. In the autumn of the very year in which the Kansas-Nebraska Bill was carried through the House of Representatives (1854), the majority which had carried it was destroyed. All "Anti-Nebraska men" drew away from it to destroy it. They did not draw together. Though "Free-Soilers," they did not relish as yet the idea of connecting themselves with the separate and avowed Free-Soil party; but joined themselves for the nonce to any independent group which promised them the satisfaction of uttering their protest against what the Democrats were doing, without withdrawing them wholly from their old allegiance. It was then that the Know-Nothings had their opportunity. A great many of the most deeply discontented voters were Whigs. They were still sensible of the compulsion of their lifelong party feeling; and it was more palatable to them to be Know-Nothings than to join with radicals who seemed inclined still further to jeopardize the peace of the country by forcing the formation of a party of revolt, upon the single and dangerous issue of slavery. In the elections of 1854, therefore, the Know-Nothings not only secured a number of seats in Congress but also elected their candidates for the governorship in Massachusetts and Delaware; and within another year they had actually carried the States of New Hampshire, Massachusetts, Rhode Island, Connecticut, New York, Kentucky, and California, besides polling votes which fell very little short of being majorities in no less than six of the Southern States, where the proper issues of the "American" party had no natural place or significance at all.

The contest for the presidency narrowed itself at once to a struggle between the Democrats and this new union of their opponents. The Know-Nothings met in convention in February, and nominated Fillmore; but when it came to the vote in November they succeeded in choosing their electors nowhere but in the little State of Delaware. The Republicans could not hold a really national convention: no States south of Delaware, Maryland, and Kentucky sent delegates to assist them at their nomination; and they nominated no statesman of their new faith, but John C. Fremont, a popular young soldier who had aided very efficiently in the conquest of California in the war with Mexico, and who had hitherto been reckoned a Democrat. In the election, nevertheless, they secured one hundred and fourteen electoral votes for their candidate, as against one hundred and seventy-four for the Democratic nominee. They carried every State of the north and north-west except Pennsylvania, New Jersey, Indiana, and Illinois; showed themselves practically the only party of opposition in the north-west; and polled a popular vote of 1,341,264 to their opponents' 1,838,169. The political field of battle was once more ordered and in set array. The issue had been very definitely joined. The Democrats had nominated James Buchanan, of Pennsylvania, who was then the Minister of the United States in London. He had been out of the country during these last years of heat and bitterness; but the platform of principles adopted by the convention which nominated him had endorsed the Compromise legislation of 1850 and what was now known to be its natural corollary, the repeal of the Missouri Compromise, as explicitly as the Republicans had repudiated them; and Buchanan himself had joined with the American ministers in France and Spain (October 18, 1854) in advising the government of the United States to acquire the island of Cuba, by purchase if possible, by force if necessary. That was in substance to advise, as the country then looked at it, the addition of more slave territory; and the advice had been tendered just after the Gadsden purchase in the south-west, and at a time, as it presently appeared, when lawless men were planning and organizing armed expeditions for the conquest of still more slave territory in central America. Buchanan's election to the presidency meant the ascendancy, at least for a time, of the party which, frankly enough, supported the Southern interest.

☆ ☆ ☆

President Buchanan's inauguration occurred in the very midst of the troubled times in Kansas, when the struggle there still hung in a doubtful balance; and he had been in office but a few days when the Supreme Court of the United States pronounced a decision which added a new and deeply significant element both to the importance and to the excitement of the contest in the unhappy Territory. This was its decision in the case of Dred Scott v. Sandford. Dred Scott was a Negro slave whose master, an army surgeon, had carried him for a brief period of residence first into the State of Illinois, where slavery was illegal, and than to a military post situated in the public domain further to the westward from which slavery had been excluded by the Compromise legislation of 1820; afterwards returning with him to Missouri, his home. The Negro claimed that his residence in the free State of Illinois had operated to destroy his master's right over him; and the case instituted in his behalf before the Courts had come at this critical juncture, by appeal, to the Supreme Court. That tribunal held that the lower Court had had no jurisdiction: that Dred Scott, at any rate after his return with his master to Missouri, was a slave, and not a citizen, and had no standing in the Courts. That was the only point it was necessary to decide, and might have ended the matter. But a majority of the judges persuaded themselves that they should go further and expound the whole question of the status of slavery in the Territories of the United States, though they must in doing so, in the opinion of every discriminating lawyer, be speaking *obiter.* Chief Justice Taney, speaking for a majority of his colleagues, declared in the opinion of the Court that it was not within the constitutional power of Congress to forbid citizens of any of the States to carry their property, no matter of what sort, into the public domain, or even to authorize the regularly constituted legislature of an organized Territory to forbid this, though it were property in slaves: that only States could regulate that matter. If this were law, the Missouri Compromise had been invalid from the first; even "popular sovereignty," to which Douglas looked for the settlement of the question, could do no authoritative thing until it spoke its purpose in a State constitution. The Free-Soilers were beyond their right at every point.

To the Republicans the decision could seem nothing less than a stinging blow in the face. They were made to feel the smart of being stigmatized as disloyal to the Constitution. No doubt the judges had thought to quiet opinion and sustain the legislation of 1854; but instead they infinitely exasperated it. Their judgment gave the last touch of dramatic interest to the struggle in Kansas, now nearing its turning-point and culmination. In October, 1857, the Free-Soil settlers of Kansas got control of the territorial legislature at the polls; but not before the pro-slavery men, hitherto in power, had made a last attempt to fix slavery upon the future State. They had hastened before the autumn elections came on to assemble a convention and frame a constitution (September, 1857), and to see that their application for admission to the Union was at Washington in due form before the Free-Soil men could intervene and undo their work. President Buchanan decided to sustain them, judging at least the formal right of application to be really theirs. But Congress would not go with him. It was Democratic in both houses; but Douglas remembered his principles with manly consistency. It was known before Congress acted that a majority of the voters of the Territory did not in fact desire a pro-slavery State constitution; and he would not force a constitution upon a majority. There were members enough in his immediate following to control the action of the Houses, and Kansas was refused admission to the Union—pending the further contest of parties.

President Buchanan's Administration inevitably incurred the suspicion, throughout all this trying business, of being conducted in the Southern interest; and in the excitement of the time the President was suspected of things of which he was quite incapable. It was charged and believed that the decision of the Supreme Court in the Dred Scott case had been a thing concerted between the President and the Chief Justice, though the President's character made such a calumny inexcusable. He was a man of unsullied integrity, and punctilious in the performance of what he considered to be his duty. He was past the prime of life, had never possessed great courage or any notable gifts of initiative, and of course suffered himself to be guided by the men whom he regarded, and had good reason to regard, as the real leaders of the Democratic party. Only two States in the North had voted for him, and only two in the North-west: the Democratic party, which had chosen him President, was, happily or unhappily, in fact a party chiefly manned and guided from the South. He had called Southern men of influence into his Cabinet in whose character and capacity he justly and implicitly believed. He took their advice because he believed it to be honest and authoritative. But the country grew infinitely restive and uneasy to see one section rule. It was Mr. Buchanan's chief fault, if fault it was, not that he yielded to improper influences, as his opponents unjustly believed, but that he did not judge and act for himself. He was weak; and weakness was under the circumstances fatal.

The year 1858 brought abundant signs of a great reaction, and it soon became only too plain that the Democratic party was driving the bulk of the country into opposition. It was the year of a general election. As the autumn approached, those who watched affairs found the critical issues of the time more and more sharply fixed and determined in their thought, and their convictions grew more and more vivid and definite. Nothing conduced more to this result than a notable debate reported from Illinois. The Republicans of Illinois had made a determined effort to keep Douglas from re-election to the Senate. They had announced that, should they succeed in obtaining a majority in the State legislature, they meant to send Abraham Lincoln to the Senate in Douglas' stead; and the autumn campaign in Illinois became for every memorable because in its course Douglas and Lincoln went about the State together and argued their claims for support face to face, upon city platforms and upon country platforms, in the presence of the voters. The striking individuality of the two men gave singular piquancy to the contest as well as their power of straightforward, unmistakable definiteness of speech. Douglas was a national character, one of the acknowledged leaders of a great party; Lincoln was a comparatively unknown man, a shrewd lawyer and local politician. His long, gaunt, ungainly figure, his sloughing gait, his homely turns of phrase marked him a frontiersman. His big, bony hands had wrought at the hard tasks of the forest and the farm. But his rough exterior did not repel the plain people to whom he spoke, alongside the more adroit and finished Douglas; and no one could hear his speech and think him common. He had taken his own way of learning to the bar. The passion for letters had been strong upon him since a boy, and his self-training had with unerring instinct followed a fine plan of mastery. By reasoning upon the principles of the law, as they came to him out of a few text-books, by poring upon books of mathematics, by reading up and down through such books of history or adventure as fell in his way in search of the experience of other men, by constant intimacy of talk and play of argument with men of every kind to whom he had access, he had made himself a master of brief and careful statement, of persuasion, and of oral debate: thoughtful, observant, steering in what he said by an unfluctuating compass of logical precision, and able all lucid, full of homely wit and anecdote such as was fit to illuminate practical subjects, and uttering phrases which found the heart of what he talked of, sometimes phrases which found the heart of what he talked of, sometimes phrases which struck his opponent like a blow, but fair, unmalicious, intellectual, not passionate.

His definition of the matter to be settled between the parties was characteristic of him. "A house divided against itself," he said, "cannot stand. I believe this government cannot endure half slave and half free. I do not expect the house to fall, but I expect it will cease to be divided. It will become all one thing or all the other." Douglas found him a very uncomfortable antagonist, who drove him to awkward admissions. Before their debate was over Douglas was no longer within reach of the presidency; and Abraham Lincoln had won the ear of the whole country. The Southern men could not vote for Douglas as the nominee and spokesman of their party. He had been forced under Lincoln's fire to admit that Congress could not empower a territorial legislature, its own creature, to do what, if the Dred Scott decision spoke true law, it was itself unable to do; that Southern settlers, therefore, could no more legalize slavery within a territory than Northern settlers could exclude it: that "popular sovereignty" was no solution, after all. The Republicans did not obtain a majority in the Illinois legislature; Douglas went back to the Senate; but he went back weakened and with loss of authority. The elections of the autumn, taking the country as a whole, gave the Republicans success enough to show how near at hand a crisis was. They increased their numbers materially in both House and Senate, carried Buchanan's own state of Pennsylvania by a handsome majority, and made it very evident that opinion was swinging their way. In the House of Representatives, indeed, they were put in a position of virtual control: for no coherent party had a working majority there. The "Douglas Democrats," who had refused to vote for the admission of Kansas with a pro-slavery constitution, were not hardly an integral part of the Democratic party; there was still a group of twenty-two Know-Nothings; and the Republicans held the balance of power.

☆ ☆ ☆

As if the crisis were not already sharp enough, conspiracy was added to the open battle of politics. On the night of Sunday, October 17, 1859, one John Brown, at the head of a little band of less than twenty followers, seized the United States arsenal at Harper's Ferry in Virginia, meaning to strike there a sudden blow for the freedom of the slaves, and, having set a servile insurrection aflame, make good his retreat to the mountains. It was the mad folly of an almost crazed fanatic; the man was quickly taken and promptly hanged; his flame of war had flickered and died in the socket. But that was not all. Brown was from Kansas; he had come to Virginia, at midsummer in that anxious year 1859, with the stain still fresh upon him of some of the bloodiest of the lawless work done there in the name of freedom: a terrible outlaw, because an outlaw for conscience' sake; intense to the point of ungovernable passion; heeding nothing but his own will and sense of right; a revolutionist upon principle; lawless, incendiary, and yet seeking nothing for himself. He brought arms and means to Virginia with which he had been supplied out of New England, not for use in the South, but for use in Kansas. But Southern men were not in a temper to discriminate. If Northern men would pay for the shedding of blood in Kansas, why not for the shedding of blood in Virginia also? Slavery was the object of the attack, and the slaveholders saw little difference, great as the difference was, between abolitionists and Free-Soilers. And this terrible warning at Harper's Ferry was of a sort to put even cool men out of temper for just and sober thinking. A slave insurrection meant what it maddened Southern men to think of; massacre, arson, an unspeakable fate for women and children. If this was what "anti-slavery" meant, it must be met and fought to the death, Union or no Union.

It was in such a season of disturbed and headstrong judgment that the presidential campaign of 1860 came on. The Democrats were the first to attempt a nomination; but their convention proved a house divided against itself and went hopelessly to pieces; and the outcome was two "Democratic" nominations. One section of the party nominated Douglas for the presidency; the other, which was the Southern Section, named John C. Breckinridge of Kentucky as its candidate. A new party sprang into existence, the "Constitutional Union" party, made up of those who had been Know-Nothings until the Know-Nothing party died of inanition, and of those who had left the other parties but had found it impossible to digest the Know-Nothing creed—of all who feared alike the Democratic and the Republican extremes of policy and doctrine, and still hoped the quarrel might be composed. These nominated John Bell of Tennessee, and declared in a platform of great simplicity and dignity that they recognized "no political principle other than the Constitution of the country, the union of the States, and the enforcement of the laws." The Republicans alone were united and confident. They warmly disavowed all sympathy with attempts of any kind to disturb slavery where it was established by law; but they declared as flatly as ever against the extension of slavery to the Territories; and they nominated not Mr. Seward, the chief figure of their party, for many felt a distrust of him as a sort of philosophical radical, but Abraham Lincoln of Illinois, the shrewd, persuasive, courageous, capable man who had loomed so big in the memorable debates with Douglas three years before. Their convention had sat at Chicago, in Mr. Lincoln's own State. The cheers of the galleries and the astute combinations and diplomacy of his friends in their work among the delegates had played as great a part as his own gifts and popularity in obtaining for him the nomination. But when once he had been named the whole country began to see how wise the choice had been. Eastern men for a little while looked askance upon this raw Western lawyer and new statesman; but not after they had heard him. And when the votes were counted it was found that he had been elected President of the United States. One hundred and eighty of the electoral votes went to him; only one hundred and three to his three opponents combined.

It was a singular result, when analyzed. The electoral votes of Virginia, Tennessee, and Kentucky had gone to John Bell, the nominee of the "Constitutional Union" party; the rest of the Southern votes had gone to

Breckinridge; Douglas had received only the votes of Missouri and three of the nine votes of New Jersey. And yet, although these amounted to but one hundred and three votes altogether in the electoral college, the total popular vote at the back of them was 2,823,741, as against a popular vote for Lincoln of only 1,866,452, a popular majority of almost a million votes against the Republicans, so large was the aggregate minority in the States whose electoral votes the Republicans had won. It was a narrow victory, no popular triumph; and Lincoln, like the other leaders of his party, was disposed to use it with the utmost good temper and moderation.

But Southern men took no comfort from the figures and did not listen to protestations of just purpose. They looked only at the result, saw only that the government was to be in the hands of the Republicans, regarded the defeat as final and irreparable. Their pride was stung to the quick by the unqualified moral censures put upon them by those who were now to be in power. "The whole course of the South had been described as one of systematic iniquity." Mrs. Stowe's striking and pathetic picture of what slavery sometimes led to, in her *Uncle Tom's Cabin* (1852), had been accepted in the North and by the English-speaking world at large as a picture of what it usually led to. "Southern society had been represented as built upon a willful sin; the Southern people had been held up to the world as those who deliberately despised the most righteous commands of religion. They knew that they did not deserve such reprobation. They knew that they lives were honorable, their relations with their slaves humane, their responsibility for the existence of slavery amongst them remote"; and that now those who had most bitterly and unjustly accused them were to become their rulers. It seemed to them, too, that the North itself had of late practiced nullification in its fight against them. More than a score of the States had passed "personal liberty" laws which were confessedly intended to bar and render impracticable the enforcement of the Fugitive Slave Law. The South Carolina legislature, which itself chose the presidential electors of the State, had remained in session to learn the result of the election. When it knew that Lincoln was to be President, it summoned a Constitutional Convention, which severed the State's connection with the Union; and before Lincoln was inaugurated six other Southern States had followed South Carolina out of the Union.

The inevitable disintegration of the Union, by reason of the operation of the institution of slavery, had worked its perfect work. The South, which did not change, had become a region apart; and it now put the union aside in accordance with the theory with respect to its authority which it conceived to have obtained at its constitution. There was here nothing of the contradiction which seemed to lie at the heart of nullification; the South was not resisting the Union and yet purposing to remain within it. It had taken the final step of withdrawal: the partnership was dissolved. If that were revolution it was at least revolution within the original theory of the law as the South had learned it.

The issue was—slavery? Yes, upon the surface. Perhaps it need never have come to this, had Douglas kept his hand from the law. The movement against slavery had been weak, occasional, non-partisan until the Missouri Compromise was repealed, ten years before. It was that which had brought the Republican party into existence and set the sections by the ears. But now that the breach had come, it did not seem to men in the South merely a contest about slavery: it seemed, rather, so far as the South was concerned, a final question and answer as to the fundamental matter of self-government. There were many men in the South who, while they had no love for slavery, had a great love, a deep inherited veneration even, for the Union, but with whom the passion for the ancient principles, the ancient sentiment, of self-government was greater even than these, and covered every subject of domestic policy. It was this they deemed threatened now. Slavery itself was not so dark a thing as it was painted. It held the South at a standstill economically, and was her greatest burden, whether she felt it to be so or not. Bad men, too, could shamefully abuse the boundless powers of a master. But humane sentiment held most men steadily and effectually off from the graver abuses. The domestic slaves, at any rate, and almost all who were much under the master's eye, were happy and well cared for; and the poor creatures who crowded the great plantations where the air was malarial and where the master was seldom present to restrain the overseer, were little worse off than free laborers would have been in a like case, or any laborers who could live there. Those who condemned slavery as it existed in the South condemned it unjustly because they did so without discrimination; and those who attacked it with adverse laws seemed to invade the privileges of self-government States under the Constitution. Thus it was that Lincoln's election meant secession, and that the state was set for the tragedy of civil war.

For the whole country it was to be the bitterest of all ordeals, an agony of struggle and a decision by blood; but for one party it was to be a war of hope. Should the South win, she must also lose—must lose her place in the great Union which she had loved and fostered, and must in gaining independence destroy a nation. Should the North win, she would confirm a great hope and expectation, establish the Union, unify it in institutions, free it from interior contradictions of life and principle, set it in the way of consistent growth and unembarrassed greatness. The South fought for a principle, as the North did: it was this that was to give the war dignity, and supply the tragedy with a double motive. But the principle for which the South fought meant standstill in the midst of change; it was conservative, not creative; it was against drift and destiny; it protected an impossible institution and a belated order of society; it withstood a creative and imperial idea, the idea of a united people and a single law of freedom. Overwhelming material superiority, it turned out, was with the North; but she had also another and greater advantage: she was to fight for the Union and for the abiding peace, concord, and strength of a great nation.

The Reconstruction of the Southern States

Concerning Reconstruction, Wilson insisted we should "speak of it, not as partisans, but historians." His effort at objectivity was less than successful. Like most historians of his generation, North and South, Wilson wrote of the "dark chapter of history" picturing the South, ravaged by carpetbaggers and Blacks and punished to satisfy the Radical Republican desire for revenge. The view conforms to the interpretations crafted by William A. Dunning and his graduate students at Columbia University, which dominated the writing of post–Civil War history until at least the 1930s, and some of their ideas remained influential longer. The resulting histories tended to ignore the importance of the enactment of the Black Codes in the southern states when the war ended, the southern resistance to civil rights legislation, and the refusal of the South to ratify the Fourteenth Amendment. It was then that Congress wrested control of the Reconstruction process from an uncooperative President Andrew Johnson. Modern scholarship, examining the details of Reconstruction in the individual states and carefully analyzing congressional actions and motives, rejects the older interpretations and yields a more balanced history of the era. Wilson's account appeared in the *Atlantic Monthly* in January 1901.

It is now full thirty years, and more, since the processes of Reconstruction were finished, and the southern states restored to their place in the Union. Those thirty years have counted for more than any other thirty in our history, so great have been the speed and range of our development, so comprehensive and irresistible has been the sweep of change amongst us. We have come out of the atmosphere of the sixties. The time seems remote, historic, not of our day. We have dropped its thinking, lost its passion, forgot its anxieties, and should be ready to speak of it, not as partisans, but as historians.

☆ ☆ ☆

The war had been fought to preserve the Union, to dislodge and drive out by force the doctrine of the right of secession. The southern states could not legally leave the Union, such had been the doctrine of the victorious states whose armies won under Grant and Sherman, and the federal government had been able to prevent their leaving, in fact. In strict theory, though their people had been in revolt, under organizations which called themselves states, and which had thrown off all allegiance to the older Union and formed a new confederation of their own. Virginia, North Carolina, South Carolina, Florida, Georgia, Mississippi, Alabama, Louisiana, Texas, Arkansas, and Tennessee, the historic states once solemnly embodied in the Union, had never gone out of it, could never go out of it and remain states. In fact, nevertheless, their representatives had withdrawn from the federal House and Senate; their several governments, without change of form or personnel, had declared themselves no longer joined with the rest of the states in purpose or allegiance, had arranged a new and separate partnership, and had for four years maintained an organized resistance to the armies of the Union which they renounced. Now that their resistance had been overcome and their confederacy destroyed, how were they to be treated? As if they had been all the while in the Union, whether they would or no, and were now at last simply brought to their senses again, to take up their old-time rights and duties intact, resume their familiar functions within the Union as if nothing had happened? . . .

Had Mr. Lincoln lived, perhaps the whole of the delicate business might have been carried through with dignity, good temper, and simplicity of method; with all necessary concessions to passion, with no pedantic insistence upon consistent and uniform rules, with sensible irregularities and compromises, and yet with a straightforward, frank, and open way of management which would have assisted to find for every influence its natural and legitimate and quieting effect. It was of the nature of Mr. Lincoln's mind to reduce complex situations to their simples [*sic*], to guide men without irritating them, to go forward and be practical without being radical, to serve as a genial force which supplied heat enough to keep action warm, and yet minimized the friction and eased the whole progress of affairs.

It was characteristic of him that he had kept his own theory clear and unconfused through the whole struggle to bring the southern people back to their allegiance to the Union. He had never recognized any man who spoke or acted for the southern people in the matter of secession as the representative of any government whatever. It was, in his view, not the southern states which had taken up arms against the Union, but merely the people dwelling within them. State lines defined the territory within which rebellion had spread and men had organized under arms to destroy the Union; but their organization had been effected without color of law; that could not be a state, in any legal meaning of the term, which denied what was the indispensable prerequisite of its every exercise of political functions, its membership in the Union. He was not fighting states, therefore, or a confederacy of states, but only a body of people who refused to act as states, and could not, if they would, form another Union. What he wished and strove for, without passion save for the accomplishment of his purpose, without enmity against persons, and yet with burning hostility against what the southerners meant to do, was to bring the people of the southern states once more to submission and allegiance; to assist them, when subdued, to rehabilitate the states whose territory and resources, whose very organization, they had used to effect a revolution; to do whatever the circumstances and his own powers whether as President or merely as an influential man and earnest friend of peace, might render possible to put them back, defeated but not conquered or degraded, into the old-time hierarchy of the Union.

There were difficulties and passions in the way which possibly even Mr. Lincoln could not have forced within any plan of good will and simple restoration; but he had made a hopeful beginning before he died. He had issued a proclamation of amnesty so early as 1863, offering pardon and restoration to civil rights to all who would abandon resistance to the authority of the Union, and take the oath of unreserved loyalty and submission which he prescribed; and as the war drew to an end, and he saw the power of the Union steadily prevail, now here, now there, throughout an ever increasing area, he earnestly begged that those who had taken the oath and returned to their allegiance would unite in positive and concerted action, organize their states upon the old footing, and make ready for a full restoration of the old conditions. Let those who had taken the oath, and were ready to bind themselves in all good faith to accept the acts and proclamations of the federal government in the matter of slavery, let all, in short, who were willing to accept the actual results of the war, organize themselves and set up governments made conformable to the new order of things, and he would recognize them as the people of the states within which they acted, ask Congress to admit their representatives, and aid them to gain in all respects full acknowledgment and enjoyment of statehood, even though the persons who thus acted were but a tenth part of the original voters of their states. He would not insist upon even so many as a tenth, if only he could get some body of loyal citizens to deal and cooperate with in this all-important matter upon which he had set is heart; that the roster of the states might be complete again, and some healing process follow the bitter anguish of the war.

Andrew Johnson promptly made up his mind, when summoned to the presidency, to carry out Mr. Lincoln's plan, practically without modification; and he knew clearly what Mr. Lincoln's plan had been for he himself had restored Tennessee upon that plan, as the President's agent and representative. As military governor of the state, he had successfully organized a new government out of abundant material, for Tennessee was full of men who had had no sympathy with secession; and the government which he had organized had gone into full and vigorous operation during that very spring which saw him become first Vice President, and then President. In Louisiana and Arkansas similar governments had been set up even before Mr. Lincoln's death. Congress had not recognized them, indeed; and it did not, until a year had gone by, recognize even Tennessee, though her case was the simplest of all. Within her borders the southern revolt had been, not solid and of a piece, but a thing of frayed edges and a very doubtful texture of opinion. But, though Congress doubted, the plan had at least proved practical, and Mr. Johnson thought it also safe and direct.

☆ ☆ ☆

Throughout 1865 Mr. Johnson pushed the presidential process of reconstruction successfully and rapidly forward. Provisional governors of his own appointment in the South saw to it that conventions were elected by the voters who had taken the oath prescribed in the amnesty proclamation, which Mr. Johnson had reissued, with little change either of form or of substance; those conventions proceeded at once to revise the state constitutions under the supervision of the provisional governors, who in their turn acted now and again under direct telegraphic instructions from the President in Washington; the several ordinances of secession were repealed, the war debts of the states were repudiated, and the legislatures set up under the new constitutions hastened to accept and ratify the

Thirteenth Amendment, abolishing slavery, as the President demanded. By December of the very year of his inauguration, every southern state except Florida and Texas had gone through the required process, and was once more, so far as the President was concerned, in its normal relations with the federal government. The federal courts resumed their sessions in the restored states, and the Supreme Court called up the southern cases from its docket. On December 18, 1865, the Secretary of State formally proclaimed the Thirteenth Amendment ratified by the vote of twenty-seven states, and thereby legally embodied in the Constitution, though eight of the twenty-seven were states which the President had thus of his own motion reconstructed. Without their votes the amendment would have lacked the constitutional three-fourths majority.

The President had required nothing of the new states with regard to the suffrage; that was a matter, as he truly said, in respect of which the several states had "rightfully exercised" their free and independent choice "from the origin of the government to the present day"; and of course they had no thought of admitting the Negroes to the suffrage. Moreover, the new governments, once organized, fell more and more entirely into the hands of the very persons who had actively participated in secession. The President's proclamation of amnesty had, indeed, excepted certain classes of persons from the privilege of taking the oath which would make them voters again, under his arrangements for reconstruction: those who had taken a prominent official part in secession, or who had left the service of the United States for the service of the Confederate government. But a majority of the southerners were still at liberty to avail themselves of the privilege of accepting the new order of things; and it was to their interest to do so, in order that the new arrangements might be shaped as nearly as possible to their own liking. What was to their liking, however, proved as distasteful to Congress as had been expected. The use they made of their restored power brought absolute shipwreck upon the President's plans, and radically altered the whole process of reconstruction.

An extraordinary and very perilous state of affairs had been created in the South by the sudden and absolute emancipation of the Negroes, and it was not strange that the southern legislatures should deem it necessary to take extraordinary steps to guard against the manifest and pressing dangers which it entailed. Here was a vast "laboring, landless, homeless class," once slaves, now free; unpracticed in liberty, unschooled in self-control; never sobered by the discipline of self-support, never established in any habit of prudence; excited by a freedom they did not understand, exalted by false hopes; bewildered and without leaders, and yet insolent and aggressive; sick of work, covetous of pleasure, a host of dusky children untimely put out of school. In some of the states they outnumbered the whites, notably in Mississippi and South Carolina. They were a danger to themselves as well as to those whom they had once served, and now feared and suspected; and the very legislatures which had accepted the Thirteenth Amendment hastened to pass laws which should put them under new restraints. Stringent regulations were adopted with regard to contracts for labor, and with regard to the prevention of vagrancy. Penalties were denounced against those who refused to work at the current rates of wages. Fines were imposed upon a great number and variety of petty offenses, such as the new freemen were most like to commit; and it was provided that, in the (extremely probably) event of the non-payment of these fines, the culprits should be hired out to labor by judicial process. In some instances an elaborate system of compulsory apprenticeship was established for Negroes under age, providing that they should be bound out to labor. In certain states the Negroes were required to sign written contracts of labor, and were forbidden to do job work without first obtaining licenses from the police authorities of their places of residence. Those who failed to obtain licenses were liable to the charge of vagrancy, and upon that charge could be arrested, fined, and put to compulsory labor. There was not everywhere the same rigor; but there was everywhere the same determination to hold the Negroes very watchfully, and, if need were, very sternly, within bounds in the exercise of their unaccustomed freedom; and in many cases the restraints imposed went the length of a veritable "involuntary servitude."

Congress had not waited to see these things done before attempting to help the Negroes to make use of their freedom, and self-defensive use of it, at that. By an act of March 3, 1965, it established, as a branch of the War Department, a Bureau of Refugees, Freedmen, and Abandoned Lands, which was authorized and empowered to assist the one-time slaves in finding means of subsistence, and in making good their new privileges and immunities as citizens. The officials of this bureau, with the War Department behind them, had gone the whole length of their extensive authority; putting away from the outset all ideas of accommodation, and preferring the interests of their wards to the interests of peaceable, wholesome, and healing progress. No doubt that was inevitable. What they did was but the final and direct application of the rigorous, unsentimental logic of events. The Negroes, at any rate, had the full advantage of the federal power. A very active and officious branch of the War Department saw to it that the new disabilities which the southern legislatures sought to put upon them should as far as possible be rendered inoperative.

That, however, did not suffice to sweeten the temper of Congress. The fact remained that Mr. Johnson had rehabilitated the governments of the southern states without asking the leave of the houses. . . .

Congress, accordingly, determined to take matters into its own hands. With the southern representatives excluded, there was a Republican majority in both houses strong enough to do what it pleased, even to the overriding, if necessary of the President's vetoes.

☆ ☆ ☆

The essential point was that Congress, the lawmaking power, should be in control. The President had been too easy to satisfy, too prompt, and too lenient. . . .

The year 1866 passed, and with all things at sixes and sevens. So far as the President was concerned, most of the southern states were already reconstructed, and had resumed their places in the Union. Their assent had made the Thirteenth Amendment a part of the Constitution. And yet Congress forbade the withdrawal of the troops, refused admittance to the southern representatives, and set aside southern laws through the action of the Freedmen's Bureau and the military authorities. By 1867 it had made up its mind what to do to bring the business to a conclusion. 1866 had at least cleared its mind and defined its purposes. Congress had still further tested and made proof of the temper of the South. In June it had adopted a Fourteenth Amendment, which secured to the blacks the status of citizens, both of the United States and of the several states of their residence, authorized a reduction in the representation in Congress of states which refused them the suffrage, excluded the more prominent servants of the Confederacy from federal office until Congress should pardon them, and invalidated all debts or obligations "incurred in aid of insurrection or rebellion against the United States"; and this amendment had been submitted to the vote of those represented in the houses. Tennessee had promptly adopted it, and had been as promptly admitted to representation. But the other southern states, as promptly as they could, had begun, one by one, to reject it. Their action confirmed the houses in their attitude toward Reconstruction.

Congressional views and purposes were cleared the while with regard to the President, also. He had not been firm; he had been stubborn and bitter. He would yield nothing; vetoed the measures upon which Congress was

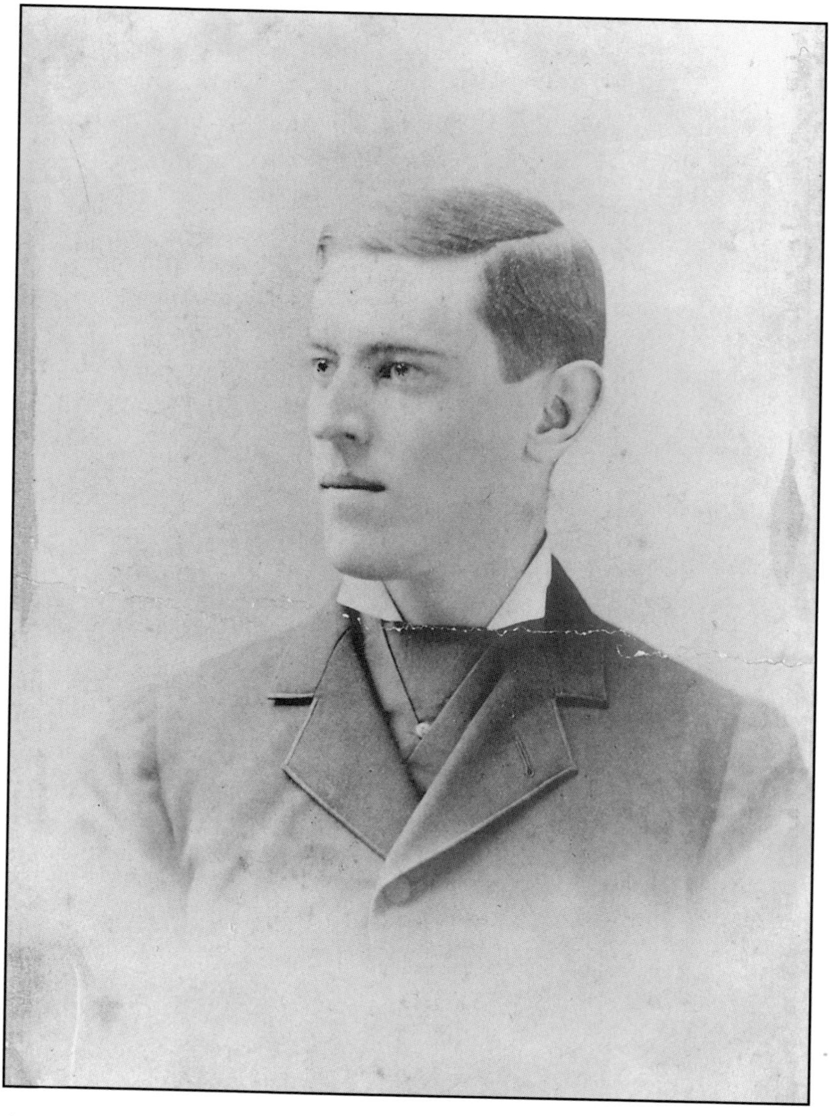

A youthful Woodrow Wilson, ca. 1880 *(Library of Congress)*.

Ellen Axon Wilson, the president's first wife, who died in August 1914 *(Library of Congress).*

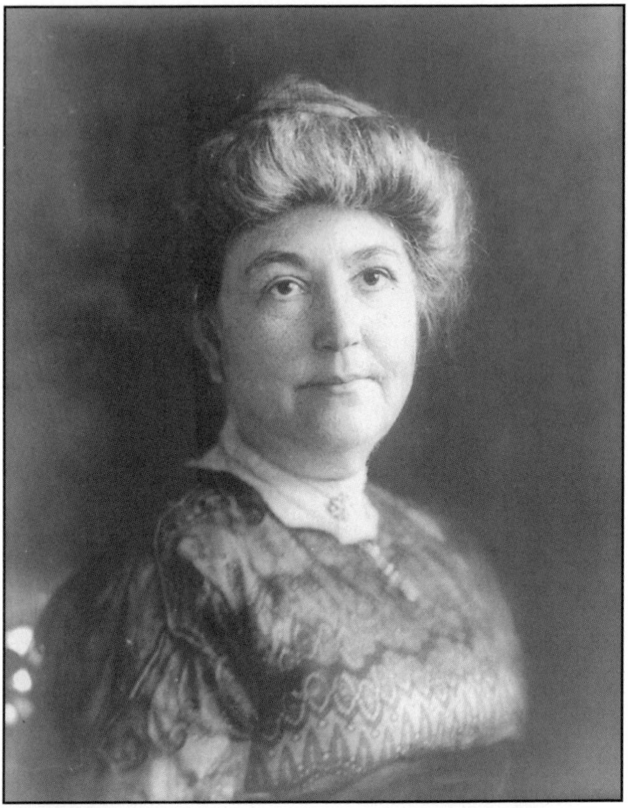

The Wilson family. From left: Jessie, Margaret, Mrs. Ellen Wilson, and Eleanor *(Library of Congress).*

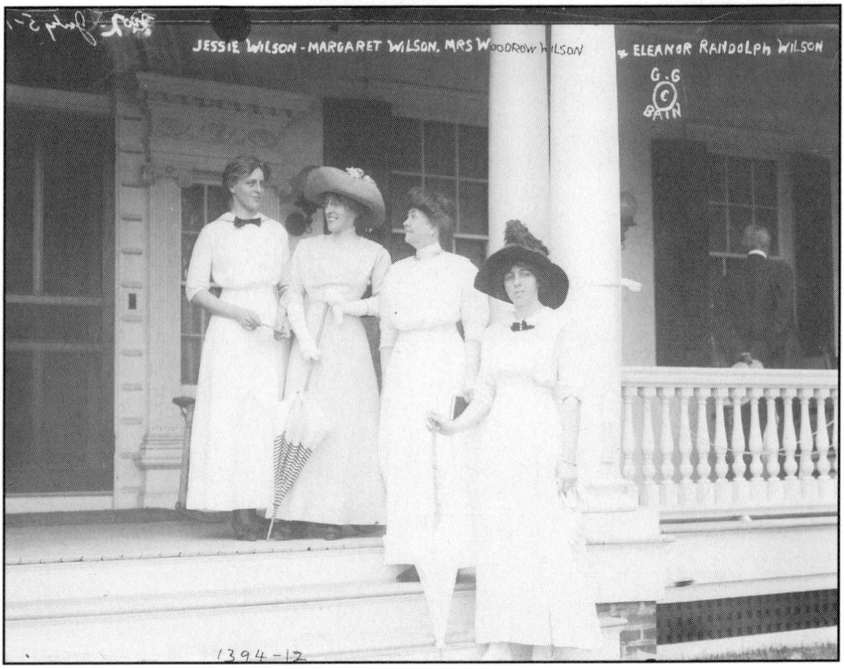

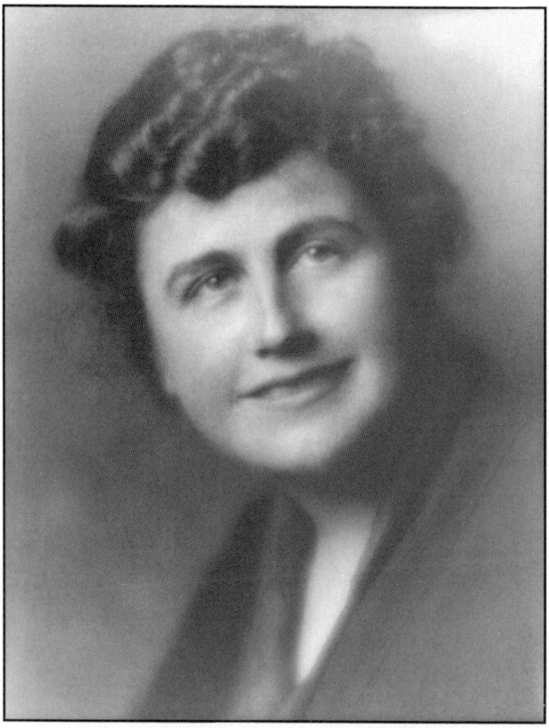

Edith Bolling Wilson became the second Mrs. Wilson in December 1915 *(Library of Congress).*

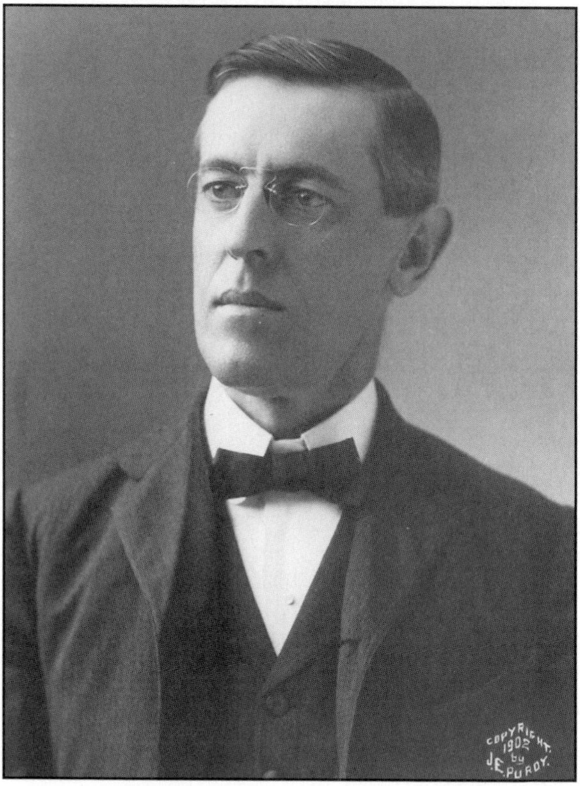

Wilson as president of Princeton *(Library of Congress).*

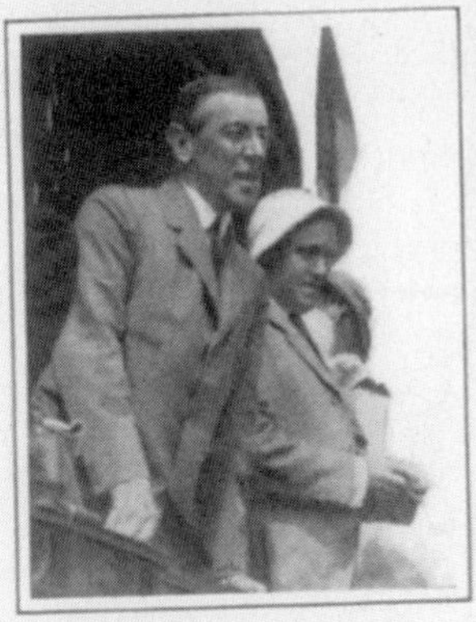

Addressing a crowd at Bradford, Ohio

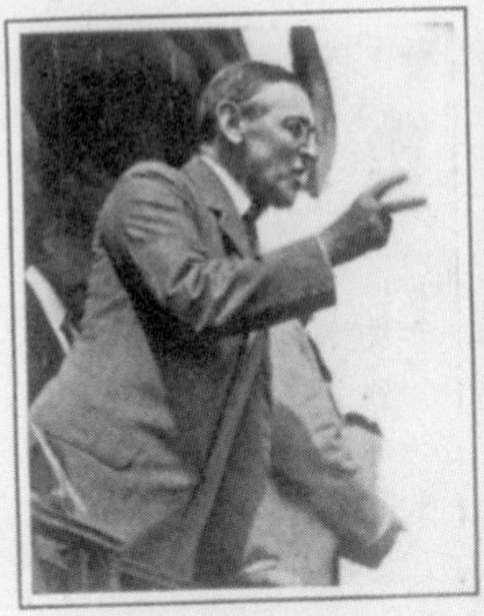

A remarkable gesture of restrained enthusiasm

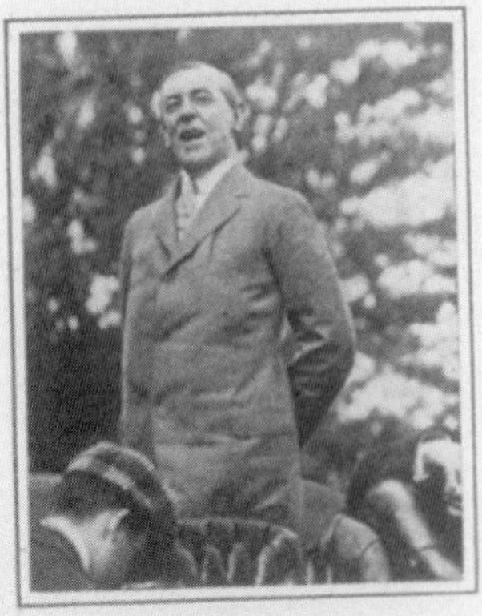

A characteristic expression of resolution

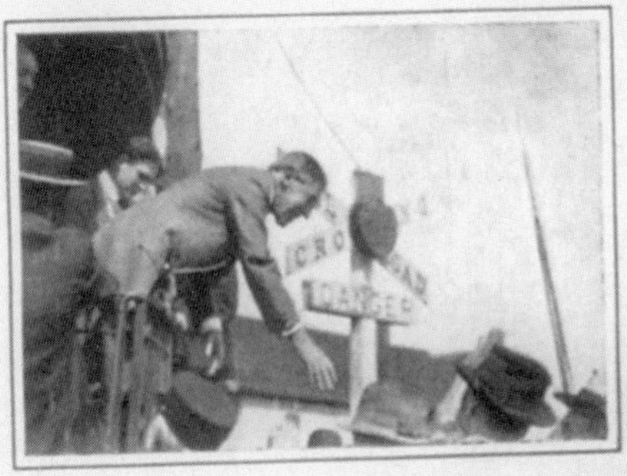

Welcoming the citizens of Marion, Indiana

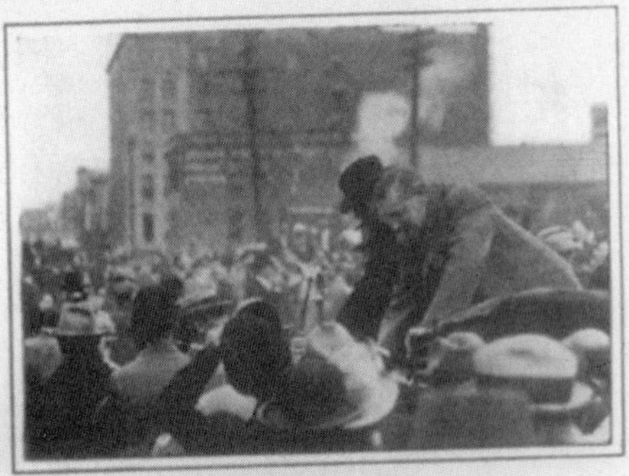

Greeting a Sioux City delegation from an automobile

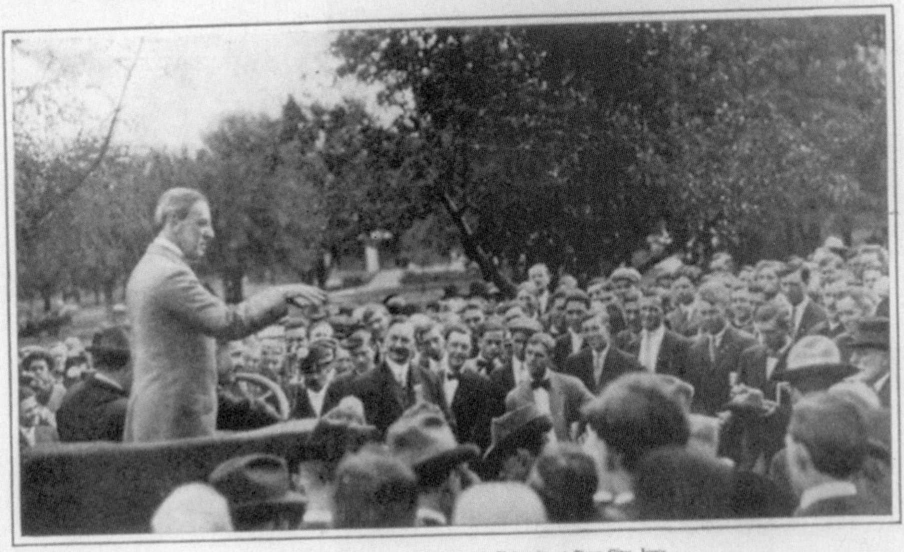

A serious speech to students of Morningside University at Sioux City, Iowa

GOVERNOR WILSON IN THE WEST

Snapshots of the Democratic candidate for the Presidency made during his recent tour

Candidate Wilson at various campaign stops in the Midwest in 1912 *(Library of Congress).*

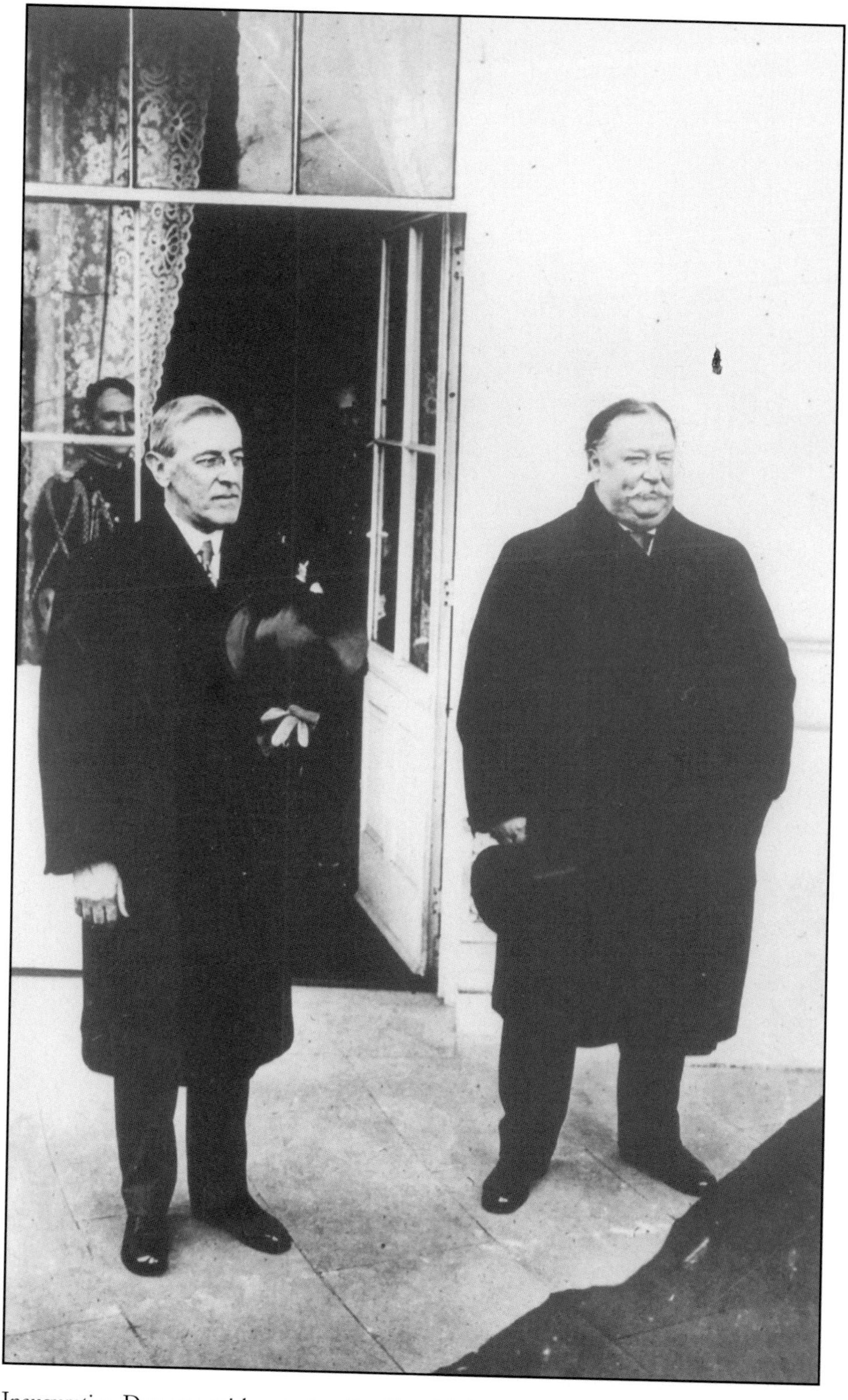

Inauguration Day, 1913, with outgoing President William Howard Taft *(Library of Congress).*

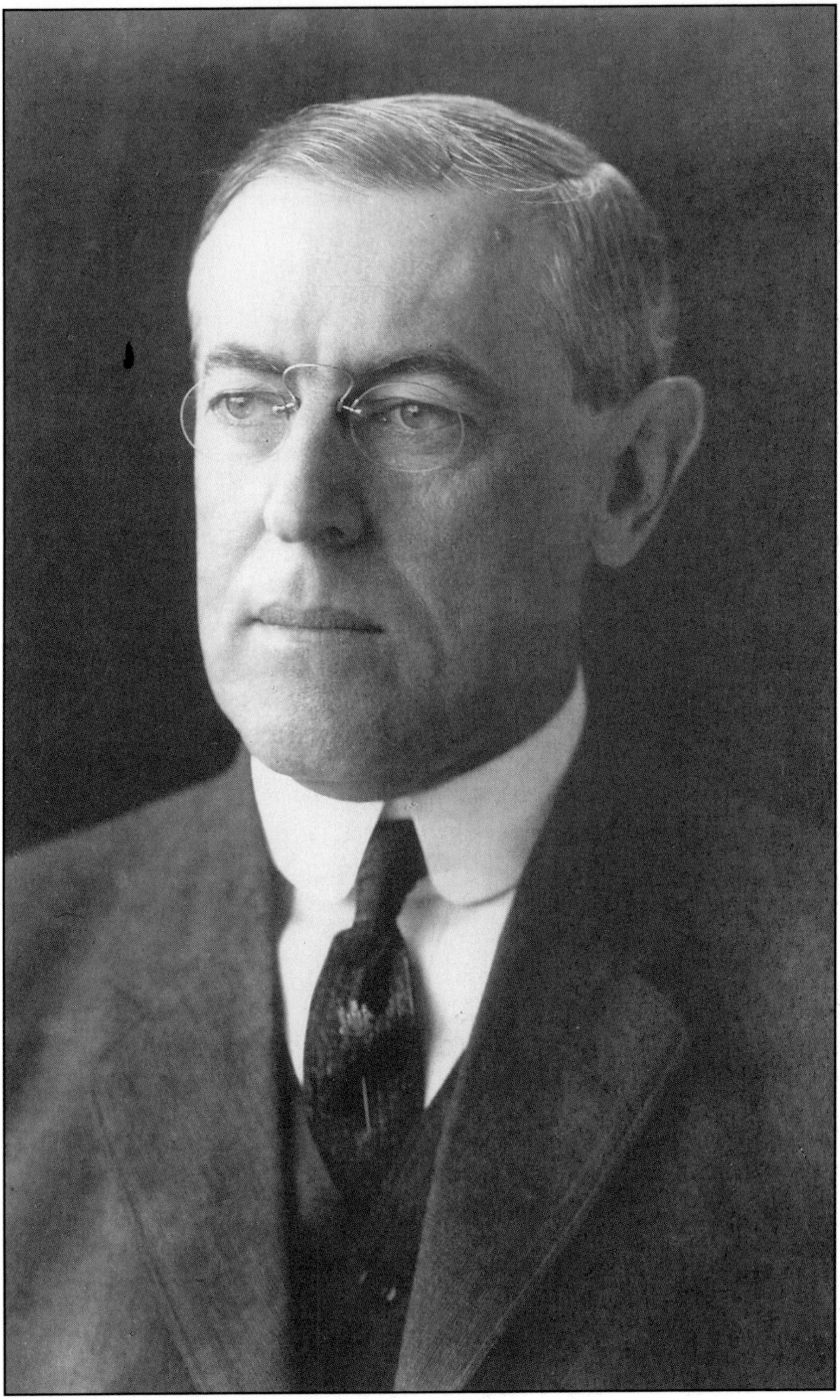

President Woodrow Wilson *(Library of Congress).*

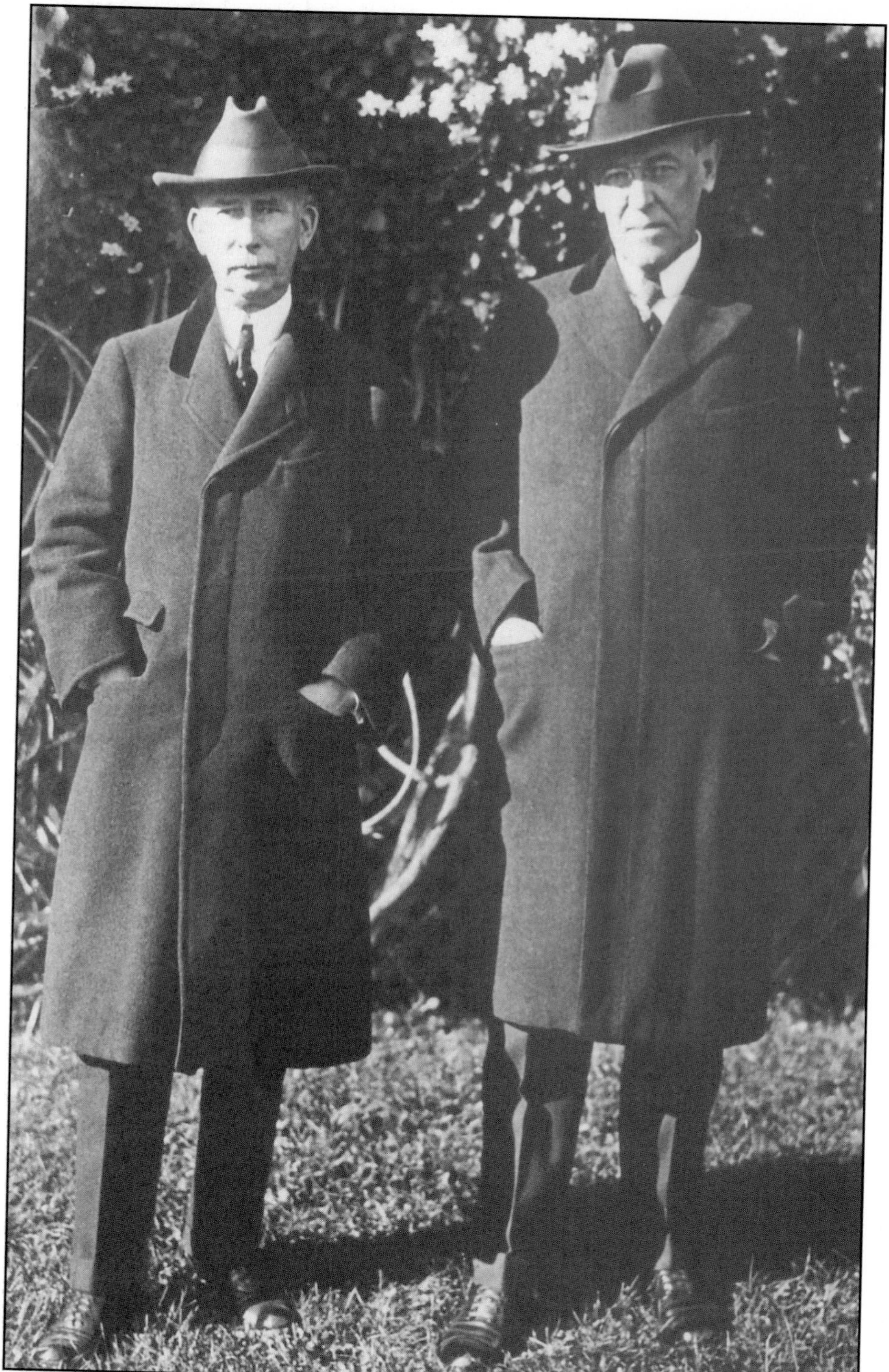

Wilson with close friend and adviser, Edward M. (Colonel) House *(Yale University).*

The president with members of his administration at the State Department on Flag Day, June 1914. On the far right is a young Franklin Delano Roosevelt, Assistant Secretary of the Navy *(Library of Congress).*

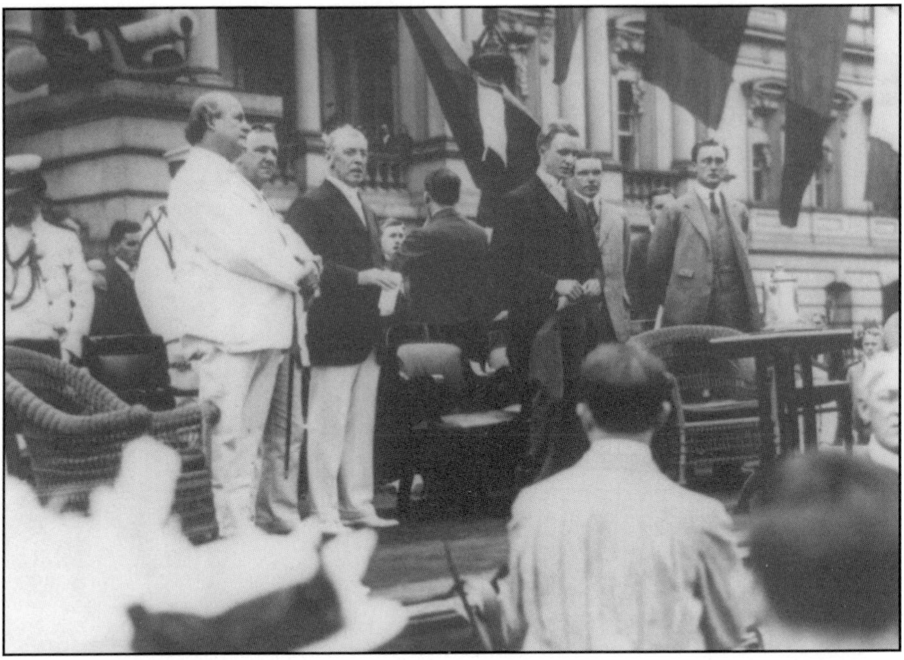

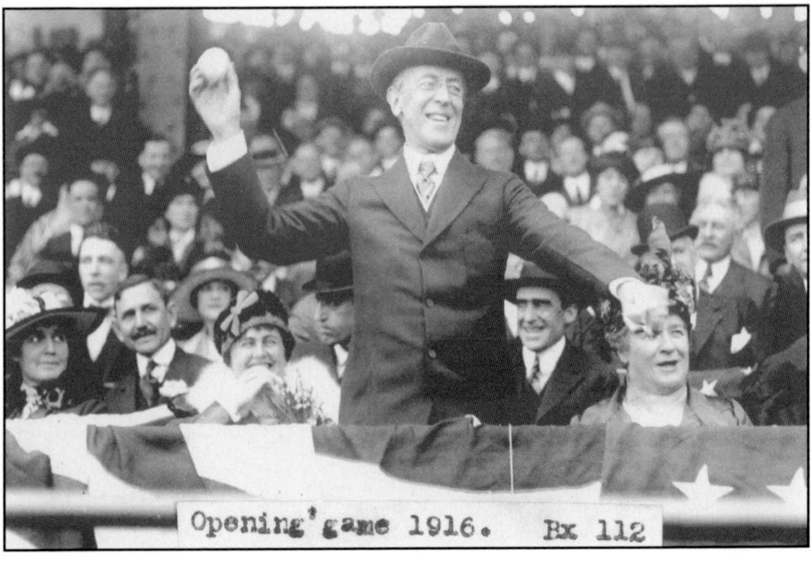

Wilson tossing the first ball for the opening game of the 1916 baseball season *(Library of Congress).*

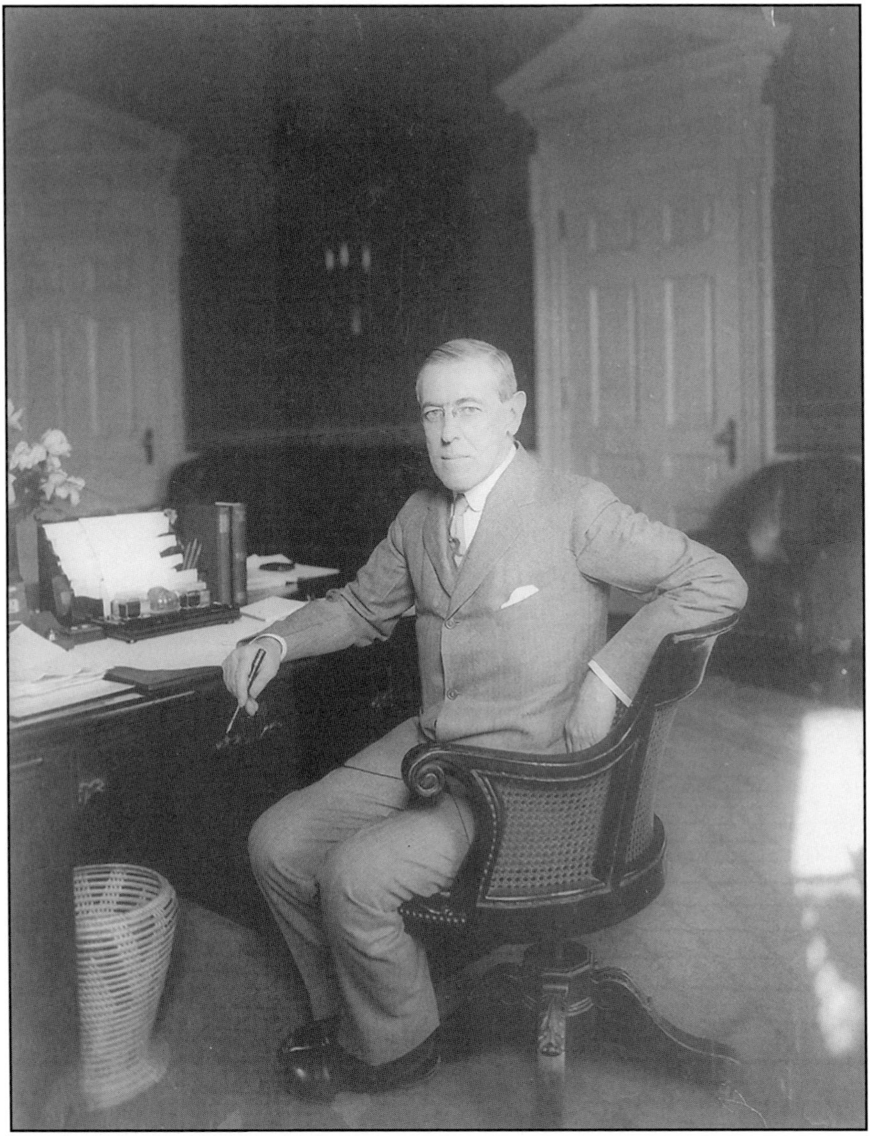

Wilson working at his desk *(Library of Congress)*.

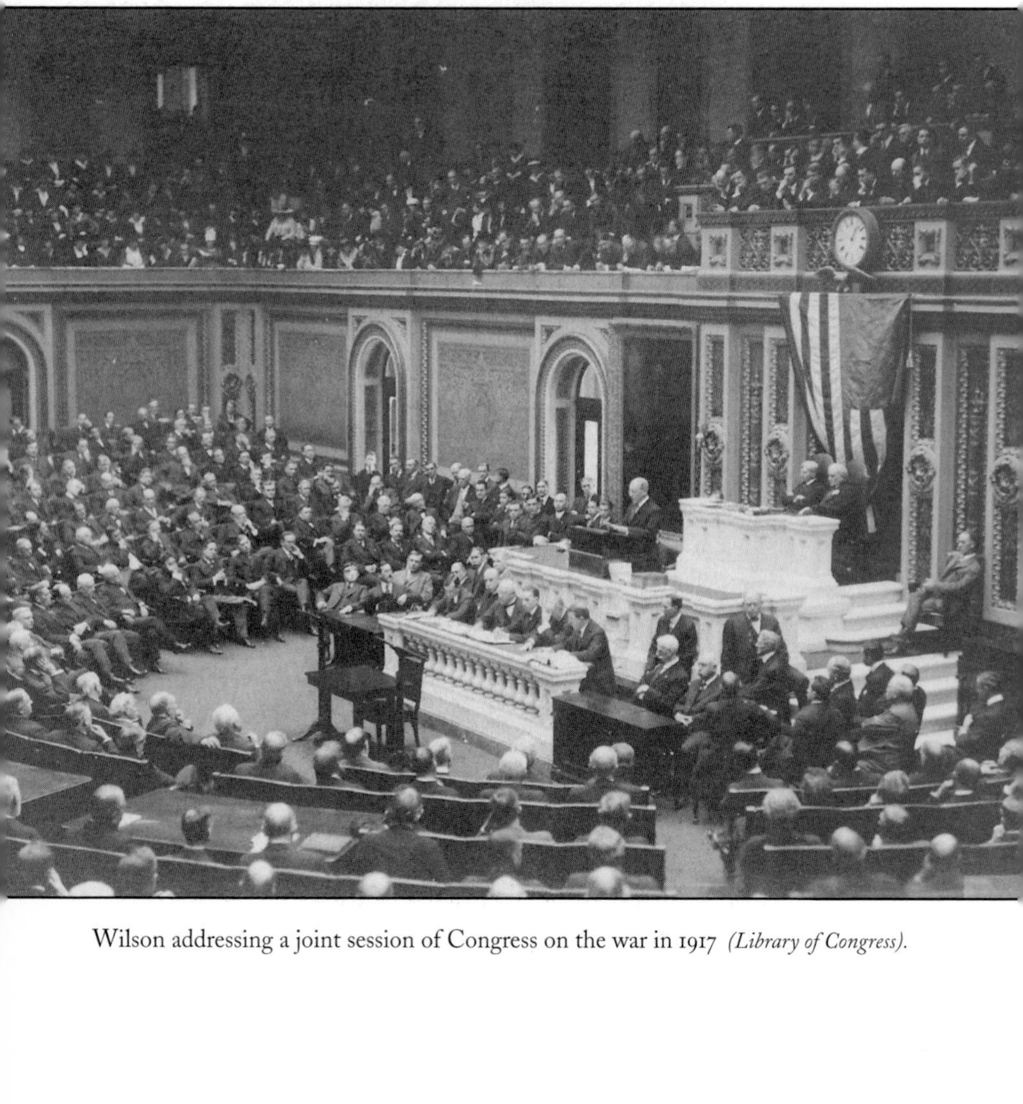

Wilson addressing a joint session of Congress on the war in 1917 *(Library of Congress).*

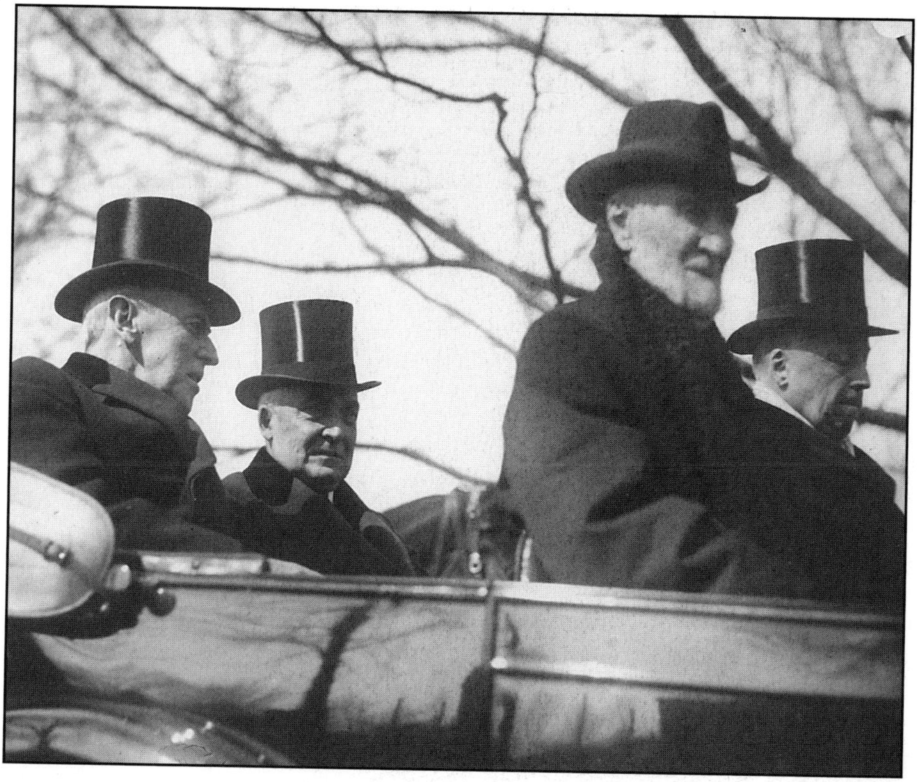

Riding to the inauguration on March 4, 1921, with Warren G. Harding. In the front seat are Congressman and former Speaker Joseph Cannon and Senator Philander Knox *(Library of Congress).*

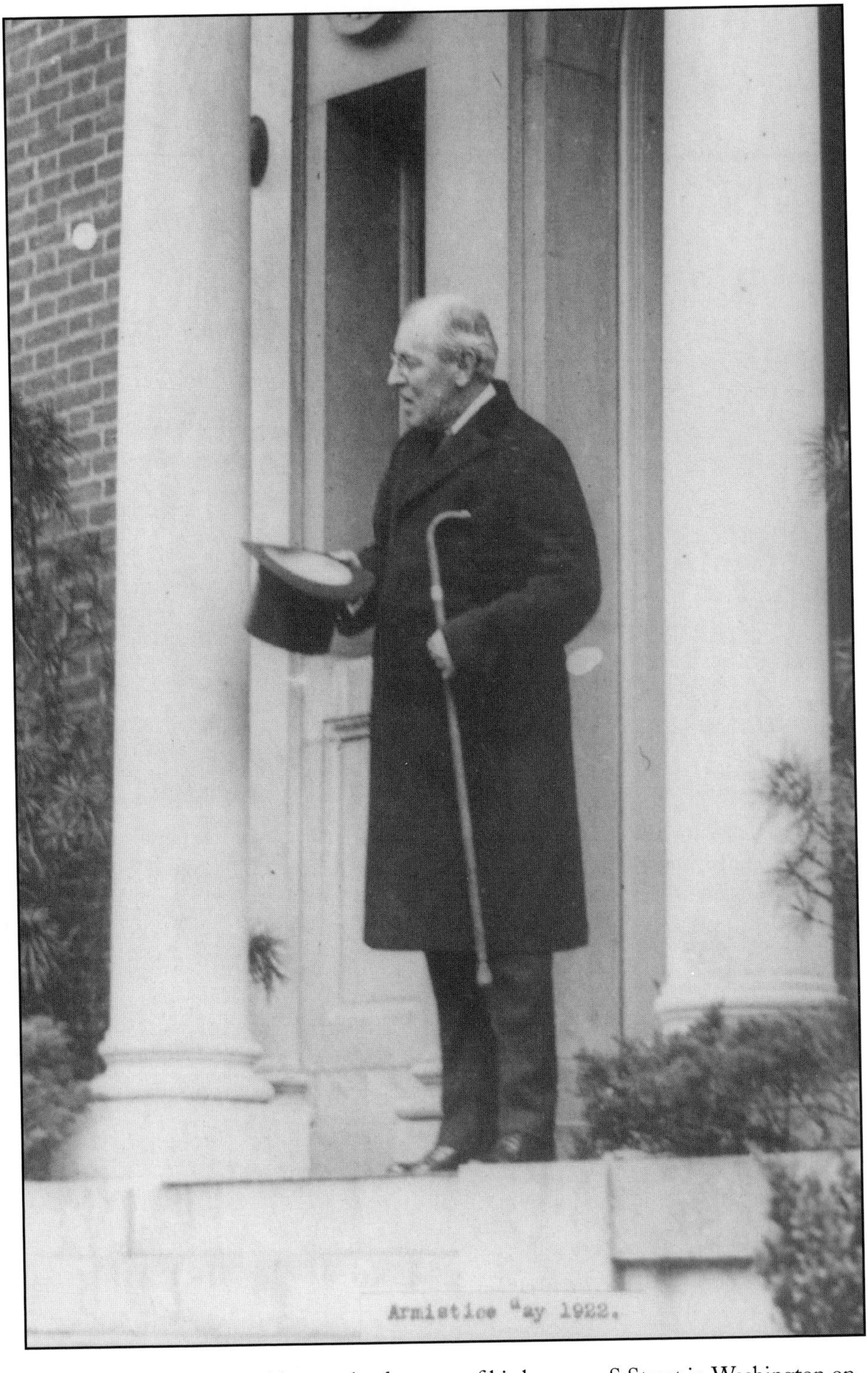

The retired and ailing president at the doorway of his home on S Street in Washington on Armistice Day, 1922 *(Library of Congress).*

most steadfastly minded to insist; alienated his very friends by attacking Congress in public with gross insult and abuse; and lost credit with everybody. It came to a direct issue, the President against Congress: they went to the country with their quarrel in the congressional elections, which fell opportunely in the autumn of 1866, and the President lost utterly. Until then some had hesitated to override his vetoes, but after that no one hesitated. 1867 saw Congress go triumphantly forward with its policy of reconstruction *ab initio.*

☆ ☆ ☆

Whatever their mistakes or weaknesses of temper or of judgment, what followed the reconstruction they affected was in almost every instance much worse than what had had to be endured under military rule. The first practical result of reconstruction under the acts of 1867 was the disfranchisement, for several weary years, of the better whites, and the consequent giving over of the southern governments into the hands of the Negroes. And yet not into their hands, after all. They were but children still; and unscrupulous men, "carpetbaggers,"—men not come to citizens, but come upon an expedition of profit, come to make the name Republican forever hateful in the South, came out of the North to use the Negroes as tools for their own selfish ends; and succeeded, to the utmost fulfillment of their dreams. Negro majorities for a little while filled the southern legislatures; but they won no power or profit for themselves, beyond a pittance here and there for a bribe. Their leaders, strangers and adventurers, got the lucrative offices, the handling of the state moneys raised by loan, and of the taxes spent no one knew how. Here and there an able and upright man cleansed administration, checked corruption, served them as a real friend and an honest leader; but not for long. The Negroes were exalted; the states were misgoverned and looted in their name; and a few men, not of their number, not really of their interest, went away with the gains. They were left to carry the discredit and reap the consequences of ruin, when at last the whites who were real citizens got control again.

But that dark chapter of history is no part of our present story. We are here concerned, rather, with the far-reaching constitutional and political influences and results of Reconstruction. That it was a revolutionary process is written upon its face throughout; but how deep did the revolution go? What permanent marks has it left upon the great structure of government, federal, republican; a partnership of equal states, and yet a solidly coherent national power, which the fathers erected?

First of all, it is clear to every one who looks straight upon the facts, every veil of theory withdrawn, and the naked body of affairs uncovered to meet the direct question of the eye, that civil war discovered the foundations of our government to be in fact unwritten; set deep in a sentiment which constitutions can neither originate nor limit. The law of the Constitution reigned until war came. Then the stage was cleared, and the forces of a mighty sentiment, hitherto unorganized, deployed upon it. A thing had happened for which the Constitution had made no provision. In the Constitution were written rules by which the associated states should live in concert and union, with no word added touching days of discord or disruption; nothing about the use of force to keep or to break the authority ordained in its quiet sentences, written, it would seem, for lawyers, not for soldiers. When the war came, therefore, and questions were broached to which it gave no answer, the ultimate foundation of the structure was laid bare; physical force, sustained by the stern love and rooted predilections of masses of men, the strong ingrained prejudices which are the fibre of every system of government. What gave the war its passion, its hot energy as of a tragedy from end to end, was that in it sentiment met sentiment, conviction conviction. It was the sentiment, not of all, but of the efficient majority, the conviction of the major part, that won. A minority, eager and absolute in another conviction, devoted to the utmost pitch of self-sacrifice to an opposite and incompatible ideal, was crushed and overwhelmed. It was that which gave an epic breadth and majesty to the awful clash between bodies of men in all things else of one strain and breeding; it was that which brought the bitterness of death upon the side which lost, and the dangerous intoxication of an absolute triumph upon the side which won. But it unmistakably uncovered the foundations of force upon which the Union rested.

It did more. The sentiment of union and nationality, never before aroused to full consciousness or knowledge of its own thought and aspirations, was henceforth a new thing, aggressive and aware of a sort of conquest. It had seen its legions and felt its might in the field. It saw the very Constitution, for whose maintenance and defense it had acquired the discipline of arms, itself subordinated for a time to the practical emergencies of war, in order that the triumph might be the more unimpeded and complete; and it naturally deemed nationality henceforth a thing above law. As much as possible, so far as could be without serious embarrassment, the forms of the fundamental law had indeed been represented and observed; but wherever the law clogged or did not suffice, it had been laid aside and ignored. It was so much easier, therefore, to heed its restrictions lightly, when the war was over, and it became necessary to force the southern states to accept the new model. The real revolution was not so much in the form as in the spirit of affairs. The spirit and temper and method of a federal Union had given place, now that all the spaces of the air had been swept and changed by the merciless winds of war, to a spirit which was consciously national and of a new age.

☆ ☆ ☆

A government which had been in its spirit federal became, almost of a sudden, national in temper and point of view. The national spirit had long been a-making. Many a silent force, which grew quite unobserved, from generation to generation, in pervasiveness and might, in quiet times of wholesome peace and mere increase of nature, had been breeding these thoughts which now sprang so vividly into consciousness. The very growth of the nation, the very lapse of time and uninterrupted habit of united action, the mere mixture and movement and distribution of populations, the mere accretions of policy, the mere consolidation of interests, had been building and strengthening new tissue of nationality the years through, and drawing links stronger than links of steel round about the invisible body of common thought and purpose which is the substance of nations. When the great crisis of secession came, men knew at once how their spirits were ruled, men of the South as well as men of the North, in what institutions and conceptions of government their blood was fixed to run; and a great and instant readjustment took place, which was for the South, the minority, practically the readjustment of conquest and fundamental reconstruction, but which was for the North, the region which had been transformed, nothing more than an awakening.

☆ ☆ ☆

We realize it now, in the presence of novel enterprises, at the threshold of an unlooked-for future. It is evident that empire is an affair of strong government, and not of the nice and somewhat artificial poise or of the delicate compromises of structure and authority characteristic of a mere federal partnership. Undoubtedly, the impulse of expansion is the natural and wholesome impulse which comes with a consciousness of matured strength; but it is also a direct result of that national spirit which the war between the states cried so wide awake, and to which the processes of Reconstruction gave the subtle assurance of practically unimpeded sway and a free choice of means. The revolution lies there, as natural as it was remarkable and full of prophecy. It is this which makes the whole period of Reconstruction so peculiarly worth of our study. Every step of the policy, every feature of the time, which wrought this subtle transformation, should receive our careful scrutiny. We are now far enough removed from the time to make that scrutiny both close and dispassionate. A new age gives it a new significance.

The Significance of American History

The special character of American history was Wilson's topic here. American settlers built a new community in wilderness conditions, and the experience created a new man with a new understanding of liberty and of government. Like his contemporary, Frederick Jackson Turner, Wilson emphasized the differences between the American experience and that of England and Europe. Wilson also challenged the racial views of many of his contemporaries, views which tied American progress to Nordic or Anglo-Saxon superiority. His ideas can be contrasted with those of Theodore Roosevelt, whose *Winning of the West* reflected his conviction about the superior qualities of Nordic peoples, a rather common view among intellectuals in the age of Social Darwinism. The experience of the United States, Wilson argued, demonstrated that "nations grow by spirit, not by blood." He makes a fervent argument for the exceptional character of the American experience and concludes with a forecast of the twentieth as the American century. The article was part of *Harper's Encyclopaedia of United States History* (1902).

The study of American history has changed its whole tone and aspect within a generation. Once a plain and simple tale, though heroic withal, of a virgin continent discovered in the West, new homes for the English made upon it, a new polity set up, a new nation made of a sudden in the hot crucible of war, a life and a government apart, a thing isolated, singular, original, as if it were the story of a separate precinct and parish of the great world, the history of the United States has now been brought at last into perspective, to be seen as what it is, an integral portion of the general history of civilization; a free working-out upon a clear field, indeed, of selected forces generated long ago in England and the old European world, but no irregular invention, no histrionic vindication of the Rights of Man. It has not lost its unique significance by the change, but gained, rather, a hundred-fold both in interest and in value. It seemed once a school exercise in puritan theory and cavalier pride; it seems now a chapter written for grown men in the natural history of politics and society, a perfect exposition of what the European civilization of the seventeenth and eighteenth centuries was to produce in the nineteenth century. What formerly appeared to be only a by-product of the creative forces of society is now clearly enough seen to be the epitome of a whole age. We see it all, now that America, having come out of her days of adolescence and preparation, has taken her place among the powers of the world, fresh and still in her youth, but no stranger among the peoples, a leader, rather, and pacemaker in the wide field of affairs.

The history of the United States is modern history in broad and open analysis, stripped of a thousand elements which, upon the European stage, confuse the eye and lead the judgment astray. It spans a whole age of the world's transformation, from the discoveries, the adventure, the romance of the sixteenth century, with its dreams of unbounded wealth in the far Indies and marvels at the ends of the earth, to the sober commerce and material might of the twentieth, with its altered dreams, of a world mastered, if not united, by the power of armed fleets patrolling it from end to end, in the interests of peace and European and American trade.

At its outset American history discloses a novel picture of men out of an old world set upon the coasts of a new to do the work of pioneers, without suitable training either of thought or hand, men schooled in an old civilization, puzzled, even daunted, by the wilderness in which they found themselves as by a strange and alien thing, ignorant of its real character, lacking all the knowledge and craft of the primitive world, lacking everything but courage, sagacity, and a steadfast will to succeed. As they pushed their gigantic task they were themselves transformed. The unsuitable habits of an old world fell away from them. Their old blood bred a new stock, and the youth of the race to which they belonged was renewed. And yet they did not break with the past, were for long scarcely conscious of their own transformation, held their thoughts to old channels, were frontiersmen with traditions not of the frontier, traditions which they cherished and held very dear, of a world in which there were only ancient kingdoms and a civilization set up and perfected time out of mind. Their muscles hardened to the work of the wilderness, they learned woodcraft and ranged the forests like men with the breeding, the quick instincts, the ready resource in time of danger of the Indian himself, and yet thought upon deep problems of religion, pondered the philosophy of the universities, were partisans and followers of statesmen and parties over sea, looked to have their fashions of dress sent to them, with every other old-world trapping they could pay for, by the European ships which diligently plied to their ports. Nowhere else, perhaps, is there so open and legible a record of the stiffness of thought and the flexibility of action in men, the union of youth and age, the dominion of habit reconciled with an unspoiled freshness of bold initiative.

And with the transplantation of men out of the old world into a wilderness went also the transplantation of institutions, with the same result. The new way of life and association thrust upon these men reduced the complex things of government to their simples. Within those untouched forests they resumed again, as if by an unconscious instinct, the simple organization of village communities familiar to their race long centuries before, or here and there put palisades about a group of huts meant to serve for refuge and fortress against savage enemies lurking near at hand in the coverts, and lived in their "hundreds" again under captains, to spread at last slowly into counties with familiar sheriffs and quarter-sessions. It was as if they had brought their old-time polity with them, not in the mature root nor even in the young cutting, but in the seed merely, to renew its youth and yield itself to the influences of a new soil and a new environment. It was drawn back to its essential qualities, stripped of its elaborate growth of habits, as they themselves were. All things were touched, as it were, by the light of an earlier age returned. The study of American history furnishes, as a consequence, materials such as can be found nowhere else for discrimination between what is accidental and what is essential in English political practice. Principles developed by the long and intricate processes of the history of one country are here put to experimental test in another, where every element of life is simplified, every problem of government reduced to its fundamental formulae. There is here the best possible point of departure, for the student who can keep his head and who knows his European history as intimately as he knows his American, for a comparative study of institutions which may some day yield us a sane philosophy of politics which shall forever put out of school the thin and sentimental theories of the disciples of Rousseau.

This is the new riches which the study of American history is to afford in the light that now shines upon it: not national pride merely, nor merely an heroic picture of men wise beyond previous example in building States, and uniting them under a government at once free and strong, but a real understanding of the nature of liberty, of the essential character and determining circumstances of self-government, the fundamental contrasts of race and social development, of temper and of opportunity, which of themselves make governments or mar them. It may well yield us, at any rate, a few of the first principles of the natural history of institutions.

The political history of America was the outcome of a constitutional struggle which concerned Englishmen in England no less deeply than it concerned Englishmen in the colonies, struggle whose motives were compounded both of questions of conscience and of questions of civil liberty, of longings to be free to think and of longings to be free to act. And Englishmen on the two sides of the sea were not wholly divorced in the issue of that struggle. Not America alone, but the power to rule without principle and restraint at home as well, was once for all cut off from the crown of England. But there was a sharp contrast, too, between the effects wrought in England and the effects wrought in America. On one side of the sea an ancient people won their final battle for constitutional government; on the other side a new people was created, a people set free to work out a new experience both in the liberty of its churches and in its political arrangements, to gain a new consciousness, take on a distinctive character, transform itself from a body of loosely associated English colonies merely, but transmuted, within little more than a generation, into a veritable nation, marked out for an independent and striking career.

At the Revolution the American States did hardly more than disengage themselves from the English dominion. Their thoughts, their imaginations, were still held subject to policy and opinion over sea. By the close of the War of 1812, these last, impalpable bonds were also thrown off. American statesmen had got their freedom of thought, and, within a generation, were the leaders of a nation and a people apart. One has only to contrast the persistent English quality and point of view of the English colonies of today, self-governing communities though most of them are, which had led their own lives for generations together under parliaments and ministers of their own free choosing, with the distinctive character of the United States to realize how much of the history of nations is spiritual, not material, a thing, not of institutions, but of the heart and the imagination. This is one of the secrets American history opens to the student, the deepest of all secrets, the genesis of nationality, the play of spirit in the processes of history.

Of course the present separateness and distinctive character of the United States among the nations is due in part to the mixture of races in the make-up of their people. Men out of every European race, men out of Asia, men out of Africa have crowded in, to the bewilderment alike of the statesmen and of the historian. An infinite crossing of strains has made a new race. And yet there is a mystery here withal. Where, when, in what way, have our institutions and our life as a people been turned to new forms and into new channels by this new union and chemistry of bloods? There has been no break in our constitutional development. Nothing has been done of which we can confidently say, This would not have been done had we kept the pure Saxon strain. All peoples have come to dwell among us, but they have merged their individuality in a national character already formed; have been dominated, changed, absorbed. We keep until now some of the characteristic differences of organization and action transplanted to this continent when races were separate upon it. We single out the Dutch element in the history of New York, the French element in the history of Louisiana, the Spanish influence in the far West. But these things remain from a time when Dutch and French and Spanish had their seats and their power apart and were independent rivals for the possession of the continent. Since they were fused they have given us nothing which we can distinguish as their own. The French who have come to us since that final settlement on the heights of Quebec have contributed nothing distinctive to our civilization or our order of government. The Dutch who have been immigrants amongst us since New Netherlands became New York have no doubt strengthened our stock, but they have adopted our character and point of view. No foreign stock long keeps its identity in our affairs.

The fact should a little daunt those who make much of physical heredity and speak of the persistence of race characteristics as a thing fixed and invariable, if they are to apply their theory to communities which are dominated by one and the same national idea, and fused to make a common stock. It is where races act separately that they act in character and with individual distinction. In this again the history of the United States demonstrates the spiritual aspects of political development. Nations grow by spirit, not by blood; and nowhere can the significant principle of their growth be seen more clearly, upon a more fair and open page, than in the history of the United States. It is this principle which throws a light as if of veritable revelation upon the real nature of liberty, as a thing bred, not of institutions nor of the benevolent inventions of statesmen, but of the spiritual forces of which institutions themselves are the offspring and creation. To talk of giving to one people the liberties of another is to talk of making a gift of character, a thing built up by the contrivance of no single generation, but by the slow providence which binds generations together by a common training.

From whatever point of view you approach it, American history gives some old lesson a new plainness, clarification, and breadth. It is an offshoot of European history and has all its antecedents on the other side of the sea, and yet it is so much more than a mere offshoot. Its processes are so freshened and clarified, its records are so abundant and so accessible, it is spread upon so wide, so open, so visible a field of observation, that it seems like a plain first chapter in the history of a new age. As a stage in the economic development of modern civilization, the history of America constitutes the natural, and invaluable, subject-matter and book of praxis of the political economist. Here is industrial development worked out with incomparable logical swiftness, simplicity, and precision,—a swiftness, simplicity, and precision impossible amidst the rigid social order of any ancient kingdom. It is a study, moreover, not merely of the make-up and setting forth of a new people, but also of its marvelous expansion, of processes of growth, both spiritual and material, hurried forward from stage to stage as if under the experimental touch of some social philosopher, some political scientist making of a nation's history his laboratory and place of demonstration.

The twentieth century will show another face. The stage of America grows crowded like the stage of Europe. The life of the new world grows as complex as the life of the old. A nation hitherto wholly devoted to domestic development now finds its first tasks of the great world at large, seeking its special part and place of power. A new age has come which no man may forecast. But the past is the key to it; and the past of America lies at the center of modern history.

5

The Political Scientist

Cabinet Government in the United States

Anticipating some of the ideas he would develop later in his book *Congressional Government,* Wilson wrote this essay in his senior year at Princeton. In it he displayed a maturity of style and a prodigious aptitude for political analysis which was remarkable in one still an undergraduate. He proposed a transformation of the structure of Congress to permit a greater role for the executive in the legislature. Blurring the lines of separation of powers, Wilson argued for the presence of cabinet officers in Congress for a more effective and responsive governing process. The essay clearly illustrated Wilson's admiration for the British parliamentary system, a prejudice he sustained throughout his academic career. It also stood as a sharp critique of the American Congress in the Gilded Age, which did not produce a body of impressive legislation even at a time when the character of the nation was undergoing important economic and social change. The essay was published in the August 1879 issue of the influential journal *International Review* after he graduated. It is one of those oddities of history which enchants the reader that the editor who approved the piece for publication was a young scholar named Henry Cabot Lodge.

Our patriotism seems of late to have been exchanging its wonted tone of confident hope for one of desponding solicitude. Anxiety about the future of our institutions seems to be daily becoming stronger in the minds of thoughtful Americans. A feeling of uneasiness is undoubtedly prevalent, sometimes taking the shape of a fear that grave, perhaps radical, defects in our mode of government are militating against our liberty and prosperity. A marked and alarming decline in statesmanship, a rule of levity and folly instead of wisdom and sober forethought in legislation, threaten to shake our trust not only in the men by whom our national policy is controlled, but also in the very principles upon which our government rests. Both State and National legislatures are looked upon with nervous suspicion, and we hail an adjournment of Congress as a temporary immunity from danger. In casting about for the chief cause of the admitted evil, many persons have convinced themselves that it is to be found in the principle of universal suffrage. . . . The existence of such sentiments is in itself an instructive fact. But while it is indisputably true that universal suffrage is a constant element of weakness, and exposes us to many dangers which we might otherwise escape, its operation does not suffice alone to explain existing evils. Those who make this the scapegoat of all our national grievances have made too superficial an analysis of the abuses about which they so loudly complain.

What is the real cause of this solicitude and doubt? It is, in our opinion, to be found in the absorption of all power by a legislature which is practically irresponsible for its acts. But even this would not necessarily be harmful, were it not for the addition of a despotic principle which it is my present purpose to consider.

At its highest development, *representative* government is that form which best enables a free people to govern themselves. The main object of a representative assembly, therefore, should be the discussion of public business. They should legislate as if in the presence of the whole country, because they come under the closest scrutiny and fullest criticism of all the representatives of the country speaking in open and free debate. Only in such an assembly, only in such an atmosphere of publicity, only by means of such a vast investigating machine, can the different sections of a great country learn each other's feelings and interests. It is not enough that the general course of legislation is known to all. Unless during its progress it is subjected to a thorough, even a tediously prolonged, process of public sifting, to the free comment of friend and foe alike, to the ordeal of battle among those upon whose vote its fate depends, an act of open legislation may have its real intent and scope completely concealed by its friends and undiscovered by its enemies, and it may be as fatally mischievous as the darkest measures of an oligarchy or a despot. Nothing can be more obvious than the fact that the very life of free, popular institutions is dependent upon their breathing the bracing air of thorough, exhaustive, and open discussions, or that select Congressional committees, whose proceedings must from their very nature be secret, are, as means of legislation, dangerous and unwholesome. Parliaments are forces for freedom; for "talk is persuasion, persuasion is force, the one force which can sway freemen to deeds such as those which have made England what she is," or our English stock what it is.

Congress is a deliberative body in which there is little real deliberation; a legislature which legislates with no real discussion of its business. Our Government is practically carried on by irresponsible committees. Too few Americans take the trouble to inform themselves as to the methods of

Congressional management; and, as a consequence, not many have perceived that almost *absolute* power has fallen into the hands of men whose irresponsibility prevents the regulation of their conduct by the people from whom they derive their authority. The most important, most powerful man in the government of the United States in time of peace is the Speaker of the House of Representatives. Instead of being merely an executive officer, whose principal duties are those immediately connected with the administration of the rules of order, he is a potent party chief, the only chief of any real potency, and must of necessity be so. He must be the strongest and shrewdest member of his party in the lower House; for almost all the real business of that House is transacted by committees whose members are his nominees. Unless the rules of the House be suspended by a special two-thirds vote, every bill introduced must be referred, without debate, to the proper Standing Committee, with whom rests the privilege of embodying it, or any part of it, in their reports, or of rejecting it altogether. The House very seldom takes any direct action upon any measures introduced by individual members; its votes and discussions are almost entirely confined to committee reports and committee dictation. The whole attitude of business depends upon forty-seven Standing Committees. Even the discussions upon their directive reports are merely nominal, liberal forms, at most. Take, as an example of the workings of the system, the functions and privileges of the Committee of Ways and Means. To it is intrusted the financial policy of the country; its chairman is, in reality, our Chancellor of the Exchequer. With the aid of his colleagues he determines the course of legislation upon finance; in English political phrase, he draws up the *budget.* All the momentous questions connected with our finance are debated in the private sessions of this committee, and there only. For, when the budget is submitted to the House for its consideration, only a very limited time is allowed for its discussion; and, besides the member of the committee to whom its introduction is intrusted, no one is permitted to speak save those to whom he through courtesy yields the floor, and who must have made arrangements beforehand with the Speaker to be recognized. Where, then, is there room for thorough discussion, for discussion of any kind? If carried, the provisions of the budget must be put into operation by the Secretary of the Treasury, who may be directly opposed to the principles which it embodies. If lost, no one save Congress itself is responsible for the consequent embarrassment into which the nation is brought, and Congress as a body is not readily punishable.

It must at once be evident to every thinking man that a policy thus regulated cannot be other than vacillating, uncertain, devoid of plan or consistency. This is certainly a phase of representative government peculiar to ourselves. And yet its development was most natural and apparently necessary. It is hardly possible for a body of several hundred men, without official or authoritative leaders, to determine upon any line of action without interminable wrangling and delays injurious to the interests under their care. Left to their own resources, they would be as helpless as any other mass meeting. Without leaders having authority to guide their deliberations and give a definite direction to the movement of legislation; and, moreover, with none of that sense of responsibility which constantly rests upon those whose duty it is to work out to a successful issue the policies which they themselves originate, yet with full power to dictate policies which others must carry into execution, a recognition of the need of some sort of leadership, and of a division of labor, led to the formation of these Standing Committees, to which are intrusted the shaping of the national policy in the several departments of administration, as well as the prerogatives of the initiative in legislation and leadership in debate. When theoretically viewed, this is an ingenious and apparently harmless device, but one which, in practice, subverts that most fundamental of all the principles of a free State, the right of the people to a potential voice in their own government. Great measures of legislation are discussed and determined, not conspicuously in public session of the people's representatives, but in the unapproachable privacy of committee rooms.

☆ ☆ ☆

What, then, is Cabinet government? What is the change proposed? Simply to give to the heads of the Executive departments, the members of the Cabinet, seats in Congress, with the privilege of the initiative in legislation and some part of the unbounded privileges now commanded by the Standing Committees. But the advocates of such a change, and they are now not a few, deceive themselves when they maintain that it would not necessarily involve the principle of ministerial responsibility, that is, the resignation of the Cabinet upon the defeat of any important part of their plans. For, if Cabinet officers sit in Congress as official representatives of the Executive, this principle of responsibility must of necessity come sooner or later to be recognized. Experience would soon demonstrate the practical impossibility of their holding their seats, and continuing to represent the Administration, after they had found themselves unable to gain the consent of a majority to their policy. Their functions would be peculiar. They would constitute a link between the legislative and executive branches of the general Government, and, as representatives of the Executive, must hold the right of the initiative in legislation. Otherwise their position would be an anomalous one, indeed. There would be little danger and evident propriety in extending to them the first right of introducing measures relative to the administration of the several departments; and they could possess such a right without denying the fullest privileges to other members. But, whether granted this initiative or not, the head of each department would undoubtedly find it necessary to take a decided and open stand for or against every measure bearing upon the affairs of his department, by whomsoever introduced. No high-spirited man would long remain in an office in the business of which he was not permitted to pursue a policy which tallied with his own principles and convictions. If defeated by both Houses, he would naturally resign; and not many years would pass before resignation upon defeat would have become an established precedent, and resignation upon defeat is the essence of responsible government. In arguing, therefore, for the admission of Cabinet officers into the legislature, we are logically brought to favor *responsible Cabinet government* in the United States.

But, to give to the President the right to choose whomsoever he pleases as his constitutional advisers, after having constituted Cabinet officers *ex officio* members of Congress, would be to empower him to appoint a limited number of representatives, and would thus be plainly at variance with republican principles. The highest order of responsible government could, then, be established in the United States only by laying upon the President the necessity of selecting his Cabinet from among the number of representatives already chosen by the people, or by the legislatures of the States.

Such a change in our legislative system would not be so radical as it might at first appear: it would certainly be very far from revolutionary. Under our present system we suffer all the inconveniences, are hampered by all that is defective in the machinery, of responsible government, without securing any of the many benefits which would follow upon its complete establishment. Cabinet officers are now appointed only with the consent of the Senate. Such powers as a Cabinet with responsible leadership must possess are now divided among the forty-seven Standing Committees, whose prerogatives of irresponsible leadership savor of despotism, because exercised for the most part within the secret precincts of a committee room, and not under the eyes of the whole House, and thus of the whole country. These committees, too, as has been said, rule without any of that freedom of public debate which is essential to the liberties of the people. Their measures are too often mere partisan measures, and are hurried through the forms of voting by a party majority whose interest it is that all serious opposition, all debate that might develop obstructive antagonism, should be suppressed. Under the conditions of Cabinet government, however, full and free debates are sure to take place. For what are these conditions? According as their policy stands or falls, the ministers themselves stand or fall; to the party which supports them each discussion involves a trial of strength with their opponents; upon it depends the amount of their success as a party: while to the opposition the triumph of ministerial plans means still further exclusion from office; their overthrow, accession to power. To each member of the assembly every debate offers an opportunity for placing himself, by able argument, in a position to command a place in any future Cabinet that may be formed from the ranks of his own party; each speech goes to the building up (or the tearing down) of his political fortunes. There is, therefore, an absolute certainty that every phase of every subject will be drawn carefully and vigorously, will be dwelt upon with minuteness, will be viewed from every possible standpoint. The legislative, holding full power of final decision, would find itself in immediate contact with the executive and its policy. Nor would there be room for factious government or factious opposition. Plainly, ministers must found their policies, an opposition must found its attacks, upon well-considered principles; for in this open sifting of debate, when every feature of every measure, even to the motives which prompted it, is the subject of outspoken discussion and keen scrutiny, no chicanery, no party craft, no questionable principles can long hide themselves. Party trickery, legislative jobbery, are deprived of the very air they breathe, the air of secrecy, of concealment. The public is still surprised whenever they find that dishonest legislation has been allowed to pass unchallenged. Why surprised? As things are, measures are determined in the interests of corporations, and the suffering people know almost nothing of them until their evil tendencies crop out in actual execution. Under lobby pressure from interested parties, they have been cunningly concocted in the closet sessions of partisan committees, and, by the all-powerful aid of party machinery, have been hurried through the stages of legislation without debate; so that even press correspondents are often as ignorant of the real nature of such special measures as the outside public. Any searching debate of such questions would at once have brought the public eye upon them, and how could they then have stood? Lifting the lid of concealment must have been the discovery to all concerned of their un-savory character. Light would have killed them.

We are thus again brought into the presence of the cardinal fact of this discussion, that *debate* is the essential function of a popular representative body. In the severe, distinct, and sharp enunciation of underlying principles, the unsparing examination and telling criticism of opposite positions, the careful, painstaking unraveling of all the issues involved, which are incident to the free discussion of questions of public policy, we see the best, the only effective, means of educating public opinion. Can anyone suppose for one moment that, in the late heated and confused discussions of the Bland silver bill, the Western papers would have had any color of justification in claiming that the Resumption Act of 1875 was passed secretly and without the knowledge of the people, if we had then had responsible government? Although this all-important matter was before the country for more than a year; was considered by two Congresses, recommended by more than one Congressional committee; was printed and circulated for the perusal of the people; was much spoken of, though little understood by the press at the time, the general mass of our population knew little or nothing about it, for it elicited almost no statesmanlike comment upon the floor of Congress, was exposed to none of the analysis of earnest debate. What, however, would have been its history under a well-ordered Cabinet government? It would have been introduced, if introduced at all, to the House by the Secretary of the Treasury as a part of the financial policy of the Administration, supported by the authority and sanction of the entire Cabinet. At once it would have been critically scanned by the leaders of the opposition; at each reading of the bill, and especially in Committee of the Whole, its weak points would have been mercilessly assailed, and its strong features urged in defense; attacks upon its principle by the opposition would have been met by an unequivocal avowal of "soft money" principles from the majority; and, defended by men anxious to win honors in support of the ministry, it would have been dissected by all those who were at issue with the financial doctrines of the majority, discussed and re-discussed until all its essential, all its accidental features, and all its remotest tendencies, had been dinned into the public ear, so that no man in the nation could have pretended ignorance of its meaning and object. The educational influence of such discussions is two-fold, and operates in two directions, upon the members of the legislature themselves, and upon the people whom they represent. . . .

Only a single glance is necessary to discover how utterly Committee government must fail to give effect to public opinion. In the first place, the exclusion of debate prevents the intelligent formation of opinion on the part of the nation at large; in the second place, public opinion, when once formed, finds it impossible to exercise any immediate control over the action of its representatives. There is no one in Congress to speak for the nation. Congress is a conglomeration of inharmonious elements; a collection of men representing each his neighborhood, each his local interest; an alarmingly large proportion of its legislation is "special"; all of it is at best only a limping compromise between the conflicting interests of the innumerable localities represented. There is no guiding or harmonizing power. Are the people in favor of a particular policy, what means have they of forcing it upon the sovereign legislature at Washington? None but the most imperfect. If they return representatives who favor it (and this is the most they can do), these representatives being under no directing power will find a mutual agreement impracticable among so many, and will finally settle upon some policy which satisfies nobody, removes no difficulty, and makes little definite or valuable provision for the future. They must, indeed, be content with whatever measure the appropriate committee chances to introduce. Responsible ministries, on the other hand, form the policy of their parties; the strength of their party is at their command; the course of legislation turns upon the acceptance or rejection by the houses of definite and consistent plans upon which they determine. In forming its judgment of their policy, the nation knows whereof it is judging; and, with biennial Congresses, it may soon decide whether any given policy shall stand or fall. The question would then no longer be, What representatives shall we choose to represent our chances in this haphazard game of legislation? but, What plans of national administration shall we sanction? Would not party programs mean something then? Could they be constructed only to deceive and bewilder?

But, above and beyond all this, a responsible Cabinet constitutes a link between the executive and legislative departments of the Government which experience declares in the clearest tones to be absolutely necessary in a well-regulated, well-proportioned body politic. None can so well judge of the perfections or imperfections of a law as those who have to administer it. Look, for example, at the important matter of taxation. The only legitimate object of taxation is the support of Government; and who can so well determine the requisite revenue as those who conduct the Government? Who can so well choose feasible means of taxation, available sources of revenue, as those who have to meet the practical difficulties of tax collection? And what surer guarantee against exorbitant estimates and unwise taxation, than the necessity of full explanation and defense before the whole House? The same principles, of course, apply to all legislation upon matters connected with any of the Executive departments.

Thus, then, not only can Cabinet ministers meet the needs of their departments more adequately and understandingly, and conduct their administration better than can irresponsible committees, but they are also less liable to misuse their powers. Responsible ministers must secure from the House and Senate an intelligent, thorough, and practical treatment of their affairs; must vindicate their principles in open battle on the floor of Congress. The public is thus enabled to exercise a direct scrutiny over the workings of the Executive departments, to keep all their operations under a constant stream of daylight. Ministers could do nothing under the shadow of darkness; committees do all in the dark. It can easily be seen how constantly ministers would be plied with questions about the conduct of public affairs, and how necessary it would be for them to satisfy their questioners if they did not wish to fall under suspicion, distrust, and obloquy.

But, while the people would thus be able to defend themselves through their representatives against malfeasance or inefficiency in the management of their business, the heads of the departments would also have every opportunity to defend their administration of the people's affairs against unjust censure or crippling legislation. Corruption in office would court concealment in vain; vicious trifling with the administration of public business by irresponsible persons would meet with a steady and effective check. The ground would be clear for a manly and candid defense of ministerial methods; wild schemes of legislation would meet with a cold repulse from ministerial authority. The salutary effect of such a change would most conspicuously appear in the increased effectiveness of our now crumbling civil, military, and naval services; for we should no longer be cursed with tardy, insufficient, and misapplied appropriations. The ministers of War, of the Navy, of the Interior, would be able to submit their estimates in person, and to procure speedy and regular appropriations; and half the abuses at present connected with appropriative legislation would necessarily disappear with the present committee system. Appropriations now, though often inadequate, are much oftener wasteful and fraudulent. Under responsible government, every appropriation asked by an Executive chief, as well as the reasons by which he backed his request, would be subjected to the same merciless sifting processes of debate as would characterize the consideration of other questions. Always having their responsible agents thus before them, the people would at once know how much they were spending, and for what it was spent.

☆ ☆ ☆

To supply the conditions of statesmanship is, we conclude, beyond our power; for the causes of its decline and the means necessary to its development are beyond our ken. Let us take a new departure. Let us, drawing light from every source within the range of our knowledge, make a little independent analysis of the conditions of statesmanship, with a view of ascertaining whether or not it is in reality true that we cannot contribute to its development, or even perchance give it a perennial growth among us. We learn from a critical survey of the past, that, so far as political affairs are concerned, great critical epochs are the man-making epochs of history, that revolutionary influences are man-making influences. And why? If this be the law, it must have some adequate reason underlying it; and we seem to find the reason a very plain and conspicuous one. Crises give birth and a new growth to statesmanship because they are peculiarly periods of action, in which talents find the widest and the freest scope. They are periods not only of action, but also of unusual opportunity for gaining leadership and a controlling and guiding influence. It is opportunity for transcendent influence, therefore, which calls into active public life a nation's greater minds, minds which might otherwise remain absorbed in the smaller affairs of private life. And we thus come upon the principle, a principle which will appear the more incontrovertible the more it is looked into and tested, that governmental forms will call to the work of administration able minds and strong hearts constantly or infrequently, according as they do or do not afford them at all times an opportunity of gaining and retaining a commanding authority and an undisputed leadership in the nation's councils. Now it certainly needs no argument to prove that government by supreme committees, whose members are appointed at the caprice of an irresponsible party chief, by seniority, because of reputation gained in entirely different fields, or because of partisan shrewdness, is not favorable to a full and strong development of statesmanship. Certain it is that statesmanship has been steadily dying out in the United States since that stupendous crisis during which its government felt the first throbs of life. In the government of the United States there is no place found for the leadership of men of real ability. Why, then, complain that we have no leaders? The President can seldom make himself recognized as a leader; he is merely the executor of the sovereign legislative will; his Cabinet officers are little more than chief clerks, or superintendents, in the Executive departments, who advise the President as to matters in most of which he has no power of action independently of the concurrence of the Senate. The most ambitious representative can rise no higher than the chairmanship of the Committee of Ways and Means, or the Speakership of the House. The cardinal feature of Cabinet government, on the other hand, is responsible leadership, the leadership and authority of a small body of men who have won the foremost places in their party by a display of administrative talents, by evidence of high ability upon the floor of Congress in the stormy play of debate. None but the ablest can become leaders and masters in this keen tournament in which arguments are the weapons, and the people the judges. Clearly defined, definitely directed policies arouse bold and concerted opposition; and leaders of oppositions become in time leaders of Cabinets. Such a recognized leadership it is that is necessary to the development of statesmanship under popular, republican institutions; for only such leadership can make politics seem worthy of cultivation to men of high mind and aim.

And if party success in Congress, the ruling body of the nation, depends upon power in debate, skill and prescience in policy, successful defense of or attacks upon ruling ministries, how ill can contending parties spare their men of ability from Congress! To keep men of the strongest mental and moral fibre in Congress would become a party necessity. Party triumph would then be a matter of might in debate, not of supremacy in subterfuge. The two great national parties—and upon the existence of two great parties, with clashings and mutual jealousies and watchings, depends the health of free political institutions—are dying for want of unifying and vitalizing principles. Without leaders, they are also without policies, without aims. With leaders there must be followers, there must be parties. And with leaders whose leadership was earned in an open war of principle against principle, by the triumph of one opinion over all opposing opinions, parties must from the necessities of the case have definite policies. Platforms, then, must mean something. Broken promises will then end in broken power. A Cabinet without a policy that is finding effect in progressive legislation is, in a country of frequent elections, inviting its own defeat. Or is there, on the other hand, a determined, aggressive opposition? Then the ministry have a right to ask them what they would do under similar circumstances, were the reins of government to fall to them. And if the opposition are then silent, they cannot reasonably expect the country to intrust the government to them. Witness the situation of the Liberal party in England during the late serious crisis in Eastern affairs. Not daring to propose any policy, having indeed, because of the disintegration of the party, no policy to propose, their numerical weakness became a moral weakness, and the nation's ear was turned away from them. Eight words contain the sum of the present degradation of our political parties: No *leaders, no principles; no principles, no parties.* Congressional leadership is divided infinitesimally; and with divided leadership there can be no great party units. Drill in debate, by giving scope to talents, invites talents; raises up a race of men habituated to the methods of public business, skilled parliamentary chiefs. And, more than this, it creates a much-to-be-desired class who early make attendance upon public affairs the business of their lives, devoting to the service of their country all their better years. Surely the management of a nation's business will, in a well-ordered society, be as properly a matter of life-long training as the conduct of private affairs.

☆ ☆ ☆

The apparently necessary existence of a partisan Executive presents itself to many as a fatal objection to the establishment of the forms of responsible Cabinet government in this country. The President must continue to represent a political party, and must continue to be anxious to surround himself with Cabinet officers who shall always substantially agree with him on all political questions. It must be admitted that the introduction of the principle of ministerial responsibility might, on this account, become at times productive of mischief, unless the tenure of the presidential office were made more permanent than it now is. Whether or not the presidential term should, under such a change of conditions, be lengthened would be one of several practical questions which would attend the adoption of a system of this sort. But it must be remembered that such a state of things as now exists, when we find the Executive to be of one party and the majority in Congress to be of the opposite party, is the exception, by no means the rule. Moreover we must constantly keep before our minds the fact that the choice now lies between this responsible Cabinet government and the rule of irresponsible committees which actually exists. It is not hard to believe that most presidents would find no greater inconvenience, experience no greater unpleasantness, in being at the head of a Cabinet composed of political opponents than in presiding, as they must now occasionally do, over a Cabinet of political friends who are compelled to act in all matters of importance according to the dictation of Standing Committees which are ruled by the opposite party. In the former case, the President may, by the exercise of whatever personal influence he possesses, affect the action of the Cabinet, and, through them, the action of the Houses; in the latter he is absolutely helpless. Even now it might prove practically impossible for a President to gain from a hostile majority in the Senate a confirmation of his appointment of a strongly partisan Cabinet drawn from his own party. The President must now, moreover, acting through his Cabinet, simply do the bidding of the committees in directing the business of the departments. With a responsible Cabinet, even though that Cabinet were of the opposite party, he might, if a man of ability, exercise great power over the conduct of public affairs; if not a man of ability, but a *mere* partisan, he would in any case be impotent. From these considerations it would appear that government by Cabinet ministers who represent the majority in Congress is no more incompatible with a partisan Executive than is government by committees representing such a majority. Indeed, a partisan President might well prefer legislation through a hostile body at whose deliberations he might himself be present, and whose course he might influence, to legislation through hostile committees over whom he could have no manner of control, direct or indirect. And such conditions would be exceptional.

But the encroachment of the legislative upon the executive is deemed the capital evil of our Government in its later phases; and it is asked, Would not the power of Congress be still more dangerously enlarged, and these encroachments made easier and surer, by thus making its relations with the Executive closer? By no means. The several parts of a perfect mechanism must actually interlace and be in strong union in order mutually to support and check each other. Here again permanent, dictating committees are the only alternative. On the one hand, we have committees directing policies for whose miscarriage they are not responsible; on the other, we have a ministry asking for legislation for whose results they are responsible. In both cases there is full power and authority on the part of the legislature to determine all the mainlines of administration: there is no more real control of Executive acts in the one case than in the other; but there is an all-important difference in the character of the agents employed. When carrying out measures thrust upon them by committees, administrative officers can throw off all sense of responsibility; and the committees are safe from punishment, safe even from censure, whatever the issue. But in administering laws which have passed under the influence of their own open advocacy, ministers must shoulder the responsibilities and face the consequences. We should not, then, be giving Congress powers or opportunities of encroachment which it does not now possess, but should, on the contrary, be holding its powers in constant and effective check by putting over it responsible leaders. A complete separation of the executive and legislative is not in accord with the true spirit of those essentially English institutions of which our Government is a characteristic offshoot. The Executive is in constant need of legislative co-operation; the legislative must be aided by an Executive who is in a position intelligently and vigorously to execute its acts. There must needs be, therefore, as a binding link between them, some body which has no power to coerce the one and is interested in maintaining the independent effectiveness of the other. Such a link is the responsible Cabinet.

Again, it is objected that we should be cursed with that instability of government which results from a rapid succession of ministries, a frequent shifting of power from the hands of one party to the hands of another. This is not necessarily more likely to occur under the system of responsibility than now. We should be less exposed to such fluctuations of power than is the English government. The elective system which regulates the choice of United States Senators prevents more than one third of the seats becoming vacant at once, and this third only once every two years. The political complexion of the Senate can be changed only by a succession of elections.

But against such a responsible system the alarm-bell of *centralization* is again sounded, and all those who dread seeing too much authority, too complete control, placed within the reach of the central Government sternly set their faces against any such change. They deceive themselves. There could be no more despotic authority wielded under the forms of free government than our national Congress now exercises. It is a despotism which uses its power with all the caprice, all the scorn for settled policy, all the wild unrestraint which mark the methods of other tyrants as hateful to freedom.

Few of us are ready to suggest a remedy for the evils all deplore. We hope that our system is self-adjusting, and will not need our corrective interference. This is a vain hope! It is no small part of wisdom to know how long an evil ought to be tolerated, to see when the time has come for the people, from whom springs all authority, to speak its doom or prescribe its remedy. If that time be allowed to slip unrecognized, our dangers may overwhelm us, our political maladies may prove incurable.

Congressional Government

Begun as his doctoral thesis at Johns Hopkins, *Congressional Government* was Wilson's first and most important book. Published by Houghton Mifflin in January 1885, it was greeted with rave reviews and marked as one of the most important books on the subject yet published. As in his earlier work, his analysis of the American system reflected his admiration for British parliamentary government in which prime minister and cabinet officers served in the legislature. The absence of such executive leadership in Congress was one of his targets, and he saw the American presidency as a weak office. The presence in Congress of a kind of boss system was undoubtedly an influence. For inspiration and some ideas, Wilson owed a debt in this work to the English political writer, critic, and editor of the *Economist* Walter Bagehot (1826–1877) who wrote a classic study, *The English Constitution* (1864). The stature of *Congressional Government* as an important book has diminished with time, but it remained in print for decades and still offers important clues to Wilson's thought extending into his political career. Its publication assured him a respected place in the academy.

Introductory

It would seem as if a very wayward fortune had presided over the history of the Constitution of the United States, inasmuch as that great federal charter has been alternately violated by its friends and defended by its enemies. It came hard by its establishment in the first place, prevailing with difficulty over the strenuous forces of dissent which were banded against it. While its adoption was under discussion the voices of criticism were many and authoritative, the voices of opposition loud in tone and ominous in volume, and the Federalists finally triumphed only by dint of hard battle against foes, formidable both in numbers and in skill. But the victory was complete, astonishingly complete. Once established, the new government had only the zeal of its friends to fear. Indeed, after its organization very little more is heard of the party of opposition; they disappear so entirely from politics that one is inclined to think, in looking back at the party history of that time, that they must have been not only conquered but converted as well. There was well-nigh universal acquiescence in the new order of things. Not everybody, indeed, professed himself a Federalist, but everybody conformed to federalist practice. There were jealousies and bickerings, of course, in the new Congress of the Union, but no party lines, and the differences which caused the constant brewing and breaking of storms in Washington's first cabinet were of personal rather than of political import. Hamilton and Jefferson did not draw apart because the one had been an ardent and the other only a lukewarm friend of the Constitution, so much as because they were so different in natural bent and temper that they would have been like to disagree and come to drawn points wherever or however brought into contact. The one had inherited warm blood and a bold sagacity, while in the other a negative philosophy ran suitably through cool veins. They had not been meant for yoke-fellows.

There was less antagonism in Congress, however, than in the cabinet; and in none of the controversies that did arise was there shown any serious disposition to quarrel with the Constitution itself; the contention was as to the obedience to be rendered to its provisions. No one threatened to withhold his allegiance, though there soon began to be some exhibition of a disposition to confine obedience to the letter of the new commandments, and to discountenance all attempts to do what was not plainly written in the tables of the law. It was recognized as no longer fashionable to say aught against the principles of the Constitution; but all men could not be of one mind, and political parties began to take form in antagonistic schools of constitutional construction. There straightway arose two rival sects of political Pharisees, each professing a more perfect conformity and affecting greater "ceremonial cleanliness" than the other. The very men who had resisted with might and main the adoption of the Constitution became, under the new division of parties, its champions, as sticklers for a strict, a rigid, and literal construction.

They were consistent enough in this, because it was quite natural that their one-time fear of a strong central government should pass into a dread of the still further expansion of the power of that government, by a too loose construction of its charter; but what I would emphasize here is not the motives or the policy of the conduct of parties in our early national politics, but the fact that opposition to the Constitution as a constitution, and even hostile criticism of its provisions, ceased almost immediately upon its adoption; and not only ceased, but gave place to an undiscriminating and almost blind worship of its principles, and of that delicate dual system of sovereignty, and that complicated scheme of double administration which it established. Admiration of that one-time so much traversed body of law became suddenly all the vogue, and criticism was estopped. From the first, even down to the time immediately preceding the war, the general scheme of the Constitution went unchallenged; nullification itself did not always wear its true garb of independent state sovereignty, but often masqueraded as a constitutional right; and the most violent policies took care to make show of at least formal deference to the worshipful fundamental law. The divine right of kings never ran a more prosperous course than did this unquestioned prerogative of the Constitution to receive universal homage. The conviction that our institutions were the best in the world, nay more, the model to which all civilized states must sooner or later conform, could not be laughed out of us by foreign critics, nor shaken out of us by the roughest jars of the system.

Now there is, of course, nothing in all this that is inexplicable, or even remarkable; anyone can see the reasons for it and the benefits of it without going far out of his way; but the point which it is interesting to note is that we of the present generation are in the first season of free, outspoken, unrestrained constitutional criticism. We are the first Americans to hear our own countrymen ask whether the Constitution is still adapted to serve the purposes for which it was intended; the first to entertain any serious doubts about the superiority of our own institutions as compared with the systems of Europe; the first to think of remodeling the administrative machinery of the federal government, and of forcing new forms of responsibility upon Congress.

The evident explanation of this change of attitude towards the Constitution is that we have been made conscious by the rude shock of the war and by subsequent developments of policy, that there has been a vast alteration in the conditions of government; that the checks and balances which once obtained are no longer effective; and that we are really living under a constitution essentially different from that which we have been so long worshiping as our own peculiar and incomparable possession. In short, this model government is no longer conformable with its own original pattern. While we have been shielding it from criticism it has slipped away from us. The noble charter of fundamental law given us by the Convention of 1787 is still our Constitution; but it is now our *form* of *government* rather in name than in reality, the form of the Constitution being one of nicely adjusted, ideal balances, whilst the actual form of our present government is simply a scheme of congressional supremacy. National legislation, of course, takes force now as at first from the authority of the Constitution; but it would be easy to reckon by the score acts of Congress which can by no means be squared with that great instrument's evident theory. We continue to think, indeed, according to long-accepted constitutional formulae, and it is still politically unorthodox to depart from old-time phraseology in grave discussions of affairs; but it is plain to those who look about them that most of the commonly received opinions concerning federal constitutional balances and administrative arrangements are many years behind the actual practices of the government at Washington, and that we are farther than most of us realize from the times and the policy of the framers of the Constitution. It is a commonplace observation of historians that, in the development of constitutions, names are much more persistent than the functions upon which they were originally bestowed; that institutions constantly undergo essential alterations of character, whilst retaining the names conferred upon them in their first estate; and the history of our own Constitution is but another illustration of this universal principle of institutional change. There has been a constant growth of legislative and administrative practice, and a steady accretion of precedent in the management of federal affairs, which have broadened the sphere and altered the functions of the government without perceptibly affecting the vocabulary of our constitutional language. Ours is, scarcely less than the British, a living and fecund system. It does not, indeed, find its rootage so widely in the hidden soil of unwritten law; its tap-root at least is the Constitution; but the Constitution is now, like Magna Carta and the Bill of Rights, only the sap-center of a system of government vastly larger than the stock from which it has branched, a system some of whose forms have only very indistinct and rudimental beginnings in the simple substance of the Constitution, and which exercises many functions apparently quite foreign to the primitive properties contained in the fundamental law.

The Constitution itself is not a complete system; it takes none but the first steps in organization. It does little more than lay a foundation of principles. It provides with all possible brevity for the establishment of a government having, in several distinct branches, executive, legislative, and judicial powers. It vests executive power in a single chief magistrate, for whose election and inauguration it makes carefully definite provision, and whose privileges and prerogatives it defines with succinct clearness; it grants specifically enumerated powers of legislation to a representative Congress, outlining the organization of the two houses of that body and definitely providing for the election of its members, whose number it regulates and the conditions of whose choice it names; and it establishes a Supreme Court with ample authority of constitutional interpretation, prescribing the manner in which its judges shall be appointed and the conditions of their official tenure. Here the Constitution's work of organization ends, and the fact that it attempts nothing more is its chief strength. For it to go beyond elementary provisions would be to lose elasticity and adaptability. The growth of the nation and the consequent development of the governmental system would snap asunder a constitution which could not adapt itself to the new conditions of an advancing society. If it could not stretch itself to the measure of the times, it must be thrown off and left behind, as a bygone device; and there can, therefore, be no question that our Constitution has proved lasting because of its simplicity. It is a corner-stone, not a complete building; or, rather, to return to the old figure, it is a root, not a perfect vine.

☆ ☆ ☆

The balances of the Constitution are for the most part only ideal. For all practical purposes the national government is supreme over the state governments, and Congress predominant over its so-called coordinate branches. Whereas Congress at first overshadowed neither President nor federal judiciary, it now on occasion rules both with easy mastery and with a high hand; and whereas each State once guarded its sovereign prerogatives with jealous pride, and able men not a few preferred political advancement under the governments of the great commonwealths to office under the new federal Constitution, seats in state legislatures are now no longer coveted except as possible approaches to seats in Congress; and even governors of States seek election to the national Senate as a promotion, a reward for the humbler services they have rendered their local governments.

What makes it the more important to understand the present mechanism of national government, and to study the methods of congressional rule in a light unclouded by theory, is that there is plain evidence that the expansion of federal power is to continue, and that there exists, consequently, an evident necessity that it should be known just what to do and how to do it, when the time comes for public opinion to take control of the forces which are changing the character of our Constitution. There are voices in the air which cannot be misunderstood. The times seem to favor a centralization of governmental functions such as could not have suggested itself as a possibility to the framers of the Constitution. Since they gave their work to the world the whole face of that world has changed. The Constitution was adopted when it was six days' hard traveling from New York to Boston; when to cross East River was to venture a perilous voyage; when men were thankful for weekly mails; when the extent of the country's commerce was reckoned not in millions but in thousands of dollars; when the country knew few cities, and had but begun manufactures; when Indians were pressing upon near frontiers; when there were no telegraph lines, and no monster corporations. Unquestionably, the pressing problems of the present moment regard the regulation of our vast systems of commerce and manufacture, the control of giant corporations, the restraint of monopolies, the perfection of fiscal arrangements, the facilitating of economic exchanges, and many other like national concerns, amongst which may possibly be numbered the question of marriage and divorce; and the greatest of these problems do not fall within even the enlarged sphere of the federal government; some of them can be embraced within its jurisdiction by no possible stretch of construction, and the majority of them only by wresting the Constitution to strange and as yet unimagined uses. Still there is a distinct movement in favor of national control of all questions of policy which manifestly demand uniformity of treatment and power of administration such as cannot be realized by the separate, unconcerted action of the States; and it seems probable to many that, whether by constitutional amendment, or by still further flights of construction, yet broader territory will at no very distant day be assigned to the federal government. It becomes a matter of the utmost importance, therefore, both for those who would arrest this tendency, and for those who, because they look upon it with allowance if not with positive favor, would let it run its course, to examine critically the government upon which this new weight of responsibility and power seems likely to be cast, in order that its capacity both for the work it now does and for that which it may be called upon to do may be definitely estimated.

☆ ☆ ☆

The House of Representatives

Like a vast picture thronged with figures of equal prominence and crowded with elaborate and obtrusive details, Congress is hard to see satisfactorily and appreciatively at a single view and from a single stand-point. Its complicated forms and diversified structure confuse the vision, and conceal the system which underlies its composition. It is too complex to be understood without an effort, without a careful and systematic process of analysis. Consequently, very few people do understand it, and its doors are practically shut against the comprehension of the public at large. If Congress had a few authoritative leaders whose figures were very distinct and very conspicuous to the eye of the world, and who could represent and stand for the national legislature in the thoughts of that very numerous, and withal very respectable, class of persons who must think specifically and in concrete forms when they think at all, those persons who can make some thing out of men but very little out of intangible generalizations, it would be quite within the region of possibilities for the majority of the nation to follow the course of legislation without any very serious confusion of thought. I suppose that almost everybody who just now gives any heed to the policy of Great Britain, with regard even to the reform of the franchise and other like strictly legislative questions, thinks of Mr. Gladstone and his colleagues rather than of the House of Commons, whose servants they are. The question is not, What will Parliament do? but, What will Mr. Gladstone do? And there is even less doubt that it is easier and more natural to look upon the legislative designs of Germany as locked up behind Bismarck's heavy brows than to think of them as dependent upon the determinations of the Reichstag, although as a matter of fact its consent is indispensable even to the plans of the imperious and domineering Chancellor.

But there is no great minister or ministry to represent the will and being of Congress in the common thought. The Speaker of the House of Representatives stands as near to leadership as anyone; but his will does not run as a formative and imperative power in legislation much beyond the appointment of the committees who are to lead the House and do its work for it, and it is, therefore, not entirely satisfactory to the public mind to trace all legislation to him. He may have a controlling hand in starting it; but he sits too still in his chair, and is too evidently not on the floor of the body over which he presides, to make it seem probable to the ordinary judgment that he has much immediate concern in legislation after it is once set afoot. Everybody knows that he is a staunch and avowed partisan, and that he likes to make smooth, whenever he can, the legislative paths of his party; but it does not seem likely that all important measures originate with him, or that he is the author of every distinct policy. And in fact he is not. He is a great party chief, but the hedging circumstances of his official position as presiding officer prevent his performing the part of active leadership. He appoints the leaders of the House, but he is not himself its leader.

The leaders of the House are the chairmen of the principal Standing Committees. Indeed, to be exactly accurate, the House has as many leaders as there are subjects of legislation; for there are as many Standing Committees as there are leading classes of legislation, and in the consideration of every topic of business the House is guided by a special leader in the person of the chairman of the Standing Committee, charged with the superintendence of measures of the particular class to which that topic belongs. It is this multiplicity of leaders, this many-headed leadership, which makes the organization of the House too complex to afford uninformed people and unskilled observers any easy clue to its methods of rule. For the chairmen of the Standing Committees do not constitute a cooperative body like a ministry. They do not consult and concur in the adoption of homogeneous and mutually helpful measures; there is no thought of acting in concert. Each Committee goes its own way at its own pace. It is impossible to discover any unity or method in the disconnected and therefore unsystematic, confused, and desultory action of the House, or any common purpose in the measures which its Committees from time to time recommend.

And it is not only to the unanalytic thought of the common observer who looks at the House from the outside that its doings seem helter-skelter, and without comprehensible rule; it is not at once easy to understand them when they are scrutinized in their daily headway through open session by one who is inside the House. The newly-elected member, entering its doors for the first time, and with no more knowledge of its rules and customs than the more intelligent of his constituents possess, always experiences great difficulty in adjusting his preconceived ideas of congressional life to the strange and unlooked-for conditions by which he finds himself surrounded after he has been sworn in and has become a part of the great legislative machine. Indeed there are generally many things connected with his career in Washington to disgust and dispirit, if not to aggrieve, the new member. In the first place, his local reputation does not follow him to the federal capital. Possibly the members from his own State know him, and receive him into full fellowship; but no one else knows him, except as an adherent of this or that party, or as a new-comer from this or that State. He finds his station insignificant, and his identity indistinct. But this social humiliation which he experiences in circles in which to be a congressman does not of itself confer distinction, because it is only to be one among many, is probably not to be compared with the chagrin and disappointment which come in company with the inevitable discovery that he is equally without weight or title to consideration in the House itself. No man, when chosen to the membership of a body possessing great powers and exalted prerogatives, likes to find his activity repressed, and himself suppressed, by imperative rules and precedents which seem to have been framed for the deliberate purpose of making usefulness unattainable by individual members. Yet such the new member finds the rules and precedents of the House to be. It matters not to him, because it is not apparent on the face of things, that those rules and precedents have grown, not out of set purpose to curtail the privileges of new members as such, but out of the plain necessities of business; it remains the fact that he suffers under their curb, and it is not until "custom hath made it in him a property of easiness" that he submits to them with anything like good grace.

☆ ☆ ☆

One very noteworthy result of this system is to shift the theater of debate upon legislation from the floor of Congress to the privacy of the committee-rooms. Provincial gentlemen who read the Associated Press dispatches in their morning papers as they sit over their coffee at breakfast are doubtless often very sorely puzzled by certain of the items which sometimes appear in the brief telegraphic notes from Washington. What can they make of this for instance: "The House Committee on Commerce today heard arguments from the congressional delegation from" such and such States "in advocacy of appropriations for river and harbor improvements which the members desire incorporated in the River and Harbor Appropriations Bill"? They probably do not understand that it would have been useless for members not of the Committee on Commerce to wait for any opportunity to make their suggestions on the floor of Congress, where the measure to which they wish to make additions would be under the authoritative control of the Committee, and where, consequently, they could gain a hearing only by the courteous sufferance of the committee-man in charge of the report. Whatever is to be done must be done by or through the Committee.

It would seem, therefore, that practically Congress, or at any rate the House of Representatives, delegates not only its legislative but also its deliberative functions to its Standing Committees. The little public debate that arises under the stringent and urgent rules of the House is formal rather than effective, and it is the discussions which take place in the Committees that give form to legislation. Undoubtedly these siftings of legislative questions by the Committees are of great value in enabling the House to obtain "undarkened counsel" and intelligent suggestions from authoritative sources. All sober, purposeful, business-like talk upon questions of public policy, whether it take place in Congress or only before the Committees of Congress, is of great value; and the controversies which spring up in the committee-rooms, both amongst the committee-men themselves and between those who appear before the Committees as advocates of special measures, cannot but contribute to add clearness and definite consistency to the reports submitted to the House.

There are, however, several very obvious reasons why the most thorough canvass of business by the Committees, and the most exhaustive and discriminating discussion of all its details in their rooms, cannot take the place or fulfill the uses of amendment and debate by Congress in open session. In the first place, the proceedings of the Committees are private and their discussions unpublished. The chief, and unquestionably the most essential, object of all discussion of public business is the enlightenment of public opinion; and of course, since it cannot hear the debates of the Committees, the nation is not apt to be much instructed by them. Only the Committees are enlightened. There is a conclusive objection to the publication of the proceedings of the Committees, which is recognized as of course by all parliamentary lawyers, namely, that those proceedings are of no force till confirmed by the House. A Committee is commissioned, not to instruct the public, but to instruct and guide the House.

Indeed it is not usual for the Committees to open their sittings often to those who desire to be heard with regard to pending questions; and no one can demand a hearing as of right. On the contrary, they are privileged and accustomed to hold their sessions in absolute secrecy. It is made a breach of order for any member to allude on the floor of the House to anything that has taken place in committee, "unless by a written report sanctioned by a majority of the Committee"; and there is no place in the regular order of business for a motion instructing a Committee to conduct its investigations with open doors. Accordingly, it is only by the concession of the Committees that arguments are made before them.

☆ ☆ ☆

Why is it that many intelligent and patriotic people throughout this country, from Virginia to California, people who, beyond all question, love their State and the Union more than they love our cousin state over sea, subscribe for the London papers in order to devour the parliamentary debates, and yet would never think of troubling themselves to make tedious progress through a single copy of the "Congressional Record"? Is it because they are captivated by the old-world dignity of royal England with its nobility and its court pageantry, or because of a vulgar desire to appear better versed than their neighbors in foreign affairs, and to affect familiarity with British statesmen? No; of course not. It is because the parliamentary debates are interesting and ours are not. In the British House of Commons the functions and privileges of our Standing Committees are all concentrated in the hands of the Ministry, who have, besides, some prerogatives of leadership which even our Committees do not possess, so that they carry all responsibility as well as great power, and all debate wears an intense personal and party interest. Every important discussion is an arraignment of the Ministry by the Opposition, an arraignment of the majority by the minority; and every important vote is a party defeat and a party triumph. The whole conduct of the government turns upon what is said in the Commons, because the revelations of debate often change votes, and a Ministry loses hold upon power as it loses hold upon the confidence of the Commons. This great Standing Committee goes out whenever it crosses the will of the majority. It is, therefore, for these very simple and obvious reasons that the parliamentary debates are read on this side of the water in preference to the congressional debates. They affect the ministers, who are very conspicuous persons, and in whom, therefore, all the intelligent world is interested; and they determine the course of politics in a great empire. The season of a parliamentary debate is a great field day on which Liberals and Conservatives pit their full forces against each other, and people like to watch the issues of the contest.

Our congressional debates, on the contrary, have no tithe of this interest, because they have no tithe of such significance and importance. The committee reports, upon which the debates take place, are backed by neither party; they represent merely the recommendations of a small body of members belonging to both parties, and are quite as likely to divide the vote of the party to which the majority of the Committee belong as they are to meet with opposition from the other side of the chamber. If they are carried, it is no party triumph; if they are lost, it is no party discomfiture. They are no more than the proposals of a mixed Committee, and may be rejected without political inconvenience to either party or reproof to the Committee; just as they may be passed without compliment to the Committee or political advantage to either side of the House. Neither party has any great stake in the controversy. The only importance that can attach to the vote must hang upon its relation to the next general election. If the report concern a question which is at the time so much in the public eye that all action upon it is likely to be marked and remembered against the day of popular action, parties are careful to vote as solidly as possible on what they conceive to be the safe side; but all other reports are disposed of without much thought of their influence upon the fortunes of distant elections, because that influence is remote and problematical.

In a word, the national parties do not act in Congress under the restraint of a sense of immediate responsibility. Responsibility is spread thin; and no vote or debate can gather it. It rests not so much upon parties as upon individuals; and it rests upon individuals in no such way as would make it either just or efficacious to visit upon them the iniquity of any legislative act. Looking at government from a practical and business-like, rather than from a theoretical and abstractly ethical point of view, treating the business of government as a business, it seems to be unquestionably and in a high degree desirable that all legislation should distinctly represent the action of parties as parties. I know that it has been proposed by enthusiastic, but not too practical, reformers to do away with parties by some legerdemain of governmental reconstruction, accompanied and supplemented by some rehabilitation, devoutly to be wished, of the virtues least commonly controlling in fallen human nature; but it seems to me that it would be more difficult and less desirable than these amiable persons suppose to conduct a government of the many by means of any other device than party organization, and that the great need is, not to get rid of parties, but to find and use some expedient by which they can be managed and made amenable from day to day to public opinion. Plainly this cannot be effected by punishing here and there a member of Congress who has voted for a flagrantly dishonest appropriation bill, or an obnoxious measure relating to the tariff. Unless the punishment can be extended to the party—if any such be recognizable—with which these members have voted, no advantage has been won for self-government, and no triumph has been gained by public opinion. It should be desired that parties should act in distinct organizations, in accordance with avowed principles, under easily recognized leaders, in order that the voters might be able to declare by their ballots, not only their condemnation of any past policy, by withdrawing all support from the party responsible for it; but also and particularly their will as to the future administration of the government, by bringing into power a party pledged to the adoption of an acceptable policy.

It is, therefore, a fact of the most serious consequence that by our system of congressional rule no such means of controlling legislation is afforded. Outside of Congress the organization of the national parties is exceedingly well-defined and tangible; no one could wish it, and few could imagine it, more so; but within Congress it is obscure and intangible. Our parties marshal their adherents with the strictest possible discipline for the purpose of carrying elections, but their discipline is very slack and indefinite in dealing with legislation. At least there is within Congress no *visible*, and therefore no *controllable* party organization. The only bond of cohesion is the caucus, which occasionally whips a party together for cooperative action against the time for casting its vote upon some critical question. There is always a majority and a minority, indeed, but the legislation of a session does not represent the policy of either; it is simply an aggregate of the bills recommended by Committees composed of members from both sides of the House, and it is known to be usually, not the work of the majority men upon the Committees, but compromise conclusions bearing some shade or tinge of each of the variously- colored opinions and wishes of the committeemen of both parties.

It is plainly the representation of both parties on the committees that makes party responsibility indistinct and organized party action almost impossible. If the Committees were composed entirely of members of the majority, and were thus constituted representatives of the party in power, the whole course of congressional proceedings would unquestionably take on a very different aspect. There would then certainly be a compact opposition to face the organized majority. Committee reports would be taken to represent the views of the party in power, and, instead of the scattered, unconcerted opposition, without plan or leaders, which now sometimes subjects the propositions of the Committees to vexatious hindrances and delays, there would spring up debate under skillful masters of opposition, who could drill their partisans for effective warfare and give shape and meaning to the purposes of the minority. But of course there can be no such definite division of forces so long as the efficient machinery of legislation is in the hands of both parties at once; so long as the parties are mingled and harnessed together in a common organization.

It may be said, therefore, that very few of the measures which come before Congress are party measures. They are, at any rate, not brought in as party measures. They are indorsed by select bodies of members chosen with a view to constituting an impartial board of examination for the judicial and thorough consideration of each subject of legislation; no member of one of these Committees is warranted in revealing any of the disagreements of the committee room or the proportions of the votes there taken; and no color is meant to be given to the supposition that the reports made are intended to advance any party interest. Indeed, only a very slight examination of the measures which originate with the Committees is necessary to show that most of them are framed with a view to securing their easy passage by giving them as neutral and inoffensive a character as possible. The manifest object is to dress them to the liking of all factions.

☆ ☆ ☆

The British system is perfected party government. No effort is made in the Commons, such as is made in the House of Representatives in the composition of the Committees, to give the minority a share in law-making. Our minorities are strongly represented on the Standing Committees; the minority in the Commons is not represented at all in the cabinet. It is this feature of closely organized party government, whereby the responsibility for legislation is saddled upon the majority, which, as I have already pointed out, gives to the debates and action of parliament an interest altogether denied to the proceedings of Congress. All legislation is made a contest for party supremacy, and if legislation goes wrong, or the majority becomes discontented with the course of policy, there is nothing for it but that the ministers should resign and give place to the leaders of the Opposition, unless a new election should procure for them a recruited following. Under such a system mere silent voting is out of the question; debate is a primary necessity. It brings the representatives of the people and the ministers of the Crown face to face. The principal measures of each session originate with the ministers, and embody the policy of the administration. Unlike the reports of our Standing Committees, which are intended to be simply the digested substance of the more sensible bills introduced by private members, the bills introduced into the House of Commons by the cabinet embody the definite schemes of the government; and the fact that the Ministry is made up of the leaders of the majority and represents always the principles of its party, makes the minority only the more anxious to have a chance to criticize its proposals. Cabinet government is a device for bringing the executive and legislative branches into harmony and co-operation without uniting or confusing their functions. It is as if the majority in the Commons deputized its leaders to act as the advisers of the Crown and the superintendents of the public business, in order that they might have the advantage of administrative knowledge and training in advising legislation and drafting laws to be submitted to parliament. This arrangement enlisted the majority in behalf of successful administration without giving the ministers any power to coerce or arbitrarily influence legislative action. Each session of the Lords and Commons becomes a grand inquest into the affairs of the empire. The two estates sit as it were in committee on the management of the public business, sit with open doors, and spare themselves no fatigue in securing for every interest represented a full, fair, and impartial hearing.

☆ ☆ ☆

This indifference of the country to what is said in Congress pointing, as it obviously does, to the fact that, though the Committees lead in legislation, they lead without concert or responsibility, and lead nobody in particular, that is, no compact and, organized party force which can be made accountable for its policy, has also a further significance with regard to the opportunities and capacities of the constituencies. The doubt and confusion of thought which must necessarily exist in the minds of the vast majority of voters as to the best way of exerting their will in influencing the action of an assembly whose organization is so complex, whose acts are apparently so haphazard, and in which responsibility is spread so thin, throws constituencies into the hands of local politicians who are more visible and tangible than are the leaders of Congress, and generates, the while, a profound distrust of Congress as a body whose actions cannot be reckoned beforehand by any standard of promises made at elections or any programs announced by conventions. Constituencies can watch and understand a few banded leaders who display plain purposes and act upon them with promptness; but they cannot watch or understand forty odd Standing Committees, each of which goes its own way in doing what it can without any special regard to the pledges of either of the parties from which its membership is drawn. In short, we lack in our political life the conditions most essential for the formation of an active and effective public opinion. "The characteristics of a nation capable of public opinion," says Mr. Bagehot, most sagacious of political critics, "is that . . . parties will be *organized;* in each there will be a leader, in each there will be some looked up to, and many who look up to them; the opinion of the party will be formed and suggested by the few, it will be criticized and accepted by the many." And this is just the sort of party organization which we have not. Our parties have titular leaders at the polls in the persons of candidates, and nominal creeds in the resolutions of conventions, but no select few in whom to trust for guidance in the general policy of legislation, or to whom to look for suggestions of opinion. What man, what group of men, can speak for the Republican party or for the Democratic party? When our most conspicuous and influential politicians say anything about future legislation, no one supposes that they are speaking for their party, as those who have authority; they are known to speak only for themselves and their small immediate following of colleagues and friends.

☆ ☆ ☆

The voter, moreover, feels that his want of confidence in Congress is justified by what he hears of the power of corrupt lobbyists to turn legislation to their own uses. He hears of enormous subsidies begged and obtained; of pensions procured on commission by professional pension solicitors; of appropriations made in the interest of dishonest contractors; and he is not altogether unwarranted in the conclusion that these are evils inherent in the very nature of Congress, for there can be no doubt that the power of the lobbyist consists in great part, if not altogether, in the facility afforded him by the Committee system. He must, in the natural course of things, have many most favorable opportunities for approaching the great money-dispensing Committees. It would be impracticable to work up his schemes in the broad field of the whole House, but in the membership of a Committee he finds manageable numbers. If he can gain the ear of the Committee, or of any influential portion of it, he has practically gained the ear of the House itself; if his plans once get footing in a committee report, they may escape criticism altogether, and it will, in any case, be very difficult to dislodge them. This accessibility of the Committees by outsiders gives to illegitimate influences easy approach at all points of legislation, but no Committees are affected by it so often or so unfortunately as are the Committees which control the public moneys. They are naturally the ones whose favor is oftenest and most importunately, as well as most insidiously, sought; and no description of our system of revenue, appropriation, and supply would be complete without mention of the manufacturers who cultivate the favor of the Committee of Ways and Means, of the interested persons who walk attendance upon the Committee on Rivers and Harbors, and of the mail-contractors and subsidy-seekers who court the Committee on Appropriations.

My last point of critical comment upon our system of financial administration I shall borrow from a perspicacious critic of congressional methods who recently wrote thus to one of the best of American journals: "*So* long as the debit side of the national account is managed by one set of men, and the credit side by another set, both sets working separately and in secret, without any public responsibility, and without any intervention on the part of the executive official who is nominally responsible; so long as these sets, being composed largely of new men every two years, give no attention to business except when Congress is in session, *and thus spend in preparing plans the whole time which ought to be spent in public discussion of plans already matured,* so that an immense budget is rushed through without discussion in a week or ten days, just so long the finances will go from bad to worse, no matter by what name you call the party in power. No other nation on earth attempts such a thing, or could attempt it without soon coming to grief, our salvation thus far consisting in an enormous income, with practically no drain for military expenditure." Unquestionably this strikes a very vital point of criticism. Congress spends its time working, in sections, at preparing plans, instead of confining itself to what is for a numerous assembly manifestly the much more useful and proper function of debating and revising plans prepared beforehand for its consideration by a commission of skilled men, old in political practice and in legislative habit, whose official life is apart from its own, though dependent upon its will. Here, in other words, is another finger pointing to Mr. Mill's question as to the best "legislative commission." Our Committees fall short of being the best form of commission, not only in being too numerous but also in being integral parts of the body which they lead, having no life apart from it. Probably the best working commission would be one which should make plans for government independently of the representative body, and in immediate contact with the practical affairs of administration, but which should in all cases look to that body for the sanctioning of those plans, and should be immediately responsible to it for their success when put into operation.

☆ ☆ ☆

The Senate

The Senate of the United States has been both extravagantly praised and unreasonably disparaged, according to the predisposition and temper of its various critics. In the eyes of some it has a stateliness of character, an eminency of prerogative, and, for the most part, a wisdom of practice such as no other deliberative body possesses; whilst in the estimation of others it is now, whatever it may have been formerly, but a somewhat select company of leisurely "bosses," in whose companionship the few men of character and high purpose who gain admission to its membership find little that is encouraging and nothing that is congenial. Now of course neither of these extreme opinions so much as resembles the uncolored truth, nor can that truth be obtained by a judicious mixture of their milder ingredients. The truth is, in this case as in so many others, something quite commonplace and practical. The Senate is just what the mode of its election and the conditions of public life in this country make it. Its members are chosen from the ranks of active politicians, in accordance with a law of natural selection to which the state legislatures are commonly obedient; and it is probable that it contains, consequently, the best men that our system calls into politics. If these best men are not good, it is because our system of government fails to attract better men by its prizes, not because the country affords or could afford no finer material.

It has been usual to suppose that the Senate was just what the Constitution intended it to be; that because its place in the federal system was exalted the aims and character of its members would naturally be found to be exalted as well; that because its term was long its foresight would be long also; or that because its election was not directly of the people demagogy would find no life possible in its halls. But the Senate is in fact, of course, nothing more than a part, though a considerable part, of the public service, and if the general conditions of that service be such as to starve statesmen and foster demagogues, the Senate itself will be full of the latter kind, simply because there are no others available. There cannot be a separate breed of public men reared specially for the Senate. It must be recruited from the lower branches of the representative system, of which it is only the topmost part. No stream can be purer than its sources. The Senate can have in it no better men than the best men of the House of Representatives; and if the House of Representatives attract to itself only inferior talent, the Senate must put up with the same sort. I think it safe to say, therefore, that, though it may not be as good as could be wished, the Senate is as good as it can be under the circumstances. It contains the most perfect product of our politics, whatever that product may be.

☆ ☆ ☆

In a country which governs itself by means of a public meeting, a Congress or a Parliament, a country whose political life is representative, the only real leadership in governmental affairs must be legislative leadership-ascendency in the public meeting which decides everything. The leaders, if there be any, must be those who suggest the opinions and rule the actions of the representative body. We have in this country, therefore, no real leadership; because no man is allowed to direct the course of Congress, and there is no way of governing the country save through Congress, which is supreme. The chairman of a great Committee like the Committee of Ways and Means stands, indeed, at the sources of a very large and important stream of policy, and can turn that stream at his pleasure, or mix what he will with its waters; but there are whole provinces of policy in which he can have no authority at all. He neither directs, nor can often influence, those other chairmen who direct all the other important affairs of government. He, though the greatest of chairmen, and as great, it may be, as any other one man in the whole governmental system, is by no means at the head of the government. He is, as he feels every day, only a big wheel where there are many other wheels, some almost as big as he, and all driven, like himself, by fires which he does not kindle or tend.

In a word, we have no supreme executive ministry, like the great "Ministry of the Crown" over sea, in whose hands is the general management of legislation; and we have, consequently, no great prizes of leadership such as are calculated to stimulate men of strong talents to great and conspicuous public services. The Committee system is, as I have already pointed out, the very opposite of this. It makes all the prizes of leadership small, and nowhere gathers power into a few hands. It cannot be denied that this is in ordinary times, and in the absence of stirring themes, a great drawback, inasmuch as it makes legislative service unattractive to minds of the highest order, to whom the offer of really great place and power at the head of the governing assembly, the supreme council of the nation, would be of all things most attractive. If the presidency were competitive, if it could be won by distinguished congressional service, who can doubt that there would be a notable influx of talents into Congress and a significant elevation of tone and betterment of method in its proceedings; and yet the presidency is very far from being equal to a first-rate premiership.

☆ ☆ ☆

But it must be said, on the other hand, that even if the Senate were made up of something better than selections from the House, it would probably be able to do little more than it does in the way of giving efficiency to our system of legislation. For it has those same radical defects of organization which weaken the House. Its functions also, like those of the House, are segregated in the prerogatives of numerous Standing Committees. In this regard Congress is all of a piece. There is in the Senate no more opportunity than exists in the House for gaining such recognized party leadership as would be likely to enlarge a man by giving him a sense of power, and to steady and sober him by filling him with a grave sense of responsibility. So far as its organization controls it, the Senate, notwithstanding the one or two special excellences which make it more temperate and often more rational than the House, has no virtue which marks it as of a different nature.

☆ ☆ ☆

In discussing the Senate's connection with the civil service and the abuses surrounding that connection, one is . . . discussing a phase of congressional government which promises soon to become obsolete. A consummation devoutly to be wished!—and yet sure when it comes to rob our politics of a feature very conspicuous and very characteristic, and in a sense very entertaining. There are not many things in the proceedings of Congress which the people care to observe with any diligence, and it must be confessed that scandalous transactions in the Senate with reference to nominations were among the few things that the country watched and talked about with keen relish and interest. This was the personal element which always had spice in it. When Senator Conkling resigned in a huff because he could not have whom he liked in the collectorship of the port of New York, the country rubbed its hands; and when the same imperious politician sought reelection as a vindication of that unconstitutional control of nominations which masqueraded as "the courtesy of the Senate," the country discussed his chances with real zest and chuckled over the whole affair in genuine glee. It was a big fight worth seeing. It would have been too bad to miss it.

Before the sentiment of reform had become strong enough to check it, this abuse of the consultative privileges of the Senate in the matter of nominations had assumed such proportions as to seem to some the ugliest deformity in our politics. It looked as if it were becoming at once the weakest and the most tried and strained joint of our federal system. If there was to be a break, would it not be there, where was the severest wear and tear? The evil practices seemed the more ineradicable because they had arisen in the most natural manner. The President was compelled, as in the case of treaties, to obtain the sanction of the Senate without being allowed any chance of consultation with it; and there soon grew up within the privacy of "executive session" an understanding that the wishes and opinions of each Senator who was of the President's own party should have more weight than even the inclinations of the majority in deciding upon the fitness or desirability of persons proposed to be appointed to offices in that Senator's State. There was the requisite privacy to shield from public condemnation the practice arising out of such an understanding; and the President himself was always quite out of earshot, hearing only of results, of final votes.

All through the direct dealings of the Senate with the President there runs this characteristic spirit of irresponsible dictation. The President may tire the Senate by dogged persistence, but he can never deal with it upon a ground of real equality. He has no real presence in the Senate. His power does not extend beyond the most general suggestion. The Senate always has the last word. No one would desire to see the President possessed of authority to overrule the decisions of the Senate, to treat with foreign powers, and appoint thousands of public officers, without any other than that shadowy responsibility which he owes to the people that elected him; but it is certainly an unfortunate feature of our government that Congress governs without being put into confidential relations with the agents through whom it governs. It dictates to another branch of the government which was intended to be coordinate and coequal with it, and over which it has no legalized authority as of a master, but only the authority of a bigger stockholder, of a monopolist indeed, of all the energetic prerogatives of the government. It is as if the Army and Navy Departments were to be made coordinate and coequal, but the absolute possession and control of all ammunition and other stores of war given to the one and denied the other. The executive is taken into partnership with the legislature upon a salary which may be withheld, and is allowed no voice in the management of the business. It is simply charged with the superintendence of the employees.

It was not essentially different in the early days when the President in person read his message to the Senate and the House together as an address, and the Senate in a body carried its reply to the executive mansion. The address was the formal communication of an outsider just as much as the message of today is, and the reply of the Senate was no less a formal document which it turned aside from its regular business to prepare. That meeting face to face was not consultation. The English Parliament does not consult with the sovereign when it assembles to hear the address from the throne.

It would, doubtless, be considered quite improper to omit from an essay on the Senate all mention of the Senate's President; and yet there is very little to be said about the Vice-President of the United States. His position is one of anomalous insignificance and curious uncertainty. Apparently he is not, strictly speaking, a part of the legislature, he is clearly not a member, yet neither is he an officer of the executive. It is one of the remarkable things about him, that it is hard to find in sketching the government any proper place to discuss him. He comes in most naturally; along with the Senate to which he is tacked; but he does not come in there for any great consideration. He is simply a judicial officer set to moderate the proceedings of an assembly whose rules he has had no voice in framing and can have no voice in changing. His official stature is not to be compared with that of the Speaker of the House of Representatives. So long as he is Vice-President, he is inseparable officially from the Senate; his importance consists in the fact that he may cease to be Vice-President. His chief dignity, next to presiding over the Senate, lies in the circumstance that he is awaiting the death or disability of the President. And the chief embarrassment in discussing his office is, that in explaining how little there is to be said about it one has evidently said all there is to say.

☆ ☆ ☆

The Executive

It is at once curious and instructive to note how we have been forced into practically amending the Constitution without constitutionally amending it. The legal processes of constitutional change are so slow and cumbersome that we have been constrained to adopt a serviceable framework of fictions which enables us easily to preserve the forms without laboriously obeying the spirit of the Constitution, which will stretch as the nation grows. It would seem that no impulse short of the impulse of self-preservation, no force less than the force of revolution, can nowadays be expected to move the cumbrous machinery of formal amendment erected in Article Five. That must be a tremendous movement of opinion which can sway two thirds of each House of Congress and the people of three fourths of the States. Mr. Bagehot has pointed out that one consequence of the existence of this next to immovable machinery "is that the most obvious evils cannot be quickly remedied," and "that a clumsy working and a curious technicality mark the politics of a rough-and-ready people. The practical arguments and legal disquisitions in America," continues he, "are often like those of trustees carrying out a misdrawn will, the sense of what they mean is good, but it can never be worked out fully or defended simply, so hampered is it by the old words of an old testament." But much the greater consequence is that we have resorted, almost unconscious of the political significance of what we did, to extra-constitutional means of modifying the federal system where it has proved to be too refined by balances of divided authority to suit practical uses, to be out of square with the main principle of its foundation, namely, government by the people through their representatives in Congress.

☆ ☆ ☆

Each branch of the government is fitted out with a small section of responsibility, whose limited opportunities afford to the conscience of each many easy escapes. Every suspected culprit may shift the responsibility upon his fellows. Is Congress rated for corrupt or imperfect or foolish legislation? It may urge that it has to follow hastily its Committees or do nothing at all but talk; how can it help it if a stupid Committee leads it unawares into unjust or fatuous enterprises? Does administration blunder and run itself into all sorts of straits? The Secretaries hasten to plead the unreasonable or unwise commands of Congress, and Congress falls to blaming the Secretaries. The Secretaries aver that the whole mischief might have been avoided if they had only been allowed to suggest the proper measures; and the men who framed the existing measures in their turn avow their despair of good government so long as they must intrust all their plans to the bungling incompetence of men who are appointed by and responsible to somebody else. How is the schoolmaster, the nation, to know which boy needs the whipping?

Moreover, it is impossible to deny that this division of authority and concealment of responsibility are calculated to subject the government to a very distressing paralysis in moments of emergency. There are few, if any, important steps that can be taken by any one branch of the government without the consent or cooperation of some other branch. Congress must act through the President and his Cabinet; the President and his Cabinet must wait upon the will of Congress. There is no one supreme, ultimate head—whether magistrate or representative body—which can decide at once and with conclusive authority what shall be done at those times when some decision there must be, and that immediately. Of course this lack is of a sort to be felt at all times, in seasons of tranquil rounds of business as well as at moments of sharp crisis; but in times of sudden exigency it might prove fatal, fatal either in breaking down the system or in failing to meet the emergency. Policy cannot be either prompt or straightforward when it must serve many masters. It must either equivocate, or hesitate, or fail altogether. It may set out with clear purpose from Congress, but get waylaid or maimed by the Executive.

If there be one principle clearer than another, it is this: that in any business, whether of government or of mere merchandising, *somebody must be trusted,* in order that when things go wrong it may be quite plain who should be punished. In order to drive trade at the speed and with the success *you* desire, you must confide without suspicion in your chief clerk, giving him the power to ruin you, because you thereby furnish him with a motive for serving you. His reputation, his own honor or disgrace, all his own commercial prospects, hang upon your success. And human nature is much the same in government as in the dry-goods trade. *Power and strict accountability for its use* are the essential constituents of good government. A sense of highest responsibility, a dignifying and elevating sense of being trusted, together with a consciousness of being in an official station so conspicuous that no faithful discharge of duty can go unacknowledged and unrewarded, and no breach of trust undiscovered and unpunished, these are the influences, the only influences, which foster practical, energetic, and trustworthy statesmanship. The best rulers are always those to whom great power is intrusted in such a manner as to make them feel that they will surely be abundantly honored and recompensed for a just and patriotic use of it, and to make them know that nothing can shield them from full retribution for every abuse of it.

It is, therefore, manifestly a radical defect in our federal system that it parcels out power and confuses responsibility as it does. The main purpose of the Convention of 1787 seems to have been to accomplish this grievous mistake. The "literary theory" of checks and balances is simply a consistent account of what our constitution-makers tried to do; and those checks and balances have proved mischievous just to the extent to which they have succeeded in establishing themselves as realities. It is quite safe to say that were it possible to call together again the members of that wonderful Convention to view the work of their hands in the light of the century that has tested it, they would be the first to admit that the only fruit of dividing power had been to make it irresponsible. It is just this that has made civil service reform tarry in this country and that makes it still almost doubtful of issue. We are in just the case that England was in before she achieved the reform for which we are striving. The date of the reform in England is no less significant than the fact. It was not accomplished until a "distinct responsibility of the Ministers of the Crown to one, and to only one, master had been established beyond all uncertainty. This is the most striking and suggestive lesson to be gathered from Mr. Eaton's interesting and valuable history of Civil Service in Great Britain. The Reform was originated in 1853 by the Cabinet of Lord Aberdeen. It sprang from the suggestion of the appointing officers, and was carried through in the face of opposition from the House of Commons, because, paradoxically enough, the Ministry had at last come to feel their responsibility to the Commons, or rather to the nation whom the Commons represented.

Those great improvements which have been made in the public service of the British empire since the days of Walpole and Newcastle have gone hand in hand with the perfecting of the system now known as responsible Cabinet government.

☆ ☆ ☆

In this country the course of the reform was quite the reverse. Neither the Executive nor Congress began it. The call for it came imperatively from the people; it was a formulated demand of public opinion made upon Congress, and it had to be made again and again, each time with more determined emphasis, before Congress heeded. It worked its way up from the convictions of the many to the purposes of the few. Amongst the chief difficulties that have stood in its way, and which still block its perfect realization, is that peculiarity of structure which I have just now pointed out as intrinsic in the scheme of divided power which runs through the Constitution. One of the conditions precedent to any real and lasting reform of the civil service, in a country whose public service is molded by the conditions of self-government, is the drawing of a sharp line of distinction between those offices which are political and those which are non-political. The strictest rules of business discipline, of merit-tenure and earned promotion, must rule every office whose incumbent has naught to do with choosing between policies; but no rules except the choice of parties can or should make and unmake, reward or punish, those officers whose privilege it is to fix upon the political purposes which administration shall be made to serve. These latter are not many under any form of government. There are said to be but fifty such at most in the civil service of Great Britain; but these fifty go in or out as the balance of power shifts from party to party. In the case of our own civil service it would, I take it, be extremely hard to determine where the line should be drawn. In all the higher grades this particular distinction is quite obscured. A doubt exists as to the Cabinet itself. Are the Secretaries political or non-political officers? It would seem that they are exclusively neither. They are at least semi-political. They are, on the one hand, merely the servants of Congress, and yet, on the other hand, they have enough freedom of discretion to mar and color, if not to choose, political ends. They can wreck plans, if they cannot make them. Should they be made permanent officials because they are mere Secretaries, or should their tenure depend upon the fortunes of parties because they have many chances to render party services? And if the one rule or the other is to be applied to them, to how many, and to which of their chief subordinates, is it to be extended? If they are not properly or necessarily party men, let them pass the examinations and run the gauntlet of the usual tests of efficiency, let errand-boys work up to Secretaryships; but if not, let their responsibility to their party be made strict and determinate. That is the cardinal point of practical civil service reform.

This doubt as to the exact *status* in the system of the chief ministers of state is a most striking commentary on the system itself. Its complete self is logical and simple. But its complete self exists only in theory. Its real self offers a surprise and presents a mystery at every change of view. The practical observer who seeks for facts and actual conditions of organization is often sorely puzzled to come at the real methods of government. Pitfalls await him on every side. If constitutional lawyers of strait-laced consciences filled Congress and officered the departments, every clause of the Constitution would be accorded a formal obedience, and it would be as easy to know beforehand just what the government will be like inside tomorrow as it is now to know what it was like outside yesterday. But neither the knowledge nor the consciences of politicians keep them very close to the Constitution; and it is with politicians that we have to deal nowadays in studying the government. Every government is largely what the men are who constitute it. If the character or opinions of legislators and administrators change from time to time, the nature of the government changes with them; and as both their characters and their opinions do change very often it is very hard to make a picture of the government which can be said to have been perfectly faithful yesterday, and can be confidently expected to be exactly accurate tomorrow. Add to these embarrassments, which may be called the embarrassments of human nature, other embarrassments such as our system affords, the embarrassments of subtle legal distinctions, a fine theoretical plan made in delicate hairlines, requirements of law which can hardly be met and can easily and naturally be evaded or disregarded, and you have in full the conception of the difficulties which attend a practical exposition of the real facts of federal administration. It is not impossible to point out what the Executive was intended to be, what it has sometimes been, or what it might be; nor is it forbidden the diligent to discover the main conditions which mold it to the forms of congressional supremacy; but more than this is not to be expected.

Conclusion

Congress always makes what haste it can to legislate. It is the prime object of its rules to expedite law-making. Its customs are fruits of its characteristic diligence in enactment. Be the matters small or great, frivolous or grave, which busy it, its aim is to have laws always a-making. Its temper is strenuously legislative. That it cannot regulate all the questions to which its attention is weekly invited is its misfortune, not its fault; is due to the human limitation of its faculties, not to any narrow circumscription of its desires. If its committee machinery is inadequate to the task of bringing to action more than one out of every hundred of the bills introduced, it is not because the quick clearance of the docket is not the motive of its organic life. If legislation, therefore, were the only or the chief object for which it should live, it would not be possible to withhold admiration from those clever hurrying rules and those inexorable customs which seek to facilitate it. Nothing but a doubt as to whether or not Congress should confine itself to law-making can challenge with a question the utility of its organization as a facile statute-devising machine.

The political philosopher of these days of self-government has, however, something more than a doubt with which to gainsay the usefulness of a sovereign representative body which confines itself to legislation to the exclusion of all other functions. Buckle declared, indeed, that the chief use and value of legislation nowadays lay in its opportunity and power to remedy the mistakes of the legislation of the past; that it was beneficent only when it carried healing in its wings; that repeal was more blessed than enactment. And it is certainly true that the greater part of the labor of legislation consists in carrying the loads recklessly or bravely shouldered in times gone by, when the animal which is now a bull was only a calf, and in completing, if they may be completed, the tasks once undertaken in the shape of unambitious schemes which at the outset looked innocent enough. Having got his foot into it, the legislator finds it difficult, if not impossible, to get it out again. . . .

Legislation unquestionably generates legislation. Every statute may be said to have a long lineage of statutes behind it; and whether that lineage be honorable or of ill repute is as much a question as to each individual statute as it can be with regard to the ancestry of each individual legislator. Every statute in its turn has a numerous progeny, and only time and opportunity can decide whether its offspring will bring it honor or shame. Once begin the dance of legislation, and you must struggle through its mazes as best you can to its breathless end, if any end there be.

It is not surprising, therefore, that the enacting, revising, tinkering, repealing of laws should engross the attention and engage the entire energy of such a body as Congress. It is, however, easy to see how it might be better employed; or, at least, how it might add others to this overshadowing function, to the might they would not make a George III. They would conquer, by dividing, the power they so much feared to see in any single hand.

"The English Constitution, in a word," says our most astute English critic, "is framed on the principle of choosing a single sovereign authority, and making it good; the American, upon the principle of having many sovereign authorities, and hoping that their multitude may atone for their inferiority."

☆ ☆ ☆

Our Constitution, like every other constitution which puts the authority to make laws and the duty of controlling the public expenditure into the hands of a popular assembly, practically sets that assembly to rule the affairs of the nation as supreme overlord. But, by separating it entirely from executive agencies, it deprives it of the opportunity and means for making its authority complete and convenient. The constitutional machinery is left of such a pattern that other forces less than that of Congress may cross and compete with Congress, though they are too small to overcome or long offset it; and the result is simply an unpleasant, wearing friction which, with other adjustments, more felicitous and equally safe, might readily be avoided.

☆ ☆ ☆

The dangers of this serious imperfection in our governmental machinery have not been clearly demonstrated in our experience hitherto; but now their delayed fulfillment seems to be close at hand. The plain tendency is towards a centralization of all the greater powers of government in the hands of the federal authorities, and towards the practical confirmation of those prerogatives of supreme overlordship which Congress has been gradually arrogating to itself. The central government is constantly becoming stronger and more active, and Congress is establishing itself as the one sovereign authority in that government. In constitutional theory and in the broader features of past practice, ours has been what Mr. Bagehot has called a "composite" government. Besides state and federal authorities to dispute as to sovereignty, there have been within the federal system itself rival and irreconcilable powers. But gradually the strong are overcoming the weak. If the signs of the times are to be credited, we are fast approaching an adjustment of sovereignty quite as "simple" as need be. Congress is not only to retain the authority it already possesses, but is to be brought again and again face to face with still greater demands upon its energy, its wisdom, and its conscience, is to have ever-widening duties and responsibilities thrust upon it, without being granted a moment's opportunity to look back from the plough to which it has set its hands.

The sphere and influence of national administration and national legislation are widening rapidly. Our populations are growing at such a rate that one's reckoning staggers at counting the possible millions that may have a home and a work on this continent ere fifty more years shall have filled their short span. The East will not always be the center of national life. The South is fast accumulating wealth, and will faster recover influence. The West has already achieved a greatness which no man can gainsay, and has in store a power of future growth which no man can estimate. Whether these sections are to be harmonious or dissentient depends almost entirely upon the methods and policy of the federal government. If that government be not careful to keep within its own proper sphere and prudent to square its policy by rules of national welfare, sectional lines must and will be known; citizens of one part of the country may look with jealousy and even with hatred upon their fellow-citizens of another part; and faction must tear and dissension distract a country which providence would bless, but which man may curse. The government of a country so vast and various must be strong, prompt, wieldy, and efficient. Its strength must consist in the certainty and uniformity of its purposes, in its accord with national sentiment, in its unhesitating action, and in its honest aims. It must be steadied and approved by open administration diligently obedient to the more permanent judgments of public opinion; and its only active agency, its representative chambers, must be equipped with something besides abundant powers of legislation.

As at present constituted, the federal government lacks strength because its powers are divided, lacks promptness because its authorities are multiplied, lacks wieldiness because its processes are roundabout, lacks efficiency because its responsibility is indistinct and its action without competent direction. It is a government in which every officer may talk about every other officer's duty without having to render strict account for not doing his own, and in which the masters are held in check and offered contradiction by the servants. Mr. Lowell has called it "government by declamation." Talk is not sobered by any necessity imposed upon those who utter it to suit their actions to their words. There is no day of reckoning for words spoken. The speakers of a congressional majority may, without risk of incurring ridicule or discredit, condemn what their own Committees are doing; and the spokesmen of a minority may urge what contrary courses they please with a well-grounded assurance that what they say will be forgotten before they can be called upon to put it into practice. Nobody stands sponsor for the policy of the government. A dozen men originate it; a dozen compromises twist and alter it; a dozen offices whose names are scarcely known outside of Washington put it into execution.

☆ ☆ ☆

An intelligent observer of our politics has declared that there is in the United States "a class, including thousands and tens of thousands of the best men in the country, who think it possible to enjoy the fruits of good government without working for them." Everyone who has seen beyond the outside of our American life must recognize the truth of this; to explain it is to state the sum of all the most valid criticisms of congressional government. Public opinion has no easy vehicle for its judgments, no quick channels for its action. Nothing about the system is direct and simple. Authority is perplexingly subdivided and distributed, and responsibility has to be hunted down in out-of-the-way corners. So that the sum of the whole matter is that the means of working for the fruits of good government are not readily to be found. The average citizen may be excused for esteeming government at best but a haphazard affair, upon which his vote and all of his influence can have but little effect. How is his choice of a representative in Congress to affect the policy of the country as regards the questions in which he is most interested, if the man for whom he votes has no chance of getting on the Standing Committee which has virtual charge of those questions? How is it to make any difference who is chosen President? Has the President any very great authority in matters of vital policy? It seems almost a thing of despair to get any assurance that any vote he may cast will even in an infinitesimal degree affect the essential courses of administration. There are so many cooks mixing their ingredients in the national broth that it seems hopeless, this thing of changing one cook at a time.

The charm of our constitutional ideal has now been long enough wound up to enable sober men who do not believe in political witchcraft to judge what it has accomplished, and is likely still to accomplish, without further winding. The Constitution is not honored by blind worship. The more open-eyed we become, as a nation, to its defects, and the prompter we grow in applying with the unhesitating courage of conviction all thoroughly-tested or well-considered expedients necessary to make self-government among us a straightforward thing of simple method, single, unstinted power, and clear responsibility, the nearer will we approach to the sound sense and practical genius of the great and honorable statesmen of 1787. And the first step towards emancipation from the timidity and false pride which have led us to seek to thrive despite the defects of our national system rather than seem to deny its perfection is a fearless criticism of that system. When we shall have examined all its parts without sentiment, and gauged all its functions by the standards of practical common sense, we shall have established anew our right to the claim of political sagacity; and it will remain only to act intelligently upon what our opened eyes have seen in order to prove again the justice of our claim to political genius.

Socialism and Democracy

Although Wilson recognized a kinship between democracy and socialism, he rejected a socialist solution for the problems of modern capitalism as impractical. His position here was consistent with the conservative cast of his political views, which moved in a progressive direction only with his entrance into active politics. While Wilson conceded a possible kinship between socialism and democracy, he rejected the former absolutely as a course of policy for a democratic government. He considered socialist ideas to be formulaic, impractical, and pernicious. At this stage Wilson showed little thoughtful concern for the economic barbarism of the times, and while he was a sharp critic of politics, he gave little energy to the analysis of the intersection of economics and politics. This unpublished essay was probably written in 1887 while he was at Bryn Mawr.

Is it possible that in practical America we are becoming sentimentalists? To judge by much of our periodical literature, one would think so. All resolution about great affairs seems now "sicklied o'er with a pale cast of thought." Our magazine writers smile sadly at the old-time optimism of their country; are themselves full of forebodings; expend much force and enthusiasm and strong (as well as weak) English style in disclosing social evils and economic bugbears; are moved by a fine sympathy for the unfortunate and a fine anger against those who bring wrong upon their fellows: but where amidst all these themes for the conscience is there a theme for the courage of the reader? Where are the brave plans of reform which should follow such prologues?

No man with a heart can withhold sympathy from the laborer whose strength is wasted and whose hope is thwarted in the service of the heartless and close-fisted; but, then, no man with a head ought to speak that sympathy in the public prints unless he have some manly, thought-out ways of betterment to propose. One wearies easily, it must be confessed, of woeful-warnings: one sighs often for a little tonic or actual thinking grounded in sane, clear-sighted perception of what is possible to be done. Sentiment is not despicable, it may be elevating and noble, it may be inspiring, and in some mental fields it is self-sufficing, but when uttered concerning great social and political questions it needs the addition of practical, initiative sense to keep it sweet and to prevent its becoming insipid.

I point these remarks particularly at current discussions of socialism, and principally of "state socialism," which is almost the only form of socialism seriously discussed among us, outside the Anti-Poverty Society. Is there not a plentiful lack of nerve and purpose in what we read and hear nowadays on this momentous topic. One might be excused for taking and keeping the impression that there can be no great need for haste in the settlement of the questions mooted in connection with it, inasmuch as the debating of them has not yet passed beyond its rhetorical and pulpit stage. It is easy to make socialism, as theoretically developed by the greater and saner socialistic writers, intelligible not only, but even attractive, as a conception; it is easy also to render it a thing of fear to timorous minds, and to make many signs of the times bear menace of it; the only hard task is to give it validity and strength as a program in practical politics. Yet the whole interest of socialism for those whose thinking extends beyond the covers of books and the paragraphs of periodicals lies in what it will mean in practice. It is a question of practical politics, or else it is only a thesis for engaging discourse.

Even mere discoursers, one would think, would be attracted to treat of the practical means of realizing for society the principles of socialism, for much the most interesting and striking features of it emerge only when its actual applications to concrete affairs are examined. These actual applications of it are the part of it which is much the most worth talking about, even for those whose only object is to talk effectively.

Roundly described, socialism is a proposition that every community, by means of whatever forms of organization may be most effective for the purpose, see to it for itself that each one of its members finds the employment for which he is best suited and is rewarded according to his diligence and merit, all proper surroundings of moral influence being secured to him by the public authority. "State socialism" is willing to act through state authority as it is at present organized. It proposes that all idea of a limitation of public authority by individual rights be put out of view, and that the State consider itself bound to stop only at what is unwise or futile in its universal superintendence alike of individual and of public interests. The thesis of the state socialist is, that no line can be drawn between private and public affairs which the State may not cross at will; that omnipotence of legislation is the first postulate of all just political theory.

Applied in a democratic state, such doctrine sounds radical, but not revolutionary. It is only an acceptance of the extremest logical conclusions deducible from democratic principles long ago received as respectable. For it is very clear that in fundamental theory socialism and democracy are almost if not quite one and the same. They both rest at bottom upon the absolute right of the community to determine its own destiny and that of its members. Men as communities are supreme over men as individuals. Limits of wisdom and convenience to the public control there may be: limits of principle there are, upon strict analysis, none.

It is of capital importance to note this substantial correspondence of fundamental conception as between socialism and democracy: a whole system of practical politics may be erected upon it without further foundation. The germinal conceptions of democracy are as free from all thought of a limitation of the public authority as are the corresponding conceptions of socialism; the individual rights which the democracy of our own century has actually observed, were suggested to it by a political philosophy radically individualistic, but not necessarily democratic. Democracy is bound by no principle of its own nature to say itself nay as to the exercise of any power. Here, then, lies the point. The difference between democracy and socialism is not an essential difference, but only a practical difference, [it] is a difference of *organization* and *policy*, not a difference of primary motive. Democracy has not undertaken the tasks which socialists clamor to have undertaken; but it refrains from them, not for lack of adequate principles or suitable motives, but for lack of adequate organization and suitable hardihood: because it cannot see its way clear to accomplishing them with credit. Moreover it may be said that democrats of today hold off from such undertakings because they are of today, and not of the days, which history very well remembers, when government had the temerity to try everything. The best thought of modern time having recognized a difference between social and political questions, democratic government, like all other governments, seeks to confine itself to those political concerns which have, in the eyes of the judicious, approved themselves appropriate to the sphere and capacity of public authority.

The socialist does not disregard the obvious lessons of history concerning overwrought government: at least he thinks he does not. He denies that he is urging the resumption of tasks which have been repeatedly shown to be impossible. He points to the incontrovertible fact that the economic and social conditions of life in our century are not only superficially but radically different from those of any other time whatever. Many affairs of life which were once easily to be handled by individuals have now become so entangled amongst the complexities of international trade relations, so confused by the multiplicity of news-voices, or so hoisted into the winds of speculation that only powerful combinations of wealth and influence can compass them. Corporations grow on every hand, and on every hand not only swallow and overawe individuals but also compete with governments. The contest is no longer between government and individuals; it is now between government and dangerous combinations and individuals. Here is a monstrously changed aspect of the social world. In face of such circumstances, must not government lay aside all timid scruple and boldly make itself an agency for social reform as well as for political control?

"Yes," says the democrat, "perhaps it must. You know it is my principle, no less than yours, that every man shall have an equal chance with every other man: if I saw my way to it as a practical politician, I should be willing to go farther and superintend every man's use of his chance. But the means? The question with me is not whether the community has power to act as it may please in these matters, but how it can act with practical advantage, a question of *policy.*"

A question of policy primarily, but also a question of organization, that is to say of *administration.*

The State

In 1889 Wilson published *The State,* the first textbook in comparative government. Considered one of his best scholarly works, it was hugely successful. It remained in use in university classrooms for a generation and was translated into several languages, including Japanese, French, Russian, Italian, Spanish, and German. The sections that follow contain ideas on government which Wilson carried with him into his political career, particularly with regard to the regulatory function of the state. It is interesting that Wilson's analysis of government here relied little on the Enlightenment theories of Hobbes, Locke, Rousseau, Montesquieu, whom he knew well, but heavily on Aristotle and the historical evolution of government forms and practices. He emphasized individual freedom limiting the reach of the state and saw the roots of the idea of freedom in the Christian idea of the individual's free relation to God. The last is an idea recently explored and affirmed by Orlando Patterson in his *Freedom in the Making of Western Culture* (1991).

Government Rests upon Authority and Force. The essential characteristic of all government, whatever its form, is authority. There must in every instance be, on the one hand, governors, and, on the other, those who are governed. And the authority of governors, directly or indirectly, rests in all cases ultimately on *force.* Government, in its last analysis, is organized force. Not necessarily or invariably organized armed force, but the will of one man, of many men, or of a community prepared by organization to realize its own purposes with reference to the common affairs of the community. Organized, that is, to rule, to dominate. The machinery of government necessary to such an organization consists of instrumentalities fitted to enforce in the conduct of the common affairs of a community the will of the sovereign man, the sovereign minority, or the sovereign majority.

Not necessarily upon Obvious Force. This analysis of government, as consisting of authority resting on force, is not, however, to be interpreted too literally, too narrowly. The force behind authority must not be looked for as if it were always to be seen or were always being exercised. That there is authority lodged with ruler or magistrate is in every case evident enough; but that that authority rests upon force is not always a fact upon the surface, and is therefore in one sense not always practically significant. In the case of any particular government, the force upon which the authority of its officers rests may never once, for generations together, take the shape of armed force. Happily there are in our own day many governments, and those among the most prominent, which seldom coerce their subjects, seeming in their tranquil noiseless operations to run themselves. They in a sense operate without the exercise of force. But there is force behind them none the less because it never shows itself. The strongest birds flap their wings the least. There are just as powerful engines in the screw-propeller, for all she glides so noiselessly, as in the side-wheeler that churns and splashes her way through the water. The better governments of our day, those which rest, not upon the armed strength of governors, but upon the free consent of the governed, are without open demonstration of force in their operations. They are founded upon constitutions and laws whose source and sanction are the will of the majority. The force which they embody is not the force of a dominant dynasty nor of a prevalent minority, but the force of an agreeing majority. And the overwhelming nature of this force is evident in the fact that the minority very seldom challenge its exercise. It is latent just because it is understood to be omnipotent. There is force behind the authority of the elected magistrate, no less than behind that of the usurping despot, a much greater force behind the President of the United States, than behind the Czar of Russia. The difference lies in the *display* of coercive power. Physical force is the prop of both, though in the one it is the last, while in the other it is the first resort.

The Governing Force in Ancient and in Modern Society. These elements of authority and force in government are thus quite plain to be seen in modern society, even when the constitution of that society is democratic; but they are not so easily discoverable upon a first view in primitive society. It is common nowadays when referring to the affairs of the most progressive nations to speak of "government by public opinion," "government by the popular voice"; and such phrases possibly describe sufficiently well all full-grown democratic systems. But no one intends such expressions to conceal the fact that the majority, which utters "public opinion," does not prevail because the minority are convinced, but because they are outnumbered and have against them not the "popular voice" only, but the "popular power" as well, that it is the potential might rather than the wisdom of the majority which gives it its right to rule. When once majorities have learned to have opinions and to organize themselves for enforcing them, they rule by virtue of power no less than do despots with standing armies or concerting minorities dominating unorganized majorities. But, though it was clearly opinion which ruled in primitive societies, this conception of the might of majorities hardly seems to fit our ideas of primitive systems of government. What shall we say of them in connection with our present analysis of government? They were neither democracies in which the will of majorities chose the ways of government, nor despotisms, in which the will of an individual controlled, nor oligarchies, in which the purposes of a minority prevailed. Where shall we place the force which lay behind the authority exercised under them? Was the power of the father in the patriarchal family power of arm, mere domineering strength of will? What was the force that sustained the authority of the tribal chieftain or of that chief of chiefs, the king? That authority was not independent of the consent of those over whom it was exercised; and yet it was not formulated by that consent. That consent may be said to have been involuntary, *inbred.* It was born of the habit of the race. It was congenital. It consisted of a custom and tradition, moreover, which bound the chief no less than it bound his subjects. He might no more transgress the unwritten law of the race than might the humblest of his fellow-tribesmen. He was governed scarcely less than they were. All were under bondage to strictly prescribed ways of life. Where then lay the force which sanctioned the authority of chief and subchief and father in this society? Not in the will of the ruler: that was bound by the prescriptions of custom. Not in the popular choice: over that too the law of custom reigned.

The Force of the Common Will in Ancient Society. The real residence of force in such societies as these can be most easily discovered if we look at them under other circumstances. Nations still under the dominion of customary law have within historical times been conquered by alien conquerors; but in no such case did the will of the conqueror have free scope in regulating the affairs of the conquered. Seldom did it have any scope at all. The alien throne was maintained by force of arms, and taxes were mercilessly wrung from the subject populations; but never did the despot venture to change the customs of the conquered land. Its native laws he no more dared to touch than would a prince of the dynasty which he had displaced. He dared not play with the forces latent in the prejudices, the fanaticism of his subjects. He knew that those forces were volcanic, and that no prop of armed men could save his throne from overthrow and destruction should they once break forth. He really had no authority to govern, but only a power to despoil, for the idea of government is inseparable from the conception of *legal regulation.* If, therefore, in the light of such cases, we conceive the throne of such a society as occupied by some native prince whose authority rested upon the laws of his country, it is plain to see that the real force upon which authority rests under a government so constituted is after all the force of public opinion, in a sense hardly less vividly real than if we spoke of a modern democracy. The law inheres in the common will: and it is that law upon which the authority of the prince is founded. He rules according to the common will: for that will is, that immemorial custom be inviolably observed. The force latent in that Common will both backs and limits his authority.

☆ ☆ ☆

The True Nature of Government. What, then, in the last analysis, is the nature of government? If it rests upon authority and force, but upon authority which depends upon the acquiescence of the general will and upon force suppressed, latent, withheld except under extraordinary circumstances, what principle lies behind these phenomena, at the heart of government? The answer is hidden in the nature of Society itself. Society is in no sense artificial; it is as truly natural and organic as the individual man himself. As Aristotle said, man is by nature a social animal; his social function is as normal with him as is his individual function. Since the family was formed, he has not been without politics, without political association. Society, therefore, is compounded of the common habit, an evolution of experience, an interlaced growth of tenacious relationships, a compact, living, organic whole, structural, not mechanical.

Society an Organism, Government an Organ. Government is merely the executive organ of society, the organ through which its habit acts, through which its will becomes operative, through which it adapts itself to its environment and works out for itself a more effective life. There is clear reason, therefore, why the disciplinary action of society upon the individual is exceptional; clear reason also why the power of the despot must recognize certain ultimate limits and bounds; and clear reason why sudden or violent changes of government lead to equally violent and often fatal reaction and revolution. It is only the exceptional individual who is not held fast in his obedience to the common habit of social duty and comity. The despot's power, like the potter's, is limited by the characteristics of the materials in which he works, of the society which he manipulates; and change which roughly breaks with the common thought will lack the sympathy of that thought, will provoke its opposition, and will inevitably be crushed by that opposition. Society, like other organisms, can be changed only by evolution, and revolution is the antipode of evolution. The public order is preserved because order inheres in the character of society.

The Forms of Government: Their Significance. The forms of government do not affect the essence of government: the bayonets of the tyrant, the quick concert and superior force of an organized minority, the latent force of a self-governed majority, all these depend upon the organic character and development of the community. "The obedience of the subject to the sovereign has its root not in contract but in force, the force of the sovereign to punish disobedience"; but that force must be backed by the general habit. The forms of government are, however, in every way most important to be observed, for the very reason that they express the character of government, and indicate its history. They exhibit the stages of political development, and make clear the necessary constituents and ordinary purposes of government, historically considered. They illustrate, too, the sanctions upon which it rests.

Aristotle's Analysis of the Forms of Government. It has been common for writers on politics in speaking of the several forms of government to rewrite Aristotle, and it is not easy to depart from the practice. For, although Aristotle's enumeration was not quite exhaustive, and although his descriptions will not quite fit modern types of government, his enumeration still serves as a most excellent frame on which to hang an exposition of the forms of government, and his descriptions at least furnish points of contrast between ancient and modern governments by observing which we can the more clearly understand the latter.

Aristotle considered Monarchy, Aristocracy, and Democracy (Ochlocracy) the three standard forms of government. The first he defined as the rule of One, the second as the rule of the Few, the third as the rule of the Many. Off against these standard and, so to say, *healthful* forms he set their degenerate shapes. Tyranny he conceived to be the degenerate shape of Monarchy, Oligarchy the degenerate shape of Aristocracy, and Anarchy (or mob-rule) the degenerate shape of Democracy. His observation of the political world about him led him to believe that there was in every case a strong, an inevitable tendency for the pure forms to sink into the degenerate.

The Cycle of Degeneracy and Revolution. He outlined a cycle of degeneracies and revolutions through which, as he conceived, every State of long life was apt to pass. His idea was this. The natural first form of government for every state would be the rule of a monarch, of the single strong man with sovereign power given him because of his strength. This monarch would usually hand on his kingdom to his children. They might confidently be expected to forget those pledges and those views of the public good which had bound and guided him. Their sovereignty would sink into tyranny. At length their tyranny would meet its decisive check at some Runnymede. There would be revolt; and the princely leaders of revolt, taking government into their own hands, would set up an Aristocracy. But aristocracies, though often public-spirited and just in their youth, always decline, in their later years, into a dotage of selfish oligarchy. Oligarchy is even more hateful to civil liberty, is even a graver hindrance to healthful civil life than tyranny. A class bent upon subserving only their own interests can devise injustice in greater variety than can a single despot: and their insolence is always quick to goad the many to hot revolution. To this revolution succeeds Democracy. But Democracy too has its old age of degeneracy, an old age in which it loses its early respect for law, its first amiability of mutual concession. It breaks out into license and Anarchy, and none but a Caesar can bring it back to reason and order. The cycle is completed. The throne is set up again, and a new series of deteriorations and revolutions begins.

Modern Contrasts to the Aristotelian Forms of Government. The confirmations of this view furnished by the history of Europe since the time of Aristotle have been striking and numerous enough to render it still oftentimes convenient as a scheme by which to observe the course of political history even in our own days. But it is still more instructive to contrast the later facts of political development with this ancient exposition of the laws of politics. Observe, then, the differences between modern and ancient types of government, and the likelihood that the historian of the future, if not of the present and the immediate past, will have to record more divergences from the cycle of Aristotle than correspondences with it.

The Modern Absolute Monarchy. Taking the Russian government of today as a type of the vast absolute Monarchies which have grown up in Europe since the death of Aristotle, it is evident that the modern monarch, if he be indeed monarch, has a much deeper and wider reach of power than had the ancient monarch. The monarch of our day is a Legislator; the ancient monarch was not. Ancient society may be said hardly to have known what legislation was. Custom was for it the law of public as well as of private life: and custom could not be enacted. At any rate ancient monarchies were not legislative. The despot issued edicts, imperative commands covering particular cases or affecting particular individuals: the Roman emperors were among the first to promulgate "constitutions," general rules of law to be applied universally. The modern despot can do more even than that. He can regulate by his command public affairs not only but private as well, can even upset local custom and bring all his subjects under uniform legislative control. Nor is he in the least bound to observe his own laws. A word, and that his own word, will set them aside: a word will abolish, a word restore, them. He is absolute over his subjects not only, ancient despots were that, but over all laws also, which no ancient despot was.

Of course these statements are meant to be taken with certain important limitations. The modern despot as well as the ancient is bound by the habit of his people. He may change laws, but he may not change life as easily; and the national traditions and national character, the rural and commercial habit of his kingdom, bind him very absolutely. The limitation is not often felt by the monarch, simply because he has himself been bred in the atmosphere of the national life and unconsciously conforms to it.

The Modern Monarchy Usually "Limited." But the present government of Russia is abnormal in the Europe of today, as abnormal as that of the Turk, a belated example of those crude forms of politics which the rest of Europe has outgrown. Turning to the other monarchies of today, it is at once plain that they present the strongest contrast possible to any absolute monarchy ancient or modern. Almost without exception in Europe, they are "limited" by the resolutions of a popular parliament. The people have a distinct and often an imperative voice in the conduct of public affairs.

Is Monarchy Now Succeeded by Aristocracy? And what is to be said of Aristotle's cycle in connection with modern monarchies? Does anyone suppose it possible that when the despotism of the Czar falls it will be succeeded by an aristocracy; or that when the modified authority of the emperors of Austria and Germany or the king of Italy still further exchanges substance for shadow, a limited class will succeed to the reality of power? Is there any longer any place between Monarchy and Democracy for Aristocracy? Has it not been crowded out?

English and Ancient Aristocracy Contrasted. Indeed, since the extension of the franchise in England to the working classes, no example of a real Aristocracy is left in the modern world. At the beginning of this century the government of England, called a "limited monarchy," was in reality an Aristocracy. Parliament and the entire administration of the kingdom were in the hands of the classes having wealth or nobility. The members of the House of Lords and the crown together controlled a majority of the seats in the House of Commons. England was "represented" by her upper classes almost exclusively. That Aristocracy has been set aside by the Reform Bills of 1832, 1867, and 1885; but it is worth while looking back to it, in order to contrast a modern type of Aristocracy with those ancient aristocracies which were present to the mind of Aristotle. An ancient Aristocracy *constituted* the state; the English aristocracy merely controlled the state.

Under the widest citizenship known even to ancient democracy less than half the adult male subjects of the state shared the franchise. The ancient Democracy itself was a government by a minority. The ancient Aristocracy was a government by a still narrower minority; and this narrow minority monopolized office and power not only, but citizenship as well. There were no citizens but they. They were the State. Everyone else existed for the state, only they were part of it. In England the case was very different. There the franchise was not confined to the aristocrats; it was only controlled by them. Nor did the aristocrats of England consider themselves the whole of the State. They were quite conscious, and quite content, that they had the State virtually in their possession; but they looked upon themselves as holding it in trust for the people of Great Britain. Their legislation was, in fact, class legislation, after a very narrow sort; but they did not think that it was. They regarded their rule as eminently advantageous to the kingdom; and they unquestionably had, or tried to have, the real interests of the kingdom at heart. They led the state, but did not constitute it.

Present and Future Prevalence of Democracy. If Aristocracy seems about to disappear, Democracy seems about universally to prevail. Ever since the rise of popular education in the last century and its vast development since have assured a thinking weight to the masses of the people everywhere, the advance of democratic opinion and the spread of democratic institutions have been most marked and most significant. They have destroyed almost all pure forms of Monarchy and Aristocracy by introducing into them imperative forces of popular thought and the concrete institutions of popular representation; and they promise to reduce politics to a single pure form by excluding all other governing forces and institutions but those of a wide suffrage and a democratic representation by reducing all forms of government to Democracy.

Differences of Form between Ancient and Modern Democracies. The differences of form to be observed between ancient and modern Democracies are wide and important. Ancient Democracies were "immediate"; ours are "mediate," that is to say, *representative.* Every citizen of the Athenian State, to take that as a type, had a right to appear and vote in proper person in the popular assembly, and in those committees of that assembly which acted as criminal courts; the modern voter votes for a representative who is to sit for him in the popular chamber, he himself has not even the right of entrance there. This idea of representation, even the idea of a vote by proxy, was hardly known to the ancients; among us it is all-pervading.

Even the elected magistrate of an ancient Democracy was not looked upon as a representative of his fellow-citizens. *He was the State,* so far as his functions went, and so long as his term of office lasted. He could break through all law or custom, if he dared. It was only when his term had expired and he was again a private citizen that he could be called to account. There was no impeachment while in office. To our thought all elected to office, whether Presidents, ministers, or legislators, are representatives. The limitations as to the size of the state involved in the absence from ancient conception of the principle of representation is obvious. A State in which all citizens were also legislators must of necessity be small. The modern representative state has no such limitation. It may cover a continent.

Nature of Democracy, Ancient and Modern. The differences of nature to be observed between ancient and modern Democracies are no less wide and important. The ancient Democracy was a class government. As already pointed out, it was only a broader Aristocracy. Its franchise was at widest an exclusive privilege, extending only to a minority. There were slaves under its heel; there were even freedmen who could never hope to enter its citizenship. Class subordination was of the essence of its constitution. From the modern Democratic State, on the other hand, both slavery and class subordination are excluded as inconsistent with its theory, not only, but, more than that, as antagonistic to its very being. Its citizenship is as wide as its native population; its suffrage as wide as its qualified citizenship, it knows no non-citizen class. And there is still another difference between the Democracy of Aristotle and the Democracy of de Tocqueville and Bentham. The citizens of the former lived for the State; the citizen of the latter lives for himself, and the State is for him. The modern Democratic State exists for the sake of the individual; the individual, in Greek conception, lived for the State. The ancient State recognized no personal rights, all rights were State rights; the modern State recognizes no State rights which are independent of personal rights.

Growth of the Democratic Idea. In making the last statement embrace "the ancient State" irrespective of kind and "the modern State," of whatever form, I have pointed out what I conceive to be the cardinal difference between all the ancient forms of government and all the modern. It is a difference which I have already stated in another way. The *democratic idea* has penetrated more or less deeply all the advanced systems of government, and has penetrated them in consequence of that change of thought which has given to the individual an importance quite independent of his membership of a State. I can here only indicate the historical steps of that change of thought; I cannot go at any length into its causes.

Subordination of the Individual in the Ancient State. We have seen that, in the history of political society, if we have read that history aright, the rights of government, the magistracies and subordinations of kinship, antedate what we now call the rights of the individual. A man was at first nobody to himself; he was only the kinsman of somebody else. The father himself, or the chief, commanded only because of priority in kinship: to that all rights of all men were relative. Society was the unit; the individual the fraction. Man existed for society. He was all his life long in tutelage; only society was old enough to take charge of itself. The state was the only Individual.

Individualism of Christianity and Teutonic Institutions. There was no essential change in this idea for centuries. Through all the developments of government down to the time of the rise of the Roman Empire the State continued, in the conception of the western nations at least, to eclipse the individual. Private rights had no standing as against the State. Subsequently many influences combined to break in upon this immemorial conception. Chief among these influences were Christianity and the institutions of the German conquerors of the fifth century. Christianity gave each man a magistracy over himself by insisting upon his personal, individual responsibility to God. For right living, at any rate, each man was to have only his own conscience as a guide. In these deepest matters there must be for the Christian an individuality which no claim of his State upon him could rightfully be suffered to infringe. The German nations brought into the Romanized and partially Christianized world of the fifth century an individuality of another sort, the idea of allegiance to individuals. Perhaps their idea that each man had a money-value which must be paid by anyone who might slay him also contributed to the process of making men units instead of state-fractions; but their idea of personal allegiance played the more prominent part in the transformation of society which resulted from their western conquests. The Roman knew no allegiance save allegiance to his State. He swore fealty to his *imperator* as to a representative of that State, not as to an individual. The Teuton, on the other hand, bound himself to his leader by a bond of personal service which the Roman either could not understand or understood only to despise. There were, therefore, individuals in the German State: great chiefs or warriors with a following *(comitatus)* of devoted volunteers ready to die for them in frays not directed by the state, but of their own provoking. There was with all German tribes freedom of individual movement and combination within the ranks, a wide play of individual initiative. When the German settled down as master amongst the Romanized populations of western and southern Europe, his thought was led captive by the conceptions of the Roman law, as all subsequent thought that has known it has been, and his habits were much modified by those of his new subjects; but this strong element of individualism was not destroyed by the contact. It lived to constitute one of the chief features of the Feudal System.

The Transitional Feudal System. The Feudal System was made up of elaborate gradations of personal allegiance. The only State possible under that system was a disintegrate [*sic*] state embracing not a unified people, but a nation atomized into its individual elements. A king there might be, but he was lord, not of his people, but of his barons. He was himself baron also, and as such had many a direct subject pledged to serve him; but as king the barons were his only direct subjects; and the barons were heedful of their allegiance to him only when he could make it to their interest to be so, or their peril not to be. They were the kings of the people, who owed direct allegiance to them alone, and to the king only through them. Kingdoms were only greater baronies, baronies lesser kingdoms. One small part of the people served one baron, another part served another baron. As a whole they served no one master. They were not a whole: they were jarring, disconnected segments of a nation. Every man had his own lord, and antagonized everyone who had not the same lord as he.

Rise of the Modern State. Such a system was, of course, fatal to peace and good government, but it cleared the way for the rise of the modern State by utterly destroying the old conception of the State. The State of the ancients had been an entity in itself, an entity to which the entity of the individual was altogether subordinate. The Feudal State was merely an aggregation of individuals, a loose bundle of separated series of men knowing no common aim or action. It not only had no actual unity: it had no thought of unity. National unity came at last, in France, for instance, by the subjugation of the barons by the king; in England by the joint effort of people and barons against the throne, but when it came it was the ancient unity with a difference. Men were no longer State fractions; they had become State integers. The State *seemed* less like a natural organism and more like a deliberately organized association. Personal allegiance to kings had everywhere taken the place of native membership of a body politic. Men were now subjects, not citizens.

Renaissance and Reformation. Presently came the thirteenth century with its wonders of personal adventure and individual enterprise in discovery, piracy, and trade. Following hard upon these, the Renaissance woke men to a philosophical study of their surroundings, and above all of their long-time unquestioned systems of thought. Then arose Luther to reiterate the almost forgotten truths of the individuality of men's consciences, the right of individual judgment. Ere long the new thoughts had penetrated to the masses of the people. Reformers had begun to cast aside their scholastic weapons and come down to the common folk about them, talking their own vulgar tongue and craving their acquiescence in the new doctrines of deliverance from mental and spiritual bondage to Pope or Schoolman. National literatures were born. Thought had broken away from its exclusion in cloisters and universities and had gone out to challenge the people to a use of their own minds. By using their minds, the people gradually put away the childish things of their days of ignorance, and began to claim a part in affairs. Finally, systematized popular education has completed the story. Nations are growing up into manhood. Peoples are becoming old enough to govern themselves.

The Modern Force of Majorities. It is thus no accident, but the outcome of great permanent causes, that there is no more to be found among the civilized races of Europe any satisfactory example of Aristotle's Monarchies and Aristocracies. The force of modern governments is not now often the force of minorities. It is getting to be more and more the force of majorities. The sanction of every rule not founded upon sheer military despotism is the consent of a thinking people. Military despotisms are now seen to be necessarily ephemeral. Only monarchs who are revered as seeking to serve their subjects are any longer safe upon their thrones. Monarchies exist only by democratic consent.

New Character of Society. And, more than that, the result has been to give to society a new integration. The common habit is now operative again, not in acquiescence and submission merely, but in initiative and progress as well. Society is not the organism it once was, its members are given freer play, fuller opportunity for origination; but its organic character is again prominent. It is the Whole which has emerged from the disintegration of feudalism and the specialization of absolute monarchy. The Whole, too, has become self-conscious, and by becoming self-directive has set out upon a new course of development.

☆ ☆ ☆

The Objects of Government

Character of the Subject. Political interest and controversy center nowhere more acutely than in the question, What are the proper objects of government? This is one of those difficult questions upon which it is possible for many sharply opposed views to be held apparently with almost equal weight of reason. Its central difficulty is this, that it is a question which can be answered, if answered at all, only by the aid of a broad and careful wisdom whose conclusions are based upon the widest possible inductions from the facts of political experience in all its phases. Such wisdom is of course quite beyond the capacity of most thinkers and actors in the field of politics; and the consequence has been that this question, perhaps more than any the few selected by society itself but the few selected by arbitrary fortune, must be under either the direct or the indirect control of society. To society alone can the power of dominating combination belong: and society cannot suffer any of its members to enjoy such a power for their own private gain independently of its own strict regulation or oversight.

☆ ☆ ☆

Control not necessarily Administration. Society can by no means afford to allow the use for private gain and without regulation of undertakings necessary to its own healthful and efficient operation and yet of a sort to exclude equality in competition. Experience has proved that the self-interest of those who have controlled such undertakings for private gain is not coincident with the public interest: even enlightened self-interest may often discover means of illicit pecuniary advantage in unjust discriminations between individuals in the use of such instrumentalities. But the proposition that the government should control such dominating organizations of capital may by no means be wrested to mean by any necessary implication that the government should itself administer those instrumentalities of economic action which cannot be used except as monopolies. . . . Government regulation may in most cases suffice. Indeed, such are the difficulties in the way of establishing and maintaining careful business management on the part of the government, that control ought to be preferred to direct administration in as many cases as possible, in every case in which control without administration can be made effectual.

Equalization of Competition. There are some things outside the field of natural monopolies in which individual action cannot secure equalization of the conditions of competition; and in these also, as in the regulation of monopolies, the practice of governments, of our own as well as of others, has been decisively on the side of governmental regulation. By forbidding child labor, by supervising the sanitary conditions of factories, by limiting the employment of women in occupations hurtful to their health, by instituting official tests of the purity or the quality of goods sold, by limiting hours of labor in certain trades, by a hundred and one limitations of the power of unscrupulous or heartless men to out-do the scrupulous and merciful in trade or industry, government has assisted equity. Those who would act in moderation and good conscience in cases where moderation and good conscience, to be indulged, require an increased outlay of money, in better ventilated buildings, in greater care as to the quality of goods, etc., cannot act upon their principles so long as more grinding conditions for labor or more unscrupulous use of the opportunities of trade secure to the unconscientious an unquestionable and sometimes even a permanent advantage; they have only the choice of denying their consciences or retiring from business. In scores of such cases government has intervened and will intervene; but by way, not of interference, by way, rather, of making competition equal between those who would rightfully conduct enterprise and those who barely conduct it. It is in this way that society protects itself against permanent injury and deterioration, and secures healthful equality of opportunity for self-development.

Society greater than Government. Society, it must always be remembered, is vastly bigger and more important than its instrument, Government. Government should serve Society, by no means rule or dominate it. Government should not be made an end in itself; it is a means only, a means to be freely adapted to advance the best interests of the social organism. The State exists for the sake of Society, not Society for the sake of the State.

Natural Limits to State Action. And that there are natural and imperative limits to state action no one who seriously studies the structure of society can doubt. The limit of state functions is the limit of *necessary co-operation* on the part of Society as a whole, the limit beyond which such combination ceases to be imperative for the public good and becomes merely convenient for industrial or social enterprise. Co-operation is necessary in the sense here intended when it is indispensable to the equalization of the conditions of endeavor, indispensable to the maintenance of uniform rules of individual rights and relationships, indispensable because to omit it would inevitably be to hamper or degrade some for the advancement of others in the scale of wealth and social standing.

There are relations in which men invariably have need of each other, in which universal co-operation is the indispensable condition of even tolerable existence. Only some universal authority can make opportunities equal as between man and man. The divisions of labor and the combinations of commerce may for the most part be left to contract, to free individual arrangement, but the equalization of the conditions which affect all alike may no more be left to individual initiative than may the organization of government itself. Churches, clubs, corporations, fraternities, guilds, partnerships, unions have for their ends one or another special enterprise for the development of man's spiritual or material well-being: they are all more or less advisable. But the family and the state have as their end a general enterprise for the betterment and equalization of the conditions of individual development: they are indispensable.

The point at which public combination ceases to be imperative is of course not susceptible of clear indication in general terms; but it is not on that account indistinct. The bounds of family association are not indistinct because they are marked only by the immaturity of the young and by the parental and filial affections, things not all of which are defined in the law. The rule that the state should do nothing which is equally possible under equitable conditions to optional associations is a sufficiently clear line of distinction between governments and corporations. Those who regard the state as an optional, conventional union simply, a mere partnership, open wide the doors to the worst forms of socialism. Unless the state has a nature which is quite clearly defined by that invariable, universal, immutable mutual interdependence which runs beyond the family relations and cannot be satisfied by family ties, we have absolutely no criterion by which we can limit, except arbitrarily, the activities of the state. The criterion supplied by the native necessity of state relations, on the other hand, banishes such license of state action.

The state, for instance, ought not to supervise private morals because they belong to the sphere of separate individual responsibility, not to the sphere of mutual dependence. Thought and conscience are private. Opinion is optional. The state may intervene only where common action, uniform law are indispensable. Whatever is merely convenient is optional, and therefore not an affair for the state. Churches are spiritually convenient; joint-stock companies are capitalistically convenient; but when the state constitutes itself a church or a mere business association it institutes a monopoly no better than others. It should do nothing which is not in any case both indispensable to social or industrial life and necessarily monopolistic.

The Family and the State. It is the proper object of the family to mold the individual, to form him in the period of immaturity in the practice of morality and obedience. This period of subordination over, he is called out into an independent, self-directive activity. The ties of family affection still bind him, but they bind him with silken, not with iron bonds. He has left his "minority" and reached his "majority." It is the proper object of the state to give leave to his individuality, in order that that individuality may add its quota of variety to the sum of national activity. Family discipline is variable, selective, formative: it must lead the individual. But the state must not lead. It must create conditions, but not mold individuals. Its discipline must be invariable, uniform, impersonal. Family methods rest upon individual inequality, state methods upon individual equality. Family order rests upon tutelage, state order upon franchise, upon privilege.

The State and Education. In one field the state would seem at first sight to usurp the family function, the field, namely, of education. But such is not in reality the case. Education is the proper office of the state for two reasons, both of which come within the principles we have been discussing. Popular education is necessary for the preservation of those conditions of freedom, political and social, which are indispensable to free individual development. And, in the second place, no instrumentality less universal in its power and authority than government can secure popular education. In brief, in order to secure popular education the action of society as a whole is necessary; and popular education is indispensable to that equalization of the conditions of personal development which we have taken to be the proper object of society. Without popular education, moreover, no government that rests upon popular action can long endure: the people must be schooled in the knowledge, and if possible in the virtues, upon which the maintenance and success of free institutions depend. No free government can last in health if it lose hold of the traditions of its history, and in the public schools these traditions may be and should be sedulously preserved, carefully replanted in the thought and consciousness of each successive generation.

Historical Conditions of Governmental Action. Whatever view be taken in each particular case of the rightfulness or advisability of state regulation and control, one rule there is which may not be departed from under any circumstances, and that is the rule of historical continuity. In politics nothing radically novel may safely be attempted. No result of value can ever be reached in politics except through slow and gradual development, the careful adaptations and nice modifications of growth. Nothing may be done by leaps. More than that, each people, each nation, must live upon the lines of its own experience. Nations are no more capable of borrowing experience than individuals are. The histories of other peoples may furnish us with light, but they cannot furnish us with conditions of action. Every nation must constantly keep in touch with its past: it cannot run towards its ends around sharp corners.

Summary. This, then, is the sum of the whole matter: the end of government is the facilitation of the objects of society. The rule of governmental action is necessary cooperation; the method of political development is conservative adaptation, shaping old habits into new ones, modifying old means to accomplish new ends.

The English Constitution

Wilson combined his talents as historian and political scientist in this essay on the development of the English constitution. His admiration for the British system of government is clear here, as it is in much of his other writing. Wilson had been a careful student and admirer of Walter Bagehot's work on the English constitution and doubtless had him in mind during this effort. He traced the roots of the English constitution back to Teutonic law and custom and its evolution in the centuries after the Norman conquest. He judged the unwritten English constitution as stable as the American and noted that the relative ease with which it could be altered gave it more flexibility. The essay was published in installments from October 1890 to January 1891 in *The Chautauquan.*

Take it all in all, the English Constitution must be conceded to be at once the most interesting and the most important in existence, whether for the student of history or for the student of politics. It has certain irresistible claims to preeminence. It is by many centuries the oldest among free constitutions. Its history leads the student by slow, orderly, and easily distinguishable stages, out of the antique polity of the Teutonic races, through the complex order of the Middle Ages, to the institutions now everywhere in vogue among advanced nations, as if it had been planned beforehand as an object-lesson in normal political development. And its structure and principles have accordingly become models for the imitation of all who, less privileged in the conditions of growth, have in these latest times felt it needful to have like generous measure of political liberty and to adopt like open and efficient organization of popular power.

It was natural that the Constitution of England should be chosen as a model by European reformers. It is in one sense essentially a European constitution; it differs from other European constitutions chiefly in having been left freer to grow along normal lines than they were. It got its full development before the age of railways and steam navigation brought nations close together despite distances once formidable and seas once dangerous, before there was talk of bridging or tunneling the Channel; there had been water enough, therefore, between it and the Continent to give it leave to be independent and individual in its growth. It was not separated from European influences; these reached it and enriched its life in as great abundance and with as complete potency as could have been desired; but it was separated from European disaster. A sea stood between it and the fell sweep of European wars and revolutions. It sufficed that England should become a naval power; it was not necessary that she should become a military encampment. Civil war she did not escape; revolutions she did undergo; but she was delivered by nature from that international compulsion which forced France to become a centralized military despotism. The parties which contended for supremacy within her sea borders were not able to get effectual foreign assistance such as every civil war on the Continent showed to be inevitable where impassible [*sic*] natural barriers did not give imperative pause to neighborly jealousy and rivalry. In short, England had the inestimable advantage of being an easily defensible island, and of being privileged, in consequence, to live her own life in her own way.

☆ ☆ ☆

The history of the English Constitution, as has already been said, begins with primitive Teutonic institutions. Of the character of these we have no detailed information. Caesar, in a few compact sentences of his Commentaries, sums up what he had learned from the Gauls of the institutions of the German tribes; Tacitus, writing a century and half later, gives a much fuller, though generalized, account of the life and government of the Germans, who were much better known in his time than in Caesar's; we have the accounts of much later writers like Bede and Nithard of the knowledge current in their day of Saxon institutions; we have codes of law possessed by Teutonic peoples in times near enough the century in which the Angles and Saxons conquered Britain to render it safe to search them for fragments and suggestions of a polity still more antique. Viewed in the light of such sources of information, it is plain that the Teutonic peoples that conquered Britain in the fifth and sixth centuries, had been organized in their homelands into more or less distinct and independent tribes, often cooperating, sometimes confederated, conscious of kinship, and gradually suffering themselves to be forced into some sort of coalescence or consolidation by pressure from without or by common efforts of conquest; but still separately organized, in some points differently organized, and maintaining each its virtual independence.

Each tribe, when maintaining a life of its own, possessed its distinct domain, its own broad clearings, round about which the country was laid waste, to hold all rival neighbors at arm's length. The characteristic unit of organization within the tribe was the village community, a settlement, doubtless, of a group of kinsmen or of closely related families whose lands were cultivated in accordance with the customary rules of some equitable system of apportionment, as common property allotted for certain periods to individual freemen for their separate use. Each village had its own assembly, through which the land allotments were effected, local by-laws passed, and all strictly communal administrative affairs attended to. But, although thus freely self-governed in small things touching only its own interests, it was in all larger matters subject to the authority of the tribe. Some tribes had kings, others had none; and even where there were kings the kingly office was one of more dignity than power. The king, of course, took precedence of all others in dignity; he presided in the general council, for he represented the unity of the tribe; he received special gifts, and was distinguished by a special retinue. But, whether there were a king in the tribe or not, authority rested with the great tribal council. This consisted of all the free men of the tribe, gathered, with their arms in their hands, in the open air at some sacred rendezvous. It elected the magistrates, or chiefs, who were to preside over the administration of the several villages and other divisions of the tribal domain. It chose the king himself, as the tribe's general representative head. It made sovereign decision of all great questions. Trivial matters of mere administration were determined by the elected chiefs of the several districts, acting as a sort of national board; and to this board belonged also the function of preparing the business which was to come before the council itself.

For judicial purposes, the villages were combined into areas larger than the single villages, areas which the Latin writers call *pagi* and which resemble the later "hundreds" which we shall find in England. For each of these districts a court sat, whose president was one of the local magistrates elected by the tribal council and in which committees of the whole body of free landowners of the district served as judges and jurors combined. In such courts, made up of the representative free villagers, were all important disputes between man and man adjudged, all crimes declared and punished.

We have here, certainly, a very attractive type of free constitution. It shows us a manly, self-reliant race, observant of individual equality and independence, combining for common purposes without subserviency to a central power, possessing an easy capacity of informal and yet efficient combination, wedded to communal self-government and yet conscious of tribal unity and subordinated in all major interests to tribal authority, singularly cohesive and yet notably free.

Free and democratic as was the primitive Teutonic constitution it early developed germs of change which were to give it a character of a very different sort. The village assembly, the district court, the tribal council, were all bodies of free men and spoke a direct democratic power. But not everyone was free even in those primitive communities. There were those who, though not slaves, were not their own masters but were bound to the soil which they cultivated, forced tenants, so to say; bound to their holdings and obliged to turn over to the masters of the soil a fixed proportion of its produce. Below this half servile class, again, were numbers of veritable slaves, prisoners of war or men condemned for debt or crime.

Nor were all free men equal in social status or privilege. Some were *eorls,* distinguished by reason of descent from god or hero or by reason of special service to the tribe; others were *ceorls* merely, simple freemen, of the rank and file of freedom. The *eorl* received more land in the allotment than did the *ceorl* and probably commanded the services of a larger number of the half servile class by which the land was tilled. It was doubtless generally an *eorl* who was picked out by the tribal assembly to exercise magisterial authority in the village or to preside over the courts. Although thus privileged and distinguished, however, in virtue of his noble blood, the *eorl* was not more free than the *ceorl.* His privileges were vouchsafed him by custom and election only, and his political rights were no whit greater than those of the humblest *ceorl.* His precedence was honorary, like that of the king. Whoever was elected by the tribal assembly, however, to be chief magistrate of his village, president of his neighborhood court, at once attained to privileges of very substantial advantage. He could maintain his *comitatus,* his household of personal followers. It was the habit of the young men of the tribe to attach themselves to such chiefs as their personal following, apprentices in arms and in the public service. The relationship thus established was exceedingly close and intimate. The members of a *comitatus* entered the household of their leader, ate at his board, did him household service. He fitted them out for the field of battle, where they were at once defenders of his person and rivals of his prowess in arms. Their adhesion to him was voluntary; the chief of most liberality and repute had the largest *comitatus,* and herein was the germ of an ascendency which needed only opportunity to overwhelm the democratic principle of the older polity.

When the tribal assembly declared war it also elected a commander of the host and gave him authority for the campaign. Commonly, no doubt, the man chosen was already a chief, the trusted leader of a numerous *comitatus.* His election to supreme command would naturally swell his following and increase his opportunity for influence and power. Similar elections picked out the leaders who were to head organized expeditions for plunder or in search of new settlements. Hengest and Horsa the notable chiefs of the great expedition which represents for us the beginning of the conquest of Britain by the tribes which were to make it English land, we may regard as just such leaders, men of first repute in arms, of tested courage and unfailing resources, of quick, unhesitating, unerring initiative, and therefore chosen leaders, followed with devoted ardor, heeded with trustful obedience, and yet fellows among the men of their host, not masters.

But conquest quickened many momentous tendencies and inaugurated a profound transformation of the entire polity of the conquerors. The authority of the leaders could not be taken away so soon as the first struggle for a foothold on the island was over: it was necessary that it should continue undiminished in order that the work of conquest might be extended and made good. The invaders were for a long time an encamped host in the new land, not peaceful settlers privileged to resume their wonted practices of simple communal self-rule. Their leaders were virtual kings from the first; they established kingdoms, not commonwealths, in Britain; and the polity which they founded there has ever since been crowned by a throne.

The change was not sudden, but gradual, no doubt at the time imperceptible. Every freeman of the host received his share, of course, of the land he had helped to win, and the old forms of settlement and government were very faithfully continued. The territory was divided upon the basis of the immemorial division of the host into hundreds, to every hundred warriors and their families so great a district; and this districting of the land among the hundreds served to reproduce the old judicial system. The districts themselves came to be called "hundreds," and for each hundred there was a court to try all cases whether civil or criminal. Within the hundred, as its constituent parts, were "townships," in whose organization and functions the primitive self-governing village-community re-appears. Each township had its own town *moot,* or meeting, and its own elected magistrate, the reeve, and was in all things of local concern self-directed, a wee democratic commonwealth. Its priest, its reeve, and four men selected in town-meeting represented it in the membership of the hundred court. Above and combining township and hundred was the great *folkmoot,* the assembly of the kingdom to which all freemen were at liberty to go, in which every freeman was at liberty to vote.

☆ ☆ ☆

Meanwhile the national parts of the English Constitution were growing, and these were destined after a while to give to the old principles of popular self-rule a new life and potency. When the Angles and Jutes and Saxons first made their settlements in Britain they established, not one kingdom, of course, but a group of small kingdoms. To these the Danes afterward added others. The great problem of the early centuries of English history, as everybody knows, was how to make out of these several separate and hostile powers a single national whole. Before the Normans came, in 1066, that problem had been solved: England had been united and needed only the compulsion and the organizing skill of the greater kings of the new foreign line, like William the Conqueror and Henry II, to give to her life and her politics a veritable national unity. Each petty Saxon or Anglian kingdom had had its *folkmoot;* when the several kingdoms were united there sprang into existence, as the council of the united realm, a great *Witenagemot.* The constituent kingdoms, many of which became the modern shires of England, retained their own councils, but these were presided over by ealdormen, chosen by the Witenagemot and by sheriffs who were deputies of the king. The Witenagemot (whose name signifies a meeting of the *Witan,* wise) consisted, possibly, in theory at least, of all the possessors of freehold land who chose to attend, after the model of the folkmoot of the smaller kingdoms; but, as a matter of fact, it was attended only by the king, the ealdormen, or governors of shires, the king's thegns, the bishops, abbots, and generally the *principes* and *sapientes* of the kingdom," who often made up a body of from ninety to a hundred members. Ecclesiastical members had been very early admitted to such councils. The church, with its uniform and centralized organization, unbroken by any line of division between kingdom and kingdom, had been England's first pattern of unity. Churchmen had become extensive landholders, and the bishop as well as the ealdorman had his thegns. Bishops and abbots were in reality of the nobility, as well as of the hierarchy of the church. The bishops were even associated with the ealdorman and the sheriff in the presidency of the *shiremoots*.

The powers of the Witenagemot were very great in theory, and in the presence of a weak or complaisant king very great, no doubt, in practice also. The old principle was persistently maintained that the king must owe his throne to election, and sometimes the election was more than a form. There were grants to be made from the public lands; there were great offices, like that of ealdorman, to be filled; there were taxes to be levied, high crimes and misdemeanors to be tried, disputes among the greater nobles to be adjudged; there was law to be created, and in all these things the advice of the Witenagemot carried more or less imperative weight. The king, however, grew more and more powerful; the common lands, once known as folk land, gradually came to be known as *crown* lands; such great offices as did not become hereditary were filled generally as the king would; in most matters the Witenagemot had only a power of sanction instead of a power of determination; still it did not become a mere shadow, and it was in the fullness of time to grow into a parliament.

When the Normans came they changed the substance of many things but they preserved the old forms. William wished to seem to come to the throne by lawful succession and submitted to the form of election by the Witenagemot. He hastened and completed the feudalization which already had gone so far, establishing the principle that every man held his land of the king; and by wholesale confiscation of the estates of all Englishmen who seriously resisted the establishment of his rule he filled the chief holdings with Normans. The council he drew about him, therefore, and in which he doubtless sought to preserve the organization of the Witenagemot, was a council of Norman barons and of the chief officers of the Norman court, more like a continental gathering of great feudatories than like the Saxon body which it had displaced. This Council, however, whether we see in it a continuation of the Witenagemot or not, is in one sense the most interesting and important body of English constitutional history. It contained within itself, in germ at least, all the chief parts of the present English Constitution. From it were to spring, in course of time, the Courts of Law, Parliament, and the Cabinet of Ministers which directs the business of Parliament and is the responsible executive body of the modern realm, the modern empire of England.

An outline of this evolution may be briefly given. Although the custom of summoning the Great Council, as we must now call the successor to the Witenagemot, continued to be observed reign after reign, it was manifestly impossible, on grounds of convenience, that so large and miscellaneous a body should be frequently summoned or made to serve as an ordinary council to give advice upon the daily conduct of the public business. It very naturally came to be the practice of the king to consult upon such matters those members of the Great Council who were constantly near his person, the thegns and officials of the court. These advisers were constantly accessible, not only, but were also, of course, familiarly acquainted with the greater part of the affairs to be decided. There sprang up thus, almost inevitably, an inner circle of councilors, a smaller Permanent Council. Scarcely had this Permanent Council come into existence, moreover, when again naturally and in obedience to the dictates of convenience, a further specialization of functions began. Some members of the Council were assigned specially to business connected with the finances; others were given separate charge of the judicial determination of cases coming up to the king for decision; and the several high officers of the Royal Household began to be associated with these several committees according as their functions were of the one kind or the other. It was in this way that the courts of law as we know them sprang into existence. At first very much resembling committees of the Permanent Council, they gradually acquired a complete separateness from that body and a complete independence of it, having a membership peculiarly their own and a jurisdiction much enlarged beyond that of the body to which they had once belonged. They were, moreover, separate from and independent of one another. A Court of King's Bench followed the king wherever he went within the kingdom, hearing all cases not specially assigned to other tribunals and supervising the local administration of justice; a Court of Common Pleas heard all suits between subject and subject; a Court of Exchequer all suits in which the Crown was directly interested, and a Court of Chancery supplied all with remedies for whom the other courts had no means of redress.

The Cabinet of Ministers was evolved out of the Permanent Council in a very similar manner. Even the Permanent Council proved to be inconveniently large for frequent consultation; some of its members, moreover, enjoyed the king's confidence in a higher degree than did others and were often selected by him as his advisers in affairs of special secrecy or importance. He thus, by slow, almost insensible, accretions of practice, drew about him still another "inner circle"—this time an inner circle of the Permanent Council, not of the Great Council—which was in course of time distinguished as the Privy Council. The permanent Council as a council thus disappears, superseded on the several sides of its activity by its parts. Nor was that the end of the differentiation process. The same forces that created within the Permanent Council a Privy Council produced within the Privy Council a Cabinet which in course of time has absorbed all executive function and left the greater body from which it was derived without any thing to do which it as a whole can insist upon doing. The Cabinet, like the Privy Council, was at first simply a small body of persons selected by the sovereign for special confidences out of the general body of his accredited counselors. Its name came to it because of the fact that this committee of special advisers was generally closeted with the king in a small room, or "cabinet," apart from the large chamber in which sat the Council itself. To this day, although the Privy Council, which still exists in name, is never called together as a whole or consulted in any matter, the Cabinet in theory owes its authority in executive matters to the fact that its members are members also of the Privy Council.

None of these developments took place suddenly or abruptly, of course, but in the slowness of time. The differentiation and development of the courts began early in the twelfth century and were not complete till the middle of the fourteenth. The Privy Council does not emerge from the Permanent Council until about the middle of the fifteenth century (time of Henry VI). The Cabinet comes very slowly into view. It does not assume definite shape before the reign of Charles I, does not assume its present functions before the time of Sir Robert Walpole, and has not attained its present organization and importance or been subjected to its present complete responsibility to Parliament before the close of our own revolution. It was the Cabinet as a link between the Crown and the legislature that our constitution-makers did not understand when they copied the English Constitution in the Convention of 1787.

Meanwhile the Great Council from whose history we turned to trace the development of the Permanent and Privy Councils and of the Courts of Law, had had its own growth, its own changes of composition and character, and that enlargement of sphere and power which were to make it over into the modern Parliament. The Great Council was at first, so to say, all House of Lords; there were no commoners in it, but only the earls and the greater barons, and the high officials of state and church; and this constitution of the national body was suffered to suffice for more than a century. Then, however, a distinct effort was made to bring the rest of the nation into representation in it. The barons made John promise in Magna Charta (A.D. 1215) that he would summon the lesser nobles, as well as the greater, to his parliaments; but the lesser barons would not come; they were not interested enough, and it was too expensive. Representation was resorted to, therefore. The county courts (the successors of the old shire-moots) elected representatives from the county gentry to go up as "Knights of the Shire" and attend Parliament. In 1265 Simon of Montfort, having temporarily triumphed over Henry III and assumed control of the government, summoned Parliament and directed that representatives (burgesses) be sent from the towns as well as from the counties, because he knew that the towns-people would support him. Edward I continued the arrangement because he wanted representatives of the towns to be present in Parliament to promise him taxes. It was in this way, not at all deliberately planned beforehand, that Parliament obtained the present elements of its membership. At first the lesser clergy also were privileged to send representatives to Parliament, but the privilege was not much or long used. The clergy preferred to sit apart in their own separate "convocations" and there vote the taxes they were called upon to contribute. Only the bishops retained their place in Parliament.

The evolution of the part played by Parliament in legislation is both curious and interesting. In the early days the laws were said to be enacted by the sovereign with consent of his Great Council. It is still, indeed, the form in England to regard the Crown as the source of law and to describe Parliament, not as making, but as assenting to legislation, although it has now been a very long time since this form corresponded with the facts. At first it did correspond with the facts fairly well; it came to be an established principle that all laws which the king proposed should be sanctioned by the lay and ecclesiastical magnates of the kingdom gathered in the Great Council. And when the representatives of the counties and towns were called to Parliament they were not at once put upon a footing of equality with the bishops and barons in this great function. It was not until the fourteenth century that two separate Houses were developed, a House of Lords and a House of Commons. During a long transitional period the several classes of members, new and old, would seem to have sat together. Probably, however, they did not vote as a single body; and not even after their differentiation into two Houses were the knights and burgesses who composed the Commons participants in law-making. It was still for a long time the Lords, and the Lords only, who assented to laws. The Commons only assented to taxation and petitioned for such laws as they desired to see enacted. In due course, however, the power of the Commons increased, for they could withhold taxes till their wishes were heeded; and English constitutional history became a history of the rise of the Commons to that pre-eminence of power in the state which has made it the most influential legislative body in the world.

The stages of the rise of the Commons to pre-eminence of power in the state are well enough marked. Petitions for legislation could be made effective by withholding grants of money to the Crown, and were well enough when heeded in good faith; but it very often happened that after a petition had been favorably answered by the king and a grant of taxes voted, the legislation, actually drawn up in accordance with it and promulgated in the name of the king and lords, differed in essential points from that which had been asked and promised. Statutes were even sometimes collusively changed in phraseology by the judges whose duty it was to transcribe them into the statute book. Aroused at length by such frauds, the Commons again used their money-grant weapon and forced the Crown to accede to the demand that their petitions should be carried out without change or addition, and the statutes thus framed accurately transcribed by the judges. Still, however, they had no real control over the matter; the statutes were promulgated after their money votes had been passed.

It was necessary to occupy and hold a still more advanced position. The Commons, therefore, demanded that no statute should be passed without consent of the whole Parliament, the Commons included; and, after a struggle, gained what they demanded, as usual. Only two more steps and the omnipotence of Parliament, together with the full participation of the Commons in that omnipotence, would be fully established. As a still further security against fraudulent practices by the judges in transmuting petitions into formal statute by transcription into the statute book, the practice was established of submitting proposed laws to Parliament in the form of bills, in the form, that is, which it was proposed they should retain when made into statutes by vote of Parliament, so that Parliament might examine even the phraseology which the law was to wear, and, if it chose, change it until it was to its mind before giving it a vote of sanction.

These steps had all been taken by the end of the fifteenth century. The final step was taken in the celebrated Bill of Rights, whose date is 1689. The Tudors and Stuarts had assumed great and arbitrary powers as toward the laws. So old a writer as Bracton had said that it was part of the Constitution of England that the king himself should be subject to the laws. But the more arbitrary monarchs had claimed the right to suspend what laws they chose (the right of *dispensation*, it was called) and their pretensions in this matter were given additional color by the fact that the Reformation in England had made the king head of the church in the place of the pope, and had thus made him apparent successor to the pretended right of the pope to dispense with obedience to human law. But after James II had been thrust out in 1688, Parliament gave an imperative and final negative to all that. No law, said the Bill of Rights, can be either suspended or in any way changed except by the same authority as that which enacted it. It had taken a long while to establish the principle, but henceforth Parliament was omnipotent.

The Revolution of 1688, as we have seen, finally established the supremacy of Parliament. It is evident to anyone who considers the details, or even the general features, of the long process by which this result was brought about, that what had been growing all the while was the power and influence of the Commons rather than of the House of Lords. It was the Lower House that had all along forced the fighting and won the victories. Indeed, the fighting was at first as much against the exclusive privileges of the Lords in law-making as against the power of the Crown. The Commons began by forcing its way to a place of equality beside the Upper House and then straightway proceeded to use its power to gain complete ascendancy over that House and become itself to all intents and purposes the whole of Parliament. It was from the first equipped with a power which was in the long run always irresistible. It represented the great body of the tax-payers and could withhold supplies from the government. It was necessary to keep it always in a good humor; and it was in a good humor only so long as its power was growing. Sunderland, when minister of William III., showed that eye for essential fact and commanding tendency which marks the statesman, by advising the new sovereign brought from over seas, to recognize the Commons as the vital member, the active partner, in Parliament, and choose his ministers from the party which had the majority in that House. William took the advice, and so set in motion by a single practical act one of those slow revolutions so characteristic of English constitutional history.

The English Cabinet Ministers are now always chosen from the majority in the House of Commons, whether that majority consist of the adherents of a single political party, or of one party and a wing of another combined, as at present. If defeated, that is outvoted, upon any important matter, they must resign their offices and give place to others who shall represent the new majority. The old weapon of the Commons was *impeachment.* When they did not like the course taken by a minister they accused him of "high crimes and misdemeanors" and he was tried by the House of Lords, the inheritor of the judicial prerogatives of the Great Council from which it directly, the Commons only by adoption, is descended. It was this great and formal process of impeachment that fixed the attention of our constitution-makers in 1787 and was borrowed by them to be put among our own constitutional machinery, to be used, if necessary, even upon the head of the state, as it could not be used in England. They did not perceive that the new and less drastic way of controlling ministers was to outvote them in Parliament, after making it necessary for them to act always through Parliament.

☆ ☆ ☆

The outline I have given of the historical development and the existing organs of the English Constitution, I hope will prove sufficient to display the general features of that singular system of law and precedent. In the main, its foundations are laid in tradition rather than in statute; its strength lies in national habit and the precedents of immemorial practice rather than in the commands of written law. So far as it rests upon written law, its history may be said to begin with the Great Charter which the barons wrung from John in 1215. There had been charters before, but none so specific as this. Henry I had assented to a charter of liberties; many there were, indeed, who in the days of oppression which followed the Conquest, looked back with longing to the "laws of Edward the Confessor," at whose hands men had received justice and a recognition of their liberties. Those liberties, should habit and tradition be received as authoritative, were as old as English history. But not till John's day did they receive exact and specific enumeration and statement. The charter obtained from John stated at length the rights of Englishmen, "their right to justice, to security of person and property, to good government." It set forth how and where the courts should sit, under what conditions Englishmen should be put in jeopardy of life, liberty, or property. It directed how the Great Council should be constituted, and denied the right of the king to tax without that Council's consent. It abolished abuses and re-constituted orderly government. It may, thus, be said to stand at the center of the first period of constitutional development in England, not creating new law, but summing up what had gone before, and preparing what was to follow. Among the most noteworthy of the documents which preceded it were the so-called Constitutions of Clarendon (laws passed in the Council at Clarendon, A.D. 1164), in which the supremacy of the Crown over the church, already more than once asserted, was re-established, and the ecclesiastical made subordinate to the civil courts, and the Assize of Clarendon (1166) concerning the organization and action of the civil courts, by which the system of presentment by grand jury, now so central to our administration of criminal justice, was established.

Besides the Great Charter, the most important fundamental documents of English constitutional history are (I) The Petition of Right, presented by Parliament to Charles I. in 1628, in which those rights and liberties are set forth which the Stuarts had wantonly violated and prayer is made that the laws be observed; (2) The Habeas Corpus Act, passed by Parliament in 1679, in which provision is made against the arbitrary imprisonment of any person without speedy trial and legal proof of his guilt; (3) The Bill of Rights, passed in 1689, which summed up as law the rights which James II. and his predecessors had violated, and swept away as illegal all the powers which they had assumed for the purposes of their tyranny; and (4) The Act of Settlement, of 1700, whereby the Roman Catholic branch of the Stuart family was denied succession to the throne, and the Protestant branch of Hanover substituted which was to give England, Anne and the four Georges, William IV. and Victoria. Perhaps there should be added to these great documents the reform bills of the present century (1832, 1867, and 1884) by which the House of Commons has been made the governing power in England by being made the truly representative organ of the constitution.

These documents one and all differ conspicuously from our own constitutional laws in this, that they are either royal ordinances, like Magna Charta, or acts of Parliament, like the Bill of Rights or the laws reforming the system of representation in Parliament. Our own constitutional provisions of like character and importance are invariably contained in documents which have been submitted to a vote of the people, and, by reason of adoption by them, given a specially formal and sacred character. An act passed by Parliament may also be repealed by Parliament; a royal ordinance also may be set aside by statute; our fundamental laws can be altered only under certain conditions and by special assent of the people to the change. This difference between our constitutional provisions and the laws which underlie the English Constitution have seemed to many to render English institutions unstable as compared with ours. Such an inference, however, is for the most part false and misleading. Parliament dare not tamper with any fundamental law which public opinion regards as sacred, for Parliament is dependent upon public opinion. That opinion is very conservative in matters of fundamental principle; the constitution is, therefore, very stable, resting upon the common thought and the common habit as fully and truly as ours.

This is nowhere more conspicuously evident than in those parts of the English system which rest wholly upon precedent, such, for example, as the practices of ministerial responsibility to the House of Commons. Such parts of the system have proved quite as lasting and quite as safe from sudden or whimsical change as have those other parts which rest upon written law, quite as stable as our own constitutional provisions. The institutions of any people, if derived from, and carefully adjusted to their historical circumstances and character, will be found to change, in the absence of passionate revolution, as slowly or as fast as the people themselves and their habits of life and thought.

In one sense the English is the most practical of existing constitutions. So soon as you formulate a constitutional system as a whole, in a single document or group of related contemporaneous documents, you subject yourself to certain necessities of logic: you must prove every subsequent change proposed to be, not incompatible but harmonious and consistent with the symmetry of the whole. English institutions have enjoyed an incomparable flexibility and freedom of development because they have not been subject to this law of theoretical consistency, but have been put together piece by piece as practical conditions and new needs have demanded. They have been put together by the forces of national development, not in accordance with the suggestions of any abstract logic of political theory.

Democracy

By 1890 Wilson was much in demand as a lecturer in civic and academic settings. He delivered this kind of lecture more often than any other. In it he produced an unsentimental analysis of modern democracy and its demands. He anticipated the Churchillian quip in conceding that democracy was a "clumsy" form of government, but to be preferred over any other. Wilson rejected the notion that democracy means that the people govern, emphasizing instead the "representative" character of democracy. His approach is marked by a realism and recognized that liberty in a democracy requires a measure of order.

Nothing has ever come so near making poets of certain of our duller historians as thought of those little democracies that lie snug about quiet Luzern, on the northern slopes of the Alps, in that rugged Switzerland where liberty and valor have grown old together. A delicate bloom appears upon the surface of their arid style as it approaches the history of those old and staunch confederates in freedom. Their adjectives begin to glow with a rich, unwonted color, their verbs quicken into a sudden life. They speak always with a certain warmth and fervor of those quiet self-respecting yeomen of the mountains, time out of mind self-governed and self-defended. Be their political principles what they may for *other* times and places, they are democrats in Switzerland. Even German sentences soften and succumb to this charm of rural liberty. They cannot resist the attractions of gatherings of freemen in political assembly "under God's free heaven upon a Springtide Sabbath-day." Without the circle stand the wives and children and those who cannot take part. The magistrates sit upon the Tribune. The proceedings open with prayer and song and a quiet, solemn address by the presiding magistrate. After that the officers of the year are elected and the legislative proposals voted upon, all with a simple show of hands, seldom formally counted, merely reckoned from the Tribune. And then the proceedings close, devoutly as they opened, with a covenant read by the clerk and taken, in accordance with hallowed ancient forms, first by the magistrates and then by all the people. This done, the assembly quietly breaks up, and everyone goes his own way. So comely is freedom when you behold its features thus decked in simplicity and demeaned with quietness!

Much the same thing has happened to those who have written of our American town-meeting. We have discovered a most interesting pedigree for it, and that pedigree has greatly excited our fancy. We look in at the doors of some unpretentious town hall one day in the Spring upon tradesmen and farmers, hard, weather-stained faces, and faces carved bargainwise by traffic; the doctor with his sanitary notions, and the parson with his plans of reform, note the self-important dignity of the Moderator, and the wise glasses upon the nose of the clerk; hear the report of the Selectmen made and pricked with comments; unconsciously get warmed by the shrewd rigor of the debate that springs up about taxes and town improvements; watch the elections to their close; and then, even as we stand there, all the long lineage of this business steals into our thoughts.

☆ ☆ ☆

Those who framed our federal government planned no *revolution:* they did not mean to invent an American government, but only to Americanize the English government, which they *knew,* and knew to be a government fit for free men to live under, if only narrow monarchical notions could be got out of it and its spirit liberalized. They thought (what Sydney and Locke had thought before them), that, in order to be pure and efficient, government ought to exist for the people, ought to serve their determinate purposes and all their permanent interests. But they thought also that it ought to be *guarded* against the heats and the hastes, the passions and the thoughtless impulses of *the people,* no less than against selfish *dynasties* and hurtful *class intrigues.* Accordingly they made it only in part a directly democratic government. They carefully sought to break the force of *sudden majorities.* They made only one Chamber the direct choice of the people, and only to that one Chamber did they assign a short term of tenure. The choice of the other Chamber they made to depend only indirectly upon the preferences of the people; and they extended the terms of *its* membership much beyond that of the popular House. They arranged that the *Presidential* term also should span twice the life of the people's chamber. And, above all, crowning and steadying the whole structure, they placed *the Supreme Court,* with its *life* tenure, made independent of parties, pledged only to preserve the fundamental law in its integrity. They meant the government they were building to stand firm, whatever storms of passion, whatever sudden tumults of party, whatever keen ardors of too sanguine reform might for a time prevail.

We have in a measure *undone* their work. A century has led us very far along upon the road of change. Year by year we have sought to bring government nearer to the people, despite the original plan. We nominate the President now in popular convention: we seek to determine at the ballot box who our federal Senators shall be when our state legislators shall have met to register our preferences; and we warn the Senators, when once they are fairly chosen, not to brave too rashly the displeasure of the triumphant majority which the people have sent to the lower House. We grow daily more and more uneasy because a man may be made President who has not received a popular majority in the vote for electors. We declare, and most of us believe, *that the people are sovereign,* and we diligently endeavor to make their sovereignty real and operative in all things.

☆ ☆ ☆

We hold that the people are sovereign, that voting is a *governing* act, not a *consenting* act, merely: that majorities speak, and that majorities effectuate *purposes of their own.* In order to hold this view intelligently we must assume, in the first place, that there always comes into existence *one prevalent opinion* upon each question that arises: a prepared judgment which the people can confidently be called upon to express whenever there is occasion or desire to appeal to them. Now the moment we state this we know that it is ridiculous: that it is even particularly ridiculous when applied to this age of ours. For this is preeminently an age of absorbing labor, "and the necessary effect of all this labor," to quote Mr. Bagehot, "is, that those subject to it have no opinions. It requires a great deal of time," he adds, "to have opinions. . . . If you chain a man's head to a ledger, and keep him constantly adding up, and take something off his salary whenever he stops, you cannot expect him to have a sound conviction" on the silver question, substantial views on the Behring Sea controversy, or original ideas upon the situation in Brazil. We know that the making and the modification of laws is fit matter for study; that questions of policy, whether domestic or foreign, are full of intricacy: we know that there is almost no subject upon which there can be said to be in any community a *single* prevalent opinion, at once diffused and intelligent: and yet we assume that the people are constantly getting definite convictions ready for the measurement of each question of government!

If we do *not* assume *this,* we are driven to other assumptions no less remarkable, and no less awkward to defend. Since we cannot believe that the complicated questions which arise in connection with the conduct of the affairs of a great nation are always intelligible, or often generally understood: if we know that they are very difficult questions, many of them, and demand a certain mastery of details for their comprehension; we are forced to assume that there is, at any rate, *an average judgment* which is to be trusted, an unstudied and instinctive opinion touching the larger bearings of the more general questions of politics which is a good and even final opinion. We take leave to assume that when such matters are put *in a broad and general way,* in the newspapers and on the stump, there will be a sort of average impression produced concerning them which will prove to be a safe enough impression in the long run: that a species of instinctive common sense on the part of ordinary people will perceive the points at issue in their just proportions; and that the politicians will, as a consequence, get a safe mandate from the vote. Do we indeed know the facts of party division and party action: the old prejudices that hold parties together; the persistent sympathies and antipathies that stiffen their separate organization; the *personal* forces that are at work within them; the interlaced jealousies and cupidities that knit them into wholes: and do we, nevertheless, believe that the political action of majorities embodies an *independent average conviction* upon questions *considered in some sort upon their merits?* It seems incredible! And yet we talk as if we *did!*

☆ ☆ ☆

What, then? Am I a political pessimist? Do I distrust the foundations, question the most essential conceptions, of the government under which we live? Do I suspect the people of blindness and all their leaders of charlatanry, and hold up popular government to be laughed at as a farce? By no means. I simply take the liberty of believing in democratic institutions *as* I *understand them.* I *believe* in the people: in their *honesty* and *sincerity* and *sagacity;* but I do not believe in them *as my governors.* I believe in them, rather, as the wholesome stuff out of which the fabric of government, wherever and whenever constructed, is woven, in homely, but also in most useful and beneficent wise. Let me give you at once an example that will illuminate my meaning. I believe, as I feel sure you also believe, that that reform of the civil service for which we have so long been struggling, with varying degrees of success, is imperatively necessary, and that it embodies eminently wise principles of government. *But it is not democratic in idea:* by which I mean that it is not consistent with those *modern assumptions* touching the nature of democratic government which we have just been discussing. It rejects the average man and the average training: it rejects the idea of constantly renewing the official *personnel* of the government from out the general body of the people. It seeks to substitute for the person whom we call "the man of the people," so far as possible, *the men* of *the schools,* the trained, instructed, *fitted* men: the men who will study their duties and master the principles of the business of their Departments. The ordinary politician is *right* when he says that this is not democratic. It is *not* democratic in the sense in which we have taught our politicians wrongly to understand democracy. It *is,* nevertheless, *eminently democratic,* if we understand democracy as history has given it to us. It is democratic in this sense, *that it draws all the governing material from the people, from such part* of the people as will fit themselves for the function. It thus plans to renew from generation to generation the youth and the variety and the integrity of the administrative capacity employed in the public service. It avoids the narrowness of aristocracy, and the degeneracy of the monarchical polity, by selecting its instruments from the widest, richest, most perennial sources. It is *but another process of representation.*

☆ ☆ ☆

Democratic nations are not made in a day; and they have never been made at all save in Switzerland, in England, and in the United States. France, possibly, will become one, bye and bye, after she shall have had still other discipline, a few more hard lessons in self-control. Even in England there are some rebellious pulses, beating still from old days of discord and insubordination: the drill of liberty has not extended to all classes. But it was her drilled classes that she sent to America: and that first blood has so far kept its advantage. We have many things to fear; but we have, nevertheless, *a mighty fund* of *unsurpassed civil capacity:* we can impart it to the best of those who come to us with other blood in their veins. Think what it is that you have in a democratic nation, made as ours has been. You have an adult, disciplined, self-possessed nation, with a self-possession born of long experience. Other polities belong to *the long days* of *preparation* for freedom: freedom to choose what causes and what leaders the people will. The strict, severe forms of monarchical authority belong to the season of schooling: *all* hereditary systems of rulership, to seasons of immaturity or of unstable, wayward choice. These sterner and more disciplinary systems belong also to those parts of the world where nations are pressed against nations, and there is friction and hazardous rivalry: where, accordingly, peoples must have the union, the organization, and the promptitude of armies. When days of tutelage and of discipline are passed: when a nation has been kept from rash excesses, though not from all exercises of liberty, until its sinews are firm and it has learned conduct, then it may be trusted to make its own choices, to live its own life.

True, its very freedom may turn out to be its danger: but not so long as it retains that love of order, and that consciousness of the need for law, in which it has been bred in its youth: its ineradicable feeling for institutions is its equipoise: *and with that equipoise it has attained its sovereignty.* This is the sovereignty over itself, the sovereignty of self-respect and self-control;

which is a power over self, not only, but over others as well. The good-natured but earnest audience, that sits in the seats and boxes and hears the play, is sovereign: makes sovereign disposition of its favors: damns play and author, or else gives them vogue and success. Our nation is not our audience: for what we do is not a play in its eyes, but part of its own life, significant for its fortunes. It must and does have a care in its applause: it is sovereign in its condemnation, even though it condemn by silence or by inattention.

The freedom of the democratic nation consists, let me repeat, not in governing itself: for that it cannot do; but in making undictated choice of the things it will accept and of the men it will follow. It need no longer always accept and always like the things it is told to like. It makes adult choice.

☆ ☆ ☆

When I take this view of the life of a free nation,—a people, not self-directed, but directed by its boldest, most prevalent minds,—I can justify my tolerance of *parties,* and my impatience with those that scorn them and make as if they could do without them. Parties preserve impulses, which would otherwise be diffused and lost. They are the whippers-in for those who plan and originate, and render the impression which these make upon their generation permanent. They perpetuate approved opinions, energize accepted convictions. They must be forgiven much of their worship of "dead issues": for they can keep their corporate feeling, their sense of *identity,* only by remembering old struggles, maintaining old comradeships; only by a keen pride in what they *have* done. It is thus that continuity of consciousness is preserved in a nation *in respect* of *the abstract things* of *its life,* the invisible things that are eternal, the principles which are the secret springs of action. They prove, at the same time that they make possible, the organic operation of state life.

Of course parties are often blind and intractable: and they almost always take ideas slowly and reluctantly; but inasmuch as they accept convictions for the organism as a whole, whose active life they embody, it is just as well that they *should* accept them slowly. Close knit fibers and a certain stubbornness of structure hold a nation together, as they do every other organism. When we come on the field it is already occupied. Habit, prejudice, established conventions, fixed systems of thought are in possession, and it will be fighting work to dislodge them. Else, society would not long endure. It cannot get along without institutions and steadfast beliefs. But I think that you will agree with me that this only makes it the more certain that we shall have vigor in our growth, and consistency in our reforms.

☆ ☆ ☆

Progress in politics is progress in social justice. The object of forms of government is clear: it is, to repose confidence wisely, or to fix responsibility distinctly. The *test* of *excellence* for forms of government is the character of the order and of the individual service which they secure. There must be character on the part of the people to judge character on the part of the official. That is the condition precedent to democracy. If there be not popular capacity, why then Nature must herself cast the parts of ruler and subject: they must be determined by blood and inheritance. A polity of free popular choice, like our own, depends for its success upon the permanency of a certain character on the part of the people. Without a firm love for order on their part, a sagacious insight into the character of men, and a steady preference for openness and honesty in the conduct of affairs, the whole structure would go presently to pieces. This law of liberty is not enough studied among us. It is not the law of doing what we please, but the law of *pleasing to do what is right.* It is a sort of sublimated principle of expediency.

We have fallen into the habit of identifying it with a large *freedom of individual action,* and that side of it unquestionably deserves the emphasis which it has received. Liberty, nevertheless, is not identical with individual privilege. It is a thing of *social organization.* A man's freedom is lost the moment he is cut off from society and thrown upon his own resources, to do everything for himself. Instantly he becomes a slave to Nature. His strength lies of course in cooperation, in combined and regulated social effort. It is not in being let alone by government that my liberty consists, but in being assisted by government to maintain *my equal place* among my fellows. Some power stronger than I am must define my rights; else they are measured by my might and not by my right: I must depend upon my own wits in a general struggle. Liberty is like steam, effective only when confined. It is the order of society that make me free, just as it is the order of nature that keeps me alive. The one keeps my organs in their places and at their functions; without pause or miscarriage, holds my house erect about me, entitles me to call what damage I suffer *accident.* The other enables me to count upon what *you will do,* to get help upon the terms of giving it, to make reasonable reckonings and confident plans. If I make breach of this order, I lose my liberty. I break bounds, and am an outlaw; I forfeit bond and must yield myself up. "Law is the *external organism of human freedom.*"

☆ ☆ ☆

The best administered tyranny, the most nicely executed injustice the world ever saw, did not compare in excellence of result with the clumsiest system of self-government. For what you want to produce is *not administrative acts,* but *happy and prosperous populations.* Government is the art of producing high averages in independence and happiness.

Observe that my ideal *reverses the order of the socialist.* He wants *first* a new constitution for society, new orders of authority and adjustments of organization, in order that thereby a new nature *may be wrought out* for society. I believe that the work must be carried on in the opposite direction. It must begin, not at the end of organization, but at that of *character. Organization is a product of character,* not an antecedent and cause of character. The body is not the cause, but the instrument, of the spirit. Let no one make the mistake of supposing that the cultivated and thinking class in any community, the class that squares its beliefs and its conduct by rational standards, is in any practical sense the directing and determinant portion of the community, *a commission to administer its mind* and *regulate the courses of its life.* Political ideas do not become practicable until they become virtually universal. The process of life for them is a process of *permeation.* That is the reason that ideas, *fit* from the *first* to reform abuses, have never reformed them speedily or at once. They have had to penetrate so many unprepared minds in their progress towards general acceptance, have had to be put in so many different ways to so many different men, have had to be rubbed over so often with old phrases so as to remove their suspicious appearance of newness, have had to be kneaded so laboriously into the general mass of common thought.

Presidential Address to the American Political Science Association: The Law and the Facts

In 1910 Wilson served a term as president of the American Political Science Association. His presidential address presented an analysis of the young discipline and appealed for the objective study of politics as human experience, which must be felt and understood and not merely confined to a catalog of facts. He reflected his long-held views on liberal learning when he prescribed new syntheses that would direct students of politics to the use of history, literature, art, and other disciplines to illuminate that experience. He used the occasion to comment on the relationship between politics and the private business sector. Speaking as he began his term as governor of New Jersey, Wilson forecast the direction of his political agenda when he said, "Business is no longer in any proper sense a private matter," and he called for the statesmanship of action. The address was published in the *American Political Science Review* in February 1911.

The life of society is a struggle for law. Where life is fixed in unalterable grooves, where it moves from day to day without change or thought of change, law is also, of course, stationary, permanent, graven upon the face of affairs as if upon tables of stone. But where life changes law changes, changes under the impulse and fingering of life itself. For it records life; it does not contain it; it does not originate it. It is subsequent to fact; it takes its origin and energy from the actual circumstances of social experience. Law is an effort to fix in definite practice what has been found to be convenient, expedient, adapted to the circumstances of the actual world. Law in a moving, vital society grows old, obsolete, impossible, item by item. It is not necessary to repeal it or to set it formally aside. It will die of itself, for lack of breath, because it is no longer sustained by the facts or by the moral or practical judgments of the community whose life it has attempted to embody.

There is, indeed, a sort of law which pushes ahead of fact, or seems to. I mean the law, so common in our day, which attempts to correct the habits or to guide the tendencies of society. Take our sanitary laws, for example. They do not record habit; they try to alter it. They are not a reduction to rule, merely, of practices into which society has naturally or instinctively settled. They seek to impose upon us, rather, habits and practices which we would not without their duress have adopted. They are based oftentimes upon scientific facts and principles which are not of common observation. We are very obedient to our men of science. We accept the conclusions of their laboratories without question or criticism and embody them in our rules of life, in our laws, with great benefit to our health, but in obedience to authority, not to experience, at any rate not to experience which is of our own development or discovery.

But even this is only an apparent exception. Law is still subsequent to the facts. Though they be not of our own discovery and we receive them on faith, they are none the less facts. Law follows them; it does not precede or predict or invent them. It is obedient to experience. It accepts the ascertained, the accomplished, the proved and established circumstance, and frames it into an imperative rule of conduct under the compulsion of what men have found to be true.

I take the science of politics to be the accurate and detailed observation of these processes by which the lessons of experience are brought into the field of consciousness, transmuted into active purposes, put under the scrutiny of discussion, sifted, and at last given determinate form in law. Nothing that forms or affects human life seems to me to be properly foreign to the student of politics.

I do not know how some students of politics get along without literature, as some of them make shift to do, without interpretations of poetry or of any of the other imaginative illuminations of life, or without art, or any of the means by which men have sought to picture to themselves what their days mean or to represent to themselves the voices that are forever in their ears as they go their doubtful journey. They read history, indeed, in search of the "facts"; but if they miss the deepest facts of all, the spiritual experiences, the visions of the mind, the aspirations of the spirit that are the pulse of life, I do not see how they can understand the facts or know what really moves the world. Very often they do not.

Politics is of the very stuff of life. Its motives are interlaced with the whole fibre of experience, private and public. Its relations are intensely human, and generally intimately personal. It is very dangerous to reason with regard to it on principles that are fancied to be universal; for it is local. Its items are of the time and place. What happens in its field is shot through with a thousand accidental elements which you will not find again upon another occasion, because occasions are not similar. And yet there is a large movement in it all which is independent in some strange way of time and place and accidental elements. There are big facts and tendencies to be picked out. There are circumstances which link whole communities together, make them feel their common interest, reveal to them their common relations, and push them forward into the field of law. They must seek a common order, whether they will or not; they must shape institutions to suit their lives and give vent to their common purposes; they must drive a strong, steadfast peg of law in at each step of their struggle forward to hold them where they are.

This study becomes more and more complex because society changes under our very eyes. I suppose there never was a time when things were actually simple. They look so to us in very ancient times of which we have scant record, no doubt, because we know very little about them. They were complex enough, even then, it may be; but we see them only in bulk, and the mass looks simple and easy of description. But manifestly affairs have grown more and more complex as civilization has deployed upon the modern stage.

There was a time, for example, when societies, when nations, seemed to move forward in mass, all together, their internal interest, at any rate, liked and interrelated in some reasonably manifest fashion. Their law was all of one weaving. The classes of which they were made up were formed in one common mold, were at least continuously conscious of one another and united in a single nexus of forces. In our day, on the contrary, there is an extraordinary, an unprecedented differentiation. There is a perceptible movement in distinct economic and therefore distinct social sections. Society is too various to see itself as a whole, and the vision of those who study it is confused. Interests have their own separate and complicated development, and must, it has seemed, be made separately and individually the subject of legal regulation and adjustment. The relations which have come to rule in our day in the field of law seem to be the relations of interests, of vast and powerful economic sections of society, rather than of individuals. Laws intended to affect one set of interests directly and vitally are not only not meant to affect other interests directly but other interests are often ignorant of them, wholly indifferent to them. They do not touch their comprehension, do not enter into their calculations, are not permitted to affect their development.

For these sections and interests are powerfully organized, for the management, defense, and expansion of their own enterprises, personnel, and properties. Their power and their resources are concentrated, their management centered in definite and active agencies. They are equipped to take care of themselves, and are alert for every advantage.

☆ ☆ ☆

And so the field, almost the subject matter, of our study has changed. It is still the object of political science to see how the forces move, to note how experience develops into law. But experience does not move with an even front, and law responds to it after its own variety, in sections, in special channels, in segments fitted to special interests. Our search is for the common interest, but where shall we find it? It is displayed in no common phenomena, at any rate in one that can be easily discerned. If we would discover it, we must compound it for ourselves out of scattered and disparate elements. We must look away from the piecemeal law books, the miscellaneous and disconnected statutes and legal maxims, the court decisions, to the life of men, in which there is always, of necessity, an essential unity, which, whether it will or no, whether it is conscious of it or not, *must* be of a piece, *must* have a pattern which can be traced. Here are the fragments: the laws, the separate forces, the eager competing interests, the disordered *disjecta membra* of a system which is no system, which does not even suggest system, but which must somehow be built together into a whole which shall be something more than a mere sum of the parts.

This is the task, the difficult, elusive, complex, and yet imperative task of political science. It is also the task of the new statesmanship, which must be, not a mere task of compromise and makeshift accommodation, but a task of genuine and lasting adjustment, synthesis, coordination, harmony, and union of parts.

☆ ☆ ☆

Perhaps we can find a starting point for the new synthesis which this latest enterprise of our thinking must seek to accomplish in two definitions which I have recently ventured to suggest in another place. We are dealing, in our present discussion, with business and we are dealing with life as an organic whole, and modern politics is an accommodation of these two. Suppose we define business as the economic service of society for private profit, and suppose we define politics as the accommodation of all social forces, the forces of business of course included, to the common interest. We may thus perceive our task in all its magnitude and extraordinary significance. Business must be looked upon, not as the exploitation of society, not as its use for private ends, but as its sober service; and private profit must be regarded as legitimate only when it is in fact a reward for what is veritably serviceable, serviceable to interest which are not single but common, as far as they go; and politics must be the discovery of this common interest in order that the service may be tested and exacted.

In this conception society is the senior partner in all business. It must be first considered, society as a whole, in its permanent and essential, not merely in its temporary and superficial, interests. If private profits are to be legitimized, private fortunes made honorable, these great forces which play upon the modern field must, both individually and collectively, be accommodated to a common purpose. Politics has to deal with and harmonize many other forces besides those of business merely. Business serves our material needs, but not often our spiritual. But the business forces are nowadays the most powerful (perhaps the have always been the most powerful) with which politics has to deal. They are the hardest to correlate, tame, and harness; and for the time being our anxious interest centers upon them. Let us extract from them, if we can, the new term of peace and prosperity which will be found in their genuine and successful synthesis.

The economist cannot help us, I fear. They must segregate these great phenomena of which I have spoken, I suppose, and study them in their pure and separate force, as they are; whereas segregation is just what we, as students of political science, are seeking to offset and correct. We wish to study them, not separately, nor even in combination only with one another, but in combination with the influences, the interests, the aspects of life which are not economic, but stuff of fortune, of peace of mind, of fair and generous dealing, of good will and enlightenment and public service.

There is the statesmanship of thought and there is the statesmanship of action. The student of political science must furnish the first, out of his full store of truth, discovered by patient inquiry, dispassionate exposition, fearless analysis, and frank inference. He must spread a dragnet for all the facts, and must then look upon them steadily and look upon them whole. It is only thus that he can enrich the thinking and clarify the vision of the statesman of action, who has no time for patient inquiry, who must be found in his facts before he can apply them in law and policy, who must have stuff of truth for his conscience and his resolution to rely on.

I know that the statesman and the student of political science have not hitherto often been partners. The statesman has looked askance upon the student, at any rate in America, and has too often been justified because the student did not perceive the real scope and importance of what he was set to do and overlooked much of the great field from which he should have drawn his facts, was not a student of thought and of affairs but merely a reader of books and documents. But the partnership is feasible, with a change in the point of view; and the common interest must somehow be elucidated and made clear, if the field of action is not to be as confused as the field of thought.

I do not mean that the statesman must have a body of experts at his elbow. He cannot have. There is no body of experts. There is no such thing as an expert in human relationships. I mean merely that the man who has the time, the discrimination, and the sagacity to collect and comprehend the principal facts and the man who must act upon them must draw near to one another and feel that they are engaged in a common enterprise. The student must look upon his studies more like a human being and man of action, and the man of action must approach his conclusions more like a student.

Business is no longer in any proper sense a private matter. It is not in our day usually conducted by independent individuals, each acting upon his own initiative in the natural pursuit of his own economic wants. It is pursued by great companies, great corporations, which exist only by express license of law and for the convenience of society, and which are themselves, as it were, little segments of society. Law is not accommodating itself, therefore, to the impulses and enterprises of individuals, as experience pushes it forward from change to change; but is accommodating itself, rather, to the impulses of bodies of men, to the aggregate use of money drawn from a myriad of sources as if from the common savings of society at large. The processes of change will be organic, institutional, constructive. It is a study in the correlation of forces.

After all, it is not purely intellectual process, this interpretation of experience, this translation of experience into law. I said just now that I did not see how the student of political science could make shift to know what he was about without the lamps of literature to light his way, those flames, those lambent spirits of men, that burn in the pages of books that some of you are apt to put away from you as having no significance as of science and of fact in them. Nothing interprets but vision, and ours is a function of interpretation. Nothing perceives but the spirit when you are dealing with the intricate life of men, shot through the passion and tragedy and ardor and great hope. That is the reason that I said that there were no experts in human relationships. Sympathy is your real key to the riddle of life. If you can put yourself in men's places, if you can see the same facts from the points of view of many scores of men of as many different temperaments, fortunes, environments, if you have Shakespearian range and vision, then things fall into their places as you look upon them and are no longer confused, disordered, scattered abroad without plan or relation. You must not classify men too symmetrically; you must not gaze dispassionately upon them with scientific eye. You must yield to their passion and feel the pulse of their life when you are studying them no less than when you are acting for them. Organic processes of thought will bring you organic processes of law. Nothing else will.

Let us break with our formulas, therefore. It will not do to look at men congregated in bodies politic through the medium of the constitutions and traditions of the states they live in, as if that were the glass of interpretation. Constitutions are vehicles of life, but not sources of it. Look at all men everywhere first of all as at human beings struggling for existence, for a little comfort and ease of heart, for happiness amidst the things that bind and limit them. Such and such are the conditions of law and effort and rivalry amidst which they live, such and such are their impediments, their sympathies, their understandings with one another. See them in their habits as they live and perhaps you will discern their errors of method, their errors of motive, their confusions of purpose, and the assistance the wise legislator might afford them.

I do not like the term political science. Human relationships, whether in the family or in the state, in the counting house or in the factory, are not in any proper sense the subject-matter of science. They are stuff of insight and sympathy and spiritual comprehension. I prefer the term Politics, therefore, to include both statesmanship of thinking and the statesmanship of action. Your real statesman is first of all, and chief of all, a great human being, with an eye for all the great field upon which men like himself struggle, with unflagging pathetic hope, towards better things. He is a man big enough to think in the terms of what others than himself are striving for and living for and seeking steadfastly to keep in heart till they get. He is a guide, a comrade, a mentor, a servant, a friend of mankind. May not the student of politics be the same? May not his eye, too, follow the dusty roads, scan the scattered mass, observe the crowded homes, heed the cry of the children as well as the silent play of the busy fingers that toil that they may be fed, follow the lines of strain, of power, of suffering, get a vision of all the things that tell; and then, with no precise talk of phenomena or of laws of action, interpret what he feels no less than what he sees to the man of action, too much engrossed, it may be, to see so much or over so wide a field, too much immersed to hear any but the nearby cries and clamors, too eagerly bent upon his immediate task to scan the distant view?

Know your people and you can lead them; study your people and you may know them. But study them, not as congeries of interests, but as a body of human souls, the least as significant as the greatest, not as you would calculate forces, but as you would comprehend life. In such an atmosphere of thought and association even corporations may seem instrumentalities, not objects in themselves, and the means may presently appear whereby they may be made the servants, not the masters, of the people. The facts are precedent to all remedies; and the facts in this field are spiritually perceived. Law is subsequent to the facts, but the law and the facts stand related, not as cause and effect, but, rather, as life and its interpretation.

6

New Jersey Politics

Government and Business

In this discussion of government and business, Wilson did not prefigure his role as governor and president. Wilson had long held rather conservative views with regard to government, business, and labor, views which gradually shifted in a progressive direction as he became more active in politics and especially when he became a candidate for office. Here he referred to the "mania for regulation." Business big and small had at this point little to fear from a political leader who equated government regulation with the slippery slope to socialism. He seemed to attribute the excesses of the business corporations to individual wrongdoers, who should be prosecuted, but offered little to suggest a sweeping vision of reform. The views expressed here, perhaps with the initiatives of the Roosevelt administration in mind, help in understanding why New Jersey progressives were not enthusiastic about his candidacy for governor in 1910, and why he appeared to be acceptable to the "regulars" of the state Democratic party. The speech was delivered to the Commercial Club of Chicago in March 1908.

... I do not feel that I come here tonight as a college president but rather as one of the citizens of the United States, interested in this question, because every man of public spirit, conscientiousness and intelligence must be interested in it. And every man must accept any opportunity that is offered to take part in the universal public counsel now going on regarding it, for certainly we stand very much in need to take counsel with each other.

We are being governed by many impulses; but we are not being governed by well thought out conclusions. It is certainly a time of excitement, of excited action which is being made more excited by excited speech; and in such a time there is special need that we should take counsel with one another as to what it is wise to do.

☆ ☆ ☆

A perfect mania for regulation has taken hold of us. We have got in a fever of activity with regard to legislation; and I suspect that after having acted we shall think; after having attempted a dozen remedies we shall then carefully set our selves down and ascertain whether any of the remedies remedy. Is it not the wiser part to ask what it is that we want to remedy and what will be likely to remedy it?

Of course it is no longer debatable that there are a great many things to remedy. It is no longer debatable that a great many practices have sprung up under the modern conditions of business which are very undesirable practices indeed, very demoralizing to the public welfare, and very demoralizing to the men who engage in them—things not founded in righteousness, not founded in fair dealing, not founded in the right interpretation of law. And these things have been done under the cover of corporate organization. They do not seem to have been done so much by individuals as by combinations of individuals, which, in the old phrase, have no bodies to be kicked or souls to be damned—intangible, invisible, multiple persons, given their existence only by the theory of law, and not susceptible to ordinary moral standards.

In fact, we feel that we have lost the wrongdoers in the complex organization of modern business, and, instead of undertaking to find them again, we are undertaking to handle the organizations and not the persons, and so are changing the whole theory and practice of our legal system. For in respect of all things hitherto punishable it has been regarded as the sound theory of the law that the persons responsible should be punished, and not the business of the country. We have been trying to regulate the business when we should have been trying to regulate transactions. We have been trying to regulate the affirmative constructive administrative conduct of business when we should have been discriminating between those transactions which are detrimental to the public welfare and those which are not, seeking to check the one and to let the other go free of restraint.

Now the pursuit of the responsible person has become necessary, because in his concealment he has brought reproach and suspicion upon all other persons similarly circumstanced with himself. We hear a great deal about dishonest transactions, but we do not hear the names of the men who have conceived the dishonesty. It will not do to cast suspicion upon hundreds of thousands of honest men because you can not find half a score of dishonest men. No man in his senses will believe that the business of this country is essentially corrupt. No man who has any experience in dealing with men of affairs in this country will suppose that the majority of them are dishonest. Everybody knows that, upon the practiced philosophy of business, business would break down if the majority of the men who conducted it were dishonest. If men could not trust each other they would not enter into transactions with each other. . . .

There is no doubt such a thing as predatory wealth but if wealth were all of it predatory, if every man were preying on every other man, a condition of things would arise which would be a condition of warfare and not of peace, a condition not of organization but of confusion and disorganization. Such a condition has not arisen, but there are undoubtedly bad practices and it is none the less necessary, if we would moralize our business, that we return to a possible basis of morality.

Now morality is never corporate. Morality is never aggregate. The only way you get honest business is from honest men. I know that there are methods by which men cover the uncomfortable emotions of their consciences. I know that men accept in business which is corporate certain compromises which they conceive to have been forced upon them by the action of those with whom they must act in corporate transactions. I know that men salve their consciences by saying it was necessary to do this, that, or the other thing because they bad to do it by way of compromise and in combination with others. But in the long run a man's conscience never lies easy under that kind of salve. It is necessary for everyone of us, sooner or later, to go to bed. It is necessary for every one of us, sooner or later, to put out the light and lie down with our consciences. It is necessary, if men would retain the momentum of their best energy, that they should retain their respect for themselves when they are alone and closeted with their own consciences; and society itself cannot exist upon any other basis. Men know they are not going to be saved from responsibility by those who judge of the essence of the matter by any combination with others. They know they must be judged separately and individually, and there is no valid system of law which can be based upon any other feeling than that.

What I want particularly to point out this evening is this: We are making in our generation a radical choice by choosing between various sorts of practices. We are choosing between opposite sorts of principles. The principle upon which we shall choose our course of action, we of this generation, is a principle which will either retain or alter the character of our government. That is the serious aspect of the whole matter.

I have heard it said that certain kinds of governmental regulations must be adopted in order to stop the drift towards socialism in this country, and yet the very kinds of governmental regulation which are contemplated in such arguments are regulations which are themselves essentially socialistic in principle. After you start a little way on that road it is merely a question of time and choice as to how far you will go upon it. You can not, after you have got on the road, arbitrarily call a halt at any one point upon it. Let me proceed at once and tell you what I mean. . . .

Now in principle there is no difference whatever between that and government ownership, no difference whatever between the direct regulation of business and the ownership of business enterprises. For the only safe way by which the government can pick its steps is by picking them upon the basis of experience, and the only thing that experience can yield is the revelation, item by item, of the things, the particular transactions, which society wishes to control.

What is it that is wrong with the business of this country? In the first place, certain monopolies, or virtual monopolies, have been established in ways which have been unrighteous and have been maintained in ways that were unrighteous; and have been used and intended for monopolistic purposes. In the second place, the business of the country has come near to being regulated, at one crisis and another, by what is no business at all, but the mere manipulation of those securities which represent business. The chief things that have gone wrong with the business of the country have not been based upon monopolistic undertakings at all, but have been based upon such things as over-capitalization and the foisting upon the public, that does not know the process by which this thing has been done, of securities that were not worth the purchase price that was paid for them. At the same time that purchase price, a perfectly artificial thing in itself, brought millions of dollars into the pockets of men who had managed the unrighteous transaction. Now the men who did these things are not always the men who administer the actual business of the country. In most instances they are not.

☆ ☆ ☆

At present we say in our law that we want every great corporation to be broken up. For more than twenty years a large number of states in the Union have been engaged in the attempt to prevent the formation of corporations which might operate their businesses as a monopoly. They have not required in those laws that they should operate them as a monopoly in order to become obnoxious to the law. It is only sufficient that they are of a kind to have power to operate as a monopoly, and if they are of that kind they are illegal.

What has been the consequence? Have those corporations been broken up? On the contrary they have multiplied. They have enormously multiplied. Have you heard any man who knew the way in which business was conducted and must be conducted in this country suggest that we should go back to the operation of business by small individual firms? Have you heard anybody suggest that we should go back from the corporate organization and attempt an entirely different one? You have heard nobody who knew anything about business suggest anything of that kind; but you continue to try to break up organizations which have the opportunity to be monopolistic without inquiring whether they have become monopolistic or not. Have you ever defined in your law what a monopoly is? Have you ever defined under the law what kind of restraint of trade you regard as undesirable? Have you ever defined under the law what constitutes overcapitalization and what kind of capitalization you regard as desirable, what process of capitalization you regard as desirable? Have you ever tried to define under the law what you mean by unfair competition? Have you ever defined under the law what you mean by the kind of business which must not be forced out of operation by competition, and the kind that ought to be forced out of operation by competition? Do you wish to save men from being forced out of business if they won't operate their business in the way that is best or most serviceable for the public? Do you wish to save the weak and check and discourage the strong? Do you mean to keep business on a level as low as that to which some trade unions try to depress their members by keeping it down to the level of that which is worst conducted? Have you ever determined any of those things? Has any legislator ever attempted to define them?

☆ ☆ ☆

Now history is inexorable. History does not indulge populistic parties. History has no atom of encouragement for socialistic processes. History says power, if you accumulate it in governors, will certainly sooner or later become oppressive and impossible to be borne. The only reign under which any self-respecting men can live is the reign, not of authority, but of law, the exact definition alike of his rights and of his obligations; definitions enforced by men whose object and interest are not political but judicial, who determine without administrative bias what is the true and ancient and lasting intent of the law of the land. The twenty-ninth clause of Magna Charta is just as permanent as any law of human nature, because it is founded in human nature.

There is no liberty unless a man's privileges be determined by the judgment of his peers and the law of the land. So soon as I have to go to Washington to ask how I may conduct my business I have ceased to live under an American polity. There is then no longer any difference between the polity which we established this government to escape and the polity which we ourselves, childishly, have returned to.

Government regulation? Yes, but through the ancient, the stable, the incorruptible instrumentality of law, not through the choice of executive officials. A country not to be upset by the scolding of magistrates but only to be upset by the corruption of its citizens, a country that knows its own mind, knows its own law, upholds its own magistrates is sure of the future because it is sure of its own principles.

Gentlemen, we shall not escape the necessity of making a fundamental choice. Wrong practices must be stopped, but they must be stopped in such a way that we shall not substitute the wrong of tyranny for the wrong of private oppression. I can resist my neighbor but I can not resist the government; and when the government is made strong against me and interferes in everything that I attempt to do, then my life is the life of a man enslaved and not of a man standing upon the ancient privileges of a free race. Have we not the self-possession to diagnose the case? Have we not the self-possession to determine exactly what it is that is the matter with us and that we want to correct? Have we not the intelligence and capacity to define the remedy in law? Have we not had courts which could be depended upon to enforce the law? I would despair of the intelligence of this people if I thought that there was more than one answer to that question.

The answer may not come soon. I admit to you in this presence that I am not hopeful of the immediate future; but I would be deeply hopeless of any future, immediate or remote, if we did not begin now to think straight about these things. We are going, apparently, to act first and think afterward; and God help us in the process of saving the fragments. But the sooner we begin to think the less the fragments will be scattered and the less impossible it will be to put them together again. The sooner we make up our minds that we are going to act upon tested principles and not upon doubtful experiments, the sooner we strip ourselves of individual interests and prejudices in the matter, the better.

Look what has been taking place in Washington: Conference after conference with regard to the amendment of the Sherman Act, not leading anywhere in particular, so far as I can learn, because of several sets of opposing interests; somebody afraid that somebody else is going to get the advantage of him; the manufacturer and the railway man afraid that the law will be so changed that they can not control the labor organizations; the labor organizations afraid that the law will be so changed that the corporations will get the upper hand of them; every man standing off for fear he cannot get as much advantage out of the new law as he can get out of the present law. That temper is the certain precursor of revolution. If you want to save this country from revolution, forget your own interests and think for a little while upon the public interest. Forget your antagonisms. Forget that there is somebody that you want to get the better of, some organization that you want to keep under your hand, and ask yourself what ought to be the position of the organization that you are interested in. Think of your common partnership, that liberal principle of give and take which is the only foundation of any lively commonwealth.

The real thing which a gathering of gentlemen like this should realize is that they must, for the salvation of their country, adjourn their own individual and particular interests for a very serious effort of public counsel; for we are on the eve of a political choice in this country which may be a permanent choice. We are upon the eve of a critical choice which may turn us in this direction or in that; and God help us if we do not know which direction we have chosen. We stand in the presence of the necessity of choosing a direction. We must recover by one process or another the ancient principles of morality, the ancient principles of public spirit, the ancient principles of common purpose, and then there will be no difficulty in putting a stop to the things which are against the public welfare.

Conservatism: True and False

At a time when the ranks of progressive reformers in American politics were growing, Wilson presented himself as a conservative in Jeffersonian terms: distrust of government, support for states' rights, and opposition to business regulation. His was a classic conservatism not in tune with what passed for conservative thought in the Gilded Age and the early years of the century, a distortion of that ideology in the service of privilege and narrow corporate interests. It was in part his conservative posture which called for change to be considered carefully and executed deliberately that made Wilson attractive as a candidate for governor to leaders of the New Jersey Democratic party. The talk was delivered to the New York Southern Society in December 1908. In the months that followed, Wilson adjusted some of his ideas to fit his developing understanding of the practical political issues of the day and consequently broadened his appeal to New Jersey voters.

The campaign is over but it was not a campaign which settled anything. Each party offered to the people in its platform a miscellaneous body of policies drawn together by no discernible principle and intended to command immediate attention rather than to form the basis of consistent co-operative action on the part of those who are most concerned to find for the country a program which will be a real solution of existing difficulties and a real guide for the future. No one can feel that that campaign settled anything or that its issues were satisfactorily concluded. Indeed, there is no clear indication that the country considered it a settlement of anything, except of the question who should be President of the United States.

Such a campaign, therefore, must have set men thinking very seriously of the future of parties and of the whole question of consistent and intelligible party program. Men cannot long be united in strong and co-operative bodies unless they are united upon principle, unless they have set before themselves some certain goal and have formed some definite idea of the course they shall take to reach that goal. It is inevitable, therefore, that we should follow up the campaign which has just closed with a great deal of conference upon political programs and party organization. We are conscious of a sort of dissolution of parties, of a confusion of issues, of singular intersection of opinion and interminglings of impulse, and of a notable absence of leadership, not of leadership of the political organizations to which we happen to belong, but of leadership of the constructive thought and purpose of the country. . . .

Not only are the circumstances of our time new circumstances, whether in the field of economic or of political conditions, but they are peculiarly new in America because the great combinations of capital and of labor and the new complexities of economic organization and of enterprise which have been set up in America have been set up under conditions quite different from those which obtain elsewhere, because of the still inexhaustible and no doubt in part still undiscovered resources of this great continent. Perhaps it will never again be possible as it has been during the past generation to pile up wealth with extraordinary rapidity in this country and to enrich the commerce of the world with unlimited supplies of ore and coal, but it will for a long time be true that America more than any other country is a place in which the development of resources and their use will proceed upon a very great scale and at a very rapid pace. Our conditions must for long remain less settled, and therefore less controllable, less calculable, less predictable than those of older countries whose resources are known and whose methods of exploitation are measurably established. America will, therefore, continue to be a scene of changeful conditions for at least another generation, and it will throughout that generation be more difficult in America than elsewhere to adjust action to definite principle in the field of politics and of enterprise. The temptations to irregular action will be greater and the difficulties of controlling it much more complex than elsewhere.

It is for this reason that it has been so easy to make the voters of this country impatient of any form of conservatism. The problems to be met are so great and perplexing that we have been in a temper to approach them boldly and with very radical proposals, and we have been easily rendered impatient of any who have cried a warning to us or who have tried to draw us back to slower, safer and better tested processes. There is a false conservatism which justifies impatience in our existing circumstances, namely, that sort of conservatism which proposes a return to old measures and expedients intended for other circumstances or to old formulas now in large part emptied of their meaning. For example, the old formula "tariff for revenue only" has a barren sound to our ears in existing circumstances, because the tariff as we now know it is not a system of taxation; it is rather a vast body of economic expedients which have been used, under the guise of taxation, for the purpose of building up various industries, great and small, and enriching the nation as a body of individuals rather than as a government. It would be perfectly futile to propose out of hand a tariff for revenue only, because you cannot get out of a system except by systematic effort and adjustment, and the point to determine at present is not, How may we best secure the necessary revenue for the maintenance and conduct of our government by means of duties on imports, but How shall we adjust our duties on imports to the present real circumstances of the nation and the present interests of our economic development as a whole. Let the one example serve for many. What we want is not a set of issues which will sound like echoes of circumstances which no longer exist, but a set of issues arising out of and intended for the present.

The conservatism which should be sharply distinguished from this false and bastard conservatism, which is merely reactionary, is the conservatism which seeks a return to old and well recognized principles, but a return to them in such a way as will give them a new interpretation and a new meaning for the time we live in. The true conservatism consists in re-examining old principles, seeking such a reformulation of them as will adapt them to the circumstances of a new time. There is no danger that the tested principles of government which we have derived from the long experience of our race will be discredited, if we understand their present application. They will be discredited only by applying them in some inadequate or pedantic way. The true way to keep our principles is to keep our heads; is not to be confused by new circumstances, but to see how and where they square with the principles by which we are trying to be guided.

Let me take a few examples. Let my first example be drawn again from the question of the tariff, which after all is central to half the questions which now perplex us in regard to the reform of our economic structure and processes. The principle for which we should seek a new interpretation and application is this: That the power of government to tax ought never to be used to confer privileges upon individuals or groups of individuals, but should be used always and only to secure general benefits, the benefit of the tax-payers as a whole or of the nation as organism.

This general benefit and development was the object sought by our policy of protective tariff as it was originally conceived by Alexander Hamilton, and all valid arguments for that system are simply reiterations of his argument in his masterly Report on Manufactures. But there came a time, and it came very early in the history of our actual tariff legislation, when the adjustment of import duties became a matter of contest and bargain, of give and take, amongst the various interests which sought advantages. The tariff of 1828 was called the Tariff of Abominations, because it was thought not to be made in the general interest but to be a miscellaneous piling together of the various duties which manufacturers of different kinds desired. Tariffs of more recent date have been touched with the same disfigurement alike of symmetry and of principle. We need not stop to inquire when and where the line was crossed. Suffice it to say that it is the present general conviction that our more recent tariff legislation has been a doling out of privileges on the part of the government and that certain protected interests have been built up with no particular regard to the interests of the nation as a whole.

When privileges have been created, governmental oversight and regulation are necessary. Those who act upon privilege or enjoy any artificial advantage must be controlled. Those who act upon right need not be. Half our present difficulties arise from the fact that privileged interests have threatened to become too strong for the general interest, and that therefore the government has had to step in to restrain those who enjoyed the very privilege which it itself had granted. Reform, therefore, must come, not in the shape of a new adjustment of interests, but in the shape of a reconsideration of the general policy of the government in these matters which shall square it with the general interest. And this reform must proceed without injustice and with as little injury as possible. It must proceed, also, gradually and with a due regard to a maintenance of economic stability. But it must proceed fearlessly and it must proceed upon the principle, not that all protection is to be withdrawn, but that all protection is to be adjusted to the general interest and withdrawn from the field of the granting of special privileges and advantages.

Take another principle which true conservatism demands should be revived and retranslated into the terms of our present life. The control of the government should be exercised by processes of law and not by administrative discretion. This does not necessarily mean that the control of the government should be exercised only through the courts as we have known them, that is, only through the formal, elaborate, and somewhat tedious judicial processes which we have come to think of as characteristic of judicial action. The government may act less formally, more summarily, through commissions, without the violation of any fundamental principle of liberty, provided only the action of the commissions be made real process of law and not a process of mere discretionary practical judgment on the part of those who compose them. This is the true meaning for us of the old Jeffersonian principle "as little government as possible." For us that maxim means as little government by executive choice and preference, as little government as possible of the kind that varies the footing upon which interests are dealt with, which chooses its measures differently, instance by instance, leaves some untouched and brings others up with a sharp turn. It means as little government by discretionary authority as possible. It is not hostile to regulated and equalized freedom or to any process of law which is a calculable process of rule and proceeds by definite standards.

Take again the question of the power of the general government as against the power of the governments of the States. We should not waste our time upon any pedantic discussion of what constitutes State rights. We know that we still have a singularly various country, that it would be folly to apply uniform rules of development to all parts of the country, that our strength has been in the elasticity of our institutions, in the almost infinite adaptability of our laws, that our vitality has consisted largely in the dispersion of political authority, in the necessity that communities should take care of themselves and work out their own order and progress, and we know that in stating these things we are dealing with facts, not with abstract principles, and that out of these facts we can draw a very definite rule of action, namely, that in all that we do we should prefer a dispersion of governmental power to a concentration of it, that "home rule" should be the normal rule of life with us and that centralized authority should be the exception. We should not be afraid of it, as of a bugaboo, but we should not be in haste to set it up and should be very sure that we were ready for a general rule before we set up a general authority.

And then, to take a final instance, I think that we can be sure that we are not done with the principle of individual initiative, of individual right. We can still be very sure that any set of measures based upon the purpose of allowing the government to coach or dictate to the individual unnecessarily, where individual action is still possible, will certainly turn out to be measures for the impoverishment of the nation in respect of everything that goes to make for its variety and energy and enrichment. It is hard to find the individual in many cases amidst the present confusion of conditions, but we know that he is the source of energy for the nation nevertheless, and that to smother him is to produce a general mediocrity and inertia. Any form of collectivism which submerges him will certainly be fatal to our progress no less than to our liberty. Whatever laws we may devise, we must make sure not to lose him by any collective process.

Such should be our handling of old principles. In this way should they be made our guides, not to recovering the past; for we are not going in that direction and do not wish to recover it, but to threading the present and making sure of a wholesome and secure development in the future.

The Democratic Opportunity

By 1909 Wilson had his eyes on the governorship of New Jersey, and by late in the year he muted some of his more conservative ideas. He recognized more clearly that some of the problems of the day were national in scale and might require national action. He devoted particular attention to the intractable problem of the trusts and corporation malfeasance. In this article, written in

November and printed in the *National Monthly* in January, he threaded a fine line suggesting the blending of increasing federal action with respect for states' rights. The essay was somewhat technical in its analysis, and while he referred directly to Democratic party policy, his tone was not as explicitly partisan as it would soon become.

The Democratic party is now facing an unusual opportunity and a very great duty. The party in power has become entangled with all sorts of interests, great and small, has lost its freedom of choice in a hundred ways, and may be said by reason of its peculiar policies to have allied itself with something less than the nation as a whole. The Democratic party, on the other hand, is free from entanglements and is at liberty to choose policies suited to national conditions as a whole and to all the new aspects of politics which have revealed themselves in recent years. It is free to make a program for the general good, if it will, with perfect candor and simplicity.

It should do this without allowing itself to be embarrassed by old formulas. Most of the old formulas of our politics are worn thread-bare and have lost their significance, having been formulated for another age which had other and very different questions to settle, and which settled them with a sincerity which we can imitate only by translating our principles into new forms and statements.

Take, for example, the old formulas with regard to strict construction and the old ideal of "as little government as possible." The indisputable fact is that the Federal Government has in recent years been launched into many fields of activity even the existence of which previous generations did not foresee. We should not now stop to be pedantic about the way in which we shall construe the fundamental law of our Government or attempt the impossible task of forcing its present activities into the framework of old statements. We should seek the best construction, should direct the activities of the Federal Government toward the objects which clearly lie within its province by means which we are convinced to be just and efficient.

It was inevitable, in our changed conditions, that the Federal Government should come out into many new fields of power. I for one, am very zealous for the maintenance of the separate powers and authority of the individual States of the Union. But it is no longer possible with the modern combinations of industry and transportation to discriminate the interests of the several States as they could once be discriminated. Interests once local and separate have become unified and national. They must be treated upon a national scale, in a national spirit, and by the national Government. The Federal Government must, if possible, be kept to its old temper of restraint and carefully studied constitutional right, but it cannot be kept to a little field when the field is in fact great and must be occupied by some common authority. Our principles are not new, but the forms in which we should express them must of necessity be new. They are so novel, indeed, as often to make the principles themselves bear an appearance of radical novelty. There should be no limitation of functions of the Federal Government by number, but only limitation by carefully considered principle and carefully adopted instrumentalities of action.

The Democratic party has always stood for a careful restraint of the powers of government, and the position I am advocating is not in derogation of its ancient principles in this matter. But it should, whenever national action is necessary, be shy, not of governmental power, but of its organization in the wrong way and its use to the wrong ends. The debates of our coming campaigns must center upon the means we are to use in accomplishing ends which the whole country sees that it is necessary to accomplish. There are Democratic means which we can conscientiously and earnestly advocate, and there are radically undemocratic means which we should oppose with every ardor and power that is in us.

Undemocratic methods and means are those which serve the interest of parties or of groups of men and which ignore the general interest and the essential rights and opportunities and responsibilities of individuals. The Democratic principle is that government should study not only regulation but individual liberty and individual responsibility and that no regulation incompatible with the freedom and development of the individual is tolerable. This principle, rightly interpreted, leads to many interesting conclusions.

Stated in general terms, our principle should be: Government, not for the sake of success at whatever cost and the multiplication of material resources by whatever process, but for the sake of discriminating justice and a wholesome development as well as regulation of the national life.

☆ ☆ ☆

Apply our principle of government for the sake of justice and development to the trust question and observe what it will yield. We are at present trying the very hazardous experiment of regulation trusts in one or other of two ways. In the first place, we are attempting to restrain them from forms of organization and course of action which are against the general interest by the compulsion of fines and penalties. These fines and penalties generally fall, if paid, not upon the individuals responsible, but upon the stockholders, who under our present extraordinary administration of the law, are without any real power to control the business they nominally own. Fines also operate to take out of legitimate business large sums of money of which the public treasury is not in need and whose withdrawal embarrasses the general processes of trade and manufacture. It is a means of regulating which so far has certainly not accomplished its objects.

The other means by which we seek control is the government of public service corporations, as we have come to call them, through commissions. We have carried this method so far that we have virtually gone the length of dictating their management, which carries us very much beyond the point of mere control. We undertake through commissions to dictate to those corporations the methods and means by which they shall conduct their business and we threaten them with penalties of the severest sort if they do not obey the directions given them. These directions may or may not have regard to the possibilities of the case, may force upon those corporations policies and measures which will render their business unprofitable, and yet the government which dictates consents to no responsibility in the matter and has calmly adopted the policy of rule even if it involves ruin.

We do not see the significance of this method of control at present because the commissions so far appointed have generally consisted of men of some wisdom and great honesty, and public opinion has watched the processes of control with a constant critical scrutiny. But the method is only in its infancy. The opportunities it offers for political influence and individual tyranny, which are the bases of graft, every man who is well read in the history of government can easily perceive. By this method of control we shall presently run into choices we never dreamed of, into nothing less than the fundamental choices of government ownership and direction, so that responsibility shall not be divided from power.

There is only one principle in regard to these matters which the Democratic party can consistently or conscientiously adopt. It is this. That control shall not be managed in such a way as to increase the powers and temptations of those who administer government, but in such a way as shall make law supreme through judicial instrumentalities, by making it operate directly upon individuals and emphasizing in every item of legislation the responsibility of individuals. It is perfectly possible to make all corporations so disclose the detail of their organization as to make it evident to the officers of the law which official, which authority, from its board of directors down to its most subordinate responsible officer, is responsible for the acts of the corporation with which the law chooses to deal. That being done, it is perfectly feasible for the law to punish the person or persons directly who ordered any illegal thing done. Such a process would check and correct illegal and unconscientious practices as no fine or corporate penalty ever can, and is as feasible in the case of public service corporations as of those which perform a less direct and obvious public function. Here is something which lawyers can work out and which will clear the whole air of chicane and evasion, which will moreover, remove from the government the burden and the temptation of the actual administration or corporate undertakings. One conspicuous responsible person sent to the penitentiary for ignoring the public interest would do more to correct recent abuses than a thousand fines piled high upon one another or a thousand corporate penalties for disobeying the orders of commissions.

There is one way of keeping such principles in constant vigor and increasing the likelihood of their adoption and operation. That is to put public opinion in control. This can be done in only one way, but can in that way be completely and easily done. It can be done by a few fearless men who will take it upon themselves to give the public full information about everything of which they have any knowledge in connection with the management of parties, the making of laws, and the conduct of every part of the public business, by fearless and consistent candor with regard to everything the Government is handling and with regard to the ways in which it is being handled. It is an absolute dereliction of public duty on the part of anyone responsible for public affairs to regard anything done by governmental authority in the field of law or policy as a private transaction, to be determined by secret conferences upon grounds not disclosed to the public view. One of the most wholesome things that has been suggested with regard to the control of corporations is that there should be the utmost publicity in respect of their operations and obligations. It is strange that we have not seen that this is also the way to purify and control government.

We live in an age in which old things are passing away, in which all things are under scrutiny, in which the renaissance of government by opinion and the general interest is as plainly forecast by every sign of the times as it was in the period preceding the French Revolution. The world has learned self-control in the time which separates us from that revolution, and America of all countries is not apt to follow the hysterical ways which then set Europe in turmoil. It will use the ordinary instrumentalities of peace and counsel to bring the radical changes about which are now inevitable. The question I wish to leave with you is: "Will the Democratic party offer its services in the great enterprise?"

Campaign Speech for Governorship

This sample of Wilson on the campaign trail in New Jersey revealed his skill in mixing political analysis and partisanship. He first lashed out at the Republican bosses in Congress who were controlling national policy and then shifted the discussion to boss influence in New Jersey with a call for reform. It was an agile performance without reference to the key New Jersey Democratic machine leaders who supported his candidacy. His voice here became more frankly partisan, as in his attack on the Payne-Aldrich tariff law. He focused his attack on Senator Nelson Aldrich of Rhode Island and House Speaker Joseph Cannon, who seemed to wield more influence over national policy than President Taft. Clearly, he adjusted his writing style to fit the demands of a stump speech, repeatedly addressing his audience with pregnant questions. The speech was delivered in Elizabeth on October 28, 1910.

I wonder if you realize how great a change has taken place in American politics since the adjournment of Congress. It is very difficult to throw our minds back to the state of affairs which existed before the last Congress of the United States adjourned. At that time the politics of the country and the policy of the country were in the control of a small group of men at one end of the capitol combined in action and purpose with a small group of men at the other end of the capitol. It is possible to name a little handful of Senators who were the masters of the Senate and a little handful of representatives clustered about the speaker of the house who were masters of the house.

The President of the United States after the adjournment of Congress admitted in the public speech that it was impossible for him to guide the policy of his party without the consent and the cooperation, not of the rest of the party, but of this little group of men. He said that in order to get the policies which he thought absolutely necessary through this house, it was necessary to give these men what they wanted in the matter of the tariff.

And what did they want? Did they want to promote the interests of the country? Did the President himself intimate that they wanted to promote the interests of the country. Nothing of the kind, for he knew that the country was aware that these gentlemen were arranging a tariff policy for the country with regard to certain groups of men in the manufacturing and commercial world.

You have been reading no doubt the magazines and newspapers since the Payne-Aldrich tariff bill was passed, how it has been disclosed that most of the clauses contained in them what has been called, in bitter jest, a joker, the meaning of which has not been disclosed to the houses themselves, and which altered the tariff and adjusted it in a way in which the interests would never dare to argue their case in public the way they granted it adjusted.

Upon the floor of the Senate, Senators were unable to get explanations from the chairman of the finance committee, Mr. Aldrich of Rhode Island, concerning some of the most important features of the bill, and submitting to his refusal to give them information. That was only a very short time ago. Have you realized how short a time ago? Now, it is not only ancient history, but it is history impossible of repetition.

These gentlemen have—at least one of them has—retired or announced his retirement from public life. He was able to see the signs of the times, and knew it was more graceful to retire when you may than when you must. A gentleman at the other end of the capitol, the indomitable speaker of the last house of Representatives, has been showing a spirit which I must say, as a sportsman, I admire. He has not admitted his defeat, and he has defied his enemies and he has been deserted by his friends.

If I stood by Mr. Cannon in the fight he made against the House of Representatives last spring, I would not have deserted him this autumn. Either he was right or he was wrong. If he was right, the men who stood by him ought to stand by him now, and ought not come, when they feel the wind of public opinion blowing hot against him, and say that under no circumstances would they vote for Mr. Cannon as speaker.

I want to say very frankly that I do not understand, and I have contempt for, that kind of politics. But you know what it means. It means that Cannonism in these few months has become impossible, and men know it.

See how the plot of the play has changed. These men have had their brief time upon the stage and the play has read, "Exit, Aldrich, Exit, Cannon." Why have they withdrawn? They have withdrawn because, as I have just said, the plot of the play demands it. There is no place for them any longer in our politics. The public opinion of this country has awakened, and it is impossible that those men should play the part again that they have played in the past.

What is the part that they have played? I have already intimated; it is the part of private arrangement. I do not know anything duller than the politics of this country has been in recent years, and I do not know anything more interesting than the politics of this country right now. It is infinitely dull to go like driven cattle to the polls and pretend that you are exercising the sovereign right of ballot, to give to man a chance to do something that they never tell us about, and that we cannot understand.

That is a beautiful exercise of independence on the part of self-governing people, when our representatives are told in unmistakable terms that what they are voting for is that business of private arrangement, which is none of their business. Now, I have talked with gentlemen, with my fellow citizens, about this sort of thing. They have shrugged their shoulders and said that the legislative business chiefly affects the large money interests, and you cannot blame them for seeing that they are represented in our legislature. You cannot blame them for seeing that they are represented?

Are these men that we go through the motions of electing our representatives or the representatives of special interests? They are the representatives of private interest—a great many of them—and not of the public. But something has happened during the summer. I didn't notice anything particular or unusual about the weather last summer, but this autumn looks like another age in the politics of America.

Look at the personnel of the play as changed. Look at the extraordinary number of new men or made-over men that have come to the front. Now, I do not want to display any lack of modesty as a Democrat, and I want to call your attention to the fact that most of the new men have appeared on the Democratic side, and that most of the prominent men in the Republican ranks are made over. For example, take the leading insurgent, I have nothing to say against Mr. Record. He did me a great service.

But take the leading Insurgents of the Middle West. They are men who used to follow the leadership of Mr. Aldrich without question: but they have broken away from the leadership, and I suspect—I won't speak with undue confidence—but I suspect that they are following the people rather than leading them. They have heard things, and they have felt currents in that great wide western country which they do not dare resist, and they have made themselves, whether they would or not, spokesmen of the new spirit that is in America. But whether we regard them as genuine converts, or unwilling converts, they are converts, and their very conversion is proof of the point that I am making, that they have recognized that new spirit when men can face in a different direction and have another attitude than they have hitherto had in matters of politics.

What does it all mean? Why, it means that one thing that we ought to know, which only one party has recognized in New Jersey, the change. There is no apparent change whatever on the part of the leaders of the Republican party in this State. They held a convention on the twentieth day of September in the city of Trenton at which strenuous efforts were made to apprise them of the change of climate. They were urged to put into the platform and to express in their nominations the new spirit of the Republican party, and they refused to do so and heaped insult upon insult upon those who suggested it, and since that nomination their chief spokesman has been the spokesman for the unorganized Republican party, for I want to say that Republican party in most parts of this country has renewed itself, as the Democratic party has renewed itself—except in New Jersey. There are no symptoms upon the surface of these changes which I have been speaking of so far as the organized Republican party in this State is concerned. The symptoms are all on the Democratic side.

Well, what does it mean? Well, if you wish to put the lowest construction upon it, it means that the Democratic party has seen the handwriting on the wall; it means that the Democratic party knows enough to get in under cover when it rains. But I don't believe that that is all there is to it, because the Democratic party has not sought a leader whose habit is to get under cover. There are symptoms that the Democratic party wants new leaders and actually wants to be led; led in a different spirit from that which has obtained hitherto; led in the spirit of a new age, led in the spirit of new processes, of new politics altogether.

Now what does this all mean? Why it is a very happy thing to state what it means. It means the end of the boss system. By the boss system I don't mean merely the system of organized politics, for parties, in order to be cooperative, must be organized, and we must not heap contempt upon the men who do the hard work in maintaining that organization.

The boss system means that the boss is used for private ends. That is the heart of the boss system. The boss system does not mean the organization, but that the organization determines the policies, not from the point of view of the public, but from the point of view of certain private interests.

What is it that is galling to a member of the legislature? To find that the organization to which he belongs in his home country has this kind of a grip upon him. It is because he is told that he must vote for a particular bill. He had not been told anything about that bill when he was elected. He supposed he was elected as a representative of the people, but it seems not. The bosses have let him know that he will sacrifice their friendship, that he will no longer enjoy their political contributions if he does not order his men to vote for them.

His men! Why his men? Because he can prevent their renomination if he chooses and they are in his grip. Because they have done something in violation of the party? Not at all. Because they have done something which the boss does not like. There is where the pinch comes. Not because it is politics at all, but because it is private business. That is the boss system.

Have you not noticed how little politics there is in the boss system for public policy, for the things we discuss? Discussion! Why, that is the dress parade on the platform. It does not follow that because gentlemen walk up and down the stage and pledge you when they go to the State capitol they are going to vote as they talk, as much as they may wish to do so, because their political fortunes are sometimes held in the hollow of a man's hand, because of the private understanding that man has had with particular interests.

That is the terror of the boss system, for it is not politics at all and absolutely deprives us of representative government. Very well, that act is over; the curtain has fallen. That kind of so-called politics has been smoked out and we are so hot on the trail of it that capture of it is instantaneously probable. It is not seen in the open; it is seen only when it is in its burrow; and when politics consists of burrows and underground passages and places of concealment then it is neither interesting nor profitable. It is both interesting and profitable when it is brought out into the open and becomes a matter of common knowledge and common discussion.

Now this change means the discussion of public questions on their merits. You are to have a novel experience—the settlement of public questions on their merits, on the basis of real solid permanent public opinion, of people whose lives are affected by everything that is best and purest in the way of legislation, so that hereafter you will ask your representatives not "Whom do you serve?" but "What do you think?"

☆ ☆ ☆

Leaving individual personal merits entirely out of the question it does seem to me this is an opportune time in which to turn for a new deal, always provided however, always provided you do your part. If the people themselves don't think, if the people themselves don't see through public questions and make a point of supporting those who show the best disposition to serve them and the most enlightened method in serving, then there is nothing in the politics of free people.

You are not to entrust your government to someone and take your eyes and your attention and interest off of it, even if the men you entrust in that fashion did what they thought right. They would be without the necessary guidance, for the men who represent you must constantly know what you are thinking about; they must constantly be in touch with your thoughts and your knowledge, and with your determination, with your devotion to those things which are for the public interest, for we are seeking a very rare and a very great thing.

We are seeking to substitute for politics old and ancient and handsome things which we call statesmanship. A very clever writer once defined a statesman as a man of ordinary opinions and of extraordinary ability. Now, in my opinion, it is absolutely necessary for a statesman to be in constant touch with the general body of opinion and if he does not share that opinion, if he cannot form it, if he cannot lead it, if he cannot inspire it, then he is no statesman at all. He may be a prophet; he may be a great thinker; he may be a very inspiring person, but he is not a statesman.

A statesman is a man who, with his intimate connection whether he knows it or not, is with the great average body of thinking men. Men do think in this country; they do observe the course of affairs; they are full of the ardor of hope that they have entered upon a new age, and they are ready therefore, to breathe that breath which distilled will make public opinion; which understood will make statesmen and which will lift the level of politics until America will feel again the exhilaration of the age in which politics is a great altruistic undertaking, in which men's veins will throb with all those unselfish purposes which after all underlie all the great accomplishments of the human race, for the standard of statesmen is the common interest, and the common interest cannot be thought out interest by interest.

If capitalists think only of the interests of capitalists, and if merchants think only of the interests of commerce, if men in retail trade think only of the retail trader in the particular community, if the workingman thinks only of the interest of the workingman, we cannot make any progress.

Each class must think also of the interest of the rest; they must try to come to a common understanding, in a common sympathy, with a common thought and purpose, and then if we can get a spokesman, and honest man, to lead them, we will recover the prestige and hope and accomplishment of American politics.

Is it not a heartening prospect? Is it not like recovering some of the breath of that age in which America becomes a nation, when men thought not only in the terms of neighborhoods and trades and occupations, but that of the leadership of the world? What was in the writings of the men that founded America—to serve the selfish interests of America? Do you find that in their writings? No; to serve the cause of humanity, to bring liberty to mankind. They set up their standards here in America in the tenet of hope, as a beacon of encouragement to all the nations of the world, and men came thronging to these shores with a hope that never existed before, with a confidence they never dared feel before, and found here for generations together a haven of peace, of opportunity, of equality. God send that in the complicated state of modern affairs we may recover the standards and recover the achievements of that heroic age.

Inaugural as Governor

In contrast to the rhetoric of the campaign, there was a shift of tone appropriate to the occasion in the new governor's inaugural delivered at Trenton on January 17, 1911. The address was delivered to a joint session of the state legislature convened at the Taylor Opera House to accommodate spectators. The conservative Princeton president is difficult to recognize in this call for thoroughgoing progressive reform. Listing corporate regulation, friendly labor law, a public utilities commission, and the conservation of natural resources, the inaugural announced a reform agenda whose successful completion propelled Wilson toward the presidency. The Democratic party machine in New Jersey did much to make Wilson governor. The regulars would soon learn that Wilson was serious about reform, including the reduction of machine political influence by the adoption of new primary and election laws already enacted in more progressive states. New Jersey progressives were delighted.

Gentlemen of the Legislature: I assume the great office of Governor of the State with unaffected diffidence. Many great men have made this office illustrious. A long tradition of honorable public service connects each incumbent of it with the generation of men who set up our governments here in free America, to give men perpetual assurance of liberty and justice and opportunity. No one dare be sure that he is qualified to play the part expected of him by the people of the commonwealth in the execution of this high trust. It is best for him, as he sets out, to look away from himself and to concentrate his thought upon the people whom he serves, the sacred interests which are entrusted to his care, and the day in which he is to work, its challenge, its promise, its energies of opinion and of purpose, its sustaining hopes and exciting expectations. The scene will inspire him, not thought of himself.

The opportunity of our day in the field of politics no man can mistake who can read any, even the most superficial, signs of the times. We have never seen a day when duty was more plain, the task to be performed more obvious, the way which to accomplish it more easy to determine. The air has in recent months cleared amazingly about us, and thousands, hundreds of thousands, have lifted their eyes to look about them, to see things they never saw before, to comprehend things that once seemed vague and elusive. The whole world has changed within the lifetime of men not yet in their thirties; the world of business, and therefore the world of society and the world of politics. The organization and movement of business are new and upon a novel scale. Business has changed so rapidly that for a long time we were confused, alarmed, bewildered, in a sort of terror of the things we had ourselves raised up. We talked about them either in sensational articles in the magazines which distorted every line of the picture, or in conservative editorials in our newspapers, which stoutly denied that anything at all bad happened, or in grave discourses which tried to treat them as perfectly normal phenomena, or in legislative debates which sought to govern them with statutes which matched them neither in size nor shape.

☆ ☆ ☆

No wise man will say, of course, that he sees the whole problem of reform lying plain before him, or knows how to frame the entire body of law that will be necessary to square business with the general interest, and put right and fairness and public spirit in the saddle again in all the transactions of our new society but some things are plain enough, and upon these we can act.

In the first place, it is plain that our laws with regard to the relations of employer and employee are in many respects wholly antiquated and impossible. They were framed for another age, which nobody now living remembers, which is, indeed, so remote from our life that it would be difficult for many of us to understand it if it were described to us. The employer is now generally a corporation or huge company of some kind; the employee is one of hundreds or of thousands brought together, not by individual masters whom they know and with whom they have personal relations, but by agents of one sort or another. Workingmen are marshaled in great numbers for the performance of a multitude of particular tasks under a common discipline. They generally use dangerous and powerful machinery, over whose repair and renewal they have no control. New rules must be devised with regard to their obligations and their rights, their obligations to their employers and their responsibilities to one another. New rules must be devised for their protection, for their compensation when injured, for their support when disabled.

We call these questions of employers' liability, questions of workingmen's compensation, but those terms do not suggest quite the whole matter. There is something very new and very big and very complex about these new relations of capital and labor. A new economic society has sprung up, and we must effect a new set of adjustments. We must not pit power against weakness. The employer is generally in our day, as I have said, not an individual, but a powerful group of individuals, and yet the workingman is still, under our existing law, an individual when dealing with his employer, in case of accident, for example, or of loss or of illness, as well as in every contractual relationship. We must have a workingman's compensation act which will not put upon him the burden of fighting powerful composite employers to obtain his rights, but which will give him his rights without suit, directly, and without contest, by automatic operation of law, as if of a law of insurance.

This is the first adjustment needed, because it affects the rights, the happiness, the lives and fortunes of the largest number, and because it is the adjustment for which justice cries loudest and with the most direct appeal, to our hearts as well as to our consciences.

But there is regulation needed which lies back of that and is much more fundamental. The composite employer himself needs to have his character and powers overhauled, his constitution and rights reconsidered, readjusted to the fundamental and abiding interests of society. If I may speak very plainly, we are much too free with grants of charters to corporations in New Jersey. A corporation exists, not of natural right, but only by license of law, and the law, if we look at the matter in good conscience, is responsible for what it creates. It can never rightly authorize any kind of fraud or imposition. It cannot righteously allow the setting up of a business which has no sound basis, or which follows methods which in any way outrage justice of fair dealing or the principles of honest industry. It thereby authenticates what it ought of right to forbid.

I would urge, therefore, the imperative obligation of public policy and of public honesty we are under to effect such changes in the law of the State as will henceforth effectually prevent the abuse of the privilege of incorporation which has in recent years brought so much discredit upon our State. In order to do this it will be necessary to regulate and restrict the issue of securities to enforce regulations with regard to bona fide capital, examining very vigorously the basis of capitalization, and to prescribe methods by which the public shall be safeguarded against fraud, deception, extortion, and every abuse of its confidence.

And such scrutiny and regulation ought not to be confined to corporations seeking charters. They ought also to be extended to corporations already operating under the license and authority of the State. For the right to undertake such regulation is susceptible of easy and obvious justification.

☆ ☆ ☆

Such regulation, based on thorough and authoritative inquiry, will go far towards disclosing and establishing those debatable values upon which so many questions of taxation turn. There is an uneasy feeling throughout the State, in which, I dare say, we all share, that there are glaring inequalities in our system or, at any rate, in our practice of taxation. The most general complaint is, that there is great inequality as between individuals and corporations. I do not see how anyone can determine whether there are or not, for we have absolutely no uniform system of assessment. It would seem that in every locality there is some local variety of practice, in the rate, the ratio of assessment value to market value, and that every assessor is a law unto himself. Our whole system of taxation, which is no system at all, needs overhauling from top to bottom. There can be no system, no safety, no regulation in a multitude of boards. An efficient Public Utilities Commission will be a beginning towards a system of taxation as well as toward a system of corporate control. We cannot fairly tax values until we have ascertained and established them.

And the great matter of conservation seems to me like part of the same subject. The safeguarding of our water supply, the purification of our streams in order to maintain them as sources of life, and the protection against those who would divert them or diminish their volume for private profit, the maintenance of such woodlands as are left us and the reforestation of bare tracts more suited for forest than for field, the sanitation of great urban districts such as cover the northern portions of our State, by thorough systems of drainage and of refuse disposal; the protection of the public health and the facilitation of urban and suburban life—these are all public obligations which fall sooner or later upon you as lawmakers of the commonwealth, and they are all parts of the one great task of adjustment which has fallen to our generation.

☆ ☆ ☆

Back of all reform lies the method of getting it. Back of the question what you want lies the question, the fundamental question of all government, how are you going to get it? How are you going to get public servants who will obtain it for you? How are you going to get genuine representatives who will serve your real interests, and not their own or the interests of some special group or body of your fellow-citizens whose power is of the few and not of the many? These are the queries which have drawn the attention of the whole country to the subject of the direct primary, the direct choice of representatives by the people, without the intervention of the nominating machine, the nominating organization.

I earnestly commend to your careful consideration in this connection the laws in recent years adopted in the State of Oregon, whose effect has been to bring government back to the people and to protect it from the control of the representatives of selfish and special interests. They seem to me to point the direction which we must also take before we have completed our regeneration of a government which has suffered so seriously and so long as ours has here in New Jersey from private management and organized selfishness. Our primary laws, extended and perfected, will pave the way. They should be extended to every elective office, and to the selection of every party committee or official as well, in order that the people may once for all take charge of their own affairs, their own political organization and association; and the methods of primary selection should be so perfected that the primaries will be put upon the same free footing that the methods of election themselves are meant to rest upon.

We have here the undoubtedly sound chain and sequence of reforms: an actual direct choice by the people of the men who are to organize alike their parties and their government, and those measures which true representatives of the people will certainly favor and adopt—systematic compensation for injured workingmen; the careful regulation in the common interest of all corporations, both in respect of their organization and of their methods of business, and especially of public service corporations; the equalization of taxes; and the conservation of the natural resources of the State and of the health and safety of its people.

Another matter of the most vital consequence goes with all these: namely, systematic ballot reform and thorough and stringent provisions of law against corrupt practices in connection alike with primaries and with elections. We have lagged behind our sister States in these important matters, and should make haste to avail ourselves of their example and their experience. Here, again, Oregon may be our guide.

This is a big program, but it is a perfectly consistent program, and a perfectly feasible program, and one upon whose details it ought to be possible to agree even within the limits of a single legislative session. You may count upon my co-operation at every step of the work.

☆ ☆ ☆

I shall take the liberty from time to time to make detailed recommendations to you on the matters I have dwelt upon, and on others, sometimes in the form of bills if necessary.

We are servants of the people, of the whole people. Their interest should be our constant study. We should pursue it without fear or favor. Our reward will be greater than that to be obtained in any other service: the satisfaction of furthering large ends, large purposes, of being an intimate part of that slow but constant and ever hopeful force of liberty and of enlightenment that is lifting mankind from age to age to new levels of progress and achievement, and of having been something greater than successful men. For we shall have been instruments of humanity, men whose thought was not for themselves, but for the true and lasting comfort and happiness of men everywhere. It is not the foolish ardor of too sanguine or too radical reform that I urge upon you, but merely the tasks that are evident and pressing, the things we have knowledge and guidance enough to do; and to do with confidence and energy. I merely point out the present business of progressive and serviceable government, the next stage on the journey of duty. The path is as inviting as it is plain. Shall we hesitate to tread it? I look forward with genuine pleasure to the prospect of being your comrade upon it.

7

Road to the White House

A Labor Day Address in Buffalo

Woodrow Wilson launched his presidential campaign with a Labor Day address in Buffalo, New York, on September 2, 1912. When he failed to win his party's nomination, Theodore Roosevelt had bolted the Republican party and ran as a Bull Moose Progressive, promising a program of broad reform action. Reflecting the spirit of his own presidency and some of the ideas of Herbert Croly's *Promise of American Life,* Roosevelt called for a "New Nationalism," prosecuted by strong leaders managing a powerful government. Challenging Roosevelt in his home state with its forty-five electoral votes, Wilson here spoke with a Jeffersonian voice to attack Theodore Roosevelt's ideas. Though calling for progressive reform, Wilson cited the dangers of placing a strong government in the hands of a few powerful men, the very condition against which history records rebellions. Reform, he argued, was essential, but not with such changes as would pose a threat to liberty. On that Labor Day he addressed workingmen's concerns and attacked Republican leaders for their partnerships with special interests, but his main target was Roosevelt, who would prove a more formidable threat than the sitting president, William Howard Taft.

When I was engaged in the campaign before my election as Governor of New Jersey, I made a good many promises, and I think that a great many people who heard me supposed that it was the usual thing that these promises were made in order to get votes, and that the man who made them would not feel the full responsibility of keeping them after he was elected. I don't know what the reason is—perhaps because I went into politics rather late in life—but I felt that every promise that I made in that campaign I was bound to try to fulfill. No man can promise more than that he will do his best. I had not tried my hand at politics. I did not know, and I told my friends in New Jersey that I did not know, whether I could bring those things to pass or not, but I did tell them that there was one thing I did know: that I would make everybody very uncomfortable if these things were not done. And I did not except the members of my own party. I promised to make the men of the Democratic party , as well as the men of the Republican party, very uncomfortable if the promises of the campaign were not fulfilled; and it was more the dread of discomfort than anything else that brought about the passage of the bills which constituted one of the most extraordinary programs of reform that we have seen in modern times in a single state.

I don't claim any credit for that. I speak of it in order to point a moral which seems to me the most important moral in politics. The only strength I had was that I was known to be, in the circumstances, the spokesman of the people of New Jersey, and the only reason I was dreaded was not that I had offices to give away, for I would not condescend to give an office in order to accomplish a political end, but because it was known that all I had to do was to ask the people of New Jersey what they thought, and they would say what they thought. . . .

I want to speak upon this occasion of course on the interests of the workingman, of the wage earner, not because I regard the wage earners of this country as a special class, for they are not. After you have made a catalogue of the wage earners of this country, how many of us are left? The wage earners of this country, in a broad sense, constitute the country, and the most fatal thing that we can do in politics is to imagine that we belong to a special class and that we have an interest which isn't the interest of the whole community. Half of the difficulties, half of the injustices of our politics, have been due to the fact that men regarded themselves as having separate interests which they must serve even though other men were done a great disservice by their promoting them. We are not afraid of those who pursue legitimate pursuits, provided they link those pursuits in at every turn with the interest of the community as a whole; and no man can conduct a legitimate business if he conducts it in the interest of a single class. I want, therefore, to look at the nation as a whole today. I would like always to look at it as a whole, not divided up into sections and classes. But I want particularly to discuss with you today the things which interest the wage earner. That is merely looking at the country as a whole from one angle, from one point of view, to which for the time being we will confine ourselves.

I want, as a means of illustration, not as a means of contest, to use the platform of the third party as the means of expounding what I have to say today. I want you to read that platform very carefully, and I want to call your attention to the fact that it really consists of two parts. In one part of it, it declares the sympathy of the party with a certain great program of social reform and promises that all the influence of that party, of the members of that party, will be used for the promotion of that program of social reform. In the other part, it itself lays down a method of procedure, and what I want you to soberly consider is whether the method of procedure is a suitable way of laying the foundation for the realization of that social program. With regard to the social program, the betterment of the condition of men in this occupation and the other, the protection of women, the shielding of children, the bringing about of social justice here, there, and elsewhere, with that program, who can differ in his heart, who can divorce himself in sympathy from the great project of advancing the interests of human beings wherever it is possible to advance them?

But there is a central method, a central purpose, in that platform from which I very seriously dissent. I am a Democrat as distinguished from a Republican because I believe, and I think that it is generally believed, that the leaders of the Republican party, for I always distinguished them from the great body of Republican voters who have been misled by them, I say not the Republican party, but the leaders of the Republican party, have allowed themselves to become so tied up in alliances with special interests that they are not free to serve us all. And that the immediate business, if you are to have any kind of reform at all, is to set your government free, is to break it away from the partnerships and alliances and understandings and privileges which have made it impossible for it to look at the country as a whole and made it necessary for it to serve special interests one at a time. Until that has been done, no program of social reform is possible, because a program of social reform depends upon universal sympathy, universal justice, universal cooperation. It depends upon our understanding one another and serving one another.

What is this program? What is the program of the third party with regard to the disentanglement of the government? Mr. Roosevelt has said, and up to a certain point I sympathize with him, that he does not object, for example, to the system of protection, except in this circumstance, that it has not inured to the benefit of the workingmen of this country. It is very interesting to have him admit this, because the leaders of the Republican party have been time out of mind putting this bluff upon you men that the protective policy was for your sake. I would like to know what you ever got out of it that you didn't get out of it by the better effort of organized labor. I have yet to learn of any instance where you got anything without going and taking it. The process of our society, instead of being a process of peace, has sometimes too much resembled a process of war, because men felt obliged to go and insist in organized masses upon getting the justice which they couldn't get any other way. It is interesting, therefore, to have Mr. Roosevelt admit that not enough of the "prize" money, as he frankly calls it, has gone into the pay envelope. I admit that not enough of the money has gone into the envelope. I wish it were not "prize" money, because dividing up "prize" money and dividing up earnings are two very different things. And it is very much simpler to divide up earnings than to divide up "prize" money, because the money is "prize" money for the reason that a limited number of men got together and obtained it from the Ways and Means Committee of the House and the Finance Committee of the Senate, and we paid the bills.

But Mr. Roosevelt says that his object will be to see that a larger proportion gets into the pay envelope. How does he propose to do it? I am here, not to make a speech, I am here to argue this thing with you gentlemen. How does he propose to do it? I don't find any suggestion anywhere in that platform of the way in which he is going to do it, except in one plank. One plank says that the party will favor a minimum wage for women and then it goes on to say that by a "minimum wage" it means a living wage, enough to live on. I am going to assume, for the sake of argument, that it proposes more than that, that it proposes to get a minimum wage for everybody, men as well as women, and I want to call your attention to the fact that just as soon as a minimum wage is established by law, the temptation of every employer in the United States will be to bring his wages down as close to that minimum as he dare, because you can't strike against the Government of the United States, you can't strike against what is in the law. You can strike against what is in your agreement with your employer, but if underneath that agreement there is the steel and the adamant of federal law, you cannot tamper with that foundation. And who is going to pay these wages? Do you know that one of the great difficulties about wages now is that the control of industry is getting into fewer and fewer hands, and that therefore a smaller and smaller number of men are able to determine what wages shall be? In other words, one of the entanglements of our government is that we are dealing not with a community in which men may take their own choice in what they shall do, but with a community whose industry is very largely governed by great combinations of capital in the hands of a comparatively small number of men; in other words, we are in the hands in many industries of monopoly itself. And the only way in which the workingman can get more wages is by getting it from the monopoly.

Very well, then. What does this platform propose to do? Break up the monopolies? Not at all. It proposes to legalize them. It says in effect, "You can't break them up. The only thing you can do is to put them in charge of the federal government." It proposes that they shall be adopted and regulated, and that looks to me like a consummation of the partnership between monopoly and government, because when once the government regulates the monopoly, then monopoly will have to see to it that it regulates the government. This is a beautiful circle of change.

We now complain that the men who control these monopolies control the government, and it is in turn proposed that the government should control them. I am perfectly willing to be controlled if it is I myself who controls me. If this partnership can be continued, then this control can be manipulated and adjusted to its own pleasure. Therefore I want to call your attention to this fact, that these great combined industries have been more inimical to organized labor than any other class of employers in the United States. Is not that so? These monopolists that the government, it is proposed, should adopt are the men who have made your independent action most difficult. They have made it most difficult that you should take care of yourselves, and let me tell you that the old adage that God takes care of those who take care of themselves is not gone out of date. No federal legislation can change that thing. The minute you are taken care of by the government, you are wards, not independent men. And the minute they are legalized by the government, they are proteges and not monopolists. They are the guardians and you are the wards. Do you want to be taken care of by a combination of the government and the monopolies? Because the workingmen of this country are perfectly aware that they sell their commodity, that is to say labor, in a perfectly open market. There is free trade in labor in the United States. The workingmen of all the world are free to come and offer their labor here, and you are similarly free to go and offer your labor in most parts of the world; and the world demand is what establishes for the most part the rate of wages. At the same time, these gentlemen who are paying wages in a free-trade market are protected by an unfree market against competition that would make them bid higher because bid in competition and not bid under protection. If I am obliged to refrain from going into a particular industry by reason of the combination that already exists in it, I can't become an employer of labor and I can't compete with these gentlemen for the employment of labor, and the whole business of the level of wages is artificially and arbitrarily determined.

Now I say, gentlemen, that a party that proposes that program cannot, if it carries out that program, put forward these other handsome purposes of social regeneration, because they have crystallized, they have hardened, they have narrowed the government which is to be the source of this thing. After all this is done, who is to guarantee to us that the government is to be pitiful, that the government is to be righteous, that the government is to be just? Nothing will then control the powers of the government except open revolt, and God forbid that we should bring about a state of politics in which open revolt should be substituted for the ballot box! I believe that the greatest force for peace, the greatest force for righteousness, the greatest force for the elevation of mankind, is organized opinion, is the thinking of men, is the great force which is in the soul of men, and I want men to breathe a free and pure air. And I know that these monopolies are so many cars of Juggernaut which are in our very sight being driven over men in such ways as to crush their life out of them. And I don't look forward with pleasure to the time when the Juggernauts are licensed. I don't look forward with pleasure to the time when the Juggernauts are driven by commissioners of the United States. I am willing to license automobiles, but not Juggernauts, because if any man ever dares take a joy ride in one of them, I would like to know what is to become of the rest of us, because the road isn't wide enough for us to get out of the way. We would have to take to the woods and then set the woods on fire.

I am speaking partly in pleasantry, but underneath, gentlemen, there is a very solemn sense in my mind that we are standing at a critical turning point in our choice.

Now you say, on the other hand, what do the Democrats propose to do? I want to call your attention to the fact that those who wish to support these monopolies by adopting them under the regulation of the Government of the United States are the very men who cry out that competition is destructive. And they ought to know, because it is competition as they conducted it that destroyed our economic freedom. They are certainly experts in destructive competition, and the purpose of the Democratic leaders is this, not to legislate competition into existence again, because statutes can't make men do things, but to regulate competition. What has created these monopolies? Unregulated competition. It has permitted these men to do anything that they chose to do to squeeze their rivals out and to crush their rivals to the earth. We know the processes by which they have done these things. We can prevent those processes by remedial legislation, and that remedial legislation will so restrict the wrong use of competition that the right use of competition will destroy monopoly. In other words, ours is a program of liberty and theirs is a program of regulation. Ours is a program by which we say we know the wrongs that have been committed and we can stop those wrongs, and we are not going to adopt into the governmental family the men who have done the wrongs and license them to do the whole business of the country.

I want you men to grasp the point because I want to say to you right now the program that I propose doesn't look quite as much like acting as a Providence for you as the other program looks. But I want to frankly say to you that I am not big enough to play Providence, and my objection to the other program is that I don't believe there is any other man that is big enough to play Providence. I have never known any body of men, any small body of men, that understood the United States. And the only way the United States is ever going to be taken care of is by having the voices of all the men in it constantly clamorous for the recognition of what is justice as they see the light. A little group of men sitting every day in Washington City is not going to have a vision of your lives as a whole. You alone know what your lives are. I say, therefore, take the shackles off of American industry, the shackles of monopoly, and see it grow into manhood, see it grow out of enshackled childishness into robust manliness, men being able to take care of themselves and reassert the great power of American citizenship. These are the ancient principles of government the world over. For when in the history of labor here in this country, or in any other, did the government present its citizens with freedom and with justice? When has there been any fight for liberty that wasn't a fight against this very thing, the accumulation of regulative power in the hands of a few persons?

I in my time have read a good deal of history and, if I were to sum up the whole history of liberty, I should say that it consisted at every turn in human life in resisting just such projects as are now proposed to us. If you don't believe it, try it. If you want a great struggle for liberty that will cost you blood, adopt this program, put yourselves at the disposal of a Providence resident in Washington and then see what will come of it. Ah, gentlemen, we are debating very serious things, and we are debating this: Are we going to put ourselves in a position to enter upon a great program of understanding one another and helping one another? I can't understand you unless you talk to me. I can't understand you by looking at you. I can't understand you by reading books. With apologies to the gentlemen in front of me, I couldn't even understand you by reading the newspapers. I can understand you only by what you know of your own lives and make evident in your own actions. I understand you only in proportion as you . . . take care of yourselves, and make your force evident in the course of politics. And, therefore, I believe in government as a great process of getting together, a great process of debate.

☆ ☆ ☆

It is amazing to me that public-spirited, devoted men in this country have not seen that the program of the third party proclaims purposes and in the same breath provides an organization of government which makes the carrying out of those purposes impossible.

I would rather postpone my sympathy for social reform until I had got in a position to make things happen. And I am not in a position to make things happen until I am part of a free organization which can say to every interest in the United States: "You come into this conference room on an equality with every other interest in the United States, and you are going to speak here with open doors; there is to be no whispering behind the hand; there is to be no private communication; what you can't afford to let the country hear had better be left unsaid."

What I fear, therefore, is a government of experts. God forbid that in a democratic country we should resign the task and give the government over to experts. What are we for if we are to be scientifically taken care of by a small number of gentlemen who are the only men who understand the job? Because if we don't understand the job, then we are not a free people. We ought to resign our free institutions and go to school to somebody and find out what it is we are about.

☆ ☆ ☆

It is very embarrassing to me, I will tell you frankly, to appear as one who solicits your votes. I would a great deal rather get elected first and then come back to you and say, "Now, what are we going to do?" Because before election a man is in this unpleasant position: he is as much as saying "Elect me, and you just see what I will do." Now, no man is big enough to say that truthfully. He can say it, but he oughtn't to say it. But after the election the point is not what will he do, but what will you back him up in doing?—what will *we* do? I had rather argue politics in the plural than in the singular. It is a lonely business arguing it in the singular. All that you can promise in the singular is that there'll be a good deal doing, that you won't allow yourself to be fooled, even by your own party, and that the pledges you take upon yourself individually you will do your best to carry out, whether anybody else goes with you or not. But I am not afraid of that. If the American people elect a man President and say, "You go on and do those things," nobody is going to head him off, because there is a force behind him which nobody dares resist,—that great impulse of just opinion without which there is no pure government at all.

I don't know any other appeal, therefore, than this appeal to you as Americans, as men who constitute the bone and sinew of American citizenship and who, when you address yourselves to the discussion of public affairs, know what the realities are, and are not deceived by the appearances. Let us get together and serve the Government of the United States.

The New Freedom

As his presidential campaign proceeded, Wilson's focus went beyond criticism of Republican rule to emphasis on distinguishing his positions from those of Roosevelt. He avoided using the label "Progressive party" for Roosevelt's campaign and referred instead to the two branches of the Republican party. Minimizing the obvious differences between Taft and Roosevelt, Wilson lumped them together as Tweedledum and Tweedledee Republicans responsible for the failures of past policies. The Democrats, he argued, offered new hope, but there was little mention of specific proposals for change. Details about economic matters and the need for new initiatives against the trusts came in the days that followed. In this speech on October 3 in Indianapolis, Wilson referred to a "new freedom" for America. The phrase struck a responsive chord and served the campaign as an alternative slogan to Roosevelt's "New Nationalism."

Mr. Chairman, fellow citizens: It would move any man very deeply, I think, to face a vast concourse like this, and certainly it constitutes for me one of the supreme privileges of my life. I cannot see you, and inasmuch as I am not boastful of my beauty, I trust you cannot see me! But I would, if I could, convey to you some of the thoughts that are suggested to my mind by this vast concourse of people.

It is impossible that a great body of people like this has come together merely out of curiosity, merely out of the habit of political rally, merely in order to show their interest in a political campaign of the ordinary kind. I believe that there is abroad in this country a very profound interest in the fundamental issues of this campaign, and I do not wonder that that interest is profound, for those issues are the issues of life and of death.

I do not believe that any speaker can exaggerate for you the critical character of the present political situation. We talk, and we talk in very plausible phrases, indeed, about returning the government of this country to the people of this country. . . . Because, as I think of the great Democratic party which has entrusted me with the responsibility of leading it, I ask myself, "What is the thing that is expected by the people of the United States of this great party?"

Because the thing that we are proposing to do, ladies and gentlemen, is, as I have just now said, to restore the Government of the United States to the people. And this issue has arisen because it is sadly true that the Government of the United States has not been under the control of the people in recent decades. We have found something intervening between us and the government which we supposed belonged to us, something intangible, something that we felt we could not grapple with, something that it was impossible to tear away from, a space that lay between us and the government at Washington. And the thing I want to impress upon your thought tonight is merely this: The Democratic party is the only party that is now proposing to take away the influences which have governed the administration of this country and kept it out of sympathy with the great body of the people.

I want you particularly to notice that there are only two parties in the present campaign, or rather that there is one party and two fragments of another party. Because it is not Democrats that have gone over into the new party, it is almost exclusively Republicans. And what we are facing, therefore, is two segments of a great disrupted party, and those two segments are made up in this way. You know that on the one hand are those who call themselves the regular Republicans, and those on the other hand who try to arrogate to themselves entirely the name of Progressives. But what I want you to realize is that these Progressives have not drawn to themselves the old force, the old insurgent force, of the Republican party.

You know that for a long time we have been seeing this split about to occur in the Republican party. For a long time there have been men showing their courage, here, there, and elsewhere, who, though they still called themselves Republicans, protested against the prevalent policy of the Republican party. These men for a long time were called by different names. In New Jersey we called them the New Idea Republicans, when being fair to the people was a new idea among Republicans. And in other parts of the country they were called by other designations, but presently we began to call them insurgents.

Now, what I want to call your attention to is the fact that the new party, the third party, has not drawn to itself the full strength, or even all the principal leaders, of the insurgent Republicans, because this circumstance appeals to every man who thinks the present situation over. The very things that we are protesting against, the very conditions that we are trying to alter, are conditions which were created under the two leaders of the two branches of the present Republican party, because it is true that these conditions were just as much created under Mr. Roosevelt as they have been created under Mr. Taft. There was a growth during his administration of the great monopolies, which we call trusts, upon a scale never before dreamed of and upon a greater scale than has been characteristic of the administration of his successor.

Some time ago, during the campaign which preceded the two Republican political conventions, you remember that there was a very interesting campaign between Mr. Taft and Mr. Roosevelt. And everything that anybody could say against Mr. Taft, Mr. Roosevelt said. And everything that anybody could say against Mr. Roosevelt, Mr. Taft said. And the Democrats were inclined to believe both of them, for the truth was that Mr. Taft was merely the successor of Mr. Roosevelt in the prosecution of policies which Mr. Taft did not alter but merely sought to confirm and establish.

You have therefore this extraordinary spectacle of the two branches of the Republican party, both of them led by men equally responsible for the very conditions which we are seeking to alter. And the reason that some of the insurgent Republicans are not following Mr. Roosevelt, the reason that men like Mr. La Follette, for example, are not following Mr. Roosevelt, is that they have already tested Mr. Roosevelt when he was President and have found that he was not willing to cooperate with them along any line that would be efficient in the checking of the evils of which we complain. So that the leader of the very movement which is proposed for our emancipation is a man who has been tried in this very matter and not found either willing or competent to accomplish the objects that we now seek.

In order to confirm my view of the matter, you have only to read Mr. La Follette's autobiography, and I advise everyman who can lay his hands on a copy of the *American Review* to read that extraordinary narrative. There, in detail, it is told how Mr. La Follette and others like him carried proposals to the then President, Mr. Roosevelt, which would have made this campaign inconceivable. And after he had, following his first generous impulse, consented to cooperate with them, he subsequently drew back and refused to cooperate with them, under what influences I do not care to conjecture, because it is not my duty and it would be very distasteful to me to call in question the motives of these gentlemen. That is not my object or my desire. My object is merely to point out the fact that the very conditions we are trying to remedy were built up under these two gentlemen who are the opponents of the Democratic party. Therefore, to my mind it is a choice between Tweedledum and Tweedledee to choose between the leader of one branch of the Republican party and the leader of the other branch of the Republican party, because what the whole country knows to be true, these gentlemen deny.

The whole country knows that special privilege has sprung up in this land. The whole country knows, except these gentlemen, that it has been due chiefly to the protective tariff. These gentlemen deny that special privilege has been caused by the administration of the protective tariff. They deny what all the rest of the country has become convinced is true. And after they have denied the responsibility of the tariff policy for special privilege, they turn about to those creatures of special privilege which we call the trusts, those organizations which have created monopoly and created the high cost of living in this country, and deny that the tariff created them. Not only that, but deny that it is possible to reverse the process by which that monopoly was created, because in the very platform of the third party (if I had thought there would be light enough to read it to you, I would have brought it and read it), in the very platform of the third party, it is not said that they intend to correct the conditions of monopoly, but merely that they intend to assuage them, to render them less severe, to legalize and moderate the processes of monopoly. So that the two things we are fighting against, namely, excessive tariffs and almost universal monopoly, are the very things that these two branches of the Republican party both decline to combat. They do not so much as propose to lay the knife at anyone of the roots of the difficulties under which we now labor. On the contrary, they intend to accept these evils and stagger along under the burden of excessive tariffs and intolerable monopolies as best they can through administrative commissions. I say, therefore, that it is inconceivable that the people of the United States, whose instinct is against special privilege and whose deepest convictions are against monopoly, should turn to either of these parties for relief when these parties do not so much as pretend to offer them relief.

It is this circumstance that puts me in a very sober mood. It is this process which makes me feel that great bodies of men of this sort have come together, not in order to whoop it up for a party, not in order to merely look at a candidate, but to show there is a great uprising in this country against intolerable conditions which only the Democratic party proposes to attack and to alter. Only the Democratic party is ready to attack and alter these things. Do you see any breach anywhere in the Democratic ranks? Don't you know that wherever you live men are coming as volunteers, recruits into the ranks of the Democrats? Don't you know that everywhere that you turn men are taking it for granted that the country must follow this party or else wander for another four years in the wilderness?

There are some noble people, there are some people of very high principle, who believe that they can turn in other quarters for relief, but they do so simply because there is one of these parties that blows beautiful bubbles for them to see float in the air of oratory, men who paint iridescent dreams of uplifted humanity, men who speak of going to the rescue of the helpless, men who speak of checking the oppression of those who are overburdened, men who paint the picture of the redemption of mankind and don't admit who they are, who are preaching this doctrine. They are the men whom we have seen and tested, and their conversion is after the time when they possessed the power to do these things and refused to do them.

Is humanity burdened now for the first time? Are men in need of succor now who were not in need of succor ten years ago? Are men now in need of protection by the government who did not need protection when these gentlemen exercised the tremendous power of the office of President? Is it not true that when Theodore Roosevelt was President of the United States the people of the United States were willing to follow him wherever he led? And where did he lead them? When did he turn in the direction of this great uplift of humanity? How long was the vision delayed? How impossible was it for him to see it when his arm was strong to come to the succor of the weak! And now he has seen it, when he wishes to regain their confidence, which by his failure to act he had forfeited!

And so I say it is not as if novices had come before us. It is not as if men had come before us who had seen these things all their lives and waited, waited in vain for an opportunity to do them. For we know the men we are dealing with, and we know that there are men in this third party who are following that leader notwithstanding the fact that they do not believe in him. They simply want a third party because they do not yet find themselves ready to trust the Democratic party and yet are unwilling to trust the regulars among the Republican party. So that they are hoping that something may happen, even under a leader whom they do not have full confidence in, that will enable mankind to find an opportunity to cast its masses against the gates of opportunity and at least burst them open by the great rush of their gathering multitudes. They do not look for guidance. They merely hope for the consummation of their united power in a blind effort to escape something that they fear and dread.

Ah, gentlemen, shall they go under such shepherds? Shall they go deliberately so shepherded? Shall mankind follow those who could have succored them and did not?

Now, on the other hand, what can we say in all honesty and truth of the Democratic party? Why, gentlemen, the Democratic party was preaching these doctrines and offering you leaders to carry them out before these gentlemen ever admitted that anything was wrong or had any dream of the hopes of humanity. We didn't wait until the year 1912 to discover that the plain people in America had nothing to say about their government. We have been telling you that for half a generation and more. We have been warning you of the very things that have come to pass, in season and out of season. We have kept a straight course. We have never turned our faces for one moment from the faith that was in us, the faith in the common people of this great commonwealth, this great body of commonwealths, this great nation. And now what is happening? Why, with renewed hope, with renewed confidence, with renewed ardor of conviction, under leaders chosen after the freest fashion that our politics have ever witnessed—chosen freely at Baltimore, chosen yesterday freely for perhaps the first time within our recollection in the Empire State of New York—untrammeled leaders, leaders who have no obligations except to those who have trusted and believed in them, are now asked to lead the Democratic party along those paths of conviction which these other gentlemen have so recently found, which they have found only now that they see that these are the paths perhaps to a renewal of their power.

I would not speak, I would not say, one word of bitterness, but I do utter my profound protest against the idea that it is possible to do these things through the instrumentality of new converts. I say that those who are rooted and grounded in this faith, those who have been willing to stay out in the cold as minorities through half a generation, are men tried to the bottom of all that is in them. Their stuff is tried out in the furnace, and they are now ready to serve you, and they are ready as an absolutely united team. Where will you find any disinclination to take the signals from the leader? Where will you find any clefts in the Democratic ranks? Is it not true that this solid phalanx, with its banners now cast to the wind, is marching with a tread that shakes the earth to take possession of the government for the people of the United States? This is what heartens the men who are in this fight. This is what quickens their pulses. This is what makes everything worthwhile that has to be done in the honest conduct of a frank campaign.

For our object, as we call you to witness, throughout this campaign is to discuss not persons, but issues. We are not interested in persons. I tell you frankly, I am not interested even in the person who is the Democratic candidate for President. I am sorry for him. I am sorry for him because I believe he is going to be elected and I believe that there will rest upon him the duty of carrying out these fundamental tasks. And there will be no greater burden in our generation than to organize the forces of liberty in our time in order to make conquest of a new freedom for America. It will be no child's play, but I believe that it will be possible. Because a man is not as big as his belief in himself. He is as big as the number of persons who believe in him. He is as big as the force that is back of him. He is as big as the convictions that move him. He is as big as the trust that is reposed in him by the people of the country. And with that trust, with that confidence, with that impulse of conviction and hope, I believe that the task is possible, and I believe that the achievement is at hand. . . .

For the business in hand, my fellow citizens, is very serious business indeed. Any state which does not now get into the procession for the renewal of the rights of man will be sorry for it a generation from now. But if their vote is recorded on the right side on the fifth of November, they will sometimes say to their children, "Yes, we took part in the re-emancipation of America on the fifth of November 1912." And I pray God that no man whom you trust on the fifth of November 1912 will ever be coward enough to betray you to your enemies, because with this great people behind them, those who surrendered again to the malign influences which have been governing the administration at Washington would indeed be cowards and renegades.

I beg that when you go to the polls on the fifth of November, you will go with quiet minds and very sober thoughts. For you are then to make your choice whether you will live under legalized monopoly for the rest of your lives or seek the way of release, which it is perfectly possible to find, by seeing to it that those who have oppressed you open again the fields of competition, so that new men with brains, new men with capital, new men with energy in their veins, may build up enterprises in America. And, amidst a nation stimulated to every kind of new endeavor, we shall find again the paths of liberty, the paths of peace, the paths of common confidence, and therefore the only paths that lead to prosperity and success.

Appeal to Republicans

What was probably Wilson's best effort in the presidential campaign came on October 28, at the Philadelphia Academy of Music. To an audience largely composed of Republicans disaffected with both Taft and Roosevelt, Wilson accused Republican leaders of neglecting their rank-and-file to serve the interests of privilege and to restrict competition. He proposed a program of economic and political liberty. Knowing his audience, he appealed to their progressive sympathies, defending American enterprise now endangered by powerful monopolists and financiers who were stifling competition. During the campaign, Wilson drew counsel on the trust problems from Louis D. Brandeis, on whom he would continue to rely for help during his presidency. One may note that in this speech, when he again warned of too much government, Wilson referred to "big brother" government years before George Orwell famously used the term.

Mr. Chairman and my fellow citizens:

You have certainly given me a welcome which makes my heart very warm indeed. I consider it a great privilege to be allowed to face an audience like this and declare the faith that is in me. Perhaps you think it is personally agreeable to me to have it proved that I am the logical choice for President of the United States, though it gives one a rather abstract feeling to be reduced to a logical conclusion. But I want to assure you that it is only upon one condition that that conclusion is gratifying to me. It is always, provided I entertain and speak and represent your thoughts, because no man can consider himself big enough to stand alone as President of the United States. He is big and. strong in proportion to the faith lodged in him, to his power to express the general thought, to his courage to execute the general purpose.

Throughout this campaign, ladies and gentlemen, I have again and again insisted before every audience that I have faced that there is no personal question involved in this campaign. It is not a comparison of persons; it is a comparison of purposes, of conceptions, of programs. You must vote next week according to what you want done, and what you regard as the most feasible means of getting those things done, for this is in one very deep sense a business campaign. We are now about to transact the affairs of America. That is the reason that great audiences like this assemble; great audiences of men who have thrown off the trammels of party control, but have taken on the obligations of public conviction; who know that conscience takes precedence of tradition; who know that men and measures are to be judged according to their individual character and not according to their nominal associations; who know, moreover, that things are to be done by men habituated to doing and not by men who have repented of not having done them.

I have been very much interested in seeing the slowly gripping and gathering paralysis of the regular Republicans, because they started out when they had their convention with a hopeful program of reform. They spoke our language. They admitted that things were wrong and said they ought to be changed, but now everywhere that I go I see spread upon the billboards warnings against doing anything, and everywhere the motto: "It is better to be safe than to be sorry." I know what that means. I know that it means that the same misgiving and paralysis is upon that branch of the Republican party that lay upon it just before and just after the last presidential election. These gentlemen then proposed a program of reform, but they did absolutely nothing to carry out that program of reform, and whenever it was proposed from any quarter they said: "No, it ought to be done, but that isn't exactly the way to do it, and it is better to be safe than to be sorry."

And now, after other hopeful promises, after giving us additional assurances, they draw back and say: "Beware! If the Democrats are chosen, they will do something, and God forbid that any man should disturb anything in America; things have happened that are bad, but they have happened; they have come to stay; they are inevitable; to disturb them is to destroy our equipoise; is to endanger a cataclysm, is to threaten a panic." Think of the American people being panic-stricken at the idea of reforming their own government! It is the logical conclusion of the uses that have recently been made of the protective system, because that protective system says you can't do anything for yourselves, the government has to do it all for you. It has sapped the originative powers; it has sapped the independence; it has checked the energy of America, and now we are asked not to venture to exercise our energy at all. There is no serious dispute among thoughtful men as to what have been the consequences of the recent *uses* to which the protective policy has been put, because, as your chairman said, we are not debating radical changes. . . .

Now, with regard to radical changes in the national program nobody is proposing to upset business, and the very gentlemen who are threatening you with the upturning of the foundations of business know that nobody is proposing to do more than they promised to do and broke their promise. I want to ask you to face very frankly the actual circumstances in which we stand and then ask yourselves what we ought to do.

The so-called tariff system has ceased to be a system of protection. It has become a system of extortion, of special favors and of monopoly, and it is extortion and special favors and monopoly that we propose to root out and nothing else. In the meantime, what has happened? Trade in this country has been checked, not fostered. Anybody who studies the figures will see that America, so far as the merchant is concerned, and the manufacturer, is now in a sort of straitjacket; she is almost bursting the bands that hold her because she is producing a great deal more than the domestic market can take up. And if you do not open the gates of foreign commerce, America will presently come to a case of very serious difficulty and congestion indeed. And while we have been provincial and domestic and have turned all our energies in upon ourselves, until we have grown too big for the very territory that we occupy, what have we done?

We have destroyed the means of commerce. We have allowed our merchant marine to go absolutely to decay, and now we are in this case: Suppose that a great department store did not maintain any delivery system at all and depended upon the wagons of another rival department store to deliver all their goods, how satisfactory do you think that would be to the customers or the owners of the department store?

☆ ☆ ☆

Domestic competition used to take care of the prices; domestic competition used to keep America quickened with life; domestic competition used to beckon new men on all the time to the handsome adventures of American enterprise; but more and more the processes of monopoly are quenching the fires that burned in us of energy and of originative power; and that, under the aegis, under these protecting, outstretched wings of a tariff policy devised by these gentlemen who have built up the trusts, not devised in the interest of the general stimulation of American industry, but devised in order to contain, hidden in the secret phrases of selected schedules, the very favors by which these men have thriven and built up their own power.

That is the so-called protective policy that we have entered the lists against. We have entered the lists in order to free the average man of enterprise in America and make ourselves masters of our own fortunes once again, because what I want to impress upon every thoughtful voter is this: The trusts lie like a great incubus on the productive part of American brains.

☆ ☆ ☆

Safeguard American men against unfair competition and they will take care of themselves. We do not want a big-brother government. I do not know what may be your preference, but I do not want a government that will take care of me. I want a government that will make other men take their hands off so I can take care of myself. What have these gentlemen wrought? What have they brought about? They have brought about a closed field of industry and a closed market for credit. That is what they have brought about. Of course, if I can't get credit, I can't begin. No man produces capital out of his own brains. I do not exude capital, and no man exudes capital.

The basis of all credit is what the man who has money believes that I can do if he lends me the money. That is the ultimate basis for credit. But if he doesn't know me, or if he knows me only to fear me, he doesn't extend his credit to me at all, and in order to get credit in America it is not sufficient that your neighbor should know you. You have to be known either in New York or Chicago or St. Louis or San Francisco, and if you are not recognized there by your financial backing, not your character, you can't get any big credit at all.

We have had disclosed in recent years all the processes by which monopoly is established and competition prevented, and I say that we can remove those obstacles one by one as they disclose themselves by directing the criminal statutes of the federal law against it. I heard an amazing statement the other day. I heard that some prominent businessman said about me that he didn't like this idea of putting everybody in jail. Everybody? Has it come to that? Do these gentlemen think there are so many persons who have laid themselves open to incarceration?

I am not desirous of putting everybody in jail; selected specimens will do. Laws in the United States are not retroactive. Anybody can keep out of jail who knows what the law is, and knows that there are men behind it who will enforce it. If you make the processes by which small men, small beginners, are undersold in particular markets, criminal; if you penalize in the same way those discriminations by which retail dealers are punished if they deal in the goods of anybody except the big manufacturers; if you see to it that raw materials are sold, not upon terms which you prescribe, but upon the same terms to everybody; if you see that the closed market for credit is opened by a very different and radically different banking system, then you have freed America. And I, for my part, am willing to stop there and see who has the best brains.

I am not interested in helping the man who cannot get to the top of his own force of character and of mind. I am merely interested in seeing that every man is free to make the most of himself. I have said again and again that I have no pill against an earthquake. I have no patent remedy for anything.

I have no knowledge of the methods, the various methods, by which water could be squeezed out of stock. I am not of an inventive turn of mind and do not know the machinery by which the water could be removed. But I am perfectly willing to see these gentlemen try to carry the water in a free competitive market. They had better begin now like the fabled man who began by carrying a calf and carried it every day until he carried a full-grown bull. They will need muscle; they will need steadiness of knee; they will need sturdiness of physical make-up; but if they can do it, I shall applaud. Because, if they can economize their processes and concentrate their energy so that by brains and efficiency they can beat anybody else, I will take off my hat to them as an American.

Now they are afraid to set their brains against others. It is their cowardice that strikes me as much as their power. They dare not let other men come into the field of competition. I challenge them, if they don't want changes made, voluntarily to open the field of competition. We won't touch it if they will in good faith voluntarily open it, for we have no commission to disturb anything that is able or honest or sound in America.

☆ ☆ ☆

And what strikes me about both branches of the Republican party is this: They say, as I intimated at the beginning, these things that have happened, these unfortunate things that have happened, cannot be reversed. There is no remedy. There is only an alleviation. All you can do is to regulate them, to modulate them, to take the sting out of them, to see that our masters are pitiful and kind; you can't divest yourselves of their mastery, neither can you conduct a government except upon the advice of your masters. These gentlemen commit themselves to the processes which are approved of by the men who have gained a mastery in American industry and in American credit, and therefore they say: "We can deal with these masters; we are in their confidence; they are patriotic men; they will do us no harm if we ask them to do us no harm; if we associate ourselves with them, they will perhaps be obedient to our behests, but we are not going to even suggest anything that goes to the root of any evil that we have suffered—we have no remedy to propose."

They are like doctors who say, "Yes, my dear friend, you are in a bad way; you are dying; but I will see to it that your closing hours are without pain. I will see to it that you are amused and employed. I will see to it that all the air is full of benevolent enterprises and that you are properly taken care of until the end comes." Did you ever reflect upon the basis of privilege? Benevolence doesn't consist in those who are prosperous pitying and helping those who are not. Benevolence consists in a fellow feeling that puts you upon actually the same level with the fellow who suffers. And I want to see a government the conscience of which does not originate with the prosperities of the country, with the bounties of the country, with the benevolence of those who have power and who have wealth. I want to see a government rooted also in the pains and sufferings of mankind. I want to see a government which is not pitiful but full of human sympathy.

I want to see a government which does not condescend, but takes part in the common life. I want to see a government that feels the thrill of the men who are struggling and does not lean down and lend them a helping hand, but walks with them in the common way and says, "Men and brethren, it is a common life; we must live it together; we must do one another justice." Privilege from above? There is no such benevolence. I say it with all reverence, but I believe that the benevolence of God does not consist in pitying us as weak creatures, but in understanding us and putting the whole Providence of God behind the best things that are in us. And so with government, which ought not to be a Providence, but should be merely the expression of the common life. It cannot lend a helping hand to mankind; it must speak for mankind.

And, ladies and gentlemen, is not that the American enterprise? America was created to illuminate the path of progress for the ordinary man. Any country in the world can show you examples of great and powerful and rich men who have prevailed and made their power felt. America is not distinguished for being rich; other countries have been rich and other countries have been disgraced, disgraced in their very heartless use of their wealth and of their power. America will have lost her title deed unless she shows that she is devoted to the interests of the rank and file of humanity.

What I have come tonight, therefore, to urge upon you as an enterprise in which we can all sink our party traditions and unite with the thought of the people, is to propose to you that as Americans we band ourselves together to restore America. And these gentlemen who offer to rescue us have not been associated with America. The men under whom trusts multiplied from forty to a thousand, from forty to ten thousand, have become accustomed to the multiplication of trusts; it is actually come to the pass that they regard monopoly as the law of nature in business. And if that is the law of nature, then America as a free government just goes out of business. Because the statement of the Democratic platform is the statement that sums up history: that private monopoly is absolutely indefensible and intolerable. If it is any monopoly, it must be a public monopoly and not a private monopoly.

You know what the processes of modern society are. They are not individualistic. They are processes of association, and those processes contain in them a danger that governments never saw before. Because men never before had the means or the genius for association that they have now, and the danger at the present moment is that private association will become stronger than public association, and that there will be combinations of men and of money stronger than the government itself. If we take this thing in hand now, it may be that we shall prevail. If we do not take it in hand now, it may be that we shall not prevail. The time is all too long postponed. The danger is so great that it will need all the prudence, all the moderation, all the intelligence, all the good nature of America to revive her ancient standards and repractice her ancient principles. If we postpone it, our temper may change. And we shall postpone it if we do not put the Democratic party in power.

I beg you to believe that I do not say that as a partisan. I want to call every man's attention here to the fact that that is the only party, as an organized and united force, that can, in the circumstances, be put in charge of all the branches of the government of the United States. Isn't that true? That is true as a practical proposition. If you want a united and organized force, led by men who are in entire sympathy with this practical program, and who will be in a position to carry the program out, there is nothing to do in the year 1912 except to put the Democrats in power from the top to the bottom.

Look what the country has done! It has carried its wave of impulse forward a little way, but never the whole way. The most interesting thing about the government of the United States is that under its constitutional balances it postpones everything. You can capture your House of Representatives in any second-year period, but you cannot capture your Senate in two years; and it may be that at the time you capture your House you haven't a chance to capture your Presidency. The present House of Representatives is Democratic because the Republican party broke its promises. But, even with the assistance of the independent Republicans in the Senate of the United States, it wasn't possible to put the program for which the country had been waiting past the veto of the President. So that you have an arrested government. You have a government that is not responding to the wishes of the people. You have a government that is not functioning, a government whose very energies are stayed and postponed. If you want to release the force of the American people, you have got to get possession of the Senate and the Presidency as well as of the House.

The only question, therefore, is do you trust the men who are now leading the Democratic party? If you believe that they are the enemies of legitimate business, do not vote for them. If you believe that they are wild-eyed reformers who do not know the prudent courses of change, do not vote for them. If you believe that they are inexperienced tyros who do not know right from wrong, who do not know the practicable from the impracticable, do not vote for them. Vote as you trust; vote as you believe; and if you see anybody else proposing to do these things and in a position to say that he knows how to do them, vote for him. I am not here as a partisan at all. I am perfectly willing to be set aside if there is somebody else who can and will do the job. . . .

I have a very deep sympathy with the next President of the United States, whoever he may be. Because I believe that we have come to the parting of the ways. I believe that as America acts now, as America determines next week, so will be the fortunes of the present and of the next generation. And, therefore, a very great solemnity comes into my thought as I face an audience like this. I am bound to be frank with you. I would be ashamed of myself if I were not. If I pretended to know it all, I would wish you to think me a fraud. If I pretended to do anything except to attempt to interpret your knowledge of affairs and your purposes, I should wish you to turn away from me. For this is a time when the common thought of the nation must determine her destiny.

We have been in the hands of trustees long enough. We have been in the hands of receivers when we were not bankrupt. The business is perfectly solid, and the stockholders are going to resume control. And the stockholders are those who have their souls in their own charge, the fortunes of their sons and daughters at their hearts, their knowledge of the general energies of America that are being checked at their consciences. These are the stockholders; for the stock of America is spiritual, not material. The only stock that America has that she can't sell everywhere in the world consists in her political ideals, in her willingness to sacrifice some material advantage.

If only a larger number of persons may be free and happy, that is the only thing that gives us the dignity and the pride to which we hope we are entitled among the nations of the world, and so, in this closing week of the campaign, I hope that every independent Republican, not only, but every Democrat, will think of the nation and of nothing else; will not think of his own business particularly.

Do you not see what happens? You take a straw vote and men vote their real individual preference. Then when it comes to election day they say: "Yes, he is the man I think qualified to be President, but somebody is going to squeeze me if I vote for him. My interest, my weakness, my cowardice, my dependence, lie that way." And thousands of men vote against their convictions for fear of the things that may happen to them.

But, thank God! that kind of man is no longer in a controlling number in America. We have been fooled just as often as we are going to be fooled. We have been misled just as often as we are going to be misled. The only reason that the Republican party has gone to pieces is that the leaders of the Republican party did not know what the voters of the Republican party were thinking about. . . . Audiences like this have gathered together because they know that the Republican leaders do not know the Republican party, and the Republican party is now seeking to rid itself of the mistakes, not of its rank and file, but of the men who have too long postponed consulting them, the men who have not regarded their votes and who have broken all the promises that they have made to them.

So that I am not appealing to you as a Democrat only; I am appealing to you as nearly as I can define it in this way, as myself, a free American, connected with an organization that has set itself free, proposing a program which every free and self-respecting man can vote for.

It doesn't make any difference how you are going to vote four years from now. We will wait and see. It doesn't make any difference whether you are permanently breaking your connections with the old Republican party or not. It may be that they will repent. It may be that they will see the light. It may be that they will consult a larger number of persons. It may be that they will understand America. It may be that they will know that the year 1912 was not like the year 1812. It may be that some intimation of history, some suggestion of an old ideal, will steal into their thoughts again. And then you can go back to them. But we will take our chances on what happens four years from now. We aren't voting in 1916. We are voting in 1912. And in 1912 all Americans who desire to restore America must join together in a great renaissance of those ideals which quicken the blood.

☆ ☆ ☆

I hope I haven't been giving you any reminiscence of the talk of the stump tonight. Nothing that has all its essence in rhetoric, but the hard business of life, the fortunes of the men who are in the midst of the struggle, the pulses of the men who are swimming against the stream, all the hard things that happen from the time you go to work until the time you drop exhausted into bed. These are the essentials of America. And if our eyes grow dull and the lamp of hope flickers in us and goes out, if we say we will live under masters and must be submissive, if we say we have no right to initiate our own affairs, if we say we must follow our party discipline and not choose our own course, then how dull will the days grow in America! How the world will look on and say, "The light has gone out; liberty has forgotten her children; America was to lead us and she has betrayed us! We know no whither to which to turn. Republics are springing up in ancient incrusted China, and America hasn't even recognized the new form of government!"

Have we forgotten our children? Have we lost the touch of our own birthright? Are we not the children of light any more? We must now band ourselves together in a new corporate entity, the sons and lovers and champions of economic and political liberty.

8

President Wilson

Presidential Inaugural Address

On the morning of March 4, 1913, Wilson and his vice president, Thomas R. Marshall, met with President Taft at the White House, and from there the inaugural party motored to the Capitol. The president-elect was greeted by a cheering crowd at the east front of the building, where Chief Justice Edward D. White administered the oath of office. Only one other Democrat, Grover Cleveland, had taken the oath since James Buchanan in 1857. Taking control of the government with Democrats in the majority in both houses of Congress, Wilson recognized this rare opportunity and promised a government of reform and renewal. The new president's inaugural address suggested the progressive thrust of his administration. Noting that material success, moral strength, and democracy had come at the price of corruption, waste, and great human cost, now a new vision called for action in the service of the nation and its people. His appeal was to the spirit of the nation with a moving call for an era "where justice and mercy are reconciled, and the judge and the brother are one."

There has been a change of government. It began two years ago, when the House of Representatives became Democratic by a decisive majority. It has now been completed. The Senate about to assemble will also be Democratic. The offices of President and Vice President have been put into the hands of Democrats. What does the change mean? That is the question I am going to try to answer, in order, if I may, to interpret the occasion.

It means much more than the mere success of a party. The success of a party means little except when the nation is using that party for a large and definite purpose. No one can mistake the purpose for which the nation now seeks to use the Democratic party. It seeks to use it to interpret a change in its own plans and point of view. Some old things with which we had grown familiar, and which had begun to creep into the very habit of our thought and of our lives, have altered their aspect as we have latterly looked critically upon them, with fresh, awakened eyes; have dropped their disguises and shown themselves alien and sinister. Some new things, as we look frankly upon them, will to comprehend their real character, have come to assume the aspect of things long believed in and familiar, stuff of our own convictions. We have been refreshed by a new insight into our own life.

We see that in many things that life is very great. It is incomparably great in its material aspects, in its body of wealth, in the diversity and sweep of its energy, in the industries which have been conceived and built up by the genius of individual men and the limitless enterprise of groups of men. It is great also, very great, in its moral force. Nowhere else in the world have noble men and women exhibited in more striking forms the beauty and the energy of sympathy and helpfulness and counsel in their efforts to rectify wrong, alleviate suffering, and set the weak in the way of strength and hope. We have built up, moreover, a great system of government, which has stood through a long age as in many respects a model for those who seek to set liberty upon foundations that will endure against fortuitous change, against storm and accident. Our life contains every great thing, and contains it in rich abundance.

But the evil has come with the good, and much fine gold has been corroded. With riches has come inexcusable waste. We have squandered a great part of what we might have used, and have not stopped to conserve the exceeding bounty of nature without which our genius for enterprise would have been worthless and impotent, scorning to be careful, shamefully prodigal as well as admirably efficient. We have been proud of our industrial achievement, but we have not hitherto stopped thoughtfully enough to count the human cost, the cost of lives snuffed out, of energies overtaxed and broken, the fearful physical and spiritual cost to the men and women and children upon whom the dead weight and burden of it all has fallen pitilessly the years through. The groans and agony of it all had not yet reached our ears, the solemn, moving undertone of our life, coming up out of the mines and factories and out of every home where the struggle had its intimate and familiar seat. With the great government went many deep secret things which we too long delayed to look into and scrutinized with candid, fearless eyes. The great government we loved has too often been made use of for private and selfish purposes, and those who used it had forgotten the people.

At last a vision has been vouchsafed us of our life as a whole. We see the bad with the good, the debased and decadent with the sound and vital. With this vision we approach new affairs. Our duty is to cleanse, to reconsider, to restore, to correct the evil without impairing the good, to purify and humanize every process of our common life without weakening or sentimentalizing it. There has been something crude and heartless and unfeeling in our haste to succeed and be great. Our thought has been "Let every man look out for himself; let every generation look out for itself," while we geared giant machinery which made it impossible that any but those who stood at the levers of control should have a chance to look out for themselves. We had not forgotten our morals. We remembered well enough that we had set up a polity which was meant to serve the humblest as well as the most powerful, and remembered it with pride. But we were very heedless and in a hurry to be great.

We have come now to the sober second thought. The scales of heedlessness have fallen from our eyes. We have made up our minds to square every process of our national life again with the standards we so proudly set up at the beginning and have always carried in our hearts. Our work is a work of restoration.

We have itemized with some degree of particularity the things that ought to be altered, and here are some of the chief items: A tariff which cuts us off from our proper part in the commerce of the world, violates the just principles of taxation, and makes the government a facile instrument in the hands of private interests; a banking and currency system based upon the necessity of the government to sell its bonds fifty years ago and perfectly adapted to concentrating cash and restricting credits; an industrial system which, take it on all its sides, financial as well as administrative, holds capital in leading strings, restricts the liberties and limits the opportunities of labor, and exploits without renewing or conserving the natural resources of the country; a body of agricultural activities never yet given the efficiency of great business undertakings or served as it should be through the instrumentality of science taken directly to the farm, or afforded the facilities of credit best suited to its practical needs; watercourses undeveloped, waste places unreclaimed, forests untended, fast disappearing without plan or prospect of renewal, unregarded waste heaps at every mine. We have studied as perhaps no other nation has the most effective means of production, but we have not studied cost or economy as we should either as organizers of industry, as statesmen, or as individuals.

Nor have we studied and perfected the means by which government may be put at the service of humanity, in safeguarding the health of the nation, the health of its men and women and its children, as well as their rights in the struggle for existence. This is no sentimental duty. The firm basis of government is justice, not pity. These are matters of justice. There can be no equality of opportunity, the first essential of justice in the body politic, if men and women and children be not shielded in their lives, their very vitality, from the consequences of great industrial and social processes which they cannot alter, control, or singly cope with. Society must see to it that it does not itself crush or weaken or damage its own constituent parts. The first duty of law is to keep sound the society it serves. Sanitary laws, pure food laws, and laws determining conditions of labor which individuals are powerless to determine for themselves are intimate parts of the very business of justice and legal efficiency.

These are some of the things we ought to do, and not leave the other undone, the old-fashioned, never to be neglected, fundamental safeguarding of property and of individual right. This is the high enterprise of the new day: to lift everything that concerns our life as a nation to the light that shines from the hearth-fire of every man's conscience and vision of the right. It is inconceivable that we should do this as partisans; it is inconceivable we should do it in ignorance of the facts as they are or in blind haste. We shall restore, not destroy. We shall deal with our economic system as it is and as it may be modified, not as it might be if we had a clean sheet of paper to write upon; and step by step we shall make it what it should be, in the spirit of those who question their own wisdom and seek counsel and knowledge, not shallow self-satisfaction or the excitement of excursions whither they cannot tell. Justice, and only justice, shall always be our motto.

And yet it will be no cool process of mere science. The nation has been deeply stirred, stirred by a solemn passion, stirred by the knowledge of wrong, of ideals lost, of government too often debauched and made an instrument of evil. The feelings with which we face this new age of right and opportunity sweep across our heartstrings like some air out of God's own presence, where justice and mercy are reconciled and the judge and the brother are one. We know our task to be no mere task of politics but a task which shall search us through and through, whether we be able to understand our time and the need of our people, whether we be indeed their spokesmen and interpreters, whether we have the pure heart to comprehend and the rectified will to choose our high course of action.

This is not a day of triumph; it is a day of dedication. Here muster, not the forces of party, but the forces of humanity. Men's hearts wait upon us, men's lives hang in the balance; men's hopes call upon us to say what we will do. Who shall live up to the great trust? Who dares fail to try? I summon all honest men, all patriotic, all forward-looking men, to my side. God helping me, I will not fail them, if they will but counsel and sustain me!

Address at Gettysburg

On the fiftieth anniversary of the battle, July 4, 1913, Wilson delivered this address at Gettysburg. After a tribute to the men who fell in battle, the president reflected on the past fifty years, which, he said, had brought the nation security and great strength. But the work was not done. Using military metaphor, he called on Americans to enlist in a continuing campaign of nation building. He urged action to do the "harder things" necessary to fulfill the country's destiny.

Friends and Fellow Citizens: I need not tell you what the battle of Gettysburg meant. These gallant men in blue and gray sit all about us here. Many of them met here upon this ground in grim and deadly struggle. Upon these famous fields and hillsides their comrades died about them. In their presence it were an impertinence to discourse upon how the battle went, how it ended, what it signified! But fifty years have gone by since then, and I crave the privilege of speaking to you for a few minutes of what those fifty years have meant.

What have they meant? They have meant peace and union and vigor, and the maturity and might of a great nation. How wholesome and healing the peace has been! We have found one another again as brothers and comrades in arms, enemies no longer, generous friends rather, our battles long past, the quarrel forgotten—except that we shall not forget the splendid valor, the manly devotion of the men then arrayed against one another, now grasping hands and smiling into each other's eyes. How complete the union has become and how dear to all of us, how unquestioned, how benign and majestic, as state after state has been added to this our great family of free men! How handsome the vigor, the maturity, the might of the great nation we love with undivided hearts; how full of large and confident promise that a life will be wrought out that will crown its strength with gracious justice and with a happy welfare that will touch all alike with deep contentment! We are debtors to those fifty crowded years; they have made us heirs to a might heritage.

But do we deem the nation complete and finished? These venerable men crowding here to this famous field have set up a great example of devotion and utter sacrifice. They were willing to die that the people might live. But their task is done. Their day is turned into evening. They look to us to perfect what they established. Their work is handed on to us, to be done in another way but not in another spirit. Our day is not over; it is upon us in full tide.

Have affairs paused? Does the nation stand still? Is what the fifty years have wrought since those days of battle finished, rounded out, and completed? Here is a great people, great with every force that has ever beaten in the lifeblood of mankind. And it is secure. There is no one within its borders, there is no power among the nations of the earth, to make it afraid. But has it yet squared itself with its own great standards set up at its birth, when it made that first noble, naive appeal to the moral judgment of mankind to take notice that a government had now at last been established which was to serve men, not masters? It is secure in everything except the satisfaction that its life is right, adjusted to the uttermost to the standards of righteousness and humanity. The days of sacrifice and cleansing are not closed. We have harder things to do than were done in the heroic days of war, because harder to see clearly, requiring more vision, more calm balance of judgment, a more candid searching of the very springs of right.

Look around you upon the field of Gettysburg! Picture the array, the fierce heats and agony of battle, column hurled against column, battery bellowing to battery! Valor? Yes! Greater no man shall see in war; and self-sacrifice, and loss to the uttermost; the high recklessness of exalted devotion which does not count the cost. We are made by these tragic, epic things to know what it costs to make a nation—the blood and sacrifice of multitudes of unknown men lifted to a great stature in the view of all generations by knowing no limit to their manly willingness to serve. In armies thus marshaled from the ranks of free men you will see, as it were, a nation embattled, the leaders and the led, and may know, if you will, how little except in form its action differs in days of peace from its action in days of war.

May we break camp now and be at ease? Are the forces that fight for the nation dispersed, disbanded, gone to their homes forgetful of the common cause? Are our forces disorganized, without constituted leaders and the might of men consciously united because we contend, not with armies, but with principalities and powers and wickedness in high places? Are we content to lie still? Does our union mean sympathy, our peace contentment, our vigor right action, our maturity self-comprehension and a clear confidence in choosing what we shall do? War fitted us for action, and action never ceases.

I have been chosen the leader of the nation. I cannot justify the choice by any qualities of my own, but so it has come about, and here I stand. Whom do I command? The ghostly hosts who fought upon these battlefields long ago and are gone? These gallant gentlemen stricken in years whose fighting days are over, their glory won? What are the orders for them, and who rallies them? I have in my mind another host, whom these set free of civil strife in order that they might work out in days of peace and settled order the life of a great nation. That host is the people themselves, the great and the small, without class or difference of kind or race or origin; and undivided in interest, if we have but the vision to guide and direct them and order their lives aright in what we do. Our constitutions are their articles of enlistment. The orders of the day are the laws upon our statute books. What we strive for is their freedom, their right to lift themselves from day to day and behold the things they have hoped for, and so make way for still better days for those whom they love who are to come after them. The recruits are the little children crowding in. The quartermaster's stores are in the mines and forests and fields, in the shops and factories. Every day something must be done to push the campaign forward; and it must be done by plan and with an eye to some great destiny.

How shall we hold such thoughts in our hearts and not be moved? I would not have you live even today wholly in the past, but would wish to stand with you in the light that streams upon us now out of that great day gone by. Here is the nation God has builded by our hands. What shall we do with it? Who stands ready to act again and always in the spirit of this day of reunion and hope and patriotic fervor? The day our country's life has but broadened into morning. Do not put uniforms by. Put the harness of the present on. Lift your eyes to the great tracts of life yet to be conquered in the interest of righteous peace, of that prosperity which lies in a people's hearts and outlasts all wars and errors of men. Come, let us be comrades and soldiers yet to serve our fellow men in quiet counsel, where the blare of trumpets is neither heard nor heeded and where the things are done which make blessed the nations of the world in peace and righteousness and love.

Addressing Congress on Tariff and Anti-Trust Reforms

Breaking precedent by addressing Congress in person for the first time since Jefferson abandoned the practice, Wilson appeared repeatedly to exhort legislators to action, and, knowing press coverage of such visits was guaranteed, to build public support for tariff reductions and anti-trust action. Import tariffs had not been significantly lowered in over fifty years. High tariffs working to the advantage of American industries that no longer needed protection generously increased profits at the expense of consumers. Progressives had long urged lower duties, but the Payne-Aldrich tariff law of 1909 actually raised the burden of American consumers. Anti-trust action since the passage of the Sherman Anti-Trust Act of 1890 had not stemmed the growth or power of the great corporations. Wilson went personally to Congress to keep his campaign promises to lower tariffs and curb the trusts. He was careful not to engage in business bashing, but rather emphasized the benefits to business and the economy from reforms in these critical areas.

An Address on Tariff Reform to a Joint Session of Congress, April 8, 1913

Mr. Speaker, Mr. President, Gentlemen of the Congress:

I am very glad indeed to have this opportunity to address the two Houses directly and to verify for myself the impression that the President of the United States is a person, not a mere department of the Government hailing Congress from some isolated island of jealous power, sending messages, not speaking naturally and with his own voice—that he is a human being trying to cooperate with other human beings in a common service. After this pleasant experience I shall feel quite normal in all our dealings with one another.

I have called the Congress together in extraordinary session because a duty was laid upon the party now in power at the recent elections which it ought to perform promptly, in order that the burden carried by the people under existing law may be lightened as soon as possible and in order, also that the business interests of the country may not be kept too long in suspense as to what the fiscal changes are to be to which they will be required to adjust themselves. It is clear to the whole country that the tariff duties must be altered. They must be changed to meet the radical alteration in the conditions of our economic life which the country has witnessed within the last generation. While the whole face and method of our industrial and commercial life were being changed beyond recognition the tariff schedules have remained what they were before the change began, or have moved in the direction they were given when no large circumstance of our industrial development was what it is today. Our task is to square them with the actual facts. The sooner that is done the sooner our men of business will be free to thrive by the law of nature (the nature of free business) instead of by the law of legislation and artificial arrangement.

☆ ☆ ☆

It is plain what those principles must be. We must abolish everything that bears even the semblance of privilege or of any kind of artificial advantage, and put our business men and producers under the stimulation of a constant necessity to be efficient, economical, and enterprising, masters of competitive supremacy, better workers and merchants than any in the world. Aside from the duties laid upon articles which we do not, and probably can not, produce, therefore, and the duties laid upon luxuries and merely for the sake of the revenues they yield, the object of the tariff duties henceforth laid must be effective competition, the whetting of American wits by contest with the wits of the rest of the world.

It would be unwise to move toward this end headlong, with reckless haste, or with strokes that cut at the very roots of what has grown up amongst us by long process and at our own invitation. It does not alter a thing to upset it and break it and deprive it of a chance to change. It destroys it. We must make changes in our fiscal laws, in our fiscal system, whose object is development, a more free and wholesome development, not revolution or upset or confusion. We must build up trade, especially foreign trade. We need the outlet and the enlarged field of energy more than we ever did before. We must build up industry as well, and must adopt freedom in the place of artificial stimulation only so far as it will build, not pull down. In dealing with the tariff the method by which this may be done will be a matter of judgment, exercised item by item. To some not accustomed to the excitements and responsibilities of greater freedom our methods may in some respects and at some points seem heroic, but remedies may be heroic and yet be remedies. It is our business to make sure that they are genuine remedies. Our object is clear. If our motive is above just challenge and only an occasional error of judgment is chargeable against us, we shall be fortunate.

An Address on Antitrust Legislation to a Joint Session of Congress, January 20, 1914

Gentlemen of the Congress:

In my report "on the state of the Union," which I had the privilege of reading to you on the 2d of December last, I ventured to reserve for discussion at a later date the subject of additional legislation regarding the very difficult and intricate matter of trusts and monopolies. The time now seems opportune to turn to that great question, not only because the currency legislation, which absorbed your attention and the attention of the country in December, is now disposed of, but also because opinion seems to be clearing about us with singular rapidity in this other great field of action. In the matter of the currency it cleared suddenly and very happily after the much-debated Act was passed; in respect of the monopolies which have multiplied about us and in regard to the various means by which they have been organized and maintained it seems to be coming to a clear and all but universal agreement in anticipation of our action, as if by way of preparation, making the way easier to see and easier to set out upon with confidence and without confusion of counsel.

☆ ☆ ☆

What we are purposing to do, therefore, is, happily, not to hamper or interfere with business as enlightened businessmen prefer to do it, or in any sense to put it under the ban. The antagonism between business and government is over. We are now about to give expression to the best business judgment of America, to what we know to be the business conscience and honor of the land. The Government and businessmen are ready to meet each other half way in a common effort to square business methods with both public opinion and the law. The best informed men of the business world condemn the methods and processes and consequences of monopoly as we condemn them; and the instinctive judgment of the vast majority of businessmen everywhere goes with them. We shall now be their spokesmen. That is the strength of our position and the pure prophecy of what will ensue when our reasonable work is done.

☆ ☆ ☆

We are agreed that "private monopoly is indefensible and intolerable," and our program is founded upon that conviction. It will be a comprehensive but not a radical or unacceptable program and these are its items, the changes which opinion deliberately sanctions and for which business waits:

It waits with acquiescence, in the first place, for laws which will effectually prohibit and prevent such interlockings of the personnel of the directorates of great corporations—bank and railroads, industrial, commercial, and public service bodies—as in effect result in making those who borrow and those who lend practically one and the same, those who sell and those who buy but the same persons trading with one another under different names and in different combinations, and those who affect to compete in fact partners and masters of some whole field of business. Sufficient time should be allowed, of course, in which to effect these changes of organization without inconvenience or confusion.

Such a prohibition will work much more than a mere negative good by correcting the serious evils which have arisen because, for example, the men who have been the directing spirits of the great investment banks have usurped the place which belongs to independent industrial management working in its own behalf. It will bring new men, new energies, a new spirit of initiative, new blood, into the management of our great business enterprises. It will open the field of industrial development and origination to scores of men who have been obliged to serve when their abilities entitled them to direct. It will immensely hearten the young men coming on and will greatly enrich the business activities of the whole country.

In the second place, businessmen as well as those who direct public affairs now recognize, and recognize with painful clearness, the great harm and injustice which has been done to many, if not all, of the great railroad systems of the country by the way in which they have been financed and their own distinctive interests subordinated to the interests of the men who financed them and of other business enterprises which those men wished to promote. The country is ready, therefore, to accept, and accept with relief as well as approval, a law which will confer upon the Interstate Commerce Commission the power to superintend and regulate the financial operations by which the railroads are henceforth to be supplied with the money they need for their proper development to meet the rapidly growing requirements of the country for increased and improved facilities of transportation. We cannot postpone action in this matter without leaving the railroads exposed to many serious handicaps and hazards; and the prosperity of the railroads and the prosperity of the country are inseparably connected. Upon this question those who are chiefly responsible for the actual management and operation of the railroads have spoken very plainly and very earnestly, with a purpose we ought to be quick to accept. It will be one step, and a very important one, toward the necessary separation of the business of production from the business of transportation.

The business of the country awaits also, has long awaited and has suffered because it could not obtain, further and more explicit legislative definition of the policy and meaning of the existing antitrust law. Nothing hampers business like uncertainty. Nothing daunts or discourages it like the necessity to take chances, to run the risk of falling under the condemnation of the law before it can make sure just what the law is. Surely we are sufficiently familiar with the actual processes and methods of monopoly and of the many hurtful restraints of trade to make definition possible, at any rate up to the limits of what experience has disclosed. These practices, being now abundantly disclosed, can be explicitly and item by item forbidden by statute in such terms as will practically eliminate uncertainty, the law itself and the penalty being made equally plain.

And the businessmen of the country desire something more than that the menace of legal process in these matters be made explicit and intelligible. They desire the advice, the definite guidance and information which can be supplied by an administrative body, an interstate trade commission.

The opinion of the country would instantly approve of such a commission. It would not wish to see it empowered to make terms with monopoly or in any sort to assume control of business, as if the Government made itself responsible. It demands such a commission only as in indispensable instrument of information and publicity, as a clearinghouse for the facts by which both the public mind and the managers of great business undertakings should be guided, and as an instrumentality for doing justice to business where the processes of the courts or the natural forces of correction outside the courts are inadequate to adjust the remedy to the wrong in a way that will meet all the equities and circumstances of the case.

☆ ☆ ☆

Inasmuch as our object and the spirit of our action in these matters is to meet business half way in its processes of self-correction and disturb its legitimate course as little as possible, we ought to see to it, and the judgment of practical and sagacious men of affairs everywhere would applaud us if we did see to it, that penalties and punishments should fall, not upon business itself, to its confusion and interruption, but upon the individuals who use the instrumentalities of business to do things which public policy and sound business practice condemn. Every act of business is done at the command or upon the initiative of some ascertainable person or group of persons. These should be held individually responsible, and the punishment should fall upon them, not upon the business organization of which they make illegal use. It should be one of the main objects of our legislation to divest such persons of their corporate cloak and deal with them as with those who do not represent their corporations, but merely by deliberate intention break the law. Businessmen the country through would, I am sure, applaud us if we were to take effectual steps to see that the officers and directors of great business bodies were prevented from bringing them and the business of the country into disrepute and danger.

☆ ☆ ☆

I have laid the case before you, no doubt as it lies in your own mind, as it lies in the thought of the country. What must every candid man say of the suggestions I have laid before you, of the plain obligations of which I have reminded you? That these are new things for which the country is not prepared? No; but that they are old things, now familiar, and must of course be undertaken if we are to square our laws with the thought and desire of the country. Until these things are done, conscientious businessmen the country over will be unsatisfied. They are in these things our mentors and colleagues. We are now about to write the additional articles of our constitution of peace, the peace that is honor and freedom and prosperity.

Remarks on Women's Suffrage

On June 30, 1914, over five hundred women marched to the White House to present to the president a suffrage resolution from the Federation of Women's Clubs. Some states sanctioned women's suffrage, but the long struggle to amend the national Constitution had not yet succeeded. Wilson received a delegation of the women who pressed him on the issue. Twice before, delegations of women had visited the White House seeking support. Wilson had not been a supporter of women's suffrage, and on this occasion the women again left without his endorsement. He had long thought it inappropriate for women to take up active roles in political affairs. The exchange here suggests some presidential testiness at the "cross-examination," perhaps from a recognition of the weakness of his argument. Wilson was eventually persuaded and in 1918 supported the adoption of the Nineteenth Amendment.

Upon being asked as an individual whether he would use his influence to have the Bristow-Mondell Resolution put through Congress at this session, the President replied:

Mrs. Wiley, and Ladies: No one could fail to be impressed by this great company of thoughtful women, and I want to assure you that it is to me most impressive. I have stated once before the position which as the leader of a party I feel obliged to take, and I am sure that you will not wish me to state it again. Perhaps it would be more serviceable if I ventured upon the confident conjecture that the Baltimore convention did not embody this very important question in the platform which it adopted because of its conviction that the principles of the Constitution, which allotted these questions to the states, were well-considered principles from which they did not wish to depart. You have asked me to state my personal position with regard to the pending measure. It is my conviction that this is a matter for settlement by the states and not by the federal government, and therefore, that being my personal conviction and it being obvious that there is no ground on your part for discouragement in the progress you are making, and my passion being for local self-government and the determination by the great communities into which this nation is organized of their own polity and life, I can only say that since you turned away from me as a leader of a party and asked me my position as a man, I am obliged to state it very frankly, and I believe that in stating it I am probably in agreement with those who framed the platform to which allusion has been made.

I think that very few persons, perhaps, realize the difficulty of the dual duty that must be exercised, whether he will or not, by a President of the United States. He is President of the United States as an executive charged with the administration of the law, but he is the choice of a party as a leader in policy. The policy is determined by the party, or else upon unusual and new circumstances by the determination of those who lead the party. This is my situation as an individual. I have told you that I believed that the best way of settling this thing and the best-considered principles of the Constitution with regard to it is that it should be settled by the states. I am very much obliged to you.

Mrs. Dorr: May I ask you this question? Is it not a fact that we have very good precedents existing for altering the electorate by the Constitution of the United States?

The President: I do not think that that has anything to do with my conviction as to the best way that it can be done.

Mrs. Dorr: It does not, but it leaves room for the women of the country to say what they want through the Constitution of the United States.

The President: Certainly it does. There is good room, but I have stated my conviction, and I have no right to criticize the opinions of others who have different convictions, and I certainly would not wish to do so.

Ms. Wiley: Granted it is a state matter, would it not give this great movement a mighty impetus if the resolution now pending before Congress were passed?

The President: But that resolution is for an amendment to the Constitution.

Mrs. Wiley: The states would have to pass upon it before it became an amendment. Would it not be a state matter then?

The President: Yes, but by a very different process, for by that process it would be forced upon the minority; they would have to accept it.

Mrs. Door: They could reject it if they wished to; three fourths of the states would have to pass it.

The President: Yes, but the other fourth could not reject it.

Mrs. Dorr: Mr. President, don't you think that when the Constitution was made it was agreed that when three fourths of the states wanted a reform that the other fourth would receive it also?

The President: I cannot say what was agreed upon. I can only say that I have tried to answer your question, and I do not think it is quite proper that I submit myself to cross-examination.

Mrs. Wiley: Thank you, Mr. President, for the courtesy.

The President: I am very much obliged to you: It has been a pleasant occasion.

An Address on Latin American Policy

Speaking to the Southern Commercial Congress in Mobile, Alabama, on October 27, 1913, Wilson took the opportunity to outline his policy toward Latin America. The speech promised a new relationship with countries to the South based on equality and mutual respect. It was hoped that the president's remarks would signal a turn away from the interventionism and "dollar diplomacy" that had embittered hemisphere relations during the Taft administration. In this Wilson was encouraged and supported by Secretary of State William Jennings Bryan. But the new administration did not fulfill the promise of the ideals suggested at Mobile. The policy of the United States continued to be shaped by the perceived need to be dominant in the Caribean, especially to protect the security of the Panama Canal. There would be, in fact, more frequent and longer interventions in Latin America by the United States during the Wilson years and the 1920s than there had been in the past.

The future, ladies and gentlemen, is going to be very different for this hemisphere from the past. These states lying to the south of us, which have always been our neighbors, will now be drawn closer to us by innumerable ties, and, I hope, chief of all, by the tie of a common understanding of each other. Interest does not tie nations together; it sometimes separates them. But sympathy and understanding does unite them, and I believe that by the new route that is just about to be opened, while we physically cut two continents asunder, we spiritually unite them. It is a spiritual union which we seek.

☆ ☆ ☆

There is one peculiarity about the history of the Latin-American states which I am sure they are keenly aware of. You hear of "concessions" to foreign capitalists in Latin-America. You do not hear of concessions to foreign capitalists in the United States. They are not granted concessions. They are invited to make investments. The work is ours, though they are welcome to invest in it. We do not ask them to supply the capital and do the work. It is an invitation, not a privilege; and states that are obliged because their territory does not lie within the main field of modern enterprise and action, to grant concessions are in this condition—that foreign interests are apt to dominate their domestic affairs: a condition of affairs always dangerous and apt to become intolerable. What these states are going to see, therefore, is an emancipation from the subordination, which has been inevitable, to foreign enterprise and an assertion of the splendid character which, in spite of these difficulties, they have again and again been able to demonstrate. The dignity, the courage, the self-possession, the self-respect of the Latin-American states, their achievements in the face of all these adverse circumstances, deserve nothing but the admiration and applause of the world. They have had harder bargains driven with them in the matter of loans than any other peoples in the world. Interest has been exacted of them that was not exacted of anybody else, because the risk was said to be greater; and then securities were taken that destroyed the risk—an admirable arrangement for those who were forcing the terms! I rejoice in nothing so much as in the prospect that they will now be emancipated from these conditions, and we ought to be the first to take part in assisting in the emancipation. I think some of these gentlemen have already had occasion to bear witness that the Department of the State in recent months has tried to serve them in that wise. In the future, they will draw closer and closer to us because of circumstances of which I wish to speak with moderation and, I hope, without indiscretion.

We must prove ourselves their friends and champions, upon terms of equality and honor. You cannot be friends upon any other terms than upon the terms of equality. You cannot be friends at all except upon the terms of honor. We must show ourselves friends by comprehending their interest, whether it squares with our own interest or not. It is a very perilous thing to determine the foreign policy of a nation in the terms of material interest. It not only is unfair to those with whom you are dealing, but it is degrading as regards your own actions.

Comprehension must be the soil in which shall grow all the fruits of friendship, and there is a reason and a compulsion lying behind all this which is dearer than anything else to the thoughtful men of America. I mean the development of constitutional liberty in the world. Human rights, national integrity, and opportunity as against material interests—that, ladies and gentlemen, is the issue which we now have to face. I want to take this occasion to say that the United States will never again seek one additional foot of territory by conquest. She will devote herself to showing that she knows how to make honorable and fruitful use of the territory she has; and she must regard it as one of the duties of friendship to see that from no quarter are material interests made superior to human liberty and national opportunity. I say this, not with a single thought that anyone will gainsay it, but merely to fix in our consciousness what our real relationship with the rest of America is. It is the relationship of a family of mankind devoted to the development of true constitutional liberty. We know that that is the soil out of which the best enterprise springs. We know that this is a cause which we are making in common with our neighbors, because we have had to make it ourselves. . . .

I know what the response of the thought and heart of America will be to the program I have outlined, because America was created to realize a program like that. This is not America because it is rich. This is not America because it has set up for a great population great opportunities of material prosperity. America is a name which sounds in the ears of men everywhere as a synonym with individual opportunity because it is a synonym of individual liberty. I would rather belong to a poor nation that was free than to a rich nation that had ceased to be in love with liberty. But we shall not be poor if we love liberty, because the nation that loves liberty truly sets every man free to do his best and be his best, and that means the release of all the splendid energies of a great people who think for themselves. A nation of employees cannot be free any more than a nation of employers can be.

In emphasizing the points which must unite us in sympathy and in spiritual interest with the Latin-American peoples, we are emphasizing the points of our own life, and we should prove ourselves untrue to our own traditions if we proved ourselves untrue friends to them. Do not think, therefore, gentlemen, that the questions of the day are mere questions of policy and diplomacy. They are shot through with the principles of life. We dare not turn from the principle that morality, and not expediency, is the thing that must guide us, and that we will never condone iniquity because it is more convenient to do so. It seems to me that this is a day of infinite hope, of confidence in a future greater than the past has been; for I am fain to believe that, in spite of all the things that we wish to correct, the nineteenth century that now lies behind us has brought us a long stage toward the time when, slowly ascending the tedious climb that leads to the final uplands, we shall get our ultimate view of the duties of mankind. We have breasted a considerable part of the climb and shall, presently—it may be in a generation or two—come out upon those great heights where there shines, unobstructed, the light of the justice of God.

On Relations with Mexico

The forces of Victoriano Huerta and Venustiano Carranza fought a bloody struggle for control of Mexico. After a tumultuous period in Mexican politics following the overthrow of Porfirio Diaz in 1910, Huerta led a military dictatorship in 1913, a government marked by corruption and violence. Carranza, who had participated in the revolt against Diaz, now organized an insurgency against Huerta and eventually forced him from power. Wilson favored the success of Carranza as the best hope for a stable democratic government in Mexico. His address to Congress on the conflict in Mexico on August 27, 1913, suggested a vigilant neutrality, the interdiction of arms exports to Mexico, friendly advice, but no intervention. A second appearance at a joint session on April 20, 1914, came after the arrest of American sailors in Tampico by forces allied with Huerta and ended with an appeal to the Congress to approve the use of arms against the Huerta regime. Troops were sent, offending all sides in Mexico including Carranza, and Mexican-American relations remained tumultuous for several years.

An Address on Mexican Affairs to a Joint Session of Congress, August 27, 1913

Gentlemen of the Congress:

It is clearly my duty to lay before you, very fully and without reservation, the facts concerning our present relations with the Republic of Mexico. The deplorable posture of affairs in Mexico I need not describe, but I deem it my duty to speak very frankly of what this Government has done and should seek to do in the fulfillment of its obligation to Mexico herself, as a friend and neighbor, and to American citizens whose lives and vital interests are daily affected by the distressing conditions which now obtain beyond our southern border.

Those conditions touch us very nearly. Not merely because they lie at our very doors. That of course makes us more vividly and more constantly conscious of them, and every instinct of neighborly interest and sympathy is aroused and quickened by them; but that is only one element in the determination of our duty. We are glad to call ourselves the friends of Mexico, and we shall, I hope, have many an occasion, in happier times as well as in these days of trouble and confusion, to show that our friendship is genuine and disinterested, capable of sacrifice and every generous manifestation. The peace, prosperity, and contentment of Mexico mean more, much more, to us than merely an enlarged field for our commerce and enterprise. They mean an enlargement of the field of self-government and the realization of the hopes and rights of a nation with whose best aspirations, so long suppressed and disappointed, we deeply sympathize. We shall yet prove to the Mexican people that we know how to serve them without first thinking how we shall serve ourselves.

But we are not the only friends of Mexico. The whole world desires her peace and progress; and the whole world is interested as never before. Mexico lies at last where all the world looks on. Central America is about to be touched by the great routes of the world's trade and intercourse running free from ocean to ocean at the Isthmus. The future has much in store for Mexico, as for all the States of Central America; but the best gifts can come to her only if she be ready and free to receive them and to enjoy them honorably. America in particular—America north and south and upon both continents—waits upon the development of Mexico; and that development can be sound and lasting only if it be the product of a genuine freedom, a just and ordered government founded upon law. Only so can it be peaceful or fruitful of the benefits of peace. Mexico has a great and enviable future before her, if only she choose and attain the paths of honest constitutional government.

The present circumstances of the Republic, I deeply regret to say, do not seem to promise even the foundations of such a peace. We have waited many months, months full of peril and anxiety, for the conditions there to improve, and they have not improved. They have grown worse, rather. The territory in some sort controlled by the provisional authorities at Mexico

City has grown smaller, not larger. The prospect of the pacification of the country, even by arms, has seemed to grow more and more remote; and its pacification by the authorities at the capital is evidently impossible by any other means than force. Difficulties more and more entangled those who claim to constitute the legitimate government of the Republic. They have not made good their claim in fact. Their successes in the field have proved only temporary. War and disorder, devastation and confusion, seem to threaten to become the settled fortune of the distracted country. As friends we could wait no longer for a solution which every week seemed further away. It was our duty at least go volunteer our good offices—to offer to assist, if we might, in effecting some arrangement which would bring relief and peace and set up a universally acknowledged political authority there.

☆ ☆ ☆

Meanwhile, what is it our duty to do? Clearly, everything that we do must be rooted in patience and done with calm and disinterested deliberation. Impatience on our part would be fraught with every risk of wrong and folly. We can afford to exercise the self-restraint of a really great nation which realizes its own strength and scorns to misuse it. It was our duty to offer our active assistance. It is now our duty to show what true neutrality will do to enable the people of Mexico to set their affairs in order again and wait for a further opportunity to offer our friendly counsels. The door is not closed against the resumption, either upon the initiative of Mexico or upon our own, of the effort to bring order out of the confusion by friendly cooperative action, should fortunate occasion offer.

While we wait the contest of the rival forces will undoubtedly for a little while be sharper than ever, just because it will be plain that an end must be made of the existing situation, and that very promptly; and with increased activity of the contending factions will come, it is to be feared, increased danger to the noncombatants in Mexico as well as to those actually in the field of battle. The position of outsiders is always particularly trying and full of hazard where there is civil strife and a whole country is upset. We should earnestly urge all Americans to leave Mexico at once, and should assist them to get away in every way possible—not because we would mean to slacken in the least our efforts to safeguard their lives and their interests, but because it is imperative that they should take no unnecessary risks when it is physically possible for them to leave the country. We should let every one who assumes to exercise authority in any part of

Mexico know in the most unequivocal way that we shall vigilantly watch the fortunes of those Americans who can not get away, and shall hold those responsible for their sufferings and losses to a definite reckoning. That can be and will be made plain beyond the possibility of a misunderstanding.

For the rest, I deem it my duty to exercise the authority conferred upon me by the law of March 14, 1912, to see to it that neither side to the struggle now going on in Mexico receive any assistance from this side of the border. I shall follow the best practice of nations in the matter of neutrality by forbidding the exportation of arms or munitions of war of any kind from the United States to any part of the Republic of Mexico—a policy suggested by several interesting precedents and certainly dictated by many manifest considerations of practical expediency. We can not in the circumstances be the partisans of either party to the contest that now distracts Mexico, or constitute ourselves the virtual umpire between them.

I am happy to say that several of the great Governments of the world have given this Government their generous moral support in urging upon the provisional authorities at the City of Mexico the acceptance of our proffered good offices in the spirit in which they were made. We have not acted in this matter under the ordinary principles of international obligation. All the world expects us in such circumstances to act as Mexico's nearest friend and intimate adviser. This is our immemorial relation towards her. There is nowhere any serious question that we have the moral right in the case or that we are acting in the interest of a fair settlement and of good government, not for the promotion of some selfish interest of our own. If further motive were necessary than our own good will towards a sister Republic and our own deep concern to see peace and order prevail in Central America, this consent of mankind to what we are attempting, this attitude of the great nations of the world towards what we may attempt in dealing with this distressed people at our doors, should make us feel the more solemnly bound to go to the utmost length of patience and forbearance in this painful and anxious business. The steady pressure of moral force will before many days break the barriers of pride and prejudice down, and we shall triumph as Mexico's friends sooner than we could triumph as her enemies—and how much more handsomely, with how much higher and finer satisfactions of conscience and of honor!

An Address to Congress on the Mexican Crisis, April 20, 1914

Gentlemen of the Congress:

It is my duty to call your attention to a situation which has arisen in our dealings with General Victoriano Huerta at Mexico City which calls for action, and to ask your advice and cooperation in acting upon it. On the ninth of April a paymaster of the U.S.S. *Dolphin* landed at the Iturbide Bridge landing at Tampico with a whaleboat and boat's crew to take off certain supplies needed by his ship, and while engaged in loading the boat was arrested by an officer and squad of men of the army of General Huerta. Neither the paymaster nor anyone of the boat's crew was armed. Two of the men were in the boat when the arrest took place and were obliged to leave it and submit to be taken into custody, notwithstanding the fact that the boat carried, both at her bow and at her stern, the flag of the United States. The officer who made the arrest was proceeding up one of the streets of the town with his prisoners when met by an officer of higher authority, who ordered him to return to the landing and await orders; and within an hour and a half from the time of the arrest orders were received from the commander of the Huertista forces at Tampico for the release of the paymaster and his men. The release was followed by apologies from the commander and later by an expression of regret by General Huerta himself. General Huerta urged that martial law obtained at the time at Tampico; that orders had been issued that no one should be allowed to land at the Iturbide Bridge; and that our sailors had no right to land there. Our naval commanders at the port had not been notified of any such prohibition; and, even, if they had been, the only justifiable course open to the local authorities would have been to request the paymaster and his crew to withdraw and to lodge a protest with the commanding officer of the fleet. Admiral Mayo regarded the arrest as so serious an affront that he was not satisfied with the apologies offered but demanded that the flag of the United States be saluted with special ceremony by the military commander of the port.

The incident cannot be regarded as a trivial one, especially as two of the men arrested were taken from the boat itself, that is to say, from the territory of the United States; but had it stood by itself it might have been attributed to the ignorance or arrogance of a single officer. Unfortunately, it was not an isolated case. A series of incidents have recently occurred which cannot but create the impression that the representatives of General Huerta were willing to go out of their way to show disregard for the dignity and rights of this government and felt perfectly safe in doing what they pleased, making free to show in many ways their irritation and contempt. A few days after the incident at Tampico an orderly from the U.S.S. *Minnesota* was arrested at Vera Cruz while ashore in uniform to obtain the ship's mail and was for a time thrown into jail. An official dispatch from this government to its embassy at Mexico City was withheld by the authorities of the telegraphic service until peremptorily demanded by our Chargé d'Affaires in person. So far as I can learn, such wrongs and annoyances have been suffered to occur only against representatives of the United States. I have heard of no complaints from other governments of similar treatment. Subsequent explanations and formal apologies did not and could not alter the popular impression, which it is possible it has been the object of the Huertista authorities to create, that the Government of the United States was being singled out, and might be singled out with impunity, for slights and affronts in retaliation for its refusal to recognize the pretensions of General Huerta to be regarded as the constitutional provisional President of the Republic of Mexico.

The manifest danger of such a situation was that such offences might grow from bad to worse until something happened of so gross and intolerable a sort as to lead directly and inevitably to armed conflict. It was necessary that the apologies of General Huerta and his representatives should go much further, that they should be such as to attract the attention of the whole population to their significance, and such as to impress upon General Huerta himself the necessity of seeing to it that no further occasion for explanations and professed regrets should arise. I, therefore, felt it my duty to sustain Admiral Mayo in the whole of his demand and to insist that the flag of the United States should be saluted in such a way as to indicate a new spirit and attitude on the part of the Huertistas.

Such a salute General Huerta has refused, and I have come to ask your approval and support in the course I now propose to pursue.

This Government can, I earnestly hope, in no circumstances be forced into war with the people of Mexico. Mexico is torn by civil strife. If we are to accept the tests of its own constitution, it has no government. General Huerta has set his power up in the City of Mexico, such as it is, without right and by methods for which there can be no justification. Only part of the country is under his control. If armed conflict should unhappily come as a result of his attitude of personal resentment towards this government, we should be fighting only General Huerta and those who adhere to him and give him their support, and our object would be only to restore to the people of the distracted republic the opportunity to set up again their own laws and their own government.

But I earnestly hope that war is not now in question. I believe that I speak for the American people when I say that we do not desire to control in any degree the affairs of our sister republic. Our feeling for the people of Mexico is one of deep and genuine friendship, and everything that we have so far done or refrained from doing has proceeded from our desire to help them, not to hinder or embarrass them. We would not wish even to exercise the good offices of friendship without their welcome and consent. The people of Mexico are entitled to settle their own domestic affairs in their own way, and we sincerely desire to respect their right. The present situation need have none of the grave implications of interference if we deal with it promptly, firmly, and wisely.

No doubt I could do what is necessary in the circumstances to enforce respect for our government without recourse to the Congress, and yet not exceed my constitutional powers as President; but I do not wish to act in a matter possibly of so grave consequence except in close conference and co-operation with both the Senate and House. I, therefore, come to ask your approval that I should use the armed forces of the United States in such ways and to such an extent as may be necessary to obtain from general Huerta and his adherents the fullest recognition of the rights and dignity of the United States, even amidst the distressing conditions now unhappily obtaining in Mexico.

There can in what we do be no thought of aggression or of selfish aggrandizement. We seek to maintain the dignity and authority of the United States only because we wish always to keep our great influence unimpaired for the uses of liberty, both in the United States and wherever else it may be employed for the benefit of mankind.

An Appeal for Neutrality in World War I

With the rest of the world, Americans were stunned that reason and diplomacy had failed to stop the engines of war in Europe in the summer of 1914. The assassination of Archduke Franz Ferdinand in late June had not been judged in itself a sufficient cause for war. But the hypernationalist pressures that had been mounting for years swept reason aside in August. On August 18, Wilson defined the posture of the United States, calling on Americans to be neutral in "thought as well as in action." It was a policy more easily proclaimed than prosecuted. As hopes for a short war faded, remaining neutral became more complex and more difficult, and to be "impartial" in thought and action, as Wilson suggested, became impossible. In part, Wilson's motive in remaining officially neutral was the hope that the United States might play a mediating role for a just and enduring peace.

My fellow countrymen:

I suppose that every thoughtful man in America has asked himself during these last troubled weeks what influence the European war may exert upon the United States, and I take the liberty of addressing a few words to you in order to point out that it is entirely within our own choice what its effects upon us will be and to urge very earnestly upon you the sort of speech and conduct which will best safeguard the nation against distress and disaster.

The effect of the war upon the United States will depend upon what American citizens say and do. Every man who really loves America will act and speak in the true spirit of neutrality, which is the spirit of impartiality and fairness and friendliness to all concerned. The spirit of the nation in this critical matter will be determined largely by what individuals and societies and those gathered in public meetings do and say upon what newspapers and magazines contain, upon what ministers utter in their pulpits, and men proclaim as their opinions on the street.

The people of the United States are drawn from many nations, and chiefly from the nations now at war. It is natural and inevitable that there should be the utmost variety of sympathy and desire among them with regard to the issues and circumstances of the conflict. Some will wish one nation, others another, to succeed in the momentous struggle. It will be easy to excite passion and difficult to allay it. Those responsible for exciting it will assume a heavy responsibility, responsibility for no less a thing than that the people of the United States, whose love of their country and whose loyalty to its government should unite them as Americans all, bound in honor and affection, to think first of her and her interests—may become divided in camps of hostile opinion, hot against each other, involved in the war itself in impulse and opinion, if not an action. Such divisions among us would be fatal to our peace of mind and might seriously stand in the way of the proper performance of our duty as the one great nation at peace, the one people holding itself ready to play a part of impartial mediation and speak the counsels of peace and accommodation, not as a partisan, but as a friend.

I venture, therefore, my fellow countrymen, to speak a solemn word of warning to you against that deepest, most subtle, most essential breach of neutrality which may spring out of partisanship, out of passionately taking sides. The United States must be neutral in fact as well as in name during these days that are to try men's souls. We must be impartial in thought as well as in action, must put a curb upon sentiments as well as upon every transaction that might be construed as a preference of one party to the struggle before another.

My thought is of America. I am speaking, I feel sure, the earnest wish and purpose of every thoughtful American that this great country of ours, which is, of course, the first in our thoughts and in our hearts, should show herself in this time of peculiar trial a nation fit beyond others to exhibit the fine poise of undisturbed judgment, the dignity of self-control, the efficiency of dispassionate action; a nation that neither sits in judgment upon others nor is disturbed in her own counsels and which keeps herself fit and free to do what is necessary and disinterested and truly serviceable for the people of the world.

Shall we not resolve to put upon ourselves the restraints which will bring to our people the happiness and the great and lasting influence for peace we covet for them?

Essential Terms for Peace in Europe

Almost from the start of the World War, Wilson sought to bring about a truce. He saw himself leading the United States as a mediating force to end the slaughter and to establish a stable peace. Frustrated in his effort by the stubborn refusal of both sides to consider any peace short of victory and apprehensive about the United States being drawn into the conflict, he took the initiative in December 1916 with notes to the warring parties calling for an end to the fighting. On January 22, 1917, he addressed the Senate to explain his formula for a settlement. The speech forecast some of the provisions which would be embodied in his famous Fourteen Points, enunciated later as war aims and peace conference goals. Most important for Wilson was the establishment of a league for peace, for which he fought with all his energy.

Gentlemen of the Senate:

On the eighteenth of December last, I addressed an identic note to the governments of the nations now at war requesting them to state, more definitely than they had yet been stated by either group of belligerents, the terms upon which they would deem it possible to make peace. I spoke on behalf of humanity and of the rights of all neutral nations like our own, many of whose most vital interests the war puts in constant jeopardy. The Central Powers united in a reply which stated merely that they were ready to meet their antagonists in conference to discuss terms of peace. The Entente Powers have replied much more definitely and have stated, in general terms, indeed, but with sufficient definiteness to imply details, the arrangements, guarantees, and acts of reparation which they deem to be the indispensable conditions of a satisfactory settlement. We are that much nearer a definite discussion of the people which shall end the present war. We are that much nearer the discussion of the international concert which must thereafter hold the world at peace. In every discussion of the peace that must end this war it is taken for granted that that peace must be followed by some definite concert of power which will make it virtually impossible that any such catastrophe should ever overwhelm us again. Every lover of mankind, every sane and thoughtful man must take that for granted.

I have sought this opportunity to address you because I thought that I owed it to you, as the counsel associated with me in the final determination of our international obligations, to disclose to you without reserve the thought and purpose that have been taking form in my mind in regard to the duty of our Government in the days to come when it will be necessary to lay afresh and upon a new plan the foundations of peace among the nations.

It is inconceivable that the people of the United States should play no part in that great enterprise. To take part in such a service will be the opportunity for which they have sought to prepare themselves by the very principles and purposes of their polity and the approved practices of their Government ever since the days when they set up a new nation in the high and honorable hope that it might in all that it was and did show mankind the way to liberty. They cannot in honor withhold the service to which they are now about to be challenged. They do not wish to withhold it. But they owe it to themselves and to the other nations of the world to state the conditions under which they will feel free to render it.

That service is nothing less than this, to add their authority and their power to the authority and force of other nations to guarantee peace and justice throughout the world. Such a settlement cannot now be long postponed. It is right that before it comes this Government should frankly formulate the conditions upon which it would feel justified in asking our people to approve its formal and solemn adherence to a League for Peace. I am here to attempt to state those conditions.

☆ ☆ ☆

No covenant of cooperative peace that does not include the peoples of the New World can suffice to keep the future safe against war; and yet there is only one sort of peace that the peoples of America could join in guaranteeing. The elements of that peace must be elements that engage the confidence and satisfy the principles of the American governments, elements consistent with their political faith and with the practical convictions which the peoples of America have once for all embraced and undertaken to defend.

I do not mean to say that any American government would throw any obstacle in the way of any terms of peace the governments now at war might agree upon, or seek to upset them when made, whatever they might be. I only take it for granted that mere terms of peace between the belligerents will not satisfy even the belligerents themselves. Mere agreements may not make peace secure. It will be absolutely necessary that a force be created as a guarantor of the permanency of the settlement so much greater than the force of any nation now engaged or any alliance hitherto formed or projected that no nation, no probable combination of nations could face or withstand it. If the peace presently to be made is to endure, it must be a peace made secure by the organized major force of mankind.

The terms of the immediate peace agreed upon will determine whether it is a peace for which such a guarantee can be secured. The question upon which the whole future peace and policy of the world depends is this: Is the present war a struggle for a just and secure peace, or only for a new balance of power? If it be only a struggle for a new balance of power, who will guarantee, who can guarantee the stable equilibrium of the new arrangement? Only a tranquil Europe can be a stable Europe. There must be, not a balance of power, but a community of power; not organized rivalries, but an organized common peace.

Fortunately we have received very explicit assurances on this point. The statesmen of both of the groups of nations now arrayed against one another have said, in terms that could not be misinterpreted, that it was no part of the purpose they had in mind to crush their antagonists. But the implications of these assurances may not be equally clear to all—may not be the same on both sides of the water. I think it will be serviceable if I attempt to set forth what we understand them to be.

They imply, first of all, that it must be a peace without victory. It is not pleasant to say this. I beg that I may be permitted to put my own interpretation upon it and that it may be understood that no other interpretation was in my thought. I am seeking only to face realities and to face them without soft concealments. Victory would mean peace forced upon the loser, a victor's terms imposed upon the vanquished. It would be accepted in humiliation, under duress, at an intolerable sacrifice, and would leave a sting, a resentment, a bitter memory upon which terms of peace would rest, not permanently, but only as upon quicksand. Only a peace between equals can last. Only a peace the very principle of which is equality and a common participation in a common benefit. The right state of mind, the right feeling between nations, is as necessary for a lasting peace as is the just settlement of vexed questions of territory or of racial and national allegiance.

The equality of nations upon which peace must be founded if it is to last must be an equality of rights; the guarantees exchanged must neither recognize nor imply a difference between big nations and small, between those that are powerful and those that are weak. Right must be based upon the common strength, not upon the individual strength, of the nations upon whose concert peace will depend. Equality of territory or of resources there of course cannot be; nor any sort of equality not gained in the ordinary peaceful and legitimate development of the peoples themselves. But no one asks or expects anything more than an equality of rights. Mankind is looking now for freedom of life, not for equipoises of power.

And there is a deeper thing involved than even equality of right among organized nations. No peace can last, or ought to last, which does not recognize and accept the principle that governments derive all their just powers from the consent of the governed, and that no right anywhere exists to hand peoples about from sovereignty to sovereignty as if they were property. I take it for granted, for instance, if I may venture upon a single example, that statesmen everywhere are agreed that there should be a united, independent, and autonomous Poland, and that henceforth inviolable security of life, of worship, and of industrial and social development should be guaranteed to all peoples who have lived hitherto under the power of governments devoted to a faith and purpose hostile to their own.

I speak of this, not because of any desire to exalt an abstract political principle which has always been held very dear by those who have sought to build up liberty in America, but for the same reason that I have spoken of the other conditions of peace which seem to me clearly indispensable—because I wish frankly to uncover realities. Any peace which does not recognize and accept this principle will inevitably be upset. It will not rest upon the affections or the convictions of mankind. The ferment of spirit of whole populations will fight subtly and constantly against it, and all the world will sympathize. The world can be at peace only if its life is stable, and there can be no stability where the will is in rebellion, where there is not tranquility of spirit and a sense of justice, of freedom, and of right.

So far as practicable, moreover, every great people now struggling towards a full development of its resources and of its powers should be assured a direct outlet to the great highways of the sea. Where this cannot be done by the cession of territory, it can no doubt be done by the neutralization of direct rights of way under the general guarantee which will assure the peace itself. With a right comity of arrangement no nation need be shut away from free access to the open paths of the world's commerce.

And the paths of the sea must alike in law and in fact be free. The freedom of the seas is the sine qua non of peace, equality, and co-operation. No doubt a somewhat radical reconsideration of many of the rules of international practice hitherto thought to be established may be necessary in order to make the seas indeed free and common in practically all circumstances for the use of mankind, but the motive for such changes is convincing and compelling. There can be no trust or intimacy between the peoples of the world without them. The free, constant, unthreatened intercourse of nations is an essential part of the process of peace and of development. It need not be difficult either to define or to secure the freedom of the seas if the governments of the world sincerely desire to come to an agreement concerning it.

It is a problem closely connected with the limitation of naval armaments and the co-operation of the navies of the world in keeping the seas at once free and safe. And the question of limiting naval armaments opens the wider and perhaps more difficult question of the limitation of armies and of all programs of military preparation. Difficult and delicate as these questions are, they must be faced with the utmost candor and decided in a spirit of real accommodation if peace is to come with healing in its wings, and come to stay. Peace cannot be had without concession and sacrifice. There can be no sense of safety and equality among the nations if great preponderating armaments are henceforth to continue here and there to be built up and maintained. The statesmen of the world must plan for peace and nations must adjust and accommodate their policy to it as they have planned for war and made ready for pitiless contest and rivalry. The question of armaments, whether on land or sea, is the most immediately and intensely practical question connected with the future fortunes of nations and of mankind.

I have spoken upon these great matters without reserve and with the utmost explicitness because it has seemed to me to be necessary if the world's yearning desire for peace was anywhere to find free voice and utterance. Perhaps I am the only person in high authority amongst all the peoples of the world who is at liberty to speak and hold nothing back. I am speaking as an individual, and yet I am speaking also, of course, as the responsible head of a great government, and I feel confident that I have said what the people of the United States would wish me to say. May I not add that I hope and believe that I am in effect speaking for liberals and friends of humanity in every nation and of every program of liberty? I would fain believe that I am speaking for the silent mass of mankind everywhere who have as yet had no place or opportunity to speak their real hearts out concerning the death and ruin they see to have come already upon the persons and the homes they hold most dear.

And in holding our the expectation that the people and Government of the United States will join the other civilized nations of the world in guaranteeing the permanence of peace upon such terms as I have named I speak with the greater boldness and confidence because it is clear to every man who can think that there is in this promise no breach in either our traditions or our policy as a nation, but a fulfillment, rather, of all that we have professed or striven for.

And in holding out the expectation that the people and Government of the United States will join the other civilized nations of the world in guaranteeing the permanence of peace upon such terms as I have named I speak with the greater boldness and confidence because it is clear to every man who can think that there is in this promise no breach in either our traditions or our policy as a nation, but a fulfillment, rather, of all that we have professed or striven for.

I am proposing, as it were, that the nations should with one accord adopt the doctrine of President Monroe as the doctrine of the world: that no nation should seek to extend its polity over any other nation or people, but that every people should be left free to determine its own polity, its own way of development, unhindered, unthreatened, unafraid, the little along with the great and powerful.

I am proposing that all nations henceforth avoid entangling alliances which would draw them into competitions of power; catch them in a net of intrigue and selfish rivalry, and disturb their own affairs with influences intruded from without. There is no entangling alliance in a concert of power. When all unite to act in the same sense and with the same purpose all act in the common interest and are free to live their own lives under a common protection.

I am proposing government by the consent of the governed; that freedom of the seas which in international conference after conference representatives of the United States have urged with the eloquence of those who are the convinced disciples of liberty; and that moderation of armaments which makes of armies and navies a power for order merely, not an instrument of aggression or of selfish violence.

These are American principles, American policies. We could stand for no others. And they are also the principles and policies of forward looking men and women everywhere, of every modern nation, of every enlightened community. They are the principles of mankind and must prevail.

Address to a Joint Session of Congress Calling for a Declaration of War

Germany began its unrestricted submarine warfare sinking American ships approaching Europe in February and March 1917. The Germans understood that this would bring the United States into the war, but they assumed that by cutting off supplies to Britain and France, the war would be won before the Americans could be ready to fight. They miscalculated. Wilson's work toward a truce sank with the ships, and neutrality was no longer possible. The president cloistered himself in the days immediately before his address, agonizing as he wrote the call to war he now felt compelled to make. Marshaling the evidence of German aggression against the United States, he argued his case to persuade the nation that better options had been exhausted and no alternative remained. His reference to recent "heartening" events in Russia referred to the Russian Revolution, not yet hijacked by Lenin and the Bolsheviks and widely welcomed as holding the hope for democracy there. Wilson called for the declaration of war on April 2, 1917. For the moment partisanship receded, and as he finished his address the assembled Congress burst into thunderous applause.

I have called the Congress into extraordinary session because there are serious, very serious, choices of policy to be made, and made immediately, which it was neither right nor constitutionally permissible that I should assume the responsibility of making.

On the third of February last I officially laid before you the extraordinary announcement of the Imperial German Government that on and after the first day of February it was its purpose to put aside all restraints of law or of humanity and use its submarines to sink every vessel that sought to approach either the ports of Great Britain and Ireland or the western coasts of Europe or any of the ports controlled by the enemies of Germany within the Mediterranean. That had seemed to be the object of the German submarine warfare earlier in the war; but since April of last year the Imperial Government had somewhat restrained the commanders of its undersea craft in conformity with its promise then given to us that passenger boats should not be sunk and that due warning would be given to all other vessels which its submarines might seek to destroy, when no resistance was offered or escape attempted, and care taken that their crews were given at least a fair chance to save their lives in their open boats. The precautions taken were meager and haphazard enough, as was proved in distressing instance after instance in the progress of the cruel and unmanly business, but a certain degree of restraint was observed. The new policy has swept every restriction aside. Vessels of every kind, whatever their flag, their character, their cargo, their destination, their errand, have been ruthlessly sent to the bottom without warning and without thought of help or mercy for those on board, the vessels of friendly neutrals along with those of belligerents. Even hospital ships and ships carrying relief to the sorely bereaved and stricken people of Belgium, though the latter were provided with safe conduct through the proscribed areas by the German Government itself and were distinguished by unmistakable marks of identity, have been sunk with the same reckless lack of compassion or of principle.

I was for a little while unable to believe that such things would in fact be done by any government that had hitherto subscribed to the humane practices of civilized nations. International law had its origin in the attempt to set up some law which would be respected and observed upon the seas, where no nation had right of dominion and where lay the free highways of the world. By painful stage after stage has that law been built up, with meager enough results, indeed, after all was accomplished that could be accomplished, but always with a clear view, at least, of what the heart and conscience of mankind demanded. This minimum of right the German Government has swept aside under the plea of retaliation and necessity and because it had no weapons which it could use at sea except these which it is impossible to employ as it is employing them without throwing to the winds all scruples of humanity or of respect for the understandings that were supposed to underlie the intercourse of the world. I am not now thinking of the loss of property involved, immense and serious as that is, but only of the wanton and wholesale destruction of the lives of non-combatants, men, women, and children, engaged in pursuits which have always, even in the darkest periods of modern history, been deemed innocent and legitimate. Property can be paid for; the lives of peaceful and innocent people cannot be. The present German submarine warfare against commerce is a warfare against mankind.

It is a war against all nations. American ships have been sunk, American lives taken, in ways which it has stirred us very deeply to learn of, but the ships and people of other neutral and friendly nations have been sunk and overwhelmed in the waters in the same way. There has been no discrimination. The challenge is to all mankind. Each nation must decide for itself how it will meet it. The choice we make for ourselves must be made with a moderation of counsel and a temperateness of judgment befitting our character and our motives as a nation. We must put excited feeling away. Our motive will not be revenge or the victorious assertion of the physical might of the nation, but only the vindication of right, of human right, of which we are only a single champion.

When I addressed the Congress on the twenty-sixth of February last I thought that it would suffice to assert our neutral rights with arms, our right to use the seas against unlawful interference, our right to keep our people safe against unlawful violence. But armed neutrality, it now appears, is impracticable. . . . The intimation is conveyed that the armed guards which we have placed on our merchant ships will be treated as beyond the pale of law and subject to be dealt with as pirates would be. Armed neutrality is ineffectual enough at best; in such circumstances and in the face of such pretensions it is worse than ineffectual: It is likely only to produce what it was meant to prevent; it is practically certain to draw us into the war without either the rights or the effectiveness of belligerents. There is one choice we cannot make, we are incapable of making: we will not choose the path of submission and suffer the most sacred rights of our Nation and our people to be ignored or violated. The wrongs against which we now array ourselves are no common wrongs; they cut to the very roots of human life.

With a profound sense of the solemn and even tragical character of the step I am taking and of the grave responsibilities which it involves, but in unhesitating obedience to what I deem my constitutional duty, I advise that the Congress declare the recent course of the Imperial German Government to be in fact nothing less than war against the government and people of the United States; that it formally accept the status of belligerent which has thus been thrust upon it; and that it take immediate steps not only to put the country in a more thorough state of defense but also to exert all its power and employ all its resources to bring the Government of the German Empire to terms and end the war.

What this will involve is clear. It will involve the utmost practicable cooperation in counsel and action with the governments now at war with Germany, and, as incident to that, the extension to those governments of the most liberal financial credits, in order that our resources my so far as possible be added to theirs. It will involve the organization and mobilization of all the material resources of the country to supply the materials of war and serve the incidental needs of the Nation in the most abundant and yet the most economical and efficient way possible. It will involve the immediate full equipment of the navy in all respects but particularly in supplying it with the best means of dealing with the enemy's submarines. It will involve the immediate addition to the armed forces of the United States already provided for by law in case of war at least five hundred thousand men, who should, in my opinion, be chosen upon the principle of universal liability to service, and also the authorization of subsequent additional increments of equal force so soon as they may be needed and can be handled in training. It will involve also, of course, the granting of adequate credits to the Government, sustained, I hope, so far as they can equitably be sustained by the present generation, by well conceived taxation.

☆ ☆ ☆

While we do these things, these deeply momentous things, let us be clear, and make very clear to all the world what our motives and our objects are. My own thought has not been driven from its habitual and normal course by the unhappy events of the last two months, and I do not believe that the thought of the Nation has been altered or clouded by them. I have exactly the same things in mind now that I had in mind when I addressed the Senate on the twenty-second of January last; the same that I had in mind when I addressed the Congress on the third of February and on the twenty-sixth of February. Our object now, as then, is to vindicate the principles of peace and justice in the life of the world as against selfish and autocratic power and to set up amongst the really free and self-governed peoples of the world such a concert of purpose and of action as will henceforth insure the observance of those principles. Neutrality is no longer feasible or desirable where the peace of the world is involved and the freedom of its peoples, and the menace to that peace and freedom lies in the existence of autocratic governments backed by organized force which is controlled wholly by their will, not by the will of their people. We have seen the last of neutrality in such circumstances. We are at the beginning of an age in which it will be insisted that the same standards of conduct and of responsibility for wrong done shall be observed among nations and their governments that are observed among the individual citizens of civilized states.

We have no quarrel with the German people. We have no feeling towards them but one of sympathy and friendship. It was not upon their impulse that their government acted in entering this war. It was not with their previous knowledge or approval. It was a war determined upon as wars used to be determined upon in the old, unhappy days when peoples were nowhere consulted by their rulers and wars were provoked and waged in the interest of dynasties or of little groups of ambitious men who were accustomed to use their fellow men as pawns and tools.

☆ ☆ ☆

Does not every American feel that assurance has been added to our hope for the future peace of the world by the wonderful and heartening things that have been happening within the last few weeks in Russia? Russia was known by those who knew it best to have been always in fact democratic at heart, in all the vital habits of her thought, in all the intimate relationships of her people that spoke their natural instinct, their habitual attitude towards life. The autocracy that crowned the summit of her political structure, long as it had stood and terrible as was the reality of its power, was not in fact Russian in origin, character, or purpose; and now it has been shaken off and the great, generous Russian people have been added in all their naïve majesty and might to the forces that are fighting for freedom in the world, for justice, and for peace. Here is a fit partner for a League of Honor.

One of the things that has served to convince us that the Prussian autocracy was not and could never be our friend is that from the very onset of the present war it has filled our unsuspecting communities and even our offices of government with spies and set criminal intrigues everywhere afoot against our national unity of counsel, our peace within and without, our industries and our commerce. Indeed, it is now evident that its spies were here even before the war began; and it is unhappily not a matter of conjecture but a fact proved in our courts of justice that the intrigues which have more than once come perilously near to disturbing the peace and dislocating the industries of the country have been carried on at the instigation, with the support, and even under the personal direction of official agents of the Imperial Government accredited to the Government of the United States. Even in checking these things and trying to extirpate them we have sought to put the most generous interpretation possible upon them because we knew that their source lay not in any hostile feeling or purpose of the German people towards us (who were, no doubt as ignorant of them as we ourselves were), but only in the selfish designs of a Government that did what it pleased and told its people nothing. But they have played their part in serving to convince us at last that that Government entertains no real friendship for us and means to act against our peace and security at its convenience. That it means to stir up enemies against us at our very doors the intercepted note to the German Minister at Mexico City is eloquent evidence.

We are accepting this challenge of hostile purpose because we know that in such a Government, following such methods, we can never have a friend; and that in the presence of its organized power, always lying in wait to accomplish we know not what purpose, there can be no assured security for the democratic Governments of the world. We are now about to accept gauge of battle with this natural foe to liberty and shall, if necessary, spend the whole force of the nation to check and nullify its pretensions and its power. We are glad, now that we see the facts with no veil of false pretense about them, to fight thus for the ultimate peace of the world and for the liberation of its peoples, the German peoples included: for the rights of nations great and small and the privilege of men everywhere to choose their way of life and of obedience. The world must be made safe for democracy. Its peace must be planted upon the tested foundations of political liberty. We have no selfish ends to serve. We desire no conquest, no dominion. We seek no indemnities for ourselves, no material compensation for the sacrifices we shall freely make. We are but one of the champions of the rights of mankind. We shall be satisfied when those rights have been made as secure as the faith and the freedom of nations can make them.

☆ ☆ ☆

It is a distressing and oppressive duty, Gentlemen of the Congress, which I have performed in thus addressing you. There are, it may be, many months of fiery trial and sacrifice ahead of us. It is a fearful thing to lead this great peaceful people into war, into the most terrible and disastrous of all wars, civilization itself seeming to be in the balance. But the right is more precious than peace, and we shall fight for the things which we have always carried nearest our hearts, for democracy, for the right of those who submit to authority to have a voice in their own Governments, for the rights and liberties of small nations, for a universal dominion of right by such a concert of free peoples as shall bring peace and safety to all nations and made the world itself at last free. To such a task we can dedicate our lives and our fortunes, everything that we are and everything that we have, with the pride of those who know that the day has come when America is privileged to spend her blood and her might for the principles that gave her birth and happiness and the peace which she has treasured. God helping her, she can do no other.

The Fourteen Points

Again addressing a joint session of Congress, on January 18, 1918, Wilson made explicit his statement of war aims, the Fourteen Points. He began by citing the talks taking place between the Germans and Russians at Brest-Litovsk, which, he argued, indicated German determination to hold all conquered territory in the east. Indeed, when Lenin made peace with the Germans weeks later, it was at a very high cost to Russia. Wilson countered by renouncing any American desire for conquest and proposed his terms for a just and enduring peace. Wilson's program was broadcast around the world and made him something of an international hero. The idealism of his proposals contrasted sharply with the greed and ambition of the other Great Power victors at the time of the Versailles peace conference.

It will be our wish and purpose that the processes of peace, when they are begun, shall be absolutely open and that they shall involve and permit henceforth no secret understandings of any kind. The day of conquest and aggrandizement is gone by; so is also the day of secret covenants entered into in the interest of particular governments and likely at some unlooked-for moment to upset the peace of the world. It is this happy fact, now clear to the view of every public man whose thoughts do not still linger in an age that is dead and gone, which makes it possible for every nation whose purposes are consistent with justice and the peace of the world to avow now or at any other time the objects it has in view.

We entered this war because violations of right had occurred which touched us to the quick and made the life of our own people impossible unless they were corrected and the world secured once for all against their recurrence. What we demand in this war, therefore, is nothing peculiar to ourselves. It is that the world be made fit and safe to live in; and particularly that it be made safe for every peace-loving nation which, like our own, wishes to live its own life, determine its own institutions, be assured of justice and fair dealing by the other peoples of the world as against force and selfish aggression. All the peoples of the world are in effect partners in this interest, and for our own part we see very clearly that unless justice be done to others it will not be done to us. The program of the world's peace, therefore, is our program; and that program, the only possible program, as we see it, in this:

I. Open covenants of peace, openly arrived at, after which there shall be no private international understandings of any kind but diplomacy shall proceed always frankly and in the public view.

II. Absolute freedom of navigation upon the seas, outside territorial waters, alike in peace and in war, except as the seas may be closed in whole or in part by international actions for the enforcement of international covenants.

III. The removal, so far as possible, of all economic barriers and the establishment of an equality of trade conditions among all the nations consenting to the peace and associating themselves for its maintenance.

IV. Adequate guarantees given and taken that national armaments will be reduced to the lowest point consistent with domestic safety.

V. A free, open-minded, and absolutely impartial adjustment of all colonial claims, based upon a strict observance of the principle that in determining all such questions of sovereignty the interests of the populations concerned must have equal weight with the equitable claims of the government whose title is to be determined.

VI. The evacuation of all Russian territory and such a settlement of all questions affecting Russia as will secure the best and freest cooperation of the other nations of the world in obtaining for her an unhampered and unembarrassed opportunity for the independent determination of her own political development and national policy and assure her of a sincere welcome into the society of free nations under institutions of her own choosing; and, more than a welcome, assistance also of every kind that she may need and may herself desire. The treatment accorded Russia by her sister nations in the months to come will be the acid test of their good will, of their comprehension of her needs as distinguished from their own interests, and of their intelligent and unselfish sympathy.

VII. Belgium, the whole world will agree, must be evacuated and restored, without any attempt to limit the sovereignty which she enjoys in common with all other free nations. No other single act will serve as this will serve to restore confidence among the nations in the laws which they have themselves set and determined for the government of their relations with one another. Without this healing act the whole structure and validity of international law is forever impaired.

VIII. All French territory should be freed and the invaded portions restored, and the wrong done to France by Prussia in 1871 in the matter of Alsace-Lorraine, which has unsettled the peace of the world for nearly fifty years, should be righted in order that peace may once more be made secure in the interest of all.

IX. A readjustment of the frontiers of Italy should be affected along clearly recognizable lines of nationality.

X. The people of Austria-Hungary, whose place among the nations we wish to see safeguarded and assured, should be accorded the freest opportunity of autonomous development.

XI. Rumania, Serbia, and Montenegro should be evacuated; occupied territories restored; Serbia accorded free and secure access to the sea; and the relations of the several Balkan states to one another determined by friendly counsel along historically established lines of allegiance and nationality; and international guarantees of the political and economic independence and territorial integrity of the several Balkan states should be entered into.

XII. The Turkish portions of the present Ottoman Empire should be assured a secure sovereignty, but the other nationalities which are now under Turkish rule should be assured an undoubted security of life and an absolutely unmolested opportunity of autonomous development, and the Dardanelles should be permanently opened as a free passage to the ships and commerce of all nations under international guarantees.

XIII. An independent Polish state should be erected which should include the territories inhabited by indisputably Polish populations, which should be assured a free and secure access to the sea, and whose political and economic independence and territorial integrity should be guaranteed by international covenant.

XIV. A general association of nations must be formed under specific covenants for the purpose of affording mutual guarantees of political independence and territorial integrity to great and small states alike.

In regard to these essential rectifications of wrong and assertions of right we feel ourselves to be intimate partners of all the governments and peoples associated together against the Imperialists. We cannot be separated in interest or divided in purpose. We stand together until the end.

For such arrangements and covenants we are willing to fight and to continue to fight until they are achieved; but only because we wish the right to prevail and desire a just and stable peace such as can be secured only by removing the chief provocations to war, which this program does not remove. We have no jealousy of German greatness, and there is nothing in this program that impairs it. We grudge her no achievement or distinction of learning or of pacific enterprise such as have made her record very bright and very enviable. We do not wish to injure her or to block in any way her legitimate influence or power. We do not wish to fight her either with arms or with hostile arrangements of trade if she is willing to associate herself with us and the other peace-loving nations of the world in covenants of justice and law and fair dealing. We wish her only to accept a place of equality among the peoples of the world, the new world in which we now live, instead of a place of mastery.

Neither do we presume to suggest to her any alteration or modification of her institutions. But it is necessary, we must frankly say, and necessary as a preliminary to any intelligent dealing with her on our part, that we should know whom her spokesmen speak for when they speak to us, whether for the Reichstag majority or for the military party and the men whose creed is imperial domination.

We have spoken now, surely, in terms too concrete to admit of any further doubt or question. An evident principle runs through the whole program I have outlined. It is the principle of justice to all peoples and nationalities, and their right to live on equal terms of liberty and safety with one another, whether they be strong or weak. Unless this principle be made its foundation no part of the structure of international justice can stand. The people of the United States could act upon no other principle; and to the vindication of this principle they are ready to devote their lives, their honor, and everything that they possess. The moral climate of this the culminating and final war for human liberty has come, and they are ready to put their own strength, their own highest purpose, their own integrity and devotion to the test.

League of Nations Address before the Second Plenary Session of the Peace Conference

Urging the necessity of a league of nations, Wilson delivered an eloquent address to a plenary session of the Paris peace conference on January 25, 1919. The United States went to war, he said, not only to defeat the Central Powers, but also to see the war followed by a more secure peace. That goal demanded an agency of collective security to superintend the peace. Wilson's call for a league was moved by a realistic understanding of history and world politics. He knew the peace treaty would be flawed; he knew that international tensions and disputes would threaten the peace. His hope was for an organization where crises could be defused by negotiation and through which collective action might deter aggression. His words and tone here suggested a greater unanimity of American opinion than he was to find on his return to the United States.

Mr. Chairman:

I consider it a distinguished privilege to be permitted to open the discussion in this conference on the league of nations. We have assembled for two purposes, to make the present settlements which have been rendered necessary by this war, and also to secure the peace of the world, not only by the present settlements, but by the arrangements we shall make at this conference for its maintenance. The league of nations seems to me to be necessary for both these purposes. There are many complicated questions connected with the present settlements which perhaps cannot be successfully worked out to an ultimate issue by the decisions we shall arrive at here. I can easily conceive that many of these settlements will need subsequent reconsideration, but many of the decisions we make shall need subsequent alteration in some degree; for, if I may judge by my own study of some of these questions, they are not susceptible of confident judgments at present.

It is, therefore, necessary that we should set up some machinery by which the work of this conference should be rendered complete. We have assembled here for the purpose of doing very much more than making the present settlements. We are assembled under very peculiar conditions of world opinion. I may say without straining the point that we are not representatives of Governments, but representatives of peoples. It will not suffice to satisfy governmental circles anywhere. It is necessary that we should satisfy the opinion of mankind. The burdens of this war have fallen in an unusual degree upon the whole population of the countries involved. I do not need to draw for you the picture of how the burden has been thrown back from the front upon the older men, upon the women, upon the children, upon the homes of the civilized world, and how the real strain of the war has come where the eye of government could not reach, but where the heart of humanity beats. We are bidden by these people to make a peace which will make them secure. We are bidden by these people to see to it that this strain does not come upon them again, and I venture to say that it has been possible for them to bear this strain because they hoped that those who represented them could get together after this war and make such another sacrifice unnecessary.

It is a solemn obligation on our part, therefore, to make permanent arrangements that justice shall be rendered and peace maintained. This is the central object of our meeting. Settlements may be temporary, but the action of the nations in the interest of peace and justice must be permanent. We can set up permanent processes. We may not be able to set up permanent decisions. Therefore, it seems to me that we must take, so far as we can, a picture of the world into our mind. Is it not a startling circumstance, for one thing, that the great discoveries of science, that the quiet studies of men in laboratories, that the thoughtful developments which have taken place in quiet lecture rooms, have now been turned to the destruction of civilization? The powers of destruction have not so much multiplied as gained facility. The enemy whom we have just overcome had at his seats of learning some of the principal centers of scientific study and discovery, and he used them in order to make destruction sudden and complete; and only the watchful, continuous cooperation of men can see to it that science as well as armed men is kept within the harness of civilization.

In a sense the United States is less interested in this subject than the other nations here assembled. With her great territory and her extensive sea borders, it is less likely that the United States should suffer from the attack of enemies than that many of the other nations here should suffer; and the ardor of the United States—for it is a very deep and genuine ardor—for the society of nations is not an ardor springing out of fear or apprehension, but an ardor springing out of the ideals which have come to consciousness in this way. In coming into this war the United States never for a moment thought that she was intervening in the politics of any part of the world. Her thought was that all the world had now become conscious that there was a single cause which turned upon the issues of this war. That was the cause of justice and of liberty for men of every kind and place. Therefore, the United States should feel that its part in this war had been played in vain if there ensued upon it merely a body of European settlements. It would feel that it could not take part in guaranteeing those European Settlements unless that guarantee involved the continuous superintendence of the peace of the world by the associated nations of the world.

☆ ☆ ☆

You can imagine, gentlemen, I dare say, the sentiments and the purpose with which representatives of the United States support this great project for a league of nations. We regard it as the keystone of the whole program which expressed our purposes and ideals in this war and which the associated nations have accepted as the basis of the settlement. If we returned to the United States without having made every effort in our power to realize this program, we should return to meet the merited scorn of our fellow citizens. For they are a body that constitutes a great democracy. They expect their leaders to speak their thoughts and no private purpose of their own. They expect their representatives to be their servants. We have no choice but to obey their mandate. But it is with the greatest enthusiasm and pleasure that we accept that mandate; and because this is the keystone of the whole fabric, we have pledged our every purpose to it, as we have to every item of the fabric. We would not dare abate a single part of the program which constitutes our instruction. We would not dare compromise upon any matter as the champion of this thing—this peace of the world, this attitude of justice, this principle that we are the masters of no people but are here to see that every people in the world shall choose its own masters and govern its own destinies, not as we wish, but as it wishes. We are here to see, in short, that the very foundations of this war are swept away. Those foundations were the private choice of small coteries of civil rulers and military staffs. Those foundations were the aggression of great powers upon the small. Those foundations were the holding together of empires of unwilling subject by the duress of arms. Those foundations were the power of small bodies of men to work their will upon mankind and use them as pawns in a game. And nothing less than the emancipation of the world from these things will accomplish peace. You can see that the representatives of the United States are, therefore, never put to the embarrassment of choosing a way of expediency, because they have never laid down for them the unalterable lines of principle. And, thank God, those lines have been accepted as the lines of settlement by all the high-minded men who have had to do with the beginnings of this great business.

I hope, Mr. Chairman, that when it is known, as I feel confident it will be known, that we have adopted the principle of the league of nations and means to work out that principle in effective action, we shall by that single thing have lifted a great part of the load of anxiety from the hearts of men everywhere. We stand in a peculiar case. As I go about the streets here I see everywhere the American uniform. Those men came into the war after we had uttered our purposes. They came as crusaders, not merely to win a war, but to win a cause; and I am responsible to them, for it fell to me to formulate the purposes for which I asked them to fight, and I, like them, must be a crusader for these things, whatever it costs and whatever it may be necessary to do, in honor, to accomplish the object for which they fought. I have been glad to find from day to day that there is no question of our standing alone in this matter, for there are champions of this cause upon every hand. I am merely avowing this in order that you may understand why, perhaps, it fell to us, who are disengaged from the politics of this great continent and of the Orient, to suggest that this was the keystone of the arch and why it occurred to the generous mind of our president to call upon me to open this debate. It is not because we alone represent this idea, but because it is our privilege to associate ourselves with you in representing it.

I have only tried in what I have said to give you the fountains of the enthusiasm which is within us for this thing, for those fountains spring, it seems to me, from all the ancient wrongs and sympathies of mankind, and the very pulse of the world seems to beat to the surface in this enterprise.

Appeal for Support of the League of Nations at Pueblo, Colorado

When Wilson returned from Paris, the peace treaty was in deep trouble in the Senate because of the league issue. Through the summer of 1919, undermined by the tactics of Henry Cabot Lodge, support for the treaty eroded. Lodge, chairman of the Senate Foreign Relations Committee, staffed the committee with senators unfriendly to the idea of American participation in the League of Nations and charged that provisions in the league's charter were dangerous to the United States. He used delaying tactics to allow time for doubts and opposition to build. In September, Wilson launched a nationwide tour trying to revive popular support. At Pueblo, Colorado, on September 25, he pleaded his case for the treaty, attacking the distortions of his critics and deftly quoted Theodore Roosevelt's early support for a league. When he closed with a tribute to the men fallen in France, Wilson was in tears. Already showing symptoms of illness, the president collapsed soon after the speech and was rushed back to Washington.

Mr. Chairman and My Fellow Countrymen:

It is with a great deal of genuine pleasure that I find myself in Pueblo, and I feel it a compliment that I should be permitted to be the first speaker in this beautiful hall. One of the advantages of this hall, as I look about, is that you are not too far away from me, because there is nothing so reassuring to men who are trying to express the public sentiment as getting into real personal contact with their fellow citizens. I have gained a renewed impression as I have crossed the continent this time of the homogeneity of this great people to whom we belong. They come from many origins, but they are all shot through with the same principles and desire the same righteous and honest things. I have received a more inspiring impression this time of the public opinion of the United States than it was ever my privilege to receive before.

The chief pleasure of my trip has been that it has nothing to do with my personal fortunes, that it has nothing to do with my personal reputation, that it has nothing to do with anything except great principles uttered by Americans of all sorts and of all parties which we are now trying to realize at this crisis of the affairs of the world. But there have been unpleasant impressions as well as pleasant impressions, my fellow citizens, as I have crossed the continent. I have perceived more and more that men have been busy creating an absolutely false impression of what the treaty of peace and the Covenant of the League of Nations contain and mean. I find, moreover, that there is an organized propaganda against the League of Nations and against the treaty proceeding from exactly the same sources that the organized propaganda proceeded from which threatened this country here and there with disloyalty, and I want to say—I cannot say too often—any man who carried a hyphen about with him carries a dagger that he is ready to plunge into the vitals of this Republic whenever he gets ready. If I can catch any man with a hyphen in this great contest I will know that I have got an enemy of the Republic. My fellow citizens, it is only . . . certain bodies of sympathy with foreign nations that are organized against this great document which the American representatives have brought back from Paris. Therefore, in order to clear away the mists, in order to remove the impressions, in order to check the falsehoods that have clustered around this great subject, I want to tell you a few very simple things about the treaty and the covenant.

Do not think of this treaty of peace as merely a settlement with Germany. It is that. It is a very severe settlement with Germany, but there is not anything in it that she did not earn. Indeed, she earned more than she can ever be able to pay for, and the punishment exacted of her is not a punishment greater than she can bear, and it is absolutely necessary in order that no other nation may ever plot such a thing against humanity and civilization. But the treaty is so much more than that. It is not merely a settlement with Germany; it is a readjustment of those great injustices which underlie the whole structure of European and Asiatic society. This is only the first of several treaties. They are all constructed upon the same plan. The Austrian treaty follows the same lines. The treaty with Hungary follows the same lines. The treaty with Bulgaria follows the same lines. The treaty with Turkey, when it is formulated, will follow the same lines. What are those lines? They are based upon the purpose to see that every government dealt with in this great settlement is put in the hands of the people and taken out of the hands of coteries and of sovereigns who had no right to rule over the people. It is a people's treaty, that accomplishes by a great sweep of practical justice the liberation of men who never could have liberated themselves, and the power of the most powerful nations has been devoted not to their aggrandizement but to the liberation of people whom they could have put under their control if they had chosen to do so. Not one foot of territory is demanded by the conquerors, not one single item of submission to their authority is demanded by them. The men who sat around that table in Paris knew that the time had come when the people were no longer going to consent to live under masters, but were going to live the lives that they chose themselves, to live under such governments as they chose themselves to erect. That is the fundamental principle of this great settlement.

And we did not stop with that. We added a great international charter for the rights of labor. Reject this treaty, impair it, and this is the consequence of the laboring men of the world, that there is no international tribunal which can bring the moral judgments of the world to bear upon the great labor questions of the day. What we need to do with regard to the labor questions of the day, my fellow countrymen, is to lift them into the light, is to lift them out of the haze and distraction of passion, of hostility, out into the calm spaces where men look at things without passion. The more men you get into a great discussion the more you exclude passion. Just as soon as the calm judgment of the world is directed upon the question of justice to labor, labor is going to have a forum such as it never was supplied with before, and men everywhere are going to see that the problem of labor is nothing more nor less than the problem of the elevation of humanity. We must see that all the questions which have disturbed the world, all the questions which have eaten into the confidence of men toward their governments, all the questions which have disturbed the processes of industry, shall be brought out where men of all points of view, men of all attitudes of mind, men of all kinds of experience, may contribute their part of the settlement of the great questions which we must settle and cannot ignore.

At the front of this great treaty is put the Covenant of the League of Nations. It will also be at the front of the Austrian treaty and the Hungarian treaty and the Bulgarian treaty and the treaty with Turkey. Every one of them will contain the Covenant of the League of Nations, because you cannot work any of them without the Covenant of the League of Nations. Unless you get the united, concerted purpose and power of the great Governments of the world behind this settlement, it will fall down like a house of cards. There is only one power to put behind the liberation of mankind, and that is the power of mankind. It is the power of the united moral forces of the world, and in the Covenant of the League of Nations the moral forces of the world are mobilized. For what purpose? Reflect, my fellow citizens, that the membership of this great League is going to include all the great fighting nations of the world, as well as the weak ones. It is not for the present going to include Germany, but for the time being Germany is not a great fighting country. All the nations that have power that can be mobilized are going to be members of this League, including the United States. And what do they unite for? They enter into a solemn promise to one another that they will never use their power against one another for aggression; that they never will impair the territorial integrity of a neighbor; that they never will interfere with the political independence of a neighbor; that they will abide by the principle that great populations are entitled to determine their own destiny and that they will not interfere with that destiny; and that no matter what differences arise amongst them they will never resort to war without first having done one or other of two things—either submitted the matter of controversy to arbitration, in which case they agree to abide by the result without question, or submitted it to the consideration of the council of the League of Nations, laying before that council all the documents, all the facts, agreeing that the council can publish the documents and the facts to the whole world, agreeing that there shall be six months allowed for the mature consideration of those facts by the council, and agreeing that at the expiration of the six months, even if they are not then ready to accept the advice of the council with regard to the settlement of the dispute, they will still not go to war for another three months. In other words, they consent, no matter what happens to submit every matter of difference between them to the judgment of mankind, and just so certainly as they do that, my fellow citizens, war will be in the far background, war will be pushed out of that foreground of terror in which it has kept the world for generation after generation, and men will know that there will be a calm time of deliberate counsel. The most dangerous thing for a bad cause is to expose it to the opinion of the world. The most certain way that you can prove that a man is mistaken is by letting all his neighbors discuss what he thinks, and if he is in the wrong you will notice that he will stay at home, he will not walk on the street. He will be afraid of the eyes of his neighbors. He will be afraid of their judgment of his character. He will know that his cause is lost unless he can sustain it by the arguments of right and of justice. The same law that applies to individuals applies to nations.

But, you say, "We have heard that we might be at a disadvantage in the League of Nations." Well, whoever told you that either was deliberately falsifying or he had not read the Covenant of the League of Nations. I leave him the choice. I want to give you a very simple account of the organization of the League of Nations and let you judge for yourselves. It is a very simple organization. The power of the League, or rather the activities of the League, lie in two bodies. There is the council, which consists of one representative from each of the principal allied and associated powers—

that is to say, the United States, Great Britain, France, Italy, and Japan, along with four other representatives of smaller powers chosen out of the general body of the membership of the League. The council is the source of every active policy of the League, and no active policy of the League can be adopted without a unanimous vote of the council. That is explicitly stated in the Covenant itself. Does it not evidently follow that the League of Nations can adopt no policy whatever without the consent of the United States? The affirmative vote of the representative of the United States is necessary in every case. Now, you have heard of six votes belonging to the British Empire. Those six votes are not in the council. They are in the assembly, and the interesting thing is that the assembly does not vote. I must qualify that statement a little, but essentially it is absolutely true. In every matter in which the assembly is given a voice, and there are only four or five, its vote does not count unless concurred in by the representatives of all the nations represented on the council, so that there is no validity to any vote of the assembly unless in that vote also the representative of the United States concurs. That one vote of the United States is as big as the six votes of the British Empire. I am not jealous for advantage, my fellow citizens, but I think that is a perfectly safe situation. There is no validity in a vote, either by the council or the assembly, in which we do not concur. So much for the statements about the six votes of the British Empire.

☆ ☆ ☆

When you come to the heart of the Covenant, my fellow citizens, you will find it in article ten, and I am very much interested to know that the other things have been blown away like bubbles. There is nothing in the other contentions with regard to the League of Nations, but there is something in article ten that you ought to realize and ought to accept or reject. Article ten is the heart of the whole matter. What is article ten? I never am certain that I can from memory give a literal repetition of its language, but I am sure that I can give an exact interpretation of its meaning. Article ten provides that every member of the league covenants to respect and preserve the territorial integrity and existing political independence of every other member of the league as against external aggression. Not against internal disturbance. There was not a man at that table who did not admit the sacredness of the right of self-determination, the sacredness of the right of any body of people to say that they would not continue to live under the Government they were then living under, and under article eleven of the Covenant they are given a place to say whether they will live under it or not. For following article ten is article eleven, which makes it the right of any member of the league at any time to call attention to anything, anywhere, that is likely to disturb the peace of the world or the good understanding between nations upon which the peace of the world depends.

☆ ☆ ☆

But you will say, "What is the second sentence of article ten? That is what gives very disturbing thoughts." The second sentence is that the council of the League shall advise what steps, if any, are necessary to carry out the guaranty of the first sentence, namely, that the members will respect and preserve the territorial integrity and political independence of the members. I do not know any other meaning for the word "advise" except "advise." The council advises, and it cannot advise without the vote of the United States. Why gentlemen should fear that the Congress of the United States would be advised to do something that it did not want to do I frankly cannot imagine, because they cannot even be advised to do anything unless their own representative has participated in the advice. It may be that that will impair somewhat the vigor of the League, but, nevertheless, the fact is so, that we are not obliged to take any advice except our own, which to any man who wants to go his own course is a very satisfactory state of affairs. Every man regards his own advice as best, and I dare say every man mixes his own advice with some thought of his own interest. Whether we use it wisely or unwisely, we can use the vote of the United States to make impossible drawing the United States into any enterprise that she does not care to be drawn into.

☆ ☆ ☆

It reassures me and fortifies my position to find how before I went over men whose judgment the United States has often trusted were of exactly the same opinion that I went abroad to express. Here is something I want to read from Theodore Roosevelt:

"The one effective move for obtaining peace is by an agreement among all the great powers in which each should pledge itself not only to abide by the decisions of a common tribunal but to back its decisions by force. The great civilized nations should combine by solemn agreement in a great world league for the peace of righteousness; a court should be established. A changed and amplified Hague court would meet the requirements, composed of representatives from each nation, whose representatives are sworn to act as judges in each case and not in a representative capacity." Now there is article ten. He goes on and says this: "The nations should agree on certain rights that should not be questioned, such as territorial integrity, their right to deal with their domestic affairs, and with such matters as whom they should admit to citizenship. All such guarantee each of their number in possession of these rights."

Now, the other specification is in the Covenant. The Covenant in another portion guarantees to the members the independent control of their domestic questions. There is not a leg for these gentlemen to stand on when they say that the interests of the United States are not safeguarded in the very points where we are most sensitive. You do not need to be told again that the Covenant expressly says that nothing in this covenant shall be construed as affecting the validity of the Monroe doctrine, for example. You could not be more explicit than that. And every point of interest is covered, partly for one very interesting reason. This is not the first time that the Foreign Relations Committee of the Senate of the United States has read and considered this covenant. I brought it to this country in March last in a tentative, provisional form, in practically the form that it now has, with the exception of certain additions which I shall mention immediately. I asked the Foreign Relations Committees of both Houses to come to the White House and we spent a long evening in the frankest discussion of every portion that they wished to discuss. They made certain specific suggestions as to what should be contained in this document when it was to be revised. I carried those suggestions to Paris, and every one of them was adopted. What more could I have done? What more could have been obtained? The very matters upon which these gentlemen were most concerned were, the right of withdrawal, which is now expressly stated; the safeguarding of the Monroe doctrine, which is now accomplished; the exclusion from action by the League of domestic questions, which is now accomplished. All along the line, every suggestion of the United States was adopted after the Covenant had been drawn up in its first form and had been published for the criticism of the world. There is a very true sense in which I can say this is a tested American document.

I am dwelling upon these points, my fellow citizens, in spite of the fact that I dare say to most of you they are perfectly well known, because in order to meet the present situation we have got to know what we are dealing with. We are not dealing with the kind of document which this is represented by some gentlemen to be; and inasmuch as we are dealing with a document simon-pure in respect of the very principles we have professed and lived up to, we have got to do one or other of two things—we have got to adopt it or reject it. There is no middle course. You cannot go in on a special-privilege basis of your own. I take it that you are too proud to ask to be exempted from responsibilities which the other members of the league will carry. We go in upon equal terms or we do not go in at all; and if we do not go in, my fellow citizens, think of the tragedy of that result—the only sufficient guaranty to the peace of the world withheld! Ourselves drawn apart with that dangerous pride which means that we shall be ready to take care of ourselves, and that means that we shall maintain great standing armies and an irresistible navy; that means we shall have the organization of a military nation; that means we shall have a general staff, with the kind of power that the general staff of Germany had; to mobilize this great manhood of the Nation when it pleases, all the energy of our young men drawn into the thought and preparation for war. What of our pledges to the men that lie dead in France? We said that they went over there not to prove the prowess of America or her readiness for another war but to see to it that there never was such a war again. It always seems to make it difficult for me to say anything, my fellow citizens, when I think of my clients in this case. My clients are the children; my clients are the next generation. They do not know what promises and bonds I undertook when I ordered the armies of the United States to the soil of France, but I know, and I intend to redeem my pledges to the children; they shall not be sent upon a similar errand.

Again and again, my fellow citizens, mothers who lost their sons in France have come to me and, taking my hand, have shed tears upon it not only, but they have added, "God bless you, Mr. President!" Why, my fellow citizens, should they pray God to bless me? I advised the Congress of the United States to create the situation that led to the death of their sons. I ordered their sons oversea. I consented to their sons being put in the most difficult parts of the battle line, where death was certain, as in the impenetrable difficulties of the forest of Argonne. Why should they weep upon my hand and call down the blessings of God upon me? Because they believe that their boys died for something that vastly transcends any of the immediate and palpable objects of the war. They believe, and they rightly believe, that their sons saved the liberty of the world. They believe that wrapped up with the liberty of the world is the continuous protection of that liberty by the concerted powers of all civilized people. They believe that this sacrifice was made in order that other sons should not be called upon for a similar gift—the gift of life, the gift of all that died—and if we did not see this thing through, if we fulfilled the dearest present wish of

Germany and now dissociated ourselves from those alongside whom we fought in the world, would not something of the halo go away from the gun over the mantelpiece, or the sword? Would not the old uniform lose something of its significance? These men were crusaders. They were not going forth to prove the might of the United States. They were going forth to prove the might of justice and right, and all the world accepted them as crusaders, and their transcendent achievement has made all the world believe in America as it believes in no other nation organized in the modern world. There seem to me to stand between us and the rejection or qualification of this treaty the serried ranks of those boys in khaki, not only these boys who came home, but those dear ghosts that still deploy upon the fields of France.

My friends, on the last Decoration Day I went to a beautiful hillside near Paris, where was located the cemetery of Suresnes, a cemetery given over to the burial of the American dead. Behind me on the slopes was rank upon rank of living American soldiers, and lying before me upon the levels of the plain was rank upon rank of departed American soldiers. Right by the side of the stand where I spoke there was a little group of French women who had adopted those graves, had made themselves mothers of those dear ghosts by putting flowers every day upon those graves, taking them as their own sons, their own beloved, because they had died in the same cause—France was free and the world was free because America had come! I wish some men in public life who are now opposing the settlement for which these men died could visit such a spot as that. I wish that the thought that comes out of those graves could penetrate their consciousness. I wish that they could feel the moral obligation that rests upon us not to go back on those boys, but to see the thing through, to see it through to the end and make good their redemption of the world. For nothing less depends upon this decision, nothing less than the liberation and salvation of the world.

Bibliography

Works by Woodrow Wilson

Congressional Government (Boston: Houghton Mifflin, 1885).
Division and Reunion (New York: Longmans, Green, 1893).
A History of the American People, 5 vols. (New York: Harper and Brothers, 1902).
Mere Literature and Other Essays (Boston: Houghton Mifflin, 1896).
An Old Master and Other Political Essays (New York: Charles Scribner's Sons, 1893).
The Papers of Woodrow Wilson, 69 vols. Arthur S. Link, ed. (Princeton, N.J.: Princeton University Press, 1966–1994).
The Public Papers of Woodrow Wilson, 6 vols. Ray Stannard Baker and William E. Dodd, eds. (New York: Harper and Brothers, 1925).
Selected Literary and Political Papers and Addresses of Woodrow Wilson, 3 vols. (New York: Grosset and Dunlap, 1925).
The State (Boston: D. C. Heath, 1889).
"Cabinet Government in the United States," *International Review,* 7 (August 1879).
"Democracy and Efficiency," *Atlantic Monthly,* 87 (March 1901).
"The Making of the Nation," *Atlantic Monthly,* 80 (July 1879).
"The Reconstruction of the Southern States," *Atlantic Monthly,* 87 (January 1901).

Selected Works on Wilson

Bailey, Thomas A., *Woodrow Wilson and the Great Betrayal* (New York: Macmillan, 1945).
———, *Woodrow Wilson and the Lost Peace* (New York: Macmillan, 1944).
Baker, Ray Stannard, *Woodrow Wilson, Life and Letters,* 8 vols. (Garden City, N.Y.: Doubleday, Page, and Co., 1927–1939).
Blum, John Morton, *Woodrow Wilson and the Politics of Morality* (Boston: Little Brown, 1956).
Bragdon, Henry Wilkinson, *Woodrow Wilson: The Academic Years* (Cambridge, Mass.: Belknap Press, 1967).
Clements, Kendrick A., *The Presidency of Woodrow Wilson* (Lawrence: University Press of Kansas, 1992).
———, *Woodrow Wilson, World Statesman* (Boston: Twayne, 1987).

Clements, Kendrick A., and Eric A. Cheezum, *Woodrow Wilson* (Washington, D.C.: Congressional Quarterly Press, 2003).

Cooper, John Milton, Jr., *The Warrior and the Priest: Woodrow Wilson and Theodore Roosevelt* (Cambridge, Mass., Belknap Press, 1983).

Cooper, John Milton, Jr., and Charles Neu, *The Wilson Era: Essays in Honor of Arthur S. Link* (Arlington Heights, Ill.: Harlan Davidson, 1991).

Ferrell, Robert H., *Woodrow Wilson and World War I* (New York: Harper and Row, 1985).

Grayson, Cary T., *Woodrow Wilson: An Intimate Memoir* (New York: Holt Rinehart and Winston, 1960).

George, Alexander L., and Juliette L. George, *Woodrow Wilson and Colonel House: A Personality Study* (New York: J. Day Co., 1956).

Hecksher, August, *Woodrow Wilson* (New York: Scribner's, 1991).

Link, Arthur S., *Wilson*, 5 vols. (Princeton, N.J.: Princeton University Press, 1947–1965).

———, *Woodrow Wilson and the Progressive Era, 1910–1917* (New York: Harper and Brothers, 1963).

Mulder, John M., *Woodrow Wilson: The Years of Preparation* (Princeton, N.J.: Princeton University Press, 1978).

Smith, Gene, *When the Cheering Stopped* (New York: William Morrow, 1964).

Thorsen, Niels Aage, *The Political Thought of Woodrow Wilson, 1875–1910* (Princeton, N.J.: Princeton University Press, 1988).

Walworth, Arthur, *Woodrow Wilson*, 2 vols. (New York: Norton, 1978).

Weinstein, Edwin A., *Woodrow Wilson: A Medical and Psychological Biography* (Princeton, N.J.: Princeton University Press, 1981).

Index

About the Editor

Mario R. DiNunzio is Professor of History at Providence College, where he has taught nineteenth- and twentieth-century U.S. history and has taught in and directed the college's innovative interdisciplinary Development of Western Civilization program. He has written on Civil War history, and previous books include *American Democracy and the Authoritarian Tradition of the West, Theodore Roosevelt: An American Mind,* and *Theodore Roosevelt.*